Barnsley's Conveyancing Law and Practice

Fourth edition

M P Thompson LL.B. (Leicester), LL.M. (Keele)
Professor of Law,
University of Leicester

Butterworths
London, Edinburgh, Dublin
1996

United Kingdom	Butterworths a Division of Reed Elsevier (UK) Ltd, Halsbury House, 35 Chancery Lane, LONDON WC2A 1EL and 4 Hill Street, EDINBURGH EH2 3JZ
Australia	Butterworths, SYDNEY, MELBOURNE, BRISBANE, ADELAIDE, PERTH, CANBERRA and HOBART
Canada	Butterworths Canada Ltd, TORONTO and VANCOUVER
Ireland	Butterworth (Ireland) Ltd, DUBLIN
Malaysia	Malayan Law Journal Sdn Bhd, KUALA LUMPUR
New Zealand	Butterworths of New Zealand Ltd, WELLINGTON and AUCKLAND
Singapore	Reed Elsevier (Singapore) Pte Ltd, SINGAPORE
South Africa	Butterworths Publishers (Pty) Ltd, DURBAN
USA	Michie, Charlottesville, VIRGINIA

A CIP Catalogue record for this book is available from the British Library.

ISBN 0 406 00489 7

Printed by Redwood Books, Trowbridge, Wiltshire

Preface to the Fourth Edition

When Professor Barnsley decided to pass on responsibility for the new edition of his widely respected book on Conveyancing and asked me to prepare the fourth edition, I must confess to having had rather mixed feelings. I was delighted to be associated with a book of such quality, but somewhat apprehensive about the size of the task. Pleasure overcame apprehension and so I decided to take on this new edition.

Much has happened since the appearance of the last edition. A new Conveyancing Protocol had been introduced, together with the introduction of the Standard Conditions of Sale (currently in their third edition) which supersede and incorporate the National Conditions of Sale and the Law Society's Conditions of Sale. I am grateful to the Law Society for giving permission to reproduce these Conditions as Appendix A. One of the features of these new Conditions is that, by a contractual term, the old rule that the risk of damage to the property between contract and completion now remains with the vendor rather than passing to the purchaser.

The legislature has also been active. Perhaps the biggest change was effected by the Law of Property (Miscellaneous Provisions) Act 1989. Section 2 of this Act, which replaced s 40 of the Law of Property Act 1925, and has already generated its fair share of case law, has enabled the section on the enforceability of contracts to be scaled down. Similarly, s 3, abolishing the rule in *Bain v Fothergill* has enabled the chapter on damages also to be pruned.

Other important ares where legislation has occurred include those of the enforceability of covenants in leases and covenants for title. Another, quite radical, piece of legislation was the Trust of Land and Appointment of Trustees Act 1996 which, at the time of writing, is yet to be brought into force. This occasioned some difficulty in incorporating it into the text, appearing as it did at a late stage in the preparation of this edition. I hope to have given its provisions sufficient coverage to be helpful, while still retaining coverage of the existing law which will continue to be relevant for some time to come.

Neither have the courts been inactive. Along with the steady flow of relevant case law, the main developments have been concerned with mortgage repossession cases, culminating with the seminal decision in *Barclays Bank plc v O'Brien* and ensuing developments. This has led to a certain recasting of the section concerned with overiding interests.

In preparing this edition, I had the considerable advantage of being given draft revisions of several chapters by Graham Barnsley. While these proved to be of considerable value, I was also given a free hand with this edition and so I am solely responsible for the final outcome. I am very grateful, however, for

the encouragement provided by him throughout. I am also extremely grateful to the editorial staff at Butterworths, who have displayed almost stoic patience in the face of continuing delays in the production of this edition, and have been very supportive throughout.

The bulk of the text was delivered to the publishers in July 1996, although it has been possible to make some further amendments thereafter. I have tried to state the law as at 31 August 1996.

M P Thompson
University of Leicester

Preface to the First Edition

'Of making many books there is no end; and
much study is a weariness of the flesh.'
(Ecclesiastes, Chap. XII, v. 12)

The opening part of this quotation could well be taken as an apt description of the steady stream of new law books currently flowing from the printer's press. Nevertheless, I make no apology for adding to this number, for I have long felt there to be a need for a book which explains the mysteries of conveyancing, especially to students who may never have seen the inside of a solicitor's office. At a time when the solicitor's monopoly on conveyancing is being challenged, it is imperative that the aspiring conveyancer is thoroughly versed in the law and practice of his calling. The practical skills, including the art of drafting documents, he can acquire in the office, but he must generally look elsewhere for an understanding of the underlying legal rules and principles. This book, which attempts to discuss the principles of conveyancing in a practical setting, has been written primarily for the undergraduate and the articled clerk, although I cherish the fond hope that the book may be of some value to the qualified practitioner. Suggestions are sometimes made (by the uninformed) that conveyancing requires no special skills or knowledge. The pages of this book should go some way towards demonstrating the falsity of such notions.

I have sought to deal with matters chronologically as they are likely to arise in a normal conveyancing transaction, whether the title to the land is registered or unregistered. Two comments should, perhaps, be made. First, I have departed from this order in one important respect. The drafting of the conveyance (or transfer) must necessarily precede the completion of the transaction. However, it seemed to me to be desirable to to have a separate section relating to conveyancing documents, rather than to attempt to slot this important subject into its correct chronological sequence. Secondly, the spread of registration of title renders it necessary to consider in detail the general principles of land registration at an early stage of the book, thus facilitating the consideration of various aspects of registered conveyancing in the subsequent pages. It is to be regretted that registration of title is not a topic which receives staisfactory treatment in real property text books, and the majority of land law courses pay but scant attention to the system. Needless to say, the solicitor of tomorrow requires a thorough understanding of the operation of the Land Registration Act 1925. Unfortunately, the need to consider two separate systems of land transfer has added considerably to the size of the book.

I have assumed that the reader has a basic knowledge of the principles of real property, equity and contract, and in the main I have refrained from covering ground that is adequately dealt with by the standard land law text books. Some overlap has been unavoidable.

Every solicitor involved in a conveyancing transaction should be familiar with the Conditions of Sale regulating the contract of sale. I have, therefore, sought to give due prominence to the terms of the National Conditions of Sale and the Law Society's Conditions of Sale. Partly because of personal preference, partly out of desire not to confuse the reader unnecessarily, I have concentrated upon the National Conditions of Sale, though in no sense have I attempted to write a commentary on these Conditions. I should like to thank Oyez Publishing Limited, the copyright owners of the National Conditions of Sale, for allowing me to reproduce the front page of their contract form and the Conditions of Sale. I am also grateful to The Law Society for granting permission to quote extracts from their Conditions of Sale.

A wind of change is now blowing over the conveyancing scene, heralding future reforms. The Law Commission are currently looking at various topics in an attempt to simplify the transfer of land. As yet, few of their recommendations have reached the statute book, but the next decade may well see the enactment of several important changes. I have sought to draw the reader's attention to the Commission's tentative proposals, where matters are still under review, though much of the information has, perforce, been relegated to the footntoes.

I am deeply indebted to my friend and former colleague, Professor M J Goodman, who has read the whole of the manuscript; his invaluable comments have saved me from many mistakes. For such errors, inconsistencies and imperfections that remain, I alone am responsible. Thanks are also due to Mr Simon Palk who has kindly read the proofs, to Mrs Barbara Abram and to my wife, both of whom rendered sterling assistance with the typing, and, by no means least, to the publishers who have so patiently endured my dilatory ways.

I have endeavoured to state the law in accordance with the material at my disposal on 30 September 1972. It has been possible, when correctng the proofs, to take account of a number of subsequent developments, mainly in the footnotes.

Finally, I should like to express the hope that, despite the length of this book, those who study its pages will not be afflicted by that 'weariness of the flesh' which seems to have plagued the Preacher of old.

January 1973   DGB

Contents

Table of statutes

References in this Table to *Statutes* are to Halsbury's Statutes of England (Fourth edition) showing the volume and page at which the annotated text of the Act may be found.

References in **bold** type indicate where the section of an Act is set out in part or in full.

xvi   **Table of statutes**

Table of cases

xxvii

PAGE

PAGE

I

M

P

PAGE

List of abbreviations

Statutes and Rules

AEA 1925	Administration of Estates Act 1925
AJA 1977	Administration of Justice Act 1977
AJA 1982	Administration of Justice Act 1982
AJA 1985	Administration of Justice Act 1985
LCA 1925	Land Charges Act 1925
LCA 1972	Land Charges Act 1972
LLCA 1975	Local Land Charges Act 1975
LPA 1922	Law of Property Act 1922
LPA 1925	Law of Property Act 1925
LP(Am)A 1926	Law of Property (Amendment) Act 1926
LPA 1969	Law of Property Act 1969
LRA 1925	Land Registration Act 1925
LRA 1986	Land Registration Act 1986
LR & LCA 1971	Land Registration and Land Charges Act 1971
LRR 1925	Land Registration Rules 1925
MHA 1983	Matrimonial Homes Act 1983
SLA 1925	Settled Land Act 1925

Books and Periodicals

Brickdale	Brickdale and Stewart-Wallace, *The Land Registration Act 1925* (4th edn, 1939).
C & B	Cheshire and Burn's *Modern Law of Real Property* (13th edn, 1982).
CLJ	Cambridge Law Journal
Co Litt	Coke's Commentary on Littleton's *Tenures* (19th edn, 1832, with notes by F Hargrave and C Butler).
Conv (NS)	The Conveyancer and Properry Lawyer (new series).
Conv Prec	The Conveyancer and Property Lawyer, Precedents for the Conveyancer.
Dart	Dart, *Treatise on the Law and Practice Relating to Vendors and Purchasers of Real Estate* (2 vols) (8th edn, 1929).

Emmet	Emmet, *Notes on Perusing Titles and on Practical Conveyancing* (19th edn, 1986).
Ency F & P	Encyclopaedia of Forms and Precedents (23 vols) (4th edn, 1966–72).
Farrand	Farrand, *Contract and Conveyance* (4th edn, 1983).
Gibson	Gibson, *Conveyancing* (21st edn, 1980).
Hallett	Hallett, *Conveyancing Precedents* (1965).
Hayton	Hayton, *Registered Land* (3rd edn, 1981).
JPL	Journal of Planning and Property Law.
K & E	Key and Elphnstone, *Precedents in Conveyancing* (3 vols) (15th edn, 1953–54).
LQR	Law Quarterly Review.
LS Gaz	The Law Society's Gazette.
MLR	Modern Law Review
M & W	Megarry and Wade, *The Law of Real Property* (5th edn, 1985).
NLJ	New Law Journal
Parker's Precedents	Parker, *Modern Conveyancing Precedents* (1964)
Potter	Potter, *Principles and Practice of Conveyancing under the Land Registration Act 1925* (1934).
Prideaux's Precedents	Prideaux, *Forms and Precedents in Conveyancing* (3 vols) (25th edn, 1958–59).
R & R	Ruoff and Roper, *Registered Conveyancing* (5th edn, 1986).
Snell	Snell, *Principles of Equity* (28th edn, 1982).
Sol Jo	Solicitor's Journal.
Walford	Walford, *Contracts and Conditions of Sale of Land* (2nd edn, 1957).
W & C	Wolstenholme and Cherry, *Conveyancing Statutes* (13th edn, 1972).
Wilkinson	Wilkinson, *Standard Conditions of Sale of Land* (3rd edn, 1982).
Williams Title	Williams on Title (4th edn, 1975).
Williams V & P	Williams, *A Treatise on the Law of Vendor and Purchaser* (2 vols) (4th edn, 1936).

Reports

Conveyancing Report	Second Report of the Conveyancing Committee, *Conveyancing Simplifications*, 1985 (The Farrand Report).
Law Com No	Law Commission Reports (various).
Royal Commission on Legal Services	The Royal Commission on Legal Services (2 vols).

Part One

Introduction

Chapter 1

Conveyancing procedures in outline

A   Introduction

Compared with other forms of property, land has always occupied a peculiar position in English law. Though not itself the subject of ownership, save in the sense dictated by the doctrine of tenure that all land is owned by the Crown, it is capable of supporting a number of estates and interests which exist quite separately from the land and which are themselves capable of ownership and alienation. For centuries land was the most important form of wealth and it has long been necessary to regulate the manner in which land, or rather estates in land, could be acquired. It is not the scheme of this chapter to consider the history of different forms of land transfer[1]. Nor is it our concern to trace the wide divergencies, which have existed in our law since the earliest times, between the law of real property, or land, and personal property. Suffice it to say that despite the assimilation of realty and personalty effected by the property legislation of 1925[2], several important differences still persist, which render it necessary to distinguish between the transfer of goods and of land.

Particularly is this true as to the mode of alienation. A contract for the sale of, say, a valuable painting may be negotiated and finalised within a few minutes. Neither the contract nor the transfer of ownership is subject to any special formalities. Physical delivery of the painting to the buyer suffices to transfer the ownership to him. But a contract for the sale of an estate in land cannot be effected so simply. Physical delivery of the subject-matter of the contract, the estate, is not possible. A transfer can only be effected by a deed[3]. The contract itself must be in writing[4]. Furthermore, the land may be subject

1   Brief mention of some of the more important forms is made in Ch 16, pp 447–448 post. See more fully Holdsworth, *A History of English Law*, Vol iii, 217–56; Vol vii, 353–87.
2   See Cheshire, 88, 93.
3   LPA 1925, s 52(1). This has not always been the rule. At common law, a feoffment with livery of seisin did not require writing to be valid, though it was not uncommon to execute a charter of feoffment as evidence of the transaction. Writing did not become essential until the Statute of Frauds 1677, s 1, but by this time the feoffment had been superseded by other more convenient forms of alienation. The system of conveyancing by deeds may be said to have sprung from the Statute of Enrolments 1535. This statute was passed to prevent the Statute of Uses 1535 operating to pass a legal estate by means of an oral bargain and sale, which in equity created a use in favour of the purchaser. It required every bargain and sale of an estate of inheritance to be made by writing, indented, sealed and enrolled in a court of record.
4   Law of Property (Miscellaneous Provisions) Act 1989, s 2.

3

to third-party rights, and unless the purchaser conducts adequate inquiries as to their existence he may find his enjoyment of the land disturbed. The procedures in complexities of our land law prompted Baron Pollock to make the following comparison during the course of his opinion delivered to the Lords in the famous case of *Bain v Fothergill*[5] – that whereas a man who sells goods must be taken to know whether they are his or not, no layman can be supposed to know what is the exact nature of his title to real property, or whether it be good against the whole world or not. Whilst this comment should now be read in the light of the simplification of our land law structure effected by the legislation of 1925, it does serve to show the need for a purchaser of land to investigate his vendor's title in order to verify that he is able to convey what he has contracted to convey. An investigation of this nature is not normally considered necessary, nor undertaken, on a sale of goods.

A transfer on sale of an estate in land is traditionally divisible into two distinct stages: (i) the contract stage, ending with the formation of an enforceable contract for sale, (ii) the conveyance stage, culminating in the legal title vesting in the purchaser by means of the appropriate instrument under seal. Often in practice the two stages almost merge into one. It may be helpful to give a brief survey of the main stages in a typical vendor-purchaser transaction[6]. It will be left to later chapters of the book to fill in the detail and explain the effects of the various steps in the chain of procedure. The position where the land is unregistered and therefore not affected by the Land Registration Act 1925, will be considered first.

B   Unregistered land

(a)   Preparation of contract[7]
Assuming the parties intend to proceed by way of a formal contract, a contract is drafted in duplicate by the vendor's solicitor and forwarded to the purchaser's solicitor for approval. It is frequently prepared on a printed form of contract, known as the Standard Conditions of Sale, which contains a host of terms which regulate the rights of the parties in relation to the transaction. The Standard Conditions of Sale, now in their third edition, were introduced in 1990 and are intended to supersede the two forms that were previously in common use, the National Conditions of Sale and the Law Society's Conditions of Sale. The contract should contain a full description of the land to be sold, the liabilities subject to which it is held and any special terms (Special Conditions of Sale) agreed upon by the parties. The title deeds or register of title should be perused and full instructions obtained from the vendor before any attempt is made to draft the contract.

5   (1874) LR 7 HL 158 at 173, p 584. See also *Re Spencer and Hauser's Contract* [1928] Ch 598 at 607, per Tomlin J.
6   For a detailed table of the usual procedure on a sale of freehold unregistered land, reference should be made to 18 Ency F & P, 374. See also the chart given in the Royal Commission's Report on Legal Services (1979), para 21.20.
7   See Ch 6.

(b)   Approval of contract

It is the responsibility of the purchaser's solicitor to approve the draft contract, subject to any desired amendments. Strictly, approval is dependent upon the results of certain searches and inquiries that are customarily made[8], as follows:

(i)   a search in the register of local land charges to ascertain the existence of any charges affecting the property;

(ii) additional inquiries of local authorities to discover details of matters within their knowledge, which are not registrable as local land charges but are of equal concern to a purchaser;

(iii) preliminary inquiries made of the vendor to elicit information about the property upon matters which the vendor is under no general duty to disclose in the contract.

At one time it was the invariable practice for the purchaser's solicitor to requisition the local search and submit his own preliminary inquiries. Nowadays it is fairly common for the local search certificate, obtained by the vendor, and replies to the standard inquiries to be forwarded by his solicitor along with the draft contract; this practice is now laid down by the National Protocol. Approval of the draft contract is signified by returning one copy to the vendor's solicitor. Each solicitor then obtains his client's signature to the contract in his possession.

(c)   Exchange of contracts[9]

No binding agreement comes into existence until contracts are exchanged. The precise way in which this exchange is effected varies in practice. As part of this procedure the purchaser is normally required to pay a deposit to the vendor's solicitor. Exchange of contracts represents the crossing of the legal Rubicon, so to speak. As a general rule, neither party can subsequently withdraw from the transaction without committing a breach of contract, unless the other party consents.

(d)   Deducing title[10]

The law has never required a vendor to furnish any evidence of his legal entitlement to the subject-matter of the contract until the parties are in a contractual relationship. After exchange of contracts he must provide the purchaser with a chronological statement of the documents and events by virtue of which he became entitled to the property. Formerly this duty was discharged by the preparation of a document, known as an abstract of title, which set out the required information in a special format. It covered a period of time fixed by the contract. Today it is standard practice to supply photographic copies of all relevant deeds within the period. In due course the vendor will be called upon to verify the contents of the abstract. This stage in

8   See Ch 7.
9   See Ch 8.
10 See Ch 9. For the meaning of this word 'title', see pp 266–269, post.

the transaction is generally termed 'deducing title'. The past two decades have witnessed significant changes in conveyancing procedures. Today it is commonplace for the vendor to deduce his title before exchange of contracts. This in turn enables the purchaser to satisfy himself as to its acceptability before he is contractually bound to buy. These new practices are seen by many solicitors as necessary developments in order to simplify, shorten and cheapen the conveyancing process.

(e)   Investigation of title[11]

The purchaser's solicitor bases his assessment of the soundness of the vendor's title on his perusal of the copy documents, and their subsequent verification by examination against the originals in the vendor's possession. In practice the examination is performed at the time of completion (as to which see the next stage). The purchaser's solicitor submits any doubts or inquiries about the state of the title to the vendor's solicitor in the form of requisitions on title which set out the purchaser's requirements for putting the title in order. If he is dissatisfied with the vendor's answers, he may submit further observations on these replies. In practice the provisions of the contract curtail a purchaser's right to raise requisitions and further observations ad infinitum. It is essential to undertake this investigation notwithstanding that the title has recently been investigated on a previous sale. A purchaser should never rely on the investigation conducted on behalf of someone else. Not only might mistakes have been made, but the previous owner might have accepted risks in relation to some matter immaterial to him, but perhaps vital to the purchaser. It is the responsibility of the purchaser's solicitor to prepare the draft conveyance which is submitted in duplicate to the vendor's solicitor normally at the same time as, and subject to, the requisitions. It is also his task to engross (ie type) the conveyance, after approval, for execution by the parties[12].

(f)   Completion[13]

This is the final step in the transaction. Completion takes place usually at the offices of the vendor's solicitor. On receipt of the balance of the purchase money, the purchaser becomes entitled to the deeds of the property, including the conveyance to him, duly executed. It is this document which operates under s 52(1) of the Law of Property Act 1925, to convey the legal estate to the purchaser. After completion various tasks, generally of a minor nature, remain to be performed but specific mention of these need not be made here.

---

11   See Ch 12.
12   Most purchases of residential property are financed with the aid of a mortgage. Where a separate solicitor acts for the mortgagee, he conducts his own investigation of the title on behalf of the mortgagee. The purchaser's solicitor deduces title and answers any requisitions raised by the mortgagee's solicitor, whose task it also is to draft the mortgage deed. Institutional lenders have their own printed forms of mortgage which merely require completing by the insertion of the mortgagor's name and address, details of the loan and a description of the property.
13   See Ch 14.

C   Registered conveyancing

1.   Historical development

The system of unregistered conveyancing is self-perpetuating. On a sale of land the purchaser investigates the title in a manner briefly described above. The same process is repeated when he comes to sell. Though we have seen that there are valid reasons why a purchaser should not rely on a previous investigation, the work involved is largely repetitive and represents a high wastage of man-hours, to say nothing of higher costs borne by the public. Attempts to reform the system of land transfer go back many years. As early as 1830 the Real Property Commissioners reported that :

> The great difficulties which occur in selling estates and obtaining money on real security, the time which usually elapses before the completion of such transactions, and the harassing expenses and disappointments which attend them, are evils universally acknowledged.

The first statutory attempt in 1862 to give certainty to the title to land and to simplify dealings with it proved to be a total failure[14]. Other Acts followed in 1875 and 1892[15]. These were eventually replaced by the Land Registration Act 1925, which introduced a number of important changes. This Act, together with the Land Registration Rules 1925, made under it, contains the bulk of the relevant law on land registration.

Compulsory registration was extended to a particular area by means of an Order in Council; thereafter, certain transactions affecting land in that area led to first registration of title[16]. At the time of the Act of 1925, it was uncertain whether registration of title was desirable on a large scale and so compulsory registration could only be introduced subject to certain safeguards, which were abolished in 1966[17]. Since then, there has been an increased commitment by the government to speed up the process of registration of title, with the result that, as of 1 December 1990, the whole of England and Wales is now subject to compulsory registration of title[18]. It is important to realise, however, that this does not mark the demise of unregistered conveyancing[19]. Herein lies a potential source of danger for practitioners, who will need to remain conversant with these principles for upward of at least 25 years. The Land Registry has estimated[20] that, even without special factors, 1% of land can continue to remain unregistered for as long as 80 years after the introduction of compulsory registration in a given area.

14   The Land Registry Act 1862.
15   The Land Transfer Acts of those years, the second of which made registration compulsory for the first time in certain parts of London.
16   LRA 1925, ss 120(1), 123(1), p 23, post.
17   LRA 1966, s 1(1), enacting that the LRA 1925, ss 120(2), 121, and 122, should cease to have effect; repealed as obsolete by the Statute Law (Repeals) Act 1995.
18   SI 1989/1347.
19   Thus in 1991/92, there were over 300,000 first registrations of title: a process that will have been preceded by the carrying out of unregistered conveyancing procedures. See Chief Land Registrar's Report 1992/93.
20   2 Conveyancing Standing Committee Report (1985), para 4.73. See, also, *Completing The Land Register in England and Wales,* Land Registry Discussion and Consultation Paper (1992).

2.   Objectives of system

The Act of 1925 has as its principal objective the simplification of land transfer. Its title is misleading, for it deals with a system, not of registration of land, but of titles to land. Basically it provides for the registration under separate and distinct titles of freehold estates and certain leasehold estates in land. The essential features of this system are:

1. The establishment of a register of title to freehold and leasehold land containing a more-or-less complete record of all matters relating to each registered title, including the name of the proprietor and the incumbrances and other interests affecting the land.
2. The provision of a facile mode of transfer by eliminating the lengthy investigation of title[1] and simplifying documents of transfer.
3. The introduction of a state indemnity scheme under which compensation is paid to a registered proprietor deprived of his title.

On a transfer of registered land it is unnecessary for the purchaser to delve into the past history of the land in order to discover whether the vendor has a good title. A once-and-for-all investigation of title has in fact been conducted by the Registry at the time of first registration[2]. All the purchaser must do is satisfy himself that the vendor is the registered proprietor subject only to those third party interests disclosed in the contract. This he can do simply by inspecting a copy of the entries in the register, which the vendor can readily supply. It should be understood that this brief explanation amounts to something of an over-simplification, and the reader will encounter exceptions and qualifications in the subsequent pages.

The advantages of land registration[3] are seen in relation to what has previously been described as the conveyance stage. The procedure leading up to exchange of contracts remains much the same. Ultimately the transaction is completed, but unlike the normal position in unregistered conveyancing the purchaser of registered land does not at this stage acquire the legal title. A further step is necessary – registration.

3.   Effect on substantive law

The purpose of the land registration legislation has been to simplify land transfer within the basic framework of the land law. It does not seek to introduce substantive changes applicable solely to registered land. A few examples taken at random may help to demonstrate this vital consideration.

---

1   For a brief judicial survey of the Act's design, see Lord Wilberforce in *Williams & Glyn's Bank Ltd v Boland* [1981] AC 487 at 503, 1980] 2 All ER 408 at 412, HL.
2   Should the title be defective in some material respect, the proprietor may be registered with an inferior grade of title; see p 35, post.
3   See HM Land Registry Explanatory Leaflet No 1, which lists 12 general characteristics and advantages, starting with its finality and certainty.

1. The Act provides for the registration of legal estates which are defined to mean 'the estates' interests and charges in or over land which are, by the Law of Property Act 1925, authorised to subsist or be created at law'[4].
2. The register of title is merely intended to be a substitute for title deeds and by and large it does not record any information not revealed in title deeds.
3. Section 82(1)(g) of the Act permits rectification of the register so as to deprive the proprietor of his title where a legal estate has been registered in the name of a person who if the land had not been registered would not have been the estate owner[5].

The reader must not conclude that the Act makes no changes in the law of real property as it affects registered land. There are important differences[6] which necessarily flow from the changes made in the machinery of conveyancing. Basic differences exist as to the method of creation of legal rights, their disposition and mode of protection. In particular it should be noted that once a title has been registered, it is registration alone that operates to vest a legal title in the transferee. A duly executed transfer of registered land does not of itself have the same effect as a conveyance of unregistered land[7].

4 Reform?

For many years it has been felt that the land registration system was in need of a thorough overhaul, a task that was naturally assigned initially to the Law Commission. Their first Working Paper (No 32), dealing mainly with leases, was circulated for comment as long ago as 1970. Others followed at regular intervals. This long period of discussion and consultation has so far not been very productive in legislative terms, which signifies, perhaps, the complexities of the problems confronting the Commission. To date, the sole product of their deliberations in the field of land registration is the Land Registration Acts 1986 and 1988. But much more is in store.

April 1987 saw the publication of their long-awaited Report (No 178) covering three major areas: overriding interests, rectification and indemnity, and minor interests. This 'substantial and significant'[8] Report will be analysed in Part II of the book. Unlike other reports, this was submitted without any appended draft Bill. Work on a comprehensive new statute was already in progress, and a draft Bill is likely to be published in the near future. However, it may be a few years yet before a new Act is in force. The operation of any new

---

4 LRA 1925, ss 2(1), 3(xi).
5 See further p 88, post.
6 Yet a purchaser cannot obtain registration without a transfer from the vendor. See pp 473–479, post.
7 For the view, by no means entirely justified, that there has in the past existed a general failure to appreciate the full impact of these changes, so retarding the development of distinctive registration principles, see (1972) 88 LQR 93, 94–97, 136–37 (D C Jackson).
8 See Law Com No 159 (21 Annual Report), para 2.43.

legislation will be dependent on a revision of the Rules of 1925, which could prove more of a headache than a redrafting of the principal Act.

D   Simplification – the future of conveyancing

The 1980s have witnessed a revolution in the conveyancing process in terms of procedures, personnel and charges. The wind of change, which this book in its first edition (1973) maintained was blowing across the conveyancing scene, has since developed into a tornado, uprooting many traditional practices. And it shows no sign of abating. Conveyancing 1990s style at times bears little resemblance to that of the 1970s, due in no small measure to the spread of land registration. Some changes have already been noted; others will be encountered throughout this book. Two important developments deserve mention here. As a result of measures by local law societies to standardise procedures within their areas of influence, the idea was mooted of producing national guidelines. This has now resulted in the production of the National Protocol intended for use in all residential conveyancing transactions. As part of this standardisation procedure, a new form of contract, the Standard Conditions of Sale, has also been produced, the intention being that this contract should replace the pre-existing alternatives. Although the use of the new Protocol and contract is not compulsory, the growing familiarity of solicitors with them has led to their widespread use.

1.   Government initiatives

Much of the impetus for change has been generated by the Conservative government, anxious to extend home ownership. One aspect of this policy has been a declared aim to simplify and cheapen house transfer, ostensibly for the benefit of the new property-owning democracy. This resulted in 1984 in the setting up of a Committee (The Farrand Committee), charged with the task of considering (inter alia) 'the scope for simplifying conveyancing practice and procedure'[9]. This committee produced a host of recommendations, some of which will never see the light of day; others are under active consideration by the Law Commission or its Standing Committee.

Their primary recommendation urged the setting up of this Standing Committee, a suggestion first proposed by the Royal Commission on Legal Services in 1979. The Committee was duly set up in October 1987 with the following terms of reference[10]:

> 'to consider matters relating to conveyancing practice and procedure, to advise the Law Commission on reform of conveyancing law, and to promote changes in practice and procedure necessary to create and maintain a cheap, simple and effective conveyancing system from the point of view of buyers and sellers of land.'

9   2 Report, paras 1.1, 1.6–8. For a not very flattering critique of their recommendations, see [1985] Conv 101 (J E Adams).

10   HL Written Answer, 31 July 1986, Vol 467, col 329.

The Committee has been working on various topics[11]: pre-contract deposits, mortgage certificates, protocols, preliminary inquiries, deposits and restrictive covenants. However, the Committee has been given an impossible brief. Their terms of reference include the primary objective to 'bring about within two years improvements' apparent to ordinary housebuyers and sellers. Apart from the ludicrously short time allowed, it is not clear how in practical terms this objective is to be achieved. Whilst some recommendations may not call for legislative backing, their implementation is governed by the willingness of conveyancers to bring them into operation. This in turn depends on their being satisfied that the proposed changes are in the best interests of their clients. Certain of the proposals have had little impact. The pre-contract deposit scheme has not been widely adopted and the plan to curb gazumping by the introduction of the Scottish system of selling houses has not been accepted. The recommendations concerned with the standardisation of preliminary enquiries have met with rather more success, the introduction of the National Protocol representing a considerable improvement on the previous position.

2.   The conveyancing monopoly

The Administration of Justice Act 1985[12], broke the solicitors' long-standing and cherished conveyancing monopoly. The Act permits all forms of conveyancing to be undertaken by a new breed of conveyancers, called licensed conveyancers and regulated by a new body, the Council for Licensed Conveyancers. Under s 12(2) of the Act, a twofold duty is laid on the Council, to ensure: (i) that standards of competence and professional conduct among licensed conveyancers are sufficient to ensure adequate protection for consumers, and (ii) that their conveyancing services are provided economically and efficiently. The Council has promulgated practice and account rules[13], similar to those that apply to solicitors. Licensed conveyancers are covered by compulsory indemnity insurance and are required to contribute to a compensation fund. They can be disqualified from practice (permanently or temporarily) on failure to comply with professional rules, or on breach of a condition attached to the licence. This is the ultimate sanction.

The first licences were granted on 1 May 1987. In their dealings with licensed conveyancers solicitors have been directed[14] to proceed on the basis that the conveyancer is a solicitor, bound by the same professional obligations. This is an important rule to observe, especially in relation to the acceptance of undertakings, and the use of various codes which The Law Society has devised to assist in the conduct of conveyancing transactions[15]. In the following pages

---

11   First Annual Report, 1985–86, Law Com No 159.
12   This development was given impetus by the House Buyers' Bill, a private member's Bill introduced in the Commons in December 1984, and surprisingly given a second reading. It was withdrawn on the Government's assurance to introduce specific measures to permit what the Bill sought to achieve.
13   As required by ss 20–23 of the Act.
14   (1987) 84 LS Gaz 1202.
15   See pp 223–225, post (exchange of contracts), pp 417–419, post (postal completions).

of this book 'solicitor' (or 'practitioner') is to be taken as including a licensed conveyancer, unless the context requires otherwise. A more fundamental inroad into the solicitors' conveyancing monopoly has been made by the Building Societies Act 1986. This enables building societies[16] to become recognised institutions for the purposes of providing conveyancing services[17]. This would facilitate the development of a 'one-stop' house-buying service whereby the purchaser could obtain conveyancing and lending services from a single source. It is envisaged[18] that the actual services would be provided by solicitors or licensed conveyancers employed by the institution, and they would continue to be amenable to the disciplinary procedures of their respective professions. One obvious area of major concern is the potential for acute conflict of interest arising when a recognised institution acts for itself and the purchaser-borrower. It is not easy to see how the institution will be in a position to offer independent advice, when the person proffering it is employed by the other party to the transaction. And what of the traditional solicitor-client relationship? This problem has been duly acknowledged. According to a Commons' statement, the rules regulating these institutions are to prohibit them from acting for persons who are also borrowing from them[19]. This difficulty apart, banks and building societies have not so far shown themselves to be desperately anxious to enter the fray. Perhaps they realise that the low profit-margins in residential conveyancing make it a rather unattractive venture. Yet it may only be a matter of time[20].

3. Conveyancing costs

The Royal Commission on Legal Services reported in 1979 that their investigations did not indicate that conveyancing charges were excessive[1]. Since then increased competition among solicitors themselves and the fear of losing work to outside bodies have resulted in a sharp decrease in charges. Moreover, buyers and sellers can now 'shop around' to find the lowest quotation[2]. A survey commissioned by The Law Society and published in January 1987,

16 And any other body corporate (eg bank, assurance company) or any unincorporated association: s 124, Sch 21, para 1(2).
17 The recognition rules will be framed by the Lord Chancellor, but the power to recognise individual institutions may be delegated to a nominated officer: Sch 21, paras 2, 5. Conveyancing services are defined by para 1(3).
18 HL Debates, 18 July 1986, Vol 478, col 1106.
19 HC Written Answer, 6 December 1985, Vol 88, col 354. The restriction would extend to the provision of services indirectly through a subsidiary company (eg a nationwide firm of estate agents) in which they hold a majority stake. See also HC Standing Committee A, 20 February 1986, cols 475–80. Will there not also be a potential conflict of interest when acting for itself and the *vendor*?
20 But note a different development. To maintain their primary role in the domestic property scene, some solicitors' firms have begun to promote a property selling service. There is now a thriving National Association of Solicitors Property Centres; see (1986) 83 LS Gaz 3321 (D Bennett), (1987) 84 LS Gaz 2992 (L Dunbow).
1   Cmnd 7648, para 21.86.
2   The Law Society has issued Notes for the guidance of solicitors on giving information about conveyancing charges: (1985) 82 LS Gaz 3058, 3065–66.

revealed[3] that even established clients were prepared to have their conveyancing work undertaken by another firm if the price were right, whilst retaining the family solicitor for other legal matters. The newly acquired liberty to advertise conveyancing charges has led some firms to offer a 'no frills' type of service at a fixed price, sometimes as low as £75 plus VAT and disbursements for a sale or purchase. These solicitors aim to have minimal direct contact with the client, and the fee charged provides no incentive to give adequate advice when problems or snags develop. This scramble for business will inevitably rebound on the profession at large[4]. Standards will drop; unprofessional practices will increase; complaints about shoddy work will abound; and insurers will constantly be settling negligence claims. Moreover, inferior conveyancing standards at lower costs can hardly be in the long term interests of the public. The old adage proclaims that one gets what one pays for, but this is no motto for any practitioner to display over his door.

There can be no doubt that cheaper and (potentially) quicker conveyancing has been facilitated by modern technological advances. The use of conveyancing support systems is now widespread. Different computer software packages have been marketed to assist with routine work. They are designed to monitor the progress of individual transactions, to collect and disseminate information, to remind of timetables and advise of outstanding matters. They are also equipped to prepare common form letters and produce standard precedents, though what effect this will have on the drafting skills of the next generation of conveyancers is a moot point. Some support packages are able to give limited guidance by suggesting what should be the next form to use. But by and large they are not sufficiently sophisticated to be able to evaluate information and act on it. Interestingly, in their evidence[5] to the Farrand Committee in 1984, the Society for Computers and Law and Technology and Law Ltd indicated that some evaluation of information might gradually become the subject of assistance by 'expert' computer systems, but this was not likely to happen for some time. The Committee themselves strongly recommended[6] that the full potential of computers should be harnessed by all participants in the conveyancing process. Conveyancing in the twenty-first century will be vastly different from conveyancing today. But it is today's law and practice with which this book is concerned.

---

3   See Lawyer, February 1987, p 15. The same survey revealed that increased competition and 'shopping-around' had within four years caused a 25% drop in fees, stated as a percentage of average house prices.
4   For expressions of concern at this and related developments, see the correspondence at (1985) 82 LS Gaz 1826–27, 2048, 3311, 3653; (1986) 83 LS Gaz 2708, 3121.
5   Reproduced at (1984) 81 LS Gaz 2687.
6   2 Report, para 9.27. Part VI of the Report considers fully the scope for the use of computers and electronic communication devices in conveyancing.

Part Two

The system of land registration

Chapter 2

General principles of land registration

A The administrative machinery

The main statutes in force relating to registration of title to land are the Land Registration Acts[1] of 1925, 1936, 1986 and 1988. The bulk of the relevant law is contained in the Act of 1925, but this is no more than a skeleton of the basic provisions. The detailed rules are left to be worked out by various Land Registration Rules[2] made under s 144 of the parent statute. These have the same force as if they had been enacted in the Act. Unfortunately, the drafting of the Act and the Rules leaves something to be desired, and inconsistencies and obscurities are not difficult to find.

1. The Land Registry

Section 126(1) of the Act of 1925 provides for the continuance of an office[3] in London to be called Her Majesty's Land Registry, the business of which is to be conducted by a registrar appointed by the Lord Chancellor and known as the Chief Land Registrar.

Section 132 enables district land registries to be created for the purposes of registration of titles to land within a particular area. The increase in the volume of business over the years has resulted in the establishment at periodic intervals of district registries, of which there are now 19 in different parts of the country[4]. Each district registry is the proper office for the registration of titles to land in its district and for the delivery of any application relating to

---

1 Except where otherwise indicated, textual references in Chs 2, 3 and 4 to 'the Act' or 'the Rules' are references to the LRA 1925, and the LRR 1925, respectively.
2 These being principally the Rules of 1925, 1976, 1977, 1978, 1986, 1989 and 1990, and the Land Registration (Open Register) Rules 1991.
3 This is in fact the same office (under a new title) as that originally established by the Land Registry Act 1862, s 108. It is located at Lincoln's Inn Fields, London, WC2.
4 At Birkenhead, Coventry, Croydon, Durham, Gloucester, Harrow, Hull, Leicester, Lytham, Nottingham, Peterborough, Plymouth, Portsmouth, Stevenage, Swansea, Telford, Tunbridge Wells, Weymouth and York. A complete and up-to-date list of the areas covered by each district registry is contained in Explanatory Leaflet No 9, obtainable from any registry.

such land. The London office is not responsible for any area and does not accept applications.

There are maintained at the various registries (in relation to land within the areas which they serve) the following:

(i) A register of title to freehold and leasehold land[5]. This comprises the sum total of all registered titles. Except where they are now held by computer, the individual particulars of each title are maintained on a vast card index system, stored in filing cabinets. The introduction of computerisation, facilitated by the Administration of Justice Act 1982[6], is now gathering pace, and the Registry hopes to be fully computerised by the end of the century.

(ii) Index maps, collectively termed the public index map, which show the position and extent of every registered estate[7]. As its name suggests, it is available for inspection by any member of the public.

(iii) An index of proprietors' names in alphabetical order, showing the numbers of the titles, charges, or incumbrances of' which the several persons mentioned therein are proprietors[8].

(iv) A list of pending applications, also open to public inspection[9].

The role played by these various documents will be more fully discussed in this chapter and elsewhere in the book.

During 1990 the structure of the Land Registry was radically changed. On 2 June it acquired executive agency status as part of the Conservative Government's policy for improving management in the Civil Service. As such it has become a separate, self-financing department. This new status, it is claimed, should enable the Registry to achieve significant improvements in the services which it provides[10].

2.   The Chief Land Registrar

At the head of this complex system is the Chief Land Registrar. He is statutorily charged with the conduct of the Registry's business[11]. However, to pave the way for the structural changes effected in 1990, he is no longer required to be legally qualified[12]. In effect the Chief Land Registrar has become the agency's

---

5   LRA 1925, s 1(1), as substituted by the AJA 1982, s 66.
6   Section 66(1), which enables the register to be kept in a non-documentary form. All of the district registries operate a computerised application processing system: see R & R, 1.11.
7   LRR 1925, r 8. See p 209, post.
8   LRR 1925, r 9.
9   LRR 1925, r 10, as substituted by the LRR 1978, r 4.
10   See HL Debates, 5 April 1990, Vol 57, col 1615; HM Land Registry Report 1989–90, paras 68–71. One benefit will be the Registry's ability to retain any surplus of receipts over expenditure, enabling it to sustain services and reduce, or avoid increasing, fees.
11   LRA 1925, s 126(1).
12   The Courts and Legal Services Act 1990, Sch 17, para 3, removed the necessity for the legal qualification introduced by the AJA 1956, s 53.

chief executive. The post is now open to any person with the requisite managerial skills and the potential to exercise them in a large legal organisation[13].

The important legal functions previously discharged by the Registrar have now largely been entrusted to a legally qualified registrar, known as the Solicitor to HM Land Registry. Those acts which he may perform are specifically laid down by statutory instrument[14]. They include rectification of the register of title under s 82 of the principal Act, and the determination of disputes affecting registered land under r 298 of the principal Rules. This jurisdiction is confined solely to disputes directly or indirectly involving an application for registration. However, the Chief Land Registrar's power to formulate forms and directions, or to allow alterations or additions to prescribed statutory forms[15] is not one that can be exercised by the Solicitor. The Registrar and those acting under his authority are exonerated from personal liability in respect of acts done or omitted to be done in good faith in the exercise or supposed exercise of their statutory powers[16].

3. The Lord Chancellor

The making of regulations for the Land Registry is vested in the Lord Chancellor[17]. He has a wide power to make general rules covering a variety of purposes contained in s 144(1) and it is under this provision that the various rules have been made. In the formulation thereof he is assisted by a body of persons known as the Rule Committee, consisting of a Judge of the Chancery Division of the High Court, the Chief Land Registrar and three others, one to be chosen by the General Council of the Bar, another by the Ministry of Agriculture and Fisheries and the third by the Council of the Law Society. He is also responsible for the appointment of the Chief Land Registrar.

B Registrable interests

In unregistered land rights in or over land fall into three main groups: (i) legal estates, (ii) legal interests which bind a purchaser of the land affected with or without notice[18] and (iii) equitable rights which are either overreachable (eg, interests under a trust for sale) or binding on the principle of notice. The Act of 1925 has a not-exactly corresponding tripartite division[19] of (i) registrable interests, (ii) overriding interests and (iii) minor interests. Only an interest

---

13 HM Land Registry Report 1989–90, para 70. The present Chief Land Registrar is a non-lawyer.
14 Land Registration (Solicitor to HM Land Registry) Regulations 1990, rr 3, 4.
15 See the LRA 1925, s 127; LRR 1925 r 74.
16 LRA 1925, s 131. As to the powers and indemnity available to district registrars, see s 133.
17 LRA 1925, s 126 (5).
18 Save for puisne mortgages which, though legal, are governed by the LCA 1972.
19 The Law Commission has recommended the creation of an additional class of interests termed general burdens: Law Com Report No 158, para 2. 15; see p 68, post.

falling within the first category is capable of being entered on the register of title under its own separate title number. This may conveniently be termed substantive registration. Interests within (ii) and (iii) are protected in the manner provided by the Act in ways to be discussed in the next chapter. This threefold classification is perhaps not entirely accurate. A hybrid group exists, consisting of legal mortgages and legal charges which partake of characteristics of groups (i) and (iii). They are not capable of substantive registration as separate titles, yet the mortgagee receives a certificate (known as a charge certificate) as evidence of his title in the same way as the proprietor of a registered interest receives a land certificate. The existence of the charge is noted on the mortgagor's register of title, which is a mode of protection applicable to minor interests[20].

As we observed in the previous chapter[1], the Act, despite its title, provides for the registration of titles to land. Section 2(1) enacts that:

> After the commencement of this Act estates capable of subsisting as legal estates shall be the only interests in land in respect of which a proprietor can be registered and all other interests in registered land (except over-riding interests and interests entered on the register at or before such commencement) shall take effect in equity as minor interests...

Just as there may be several legal estates existing in relation to a particular plot of land, so there may be several registered titles affecting the one plot. The expression 'legal estates' is defined by s 3(xi) to cover those interests capable of existing as legal interests within the Law of Property Act 1925, s 1(2). Section 2(1) merely limits the boundaries of registrable estates. It does not say that they must be registered; the need to register the title to any particular estate is governed by other provisions.

1.   Freehold estates

By virtue of s 4 of the Act an estate owner holding a legal estate in fee simple, whether entitled beneficially or as limited owner, or a person entitled to require such an estate to be vested in him[2] may apply to be registered in respect of that estate. An estate subject to a subsisting right of redemption and the equitable interest arising under a contract for sale cannot be the subject of any substantive registration. Parts of a house or building, such as a freehold flat, can be separately registered. 'Land' includes mines and minerals whether or not held with the surface, so that mines and minerals that have been horizontally severed from the surface can be registered. Registration of a freehold title automatically extends to the mines and minerals under the land (other than coal), unless they have previously been severed, in which case the Registrar is bound to record the fact on the register[3]. An undivided share in

---

20   Mortgages are more fully considered in Ch 15. For land certificates, see p 42, post.
1   Pages 7–8, ante.
2   Eg, a remainderman who becomes beneficially entitled on the death of the life tenant.
3   LRR 1925, r 196.

land is expressly excluded from the statutory definition of 'land' and is not capable of substantive registration[4].

2.   Leasehold estates

The title to a term of years absolute is registrable, except as follows[5].

(i) *A lease for a term of which 21 years or less are unexpired.*   Careful note needs to be taken of the way in which the Act deals with leases. This category prevents the substantive registration of two classes of lease: (i) a lease granted for not more than 21 years[6]; (ii) a lease for a longer term of which less than 21 years remain unexpired at the time of the application for first registration[7]. This exception does not affect the need to complete by registration the transfer of an *existing registered* leasehold title with a term of less than 21 years unexpired at the time of the transfer.

(ii) *An equitable lease.*   Notwithstanding the fact that s 3(x) of the Act defines 'lease' as including an agreement for a lease, a person entitled to an equitable lease cannot apply for substantive registration of his lease. An applicant for registration must be the owner of a *legal* estate[8]. Nor does the lessee come within the category mentioned in s 8(1)(b) of a person entitled to require a legal leasehold estate, *held* under such a lease, to be vested in him. The word 'held' indicates that the leasehold estate is already in existence. A mere right to require its creation is insufficient[9].

(iii) *A term of years demised by way of mortgage whilst there is a subsisting right of redemption.*   The mortgagee cannot register his mortgage term as a title with its own title number separately from that of the mortgagor's freehold.

Originally s 8(2) of the Act of 1925 precluded the registration of any lease containing an absolute prohibition against inter vivos dealings. Since registered conveyancing is concerned to simplify dealings with land, it was imagined that nothing could be achieved by registering an inalienable estate. Such reasoning failed to impress the Law Commission[10]. Their recommen-dation to remove

---

4   LRA 1925, s 3(viii).
5   LRA 1925, s 8(1), and (1A) (added by the LRA 1986, s 2(2)). For the meaning of 'term of years absolute', see s 3 (xxvii). Leasehold titles are further considered in Ch 15.
6   Considered by the Law Commission to be an acceptable dividing line between registrable and unregistrable leases: Law Com Report No 125, para 4.27–29.
7   Subject in the cases of leases granted or assigned after 31 December 1986 to the LRA 1925, s 8(1A). Legal leases falling within (i) rank as overriding interests. As to a reversionary lease, see LRR 1925, r 47.
8   LRA 1925, ss 3(iv), 4(1)(a).
9   Brickdale, 87.
10   Law Com No 125, para 4.30. The lessor is always free to waive the prohibition. Moreover a transfer in breach of the restriction is nonetheless effective to vest the legal title in the assignee (subject to the lessor's rights of forfeiture, if any): *Old Grovebury Manor Farm Ltd v W Seymour Plant Sales and Hire Ltd (No 2)* [1979] 3 All ER 504, CA.

the bar was implemented by the Land Registration Act 1986. By virtue of a new s 8(2) a so-called inalienable lease may now be registered, but only if provision is made in the prescribed manner for preventing any dealing with it in contravention of the prohibition by an entry to that effect on the register. This amendment applies to inalienable leases whenever created. Any such lease granted before the commencement of the Act (on 1 January 1987) will not become compulsorily registrable (if at all[11]) until the first assignment for value thereafter.

3. Easements

It should be remembered that easements possess a double aspect, as appurtenant to the dominant land and as obligations binding the servient land. Here we are concerned with the rights of the dominant owner. An easement is within the definition of a legal estate for the purposes of s 2(1) of the Act, but it is not possible for the dominant owner to register his easement separately from the dominant land[12]. Registration of easements as a separate species of property is, of course, unnecessary. They can exist only for the benefit of the dominant land and cannot be dealt with separately from that land. Furthermore, on first registration the Registrar does not automatically register appurtenant easements. This is technically unnecessary. Registration of a person as proprietor of land vests in him the legal estate together with all rights, privileges and appurtenances belonging thereto[13]. This reveals a minor defect in the system. The description of the registered estate appearing in the proprietor's property register may thus be incomplete, and a purchaser can ascertain the existence of appurtenant easements only by making specific inquiries.

It is always open for the applicant for first registration, or any proprietor of a registered estate, to apply in writing for a specific entry to be made on the register of any appurtenant legal easement. He will be required to furnish evidence of its existence[14]. Entry of the easement as part of the description of the registered land confers a title to it corresponding to the nature of the title granted in respect of the land[15]. This differentiates an easement entered as an appurtenant right from one the benefit of which simply vests in the proprietor by virtue of the general vesting provisions of the Act. So, if the dominant land is registered with an absolute title, the proprietor also obtains an absolute title to the appurtenant easement itself, even though under the general law it may

---

11   It must still be capable of substantive registration under s 8(1). It may be immediately eligible for voluntary registration (p 26, post).

12   LRR 1925, r 257. For s 2(1), see p 20, ante.

13   LRA 1925, ss 5, 20(1); LRR 1925, r 251; *Re Evans's Contract, Evans v Deed* [1970] 1 All ER 1236.

14   LRR 1925, rr 252(1), (2), 257. But see r 199. The evidence required is usually evidence of the title of the grantor.

15   LRR 1925, r 254(1). If the Registrar is not satisfied that the right is appurtenant, he may enter notice of the fact that the proprietor claims it. This usually occurs if the title of the grantor cannot be shown.

have become unenforceable for some reason[16]. The easement attracts the indemnity provisions contained in s 83 of the Act[17], and the proprietor will be entitled to claim compensation should he subsequently lose the benefit of the easement through rectification.

C   Compulsory and voluntary registration

The title to land may be registered either because it has to be, or because the owner has registered it voluntarily. From 1 December 1990 compulsory registration of title extends to the whole of England and Wales[18]. As at that date it was estimated that around nine million property titles were unregistered.

1.   Compulsory registration

(a) Land Registration Act 1925, s 123
Even though registration of title is now compulsory within all areas, the registration of individual titles is statutorily provided for only after certain specified transactions. Property may, therefore, remain unregistered for many years after the system became operative in the locality. Section 123(1) lists those transactions giving rise to compulsory registration as follows:

(a) every conveyance on sale of freehold land;
(b) every grant of a term of years absolute of more than 21 years from the date of delivery of the grant;
(c) every assignment on sale of leasehold land held for a term of years absolute having more than 21 years to run from the date of delivery of the assignment[19].

While it is customary to speak of registration being compulsory (as the section itself does), there is no such mandatory requirement. Instead it provides a sanction against non-registration by enacting that the conveyance, grant or assignment (as the case may be) shall:

> ... on the expiration of two months from the date thereof or of any authorised extension of that period, become void so far as regards the grant or conveyance of the legal estate in the freehold or leasehold land comprised in the conveyance, grant or assignment ... unless the grantee (that is to say the person who is entitled to be registered as proprietor of the freehold or leasehold land) or his successor in title or assign has in the meantime applied to be registered as proprietor of such land ...

---

16   Cf *Meek v Clarke* [1982] CA Transcript 312 (easement entered as appurtenant after execution of release by dominant owner); *Jones v Robert Russell Developments Ltd* (21 May 1985, unreported), Ch D.
17   See further Ch 4.
18   By virtue of the Registration of Title Order 1989. Parts of Essex, Suffolk, and Hereford and Worcester were the last areas to be brought within the system.
19   Following a Law Commission recommendation, the term of 21 years in (b) and (c) was substituted for the original period of 40 years as from January 1987: LRA 1986, s 2(1). See Law Com Report No 125, para 4.32ff.

The prospective loss of the legal estate is an effective sanction to compel any grantee to apply for registration, so that, in effect, the provisions of s 123 are mandatory. They will be regarded as having been complied with even if only part of the land comprised in a conveyance is lodged for registration[20]. The Registrar (or the court on an appeal from him) can extend the period if satisfied that an application cannot be made within the time limit, or can only be so made by incurring unreasonable expense, or that some accident or other sufficient cause has prevented the application from being submitted within the period. If the registrar grants an extension, which, in practice, he is usually willing to do[1], then the effect of this is to nullify the effect of s 123 and to re-vest the legal estate in the grantee from the date of the conveyance or transfer[2]. In certain special cases, Parliament has decreed that s 123 should apply to land not situated within an area of compulsory registration. A notable occasion arose under s 154 of the Housing Act 1985, governing the sale or grant of a lease of a council house under the statutory right to buy provisions of that Act[3]. Where, however, a council house was conveyed otherwise than in pursuance of the statutory right to buy[4], the transaction did not attract the provisions of s 123. This may constitute a trap for the purchaser from the original buyer. Unless the initial conveyance recited that the sale was made under the Act's provisions, he will have no means of knowing whether the title ought to have been compulsorily registered on the occasion of that sale.

Compulsory registration of title does not apply to any area of land declared by the Registrar to be subject to a souvenir land scheme[5].

(b) Meaning of 'on sale'
Not every change of estate ownership results in a compulsory registration, only conveyances and certain assignments on sale, and the grant of a legal lease for more than 21 years. 'Conveyance on sale' and 'assignment on sale' are defined to mean an instrument made on sale by virtue of which there is conferred or completed[6] a title under which an application for first registration may be made[7]. There is no general definition of 'sale'[8]. Some transactions are clearly excluded: a gift of property, an assent vesting property in a devisee, the appointment of a new trustee. Other transactions are statutorily exempted from the compulsory provision[9], including those involving incorporeal hereditaments (such as a conveyance of a legal rentcharge) and mines and minerals apart from the surface. The definition of 'assignment on sale'

20   *Proctor v Kidman* (1986) 51 P & CR 67.
1   See R & R 11.13.
2   *Pinekerry Ltd v Kenneth Needs (Contractors) Ltd* (1992) 64 P & CR 245 at 247.
3   See also the Commons Registration Act 1965, s 12; Housing Act 1988, Sch 12, para 2(2)(a).
4   Eg, a conveyance to a person not qualifying as a secure tenant within s 118(1) of the Act.
5   LR & LCA 1971, s 4; Land Registration (Souvenir Land) Rules 1972. For the background to this provision, see 35 Conv (NS) 390 (T B F Ruof).
6   This prevents evasion of s 123 by splitting up the conveyance (or assignment) into two stages so expressed that neither of them by itself is within the definition: Brickdale, 277.
7   LRA 1925, s 123(3).
8   Cf LPA 1925, s 205(1)(xxiv) (means a sale properly so called).
9   LRA 1925, s 120(1), proviso.

expressly excludes an assignment on surrender of a lease to the reversioner containing a declaration that the term is to merge. A conveyance or assignment by way of exchange *provided money is paid for equality of exchange* is specifically included[10].

In ordinary legislative usage the word 'sale' denotes an exchange of property for cash, in the absence of a special context to the contrary[11]. This general rule would appear to govern the construction of s 123. Despite the opposing view advocated by some commentators[12], a conveyance of land for a consideration which takes the form of money's worth rather than money, such as the transfer of shares or the extinguishment of a debt[13], would not, it is submitted, be caught by s 123. Weight is given to this view by the express inclusion within the section of exchanges where equality of money is paid. This clearly infers that a straight exchange of land for land (money's worth) or an exchange where part of the consideration is in some other form of money's worth is not intended to lead to compulsory first registration. Similarly excluded would be an appropriation of reality by a personal representative on satisfaction of a legacy or share of residue. It is a matter of some concern that the Act fails to regulate the point specifically. Inexplicably, the Law Commission's draft Land Registration Bill fails to resolve the uncertainty satisfactorily[14].

A transaction does not cease to be 'on sale' simply because no money is actually handed over on completion; thus a conveyance of land where the whole of the purchase price is left outstanding on mortgage is caught by the Act. In relation to newly created leases, it will be observed that no reference is made to a grant 'on sale'. The payment of a premium by the lessee or even of rent is not a prerequisite for attracting the provisions of s 123.

Finally it must be stressed that s 123 provides machinery for the *first registration* of titles *hitherto unregistered*. Once a title has been registered, subsequent dealings authorised by the Act must be registered whether the transaction constitutes a sale or not. So, a donee of registered property must be registered as the proprietor in place of the donor, if the legal title is to become vested in him[15].

(c) Compulsory registration of leases
The rules governing the substantive registration of leases were simplified by the Land Registration Act 1986. As we have just seen, a lease of unregistered

---

10   LRA 1925, s 123(3).
11   *Simpson v Connolly* [1953] 2 All ER 474; *IRC v Littlewoods Mail Order Stores Ltd* [1963] AC 135, [1962] 2 All ER 279, HL; *Re Westminster Property Group plc* [1985] 2 All ER 426, CA.
12   See Brickdale, 56; R & R 201, adopting by analogy the interpretation given to 'sale' in the Stamp Act 1891, ss 54, 55: *J & P Coat's Ltd v IRC* [1897] 2 QB 423, CA. But contrast *Jopling v IRC* [1940] 2 KB 282, [1940] 3 All ER 279.
13   See *Simpson v Connolly*, supra; *Thorndike v Hunt* (1859) 3 De G F & J 563.
14   See cl 13(6)(b), which, for instance, provides that 'conveyance on sale' includes a conveyance by way of exchange, whether equality money is paid *or not*. The words in italics suggest that an exchange of land for land would be caught; but does it follow from this that a conveyance for a non-pecuniary consideration other than land would be treated as 'on sale'?
15   LRA 1925, s 19(1): see p 478, post.

land for more than 21 years falls within the modified s 123(1). The term of 21 years replaces the period of 40 years originally prescribed by sub-s (1). This change applies only to transactions occurring after the Act became operative on 1 January 1987. So, for example, a lease for 30 years granted in 1986 will become compulsorily registrable on an assignment for value in 1993. On the other hand, if the first such assignment were to occur in 1996, then s 8(1) of the main Act would come into play[16]. Registration would not be possible since fewer than 21 years of the term would remain unexpired.

This reduction in the length of term laid down as the criterion for registrability necessitated a consequential amendment to s 8(1). Suppose a legal lease for 30 years is assigned for value in July 1993 at a time when there are 21 years and three days of the term to run. The transaction is caught by s 123(1). However, unless the transferee applies for registration within two days of the assignment (a virtual impossibility in practice), he will be excluded by s 8(1). The two conflicting provisions have been reconciled by the insertion of a new s 8(1A)[17]. This expressly permits an application for registration within the two months allowed by s 123, or any authorised extension thereof, notwithstanding that less than 21 years remain unexpired at the relevant time. Thus an application for registration submitted in August 1993 will be saved by s 8(1A).

The point made at the close of section (b) above is also relevant to leases. The grant of a lease for more than 21 years by a *registered proprietor* requires substantive registration for reasons quite apart from s 123. Such a lease ranks as a disposition of registered land. It must be completed by registration of the lessee as the proprietor of the new leasehold title, without which he cannot obtain a legal estate[18].

2.   Voluntary registration

Until compulsory registration of title was extended to the whole of the country, it was possible for a voluntary application for first registration to be made in two different situations: (i) in relation to land in a non-compulsory area; (ii) in relation to land within a compulsory area, but not founded on a transaction falling within s 123 of the Act. During the 1960s it became necessary to suspend voluntary applications in situation (i), except in certain cases specified by the Registrar[19]. Since 1 December 1990, however, this restriction ceases to be effective. Nevertheless, the Registry does not appear to be actively encouraging voluntary registrations[20].

16   See p 21, ante.
17   By s 2(2) of the LRA 1986.
18   See the LRA 1925, ss 18(1)(e), 19(2), and 22(1)(d), 22(2) (underleases). The two months'
      time limit imposed by s 123(1) does not apply to a dispositionary lease.
19   LRA 1966, s 1(2); repealed as obsolete by the Statute Law (Repeals) Act 1995. See Practice
      Leaflet No 12 for the permissible voluntary applications. These leaflets are issued by the
      Registry for the benefit of practitioners.
20   See (1990) 87/14 LS Gaz 14, 15 (E J Pryer). The Land Registration Fee Order 1990 did,
      however, abolish the additional fee payable on voluntary applications: ibid.

D   Classes of title and the effect of first registration

An estate in land may be registered with one of four different classes of title: absolute, possessory, qualified or good leasehold, the latter being as its name indicates confined solely to leasehold estates. It is necessary to consider what is the effect of *first registration* with a particular class of title. This section does not profess to deal with the effect of registration on a transfer of land already registered[1], though the position is similar to that on first registration.

1.   Absolute title

(a) Freehold land

An absolute title cannot be granted unless and until the title submitted by the applicant has been approved by the Registrar[2]. He is invested with a wide discretionary power to approve a title which is open to objection, provided he is satisfied that the owner will not be disturbed in his enjoyment of the estate[3]. In this way he can ignore minor blemishes and defects in title, so conferring on the applicant an absolute title with all its advantages. The Registrar is, in effect, in the same position as that of a willing but prudent purchaser under an open contract[4]. In *Dennis v Malcolm*[5] it was held that no appeal lies from his refusal to grant an absolute title. The court has no jurisdiction to make a declaration that a particular title is fit to be registered with an absolute title and unconditionally[6]. Nevertheless, once the court has declared that an incumbrance affecting land is no longer enforceable and in consequence a vendor of that land is able to establish a good marketable title to it, the Registrar will, presumably, act on the court's decision and refrain from entering the erstwhile adverse right as an incumbrance against the title when the land is subsequently registered for the first time.

Exceptionally the need for any investigation of title prior to first registration is statutorily dispensed with. A special procedure operates in the case of certain transactions effected by local housing authorities, new town corporations and other public sector landlords[7]. As sufficient evidence of the various facts stated therein, the Registrar is obliged to accept a certificate given to the transferee to the effect that the transferor is entitled to convey the freehold subject only to such adverse rights as are mentioned in the conveyance or summarised in the certificate. If as a result of acting on the certificate he has to meet a claim under the Act of 1925, the transferor is liable to indemnify him.

1   See Ch 15.
2   LRA 1925, s 4.
3   LRA 1925, s 13(c). See (1976), 40 Conv (NS) 122 (C T Emery).
4   Brickdale, 6. For open contracts see p 147, post.
5   [1934] Ch 244. His decision is amenable to judicial review. See *Quigly v Chief Land Registrar* [1993] 4 All ER 82.
6   *MEPC Ltd v Christian-Edwards* [1978] Ch 281, [1978] 3 All ER 795, CA (abandoned contract for sale): affd [1981] AC 205, [1979] 3 All ER 752, HL.
7   See the Housing Act 1985, s 154(2), (5); Housing Act 1988, Sch 12, para 2(2)(b), (3); Local Government and Housing Act 1989, s 172 and the New Towns (Transfer of Housing Stock) Regulations 1990, r 7(2).

The effect of first registration with an absolute freehold title is set out in s 5 of the Act which provides:

> Where the registered land is a freehold estate, the registration of any person as first proprietor thereof with an absolute title shall vest in the person so registered an estate in fee simple in possession in the land, together with all rights, privileges and appurtenances belonging or appurtenant thereto, subject to the following rights and interests[8] but free from all other estates and interests whatsoever, including estates and interests of His Majesty[9].

Normally this vesting which s 5 effects simply confirms the existing position. The legal title to the land will already have passed to the applicant by virtue of the conveyance from the vendor, but as will shortly be seen first registration may have a curative effect and achieve what the conveyance could not do. Appurtenant rights such as easements automatically vest in the applicant without express mention on the register of title[10], even though he cannot adduce satisfactory evidence of their enforceability. Section 72 provides that if before the registration of any freehold land with an absolute title, any easement, right or privilege has been acquired for the benefit thereof, then on registration the easement etc shall become appurtenant to the registered land in like manner as if it had been granted to the registered proprietor. On a literal interpretation, the section would appear to revive interests previously avoided[11]. The section is presumably intended to preserve enforceable easements only, and it is conceived that the courts will so construe the provision[12].

(i) *Adverse rights.*   Registration takes effect subject to:

(a) *Incumbrances and other entries appearing on the register.*   The drafting here is somewhat elliptical. An entry is not a right or interest, so that para (a) must be interpreted as meaning subject to rights and interests created by any document or transaction recorded as an entry[13]. This paragraph relates to enforceable third party rights subsisting at the time of registration and noted on the register as part of the registration process[14], such as restrictive covenants, adverse easements, certain leases, estate contracts. Entry on the register does not operate to revive a right or interest which has ceased to be enforceable prior to first registration of title because of non-registration as a land charge[15], or because it had been released by the grantee or was void ab initio.

---

8   As to which see below.
9   *Re Suarez (No 2)* [1924] 2 Ch 19 (Crown's claim to escheat barred under Land Transfer Act 1875, s 7, the precursor of s 5).
10   See p 22, ante, for the right to apply for entry on the register of an appurtenant right.
11   Eg, an equitable easement formerly appurtenant to the land, which has previously become unenforceable against the servient land for want of registration as a land charge.
12   Cf *Kitney v MEPC Ltd* [1978] 1 All ER 595, CA, post.
13   *Kitney v MEPC Ltd*, supra, at 602, per Goff LJ.
14   A third party anxious to ensure that his rights will be duly protected can lodge a caution against first registration (not to be confused with a caution *against dealings*, p 73, post). This entitles him to receive notification of any application to register the land, and to substantiate his claim before the Registrar. See the LRA 1925, s 53; R & R, 13.01–13.11; (1956) 20 Conv (NS) 3.
15   *Kitney v MEPC Ltd*, a case involving an unregistered option to renew an underlease. The underlease (but not the option) was noted against the superior title.

(b) *Overriding interests*[16] unless the contrary is expressed on the register.

(c) *Minor interests*[17] but only if the proprietor is not entitled to the land for his own benefit, in which event he takes subject to such minor interests of which he has notice. This restriction applies to a first proprietor who is, for instance, a tenant for life of settled land. It has been suggested[18] that the words 'not entitled for his own benefit' are wide enough to cover all cases where a person has become a constructive trustee, as where he purchases from his beneficiary, or the purchase price is provided by some third person in circumstances where there is no presumption of advancement or intention of gift.

Section 5 may operate to defeat an incumbrance, eg a restrictive covenant, enforceable against the estate prior to first registration, but which, through some error on the Registry's part, is not noted on the register. The person formerly entitled to the benefit of the covenant may be able to obtain rectification of the register, failing which he would be able to claim an indemnity under the Act[19], but this pecuniary recompense may be inadequate compensation for the loss of his rights. Since the section only refers to 'estates and interests', it does not seem to defeat purely contractual rights, where they exist. Notwithstanding the omission of the covenant from the register, an original covenantee may still be able to enforce a restrictive covenant against the registered proprietor, if *the original covenantor*, even by injunction. He can rely on his contractual claim without having recourse to any proprietary interest. In practice, this situation will rarely occur; the first registered proprietor will usually be a purchaser from the original covenantor, or from some remoter predecessor in title.

(ii) *Curative effect of registration.* Section 7 is an important and far-reaching provision, the precise effects of which have not yet been fully explored by the courts. Registration defines the estate vested in the registered proprietor, whether that estate is identical with the estate vested in him before registration or not[20]. In other words, first registration operates to cure defects in the title existing prior to first registration. Section 69(1) of the Act[1] contains a complementary provision which deems a registered proprietor of freehold land to have the legal estate in fee simple in possession vested in him without any conveyance. Thus a first registered proprietor obtains the legal title even though the conveyance to him was a forged document[2], or was otherwise incapable of transferring a good title. The Act, therefore, contains a striking

---

16 See pp 50–70, post.
17 See pp 71–80, post.
18 Brickdale, 83.
19 LRA 1925, ss 82(1)(b), 83(2), discussed in Ch 4, post. See *Freer v Unwins Ltd* [1976] Ch 288, [1976] 1 All ER 634, p 92, post, where, surprisingly, the covenantee obtained rectification despite the proprietor being in possession of the land. Rectification will not necessarily enable the covenantee to enforce the covenant against the registered proprietor; this will depend on the date when rectification becomes effective: ibid.
20 *Kitney v MEPC Ltd* [1978] 1 All ER 595 at 606, CA, per Buckley LJ.
1 See *Spectrum Investment Co v Holmes* [1981] 1 All ER 6.
2 Cf *Argyle Building Society v Hammond* (1984) 49 P & CR 148, CA (land already registered).

exception to the general principle of *nemo dat quod non habet*[3]. Take the case of *Re 139 High Street, Deptford*[4], where V conveyed a freehold shop and annex to P who became the first registered proprietor with an absolute title. In fact the annex belonged to X who obtained rectification of the register by excluding the annex from P's title. However, s 5 had operated to vest in P the freehold estate in the entirety of the land. He was entitled to compensation for his loss[5], notwithstanding that the conveyance itself did not vest in him any title to the annex, as V himself had no title to it[6]. So long as the proprietor remains registered as such, he has full power to transfer the registered estate, and to create valid mortgages.

(iii) *Extent of statutory vesting.*   Section 7 leaves one vital question tantalisingly unanswered. Registration is stated to vest in the proprietor 'an estate in fee simple in possession in the land'. Is the curative effect of s 5 limited to vesting in the proprietor the *legal* title[7] but no more in a case where the conveyance leading to first registration failed for some reason to vest in him the equitable title to land with which he is subsequently registered? This problem occurs, for example, where a vendor has inadvertently conveyed the same plot of land to different purchasers at different times, the second conveyance leading to first registration of title. Consider the facts of *Re 139 High Street, Deptford.* Was P's registration as proprietor of the annex effective to vest in him not only X's legal estate but also his beneficial (ie equitable) interest in that land? The difficulty was not raised in this case. In *Epps v Esso Petroleum Co Ltd*, another case concerning a double conveyance of land, Templeman J took the view that s 5 merely vests the legal estate in the first proprietor, P, leaving the equitable title undisturbed in the prior owner, X[8]. With respect, it is submitted that s 5 ought not to be construed in these situations as clothing the registered proprietor with nothing more than the outer cloak of legal ownership. It should be held to vest in him any outstanding equitable interest as well. To exclude from the operation of s 5 an outstanding equitable interest is plainly

---

3   For a good example, see *London Borough of Hounslow v Hare* (1990) 24 HLR 9 (Transfer of leasehold land void under Charities Act 1960, s 29).

4   [1951] Ch 884, [1951] 1 All ER 950.

5   A sum of £1,278 was paid to P (see (1954) 18 Conv (NS) 138). For rectification and indemnity, see Ch 4, post.

6   Registration may also revest an estate that has been forfeited: *Morrelle Ltd v Wakeling* [1955] 2 QB 379 at 410, [1955] 1 All ER 708 at 720, CA, per Evershed MR: on appeal, see *A-G v Parsons* [1956] AC 421, [1956] 1 All ER 65, HL. It is also arguable that s 5 operates to vest a legal title in a minor, even though a minor is not an estate owner within s 3(iv) of the Act. Contrast R & R, 10.05. The point is more fully discussed in the 2nd edn, p 20, note 16.

7   Bearing in mind that the only freehold estate capable of registration under the Act is a legal estate: s 2(1), p 20 ante. See also s 69(1). The Law Commission's draft Bill does not clarify the issue; see cl 12, which would replace s 5.

8   [1973] 2 All ER 465 at 468, 472. To dismiss these observations as mere dicta overlooks the fact that in considering whether the plaintiff was in actual occupation of the disputed land, the learned judge accepted the proposition that, notwithstanding the conveyance, the plaintiff possessed 'rights' (ie, an equitable interest in fee simple) capable of protection under s 70(1)(g) of the Act by virtue of that alleged occupation. Cf the somewhat equivocal statement in *Re Sea View Gardens* [1966] 3 All ER 935 at 941, per Pennycuick J, that the effect of registration is 'to displace the true owner with a valid prior title'.

inconsistent with the words 'free from all other estates and interest whatsoever'. This expression clearly envisages a comprehensive vesting, subject only to those third party rights falling within paras (a)-(c) of s 5, of rights that were already existing and binding on the proprietor before first registration. It is not the scheme of s 5 to create by the fact of registration alone adverse rights which become binding on the proprietor. The view adopted by Templeman J, if correct, exposes a flaw in the Act, which goes to the roots of the system[9], and casts into the arena of speculation the reliability of the register of title.

Any notion that s 5 should be restrictively interpreted in order to preserve X's rights is unfounded. Even though the Act does divest X of his equitable interest in the disputed land, he is in no way debarred from seeking rectification of the register, and the court can uphold his claim by exercising its discretion to order rectification[10]. On the other hand, the indemnity provisions of the Act appear to break down should the contrary opinion be well-founded[11]. These are additional grounds for doubting Templeman J's view.

(iv) *How absolute?* How absolute is this absolute title? A leading work on registered land conveyancing stated that an absolute title is without question the most reliable and marketable title that exists, because it is virtually indefeasible and cannot be bettered[12]. Whilst perhaps such a title cannot be bettered, some commentators[13] have grave misgivings as to its indefeasibility. Only if registration confers immunity from attack can the title be said to be indefeasible. However, the proprietor registered with an absolute title is safe only so long as the register is not rectified against him, and it will be seen that his title is open to attack on the widest of discretionary grounds[14]. The absoluteness of his title is only relative. He can never be completely sure that an adverse claim against him will not be upheld, as occurred in *Re 139 High Street, Deptford* or in *Bridges v Mees*[15] where the claim of a squatter was upheld. It might be more accurate to say that the strength of an absolute title depends not on its virtual indefeasibility but on the statutory indemnity behind it; and it by no means follows that a proprietor suffering rectification is entitled to

9 Thus, in relation to the disputed land, registration would be no more than an empty act; see (1974) 38 Conv (NS) 236 (S N Palk). See also R & R, 40.09, who do not advert to the problem, though their discussion of the *Deptford* case at 40.18 suggests that they accept that s 5 effects a complete vesting. Moreover, it appears to be the Registry's policy in appropriate cases to award indemnity to a registered proprietor deprived of the disputed land through rectification: see note 5, ante, and the Annual Reports of HM Land Registry detailing indemnity payments. Yet he can hardly be said to have suffered loss within s 83(1) (p 97, post) if all that he loses is the bare legal estate which he previously held in trust for the former legal owner, X. And, if he is simply a trustee for X, should he not be obliged to account to X for the indemnity paid to him?

10 Eg, under LRA 1925, s 82(1)(b), (g) or (h), p88, post. But it must be conceded that rectification is unlikely if P is a proprietor in possession, p 89, post.

11 See p 97, post.

12 R & R, 81.

13 See (1972) 88 LQR 93, 126–33 (D C Jackson); Farrand, 145–46.

14 See LRA 1925, ss 82(1)(h), (3)(c), pp 84–95, post.

15 [1957] Ch 475, [1957] 2 All ER 577, p 54, post. For another startling example, see *Argyle Building Society v Hammond* (1984) 49 P & CR 148, CA (forgery).

claim an indemnity[16]. Furthermore, it is difficult to reconcile the view of Templeman J in *Epps v Esso Petroleum Co Ltd*[17] with the notion of indefeasibility. A registered title which professes to be absolute, and yet may leave the beneficial interest in the land outstanding in some third party, is a contradiction in terms, particularly if no right to compensation arises under the Act when the registered proprietor is deprived through rectification of what the statute does vest in him.

(b) Leasehold land

Under s 9 of the Act, registration with an absolute leasehold title is deemed[18] to vest in the first proprietor the possession of the leasehold interest with all implied or expressed rights, privileges and appurtenances. The wording of this section differs somewhat from its freehold counterpart, s 5, but the effect is thought to be similar. Thus, registration should operate to vest in the registered lessee the legal and equitable interests in the leasehold term. The reference to 'vesting the possession' is taken from the Land Transfer Act 1875, s 13, enacted in the heyday of the doctrine of interesse termini. In view of that doctrine's subsequent abolition[19] there appears to be no justification for the retention of these words. What has previously been said of s 72 in relation to freehold land applies equally to leasehold titles.

The vesting is subject to the same rights as those affecting freeholds, ie incumbrances and other entries on the register, overriding and minor interests, but in addition it is *subject to all implied and express covenants, obligations and liabilities incident to the registered land.* Save for these, the registered lessee takes free from all other estates and interests. One point peculiar to leaseholds arises in relation to incumbrances and entries on the register. The register referred to is not simply the lessee's own register; it includes the register of any superior title. Thus, the lessee takes subject to restrictive covenants registered against the title of any freeholder, even though he has no notice of them[20].

An absolute leasehold title guarantees that the lease has been validly granted. It is not, therefore, possible for an applicant to be registered with an absolute leasehold title without the titles to both the freehold and the leasehold (including intermediate leaseholds) being approved[1]. Unless the freehold title is already registered (in which case it will have been previously approved), the applicant must deduce title to the freehold. Despite the absence of a statutory entitlement to investigate the freehold title, an intending lessee, or the purchaser of a lease, may have a contractual right to do so by virtue of the new

16   See pp 97–104, post.
17   [1973] 2 All ER 465.
18   A word apparently without significance: *Morelle Ltd v Wakeling* [1955] 2 QB 379 at 414, [1955] 1 All ER 708 at 723, CA, per Lord Evershed MR.
19   LPA 1925, s 149(1). Under the doctrine a lessee did not acquire a legal estate until actual entry on the land demised. Section 13 vested the legal title in him irrespective of entry into possession.
20   See p 342, post. In practice, covenants affecting the freehold title are normally noted against an absolute leasehold title.
 1   LRA 1925, s 8(1) proviso (i).

Standard Conditions of Sale[2]. As a result, the incidence of absolute leasehold titles will increase in the future. Indeed, the Registry has been anxious to encourage their registration. Should the lessor himself be registered with an absolute freehold title, the Registry will, of its own volition, treat an application for registration with a good leasehold as being one for an absolute leasehold title[3].

2. Good leasehold title

This type of title is confined solely to leasehold estates and is intended to cover those leasehold titles not supported by any documentary evidence of the freehold title. Where a good leasehold title is required, the leasehold (though not the freehold) title must be approved by the Registrar[4]. Under s 10 of the Act, the effect of first registration with this title is the same as for an absolute leasehold, but with this important exception. The title does not affect or prejudice the enforcement of any estate, right or interest affecting or in derogation of the lessor's title to grant the lease. Since the Registrar does not see the freehold title he cannot guarantee that the lessor was in a position validly to grant the lease. This is the basic difference between absolute leasehold and good leasehold titles. Suppose that the lessor has acquired the freehold title by fraud, or, being a mortgagor, leased the property contrary to the terms of the mortgage. Should a valid third party claim result in the register being rectified against the lessee, he is entitled to be indemnified under the Act if he has an absolute leasehold title, since the Registrar has warranted the lease's validity, but not if he merely has a good leasehold. Despite the significant difference in the scope of the guarantee attaching to a good leasehold title compared with an absolute title, it must not be thought that these titles are not sound marketable titles which a purchaser should avoid at all costs. They have their counterparts (lacking, of course, the statutory guarantee) in the unregistered system of land transfer. There are in various parts of the country numerous unregistered long leasehold titles which have been, and will continue to be, freely saleable on the open market, although the vendor does not deduce the freehold title[5]. Nevertheless, there seems to be a general preference on the part of institutional lenders for absolute leaseholds, wherever possible[6].

3. Possessory title

A possessory title is granted where the applicant's title is based solely on occupation as a squatter by himself and his predecessors in title, or where he

2   See further p 291, post. For the statutory position, see the LPA 1925, s 44, p 290, post.
3   Registered Land Practice Note, A2. These Notes, published by the Longman Group (2nd edn, 1986), are the result of discussions held regularly by the Joint Advisory Committee of the Law Society and the Land Registry. Whilst without any binding effect, they provide helpful guidance on problems likely to arise in practice.
4   LRA 1925, s 8(1) proviso (ii).
5   For the position where the contract is subject to the Standard Conditions of Sale, see p 291, post.
6   See (1977) 121 Sol Jo 161; R & R, 5-09.

is unable to produce the documents of title which ought to be in his custody[7]. The application must be supported by such evidence of title as is from time to time prescribed[8]. If there are documents of title these must be forwarded; if the applicant relies on adverse possession, a statutory declaration may constitute prima facie evidence of his right to seek registration[9]. It occasionally happens that a proprietor's title is partly absolute (or good leasehold) and partly possessory, as where a previous owner has encroached upon adjacent land and made it part of his own. In this situation two separate titles will be registered, each with its own title number. If, on an application for registration with possessory title, the Registrar is satisfied as to the title to the estate, he may register it as absolute or good leasehold[10] as the case may be, though conversely an applicant for an absolute title may find he is registered with a possessory title.

First registration with a possessory title is similar in effect to registration with a corresponding absolute freehold or leasehold title. However, the title is also made subject to any estate, right or interest (whether, in the case of leasehold land, in respect of the lessor's title or otherwise) adverse to or in derogation of the first proprietor's title and subsisting or capable of arising at the time of registration[11]. So a proprietor of a possessory title takes subject to any enforceable restrictive covenants affecting the land, even though no mention of them can be made on the register[12]. In effect, a possessory title gives no guarantee as to the title prior to first registration. The previous owner may be able to upset the title, on the ground that the evidence does not establish that the proprietor's possession was sufficiently adverse to support a possessory title[13]. The proprietor cannot recover any indemnity if the register is rectified to give effect to a superior title or claim.

Section 75(1) of the Act provides for the Limitation Act 1980 to apply to registered land in the same manner as it does to unregistered land, but with one significant difference. On the expiration of the 12 years' limitation period, the estate of the registered proprietor is not extinguished. Instead, he is deemed to hold it in trust for the person who has acquired title against him. The squatter appears to become the equitable owner under a statutory trust pending his own registration with a possessory title. The precise effect of s 75(1) and the extent to which it creates a divergence in the substantive law governing registered and unregistered land transfer are disputed[14]. The express reference

---

7   Provided the loss or destruction of deeds can be satisfactorily explained, the Registrar may be willing to grant an absolute or good leasehold title: Practice Leaflet No 4.
8   LRA 1925, s 4 proviso (ii) (freeholds), s 8(1) proviso (iii) (leaseholds).
9   LRR 1925, rr 37, 38.
10   LRA 1925, ss 4 proviso (iii), 8(1) proviso (iv).
11   LRA 1925, s 6 (freeholds), s 11 (leaseholds).
12   It is the practice to enter a note on the register to the effect that the title is subject to such restrictive covenants as may have been imposed on the land prior to the date of first registration so far as they are still legally enforceable; see R & R, 5-05. For the enforceability of covenants against a squatter, see *Re Nisbet and Potts' Contract* [1906] 1 Ch 386, CA.
13   *Tester v Harris* (1964) 189 EG 337.
14   *Fairweather v St Marylebone Property Co Ltd* [1963] AC 510 at 548, [1962] 2 All ER 288 at 299, HL, per Lord Denning (machinery only); *Jessamine Investment Co v Schwartz* [1978] QB 264 at 275, [1976] 3 All ER 521 at 530, CA, per Sir John Pennycuick (conveyancing device).

in sub-s (1) to the squatter's acquisition of title has been said to achieve a 'parliamentary conveyance', contrary to the rule applicable to unregistered land[15].

Some divergence in the substantive law seems inescapable from the wording of sub-s (1). *Spectrum Investment Co v Holmes*[16] illustrates the point. After the defendant, S, had been registered with a possessory leasehold title of a house, the documentary lessee, T, purported to surrender her lease to the plaintiff freeholder, F, to enable F to obtain possession of it. The claim failed in limine. S was the registered proprietor of the leasehold term, not T whose own registered title had been closed. T was incapable of effecting any dealing with the title. Had the land been unregistered, the ploy would have succeeded[17]. Indeed, in the *Spectrum* case Browne-Wilkinson J inclined to the view (at p 17) that pending S's registration under the Act, F and T could have dealt with the leasehold estate without reference to a squatter's rights, thereby defeating S's interest. But, with respect, this dictum overlooks the fact that S's rights constituted an overriding interest under s 70(1)(f) of the Act[18], binding upon F.

4. Qualified title

It may sometimes appear on an application for registration with an absolute freehold title that the title can be established only for a limited period or subject to certain reservations, or in the case of an application in relation to leasehold land (either for absolute or good leasehold titles) that the lessor's title to the reversion or the lessee's title to the leasehold are subject to similar qualifications. On such rare occasions the Registrar may except from the effect of registration any estate, right or interest arising before a specified date, or arising under a specified instrument or otherwise particularly described in the register[19]. Though a qualified title cannot in the first instance be applied for, the Registrar cannot grant such a title of his own accord, but only with the consent of the person seeking first registration.

A qualified title may be granted where, for example, the applicant's predecessor in title (being a trustee) acquired the land from his co-trustees in breach of trust. An entry would be made in the register to the effect that the rights and interests of the beneficiaries under the trust were excluded from the effect of registration. Consequently, should the title subsequently be upset by the beneficiaries, the proprietor could claim no indemnity under the Act. The specific defect of title appears on the face of the register, so differentiating the qualified title from the possessory title which is subject to all adverse estates, rights and interests existing at the time of first registration. Except for the specified defect, registration with a qualified title has the same effect as

15   *Fairweather's* case, at 542, 295, per Lord Radcliffe; *Tichborne v Weir* (1892) 67 LT 735, CA.
16   [1981] 1 All ER 6.
17   *Fairweather v St Marylebone Property Co Ltd*, supra.
18   Page 54, post. Also, presumably, under s 70(1)(g) (occupiers' rights). See R & R, 29-05.
19   LRA 1925, s 7 (freeholds), s 12 (leaseholds).

registration with an absolute title or a good leasehold title, as the case may be. Very few qualified titles have been registered.

5.   Conversion of titles

The superiority of the absolute title over its lesser brethren is easily demonstrated and provision is made for the subsequent upgrading of inferior titles. The Land Registration Act 1986, s 11, replaces s 77 of the Act of 1925, and gives effect to various recommendations of the Law Commission[20] designed to simplify the rules regulating the conversion of titles. The position may be summarised as follows:

(1) *A good leasehold title* is capable of conversion to absolute leasehold if the Registrar is satisfied as to the reversionary freehold title (and any intermediate leasehold title) (s 77(1)). This could occur after the intervening registration of the freehold with an absolute title.

(2) *A possessory* title may be registered as absolute freehold or good leasehold[1] (as the case may be) if either (a) the Registrar is satisfied as to the title, or (b) the land has been so registered for at least 12 years after the commencement of the Act[2] and the Registrar is satisfied that the proprietor is in possession (s 77(2)).

(3) *A qualified* title may be converted into an absolute freehold (or good leasehold) if the Registrar is satisfied about the title (s 77(3)).

No conversion can be effected so long as any claim adverse to the title remains outstanding (s 77(4)). Subject to this qualification, the Registrar is free to act on his own initiative in all three situations. Alternatively, the proprietor may apply for his title to be upgraded, using the new combi Form 6[3]. Any person suffering loss by reason of a conversion of a title is entitled to be indemnified (s 77(6)).

6.   A new estate?

The Land Registration Act 1925 is a statute designed to simplify the processes of making and investigating title[4]. However, a not inconsiderable body of

---

20   Law Com No 125, Pt III.

  1   If the Registrar is also satisfied as to the reversionary title, the leasehold may be converted to absolute title under sub-s (1).

  2   See the LRA 1986, s 1(2)(a). For the position when a period of registration has started to run before the commencement of the Act, see s 1(2)(b), and explanatory notes to cl 1 of the draft Bill in Report No 125, p 51.

  3   Prescribed by the Land Registration Rules 1986, r 5.

  4   *National Provincial Bank Ltd v Hastings Car Mart Ltd* [1964] Ch 665 at 696, [1964] 1 All ER 688 at 701, CA, per Russell, LJ; revsd sub nom *National Provincial Bank Ltd v Ainsworth* [1965] AC 1175, [1965] 2 All ER 472, HL.

opinion exists which asserts that the Act goes much further; it creates a new estate in land, a statutory or registered estate which on first registration replaces or even destroys the common law legal estate[5]. Support for this theory is derived largely from the Act itself, a passing reference to 'a statutory title' by Lord Hanworth MR, in a case where the Court of Appeal was dealing with a claim to rectify the register[6], and a sizeable weight of judicial authority from Australia, where a somewhat different system of land registration operates. Can this theory be justified?

(a) Some arguments considered

There is no specific provision in the Act purporting to destroy the common law estate; its demise is presumed from a construction of various sections of the Act. Thus, in relation to freehold land s 5 enacts that registration of a person as first proprietor with an absolute title vests in him an estate in fee simple in possession. Seeing that in normal cases he already has the fee simple estate by virtue of the conveyance from the vendor, what is the purpose of the section unless it is to vest in him something different from what he already possesses? The argument fails to account for the curative effect of first registration. The scheme of registration is not to be hindered by technical defects in title. Even assuming the conveyance was ineffective to pass any legal estate on account of some flaw in the title, yet the subsequent registration[7] cures that defect and achieves what the conveyance failed to do. Registration is complete in itself. Under s 69(1) of the Act, the proprietor is deemed to have the legal estate vested in him without any conveyance. He does not have to obtain any further assurance to cure any defect in title before he can be registered. It has been argued[8] that the words in s 69(1) 'legal estate' and 'registered estate' imply a distinction, justifying the existence of a separate statutory estate. On the contrary, however, the respective definitions of these two expressions rather suggest they are one and the same[9].

A further argument advanced in support of the demise of the common law estate is the provision in s 69(4) that the estate vested in the proprietor can only be disposed of or dealt with by him in the manner authorised by the Act. If the common law estate has been replaced, what is more vital than a definition of the proprietor's powers in relation to this statutory estate? However, the better view is that the draftsman was compelled to specify the

---

5   The main proponents are Potter, *Principles of Land Registration*, 30, R C Connell (1947) 11 Conv (NS) 183, 232, and D C Jackson (1972) 88 LQR 93. The view has in the past found favour with Registry officials (see Caswell's edn of Professor Potter's book, 3 K & E, 34) but is not adopted by R & R, 75–76. Professor Potter's chief opponent was A D Hargreaves; see the Hargreaves–Potter controversy in (1949), 12 MLR 139, 205, 477. See also Farrand, 154–56, who suggests that the problem is appellative rather than substantive.

6   *Chowood Ltd v Lyall (No 2)* [1930] 2 Ch 156 at 163, CA.

7   Pages 30–32, ante.

8   Connell, loc cit, 235.

9   'Registered estate' means 'the *legal estate* . . . as respects which a person is for the time being registered as proprietor', and 'legal estates' mean 'the estates which are by the LPA 1925, authorised to subsist or to be created at law': LRA 1925, s 3(xxiii), (xi).

powers, not to define or create them, but as a matter of conveyancing machinery to indicate the manner of their exercise[10].

(b) The judicial view

However attractive might be the arguments advanced by the proponents of the new statutory estate, it has received no direct support from English judges. The tenor of their judgments clearly indicates that the Act had no such revolutionary effect. For example in *Lee v Barrey*[11] Lord Evershed MR spoke of s 69 as being 'directed to bringing registered land into the general scheme of the property legislation of 1925'. More recently Lord Oliver has said that the provisions of the Land Registration Acts were designed to operate in parallel and consistently with the property legislation governing unregistered land[12].

This is not to say that the Act of 1925 has not made important alterations to the law of real property as applied to registered land. But as we noted in the previous chapter[13], these all stem as a necessary consequence from the changes made in conveyancing machinery.

E   The register and certificates of title

The term 'register', used in both the Act of 1925 and the Rules, is somewhat misleading as it describes three different things. Section 1 of the Act requires the keeping of a register of title to freehold and leasehold land, which need not be in documentary form[14]. In this context the register connotes the global record of all registered titles. The register[15] may also denote the record of title of each individual proprietor; this record is itself divided into three parts, each known as a register: the property register, the proprietorship register and the charges register. This section is concerned with the individual proprietor's register of title and its component parts. Each registered title has its own separate title number.

This register of title acts as a mirror; it reflects the state of the proprietor's title. In truth this is merely an approximation, for not all matters in which a

10   See (1949), 12 MLR 139, 140 (A D Hargreaves). Potter tentatively suggested (see 12 MLR 207) that some 'sort of ghost of a common law estate' might remain for the purposes of enjoyment as distinct from disposition. But see Hargreaves's reply at 12 MLR 477–8.

11   [1957] Ch 251 at 261, [1957] 1 All ER 191 at 195, CA; *Re White Rose Cottage* [1965] Ch 940 at 952, [1965] 1 All ER 11 at 16, CA, per Harman LJ (necessity 'radically to reform the land registration system to match with' the new real property regime introduced by the LPA 1925).

12   *Abbey National Building Society v Cann* [1991] 1 AC 56 at 77, [1990] 1 All ER 1085 at 1088, HL, per Lord Oliver, adding, rather interestingly, that a registered proprietor's powers to dispose of or create legal estates rest entirely on statute, citing the LRA 1925, s 69(4).

13   Pages 8–9, ante. In proposing its new scheme for registered land in Report No 158, the Commission was not constrained by the fact that it might be creating or perpetuating distinctions from unregistered land: para 2.5.

14   Section 1(2), as substituted by the AJA 1982, s 66(1). This paved the way for computerisation.

15   See, eg, s 5 of the LRA 1925. For a case where the correct meaning was crucial, see *A J Dunning & Sons (Shopfitters) Ltd v Sykes & Son (Poole) Ltd* [1987] Ch 287, [1987] 1 All ER 700, CA (LRR 1925, r 77(1)(a) and covenants for title).

prospective purchaser will be interested are recorded on the register. Overriding interests constitute the major exception to the mirror principle[16]. At the same time, the register operates as a curtain which ensures that a purchaser need not concern himself with trusts and equities that exist behind the curtain. So, s 74 of the Act enacts that no person dealing with a registered estate is to be affected with notice of any trust and references to trusts shall, so far as possible, be excluded from the register. Nevertheless, we shall see that even the curtain principle is not inviolate[17]. Occasionally it may be necessary to go behind a registered entry in order to inquire into the validity of some right or interest which the entry purports to protect[18].

1. Property register

The property register contains a verbal description of the registered property by reference to a plan. A typical description is as follows:

> The freehold land shown edged with red on the plan of the above Title filed at the Registry and being ...[19]

The description may include a reference to appurtenant easements, if an application therefor has been made, though, as previously seen, registration vests in the proprietor all appurtenant rights and privileges without express mention. Where mines and minerals have previously been excepted, a note to this effect appears in the property register. Exemptions from overriding interests are also mentioned here. If part of the land comprised in a registered title is later transferred, a note is made in the register that the land edged and numbered in green on the plan has been removed from the title and registered under its own title number shown in green on the plan.

In the case of leaseholds, short particulars of the lease (date, parties, term, date of its commencement and rent) are included, together with a statement (if applicable) excepting all rights arising from unlicensed dealings[20].

2. Proprietorship register

This states the nature of the title, the name, address and description of the proprietor and any entries affecting his right of disposal. For example, when trustees for sale are registered as joint proprietors, a statement may be added that no disposition by a sole proprietor of the land under which capital money arises is to be registered except under an order of the Registrar or of the

---

16 Rectification also constitutes a 'crack' in the mirror principle, 'wider but shallower' than that opened by overriding interests: Law Com No 158, para 2.10.
17 Page 56, post.
18 See *Kitney v MEPC Ltd* [1978] 1 All ER 595, CA, p 28, ante.
19 This is the wording used for a register in computerised form. In the case of a title still kept on card (ie, a manual register) the description reads: 'The freehold land shown and edged ... at the Registry registered on ... known as ...'.
20 See LRR 1925, r 45.

court[1]. Any caution[2] registered to protect a claim adverse to the proprietor's title appears in this register, and also miscellaneous matters required by the Rules to be entered on the register without any particular part being specified, eg, any modification of the implied covenants for title. On a change of proprietor consequent upon, for example, a transfer for value, the name of the vendor is deleted and the purchaser's particulars substituted.

3.   Charges register

Details of charges, incumbrances and other obligations adversely affecting the land from time to time appear in the charges register, such as: restrictive covenants, rentcharges, leases (not being overriding interests), and easements. The practice in relation to restrictive covenants varies. In the case of covenants created prior to first registration, short particulars of the deed of creation are entered in the register and a copy of the covenants are set out in a separate schedule. Where they are imposed on a transfer of registered land, the charges register merely records that the transfer contains restrictive covenants and adds a note that a copy of the transfer appears in the land certificate.

Details of a mortgage or charge are also entered in the charges register together with the name and address of the mortgagee, the proprietor of the registered charge. On its repayment the entry is cancelled, as also is the entry relating to any lease, or other incumbrance that is determined.

4.   Privacy of register

Until recently, and unlike most other countries where a register of title or of land is maintained, a proprietor's register of title was not open to inspection by the general public. It was private. As a basic rule, no-one could inspect the register or any document referred to in it without the written authority of the proprietor or his solicitor[3]. This compared roughly with the position in relation to unregistered land, for an estate owner is not under any general obligation to produce his title deeds the contents of which are private[4].

During the early 1980s the issue of opening the register of title to public inspection was thoroughly investigated by the Law Commission. After appropriate consultations which indicated widespread support for a change in the law, the Commission recommended that the register should become public. Effect was given to this 'welcome modernisation of the law'[5] by the Land Registration Act 1988, which substituted a new s 112 for ss 112 to 112C

---

1   See further p 76, post.
2   For cautions, see pp 73–76 , post.
3   See the original s 112 of the LRA 1925. Several exceptions were enacted by the Act itself; others were added later. See ss 112A, 112AA, 112B and 112C, inserted by various statutes.
4   But it is possible to search for land charges affecting the land without the owner's consent or knowledge, solely on payment of the fee.
5   Law Com Report No 148, para 20, which represented a radical shift from their provisional attitude. See Working Paper No 32, paras 70–94 (wholly open register not feasible).

of the main Act. As a result any person can now apply to inspect the register and obtain office copies of (a) entries in the register (including the filed plan), and (b) documents referred to in the register (including the filed plan), and (c) documents referred to in the register and in the Registrar's custody (sub-s (1)). The relevant prescribed form must be used: form 109 to obtain copy entries, and form 110 for copy documents[6]. Moreover, a separate fee (currently £6) must be paid. An application can still be made on form 109, even if the relevant title number cannot be quoted. In this case an additional fee (£6) is payable[7], and this will be retained irrespective of whether or not the land is registered.

(a) Exclusions
The right to obtain copy documents does not extend to copies of mortgages or leases. Apart from the fact that the originals of registered mortgages and registered leases are not retained in the Registry, though copies may sometimes be filed, it was thought desirable to exclude the right to inspect copy mortgages because of the strength of opinion against making financially sensitive information publicly available. Therefore, neither the amount of any mortgage loan nor the rate of interest will be disclosed, only the existence of the mortgage, its date and date of registration, and the mortgagee's name. Copy leases need not normally be made available, since persons interested in their contents should often have ready access to them.

Section 112(2) excludes the right to inspect and obtain copies of *documents held by the Registrar* but falling outside s 112(1)(b), save (i) as of right in certain exceptional situations, and (ii) at the Registrar's discretion[8]. Cases coming within (i) are limited to inspections required in connection with criminal proceedings, or receivership or insolvency matters[9]. In these instances the applicant is also entitled to request a search of the index of proprietors' names, a right which is not available to the general public[10].

(b) Reasons for inspection
It remains to be seen how frequently[11] and for what reasons applications to inspect the register are made otherwise than in connection with a conveyancing transaction. Various purposes come to mind. For example, a builder may find the power useful when seeking to discover the ownership of land which he wishes to develop. Adjoining landowners involved in a boundary dispute will

6 Land Registration (Open Register) Rules 1992, rr 2, 3. Inspection of the register may be undertaken personally: ibid, r 4. Applications may also be made by fax, but at present only to the Plymouth Registry; see (1990) 87 LS Gaz 41/19.
7 To cover the cost of checking the public index map. Strictly speaking, an applicant unsure of whether the title to land is registered or not ought initially to request such a search, but this is rather time-consuming.
8 (1990) 87 LS Gaz 41/19.
9 Land Registration (Open Register) Rules 1990, r 6, and Sch 2.
10 LRR 1925, r 9 (as substituted by LRR 1976, r 2).
11 By March 1991 about 1,000 copy registers were being issued daily to applicants: HM Land Registry Report, 1990–91, p 10. The Report does not reveal how many of these were for strictly conveyancing purposes.

be able to ascertain if the disputed land is within his neighbour's registered title. The Law Commission felt that an open register could contribute significantly to the simplification of house transfer[12], though in many transactions the supposed benefits are likely to be marginal. However, it will prove very beneficial for purchasers of long leases to be able to discover whether the freehold reversion is registered or not[13], and if so, what covenants and incumbrances affect the superior title. One possible consequence of the register being made public may be an increase in the number of applications to register transfers and other dealings in the name of a nominee, in an attempt to conceal the true ownership of the land.

5.   Certificates of title

As evidence of his title, the registered proprietor receives a land certificate which contains replicas of the register of title to which it relates, and a copy of the plan. Any inaccuracy in the plan or the copy entries appearing in the certificate of title entitles a person suffering loss by reason thereof to be indemnified under the Act[14]. An illustration of the contents of a land certificate, showing some typical entries, appears at the end of this chapter. Under s 68 of the Act the certificate is admissible as evidence of the several matters it contains, without it being necessary to produce the actual records maintained in the Registry[15].

    The land certificate certifies that the land described in the property register and shown on the official plan is registered at HM Land Registry with the title number and class of title stated in the Register. It also states that office copies of the entries in the register and of the plan are contained in the certificate[16]. The certificate bears the official Registry seal and shows the date (stamped in one of the panels printed inside the front cover) when it was last examined with the register at the Registry. Since the certificate contains copies of the official register, it is preferable that it is kept up to date. It is always made to agree with the register on production at the Registry. However, certain entries can be recorded against the title without production of the proprietor's certificate (as to which see below), so there is no guarantee that at any given time it corresponds with the official register. The Registrar will on application make it correspond without the payment of a fee.

    When land is subject to a registered mortgage, the mortgagee receives a charge certificate. This certifies that the charge within is registered at the Registry against the title number referred to. To all intents and purposes it is the same as a land certificate. It contains office copies of the entries in the

---

12   Para 18(v), citing aspects identified in 2 Conveyancing Report, para 4.49.

13   Particularly important in view of SCS 8.1.3, discussed p 341, post.

14   LRA 1925, s 113; see also (1975) 39 Conv (NS) 315–17.

15   LRA 1925, s 68.

16   The wording of a land certificate in computerised form, given in the text, differs from that prescribed by the LRR 1925, r 261, and Sch, Form 78. Also, the outer cover of such certificates is in a new design.

register and of the official plan[17]; the original mortgage deed is bound up inside. Section 67 of the Act requires the land certificate to be retained in the Registry during the subsistence of the mortgage. However, this retention is purely nominal. On a contemporaneous transfer and mortgage of registered land, no separate land certificate is prepared for the new transferee[18], but the Registry always acts as if there were such a certificate deposited with it.

(a)   Production of certificates
It has been said that the land certificate relating to an absolute title constitutes conclusive evidence of the registered proprietor's title to the land and replaces the title deeds which he normally holds in unregistered conveyancing[19]. This evidence of title will need to be made available whenever production of the deeds would be necessary in unregistered conveyancing, such as on a sale. He is required to produce it to the Registrar on a number of specified occasions[20], the most important of these being:

(i) a disposition of the registered land, such as a transfer of the whole or part only, the grant of an easement, or creation of a mortgage;
(ii) a transmission relating to the land, such as that occurring on the death of the proprietor;
(iii) the noting of any adverse estate, right, claim or restriction;
(iv) any rectification of the register unless the Registrar orders to the contrary.

Production of the certificate is not required on lodgment of a caution or inhibition, nor, exceptionally, on the entry of certain notices, including[1] a spouse's statutory rights to occupy the matrimonial home[2]. The Law Commission have advocated various amendments to the rules governing production of land certificates, consequent upon their recommended reforms for the protection of third party rights affecting registered land[3]. These are discussed more fully in the following chapter. In like manner, a mortgagee's charge certificate is roughly equivalent to possession of the deeds in unregistered conveyancing. Production of the certificate is required for dispositions or transmissions of the registered charge, for the entry of notices, restrictions, etc.

---

17 No copy of the plan is included in a charge certificate of a second, or subsequent, mortgage.
18 When a first charge is created by an existing registered proprietor, his land certificate is destroyed once it is lodged at the Registry.
19 R & R, 3-26; *Williams and Glyn's Bank Ltd v Boland* [1981] AC 487 at 504, [1980] 2 All ER 408 at 412, HL, per Lord Wilberforce.
20 LRA 1925, ss 64(1), 82(6).
1 Others being (see s 64(1)(c), as amended) a charge for inheritance tax, and a lease at a rent without taking a fine (premium) (though the Law Commission recommend that this exception should be abolished for the sake of fraud prevention: Report No 158, para 4.110).
2 Ibid, s 64(5), inserted by the Matrimonial Homes and Property Act 1981, s 4(1) (as amended by the MHA 1983, Sch 2). See also s 64(6), added by L & TA 1987, Sch 4, para 2; and s 64(7), added by the Access to Neighbouring Land Act 1992, s 5(3).
3 Law Com No 158, paras 4.105 ff.

(b) Conclusiveness of certificates

According to the theory, the land certificate replaces the title deeds. Yet it must not be thought that reference to them is rendered otiose once a title has been registered, or that the certificate contains all the information ascertainable by perusing the deeds. In the case of leasehold land reference to the lease is essential to discover what covenants, provisions and conditions affect the property. Where the title is possessory or qualified, the title deeds are still important in relation to any pre-registration rights or interests excepted from the effect of registration.

It is doubtless in the realm of the absolute title that the certificate comes nearest to a satisfactory replacement of the title deeds. Even here, however, it does not contain all the desired information. Appurtenant easements may not have been entered in the property register on first registration. Moreover, adverse rights taking effect as overriding interests are not usually revealed, though these are interests that mainly concern matters which would not ordinarily be discoverable by a perusal of title deeds relating to unregistered land[4]. Nevertheless, it means that the registered land system is no improvement on, as opposed to a replacement of, the system based on deeds.

Positive covenants existing at the time of first registration are not recorded in the register of title of the burdened land. Whilst a positive covenant affecting freehold land does not bind the covenantor's successors in title[5], it does not follow that they can be ignored. When he later comes to sell the land, the first registered proprietor needs to know of their existence because of the possibility of taking an indemnity covenant from the purchaser, but he must turn to the deeds, not to his land certificate, to ascertain if any exist. This defect is acknowledged and mitigated to some extent by a note printed inside the cover of the land certificate, warning of the need to inquire into the existence of positive covenants. If the matter is sufficiently important to warrant an express warning, it would seem that the proper place to mention them is somewhere in the register rather than on the cover. As a concession, a note is made in the proprietorship register of the existence of positive covenants created *after* the date of the first registration and a copy of them is sewn into the certificate of title[6].

The land certificate as a document of title is also defective in that it is not required to record matters of legal consequence contained in a transfer of registered land, which is permanently retained in the Registry and not returned to the transferee with the land certificate. The transfer may assign the benefit of positive or negative covenants[7] but this information does not appear in the

---

4   See p 50, post.
5   Unless the principle of *Halsall v Brizell* [1957] Ch 169, [1957] 1 All ER 371, applies.
6   See Registered Land Practice Note 0.1. The reason alleged for not noting positive covenants on first registration is the immense task involved in examining all documents lodged to ascertain their existence. Yet a similar operation is undertaken to discover restrictive covenants. Furthermore, if positive and negative covenants are intermixed, the positive ones are rarely edited out. The problem with positive covenants is compounded by the use on first registration of a transfer pursuant to r 72 (p 544, post) without incorporating any indemnity covenant.
7   See further on this issue, pp 499–500, post.

land certificate. Nor is it possible to tell from the certificate whether property vested in joint tenants is held by them upon the terms of an express or a statutory trust for sale. Again, the transfer may contain an express indemnity covenant in relation to existing covenants. Neither the Act nor the Rules require its existence to be noted in the register, though as a concession a note of any indemnity covenant is included in the certificate[8]. There is an argument in favour of the transfer (or a copy) being incorporated into the certificate, not as evidence of the proprietor's title, for this is established by the certificate, but as evidence of special matters in the transfer.

6.   Maps and plans[9]

It has previously been seen that the registered property is in part described by reference to an accurately prepared plan. This is one of the obvious advantages of the registered system over its unregistered counterpart, where plans are notoriously inaccurate and often inserted solely for identification purposes. Nevertheless, the alleged benefits of Land Registry plans, namely their great clarity and exactitude[10], are not always apparent in reality. Furthermore, as the plans are drawn to a scale of $1/1,250$ (104.2 feet to one inch), they should not be used when identification of precise boundaries is required, especially on a sub-division of land[11].

Of the various modes of description permitted by s 76 of the Act, the one invariably adopted today is the verbal description referring to a filed plan. This plan shows the extent of the registered land by red edging drawn along the inside of the lines demarcating the property's physical boundaries. Where the boundary does not follow a physical feature, it is shown on the plan by a dotted line. The filed plan is an individual plan, prepared by the Registry and based on the Ordnance Survey (OS) map, for use with one particular title. This enables matters peculiar to that title to be shown, such as the route of a right of way affecting the land, indicated on the plan by blue tinting[12]. An applicant for first registration is obliged to furnish sufficient particulars by plan or otherwise to enable the land to be fully identified on the OS map or the Land Registry general map[13]. Alas, the Registry often experiences difficulty

---

8 Registered Land Practice Note 0.1. See further p 498, post.
9 See also pp 542–544, post.
10 See (1980) 130 NLJ 1166.
11 In *Scarfe v Adams* [1981] 1 All ER 843 the Court of Appeal was heavily critical of the use of such a plan when a house was subdivided. Various scales are employed for different types of land. A scale of $1/2,500$ is adopted for areas of land with little or no development, and $1/10,000$ for large tracts of open and unpopulated land (eg, moorland).
12 Different modes of coloration are used by the Registry. Besides red edging, green edging indicates land removed from the title and green tinting relates to islands of land within the land edged red not belonging to the proprietor; blue and brown tinting mark the route of adverse or appurtenant rights of way.
13 LRR 1925, r 20(iii). The general map is a composite map covering numerous properties. Because of its inflexibility compared with the filed plan, it is no longer used as a means to describe registered land. It is still the basis for the public index map (p 209, post).

in identifying the land conveyed[14]. Exceptionally, the parties' own deed plan may be used as the filed plan, eg, where the property comprises overlapping floors.

Since 1969 new and revised OS maps have been in metric measurements. However, for the time being the Registry is prepared to accept either metric or imperial measurements on plans attached to conveyancing documents lodged for registration. When figured dimensions are shown on official title plans, they are reproduced in the same form (whether metric or imperial) as those appearing on the deed plan[15].

7.   General boundaries rule

Rule 278 requires the filed plan to indicate the general boundaries only[16] of the registered plot. It does not profess to determine the exact line of the boundary. So, no guarantee is given that the legal boundary is the centre of a fence, hedge or ditch, or whether the land includes the whole or any part of an adjoining road. The plan is, therefore, of little help in solving boundary disputes. A doubt or dispute as to boundaries may be resolved by a hearing before the Registrar[17]. The Law Commission has expressed its satisfaction with the general boundaries rule and advised its retention[18]. The alternative would be to have a system for defining precisely the exact boundaries of each registered plot. Whilst r 276 does lay down a cumbersome procedure for this (at the applicant's own expense), it is hardly ever used in view of the costs involved. In the circumstances, the Commission saw no need to simplify this procedure so as to make it of more general application.

Where in a particular case the filed plan does not assist in determining the true extent of the property, reference has to be made to the conveyance preceding registration[19]. Other factors may occur which result in the filed plan not revealing the true extent of the land vested in the proprietor. One such situation arose in *Proctor v Kidman*[20]. Here a strip of land inadvertently omitted from both the plan on the conveyance leading to first registration and the filed plan was nevertheless held to be part of the proprietor's registered title because it was the parties' clear intention that the conveyance should pass it to him.

---

14   Law Com No 125, para 2.7; R & R, 12–23; And see (1987) 84 LS Gaz 635 (E J Pryer).

15   See Practice Leaflet No 11 (Introduction of Metrication).

16   Refer generally to Practice Leaflet No 16 (Boundaries in Land Registration), reproduced in [1990] Conv 403–09.

17   Under the LRR 1925, r 298. And see Practice Leaflet No 11, para 6.

18   Law Com No 125, Pt II.

19   *Re St Clement's, Leigh-on-Sea* [1988] 1 WLR 720; *Lee v Barrey* [1957] Ch 251, [1957] 1 All ER 191, CA (conflict between transfer plan and filed plan; transfer plan prevailing).

20   (1986) 51 P & CR 67, CA, p 484, post. There was no suggestion that the omitted land was to be regarded as included by virtue of the general boundaries rule.

8. Form of entries in land certificate

The illustration given in the following pages will give some impression of the nature and form of the entries which may appear in a typical non-computerised land certificate relating to freehold land registered with an absolute title[1]. The names, addresses and documents referred to are purely fictional.

---

1 Practice Leaflet No 19 contains examples of specimen registers of title for freehold and leasehold land, including a computerised register printout.

	H.M. LAND REGISTRY

TITLE NUMBER LT9876

Edition 1 opened 20.5.80 This register consists of 2 pages

A. PROPERTY REGISTER

containing the description of the registered land and the estate comprised in the Title

COUNTY	DISTRICT
LEICESTER	OADBY

The freehold land shown and edged with red on the plan of the above Title filed the Registry registered on 20 May 1980 known as 'Redacres', Blackthorn Lane, together with the rights granted by but subject to the exceptions and reservations continued in the transfer dated 5 May 1980 referred to in Entry No 1 of the Charges Register.

NOTE: A Conveyance dated 8 April 1951 made between (1) Samuel White and (2) James Black contains the following exception and reservation and this registration takes effect subject thereto:–

> 'EXCEPT AND RESERVING unto the Vendor all mines and mineral substances in or under the property hereby conveyed with full power and authority to work and get such mines minerals and mineral substances but by underground workings only including power to let down the surface whether built upon or not proper compensation being paid to the Purchaser and his successors in title for all damage done by subsidence to the surface or any buildings or erections thereon.'

B. PROPRIETORSHIP REGISTER

stating nature of the Title, name, address and description of the proprietor of the land and any entries affecting the rights of disposal thereof

TITLE ABSOLUTE

Entry number	Proprietor, etc.
1.	~~PETER BROWN of 12 Ivy Drive, Leicester, Headmaster, registered on 20 May 1980.~~[2]
2.	HENRY GREEN, Accountant, and ENID GREEN, his wife, both of 'Redacres', Blackthorn Lane, Oadby, registered on 16 January 1990.
3.	RESTRICTION registered on 16 January 1980: No disposition by a sole proprietor of the land (not being a trust corporation) under which capital money arises is to be registered except under an order of the Registrar or of the Court.

2   When the register of title is computerised, former owners are not shown; evidence of previous ownership may be available from the Registry. Also the date of registration is given in brackets at the beginning of each entry, thus: '(16 January 1990) HENRY GREEN ...'

C. CHARGES REGISTER		
containing charges, incumbrances, etc, adversely affecting the land and registered dealings therewith		
Entry number	The date at the beginning of each entry is the date on which the entry was made on and this edition of the register	Remarks
1.	20 May 1980–A transfer of the land in this title dated 5 May 1980 by Grey (Estates) Ltd to Peter Brown contains restrictive covenants.	Copy in Certificate
2.	16 January 1990–CHARGE dated 4 January 1990 registered on 16 January 1980 to secure the moneys including the further advances therein mentioned.	
3.	PROPRIETOR STANFORD BUILDING SOCIETY of High Street, Stanford.	

Chapter 3

Third party rights affecting registered land

In the previous chapter we were principally concerned with those interests which are capable of substantive registration, in what circumstances and with what consequences. Only incidental reference was made to third party rights which may affect a registered title. The student of real property is accustomed to divide such rights into legal and equitable, and to regard the enforceability of the latter as being governed (in the main) by registration as a land charge, which constitutes actual notice under s 198(1) of the Law of Property Act 1925. Under the Land Registration Act 1925, third party rights (other than mortgages which form a special group[1]) are classified into (i) overriding interests and (ii) minor interests. Both categories contain interests which are legal and equitable, a fusion which has prompted the suggestion[2] that the Act has tacitly abandoned the distinction between legal and equitable interests as the chief basis of the classification of incumbrances. A detailed examination of the rights falling within these two classes must now be undertaken.

A Overriding interests

1. General nature and characteristics

Section 3(xvi) of the Act defines overriding interests to mean all the incumbrances, interests, rights and powers not entered on the register but subject to which registered dispositions are by the Act to take effect. This definition has been judicially criticised as being 'a little less than satisfactory'; it simply means that 'overriding interests' are overriding interests[3]. The main subject of interests afforded this exalted status is contained in s 70(1) of the Act. As their name indicates, these interests do not depend for their enforceability on being noted on the register; they bind a registered proprietor even though he is completely unaware of their existence. To this extent, they partake of the character of a legal interest affecting unregistered land. Rights falling within the list of overriding interests may, however, be entered on the

---

1 Page 20, ante.
2 (1958) 22 Conv (NS) 14, 17 (F R Crane).
3 *Abbey National Building Society v Cann* [1991] 1 AC 56 at 84, [1990] 1 All ER 1085 at 1094, HL, per Lord Oliver.

register of title. In this event, as s 3(xvi) shows, they do not take effect as such in relation to that particular title. They acquire their protection by virtue of being noted on the register.

In *National Provincial Bank Ltd v Hastings Car Mart Ltd*[4] Cross explained the general nature of overriding interests in these terms:

> Overriding interests are, speaking generally, matters which are not usually shown on title deeds or mentioned in abstracts of title and as to which, in consequence, it is not possible to form a trustworthy record on the register. As to such matters, persons dealing with registered land must obtain information outside the register in the same manner and from the same sources as people dealing with unregistered land would obtain it.

It does not follow that because these interests are designated overriding a vendor of registered land owes no duty to his purchaser in respect of them. Save where the existence of the interest is apparent, they constitute defects in his title which require disclosure in the contract of sale[5]. A purchaser who discovers the existence of undisclosed overriding interests prior to completion of the transaction may be entitled to rescind the contract. On registration as proprietor, the purchaser takes subject to them, irrespective of his lack of notice, and his rights are limited to suing the vendor on the covenants for title[6]. It should not be imagined that amongst the conglomeration of rights and interests included within the statutory list there lurk strange monsters unknown to unregistered conveyancing. These interests are in no way peculiar to registered land, though their nomenclature is[7]. According to Lord Wilberforce[8]:

> The whole frame of section 70 ... shows that it is made against a background of interests or rights whose nature and whose transmissible character is known, or ascertainable, aliunde, ie, under other statutes or under the common law.

It is not the scheme of the Act to create a difference as to the nature of the rights by which a purchaser may be bound, according to whether the land is registered or unregistered. Yet it will be seen that some rights enjoy a greater (or lesser) measure of protection under one system of conveyancing than the other. In some cases the position is more favourable to third parties, in others the position is worsened[9]. After years of deliberation and consultation the Law Commission has produced its recommendations for the much needed reform of overriding interests[10]. For the moment, we must confine our attention to s 70(1) as at present enacted, leaving consideration of the Commission's Report until later.

4   [1964] Ch 9 at 15, [1963] 2 All ER 204 at 207.
5   See pp 153–161, post, as to this duty of disclosure, and SCS 3.1.2, 3.1.3.
6   But see pp 678–682, post, where it will be shown that in relation to registered land the covenants for title are of reduced value with regard to overriding interests.
7   *Lloyds Bank plc v Rosset* [1989] Ch 350 at 371, [1988] 3 All ER 915 at 921, CA, per Nicholls LJ.
8   *National Provincial Bank Ltd v Ainsworth* [1965] AC 1175 at 1261, [1965] 2 All ER 472 at 503, HL.
9   Contrast *Williams & Glyn's Bank Ltd v Boland* [1981] AC 487, [1980] 2 All ER 408, HL, a favourable case, with *Freer v Unwins Ltd* [1976] Ch 288, [1976] 1 All ER 634.
10   Law Com No 158, Pt II, pp 66–69, post. See also (1972) 88 LQR 93, 104–20 (D C Jackson).

Overlapping categories

The Act does not draw a clear distinction between overriding interests, which are protected without being entered on the register, and other interests which are required to be protected by substantive registration or noting on the register. Interests strictly falling within the latter two categories are capable of being protected as overriding interests. One specific example will suffice to illustrate the point, though others will be encountered in the ensuing pages. In Chapter 2 we saw that the grant by a registered proprietor of a lease for a term exceeding 21 years ranks as a disposition of registered land, and to obtain a legal estate the lessee must seek substantive registration of himself as proprietor of the leasehold title. Nevertheless, despite the failure to register the lease, his interest (which perforce can subsist as an equitable interest only) may still be protected as an overriding interest under s 70(1)(g), which protects the rights of persons in actual occupation of the land[11].

Nor does the Act deal satisfactorily with burdens, whether imposed by legislation or the common law, which affect land owners generally, such as the consequences of the planning laws, or criminal or tortious liability (eg under the law of nuisance) in relation to land. The Commission see this as a defect which needs to be remedied in future legislation[12].

2.   Specific heads of overriding interest

Section 70(1) of the Act lists 12 distinct categories of overriding interest, and subsequent statutes have added to the number. The opening words of the section reiterate what has been stated in general terms in previous sections of the Act, namely, that all registered land is, unless the contrary is expressed on the register, deemed to be subject to such of the following overriding interests *as may be for the time being subsisting in reference thereto.* The italicised words are important. The section secures the continuing enforceability of existing third party rights. It does not purport to revive or resurrect rights that for some reason have already ceased to be enforceable prior to the relevant date for determining what rights bind on the proprietor. Particular consideration will be given to those groups likely to be encountered in practice.

A disposition of freehold registered land operates, when registered, to confer on the transferee the legal fee simple estate subject to (inter alia) overriding interests, if any, affecting the estate transferred (unless the contrary is expressed on the register)[13]. The relevant date for determining the existence of overriding interests is the date of registration[14].

---

11   Some commentators consider this 'longstop' effect to be an advantage of registered land. See M & W, 207.
12   Report No 158, paras 2.1, 2.15, p 68, post.
13   LRA 1925, ss 20(1), 23(1) (leaseholds). See also s 5(b) (first registration), p 28, ante.
14   *Abbey National Building Society v Cann* [1991] 1 AC 56, [1990] 1 All ER 1085, p 59, post.

(a) Rights of common[15], drainage rights, customary rights (until extinguished), public rights, profits à prendre, rights of sheepwalk, rights of way, watercourses, rights of water, and other easements not being equitable easements required to be protected by notice on the register

A more motley collection of rights can hardly be imagined. Basically para (a) is concerned with easements and profits and various public rights. Many of the interests listed are merely examples of easements or profits (eg drainage rights, rights of way). The Law Commission quite rightly maintains that they can be disregarded as superfluous[16]. Rights arising from custom and enjoyed by the inhabitants of a defined locality (such as a town or parish) will continue to exist as overriding interests, but as a separate heading of customary rights[17]. Examples of such rights include the right for parishioners to cross private land to go to and from church[18], and the right of the inhabitants of a borough to use land for sports and pastimes[19]. A customary right is not a public right, since it is not one which exists throughout the whole realm. Until recently, the major uncertainty of para (a) revolved around the eligibility of *equitable* easements to rank as overriding interests. The general consensus of extra-judicial opinion favoured their exclusion, despite the fact that there is nothing in the Act which *requires* them to be protected by notice, save in the sense that they ought to be so protected if they are to bind a registered proprietor[20]. However, in *Celsteel Ltd v Alton House Holdings Ltd*[1] Scott J held that equitable easements are within (a) by virtue of r 258 of the 1925 Rules. This rule provides that adverse rights, privileges and appurtenances occupied or enjoyed with land are overriding interests within s 70. The language of r 278, which is reminiscent of the Law of Property Act 1925, s 62, suggests that its purpose was to preserve the continuing enforceability of rights arising under the general words or the rule in *Wheeldon v Burrows*[2]. Whether it was intended to relate to easements expressly created is questionable. Additionally, the learned judge took the view that an equitable easement which qualified for protection under para (g) as part of the rights of a person in actual occupation would rank as an overriding interest[3].

---

15 See the Commons Registration Act 1965, s 1(1), (2).
16 Report No 158, para 2.19.
17 Ibid, paras 2.71–73. See generally 12 *Halsbury's Laws*, (4th edn), Custom and Usage.
18 *Brocklebank v Thompson* [1903] 2 Ch 344.
19 *New Windsor Corpn v Mellor* [1975] Ch 380, [1975] 3 All ER 44, CA; contrast *Alfred F Beckett Ltd v Lyons* [1967] Ch 449, [1967] 1 All ER 833, CA (alleged custom to take sea coal from foreshore not upheld).
20 LRA 1925, ss 49(1)(c), 59(2). See Brickdale 192; R & R, 6-06; Emmet, para 5.194. Contra Potter, 11, 268. But what then is the justification for not excluding equitable profits?
1 [1985] 2 All ER 562 (easement granted by dispositionary lease not completed by registration); reversed in part, not affecting this point, [1986] 1 All ER 608, CA. His reference (at 575) to the right being *openly* exercised should not be construed as excluding easements lacking visible enjoyment, such as a right of underground drainage. See M P Thompson [1986] Conv 31.
2 (1879) 12 Ch D 31, CA. For r 258, see R & R, 6-07.
3 At 575. It is difficult to envisage a realistic situation when this might occur in practice.

(b) Liability to repair highways by reason of tenure, quit-rents, crown rents, heriots and other rents and charges (until extinguished) having their origin in tenure
Most of these tenurial rights are now obsolete and nothing further need be said about them. Liability to repair highways *ratione tenure* may still survive[4], but it is rarely encountered.

(c) Liability to repair the chancel of any church[5]

(d) Liability in respect of embankments, and sea and river walls
This paragraph relates to subsisting liabilities arising by reason of tenure or custom. Liability existing under a covenant to repair or maintain is outside this paragraph, otherwise positive covenants, the burden of which does not run with freehold land, would assume a proprietary nature.

(e) Land tax, tithe rentcharge, payments in lieu of tithe, and charges or annuities payable for the redemption of tithe rentcharges
These various financial charges have now been statutorily extinguished. Land tax was abolished by the Finance Act 1963, s 68. Tithe rentcharges were extinguished by the Tithe Act 1936, and the annuities which replaced them ceased to be payable as from 2 October 1977[6].

(f) Subject to the provisions of this Act, rights acquired or in course of being acquired under the Limitation Acts
The way in which the Limitation Act 1980 applies to registered land has been considered on page 35. This paragraph protects the squatter's rights even when he has taken no steps to regularise his position by the registration of a possessory title. The operation of para (f) is well illustrated by *Bridges v Mees*[7].

> In 1936 X orally contracted to purchase a strip of registered land at the rear of his garden from Y Co for £7. He paid a deposit of £2 and entered into occupation. The following year he paid the balance of £7, but did not take any transfer of the land nor protect his rights by an entry on the register. In 1977 Y Co went into liquidation. Later the liquidator conveyed the strip of land with other adjoining land to Z who was subsequently registered as proprietor with an absolute title.

It was held that Z's title was subject to X's rights acquired by virtue of his adverse possession of the land for almost 20 years. Z was a trustee of the land for X who was entitled to a transfer of it or to rectification of the register[8]. Had

---

4   See Pratt and MacKenzie, *Law of Highways* (21st edn), 76.
5   See generally, 14 *Halsbury's Laws* (4th edn), para 1100; *Hauxton Parochial Church Council v Stevens* [1929] P 240. See Law Com No 152, advocating abolition after ten years. Pending implementation of this, chancel repairs liability would subsist as a general burden, not as an overriding interest: Law Com No 158, para 2.81.
6   Finance Act 1977, s 56. See Law Com No 158, paras 2.88–93.
7   [1957] Ch 475, [1957] 2 All ER 577; *Chowood Ltd v Lyall (No 2)* [1930] 2 Ch 156, CA.
8   The equitable interest arising under the contract of 1936 also constituted an overriding interest within para (g); see below.

X's occupation commenced ten years later, he would not by 1976 have acquired any adverse title, but since para (f) includes *rights in course of acquisition*, Z could not have alleged that the transfer to him started time running again. X would have acquired a title if Z had allowed the remainder of the limitation period to expire without challenging X's occupation.

(g) The rights of every person in actual occupation of the land or in receipt of the rents and profits thereof, save where inquiry is made of such person and the rights are not disclosed

This is the most extensive and controversial category of overriding interest–frequently asserted to be the counterpart in a modified statutory form of the equitable rule of constructive notice[9]. In other words, it is a statutory application of the rule in *Hunt v Luck*[10]. However, it has been persuasively shown[11] that para (g) cannot be convincingly justified by reference to this rule. The paragraph also protects the rights of persons in receipt of the rents and profits of the land. Several points arise for discussion.

(i) *Rights.* The Act protects the *rights* of the occupant. This point should not be overlooked. Actual occupation is not a right or interest in itself. To constitute an overriding interest under (g), there must be a combination of an interest which justifies continuing occupation plus actual occupation[12]. Furthermore, the right need not be one in virtue of which the claimant is in occupation. In *Webb v Pollmount Ltd*[13] an occupying tenant's option to purchase the reversion was held to be an overriding interest enforceable against a purchaser of the freehold. In order to ascertain what rights are within the paragraph one must look outside the Act to see what rights affect purchasers under the general law[14]. It is sometimes said that the right must be 'an interest in land'[15]. However, the opening words of s 70(1) speak merely of rights 'subsisting in reference [to the land]', a phrase wider in meaning than 'interest in land'. Thus, in *Williams & Glyn's Bank Ltd v Boland*[16] the House of Lords held that the beneficial interest of an occupying tenant in common fell within the paragraph despite the imposition of the statutory trust for sale under s 37 of the Law of Property Act 1925.

9 See, eg, *National Provincial Bank Ltd v Ainsworth* [1965] AC 1175 at 1259, [1965] 2 All ER 472 at 502, HL, per Lord Wilberforce, a view he repeated in *Williams & Glyn's Bank Ltd v Boland* [1981] AC 487 at 504, [1980] 2 All ER 408 at 412, HL; *Abbey National Building Society v Cann* [1991] 1 AC 56 at 88, [1990] 1 All ER 1085 at 1097, per Lord Oliver.
10 [1902] 1 Ch 428, CA. For constructive notice, see pp 376–380, post.
11 See Law Com No 158, paras 2.61–2. But see P Sparkes [1989] Conv 342.
12 *City of London Building Society v Flegg* [1988] AC 54 at 74, [1987] 3 All ER 435 at 441, HL, per Lord Templeman.
13 [1966] Ch 584, [1966] 1 All ER 481. See also *London and Cheshire Insurance Co Ltd v Laplagrene Property Co Ltd* [1971] Ch 499, [1971] 1 All ER 766 (vendor's lien for unpaid purchase money); *Lee-Parker v Izzet* [1971] 3 All ER 1099 (occupying purchaser's lien for deposit).
14 *National Provincial Bank Ltd v Ainsworth*, supra, at 1261, 503, per Lord Wilberforce.
15 Ibid, at 1237 and 488, and adopted by Ungoed-Thomas J in *Webb v Pollmount Ltd*, supra, at 596, 485.
16 [1981] AC 487, [1980] 2 All ER 408, HL; distinguished in *City of London Building Society v Flegg* [1988] AC 54, [1987] 3 All ER 435, HL (mortgage by two trustees for sale).

In many cases the claimant's interest will clearly come within para (g) because it constitutes a recognised legal or equitable interest in land. Such interests possess the quality of being capable of enduring through different ownerships of the land according to normal conceptions of title to land[17]. On the other hand, personal rights are outside the scope of the protection, such as a mere contractual licence[18], or a collateral agreement whereby a tenant, on signing a lease, deposited with his landlord a sum of money as security for due payment of rent[19]. Similarly, a right to claim financial relief under the Matrimonial Causes Act 1973, s 37(2), cannot qualify as an overriding interest[20].

In between, there exists a variety of equitable rights, sometimes called equities or mere equities, in respect of which it must be regarded as debatable to what extent they can come within para (g). Thus, an equity which is ancillary to, or dependent on, an equitable interest in land (eg, an equity to have a deed[1] or contract rectified) may constitute a s 70(1)(g) right, but not, according to Lord Upjohn[2], a 'mere equity standing naked and alone'; for under the general law such a right is incapable of binding successors in title. None of the cases involving an equity arising from expenditure, acquiescence or estoppel have as yet involved registered land. According to Lord Denning MR[3], the equity arising from expenditure on land is an 'obvious example' of a right within the paragraph. This would surely be true where the licensee's right of occupation has been established by the courts[4]. Where the equity that has arisen has yet to be litigated, and so the extent of the remedy to be afforded is unknown, the position is less clear[5]. Such rights are, until litigated, inchoate but have been held, in a number of cases, to bind successors in title[6]. It is submitted that such rights can be categorised as equities and so, if the possessor of the right is in actual occupation of the land[7], they should, in principle, be held to be overriding interests[8].

17   *National Provincial Bank Ltd v Hastings Car Mart Ltd* [1964] Ch 665 at 696, [1964] 1 All ER 688 at 701, CA, per Russell LJ; on appeal, see note 14, ante.
18   *Ashburn Anstalt v Arnold* [1989] Ch 1, [1988] 2 All ER 147, CA, obiter. The court rejected Lord Denning MR's statement of principle in *Errington v Errington and Woods* [1952] 1 KB 290, [1952] 1 All ER 149, CA, that a contractual licence to occupy land constituted an equitable interest in land as being 'not supported by authority, nor necessary for the decision of the case and per incuriam': per Fox LJ at 22, 164.
19   *Eden Park Estates Ltd v Longman* [1982] CA Transcript 417. Cf *Hua Chiao Commercial Bank Ltd v Chiaphua Industries Ltd* [1987] AC 99, [1987] 1 All ER 1110, PC.
20   *Kemmis v Kemmis* [1988] 1 WLR 1307 at 1332, CA, per Nourse LJ.
1   Cf *Blacklocks v JB Developments (Godalming) Ltd* [1982] Ch 183, [1981] 3 All ER 392, p 85, post.
2   *National Provincial Bank Ltd v Ainsworth*, supra, at 1238, 488.
3   *National Provincial Bank Ltd v Hastings Car Mart Ltd*, supra, at 689, 697. Cf *Lee-Parker v Izzet (No 2)* [1972] 2 All ER 800, where the point was conceded.
4   *Williams v Staite* [1979] Ch 291, [1978] 2 All ER 928, CA.
5   See S Baughen (1994) 12 LS 147.
6   *Inwards v Baker* [1965] 2 QB 29, [1965] 1 All ER 446, CA (beneficiary under a will); *E R Ives Investments Ltd v High* [1967] 2 QB 379, [1967] 1 All ER 504, CA (purchaser with express notice); *Voyce v Voyce* (1991) 62 P & CR 290, CA (donee).
7   The right of drainage upheld in *Ward v Kirkland* [1967] Ch 194, [1966] 1 All ER 609 would not have come within para (g) as the person was not in actual occupation. Query whether it could have come within para (a).
8   Although see the doubt, expressed *obiter*, in *Canadian Imperial Bank of Commerce v Bello* (1991) 64 P & CR 48 at 52, per Dillon LJ.

The paragraph simply protects existing rights. It does not extend or alter them. Nor does it invest them with an enforceability which they are incapable of possessing under the general law. Thus, the interest of a beneficiary under a trust for sale is overreached on a sale or mortgage by two trustees for sale, and s 70(1)(g) does not enable the beneficiary, though in occupation, to enforce any rights against the purchaser or mortgagee[9]. *Paddington Building Society v Mendelsohn*[10] provides another illustration. Here an occupying equitable tenant in common was estopped from asserting her interest against the plaintiff society because in the circumstances she was taken to have intended the mortgagee to have priority. Since her rights did not enjoy priority under the general law, s 70(1)(g) could not change them into different and greater rights. Similarly, a third party right, void against a purchaser for non-registration as a land charge, is not rendered enforceable after first registration by virtue of s 5 of the Act because the claimant happens to be in actual occupation of the land[11].

Parliament has expressly enacted that a spouse's statutory rights of occupation under the Matrimonial Homes Act 1983[12], and a tenant's statutory right to acquire the freehold or apply for an extended lease[13], do not rank as overriding interests, despite the claimant's actual occupation. These rights require protection in the appropriate manner on the register of title.

(ii) *Occupation.*   The section protects the rights of the person in *actual occupation* of the land, ie, of the physical land[14]. Further, he must be in occupation of some part[15] of the land which is affected by his rights[16]. Occupation is a matter of fact, not of law[17]. The word 'actual' simply emphasises that what is required is physical presence, not some entitlement in law[18]. It involves some degree of permanence and continuity; this rules out mere fleeting presence[19]. Actual occupation will not necessarily be negatived by regular and repeated absence. So, if a person lives in a house, a temporary absence there from on the relevant date (eg because

9   *City of London Building Society v Flegg* [1988] AC 54, [1987] 3 All ER 435, HL.
10   (1985) 50 P & CR 244, CA, applying *Bristol and West Building Society v Henning* [1985] 2 All ER 606, CA; *Equity and Law Home Loans Ltd v Prestidge* [1992] 1 All ER 909, CA (remortgage). For criticism, see M P Thompson [1992] Conv 206. See also *Castle Phillips Finance v Piddington* [1995] 1 FLR 783, CA.
11   Eg, first registration of freehold land subject to a lease granting an unregistered option to purchase. Cf *Webb v Pollmount Ltd* [1966] Ch 584, [1966] 1 All ER 481, where the freehold title was already registered when the lease and option were created.
12   Section 2(8)(b).
13   Leasehold Reform Act 1967, ss 1, 5(5).
14   *Webb v Pollmount Ltd* [1966] Ch 584 at 593, [1966] 1 All ER 481 at 483, per Ungoed Thomas J.
15   *Hodgson v Marks* [1971] Ch 892 at 916, [1970] 3 All ER 513 at 527, per Ungoed Thomas J ('land' refers to 'land or any part thereof').
16   *Celsteel Ltd v Alton House Holdings Ltd* [1985] 2 All ER 562 at 574, per Scott J (garage occupant unable to assert under (g) equitable easement over driveway leading to garage because of non-occupation of drive).
17   *Boland's* case [1979] Ch 312 at 332, [1979] 2 All ER 697 at 705, CA, per Lord Denning MR.
18   *Boland's* case [1981] AC 487 at 505, [1980] 2 All ER 408 at 413, HL, per Lord Wilberforce.
19   *Abbey National Building Society v Cann* [1991] 1 AC 56 at 93, [1990] 1 All ER 1085 at 1101, HL, per Lord Oliver. Cf *Kingsnorth Finance Ltd v Tizard* [1986] 2 All ER 54 (spouse sleeping elsewhere but visiting house daily and leaving belongings there; sufficient for para (g): per Judge Finlay QC, at 59, obiter).

the claimant is away on holiday or ill in hospital[20]) will not defeat the available protection. A long period of absence may, however, indicate that the claimant has ceased to live there, as where an elderly relative in hospital is too ill to return home. It should not be overlooked that the occupation of the vendor or mortgagor in no way excludes the possibility of occupation by another person, such as a spouse, cohabitee, mother or other third party[1].

The acts which suffice to constitute actual occupation will vary according to the nature of the property involved. In the case of a house, occupation will normally be shown by living there. With woodland, the performance of acts of ownership, such as lopping branches, clearing brushwood and planting saplings, would be enough. The regular parking of a vehicle on an unfenced strip of land, apparently comprised in garage premises, has been held not to amount to actual occupation[2]. In *Lloyds Bank plc v Rosset*[3] the Court of Appeal held that there could be actual occupation of a semi-derelict house by virtue of daily presence there in order to execute works of renovation and rebuilding. However, where the house is fit for habitation, the taking of preparatory steps leading to the assumption of actual residential occupation on or after completion of the purchase is inadequate. In *Abbey National Building Society v Cann*[4] the claimant's agent, by courtesy of the vendor, began to move furniture into the house and to lay carpets approximately half an hour before completion. The House of Lords declined to uphold such activity as amounting to actual occupation. It does not follow from this ruling that a third party claimant can never be in actual occupation prior to completion. It is a question of evidence. Nevertheless, for there to be such occupation, it would seem to be necessary to establish that the moving-in process had finished and residence actually commenced, eg by sleeping in the house (with the vendor's consent) during the night preceding completion day[5].

Actual occupation does not necessarily involve the claimant's personal presence. A person may be in occupation through another, such as a resident caretaker or an employer, or a builder employed to renovate an uninhabitable house[6], or even by means of personal effects, such as furniture[7].

(iii) *Discoverability of occupation?*   There appears to be considerable judicial uncertainty as to whether or not the occupation, to suffice for the purposes of

20   *Chhokar v Chhokar* [1984] FLR 313.
1   *Boland's* case, supra (wife); *Bull v Bull* [1955] 1 QB 234, [1955] 1 All ER 253, CA (mother); *Hodgson v Marks* [1971] Ch 892, [1971] 2 All ER 684, CA (non-relative); *Hussey v Palmer* [1972] 3 All ER 744, CA (mother-in-law); *Re Sharpe* [1980] 1 All ER 198 (aunt).
2   *Epps v Esso Petroleum Co Ltd* [1973] 2 All ER 465; cf *Kling v Keston Properties Ltd* (1983) 49 P & CR 212 at 219, per Vinelott J (car in lock-up garage).
3   [1989] Ch 350, [1988] 3 All ER 915; reversed on appeal on the ground that the claimant, a wife, possessed no beneficial interest in the house: [1991] 1 AC 107, [1990] 1 All ER 1111, HL.
4   [1991] 1 AC 56, [1990] 1 All ER 1085, HL, discussed in (1990) 106 LQR 545 (R J Smith), [1991] Conv 116 (S Baughen), 155 (P T Evans), [1990] CLJ 397 (A J Oakley).
5   It is quite another issue whether the claimant's rights could be enforced against the purchaser's mortgagee. See further, pp 361–372.
6   *Lloyds Bank plc v Rosset* [1989] Ch 350, [1988] 3 All ER 915, CA. In view of its decision the House of Lords had no need to discuss the issue of actual occupation.
7   *Chhokar v Chhokar* [1984] FLR 313 at 317, per Ewbank J (wife in hospital).

para (g), must be such as to put the purchaser on inquiry. Is the discoverability or apparency of the occupation a relevant factor to take into account? In *Boland's* case[8] Lord Scarman took the view that the occupation does not have to be of such a nature as would necessarily put an intending purchaser on notice of an adverse claim. On this view a person can be in actual occupation, even though a purchaser or mortgagee fails to discover his presence there after the most searching of inquiries[9]. Despite this decisive rejection of the relevance of the doctrine of notice, two of the Court of Appeal judges in *Rosset*[10] inclined to a notice-based test. The difficulty appears to be created by the closing words of para (g), which deprive rights of overriding status if inquiry is made of the occupier and the rights are not disclosed. According to Mustill LJ in *Rosset*[11], these words 'at least hint' that Parliament principally had in mind that the acts constituting actual occupation must be such that a purchaser who goes to the land and investigates will discover the fact of occupation and thereby be put on inquiry. But, with respect, this does not follow. Section 70 (1) is concerned with the enforceability of various third party rights, and it should be viewed from the stand point of the third party claimant, rather than that of the purchaser or mortgagee. So far as para (g) is concerned, what matters is the claimant's actual occupation. This operates to protect his rights. But if he fails to disclose them when asked, the section, creating a kind of limited statutory estoppel, deprives those rights of their enforceability. So interpreted, there is nothing in s 70(1)(g) which demands that the occupation must be discoverable or apparent in order to confer protection. To resurrect the doctrine of notice in this context would be a retrograde step. As Lord Scarman observed in *Boland*, it would substitute the uncertainties of notice, actual or constructive, for 'a plain factual situation' as the determinant of an overriding interest[12]. This must, surely, be the preferred view.

(iv) *Date of occupation.* After some judicial and academic uncertainty on the point, the House of Lords decided in *Cann*[13] that the relevant date for determining the question of actual occupation is *the date of completion* of the transaction giving rise to the right to be registered. According to Lord Oliver, this conclusion makes good conveyancing sense. It produces a result which is just, convenient and certain, as opposed to one that is capable of leading to

8 [1981] AC 487 at 511, [1980] 2 All ER 408 at 417, HL. See also Lord Wilberforce at pp 504, 412 (notice no application even by analogy to registered land).

9 *Kling v Keston Properties Ltd* (1983) 49 P & CR 212 at 222, per Vinelott J; *Hodgson v Marks* [1971] Ch 892 at 932, [1971] 2 All ER 684 at 688, CA, per Russell LJ.

10 Per Mustill LJ at [1989] Ch 350 at 394, 397, [1988] 3 All ER 915 at 938–39, 941; per Purchas LJ at 405, and 946, 947, respectively. See also *Abbey National Building Society v Cann* (1989) 57 P & CR 381 at 398–95, CA, per Ralph Gibson LJ. The House of Lords in *Cann* did not consider this controversial point.

11 Note 6, supra.

12 [1981] AC 487 at 511, [1980] 2 All ER 408 at 417. See also Law Com Report No 158, para 2.57, rejecting the relevance of the doctrine of notice; [1991] Conv 155, 165; contra, [1989] Conv 342 (P Sparkes).

13 [1991] 1 AC 56, [1990] 1 All ER 1085, adopting Nicholls LJ's analysis in *Rosset's* case [1989] Ch 350 at 374, [1988] 3 All ER 915 at 923. For the pre-*Cann* authorities, see the 3rd edn of this work, p 53, n 3. For completion, see ch 14.

manifest injustice and absurdity[14]. In the usual domestic conveyancing transaction it is on completion that the purchaser and his mortgagee become irrevocably committed to the transaction. The ruling eliminates, for example, the possibility of a mortgagee, who after making appropriate inquiries parts with the mortgage advance on completion, being bound by an adverse interest asserted by an occupier who moves in between completion and registration of the mortgage.

Of course, the overriding interest must still be subsisting at the date of registration, if it is to bind the transferee or mortgagee under s 20(1) of the Act. However, the protection of rights under para (g) is not dependent on the duration of occupation. If the claimant is in actual occupation at the relevant time, his rights remain enforceable against the proprietor although he later ceases to occupy the land, provided this does not occur before registration[15].

A question not considered in *Cann* is when first registration of title is in issue. It might be thought that the relevant date for determining actual occupation would be the date of registration rather than the date of the conveyance leading to first registration of title, the concept of overriding interests having no role to play where title is unregistered. While this is correct in principle, the point may be academic. This is because, if the person claiming the interest is not in actual occupation at the time of the conveyance, then the purchaser is likely to take free of that interest as a bona fide purchaser. If the claimant is then in actual occupation at the time of registration, there will be no right in existence to take effect as an overriding interest; the pre-existing equitable interest will have been overridden.

(v) *Land occupied.* The rights which para (g) protects relate only to the land occupied by the claimant. In *Ashburn Anstalt v Arnold*[16] the tenant of a shop on part of a development site enjoyed a contractual right in certain circumstances to a lease of a new shop at some unspecified location on the site. It was held that his overriding interest, ie his right to a new lease, did not extend to the remainder of the proprietor's title of which the shop that he occupied formed but part. This illustrates a weakness of the protection provided by s 70(1)(g). Had the tenant protected his estate contract by notice on the register, his rights would have been enforceable over the entirety of the registered title.

(vi) *Rights of other persons.* Not only is the actual occupier protected, but also the person in receipt of the rents and profits. So, failing any inquiry, the occupation of a tenant operates to preserve the rights of the landlord. A person who allowed his step-daughter and her family to occupy a flat on a rent free basis has been held to be outside para (g)[17]. According to the obiter opinion

---

14 At 83 and 1093. Lord Jauncey spoke of 'the date of execution of the mortgage' as the appropriate date, at 104, 1109, but this should not be understood as referring to a date different from the date of completion.

15 *London and Cheshire Insurance Co Ltd v Laplagrene Property Co Ltd* [1971] Ch 499, [1971] 1 All ER 766 at 771, per Brightman J.

16 [1989] Ch 1, [1988] 2 All ER 147, CA.

17 *Strand Securities Ltd v Caswell* [1965] Ch 958, [1965] 1 All ER 820, CA. Payment of a nominal rent of a penny a week would have made all the difference; see Russell LJ at 983, 829.

expressed in *E S Schwab & Co Ltd v McCarthy*[18], a landlord does not qualify if the rent reserved is not paid, despite his having taken a deposit as security for it. In this case the landlord never received any rent.

(vii) *Protection of derivative interests.* Authority exists for saying that the protection accorded to an overriding interest by para (g) extends to a derivative interest carved out of that overriding interest. In *Marks v Attallah*[19] a beneficiary under a bare trust, who was in occupation at the time of completion of the plaintiff's purchase, was held able to create a lease (necessarily equitable) binding on the plaintiff, despite the lease being granted a year after the plaintiff's registration as proprietor. According to Ungoed Thomas J, s 20(1) of the Act provides that a registered disposition is subject to overriding interests, not subject to overriding interests in any particular person. The tenant, claiming under the occupying beneficiary, was entitled to shelter behind her overriding interest. It mattered not that he could establish no protection in his own right. It is doubtful whether s 20 should be interpreted this way. The decision means that in s 20(1) 'overriding interests' are to be understood as including derivative non-overriding and non-protected interests created *after registration*. This is a startling proposition, having no counterpart in unregistered land. It is thought, with respect, that the decision is wrong[20].

(viii) *Inquiry.* A purchaser takes free from any overriding interest where inquiry is made of the occupier and his rights are not disclosed. Yet this may be of little consolation to the purchaser, if the view discussed on page 59 is correct that the occupier need not be a readily discoverable person. There appears to be no reported instance where a purchaser or mortgagee has taken free from the occupier's rights because inquiry of him failed to reveal them. Since, presumably, the inquiry is one 'for the purposes of the intended disposition'[1], it should be made no later than the date of completion of the purchase or mortgage. It was this consideration that led the House of Lords in the *Cann* case to hold that it is the date of completion, not that of subsequent registration, that determines whether there is actual occupation for the purposes of para (g). It is the only date at which the inquiry can realistically be made and be relevant[2]. Yet in practice, the only inquiries that are normally made are raised before exchange of contracts[3], and these tend to be with the

---

18 (1975) 31 P & CR 196 at 213 and 215, CA. What if the landlord has not collected the rent for a long time? The Law Commission feels that the rights of these other persons should not continue to have overriding status: Report No 158, para 2.70; draft Bill, cl 7(2)(d).
19 (1966) 198 EG 685. The existence of the beneficiary's interest was conceded, a point subsequently shown to have been properly made: *Hodgson v Marks* [1971] Ch 892, [1971] 2 All ER 684, CA. *Marks v Attallah* is ignored by R & R and by Emmet. It is accepted as correctly decided, without question, by Hayton, 139, and Gray, *Elements of Land Law*, (2nd edn), 206.
20 The decision also runs counter to s 101 of the Act, which regulates dealings off the register. The effect of the ruling is that unprotected minor interests can be elevated to the status of overriding interests by virtue of some other person's occupation.
1 *London and Cheshire Insurance Co Ltd v Laplagrene Property Co Ltd* [1971] Ch 499 at 505, [1971] 1 All ER 766 at 771–72, per Brightman J.
2 [1991] 1 AC 56 at 88, [1990] 1 All ER 1085 at 1097, per Lord Oliver.
3 See p 183, post, discussing the standard form preliminary inquiry.

vendor rather than with the occupier, which is what the Act requires. Reliance is placed on the vendor's (or borrower's) replies, and any necessary consents or waivers are sought from occupiers who are disclosed. As the Law Commission observed, a risk is undertaken, no inquiries are made on the spot and reliance is placed on conveyancing being conducted on a basis of good faith[4].

The conclusion that this proviso in para (g) performs no useful purpose because it is worthless in practice must surely be correct. Under the existing legislation only non-disclosure on inquiry can, seemingly, bar the occupier from enforcing his rights[5]. The recommended repeal of the proviso will enable the courts to decline to uphold an occupier's rights in a suitable case of fraud or estoppel. This jurisdiction will apply to all categories of overriding interests[6].

(ix) *Occupiers within para (g).*   It is now necessary to have a brief look at different occupiers who may come within the paragraph, always remembering that it is the occupier's rights, not merely his occupation, that are protected. A purchaser in occupation under an enforceable contract for sale[7], or a tenant occupying by virtue of an agreement for a lease are within the provision. Similarly, para (g) extends to protect a transferee of registered land, or a lessee of a registrable lease, who fails to apply for substantive registration, provided he enters into actual occupation. Its operation is illustrated by the case of *Kling v Keston Properties Ltd*[8]. The plaintiff, X, was in occupation of a garage, qua licensee, but with the benefit of a right of pre-emption should Y, the owner, sell it on long lease. Y agreed to lease it to Z. Thereupon X's right was converted into an option to purchase[9]. This constituted an equitable interest in the land which by virtue of X's occupation was binding on Z's registered title.

The decision in *Hodgson v Marks*[10] establishes that a beneficiary entitled to the fee simple estate in equity under a bare trust can rely on para (g) to enforce his rights against a purchaser from the trustee. Following the House of Lords' ruling in *Boland's* case, the position of an occupying beneficiary under a trust for sale is the same, so long as his interest is not overreached on a sale or mortgage of the property[11]. The general application of s 70(1)(g) to beneficiaries under a bare trust or a trust for sale is not curtailed by s 74 of the Act. This section, which provides that no one dealing with a registered estate is to be affected with notice of any trust, express, implied or constructive, does

---

4   Law Com No 158, para 2.59; and see its Report No 115, paras 39–41. To rely on inaccurate information supplied by the vendor will not protect the purchaser vis-à-vis an occupier enjoying rights. It may give rise to a claim against the vendor for misrepresentation.

5   An argument based on estoppel failed at first instance in *Hodgson v Marks* [1971] Ch 892, [1970] 3 All ER 513.

6   See the Commission's draft Bill, cll 7(2)(d), 9(7). For the view that the inquiry rule itself operates as a restricted form of statutory estoppel, see p 59, ante.

7   *Bridges v Mees* [1957] Ch 475, [1957] 2 All ER 577, p 54, ante. Or an unregistered donee in occupation by virtue of a fully effective voluntary transfer; cf *Mascall v Mascall* (1984) 50 P & CR 119, CA.

8   (1983) 49 P & CR 212.

9   Following *Pritchard v Briggs* [1980] Ch 338, [1980] 1 All ER 294, CA, p 387, post.

10   [1971] Ch 892, [1971] 2 All ER 684, CA; *Bridges v Mees*, supra (the vendor was in fact a bare trustee for the purchaser who had paid all the purchase money).

11   *City of London Building Society v Flegg* [1988] AC 54, [1987] 3 All ER 435, HL.

not affect the enforcement of any interest or right existing as an overriding interest[12]. Conversely, a beneficiary in occupation of settled land cannot claim an overriding interest; s 86(2) of the Act expressly enacts that interests arising under a settlement take effect as minor interests *and not otherwise*. Presumably, this provision will extend to equitable interests under which a licensee has an equity to reside in a house for the rest of his life. However, the courts have yet to resolve the doubt as to whether these cases attract the provisions of the Settled Land Act 1925[13]. The frequency with which unintended and informal settlements occur has prompted a Law Commission recommendation to upgrade into overriding interests the proprietary rights of beneficiaries in occupation under a strict settlement[14].

One final and important point needs to be stressed. The fact that an overriding interest claimed by an occupier is also capable of being protected on the register in the proper manner, which he has failed to do, is quite irrelevant. Several cases involving para (g), including *Boland's* case, affirm this principle[15].

The decision in *Boland* was one of the more important ones affecting registered land in recent years and generated a considerable literature and subsequent case law. Its main effect has been in the context of possession actions by mortgagees and so a detailed consideration of the conveyancing implications of it, and the other decisions related to this matter, will be deferred until the subject of mortgages is considered[16].

(h) In the case of a possessory, qualified or good leasehold title, all estates, rights, interests and powers excepted from the effect of registration
As we saw in the previous chapter[17], registration with less than an absolute title does not prejudice various interests; these take effect as overriding interests.

(i) Rights under local land charges unless and until registered or protected on the register in the prescribed manner
Local land charges are not generally protected on the register, except in the case of a charge securing the payment of money which requires registration before realisation[18]. Consequently, the same searches in the registers maintained by local authorities must be undertaken as in unregistered conveyancing. As to what constitute local land charges see the Local Land Charges Act 1975, s 1, discussed in Chapter 7.

---

12   *Boland's* case, [1981] AC 487 at 508, [1980] 2 All ER 408, 415, per Lord Wilberforce.
13   The questions are: is there a settlement within the Act? Is the court order establishing the equity an 'instrument' for the purpose of s 1(1)? See *Griffiths v Williams* (1977) 248 EG 947 at 949, CA, per Goff LJ; *Ivory v Palmer* [1975] ICR 340 at 347, CA, per Cairns LJ. Contrast *Binions v Evans* [1972] Ch 359, [1972] 2 All ER 70, CA; *Dodsworth v Dodsworth* (1973) 228 EG 1115, CA; *Ungurian v Lesnoff* [1990] Ch 206; *Costello v Costello* [1994] EGCS 40. And see [1978] Conv 229 (P W Smith).
14   Law Com No 158, para 2.69; draft Bill, cll 7(2)(d), 47.
15   See also *Bridges v Mees*, supra; *Hodgson v Marks*, supra; *Kling v Keston Properties Ltd*, supra.
16   See pp 361–372, post.
17   Pages 33–36, ante.
18   LRA 1925, s 59(2); LRR 1925, r 155.

(j) Rights of fishing and sporting, seigniorial and manorial rights of all descriptions (until extinguished), and franchises
This relates to a very limited class of manorial incidents formerly attaching to copyhold land and indefinitely preserved by the Law of Property Act 1922[19].

(k) Lease granted for a term not exceeding 21 years
A lease does not have to take effect in possession to be within this paragraph. An agreement for a lease is not, however, protected. The word 'granted' imports the actual creation of a term of years taking effect at law[20]. The same word also implies the express creation of a term by the act of the parties, either by deed, or by signed writing or parol in the case of leases that can be created informally. A lease arising by implication of law does not seem to be within this paragraph. The scope of para (k) has been widened by the Land Registration Act 1986, s 4(1), which removed the previous qualification that operated to exclude leases granted at a fine (or premium)[1]. The paragraph protects 'leases'. To what extent the lessee's rights (other than that of possession) are similarly protected is not stated. The problem is only likely to be material where the lessee cannot bring himself within para (g). It seems that para (k) enables the lessee to enforce all the terms having reference to the subject matter of the lease, but not those that are merely collateral to the relationship of landlord and tenant, eg an option to purchase the freehold reversion[2].

(l) Mines and minerals
This paragraph, the lengthy wording of which has not been reproduced, deals with rights to mines and minerals relating to land registered prior to 1926. When land is first registered after 1925, the proprietor of an absolute freehold title obtains title to the mines and minerals (since they are included within the definition of land), unless they have been severed and the Registrar makes a note on the register that they are excepted from the registration[3]. They do not take effect as overriding interests, except in the case of coal and coal mines vested in the British Coal Corporation[4] and manorial rights to mines and minerals protected under para (j).

According to s 70(1) of the Act, registered land is deemed to be subject to such overriding interests 'as may be for the time subsisting in reference thereto'. This raises a question of considerable importance: what is the relevant date to determine whether an overriding interest subsists so as to be binding upon a

---

19   Section 128, Sch 12, paras 5 and 6.
20   *City Permanent Building Society v Miller* [1952] Ch 840, [1952] 2 All ER 621, CA. The context displaces the definition in s 3(x) that lease includes an agreement for a lease.
1   See *Skipton Building Society v Clayton* (1993) 25 HLR 596, CA.
2   See *Woodall v Clifton* [1905] 2 Ch 257. Cf *Webb v Pollmount Ltd* [1966] Ch 584, [1966] 1 All ER 481, p 55, ante, (option enforceable under s 70(1)(g)).
3   LRR 1925, r 196. See p 20, ante. See generally R & R, 6–26, 9–18.
4   Coal Act 1938, s 41; Coal Industry Nationalisation Act 1946, ss 5, 8. Coal Industry Act 1987, s 1.

purchaser? This was considered in *Abbey National Building Society v Cann*[5], where the House of Lords held that, in general, the crucial date for all overriding interests is the date of registration. This is, with respect, the only feasible ruling that could have been given, and seems to be dictated by ss 20(1) and 23(1) of the Act. The problem with this is that a transferee could find himself bound by an overriding interest created after completion and before registration[6]. It was precisely this consideration that led the House to hold that, in the case of interests coming within para (g), the relevant time should be the date of completion and not the date of registration. In respect of other interests, such as the grant of an easement or a lease, or the maturing of a squatter's rights between completion and registration, the transferee will be bound. Similarly, the ruling ensures the enforceability of a local land charge arising after completion; a matter of considerable concern to their Lordships[7].

3.   Overriding interests on the register

As defined, overriding interests do not include matters entered on the register. Once entered on the register, protection as an overriding interest becomes superfluous; the entry itself confers protection, for registration always takes effect subject to entries appearing on the register[8]. Rights and interests included within the list of overriding interests may find their way on to the register for a variety of reasons. Those interests which are duly protected by means of a notice, caution[9] or restriction constitute the commonest examples of s 70(1) rights entered on the register. In addition, s 70(2) of the Act requires adverse easements created by an instrument to be noted on the register at the time of first registration provided they appear on the title[10], whilst s 70(3) empowers the Registrar to enter notice of any overriding interest proved to his satisfaction or admitted. This latter provision is not limited to first registrations, and an interested party has an independent right by virtue of r 197 to apply for notice of an overriding interest to be entered on the register. An entry may also be made on the register recording the fact that the title is *not* subject to a particular overriding interest. However, the view has been judicially expressed that this provision merely enables the cancellation of a previous entry noting the existence of some liability[11].

5   [1991] 1 AC 56, [1990] 1 All ER 1085, HL.
6   And by a derivative interest carved out of an overriding interest *after* registration, if *Marks v Attallah* (1966) 198 EG 685, p 61, ante, is correct.
7   See [1991]1 AC 56 at 85–87, [1990] 1 All ER 1085 at 1095–96, per Lord Oliver; [1991] AC at 105–6, [1990] 1 All ER at 1110, per Lord Jauncey.
8   See eg LRA 1925, ss 5(a), 9(b), 20(1)(a), 23(1)(b).
9   What if the caution is later removed after warning-off (p 74, post)? Will the claimant's occupation still protect his rights under para (g)? Section 55(1) suggests so, provided 'may' has mandatory force. And see Law Com No 158, para 2.2, note 6, citing *Re Dances Way West Town, Hayling Island* [1962] Ch 490, [1962] 2 All ER 42, CA.
10   Other than those of a trivial or obvious nature: LRR 1925, r 199. See also r 41.
11   LRR 1925, r 197; *Re Dances Way West Town, Hayling Island*, supra, at 510, 53, per Diplock LJ. Cf R & R, 6–29.

4.   Reform–the way ahead?

(a) Continued existence justified

The existence of many overriding interests not appearing on the register of title inevitably means that it does not contain a complete record of all matters affecting the title to land. In this major area, therefore, reliance on the register may prove to be misplaced. They have been branded as 'the stumbling block' to land registration[12], and 'inconsistent with the whole concept of registered title'[13]. Viewed from the purchaser's standpoint, overriding interests are doubly odious. Not only is he obliged to make inquiries outside the register, he is denied any right of indemnity under the Act[14] if it is rectified against him to give effect to some overriding interest which perhaps he did not, and could not, discover. Yet their existence can be defended, as the Law Commission was at pains to show in Report No 158. Some rights are too transient to be worth recording. Others arise under an informal arrangement without professional advice; to require such to be protected by registration on pain of deprivation would be too harsh and unjust a penalty (para 2.6). Though at one time the notion of total abolition was canvassed, the Commission eventually concluded that they should be retained, but reduced in number. In deciding which of the existing categories should keep their privileged status, two principles were adopted, the first being subject to the second: (1) in the interests of certainty and of simplifying conveyancing, the class of right automatically binding a purchaser should be as narrow as possible; but (2) interests should be overriding where protection against purchasers was needed, yet to require entry on the register was either not reasonable to expect or not sensible to require. Lest this be interpreted as undue bias towards the conveyancer and his client, the indemnity provisions of the Act are to be extended to claims occasioned by overriding interests[15].

(b) The privileged group

Consideration of these two principles left only five candidates remaining for continued overriding interest status: (i) easements and profits, (ii) rights by adverse possession, (iii) short leases, (iv) occupiers' rights, and (v) customary rights[16]. Those interests scheduled for relegation will become minor interests, or in a few cases, general burdens. The Commission rejected the idea that during a transitional period those interests demoted to minor interests should be registrable as of right so as to bind subsequent new proprietors. In reality, there will be an indeterminate period when the current registered proprietor will continue to be bound, and his successors in title, except a transferee in good faith and for value. He will not be bound unless the right has been

12   Brickdale, 32.
13   *Law Reform Now* (1964), 81, cited in Law Com No 158, para 2.2.
14   Page 97, post.
15   Para 2.6; see further, p 103, post.
16   Para 2.24; draft Bill, cl 7(2).

protected on the register in the proper manner[17]. Further comment on the detailed proposals of some of the five categories is necessary.

(i) *Easements and profits*[18]. The extent of this grouping is to be reduced. It will be confined to legal rights only and will embrace easements arising by operation of law, eg under s 62 of the Law of Property Act 1925, by implied grant or reservation or through the doctrine of non-derogation of grant. Also included will be adverse legal easements existing at the time of first registration of the servient land, unless entered on the register as part of the registration process. Unlike the present para (a), there will be no need to mention specifically rights of sheepwalk, watercourses etc. *Excluded* from overriding status will be (i) equitable easements, and, importantly, (ii) easements expressly created after first registration. The latter already require completion by registration[19], and until then they will, under the new regime, rank as minor interests only.

(ii) *Short leases.* This head of overriding interest will cover legal leases for a continuous term not exceeding 21 years, taking effect in possession immediately or within one month of its creation. The tenant's rights having reference to the subject matter of the lease (eg an option to renew) will be expressly included. Two points deserve mention. The need for the lease to be continuous will exclude discontinuous terms, including 'time share' arrangements, whilst the immediacy of possession requirement rules out reversionary leases (paras 2.44, 2.46). The one month's latitude is intended to catch (eg) short tenancies granted today, but to commence at the start of next week. Equitable leases will, as at present, not qualify for overriding status. Such leases will usually be protected under (iii) below.

(iii) *Rights of actual occupiers.* As we have noticed, the Commission rejected the view that s 70(1)(g) was the statutory offspring of the rule in *Hunt v Luck*[20], despite the accumulated judicial support for the proposition. Nevertheless, it was firmly convinced of the necessity to retain this favoured category. The rights of actual occupiers, including most beneficial interests in dwelling-houses, are often of the kind which arise informally, without the acquirer having the benefit of legal advice (para 2.64). Consequently, they were considered to be eligible for automatic protection on the basis of the second of the Commission's two fundamental principles.

---

17 Paras 2.16–2.18. This savours of the private expropriation of property rights without compensation. No consideration appears to have been given to the possibility of compensation from public funds, assessed in accordance with principles including the gravity of the loss to the claimant and the extent to which he could realistically be held to have been negligent in failing to protect his rights. The Commission merely contented themselves by saying that the unprotected right would not necessarily be worthless as there might well be remedies against the previous proprietor. Such situations would in practice be confined to cases where the proprietor had granted the interest, so that a contractual remedy might be available.

18 See paras 2.25–2.35. In the following discussion easements include profits.

19 As a disposition of registered land under ss 18 (1)(c), 21(1)(b); see ss 19(2), 22(2). And see further Ch 15; [1987] Conv 328 (AM Prichard).

20 [1902] 1 Ch 428, CA; see p 55, ante.

Apart from some minor modifications[1], the scope and operation of para (g) will remain unabated. All the occupier's rights will continue to be protected, not merely those by virtue of which he is actually in occupation. In many respects the Commission's recommendations are less radical than the provisional proposals outlined in its 1971 Working Paper. This is attributable to the undermining influence of the Lords' decision in *Boland's* case[2]. They declined to introduce any element of apparency into the concept of actual occupation. So to do would be to revive the doctrine of notice[3]. They summarily dismissed a suggestion to exclude rights capable of protection on the register by an appropriate entry (para 2.66). To have adhered to their previous contrary view would, in effect, have been to counsel the reversal of *Boland*, which would not be socially acceptable[4]. Occupiers' rights will potentially continue to enjoy dual protection status: either as overriding interests *or as minor interests*, depending on the circumstances. Some commentators will, justifiably, see this failure to eliminate the overlap between different classes of interests and their mode of protection as an unwelcome perpetuation of a principle that was probably not intended by the framers of the 1925 Act[5]. One way to limit the operation of the rule in this respect was canvassed and rejected. The Commission did not consider it to be feasible to exclude proprietary rights that had been acquired with all due formality, even though the additional requirement of protection by entry on the register could reasonably be expected in such situations (para 2.67).

(c) General burdens

The Commission's draft Bill creates a new class of rights – burdens of general incidence, whether imposed by legislation or the common law. They will bear a superficial resemblance to overriding interests in that they are to be automatically binding on all proprietors; but their very nature will exclude them from the rectification and indemnity provisions of the Act. Certain existing overriding interests will be brought within this new category[6]: (i) public rights (a); (ii) chancel repairs liability (c); (iii) local land charges (i); (iv) mineral rights vested in British Coal (l); and franchises (principally markets and fairs) (j)[7]. Also included in the list is a statutory tenancy under the Rent Act 1977.

---

1 The deletion of the inquiry proviso, and withdrawal of automatic protection for those in receipt of rents, offset by the more significant inclusion of beneficiaries under strict settlements.

2 [1981] AC 487, [1980] 2 All ER 408, HL; Report No 158, para 2. 7. See also pp 55, post.

3 But see p 59, ante, as to the judicial uncertainty on this issue.

4 Particularly in the light of the unfavourable responses to their 1982 Report (No 115), which adopted an anti-*Boland* stance; see Report No 158, para 2.7.

5 See the issue more fully explored in Working Paper No 37 (1971), paras 15ff.

6 Draft Bill, cl 5(3). The existing s 70(1) classification is given in brackets. It is envisaged that the Registrar would have a discretion to note a general burden on the register: Report No 158, para 2.15.

7 See para 2.100, and App F.

(d) New minor interests
The following interests are to be relegated to minor interests and require protection as such: (i) highway liability arising from tenure (b); (ii) liability in respect of embankments, sea and river walls (d); (iii) crown rents (b); (iv) payments in connection with tithes (e); (v) manorial rights (j).

One existing s 70(1) group has not hitherto been mentioned – para (h) rights. The Commission concluded that rights expressly excluded from the effect of registration stand and take effect outside the register. There is no need to make further provision for any excepted matter in the register. On this basis alone continuing overriding interest status was not warranted.

(e) Conclusion
Compared with the extremely radical proposals which were at one time being actively debated[8], the Commission's final recommendations are somewhat tame and low-key. Apart from the much-needed legislative re-drafting of s 70(1), it is an exercise in cosmetic surgery (para 2.23), Part II of the Report essentially preserves the status quo. The only practically important categories within sub-s (1) are (a), (f), (g) and (k). All will continue to apply with minor modifications more or less as at present. There are, however, two significant and beneficial changes which will apply to *all* five remaining categories of overriding interests. These are: (i) that they will be expressly subject to a general provision regarding fraud and estoppel, and (ii) that indemnity will be available.

The Law Commission urged another change which it saw as vital. To solve the so-called registration-gap problem, it recommended that the relevant date to determine the enforceability of all overriding interests should be the date of completion of the disposition, not of registration. This solution has been overtaken by the decision in *Abbey National Building Society v Cann*[9], and it remains to be seen whether the Commission will still press for their preferred reform[10].

B   Minor interests

In contrast to overriding interests which are binding even though not appearing on the register, numerous third party rights and interests exist which are liable to be defeated on a registered disposition for value of the burdened land unless they are protected by an entry on the proprietor's register of title. These are known as minor interests, defined by s 3(xv) of the Act to mean:

8   See para 2.71, and the 21 items listed in footnote 36.
9   [1991] 1 AC 56, [1990] 1 All ER 1085, p 60, ante.
10   Interestingly, their proposal appears not to have been carried into the draft Bill. See, eg, cl 17(2), which in this respect is drafted in terms similar to s 20(1) of the Act. Consideration ought, perhaps, to be given to a more radical suggestion. Would any adverse practical consequences ensue, if an application for registration were to be deemed to be completed (and, therefore, the legal title acquired) as from the date of completion of the transaction?

... the interests not capable of being disposed of or created by registered dispositions and capable of being overridden (whether or not a purchaser has notice thereof) by the proprietors unless protected as provided by this Act, and all the rights and interests which are not registered or protected on the register and are not overriding interests.

Specificially included within the definition are interests and powers capable of being overridden either by trustees for sale, or by a tenant for life or statutory owner of settled land. Section 2(1) provides that apart from legal estates which are capable of substantive registration and overriding interests, all other interests in registered land take effect *in equity as minor interests*.

1.   Classification of minor interests

This long and obscure definition clause embraces three categories of interests.

(a) Equitable interests under settlements and trusts for sale
Within this group come the beneficial interests existing behind a settlement or trust for sale, which are protected by means of an appropriate restriction entered against the registered proprietor. This restriction warns a purchaser of the land to comply with the overreaching provisions of the Settled Land Act 1925, and the Law of Property Act 1925, so protecting the interests of the beneficiaries[11]; but he will take free from these provided the overreaching machinery is carried out[12].

(b) Dispositions of registered land
A disposition of registered land, such as the creation of a mortgage or the grant of a registrable lease, ranks as a minor interest until the disposition is completed by registration in the prescribed manner. Take the case of a dispositionary lease which A, a registered proprietor, grants to B for a term exceeding 21 years. B does not obtain a legal lease until the disposition is completed by substantive registration under s 19(2) of the Act[13]. Pending registration, his lease ranks merely as a minor interest, unless he brings himself within s 70(1)(g). As such it will be defeated on a transfer for value of the freehold reversion if not protected on the register. The status of the lease as a minor interest is, in practice, temporary only; it ceases to be such on substantive registration as a separate title. The position of a transferee of registered land until he is registered as the new proprietor is similar.

This class of minor interests, comprising what might be termed inchoate legal estates or interests awaiting their full recognition as such by completion of the registration process, has no corresponding counterpart in unregistered conveyancing. Here the full legal title passes under the conveyance, lease or mortgage, and nothing further has to be done before it vests in the grantee.

11   See further post, pp 302–306 (settlements), pp 306–317 (trusts for sale).
12   Cf *Ahmed v Kendrick* (1987) 56 P & CR 120, CA (no overreaching; forged transfer).
13   There is no obligation on B to register, but the lessee usually does to obtain a legal title.

(c) Non-registrable interests[14] *requiring protection on the register*

This group resembles most closely that class of interests known as land charges in unregistered conveyancing, eg estate contracts and restrictive covenants. These minor interests cannot be registered as separate titles but require to be protected on the register, and if not protected they become unenforceable against a subsequent purchaser for value. To this extent, they partake of the character of equitable interests in unregistered conveyancing, whose enforceability depends on notice, usually by means of registration under the Land Charges Act 1972.

2. Methods of protection

Minor interests can be protected on the register by the entry of a notice, caution, inhibition or restriction[15]. These are not mutually exclusive methods; some interests may be protected by a notice, caution or restriction[16]. And it should not be forgotten that an interest which has not been properly protected as a minor interest may nevertheless be enforceable as an overriding interest by virtue of s 70(1)(g)[17]. Subject to this one point, a transferee for valuable consideration of an absolute freehold title takes free from any minor interest not entered on the register[18], even, it seems, an interest to which he is party or privy[19]. Conversely, a transferee otherwise than for value, such as a donee or transferee for a nominal consideration of £1[20], is bound by all minor interests subject to which the transferor held the land[1], despite their lack of protection.

(a) Notice

(i) *Interests protected.* A notice (or note as it is sometimes termed) is a specific entry on the register of the interest which it protects. It appears in the charges register of the registered proprietor. The Act specifies[2] those interests capable of being protected by notice, the main ones being leases (other than those qualifying as overriding interests), restrictive covenants, and other land charges

---

14 Including certain leases *not* converted into overriding interests by the LRA 1986, because they were created before the Act became operative, eg gratuitous leases and leases granted at a premium for 21 years or less. See pp 481–485, post. They will also embrace those interests destined to lose overriding interest status under the Law Commission's revised scheme.

15 LRA 1925, s 101(3). The statutory provisions are ambiguous, overlapping and out of balance; the subject appears to have been treated in a rather aimless way: Law Com No 158, para 4.34.

16 See R & R, (5th edn) 786, 787, for a list of the normal and possible alternative methods of protection for interests which constitute land charges within the LCA 1972.

17 See p 63, ante.

18 LRA 1925, ss 20(1), 23(1), (2) (leasehold titles). On the question whether notice of the existence of an unprotected interest affects the position, see p 77, post.

19 *Orakpo v Manson Investments Ltd* [1977] 1 All ER 666 at 687, CA, per Goff LJ (obiter); affd on other grounds [1978] AC 95, [1977] 3 All ER 1, HL. Contrast *Jones v Lipman* [1962] 1 All ER 442 (unprotected contract not defeated by sham transaction).

20 *Peffer v Rigg* [1978] 3 All ER 745, p 77, post; LRA 1925, s 3(xxxi).

1 LRA 1925, ss 20(4), 23(5).

2 See ss 48–51, 59(2), (5).

until the land charge is registered as a registered charge[3]. An entry protecting a contract for the sale of land might read: '6 April 1988–Contract dated 17 March 1988 for sale to AB for £20,000'.

The date at the beginning of the entry indicates when it was made on the register.

(ii) *Production of land certificate.*   So long as the proprietor's land certificate is outstanding, a notice protecting a minor interest cannot be entered on the register unless the certificate is lodged at the Registry. There are exceptions to this requirement, the most important being a spouse's charge in respect of rights of occupation under the Matrimonial Homes Act 1983[4]. The co-operation of the registered proprietor is thus necessary, at least in theory, and having created the interest he will not normally object to the lodgment of the certificate, provided he is able to do so. If, for instance, he has already deposited the certificate with a third party as security for a loan, protection by way of notice is not possible without the chargee's unlikely co-operation. However, the Registry do not regard the certificate as being outstanding when it is already there for any reason, even one wholly unconnected with the application to enter the notice. The need for the proprietor's concurrence is, therefore, rendered illusory, particularly when the land is subject to a registered charge. In this situation the land certificate will always be deposited at the Registry[5], thereby facilitating entry of the notice. In practice, the Registry take steps to notify the proprietor of the receipt of any application to enter a notice[6], which affords him an opportunity to object. Should the registered proprietor refuse to deposit his certificate because (eg) of a dispute relating to the minor interest, the incumbrancer can protect his (alleged) interest by lodging a caution.

An application to register a notice[7] which is not accompanied by an outstanding land certificate will be accepted by the Registry, albeit provisionally, but no entry will be made against the title until the certificate is lodged there. Nevertheless, as a result of r 83 of the 1925 Rules[8], the application has priority as from the date of its delivery at the Registry, even though it was not then in order. The application will be revealed on any search certificate issued to an intending transferee. Where, however, entry of a notice is applied for during the priority period conferred by an official search certificate, the application is temporarily held in abeyance by the Registry to await the outcome of events. Thus, if a dealing with the land (such as a transfer) is completed within that priority period and so protected by virtue of the Land Registration (Official

3   A reference to puisne mortgages registrable as substantive charges under s 26 of the Act.
4   Matrimonial Homes and Property Act 1981, s 4(1), adding a new sub-s (5) to s 64 of the main Act. For the other cases, see s 64(1)(c), p 43, ante.
5   Pursuant to the LRA 1925, s 65. See p 20, ante.
6   Except a notice protecting the charge arising under the MHA 1983 a procedure that has evoked strong judicial criticism: *Watts v Waller* [1973] QB 153 at 176, [1972] 3 All ER 257 at 269, CA, per Orr LJ; *Wroth v Tyler* [1974] Ch 30 at 39, [1973] 1 All ER 897 at 903, per Megarry J. For the reason why, see R & R, 39–11.
7   Form 59, accompanied by evidence in support of the claim: LRR 1925, r 190.
8   As substituted by the LRR 1978, r 8, and amended by the LRR 1990, r 9. See also *Smith v Morrison* [1974] 1 All ER 957 at 965.

Searches) Rules 1990[9], the notice application is re-dated administratively so that it loses its priority to the protected dealing.

(iii) *Effect of entry.* From the incumbrancer's point of view a notice is the most efficient form of protection. No further action is needed to ensure that later purchasers are bound by it. However, whilst a disposition of registered land takes effect subject to the estate or interest protected by the notice, it does so only if and so far as such estate or interest may be valid. The entry operates merely by way of notice[10]. It does not render enforceable an interest which is unenforceable under the general law. Thus, notation of a restrictive covenant satisfies one of the requirements which must be established if the burden of the covenant is to pass in equity; to enforce the covenant, the covenantee must still show, for example, that he owns or retains land benefited by it[11]. An entry that land is subject to a positive covenant does not cause that covenant to run with the land[12], any more than a purchaser of unregistered land is bound by a positive covenant of which he has express notice. Similarly, entry of a notice cannot revive an interest (such as an option to purchase) that has previously become void for want of registration under the Land Charges Act 1972[13].

(b) Caution

(i) *Cautionable interests.* Section 54(1) of the Act enables any person interested under an unregistered instrument, or as a judgment creditor or otherwise howsoever, in any registered land to lodge a caution to the effect that no dealing with the land by the proprietor is to be registered until notice has been served upon the cautioner. The provision facilitates the protection of a variety of rights. Thus the cautioner may be a purchaser under a contract for sale, a lessee under an agreement for a lease, a person having the benefit of a writ or order affecting land[14], a person entitled to a lien on land[15], or claiming an equity arising out of acquiescence – these are merely illustrations. An interest in the proceeds of sale of land held on trust for sale is a minor interest by virtue of the definition in s 3(xv) of the Act, so that an equitable tenant in common is entitled to lodge a caution[16]. The applicant need not be interested

---

9   Rule 6. See further for official certificates of search, pp 407–411, post.
10   LRA 1925, ss 50(2), 52(1), (2). Cf the puzzling statements in *Kashmir Kaur v Gill* that entry of a notice gives constructive notice to a purchaser without actual knowledge of it: [1988] 2 All ER 288, 289, 295, CA, per Dillon LJ and Sir Denys Buckley.
11   *LCC v Allen* [1914] 3 KB 642, CA.
12   *Cator v Newton and Bates* [1940] 1 KB 415, [1939] 4 All ER 457, CA.
13   *Kitney v MEPC Ltd* [1978] 1 All ER 595, CA, p 28, ante.
14   LRA 1925, s 59(1). Cf *Sowerby v Sowerby* (1982) 44 P & CR 192; *Belcourt v Belcourt* [1989] 2 All ER 34 (caution in respect of appeal against court order).
15   *Lee v Olancastle Ltd* [1987] NPC 66 (lien for return of deposit); contrast *Woolf Project Management Ltd v Woodtrek Ltd* (1987) 56 P & CR 134.
16   *Elias v Mitchell* [1972] Ch 652, [1972] 2 All ER 153. For s 3(xv), see p 70, ante. Contrast *Lynton International Ltd v Noble* (1991) 63 P & CR 452 (contractual right to share profits on a re-sale not an interest in land).

in land in the sense of having a true proprietary interest capable of binding purchasers. In *Clayhope Properties Ltd v Evans*[17] a tenant obtaining an order appointing a receiver to manage the demised premises was held entitled to lodge a caution against the landlord's title. On the other hand, rights of a purely personal nature are not cautionable, such as a right of pre-emption which on its construction is binding on the grantor only during his lifetime[18]. The statutory charge under the Matrimonial Homes Act 1983 can no longer be protected by means of a caution: s 2(9). The Registrar has no power to enter a caution of his own motion, nor can a caution be lodged without his consent if the claimant's interest is already protected by a notice or restriction[19].

An application for a caution should be made on Form 53, and should be accompanied with a statutory declaration which specifies the nature of the interest claimed[20]. However, the entry itself, which is recorded in the proprietorship register, gives no indication of the claim which the caution protects. It simply says, for example, 'Caution dated 2 May 1992 registered on 9 May 1992 in favour of AB'. Production of the proprietor's land certificate is not required.

A caution is not transferable. On the assignment of an interest already protected, the assignee should lodge a fresh caution. After the death of the cautioner, his personal representative may exercise his rights under the caution[1].

(ii) *Nature of protection afforded.*   Lodging a caution secures interim protection for the cautioner who is entitled to receive notice of any intended dealing with the land. This notice warns him that his caution will cease to have effect on the expiration of a specified period (usually 14 days) unless he shows cause why the caution should continue to have effect or why the dealing should not be registered[2]. Whether it is cancelled, or registration of the dealing is refused or completed subject to the cautioner's interest, depends on the validity of his claim, and this is determined at a hearing before the Registrar. If the cautioner takes no further steps after receipt of the 'warning-off' notice, the caution automatically lapses. Thereupon the land may be dealt with in the same manner as if no caution had been lodged[3].

According to s 76(2) of the Act, a caution has no effect except as is therein mentioned. The protection which it secures is inferior to that afforded to a person who registers a notice. A notice establishes priority and ensures that the interest protected (assuming it is otherwise enforceable) will bind a subsequent transferee without further inquiry. On the other hand, a caution

---

17   [1986] 2 All ER 795, CA. See the Supreme Court Act 1981, s 37.
18   *Murray v Two Strokes Ltd* [1973] 3 All ER 357; aliter if it is capable of creating a proprietary interest. See *Pritchard v Briggs* [1980] Ch 338, [1980] 1 All ER 294, CA (unregistered land).
19   Section 54(1) proviso. See R & R, 36.13, for a case where consent might be forthcoming.
20   LRR 1925, r 215(1), (4) (prescribing Form 14 for the declaration).
 1   LRA 1925, s 56(4): R & R, 36.15. The Law Commission advocate that this clumsy rule should be changed: Report No 158, para 4.47; draft Bill, cl 34(7).
 2   LRA 1925, s 55; LRR 1925, r 219. See generally rr 215–22.
 3   But see p 71, note 16, ante.

does not of itself confer any priority[4]. It merely warns that some right is claimed, and affords a right to be heard in opposition to an application to register a dealing[5]. The cautioner will not be able to enforce his interest against a transferee, unless he first establishes the validity of his claim at the hearing.

A caution's greatest effect has been said to be informal. It acts as a deterrent to prospective purchasers and mortgagees, who will not usually proceed with the transaction until satisfied that they will take free from the protected interest. Nevertheless, entry of a caution will not prevent overreaching occurring on a sale or mortgage by two trustees for sale[6].

(iii) *Improper cautions.* As production of the proprietor's land certificate is not required, lodging a caution is regarded as a hostile act, though protection by means of a caution instead of a notice does not necessarily indicate that the interest is disputed by the proprietor. The land certificate may be deposited with a third party by way of security, so preventing registration of a notice. Under s 56(3) a person lodging a caution without reasonable cause is liable to compensate any person who thereby sustains damage. In the context of this provision the phrase 'without reasonable cause' does not appear to have been judicially considered. It is thought that it covers a case where a caution is lodged maliciously for an ulterior motive, eg to hold up a transaction relating to the land affected, or there are no substantial grounds for supporting it, but not where the cautioner has a genuine belief based on reasonable grounds that an enforceable right or claim exists[7]. Section 76(3) does not provide an exhaustive remedy; it does not, for instance, oust the inherent jurisdiction of the court to vacate improperly lodged cautions[8]. The court is prepared to take a robust attitude in respect of such applications and may order the vacation of the caution unless the cautioner is prepared to give an undertaking to pay damages to the proprietor should it later transpire that the entry was unjustified[9].

The section speaks only of lodging a caution. No sanction is imposed for unreasonably *maintaining* a caution. Yet this may just as likely cause embarrassment to the registered proprietor as the initial wrongful registration, as where a purchaser fails to remove a caution after the vendor has validly terminated the contract for sale. There is no comparable provision regulating the registration of notices without reasonable cause. Such a provision is not

4 *Clark v Chief Land Registrar* [1994] Ch 370, [1994] 4 All ER 96, CA.
5 *Smith v Morrison* [1974] 1 All ER 957 at 978, per Plowman J, but only if the caution is actually entered on the register: *Smith v Morrison* (caution cancelled on purchaser's application to register within priority period of clear search certificate).
6 Law Com Report No 188, paras 2.27, 2.32; R & R, 36–13, n 2. See further, p 362, post.
7 Cf the Australian cases of *Frankcombe v Foster Investments Pty Ltd* [1978] 2 NSWLR 41; *Bedford Properties Pty Ltd v Surgo Pty Ltd* [1981] 1 NSWLR 106. See also *Clearbrook Property Holdings Ltd v Verrier* [1973] 3 All ER 614 at 617, per Templeman J. This is better than the system in unregistered land, although the courts have effectively achieved a similar result by means of undertakings given on motion to vacate registered land charges. See p 403, post.
8 *Clearbrook Property Holdings Ltd v Verrier*, supra.
9 See *Tiverton Estates Ltd v Wearwell* [1975] Ch 146, [1974] 1 All ER 209, CA; *Tucker v Hutchinson* (1987) 54 P & CR 106.

required. The need for the proprietor's consent means, in theory, that entry of a notice can never be unreasonable, but as has been seen, his concurrence is rendered something of a myth when the certificate is already at the Registry[10].

(c) Inhibition

Except in relation to bankruptcy[11] an inhibition, which can only be entered on the register by order of the Registrar or the court, is an unusual form of protection. It can be used when 'extremely rigorous precautionary measures' are needed, for example, in cases of suspected fraud or forgery[12]. It prevents the registration of any dealing with the registered land during a specified period or until the occurrence of a specified event[13].

(d) Restriction

A restriction (like an inhibition) does not directly protect third party rights in registered land, but it may have this effect indirectly. It operates to prevent a disposition of the land taking effect without prior conformity to some specified requirement, such as the obtaining of a named person's consent to the transaction[14]. In effect, it limits a registered proprietor's powers of disposition. Entry of a restriction requires production of the land certificate if it is not already in the Registry[15]. It may be applied for by the proprietor himself or by a person having sufficient interest in the land[16]. The restriction is the proper and most efficient method of protecting beneficial interests under a trust for sale of land, though a notice or a caution (more commonly) are also used as alternatives. In certain circumstances, the Registrar is obliged to enter a restriction at the time of registration. This occurs, for example, where land is vested in joint proprietors[17], or is held on charitable trusts (including property vested in trustees on behalf of a church or chapel), or for educational purposes[18].

Provided a dealing with registered land is effected in accordance with the terms of the restriction, the transferee will be registered as proprietor in the normal manner. If the restriction is not intended to continue in force he should ensure that the person whose interest it protects applies for its withdrawal. No statutory provision exists for the automatic cancellation of a restriction on dealing which complies with its requirements. Obligatory restrictions cannot be withdrawn on the mere application of an interested party[19].

---

10   This will cease to be even a theoretical problem under the Law Commission's revised scheme.
11   LRA 1925, s 61.
12   R & R, 37–03; *Ahmed v Kendrick* (1987) 56 P & CR 120, CA (forgery).
13   Ibid, s 57.
14   Ibid, s 58(1). The consent may be given in the document to be registered.
15   Ibid, s 64(1)(c).
16   Ibid, s 58(5): LRR 1925, rr 235, 236. Form 75 should be used.
17   LRA 1925, s 58(3), unless the survivor can give a valid receipt for purchase money. See the example given in entry no 3 in the proprietorship register appearing on p 48, ante.
18   LRR 1925, rr 60-62, 123(2). See R & R, 38–15 et seq, for a detailed list of voluntary and compulsory restrictions and the form of the restriction applicable to each occasion.
19   LRA 1925, s 58(4).

3.   Knowledge of unprotected interest

Actual knowledge or notice of an unprotected minor interest does not affect a purchaser's entitlement to take free from the interest. Section 79(6) of the Act enacts that a purchaser acquiring title under a registered disposition is not to be concerned with any matter or claim (not being an overriding interest) which is not protected on the register, whether he has or has not notice thereof express, implied or *constructive*. Similarly, by virtue of s 20(1) a transferee for value under a registered disposition of an absolute freehold title takes free of 'all estates and interests whatsoever' unless they are protected on the register or take effect as overriding interests. So in *De Lusignan v Johnson*[20] a registered chargee took free from an unprotected estate contract of which he had express knowledge. In *Boland's* case[1] Lord Wilberforce asserted categorically that the land registration system is designed to free the purchaser from the hazards of the doctrine of notice; it has no application even by analogy to registered land. The contrary decision in *Peffer v Rigg*[2] cannot, it is thought, be sustained. Here, as part of a divorce settlement X transferred a house, which he held on an express trust for himself and Y, to his ex-wife, W, for £1. Y's interest was not protected on the register, nor was he in actual occupation of the house. Graham J held that since W was aware of Y's beneficial interest, she was bound by it and took the house on trust for herself and Y as beneficial tenants in common. Surprisingly, the learned judge did not consider the vital exclusion of the effect of notice in s 59(6)[3]. To introduce the doctrine of notice further than the Act itself allows[4] destroys the certainty (albeit not total) which the register of title currently affords.

   In appropriate circumstances, the court may impose a trust to give effect to an unprotected interest, but only if it is satisfied that the conscience of the registered proprietor is affected. There has to be conduct which, in equity's eyes amounts to fraud[5]. Conveyancers will surely applaud Fox LJ's observation that, in matters relating to title to land[6], certainty is of prime importance. The courts should not impose a constructive trust based on inferences from slender materials. Mere knowledge of the unprotected interest does not suffice, nor does the mere taking of a conveyance or transfer expressly 'subject to' such interest[7]. There needs to be the assumption of an obligation – by contract or collateral obligation – to give effect to the interest; and this may be reflected by paying a reduced price for the property[8]. A constructive trust was imposed

20   (1973) 230 EG 499. See also the LRA 1925, s 3(xv), p 71, ante.
 1   [1981] AC 487 at 504, [1980] 2 All ER 408 at 412; *Strand Securities Ltd v Caswell* [1965] Ch 373 at 390, [1964] 2 All ER 956 at 967, per Cross J.
 2   [1978] 3 All ER 745.
 3   Which makes it clear that notice is not to be equated with lack of good faith, contrary to what Graham J held. On the basis that the nominal sum of £1 was to be treated as the consideration for the transfer (see at 751), W took subject to Y's interest under s 20(4).
 4   Eg, ss 5(c), 70(1)(g); LRR r 77(1)(b).
 5   See, for example, *Du Boulay v Raggett* (1988) 58 P & CR 138 at 154. See, generally, M P Thompson [1985] CLJ 280.
 6   *Ashburn Anstalt v Arnold* [1989] Ch 1 at 26, [1988] 2 All ER 147 at 167, CA.
 7   See Fox LJ's discussion of the relevant cases at 22–26, 164–167 respectively.
 8   As in *Binions v Evans* [1972] Ch 359, [1972] 2 All ER 70, CA (unregistered land).

upon a purchaser of registered land in *Lyus v Prowsa Developments Ltd*[9], because the contract of sale was construed as requiring the purchaser to give effect to the plaintiff's prior contract of sale. Since the fraud which prompts equity's intervention consists in the purchaser's unconscionable attempt to deny the unprotected interest, it is not thought that s 74 of the Act can operate to prohibit effect being given to the trust.

The problem of knowledge of an unprotected interest was an obvious issue that confronted the Law Commission. Its solution, which is in marked contrast to the position with regard to the Land Charges Act 1972[10], has been to require the purchaser to be in good faith and for valuable consideration, if he is to take free from an unprotected minor interest. Its draft Bill contains no definition of good faith[11]. The onus of establishing a lack of good faith would rest with the minor interest holder. It would not suffice simply to establish that the purchaser was aware of the interest[12]. What more would have to be established would depend on the court's interpretation of good faith in each case. Implementation of this proposal would clearly lead to uncertainty as case law would need to develop to provide guidance as to when a purchaser would be bound by an unprotected interest. While the desire to prevent unmeritorious purchasers from taking free of unprotected interests, which are known about prior to the transfer, is understandable, it is suggested that it would nevertheless be preferable for the concept of good faith to be excluded from the system of registered land.

4.   Priority between minor interests[13]

In section 2 above we looked at what steps should be taken to ensure that a minor interest is enforceable against a transferee under a registered disposition. When it comes to the related question of priorities between competing minor interests, the Act affords little clear guidance. Problems of priority arise most commonly in relation to financial charges on land[14]. They can also occur in cases involving non-financial interests (eg a contest between a Class F charge and an estate contract), or between a financial and a non-financial interest, as in the case of *Barclays Bank Ltd v Taylor*[15].

9   [1982] 2 All ER 953 (sale by a mortgagee not bound by prior contract), approved in *Ashburn Anstalt v Arnold*, supra, at 24, 166. See also *Bahr v Nicolay (No 2)* (1988) 164 CLR 604; *Peffer v Rigg*, supra, where as an alternative ground for decision, Graham J imposed a constructive trust because the transferee knew that the house was trust property. *Sed quaere.* Constructive trusts were disallowed in *Miles v Bull (No 2)* [1969] 3 All ER 1585 and in the *Ashburn* case. For criticism of the employment of the constructive trust in this context, see M P Thompson [1988] Conv 201 at 205, 206.

10   See *Midland Bank Trust Co Ltd v Green* [1981] AC 513, [1981] 1 All ER 153, HL; p 399, post.

11   See R J Smith [1987] Conv 334 at 347.

12   See Law Com No 158, paras 4.14–17; draft Bill cll 9(3), (4), 70(1). In its Report, the Commission saw no harm in linking good faith to the concept of honesty, as in the Sale of Goods Act 1979, s 61(3): para 4.15; but Bill does not adopt this definition.

13   See generally (1971) 35 Conv (NS) 100, 168 (S Robinson); (1977) 93 LQR 542 (R J Smith).

14   The priority of registered charges is determined by the order in which they are entered on the register: LRA 1925, s 29, CA.

15   [1974] Ch 137, [1973] 1 All ER 752, CA. *Mortgage Corpn Ltd v Nationwide Credit Corpn Ltd* [1994] Ch 49, [1993] 4 All ER 623, CA.

X by deed mortgaged his land to the bank. The mortgage was not registered nor protected in the then appropriate manner[16]; it took effect only in equity. Later X contracted to sell the land to Y who paid the purchase money without obtaining a transfer. Y lodged a caution against dealings, and when the bank applied to register its mortgage Y objected.

The Court of Appeal held that as this was a contest between two equitable interests, priority was to be determined by the order of their creation. Where the equities are equal, the first in time prevails. The bank's charge, therefore, had priority, there being nothing in its conduct to justify postponement of its interest. It was of no consequence that the bank had failed to protect its interest, nor could Y, by lodging a caution, secure priority for his contract.

Priority disputes will often come to light and be determined once the warning-off procedure has come into operation, as happened in the case just discussed. They can arise in other situations, as where applications to protect competing minor interests are received at the Registry on the same day. Fortunately, however, potential disputes are normally still-born because of the effect of ss 20(1) and 23(1) of the Act. Similarly the Land Registration (Official Searches) Rules 1990, r 6, confers priority on a purchaser who applies for substantive registration of his transfer within the priority period allowed by his official certificate of search. He takes free from any minor interest, an application for entry of which is received at the Registry during such period. The fact that the purchaser's contract was not protected as a minor interest has no bearing on priority. Conversely, if the priority period expires before he applies for registration, it will take effect under s 20(1) subject to the minor interest, even though his own contract was protected on the register before that interest.

The scheme for the future
Despite doubts expressed in some quarters[17], the ruling in *Taylor's* case appears to be of general application. However, the Law Commission's draft Bill contains a new comprehensive scheme[18] regulating the priority of competing interests, including minor interests. Basically, priority is to be governed by what is termed the 'protection date'; the interest that has the earlier protection date will have priority: cl 9(1). Different protection dates are specified for different classes of interest. In the case of a minor interest protected on the register (termed a protected interest), priority is determined by the date of entry on the register. For an unprotected minor interest, the date of its creation is the vital date: cl 9(5)[19]. The general rule will not apply in certain situations. For example, suppose two minor, ie unprotected, interests, A & B. The earlier (A) will have priority over the later (B). If A subsequently is protected on the register, its protection date as a protected interest will be later than B's as an unprotected

16 Ie, a special mortgage caution under LRA 1925, s 106, abolished by AJA 1977, s 26.
17 See Smith, op cit, 548–50.
18 Giving effect to recommendations in Report No 158, paras 4.94–104.
19 In the Bill the term 'minor interest' is reserved for non-overriding interests not protected on the register: cl 7(1). The protection date for an overriding interest is the date when it became such an interest.

minor interest. Nevertheless, A will retain its original priority over B[20]. The two minor interest holders will be free to vary the order of priority, but a note on the register to this effect will be necessary. The priority rules are to apply without regard to the doctrine of notice[1], but not so as to prevent the operation of fraud or estoppel principles: cl 9(6)(b), (7).

These new rules will be prospective only, determining priority issues between interests both or all of which are created after it becomes operative. The existing equitable rules will continue to apply for several years yet, an extra burden for conveyancers who will be faced with the task of operating two different sets of rules[2]. This is unavoidable. The Commission could hardly have suggested retrospective effect for its new rules, since this might have operated to alter property rights established under the existing law.

5.   Cancellation of entries

There exists both an inherent and a statutory jurisdiction for the court to vacate entries protecting third party rights. The court has a general power to make orders in personam against parties interested in property or under contracts. This inherent jurisdiction, to be exercised (where necessary) to avoid injustice[3], subsists notwithstanding that s 82(1) of the Land Registration Act 1925 also confers a wide jurisdiction to rectify the register. Apparently, the two jurisdictions can be exercised concurrently[4]. When acting under its inherent jurisdiction the court may make an order in a personal form, ordering (eg) a cautioner to remove his caution[5]. An order in impersonal form, ie one that simply requires the entry to be removed, is preferable; it can safely be acted upon by the Registrar without waiting for the cautioner to take steps to give effect to the order[6]. It also obviates any difficulties that might otherwise arise should a personal order be disobeyed by the cautioner. An order under s 82 directs the Registrar to make the necessary alteration to the register.

The courts recognise that the presence on the register of a wrongful or erroneous entry (particularly a caution) may well jeopardise a prospective dealing with the land by the proprietor. In a proper case, the court will order the entry to be vacated in interlocutory. proceedings on motion, without waiting for the dispute between the parties to be finally resolved at the trial of the action. This speedy remedy is, in general, available only where there is no

---

20   See the explanatory note to cl 9(2) of the Bill. Clause 9(3) gives additional priority to the purchaser of a registered, protected or overriding interest.

 1   So ensuring that unregistered land concepts will not infiltrate the determination of registered land priority questions.

 2   But the equitable rules will gradually cease to be of practical relevance as time progresses; see paras 4.98(vii), 4.100.

 3   *Hynes v Vaughan* (1985) 50 P & CR 444 at 462, per Scott J.

 4   *Hynes v Vaughan,* supra (caution ordered to be vacated), but which Goulding J denied he had power to do because of the different form of the orders: *Lester v Burgess* (1973) 26 P & CR 536 at 543.

 5   As in *Rawlplug Co Ltd v Kamvale Properties Ltd* (1968) 20 P & CR 32, where the proprietor sought an order in the personal form.

 6   *Calgary and Edmonton Land Co Ltd v Dobinson* [1974] Ch 102, [1974] 1 All ER 484.

triable issue or arguable point in support of the registration, otherwise the matter must go to trial in the normal way[7]. Examples of the use of this procedure are quite common. In *Tiverton Estates Ltd v Wearwell Ltd*[8] the court on motion ordered a caution to be vacated under s 82(1), because the defendant purchasers had failed to make out a prima facie case that any enforceable contract for sale ever existed. Similarly, the courts have vacated cautions protecting contracts for sale that have ceased to be enforceable[9], and cautions lodged by cautioners claiming some right considered by the court not to constitute a cautionable interest[10]. Nevertheless, in all such cases the court seeks to maintain a fair balance between the parties in dispute. For, although registration can be a weapon of considerable nuisance value in the cautioner's hands, simply to vacate the caution without more deprives him of his protection and leaves the proprietor free to act in a way detrimental to his claim. Where, therefore, there is a triable issue, the court may allow the caution to remain, but only on condition that the cautioner gives an undertaking to pay the registered proprietor any damages sustained by its continued presence, in case it is subsequently held to have been wrongly entered[11]. Under an alternative, but no longer favoured procedure[12], the caution is vacated and replaced by an injunction restraining the proprietor from dealing with the land inconsistently with the cautioner's claim, but coupled with the latter's cross-undertaking as to damages[13].

6. Proposals for reform

The Law Commission's draft Bill, cl 33, incorporates its recommendations for the reform of the law governing the protection of minor interests. Despite the flaws in the existing provisions, it viewed the present system, in operation, as basically sound and working reasonably well. The new provisions will have prospective effect only. When in force, they will permit a clearer distinction to be drawn between acknowledged and disputed entries. Protection on the register will normally be by notice or by caution, except for certain excluded interests, when protection by restriction is to be the *sole* permitted method. Whatever form the entry takes, it will not in itself confer validity on the interest. This is the present rule. The choice between notice or caution will depend on whether the proprietor acknowledges the interest. A notice will not be

---

7 *Clearbrook Property Holdings Ltd v Verrier* [1973] 3 All ER 614 at 615, per Templeman J.
8 [1975] Ch 146, [1974] 1 All ER 209, CA.
9 *Rawlplug Co Ltd v Kamvaler Properties Ltd*, supra; *Lester v Burgess*, supra; *Clearbrook Property Ltd v Verrier*, supra; *Hynes v Vaughan*, supra; *Bechal v Kitsford Holdings Ltd* [1988] 3 All ER 985 (contract rescinded due to non-compliance with completion notice).
10 *Calgary and Edmonton Land Co Ltd v Dobinson*, supra (creditor of company in liquidation, not being a beneficiary under a trust for sale, has no minor interest in its land); *J Williams v Andrews* (1971) 221 EG 1158 (non-proprietary right of pre-emption).
11 *Alpenstow Ltd v Regalian Properties plc* [1985] 2 All ER 545; *Tucker v Hutchinson* (1987) 54 P & CR 106, CA.
12 *Tucker v Hutchinson*, supra, at 110, per Balcombe LJ.
13 *Clearbrook Property Ltd v Verrier*, supra; *Blue Town Investments Ltd v Higgs and Hill plc* [1990] 2 All ER 897 at 901, per Browne-Wilkinson V-C.

entertained without the proprietor's consent, evidenced in the prescribed manner[14]. A disputed entry will result in a caution only. The warning-off procedure remains unchanged. Both methods of protection will confer the same priority. Inhibitions are to be retained. They are seen as being potentially useful to protect Mareva or similar injunctions on the register.

As for restrictions, they will, in future, be employed primarily to protect those interests that are overreachable by trustees or by a tenant for life. Production of the land certificate is to be dispensed with: see cl 40(1)(b). However, an application for entry of a restriction will be accepted only if made with the proprietor's consent, except when the interest to be protected is overreachable or a floating charge: cl 35(3).

---

14   Eg by lodging the land certificate, or giving written consent if it is on deposit. Consent will not be required for notices relating to charging orders. Being statutory creatures, they warrant exceptional treatment. For them, protection by caution is also to be prohibited: cl 33(3).

Chapter 4
Rectification and indemnity

A Introduction

One of the main advantages of the system of land registration is the curative effect of registration. However defective the grantor's title might be, registration with an absolute title vests in the first proprietor of freehold land the estate in fee simple in possession in the land[1]. Yet there is no guarantee that a proprietor registered with an absolute title will always be entitled to retain what the statute has vested in him, even though there is no suspicion of fraud or improper conduct on his part. His title may be absolute; it is not indefeasible. It may be wrong, unjust or impossible to recognise him as proprietor according to the general law[2], in which event he may be deprived of his title through rectification of the register. It is interesting to note that successive statutes have progressively widened the scope of rectification. Under the Land Registry Act 1862, it was not contemplated save in relation to entries procured by fraud. Rectification was completely foreign to the system as originally devised, which did not countenance the registration of any title not shown to be perfect. But by the time of the 1925 Act this cardinal rule had been abandoned. Section 82(1) lists eight specific grounds on which rectification can be ordered, whilst s 83 defines the limits of the statutory insurance scheme established to compensate proprietors who become the victims of rectification.

The legislative movement away from the principle of indefeasibility throws into sharp relief the previously expressed view of the Chief Land Registrar that an absolute title 'is virtually indefeasible and cannot be bettered'[3]. The second of these two claims has, however, more foundation. The proprietor of an absolute title can rely on his registered title with greater security than an owner can rely on his unregistered estate. At the most, the latter, in the event of a defect in his title being established, can only seek the protection afforded by the covenants for title. The registered proprietor has the benefit of the State guarantee of title. This is not a statutory expression, but it satisfactorily explains[4] the compensation scheme operative under the Act. Nevertheless, despite the counter-balancing effect of this scheme, defeasibility through the ready availability of rectification has been said to be 'productive of future

1 LRA 1925, ss 5, 9 (leaseholds). Registration of a disposition of registered land has a similar effect: ss 20(1) (freeholds) , 23(1) (leaseholds). For titles less than absolute; see pp 33–36, ante.
2 R & R, 40-03.
3 R & R (5th edn), 81. See now 5-02.
4 See *Re 139 High Street, Deptford, ex p British Transport Commission* [1951] Ch 884 at 888, [1951] 1 All ER 950 at 952, per Wynn-Parry J.

uncertainty and contrary to the raison d'être' of the system[5]. It remains to be considered later in this chapter to what extent rectification and indemnity are complementary remedies.

B   Rectification

1.   What is meant by rectification?

The Act nowhere defines what it means by rectification. It has been explained[6] as denoting any amendment to the register or the plan for the purpose of putting right any substantive error of omission or commission or any legally recognised grievance. In effect, it is a method of asserting an unregistered interest against a registered proprietor. It enables, for instance, land to be removed from a proprietor's title in order to give effect to some adverse claim. Various powers of rectification are conferred upon the Registrar, which appear to be of a somewhat different nature. He is empowered to amend the register to correct clerical and such like errors which can be altered without detriment to any registered interest, or to rectify the register where land has been registered in error[7], an apparently unlimited power which entitles the Registrar to effect rectification[8] of his own accord subject to certain safeguards.

2.   Grounds for rectification under s 82(1)

The opening words of s 82(1) are as follows :

> The register may be rectified pursuant to an order of the court or by the Registry, subject to an appeal to the court, in any of the following cases, but subject to the provisions of this section ...

The first point to observe is that rectification is discretionary. A claimant who succeeds in bringing his claim within one (or more) of the statutory cases is not entitled as of right to rectification. Secondly, and importantly, s 82(2) of the Act provides that the register may be rectified notwithstanding that rectification may affect any estates, rights, charges or interests acquired or protected by registration, or by any entry on the register, or otherwise. The effect of rectification may, therefore, be to cause loss to an innocent party.

Section 82(1) lists eight cases when rectification may be ordered. Of these, rectification under grounds (a) and (b) is available only if the court makes an order to that effect; in the remaining cases either the court or the Registrar may order it. Legal proceedings are instituted by means of an originating summons to a single judge of the Chancery Division[9]. No particular form of

---

5   Law Com No 158, para 3.4.
6   R & R, 881.
7   LRR 1925, rr 13, 14.
8   Presumably subject to payment of indemnity (where appropriate) but, seemingly, free from the restrictions imposed by s 82(3) (pp 89–93, post). See *Chowood Ltd v Lyall (No 2)* [1930] 1 Ch 426 at 439, per Luxmoore J; affd [1930] 2 Ch 156, CA; Law Com No 158, para 3.3.
9   RSC Ord 93, r 10.

application to the Registrar for rectification is prescribed; in practice it will be in writing and set out the grounds on which it is sought. These eight grounds are not mutually exclusive. A claimant may well be able to bring his case within several paragraphs[10]. The court also possesses an inherent jurisdiction to rectify the register[11].

The case of *Blacklocks v JB Developments (Godalming) Ltd*[12], is authority for the proposition that a right to claim rectification of the register constitutes an overriding interest, if coupled with actual occupation of the disputed land. This is, with respect, an unfortunate ruling. It brings the statutory scheme of rectification into the arena of overriding interests. The decision on this point was clearly not necessary in order to do justice between the litigants, for s 82(1) contains ample power to award rectification in a wide variety of situations.

(a) '… Where a court of competent jurisdiction has decided that any person is entitled to any estate right or interest in or to any registered land or charge, and such court is of opinion that a rectification of the register is required, and makes an order to that effect'
This paragraph confers on the court a wide power to order rectification when the court considers this is required. The wording of para (a) suggests that it is not intended to be a ground on which an applicant can himself base a claim for rectification[13]. For instance, it enables the court to order rectification against a plaintiff in proceedings which he has brought for some other form of relief. In *Chowood Ltd v Lyall (No 2)*[14] the court ordered rectification to give effect to the defendant's overriding interest in proceedings brought by the plaintiff for trespass and an injunction. Similarly, in *Ahmed v Kendrick*[15], in an action for possession of a house, the court rectified the register by deleting the plaintiff's inhibition, and substituting the defendant as co-proprietor in place of the plaintiff's husband. Equally, however, the court has jurisdiction under (a) to rectify the register in favour of a plaintiff in proceedings instituted by him to secure some quite different remedy[16], whether or not he also seeks rectification by way of secondary[17] or consequential relief.

Paragraph (a) does not give any substantive cause of action where none previously existed[18]. This means that the claimant has been the victim of a

10   *Argyle Building Society v Hammond*, supra, at 151, per Slade LJ, indicating that jurisdiction existed under paras (a),(b),(d), (g) and (h).
11   See pp 80–81, ante.
12   [1982] Ch 183, [1981] 3 All ER 392 (land by common error transferred to and registered in name of defendant's predecessor, though remaining in plaintiff's occupation). The true ratio is hotly disputed. The case is exhaustively examined by the author in [1983] Conv 361. See also ibid, 257, and contra, ibid, at 169. The learned judge spoke about a *right* to rectify, without seeming to realise that, strictly, the entitlement to rectification is discretionary only.
13   Contrast s 82(1)(b), where the court makes an order on the application of an aggrieved person.
14   [1930] 2 Ch 156, CA. The defendant counterclaimed for rectification.
15   (1987) 56 P & CR 120, CA (husband forging plaintiff wife's signature to transfer).
16   *Rennie v Proma Ltd* (1990) 17 EG 69 (vacation of defendant's restriction in plaintiff's action for declaration of entitlement to buy freehold).
17   Cf *Proctor v Kidman* (1986) 51 P & CR 67, CA.
18   *Norwich and Peterborough Building Society v Steed (No 2)* [1993] Ch 116 at 33, [1993] 1 All ER 330 at 343, CA.

forged conveyance or transfer, has established the requisite period of adverse possession, or can establish that land to which he is entitled has been erroneously included in another person's title. In *Orakpo v Manson Investments Ltd*[19], Buckley LJ indicated, obiter, that the court has jurisdiction under this paragraph to order rectification against the registered proprietor in favour of a person claiming an adverse interest which, though created by the registered proprietor, has by virtue of s 20(1) of the Act become void against him for want of protection on the register. This proposition seems to be incorrect. A court can hardly decide that the claimant is entitled to an interest which the statute has expressly declared to be unenforceable against him[20]. The precise form which rectification takes is determined by what the court considers is necessary in order to give effect to the estate, right or interest which it has recognised. It may result in the disputed land being removed from, or added to[1], the proprietor's title, or the plaintiff's name being entered on the proprietorship register in place of the defendant's[2], or the vacation of a notice or caution which has been improperly registered against the proprietor's title[3].

(b) '…Where the court, on the application in the prescribed manner[4] of any person who is aggrieved by any entry made in, or by the omission of any entry from, the register makes an order for the rectification of the register'

A case would arise within this paragraph where on first registration the Registrar had omitted to enter in the charges register some third party incumbrance, such as a restrictive covenant. The incumbrancer would be a person aggrieved by the omission, for under s 5 of the Act registration would vest in the proprietor a title free from the restriction. Another example occurred in *Hynes v Vaughan*[5], where the court ordered vacation of a caution protecting a contract for sale that was no longer enforceable. The word 'entry' needs to be widely interpreted. It covers, for instance, an error in the filed plan which wrongly incorporates land of an adjacent owner. It may be that para (b) applies not only to mistakes by the Registry, but also to a mistake made or induced by one of the parties to the dispute[6]. Yet it is not thought that an incumbrancer who has failed to

---

19   [1977] 1 All ER 666 at 678, CA; affd without reference to this point [1978] AC 95, [1977] 3 All ER 1, HL.

20   See D C Jackson (1978) 94 LQR 239, 243.

 1   *Proctor v Kidman* (1986) 51 P & CR 67, CA.

 2   Cf *Tester v Harris* (1964) 189 EG 337 (insufficient evidence to support registered possessory title; paper title not displaced). It is unclear what para of s 82(1) was relied on.

 3   *Calgary and Edmonton Land Co Ltd v Discount Bank (Overseas) Ltd* [1971] 1 All ER 551.

 4   Proceedings are begun by originating summons: RSC Ord 5, r 3.

 5   (1985) 50 P & CR 444; *Price Bros (Somerford) Ltd v J Kelly Homes (Stoke-on-Trent) Ltd* [1975] 3 All ER 369, CA. It has been suggested that an improperly registered caution can be vacated under para (a) as well as (b): *Tiverton Estates Ltd v Wearwell Ltd* [1975] Ch 146 at 156, [1974] 1 All ER 209 at 213, CA, per Lord Denning MR. This would appear to be because a negative decision that a defendant has no cautionable interest necessarily imports a decision that the proprietor has a title free from the alleged interest: *Watts v Waller* [1973] QB 153 at 171, [1972] 3 All ER 257 at 265–66, CA, per Orr LJ. This suffices to confer jurisdiction under para (a): ibid.

 6   *Chowood Ltd v Lyall (No 2)* [1930] 2 Ch 156 at 168–69, CA, per Lawrence LJ, who declined to express a concluded opinion on the point.

protect his interest on the register, so that it becomes unenforceable against a subsequent registered proprietor, can maintain that he is a person aggrieved by the omission for the purposes of this paragraph[7].

(c) 'In any case and at any time with the consent of all persons interested'
Rectification should normally follow as matter of course, but not necessarily in every case[8].

(d) 'Where the court or the Registrar is satisfied that any entry in the register has been obtained by fraud'
This paragraph covers a case where registration has been obtained as a result of fraud practised on the Land Registry[9]. Thus, if a forged conveyance or transfer is lodged for registration, *by the forger*, this will amount to fraud on the Registry and the victim of the forgery will be able to apply for rectification of the register under this paragraph[10]. Contrary to what was previously thought[11], however, the fact that fraud was practised on the previous proprietor in order to obtain a transfer of the land will not enable rectification to be sought under this paragraph. The leading case is *Norwich and Peterborough Building Society v Steed (No 2)*[12]. The registered proprietor of land had emigrated to the United States and gave his mother a power of attorney. By means of fraud, the proprietor's sister and brother in law got the mother to transfer the land to them for £24,500, £15,000 of that sum being raised by means of a mortgage with the plaintiff. They were registered as proprietors of the land. When there was default on the mortgage, and possession proceedings were brought, the previous proprietor sought rectification of the register, to have himself reinstated as proprietor and to have the legal charge removed from the register. The Court of Appeal held there to be no jurisdiction to order rectification as against the mortgagee.

It was accepted that, had the transfer been void, either because it had been forged, or the mother could have established a plea of *non est factum*, then the claim for rectification would have succeeded under either paragraph (a) or (g). On the facts, however, the transfer was voidable and not void. A claim for rectification against the mortgagee, under paragraph (a), could not succeed as it was a bona fide purchaser who had, by registration, acquired a legal estate. Neither could any claim under paragraph (d) succeed because no fraud had been practised on the Registry[13].

---

7   See (1976) 92 LQR 338, 342. Yet para (h) might apply, p 88, post.
8   Law Com No 158, para 3.7; cf [1983] Conv 361, 363 (D G Barnsley).
9   *Norwich and Peterborough Building Society v Steed (No 2)* [1993] Ch 116 at 134, [1993] 1 All ER 330 at 344, CA.
10   *Ibid* at 134, 344. Rectification could also be sought under paras (a) and (g).
11   See the 3rd edition of this work, p 84.
12   Supra.
13   Dicta to the contrary in earlier proceedings *sub nom Argyle Building Society v Hammond* (1984) 49 P & CR 148, CA were disapproved.

(e) 'Where two or more persons are, by mistake, registered as proprietors of the same registered estate or of the same charge'
In this unlikely situation[14] it seems that the second or later of the two proprietors will be the one who technically has the legal estate vested in him[15]. Whether he will be the one who is ultimately allowed to retain the land may well depend on which of the rival proprietors is in possession for the purposes of s 82(3).

(f) 'Where a mortgagee has been registered as proprietor of the land instead of as proprietor of a charge and a right of redemption is subsisting'[16]

(g) 'Where a legal estate has been registered in the name of a person who if the land had not been registered would not have been the estate owner'
This paragraph apparently has a wide application. Jurisdiction to order rectification was exercised in *Chowood Ltd v Lyall (No 2)*[17], to give effect to a squatter's title, and in *Re 139 High Street, Deptford*[18], where on first registration land belonging to an adjoining owner was erroneously included in the proprietor's title. It also applies when registration follows a forged transfer[19].

(h) 'In any other case where, by reason of any error or omission in the register, or by reason of any entry made under a mistake, it may be deemed just to rectify the register'
Paragraph (h) confers a power to rectify the register in any case not expressly provided for in the preceding grounds. Although this might, on the face of it, appear to confer a general discretion to rectify[20], in *Norwich and Peterborough Building Society v Steed (No 2)*[1], the Court of Appeal held that rectification, under this paragraph, can only be done in the event of some error made in the Registry and that, as the legal charge had not been registered due to any mistake in the Registry, there was no jurisdiction under this paragraph to order rectification. In the light of this, the statement of opinion by Buckley LJ in *Orakpo v Manson Investments Ltd*[2] that paragraph (h) can be relied upon where there is an omission in the register of some entry which ought to be there for the applicant's protection, notwithstanding that the omission is due to the applicant's failure to ensure that the interest claimed has been properly protected, cannot be relied upon.

---

14   Apparently it has occurred; see (1956), 20 Conv (NS) 302, 313–14.
15   By virtue of the LRA 1925, ss 20(1) (freeholds), 23(1) (leaseholds).
16   This has ceased to be of any practical importance. It covered a case where an attempt was made to create a mortgage in the pre-1926 manner.
17   [1930] 2 Ch 156, CA.
18   [1951] Ch 884, [1951] 1 All ER 950. Cf *Epps v Esso Petroleum Co Ltd* [1973] 2 All ER 465.
19   *Norwich and Peterborough Building Society v Steed (No 2)*, supra. Under the general law a forged conveyance, being void, passes no title.
20   See Law Com No 158, para 3.7, W & C, 77 (a virtually uncontrollable power).
1   Supra at 135, 145.
2   [1977] 1 All ER 666 at 679, CA, obiter; see also Goff LJ at 687. The case concerned on this point an unprotected vendor's lien allegedly subrogated to the mortgagee.

It enables the Registrar to cancel notice of an adverse easement entered on the Register[3]. In *Chowood Ltd v Lyall (No 2)*[4], Lawrence LJ expressed the view that an error made in derogation of the right of the true owner was an entry made by mistake within para (h). This comment must now, also, be read with caution in that regard should now be had to who was responsible for the error. In the case, itself, rectification could have been ordered under other paragraphs.

3.   Restrictions upon right to rectify[5]

Rectification of the register under s 82(1) of the Act is expressed to be 'subject to the provisions contained in sub-s (3), as amended by the Administration of Justice Act 1977, s 24'. Section 82(3) now reads as follows:

> The register shall not be rectified, except for the purpose of giving effect to an overriding interest or an order of the court, so as to affect the title of the proprietor who is in possession–
> (a)   unless the proprietor has caused or substantially contributed to the error or omission by fraud or lack of proper care; or
> (b)   ...
> (c)   unless for any other reason, in any particular case, it is considered it would be unjust not to rectify the register against him.

(a) Possession
The privileged position accorded to the registered proprietor in possession has been said to represent the last vestiges of the concept of indefeasibility of title[6]. Possession is the key that brings s 82(3) into operation. Unfortunately, it is not clear what is meant by possession. While, clearly, it covers actual occupation of the land, the question is whether its meaning is wider than this. Possession, unless the context otherwise requires, is defined by s 3(xviii) of the Act to include the receipt of rents and profits or the right to receive the same, if any. The issue is whether the present context requires modification to this definition. Although it was accepted in *Freer v Unwins*[7] that a freeholder in receipt of rents and profits was in possession, the point was not argued. It is thought that the better view is that possession should only extend to physical possession. Otherwise, a registered proprietor not in possession could resist rectification on the ground that he was in possession by virtue of a proprietary right and that, if he could show such a right there would be no question of rectification to deprive him of it[8]. Beyond that, it will be a matter of fact and

3   See *Re Dances Way, West Town, Hayling Island* [1962] Ch 490, [1962] 2 All ER 42, CA; *Re Sunnyfield* [1932] 1 Ch 79, (restrictive covenants no longer enforceable).
4   [1930] 2 Ch 156 at 168, CA.
5   See (1968) 84 LQR 528 (S Cretney & G Dworkin).
6   Law Com Working Paper, No 45, para 28; cf Law Com No 158, para 3.12.
7   [1976] Ch 288, 294, [1976] 1 All ER 634 at 636–637.
8   Emmet 20.024 where s 83(4) is used to buttress the argument. For the contrary view, see the 3rd edition of this work, p 86. According to the Law Commission's draft Bill, cl 44(3), the proprietor would have to be a purchaser in actual occupation. And see Report No 158, para 3.12.

degree as to whether a proprietor is in possession. A dictum of Lord Hanworth MR[9] suggests that a proprietor is in possession if he exercises acts of ownership on the land. It is conceived, however, that sporadic or isolated acts of ownership would not suffice[10].

The Act does not state at what date the proprietor must be in possession for the purposes of s 82(3). In a case where rectification is granted by the Registrar, the relevant date would appear to be the deemed date of the application to him for rectification[11]. When ordered by the court, the relevant date is thought to be either the date of the trial[12], or, more probably, the date when court proceedings are commenced. In practice, the proprietor will be in possession at all material times. He is not likely to move out of possession once he is aware of the existence of a dispute likely to lead to a claim for rectification.

Rectification against the proprietor in possession is confined to four cases, of which two appear in the opening part of the subsection. The other two are provided for by paras (a) and (c). Section 82(3)(b) was repealed by the Administration of Justice Act 1977. Paragraphs (a) and (c) will be considered first.

(b) Fraud or lack of proper care: s 82(3)(a)

Section 24 of the 1977 Act was enacted in its present form in order to overturn the effect of certain decisions which had interpreted the original provision in a way that effectively deprived the proprietor of the protection which he was meant to have[13]. The intention behind the new para (a) is obvious. It is not to be applicable unless the proprietor has in some way been at fault, either because of fraud or carelessness. 'Fraud' is to be understood as having the same meaning as 'fraud' in s 82(1)(d), though, as has been noticed, this is a word of uncertain scope. The expression lack of *proper* care[14] (as distinct from reasonable care) is not altogether welcome. It has been criticised on the ground that it is not a technical expression familiar to conveyancers[15]. The proprietor may be guilty of lack of proper care if an inspection of the land could have revealed the discrepancy in its area, or the deeds ought to have put him (or his adviser) on

---

9   *Chowood Ltd v Lyall (No 2)* [1930] 2 Ch 156 at 164, CA; *Epps v Esso Petroleum Co Ltd* [1973] 2 All ER 465 (proprietor treating disputed land in same way as his adjacent premises held to be in possession).

10 *Epps v Esso Petroleum Co Ltd*, supra, (sporadic parking of a car on the disputed strip did not amount to possession).

11 This is the date when rectification takes effect: LRR 1925, rr 1(5B), 83(1), (2), p 94, post.

12 Cf *Epps v Esso Petroleum Ltd* [1973] 2 All ER 465, per Templeman J.

13 See *Chowood Ltd v Lyall (No 2)* [1930] 1 Ch 426; affd on other grounds [1930] 2 Ch 156, CA; *Re 139 High Street, Deptford* [1951] Ch 884, [1951] 1 All ER 950, p 13, ante; *Re Sea View Gardens Claridge v Tingey* [1966] 3 All ER 935 in all of which the proprietor lost the protection of para (a) because of the voluntary, but quite innocent, act of lodging a deed containing a defective plan or property description, resulting in too much land being registered.

14 The phrase is taken from the LR & LCA 1971, s 3(1), a provision relating to indemnity. See LRA 1925, s 83(5), p 98, post.

15 Law Com Report No 158, para 3.14. See further, p 103, post.

inquiry that something might be amiss[16], or where a non-fraudulent failure on first registration to lodge all relevant documents of title results in some third party interest (eg a restrictive covenant) being omitted from the register of title. A subsequent transferee will not normally be responsible for the mistake in registration; to this extent he is in a better position than a first registered proprietor[17].

Cases falling within the discarded para (b), which permitted rectification if the immediate disposition to the proprietor in possession was void, are now embraced by the new para (a). A person who procures his registration by means of a forged transfer is guilty of fraud within para (a). Equally, a subsequent proprietor who knows of the forgery displays a lack of proper care. On the other hand, no such fault can be attributed to a subsequent transferee in possession (whether for value or not[18]) who is unaware of the forgery or other suspicious circumstances surrounding the original registration.

(c) Unjust not to rectify (s 82(3)(c))

While this paragraph appears to confer a wide general discretion to order rectification, it should be read as an additional hurdle that the applicant must surmount before rectifications should be ordered. A claim for rectification under one of the preceding paragraphs will still need to be made out. All the circumstances of the case, including matters such as how long the proprietor has lived in the property can then be considered in deciding whether it would be unjust not to rectify the register[19].

Though there appears to be no reported decision where rectification has been ordered on the basis of s 82(3)(c), the provision has been the subject of judicial consideration. Luxmoore J[20] expressed the view that it would be unjust not to rectify where the effect of registration had been to deprive an owner of land without his assent or knowledge. If this alone is considered sufficient to apply para (c), it renders somewhat illusory the curative effects of first registration[1]. This interpretation has not found favour with later judges. The cases indicate that an applicant for rectification is unlikely to succeed under para (c) where he is guilty of conduct which the court considers in some way to be reprehensible. In *Re Sea View Gardens, Claridge v Tingey*[2] Pennycuick J thought it 'abundantly clear' that it would not be just to order rectification where the applicant (who claimed to be the owner of a disputed plot of land

---

16 Such as the vendor's failure to comply with a covenant to build a wall which, if built, would have indicated the true boundary: see *Epps v Esso Petroleum Co Ltd* [1973] 2 All ER 465, where this was an important factor in determining the application of s 82(3)(c). Quaere whether the use of an inadequate plan would suffice; see *Scarfe v Adams* [1981] 1 All ER 843, CA.

17 *Epps v Esso Petroleum Co Ltd*, supra, at 472, per Templeman J.

18 Under the old para (b) a proprietor in possession claiming otherwise than for value was denied protection. The new para (a) omits this exclusion.

19 See *London Borough of Hounslow v Hare* (1990) 24 HLR 9.

20 *Chowood Ltd v Lyall (No 2)* [1930] 1 Ch 426 at 438. The Court of Appeal held that s 82(3) was not relevant because the proprietor was not in possession: [1930] 2 Ch 156, CA.

1 Cretney & Dworkin, op cit, p 538.

2 [1966] 3 All ER 935 at 941.

prior to registration) had stood by and knowingly allowed the registered proprietor to do work on the land before he intervened with his application. In *Epps v Esso Petroleum Co Ltd*[3] Templeman J declined to order rectification in favour of a plaintiff who, by failing to make proper inquiries before completion, did not discover the true boundaries of the land he had contracted to buy. In the circumstances, justice lay wholly with the defendant registered proprietors in whom the disputed strip of land was vested. Furthermore, the fact that they would be entitled to an indemnity on rectification, whereas the plaintiff would obtain nothing if his claim were to be rejected[4], did not suffice to tip the scales in his favour. This decision clearly demonstrates that rectification and indemnity are by no means complementary remedies.

In determining whether it is unjust not to rectify, different considerations may apply depending upon whether the proprietor in possession is the first registered proprietor or a subsequent transferee for value. Suppose application is made for the entry of restrictive covenants inadvertently omitted from the register on first registration. It may be unjust not to rectify the register against a first registered proprietor, particularly if he purchased the land knowing that it was burdened by those restrictions. Conversely, it might be unjust to order rectification against a transferee who in reliance upon the register purchased the property on the basis that it was not subject to any restrictions[5]. The fact that the claimant for rectification, or the proprietor in possession, derived title otherwise than for value, would also be a relevant factor to take into account. The Law Commission does not support the retention of para (c); it introduces too great an element of uncertainty into the system[6]. Nothing will be lost by its demise.

(d) Overriding interests
The opening words of sub-s (3) provide for rectification against a registered proprietor in possession 'for giving effect to an overriding interest ...'. This is an important exception, which calls for little further comment. Registration is subject to overriding interests. Rectification to give effect to such an interest merely records on the register what is the true situation; it does not alter the proprietor's position. When the registered proprietor is in possession, the applicant for rectification will not normally be able to claim an overriding interest by virtue of s 70(1)(g) of the Act, since he himself will not be in actual occupation of the land[7]. Nevertheless, such a claim is not entirely incompatible with the proprietor's reliance on s 82(3). The relevant time for determining the applicant's occupation for the purposes of s 70(1)(g) is the date of completion of the transaction, and he may have vacated the land, without

---

3   [1973] 2 All ER 465. For the relevance of the value of any indemnity, see also *London Borough of Hounslow v Hare*, supra, at 27.
4   Because of the LRA 1925, s 83(11), considered p 100, post.
5   See *Freer v Unwins Ltd* [1976] Ch 288 at 299, [1976] 1 All ER 634 at 637, per Walton J.
6   Report No 158, para 3.15. See their draft Bill, cl 44(3), (4).
7   *Epps v Esso Petroleum Co Ltd*, supra, at 472. This does, however, emphasise the difference between occupation and possession.

prejudicing his claim to an overriding interest[9], long before the registered proprietor took possession.

(e) Court order

The register may also be rectified against the proprietor in possession so as to give effect to an order of the court. This somewhat puzzling provision, introduced by s 24 of the Act of 1977, must be understood to refer to a court order other than an order for rectification made pursuant to s 82(1)[10]. Unless it is so construed, this new ground for rectification against the proprietor in possession appears to remove completely the special protection which s 82(3) confers on him – a result Parliament can hardly have intended.

(f) Rectification always discretionary

Section 82(3) enacts that: 'The register shall not be rectified ...' unless one of the conditions there stated is fulfilled. This provision should not be interpreted as meaning that rectification must be ordered when one of these conditions is shown to exist. This point has sometimes been overlooked in relation to s 82(3)[11]. The court's power of rectification given by s 82(1) never ceases to be discretionary[12]. Thus, the court may refuse to rectify notwithstanding that the requirements of s 82(3)(a) are shown to have been satisfied. Seemingly, the court has jurisdiction to deny rectification, even when it is sought to give effect to an overriding interest. Since registration is always subject to these interests, the dismissal of the claim means, in effect, that the court considers that the claimant has forfeited his right to enforce the interest because of his conduct. In such a situation it would seem to be essential for the court to direct the Registrar to note on the register that the land is free from the interest claimed[13]. Otherwise, it will remain binding on the proprietor.

When deciding how to exercise the discretion under s 82(1), the courts have shown a willingness on occasions to resort to general principles which govern priority disputes affecting unregistered land. This is seen especially in cases where it has been necessary to decide which of two innocent parties will suffer loss for the wrongdoing of a third person[14].

---

9   Page 65, ante. As to the relevant date for s 82(3) purposes, see p 90, ante.

10   26 *Halsbury's Laws* (4th edn), para 1058, note 2. Examples would include an order under the Matrimonial Causes Act 1973, s 24 (property adjustment orders); s 37(2)(b) (avoidance of dispositions of property to defeat claim for financial relief) ; the Inheritance (Provision for Family and Dependants) Act 1975, s 2(1)(c) (transfer of property in deceased's estate). Contrast the Law Commission's understanding of the reason for this exception; see Report No 158, para 3.13 (preservation of rights of trustee in bankruptcy) and draft Bill, cl 44(4)(d).

11   See *Re 139 High Street, Deptford* [1951] Ch 884 at 889, [1951] 1 All ER 950 at 952, per Wynn-Parry J.

12   *Epps v Esso Petroleum Co Ltd* [1973] 2 All ER 465 at 472, per Templeman J. Presumably, no element of discretion can exist when rectification is required to give effect to a court order.

13   By virtue of the power conferred by the LRR 1925, r 197. But see p 65, ante.

14   *Argyle Building Society v Hammond* (1984) 49 P & CR 148 at 160, CA, per Slade LJ, discussing *Re Leighton's Conveyance* [1937] Ch 149, [1936] 1 All ER 667; *Argyle Building Society v Steed* (15 December 1989, unreported).

4.   Effect of rectification

As we have already observed, s 82(2) of the Act permits the register to be rectified, notwithstanding that it may affect any estates, rights, charges, or interests acquired or protected by registration, or by any entry on the register. The effect of rectification in any particular case will depend largely on the nature of the order that is made. For example, rectification may take the form of removing land from X's title and including it in Y's registered title. Y's registration as proprietor will automatically vest the legal title in him. But what if rectification is ordered in favour of Y, who is not a proprietor of any registered land, by the removal from X's title of land which is held to belong to Y? This situation occurred in *Chowood Ltd v Lyall (No 2)*[15] and in *Re 139 High Street, Deptford*[16]. In both cases the disputed land in respect of which rectification was ordered was unregistered land whilst in Y's ownership. In neither case does it appear that the court ordered any consequential relief for the re-vesting of the legal title. There is nothing in the Act of 1925 to warrant the view that 'de-registration' automatically operates to re-vest the legal title in Y. The Registry takes the view[17], however, that removal of the land from X's title, by necessary implication, perfects Y's unregistered title, and he can, without more, rely on his documentary title to establish his legal title to the land. Whilst this would seem to be implicit in the two decisions, it is thought that the point should be expressly provided for in any future Land Registration Act.

A further problem merits discussion. From what date does rectification take effect? According to the modified r 83(2) of the Land Registration Rules 1925, an application[18] for rectification of the register 'shall be completed by registration' as of the day on which it is deemed to have been delivered at the Registry. This rule does not envisage rectification operating retrospectively as from the date when X was erroneously registered as proprietor. Y's entitlement to recover any rents and profits of the land received by X, or an occupation rent if X himself has been in possession, is uncertain, save that such loss would not be recoverable by Y under the existing indemnity provisions of the Act. However, r 83(2) does not govern any situation where rectification is claimed and ordered in court proceedings not preceded by an application therefor to the Registrar. The court would be free, in a suitable case, to order retrospective rectification; s 82(2) of the Act contains nothing to suggest that the effect of a court order for rectification is limited in the manner laid down by s 83(2). This interpretation of the scope of s 82(2) has the support of the Law

---

15   [1930] 2 Ch 156 (successful claim to squatter's rights under s 70(1)(f). Cf *Tester v Harris* (1964) 189 EG 337, where X's possessory title was upset by Y, the unregistered paper title owner, due to insufficient evidence to establish X's adverse possession. Y was declared entitled to the disputed land, and an order made for rectifying the register to give effect to the declaration.

16   [1951] Ch 884, [1951] 1 All ER 950, p 88, ante.

17   I am indebted to Mr M L Wood, Land Registrar, of HM Land Registry, for this information.

18   'Application' in r 83(2) is defined to mean 'an application for ... rectifying ... any entry in the register': LRR 1925, r 1(5B), inserted by LRR 1978, r 2.

Commission, which takes the view that both the court and the Registrar should have as full and ample a power of rectification as is needed to achieve justice. This must include the power to rectify with retrospective effect[19].

The provisions of the Act produce some interesting anomalies when rectification is ordered to give effect to a restrictive covenant omitted from the register. If X, a registered proprietor of freehold land, suffers rectification by the entry on his register of title of a restrictive covenant, he becomes bound by it. By virtue of s 70(2), where notice of a restrictive covenant is entered on the register, *the proprietor* and persons deriving title under him are deemed to be affected with notice of it as an incumbrance. But suppose that before rectification is sought X has already leased the land to T for 21 years and T has assigned it to A. This was, in effect, the situation that occurred in *Freer v Unwins Ltd*[20]. Walton J held that the assignee was not bound. Section 70(2) also provides that entry of a notice does not affect incumbrancers and other persons who at the time when it is entered may not be bound by the covenant. The words 'other persons' included lessees, and both T and A were within the exception since the rectifying entry on the freehold title was made after the date of the lease and the assignment to A[1]. In the end result the rectification which the plaintiff-covenantee obtained in *Freer v Unwins Ltd* assisted him not one iota. He could neither enforce the covenant against A (the defendant) during the remainder of the lease[2], nor obtain any indemnity under the Act for his inability to do so[3]. Had rectification been made retrospective to the date when the omission first occurred, then presumably A would have been bound, though it has been suggested that the wording of s 50(2) rules out the possibility of retrospective rectification, at least in the case of restrictive covenants[4].

In *Freer's* case, the lease, not being for a term exceeding 21 years, was not registrable. Had A been the assignee under a registered lease, he would still have not been bound by the covenant, unless the plaintiff-covenantee had also been able to obtain rectification of the leasehold title.

---

19   Law Com No 158, para 3.8. Identical jurisdiction for court and Registrar is urged: ibid, para 3.19. See the draft Bill, cl 44(1).
20   [1976] Ch 288, [1976] 1 All ER 634; noted (1976) 40 Conv (NS) 304, [1976] CLJ 211, (1976) 92 LQR 338; see also R & R, 890.
1   It is misleading to assert that *Freer v Unwins Ltd* held that the power to rectify cannot be exercised with retrospective effect: see Report No 158, para 3.8. Rectification had already been ordered by the Registry on an application to it, and a new edition of the freehold title opened on a date subsequent to the T-A transaction. Walton J was merely called upon to determine the legal consequences of that rectification in the light of the Act's provisions. Consequent upon his decision, r 83(2) was revised so as to deal with applications, not simply registrations as before. The amendment gave statutory backing to what was the Registry's practice, applied in *Freer's* case, as to the dating of rectified entries.
2   Seemingly an assignee from A would be bound (unless all derivative interests out of the lease take free from it), in which event A could claim an indemnity under s 83(1) since rectification had deprived him of the right to assign his estate free from a burdensome restriction.
3   Page 98, post.
4   Hayton, *Registered Land* (3rd edn), p 182.

C Indemnity

1. Entitlement to indemnity

It is the general scheme of the Act to compensate persons who suffer loss by reason of some error in or omission from the register. It is claimed[5] that rectification and indemnity are essentially complementary remedies, but the Act itself imposes some important qualifications on the principle, which the courts have not been slow to recognise[6]. The main grounds on which a claim for indemnity may be founded are contained in s 83. For details of indemnity claims which the Registry meets, and the grounds on which they are based, reference should be made to the Reports on HM Land Registry, submitted annually to the Lord Chancellor by the Chief Land Registrar.

(a) Loss suffered by rectification (s 83(1))
A person suffering loss by reason of any rectification of the register is entitled to be indemnified, subject to certain exceptions to be considered later. Compensation is, therefore, recoverable by a registered proprietor where land included in error within his title is removed on rectification, a situation illustrated by the *Deptford* case[7]. At first sight it may seem illogical that a person can recover compensation for the loss of land to which he had no title prior to registration. But this result is a necessary consequence of the statutory effect of first registration which operates to vest a title in him. Annual Reports show that claims made under s 83(1) have been made in respect of: errors in recording rights of way and restrictive covenants; mapping errors; the registration of forged transfers and charges; the erroneous cancellation of a charge later reinstated, and fraudulent applications to replace a lost land certificate. When rectification is ordered consequent upon the Registry's failure on first registration to record an adverse interest, such as an easement or restrictive covenant, the first proprietor can still claim an indemnity, even though that interest was, to his knowledge, binding on him prior to his registration. As a result of its omission from the register, he acquires a title free from the interest, whereas rectification denies him an unincumbered title.

(b) Non-rectification (s 83(2))
Subject again to certain exceptions, where an error or omission has occurred in the register, but the register is not rectified, any person suffering *loss* by reason of the error or omission is entitled to be indemnified. Although the wording of s 83(2) appears to make it clear that an indemnity is available only after an unsuccessful claim to rectification has been made, it seems that a

---

5   R & R, 40-01.
6   *Epps v Esso Petroleum Co Ltd* [1973] 2 All ER 465; *Freer v Unwins Ltd* [1976] Ch 288 at 295–96, [1976] 1 All ER 634 at 637, per Walton J.
7   [1951] Ch 884, [1951] 1 All ER 950, p 31, ante. The registered proprietor was ultimately awarded £1,278; see (1954) 18 Conv (NS) 130, 138. If the case arose today, rectification might not be ordered; see p 90, ante. See also *Re Boyle's Claim* [1961] 1 All ER 620.

claimant can simply make a claim for an indemnity without, first, having sought rectification[8]. According to Annual Reports, indemnity has been paid under sub-s (2) for loss resulting from: registration of the wrong amount of land; the erroneous cancellation of a caution or registered charge; failure to enter notice of covenants on first registration, and errors resulting from fraud. The right to compensation is not dependent upon the claimant's own title being registered.

(c) Other cases

The Act also provides for the payment of compensation in a number of other situations which can usefully be considered together. Indemnity can be claimed for loss suffered by reason of the destruction or loss of any document lodged at the Registry, or because of any error, omission or inaccuracy in an official search[9], filed abstract, copy or extract of a filed document, or an office copy of the register or filed plan[10]. A trustee in bankruptcy is entitled to an indemnity where loss is suffered by the estate of a bankrupt proprietor because of the omission to register a creditor's notice or bankruptcy inhibition[11].

2. No indemnity payable

A claimant may be denied an indemnity under the Act for a variety of reasons.

(a) No loss suffered

To be entitled to an indemnity by virtue of s 83(1)–(3) of the Act, the claimant must have suffered loss by reason of the rectification, or the error or omission, as the case may be. In this context 'loss' has a special meaning. It has been held that no loss is suffered for the purposes of s 83(1) where rectification is ordered to give effect to an overriding interest[12]. As we have seen, in such a case rectification does not alter the proprietor's real position; he cannot, therefore, be said to suffer loss by reason of it. This obviously constitutes qualification to the principle of indemnity and highlights an inherent weakness in our system of land registration. It is part of the Law Commission's recommended overhaul of the system that there should be greater flexibility in the availability of indemnity. In future, the statutory guarantee should embrace losses suffered by reason of overriding interests[13].

Where the register is rectified on account of a forged disposition, a proprietor of any land or charge claiming in good faith thereunder is deemed

---

8   *Clark v Chief Land Registrar* [1993] Ch 294, [1993] 2 All ER 936; affd [1994] Ch 370, [1994] 4 All ER 96, CA.

9   LRA 1925, s 83(3); *Parkash v Irani Finance Ltd* [1970] Ch 101 , [1969] 1 All ER 930.

10   LRA 1925, ss 110(4), 113.

11   Section 61(7), as amended by the Insolvency Act 1985, Sch 8, para 5(3)(c). For another example, see LRA 1925, s 77(6) (loss on conversion of title), p 36, ante.

12   *Re Chowood's Registered Land* [1933] Ch 574.

13   Law Com No 158, para 3.21. See further p 103, post.

by s 83(4)[14] to have suffered loss by reason thereof and to be entitled to an indemnity.

(b) Rectification obtained

No provision is made for the payment of compensation in cases where a claim to rectification has been upheld. Yet the decision in *Freer v Unwins Ltd*[15] demonstrates that rectification by itself may not always be an adequate remedy. This deficiency in the Act has been recognised by the Law Commission, and it has recommended that there should be power to award compensation in addition to rectification in appropriate circumstances[16]. Any personal action for damages for loss suffered despite rectification is ruled out by the indemnity afforded to Registry officials by s 131 of the Act, except in the unlikely event of bad faith being established.

(c) Statutory exclusions

The Land Registration Act 1925 contains a number of provisions which exclude the right to an indemnity in various cases. The most important of these[17] arises under s 83(5)(a), as substituted by s 3(1) of the Land Registration and Land Charges Act 1971. No indemnity is payable:

> ... where the applicant or a person from whom he derives title (otherwise than under a disposition for valuable consideration which is registered or protected on the register) has caused or substantially contributed to the loss by fraud or lack of proper care.

A claimant is not allowed to profit from his own wrongdoing or carelessness. The words 'fraud or lack of proper care' have been encountered before in s 82(3)(a), and they should, of course, be similarly interpreted. A lack of proper care sufficient to justify an order for rectification against a proprietor in possession will automatically deprive him of any indemnity for loss suffered thereby. This statutory exclusion operates howsoever the loss is alleged to have been caused – whether by rectification or non-rectification. In view of the high incidence of fraud and forgery in mortgage transactions, a mortgagee who lends on the security of a charge without seeking adequate identification evidence of the borrower may well be unable to establish that he has exercised proper care, if he later suffers loss because the borrower, or one of joint borrowers, turns out to be an imposter[18].

The fraud or lack of proper care need not necessarily be that of the applicant. No indemnity is payable where he is a volunteer who derives title from a person guilty of such conduct. In this respect s 83(7)(a) differs from s 82(3)(a), which does not make the volunteer vicariously liable for his

---

14   But 'subject as herein after provided', a reference to (inter alia) s 83(5), (11).
15   [1976] Ch 288, [1976] 1 All ER 634, p 95, ante.
16   Law Com No 158, para 3.28; draft Bill, cl 45(1)(b).
17   For other instances see s 42(2) (disclaimers by trustee in bankruptcy), s 60(2) (company dispositions free from unprotected incumbrances), s 83(5)(b) (mines and minerals).
18   See the Annual Report for 1990–91, para 43, where this suggestion is made.

predecessor's shortcomings[19]. But to conclude that the revised wording of s 82(3)(a) effects an improvement in a volunteer's position under s 83(7)(a) as regards indemnity is a mistake. Suppose X is registered as proprietor of land in circumstances where there has been a lack of proper care on his part. X gives the property to Y, who is registered as proprietor and enters into possession. Assuming there is no personal lack of care by Y, rectification cannot be awarded against him on the basis of s 82(3)(a). It may nevertheless be ordered under s 82(3)(c), in which event Y is debarred by s 83(7)(a) from recovering any indemnity under the Act. He claims through X whose lack of proper care has (in the circumstances) caused or contributed to the loss.

A transferee under a *disposition for valuable consideration which is registered*[20] *or protected on the register* is never prejudiced in relation to any indemnity by his predecessor's fraud or lack of care. The words in italics are significant. In some situations even a transferee for value would appear to be affected by his transferor's fraud or lack of care. Suppose that V conveys to P for value an unregistered plot of land. Later V conveys an adjacent plot to P2, who is registered as first proprietor with an absolute freehold title. Owing to an error attributable to V's lack of proper care, part of P's land is included within P2's title. Should P seek rectification and this is refused, it seems that s 83(5)(a) bars his entitlement to an indemnity. Though P is not a volunteer, the V-P conveyance is not a *registered disposition*[1].

A claimant who is caught by s 83(7)(a) is wholly disqualified from obtaining statutory compensation. This is as it should be on the present wording of the section. Where the contribution to the loss is less than substantial, the claimant can, it seems, recover the full amount of the indemnity which the Act permits, even though he is partly (albeit not substantially) to blame. Whether he should be able to do so is questionable. A good case can be made for the introduction of a scheme for the apportionment of responsibility. So, an indemnity would be reduced when the applicant was at fault to such a degree as was thought just and equitable, having regard to his share in the responsibility for the loss[2].

(d) Claim statute-barred

The provisions of s 83(11)[3] defining the liability to pay indemnity under the Act operate unfairly to restrict a claimant's right to compensation. Liability to pay constitutes a simple contract debt. The basic limitation period is, therefore, six years. The cause of action is deemed to accrue 'when the claimant knows or but for his own default might have known, of the existence of his claim'. In

---

19   See p 91, ante.
20   Including a lessee under a non-registrable lease which takes effect as if it were a registered disposition: LRA 1925, s 19(2). But what of his assignee? See p 89, ante.
1   On a strict wording of para (a), it is immaterial that V's lack of care arose in relation to the V-P conveyance, or the V-P2 transaction. Can this be correct?
2   See Law Com No 158, para 3.27; draft Bill, cl 45(6).
3   As amended by the Limitation Act 1980, s 40(2), Sch 3, para 1.

Argyle Building Society v Steed [4] Knox J held that the words 'his claim' referred to the applicant's claim for rectification, not the claim for indemnity after refusal of rectification. So interpreted[5], the subsection constitutes something of a trap for the unwary as Knox J recognised. For, if the claim for rectification is resisted, its outcome may not be determined until after the six years have elapsed, so defeating any entitlement to statutory compensation.

The proviso to sub-s (11) imposes a further restraint on the claimant's rights. Where the claim to an indemnity arises in consequence of the registration of an absolute or good leasehold title[6], it must be made within six years of *the date of registration*, whether the claimant knew about the registration or not. A claimant who does not learn about the erroneous registration until more than six years after the date of registration may find himself without any remedy. Not only is he denied any right to indemnity, his claim to rectification is likely to be defeated by s 82(3) if the registered proprietor is in possession. This is precisely what occurred in the *Epps* case[7], where the fact that the plaintiffs right to any indemnity would be time-barred was not sufficient to tilt the balance of justice in favour of rectification. More recently, Knox J indicated in the *Steed* case that when deciding whether or not to order rectification, the absence through lapse of time of a good claim to indemnity ought not to be a consideration of very great weight.

The harshness of the principle adopted in *Epps* has been recognised by the Law Commission[8]. The draft Bill, attached to the Commission's fourth Report on Land Registration (Law Com No 173), contains a much simpler and fairer clause (44(12)) relating to limitation. Under it the cause of action relating to a claim for loss suffered by rectification would be deemed to arise on rectification. In other claims for indemnity it would be deemed to arise when the claimant knew, or ought to have known, of the existence of his claim.

The proviso to s 83(11) expressly extends the period for claiming indemnity in four special cases[9], one of which deserves passing mention. A claim to indemnity in respect of a breach of a restrictive covenant affecting freehold land is enforceable within six years from its breach, where it was binding on the first proprietor at the time of first registration. Where the claim to an indemnity arises by reason of rectification pursuant to a court order, time begins to run from the date of the order, not from some earlier date from which the rectification takes effect[10]. There is no express limitation period for claims for rectification.

---

4   (15 December 1989, unreported), Ch D. The judgment is taken from the Lexis transcript; affd without reference to this point *sub nom Norwich and Peterborough Building Society v Steed (No 2)* [1993] Ch 116, [1993] 1 All ER 330, CA.

5   Support for this construction can be found in sub-s (11) itself; the immediately following proviso opens with the words, 'Where a claim to indemnity arises ...'

6   The expression 'absolute title ... title' embraces absolute freehold and absolute leasehold titles.

7   [1973] 2 All ER 465, p 92, ante. Cf the approach of Wynn-Parry J in *Re 139 High Street, Deptford* [1951] Ch 884 at 892, [1951] 1 All ER 950 at 954.

8   Law Com Report No 158, para 3.32, adopting a recommendation of the Law Reform Committee: 21st Report (Limitation of Actions) (1977), Cmnd 6923, paras 3.76–77.

9   Paragraphs (a)–(d). The remaining three cases relate to infants, settled land and mortgages.

10   Eg by virtue of the LRR 1925, r 83(2), p 93, ante.

3. Claiming compensation

(a) Determination of claim
The Land Registration and Land Charges Act 1971, s 1, abolished the insurance fund established by the Land Transfer Act 1897[11]. Any indemnity is now payable by the Chief Land Registrar out of moneys provided by Parliament. In theory, an insurance premium element is built into the fees payable for registering dealings with registered titles. In reality, this premium element comprises an insignificant proportion of the total fee which is calculated by reference to the value of the land. By virtue of s 2(1) of the Act of 1971, the court decides any question as to a claimant's right to an indemnity, or its amount. The Registrar's power to determine such matters has been abolished, but without prejudice to his power to settle claims for indemnity by agreement[12]. It, therefore, seems advisable to submit any claim to the Registrar in the first instance[13], and to refer the matter to the court only if he rejects the claim.

(b) Amount of indemnity
Section 83(6) of the Act limits the payment of indemnity where it is awarded in respect of the loss of an estate or interest in or charge on land. Two situations are covered: (a) where the register is not rectified, the amount is not to exceed the value of the estate or charge at the time when the error or omission causing the loss was made; (b) where the register is rectified, the indemnity is limited to its value (assuming there had been no rectification) immediately before rectification. Under (b) the applicant is enabled to recover the value of any expenditure on the property which has increased its value. It is uncertain whether a claimant can recover consequential loss, ie loss additional to the value of any estate or interest lost as a result of rectification or a refusal to rectify, though the Act does not in terms exclude such loss. Reasonable costs and expenses properly incurred by an applicant in relation to his claim are recoverable, notwithstanding that no other indemnity is payable[14].

These arbitrary limitations can cause hardship, especially when the register is not rectified (case (a)). The Law Commission[15] favours the repeal of s 83(6), which is seen as wrong in principle. Yet the claimant's own conduct ought not to be totally ignored. In accordance with ordinary principles of assessment of damages, the indemnity payable should be limited if he has failed to mitigate his loss or stood by, hoping that it might increase.

A person who has caused or substantially contributed to the loss by his fraud is liable to the Registrar (on behalf of the Crown) for the amount of any indemnity paid in respect of such loss[16]. No right of recovery exists from a person merely contributing to the loss through lack of proper care. In addition,

11 Section 21. For the history of this fund, consult Law Com No 158, paras 3.23–24. See generally (1971) 35 Conv (NS) 390 (T B F Ruoff and P Meehan).
12 LR & LCA 1971, s 2(5); s 14(2)(b), Sch 2, repealed the LRA 1925, s 83(7).
13 The most simple, cheap and logical solution: per Ruoff & Meehan, op cit, p 395.
14 LRA 1925, s 83(8), as substituted by the LR & LCA 197 1, s 2(4).
15 Report No 158, para 3.30. The draft Bill does not reproduce sub-s (6).
16 LRA 1925, s 83(9).

the Registrar is entitled to enforce any express or implied covenant (eg for title) or other right which the person indemnified could have enforced in relation to the matter in respect of which indemnity has been paid[17].

It is worth noting that despite the large volume of business conducted by the Land Registry, the annual amounts paid by way of compensation are incredibly small. For the year 1993–94[18], the indemnity payments (including costs) totalled £1,521,836.01, which reflects the high standard of the Registry's work. Of course, the various limitations on the right to an indemnity must not be overlooked, especially that concerning overriding interests. To what extent the annual level of payments is depressed by these restrictions is impossible to assess.

D Proposals for reform

The Law Commission's draft Bill, attached to the Fourth Report on Land Registration, No 173, seeks to give effect to recommendations put forward in the Third Report (No 158). In the earlier Report the Commission accepted that the jurisdiction to rectify should be consistent with the basic principle that the registered land system is not intended to effect alterations to the substantive law. As to the powers of rectification, the Bill provides that it would be available when (a) there is an error or omission from a register, *and* (b) that error or omission relates to an overriding interest, *or* rectification would be just in all the circumstances (cl 44(1)). If both requirements are satisfied, rectification becomes mandatory, save as against an occupying proprietor. Wisely, the Bill makes no attempt to elaborate the concept of justice, although in the Third Report (para 3.6) the Commission envisaged that this issue would be determined on a consideration of such matters as fraud, lack of good faith, or absence of value. The requirement of justice is not applied in relation to overriding interests; to decline to rectify in respect of such an interest would not affect its existence, and it would continue to bind the land[19]. The Bill does, however, contain a supplementary provision (cl 46(2)), to the effect that an error or omission occurs when the register shows that the title to a registered interest does not accurately reflect the title to the land according to established rules of land law[20]. This reformulation of the jurisdictional basis of rectification will produce an anomalous, and unfortunate, consequence. It will be necessary to know and apply unregistered land law principles long after they have ceased to play any practical role in conveyancing transactions. The superseded common law system of land transfer will continue to haunt conveyancers, Registry officials and the courts well into the next century. Might

17 LRA 1925, s 83(10). Would the reference to 'other right' permit recourse against a negligent solicitor? Clause 45(11)(b) of the Bill replaces 'other right' by 'any right of action'. The sums recovered under s 83(10) tend to be very small.
18 Annual Report for 1993–94, para 25. The largest single claim was for £200,000.
19 See the explanatory note to cl 44. Yet it would be possible to enter on the register a note as to freedom from the interest: LRR 1925, r 197, p 93, ante, discussing a similar issue raised in relation to s 82(3).
20 Report No 158, paras 3.6, 3.18 and 3.34(2).

it not have been better to seek a formula that was not so heavily dependent on unregistered land rules?

The need to strengthen the ailing concept of indefeasibility of title in the interests of 'confident and secure conveyancing' (para 3.17) was also uppermost in the Commission's mind. The privileged status of the proprietor in possession is to be enhanced. Rectification is not to be ordered against a registered proprietor who has been a prudent purchaser and who is in actual occupation of the land, *unless* it is in favour of a trustee in bankruptcy or gives effect to an overriding interest. The immunity conferred by the Bill would be narrower than that presently available under s 82(3), since it will not cover any proprietor who is not a purchaser[1]. The discretionary power to rectify under s 82(3)(c) of the Act will disappear. However, the exception for fraud or lack of proper care is retained, though the Bill purports to define 'lack of proper care' in 'more familiar terms'[2].

The Commission has quite properly recognised the force of calls for more flexibility in the availability of indemnity. So long as compensation is denied to a proprietor suffering rectification to give effect to an overriding interest, rectification and indemnity can never truly be said to be complementary remedies. Having accepted the inevitability that reduced number of third party rights should retain their exalted status as overriding interests, the Commission felt constrained to offer some consolation to disappointed purchasers bound by them. The availability of an indemnity to cover overriding interests was seen as a way to establish an acceptable balance between competing innocent interests (para 2.12). When such compensation is paid, the Registrar is to be required to make whatever entries relating to the interest are considered expedient[3]. In other words, he can rectify the register by entering the overriding interest on it. This procedure should achieve two beneficial results. It should encourage the creation of a more complete register of title, and also facilitate a proper consideration of the claim before paying any indemnity. Moreover, under the Bill a claim would not always succeed in full, and perhaps not at all, if the proprietor had contributed to his loss by his own lack of proper care[4]. This was one consideration which prompted the Commission's expectation that an extension of indemnity to overriding interests would not prove very expensive[5]. Other more minor modifications to the statutory compensation system have already been noted when considering the existing provisions of the Act.

On balance, the Commission's various recommendations are to be welcomed. They will, when given statutory effect, make the operation of the

1 See cl 44(3), (4). 'Purchaser' is defined traditionally, to mean a person in good faith and for valuable consideration, including a lessee and mortgagee: cl 70(1).
2 Report No 158, para 3.14, and cl 46(2) which, without being exhaustive, provides that such lack exists if the proprietor has actual or constructive knowledge of the error or omission.
3 See the draft Bill, cl 45(1)(c), (2).
4 See cll 45(5), (6), 46(3).
5 Para 3.29. Since most of the remaining heads of overriding interests will involve some physical presence on the land for their validity (see p 55, ante), the purchaser would be expected to make inquiry of occupants. Failure to make proper inquiry would be indicative of a lack of adequate prudence on his part.

twin remedies of rectification and indemnity less arbitrary and more in accord with notions of justice and fairness. The one highly disturbing feature is the prominent role that unregistered land principles will have in determining the entitlement to rectification.

Part Three

The contract stage

Chapter 5

Formation of the contract of sale

A Introduction

Until the coming into force of s 2 of the Law of Property (Miscellaneous Provisions) Act 1989, it was true to say that a contract for the sale of land could be made in the same way as any other contract. What was required was a concluded agreement between the parties, supported by consideration and intended to create legal relations. Such contracts did differ from other contracts, however, in a number of important respects. First, because of the equitable doctrine of specific performance and, second, because of the difficulties of title[1]. In addition they were subject to the formal requirements of s 40 of the Law of Property Act 1925. It is mainly the difficulties of title that produce the differences. Whereas a contract for the sale of personalty may be negotiated, completed and the buyer in full possession of his new acquisition all in a matter of minutes, weeks or months may elapse between an oral agreement for the sale of land and the subsequent vesting of the legal title in the purchaser.

Not every transfer of freehold or leasehold land is preceded by a contract. In some cases, no element of sale is involved, as where property is vested in a donee, or in a devise under a testator's will, or on the appointment of new trustees. Each of these, and other similar transactions, may produce conveyancing problems and will require the preparation and execution of the appropriate document vesting title in the grantee. They are not our concern in this part of the book. Where a transfer results from a sale, there must, of necessity, be a contract prepared by the parties. This is usually embodied in a formal contract prepared by the vendor's solicitor and containing the conditions of sale. However, there is nothing sacrosanct about a formal contract prepared by the parties' legal advisers. Previously it was the case that a contract for the sale of land could arise in a number of informal ways. After the enactment of s 2 of the Law of Property (Miscellaneous Provisions) Act 1989, to be considered shortly, this is much less likely to happen today, than was previously the case. Nevertheless, it remains possible for the parties, without having obtained advice, to enter into a contract for the sale of land and they may well then encounter problems not normally arising under a formal contract; these will be considered in a later chapter.

---

1   *Sheggia v Gradwell* [1963] 3 All ER 114 at 121, CA, per Harman LJ.

B   Capacity

Before turning to the formal requirements necessary for the creation of a contract for the sale of land, something must be said concerning a person's capacity to acquire or dispose of land. The following will be considered here: minors, companies and persons suffering from mental disorder. The position on bankruptcy will be considered in Chapter 8. Disabilities formerly attaching to married women, aliens and convicts are no longer operative.

1.   Minors[2]

(a) Legal ownership

Section 1(6) of the Law of Property Act 1925, enacts that a legal estate is not capable of being held by a minor; consequently he (or she) cannot be a mortgagee[3], trustee[4], personal representative[5], tenant for life[6] or have a legal estate vested in him beneficially. Where a minor is entitled to an equitable fee simple or a term of years absolute, the legal estate will be subject to a settlement[7]. A conveyance of a legal estate to a minor does not pass the estate to him; it operates as an agreement for valuable consideration to execute a settlement by means of a principal vesting deed and a trust instrument in his favour, and in the meantime to hold the land in trust for him[8]. The ineffectiveness of the conveyance to pass the legal estate is not affected by the rebuttable presumption that parties to a conveyance are of full age at the date thereof[9]. If the mistake is not discovered until after the purchaser has attained his majority, the title can be corrected by a simple confirmatory conveyance from the vendor.

Similarly, a purported disposition of registered land to a minor does not entitle him to be registered as proprietor until he attains full age. In the meantime, it operates as a declaration binding upon the proprietor that the registered land is held in trust to give effect to minor interests[10] in his favour corresponding, as nearly as may be, with the interests which the disposition purports to transfer[11]. However, it would appear that if by mistake a minor were registered as proprietor following a transfer to him, the legal title would vest in him[12], subject to the prospect of rectification to give effect to the statutory position. Should he attain full age without the register being rectified then,

---

2   See Family Law Reform Act 1969, s 12.
3   LPA 1925, s 19(6).
4   LPA 1925, s 20.
5   Supreme Court Act 1981, s 118.
6   SLA 1925, s 19(1).
7   SLA 1925, s 1(1)(ii)(d).
8   SLA 1925, s 27(1); LPA 1925, s 19(1). A conveyance to a minor jointly with a person of full age operates to vest the legal estate in the adult on the statutory trusts: ibid, s 19(2).
9   LPA 1925, s 15.
10   For minor interests, see pp 70–71, ante.
11   LRA 1925, s 111(1).
12   By virtue of LRA 1925, ss 20(1) (freeholds), 23(1) (leaseholds). This result is contrary to the spirit of s 111(1), but the sub-s is defective in that it does not say what is to happen if a minor is *in fact* registered.

unlike the position in unregistered conveyancing, no further step would be necessary to clothe him with the legal title.

(b) Equitable ownership

The legislation of 1925 has not interfered with the minor's position in equity; he can still acquire and dispose of equitable interests in land. A devise of land to a minor is effective to vest the equitable interest in him[13], as is a purported conveyance, or lease, of a legal estate[14]. But a *contract* entered into by a minor for the purchase of land will not of itself vest any equitable interest in him[15]. Following repeal of the Infants Relief Act 1874, by the Minors' Contracts Act 1987[16], a mortgage by a minor to secure the repayment of money lent is no longer 'absolutely void'. The mortgagee can acquire no charge on the legal title which the minor does not possess. However, under s 63 of the Law of Property Act 1925, the mortgage would be effective to create an equitable mortgage on his equitable interest in the property.

(c) Repudiation

The Infants Relief Act 1874 never applied to contracts for the purchase (or sale) of an interest in land[17]. Such contracts are binding upon him unless repudiated during infancy or within a reasonable time of attaining majority. Thus, an equitable lease is binding on a minor prior to repudiation; he must pay the rent reserved[18] and observe the covenants in the lease. Repudiation terminates the minor's future liabilities; it is uncertain whether it also extinguishes accrued liabilities. An infant purchaser who repudiates after entering into a contract to buy can recover any deposit paid provided there is a total failure of consideration[19]. Once completion has been effected and possession enjoyed for a period before he elects to repudiate, no recovery of the purchase money seems possible[20].

---

13 Unless the land is sold for administration purposes, the personal representatives should vest it in trustees of the settlement under s 26(1) of SLA 1925, though usually they themselves will be such trustees: ibid s 30(3).

14 This follows from the statutory trust created in his favour by SLA 1925, s 27(1), note 11, ante. And see *Davies v Beynon-Harris* (1931) 47 TLR 424 (lease) .

15 *McFarland v Brumby* [1966] NZLR 230 at 234, per Woodhouse J. The existence of an equitable interest arising from a contract stems from the purchaser's potential entitlement to the remedy of specific performance (see pp 243–255, post), but the statutory restriction on the holding of a legal estate precludes any award in favour of a minor.

16 Section 1(a), applicable to contracts made after the Act became operative on 9 June 1987. For the prior law, see *Nottingham Permanent Benefit Building Society v Thurstan* [1903] AC 6, HL (mortgagee entitled to equitable charge by subrogation).

17 *Duncan v Dixon* (1890) 44 Ch D 211.

18 *Ketsey's Case* (16 13) Cro Jac 320; *Davies v Beynon-Harris* (1931) 47 TLR 424.

19 *Corpe v Overton* (1833) 10 Bing 252 (deposit paid prior to execution of deed of partnership recoverable).

20 Cf *Holmes v Blogg* (1818) 8 Taunt 508 (repudiation of lease after taking possession; no recovery of premium paid). And see *McFarland v Brumby*, supra (agreement to purchase by minor and adult, under which they took possession on payment of deposit by minor; minor not able to recover deposit on repudiation two months later).

A minor can dispose of an equitable interest in property to a purchaser, or assign an equitable lease[1], subject in each case to his right to repudiate the transaction. On avoidance, the equitable interest revests in him without any conveyance. He can now be required by the court to repay the purchase money, if it is just and equitable to do so[2].

2.   Companies

A company limited under the Companies Acts has power to enter into such transactions as are specifically authorised in its memorandum of association or are incidental or consequential to its main purpose[3]. A company can, therefore, buy or sell land only in accordance with the terms of its memorandum, though it is the practice to include wide powers to purchase, sell or lease land. Likewise it should be ascertained that a company has power to borrow if it is seeking to raise money on a mortgage of its property. In the absence of an express power, a company has an implied power to borrow for purposes incidental to the course and conduct of its business[4].

3.   Persons suffering from mental disorder

The legal capacity of such persons depends upon whether or not a receiver has been appointed under the Mental Health Act 1983. The appointment of a receiver renders it impossible for the person of unsound mind to exercise any power of disposition inter vivos over his own property, even during a lucid interval. On the making of the order, his property passes out of his control and an attempted disposition by him is null and void[5]. The receiver is statutorily empowered to make or concur in making all requisite dispositions for conveying or creating a legal estate in his name or on his behalf[6]. In the absence of any receiver, a contract entered into by a person of unsound mind is binding upon him if the other party is unaware of the mental disorder. Its validity is

---

1   Since a lease to a minor is binding on him until repudiation, an infant tenant still remains liable on the covenants in the lease, even after assigning it. Notwithstanding the assignment he retains, it seems, his right to repudiate the lease (as distinct from the assignment); if exercised, the lease terminates and with it the assignee's rights to possession.

2   Or transfer property representing it: Minors' Contracts Act 1987, s 3(1). The rule that on repudiation a minor can recover property transferred by him under a completed disposition has been somewhat jolted by the majority decision in *Chaplin v Leslie Frewin (Publishers) Ltd* [1966] Ch 71, [1965] 3 All ER 764, CA (copyright assigned under voidable contract not recoverable by minor on repudiation of contract). And see generally, 2 Williams V & P, 86 1–62.

3   For the protection afforded to third parties, see Companies Act 1985, as substituted by Companies Act 1989, s 108.

4   *General Auction Estate and Monetary Co v Smith* [1891] 3 Ch 432.

5   *Re Marshall, Marshall v Whateley* [1920] 1 Ch 284 (equitable charge executed after the appointment of a receiver under the Lunacy Act 1890, held null and void). For the sale of land where property is being administered by the Court of Protection, see the Mental Health Act 1983, ss 95, 96(1)(b) .

6   LPA 1925, s 22 (as substituted by the Mental Health Act 1959, Sch 7).

judged by the same standards as a contract made by a person of sound mind[7]. However, the other party's knowledge of the incapacity renders the contract voidable at the instance of the person of unsound mind, his receiver, or personal representative[8]. This rule applies not merely to contracts, but also to conveyances of property for valuable consideration[9] and, presumably, other inter vivos dispositions, except that a voluntary conveyance is absolutely void, even where no receiver is in control[10].

C Formalities

Until the coming into force of s 2 of Law of Property (Miscellaneous Provisions) Act 1989, the issue of formalities concerning contracts for the sale of land was governed by s 40 of the Law of Property Act 1925 which, in turn, had replaced the, substantially similar, s 4 of the Statute of Frauds 1677. The new Act governs contracts entered into after 27 September 1989. Contracts entered into before that date will continue to be governed by the old regime. The former law is now, of course, of considerably less importance than was previously the case. Nevertheless, it can still apply to disputes that arise today[11]. Moreover, to appreciate fully the changes wrought by the new statutory regime, it is necessary to give a summary of the previous law[12]. It should also be borne in mind that much of the previous case law concerned with s 40 will continue to be relevant to the construction of the new Act.

1. Contracts made before 27 September 1989

Section 40(1) of the Law of Property Act 1925 provides that:

> No action may be brought upon any contract for the sale or other disposition of land or any interest in land, unless the agreement upon which such action is to be brought, or some memorandum or note thereof, is in writing, and signed by the party to be charged or by some other person thereunto by him lawfully authorised.

Various points can be made about this section. First, the section dealt with the enforceability of the contract; it was not concerned with its validity. An oral contract for the sale of land was a perfectly valid contract. It simply could not

---

7 *Hart v O'Connor* [1985] AC 1000, [1985] 2 All ER 880, PC (sale of land at undervalue upheld in absence of any unconscionable conduct or equitable fraud).
8 *Beaven v M'Donnell* (1854) 9 Exch 309 (agreement for purchase of land upheld); *Imperial Loan Co v Stone* [1892] 1 QB 599, CA. In an action of specific performance the person seeking to avoid the contract has the duty of establishing incapacity: *Broughton v Snook* [1938] Ch 505, [1938] 1 All ER 411.
9 *Selby v Jackson* (1844) 6 Beav 192; *Campbell v Hooper* (1855) 3 Sm & G 153 (mortgage).
10 *Elliot v Ince* (1857) 7 De GM & G 475; *Manning v Gill* (1872) LR 13 Eq 485.
11 Equitable leases, mortgages by deposit of title deeds and options to purchase are the most likely candidates.
12 For a much fuller treatment see the 3rd edition of this work, pp 105–128.

be sued upon. It could, however, be used as a defence to an action. So, if under an oral contract of sale a purchaser had paid a deposit and subsequently defaulted, the vendor would be able to use the existence of the oral contract as justification for retaining the deposit[13].

(a) Evidenced in writing

The section did not require the contract to be in writing, for it to be enforceable. What was necessary was that there was written evidence of it, signed by the person to be charged, namely the defendant. There was never any requirement that the writing need take any particular form in order to satisfy the section. Neither was it necessary for the parties to intend to do so. The question is not one of the intention of the party who signs the document, but simply one of evidence against him[14]. A receipt for a deposit, a letter written to a solicitor[15], correspondence passing between the parties, were common examples of inadvertent memoranda held to comply with the section[16].

A somewhat contentious matter under the old law concerned whether, to be adequate as a memorandum, it was necessary for there to be written acknowledgement of the existence of a contract, or whether it was sufficient if the writing merely recorded the terms of the agreement. The authorities on this point were in conflict[17]; a conflict which had not been definitively resolved by the time the section was replaced.

A final matter to be noted was that the section did not require both parties to sign the memorandum; all that was required was that it was signed by the party to be charged. If the vendor has signed the memorandum, but the purchaser has not, then the purchaser could sue the vendor but the vendor could not sue the purchaser.

(b) Part performance

As has been noted the effect of non-compliance with the formalities prescribed by s 40(1) was not to make the contract void; it was merely unenforceable by action. Cases could arise, however, where one, or both of the parties had acted in reliance on a belief that the contract was enforceable. In such circumstances, it may be unfair, subsequently, to allow s 40 to be pleaded so that liability under the contract could effectively be avoided. To meet this difficulty, equity developed the doctrine of part performance, a doctrine which eventually, was given statutory recognition[18].

13   *Monnickendam v Leanse* (1923) 39 TLR 445.
14   *Re Hoyle, Hoyle v Hoyle* [1893] 1 Ch 84 at 99, CA, per Bowen LJ.
15   *Smith-Bird v Blower* [1939] 2 All ER 406. The letter was held not to be privileged from disclosure; it was not written to obtain legal advice, but merely to supply information.
16   See, also, *Hill v Hill* [1947] Ch 231, [1947] 1 All ER 54, CA, (note endorsed on rent book); *Dewar v Mintoft* [1912] 2 KB 373 (a letter repudiating an alleged agreement); *Johnson v Nova Scotia Trust Co* (1973) 43 DLR (3d) 222 (a clause in a revoked will); *Grindell v Bass* [1920] 2 Ch 487 (an admission in a pleading), although see *Hardy v Elphick* [1974] Ch 65, [1973] 2 All ER 914, CA.
17   See, principally, *Law v Jones* [1974] Ch 112, [1973] 2 All ER 437, CA; *Tiverton Estates Ltd v Wearwell Ltd* [1975] Ch 146, [1974] 1 All ER 209, CA.
18   LPA 1925, s 40(2).

The precise parameters of this doctrine were the subject of a certain amount of controversy[19]. The underlying rationale was, however, tolerably clear. If the plaintiff had, with the co-operation of the defendant, partly performed the contract, or had otherwise relied upon the contract being enforceable, and the acts in question pointed to the existence of a contract between the parties[20], then it became fraudulent for the defendant to plead the statute and defend an action on the contract on the basis of the lack of a written memorandum of it. An equity arose in favour of the defendant and, in satisfying that equity, the court had to choose 'between undoing what has been done (which is not always possible, or, if possible, just) and completing what has been left undone'[1]. In practice, this meant that, if a successful act of part performance was established, a classic example of which being that the purchaser had gone into possession of the property he had contracted to buy, then the, previously unenforceable, oral contract became enforceable and specific performance of the contract would be ordered.

(c) The rationale for change

This thumbnail sketch of the previous statutory regime identifies the main areas that the Law Commission felt, in its review of this area of the law[2], to be unsatisfactory. The idea of a valid, but unenforceable, contract was felt to be needlessly confusing. The possibility of a unilaterally enforceable contract, a possibility stemming from the fact that only the party to be charged need sign the memorandum, was felt to be unjust. The uncertainty as to whether the memorandum need acknowledge the existence of the contract was considered to be undesirable, as were the various uncertainties surrounding the doctrine of part performance. Reform was, therefore, thought to be appropriate. The Law Commission considered that it was desirable that contracts for the sale of land should be in writing. To this end proposals were put forward which resulted in s 2 of the Law of Property (Miscellaneous Provisions) Act 1989; a provision which is drafted in a significantly different way from the Bill put forward by the Commission in its Report.

2. Contracts made after 26 September 1989

Section 2 of the Law of Property (Miscellaneous Provisions) Act 1989 provides that:

(1) A contract for the sale or other disposition of an interest in land can only be made in writing and only by incorporating all the terms which the parties have expressly agreed in one document or, where contracts are exchanged, in each.

(2) The terms may be incorporated in a document either by being set out in it or by reference to some other document.

---

19 See 3rd edition of this work, pp 118–127.
20 See *Steadman v Steadman* [1976] AC 536, [1974] 2 All ER 977, HL.
 1 *Maddison v Alderson* (1883) 8 App Cas 467 at 476, per Earl of Selborne LC.
 2 (1987) Law Com No 164. A fuller critique can be found in (1985) Law Com WP No 92.

(3) the document incorporating the terms or, where contracts are exchanged, one of the documents incorporating them (but not necessarily the same one) must be signed by or on behalf of each party to the contract.

(4) Where a contract for the sale or other disposition of an interest in land satisfies the conditions of this section by reason only of the rectification of one or more documents in pursuance of an order of a court, the contract shall come into being, or be deemed to come into being, at such time as may be specified in the order.

Before analysing the section, one vitally important point should be made. It is that the section requires the contract to be made in writing. There is, therefore, in respect of agreements to which the Act applies, no longer any such thing as an oral contract for the sale of land. Oral agreements do not, as was previously the case, give rise to unenforceable contracts; they have no contractual effect at all. It follows from this that the doctrine of part performance has been abolished. Cases which would have been part performance cases under the old law will be dealt with below.

3.   Contracts within the section

The section speaks of '*contract for the sale or other disposition of land or any interest in land*'. Clearly the following are caught: contracts for the sale of freehold land, for the grant, assignment or surrender[3] of a lease, and for the grant of a mortgage, easement or profit[4]. An agreement for the letting of furnished rooms is also caught[5], but not a contract for lodgings[6], or for a licence to maintain an advertisement hoarding on land, since in neither case is there any interest in land created. Timber and growing crops (*fructus naturales*) are treated as land within the section, unless the contract requires their severance on sale, but not annual crops (*fructus industriales*) such as wheat, corn, hops etc[7]. A statutory contract for the sale of land arising under a compulsory purchase order does not require compliance with the section[8].

Less obvious contracts required to be in writing because they involve an interest in land have been held to include contracts relating to:

(i) fixtures, which are regarded as attached to and part of the land[9], but not a contract for a tenant to sell tenant's fixtures to his landlord, since in essence it constitutes a renunciation of his right to remove them[10];

(ii) building materials in a house to be demolished by the purchaser[11];

---

3   *Smart v Harding* (1855) 15 CB 652.
4   Land is defined to include 'an easement, right, privilege, or benefit, in, over, or derived from land'; see LPA 1925, s 205(l)(ix). And see *Webber v Lee* (1882) 9 QBD 315.
5   *Inman v Stamp* (1815) 1 Stark 12.
6   *Wright v Stavert* (1860) 2 E & E 721.
7   See *Marshall v Green* (1875) 1 CPD 35, for a review of the authorities.
8   *Munton v Greater London Council* [1976] 2 All ER 815, CA.
9   *Jarvis v Jarvis* (1893) 63 LJ Ch 10, even when sold separately from the land.
10   *Lee v Gaskell* (1876) 1 QBD 700.
11   *Lavery v Pursell* (1888) 39 Ch D 508.

(iii) slag and cinders forming part of the land[12];

(iv) an undivided share in land. Under the old law, this was regarded as not entirely free from controversy[13], but s 2(6) of the 1989 Act makes it clear that such contracts are within the ambit of the Act.

In *Daulia Ltd v Four Millbank Nominees Ltd*[14], it was held that a unilateral contract to enter into a formal written contract for the sale of land is itself a contract to dispose of an interest in land, and is unenforceable unless evidenced in writing. The unilateral contract is capable of being specifically enforced and gives the purchaser a right to the land in equity. To allow the enforcement of an oral offer to enter into a written contract would be tantamount to take the main contract out of the statute altogether. The door would then be open for the practical nullification of the section in a large variety of cases, which the court was not prepared to countenance.

A matter which generated some controversy was the position on the exercise of an option to purchase[15], it having been said to be 'evident that the draftsman of this section did not take account of options'[16]. The principal concern was whether the notice exercising the option had to comply with s 2, or in other words, it had to be signed by both parties. Much of this controversy centred around the juridical nature of an option to purchase: whether it was best categorised as being an irrevocable offer to sell the property, or whether it was a conditional contract of sale[17]. In *Spiro v Glencrown*[18] Hoffmann J considered this matter and took the view that options should be considered to be *sui generis* so that if the option, itself, satisfies the statute, it is irrelevant if the notice exercising it does not.

Certain contracts which would otherwise be caught by s 2 are expressly excluded from the formal requirements imposed by the statute. Under s 2(5) of the Act, s 2(1) does not apply to:

(i) a contract to grant such a lease as is mentioned in s 54(2) of the Law of Property Act 1925;

(ii) a contract made in the course of a public auction; and

(iii) a contract regulated under the Financial Services Act 1986.

4. The terms of the contract

The writing should contain all the terms of the contract. In particular, it should contain (a) the names of the parties, (b) a description of the parties, (c) a

---

12 *Morgan v Russell & Sons* [1909] 1 KB 357.

13 See *Cooper v Critchley* [1955] Ch 431, [1955] 1 All ER 520 and the 3rd edition of this work, pp 106, 107.

14 [1978] Ch 231, [1978] 2 All ER 557, CA (oral promise to conclude formal contract if purchaser tendered signed contract and deposit at specified place and time). Contrast *Pitt v PHH Asset Management Ltd* [1993] 4 All ER 961, CA (lock-out agreement not governed by s 2). See [1994] Conv 58 (M P Thompson). Post, p 217.

15 See (1990) 87 LSG 19 (J E Adams).

16 *Trustees of the Chippenham Golf Club v North Wiltshire District Council* (1991) 64 P & CR 527 at 530, CA, per Scott LJ.

17 See Barnsley's *Land Options*, 11–14.

18 [1991] Ch 537, [1991] 1 All ER 600.

statement of the consideration, (d) any agreed special terms and (e) the signature of both parties, or their lawfully authorised agents. Writing which does not contain all the agreed terms is, prima facie, insufficient, although, as will be seen, the courts have proved themselves willing to circumvent difficulties caused by omitted terms. In considering the adequacy of the reference to terms agreed in the contract, the previous case law that grew up in relation to s 40 of the Law of Property Act 1925 will, in general, continue to be relevant.

(a) The parties

The rule laid down by *Potter v Duffeld*[19] is that the memorandum must contain either the names of the parties or such a reasonable description of them that there cannot be any dispute as to their identity. Expressions such as 'proprietor' or 'owner' of a specified property are adequate, although the document does not actually name the vendor. Conversely, descriptions such as 'vendor' or 'client' are too uncertain to suffice[20], unless the memorandum contains other information enabling the 'vendor' or 'client' to be identified[1].

A memorandum is not inadequate simply because the vendor, being a limited company, is described by the wrong name, provided that it is clear, either from the surrounding circumstances or in the light of known facts, that the name inserted in the document as being that of the vendor is merely an inaccurate description[2]. That the parties' names appear in the document is not enough unless it also reveals their respective capacities as vendor or purchaser[3], either expressly or from surrounding circumstances[4].

There is one exception to the requirement that the contracting parties should be named or identified. In *Davies v Sweet*[5], a memorandum signed by the vendor's agent was held sufficiently to describe the vendor, although the vendor's name nowhere appeared in the memorandum and there was nothing to show that the agent signed as such. It seems rather anomalous that X can support an action for specific performance against Y by producing a document purporting to record a contract for sale between X and Z. The decision is supported by the rule of agency that an agent who contracts in his own name does not cease to be personally liable even though the other party is aware that he was acting as agent. The memorandum therefore identified two parties contractually bound to each other, and this was sufficient to render it enforceable against the principal under normal rules of agency. In situations involving agency, the contract will not bind the principal unless the agent has express or implied authority to contract on his behalf. One spouse does not as a matter of law possess implied authority to enter into a contract for the sale of

---

19   (1874) LR 18 Eq 4.
20   See *Jarrett v Hunter* (1886) 34 Ch D 182 at 184–85, per Kay J.
 1   *Commins v Scott* (1875) LR 20 Eq 11.
 2   *F Goldsmith (Sicklesmere) Ltd v Baxter* [1970] Ch 85, [1969] 3 All ER 733 (plaintiff company contracting in the name of Goldsmith Coaches (Sicklesmere) Ltd) .
 3   *Dewar v Mintoft* [1912] 2 KB 373.
 4   *Auerbach v Nelson* [1919] 2 Ch 383 ('Received from A – £10'; court assumed that person paying £10 deposit was the purchaser).
 5   [1962] 2 B 300, [1962] 1 All ER 92, CA; *Basma v Weekes* [1950] AC 441, [1950] 2 All ER 146, PC.

land owned by the other spouse[6]. An agent who, without authority, purports to contract for a principal is liable in damages for breach of an implied warranty of authority[7], unless the other contracting party knows, or is taken to have known, that he had no such authority[8].

(b) The property
As with the parties, so with the property, which should be described in such a way as to be capable of being identified with certainty. Parol evidence has been admitted to establish the identity of property described as 'Mr Ogilvie's House'[9], and 'twenty-four acres of land, freehold, at Totmonslow'[10]. A reference to 'my house' may be sufficient[11] if the vendor has only one property, but not if he owns more than one, since parol evidence cannot be adduced to establish which of two (or more) properties is the subject of the agreement.

Generally speaking all that is required is a physical description of the property. A memorandum is not insufficient because it fails to specify the precise legal interest which is to be transferred or makes no reference to incumbrances affecting the property. When no interest is mentioned, then prima facie it is implied that the agreement relates to an unincumbered freehold estate[12]. When the memorandum indicates that something less than the vendor's whole interest is to pass, it should state what exact interest the purchaser has agreed to buy. In *Dolling v Evans*[13], an agreement for the grant of an underlease did not specify the length of the term and this was held fatal.

(c) The price
Either the consideration or the means of ascertaining it[14] must be recorded. Thus a memorandum evidencing an agreement for the grant of a lease should refer to the agreed rent. Any special terms of payment must also be included[15]. Where the machinery for ascertaining the price breaks down, the court will substitute its own machinery to ensure that the agreement is performed, provided it is a subsidiary and non-essential term[16]. The parties are bound by

6   One spouse may be estopped from denying the other's lack of authority, p 113, post.
7   *Collen v Wright* (1857) 8 F & B 647 (agreement for lease of farm). An agent's awareness of his lack of authority may give rise to liability for deceit: *Polhill v Walter* (1832) 3 B & Ad 114.
8   *Halbot v Lens* [1901] 1 Ch 344.
9   *Ogilvie v Foljambe* (1817) 3 Mer 53; *Bleakley v Smith* (1840) 11 Sim 150 (the property in Cable Street); *Auerbach v Nelson*, supra (house being sold for £500 from N).
10 *Plant v Bourne* [1897] 2 Ch 281, CA; *Shardlow v Cotterell* (1881) 20 Ch D 90, CA; *Harewood v Retetse* [1990] 1 WLR 333.
11 *Cowley v Watts* (1853) 17 Jur 172.
12 *Timmins v Moreland Street Property Co Ltd* [1958] Ch 110 at 118–21, [1957] 3 All 265 at 269-70, CA, per Jenkins LJ, and the authorities there cited. If the vendor does not possess a freehold estate, or it is subject to incumbrances, the purchaser has various remedies open to him; see pp 620–621, post.
13 (1867) 31 JP 375, 36 LJ Ch 474; *Cox v Middleton* (1854) 2 Drew 209.
14 *Smith v Jones* [1952] 2 All ER 907 (sale at 'the controlled price fixed by the government'); *Brown v Gould* [1972] Ch 53, [1971] 2 All ER 1505.
15 *Neale v Merrett* [1930] WN 189.
16 *Sudbrook Trading Estate Ltd v Eggleton* [1983] 1 AC 444, [1982] 3 All ER 1, HL (option; lessor refusing to appoint his valuer); aliter if the machinery is essential (eg price to be fixed by named valuer).

a valuation given honestly and in good faith, even if the valuer is mistaken as to the property's true value[17].

(d) Other agreed terms

Aside from the essential basics, common to all contracts for the sale of land, parties, property and price, the writing must include all other terms agreed between the parties. Under the previous statutory regime, there was an exception to this rule. If the term omitted was for the exclusive benefit of the plaintiff, he could waive the term and enforce the contract as evidenced in the memorandum[18]. Conversely, if the omitted term was for the sole benefit of the defendant then the plaintiff could enforce the contract provided he submitted to perform the omitted term[19]. If, however, the term omitted from the memorandum was of mutual benefit of the parties, the term could not be waived, with the result that the memorandum was defective[20].

Because s 2 requires all the contractual terms to be in writing, waiver seems to be out of the question. Nevertheless, the courts when faced with the problem of writing which does not fully embody the whole of the agreement have shown themselves willing, by various methods, to enforce the agreement with the, somewhat paradoxical, result that the law is now more liberal than was previously the case. In *Record v Bell*[1] there was an agreement for the sale of residential property for a price of £1.3 million. Contemporaneously with this agreement, there was a separate agreement for the sale of various chattels. The day before exchange of contracts, the purchaser's solicitor wrote to his opposite number stating that the contract was conditional on office copies showing that the vendor was the registered proprietor and that this condition be attached to the contract. This occurred and contracts were exchanged. The office copies did, indeed, show the vendor to be the registered proprietor but the purchaser refused to complete the contract. In defence to an action for specific performance, the purchaser argued that s 2 had not been complied with because the condition regarding title had not been incorporated into the contract. Judge Baker QC accepted that there had not been incorporation but held that the condition as to the title was a collateral contract, the consideration for which was the exchange of contracts which followed. On this basis, he held that the contract was enforceable.

To similar effect is the decision in *Tootal Clothing Ltd v Guinea Properties Ltd*[2]. A contract for the grant of a lease stated that 'this agreement sets out the entire agreement between the parties'. This was not, in fact, true as a clause was omitted that the landlord would contribute to the cost of shop-fitting works which, it had been agreed, would be carried out by the tenant. After the lease

---

17   *Campbell v Edwards* [1976] 1 All ER 785, CA. A negligent valuation may give rise to liability in damages: *Arenson v Casson Beckman Rutley & Co* [1977] AC 405, [1975] 3 All ER 901, HL.
18   *North v Loomes* [1919] 1 Ch 378, (payment of legal fees).
19   *Scott v Bradley* [1971] Ch 850, [1971] 1 All ER 583. See, also, the 3rd edition of this work, 117, 118.
20   *Hawkins v Price* [1947] Ch 645, [1945] 1 All ER 689.
 1   [1991] 4 All ER 471. See [1991] Conv 472 (M Harwood).
 2   (1992) 64 P & CR 452, [1993] Conv 89 (P Luther).

had been granted, and the tenant had carried out the works, the landlord refused to pay his agreed contribution, pleading s 2. The Court of Appeal held for the tenant. First, it was held that s 2 applied only to executory contracts. When, as here, the contract had been completed, the section ceased to be applicable. It was further stated, obiter, that even had this not been the case, the agreement would have been enforceable as the subject matter of the dispute was a collateral agreement and was not, of itself, a land contract and so would not have needed to comply with s 2[3].

Although, in these cases there did appear to be an element of separateness in between the main contract concerning the sale of the interest in land and the other agreement, sufficient to justify the finding of a collateral contract, in other cases this may not be so. It emerges from *Wright v Robert Leonard Developments Ltd*[4], however, that the courts will still be prepared to enforce a contract even though not all of its terms are in writing. In this case the agreement concerned the sale of a leasehold flat. Prior to exchange of contracts, a schedule of fixtures and fittings had been drawn up which, it was agreed, would be included in the sale. The contracts, however, made no reference to this schedule and was entirely silent as to this matter. After contracts had been exchanged the vendor removed various fittings and an action was brought for damages. Again, s 2 was pleaded as a defence. The Court of Appeal found it to be impossible to find the existence of a collateral contract. The agreement could only be construed as a whole. Nevertheless, the award of damages was upheld. It was found that there was convincing proof[5] that there was an agreement that the various chattels were to be included in the price. This was sufficient for the court to order rectification of the written contract which became, therefore, fully enforceable.

The case is important and demonstrates that, somewhat paradoxically, the new law may be more liberal in respect of omitted terms than was previously the case. Under the old law, as has been seen, if a term had been omitted from the memorandum, that memorandum would, nevertheless, be adequate if the omitted term was for the sole benefit of either of the parties. If that was the case, the term could either be waived or an undertaking given to perform it. If, however, the omitted term was for the mutual benefit of the parties then the omission was fatal to the adequacy of the memorandum. In the case of rectification, however, where what is argued is that the written contract does not reflect what was actually agreed between the parties, the fact that the missing term is mutually beneficial to the parties is immaterial.

A second point which can be made about rectification concerns the standard of proof. Before a court will order rectification, it is necessary that there is convincing proof that the written agreement does not accurately reflect the common intention of the parties. If the proof is insufficient, then the outcome is likely to be that the contract, as written, will be enforced; the court being unpersuaded that there is, actually a term omitted from the written contract.

3   Ibid at p 456 per Scott LJ.
4   [1994] NPC 49, CA.
5   See *Joscelyne v Nissen* [1970] 2 QB 86, [1970] 1 All ER 1213, CA.

Finally, it should be noted that these difficulties will not arise if the contract does not contain a term which is implied by law, such as a term for vacant possession to be given upon completion; nor should there be a problem if an agreed term which is omitted is identical with one which the law will imply[6].

(e) Leases

A contract for the grant of a lease raises one or two special problems. Not only must it specify the parties, the property and the rent (ie the consideration), it is necessary to state the duration of the lease and the date of its commencement[7], and, subject to what has been said earlier, any express terms of the lease that have been agreed upon. If the parties have not agreed upon the duration of the lease and this is faithfully recorded in the document which they have signed, there is no concluded contract because a lease of uncertain duration cannot exist[8]. Similarly, in the absence of any agreed date for the commencement of the lease, the court will not give validity to the agreement by implying that the term is to begin within a reasonable time, or by taking the date of the agreement as the date of commencement[9].

Finally, it should be recalled, s 2 does not apply to all leases. A contract for a lease of less than three years, taking effect in possession, at the best rent reasonably available without taking a fine can be created informally.

5.   The signature

Under the previous law, a memorandum was adequate if it was signed only by the party to be charged, that is the defendant, or his agent. Consequently, X, who had not signed any memorandum, could sue Y, who had signed[10], but not vice versa. This was considered by the Law Commission to be unjust. For s 2 to be satisfied, it is necessary that both parties sign the contract.

(a) Mode of signature

In the past, the courts adopted a liberal approach to the meaning of the word 'signed'. The inclusion of initials[11] and the use of a rubber stamp[12] have been accepted as valid signatures. The test was taken to be that, provided that the name is inserted in to the document in such a manner as to have the effect of authenticating the document, the requirement that there be a signature was

---

6   *Farrell v Green* (1974) 232 EG 587. Cf *Record v Bell*, supra, where a possible argument along these lines was not raised.
7   *Dolling v Evans* (1867) 31 JP 375, 36 LJ Ch 474.
8   *Prudential Assurance Co Ltd v London Residuary Body* [1992] 2 AC 386, [1992] 3 All ER 504, HL.
9   *Harvey v Pratt* [1965] 2 All ER 786, CA. Contrast *Jenkins v Harbour View Courts Ltd* [1966] NZLR 1 (agreement specifying date of termination enforced).
10   *Farrell v Green* (1974) 232 EG 587.
11   *Chichester v Stobbs* (1866) 14 LT 433. Oral evidence is permissible to identify the signatory.
12   *Bennett v Brumfitt* (1867) LR 3 CP 28; *Tourret v Cripps* (1879) 48 LJ Ch 567 (printed letter heading).

regarded as having been complied with[13]. Consistent with this liberal approach, an unsigned memorandum in the defendant's handwriting which contained his name somewhere in the document sufficed, such as an agreement commencing 'I, A, agree'. This is known as the 'authenticated signature fiction'[14], the basis of which being, that the fact that the defendant had written his own name, was clear evidence that he recognised the existence of the contract. It has become apparent, however, that the courts, when dealing with the new Act, are not prepared to continue this liberal approach. In *Firstpost Homes Ltd v Johnson*[15] the Court of Appeal refused to accept that the typed version of one of the party's names would suffice as a signature. Moreover, the view was expressed that the old authorities should not be seen as reliable guides as to how a modern statute, aimed at reforming the law as regard to formalities, should be interpreted. This seems realistic but is unlikely to be of major significance, because the requirement that both parties sign the agreement should lead to there being fewer occasions when there will be doubt as to what constitutes a signature.

(b) Subsequent alterations
The previous position was that, if there was a variation of the contract after the memorandum had been signed, then, for the memorandum to be adequate, there should either be a fresh signature, or the existing signature should be revived by some act of acknowledgement[16]. Under the new Act, it would seem, in principle, that any alteration to the original contract should be signed by both parties because, otherwise, the court would be called upon to give contractual effect to an agreement which does not comply with the Act. This was held to be the case by the Court of Appeal in *McCausland v Duncan Lawrie Ltd*[17], where a subsequent attempt to vary a contract was disregarded when the purported variation did not, itself, comply with s 2. The contract originally entered into was enforced.

(c) Signature by agents
In determining whether an agent has been 'thereunto lawfully authorised', the ordinary rules of agency are to be applied. The authority may be given orally[18], and an unauthorised signature may be subsequently ratified by the principal. Ratification relates back to the time of the contract between the agent and the other party; a withdrawal by the latter is inoperative, even though

---

13   *Ogilvie v Foljambe* (1817) 3 Mer 53; *Hucklesby v Hook* (1900) 82 LT 117 per Buckley J.
14   *Knight v Crockford* (1794) 1 Esp 190; *Johnson v Dodgson* (1837) 2 M & W 653 ('sold "A"' held to be sufficient). In *Pi ie v Saunders* (1961) 104 CLR 149 the fiction was held to be inapplicable to a document not recognisable as a memorandum of a concluded agreement, in this case, a solicitor's instruction for the preparation of a lease.
15   [1995] 4 All ER 355, CA.
16   *New Hart Builders v Brindley* [1975] Ch 342, [1975] 1 All ER 1007; *Richards v Creighton Griffiths (Investments) Ltd* (1972) 225 EG 2104.
17   [1996] NPC 94, CA.
18   *Heard v Pilley* (1869) 4 Ch App 548.

made prior to the principal's ratification[19]. One party is not permitted to sign for the other[20]; to hold otherwise would create an obvious inducement for fraud, which the statute was designed to prevent. One person may, however, act as agent for both contracting parties.

The agent must be authorised to sign. Should the agent enter into the contract in his own name, or sign the memorandum with his own name, he incurs a personal liability. To avoid this, he should indicate when appending his signature that he is signing 'as agent' for another, or 'for' a named person[1]. A vendor may be estopped by his conduct from denying that an agent had no authority to conclude a contract or sign a memorandum of it[2].

Sometimes the law implies authority for an agent to sign. As these occasions have special relevance to sales of land, they must be looked at more closely.

(i) Auctioneers.   Where property is sold at auction, the position was that the auctioneer had authority to sign the memorandum for both parties[3]. Under the new Act, however, contracts made at a public auction need not satisfy the formal requirements stipulated for other land contracts. This point will not, therefore, arise in respect of contracts to which the Act applies.

(ii) Estate agents.   Under the old law, it was not clear to what extent an estate agent had authority to sign a memorandum on behalf of the vendor. The question now is whether he has authority to enter into a contract as agent for the vendor. According to Lord Greene MR, the making of a contract is no part of an estate agent's business, not even when he is employed to sell the property at a stated price; only express authority suffices[4].

(iii) Solicitors.   The mere existence of a solicitor-client did not confer on the solicitor implied authority to sign a contract on his client's behalf[5]. Consequently, he also lacks authority to enter into a contract[6]. He may, however, be expressly authorised to do so, or the way that the instructions are given may show by implication that he is entitled to bind his client[7]. Instructions to settle the terms of an arrangement[8] or to carry out an agreement[9] have sufficed for

19   *Bolton Partners v Lambert* (1889) 41 Ch D 295, CA, doubted in *Fleming v Bank of New Zealand* [1900] AC 577, PC. But not if the acceptance of the offer is made subject to ratification: *Watson v Davies* [1931] 1 Ch 455.

20   *Sharman v Brandt* (1871) LR 6 QB 720.

1   *Universal Steam Navigation Co Ltd v James McKelvie & Co* [1923] AC 492, HL; *Kimber Coal Co v Stone and Rolfe Ltd* [1926] AC 414, HL.

2   *Spiro v Lintern* [1973] 3 All ER 319, CA (spouse); *Worboys v Carter* (1987) 283 EG 307, CA (failure to disillusion buyer that no concluded contract due to land agent's want of authority).

3   See the 3rd edition of this work, pp 113, 114.

4   *Wragg v Lovett* [1948] 2 All ER 968 at 969, CA, obiter. See Emmet, para 2.050.

5   *Smith v Webster* (1876) 3 Ch D 49, CA, *Gudgeon v Squires* (1970) 215 EG 922.

6   Cf *Hooper v Sherman* [1994] NPC 153, CA, where this point was not pleaded and leave to amend was refused.

7   *Gavaghan v Edwards* [1961] 2 QB 220 at 226, [1961] 2 All ER 477 at 479, CA; see also *Griffiths v Young* [1970] Ch 675, [1970] 3 All ER 601, CA.

8   *Joliffe v Blumberg* (1870) 18 WR 784.

9   *North v Loomes* [1919] 1 Ch 378 at 383 per Younger J.

this purpose. Where a formal contract is signed by a solicitor, or other agent, the other party ought, as a precautionary measure, satisfy himself that the necessary authority exists. The step is rarely taken in practice when a solicitor signs.

6.   Joinder of documents

It has always been the case that the terms of the agreement need not be contained in one document. Instead, a number of documents could, when read together, constitute a sufficient memorandum. For contracts governed by s 40, the position was spelt out in *Timmins v Moreland Street Properties Ltd*[10] by Jenkins LJ, who said:

> ... there should be a document signed by the party to be charged which while not containing in itself all the necessary ingredients of the required memorandum, does contain some reference, express or implied, to some other document or transaction. Where any such reference can be spelt out of a document so signed, then parole evidence may be given to identify the other document referred to, or as the case may be, to explain the other transaction, and to identify any document relating to it.

The starting point, when joinder was in issue, was to find some document signed by the defendant. If that document contained a reference to another document then the two documents could be read together in order to piece together an adequate memorandum. While joinder remains possible under the new law because of the terms of the new section, it is unlikely that there will be many instances of it. It is noteworthy that, had the draft Bill proposed by the Law Commission been enacted, the law relating to joinder would have remained substantially the same as was previously the case. There are significant differences, however, between the actual section and the draft Bill[11], the result being that there will now be very few cases where documents can be joined so as, together, they constitute a written contract.

(i) One document.   Section 2 requires that the terms which have been agreed between the parties to be in one document signed by both parties. To this requirement, there is one exception. This refers to the practice, to be described in detail in a later chapter, of exchanging contracts. In this case identical versions of the contract are prepared and are signed, respectively by the vendor and the purchaser. The contract comes into being when the two parts are exchanged, so that the vendor has the part signed by the purchaser and vice versa. This practice is expressly catered for by the Act which, as an alternative to the terms being in one document signed by both parties, lays down that, where contracts are exchanged, the section is satisfied if all the terms agreed between the parties are contained in each part. In this case the requirement

---

10   [1958] Ch 110 at 130, [1957] 3 All ER 265 at 276, CA.
11   This is commented upon in the Parliamentary debate, but the reason for the change is not explained: HL Vol 503, Col 604.

of signature is met by the signature of each party being on the respective parts of the contract. Joinder of documents is then permitted if the document to be joined is referred to in the document signed by both parties[12]. In practice, the situation where joinder is most likely to occur is when the parties have agreed, as part of their contract, that certain chattels currently in the property are to be included in the sale. An agreed schedule is then drawn up. This will be incorporated in the contract if the document signed by both parties refers to this schedule. If it does not, the document will not satisfy the section because the document signed by the parties does not include all the terms agreed upon[13].

(ii) Contracts by correspondence.   Under the previous law, there was no need for the memorandum to take any particular form and could be created by an exchange of letters. The question has arisen as to whether this remains possible. The issue was addressed in two recent, and conflicting, cases in the Court of Appeal. In *Hooper v Sherman*[14] a couple were joint owners of a house in which they cohabited. Their relationship became troubled and she sought a non-molestation order against him. Before the application was heard, a compromise agreement was reached. It was agreed that he would transfer his share in the house to her and, in return, she would accept sole liability for the mortgage repayments. Her solicitor then wrote to his solicitor confirming the fact of agreement and stating its terms. His solicitor replied, also confirming the fact of the agreement. In a subsequent dispute between the parties, the question arose as to whether there was a contract in existence.

Had the issue been whether there was a sufficient memorandum for the purpose of s 40, the case would have presented no difficulty. Had he been seeking to enforce the agreement, the letter from her solicitor would have sufficed as the memorandum[15]. If she had been the plaintiff, the letter containing the terms of the agreement, written by her solicitor, could have been joined to the letter signed by his solicitor and, together, the two letters would have comprised an adequate memorandum. Whether s 2 was satisfied, however, presented rather greater problems.

Clearly, the terms that had been agreed did not appear in one document signed by the parties. The majority was prepared to hold, however, that there had been an exchange of contracts. This finding was based upon two important concessions: that the term 'exchange of contracts' was not a term of art and that, in accordance with the views of the Law Commission, it remained possible to form a contract by correspondence. On the basis of these concessions, it was held that if each party has possession of a document, signed by the other, which together contain all the terms of the agreement then the section is satisfied. Morritt LJ, on the other hand, dissenting with much force, held that

---

12   LP(MP)A, s 2(3).
13   See *Wright v Robert Leonard (Developments) Ltd* [1994] NPC 49, CA. Rectification of the contract was ordered.
14   [1994] NPC 153. See [1995] Conv 319 (M P Thompson).
15   The point about the authority of the solicitors to sign as agents for the parties was not taken.

the correspondence merely recorded the prior, oral agreement and was not, itself, a contract.

The facts of *Commission for New Towns v Cooper*[16] were complex but, for present purposes, the only issue was a relatively simple one: whether an exchange of faxes confirming an oral provisional agreement satisfied s 2. The Court of Appeal unanimously held that it did not. In contrast to the view taken in *Hooper v Sherman*, Stuart-Smith LJ took the view that the term 'exchange of contracts' while not technically a term of art was a process that was familiar to conveyancers. The essence of it was the swapping, either actually or constructively, of identical documents[17]. It did not include an exchange of correspondence.

The Court in *Cooper* felt free not to follow the earlier decision in *Hooper v Sherman*. This was considered an appropriate course of action because the decision in that case was based upon concessions which, it was held had wrongly been made. The first concession was that exchange of contracts was not a term of art. As has been seen, in the more recent case, the Court of Appeal held that the process did have a technical meaning. The second concession was that, consistent with the view of the Law Commission, a contract could still be made by correspondence. The difficulty with this was that the Law Commission's view as to this was based upon the contents of its draft Bill. As originally drafted, the clause in the Bill would have enabled a contract to be created by correspondence. The actual s 2, however, differs significantly from the clause drafted by the Law Commission. It is submitted that the view taken in *Commission for the New Towns v Cooper* is the correct interpretation of s 2 and that it is no longer possible to create a contract by correspondence save for the unlikely event of both parties signing one of the letters.

Although the better view as to what constitutes an exchange of contracts is that taken in *Cooper*, it remains the case that there are now two conflicting decisions of the Court of Appeal on this issue. The court in *Cooper* felt free not to follow earlier, binding, authority because it felt that the fact that the decision was made on the basis of concessions which had wrongly been made enabled it to do so. This exception to the doctrine of *stare decisis* is based upon a suggestion made in *Joscelyne v Nissen*[18] and is not a well established exception to the doctrine of precedent. The possibility remains, therefore, that a future court may prefer to accept the decision in *Hooper v Sherman* rather than that in *Cooper*, particularly if it is unsympathetic to a defendant seeking to escape liability under a concluded agreement. While this potential uncertainty is unwelcome, it is, nevertheless, submitted that *Commission for New Towns v Cooper* is the authority which should be followed.

If this view is correct, then the scope for the application of the doctrine of joinder of documents is now very much more limited than was previously the case. In the past, a s 40 memorandum could be constructed by joining together previous correspondence to make a composite whole. This will no longer be the case. The starting point in any case of joinder must be a document signed

16 [1995] Ch 259, [1995] 2 All ER 929, CA.
17 *Eccles v Bryant* [1948] Ch 93, [1947] 2 All ER 865, CA. See p 221, post.
18 [1970] 2 QB 86 at 99, [1970] 1 All ER 1213 at 1223, CA.

by both parties, which is unlikely to occur in the case of correspondence. Consequently a contract by correspondence is now highly unlikely to be a practical possibility.

D   Effect of failure to comply with statutory formalities

The most profound change in the law brought about by s 2 of the Law of Property (Miscellaneous Provisions) Act 1989 is the consequence of non-compliance with the new requirements as to writing. Until the coming into force of this section, as has been seen, a contract for the sale of land could be made in the same way as any other contract. Unless there was an adequate memorandum of it, however, then, subject to the equitable doctrine of part performance, the contract was not enforceable by action: neither party could sue upon it. There was no bar on one party using the existence of the contract as a defence; a vendor could rely on the existence of the unenforceable contract to retain a deposit paid to him by the purchaser[19].

The point that, under the old law, an oral contract could exist enabled the equitable doctrine of part performance to develop. This doctrine, which was afforded statutory recognition[20], developed on the basis that where one party to the oral contract had partially performed it, or had otherwise relied upon it being enforceable, it may be inequitable for the other side to plead the statute and argue that the contract was unenforceable because there was no adequate memorandum. In such circumstances, equity would order that the contract be carried out.

Although the underlying ethos of the doctrine of part performance was clear enough, the application of the doctrine became beset by various uncertainties and technicalities. The existence of these difficulties was one of the reasons that prompted the Law Commission to recommend the replacement of s 40 with the new statutory provision. Unfortunately, it would seem that the reform that has been introduced may bring with it problems of its own[1].

1.   Abolition of part performance

Section 2 requires contracts for the sale of land to be in writing. It follows from this that there is now no such thing as an oral contract for the sale of land. Because of this, the doctrine of part performance is, by necessary implication, abolished. It is not possible partially to perform a non-existent contract. The question which then arises is what happens in situations which would have amounted to part performance in the past.

---

19   *Monnickendam v Leanse* (1923) 39 TLR 445.
20   LPA 1925, s 40(2).
 1   See (1990) 10 LS 325 (L Bentley and P Coughlan); (1993) 13 OJLS (C Davis).

2. Estoppel

The Law Commission was, of course, perfectly well aware that the enactment of its proposal would result in the abolition of part performance. It was also conscious of situations, which involved part performance in the past, where parties had behaved upon the basis that there was a contract between them, in circumstances where it would be inequitable to allow one party, subsequently, to deny efficacy to the agreement. The Commission was keen to ensure that a party who had acted in such circumstances should not be left without a remedy. The view was taken that the existing doctrine of equitable estoppel was sufficiently flexible and well-developed to provide an appropriate remedy in this type of situation[2].

Equitable, or proprietary, estoppel, as it is commonly known, is a doctrine of some antiquity[3]. The central element of the doctrine is that one person, A, has acted in reliance on a belief or expectation that he either has, or will obtain, an interest in the property of another person, B, in circumstances where it would be unconscionable for B to rely on his strict legal rights and deny any relief to A[4]. Although the expression of the doctrine in the general terms of unconscionability may, at first sight, appear somewhat vague, various criteria have emerged. The essential task of the court, when faced with a claim based upon estoppel is to consider three issues, enumerated by Scarman LJ. These are:

> First, is there an equity established? Secondly, what is the extent of the equity if one is established? And, thirdly, what is the relief appropriate to satisfy the equity[5]?

These issues will be considered in turn.

(a) Establishing an equity
At the risk of some over generalisation, estoppel cases fall into two basic types. The first is where B has actively encouraged A to believe that he has or will have rights over B's land and A relies upon this expectation. These two elements of encouragement and reliance will then be sufficient to raise an equity. A classic example of this is provided by *Plimmer v City of Wellington Corpn*[6]. The plaintiff's predecessor in title had built a jetty on his own land. Later, at the request of the government, he was persuaded to extend the jetty onto the government's land. This he did, at considerable expense. When that land was acquired by the defendant, the issue was whether or not the plaintiff had any rights in that land. The Privy Council held that he did. As there had been active encouragement to extend the jetty, there must have been an implicit

---

2 See (1987) Law Com No 164, paras 5.4–5.5.
3 See *Hobbs v Nelson* (1649) Nels 47.
4 See *Taylor Fashions Ltd v Liverpool Victoria Trustees Co Ltd* [1982] QB 133n, [1981] 1 All ER 897; *Habib Bank Ltd v Habib Bank AG Zurich* [1981] 2 All ER 650, [1981] 1 WLR 1265, CA; *Lim Teng Huan v Ang Swee Chaun* [1992] 1 WLR 113, PC.
5 *Crabb v Arun District Council* [1976] Ch 179 at 193, [1975] 3 All ER 865 at 875, CA.
6 (1884) 9 App Cas 699, PC.

understanding that rights would be obtained in consequence of that expenditure. In these circumstances it would be inequitable to deny the plaintiff some remedy[7].

A more modern example is provided by *Pascoe v Turner*[8]. An unmarried couple were cohabiting in a house owned by the male partner. He purported to give her the house and its contents. In reliance on this, she spent several hundred pounds by way of repairs and improvements. On the breakdown of their relationship, he sought to evict her from the house. It was held that she had acquired rights through estoppel and the equity that had arisen was satisfied by the court ordering him to convey the house to her.

In this type of case, there is a clear link between the creation of the expectation by one party and the reliance by the other, so that it is quite easy to establish that an equity has arisen. The other type of case, which frequently occasions rather greater difficulty, is where there is no active encouragement for one party to act in reliance upon an expectation. In the past, strict criteria were laid down which had to be satisfied before any estoppel rights would arise[9]; the modern approach is to take a less formulaic approach to the dispute and focus on the question of unconscionability.

A good example of this type of case is provided by *E R Ives (Investment) Ltd v High*[10]. Mr High and Mr Westgate were neighbours. Mr Westgate constructed a block of flats the foundations of which, it was later discovered, encroached upon Mr High's land. Rather than seek to have the flats demolished, Mr High agreed that the foundations could stay where they were, in return for him having a right of way across Mr Westgate's land. This contract, which was effective to create an equitable easement was not registered as a land charge and, in consequence, was void against the Wrights who had purchased Mr Westgate's land. Neither Mr High nor the Wrights were aware of this and both continued on the basis that the right of way was still valid. Some time later, Mr High built a garage on his own land in such a way that it was only possible to gain access to it by using the right of way across his neighbours' land. The Wrights were aware of the building work and, indeed, complimented Mr High on it. Later they sold and conveyed their land to Ives Investment, expressly subject to Mr High's rights, 'if any'. Ives Investment then sought an injunction restraining Mr High from using the right of way.

One of the grounds for deciding in favour of Mr High was estoppel. This right had arisen from the work done in constructing the garage. Unlike the position in *Plimmer v City of Wellington Corpn*, there had been no active encouragement of Mr High to believe that he had, or would obtain, a right over the disputed land. Rather, at the material time, both parties laboured under the mistaken belief that such a right was already possessed. What caused the equity to arise was that Mr High had relied on his mistaken belief and the Wrights had acquiesced in that reliance. Accordingly, it would have been inequitable for them, having stood by while he spent money on the faith of his belief, subsequently, to deny him access over the land.

7 For a discussion of remedies, see pp 130–132, post.
8 [1979] 2 All ER 945, [1979] 1 WLR 431, CA.
9 *Willmott v Barber* (1880) 15 Ch D 96 at 105, 106.
10 [1967] 2 QB 379, [1967] 1 All ER 504, CA.

The difference between cases such as *Plimmer* and *E R Ives (Investment) Ltd v High* is that in the former there was active encouragement of an expectation while, in the latter, there was passive acquiescence in reliance upon an expectation that rights already existed. What is common to both is that the person against whom the equity arises is responsible in some way for the reliance carried out on the faith of the expectation. This is easier to establish in cases of active encouragement, with the result that, in such cases, the courts are prepared to assume that active encouragement has triggered reliance[11]. It nevertheless remains an indispensable requirement, if an equity is to be established, to show reliance upon an expectation for which the other party bears responsibility.

This element of mutuality means that unilateral actions cannot give rise to estoppel rights; an issue which generated some controversy in the old law of part performance[12]. The lack of mutuality was one of the reasons why a claim based upon estoppel failed in *Taylors Fashion Ltd v Liverpool Victoria Trustees Co Ltd*[13]. In this case, both landlord and tenant were, for a considerable period of time, unaware that an option to renew a lease was void for non-registration. The tenant argued that the landlord was estopped from denying this, basing his claim on the installation of a lift in the demised premises. The claim failed for two reasons. First, what was done, allegedly in reliance on the expectation that the option was valid, was entirely consistent with what a tenant of that particular property might have done to augment the commercial utility of the premises, even had there been no option to renew the lease. Reliance could not be established. Second, even had reliance been shown, there was no element of mutuality involved; the landlord had not asked the tenant to install the lift and there was nothing he could have done to have prevented its installation. Indeed, the installation was actually envisaged by the lease. The landlord was not responsible, therefore for the alleged act of reliance and, therefore, no equity arose against him.

(i) Examples of reliance.   It is essential, for an equity to arise, that there has been reliance on the expectation. Classically the reliance will take the form of expenditure, for example, spending money on property owned by another person, by building an extension upon it[14]. While the expenditure of money, in reliance upon an expectation, is a sufficient act of reliance, it is not a necessary one. Reliance has been held to include the selling of property without reserving a right of way[15] and the giving up of a job and a council house to live near a parent in a house provided by the parent, believing that it would be his[16]. In short, it is any conduct which would cause detriment, if the expectation in reliance upon which a person acted, is left unfulfilled.

---

11   *Greasley v Cooke* [1980] 3 All ER 710, [1980] 1 WLR 1306, CA.
12   See (1995) Law Com WP No 92, para 3.23.
13   Supra.
14   *Inwards v Baker* [1965] 2 QB 29, [1965] 1 All ER 446, CA.
15   *Crabb v Arun District Council,* supra.
16   *Jones v Jones* [1977] 2 All ER 231, [1977] 1 WLR 438.

(ii) Action by the vendor.   It has been argued that, unlike the previous position when the doctrine of part performance was still operative, a vendor may not be able to rely on the doctrine of estoppel when he has acted in the expectation that the purchaser will implement the agreement[17]. The main basis of this argument is that equitable estoppel is seen as a means of acquiring an interest in land by informal means. Because what the vendor expects to acquire under the contract is money, it is argued that estoppel will only be of value to the purchaser. This seems unduly alarmist as estoppel has been held to apply to an expectation of disposing of an interest in land as well as to acquiring an interest[18]. It is conceived that an act by the vendor which would, in the past, have constituted part performance, such as allowing the purchaser into possession or redecorating the property to the purchaser's specifications[19], will now give the vendor rights through the medium of estoppel.

(b) The extent of the equity
The second element of estoppel identified by Scarman LJ is the ascertainment of the extent of the equity. This, quite simply, means the extent of the expectation. In many estoppel cases this may not be a straightforward task, as many such cases have their background in very informal transactions, where it is not always easy to discern just what expectation a person had. In the present context, this is unlikely to be a problem as the parties will have reached an agreement; the difficulty is that the terms of s 2 are not satisfied, with the result that that agreement does not have contractual effect. The extent of the equity will be what the parties have actually agreed upon.

(c) Satisfying the equity
Once the court is satisfied that an equity has arisen, there exists considerable discretion as to what remedy is the most appropriate means of satisfying it. The maximum remedy that can be afforded is to make an order that the full expectation be satisfied. This occurred in *Pascoe v Turner*[20], where the Court of Appeal ordered the man to convey the house to his erstwhile partner. It was made clear in the decision, itself, however, that this was by no means an automatic solution, the court's role not being simply one of enforcing a promise that had been made. Thought was given to whether the woman should be given only an indefinite licence to occupy the house but, for various reasons, this was not, on the facts, considered to be the most appropriate solution[1]. In the exercise of its discretion, the court has arrived at a number of solutions, which have included simply dismissing a possession action[2], granting possession on terms that occupiers were compensated for improvements made[3], and

---

17   C Davis (1993) 13 OJLS 99.
18   *Salvation Army Trustee Co Ltd v West Yorkshire Metropolitan County Council* (1980) 41 P & CR 179.
19   See *Dickinson v Barrow* [1904] 2 Ch 339; *Rawlinson v Ames* [1925] Ch 96.
20   [1979] 2 All ER 945, [1979] 1 WLR 431, CA.
 1   Ibid at 438–439 and 950, 951 respectively.
 2   *Williams v Staite* [1979] Ch 291, [1978] 2 All ER 928.
 3   *Dodsworth v Dodsworth* [1973] EGD 233.

granting a lien over the land in respect of the outlay[4]. The court will have regard to all the circumstances of the case, including the conduct of the parties[5], to determine the most appropriate remedy to satisfy the equity that has arisen. The question which arises is whether in cases where parties have reached an agreement for the sale of land, but s 2 has not been satisfied, and estoppel rights have arisen, the courts will exercise a similar discretion.

In the past, when a party to an oral contract had performed an adequate act of part performance, the court had a choice of remedy. It could choose between 'undoing what has been done (which is not always possible, or, if possible just) and completing what has been left undone[6]'. In practice, this meant that the court would order specific performance of the contract. The question remains whether, where one of the parties to an agreement establishes rights through estoppel, the court will either order the other party to restore the actor to his original position or decide that the equity should be satisfied by implementing the oral agreement or, alternatively, arrive at some other solution.

There are indications that, when the parties have arrived at an agreement and the question of estoppel arises, the court will simply implement what the parties have agreed[7]. This has the considerable merit of certainty and resulting predictability. In *Morritt v Wonham*[8], however, in what was actually a part performance case, the judge felt able to adopt an unfettered discretionary approach. The defendant, who was in his eighties, orally agreed to leave the plaintiff his property by will in return for the latter undertaking various building works. The value of the work done was estimated to have been in the region of £15,000 to £20,000 and the value of the property, itself, was in the region of £365,000. When a dispute broke out between the parties, the judge held that there was an oral contract and that the plaintiff had carried out acts of part performance. He did not, however, enforce what the parties had actually agreed. Instead, he imposed a trust for sale, under which the defendant was to have a life interest and was also to be entitled to £40,000 to be raised either by a mortgage or selling off part of the property.

This remarkable rewriting of the parties' contract seemed to be entirely unwarranted under the now superseded doctrine of part performance. Of present relevance is that the judge considered it to be open to him to adopt this course precisely because, under the new law, cases such as this would be decided upon the principles of estoppel. It is quite true that in estoppel cases the courts do have a discretion as to how the equity that has arisen should be satisfied. Applying a general discretionary approach in the present context is, however, conducive to uncertainty and it is to be hoped that the courts will confine the exercise of their discretion to either effecting restitution or to enforcing the agreement reached between the parties. Unfortunately, it remains to be seen how the courts will react to cases which, in the past, would

---

4   *Unity Joint Stock Mutual Banking Association v King* (1858) Beav 2572.
5   See *Crabb v Arun District Council*, supra; *Williams v Staite*, supra; *J Willis & Son v Willis* [1986] 1 EGLR 62; [1986] Conv 406 (M P Thompson).
6   *Maddison v Alderson* (1883) 8 App Cas 467 at 476, HL, per Earl of Selborne LC.
7   *J T Developments Ltd v Quinn* (1990) 62 P & CR 33, CA; *Ling Teng Huan v Ang Swee Chuan* [1992] 1 WLR 113, PC.
8   [1993] NPC 2, [1994] Conv 233 (M P Thompson).

have been part performance cases but are now to be decided on estoppel principles.

E   Dangers of informal contracts

The point has previously been made that, in the majority of cases, the contracting parties are content to have their agreement recorded in a formal document prepared by solicitors, so that no contract comes into being until some time after they have completed their negotiations. Occasionally, impatient at the law's delay, they are anxious to have some tangible proof of their agreement. The purchaser may be prepared to pay a deposit, hoping to persuade the vendor from accepting a better offer elsewhere, or the vendor may insist upon a nominal deposit as a token of the purchaser's good faith. In the past, it was often a matter of chance whether any resulting cheque and receipt, or other correspondence, would constitute an adequate memorandum. Under the new law this is far less likely to happen, owing to the requirement that the signatures of both parties to the same document is satisfied before the contract is formed.

If the parties do sign the same document and, thereby, create a contract, they may encounter problems they would have avoided had they not been so hasty. The purchaser may discover, too late, that the property is subject to a road improvement scheme or scheduled for demolition; such factors will not provide him with any defence if he breaks the contract and is sued by the vendor. Had he waited until he had received the results of the customary searches and inquiries before entering a contract, he would have been able to resile without incurring any legal liability. Or again, it may just simply be that he is unable to raise a mortgage.

A vendor, too, is not immune from danger if he enters into a contract precipitously. It will be unlikely that he will have incorporated details of the tenure of the property and the incumbrances affecting it. Nevertheless, he will by law have bound himself to convey an estate in fee simple in possession free from incumbrances, for this one of the conditions that the law implies in every 'open contract'[9], unless the contrary is agreed. Should the property be leasehold, or subject to restrictive covenants, he cannot convey what he has contracted to sell. The purchaser, if he wishes, can refuse to proceed with the contract, recover his deposit and sue for damages.

F   Agreements 'subject to contract'

1.   Meaning of 'subject to contract'

Whether or not the parties to a sale and purchase of land intend to bind themselves contractually immediately will depend on the circumstances of each

---

9   An open contract arises when the parties have agreed upon the barest essentials, ie the property and price. The other terms necessary to give business efficacy to the contract are implied by the general law. See pp 147–149, post.

case. They frequently negative such intention by making or accepting an offer 'subject to contract'. This phrase makes it clear that the parties intend that 'neither of them is to be bound until a contract is signed in the usual way[10]'. Until a formal contract has been settled by the parties' legal advisers, signed and exchanged, the matter remains in a state of negotiation[11]. The parties have a *locus poenitentia*; either side is free to suggest new terms or to withdraw from the transaction. As there is no concluded contract, the purchaser, if he decides not to proceed, is entitled to the return of any money paid to the vendor[12]. On the other hand, if it is the vendor who withdraws, the purchaser cannot, ordinarily, recover from him any abortive expenditure incurred in respect of a survey or other similar fees[13].

A situation can arise where parties have agreed 'subject to contract' but both confidently expect that the exchange of contracts is a formality and act on the basis that they will be entering into a contract in due course. In such situations, it is possible that a remedy may be available. In *William Lacey (Hounslow) Ltd v Davis*[14], a builder had submitted an acceptable tender in respect of the proposed sale of a property and both sides expected contracts to be exchanged as a matter of course. At the request of the vendor's surveyors, he then performed a considerable amount of work on the property. The vendor then sold the property elsewhere and the builder was able to recover damages in respect of the work done; the basis of the award being *quantum meruit*.

A case such as this is an exception to the general rule that the purchaser cannot recover from the vendor cost incurred while the transaction is 'subject to contract'. The work done in this case was far more extensive than that which is normally done in the preparation of a tender and, moreover, it was work which had benefited the vendor. The circumstances were such that it would have been unconscionable for the vendor to retain the benefit. In most cases where pre-contractual expenditure is incurred and the planned contract does not come to fruition, such expenditure will not be recoverable[15].

A second possible source of relief for a party disappointed that a 'subject to contract' agreement has not resulted in a binding contract is estoppel. Circumstances may arise where the reliance on the expectation that contracts will be exchanged has been such that it is inequitable for the other party to refuse, subsequently, to enter into a contract[16]. Because the effect of the term 'subject to contract' is well known, however, a very strong case will need to be established for an estoppel to arise in such a situation[17]. Where the parties are

10 *Spottiswoode, Ballantyne & Co Ltd v Doreen Appliances Ltd* [1942] 2 KB 32 at 35, [1942] 2 All ER 65 at 66, CA, per Lord Greene MR.
11 *Keppel v Wheeler* [1927] 1 KB 577 at 583, CA, per Bankes LJ. For exchange of contracts, see pp 219–227, post.
12 *Chillingworth v Esche* [1924] 1 Ch 97, CA.
13 For the problem raised by gazumping see pp 216–219, post.
14 [1957] 2 All ER 712, [1957] 1 WLR 932.
15 *Regalian Properties plc v London Docklands Development Corpn* [1995] 1 All ER 1005, [1994] NPC 139, [1995] Conv 135 (M P Thompson).
16 *Salvation Army Trustee Co v West Yorkshire Metropolitan County Council* (1980) 41 P & CR 179, [1983] Conv 85 (J T Farrand). See also *Waltons Stores (Interstate) Ltd v Maher* (1988) 164 CLR 387.
17 *A-G for Hong Kong v Humphreys Estate (Queen's Gardens) Ltd* [1987] AC 114 at 128, 129, [1987] 2 All ER 387 at 395, PC, per Lord Templeman.

experienced players in the property market, it is highly unlikely that an estoppel will arise after the conclusion of a 'subject to contract' agreement.

Regrettably, the words 'subject to contract' are sometimes the victim of thoughtless and inappropriate[18] usage in legal documents. Usually the phrase prevents the creation of a contract; occasionally the words are disregarded as meaningless in the context. In *Alpenstow Ltd v Regalian Properties plc*[19], Nourse J declined to interpret them according to their clear, primary meaning; to have done so would have deprived a carefully drafted and professionally drawn agreement of any effect. Cases such as these serve as a warning, even to skilled draftsmen, of the need for care when employing the phrase in any unusual situation.

2.   Effect of lawyer's correspondence expressed to be 'subject to contract'

Prior to 1989, as has been seen, it was perfectly possible for parties to reach a concluded oral contract for the sale of land. Difficult questions could then arise when a solicitor, in writing to his opposite number to confirm the agreement, headed the letter, as it was customary to do, 'subject to contract'. The difficulty was in determining the circumstances, if any, when this correspondence could constitute a s 40 memorandum, thereby making the, previously unenforceable, oral contract enforceable[20].

Happily, these difficulties have now disappeared. It is no longer possible for there to be an oral contract for the sale of land. The issue is now, not whether there is adequate written evidence of the oral contract, but whether the writing complies with s 2 and so creates a contract. Unless the phrase 'subject to contract' has been inserted into a document by mistake, and is not, therefore, expressing the wishes of the parties, documents marked 'subject to contract' cannot create a binding contract.

3.   Problems of construction

It does not automatically follow that because the parties contemplate the execution of some other document incorporating the terms of their agreement, there can be no binding contract unless that document is subsequently signed. It is a question of construction whether

> the execution of the further contract is a condition or term of the bargain or whether it is a mere expression of the desire of the parties as to the manner in which the transaction already agreed to will in fact go through[1].

18   See, for example, their futile usage in notices served under rent review procedures: *Shirlcar Properties Ltd v Heinitz* (1983) 268 EG 362, CA; *Sheridan v Blaircourt Investments Ltd* (1984) 270 EG 1290; *British Rail Pension Trustee Co v Cardshops Ltd* [1987] 1 EGLR 127.
19   [1985] 2 All ER 545; *Michael Richards Properties Ltd v Corpn of Wardens of St Saviour's Parish, Southwark* [1975] 3 All ER 416; *Kelly v Park Hall School Ltd* [1979] IR 340.
20   See the 3rd edition of this work, pp 130, 131.
 1   *Von Hatzfeldt-Wildenburg v Alexander* [1912] 1 Ch 284 at 288, per Parker J.

In the latter case there may still be a binding contract, notwithstanding the non-execution of a more formal document. It was held there was a binding contract where a letter of acceptance stated that the writer had requested his solicitors 'to forward the agreement for purchase'[2]. Another example is furnished by the case of *Branca v Cobarro*[3]. Here a written agreement prepared by one of the parties concluded: 'This is a provisional agreement until a fully legalised agreement drawn up by a solicitor and embodying all the conditions herewith stated is signed'. The court held that the agreement constituted a binding contract. The final clause, particularly the word 'until', implied that the agreement was intended to be immediately and fully binding, and to remain so unless and until superseded by a later agreement of the same tenor but expressed in more precise and formal language. It should be appreciated that, because of the greater formality insisted upon by s 2 and, in particular, the requirement that both parties sign the same document, such cases are likely to be infrequent.

G   Conditional contracts

Care must be taken to distinguish cases where there is no contract at all because the parties' negotiations are 'subject to contract' , from situations where they have concluded a conditional contract. They may have entered into an agreement for sale subject to the consent of the Charity Commissioners, or the reversioner's licence to assign, or the purchaser's obtaining planning permission or the grant of a satisfactory mortgage. The precise effect of a condition of this type is a question of construction. The law on this topic is rather complex, and not all of the cases are easy to reconcile. The draftsman is always well advised to make his intentions abundantly clear on this issue, by indicating how and in what way the contract is affected by the condition, and providing for the consequences of its non-fulfilment.

(a) Condition precedent to contract
The condition may operate as a condition precedent to the formation of a contract for sale between the parties. A condition of this type has the same effect as a 'subject to contract' qualification. No binding agreement exists unless and until the condition is fulfilled; either party is free to withdraw without awaiting its fulfilment or non-fulfilment. In *Aberfoyle Plantations Ltd v Cheng*[4], a

---

2   *Rossiter v Miller* (1878) 3 App Cas 1124, HL; *Bonnewell v Jenkins* (1878) 8 Ch D 70, CA ('We have asked V's solicitor to prepare contract').
3   [1947] KB 854, [1947] 2 All ER 101, CA; *Bushwall Properties Ltd v Vortex Properties Ltd* [1975] 2 All ER 214; revsd on other grounds [1976] 2 All ER 283, CA.
4   [1960] AC 115, [1959] 3 All ER 910, PC, a 'very unusual and special case': *Property and Bloodstock Ltd v Emerton* [1968] Ch 94 at 1115, [1967] 3 All ER 321 at 327, CA, per Danckwerts LJ. In the *Aberfoyle* case, the entire contract was made subject to the condition, as the opening words of cl 1 of the agreement showed; yet there was also a provision for the contract to become null and void on non-fulfilment of the condition. See further 9 *Halsbury's Laws* (4th edn), para 264.

purchase of land was expressed to be conditional upon the vendor's obtaining a renewal of certain leases. The Judicial Committee of the Privy Council took the view that until the condition was satisfied no contract for sale could come into existence. Since the date fixed for completion had passed without the condition being fulfilled, the purchaser was entitled to the return of his deposit. Similarly in *Michael Richards Properties Ltd v Corpn of Wardens of St Saviour's Parish, Southwark*[5], Goff J held that a condition requiring the Charity Commissioners' consent to the sale[6] was a true condition precedent, and the contract became effective only when it was given.

(b) Condition precedent to performance

Alternatively, and more frequently, the condition is held not to prevent the formation of a binding contract. Its non-fulfilment renders the contract unenforceable by either party[7], unless the condition (being for the sole benefit of one of the parties) is waived by that party. The condition takes effect as one of the terms of the contract; apart from its non-fulfilment neither party is entitled to withdraw from the contract except by consent. Conditions falling into this category have been held to occur where the contract was made subject to the vendor arranging a satisfactory mortgage[8], to planning permission[9], to the reversioner's consent to the assignment of a lease[10], to satisfactory searches and replies to pre-contract inquiries[11], to the purchaser's solicitor approving the lease[12], and to a survey of the property[13].

(c) Time for fulfilment

The agreement may, or may not, provide a date by which the condition is to be fulfilled. The date so fixed must be strictly adhered to without any extension by reference to equitable principles. In the absence of a specified date, the condition must be satisfied within a reasonable time, judged by an objective

---

5   [1975] 3 All ER 416.
6   As required by the Charities Act 1960, s 29(1). See also *Haslemere Estates Ltd v Baker* [1982] 3 All ER 525. For exemptions, see s 29(4) and Sch 2; the Charities (Religious Premises) Regulations 1962, SI 1962 No 1421, r 1.
7   Such a condition may variously be termed a condition precedent to the performance of obligations under the contract, or a condition suspensive of the obligations thereunder. A condition may also operate as a condition subsequent, ie where the contract provides for liability to cease on the occurrence of some future event.
8   *Lee-Parker v Izzet* [1971] 3 All ER 1099, more fully reported on this point at (1971) 22 P & CR 1098. Contrast *Lee-Parker v Izzet (No 2)* [1972] 2 All ER 800. See now *Graham v Pitkin* [1992] 2 All ER 235, [1992] 1 WLR 403, PC.
9   *Batten v White* (1960) 12 P & CR 66.
10 *Property and Bloodstock Ltd v Emerton*, supra; *Brickwoods Ltd v Butler and Walters* (1970) 23 P & CR 317, CA (contract conditional on vendor procuring car parking licence). For licences to assign, see pp 272–276, post.
11 *Mason v Stapleton's Tyre Services Ltd* (1963) 186 EG 113; *Aquis Estates Ltd v Minton* [1975] 3 All ER 1043, CA (property to be free from adverse entry in local land charges register). *Ganton House Investments Ltd v Corbin* [1988] 2 EGLR 69.
12 *Caney v Leith* [1937] 2 All ER 532.
13 *Ee v Kakar* (1979) 40 P & CR 223, not following *Marks v Board* (1930) 46 TLR 424. See [1979] Conv 285 (V Callender) and [1980] Conv 446 (J E Adams).

test applicable to both parties[14], and in any event not later than the date fixed for completion[15]. In the case of a condition precedent to performance, a party who signifies his refusal to continue with the contract before the time for fulfilment has elapsed commits breach of contract. Thus in *Smith v Butler*[16]:

> V contracted to sell to P the lease of a public house which was subject to a mortgage, on condition that M, the mortgagee, consented to transfer the outstanding loan from V to P. V experienced difficulty in procuring M's consent. Before the date fixed for completion P repudiated the contract.

It was held that V had until the completion date to perform the condition so that P, being in breach of contract, could not recover his deposit.

If the condition is not satisfied in time the contract cannot be enforced. Non-fulfilment discharges the parties from their obligations under the contract[17]. So the purchaser can recover his deposit. This principle is subject to an important qualification. Where fulfilment of the condition requires action on the part of one of the parties, that party cannot rely on the non-performance unless he has taken reasonable steps to secure its fulfilment. He cannot take advantage of a state of affairs that his own default has produced[18]. Thus, where the agreement is subject to survey, the purchaser is bound to obtain a surveyor's report. Failure to do so within a reasonable (or a specified) time precludes him from resiling from the transaction. Having obtained a report, he must act bona fide in deciding whether or not to proceed with the purchase. If a reasonable man would be satisfied with the report, the purchaser will experience difficulty in persuading a court that his decision to discontinue the contract was bona fide[19].

The contract may expressly regulate the consequences of non-performance. For instance, it may provide for the contract to become null and void, though the use of this formula is not advisable bearing in mind possible difficulties surrounding the interpretation of the word 'void'. Alternatively, one or both of the parties may be entitled to serve a notice terminating the contract[20]. Such a clause ought always to specify the period within which the notice is to be given; otherwise it will be ineffective unless served within a reasonable time after the last date for fulfilment of the condition[1].

14 *Re Longlands Farm* [1968] 3 All ER 552 (planning permission not obtained by purchaser more than three years after contract; vendor discharged).
15 *Aberfoyle Plantations Ltd v Cheng* [1960] AC 115, [1959] 3 All ER 910. These rules apply equally to conditions that are precedent to performance; see *Brickwoods Ltd v Butler and Walters* (1969) 21 P & CR 256 at 264, per Megarry J; affd (1970) 23 P & CR 317, CA.
16 [1900] 1 QB 694, CA; *Batten v White*, supra.
17 When no time for performance is specified, the expiration of a reasonable period itself permits rescission without service of a prior notice calling for fulfilment or completion within a reasonable time: *Perri v Coolangatta Investment Pty Ltd* (1982) 149 CLR 537.
18 See *New Zealand Shipping Co Ltd v Société des Ateliers et Chantiers de France* [1919] AC 1, HL.
19 *Ee v Kakar*, supra, at 228, per Walton J; *Meehan v Jones* (1982) 149 CLR 571 (subject to satisfactory financial arrangements). But see p 139, post.
20 Unless his conduct bars recourse to his contractual right: *Aquis Estates Ltd v Minton* [1975] 3 All ER 1043, CA.
 1 *Brickwoods Ltd v Butler and Walters*, supra; *Pine View Developments Ltd v Napthan* (1975) 236 EG 53.

(d) Waiver

A term or condition which is for the sole benefit of one of the parties may be waived by that party who can then enforce the contract without it. In *Batten v White*[2], a vendor repudiated a contract for sale subject to planning permission at a time when the purchaser was still seeking permission; it was held that the purchaser could waive the condition and sue for specific performance. According to Brightman J in *Heron Garage Properties Ltd v Moss*[3], in the absence of any express contractual right, waiver will in general be allowed only where the stipulation (i) is in terms for his exclusive benefit because it is a power or right vested by the contract in him alone, or (ii) is by inevitable implication for his benefit alone[4]. The learned judge refused to allow the purchaser's attempted waiver of a condition relating to planning permission because it was inextricably mixed up with other contractual terms from which it could not be severed. The date for completion was geared to the date by which planning consent was obtained[5]. Furthermore, the term could not be said to be for the purchaser's sole benefit, in as much as the contract conferred on the vendors[6] (as well as the purchaser) a right to determine the agreement in the event of planning consent not being obtained within a stated period. Where the grant of planning permission is solely for the benefit of the purchaser, it may be waived by him[7].

To be valid waiver must be effected before the time fixed for fulfilment has expired. Once a condition has been duly waived by one of the parties, it is too late for the other to seek to avoid the contract under an express power on the grounds of non-fulfilment of the condition. The contractual power of termination is operative only so long as the contract is conditional.

It is not competent for either party unilaterally to waive a condition which is precedent to the formation of a contract[8]. Until the condition is satisfied, no contract exists, so that there is no right or term to waive. Moreover, to allow waiver in such circumstances would enable one party to impose on the other party without his assent a binding contract with different terms.

(e) Uncertainty

A condition that is so vague or imprecise that no definite or practical meaning can be given to it avoids the entire contract. Nevertheless, the courts are

---

2   (1960) 12 P & CR 66; *Morrell v Studd and Millington* [1913] 2 Ch 648 (provision for securing balance of purchase moneys to vendor's satisfaction).
3   [1974] 1 All ER 421, criticised at (1975) 39 Conv (NS) 251, 255 et seq.
4   For examples see *Bennett v Fowler* (1840) 2 Beav 302 (condition requiring vendor to make a good title); *Usanga v Bishop* (1974) 232 EG 835 (house to be vacated by tenants); *Ee v Kakar*, supra.
5   Waiver was similarly disallowed in *Boobyer v Thornville Properties Ltd* (1968) 19 P & CR 768 and *Federated Homes Ltd v Turner* (1974) 233 EG 845.
6   Similarly, where the contract provides for it to become null and void on non-performance. This operates to give both parties the right to act on the clause: *Meehan v Jones* (1982) 149 CLR 571.
7   *Balbosa v Ayoub Ali* [1990] 1 WLR 914, PC.
8   *Turney v Zhilko* (1959) 18 DLR (2d) 447; *Barnett v Harrison* (1975) 57 DLR (3d) 225; 9 *Halsbury's Laws* (4th edn), para 264. Contrast *Scott v Rania* [1966] NZLR 527.

reluctant to declare void on the ground of uncertainty an agreement intended to have legal effect; wherever possible they endeavour to find a reasonable interpretation for the offending clause. The issue of certainty has arisen in a number of recent cases involving mortgage conditions. In *Lee-Parker v Izzet (No 2)*[9], a contract for sale was expressly subject to 'the purchaser obtaining a satisfactory mortgage'. The concept of a satisfactory mortgage was considered to be too indefinite to be given practical meaning; it left at large two most essential matters – the amount of the loan and the terms of repayment. The contract was, therefore, void for uncertainty. Contrast with this the decision in *Janmohamed v Hassam*[10], where the contract provided that if the purchaser did not obtain a mortgage *satisfactory to him*, the contract should thereupon be rescinded. According to Slade J, the italicised words made all the difference. It was possible to import a term by necessary implication that such satisfaction should not be unreasonably withheld. With that further term imported the condition was not so vague that it could not be given a reasonable effect.

This trend of being reluctant to hold conditions void for uncertainty was continued by the Privy Council in *Graham v Pitkin*[11]. Commenting upon *Lee Parker v Izzet (No 2)*, Lord Templeman said of that case that since 'the purchaser, if he had the money, could always have declared that a mortgage of £10 from his brother-in-law was "satisfactory" their Lordships doubt the finding that there was no contract[12]'. Since the condition is for the purchaser's benefit, it is one that he will normally be able to waive. It now seems unlikely that a contract made conditional on the purchaser obtaining finance will be regarded as uncertain.

---

9   [1972] 2 All ER 800; *Re Rich's Will Trusts* (1962) 106 Sol Jo 75.
10   [1977] 1 EGLR 142, 241 EG 609; *Lee-Parker v Izzet* [1971] 3 All ER 1099 at 1105. Unlike the position in some Commonwealth jurisdictions, 'subject to mortgage' agreements are rare in this country because our 'subject to contract' procedure renders them largely otiose. See (1976) 40 Conv (NS) 37 (B Coote).
11   [1992] 2 All ER 235, [1992] 1 WLR 403, PC.
12   Ibid at 406 and 237 respectively.

Chapter 6

Contents of formal contracts

A Drafting the contract: introductory points

1. Use of standard form contracts

(a) Sale by private treaty

It is the usual practice for the parties, whenever a transaction by private treaty involves the payment of purchase money[1], to have a formal contract prepared by their legal advisers, irrespective of whether the title to the land is registered or unregistered. The vendor's solicitor drafts the contract which he submits to the purchaser's solicitor for approval. Both solicitors play their respective parts in formulating the terms of the document. The contract is prepared in duplicate. Each party will eventually sign one copy (his 'part' as it is commonly termed), after which the solicitors will exchange[2] the two parts so that each will have the other's signed part. This procedure is adopted irrespective of whether the title to the land is registered or unregistered.

Frequently the vendor's solicitor drafts the contract on a standard form containing a set of general Conditions of Sale. Frequently the vendor's solicitor drafts the contract on a standard form containing a set of general Conditions of Sale. For many years, there existed two standard forms which were in common use, The Law Society's Conditions of Sale and the National Conditions of Sale. In addition to these standard form contracts, some local law societies published their own forms, which consisted of adaptations of the Law Society's form. As part of an attempt to facilitate conveyancing, by avoiding a variety of different standard form contracts, the two main forms were conjoined in 1990 as The Standard Conditions of Sale, now in their third edition. A solicitor, when drafting the contract should use these conditions adding details, including the Special Conditions of Sale[3], appropriate to the particular transaction.

The Council of the Law Society considers that it is contrary to professional practice for a solicitor acting for a seller of property to prepare a contract which he knows will be placed before a prospective buyer for signature before

---

1 As in a conveyance of the freehold, or assignment of a long lease. It is not normal to have a formal contract on the grant or assignment of a short lease at a rack rent (ie one representing the full value of the land and buildings). There is a steady increase in the number of house owners prepared to undertake their own conveyancing work. But see the warning at the foot of the SCS form reproduced on p 148, post.
2 For exchange of contracts, see pp 219–227, post.
3 See pp 161–176 post.

that person has obtained, or has had a proper opportunity to obtain, legal advice[4].

(b) Sales by auction

When property is to be sold by auction the procedure is somewhat different. The contract and conditions of sale are prepared by the vendor's solicitor, but it is not submitted for approval to solicitors acting for intending bidders. The contract is made available for inspection at the offices of the auctioneer and of the vendor's solicitor a week or so before the date of the auction. Immediately before the auction is conducted prospective buyers are normally allowed to ask questions about the property or the contract. After its conclusion one part of the contract is signed by or on behalf of the successful bidder, who (or whose solicitor) receives in exchange the part signed by or on behalf of the vendor.

2. Taking instructions

From the vendor's point of view the contract is a most crucial document. It defines his obligations both in relation to the land and the terms upon which it is to be sold. Unfortunately the drafting of the contract does not always receive the attention that its importance deserves. It is not sufficient to adopt the contract used on the occasion of the vendor's purchase, assuming the solicitor acted on that occasion, though he should undoubtedly peruse that contract and the other documents (eg preliminary inquiries) relating to that transaction. Before preparing the contract, the solicitor should arm himself with all necessary information. This might seem axiomatic, but it is not always adhered to in practice. Inquiries should be made of the client to ascertain the need for any special terms to be inserted in the contract, the precise identity of the property especially if situated in a rural area, whether fittings are to be included in the price or taken over at a valuation, whether during his period of ownership he has entered into any agreements affecting the property[5], to mention but a few matters. Where the property is sold subject to existing leases, full details of the tenancies (ie whether contractual or statutory) and the tenants, the rents and the properties should be obtained. Unless he acted for the vendor when he acquired the property, or the title is already registered, the solicitor ought to investigate his client's title to discover any defects of title which may require some special clause in the contract. In some cases a visit to the property may be desirable. Unless specifically requested, it is not a solicitor's duty to advise his client whether the transaction he is instructed to carry through is a prudent one from the client's point of view[6].

---

4 Guide to the Professional Conduct of Solicitors (1993), para 24.03.
5 Especially those of which there may be no evidence with the deeds, eg on oral licence granted to a neighbour to lay drains, as in *Ward v Kirkland* [1967] Ch 194, [1966] 1 All ER 609.
6 *Bowdage v Harold Michelmore & Co* (1962) 183 EG 233 (no duty to advise as to reasonableness of sale price in option agreement).

To be in a position to draft the contract in a case involving unregistered land, a practitioner needs to have the title deeds in his possession, though this elementary precaution is occasionally ignored. In one case[7] a vendor's solicitors actually exchanged contracts without the deeds ever being produced to them. They later discovered that the vendor had not mislaid them, as they supposed, but had sold the property some years previously but had forgotten this. Where the property is in mortgage (eg to a building society) he will not normally be able to obtain the deeds without agreeing to hold them to the mortgagee's order. On a sale of registered land the information appearing in the land certificate is widely used as the basis of the draft contract. However, since the certificate may not disclose all the entries against the vendor's title, it is always prudent to obtain from the Registry office copies of the subsisting entries. Under the Standard Conditions of Sale, the vendor is obliged to supply office copy entries[8]. Such a contractual obligation will not be satisfied by sending the purchaser a copy of the land certificate[9].

There are authorities which indicate that entering into a contract to sell land may, of itself, operate as a representation by conduct as to the vendor's ownership, sufficient to sustain an action under s 2(1) of the Misrepresentation Act 1967[10], should the vendor have no title[11]. These cases were motivated by a desire to circumvent the rule in *Bain v Fothergill*[12], which precluded the purchaser from obtaining damages for loss of bargain in the event of the vendor having a defective title, although it is dubious whether damages for loss of bargain could be obtained under s 2(1)[13]. As the limit to the award of damages effected by the rule in *Bain v Fothergill* has now been abolished[14], this issue has become academic. Because the vendor is potentially liable in damages, however, in the event of his title proving to be defective, it is essential that every vendor's solicitor ensures that his client can implement the terms of his contract relating to title.

3.   Submission for approval and accompanying documents

Once drafted, the vendor's solicitor forwards the contract to his opposite number for approval, enclosing with it a letter expressing the sale (or proposed sale) to be 'subject to contract'. The significance of these words has already

---

7   *Errington v Martell-Wilson* (1980) 130 NLJ 545 (vendor held liable for misrepresentation).
8   SCS 4.2.1. See further p 336 post.
9   *Wood v Berkeley Homes (Sussex) Ltd* (1992) 64 P & CR 311, CA.
10   See p 660, post.
11   *Watts v Spence* [1976] Ch 165, [1975] 2 All ER 528, applied in *Errington v Martell-Wilson*, supra; Emmet, para 1.016; 42 *Halsbury's Laws*, para 270.
12   (1874) LR 7 HL 158.
13   *Sharneyford Supplies Ltd v Edge* [1986] Ch 128, [1985] 1 All ER 976; revsd on other grounds without reference to this point, [1987] Ch 305, [1987] 1 All ER 588, CA, although Balcombe LJ (at 591) did consider that the trial judge's criticisms of *Watts v Spence* were well-founded. For the proper measure of damages, see *Cemp Properties (UK) Ltd v Dentsply Research and Development Corp (Denton Hall & Burgin, third party)* [1991] 2 EGLR 197 at 199. See p 661 post.
14   Law of Property (Miscellaneous Provisions) Act 1989, s 3.

been considered[15]. To facilitate its approval it is customary to send copies of any restrictive covenants, or details of other adverse rights, disclosed in the contract, and on the assignment of leasehold land a copy of the lease.

One important point must be noted. The vendor is not, at this juncture, legally obliged to furnish documentary evidence that he is able to convey the subject matter of the contract. The complexities, at one time, affecting the title to land demanded that the deduction and investigation of title were formerly always postponed until after an exchange of contracts[16]. For many years, conditions of sale have contained a term requiring a vendor to deliver an abstract of title after exchange of contracts[17]. Over a period of time, a large body of professional opinion took the view that the abstract should accompany the draft contract. The purchaser's solicitor could thus satisfy himself that the title is sound before his client binds himself to buy; this helps reduce the time-lag between exchange of contracts and completion. This body of opinion is now reflected in the Conveyancing Protocol, so that when the Protocol is used, the vendor's solicitor should adopt the practice of sending with the draft contract an abstract of title or, when title is registered, office copy entries[18]. A related issue is whether a vendor's solicitor should also send replies to the standard form preliminary inquiries and a local land charges search certificate. Consideration of this will be deferred to the next chapter.

There are pros and cons in respect of the procedure set out in the Protocol. In favour of not adopting the recommended procedure can be cited economy; both parties are spared the time and expense of deducing and investigating the title, should negotiations between them break down and contracts are never exchanged[19]. As a means of reducing the frustration felt by the contracting parties, the Royal Commission on Legal Services advocated the change which is now enshrined in the Protocol[20]. Certainly, there can be little objection to adopting this procedure whenever the title is relatively straightforward, as it often is on the sale of a typical urban house. Whether the adoption of this practice in all cases is desirable is, however, debatable. When the title is lengthy or complicated, objections or queries are likely to be raised by the purchaser's solicitor. In these situations, early submission of the abstract may delay exchange, as the vendor's solicitor seeks to remedy the alleged defect, or satisfy the purchaser's solicitor that the title offered is sound – assuming he is prepared to go this far. Under the traditional procedure, a purchaser who discovers some defect during his post-contract investigation of title can require the vendor to rectify the matter, failing which he will often be able to terminate the contract, recover his deposit, and claim damages. But these rights may be of small consolation to a purchaser who has contracted to sell his existing property on the strength of his contract to buy. Therefore, it is urged, it is

---

15 Pages 132–135, ante.
16 *Reeve v Berridge* (1888) 20 QBD 523 at 528, CA, per Fry LJ.
17 SCS 4. For abstracts of title, see pp 281–285 post.
18 National Conveyancing Protocol (3rd edn), para 4.
19 See The Law Society's evidence to the Royal Commission on Legal Services, Memorandum No 3, Pt II, Section XII, p 122, para 11.
20 Royal Commission Report, Vol 1, 285, Annex 21.1, para 11.

better for a purchaser to discover that title is unsound before committing himself to buy and sell.

When a purchaser is supplied with an abstract of the title prior to exchange of contracts, his solicitor will normally investigate the title before exchange. He is not obliged to do so, unless the contract requires this (as sometimes happens on the sale of new houses on a building estate). If he decides to defer the investigation until afterwards, he should perhaps make it clear that exchange of contracts is not to be taken as an acceptance of the title by the purchaser. Even without this reservation it is not considered that failure to investigate the title pre-contract would fix the purchaser with constructive notice of defects in the title not disclosed by the vendor in the contract. Prima facie it is the vendor's duty to disclose the state of his title, not the purchaser's duty to make inquiry before entering into the contract[1]. A vendor cannot discharge his duty in such a facile manner.

4.   Contract races

A vendor anxious to secure a quick sale may instruct his solicitor to forward draft contracts to the solicitors acting for different prospective purchasers, stating that he will sell to the one who is the first to return a signed contract with the required deposit. The Council of The Law Society has issued a Direction setting out the various steps to adopt in such cases[2]. The vendor's solicitor must immediately disclose his client's decision direct to the solicitor of each intending purchaser. If given orally it must be confirmed in writing. A purchaser is thus warned of his involvement in a contract race, but this does not enable him to recover wasted expenditure if he is not the first past the post. Should the vendor refuse to authorise disclosure, his solicitor must cease to act for him forthwith. The Council has emphasised that the terms of the Direction are mandatory. A solicitor found to be in breach is liable to disciplinary proceedings. Arguably this is much too severe a penalty for infringement. The justification for the Direction appears to be without legal basis. Whilst a prospective purchaser may be morally entitled to be told about competing purchasers, he has no legal right to such information. Consequently, the Direction may amount to unnecessary interference with the proper freedom of solicitors to conduct to the best advantage their clients' lawful business[3].

Formerly, a vendor desirous of starting a contract race, faced a potential trap owing to the decision in *Daulia Ltd v Four Millbank Nominees Ltd*[4], where it

1   *Re White and Smith's Contract* [1896] 1 Ch 637 at 641, per Stirling J. The case was concerned with whether a purchaser of a lease had constructive notice of onerous covenants not referred to in the contract, but the principle is of general application.
2   (1977) 74 LS Gaz 834, republished in (1979) 76 LS Gaz 1177, drawing attention for the first time to its mandatory force. And see Guide to the Professional Conduct of Solicitors (1993), para 24.04. Licensed conveyancers are subject to similar obligations.
3   (1982) 79 LS Gaz 156 (J E Adams). Solicitors are divided on the issue; see the correspondence at (1980) 124 Sol Jo 51; (1980) 77 LS Gaz 36, 154; (1986) 83 LS Gaz 3210, 3389.
4   [1978] Ch 231, [1978] 2 All ER 557, CA.

was held that an offer or undertaking to exchange contracts with the first person to comply with the condition constituted a unilateral contract, the offer being irrevocable as soon as a potential purchaser started to comply with it. This meant that a vendor could bind himself to sell, without knowing that a binding contract would ensue and without being able to accept a higher price so long as his offer was open for acceptance. The unilateral contract was, however, caught by s 40(1) of the Law of Property Act 1925 and had, therefore, to be evidenced in writing. This requirement could be fulfilled by the vendor complying with the Law Society's directive to give written notification of the vendor's decision to institute a contract race. With the new requirement as to formalities introduced by s 2 of the Law of Property (Miscellaneous Provisions) Act 1989, it is difficult to envisage circumstances where a document will be produced which is sufficient to create a unilateral contract of the type held to exist in *Daulia*. The potential trap would, therefore, seem to have disappeared.

5. Acting for both parties

Prior to 1973 solicitors frequently acted for the vendor and the purchaser in the same conveyancing transaction, usually without apparent detriment to either side. But the comparatively few cases where a conflict of interest actually occurred, resulting in an allegation of professional negligence, usually ended up before the courts, and the judges were never slow to censure the practice[5]. The present position is governed by the Solicitors' Practice Rules 1987. Rule 6 prevents solicitors from acting for both vendor and purchaser or lessor and lessee in a sale or lease for value at arm's length. It also introduces[6] a prohibition against acting for lender and borrower in a private mortgage at arm's length. To this general rule there are several exceptions, the most important being where:
(i)   both parties are established clients, or associated companies;
(ii) in a transfer of land the consideration is less than £7,000;
(iii) there are no other solicitors in the vicinity whom the client can reasonably be expected to consult.

Two offices of the same firm may, subject to certain restrictions, act for the parties if the offices are in different localities. The lack of further explanation of expressions such as 'established clients' and 'vicinity' is intentional; according to The Law Society too precise a definition would merely facilitate circumvention. Each exception is subject to a vital overriding provision – *conflict of interest* must appear to exist. Immediately such conflict becomes evident, the solicitor should ask both clients in their own interests to seek

---

5   *Goody v Baring* [1956] 2 All ER 11 at 12–13, per Danckwerts J; *Smith v Mansi* [1962] 3 All ER 857 at 859–60, CA, per Danckwerts LJ; *Nash v Phillips* (1974) 232 EG 1219.
6   Following adverse comments in *Wills v Wood* (1984) 128 Sol Jo 222, CA. Basically a private mortgage is a loan from a non-institutional source: r 6(3)(b). Licensed conveyancers are not permitted to act for both parties unless it appears there is no conflict of interest between them and they have consented in writing; see para 20 of their Practice Rules 1987.

independent advice[7]. In *Nash v Phillips*[8] Foster J considered that a conflict arose where the vendor desired an early completion but the purchaser declined to sign the contract until his existing house had been sold. In a contract race a solicitor ought not to accept instructions to act for more than one prospective purchaser.

When a solicitor does act for both parties, it is common practice for him to prepare a single contract form which they both sign. In this event an exchange of contracts does not take place[9], as happens when the parties are separately represented. An exchange of parts is quite possible and frequently occurs where different branch offices of the same firm are acting for different parties.

Conflicts of interest can sometimes occur when, as is normal, the same solicitor acts for the purchaser and the mortgagee. Such a case will arise if the solicitor becomes aware of an unusual chain of sales which tends to indicate an inflated valuation of the property. If such facts come to light, the solicitor should request the purchaser's permission to communicate this to the mortgagee. If such permission is refused, the solicitor should decline to continue to act for the purchaser[10].

B   Parts of formal contract

A formal contract is in three parts: the particulars of sale, the general conditions of sale and the special conditions of sale. The proper function of the particulars is to describe the subject-matter of the contract; that of the conditions is to state the terms on which it is sold[11]. It is not clear to what extent the division into particulars and conditions is one of substance or mere traditional convenience. In an old case, it was held that a misrepresentation in the particulars could not be cured by information in the conditions of sale, which revealed the proper position[12]. More recently, in a case involving a clause precluding any annulment of the sale on account of any error in the *particulars*, Sargant J refused to construe the clause so narrowly as to exclude from its purview omissions appearing in that part of the contract headed 'Conditions of Sale'[13]. Following the recommendations of the Law Society[14], it is now standard practice today to incorporate, within the particulars, not merely a physical description of the property, but also suitable reference to the encumbrances affecting it, whether or not they are also mentioned in the particulars.

---

7 See also *Clark Boyce v Mouat* [1994] 1 AC 428, [1993] 4 All ER 268, PC, [1994] Conv 404 (R Tobin).
8 Supra, a case involving established clients. See also *The Professional Conduct of Solicitors*, para 24.01, outlining a solicitor's duty in cases of conflict.
9 *Smith v Mansi* [1962] 3 All ER 857, CA.
10 *Mortgage Express v Bowerman* [1996] 2 All ER 836, CA.
11 *Torrance v Bolton* (1872) LR 14 Eq 124 at 130 per Malins V-C, *arguendo*; affd 8 Ch App 118.
12 *Robins v Evans* (1863) 2 H & C 410.
13 *Re Courcier and Harrold's Contract* [1923] 1 Ch 565.
14 (1952) 49 LSG 29. But see *Blaiberg v Keeves* [1906] 2 Ch 175 at 184 per Warrington LJ.

The conditions of sale, themselves, may be either special, or general. The former are specially relevant to the contract in question; general conditions are very much common form, applying more or less to all contracts incorporating such terms. The Standard Conditions of Sale incorporate a number of Special Conditions relevant to most transactions, such as that the property is to be sold with vacant possession on completion. These are printed on the back page of each form and need to be completed by the draftsman. The names of the parties, the description of the property, the purchase price and the guarantee of title[15] are on the front page of the form, which must be filled in. The general conditions are contained on the inside two pages.

C   General conditions of sale

Before turning our attention to the Particulars of Sale, it will be helpful to say something at this stage about the nature and function of the General Conditions of Sale. An initial question is, why have them? The answer lies in an understanding of English land law, whose complexities are such that in any contract for the sale of land it is essential that the respective rights and duties of the parties are clearly defined. If the parties have not expressly provided for certain important matters, the law will imply terms regulating them. The term 'open contract' has already been mentioned. An enforceable contract can exist although the parties have done nothing more than state the price and identify the property in writing. This constitutes an open contract. Nevertheless, several fundamental questions remain unanswered. For what estate? What proof of title must the vendor adduce and for how long? When can the purchaser demand possession? These and other basic problems are resolved by the law through the medium of implied conditions. Every open contract is subject to a code of implied obligations, unless specific provision is made to the contrary.

These open contract conditions impose onerous terms upon the vendor, and over the years the practice has developed of incorporating within the contract express conditions, designed to facilitate the vendor's task and to cut down the purchaser's rights under an open contract. Such conditions have now become fairly stereotyped and sufficiently general in nature to be capable of being incorporated in a standard form. Every formal contract is made subject to General Conditions of Sale, but these apply only so far as they are not varied by or inconsistent with the Special Conditions[16].

General Conditions range over a variety of matters; there are provisions regulating the parties' rights of rescission, the charging of interest, the preparation and contents of the transfer deed, and the submission of requisitions. Particular clauses deal with problems raised by existing leasehold interests, undisclosed local land charges, the town planning legislation, etc. In reality, General Conditions are incorporated as an insurance measure. Some may be irrelevant to the contract which may be successfully completed without

---

15   Pages 161–174 post.
16   SCS Special Condition 1(a).

AGREEMENT
(Incorporating the Standard Conditions of Sale (Third Edition))

Agreement date   :

Seller   :

Buyer   :

Property
(freehold/leasehold)   :

Root of title/Title Number   :

Incumbrances on the Property :

Title Guarantee
(full/limited)   :

Completion date   :

Contract rate   :

Purchase price   :

Deposit   :

Amount payable for chattels :

Balance   :

The Seller will sell and the Buyer will buy the Property for the Purchase price.
The Agreement continues on the back page.

WARNING	Signed
This is a formal document, designed to create legal rights and legal obligations. Take advice before using it.	Seller/Buyer

recourse to the majority of them. Many a vendor and purchaser sign their contracts in blissful ignorance of their existence[17] – and it is perhaps as well! Nevertheless, they lurk backstage, ready to play their part should the need arise. Notwithstanding their generality, it is still incumbent upon a solicitor to consider whether the peculiar circumstances of his case are adequately covered by the General Conditions; if not, he should frame a suitable special condition. In particular, the form used is planned primarily for the sale of houses with vacant possession; consequently either form may require adaptation on the sale of building land, or agricultural, industrial or investment property.

As a means of simplifying conveyancing, the Second Report of the Conveyancing Committee suggested[18] the replacement of the, then, prevailing two sets of General Conditions by one set of conditions applicable to all contracts for the sale of land. This suggestion has been accepted by the profession and the Standard Conditions of Sale are currently in their third edition. In addition to this set of conditions, there is in existence a statutory code of conditions of sale[19], of very limited application, prescribed by the Lord Chancellor under the Law of Property Act 1925, s 46. It is confined to 'contracts by correspondence'. Owing to the enactment of s 2 of the Law of Property (Miscellaneous Provisions) Act 1989, however, it is very difficult to envisage a realistic scenario when such a contract may now be formed. Unless the parties choose to incorporate the statutory code, not something which is likely to occur in practice, the statutory conditions are likely to fall into total desuetude.

A fuller consideration of individual conditions will be postponed until discussion of the particular topic to which each relates. Though it should not be forgotten that basically most of the General Conditions are modifications or negations of some open contract term, it will be the aim of this book to concentrate upon the General Conditions as they appear in the usual forms of contract and, where appropriate, to consider by way of comparison the corresponding position under an open contract.

D   Particulars of sale

1.   Physical description

The particulars should describe the land to be sold with perfect accuracy and not leave it to inference[20]. Failure to observe this cardinal rule may entitle the purchaser to rescind the contract[1] or oblige the vendor to accept an abatement

---

17 'I cannot believe that purchasers of house property throughout the land would be overjoyed at having such lengthy explanation of the [NCS] ritually foisted on them': *Walker v Boyle* [1982] 1 All ER 634 at 640, per Dillon J.
18 Paras 6.27, 7.7, 9.36.
19 SR & O 1925, No 779. It regulates the date and place of completion, possession and apportionment of outgoings, delivery of the abstract and requisitions, preparation of the conveyance, and the vendor's right to rescind in certain cases.
20 *Swaisland v Dearsley* (1861) 29 Beav 430.
1 See *Mustafa v Baptist Union Corpn Ltd* (1983) 266 EG 812 (blocked-off room let to adjacent owner not excluded from particulars).

in the purchase price[2]. It is not uncommon for the vendor's solicitor to adopt the description of the property as it appears in the conveyance to the vendor, at least if he is selling the whole of such property. Yet he should always remember that it is not his duty simply to follow the exact terms of the description of the existing title; he ought to make full inquiry into the facts in order that he may be able to describe correctly the property[3]. The contract description should also be checked against the description in the earlier documents of title, as should the accuracy of all measurements and areas mentioned in the particulars.

(a) Plans

There seems a general reluctance to identify the property to be sold by reference to a professionally prepared plan. If a plan is to be attached to the contract, common sense dictates that it should be accurate, yet many plans are hastily prepared by junior members of the office staff, often using as a basis some out-of-date plan endorsed on an early title deed. It is advisable to have a plan wherever the vendor is selling off a portion of his land[4], particularly when the natural boundaries are not obvious. The absence of any plan increases the risk of the parties, or one of them, being mistaken as to the area of land within the contract. Similarly, on the division of a building into separate parts a large scale plan is essential, showing the rooms and dividing walls if necessary, in order to define the precise boundaries of the sub-divided lots[5]. Where the particulars describe the property by reference to a plan attached to some earlier conveyance of the property[6], a copy of the deed plan should be attached to the contract. It should be checked to ascertain that it accurately shows the property at the present time[7]. It is not unknown for adjacent landowners to alter their boundaries, and it ought always to be ascertained that the vendor has not entered into any boundary agreement with an adjoining owner. A plan stated to be for identification purposes only entitles the purchaser to a conveyance of all the land coloured on the plan[8].

The need for accuracy is highlighted by the interesting decision in *Jackson v Bishop*[9]. Estate developers selling plots by reference to a site plan were held to owe to their purchasers a duty of care in tort to ensure that the plan was

2 The nature of the purchaser's remedies are fully considered in Part V of this book.
3 Per Lord Kinnear in *Gordon-Cumming v Houldsworth* [1910] AC 537 at 547, HL.
4 *Lloyd v Stanbury* [1971] 2 All ER 267 at 273, per Brightman J.
5 Cf *Scarfe v Adams* [1981] 1 All ER 843, CA (map on a scale of 1:2500 attached to transfer of sub-divided part of house described as 'worse than useless').
6 Most suburban houses are described by reference to the plan on the first conveyance of the property as a separate entity.
7 See *Wallington v Townsend* [1939] Ch 588, [1939] 2 All ER 225, where the contract plan, though an exact copy of the plan on the conveyance to the vendor, included a strip of land on which stood part of the adjacent semi-detached property. It had been overlooked that the vendor had previously purchased the adjacent property and had made certain modifications resulting in an alteration of the boundary between the two properties.
8 *Re Lindsay and Forder's Contract* (1895) 72 LT 832.
9 (1979) 48 P & CR 57, CA (double conveyance). Liability on the covenants for title was also established, p 667, post. The surveyor who actually drew the plan owes a similar duty.

accurate and related to the existing features on the ground. There is no reason to limit this duty to house developers. It could well embrace a vendor who has a faulty plan prepared on a subdivision of his land. It may perhaps extend to a vendor who contracts to sell land by reference to an obsolete plan taken from an earlier deed without checking whether it indicates accurately the land which he is able to sell[10].

(b) Boundaries

The Standard Conditions of Sale[11] discharge the vendor from any obligation to define the ownership of boundary walls, fences and hedges, though it is usual for the purchaser to attempt to establish this before signing the contract by means of a preliminary inquiry. Where the property sold comprises land of different tenures or of different titles, the vendor does not have to identify the different parts[12] (except to the extent that he can do so from information in his possession). The basic rule appears to be the same even in the absence of such a condition[13].

(c) Conditions as to identity

The Standard Conditions of Sale also regulate a purchaser's entitlement to call for evidence of identity. The vendor has to establish identity as part of his obligation to show a good title. A comparison of the description of the land in the deeds with that in the contract must show that the property purchased is the same as or part of the property to which the deeds relate. If not, the vendor is unable to enforce the contract[14] without giving additional evidence of identity. In this event, General Condition 4.3 entitles the purchaser to require the vendor to make or obtain, or pay for and hand over a statutory declaration to support the evidence of identity. The form of the declaration is to be agreed with the purchaser, who must not unreasonably withhold his agreement. A statutory declaration may be necessary where the land sold forms part of a much larger estate, when it is not unusual to obtain a declaration from an estate agent who has collected, on behalf of the vendor, the rents and profits from the property to be sold for many years.

(d) Registered land

In a straightforward case registered land can be adequately described by adopting the description contained in the property register. A copy of the filed plan should be sent with the draft contract. The class of title (ie whether absolute, possessory, etc) can be either incorporated within the particulars or separately mentioned in the Special Conditions. The same need to have a

10 Ie a *Wallington v Townsend,* note 12, ante, situation.
11 See SCS 4.3.1(a)(b).
12 SCA 4.3.1(c).
13 *Dawson v Brinckman* (1850) 3 Mac & G 53.
14 *Flower v Hartopp* (1843) 6 Beav 476; *Re Bramwell's Contract* [1969] 1 WLR 1659; *Halsbury's Laws,* para 115.

plan exists as with unregistered land if the vendor is selling part only of his property.

2. Legal description

A description of the property cannot be considered adequate unless it states the tenure, and makes mention of the benefits and burdens affecting the property. When drafting the particulars it should always be remembered that, unless the contrary appears, the interest to be sold is to be taken as comprising the fee simple in possession free from incumbrances, and a purchaser is entitled to reject any lesser interest[15]. Where the property is not freehold or is freehold subject to incumbrances not to be discharged on or before completion, care must be taken to refer to such matters.

(a) Tenure

The vendor must not mislead the purchaser into thinking he will obtain something different from what the vendor is able to offer. The particulars should make it clear that the property is freehold or leasehold and in the case of the latter, whether the term was created by a head lease or underlease. The vendor does not show a good title to under leasehold property if the contract describes the property simply as leasehold[16]. The purchaser is entitled to know that he will be exposed to the risk of forfeiture through acts done by the under lessor. The purchaser cannot complain of the misdescription if he is aware of the true nature of the vendor's interest when he enters into the contract[17], and it ought to follow that an erroneous description should not be fatal if the contract as a whole contains adequate information to notify the purchaser that the property is held under an underlease[18]. Yet Clauson J held in *Re Russ and Brown's Contract*[19], that this does not suffice; the contract must distinctly specify that what is offered for sale is an underlease. It is submitted that this is too strict a rule. For instance, should the contract provide for the title to commence with a certain underlease, it is conceived that the court would hesitate to refuse to uphold the contract merely because the property was described in the particulars as leasehold rather than under leasehold. That a more liberal approach might prevail today is suggested by the later decision in *Becker v Partridge*[20], where it was doubted whether the description of a sub-underlease as an 'underlease' was a sufficient misdescription justifying rescission.

---

15 *Hone v Gakstatter* (1909) 53 Sol Jo 286; *Timmins v Moreland Street Property Co Ltd* [1958] Ch 110 at 118, [1957] 3 All ER 265 at 269, CA, per Jenkins LJ. But not if he had knowledge to the contrary at the time of making the contract: ibid.

16 *Re Russ and Brown's Contract* [1934] Ch 34, CA; *Re Beyfus and Master's Contract* (1888) 39 Ch D 110, CA.

17 *Flood v Pritchard* (1879) 40 LT 873.

18 See eg *Camberwell and South London Building Society v Holloway* (1879) 13 Ch D 754 at 761–62, per Jessel MR.

19 [1934] Ch 34, CA; *Re Beyfus and Master's Contract* (1888) 39 Ch D 110 at 115, CA, per Bowen LJ, doubting the view of Jessel MR, note 18, ante.

20 [1966] 2 QB 155, [1966] 2 All ER 266, CA.

Similarly, a purchaser of an underlease is entitled to be told that the head lease comprises more property than is being sold to him; there is the same risk of forfeiture arising from the acts or omissions of persons over whom he will have no control[1]. In *Becker v Partridge*, the court considered that a purchaser's objection to the lack of such notice cannot be maintained where the property sold is part of a house (eg a flat), since it is practically obvious that it will almost certainly be the subject of a letting of the whole house.

As to registered land, the exact nature of the registered title must be made known. To describe a possessory freehold title simply as 'registered freehold property' is positively misleading[2]. Likewise, it seems necessary to make it clear whether leasehold property is held under an absolute or good leasehold title.

(b) Benefits

Appurtenant easements or restrictive covenants existing for the benefit of the land sold should be mentioned in the particulars, though their omission is not fatal. The subsequent conveyance will pass all existing easements without express mention, and it is unlikely that a vendor would be unwilling to assign the benefit of restrictive covenants if his refusal to do so might result in his being unable to enforce the contract.

(c) Burdens

(i) *Duty to disclose.* The state of the vendor's title is a matter exclusively within his own knowledge, and the purchaser is generally in the dark. The vendor is, therefore, duty bound to disclose all latent defects in his *title*. In this context, the word 'defect' bears an extended meaning. He must disclose any flaw in the documentary title which might affect his ownership of the property and, therefore, his right to deal with it. Such matters are dealt with in the Special Conditions[3]. He must also disclose third party rights which prevent him from conveying free from incumbrances, ie all outstanding interests or burdens derogating from absolute ownership of the estate, irrespective of their date of creation[4]. In this sense a defect in title simply means an incumbrance[5] affecting the property. Within this category come the following: restrictive covenants,

---

1   *Creswell v Davidson* (1887) 56 LT 811; *Re Lloyds Bank Ltd and Lillington's Contract* [1912] 1 Ch 601. The same holds true of the assignment of part of the property demised by a head lease, though here the contract would provide for the rent to be apportioned, or indicate that it was subject to a rent apportioned by a previous assignment, thus notifying the purchaser of the existence of the other property.

2   *Re Brine and Davies' Contract* [1935] Ch 388.

3   See further, p 155, post.

4   Including any created before the commencement of the purchaser's investigation of title.

5   The word 'incumbrance' is commonly used nowadays to mean any adverse third party right or liability; see eg *MEPC Ltd v Christian-Edwards* [1981] AC 205 at 218, [1979] 3 All ER 752 at 756, HL, per Lord Russell speaking of a contract for sale as an incumbrance on the title. Sometimes it is employed in a narrow sense to connote a charge of a financial nature, as in LPA 1925, s 205(1)(vii).

easements, leases, local land charges, mortgages or charges, licences arising from estoppel or acquiescence. A defect is latent if it cannot be discovered by the exercise of reasonable care on an inspection of the property. With the exception of some easements (for instance, rights of way), none of the incumbrances listed are of such a nature as to be capable of being revealed on inspection. It is not thought that adverse rights of an occupier (eg a lessee) are to be treated as patent for this purpose. According to the better view, the doctrine of constructive notice has nothing to do with the rights and liabilities of vendors and purchasers between themselves[6].

The vendor's duty is occasionally expressed as a duty to disclose all material facts adversely affecting the price to be paid, such as an adverse planning decision rendering the property liable to compulsory acquisition[7]. This statement of the duty is, however, too wide. It conflicts with the basic rule of caveat emptor[8], which absolves a vendor of land from any general duty of disclosure, however material the matter may be, unless it constitutes a latent defect relating to title. In the earlier cases of *Carlish v Salt*[9] and *Beyfus v Lodge*[10], two decisions involving non-disclosure of material matters judicially described as directly affecting the value of the property, the defect concerned was plainly a latent defect in title.

No uniformity of practice exists as to the proper place in the contract for the disclosure of burdens; it ought to be a matter of no consequence[11], provided they are properly brought to the purchaser's attention. Express reference to an adverse right, though clearly preferable, is not vital. It is very common practice to use a blanket phrase such as 'subject to the covenants, conditions, restrictions and stipulations contained or referred to' in a certain deed[12]. Registered land is frequently sold 'subject to the entries on the register'. Such a generalised formula should be avoided. In many cases it will not reflect the parties' intentions; for as a matter of strict construction the phrase includes all the registered charges which the vendor is to redeem on completion[13]. When land is sold subject to, but with the benefit of a particular adverse right, this may be interpreted as an intention to confer new rights on the third party owner and operate on conveyance to create a constructive trust in his favour[14].

6   *Caballero v Henty* (1874) 9 Ch App 447 at 450, CA, per James LJ, not following *James v Lichfield* (1869) LR 9 Eq 51. See also the supporting dicta in *Rignall Developments Ltd v Halil* [1987] 3 All ER 170 at 178, per Millett J.
7   *Sakkas v Donford Ltd* (1982) 46 P & CR 290 at 302, per Lord Grantchester QC, relying on the judgment of Joyce J in *Carlish v Salt* [1906] 1 Ch 335.
8   Discussed in Ch 7.
9   [1906] 1 Ch 335 (statutory party wall notice and award resulting in liability to contribute towards repair costs); 42 *Halsbury's Laws*, para 56, note 3.
10   [1925] Ch 350 (landlord's notice to vendor to repair demised premises).
11   *Re Courcier and Harrold's Contract* [1923] 1 Ch 565. See further p 155, post. They should be listed in the space on the front page of the Standard Conditions of Sale.
12   See *Re Childe and Hodgson's Contract* (1905) 50 Sol Jo 59.
13   See *Faruqi v English Real Estates Ltd* [1979] 1 WLR 963 at 966, per Walton J.
14   *Lyus v Prowsa Developments Ltd* [1982] 2 All ER 953 (contract for sale), applying *Binions v Evans* [1972] Ch 359 at 368–69, [1972] 2 All ER 70 at 76, CA, per Lord Denning MR. See this problem considered in *Ashburn Anstalt v Arnold* [1989] Ch 1 at 25–26, [1988] 2 All ER 147 at 166–167, CA, per Fox LJ.

Failure by the vendor to discharge his obligation of disclosure may be a sufficient ground for the purchaser to terminate the contract and recover his deposit, or entitle him to seek a reduction in the price[15]. In the case of a fraudulent concealment the court may even set aside the conveyance after completion[16].

(ii) *Contractual circumventions.* This duty of disclosure imposes a heavy burden on the vendor, for it extends to defects of which he has no knowledge. It is not surprising, therefore, that in the past attempts have been made to relieve a vendor of the obligation by means of a condition to the effect that the property was sold subject to all rights and incumbrances, whether disclosed or not. The courts have not allowed such conditions to flourish. A vendor cannot put forward conditions of sale designed to force upon a purchaser latent defects in title of which he (the vendor) knows, but does not disclose in the contract. To permit reliance on such a clause would be 'nothing short of a direct encouragement to fraud'[17]. It simply affords protection to a vendor if it subsequently turns out that the property is subject to an adverse right of which he is unaware.

Under the Standard Conditions of Sale, the vendor contracts to sell free from incumbrances except for certain categories of incumbrance[18]. Incumbrances mentioned in the conditions are:

(a) those incumbrances mentioned in the agreement;
(b) those discoverable by inspection of the property before the contract;
(c) those the seller does not and could not know about;
(d) entries made before the date of the contract in any public register except those maintained by HM Land Registry or its Land Charges Department or by Companies House; and
(e) public requirements.

The condition further requires the vendor to inform the purchaser in writing, after the contract, of any new public requirements and of anything in writing which he learns about concerning any incumbrances subject to which the property is sold.

A number of comments can be made concerning this condition. Paragraph (b) exempts the vendor from disclosing incumbrances which could have been discovered by an inspection of the property before the contract. This raises the question of whether the vendor is thereby exempted from disclosing the rights of occupiers of the property. A purchaser, where title is unregistered, would certainly be held to have constructive notice of such rights, it being the case that reasonable inquiries would reveal such interests[19]. As this would mean that the vendor would be relieved from the obligation to disclose latent defects

---

15 See further as to the purchaser's remedies, pp 645–648, post.
16 See eg *Hart v Swaine* (1877) 7 Ch D 42, p 688, post.
17 *Nottingham Patent Brick and Tile Co v Butler* (1885) 15 QBD 261 at 271, per Wills J; affd (1886) 16 QBD 778, CA. See eg *Sakkas v Donford Ltd* (1982) 46 P & CR 290 (no reliance on NCS 15 (4)); *Rignall Developments Ltd v Halil* [1987] 3 All ER 170. Many of the recent cases where conditions have been declared ineffective have, significantly, involved auction sales.
18 SCS 3.1–3.4.
19 See *Kingsnorth Finance Ltd v Tizard* [1986] 2 All ER 54, [1986] 1 WLR 783.

in title, it is conceived that this paragraph should be limited to exonerating the vendor from disclosing only patent defects in title[20].

A second point concerns paragraph (c), which relieves the vendor from having to disclose incumbrances, the existence of which he neither knew about or could have known about. The potential difficulty here is the meaning to be given to the expression 'could have known about'. Under previous conditions of sale, the vendor was not required to disclose incumbrances which he did not know about[1]. The view was expressed that this meant matters of which the vendor was actually aware, rather than constructively aware[2]. Clearly, the obligation to disclose incumbrances of which the vendor could have known will extend to matters of which the vendor was constructively aware. More problematic is whether the incumbrances of which the vendor could have known about is limited by any test of reasonableness. The point can be illustrated by *William Sindall plc v Cambridgeshire County Council*[3].

A purchaser of land from the council discovered, after completion, the existence of a 9" foul pipe running underneath the land and sought rescission alleging misrepresentation, the alleged misrepresentation being a reply to a preliminary inquiry that, so far as the vendor was aware, the land was not subject to any rights not disclosed in the contract[4]. The action failed because there was no misrepresentation: the vendor was not aware of the existence of the foul pipe and could not reasonably have known about it, as the existence of the pipe was not noted against the title deeds and the relevant documents were held by the city planning department. Had the defect in title emerged before completion and the contract been governed by the Standard Conditions of Sale, arguably, the purchaser would have been entitled to rescind. The expression used is 'could have known about'; not 'should have known about'. On the facts, it was possible to have discovered the existence of the easement, albeit not by means of inquiries that a prudent conveyancer would make. Construed literally[5], therefore, under the new conditions the vendor should have disclosed this adverse right. While it is quite possible that the courts will construe the paragraph to limit the vendor's obligation to disclose matters which the vendor ought reasonably to have known about, this is not what the condition actually says. It would seem preferable to amend the clause to limit the vendor's duty of disclosure to matters which he either knew or ought reasonably to have known.

The Standard Conditions of Sale make no reference to incumbrances of which the purchaser was aware prior to entering into the contract. This is probably immaterial as, under the general law, a purchaser cannot object to

20 See p 154 ante.
  1 See NCS (20th edn) 14.
  2 *Celsteel Ltd v Alton House Holdings Ltd (No 2)* [1986] 1 All ER 598 at 607; affd [1987] 2 All ER 240, CA, without reference to this point. But see *Heywood v Mallalieu* (1883) 25 ChD 357, which was not cited (vendor's solicitor aware of rumoured existence of adverse easement but forbearing to make inquiries; vendor denied reliance on condition).
  3 [1994] 3 All ER 932, [1994] 1 WLR 1016.
  4 See pp 193–197, post.
  5 It should also be noted that, under the contra proferentem rule, clauses limiting the purchaser's right will be construed against the vendor: *Leominster Properties Ltd v Broadway Finance Ltd* (1981) 42 P & CR 372 at 387, per Slade J; Emmet, para 2.075.

an undisclosed incumbrance of which he knew when entering into the contract[6], unless the vendor contracts to convey a good title[7] (which is rare today). Registration of a land charge, not disclosed in the contract, does not count as knowledge for this purpose[8]. Nor does s 198 of the Law of Property Act 1925 exonerate a vendor of land, known to be subject to a registered local land charge, from disclosing its existence fully, despite a contractual term deeming the purchaser to have knowledge of it[9].

(d) Disclosure of particular burdens

(i) *Easements.*   Although the existence of a right of way may be patent, so that a purchaser who fails to inspect the property cannot complain of its non-disclosure in the contract[10], the courts are generally averse to holding that a right of way is patent. Inspection might reveal the existence of a track, but it may be impossible to tell whether it constitutes a public, or a private, right of way, or merely an accommodation track used by the owner of the land. It is not enough that there exists on the land an object of sense that might put the purchaser on inquiry; to be patent, the defect must be visible to the eye or arise by necessary implication from something so visible[11]. All rights of way should be disclosed, as should other easements, such as rights of drainage[12] or rights of light, but not an agreement preventing the acquisition of a right of light by prescription[13], nor, apparently, rights that may at some indefinite future time adversely affect the land[14].

(ii) *Leases.*   Existing tenancies should be revealed, for in the absence of any contrary stipulation, the purchaser is entitled to vacant possession on completion. The rent should be correctly stated[15] so that failure to disclose service of a certificate of disrepair resulting in an abatement of the rent may be fatal[16]. The receipt by the vendor of a notice to quit should be disclosed[17].

---

6   See note, p 152, ante. Aliter, if the defect is removable: *Rignall Developments Ltd v Halil,* supra, (repayable improvement grant).

7   *Cato v Thompson* (1882) 9 QBD 616, CA.

8   LPA 1925, s 24, p 208, post, which does not extend to registered *local* land charges.

9   *Rignall Developments v Halil,* supra.

10   *Bowles v Round* (1800) 5 Ves 508; *Ashburner v Sewell* [1891] 3 Ch 405 at 408, per Chitty J.

11   *Yandle & Sons v Sutton* [1922] 2 Ch 199.

12   *Re Belcham and Gawley's Contract* [1930] 1 Ch 56 (underground sewer vested in local authority).

13   *Greenhalgh v Brindley* [1901] 2 Ch 324; *Smith v Colbourne* [1914] 2 Ch 533, CA.

14   *Dorner v Solo Investments Pty Ltd* [1974] 1 NSWLR 428 (no duty to disclose possibility of gas pipe line being laid across land). See also *Aslan v Berkeley House Properties Ltd* (1990) 37 EG 81, CA.

15   *Wood v Kemp* (1858) 1 F & F 331; *Jones v Rimmer* (1880) 14 Ch D 588, CA (contract failed to mention rent of £43 17s 6d).

16   *Re Englefield Holdings Ltd and Sinclair's Contract* [1962] 3 All ER 503 (purchaser entitled to abatement in price). But see SCS 3.3.2(e) (no warranty as to amount of lawfully recoverable rent).

17   *Dimmock v Hallett* (1866) 2 Ch App 21. Cf *Davenport v Charsley* (1886) 54 LT 372 (informal intimation that tenant proposing to give up tenancy). See also *Aslan v Berkeley House Properties Ltd,* supra (break clause).

The Standard Conditions of Sale[18] require the vendor to make available to the purchaser copies or full particulars of the leases or tenancies affecting the property. The purchaser is deemed to have notice of and takes subject to the terms of all existing tenancies and the rights of the tenants, whether he inspects the documents or not. This condition does not enable a vendor to impose on the purchaser a lease different from any of those of which copies have been supplied[19].

(iii) *Exceptions and reservations.*   These are not necessarily incumbrances but must be revealed. If the vendor has no title to the mines and minerals under the surface because they have been excepted (ie retained) by a previous owner (as is not unusual), the contract should so state[20]. A vendor desiring to reserve some right over the property to be sold must expressly stipulate for it in the contract. Normally no easements will be implied in his favour, and it is too late to insist on a reservation once a contract making no provision for it has been concluded[1].

(iv) *Local land charges.*   These will be considered in the next chapter.

(v) *Overriding interests.*   There seems no reason why these should be treated any differently from third party rights affecting unregistered land. On a sale of registered land all latent overriding interests should be disclosed. Where a minor interest is protected by an entry on the vendor's register of title, he can discharge his duty by supplying the purchaser with a copy of the subsisting entries on the register[2].

(vi) *Restrictive covenants.*   The vendor must disclose every covenant affecting the property to any substantial extent[3], including those created prior to the proposed root of title[4]. The burden of showing that an adverse restriction does not substantially affect the land rests on the vendor[5].

(vii) *Sales of leasehold property.*   Some of the special problems raised by leaseholds have been mentioned[6]. In the absence of an express condition to the contrary, the vendor must disclose all unusual and onerous covenants contained in the lease, either by specifically referring to them in the contract or affording the

18   SCS 3.3.2(a).
19   *Pagebar Properties Ltd v Derby Investments Holdings Ltd* [1973] 1 All ER 65 (purchaser's discovery of undisclosed lease at time of completion). The obligation imposed on a vendor by SCS 3.3.2(c) to inform the purchaser of changes in the disclosed terms is to be taken as relating to existing leases; it does not affect the principle stated in the text.
20   See *Re Jackson and Haden's Contract* [1906] 1 Ch 412, CA.
1   *Simpson v Gilley* (1922) 92 LJ Ch 194. See also p 550, post.
2   But see *Faruqi v English Real Estates Ltd* [1979] 1 WLR 963, p 171, post.
3   *Phillips v Caldcleugh* (1868) LR 4 QB 159; *Hone v Gakstatter* (1909) 53 Sol Jo 286; *Re Stone and Saville's Contract* [1963] 1 All ER 353, CA (non-disclosure of covenant not to use land otherwise than as private house and garden rendered title 'thoroughly bad').
4   *Re Cox and Neve's Contract* [1891] 2 Ch 109. For roots of title, see pp 275–277, post.
5   *Re Ebsworth and Tidy's Contract* (1889) 42 Ch D 23 at 51, CA, per Fry LJ; *Re Higgins and Hitchman's Contract* (1882) 21 Ch D 95; *Re Stone and Saville's Contract*, supra.
6   Page 152, ante.

purchaser an opportunity of inspecting the lease[7]. The vendor's duty is generally eased by providing that the purchaser shall be deemed to have bought with full notice of the contents of the lease (or underlease), whether he inspects the document or not[8]. Such a clause does not override a positive misdescription in the particulars. In *Charles Hunt Ltd v Palmer*[9], leasehold shops described as 'valuable business premises' were subject to covenants restricting their use to a very limited class of business; it was held that the purchaser was not bound to complete though the contract incorporated a condition deeming him to have notice of the lease's contents. There may also be a condition precluding any objection by the purchaser that the covenants and conditions in an underlease do not correspond with those in the superior lease[10]. Under an open contract, non-disclosure of this fact amounts to 'a formidable objection' to the vendor's title[11]. Failure to disclose a rent review notice served by the lessor has been held to constitute a latent defect in title[12].

(viii) *Incumbrances not requiring disclosure.*   No duty exists to disclose latent defects in the physical quality of the land[13], such as a natural underground watercourse[14], or defects which are patent. It has been held that a notice served by a local authority and requiring the execution of private street works need not be disclosed; an inspection of the property would reveal that such a notice might be served at any time[15]. There is no obligation to disclose a latent incumbrance which will not remain binding on the purchaser after completion. Consequently the particulars should not refer to mortgages to be discharged on or before completion. Incumbrances that have ceased to be enforceable do not, strictly speaking, require disclosure, such as a restrictive covenant that has been openly breached for a long period of time[16]. In *MEPC Ltd v Christian-Edwards*[17], a vendor was held to have shown a good title to freehold land, despite not having disclosed the existence of a contract for sale affecting the land entered into some 60 years earlier. The court was satisfied that in the circumstances the contract had been abandoned and was no longer capable

---

7   *Reeve v Berridge* (1888) 20 QBD 523, CA. Whether a particular covenant can be classified as unusual is a question of fact, depending on, eg locality: *Flexman v Corbett* [1930] 1 Ch 672. For a recent discussion see *Chester v Buckingham Travel Ltd* [1981] 1 All ER 386 (covenants restricting user and alterations, and proviso for re-entry on breach of covenant (but not for bankruptcy) held usual at at 1971; covenant against assignment and underletting without consent (surprisingly) held unusual, following *Hampshire v Wickens* (1878) 7 Ch D 555).
8   SCS 8.1.2, in effect reversing the principle applied in *Reeve v Berridge*, supra.
9   [1931] 2 Ch 287. See also *Atlantic Estates plc v Ezekiel* [1991] 2 EGLR 202, CA.
10   NCS 11(4). SCS contains no such provision.
11   *Darlington v Hamilton* (1854) Kay 550.
12   *F and B Entertainment Ltd v Leisure Entertainment Ltd* (1976) 240 EG 455. The obligation to disclose such a notice was covered by LSC 3(2)(d). SCS contains no such provision.
13   Physical defects come within the caveat emptor rule; see pp 178–188, post.
14   *Shepherd v Croft* [1911] 1 Ch 521, yet failure to alert the purchaser to it may give rise to a misdescription, entitling him to compensation: ibid.
15   *Re Leyland and Taylor's Contract* [1900] 2 Ch 625, CA. Cf *Carlish v Salt* [1906] 1 Ch 335. And see *Spooner v Eustace* [1963] NZLR 913 (no duty to disclose that house encroaches over boundary of adjoining property).
16   *Hepworth v Pickles* [1900] 1 Ch 108.
17   [1981] AC 205, [1979] 3 All ER 752, HL.

of specific performance. However, in the case of any incumbrance of doubtful validity the vendor is best advised to regulate the position by a special condition in the contract, rather than not disclose it in the expectation that if the purchaser later raises an objection the court will uphold the title offered.

The same procedure should be adopted for an equitable interest governed by the old doctrine of notice, eg a pre-1926 restrictive covenant, or an estoppel interest, which the vendor claims is not binding on him because he purchased without notice. A purchaser will not be compelled to accept a title depending upon proof of the seller's lack of notice of an incumbrance. Whether the vendor acquired with or without notice is a question of fact and of evidence capable of being disputed and the courts will not compel the purchaser to buy a lawsuit[18]. On the other hand there is no need to disclose a third party right statutorily void against the vendor because of non-registration[19]. In this event he can pass a good title free from it.

(e) Planning matters

(i) *General position.*   It is uncertain to what extent planning matters affecting the property constitute latent defects in title which require disclosure by the vendor. For example, must he reveal that the existing use of the land is not authorised by the planning legislation, or that a building has been erected without permission? The few relevant authorities give no clear guidance on this issue. The basic principle of caveat emptor requires that in the absence of any express warranty the purchaser is responsible to satisfy himself that the premises are fit for the purpose for which he intends to use them, whether that fitness depends on the state of the structure or the state of the law[20]. A vendor would thus appear to be under no duty to disclose the permitted use of the land. This accords with the briefly reported decision in *Mitchell v Beacon Estates (Finsbury Park) Ltd*[1]. In *Gosling v Anderson*[2], Graham J expressed the view that the absence of planning permission was not in itself a matter of title nor was it apart from special circumstances a latent defect in title. More recently, however, in a ruling difficult to reconcile with general principle, Lord Grantchester QC held[3] that a vendor was obliged to disclose the existence of an adverse zoning decision by the planning authority because it was a material fact adversely affecting the value of the property.

Other remedies may be open to the purchaser. An inaccurate statement as to the permitted use of premises may amount to an actionable misrepresentation entitling him to rescind the contract, for example, if the

---

18   *Nottingham Patent Brick and Tile Co v Butler* (1886) 16 QBD 778 at 787, CA, per Lord Esher MR.
19   See LGA 1972, s 4 (5), (6). No dispute as to possible enforceability can arise, since this is determined by the statute. See further pp 397–401, post.
20   *Edler v Auerbach* [1950] 1 KB 359 at 374, [1949] 2 All ER 692 at 699, per Devlin J.
  1   (1949) 1 P & CR 32; cf *Sidney v Buddery* (1949) 1 P & CR 34.
  2   (1971) 220 EG 1117, adopting *Hill v Harris* [1965] 2 QB 601, [1965] 2 All ER 358, CA; revsd on other grounds not affecting this point (1972) 223 EG 1743, CA.
  3   *Sakkas v Donford Ltd* (1982) 46 P & CR 290 (zoning as public open space), p 54, ante.

property is described as offices whereas, in fact, there is only limited permission for this use[4], or where property has been described as a wine bar and the justices' licence has been revoked[5].

(ii) *Standard Conditions of Sale.*   It was previously the case that the National Conditions of Sale and the Law Society's Conditions of Sale differed quite appreciably as to what the vendor must disclose in respect of planning considerations[6]. The Standard Conditions of Sale are modelled on the latter set of conditions. The matter is dealt with under what is termed public requirements. This expression is defined by Condition 1.1.1(j) to mean any notice, order or proposal given or made (whether before or after the date of the contract) by a body acting on statutory authority. He is then required by Condition 3.1.2(e) to disclose all public requirements. He must then give the purchaser written details of any new public requirements and of anything in writing that he learns about concerning any incumbrances to which the property is sold. This obligation does not extend, therefore, to information communicated to him verbally from (eg) a council official or gleaned from a local newspaper. Condition 3.1.4 provides that the purchaser is to bear the cost of complying with any outstanding public requirement and to indemnify the vendor against any liability resulting from a public requirement.

A purchaser who is concerned about the planning aspects of his purchase is free to negotiate some special stipulation with the vendor. In practice, planning matters are usually investigated before exchange of contracts[7] by means of local searches and preliminary inquiries, which are considered in the next chapter.

E   Special conditions of sale

As each particular transaction differs so it is necessary for each contract to incorporate special terms appropriate to that transaction. Some special conditions are so basic as to be present in every contract. The incorporation of other special terms may be necessary because of the type or location of the property, the state of the vendor's title, or the nature of the bargain between the parties. It is the task of the vendor's solicitor when drafting the contract to consider carefully what special conditions are warranted by the transaction. In the following pages an attempt will be made to discuss some situations, selective only, when additional clauses are, or may be, desirable. Only a perusal of the various precedent books will reveal how numerous and varied special conditions can be.

---

4   *Laurence v Lexcourt Holdings Ltd* [1978] 2 All ER 810.
5   *Atlantic Estates plc v Ezekiel,* [1991] 2 EGLR 202, CA.
6   See the 3rd edition of this work, pp 154–155.
7   But see the rarely used NCS 3 and LSC 4 which enabled local searches to be made after exchange and give the purchaser a right of rescission if some adverse matter is revealed thereby. Cf the extended use of such clauses advocated in 2 Conveyancing Committee, para 2.20–21.

In the past, the standard forms contained a number of printed Special Conditions covering basic terms relevant to the majority of cases. These dealt with such matters as the date of completion, the capacity in which the vendor was selling the land, the commencement of the title, vacant possession, incumbrances affecting the property and the prescribed rate of interest for various purposes. The Standard Conditions of Sale now, with the exception of the Special Condition that the vendor will either sell the property with vacant possession or subject to a lease, as the case may be, deal with these matters on the front page of the contract and are incorporated by the Special Conditions. Any additional special conditions which the draftsman deems desirable are inserted below the printed ones.

1.   Completion date

The Standard Conditions of Sale provide for the insertion of the agreed completion date, although, in practice, it is not usually filled in until exchange of contracts. At the time the contract is first drafted the parties may have formed but a hazy idea of the completion date. In the absence of any date being expressly stated, the position is governed by the General Conditions, which is stated to be 20 working days from the date of the contract[8]. Where time is to be of the essence of the contract[9], a clause to this effect should be added.

2.   Guarantee of title

In the past, it was normal practice for the vendor to state in what capacity he was selling the property, for example, as beneficial owner. The significance of this statement was that it defined the extent of the covenants for title implied on his part by the subsequent conveyance by virtue of s 76 of the Law of Property Act 1925. The statutory covenants for title implied by the 1925 Act were, to say the least, highly convoluted in form and have been superseded by the varying guarantees of title introduced by the Law of Property (Miscellaneous Provisions) Act 1994. The front page of the Statutory Conditions of Sale includes a space for the vendor to state whether he is offering a full, or a limited, guarantee of title. The latter will be appropriate, for example, in cases where the vendor has only a possessory title to part of the land. The effect of the old covenants for title and the new guarantees of title will be considered in Chapter 23.

3.   Commencement of the title

The contract should contain a special condition stipulating the document which is to commence the purchaser's investigation of the title, thus: 'The

---

8   SCS 6.1.1.
9   See pp 423–424, post.

abstract of title shall begin with a conveyance on sale dated 16 January, 1963'[10]. This document is termed the root of title. Under an open contract a purchaser can insist on a root of title going back at least 11 years[11]. With a formal contract the vendor is free to reduce this period, though he runs the risk of the purchaser's refusal to contract on this basis[12]. When specifying the root of title, a vendor's solicitor ought to state the precise nature of the deed, eg a conveyance *on sale*. Simply to provide that 'the title shall commence with a conveyance dated ... ' infers that the document was a conveyance on sale, and that consequently the title was on that occasion investigated and approved. When a title for less than the statutory period is offered, the vendor's failure to disclose that the root of title is a voluntary conveyance makes the condition misleading. In this situation the court will not compel the purchaser to accept a title commencing with such a deed[13].

In the case of leasehold estates, the title usually commences with the lease itself and, omitting the intervening title, continues with an assignment or other document at least 15 years old. The investigation of title to leasehold land is governed by special statutory provisions. These and other problems relating to roots of title generally will be discussed in greater detail in Chapters 9 and 10.

Registered titles
The need to provide for a root of title does not arise in the case of land registered with an absolute or good leasehold title[14]. The purchaser is concerned only with the existing, not the past, state of the vendor's title. On the front page of the Standard Conditions of Sale, the vendor should insert the title number. He is then required to supply the documents specified in s 110 of the Land Registration Act 1925 (which defines the vendor's obligations as to title on a sale of registered land[15]). In the case of a possessory or qualified title, an investigation of the pre-registration title will be necessary, though the vendor is free to stipulate (and he normally does) that no evidence of such title will be adduced.

4. Vacant possession

(a) General position
The Standard Conditions of Sale contain a special condition that the property is sold with vacant possession on completion, or, as the case may be, subject to the specified leases or tenancies affecting the property[16]. The term for vacant

---

10 LSC Special Condition E; NCS Special Condition B (Title shall be deduced and shall commence as follows:—).
11 LPA 1969, s 23, reducing the period of 30 years prescribed by the LPA 1925, s 44(1).
12 For the consequences of accepting less than the statutory period, see pp 273, and 397, post.
13 See *Re Marsh and Earl Granville* (1883) 24 Ch D 11 especially at 23, CA, per Baggallay LJ.
14 In the case of registered leaseholds, only short particulars of the lease under which the land is held are given in the property register. The vendor should, therefore, make a copy or abstract of the lease available to the purchaser.
15 SCS 4.2.1.
16 SCS Special Condition 5.

possession is frequently encountered on a sale of residential property. Even in the absence of any express clause a term to this effect is implied in a contract disclosing no tenancies and silent as to vacant possession[17], but it will be displaced by the purchaser's pre-contract knowledge of subsisting tenancies[18]. The term, express or implied, imposes an obligation on the vendor to convey the land free from any claim of right to possession by a third party, such as a tenant[19], or a spouse who has registered a Class F charge. There is conflicting authority as to the position if the property is occupied by squatters. In *Cleadon Trust Ltd v Davis*[20], it was held that, where tenants had continued in possession of the property after the expiration of their lease, the vendor was in breach of his obligation to give vacant possession. On the other hand, in *Sheikh v O'Connor*[1], it was held that, when tenants had unlawfully taken occupation of a room in another part of the same building, the vendor had not failed to give vacant occupation of the room. In principle, it is submitted, the former position is correct and it should be for the vendor to take action to evict squatters. This would also be consistent with the position where, between contract and conveyance, squatters damage the property and the vendor is liable for that damage[2]. There may be a breach even though the property is unoccupied at the time of completion, as where notice of entry (not yet acted upon) has been served by an authority exercising compulsory acquisition powers[3]. It gives the purchaser not merely the right to possession in law, but the power to exercise that right in fact. So, he is entitled to enjoyment of the property free from physical impediments that substantially interfere with his occupation[4]. The courts are reluctant to allow an express term for vacant possession to be contradicted by the conditions of sale. In *Topfell Ltd v Galley Properties Ltd*[5], a house was sold with vacant possession. The contract provided that the purchaser bought subject to any notices whether registered or not and was deemed to have knowledge of matters disclosed by local searches. Unknown to him a statutory direction had been served on the vendor, which prevented occupation of the ground floor rooms. It was held that the vendor was bound to convey the property in a state in which the ground floor could be legally occupied and enjoyed, and he was not excused from doing so by the contractual

---

17 *Cook v Taylor* [1942] Ch 349 at 354, [1942] 2 All ER 85 at 87, per Simonds J.
18 *Timmins v Moreland Street Property Co Ltd* [1958] Ch 110 at 118–19, 132, [1957] 3 All ER 265 at 269, 277, CA, per Jenkins and Romer LJJ, though Pennycuick V-C, surprisingly, termed it a novel proposition in *Farrell v Green* (1974) 232 EG 587 at 589.
19 *Hissett v Reading Roofing Co Ltd* [1970] 1 All ER 122; *Sharneyford Supplies Ltd v Edge* [1987] Ch 305, [1987] 1 All ER 588, CA; *Appleton v Aspin* [1988] 1 All ER 904, [1988] 04 EG 123, CA.
20 [1940] Ch 940, 143 EG 611.
 1 [1987] 2 EGLR 269.
 2 *Davron Estates Ltd v Turnshire Ltd* (1982) 133 NLJ 937; pp 245–250, post.
 3 *Korogluyan v Matheou*(1975) 30 P & CR 309 (obiter); *James Macara Ltd v Barclay* [1945] KB 148, [1944] 2 All ER 589, CA (notice of requisition).
 4 *Cumberland Consolidated Holdings Ltd v Ireland* [1946] KB 264, [1946] 1 All ER 284, CA (rubbish left on premises), distgd in *Hynes v Vaughan* (1985) 50 P & CR 444 (accumulated rubbish piles becoming part of surrounding soil).
 5 [1979] 2 All ER 388 (purchaser entitled to specific performance with abatement in price). Contrast *Korogluyan v Matheou*, supra, where a similar condition was effective.

conditions. The term for vacant possession does not merge in the conveyance on completion[6].

The vendor's obligation is almost invariably[7] to give vacant possession on completion, ie the day when the transaction is completed. Under the Standard Conditions of Sale, it is implicit that vacant possession should be given by 2.00 pm. This is achieved by the contract stating that unless the money due on completion is received by that time, completion is to be treated as taking place on the next working day. This clause does not apply, however, unless vacant possession has been given by 2.00 pm[8]. If vacant possession is not given by this time, it would seem that the vendor is the person in default for the resultant delay[9].

(b) Matrimonial homes

By virtue of s 4 of the Matrimonial Homes Act 1983, a contract for the sale of a dwelling-house whereby the vendor agrees to give vacant possession on completion is subject to an implied term that he (or she) will before completion procure the cancellation of any registered Class F charge protecting a spouse's statutory right of occupation in relation to the property[10]. The vendor discharges this obligation by delivering to the purchaser or his solicitor[11] on completion an application by the spouse for its cancellation[12]. A purchaser's solicitor who accepts a cancellation form which is not effective to cancel the entry is in breach of duty and liable in damages to his client[13]. Section 4 does not apply if the contract expressly provides to the contrary, or it is one made by a vendor entitled to sell free from the charge, eg a prior mortgagee selling in exercise of his power of sale. The case of *Wroth v Tyler*[14] shows that this implied term operates notwithstanding that the charge is registered *after* the vendor has contracted to sell the house. A post-contract registration effects, therefore, a statutory variation of its terms, consequent upon the act of a person not a party to the contract, who is under no duty to inform the vendor about the registration. A vendor unable to procure the removal of a post-contract registered charge will be in breach of his duty to give vacant possession, and

---

6   *Hissett v Reading Roofing Co Ltd*, supra. For merger, see p 468–469, post.
7   Contrast *Desai v Harris* (1987) Independent, 16 February (possession three months after date of contract).
8   SCS 6.1.2, 6.1.3.
9   See SCS 7.3.1.
10 The Act applies to spouses only. The statutory rights exist in relation to any house that at some time has been the matrimonial home; cf *S v S* (1980) 10 Fam Law 153. A registration is effective even though the spouse is not actually living in the house: *Watts v Waller* [1973] QB 153, [1972] 3 All ER 257, CA. For further discussion of this Class F charge, see p 390, post.
11 Or licensed conveyancer: AJA 1985, s 34(2)(f).
12 Form K13 for unregistered land; Form 202 for protective notices affecting registered land, now the only permissible mode of protection: MHA 1983, s 2(9). See p 74, ante.
13 *Holmes v H Kennard & Son* (1984) 49 P & CR 202, CA (accepting form signed by solicitor without obtaining written evidence of his authority to sign).
14 [1974] Ch 30, [1973] 1 All ER 897. For consideration of some problems raised by this decision, see [1974] CLP 76 (D G Barnsley); (1974) 38 Conv (NS) 110 (D J Hayton); Law Com No 86, paras 2.74–2.90.

he may be liable to pay substantial damages to the disappointed purchaser[15]. The spouse's conduct may exceptionally operate to stop her from asserting her rights, eg by knowingly assisting while the vendor negotiates a sale with vacant possession[16].

When a charge has already been registered before exchange of contracts, it is clearly imprudent for a vendor to proceed without first ensuring the spouse's concurrence in the proposed sale by, eg obtaining a statutory release of the rights under s 6 of the Act or a signed application for cancellation of the entry. But the vendor will usually be unaware of the registration, especially in unregistered land transactions[17]. The existence of a registered Class F charge can be discovered by the simple expediency of requesting an official certificate of search. Such a step, however, represents an unwelcome departure from long established conveyancing procedures. It has not previously been considered necessary for a *vendor's* solicitor to effect a land charges search against his own client before the latter enters into a contract of sale. Nevertheless, it is conceived that a search ought to be made should the solicitor suspect matrimonial difficulties between the spouses, or where the purchaser's solicitor raises the issue in a pre-contract inquiry, as some are wont to do[18].

There seems to be little that a vendor can effectively do to guard against the consequences of a post-contract registration. It is not standard practice for a vendor's solicitor to seek to avoid the potential problems by obtaining a statutory release before exchange of contracts, or by joining the spouse in the contract to signify consent to the sale[19]. The reasons for this are obvious. A solicitor will experience difficulty in persuading spouses living happily in marital bliss of the need for a release; even its very suggestion may impair the solicitor-client relationship. The Standard Conditions of Sale contain a provision specifically regulating the parties' rights in the event of a post-contract registration.

The alarm engendered by the decision in *Wroth v Tyler* has largely evaporated. Practitioners are now much more conscious of the need to grapple with the implications of *Williams and Glyn's Bank Ltd v Boland*[20]. Unless they already know of the existence of matrimonial tension, solicitors prefer to ignore the problems raised by *Wroth v Tyler* when drafting the contract, hoping that the registration of a Class F charge will not become a live issue in the transaction. The number of these charges registered annually tends to belie the wisdom of this attitude, yet in most cases it proves well-founded in practice[1].

---

15 *Wroth v Tyler*, supra.
16 *Wroth v Tyler*, supra, at 47, 910, per Megarry J.
17 In the case of registered land, early warning will be received of any adverse entry recorded against the title before the vendor's solicitor requests office copy entries. This is one important reason for not simply photocopying the entries in the land or charge certificate, which may not be up to date.
18 See Emmet, para 11.028. If pre-contract searches became the general practice, the Land Charges Department would be unable to cope with the increase in the volume of business.
19 The purchaser's solicitor may request this in answer to a preliminary inquiry if he discovers that the spouse has an equitable interest by virtue of contribution. See p 191, post.
20 [1981] AC 487, [1980] 2 All ER 408, HL.
 1 During the year ending 31 March 1993, 2,400 were registered, which does not include the figures for registered land: HM Land Registry Report for 1992–93. Would a solicitor failing to warn his client of the possible dangers be guilty of professional negligence, if he suffered loss due to a Class F registration?

5. The deposit

The payment of a deposit on exchange of contracts is a matter regulated by the General Conditions[2] and will be considered in a later chapter.

6. Burdens

The Standard Conditions of Sale envisage that liabilities or burdens such as restrictive covenants or easements (whether subsisting or to be created) will find their way onto the front page of the form. Leases and tenancies are normally dealt with in a separate condition. It is essential to set out the precise terms of covenants and easements which the vendor proposes to create or reserve. Care must be taken to ensure that these will be enforceable and effective to protect his interests[3]. On the sale of a house on a building estate, it is usual to provide that the conveyance or transfer to the purchaser shall be in the form of the specimen document attached to the contract, and in this way the covenants, exceptions and reservations become incorporated within the contract.

7. Variations of General Conditions

The General Conditions apply only so far as they are not varied by or inconsistent with the Special Conditions. The rate of interest payable in certain circumstances is frequently raised above the rate specified in the General Conditions. The amount of the deposit may be varied by agreement. Should the purchaser desire to pay less than the required 10%, it is his solicitor's duty to ascertain beforehand that the vendor is willing to accept a smaller amount. Alas, some practitioners adopt the discourteous and unprofessional habit of sending with the purchaser's part of the contract a cheque for a smaller deposit with the request that the vendor accept it in lieu of a full deposit. For the vendor's solicitor to accept less than the prescribed 10% in such circumstances without his client's authority would amount, it seems, to professional negligence[4].

8. Fixtures and fittings

Fixtures[5] are regarded as part of the realty and so form part of the property to be sold. Subject to any contrary provision, once the contract has been signed

2 2.2.1 providing for payment of a 10% deposit; see pp 233–242, post.
3 Cf *Cordell v Second Clanfield Properties Ltd* [1969] 2 Ch 9, [1968] 3 All ER 746 (reservation of right of way over estate roads for access to vendor's retained land without imposing obligation on developer to construct road giving suitable access).
4 See *Morris v Duke-Cohan & Co* (1975) 119 Sol Jo 826.
5 As to the test for deciding whether an object is or is not a fixture, see *Holland v Hodgson* (1872) LR 7 CP 328 at 334, per Blackburn J; *Hamp v Bygrave* (1982) 266 EG 720, stressing the purpose of the annexation. See generally M & W, 730–34.

a vendor cannot remove, eg a valuable ornate door[6], or even fruit trees or rose bushes[7]. A purchaser is under no obligation to pay extra for the fixtures passing to him, unless the contract otherwise provides. Articles not constituting fixtures can therefore be taken by the vendor[8], or if the purchaser wishes to acquire them he can be asked to pay for them.

As part of the Conveyancing Protocol, the vendor is expected to complete a detailed questionnaire relating to the items in the house which are to be included, and those to be excluded, from the sale. The contract then provides for the list of chattels to be included in the sale to be set out on an attached list[9]. There is space on the front page of the contract for any separate price agreed in respect of chattels to be included. It is further provided that, irrespective of whether a separate price has been agreed for the chattels, the contract for their sale is to be a contract for the sale of goods and that ownership will pass on completion of the transaction[10].

In stating the price agreed to be paid for the chattels, the parties should resist the temptation deliberately to inflate their value, whilst reducing the price paid for the property, in a bid to save the purchaser the payment of stamp duty. This unlawful purpose may bar a claim for specific performance[11], and the practitioners knowingly involved in such a practice will be guilty of professional misconduct[12].

Where there is an indivisible contract, with a single price for the land and the chattels, writing which does not include the term relating to the chattels will not satisfy s 2 of the Law of Property (Miscellaneous Provisions) Act 1989, the result being that there will be no contract at all between the parties, unless the court is willing to rectify the document to include the missing term[13].

9.   Defects of title

The vendor's solicitor must not assume that his client's title is in apple-pie order unless perhaps he acted for the vendor when he acquired the property! There may be some defect which casts doubt on the vendor's ownership of the estate, or renders it uncertain whether he can convey free from certain incumbrances, such as a restrictive covenant believed to have become unenforceable by acquiescence. Or it may be that though the vendor has a good title, he may be unable to give proof of some matter on which it depends. Indeed, should the vendor be aware of a defect in his title, he must disclose it

6 *Phillips v Lamdin* [1949] 2 KB 33, [1949] 1 All ER 770; *Hamp v Bygrave*, supra (patio lights).
7 *Sinclair-Hill v Sothcott* (1973) 26 P & CR 490 at 494, per Graham J.
8 *Hynes v Vaughan* (1985) 50 P & CR 444 (growing frame and sprinkler system); *Deen v Andrews* (1986) 52 P & CR 17 (greenhouse; purchaser liable for conversion).
9 SCS Special Condition 4.
10 SCS 9.
11 *Glessing v Green* [1975] 2 All ER 696 at 702, CA, per Sir John Pennycuick. But not an action in tort for damages for the vendor' fraudulent misrepresentation, which is not based upon any unlawfulness of the contract: *Sauders v Edwards* [1987] 2 All ER 651, CA (purchase of a freehold flat).
12 *Sauders v Edwards*, supra at 618, per Kerr LJ.
13 *Wright v Robert Leonard Development Ltd* [1994] NPC 49, CA.

fully and frankly in the contract[14]. Subject to this, as Danckwerts LJ once observed[15]:

> I[t] here is no doubt that by a clearly drawn special condition which is put in the contract by a vendor who acts in good faith, and which discloses a possible defect in title, the purchaser may be compelled to accept the title ...

Naturally the courts scrutinise such conditions very closely. They must be clearly and unambiguously phrased; they must not mislead. Since they operate to curtail the purchaser's rights under an open contract, the contra proferentem rule will apply. In the nineteenth century case of *Williams v Wood*[16], a condition setting forth the defect in a way intelligible to a trained equity lawyer was rejected because it did not lead an ordinary purchaser to conclude that the title was defective. Perhaps a less stringent test would be adopted today when most ordinary purchasers instruct solicitors to act for them. Various attempts have been made in the past to cater for specific defects, and with varying measures of success.

(a) Assumptions

A purchaser may be required to assume the truth of something which the vendor is not in a position to establish by legal proof, such as satisfaction of a mortgage. Such a condition is valid, even though it is intended to cover a flaw which goes to the root of the title[17]. A vendor cannot require the purchaser to assume that which the vendor knows to be false[18]. Provided all the facts are fully disclosed, it is not necessary to explain in the condition the specific defect in the title which it is intended to cover[19]. On the other hand, a failure to state the legal effect of the assumption may make the condition misleading, as where the vendor frames the condition in such a way as to suggest he has a title to the property, though in fact he has none. The vendor cannot avail himself of the condition in such circumstances[20].

(b) Acceptance of vendor's title

A term, sometimes inserted in contracts for the assignment of leasehold property, that the vendor's title shall be accepted by the purchaser who shall raise no requisition or objection thereon does not absolve the vendor from

---

14 *Faruqi v English Real Estates Ltd* [1979] 1 WLR 963 at 967, per Walton J. This is an *equitable* duty in that though the vendor may not be in breach of contract at law (as was the position in the *Faruqi* case) the court will never decree specific performance if the defect is not disclosed.

15 *Becker v Partridge* [1966] 2 QB 155 at 171, [1966] 2 All ER 266 at 271, CA.

16 (1868) 16 WR 1005, applied by Walton J in the *Faruqi* case, supra.

17 *Re Sandbach and Edmondson's Contract* [1891] 1 Ch 99, CA; *Blaiberg v Keeves* [1906] 2 Ch 175 (purchaser to assume rent released); *Ashton v Sobelman* [1987] 1 All ER 755 (purchaser to assume registered lease forfeited by peaceable re-entry).

18 *Re Banister, Broad v Munton* (1879) 12 Ch D 131, CA; *Beyfus v Lodge* [1925] Ch 350.

19 *Smith v Watts* (1858) 4 Drew 338; *Re Sandbach and Edmondson's Contract*, supra.

20 *Re Cumming to Godbolt* (1884) 1 TLR 21; *Harnett v Baker* (1875) LR 20 Eq 50. See also *Rignall Developments Ltd v Halil* [1987] 3 All ER 170 (purchaser deemed to have knowledge of contents of local register ineffective).

his obligation to disclose defects of which he knows or ought to know[1]. Where the purchaser agrees to buy all the vendor's estate, right and interest (if any) in certain property, he cannot later complain that the title is bad[2], though he is entitled to the best title the vendor can produce[3]. Conditions requiring the purchaser to accept such title as the vendor has are sometimes encountered when the vendor has encroached on waste land adjoining his property.

(c) Restriction on right to inquire about earlier title
A condition which precludes the purchaser from inquiring about the title before a certain date may be effective to prevent his objecting to a defect in the title prior to that date. The effect of the condition depends in each case on its precise wording[4]. It is statutorily enacted that a purchaser shall make no requisition, objection or inquiry with respect to the title prior to the date fixed as the commencement of the title, and this provision takes effect as if it were an express stipulation in the contract[5]. A condition of this nature is subject to important limitations. A purchaser is not prevented from objecting to the title on the grounds of some undisclosed incumbrance, such as restrictive covenants, even though created before the root of title[6]. Furthermore, the courts will not award specific performance against the purchaser when its effect would be to compel him to pay his money for nothing because the title offered is so bad that he could be turned out of possession immediately. *Re Scott and Alvarez's Contract, Scott v Alvarez*[7] provides a good illustration of the application of this rule.

> Leasehold property was sold under a condition that the purchaser should not make any objection to the intermediate title between the granting of the lease and a certain assignment. The purchaser discovered *aliunde* that the intermediate title rested on a forged deed and a conveyance by a trustee purporting to convey as beneficial owner.

The Court of Appeal refused to decree specific performance against the purchaser, but held that the condition precluded him from recovering his deposit[8].

---

1   *Re Haedicke and Lipski's Contract* [1901] 2 Ch 666 (onerous covenants); *Becker v Partridge* [1966] 2 QB 155, [1966] 2 All ER 266, CA (breaches of covenant of which vendor's solicitors ought to have been aware).
2   *Hume v Pocock* (1866) 1 Ch App 379.
3   *Keyse v Hayden* (1853) 20 LTOS 244. Apart from any contrary provision, he must convey such right or interest free from an existing incumbrance (*Goold v Birmingham, Dudley and District Bank* (1888) 58 LT 560). Cf *Fowler v Willis* [1922] 2 Ch 514.
4   See *Smith v Robinson* (1879) 13 Ch D 148; *Waddell v Wolfe* (1874) LR 9 QB 515; *Re National Provincial Bank of England and Marsh* [1895] 1 Ch 190.
5   LPA 1925, s 45(1), (11), p 277, post.
6   *Phillips v Caldcleugh* (1868) LR 4 QB 159; *Nottingham Patent Brick and Tile Co v Butler* (1886) 16 QBD 778, CA.
7   [1895] 2 Ch 603, CA. Prior to this, the CA had held (see [1895] 1 Ch 596, CA) that it was not sufficient for the purchaser merely to show that the title was doubtful or open to suspicion. It was not until after judgment in the earlier proceedings that the purchaser discovered the forgery and was given leave to re-open the case.
8   Loss of the deposit is now subject to the discretion vested in the court under the LPA 1925, s 49(2); see p 621, post.

(d) Property sold subject to adverse rights whether disclosed or not
The effectiveness of this condition has been considered earlier in the chapter[9].

(e) Correct procedure
If there is a defect in the title, the wisest course is to set out in the condition all the relevant facts, remembering not to mislead the purchaser, and then to stipulate that the purchaser shall make no requisition or objection on account of the facts stated. A prudent purchaser will endeavour to probe the defect by asking preliminary inquiries. In the last resort the decision to buy must be his, and the more informative the special condition, the quicker the purchaser should be in making up his mind. From the vendor's position it is far better that the purchaser decides not to proceed before exchanging contracts than that he should rescind afterwards on the ground that the condition is misleading and does not preclude him from objecting to the defect.

The case of *Faruqi v English Real Estates Ltd*[10] is instructive on the disclosure of title defects. Registered land was sold at auction subject to the entries on the vendor's register of title. The purchaser's solicitor later called for production of a deed creating certain restrictive covenants referred to in the charges register, but the vendor was unable to comply. The court upheld the purchaser's contention that he had not deduced a good title[11]. Since he was aware of his inability to produce the vital document, it was his duty in equity to disclose the defect in a way that brought it to the purchaser's attention. Failure to do so precluded all reliance on a contractual clause deeming the purchaser to buy with full notice of the covenants. What the vendor should have done was to insert a special condition in the contract along the following lines[12]:

> The property is sold subject to the covenants and restrictions created by a deed dated ... The vendor is unable to discover the whereabouts of this deed or any copy thereof but the purchaser shall be deemed to purchase with full knowledge thereof and shall make no inquiry, objection or requisition with respect thereto.

10. Missing documents[13]

The mere fact that the vendor has lost or mislaid the title deeds does not release the purchaser from performance of the contract, but the vendor must furnish satisfactory secondary evidence of the contents and execution of the missing documents[14]. Strictly speaking there is no need to disclose in the contract the fact that they are missing[15]. It is in the vendor's interest to provide

9 See p 155, ante.
10 [1979] 1 WLR 963.
11 Return of the deposit was ordered under the LPA 1925, s 49(2), but not recovery of conveyancing costs as the vendor was not technically in breach at law. See further p 621, post.
12 This was basically the form of the clause inserted in the contract whereby the vendor had agreed to buy the property (see at 965), hence his knowledge of the defect.
13 (1949) 13 Conv (NS) 349 (E O Walford).
14 *Re Halifax Commercial Banking Co Ltd and Wood* (1898) 79 LT 536, CA.
15 *Re Stuart and Olivant and Seadon's Contract* [1896] 2 Ch 328 at 335, CA, per Kay LJ.

for missing documents by way of a special condition, setting out what secondary evidence will be provided. This may take the form of a counterpart, draft, copy, abstract, or a recital if coupled with long uninterrupted possession under the lost document[16]. Where all the deeds have been lost or destroyed, it will be necessary to obtain a statutory declaration explaining the loss and also the best secondary evidence available in the circumstances, such as an abstract of title compiled from draft documents prepared by solicitors who acted on previous transactions. It may well be advisable to obtain a declaration from the solicitor who acted for the vendor on the purchase of the property to the effect that a good and marketable title was deduced by the then vendor, that the documents of title were examined, the conveyance to the purchaser duly executed, stamped and completed, and the deeds handed to the purchaser or forwarded to the mortgagee (as the case may be). The loss of a single deed can be covered by a condition that the purchaser shall be satisfied with the production of a document purporting to be a copy of the missing deed and requiring him to assume the original was duly executed[17]. If a land or charge certificate has been lost, an application can be made for the issue of a new certificate[18].

It can be seen from the *Faruqi* case what is the proper procedure to adopt when there is with the deeds no copy of adverse restrictive covenants, or of exceptions and reservations affecting an area of land of which the property to be sold forms part (a not infrequent occurrence). Purchasers do not generally object to the usual condition precluding objection to the missing information, especially if the incumbrances have been created or reserved many years beforehand. They may not relate to the land (otherwise there would usually be a copy with the deeds) or even if they do, they are probably no longer subsisting, although legal proof is not forthcoming. Before accepting such a condition, a purchaser's solicitor should ascertain by means of a preliminary inquiry that no attempt has been made to enforce the incumbrances against the vendor.

11.   Sales-off

Special problems arise when a vendor sells part only of his land and retains adjoining property. To take a simple case, V owns a house in a large garden, part of which he proposes to sell to P. It has already been noted that as a general rule no rights will be implied in V's favour over P's adjacent plot. Apart from any express restriction, V cannot restrain P from building on his plot so as to interfere within the light to V's windows. If V decides to sell the house and retain part of the garden, the conveyance to P may operate to pass

---

16   *Moulton v Edmonds* (1859) 1 De G F & J 246.
17   Due execution of missing documents must be proved (*Bryant v Busk* (1827) 4 Russ 1), though due stamping will be presumed (*Hart v Hart* (1841) 1 Hare 1).
18   LRA 1925, s 67(2); LRR 1925, r 271. A statutory declaration explaining the loss and the efforts made to trace the certificate is required and a bond may also be necessary, indemnifying the Chief Land Registrar from any loss sustained by reason of the issue of a new certificate. See Practice Leaflet for Solicitors No 3.

to P easements under the rule in *Wheeldon v Burrows*[19] or under the Law of Property Act 1925, s 62[20] and these may seriously hamper V in his use of the retained land.

In the past there was some divergence between the National Conditions of Sale and the Law Society's Conditions of Sale as to how this matter was dealt with[1]. The former set of conditions was more vendor orientated than were the Law Society's Conditions. The Standard Conditions of Sale follow more closely the Law Society's Conditions with respect to this matter.

Standard Condition 3.4.2 provides that the purchaser will have no right to light or air over the retained land, but otherwise the vendor and the purchaser will have the rights over the land of the other which they would have had if they were two separate buyers to whom the seller had made simultaneous transfers of the property and the retained land[2]. In effect, this entitles V or P, depending on the circumstances, to claim such rights as would pass under the rule in *Wheeldon v Burrows*. The condition does not appear to negative s 62, so that P can claim any rights which would pass to him by virtue of that section. Condition 3.4.3 further provides that either party may require that the transfer contain appropriate express terms.

Despite the presence of this general condition[3], it is vital in every transaction involving a sale-off for each solicitor to decide whether the condition adequately safeguards his client's interests and, where necessary, to make suitable amendments. This point is underlined by reference to two recent decisions where consideration was given to general conditions dealing with this issue.

In *Lyme Valley Squash Club Ltd v Newcastle under Lyme Borough Council*[4], it was held, surprisingly, that P acquired an easement of light over V's retained land, notwithstanding a contractual term (not reflected in the conveyance) that he was not to be entitled to any easements. V's claim for rectification was dismissed. The learned judge felt able to go behind the small print of the contract (as he termed it). No one had given it a thought and it was contrary to the parties' presumed mutual intention. This ruling must be treated with considerable reserve. Rectification apart[5], it does not seem open to a court to disregard a term of the contract which regulates expressly the precise issue between the parties. Moreover, it is difficult to reconcile with the earlier Court

---

19   (1879) 12 Ch D 31, CA.
20   See p 551, post, as to the easements that may pass under s 62.
 1   See Wilkinson, *Standard Conditions of Sale of Land* (3rd edn) 26–30 comparing the two sets of conditions.
 2   Known as the rule in *Swansborough v Coventry* (1832) 2 Moo & S 362, whereby each grantee obtained the same easements over the other's land as he would if the grantor had retained it. This rule for simultaneous conveyances is introduced solely to give a vendor rights which he would not have acquired under the general law.
 3   Which practitioners are sometimes wont to overlook completely; see *Lyme Valley Squash Club Ltd v Newcastle under Lyme Borough Council* [1985] 2 All ER 405, considered post.
 4   Supra. Damages were awarded in lieu of an injunction. Rectification was also not available because of the intervention of third parties (mortgagees) without notice of the claim.
 5   Ie of the contract, no longer possible in this case since it had merged with the conveyance on completion.

of Appeal decision in *Squarey v Harris-Smith*[6]. Here it was reluctantly held that a term negativing any entitlement to easements was fatal to the purchaser's claim to a right of way under the doctrine of *Wheeldon v Burrows*. The *Lyme Valley* case highlights one important practical lesson. Practitioners should always ensure that the subsequent conveyance gives effect to the terms of the contract. Failure to take this elementary step may well oblige one of the parties to institute subsequent proceedings for rectification.

12.   Sales to existing tenants

Similar problems may occur when a vendor sells the freehold to his tenant. Prima facie any right or privilege, capable of existing as an easement, granted to him during the tenancy over the landlord's adjacent land may be enlarged by the conveyance into an easement by virtue of s 62. Apart from some special provision in the contract, it may be more difficult for a vendor-landlord to establish that no such right has passed, for it has to be assumed that the terms of the bargain are intended to be in accordance with the rights or privileges which the tenant has been able to enjoy in fact[7]. On the exercise by a tenant of an option to purchase, the resulting contract for sale will ordinarily constitute an open contract[8], unless the option agreement provides for it to be subject to one or other of the Standard Conditions of Sale.

Neither of these Conditions deals expressly with the effect of the contract on the tenancy. Prima facie the tenant's agreement to buy the demised premises does not operate to surrender the tenancy[9]. The terms of the contract may have this effect, such as a clause for payment of interest from the expiration of the notice exercising the option[10]. Where rent continues to be payable until the date of actual completion[11], the contract does not determine the tenancy. Consequently, the tenant's failure to complete does not allow the vendor to recover possession[12], should the tenancy be within the protection of the Rent Act 1977. This can be avoided by providing that the tenancy shall be surrendered on the making of the contract and thereafter the tenant shall remain in occupation as licensee. It may not be in the tenant's interests to agree to such a clause; a change in the character of his occupancy from statutory tenant to licensee results in loss of his statutory protection[13].

---

6 (1981) 42 P & CR 118, CA, a decision on LSC (1934 edn) 26 (similar to LSC (1973) 4(c), jettisoned from later editions because of criticism). Significantly, Lawton LJ regretted (at 130) that the decision turned on the inclusion in the contract of a condition which probably nobody had ever read.

7 *Goldberg v Edwards* [1950] Ch 247 at 257, CA, per Lord Evershed MR (privilege afforded tenant after taking possession but before execution of formal lease).

8 Rather than a contract by correspondence within the LPA 1925, s 46: *Stearn v Twitchell* [1985] 1 All ER 631.

9 *Doe d Gray v Stanion* (1836) 1 M & W 695.

10 *Cockwell v Romford Sanitary Steam Laundry Ltd* [1939] 4 All ER 370, CA; *Turner v Watts* (1928) 97 LJKB 403, CA (interest payable from date of contract).

11 See eg NCS 6(2).

12 Cf *Nightingale v Courtney* [1954] 1 QB 399, [1954] 1 All ER 362, CA.

13 *Turner v Watts* (1927) 97 LJKB 403, CA (statutory tenant).

A tenant may have a statutory right to acquire the freehold reversion under the Leasehold Reform Act 1967, aspects of which are considered in Chapter 8. The right to buy conferred on public sector tenants by the Housing Act 1985, is outside the scope of this book.

F   Conditions avoided by statute

Certain conditions are rendered void by statute. Apart from a few isolated provisions dealing with a miscellany of matters[14], these prohibited stipulations fall into two main categories: those relating to the legal estate and those designed to ensure that a purchaser is free to employ his own solicitor.

1.   Conditions relating to legal estate

The basis of post-1927 conveyancing is the legal estate. Equitable interests are to be kept off the legal title and overreached on a conveyance to a purchaser wherever possible. The Law of Property Act 1925 contains certain provisions designed to ensure that a vendor utilises this machinery.

Section 42(1) renders void a stipulation requiring a purchaser of a legal estate in land to accept a title made with the concurrence of a person entitled to an equitable interest, if a title can be made discharged from the interest without such concurrence, under a trust for sale or under any statute such as the Settled Land Act 1925, or the Law of Property Act 1925[15]. Thus a purchaser from a single trustee for sale cannot by contract be compelled to take a conveyance with the beneficiaries joining in to release their rights. The purchaser can insist upon the appointment of a second trustee[16]. Nevertheless, the subsection leaves a purchaser free to accept a title made with the concurrence of equitable owners, if he wishes[17].

As a corollary to s 42(1), it is provided that a purchaser shall not be required to pay or contribute towards the costs of obtaining any document necessary to bring into operation the appropriate overreaching machinery. A stipulation to the effect that the purchaser must bear the expense of tracing or getting in any outstanding legal estate, or preventing any objection being taken by him on account of an outstanding legal estate is similarly avoided. The enforcement by the purchaser of any right under the section does not entitle the vendor to rescind the contract[18].

---

14   Eg see Stamp Act 1891, s 117 (p 467, post); LPA 1925, s 125 (2), as amended by LP(Am)A 1926, Schedule (p 278, post) and LRA 1925, s 110 (p 335, post).
15   Equitable interests may be overreached on a conveyance of the land in any of the situations enumerated in LPA 1925, s 2(1), (2).
16   See LPA 1925, s 27, p 313, post.
17   See *Cole v Rose* [1978] 3 All ER 1121 at 1127, per Mervyn Davies QC.
18   LPA 1925, s 42(2), (3), (8).

Not all equitable interests are capable of being overreached, for some are protected by registration[19]. If the purchaser is entitled to the legal estate discharged from any equitable interest protected by registration, which will not be overreached by the conveyance to him[20], he can require, free of expense to himself, the registration to be cancelled or the equitable owner to concur in the conveyance. A stipulation to the contrary is void[1].

2.   Employment of own solicitor

Apart from some statutory prohibition, it might be an easy matter for the vendor to foist a bad title upon a purchaser by requiring him to employ the vendor's own solicitor. Section 48(1) of the Law of Property Act 1925 makes void any stipulation which restricts a purchaser in the selection of a solicitor[2] or requires the conveyance, or the registration of title, to be prepared or carried out at the purchaser's expense by the vendor's solicitor. It does not prevent the voluntary employment by the purchaser of the vendor's solicitor, but, as we have seen[3], the occasions when a solicitor can properly act for both parties have been severely curtailed. The section also expressly preserves the right for a vendor to furnish a specimen form of conveyance from which the purchaser can prepare a draft, and to charge a reasonable fee. This procedure is commonly adopted on the sale of houses on a building estate to ensure uniformity of conveyance. The Act does not alter the practice whereby, on the grant of a lease, the lease is prepared by the lessor's solicitor at the lessee's expense[4].

---

19   The enforceability of a few others is still determined by the doctrine of notice; p 391, post.
20   A limited owner's charge or general equitable charge may be overreached despite registration by means of an ad hoc trust for sale or settlement; see M & W, 408.
1   LPA 1925, s 43(1).
2   Or licensed conveyancer: AJA 1985, s 34(2)(c). Section 48(2) avoids leasehold covenants requiring assignments to be prepared by the lessor or his solicitor.
3   See p 145, ante.
4   LPA 1925, s 48(3). This must be read subject to the Costs of Leases Act 1958, which exempts a tenant from having to pay the landlord's costs, unless the parties otherwise agree in writing, thus abrogating the custom recognised by *Grissel v Robinson* (1836) 3 Bing NC 10.

Chapter 7

The purchaser's inquiries and searches

A   Introduction

In Chapter 6 we saw that the law imposes on the vendor a limited duty of disclosure only. Yet a purchaser's decision to proceed with the transaction may depend on information which the vendor is under no duty to disclose, such as the condition of the property, or of which he is not even aware. To protect himself the purchaser needs to have the property surveyed and to make searches and inquiries not only of local authorities but also of the vendor himself. This chapter considers the nature of, and need for, the following:

(i)   an independent survey of the property;
(ii) pre-contract (or preliminary) inquiries;
(iii) a search in the register of local land charges;
(iv) additional local authority inquiries;
(v)   various miscellaneous searches for particular transactions.

There may also be compelling reasons why a purchaser's solicitor ought to inspect the property, not to check its structural condition, but to view the physical features of the land[1]. These could have important legal implications. The existence of paths may be revealed, problems relating to access discovered, projections from adjoining properties spotted, and not the least is the necessity to check the accuracy of any contract plan. The existence of vacant land adjacent to the property should prompt inquiries as to the possible future development of that land, and the enjoyment of light over it[2], but without first viewing the property the practitioner cannot appreciate whether any need exists to raise these matters. An inspection may also disclose third party rights not mentioned in the contract, though a mere external observation is not

---

1   Cf The Law Society's Digest, Opinion No 127, stating that though it is the solicitor's duty to satisfy himself as to the identity of the property purchased, the method of doing so is a matter for his discretion and a personal inspection of the property is not, as a rule, necessary. But see note 3, below.
2   A contract for the sale of a house with windows overlooking land of a third person imports no warranty that the windows are entitled to the access of light over that land: *Greenhalgh v Brindley* [1901] 2 Ch 324 at 328, per Farwell J.

likely to reveal the existence of occupational rights of third parties[3]. It is not thought that many practitioners do view their client's properties, even where factors such as distance do not render this impossible. It therefore behoves a solicitor to ascertain as much as he can from his client about the layout of the property, its physical features and the occupation of persons other than the vendor.

B   The caveat emptor rule

1.   Scope of rule

(a) Physical and legal fitness

For many generations the law of this country has been that on a contract for the sale of land there is no warranty as to the habitability of the property erected on it. Defects of physical quality are regarded as patent defects which prima facie a vendor is not required to disclose. The responsibility for their discovery is placed by the law on the purchaser. The immunity operates to protect the vendor even in respect of latent structural defects of which he is aware[4]. However, he cannot shelter behind the rule if he negligently undertakes works of repair or conversion, which later cause damage to the purchaser[5]. The doctrine applied also to lettings, save that even the common law recognised the existence of an implied warranty of fitness for habitation when a furnished house was let[6].

The caveat emptor doctrine is not confined merely to the structural condition of buildings[7]. In particular, on a demise of property no condition on the lessor's part is implied that the premises are legally fit for the purpose contemplated by the parties[8]. Similarly, it appears to be the purchaser's duty to verify that the existing use of the land is authorised under the planning legislation. The vendor gives no warranty that it is[9]. A purchaser prevented

---

3   See now as to the importance of discovering these, especially on a purchase from a sole vendor, *Williams and Glyn's Bank Ltd v Boland* [1981] AC 487, [1980] 2 All ER 408, HL. See p 58, ante; pp 361–372, post.

4   Cf the Law Commission's recommendation in their Report No 40, paras 48–55, which was rejected by Parliament. But see (1942) 5 MLR 194 (G Williams), [1980] Conv 287 (E L Newsome); *McGrath v MacLean* (1979) 95 DLR (3d) 144 (recognising that a duty may exist).

5   *Hone v Benson* (1978) 248 EG 1013 (faulty construction of central heating system).

6   *Smith v Marrable* (1843) 11 M & W 5. No duty arose to keep it habitable: *Sarson v Roberts* [1895] 2 QB 395, CA. For a landlord's statutory obligations, see the Landlord and Tenant Act 1985, ss 8(1), 10–12. For the duty to ensure reasonable safety in certain circumstances, see the Defective Premises Act 1972, s 4.

7   *Cheater v Cater* [1918] 1 KB 247, CA; *Shirvell v Hackwood Estates Co Ltd* [1938] 2 KB 577, [1938] 2 All ER 1, CA. Contrast *Leakey v National Trust for Places of Historic Interest or Natural Beauty* [1980] QB 485, [1980] 1 All ER 17, CA (owner's duty to abate hazard on land).

8   *Hill v Harris* [1965] 2 QB 601, [1965] 2 All ER 358, CA (user permitted by sub-lease prohibited by head lease); *Stokes v Mixconcrete (Holdings) Ltd* (1978) 38 P & CR 488, CA (grant of right of way implies no warranty that right adequate for grantee's needs).

9   *Gosling v Anderson* (1971) 220 EG 1117; revsd on other grounds (1972) 223 EG 1743, CA; *Molton Builders Ltd v City of Westminster London Borough Council* (1975) 30 P & CR 182 (service of enforcement notice). Contrast *Watkin v Wilson* [1985] 1 NZLR 666 (sunroom not complying with building by-laws constituted latent defect in title entitling purchaser to damages); discussed [1986] Conv 297.

from using the property for the intended purpose may not necessarily be without redress. Legal unfitness stemming from an undisclosed restrictive covenant may result in a purchaser of freehold land rescinding the contract, or suing after completion for breach of the covenants for title. Alternatively, he may be entitled to rescind on the grounds of misdescription[10], or for misrepresentation, as in *Laurence v Lexcourt Holdings Ltd*[11] where premises were agreed to be let for 15 years as offices, but the lessor had forgotten the fact that permission for such use was available for only two years.

(b) Contractual clauses

The basic common law rule is given effect to in the Standard Conditions of Sale. Thus, the Conditions stipulate that the buyer accepts the property in the physical state it is in at the date of the contract unless the seller is building or converting it[12]. This term relates to the physical condition of the property at the date of the contract. It does not extend to a case where the property is unusable by reason of the presence on it of chattels which obstruct its user[13]. Nor can it be relied on when the vendor is guilty of fraud[14], or has negligently repaired or modified the property[15]. The operation of such clauses on a sale of leasehold property must be noted. When the lease contains a lessee's repairing covenant, a purchaser can call upon the vendor to repair the property in accordance with the covenant as part of his obligation to assign a good title[16]. Assuming the lease contains the usual forfeiture clause, any outstanding breach of covenant renders the interest defeasible at the lessor's option, and the court will not decree specific performance against the purchaser. The purchaser's rights are subject to any contrary contractual term. The Standard Conditions operate, therefore, to bar complaint of disrepair existing at the date of the contract[17].

(c) Liability in specific cases

Despite the absence of any general duty of disclosure, liability may arise in the circumstances of a particular case. The vendor's deliberate concealment of patent defects by words or conduct amounts to fraud[18]. The purchaser may void the contract should he have been deceived, or recover damages if with

---

10   *Re Puckett and Smith's Contract* [1902] 2 Ch 258, CA; cf *Shepherd v Croft* [1911] 1 Ch 521; *Re Belcham and Gawley's Contract* [1930] 1 Ch 56, discussed p 643, post.
11   [1978] 2 All ER 810. See also *Atlantic Estates plc v Ezekiel* [1991] 2 EGLR 202, CA.
12   SCS 3.2.1.
13   *Cumberland Consolidated Holdings Ltd v Ireland* [1946] KB 264, [1946] 1 All ER 284, CA (hardened cement sacks in cellar), distgd *Hynes v Vaughan* (1985) 50 P & CR 444 (rubbish forming part of surrounding soil).
14   *Gordon v Selico Co Ltd* [1986] 1 EGLR 71, CA.
15   *Hone v Benson* (1978) 248 EG 1013, note 5, ante.
16   *Barnett v Wheeler* (1841) 7 M & W 364; *Re Highett and Bird's Contract* [1903] 1 Ch 287, CA. The buyer's knowledge of lack of repair is immaterial. See further p 295, post.
17   Cf *Lockharts v Bernard Rosen & Co Ltd* [1922] 1 Ch 433; *Beyfus v Lodge* [1925] Ch 350; *Butler v Mountview Estates Ltd* [1951] 2 KB 563, [1951] 1 All ER 693.
18   *Ridge v Crawley* (1959) 173 EG 959, CA; (concealing cracks indicating settlement); *Gordon v Selico Co Ltd*, supra (dry rot covered up by lessor's agent).

knowledge of the deception he elects to complete the transaction. A vendor guilty of such fraud cannot maintain that the purchaser could have discovered the defect on a survey or on closer inspection of the property[19]. Fraud apart, inaccurate statements as to condition may be actionable under the Misrepresentation Act 1967.

Alternatively, a purchaser may be able to establish a collateral warranty as to fitness. The difficulty has always been to decide when a representation made during negotiations preparatory to a contract amounts to an actionable warranty. Completion of the transaction is no bar to the recovery of damages for its breach. *De Lassalle v Guildford*[20] is one case where the claim succeeded. A tenant declined to sign a lease unless the landlord assured him that the drains were sound. The assurance was given, but when they proved to be defective the landlord was obliged to pay damages. Changes made by the Misrepresentation Act 1967 will make it less necessary for a purchaser to seek to establish a collateral warranty. It is a debatable point whether the Act renders any distinction between them completely otiose.

An additional point which can be made is that it is possible, in limited circumstances, that an estate agent may be liable in tort in respect of representations made about the property. Such liability will be unusual because, in most cases, the purchaser will not rely on what the agent has said but will seek to verify the information for himself. Where the estate agent knows that this verification will not take place, and that the purchaser is relying upon him, the agent is potentially liable for negligence[1]. It can also be noted that an estate agent commits a criminal offence if he makes a false or misleading statement about a prescribed matter in the course of an estate agency business[2]. This potential criminal liability is subject to a defence of due diligence[3].

As a result of recent far-reaching judicial and statutory developments, the caveat emptor doctrine now exists in a somewhat emasculated form. The operation of the rule was extensively investigated by the Law Commission in the late 1960s[4], and, acting on some of their recommendations, Parliament passed the Defective Premises Act 1972, operative as from 1 January 1974. Contemporaneously with this legislative activity the courts were developing the common law rules relating to defective premises. The Act does not abrogate the duties enforceable at common law in relation to such premises, as s 6(2) makes abundantly clear. To these developments we must now turn.

---

19   *Gordon v Selico Co Ltd*, supra.
20   [1901] 2 KB 215, CA; see at 221 as to how a warranty may be established, per AL Smith MR. See also *Jameson v Kinmell Bay Land Co Ltd* (1931) 47 TLR 593, CA (road to be constructed); *Buchanan v Kenner* [1952] CPL 180 (assurance that dry rot eliminated). Sometimes the law implies a warranty.
 1   *McCullagh v Lane Fox & Partners Ltd* [1996] 1 EGLR 35, CA (no liability on the facts).
 2   Property Misdescriptions Act 1991, s 1. There are 33 prescribed matters: Property Misdescriptions (Specified Matters) Order 1992 (SI 1992, No 2834).
 3   Property Misdescriptions Act 1991, s 2.
 4   Law Com Report, No 40 (1970).

2. Liability of builder-vendor

(a) Contractual

The caveat emptor doctrine did not apply to the sale of a house in course of erection. For one reason the house was uncompleted, perhaps not even built, so the purchaser could have no opportunity to inspect it in its final state before deciding to buy. Prima facie, therefore, the common law implied a threefold warranty by the builder[5]: (i) to undertake the work in a good and workmanlike manner; (ii) to supply good and proper materials; and (iii) to ensure the house would be reasonably fit for human habitation. This warranty was displaced by an express term as to building[6]. Liability for breach of the warranty (implied or express) is contractual, and only the purchaser can sue for its breach.

(b) Statutory liability[7]

As from 1 January 1974, builders of new houses became subject to the statutory obligations created by the Defective Premises Act 1972. Subject to one far-ranging exception considered in paragraph (c), s 1(1) of the Act[8] imposes on a builder (and certain other people to be noted below) a statutory duty equivalent in terms to the implied warranty existing at common law, ie a duty to see that his building work is done in a workmanlike manner with proper materials so that when completed the dwelling will be fit for habitation[9]. The duty arises in relation to work done in connection with the *provision of a dwelling* whether it is provided by the erection, conversion, or enlargement of a building. It is questionable whether a mere extension to an existing house (eg by building an extra bedroom) falls within the Act, since there is no provision of a dwelling unless the result is to produce two or more separate dwellings where formerly there was only one. This statutory obligation cannot be excluded or restricted[10]. Where the dwelling is erected in accordance with plans and specifications supplied by or on behalf of the purchaser, the builder is, by virtue of s 2(2), to be regarded as having discharged his statutory obligations if he complies with his instructions in a workmanlike manner.

The duty created is of more than strictly contractual force. It is owed not merely to the original purchaser, but to every person who acquires an interest, legal or equitable, in the dwelling. Its breach is redressable, presumably, by an action for breach of statutory duty, and the damages recoverable will include all those foreseeably arising from it, including personal injuries and damage to the property. Persons outside the scope of the duty, such as visitors or

---

5 *Hancock v BW Brazier (Anerley) Ltd* [1966] 2 All ER 901, CA. But not if the house was finished at the date of the contract: *Hoskins v Woodham* [1938] 1 All ER 692.

6 *Lynch v Thorne* [1956] 1 All ER 744, CA; distgd *Basildon District Council v JE Lesser (Properties) Ltd* [1985] QB 839, [1985] 1 All ER 20 (implied term of fitness of buildings *designed* by builder).

7 See generally Holyoak and Allen, *Civil Liability for Defective Premises*, Ch 3.

8 Giving effect to recommendations of the Law Commission in Report No 40, paras 20–37.

9 See *Alexander v Mercouris* [1979] 3 All ER 305 at 308, CA, per Buckley LJ.

10 Section 6(3). No statutory duty arises in relation to industrial or commercial premises.

members of the purchaser's family[11], must seek redress at common law for damage sustained by the negligent construction of the dwelling. This option is also available to the owner, for the builder's statutory obligation exists in addition to any other duty owed by him[12].

Persons on whom duty is imposed.   The duty is imposed on any person 'taking on work for or in connection with the provision of a dwelling'. It includes not only the builder, but sub-contractors, architects and surveyors, suppliers of 'purpose built' components for installation in specific dwellings, developers and local authorities who in the course of a business or in exercise of statutory powers arrange for others to build dwellings on their behalf. It does not extend to manufacturers of general building materials or mass produced components whose obligations will continue to be governed by the law relating to the sale of goods and to negligence. The exact nature of the obligation will not be the same in every case. For example, a sub-contractor[13] who undertakes work on the terms that he adopts plans and specifications provided by the builder or main contractor will under s 1(2) discharge his duty if he executes the work in accordance therewith, but not if he substitutes sub-standard materials which cause the premises to be defective. Depending on the circumstances a purchaser could well have a cause of action against more than one person[14].

At one time, it was thought the Act was destined to have only limited effect. The first reason, which remains valid, is that it has no application to houses (by far the vast majority) covered by the NHBC scheme, discussed below. Secondly, at one time the law of tort had developed in such a way that s 1 of the Act was largely overlapped by liability at common law. These developments have, however, been reversed resulting in the statutory liability assuming greater potential importance than was previously the case.

(c) National House-Building Council's (NHBC) scheme [15]

The statutory remedy under s 1 is expressly excluded where the dwelling is sold with the benefit of the NHBC scheme, which has been approved[16] for the purposes of s 2. This scheme confers on new house-buyers rights (additional to any other rights conferred by the law) in respect of defects in the state of the building. The vast majority of builders participate in this scheme. The

---

11   Other than a spouse whose statutory rights of occupation under MHA 1983 rank as a charge on the estate as if it were an equitable interest: s 2(1).

12   Section 6(2). It may be more advantageous to pursue the common law remedy (as to which see p 184, post) because of the less favourable limitation period under the Act. See s 1(5) (time runs from *completion* of the building, not from the date of acquisition or the date of damage).

13   As to the sub-contractor's common law duty to a building owner, see *Junior Books Ltd v Veitchi Co Ltd* [1983] 1 AC 520, [1982] 3 All ER 201, HL (Sc).

14   There were compelling reasons for such an extensive duty: Report No 40, para 28.

15   See further, Tapping and Rolfe, *Guarantees for New Homes* (2nd edn): Holyoak and Allen, loc cit, paras 3.49–79. For an alternative scheme, called Foundation 15, see (1988) 132 SJ 1644.

16   House-Building Standards (Approved Scheme etc) Order 1979, SI 1979, No 381.

buyer of a house constructed by a non-registered builder will find difficulty in obtaining a mortgage from one of the usual sources. As between the Council and a registered developer, ie the vendor-builder[17], the latter is duty bound to use the standard form NHBC Agreement HB7 (1986). Failure to do so may result in disciplinary proceedings. Vis-à-vis the purchaser no such obligation exists. His adviser must ensure that the contract with the developer includes a term binding him to enter into the prescribed form. In the Agreement the developer assumes an obligation commensurate with the statutory duty imposed by s 1, ie to build in an efficient and workmanlike manner with proper materials so that the dwelling is fit for habitation (cl 2). He is required by cl 6 to make good at his own expense defects[18] arising from non-compliance with the Council's requirements and reported within two years (the 'initial guarantee period'). Thereafter the Council's insurance scheme[19] provides cover against major structural damage for a further period of eight years. Broadly this part of the scheme embraces such defects as subsidence, settlement, collapse or serious distortion of joists or roof structure. Non-structural defects are excluded, as is damage resulting from normal wear and tear. Claims must be made in writing as soon as reasonably practicable[20]. The Council's liability is confined to claims consequent upon the fault of the developer or his sub-contractor. When the developer is not the builder and the house is erected by a third party under contract with the developer, no redress is available from the Council for defective work carried out by a sub-contractor employed by the third party. Liability may arise at common law.

Persons protected. The benefits of the Agreement are intended to accrue to subsequent owners. The first purchaser purportedly contracts on behalf of himself, his successors in title and (curiously) mortgagees in possession. For his part, the developer undertakes (cl 10) not to deny liability on the basis of a lack of any assignment to a later purchaser. The legal effectiveness of these devices is suspect, though the Council is of the opinion that no express assignment is necessary[1]. There is also authority for the view that the benefit passes automatically by virtue of s 78 of the Law of Property Act 1925[2]. For the cautious practitioner an appropriate clause in the contract between the original purchaser (ie the seller) and his purchaser will be effective in equity to vest the benefit in the latter[3]. It is good conveyancing practice for the vendor's

---

17 The Agreement is entered into by 'the Developer' who sells the land to the purchaser, whether or not he is the actual builder.
18 Excluding defects from wear and tear, gradual deterioration by neglect, and normal shrinkage.
19 The developer warrants (cl 4) to secure this cover for the building.
20 Which can penalise a later purchaser if a predecessor has failed to claim. There is a complicated method of assessing the compensation payable.
1 They at one time provided a recommended form of assignment, but no longer. Membership rules forbid developers from taking the point on pain of disciplinary proceedings.
2 *Marchant v Caswell and Redgrave Ltd* (1976) 240 EG 127. Sed quaere; Holyoak and Allen, op cit, 3.65; (1980) 130 NLJ 171, 173 (J E Adams).
3 Written notice of assignment to both the registered developer and the Council would be required to effect a legal assignment of the benefit: LPA 1925, s 136.

solicitor to supply a copy of the Agreement with the draft contract, together with copies of other guarantee documents (eg relating to cavity wall insulation, or dry rot eradication). The purchaser can obtain information about matters arising under them, such as defects claims, through his preliminary inquiries.

(d) Tortious liability for defective building

(i) *Common law immunity abolished.*   The old common law rule rendered a vendor immune from liability for damage caused by a defect in property which he had negligently created[4]. Acting on a Law Commission recommendation, Parliament removed this immunity in s 3 of the Defective Premises Act 1972. Even before it became operative, the immunity from suit of builders had come under attack, the Court of Appeal having held[5] *obiter* that contrary to earlier rulings this immunity had not survived *Donoghue v Stevenson*[6]. This understanding of the legal position was endorsed unanimously by the House of Lords, again *obiter*, in *Anns v Merton London Borough Council*[7] and this remains the case, despite the overruling of *Anns* by the House of Lords in *Murphy v Brentwood District Council*[8]. What must be considered is the extent of a builder's liability.

In *Anns*, the House of Lords held that a local authority owed a duty of care to a purchaser of property in relation to the duties, powers and discretions arising under the Public Health Act 1936. This did not necessarily mean that the council had to examine the foundations in every case but a failure to do so could, in certain situations, constitute a breach of that duty of care. The cause of action would then accrue if damage to the property sustained as a result of the negligence became such that there was an imminent danger to the health and safety of persons occupying it.

The imposition of a duty of care on the local authority marked a considerable extension of the ambit of the tort of negligence and the reasoning process that led to it was of potentially wide application. Also of importance was the type of damage for which liability could ensue; the perennially difficult problem of liability for economic loss. Both of these issues were considered by a seven member House of Lords in *Murphy v Brentwood District Council* who, invoking the practice statement[9], decided not to follow *Anns*, which was considered to have been wrongly decided.

In considering the question of the potential liability of local authorities, the House rejected the approach taken in *Anns*, which adopted the 'two stage'

---

4   See *Bottomley v Bannister* [1932] 1 KB 458 at 468, CA, per Scrutton LJ.
5   *Dutton v Bognor Regis UDC* [1972] 1 QB 373, [1972] 1 All ER 462, CA.
6   [1932] AC 562, HL(Sc). *Otto v Bolton and Norris* [1936] 2 KB 46, [1936] 1 All ER 960 had confirmed the immunity, which was later restricted to builder-vendors: *Sharpe v ET Sweeting & Son Ltd* [1963] 2 All ER 455.
7   [1978] AC 728, [1977] 2 All ER 492, HL.
8   [1991] 1 AC 398, [1990] 2 All ER 908, HL. Also expressly overruled was *Dutton v Bognor Regis District Council*, supra. Cases which relied upon *Anns*, such as *Batty v Metropolitan Property Realisations Ltd* [1978] QB 554, [1978] 2 All ER 445, CA, were also overruled.
9   [1966] 3 All ER 77, [1966] 1 WLR 1234.

approach to determining whether a duty of care existed in any given situation. This approach was based largely on the question of foreseeability of harm; instead the House preferred to take an incrementalist approach to deciding whether a duty of care existed in novel situations. It was held that the local authority did not owe a duty of care to potential property owners to ensure that the building plans complied with the byelaws or were otherwise sound.

It was accepted that the builder did owe a duty of care to potential purchasers. The key question then became the extent of that duty. In *Anns*, it was held that the cause of action arose when the defect resulted in damage to the property which presented an imminent danger to health or safety. This, too, was rejected, the view being taken that such damage was, in reality, a species of pure economic loss which is not generally recoverable in an action for negligence. The potential liability of the builder[10] was held to be limited to cases of damage causing physical injury to persons or damage to other property.

The effect of the decision was subsequently summarised by Lord Keith in the following terms:

> It was the unanimous view that while the builder would be liable under the principle of *Donoghue v Stevenson* in the event of the defect, before it had been discovered, causing physical injury to persons or to property other than the building itself, there was no sound basis in principle for holding him liable for the pure economic loss suffered by a purchaser who discovered the defect, however such discovery might come about, and required him to expend money in order to make the building safe and suitable for its intended purpose[11].

The limiting of the liability of builders to cases of physical injury and damage to other property means that it will only be in rare cases that a builder will be liable to a subsequent purchaser. This is because defects which later cause damage resulting in personal injury are likely to be detectable on an inspection of the property, in which case, the builder will no longer be liable for the resulting injury.

A second point which can be made concerns limitation. It was previously the case that difficult issues arose as to when time started to run for the purposes of limitation, it being difficult to determine when the damage occurred and the cause of action accrued[12]. These problems now disappear as it will be obvious when the cause of action arises: it is either when a person is injured or neighbouring property is damaged. This means that the complex provisions of the Latent Damage Act 1986, which sought to deal with the problem of difficult to discover damage, now have a much more limited scope than was previously the case[13].

---

10   The question of whether a local authority might be held liable in case of personal injury was left open: see [1991] 1 AC 398 at 457 per Lord Mackay LC, 463 per Lord Keith; [1990] 2 All ER 908 at 912 and 917 respectively.
11   *Department of the Environment v Thomas Bates & Son Ltd* [1991] 1 AC 499 at 519, [1990] 2 All ER 943 at 946, HL.
12   See the 3rd edition of this work, pp 177–178.
13   Stanton, *The Modern Law of Tort*, p 355.

3.   Purchaser's independent survey

(a) The general position

In relation to the purchase of existing property, the Defective Premises Act 1972 made no change in the law governing a vendor's contractual position as to defects of quality. The Law Commission had considered that any alteration in the law would be undesirable, especially for house purchasers whose interests were best served by an independent survey[14]. Ideally a full structural survey should be obtained. In practice, the vast majority of purchasers with a building society mortgage[15] dispense with their own survey. They are content to rely instead on the 'survey' carried out by the society, on the basis that if there is anything seriously wrong with the house the society will either refuse a loan or require major defects to be remedied. Contrary to popular belief, this is not a survey at all. Though paid for by the borrower, the report is prepared solely for the society's benefit to enable it to assess the value of the property as a mortgage security[16]. A detailed inspection is not undertaken. Of recent years it has become. standard practice for societies to let the borrower have a copy of this report, which is normally accompanied by a clear warning that it is not, and should not be taken to be, a structural survey.

(b) Liability for negligent report

It is common knowledge amongst surveyors that house buyers frequently rely on the valuation report, especially now that a copy is forwarded to them. This raises the question whether the surveyor owes any duty of care to the borrower, as distinct from the society, in relation to his inspection of the property. This question was first raised in *Yianni v Edwin Evans* [17], where Park J held that there was such a duty and this approach has since been confirmed by the House of Lords[18] where a surveyor was held liable after failing to check that chimneys had adequate support, having noticed that the chimney breasts had been removed.

---

14   See Law Com Report, No 40, paras 17–19. From time to time suggestions are made that it should be the vendor's duty to commission a survey to be made available to prospective purchasers. Proponents of the scheme see it as a means of expediting the exchange of contracts. A provision to this effect was included in the House Buyers' Bill 1983. The proposal was considered and rejected by the Law Commission (Report No 65), paras 20–23) and the Farrand Committee (2 Report, paras 2.6–13, 9.39). The Royal Institution of Chartered Surveyors oppose the idea: ibid, para 2.10, and note the point about vendors possibly pressurising surveyors to produce a more favourable report. See also (1986) 280 EG 1068 (I V Oddy).

15   Perhaps as many as 85%–90%; see *Yianni v Edwin Evans & Sons* [1982] QB 438 at 445, [1981] 3 All ER 592 at 597. Instead of a full structural survey, a purchaser can obtain a semi-structural report and valuation, giving some detail of the property's condition and an opinion of its open market value.

16   As required by the Buildings Societies Act 1986, s 13.

17   Supra.

18   *Smith v Eric S Bush, Harris v Wyre District Council* [1990] 1 AC 831, [1989] 2 All ER 514, HL. An aggrieved borrower may also complain to the Building Society's Ombudsman under Building Societies Act 1986, s 83. See *Halifax Building Society v Edell* [1992] 3 All ER 389 (refusal to make further advances).

The extent of this duty is, however, qualified by the nature of the survey. A valuation report is not a full structural survey and so matters which would be discovered where a full survey is conducted may be missed by a valuation report, without liability arising. In inspecting the property for the purpose of making the report, the surveyor would not, ordinarily, be expected to perform tasks such as lifting carpets unless suspicions are created by other evidence of problems affecting the house[19]. Again, it should be remembered that the principal function of this type of survey is to ascertain that the house is adequate security for the amount to be borrowed. If the purchaser is making a significant contribution to the purchase price from his own resources, it will be increasingly advisable for him to commission a more detailed survey than the one carried out for inspection purposes.

(i) *Disclaimers.*   The willingness of societies to allow prospective borrowers to see the report has been accompanied, not unexpectedly, by attempts to protect them and their surveyors from liability. A mortgage applicant is required to acknowledge that it is supplied without any acceptance of liability on the surveyor's part. This disclaimer is then repeated in the report itself. The effectiveness of such disclaimers was considered by the House of Lords in *Smith v Eric S Bush*[20]. The case concerned a house at the lower end of the market where the purchaser had received a valuation report subject to a disclaimer of liability. The argument that the effect of the disclaimer was effective to prevent a duty of care arising at all was rejected, it being accepted that the surveyor knew that the purchaser was likely to rely on the report, which he had paid for, without commissioning a further survey. The question was then whether it was fair and reasonable to allow the surveyor to rely upon it[1]. It was held that it was not. This was an ordinary transaction and it was not considered to be fair and reasonable for the surveyor to be allowed to disclaim liability.

It was made clear, however, that it is not the case that all disclaimers of liability will necessarily fail to satisfy the test laid down in the Unfair Contract Terms Act 1977. Lord Griffiths reserved his opinion on whether disclaimers relating to commercial properties, larger blocks of flats and very expensive properties would be upheld[2]. Another factor which may be relevant in determining whether a disclaimer is fair and reasonable is the knowledge and experience of the purchaser. In *Stevenson v Nationwide Building Society*[3], the plaintiff was, himself, an estate agent and signed a disclaimer form in respect of a valuation report in respect of a somewhat unusual property. He fully understood the effect of the disclaimer and the different costs involved in the commissioning of different types of property inspection. The judge held that the society was not liable for the negligence of their employee in preparing

---

19   See *Roberts v Hampson & Co* [1989] 22 All ER 504, [1990] 1 WLR 94.
20   Supra.
1   Unfair Contract Terms Act 1977, ss 2(2) and 11(3). The onus is on the surveyor to uphold its reasonableness: s 11(5).
2   [1990] 1 AC 831 at 859, [1989] 2 All ER 514 at 532.
3   [1984] EGD 934.

the report; the disclaimer was considered to be fair and reasonable. This decision should be treated with a little caution, however, in that the judge seemed to take the view that such disclaimers were, as a general proposition, reasonable; an approach rejected in *Smith v Eric S Bush*. Nevertheless, on the facts, it may still be regarded as correct. In the usual type of conveyancing transaction, such disclaimers will be held to be ineffective.

(ii) *Damages.*   If the purchaser suffers loss resulting from a negligent survey, the measure of damages is the difference between the value of the property as described in the negligent report and the value of the property as it actually is[4]. In *Watts v Morrow*[5], the plaintiffs bought property for £177,500. Subsequently, major defects were found in the property, which had not been mentioned in the surveyor's report. The cost of the repairs was £33,961 and it was found that, as a result of the defects, the house was worth some £15,000 less than the plaintiffs had paid for it. The correct measure of damages was the latter figure[6]. The reason for what, at first sight, might appear to be a somewhat harsh rule is to prevent the plaintiff from obtaining a windfall as a result of the defendant's negligence. In the instant case, had the cost of repairs been awarded as damages, rather than the diminution in value, the plaintiffs would have had to pay £143,500 for a house which was found to be worth £162,500[7]. In addition to these damages, there may be a moderate award of damages in respect of the physical discomfort caused by the damage to the property. The cause of action accrues when the purchaser acts on the report and not when the damage occurs[8].

It may well be the case that, if the purchaser had known the true state of the property, he would not have completed the purchase at all, but would have withdrawn from the transaction. In such circumstances, when the damage is discovered, an effort may be made to sell the property. In this event, the purchaser would also be entitled to recover the transaction costs involved[9].

C   Pre-contract inquiries

1.   The National Conveyancing Protocol

To off-set the vendor's rather limited duty of disclosure, it was standard practice for the purchaser's solicitor, prior to his client signing the contract, to submit inquiries (termed preliminary or pre-contract inquiries) to his counterpart to elicit further information to assist the purchaser in deciding whether to proceed with the transaction. Many practitioners used a printed form of standard

---

4   For the position with respect to a claim by a lender in respect of a negligent report, see *Swingcastle Ltd v Alastair Gibson* [1991] 2 AC 223, [1991] 2 All ER 353, HL.
5   [1991] 4 All ER 937, [1991] 1 WLR 1421, CA.
6   See also *Philips v Ward* [1956] 1 All ER 874, CA; *Perry v Sidney Phillips & Son* [1982] 3 All ER 705, CA.
7   See [1991] 4 All ER 937 at 959, [1991] 1 WLR 421 at 1445, per Bingham LJ.
8   *Secretary of State for the Environment v Essex, Goodman & Suggitt* [1986] 2 All ER 69.
9   *Watts v Morrow*, supra.

inquiries, adding any further questions considered to be relevant to the particular transaction. Recent years witnessed a growth industry in the publication of these forms by different law stationers. Whilst covering the same ground, there existed some significant variations in detail between the forms. Some firms of solicitors compiled their own list of standard inquiries, whilst others adopted a set of questions advocated by their local law society.

(a) Problems of the system
Few aspects of modern conveyancing procedure have attracted as much trenchant criticism as the use of these inquiries. As long ago as 1970 it was alleged[10] that they had got completely out of hand. From that date, the position actually got worse. The indiscriminate use of preliminary inquiries as a sort of safeguard against a possible action for negligence is to be totally deprecated, yet a strong feeling exists that it was simply the task of a secretary to send out the form. Vendors' solicitors frequently complained of receiving a long list of inquiries, many of which are quite irrelevant[11]. There is no point, on a sale of a first floor flat on a housing estate, in asking about mooring rights, or whether the trees, garden sheds and ornaments are included. It may be cost effective for the purchaser's solicitor to submit his own long set of standard questions in unamended form[12], but it is the height of professional discourtesy, even arrogance, to expect the vendor's solicitor to do his work for him by deciding what is or is not relevant. Professional laziness should never be condoned. The vendor's solicitor was recommended not to answer these inquiries at all until the purchaser's solicitor submitted an amended form confined to relevant questions only[13].

(b) Conveyancing Standing Committee's response
In its review of the existing forms the Committee concluded that the questions ranged too widely. Mindful of the widespread concern at the abuse of the system, it recommended the use of a core number of basic inquiries only, in an attempt to meet the needs of efficient and cost-effective conveyancing. In compiling its list of suitable inquiries, which were confined to house purchases, the Committee adopted certain basic aims. Standard inquiries should not ask about matters which can be settled by the parties personally (eg transfer of the telephone number), or seek information more easily and reliably found elsewhere (eg planning inquiries). This latter point is to curtail unnecessary duplication. Nor should they be used as a substitute for inspecting the property. Furthermore, the Committee rightly urged that inquiries should seek

10 See (1970) 34 Conv (NS) 224, 226; and see (1961) 25 Conv (NS) 336 (I S Wickenden & S B Edell).
11 (1986) 130 Sol Jo 331 (sale of modern semi in Bath; standard form *plus* 74 extra questions received). See also letters at (1984) 81 LSG 781, 1583, 2820, 3470; vol 85, 3577; vol 86, 2128. And see 2 Conveyancing Committee, para 1.19; (1984) 128 Sol Jo 743 (T M Aldridge); ibid; 785, 817 (letters).
12 A practice defended, surprisingly, by Prof J E Adams at (1987) 137 NLJ 466, commenting lukewarmly at times on the Standing Committee's recommendations.
13 See the 3rd edition of this work, p 183.

information on questions of fact; those requiring the vendor to express an opinion are unsatisfactory, and generally unproductive[14].

The Seller's Property Information Form

The Law Society reacted positively to these recommendations and the result was the production of the National Conveyancing Protocol, now in its third edition. The Protocol envisages that the vendor will prepare an information package for use by the purchaser. Included in this package is the Seller's Property Information Form which should be sent to the purchaser, together with the draft contract and office copy entries or the epitome of title[15]. The Seller's Property Information Form is designed to replace the old system of preliminary inquiries.

The form itself is in two parts, the first part to be completed by the vendor and the second by his solicitor. In addition, there is a form to be completed which details the fixtures and fittings which are to be included in the sale. This is a comprehensive document detailing items likely to be found in any given room in a house querying whether, if present, they are to be included, or excluded from the sale.

(i) *Inquiries of the seller.*   In the introductory notes for the vendor to be read before completing the form, a number of salient pieces of advice are given. One, in effect, is, if the vendor is unaware of the answer to a particular question, he should say so. This is a likely response to question 1.3 which asks if he knows of any boundary changes during the last 20 years. Many vendors will not know the answer to this. Another is a reminder of the caveat emptor rule. The vendor is advised that the purchaser will take the property in the condition it is and that if he requires more information about it, he should get that information from his own advisers. In other words, if the purchaser raises additional inquiries about the condition of the property, the vendor is reminded that he need not answer them.

As to the questions themselves, those which the vendor is expected to answer relate to matters such as boundaries, disputes, notices, guarantees, services facilities, sharing arrangements with neighbours, restrictions, planning, fixtures, expenses attaching to the property[16], and a general final question asking if there is anything else the seller thinks that the buyer may have a right to know. A couple of these questions warrant further comment. As noted previously, the question concerning boundaries may not be answerable by the vendor as it may well relate to matters occurring before he became the owner of the property. The final question is clearly open-minded in scope and a vendor may well feel unable to answer it.

---

14   Eg please confirm that the central heating system is in good working order – which rarely evoked a clear reply (other than 'no'!) for fear of creating a warranty of soundness.
15   Protocol, para 4.3.
16   This relates to matters such as contribution to the clearing of a cess pool or septic tank and expressly excludes items such as water rates and community charge (now replaced by the council tax).

Question 7 usefully seeks details of rights or interests of an informal nature. Cases such as *Ward v Kirkland*[17] and *ER Ives Investment Ltd v High*[18] have highlighted the problem that can arise by the somewhat nebulous right, the equity arising by estoppel, or out of acquiescence. A preliminary inquiry of this kind may be the only inquiry that can reasonably be made to free the purchaser from the trammels of constructive notice, at least in relation to rights not apparent on inspection (eg underground drainage rights). Since rights of this nature frequently result from some informal neighbourly agreement, the chances of there being any record with the vendor's deeds are remote and, consequently, the contract will not normally disclose them. Question 8 attempts to deal with the *Boland* problem. It requests the names and ages (if under 18) of occupants and asks if they have any rights to stay on the property with the seller's permission[19]. In the light of the *Flegg* decision[20] it is not necessary to raise this inquiry when purchasing from legal co-owners. If on a sale by a sole legal owner, the inquiry brings to light the existence of an equitable interest, the purchaser will need to decide what steps he requires to be taken to ensure that the occupant will have no rights enforceable against him. So, he may call upon the vendor to appoint a second trustee, or obtain the occupant's concurrence in the sale by joining in the contract[1]. The question further inquires about the existence of any tenancies. If the existence of a tenancy is revealed and the tenant has security of tenure conferred by the Rent Act 1977 or the Housing Act 1988, an agreement by the tenant to give up possession on completion of the contract will not be sufficient for the statutory right to security to be lost[2].

Certain inquiries which used to be encountered in the past are now no long asked. At one time, the vendor was asked to supply information concerning matters such as details of structural or drainage defects, subsidence, woodworm dry or wet rot, or defective electrical wiring. Such questions do not appear in the new form. If these matters are raised as additional inquiries, then it is quite proper for the vendor not to reply beyond stating that these are matters for the purchaser's survey to determine.

(ii) *Inquiries of the seller's solicitor.* Part II of the Seller's Property Information Form is to be completed by the vendor's solicitor. A number of matters are raised. These are whether the information in the deeds corresponds to the vendor's reply concerning boundaries, relevant documents other than those disclosed by the vendor, whether all guarantees have been assigned to the seller, the enjoyment of services, any adverse interests affecting the property, any restrictions on the use of the property, the mechanics of sale and whether

---

17 [1967] Ch 194, [1966] 1 All ER 609.
18 [1967] 2 QB 379, [1967] 1 All ER 504, CA.
19 Inquiry of the vendor does not obviate the need for inquiry of the occupier. Reliance on the untrue ipse dixit of the vendor does not suffice: *Hodgson v Marks* [1971] Ch 892 at 932, [1971] 2 All ER 684 at 684, CA, per Russell LJ. See a letter at (1979) 123 Sol Jo 520.
1   But see pp 366–372.
2   *Appleton v Aspin* [1988] 1 All ER 904, [1988] 1 WLR 410, CA; *Woolwich Building Society v Dickman* [1996] 3 All ER 204, CA. See [1988] Conv 212 (S Bridge).

the whole or part of the deposit is to be used on a related transaction[3]. Many of these inquiries overlap with those asked of the vendor and, as the two parts are to be sent to the purchaser together, there should not be any discrepancies between the two parts. In any event, the solicitor should consult his client before answering such inquiries.

(iii) *Additional inquiries.*   Even on a sale of domestic property, it may be the case that additional inquiries are necessary. This was recognised by the Standing Committee, although it did not contemplate the addition to the standard forms of any which it considers should not be asked. The need to raise additional inquiries depends on the special circumstances of each individual transaction[4]. It may be necessary to elucidate or object to clauses in the draft contract. The purchaser's inspection of the property, or its situation or surrounding features, may call for special questions but these should not be asked until the contract and accompanying papers have been studied.

   In the past, standard inquiry forms used to be rather unhelpful when it came to sales of leasehold property. Under the National Conveyancing Protocol, there is now a Seller's Leasehold Information Form which, as is the case with the sale of a freehold property, is divided into parts to be completed by the seller and his solicitor respectively. This form is designed to be used for both commercial and residential properties with the result that not all the questions will be relevant to a particular transaction.

(d) Vendor's replies

The main problem with the previous regime with regard to preliminary inquiries was relevance. Coupled with this, there was no duty on the part of the vendor to reply to them. If, however, the parties adopt the National Protocol, this second problem is removed and, indeed, even prior to the introduction of the Protocol, it was standard conveyancing practice to answer them. Although it was standard practice to respond to preliminary inquiries, a familiar complaint related to the vague and unhelpful replies that are received[5]. Some practitioners seemed to adopt the philosophy that stereotyped questions deserved nothing better than stereotyped answers, in some occasions given without consulting their clients. This practice, which could not be condoned, should be obviated by use of the new form. The questions are written in an intelligible fashion and are expressly directed at the vendor who is expected to supply the answers and sign the form. Where the new form is not used and the vendor's solicitor is sent one of the old preliminary inquiries forms, he should consult with his client as to the answers and not anticipate what the likely response might be. It would also seem to be the case that he is under a duty to check the accuracy of information provided if it is at variance with his own knowledge[6].

3   See p 236–239, post.
4   For some esoteric inquiries prompted by various newspaper reports, see [1995] Conv 355 (H W Wilkinson).
5   See 2 Conveyancing Report, para 1.19.
6   *Computastaff Ltd v Ingledew Brown Bennison and Garrett* [1983] EGD 983 (failure to check rateable value).

(e) Effectiveness of inquiries
It is generally accepted, even by the most ardent critics, that relevant and properly worded inquiries have an important role to play in the conveyancing process. This is increasingly the case with the introduction of the new form of inquiries which have limited the inquiries to the directly relevant and so make it less likely that the procedure degenerates into little more than a meaningless and time-consuming charge. Old habits, particularly bad ones, die hard, and it is as yet unclear to what extent the new procedure has supplanted the old.

2. Purchaser's remedies for inaccurate replies

A purchaser who discovers the inaccuracy of a reply to pre-contract inquiries need only pursue legal remedies when its falsity comes to light after exchange of contracts. So long as they have not been exchanged, he can simply refuse to proceed or seek better terms. His primary remedy will be in respect of the misrepresentation contained in the replies. A purchaser will not normally be able to establish that they amount to collateral warranties sufficient to support an action for breach of contract. Whether or not the replies are intended to have contractual effect as a warranty depends on the parties' intention. This is a matter of inference to be gathered from all the relevant circumstances and, in practice, these will normally negate such an intention[7].

(a) Rights under the Misrepresentation Act 1967
Compared with his position prior to its enactment[8], and leaving aside the rare occurrence of fraud[9], the Act considerably enhances a purchaser's rights in relation to inaccurate preliminary inquiry replies. It is not intended to discuss the details of the statute, with which the reader will be familiar[10]. So far as is here relevant, its main provisions are in s 2(1), (2) and s 3 (as amended). In effect s 2(1) creates a new statutory right of action for damages[11] in respect of negligent misrepresentations inducing the contract, unless the representor (ie the vendor) or his agent[12] can establish reasonable grounds for believing the facts represented to be true[13]. A purely innocent representation (one not

7   See *Hamp v Bygrave* [1983] EGD 1000, applying *Mahon v Ainscough* [1952] 1 All ER 337, CA; *Gilchester Properties Ltd v Gomm* [1948] 1 All ER 493.
8   An innocent misrepresentation led to rescission of the contract in equity before, but not after, completion, and without any entitlement to damages unless it had become a contractual term.
9   For an example, see *Neighbour v Barker* [1992] 2 EGLR 149.
10 See further Allen, *Misrepresentation*; Treitel, *The Law of Contract*, Ch 9; (1967) 30 MLR 369 (P S Atiyah & G H Treitel); (1970) 67 LS Gaz 183, 256, 318 (J E Adams).
11 After early judicial uncertainty, authority now favours the tortious measure of damages: see *Cemp Properties (UK) Ltd v Dentsply Research and Development (Denton, Hall & Burgin, Third Party)* [1991] 2 EGLR 197; Ch 22, p 660, post, where various aspects relating to innocent and fraudulent misrepresentations are discussed.
12 Liability under s 2(1) attaches to the principal, not his agent: *Resolute Maritime Inc v Nippon Kaiji Kyokai, The Skopas* [1983] 2 All ER 1.
13 See *Laurence v Lexcourt Holdings Ltd* [1978] 2 All ER 810, p 179, ante; *Walker v Boyle* [1982] 1 All ER 634.

even made carelessly) may under s 2(2) be remedied at the court's discretion by an award of damages in lieu of rescission. Under sub-s (2), the court cannot order rescission and award damages, although the purchaser could claim an indemnity in respect of expenses necessarily incurred under the contract[14]. The Act does not affect the law relating to fraudulent misrepresentation.

Whilst enlarging the remedies available, the Act does not supersede the common law requirements that must be satisfied before an action can be maintained. the purchaser must still establish a representation of fact[15]. The Act does not cover mere puffs or representations of law. A statement of intention can, however, amount to an actionable representation. In *Goff v Gauthier*[16], a purchaser was able to rescind a contract for misrepresentation after having exchanged contracts expeditiously upon having been told by the vendor that, unless he did so, a contract of sale would be sent to another purchaser at a slightly higher price. This was untrue. The misrepresentation was that the statement of intention was genuine.

Quite often, the vendor's replies are purposefully couched in vague and inconclusive terms. In one case, where the answer was qualified by the phrase 'so far as the vendor knows', Romer J was not persuaded that it constituted a sufficiently definite statement to amount to a representation[17], although, today, it is quite likely that this doubt will not be shared[18]. More recently, it was held in *William Sindall plc v Cambridgeshire County Council*[19] that such a qualifying statement, itself, amounted to an implied representation that such inquiries have been made to determine the truth of the matter as would have been expected to have been made by a prudent conveyancer. It is clear that, despite a lawyer's caution in framing his client's replies, liability for misrepresentation may still arise.

As Bridge LJ observed in *Cremdean Properties Ltd v Nash*[20], the word 'representation' is an extremely wide term and he failed to see why a person should not be making a representation when stating his opinion or belief. To give the word when it appears in the Act a narrow or limited construction would be a retrograde step. Assuming there is a misrepresentation, the purchaser must establish that he acted on it when entering into the contract. It need only be one of several factors inducing the contract[1]. The point has already been made that a purchaser's solicitor ought to inform his client of all

---

14   *Whittington v Seale-Hayne* (1900) 82 LT 49.
15   On the question whether a vendor makes any representation as to title by entering into a contract for sale, see p 142, ante.
16   (1991) 62 P & CR 388.
17   *Gilchester Properties Ltd v Gomm* [1948] 1 All ER 493 at 495.
18   See *Gran Gelato Ltd v Richcliff (Group) Ltd* [1992] Ch 560, [1992] 1 All ER 865, where nothing was made of this point.
19   [1994] 3 All ER 932, [1994] 1 WLR 1016, CA.
20   (1977) 244 EG 547 at 551, CA; *Brown v Raphael* [1958] Ch 636, [1958] 2 All ER 79, CA; Adams, op cit, 319.
 1   For an extreme case, see *Gosling v Anderson* (1972) 223 EG 1743, CA (damages for misrepresentation that planning permission for garage granted, despite purchaser's awareness that position uncertain; effect of misrepresentation not nullified). For a case where there was no reliance, see *Swingler v Khosla* [1991] 1 EGLR 245.

replies which may affect his decision to buy[2]. Normally a contracting party cannot allege that he relied on a misrepresentation of which he was unaware. However there will usually be inferred or implied reliance sufficient to support an action, notwithstanding that his solicitor did not specifically disclose the information to him, at least where his advice to the purchaser to sign the contract was influenced by the representation.

(b) Excluding liability

The Misrepresentation Act 1967 forestalls any attempt to contract out of it. By virtue of s 3[3] a contractual term which excludes or restricts (a) any liability thereunder by reason of any misrepresentation, or (b) any remedy available to another contracting party by reason thereof, is of no effect save in so far as it satisfies the requirement of reasonableness laid down in s 11(1) of the Unfair Contract Terms Act 1977. This provides that the term must have been a fair and reasonable one to be included, having regard to the circumstances which were, or ought reasonably to have been, known to or in the parties' contemplation when the contract was made. The burden is thrown on those relying on the term to establish its reasonableness.

The courts have adopted a robust attitude to the application of s 3, which is particularly noticeable in the case of property sales by public auction[4]. Auction catalogues frequently contain a bewildering array of clauses in small print which seek to protect the vendor at the purchaser's expense. Nor are the courts willing to allow legal ingenuity, whether in drafting or argument, to frustrate the plain objective of the statute. In the *Cremdean* case the court declined to hold that the operation of s 3 had been nullified by a disclaimer the effect of which was, in law, as if no representation had ever been made because the accuracy of the replies was not guaranteed. Bridge LJ was prepared to go further[5]. A disclaimer that specifically denied to the vendor's statements the status of representations would be caught by s 3; for its intended and actual effect is simply to exclude liability.

(i) *Contractual clauses.* In the past, the National Conditions of Sale and the Law Society's Conditions of Sale both contained clauses which sought to limit liability for misrepresentation, both of which were caught by s 3. The National Conditions, cl 17(1) provided that no error in any preliminary answer should annul the sale, nor (unless it materially affected its description or value) should damages or compensation be payable. In *Walker v Boyle*[6], a purchaser bought a property affected by a boundary dispute, relying partly on the vendor's erroneous reply to a preliminary inquiry that there were no such disputes. In

---

2 A solicitor's knowledge will be imputed to his client. Consider *Strover v Harrington* [1988] 1 All ER 769 (solicitor notified of misrepresentation in sale particulars, but failed to inform purchaser; purchaser's claim for damages against vendor dismissed).
3 As substituted by the Unfair Contract Terms Act 1977, s 8.
4 See eg *South Western General Property Co Ltd v Marton* (1982) 263 EG 1090; *Sakkas v Donford Ltd* (1982) 46 P & CR 290. Cf *Swingler v Khuzla*, supra.
5 (1977) 244 EG 547 at 551, CA (alleged misrepresentation of lettable office space). Scarman LJ (at 551) found the simple logic of the main argument attractive, but not compelling.
6 [1982] 1 All ER 634; [1982] Conv 236 (K Hodkinson).

upholding the purchaser's claim to rescind the contract, Dillon J refused to give effect to condition 17(1), as it did not meet the requirement of reasonableness[7]. Neither the fact that both parties had experienced solicitors acting for them, nor the fact that it was a common term of ancient vintage in standard conditions of sale, operated to save it.

This decision led directly to a redrafting of the relevant condition. The matter is now dealt with in the following way in the Standard Conditions of Sale. Condition 7 states what remedies are available to a purchaser in the event of a misrepresentation having been made. If there is a material misrepresentation, the purchaser is entitled to damages. He is only entitled to rescind the contract if either the misrepresentation is made fraudulently or recklessly or he would be obliged, to his prejudice, to accept property differing substantially (in quantity, quality or tenure) from what the error had led him to expect. It is thought that this clause strikes a reasonable balance between the parties and is unlikely to be held not to satisfy the test of reasonableness.

(ii) *Other disclaimers.*   Although the Seller's Property Information Form makes no attempt to disclaim liability for misrepresentations but, instead, reminds the vendor that he may be liable in damages, or that the contract may be rescinded, in the event of any incorrect replies, it was not unknown for preliminary inquiries forms to seek to disclaim liability. One such disclaimer consisted of a warning that the replies were believed to be accurate (without their accuracy being guaranteed) but do not obviate the need to make appropriate searches, inquiries and inspections. Section 3 does not catch a disclaimer of liability contained in replies to inquiries; it is not a term contained in a contract. Nevertheless, not being contractual in origin, it cannot bind a purchaser[8]. Moreover, it does not, of itself, prevent the answers from being representations of fact[9]. At the most, it might assist the vendor in showing that the purchaser relied, not on the misrepresentation, but on his own investigations[10].

Printed warnings also attempted to exonerate the vendor's solicitor from any responsibility when giving the replies on his client's behalf. This extended disclaimer was introduced as a response to the decision in *Wilson v Bloomfield*[11]. Since then, it was decided in *Gran Gelato Ltd v Richcliff (Group) Ltd*[12], that the vendor's solicitor does not normally owe a duty of care to a purchaser, so such clauses are now redundant. If however, the misrepresentation is caused by the negligence of the vendor's solicitor, his client will be liable to the purchaser and the solicitor will, in turn be liable to his client.

---

7   But without really explaining why.
8   *Cremdean Properties Ltd v Nash* (1977) 244 EG 547 at 557 at 551, CA, per Bridge LJ.
9   *Walker v Boyle* [1982] 1 All ER 634 at 640, per Dillon J. See also *Cooper v Tamms* [1988] 1 EGLR 257.
10   *Cremdean Properties Ltd v Nash*, supra, at 549, per Bridge LJ.
11   (1979) 123 Sol Jo 860, CA (inaccurate reply about boundary dispute). The court refused to strike out the purchaser's claim against the vendor's solicitor.
12   [1992] Ch 560, [1992] 1 All ER 865. See also *Al-Kandari v JR Brown & Co (a firm)* [1988] QB 665, [1988] 1 All ER 833, CA.

(iii) *Denying agent's authority to make representations.* One limited loophole has been recognised by the courts as legitimate. Section 3 does not qualify the right of a principal (the vendor) to limit the otherwise ostensible authority of his agent (eg auctioneer, or estate agent) to make representations in relation to the property[13]. It makes no difference that the limitation is in a contractual document[14]. The agent may not be exposed to liability under s 2(1) of the Misrepresentation Act 1967, but he is clearly subject to the ordinary tortious liability in fraud and negligence[15]. Even where there is a denial of authority to make representations, this will not be effective if the agent makes a particular statement at the request of the vendor[16].

(c) Vendor's tortious liability
A question which has arisen is whether the relationship between a prospective vendor and purchaser is such as to create a duty of care on the vendor's part when making statements in the course of pre-contractual negotiations. Recent authorities have proceeded on the basis that there is tortious liability[17]. In any action based upon a breach of a duty of care, the vendor will not be able to take advantage of a contractual exclusion clause such as that discussed on page 196. However, in most cases involving negligent misrepresentations, a purchaser should be able to obtain ample redress under s 2 of the Misrepresentation Act 1967 without having to rely on the vendor's tortious liability under the *Hedley Byrne* principle[18] and it is not easy to see the advantage to a purchaser of pursuing both courses of action.

D   Local land charges[19]

1.   Need for search

A search should be made in the register of local land charges maintained by the appropriate local authority. The search is made with the registering

---

13   *Overbrooke Estates Ltd v Glencombe Properties Ltd* [1974] 3 All ER 511, approved by Bridge LJ in the *Cremdean* case, supra, at 549. See also *Moore v Khan-Ghauri* [1991] 2 EGLR 9, CA.
14   *Collins v Howell-Jones* (1980) 259 EG 331, CA. A common form of disclaimer printed in estate agents' sale particulars states that 'the vendor does not make or give and neither [the agents] nor any person in their employment has any authority to make or give any representation or warranty in relation to this property'.
15   *McCullah v Lane Fox Partners* [1996] 1 EGLR 35, CA.
16   *Museprime Properties Ltd v Adhill Properties Ltd* [1990] 2 EGLR 196.
17   *Cooper v Tamms,* supra at p 262, per Mr P S Crawford QC; *Gran Gelato v Richcliff (Group) Ltd* [1992] Ch 560 at 569, [1992] 1 All ER 865 at 871, per Sir Donald Nicholls V-C, who considered that the contrary could not be seriously argued.
18   *Hedley Byrne & Co Ltd v Heller & Partners Ltd* [1964] AC 465, [1963] 2 All ER 575, HL.
19   See generally Garner, *Local Land Charges* (8th edn). The system was altered radically in consequence of the Law Commission Report on Local Land Charges (Law Com No 62, 1974). This led to the enactment of the LLCA 1975, which became operative on 1 August 1977. See (1976) 40 Conv (NS) 106 (J E Adams), discussing the Act.

authority (District Councils, London Boroughs and the Common Council of the City of London). These authorities have a duty to keep the local land charges register[20].

The purpose of this search is to discover registered matters which do not require disclosure by a vendor because they do not constitute incumbrances. Merely because something is termed a local land charge, it does not automatically follow that it ranks as an incumbrance within the vendor's limited duty of disclosure. Some by their very nature do, such as a financial charge in respect of street works expenses[1], some do not, such as a resolution to prepare a town planning scheme[2], whilst the status of others is uncertain. It is equally essential to make a search where the title to the land is registered. Under the Land Registration Act 1925, s 70(1)(i), a local land charge ranks as an overriding interest unless and until registered or protected on the register. It may at any time be protected on the register by means of a notice, though this is unusual, and must, if it constitutes a financial charge, be registered as a charge before realisation[3]. Solicitors frequently do not take sufficient notice of information contained in local search certificates. Negligence claims for failing to advise purchasers of adverse entries, or to chase up ambiguous entries or replies are not uncommon[4].

The contract may deal expressly with local authority matters in the Special Conditions of Sale. A contractual term sometimes encountered on sales of land by auction deems the purchaser to have made local searches and inquiries and to have full knowledge of all matters which might be disclosed thereby. The vendor cannot rely on such a condition to excuse his failure to disclose in the contract a registered charge of which he or his solicitor was aware[5]. For contracts governed by the Standard Conditions of Sale, the matter is regulated by condition 3.4 and 3.5. Under these clauses, the land is sold subject to all matters registered in a public register except those maintained by HM Land Registry or its Land Charges Department or by Companies House. Further, the property is also sold subject to public requirements, this expression being defined to mean any notice, order, or proposal given or made (either before or after the date of the contract) by a body acting on statutory authority[6]. It is further provided that, after the contract is made, the seller is required to give the buyer written details of any new public requirement and of anything he

---

20 Ibid, s 3(1), (3) as substituted by the Local Government (Miscellaneous Provisions) Act 1982, s 34(1)(a), which permits the register to be maintained otherwise than in documentary form.

1 *Stock v Meakin* [1900] 1 Ch 683, CA; *Rignall Developments Ltd v Halil* [1987] 3 All ER 170 (improvement grant condition, breach of which causes grant to be repayable).

2 *Re Forsey and Hollebone's Contract* [1927] 2 Ch 379, CA. Town planning schemes were replaced by development plans, in turn replaced by structure and local plans under the Town and Country Planning Act 1971.

3 LRA 1925, ss 49(1)(c), 59(2) proviso. They will rank as general burdens under the Law Commission's reforms; see p 68, ante.

4 *Lake v Bushby* [1949] 2 All ER 964; *GP & P Ltd v Bulcraig and Davis* [1986] 2 EGLR 148. See also pp 213–214, post.

5 *Rignall Developments Ltd v Halil* [1987] 3 All ER 170.

6 SCS 1.1.1.(j).

learns about concerning any incumbrance subject to which the property is sold[7]. The buyer must bear the cost of complying with any outstanding public requirement and is to indemnify the seller against any liability arising from a public requirement[8]. The effect of these terms is that the purchaser is bound by all such matters. He has no redress against the vendor for any such matter not disclosed in the contract, save in respect of a warranty given by the vendor that he had informed the purchaser of the contents of any communication received by or known to him before the contract, or in respect of any misrepresentation made concerning these matters.

(a) Delays and post-contractual searches

As indicated at the beginning of this chapter, local searches are normally made before exchange of contracts. Serious delays were occasioned by the need to await the results of such searches, thereby occasioning much annoyance to practitioner and client alike. The Farrand Committee reported that the most contentious aspect of the operation of local authority registers was the delay in receiving responses to the searches, although the fault is not solely that of the authorities[9]. Happily, matters have now improved and, inordinate delays are no longer commonplace[10]. In parts of the country where delays do occur, it may be sensible to take out a local search delay insurance policy, now run by several insurance companies. Alternatively, provision can be made in the contract for a search to be made after exchange, with the purchaser being given the right of rescission if the search reveals some adverse entry. Such clauses were not commonly employed in the past and are unlikely to be encountered often today.

(b) Vendors' searches

Searches made by vendors are seen as an alternative method of combating local authority delays. It became a fairly common practice for the vendor to request the search and submit additional inquiries, and then to forward the results with the draft contract to the purchaser, who would be able to rely on the certificate[11]. This practice was, initially sanctioned by the Law Society in the National Conveyancing protocol. A difficulty with it, however, was that the search could become out of date, with the result that the purchaser would not feel able to rely upon it. Although this problem could be alleviated by insurance, the practice became unpopular with the profession, with the result that the current third edition of the Protocol has reversed the original position so that purchasers are now expected to carry out their own searches and inquiries.

---

7 SCS 3.1.3.
8 SCS 3.1.4.
9 2 Report, paras 4.78, 4.83 (delays resulting from solicitors' failure to send adequate plans). Delays of 12 weeks or more had become common in some London boroughs: (1987) 84 LS Gaz 162. In Millett J's strong words, these delays had become a scandal, threatening to impede the proper working of a free market: *Rignall's* case, supra, at 171.
10 See Law Society's Guide to the National Conveyancing Protocol, p 9.
11 By virtue of the LLCA 1975, s 10(3)(d), discussed p 204, post.

2.   What is a local land charge?

The Local Land Charges Act 1975 describes by means of inclusion (s 1) and exclusion (s 2) the general characteristics of all matters constituting local land charges. They are so diffuse in nature as to defy simple definition. Basically they comprise public matters in which local authorities, government departments and independent statutory corporations (eg water authorities) are interested. They have one vital feature in common. They bind successive owners of the land affected, hence the need for an intending purchaser to search for registrations before contracting to buy[12].

Section 1 of the Act lists five different categories of charge.

(a) Financial charges securing the payment of money for work done by an authority under various statutes relating to public health, private street works and similar enactments: s 1(1)(a).

(b) A prohibition or restriction on the use of land imposed by a local authority (eg on the grant of some consent or licence) or enforceable by it under any covenant or agreement: s 1(1)(b).

(c) A prohibition or restriction of the kind described in (b) but imposed or enforceable by a Minister of the Crown or government department, if created on or after 1 August 1977: s 1(1)(c).

(d) A positive obligation affecting land enforceable by a local authority, Minister of the Crown or government department under a covenant or agreement made on or after 1 August 1977: s 1(1)(d). Local authorities are entitled to enforce positive obligations under various local Acts.

(e) Any charge or other matter not falling within (a)-(d) which is expressly made a local land charge by statute: s 1(1)(e). This paragraph enables Parliament to bring any appropriate matter within the scope of the Act simply by declaring it to be a local land charge. Schedule 1 to the Act introduces this formula into a large number of existing statutes.

The provisions of s 1 must be read subject to s 2, which excludes certain matters that would otherwise fall within s 1. The most important of these exclusions are as follows:

(i) Any restriction or positive obligation between lessor and lessee.

(ii) Any restriction created by a covenant or agreement *made for the benefit of land* vested in a local authority or government department. This exclusion covers restrictions enforceable under the general law in accordance with the rule in *Tulk v Moxhay*[13].

---

12   They should not be confused with land charges, which are essentially private matters and are governed by LCA 1972. See Ch 13. Exceptionally the LLCA 1975 embraces two quite private matters: light obstruction notices under the Rights of Light Act 1959, and management schemes under the Leasehold Reform Act 1967, s 19.

13   (1848) 2 Ph 774. They are registrable as D(ii) land charges. Restrictions imposed statutorily by an authority not owning benefited land are local land charges under s 1(1)(b) of the Act.

(iii) Any restriction embodied in byelaws.

(iv) Conditions or limitations subject to which planning permission was granted before the Act took effect. *Post*-Act conditions and limitations subject to which planning permission is expressly granted are registrable as local land charges. The reason for this distinction is not easy to discern[14], especially as the existence of planning conditions can be readily discovered by inspection of the planning registers maintained under s 69 of the Town and Country Planning Act 1990.

Parts of the Register

To facilitate the registration of different types of charge, provision is made for the register to be divided into 12 numbered parts[15]. Brief reference will be made to each to indicate the wide variety of charges caught by the Act. Registration is against the *land* affected by the charge.

Part I General financial charges. Registration of these charges is governed by s 6 (2) of the 1977 Act. It enables a local authority, having expended money on eg street works, or maintenance of sewers and drains, to register a charge temporarily, pending calculation of the actual sum chargeable in respect of the property concerned, when a Part 2 charge can be registered. A general financial charge gives advance warning that a specific charge for an ascertained sum will in due course be registered.

Part 2 Specific financial charges. Such charges arise under several Acts where a local authority has incurred expenditure for which the owner of the premises is liable, often after he has defaulted in complying with a notice to execute certain works. A charge for street works expenses will be registered here after the final apportionment has been made in respect of the property. Numerous charges of this nature exist under the Public Health Act 1936, and related legislation, such as the cost of providing fire escapes for high buildings (s 60), or of abating statutory nuisances (ss 95, 96). A specific charge cannot be registered before the general charge relating to the same matter has been cancelled.

Part 3 Planning charges[16]. Entries in this part of the register are those most widely met in practice. They include post-Act planning conditions, orders revoking or modifying planning permission, planning agreements, tree preservation orders, enforcement notices and stop notices.

Part 4 Miscellaneous non-planning prohibitions and restrictions. A whole host of charges arising under innumerable statutes re registered here. Demolition and closing orders, control orders and improvement grant conditions, under

14 Cf Law Com Report, No 62, paras 36–39, favouring the view implicit in *Rose v Leeds Corpn* [1964] 3 All ER 618, CA, that planning conditions should not rank as local land charges.
15 See the LLC Rules 1977, SI 1977 No 985.
16 For a survey see (1983) 80 LS Gaz 2821 (C M Brand & D W Williams).

the Housing Act 1985, and improvement lines under the Highways Act 1980 – these are just a few examples. One of the more recent additions to the Part 4 list is the housing action area resolution made under the Housing Act 1985, s 239(7). The designation of a housing action area may be of concern to a *vendor* (other than an owner-occupier) of residential property within the area, because notice of intended disposal must be given to the authority at least four weeks before contracting to sell it[17]. As a means of giving notice the registration[18] will in practice be of little assistance to such a vendor, unless his solicitor makes a local search for submission to the purchaser's solicitor with the draft contract.

Part 5 Charges for improvement of fenland ways.   This relates to charges incurred in relation to the maintenance of private ways in fenlands[19].

Part 6 Land compensation orders.   This contains entries relating to certain charges falling within ss 8(4) and 72(8) of the Land Compensation Act 1973.

Part 7 New towns orders.   The first important step in the establishment of a new town is the making of an order designating the area as a proposed new town. This designation order and the compulsory purchase orders made pursuant to it are registrable here.

Part 8 Civil aviation orders.   Part 8 covers rights and orders registrable by virtue of the Civil Aviation Act 1982, s 77.

Part 9 Open cast coal and mining orders.   This covers entries relating to compulsory rights orders and compulsory purchase orders under the Opencast Coal Act 1958, whereby the National Coal Board can obtain rights to carry on opencast coal working for a temporary period.

Part 10 Lists of buildings of special architectural or historic interest.   Under s 1 of the Planning (Listed Buildings and Conservation Areas) Act 1990, the Secretary of State can compile or approve lists of buildings of special architectural or historic interest. A copy of so much of the list as relates to registering authority must be deposited with the clerk of the council and the copy becomes registrable in Part 10.

Part 11 Light obstruction notices.   Readers will be familiar with the provisions of the Rights of Light Act 1959, and no further comment will be made[20].

---

17   Section 247. The authority may compulsorily acquire the property: s 243(2).
18   Notice resulting therefrom by virtue of the LPA 1925, s 198, will not constitute knowledge sufficient to establish the requisite mens rea for the offence of failing to notify the authority under s 249 of the 1985 Act: cf *Barber v Shah* (1985) 17 HLR 584.
19   Agriculture (Miscellaneous Provisions) Act 1941, s 8(3)(d).
20   See M & W, 891–92.

Part 12 Land drainage schemes.   The Land Drainage Act 1991 empowers certain authorities to prepare a scheme for the improvement of drainage works in certain cases. The scheme becomes registrable in this part of the register.

3.   Mode of searching

A search can be effected by the applicant attending the council offices and inspecting the register in person, on payment of the prescribed fee[1]. A *personal* search is sometimes made when it is feared that there might be undue delay in the receipt of an official search certificate, or where the purchaser is anxious for a speedy exchange of contracts or proposes to buy land at an auction. These occasions apart, it is the invariable practice to take advantage of s 9 of the Act. This enacts that where a person requires an official search to be made of the register, he may on payment of the prescribed fee make a requisition therefor to the registering authority, which shall thereupon[2] make the required search and issue an official certificate setting out the result. This requisition must be in the appropriate form, signed by the applicant or his solicitor, as follows[3]:

> An official search is required in [Part of] the register of local land charges kept by the above-named registering authority for subsisting registrations against the land [defined in the attached plan and[4]] described below ...

Unlike land charges, local land charges are registered against the land. The name of the estate owner is not therefore necessary. Normally the correct postal address is adequate to identify the property, otherwise a plan drawn to scale and furnished in duplicate is required. Having made the search the authority issues a certificate, signed and dated, that:

> It is hereby certified that the search registered above reveals no subsisting registration or the registration described in the Schedule hereto[5] up to and including the date of the certificate.

The entries are revealed in schedules attached to the certificate, there being different forms of schedules laid down by the Rules for different parts of the register. A composite form (known as LLC 1) containing both the requisition and the form of certificate is employed; all that it is necessary for the solicitor and the registering authority to do is to complete the respective parts of the form.

---

1   LLCA 1975, s 8.
2   A significant word, which, surely, rules out the long delays in the issue of the certificate by some authorities.
3   LLC Rules 1977, r 13, Sch 1, prescribing Form C.
4   The inappropriate words need deleting. Usually a search in the whole of the register is requested.
5   The inappropriate words are deleted.

4.   Effect of undisclosed charges

(a) New compensation scheme

Prior to the Local Land Charges Act 1975, non-registration of a local land charge rendered it void against a purchaser of a legal estate in the land. Moreover, the official search certificate was conclusive according to its tenor, and he took free from a registered charge not revealed by it. The Act has made significant changes in the law on both these points. Now a purchaser takes subject to any unregistered charge, or to any charge which, though registered, is not disclosed by his search certificate. However, by virtue of s 10, a purchaser[6] is entitled to compensation[7] for loss suffered if: (a) he has relied on a material personal search made before the relevant time and the charge was in existence but not registered[8]; *or* (b) he has relied on a material official search made before the relevant time and the charge was in existence (whether registered or not) but was not disclosed on the official certificate: sub-s (1). For the purposes of (b) a material search is either one requisitioned by or on behalf of the buyer, or one whose contents he or his solicitor had knowledge of before the relevant time: sub-s (3)(d). This alternative is designed to facilitate the procedure, already mentioned, whereby the vendor obtains the search certificate which is later sent to the purchaser's solicitor with the draft contract. The relevant time will usually be the time when the contract is made: sub-s (3)(b)(i). Where, however, there is no prior contract, or it is a qualified liability contract[9], the relevant time is the date of acquisition (taken to be in the case of registered land when the disposition is made): sub-s 3(b)(ii).

Compensation is intended to relieve a purchaser who has been misled by the certificate. He must establish loss suffered by reason of the non-registration or omission of the charge. If he possesses information (supplied, eg by the vendor or a council official) which seemingly conflicts with the result of his search, no right to compensation appears to exist. He is put on inquiry of the need to investigate the position; he cannot later complain should he neglect to do so and yet he contracts to buy without re-negotiating the price. No statutory machinery exists for quantifying compensation, which may prove to be difficult to assess in the case of a non-financial charge. Where land is subject to a mortgage, s 11 requires the compensation to be paid to the mortgagee, and he must apply it as if it were proceeds of sale (ie in reduction of the mortgage debt).

---

6   Ie one who for valuable consideration acquires any interest in land or the proceeds of sale of land, including a lessee or mortgagee: s 10(3)(a).

7   Exceptionally compensation is excluded by the Act, eg light obstruction notices. Nor does s 10 apply to a dual status local land charge, ie one which before the Act came into force was both registrable and registered under the LCA 1925 or 1972. There is no need to re-register such under the LLCA 1975: s 5(6).

8   No right to compensation arises when a personal search does not reveal a registered charge. As to what constitutes a material search, see s 10(3)(c).

9   See ibid, s 10(3)(b). It will cover eg a contract to which SCS 3 is made to apply pp 198–199, ante.

(b) Enforcement of charges

The mode of enforcement depends on the type of local land charge. A financial charge takes effect, when registered, as a charge by way of legal mortgage. So the authority can exercise the statutory powers, including sale, without the need for a court order[10]. If the statute under which it is acquired imposes a charge on the land, it operates to confer a charge on all estates and interest in that land, not merely (where the land is already mortgaged) on the owner's equity of redemption[11].

Breach of prohibition or restriction is normally punishable by a fine, coupled with powers vested in the appropriate authority to take steps to secure compliance and to recover any expenses incurred.

(c) Discharge between vendor and purchaser

As pointed out previously[12], the Standard Conditions of Sale, cl 3.1.4, the purchaser is required to bear the cost of complying with any outstanding public requirement and is to indemnify the vendor against any liability resulting from a public requirement.

5. Value of local search certificate

As we have seen, an official search certificate confers no protection or priority in respect of charges that are unregistered or undisclosed (unlike a land charges certificate). Therefore the search is good only for the day on which the certificate is dated. The period during which it can safely be relied upon in practice is not defined, as this is not a matter that is regulated by statute[13]. Further, no entitlement to compensation arises under s 10 for a charge that comes into existence *after* the search but before the contract.

It is not to be imagined from these factors that a local land charges search is of little value; quite the contrary. The existence of a registered charge may be vital to the purchaser's decision whether or not to proceed, or to re-negotiate the asking price. Whilst it is the normal procedure for the search to be made before exchange of contracts, it is not customary to effect a second search before completion[14]. This will give up-to-date notice of any alterations, but the disclosure of a post-contract registration will not, where the Standard Conditions of Sale apply, entitle the purchaser to require the vendor to discharge it, or give him any right to rescind the contract.

---

10 LLCA 1975, s 7; *Payne v Cardiff RDC* [1932] 1 KB 241.
11 *Westminster City Council v Haymarket Publishing Ltd* [1981] 2 All ER 555, CA (unpaid rating surcharge enforceable against purchaser from mortgagee).
12 Page 199 ante.
13 See 3rd edn, p 191, suggesting that a period of two months is usually considered acceptable.
14 The Council of The Law Society is of the opinion that a mortgagee's solicitor is well advised to make a further search before completion of the mortgage (see (1952) 49 LS Gaz 501), but this is not generally done. The mortgagee's solicitor relies on the one made on behalf of the purchaser, except where there is a considerable time-lag.

E　Additional inquiries

1.　Nature of additional inquiries

Not all the information in which a prospective purchaser may be interested is capable of being entered in the register of local land charges. No logical justification seems to exist for requiring the registration of some matters whilst excluding others. It is, therefore, necessary to raise additional inquiries of the local authority at the same time as the requisition for an official search is submitted. A standard form of inquiry, varying according to the particular type of authority consulted[15], has been approved by the Council of the Law Society and the various local government bodies. These additional inquiries are not part of the statutory scheme for the registration of charges prescribed by the 1975 Act. They are, nevertheless, an essential adjunct to it. The inquiry form is divided into compulsory (Part I) and optional (Part II) questions. The former fall roughly into four categories: roads, sewers and drains, planning (the majority) and a miscellaneous group covering matters such as smoke control orders, the rating of unoccupied property and compulsory land registration areas. Much of the information sought relates to matters in the course of becoming registered charges (eg resolutions authorising service of enforcement or stop notices[16] or planning contravention notices)[17], or those of a similar but unregistrable nature (eg compulsory purchase resolutions).

　　The optional Pt II inquiries will not be answered unless the applicant initials those, if any, to which he desires a reply[18]. These include questions about, eg public paths, their stopping up or diversion, the location of pipe-lines, and other more specialised planning inquiries (eg advertisements, listed building consents). Supplementary inquiries can be added, which the authority may be willing to answer, again on payment of an increased fee. All the printed questions are designed to provide information on matters affecting the property which is the subject of the inquiry. Yet a prospective purchaser may be anxious to learn of proposals affecting neighbouring land, which could influence his decision to buy. An obvious example is the potential development of nearby vacant land. The amount of extra information which can be ascertained by means of supplementary questions is obviously limited[19]. Should a purchaser wish to know more about the prospects for a particular property, there is no

---

15　Either Con 29A (District Councils) or Con 29D (London Boroughs and the Corpn of London). The replies to various inquiries in Con 29A cover knowledge and actions of both the District Council and the County Council. See the guidance notes at (1987) 84 LS Gaz 3342–43.

16　See Town and Country Planning Act 1990, ss 172, 178.

17　Ibid, s 171C, introduced by Planning and Compensation Act 1991, s 1.

18　And pays a separate fee for each question asked. Pt I inquiries are answered for a composite fee.

19　This has prompted some practitioners to seek this kind of information in preliminary inquiries.

real substitute for a visit by him to the Council Offices. It is not customary for a vendor's solicitor who effects a local search for use by a purchaser to raise any Pt II inquiries. The need for these and any supplementary questions is a matter for the purchaser's solicitor to consider with his client on receipt of the search certificate and Pt I replies.

It should also be appreciated that the reply received may prompt the need for further inquiries to be made, in which case a failure to do this may lead to an action in negligence by the purchaser against his solicitor[20].

2. Authority's replies

Many local authorities give their replies (other than non-standard ones) by way of a separate pre-printed answer sheet attached to the inquiry form. A headnote to this explains that the replies are:

> ...furnished after appropriate inquiries and in the belief that they are in accordance with the information at present available to the officers of the respective Councils, but on the distinct understanding that neither the District Council nor the County Council, nor any officer of either Council, is legally responsible therefor, except for negligence.

The authority thus accepts liability for loss caused by negligence in answering the inquiries. This liability is expressly stated to extend to a person (being a purchaser for the purposes of s 10(3) of the Act of 1975) who or whose agent had knowledge of the replies before the relevant time as there defined. The purchaser can in an appropriate case maintain an action against the authority for an incorrect reply, notwithstanding that the inquiries were submitted by the vendor's solicitor[1]. For the purpose of liability no distinction is drawn between Pt I and II inquiries; but in relation to supplementary questions that may be raised, the authority is free to determine on what basis as regards liability its answers are given[2]. The disclaimer does not cover information supplied by letter or in the course of a telephone conversation[3].

One further point deserves mention. As the printed form warns, the replies, so far as they concern proposals, may change. Indeed, they may never materialise. This seemingly obvious point is worth drawing to the client's attention. It also needs to be recognised that not every failure to reveal details of a proposed scheme will amount to negligence, since the authority may decide that it is still at an exploratory stage and not sufficiently advanced to warrant disclosure. Authorities must be careful when making statements capable of affecting property values, and it is not always easy to preserve a proper balance between the conflicting interests of vendor and purchaser.

---

20 See *Faragher v Gerber* [1994] EGCS 122.
 1 He would in any event appear to be within the scope of the authority's duty of care under the general law. See *Coats Patons (Retail) Ltd v Birmingham Corpn* (1971) 69 LGR 356 (failure to disclose subway; liability in contract and tort established); *JGF Properties Ltd v Lambeth London Borough* [1986] 1 EGLR 179 (action failed).
 2 Any general disclaimer will be caught by the Unfair Contract Terms Act 1977.
 3 See *JGF Properties Ltd v Lambeth London Borough*, supra, illustrating the problems of basing a negligence claim on allegedly incorrect information imparted over the telephone.

3.　Inquiries on planning matters

A purchaser will depend heavily on his search certificate and the replies to inquiries to discover the planning details relating to the property. The precise nature of the information relevant to him will depend on the type of property that he is interested in buying. Some of it will be obtainable from the vendor. A purchaser of an existing house will need to check that no unauthorised extensions or alterations have been made to it. The Seller's Property Information Form makes a number of inquiries concerning planning matters. An inquiry is made as to whether the property is used as a private dwelling and whether it is a listed building or in a conservation area. An inquiry is then made as to whether any building work has been done in the past four years and, if so, whether planning permission or listed building consent was obtained. A further inquiry is made as to whether there has been any change of use in the last ten years (eg a dividing into flats or using part for business use). The reason for this inquiry over ten years as opposed to four years in a previous inquiry is that immunity exists for four years in respect of breach of planning control consisting of a change of use of any building to use as a single dwelling-house[4] but, in respect of any other breach of planning control, the period of immunity is set at ten years[5]. The vendor is also asked whether any application for planning permission or listed building consent has been made. The benefit of a planning permission runs with the land[6].

F　Miscellaneous searches[7]

1.　Land charges search

The purchaser need not make a *land charges* search before exchange of contracts. The Law of Property Act 1969, s 24 (1) enacts that where any question arises whether a purchaser[8] had knowledge, at the time of entering into a contract, of a registered land charge, it is to be determined by reference to his *actual* knowledge and without regard to the provisions of s 198 of the Law of Property Act 1925. This provision reverses the view, found on Eve J's controversial decision at first instance in *Re Forsey and Hollebone's Contract*[9],

---

4　Planning, Listed Buildings and Conservation Act 1990, s 28.
5　Ibid, s 171(B), a section introduced by Planning and Compensation Act 1991, s 4.
6　Town and Country Planning Act 1990, s 75(1).
7　See generally, Bourne, *Handbook of Conveyancing Searches*; Silverman, *Searches and Enquiries, A Conveyancer's Guide*.
8　Defined to include a lessee, mortgagee or other person acquiring or intending to acquire an estate or interest in land: sub-s (3).
9　[1927] 2 Ch 379, CA (both parties unaware of resolution to prepare town planning scheme). This was an alternative ground for his decision (see at 382–83), so his comments are in no way to be treated as obiter (as is commonly asserted). The CA upheld his decision on the alternative ground that the resolution was not an incumbrance, without hearing argument on the notice point. See also *Re Middleton and Young's Contract* [1929] WN 70. For s 198, see p 396, post. And see [1954] CLJ 89 (H W R Wade), discussing problems raised by Eve J's decision.

that s 198 operated to fix a purchaser with notice of any charge registered at the time of the contract. As a result he was barred from rescinding the contract on the ground of the vendor's non-disclosure of an irremovable registered land charge. In theory the purchaser ought to have searched for land charges before contract. Section 24(1) removes this necessity. Neither constructive nor 'statutory' notice will preclude objection to an undisclosed registered charge, only the purchaser's actual knowledge, including that of his solicitor or other agent acquired in the course of the transaction[10]. Eve J's ruling has recently been attacked by Millett J[11], who questioned the soundness of the view that 'statutory' notice was to be equated with knowledge for the purposes of the rule which prevents rescission of the contract due to an undisclosed irremovable incumbrance of which he was aware at the date of the contract[12]. He was not disposed to apply Eve J's decision to a case where the vendor himself, through his solicitor, had actual knowledge of the registered charge which he alleged the purchaser was bound to accept[13].

The limits of s 24 must be noted. It does not relate to contracts for the sale of registered land. There is no reason why it should; s 198 has no equivalent in the Land Registration Act 1925, or in the rules made thereunder. Nor does it apply to local land charges[14]. But as these are registered against the land affected, there exists no barrier to effecting a search before exchange of contracts[15].

2. Search in public index map

Rule 9 of the Land Registration (Open Register) Rules enables any person to obtain, free of charge, an official search of the index map and parcels index. One of the purposes of such a search used to be to ascertain whether the land which is the subject of the search is in an area of compulsory registration. With the spread of registration throughout the country, this reason no longer exists. Reasons remain, however, why such a search should be made. The official certificate of search reveals whether the title is registered and, if so, whether as freehold or leasehold and under what title number and, if it is not registered, whether the land is affected by a pending application for first registration or a caution against first registration or a priority notice[16]. The application is made on Form 96 and need not be accompanied by a plan if the land can be properly identified by its postal address. Every purchaser of land is well advised to effect this search before exchange of contracts on any purchase of land which will result in a first registration of title. It enables him to check that no part of the

---

10 LPA 1969, s 24(2).
11 *Rignall Developments Ltd v Halil* [1987] 3 All ER 170 (improvement grant condition).
12 See p 157, ante, and p 397, post.
13 If Eve J's ruling is correct, then it would follow that a vendor could not rely on any contractual clause purporting to excuse his non-disclosure of registered charges, since by virtue of s 198 he would himself be deemed to have actual notice of them.
14 See the definition of 'registered land charge' in s 24(3).
15 For a land charges search a purchaser needed to know the names of previous estate owners, which he would not normally have if investigation of the title took place after contract.
16 Land Registration (Open Register) Rules 1991, r 9(4), (5), Schedule.

land is registered with a title adverse to the vendor's interest (as, for example, might happen if part of the land has been previously sold off[17]). Further, if the purchaser makes a specific request for a plan on Form 96, the Registrar will supply an official plan defining the extent of the land as shown on the Ordnance Survey map provided that the extent of the land to be searched can be readily determined from an inspection of the parcels index and that it can be shown on a single page of A4 paper[18]. This official plan can be compared with the contract plan and any discrepancies in the plot boundaries as revealed by the two plans can be clarified with the vendor. Otherwise, if the inaccuracy of the contract plan is not discovered until after completion when the Registry is preparing the filed plan for the property, the purchaser may find that he is ultimately registered with a plot of land smaller in size than the one which he thought he had acquired.

3.   Search in Commons register

The Commons Registration Act 1965 creates a Commons register[19] for the registration of (i) common land and town or village greens, (ii) rights of common over such land, and (iii) persons claiming to be owners of common land (s 1). Registration could be effected by any person or authority whose application was supported by an appropriate statutory declaration (s 4(1)). No evidence of title was required. Initially registration was provisional only, pending a hearing before a Commons Commissioner into any objection thereto lodged within a prescribed time limit (s 7), which has long since expired. If no objection was made in time, the registration (whether of the land or of rights over it) became final and, generally speaking, unchallengeable (s 7)[20]. Registration is conclusive evidence of the matters registered (s 10).

The Act and the procedures established by it have provoked strong judicial criticism. It has been said to be ill-drafted, and cries out for amendment[1]. It creates pitfalls for the unsuspecting – landowners, purchasers and conveyancers alike. It permits quite groundless claims to become final, if not challenged in time. Cases are known where land has been registered as common land, on which houses have been erected for many years[2]. The statute imposed no duty on registration authorities to inform landowners of an application or provisional registration affecting their land. Consequently a person might find

---

17   See *Epps v Esso Petroleum Co Ltd* [1973] 2 All ER 465, p 92, ante. See (1987) 84 LSG 2260, para 5 (provision of search by vendor's solicitor when sending draft contract).
18   See R & R 4.13.
19   Maintained by the council of the county, metropolitan district or London borough in which the land is situated: s 2(1), amended by the Local Government Act 1985, Sch 8, para 10 (6).
20   There are limited powers of amendment (s 13) and of judicial rectification for fraud (s 14). A registration in the ownership section remains open to challenge.
1   See *Corpus Christi College, Oxford v Gloucestershire County Council* [1983] QB 360 at 370, 378, [1982] 3 All ER 995 at 1002, 1009, CA, per Lord Denning MR and Oliver LJ, respectively.
2   See (1984) LS Gaz 3401 (D Green), highlighting problems created by the legislation.

his land irrevocably registered as common land without the matter ever having been brought to his notice[3]. Land may continue to be registered as common land under the Act, even though it is no longer subject to any registered rights of common[4].

Matters entered in the register do not constitute local land charges, nor does the additional inquiries form contain any relevant question. Information can, however, be obtained by requisitioning an official search in the Commons register on Form 21[5]. In what circumstances ought a purchaser's solicitor to make such a search? In *G & K Ladenbau (UK) Ltd v Crawley and de Reya*[6] solicitors were held liable in negligence for failing to make a search on the purchase of land for factory development in Newport, Monmouthshire. There were in this case particular factors which ought to have alerted them to the need for a search[7]. Clearly there will be many occasions when a Commons search is not required, eg on the purchase of property on a well established housing estate, or of industrial or commercial premises in a city centre. On the other hand a search would seem to be prudent on the purchase of vacant (ie unbuilt upon) land in a rural area, especially if neither the solicitor nor his client has any local knowledge of the area in question.

Rights of common constitute latent defects of title falling within the vendor's duty of disclosure. He may, of course, be able to shelter behind a general condition in one of the standard form contracts if he is unaware of the registration[8].

4. Various searches

A specialised search may be desirable depending on the location or situation of the property. The following are examples.

(i) Coal Board search
This should be effected by means of inquiry to the appropriate regional office of the Board, when land is in or near to an area of coal mining activity. The search will disclose the date of past or anticipated future workings under or in the vicinity of the property, and whether it is or may be subject to subsidence.

---

3 See *Smith v East Sussex County Council* (1977) 76 LGR 332.
4 The *Corpus Christi* case, supra. Land can be registered as common land despite there being no rights of common over it, because by definition 'common land" includes 'waste land of a manor not subject to rights of common': s 22(1)(b).
5 Prescribed by the Commons Registration (General) Regulations 1966, SI 1966 No 1471, r 32 (2), Sch 1.
6 [1978] 1 All ER 682. Ironically the registration was a complete mistake, being based on an erroneous plan (see at 689).
7 An earlier conveyance had indicated that part of the land had previously belonged to the lord of the manor, so warning of the possibility that the site might be waste land of a manor (note 19, ante).
8 SCS 3.1.2(d), p 155, ante.

(ii) Water Authority search

A search[9] with the river authority should be made on the purchase of property which has a river or stream running through it or along or near its boundaries. Its purpose is to ascertain whether the authority has rights of entry for the repair or maintenance of the river banks, whether the riparian owner is liable to contribute towards the costs thereof, and, importantly, whether the property is susceptible to flooding.

(iii) Cheshire Brine Board search

Property in parts of Cheshire may be affected by underground salt mining. An inquiry of the Board will elicit relevant information, provided that the written consent of the owner (or his agent) to the disclosure of details is also submitted.

---

9   Similar inquiries should be raised of the British Waterways Board if a canal runs through or borders the property.

Chapter 8

Exchange of contracts and the parties' rights pending completion

A Introduction

1. Preliminaries to exchange

Usually the parties to the transaction are separately represented, in which case both solicitors have their respective parts to play in the preparation of the contract. The purchaser's solicitor approves the draft contract on behalf of his client, but not before he is satisfied that the local searches and answers to inquiries reveal nothing adverse. He should also ensure that it accords with his client's instructions, checking in particular the price, the description of the property and any agreed special terms. Objections to particular clauses in the draft are best dealt with by way of preliminary inquiry; it merely adds to the delay if the vendor's solicitor first learns of these when it is returned to him amended. Having approved the contract, with or without amendments, the purchaser's solicitor sends one copy to the vendor's solicitor for signature by the vendor, and retains the other for his own client's signature. Amendments of substance ought to be initialed by the parties to obviate any argument that they were added after the contract was signed[1]. Before signing the contract a vendor should satisfy himself that he will be able to perform his contract. He should, for example, ensure that vacant possession can be given on completion[2] or that a mortgagee whose mortgage is not to be redeemed has agreed to concur in the sale[3].

Solicitors should check that their client's part of the contract is properly signed by or on behalf of the appropriate person. A purchaser's solicitor should be on his guard against a contract by spouses signed by one of them only 'for self and co-owner [or spouse]'[4]. It goes without saying that he should not ask his own client to sign without first discussing the terms of the contract[5] with him and their legal effect. The purchaser should be made aware of adverse

---

1   See *Earl v Mawson* (1974) 232 EG 1315, CA, p 226, post.
2   Cf *Sharneyford Supplies Ltd v Edge* [1987] Ch 305, [1987] 1 All ER 588, CA. His solicitor may owe him a duty to ensure this: *Rumsey v Owen, White and Catlin* (1976) 241 EG 611.
3   *Baines v Tweddle* [1959] Ch 679, [1959] 2 All ER 724, CA (vendor's conduct held to bar recourse to contractual right to rescind).
4   Doubts exist as to the effectiveness of the spouse's agency: [1980] Conv 191 (P W Smith).
5   But not the General Conditions: *Walker v Boyle* [1982] 1 All ER 634 at 645, per Dillon J.

rights affecting the property[6], restrictive covenants[7], the details of any relevant planning permission[8] (or the lack of it[9]), as well as entries revealed by the local search certificate or information disclosed in answer to preliminary inquiries. Apart from special instructions, there is no duty to advise whether a transaction is a prudent one[10].

Failure to advise the client adequately may constitute breach of duty, entitling him to damages. The extent of the duty depends on the retainer which the solicitor is given. It is a duty to use reasonable care and skill in giving such advice as the particular case demands[11]. Its scope may depend on the client's apparent need for advice. A solicitor is not expected to provide the same detailed advice in matters within the knowledge or expertise of an experienced client as might be required when acting for a first-time buyer[12]. A solicitor's liability is both contractual and tortious[13], which has important consequences for limitation purposes. For whereas in contract the limitation period runs from the date of breach, in tort it begins only when damage is sustained.

2. Time

After both parties have signed their respective parts, the next step is the exchange of contracts, assuming all pre-contract aspects of the transaction have been satisfactorily dealt with. A solicitor is not, however, under a duty to ensure that his client has procured a mortgage before exchanging contracts, provided he warns him of the risks involved if any mortgage application is later rejected[14]. Strictly speaking he ought to obtain his client's instructions[15] as to the date for the exchange, though in practice the circumstances often indicate that this is desired as soon as possible. If he exchanges contracts in

---

6 *Piper v Daybell, Court-Cooper & Co* (1969) 210 EG 1047 (right of way; damages included sum for loss of privacy).
7 *Ford v White & Co* [1964] 2 All ER 755 (purchaser suffering no loss).
8 *Raintree Ltd v Holmes & Hill* (1984) 134 NLJ 522 (limited permission); *GP & P Ltd v Bulcraig & Davis* [1986] 2 EGLR 148 (conditional permission).
9 *Lake v Bushby* [1949] 2 All ER 964.
10 *Bowdage v H Michelmore & Co* (1962) 183 EG 233 (grant of option).
11 *Sykes v Midland Bank Executor and Trustee Co Ltd* [1971] 1 QB 113 at 125, [1970] 2 All ER 471 at 477, CA, per Salmon LJ. See also Supply of Goods and Services Act 1982, s 13.
12 *Carradine Properties Ltd v D J Freeman & Co* (1982) 126 Sol Jo 157, CA; *Aslan v Clintons* (1984) 134 NLJ 584 (experienced property developer).
13 *Midland Bank Trust Co Ltd v Hett, Stubbs & Kemp* [1979] Ch 384, [1978] 3 All ER 571; *Forster v Outred & Co* [1982] 2 All ER 753 at 764, CA, per Dunn LJ. But see the trenchant contrary opinion expressed by Lord Scarman in *Tai Hing Cotton Mill Ltd v Liu Chong Hing Bank Ltd* [1986] AC 80 at 107, [1985] 2 All ER 947 at 957, PC, not citing relevant English authorities. For strong criticism, see (1985) 1 PN 198 (J Holyoak); (1986) 2 PN 17 (R Martyn). According to Steyn J in *Banque Keyser Ullmann SA v Skandia (UK) Insurance Co Ltd* [1990] 1 QB 665, [1987] 2 All ER 923 at 950, Lord Scarman's observations were not intended to be of general application.
14 *Buckland v Mackesy* (1968) 112 Sol Jo 841, CA. But see *McLellan v Fletcher* [1987] NLJ Rep 593 (duty to ensure life policy forming part of mortgage security in force before completion).
15 For a ruling that a solicitor acting for spouses should not accept instructions from a wife if her husband is also available, see *Morris v Duke-Cohan & Co* (1975) 119 Sol Jo 826. *Sed quaere.*

breach of his instructions, he may be liable in damages to his client[16]. Moreover, when a client is involved in a linked sale and purchase, he must, in the absence of specific instructions to the contrary, ensure as near a simultaneous exchange of contracts in the two transactions as it is legally possible to achieve[17].

(a) Chain transactions

Contracting parties who are ready and anxious to exchange their respective contracts may find themselves thwarted by factors outside their control. This occurs frequently in domestic conveyancing when a chain of inter-dependent transactions exists[18]. Suppose a chain of linked transactions: A-B, B-C, C-D, D-E, E-F, F-? Everybody in the chain may be ready to exchange contracts, save for F who is having difficulty in selling his existing house. F's tardiness effectively holds up the other parties. These chains are a constant source of frustration to house owners and buyers alike. Popular opinion is misconceived when it asserts that solicitors are largely responsible for the delays. Many are the reasons why one person in a chain cannot proceed[19], which lawyers are powerless to do anything about. Various changes in pre-contract procedures have been mooted[20]. These may assist in reducing the time-lag between the initial 'subject to contract' accord and the eventual exchange of contracts; but they will not help F (in the example) one iota to find a suitable purchaser.

There are ways of resolving the impasse. E could exchange contracts with D, so producing a knock-on effect down the chain. However, for good reasons few buyers are prepared to undertake this step. Not only would E have to obtain a bridging loan at a high interest rate to fund the D-E purchase, he may well find himself for a short uncertain period the owner of two houses. The Conveyancing Committee acknowledged there was no simple solution available to avoid chain transactions but recommended strongly a greater use of cheaper bridging finance as the most practicable way of alleviating the difficulties. Building societies were urged to encourage more use of concurrent mortgages[1].

Many large national or regional estate developers operate exchange schemes whereby they take a buyer's existing property in part exchange for the new house. The agreed market value of the existing house is discounted by 5% or so, which is intended to cover the builder's outgoings, such as sale and legal expenses, maintenance, and rates. Buyers can recoup some of the discount by the resultant saving in estate agent's fees. Previously, this practice could also eliminate liability to pay stamp duty because stamp duty used to be

---

16 *Buckley v Lane Herdman & Co* [1977] CLY 3143 (failure to effect simultaneous exchange of sale and purchase contracts): *Simpson v Grove Tompkins & Co* (1982) 126 Sol Jo 347, CA.
17 *Morris v Duke-Cohere & Co, supra.*
18 Research among estate agents indicates that 75% of all housebuyers are involved in a chain, one in three of which is broken: The Times, 27 February 1987.
19 Eg delay in the receipt of local searches; difficulty in raising finance; a buyer withdrawing at the last moment; the vendor re-selling at a higher price (gazumping). For an interesting survey into the cause and extent of pre-contract delays, see (1985) 135 NLJ 1030.
20 See 2 Conveyancing Committee Report, ch 2, and pp 189–190, ante.
 1 Ibid, paras 5.2–7, 9.24. Most building societies will not lend on the security of a buyer's intended house whilst the loan on his existing property remains unpaid. Hence the need for bridging finance from another source, eg a bank.

payable on the difference in price between the two properties, which may well not exceed the £60,000 threshold on which stamp duty becomes payable. The position now is that there is a charge of 1% on the property sold, a charge of 50 pence being levied on the property being conveyed in part exchange. If, for example, a house is being purchased for £100,000 the consideration being the transfer of a house worth £80,000 and a cash payment of £20,000, full stamp duty is payable on the conveyance of the £100,000 house and a 50 pence charge made on the other conveyance[2]. Some nationwide estate agency firms (such as Black Horse Agencies and Prudential Property Services) provide a similar service and are prepared to buy a client's house, again at a discount (varying from 8 to 12%) of its agreed valuation[3]. It remains to be seen whether building societies will use their extensive powers under the Building Societies Act 1986, to develop a general house trade-in scheme for buyers.

One consequence of these delays in exchanging contracts is that solicitors are obliged to proceed with the post-contract conveyancing aspects of the transaction, such as perusing the title and having the conveyance or transfer executed ready for completion. It is by no means uncommon for completion to take place a mere three or four days after exchange, or even on the same day[4]. In this latter situation it is still highly desirable for a purchaser to insist on an exchange of contracts prior to completion. This is not an idle formality, for it enables him to claim the benefit of those contractual terms that survive completion, eg the term for vacant possession[5].

(b) Gazumping

As we saw in Chapter 7, when a vendor and purchaser conclude a 'subject to contract' arrangement, the law regards them as being in a state of negotiation until contracts are exchanged, and either party is free to withdraw from the bargain. The vendor may sell to another person at a higher price – a practice known as gazumping. Unless the first buyer can improve upon the increased price, he stands to lose the legal, surveying and other fees already incurred[6]. These are not recoverable from the vendor, who is not in breach of any contract. Equally the buyer, finding a more attractive property, may pull out of the deal, leaving the vendor without redress and perhaps unable to proceed with his intended purchase of another house. The similar plight of vendors in this situation is usually ignored in the clamour for reform.

Gazumping is an unwelcome feature of the private housing market in times of heavy demand and rising prices. It is an emotive issue, frequently aired in the national press. The spiralling of house prices in the early 1970s

---

2   Finance Act 1994, s 241; Inland Revenue press release, 18 April, 1994.
3   For a consideration of stock purchase schemes, see ibid, paras 5.8–18.
4   This can be a very risky business for purchasers. It is not unknown for a vendor, on receipt of a higher offer from a third person, to call the deal off on the very day that exchange and completion have been arranged to take place.
5   See p 165, ante (vacant possession); p 468, post (merger on completion).
6   For consideration of the rare situations where damages can be obtained for pre-contractual expenditure, see *Regalian Properties plc v London Docklands Development Corpn* [1995] 1 All ER 1005, [1995] 1 WLR 212; [1995] Conv 135 (M P Thompson).

prompted the government of the day to refer the matter to the Law Commission[7]. Whilst recognising that the 'subject to contract' procedure had its drawbacks and was capable of abuse, the Commission felt it was based on a sound concept[8]. It ensured that

> that 'those buying and selling houses do not find themselves irrevocably committed to a sale or purchase before being given the chance of taking advice, or making proper inquiries, searches and inspections and of making their financial arrangements.' (para 7)

Legislation was not the answer. Nor did the Commission feel able to advocate a more extensive use of option agreements or conditional contracts. Options, judicially described as 'ticklish things'[9], are quite unsuited to ordinary domestic transactions, whereas conditional contracts lack that element of binding security so vital to parties enmeshed in a conveyancing chain. Recent years have witnessed various changes in pre-contract procedures, some of a controversial nature. These have been introduced in an attempt to expedite exchange of contracts and so reduce the risk of gazumping. In truth, however, the differing causes of the delays in contract exchanges are beyond the law's power to eliminate or even control[10]. Particularly when the parties are involved in a chain of linked transactions, the threat of withdrawal is ever present, and the longer the chain the greater will be the risk. For buyers, insurance can provide some financial compensation. Some years ago, the National Association of Homeowners launched a policy for its members, enabling them for a small premium to recover expenditure lost as a consequence of being gazumped.

A recent device to prevent gazumping was considered in *Pitt v PHH Asset Management Ltd*[11]. After prolonged negotiations, the prospective vendor and purchaser agreed that the vendor would not consider any other offers on the property for an agreed period of time. It was held that this constituted a valid 'lock-out agreement'[12], which was not within the ambit of s 2 of the Law of Property (Miscellaneous Provisions) Act 1989. The vendor having sold the property elsewhere, he was, in principle[13], liable in damages for breach of this contract. It is not thought likely, however, that in most cases the vendor will be willing to enter such an agreement unless there is some corresponding promise

---

7 An unsuccessful Private Member's Bill, The Abolition of Gazumping and Kindred Practices Bill, had been introduced in 1971.
8 Law Com No 65, a view still held by the Commission's Standing Committee (see p 10, ante) more than a decade later: *Pre-Contract Deposits* (1987), para 4.
9 *Mackay v Wilson* (1947) 47 SRNSW 315 at 318, per Jordan CJ.
10 Following an upsurge in the incidence of gazumping early in 1987, the Conveyancing Standing Committee produced in September 1987 a booklet explaining how the Scottish system of house transfer (which does not give rise to gazumping) might be adapted for use in this country. No recommendation was made as to whether the Scottish system was superior. The Scottish procedure is based on the submission of sealed bids by interested buyers. These are opened on the closing date and the most satisfactory offer accepted, whereupon a binding contract comes into existence. But the system has its own disadvantages. It removes the security given by a synchronised sale and purchase, and leads to wasted expenditure (eg search and survey fees) by unsuccessful bidders.
11 [1993] 4 All ER 961, [1994] 1 WLR 327, CA; [1994] Conv 58 (M P Thompson).
12 Applying *Walford v Miles* [1992] 2 AC 128, [1992] 1 All ER 453, HL.
13 The question as to whether there was a contract at all was decided as a preliminary point.

by the purchaser subsequently to exchange contracts; an agreement which will be subject to s 2[14].

(c) Law Commission's Conveyancing Committee Scheme

In January 1987 the Conveyancing Standing Committee unveiled a widely publicised procedure which it was hoped would make a positive contribution towards alleviating the problems and uncertainties that exist before exchange of contracts. The voluntary scheme envisages that when the vendor (V) and purchaser (P) have reached a 'subject to contract' arrangement they will sign a standard form pre-contract deposit agreement. This requires each party to pay a deposit of one half per cent of the agreed price to V's solicitor as stakeholder. In no way does the agreement operate as the formal contract for sale between V and P. The Committee contemplates that V's selling agent will supply copies of the form for signature. The agreement gives a limited period, normally four weeks, for contracts to be exchanged. A party who withdraws or declines to exchange within that period forfeits his deposit to the other. It provides certain situations in which a party may withdraw without losing his deposit. These include: (i) P's discovery of some adverse matter which reduces the property's open market value[15] by more than the preliminary deposit; (ii) P's failure to obtain a mortgage of a stated amount from a specified source and, significantly and if appropriate, (iii) the inability of V or P within the period to exchange contracts in a linked transaction.

The Conveyancing Committee recognises that signature of the agreement will not deter a vendor from gazumping if someone else offers him a price substantially in excess of what he will forfeit. At best it provides a disappointed purchaser with some compensation for his wasted expenditure. The scheme has received a mixed and less than enthusiastic response from the interested professions. The National Association of Estate Agents has reluctantly declined to give its blessing[16], whilst The Law Society's Land Law and Conveyancing Committee feels that solicitors should give it a fair chance[17]. It is too early to judge how successful the scheme will prove to be. A major flaw is its failure to address fully the problems of linked transactions. In practice, a purchaser will be ill-advised[18] to enter into the agreement with his vendor unless he can at about the same time secure a similar agreement from his own purchaser. But how often will this be possible? Unfortunately the scheme raises the unwelcome spectre of synchronising the exchange of contractual documents, which already tantalisingly confronts the parties at the time of formation of the principal contract. Maybe it can only be safely operated when neither party is involved

14 *Daulia Ltd v Four Millbank Nominees Ltd* [1978] Ch 231, [1978] 2 All ER 557, CA.
15 Not the agreed purchase price. There is scope for dispute here. The information may be revealed by a local search or survey.
16 (1987) 137 NLJ 69. And see (1987) 84 LS Gaz 165 (D Perkins).
17 (1987) 84 LS Gaz 791 (N Bonham-Carter). Cf the letters at pp 458, 954.
18 The agreement proceeds on the basis that the parties will sign it without taking legal advice, unless its terms have been amended (which is permissible) or something seems unclear. But how many cautious buyers are likely to sign unadvised a form produced by the vendor's agent?

in a dependent transaction. The Standing Committee, perhaps unwittingly, has introduced a totally new stage in the pre-contract conveyancing process, which results in the parties assuming contractual obligations to each other of a financial nature before they are even legally bound to buy and sell. This can hardly be seen as a desirable development especially at a time when the aim is to simplify the conveyancing system[19], and the scheme has not proved to be popular.

In truth, it is difficult to see any workable and effective way to prevent the practice of gazumping, its root causes being the delays involved in achieving an exchange of contracts, something which is almost inevitable when a chain of any length is being constructed, and volatile house prices. In recent times, with the housing market being depressed, gazumping is a far less common phenomenon than was once the case. Because of the state of the market, ironically, somewhat more likely nowadays is the purchaser refusing to exchange unless there is a reduction in the price provisionally agreed: a practice which has been dubbed gazundering. At the end of the day a solution to the problem involving changes in law or practice seem unlikely to occur.

B Exchange of contracts

1. Role of solicitor

(a) Ostensible authority to effect exchange
A solicitor is his client's agent to perform the appropriate tasks which will result in the creation of a binding contract. The opportunities for him to act on his own initiative are rather circumscribed. In the past, it was accepted that a solicitor had no implied authority to make a contract for his client; but if the parties have already concluded an oral contract, the solicitors' correspondence could constitute the necessary statutory memorandum[1]. A solicitor who holds his client's signed part of the contract has ostensible authority to effect exchange of contracts so that if, contrary to his client's instructions, he did exchange contracts, then, *as between vendor and purchaser* a binding contract came into being, capable of being enforced by specific performance[2]. It is not entirely clear that this is still the case. Because of s 2 of the Law of Property (Miscellaneous Provisions) Act 1989, there is no longer any such thing as an oral contract for the sale of land. Solicitors' correspondence cannot, therefore, create a contract between the parties[3]. As it is no longer the case that exchange of contracts can be viewed as making a previously unenforceable, but nevertheless valid, oral contract enforceable, it could be argued that, as it is

---

19 In addition the agreement is bound to give rise to disputes about the right to forfeit or to withdraw, inevitably involving the stakeholder; see (1987) 84 LS Gaz 791; [1987] Conv 89 (J E Adams).
1 *Daniels v Trefusis* [1914] 1 Ch 788. See the 3rd edition of this work, pp 115, 116 and 208.
2 *Compass v Thomas* (1973) 117 Sol Jo 306, CA. The client would have an action for damages against his solicitor.
3 *Commission for the New Towns v Cooper (Great Britain) Ltd* [1995] 2 All ER 929, CA, which is to be preferred to *Hooper v Sherman* [1994] NPC 153, CA.

the exchange of contracts that creates the contractual relationship, and a solicitor, as has been seen, does not have implied authority to enter into a contract on behalf of his client, therefore he no longer has any kind of authority to exchange contracts on behalf of his client. It is thought, however, that the courts will continue to accept that a solicitor has ostensible authority to exchange contracts, this being the method of implementing the agreement of the parties. The other side is entitled to rely on the solicitor having authority doing what he is authorised to do, unless they are aware of suspicious circumstances (eg uninitialed amendments) suggesting a lack of authority.

In some circumstances, a solicitor may be liable in damages to the other party for breach of warranty of authority. This happened in *Chitholie v Nash & Co*[4] where a vendor's solicitor signed the contract without authority and then exchanged parts. The purchaser's claim to specific performance was doomed to failure, but he recovered damages from the solicitor for wrongfully warranting that he had authority to enter into the contract on his client's behalf.

(b) Post-signature amendments

This can be a troublesome area. A solicitor has no implied authority to alter his client's contract after he has signed it. Equally, he has no ostensible authority to exchange contracts in an uninitialled amended form[5]. The presence of unsigned alterations of substance should put a solicitor on inquiry as to the other's authority to effect an exchange. Sometimes a solicitor, anxious not to delay an exchange of contracts which his client desperately wants, agrees to a last minute alteration without obtaining his prior authority[6]. He then exchanges contracts in the expectation that his client will ratify his action. Since it will usually be in his interests to do so the client will oblige, in which case ratification relates back to the time when the alteration was made[7]. In the absence of ratification the client is not bound by the contract, hence the need to verify that uninitialled alterations have been agreed to, inconvenient though this may be at such a late stage.

2.   Mode of exchange

(a) What constitutes an effective exchange

Under s 2 of the Law of Property (Miscellaneous Provisions) Act 1989, the contract can only be made in writing and only by incorporating all the terms which the parties have expressly agreed in one document or, whether contracts are exchanged, in each. Exchange of contracts, which is the usual means of bringing a contract into being, is not a mere matter of machinery; it is the vital

---

4   (1973) 229 EG 786. See also *Suleman v Shahsavari* [1989] 2 All ER 460, [1988] 1 WLR 1181. Damages for loss of bargain were awarded.
5   *Earl v Mawson* (1974) 232 EG 1315, CA.
6   Eg reducing the amount of the deposit, as in *Harrison v Battye* [1974] 3 All ER 830, CA.
7   *Koenigsblatt v Sweet* [1923] 2 Ch 314, CA (deleting purchaser's spouse as contracting party). A withdrawal by the other party is ineffective as against a subsequent ratification: *Bolton Partners v Lambert* (1889) 41 Ch D 295.

factor which brings the contract into existence[8]. What, therefore, in law constitutes an effective exchange? According to Buckley LJ, in *Domb v Isoz*[9]:

> ...the essential characteristic of exchange of contracts is that each party shall have such a document signed by the other party in his possession or control so that, at his own need, he can have the document available for his own use. Exchange of a written contract for sale is effected so soon as each part of the contract, signed by the vendor or the purchaser is in the actual or constructive possession of the other party or his solicitor.

This dictum was recently considered by the Court of Appeal in *Hooper v Sherman*[10]. A couple, who were co-owners of a house, agreed that one of them would buy out the interest of the other. Her solicitor wrote to his counterpart confirming the fact of agreement and confirming its terms. His solicitor replied confirming the fact of agreement. the question was whether there was a contract. The majority of the Court of Appeal held that there was. Concessions made by counsel that exchange of contracts was not a term of art and that, under the new Act, it was still possible to effect a contract by correspondence were accepted by the court. On this basis, it was held that, as each party had a document signed by the other, this amounted to an exchange of contracts as described in *Domb v Isoz*.

This view was not accepted by a differently constituted Court of Appeal in *Commission for New Towns v Cooper*[11]. Among the issues to be considered in this case was whether an exchange of faxes confirming an earlier agreement amounted to an exchange of contracts, thereby satisfying s 2. The Court of Appeal held that it did not. The process of exchange was held to constitute the swapping, actually or constructively, of identical documents; it did not amount to an exchange of correspondence. The court felt free not to follow *Hooper v Sherman* on the basis that it had proceeded upon concessions which were considered to have been wrongly made[12]. In particular, the earlier court had accepted, in accordance with the view of the Law Commission, that it was possible for contracts to continue to be made by correspondence. This overlooked, however, that the Bill as drafted by the Law Commission was significantly different from what was actually enacted. Although the two Court of Appeal decisions on what constitutes an exchange are in conflict, it is submitted that the approach taken in *Commissioner for New Towns v Cooper* is to be preferred, being consistent with the long held view that exchange of contracts consists of the swapping of identical documents.

(b) Personal exchange
The once familiar ceremonial exchange of contracts by solicitors in person at the offices of the vendor's solicitor has virtually fallen into disuse[13]. This method is usually quite unsuited to the needs of modern domestic conveyancing.

---

8   *Eccles v Bryant* [1948] Ch 93, [1947] 2 All ER 865, CA.
9   [1980] Ch 548 at 557, [1980] 1 All ER 942 at 948, CA.
10 [1994] NPC 153.
11 [1995] 2 All ER 929, CA. See [1995] Conv 319 (M P Thompson).
12 *Joscelyne v Nissen* [1970] 2 QB 86 at 89, [1970] 1 All ER 1213 at 1223, CA.
13 It is still employed by firms with offices in the same building or same small provincial town.

(c) Postal exchange

Another method sometimes adopted is to exchange contracts by post. The purchaser's (P's) signed part (with the deposit) is despatched first. On its receipt the vendor's (V's) solicitor sends V's contract in return. Uncertainty can arise as to the exact moment of exchange. In *Eccles v Bryant*[14] though V's solicitor had received P's contract, he failed to send V's signed part in exchange because V had changed his mind. P's action for specific performance was dismissed. Both parts had been signed, but no exchange had taken place, so there was no contract to be enforced. This rendered it unnecessary for the court to decide whether exchange was legally complete when the second of the two documents (V's part) was put into the post, or when it was received by P's solicitor.

The Standard Conditions of Sale purport to follow the former position[15], following the normal contractual rule applicable to postal acceptances. The open contract position is obscure. However, the need for each party to have the other's signed part in his possession or control suggests that the normal postal rule should not apply to contracts for the sale of land intended to be exchanged in parts[16]. The expression of intention contained in the Standard Conditions should mean that the courts will apply the normal postal rule and not regard the condition as being a term of a non-existent contract. If contracts are exchanged by telex, then the contract is made when the second part is received[17]. Increasingly solicitors have turned to private firms for the transmission of mail. A widespread network of document exchange centres covers the country[18]. Exchange of contracts through the medium of a document exchange is expressly sanctioned by the Standard Conditions of Sale, which provide that the contract is made when the last copy is deposited at the document exchange[19]. Such an enabling clause is not, however, necessary (and is strictly without contractual effect). A solicitor has implied authority to exchange contracts on behalf of his client in this way[20]. Before a solicitor seeks to make use of document exchange, he should check that his counterpart does also, it being unsafe to assume that this is the case. A failure to do so may result in liability for negligence if documents go astray when it is known to be urgent that contracts are exchanged[1].

(d) Exchange by telephone

A party to a domestic conveyancing transaction will often be involved in a linked sale and a purchase. He will naturally look to his solicitor to synchronise

---

14   [1948] Ch 93, [1947] 2 All ER 865, CA; *Sim v Griffiths* (1963) 186 EG 541 (V's death before her part sent to P's solicitor; no contract).
15   SCS 2.1.1.
16   See, eg, per Asquith LJ in *Eccles v Bryant*, supra, at 108, 871, and Buckley LJ in *Domb v Isoz*, supra, cited above. Contra, per Templeman LJ in *Domb v Isoz* at 564, 953.
17   *Brinkibon Ltd v Sahag Stahl GmbH* [1983] 2 AC 34, [1982] 1 All ER 293, HL.
18   See (1985) 82 LSG 1306, (1986) 83 LSG 13, giving details of the Britdoc Ltd scheme.
19   SCS 2.2.1.
20   *John Willmott Homes Ltd v Read* (1985) 51 P & CR 90 at 99 per Whitford J. Any relevant rule of the exchange agency will determine when a communication is deemed to have been delivered.
 1   *Stovold v Barlows* [1995] EGCS 155, CA.

the exchange of contracts in the two transactions. Neither of the procedures discussed in paragraphs (*b*) and (*c*) is particularly well-suited to achieve this result[2]. During the 1970s solicitors developed the practice of effecting exchange by telephone, a procedure which the Court of Appeal sanctioned in *Domb v Isoz*[3], much to the relief of the profession. In this case

> V's solicitor held both parts of the contract signed by V and P. He agreed with P's solicitor over the telephone that contracts should be treated as irrevocably exchanged from that moment. V's contract was never forwarded to P's solicitor. V declined to proceed on the basis that there had been no exchange of contracts. This defence was rejected and P was awarded damages for breach of contract.

The fact that V's part of the contract was still with his solicitor was of no consequence. The Court held that from the time of the telephone conversation V's contract was in the effective control and constructive possession of P's solicitor. It had ceased to be V's document. Consequently, an exchange had been effected. There is nothing unusual in this concept of constructive possession. As Bridge LJ observed, it is 'the merest commonplace' in conveyancing transactions for one solicitor to hold documents to the order of a party not his own client. Moreover, the Court recognised that a solicitor has ostensible authority to exchange contracts in this manner. So no express contractual term purporting to authorise the procedure is required[4].

(i) *The Law Society's formulae.* Acting on a suggestion made by Templeman LJ in *Domb v Isoz*[5], The Law Society has produced two widely used formulae for adoption by the profession[6]. Formula A is for use when one solicitor (invariably in practice the vendor's) holds both signed parts of the contract. Formula B applies where each solicitor holds his own client's signed contract[7]. Their use is not obligatory. The respective solicitors must mutually agree to operate the appropriate formula. There are no restrictions on their usage when a licensed conveyancer acts for the other contracting party.

(ii) *Formula A.* This applies when the solicitor for the purchaser (P) has already forwarded to his opposite number P's signed contract and a cheque for the deposit in readiness for exchange. P's contract is held by the vendor's (V's) solicitor to the order of (ie, as agent for) P's solicitor. Pending exchange it is still P's document. Adoption of Formula A imposes on V's solicitor several significant obligations, as follows:
(1) confirmation that he holds V's contract signed by his client(s)[8];
(2) insertion of the agreed completion date in each part;

2   See *Domb v Isoz* [1980] Ch 548, 564, [1980] 1 All ER 942, 953, CA, per Buckley and Templeman LJJ.
3   Supra. For another aspect of this case, see p 226, post.
4   Though this is provided for by NCS 1(6) and LSC 10(2). But see note 222, ante.
5   Supra, at 564, 953.
6   See (1986) 83 LS Gaz 2139, replacing the earlier versions given in (1983) 80 LS Gaz 1891.
7   See (1987) 84 LS Gaz 3313 (R Castle), giving examples of misuse.
8   He thereby warrants that all necessary parties have duly signed: (1986) 83 LS Gaz 2139.

(3) confirmation that he holds V's part to the order of P's solicitor;
(4) an undertaking to send that day V's contract to P's solicitor either by first class post, personal delivery to his office or to a document exchange (if appropriate).

It is the confirmation in (3)[9] that operates to bring about the telephonic exchange of contracts. Thereupon the parties are bound. Exchange is complete. P's solicitor is deemed to have constructive possession of V's signed contract, which is tantamount to actual possession in the light of V's solicitor's undertaking to send it. Failure to honour this undertaking, even when acting under instructions from his client, can lead to serious disciplinary proceedings[10].

(iii) *Formula B.*   This involves a mutual acceptance by both solicitors of the four obligations already discussed[2]. Contracts are exchanged as from the moment when each solicitor confirms to the other that he holds his own client's part to the order of the other solicitor. If amendments have been made to the draft contract, a vital preliminary step is to check that the details of the two parts are identical[12].

(iv) *Formula C.*   With a view to facilitating the synchronisation of exchange of contracts when a chain of transactions is involved, the Law Society introduced a new Formula C[13], this Formula being slightly modified in 1991, to reflect the fact that some exchanges are conducted by fax[14]. Formula C, which has not proved to be popular[15], works on a the basis of a series of undertakings. It starts with the solicitor at one end of the chain telephoning the solicitor next in the chain telling him that he holds his client's signed part of the contract and that he will exchange contracts later in the day when requested to do so. The same undertakings are then given to other solicitors involved in the chain until the end of the chain is reached. Contracts are then exchanged using Formula B and the requests to exchange contracts are then passed down the chain. The Law Society gave the following example of how Formula C is intended to operate giving the following scenario: W sells to X, who sells to Y, who sells to Z.

10.00 am Z's solicitor telephones Y's solicitor:
Formula C, part 1 agreed
10.10 am Y's solicitor telephones X's solicitor:
Formula C, part 1 agreed
10.20 am X's solicitor telephones W's solicitor: Formula B agreed at the top of the chain with part 1 of Formula C in place further down the chain, an immediate exchange of contracts is possible.

---

 9   Combined with P's solicitor's release of P's contract to be held by V's solicitor on V's behalf.
10   See p 464, post, in relation to solicitor's undertakings.
11   The undertaking by P's solicitor includes an obligation to send the deposit.
12   As to the reason for this, see p 226, post.
13   See (1989) 86 LSG No 11, p 26.
14   (1991) 88 LSG No 45, p 15.
15   It has been described as being 'demanding, time-consuming, risky and uncertain': (1990) 87 LSG, No 22, p 19 (R Castle).

10.30 am X's solicitor telephones Y's solicitor Formula C part 2 activated – the X–Y contract is binding. 10.40 am. Y's solicitor telephones Z's solicitor Formula C part 2 activated – the Y–Z contract is binding.

Formula C also envisages the deposit on the original transaction being passed along the chain. This aspect of the Formula will be considered below[16].

(v) *Eliminating uncertainties.* To avoid the risk of misunderstandings inherent in every telephone conversation, the solicitors should agree and record identical attendance notes. The Law Society's recommended memorandum[17] records: (a) the date and time of exchange; (b) the formula used; (c) the completion date; (d) the deposit to be paid (if any); (e) the identities of the persons involved in the conversation. Rather impracticably, Templeman LJ had suggested[18] that exchange by telephone should only be carried out by a partner or proprietor of a firm of solicitors. Whilst not endorsing this limitation, The Law Society has advocated that solicitors should consider carefully who within the firm is authorised to adopt the procedure and to ensure its use is restricted to them.

Exchange by telephone greatly facilitates the same-day exchange of contracts in a long chain of conveyancing transactions. But the attendant dangers should not be forgotten. The risk of uninitialled alterations, defective signatures or unidentical parts cannot be eliminated[19], though these are also hazards that might confront a purchaser's solicitor when a postal exchange takes place. Fortunately such occurrences are comparatively rare in practice.

(e) No formal exchange
A solicitor's freedom to act for both parties is severely curtailed as we have noticed[20]. Where he does so act there is no actual or constructive exchange of contracts in the sense in which there is when different solicitors are instructed. Indeed, when only one solicitor is involved, the idea of an exchange has been judicially described as 'artificial nonsense'[1]. The procedure adopted by practitioners when acting for both parties varies. Some firms prepare the contract in duplicate; others use a single document. In either case the signatures of all parties are necessary before they become contractually bound[2]. Once a completed contract has been unconditionally signed by all parties, nothing

---

16 Pages 236–237, post.

17 (1986) 83 LS Gaz 2139, adopting the suggestion of Templeman LJ in *Domb v Isoz* [1980] Ch 548 at 564, [1980] 1 All ER 942 at 953, CA. See *Griffiths v Young* [1970] 3 All ER 601, CA, as to the problems of a disputed telephone conversation between solicitors.

18 *Domb v Isoz*, loc cit.

19 They could be if both parts were *physically exchanged* in advance to be held initially by each solicitor to the other's order. Each would then have a sight of the other's signed document before agreeing by telephone to release his own client's part to be held by the other solicitor on his client's behalf. This attractive procedure, suggested by Bridge LJ in *Domb v Isoz*, supra, at 560, 950, has not been reflected in either of The Law Society's formulae. Why?

20 See p 145, ante.

1 *Smith v Mansi* [1962] 3 All ER 857 at 861, CA, per Danckwerts LJ.

2 *Beck v Box* (1973) 231 EG 1295.

more is required to make the contract binding[3]. Other exceptional circumstances may exist which indicate that a formal exchange of contracts is not envisaged by the parties[4].

3. Identical parts

Whatever mode of exchange is adopted, no binding contract results unless the two parts exchanged are identical in all *material* respects. In *Harrison v Battye*[5] the solicitors, after their clients had signed their respective parts but before exchange, agreed to vary the amount of the deposit. The purchaser's part incorporated this amendment, but the vendor's part was inadvertently left unaltered. The purchaser's action for specific performance was dismissed as there was no concluded contract. Similarly, the addition of a new contracting party (eg a spouse joined as co-purchaser) or the insertion of a new term[6] will prima facie preclude the creation of any contract, should the amendment feature in only one signed part.

The existence of non-identical parts may not be so fatal as appears at first sight. In *Harrison v Battye* the vendor had not consented[7] to the reduction in the deposit. Where, however, there is clear evidence that both parties have themselves agreed to a last minute variation, the courts will uphold the exchange as effective on the ground that the remedy of rectification would be available to cure the discrepancy[8].

4. Agreeing the completion date

In all cases the solicitors should ascertain from their clients the desired completion date for insertion in the contract. Securing agreement on this can often prove to be of considerable difficulty when the parties are involved in a chain of transactions. Somehow all of them must agree on the same day, unless at least one party is willing to forgo synchronised completions of his sale and purchase transactions[9]. The insertion of the agreed completion date is expressly called for by the approved formulae employed on an exchange of contracts by telephone. In other situations this may be overlooked. Solicitors have no implied authority to fix the date on behalf of their clients. The insertion at the time of exchange of some date not agreed to by the parties prevents the

---

3   *Smith v Mansi*, supra.
4   *Storer v Manchester City Council* [1974] 3 All ER 824, CA (sale of council house to tenant; council intending to dispense with usual legal formalities). Contrast *Gibson v Manchester City Council* [1979] 1 All ER 972, HL (no concluded contract).
5   [1974] 3 All ER 830, CA.
6   *Earl v Mawson* (1974) 232 EG 1315, CA.
7   The contrary indication in the headnote is wrong; see at 833, per Sir Eric Sachs.
8   *Domb v Isoz* [1980] Ch 548, [1980] 1 All ER 942, CA (agreed term that sale to include fittings and fixtures).
9   This will probably entail his having to find either temporary accommodation or bridging finance, depending on whether it is his sale or purchase that is to be completed first.

formation of any binding contract, unless they both later ratify the date[10]. When no completion date is specified in a formal contract, the relevant general condition determines the position[11].

5. Subsequent variation of contract

The parties may vary the agreement *after* exchange of contracts. The position as previously understood was that, to be effective, the variation itself had to be evidenced in writing and signed or initialed[12]. The reason for this is that, after variation, the agreement between the parties is not the original contract, but that contract as varied, and there must be an adequate written record of the contract as it now stands[13]. In *McCausland v Duncan Lawrie Ltd*[14], the Court of Appeal held that a written contract which satisfied s 2 of the Law of Property (Miscellaneous Provisions) Act 1989 had not been effectively varied by correspondence between the respective solicitors with respect to the completion date. This seems to be correct in principle, otherwise the contract which the court would ultimately enforce would not satisfy the terms of s 2. On the other hand, a complete discharge of a written contract may be effected orally. Suppose V and P enter into a formal contract for the sale and purchase of plot A. Later they orally agree to buy and sell plot B instead. Their oral agreement will effectively discharge the written contract[15], but the second agreement is not a contract because it is not in writing as required by s 2.

If the contract mistakenly fails to record the true agreement between the parties, the court has jurisdiction to rectify the contract and to order its specific performance as rectified, despite all the terms of the contract not being in writing[16].

6. Protection of contract for sale

Should the purchaser's solicitor take the precaution of protecting his client's contract in the appropriate manner? With unregistered land the contract ranks as a C(iv) land charge, and will be avoided against a later purchaser of the legal estate for money or money's worth if not registered[17]. Since the majority

10 See p 220, ante.
11 See SCS 6.1.1. See p 420, post.
12 Appropriate words or gestures expressly directed to reviving the existing signature may suffice: *New Hart Builders Ltd v Brindley* [1975] Ch 342, [1975] 1 All ER 1007.
13 *Goss v Lord Nugent* (1833) 5 B & Ad 58; *Morris v Baron & Co* [1918] AC 1 at 31, HL, per Lord Atkinson; *New Hart Builders Ltd v Brindley*, supra.
14 [1996] NPC 94, CA.
15 *Morris v Baron & Co*, supra.
16 *United States of America v Motor Trucks Ltd* [1924] AC 196, PC; *Wright v Robert Leonard (Developments) Ltd* [1994] NPC 49, CA. The court has a discretion as to the date from which rectification is deemed to have taken effect: Law of Property (Miscellaneous Provisions) Act 1989, s 2(4). See further on rectification, Ch 24.
17 LCA 1972, s 4(6). On a sub-sale registration must be effected against the head-vendor (as the legal estate owner): *Barrett v Hilton Developments Ltd* [1975] Ch 237, [1974] 3 All ER 944, CA. See generally Ch 13.

of contracts are completed within a comparatively short time after exchange, it is not the practice to register the contract, unless completion is to be delayed or a dispute arises between the parties. Whatever the standard practice of the profession might be, a solicitor failing to register a contract which subsequently became void would be liable to his client for professional negligence[18]. The solicitor's liability is both contractual and tortious[19]. The precise effect of registration needs to be carefully understood. Registration gives notice. It does not determine the priority of competing equitable interests[20]. Nor does it operate to confer enforceability on an agreement which through lack of statutory formality is not contractual.

Registered land

The contract should be protected by a notice in the vendor's charges register, which will require his co-operation in lodging the land certificate at the Registry[1], otherwise the contract can only be protected by a caution. If the vendor's property is subject to a registered charge, the land certificate will already be deposited at the Registry[2]. The purchaser can thus obtain the entry of a notice without his concurrence, though the contract will not bind the chargee. Entering a notice or lodging a caution secures for the purchaser no greater measure of protection than does registration of a C (iv) land charge in the case of unregistered land. So a purchaser (P) cannot acquire priority for his contract over some other equitable right, eg a charge arising under the Matrimonial Homes Act 1983, merely because that other right is entered on the register after P has protected his contract[3]. It may even be that P will have to take subject to an adverse third party interest not protected on the register until after completion of his purchase. Normally he will not be affected by such an interest since his official search certificate (which will not disclose the interest) will confer priority, provided his transfer is lodged for registration within the period of protection afforded by the certificate. In practice, however,

---

18 See *Wroth v Tyler* [1974] Ch 30 at 64, [1973] 1 All ER 897 at 927, per Megarry J; cf *Edward Wong Finance Co Ltd v Johnson, Stokes and Master* [1984] AC 296, PC (completion procedures according to general professional practice in Hong Kong held negligent).

19 *Midland Bank Trust Co Ltd v Hett, Stubbs and Kemp* [1979] Ch 384, [1978] 3 All ER 571 (failure to register option). But see note 13, p 214, ante and contrast *Bell v Peter Browne & Co* [1990] 2 QB 495, [1990] 3 All ER 124, CA. It is particularly vital to ensure that an option to purchase (see p 229, post) is duly protected.

20 LPA 1925, s 198(1), p 396, post. Consider the competing claims of X and Y when V contracts to sell the same land first to X, then to Y. Y cannot, by being the first (or only one) to register, secure priority, even if V later conveys the land to X. Because X is first in time and prima facie entitled to specific performance free from Y's rights, Y's registration merely gives X notice of rights inferior from the point of priority to his own. Should V convey to Y (rather than X), Y will have priority, provided X has not registered his C(iv) before the V–Y conveyance.

1 LRA 1925, s 49(1)(c), see p 72, ante.

2 Ibid, s 65.

3 This question of priorities will be determined by general equitable principles, and is not thought to be affected by the equivocal provisions of s 107(1) of the Act. But see [1976] CLP 26, 40–42, 55 (D J Hayton).

this requirement is not infrequently overlooked[4], to the potential prejudice of the purchaser.

Protection of P's contract on the register will give priority over a competing legal interest which does not of itself require substantive registration (eg lease taking effect as an overriding interest) and which has been created by the vendor after completion of P's purchase but before P's registration as proprietor[5]. It should not be forgotten that a purchaser's own occupation under an enforceable contract constitutes an overriding interest, binding on a subsequent transferee for value, with or without notice[6].

C Special cases

Hitherto we have been considering the position where the usual conveyancing procedure operates. A contractual relationship between vendor and purchaser can, of course, arise in other ways. The parties themselves may have prepared a document sufficient for the purposes of s 2 of the Law of Property (Miscellaneous Provisions) Act 1989. Some other special situations must now be considered.

1. Options to purchase and rights of pre-emption

A valid option to purchase land constitutes an irrevocable offer by the grantor to sell[7] to the grantee during the period specified for its exercise. When the offer is accepted by giving notice of exercise to the grantor, a contract for the sale and purchase of the land is brought into existence, provided the terms and conditions on which it is exercisable have been completely fulfilled. In particular the time prescribed for its exercise must be strictly observed. In this respect time is of the essence of the option, which lapses if the grantee does not give his notice timeously[8]. Where the option agreement makes no provision for the resulting contract of sale to be governed by one of the standard form Conditions of Sale, exercise of the option creates an open contract[9].

An option to purchase must be distinguished from a right of pre-emption (or first refusal)[10], which merely obliges the grantor to offer the property to the grantee, should he desire to sell. It does not entitle the grantee to set in motion any machinery for the acquisition of the land. The exact legal status of

---

4 See further p 475, post.
5 LRA 1925, s 18 (3). If P fails to protect his contract he takes subject to the lease. Until P's registration as proprietor the legal title remains in the vendor (p 73, post). The situation posed in the text is hardly likely to occur in practice.
6 *Bridges v Mees* [1957] Ch 475, [1957] 2 All ER 577.
7 The option itself creates an *immediate* equitable interest in the land: *London and South Western Rly Co v Gomm* (1882) 20 Ch D 562 at 581, CA, per Jessel MR. See generally Barnsley, *Land Options*, (2nd edn) 11–12, 35–36, Ch 4.
8 *Wheatley v Burrell Enterprises Ltd* (1963) 186 EG 259, CA.
9 See pp 147, 149 ante.
10 See generally Barnsley, op cit, Ch 7.

these rights has been problematic for many years. In *Pritchard v Briggs*[11] the Court of Appeal decided by a majority that the grant of a right of pre-emption was a mere *spes*. The evolution of the relationship of vendor and purchaser depends on the grantor, of his own volition, choosing to fulfil certain specified conditions, eg to sell. This converts the pre-emption into an option and thereupon the grantee acquires an equitable interest in land. The decision has been widely attacked as being unsound in principle[12]. One of the difficulties raised by the decision is knowing precisely when the conversion process occurs.

Is it when the grantor puts the property up for sale, or makes an offer to a third party, or concludes a binding agreement to sell? Can he circumvent his obligation to the grantee by offering to create a long lease rather than selling the freehold[13]? Ultimately the answer to such questions will depend on a construction of the agreement conferring the right of pre-emption. In*Pritchard v Briggs* the grant of an option to purchase in favour of a third party was held not to be a sale of the land which operated to make a prior right of pre-emption exercisable.

2. Tenant's purchase under the Leasehold Reform Act 1967

A situation similar in effect to the exercise of an option to purchase arises when a qualifying tenant gives notice of his desire to purchase the freehold under the Leasehold Reform Act 1967. This Act enables a tenant of a house[14] held on a long lease (basically one granted for a term exceeding 21 years) to acquire the freehold[15] in certain circumstances at a price calculated as provided by the Act[16]. A qualified tenant wishing to take advantage of the Act must serve on the landlord a notice in a prescribed form. If valid it creates a contractual relationship between them, binding the landlord to make and the tenant to accept a conveyance of the freehold[17]. The notice operates as an estate contract, registrable as a C (iv) land charge or protectable by a notice or caution in the case of registered land[18]. The resulting contract for sale is governed by

11   [1980] Ch 338, [1980] 1 All ER 294, CA, applied in *Kling v Keston Properties Ltd* (1983) 49 P & CR 212. As to their registrability as land charges, see p 387, post.
12   See M & W, 605–6; (1980) 96 LQR 488, [1980] Conv 433.
13   Cf *Kling v Keston Properties Ltd*, supra, where the triggering event was the grantor's desire to sell the property on a long lease.
14   As to which see *Tandon v Trustees of Spurgeon's Homes* [1982] AC 755, [1982] 1 All ER 1086, HL (purpose-built shop with flat above); *Sharpe v Duke Street Securities NV* (1987) 283 EG 1558, CA. Rights have now been conferred on tenants of flats: Leasehold Reform, Housing and Urban Development Act 1993, Part I.
15   But see *Gratton-Storey v Lewis* [1987] 2 EGLR 108, CA (no right for resident sub-tenant who also owned freehold to acquire intervening leasehold interest).
16   See s 9. For the relevant rental and rateable value limits, see s 1(1)(a) (as amended); (5), (6), and s 4; for the residence qualification (now only three years), see s 1(1)(b) (as amended); *Poland v Earl Cadogan* [1980] 3 All ER 544, CA. The tenant may opt instead to take an extension of 50 years to his existing term.
17   The provisions of which are regulated by s 10.
18   Section 5(5). The tenant's rights do not rank as an overriding interest within the LRA 1925, s 70(1)(g). Failure to protect the notice will not be fatal since a fresh notice can be served on the purchaser of the reversion.

conditions of sale specially prescribed for these transactions[19]. Once the right to acquire has accrued, it can be released by the tenant, but mere inactivity does not deprive him of his right to enforce the notice[20] unless his conduct suffices to found an estoppel. Trustees in whom the lease is vested owe a fiduciary duty to serve a notice on behalf of a qualifying beneficiary in occupation under the trust[1].

By virtue of s 7(1) of the Act, the benefit of the rights acquired by the tenant are transmissible to his assigns. This is of importance to a prospective purchaser of a leasehold house from a vendor-tenant qualified to serve a notice but who has not done so. It is in the purchaser's interests to prevail upon him to serve a notice before exchange of contracts, the benefit of which he can agree to assign to the purchaser on completion[2]. Alternatively, the contract can include a term whereby the vendor agrees to serve a notice if the purchaser so requires within a specified period and to assign its benefit. Once a tenancy has been assigned without the benefit of the notice, it ceases to have effect (s 7(2)). It is therefore vital to ensure that the assignment of the leasehold term includes an assignment of the benefit of the notice.

3.   Sales by public auction

The form and contents of a contract for sale by auction do not differ materially from a contract for sale by private treaty. Because s 2 of the Law of Property (Miscellaneous Provisions) Act 1989 does not apply to sales made in the course of a public auction[3], a binding contract is formed when the property is knocked down to the successful bidder. Thereafter there is no opportunity for approval of the formal contracts which are signed at the end of the auction. However, the particulars of the property and special conditions are read out at the time of the auction and they can usually be inspected beforehand at the offices of the vendor's solicitor and of the auctioneer. An interested party may effect his own local searches beforehand, but it is commonplace for these to be made on the vendor's behalf and produced at the auction. Because the successful bidder will be contractually bound to buy the property when the hammer falls, it is essential that his financial arrangements have been made prior to the auction.

(a) Conditions regulating conduct of auction
The Standard Conditions of Sale contain provisions relating to the conduct of the auction, some of which are dictated by the Sale of Land by Auction Act 1867.

19   Leasehold Reform (Enfranchisement and Extension) Regulations 1967, SI No 1879.
20   *Collin v Duke of Westminster* [1985] QB 581, [1985] 1 All ER 463, CA (claim, being a speciality, subject to 12 years' limitation period under Limitation Act 1980, s 8).
1   See s 6(3); *Marsh v Gilbert* (1980) 256 EG 715.
2   For a precedent, see 18 Ency F & P, 712, Form 3:B:81. The vendor is advised to add an express denial of any warrant as to his entitlement to acquire the freehold.
3   Law of Property (Miscellaneous Provisions) Act 1989, s 2(5).

(i) *Reserve price.*   The sale may be either 'without reserve' or subject to a reserve price; this must be clearly stated in the contract[4]. The Standard Conditions of Sale state that the sale is subject to a reserve price[5]. They also enable the vendor or his agent to bid up to that price, a right which by statute must be expressly reserved, in which case the vendor, or someone on his behalf, can bid[6]. By reserving this right, the vendor is more likely to achieve the reserve price, thus reducing the chances of an abortive auction. If the sale is without reserve, it is not lawful for the vendor to employ a 'puffer', someone to bid on his behalf[7]. In the past, the Standard Conditions of Sale gave the vendor the right to withdraw the property from sale during the auction[8]. There is no such clause in the Standard Conditions of Sale and, in the absence of such a clause, it is doubtful if the vendor is free to withdraw the property if the sale is without reserve[9]. A vendor who wishes to reserve this right should, therefore, incorporate a special condition to this effect.

(ii) *Bidding.*   A bid is in the nature of an offer to buy, and the acceptance of a bid by the auctioneer does not result in a binding contract unless the property is knocked down at that price and, in the case of a reserve price, that price has been reached[10]. Subject to this the highest bidder becomes the purchaser, the general consensus being that a term that no bid shall be withdrawn is unenforceable[11]. Being merely an offer, it can be withdrawn at any time before acceptance, ie, before the fall of the hammer. The Standard Conditions of Sale do not contain such a clause. If a dispute arises as to the bidding the auctioneer has power either to determine the dispute or put up the property again at the last undisputed bid[12]. He is also empowered to refuse to accept any bid[13].

(b) Auctioneer's authority to sign contract
Because a sale by public auction is not governed by s 2 of the Law of Property (Miscellaneous Provisions) Act 1989, the contract of sale is formed when the

---

4   Sale of Land by Auction Act 1867, s 5.
5   SCS 2.3.2.
6   SCS 2.3.3; Sale of Land by Auction Act 1867, ss 5, 6. Contravention of these provisions renders the sale invalid: ibid, s 4.
7   Sale of Land by Auction Act 1867, s 4.
8   NCS 1(4); LSC 25(3)(c).
9   For a discussion of the conflicting opinions, see Williams, *Title*, 123.
10   *McManus v Fortescue* [1907] 2 KB 1, CA. Occasionally the auction takes the form of the submission by interested persons of a single bid, or tender, contained in a sealed envelope opened on a specified date. With such auctions a referential bid, one expressed as a stated amount more than any other bid, is invalid: *Harvela Investments Ltd v Royal Trust Co of Canada* [1986] AC 207, [1985] 2 All ER 966, HL (sale of shares). An offer to sell by sealed tender constitutes a unilateral contract with each offeree, which is converted into a bilateral contract when the highest bid is duly received.
11   1 Williams, V & P, 21–22; Williams, *Title*, 124; 1 Dart, 122. But see *Freer v Rimner* (1844) 14 Sim 391 (sale under court decree; retraction disallowed).
12   SCS 2.3.5. As to what amounts to a dispute. see *Richards v Phillips* [1969] 1 Ch 39, [1968] 2 All ER 859, CA.
13   SCS 2.3.4.

property is knocked down to the successful bidder. It is no longer necessary, therefore, to insert clauses in the draft contract requiring the purchaser, forthwith to sign the contract and pay the deposit. It was settled that, after the auction was completed, the auctioneer had authority to sign the contract on behalf of both vendor and purchaser[14]. As a binding contract comes into being on the fall of the hammer, this point is now academic.

D   The deposit

1.   Obligation to pay

The general law imposes no obligation on a purchaser to pay a deposit on entering into a contract to buy land. The Standard Conditions of Sale, however, stipulate for payment of a 10% deposit no later than the date of the contract[15]. Except when it is received by an auctioneer on a sale by public auction, the deposit is required to be paid to the vendor's solicitor. It normally accompanies the purchaser's signed part of the contract. The amount is often varied by agreement, especially in the case of a first-time buyer or a purchaser whose mortgagee is providing more than 90% of the purchase price. Except in areas of the country where smaller deposits are customary[16], payment of less than the standard 10% should be agreed in advance with the vendor. A vendor's solicitor has no implied authority to accept a deposit for an amount less than that provided for by the contract signed by his client[17]. The consequences of failure to obtain the contractual deposit on exchange of contracts are amply demonstrated by *Morris v Duke-Cohan & Co*[18].

Except on a sale by auction, the Standard Conditions require the deposit to be paid by banker's draft[19] or by cheque drawn on a solicitor's bank account. It is not uncommon for the purchaser's own personal cheque[20] to be sent, but a cautious practitioner is unlikely to accept this unless there is time for it to be cleared before exchange of contracts. Often this counsel of perfection has to be ignored in practice because of the need to synchronise the exchange in linked transactions. Whatever form payment takes, a deposit forwarded to the vendor's solicitor in advance of exchange should be sent on the terms that it is

---

14   *Leeman v Stocks* [1951] Ch 941, [1951] 1 All ER 1043.
15   SCS 2.2.1.
16   The Isle of Wight Conveyancing Protocol advocates 5% or £1,000, whichever is less: (1984) 81 LS Gaz 2356.
17   Cf *Harrison v Battye* [1974] 3 All ER 830, CA. The vendor can ratify the variation.
18   (1975) 119 Sol Jo 826.
19   SCS 2.2.1. Technically an order for the payment of money drawn by one bank on another, but otherwise resembling an ordinary cheque save that it is not subject to dishonour. They are normally reserved for deposits of large amounts.
20   Sometimes this may be drawn initially in favour of the purchaser's own solicitor who, if he then endorses it over to the vendor's solicitor, becomes obliged to meet it personally if it is dishonoured. Presumably it would now be regarded as within a solicitor's ordinary course of business to accept payment by cheque: *Pape v Westacott* [1894] 1 QB 272 at 283, CA, per Davey LJ; *Farrer v Lacy, Hartland & Co* (1885) 31 Ch D 42, CA (auctioneer's implied authority to take deposit cheque). And see [1979] Conv 90.

held by him as a stakeholder (ie as agent for both parties) pending exchange. This effectively prevents its use by the vendor's solicitor to fund the deposit on the vendor's own purchase before contracts have been exchanged in the transaction with the purchaser. The adoption of Formula B to effect an exchange of contracts by telephone means that a binding contract comes into existence before the deposit is received or even paid. The purchaser's solicitor undertakes to forward this on the same day, though not necessarily by banker's draft[2].

2.   Nature of deposit[3]

The deposit operates as a security for the completion of the purchase. It is more than simply a part payment; it is an earnest to bind the bargain and creates by the fear of its forfeiture a motive in the payer to perform the rest of the contract[4]. The threat of its loss operates as a potent incentive for the purchaser not to indulge in a capricious change of mind. A deposit must be distinguished from (i) a nominal payment (frequently termed a pre-contract deposit) which a prospective purchaser sometimes makes to the vendor's estate agent when he signifies his willingness to buy 'subject to contract'; (ii) the one-half per cent pre-contract 'deposit' payable under the recently introduced pre-contract deposit agreement procedure[5]; and (iii) an instalment of the purchase price made after the contract has been concluded and a contractual deposit paid. Such part payments are generally not forfeitable by the vendor. As to (i), the payment is not strictly a deposit. It does not guarantee due performance of any bargain, for as yet there is no bargain. It is simply money paid by an interested buyer as evidence of his genuine intention to negotiate. Unless and until a contract is concluded, he is entitled to require its return at any time and for any reason, but apparently, without interest[6]. On the making of the contract it stands in the same position as a deposit properly so-called.

Consequences of non-payment
Because it is a term 'of so radical a nature'[7], the purchaser's default in payment constitutes a fundamental breach of contract entitling the vendor, if he so wishes, to treat the contract as discharged and to sue for damages. This has

1   Irrespective of how it is to be held *after* exchange (p 235, post). He ought not to require it to be held to his order. This obliges the vendor's solicitor to hold the document physically to his order, not merely the proceeds: (1980) 77 LS Gaz 766. It would technically preclude enactment in readiness for use of the proceeds (if permitted) in connection with the vendor's linked purchase.
2   See p 224, ante. A client's account cheque suffices. Compare (1984) 81 LS Gaz 1891, note 2. Strictly the contract needs amendment to authorise a post-exchange payment; see note 2, ante.
3   See [1995] Conv 41, 100 (A J Oakley).
4   *Howe v Smith* (1884) 27 Ch D 89, at 98, 101, CA, per Bowen and Fry LJJ.
5   See p 218, ante.
6   *Potters v Loppert* [1973] Ch 399, [1973] 1 All ER 658 (agent expressly holding payment as stakeholder).
7   *Myton Ltd v Schwab-Morris* [1974] 1 All ER 326 at 331, per Goulding J.

now been accepted as the true rule in this country[8], bringing us into line with the Australian position[9]. On general contractual principles it ought to follow that non-payment for whatever reason justifies the vendor's immediate rescission without having to give the purchaser prior notice calling for payment within a reasonable time. Yet in *Millichamp v Jones*[10], a decision involving an option to purchase, Warner J held that in the case of an inadvertent non-payment the vendor must give the purchaser an opportunity to comply with the obligation before seeking to terminate the contract. Even assuming the case to be correctly decided, which it is respectfully submitted is not so, it will be of limited application to ordinary contracts for the sale of land. Here non-payment is likely to be intentional, resulting from a failure to send any deposit at all (eg after a telephonic exchange using Formula B) or because the cheque has been stopped or dishonoured[11].

The Standard Conditions of Sale expressly entitle a vendor to terminate the contract if the deposit cheque is dishonoured. This step must be taken within seven working days after the cheque has not been met on first presentation[12]. The Standard Conditions do not deal with the position if no deposit is paid, in which event the vendor's rights will be governed by the general law.

3. Capacity of deposit-holder

(a) Agent or stakeholder?

The contract will normally determine the question whether a deposit paid to a third party is received by him as agent for the vendor, or as a stakeholder. Subject to any variation, the Standard Conditions provide[13] for it to be held by a stakeholder, whether he be the vendor's solicitor or an auctioneer. In the absence of any express or implied capacity, the vendor's solicitor holds a deposit as agent for the vendor[14] and an auctioneer as a stakeholder[15].

A solicitor receiving the deposit as agent for the vendor must on demand pay it to the vendor together with accrued interest[16], or according to his

8 *Damon Cia Naviera SA v Hapag-Lloyd International SA* [1985] 1 All ER 475, CA, rejecting the alternative view of Goulding J in *Myton Ltd v Schwab-Morris*, supra, that payment was a condition precedent to formation of a contract.
9 *Brien v Dwyer* (1979) 141 CLR 378; and see *Watson v Healy Lands Ltd* [1965] NZLR 511 at 516, 517, per Woodhouse J.
10 [1983] 1 All ER 267 (grantee unaware of duty to pay on exercise), criticised, with justification, at (1983) 99 LQR 503 (J W Carter), but followed by Whitford J in *John Willmott Homes Ltd v Read* (1985) 51 P & CR 90, where the deposit, payable within seven days *after* exercise of option, was clearly not a security for performance.
11 *Myton Ltd v Schwab-Morris*, supra; *Pollway Ltd v Abdullah* [1974] 2 All ER 381, CA (auction deposit cheque stopped).
12 SCS 2.2.4. This covers a situation where one of two deposit cheques bounces: *Trustbridge Ltd v Bhattessa* [1985] LS Gaz R 2580, CA.
13 SCS 2.2.3.
14 *Ellis v Goulton* [1893] 1 QB 350 at 353, CA, per Bowen LJ, a rule which extends to the receipt of the entire purchase price: *Tudor v Hamid* [1988] 1 EGLR 251, [1987] NLJ Rep 79, CA.
15 *Harington v Hoggart* (1830) 1 B & Ad 577.
16 Assuming the circumstances are such that in fairness to the client interest ought to be paid to him under the Solicitor's Accounts (Deposit Interest) Rules 1987: (1987) 84 LS Gaz 899.

instructions. Consequently, though a solicitor will normally retain any deposit held as agent until completion and then deal with it in various ways, it is perfectly proper for such a deposit to be used even before completion in discharge of a second mortgage, or in payment towards a deposit on other property which the vendor has contracted to buy. If the contract goes off owing to his default the deposit should be returned to the purchaser, but he must sue the vendor, not the agent, for its recovery, even where the money is still in the agent's possession[17].

On the other hand, a stakeholder is the agent for both parties. He holds the deposit on trust to deal with it in different ways in different contingencies[18]: to pay it to the vendor on the purchaser's default, or return it to the purchaser if the vendor breaks the contract. In the normal case where the contract is completed, it becomes payable to the vendor and the purchaser should authorise the stakeholder to release it to him or his solicitor, a formality rarely observed in practice. The stakeholder assumes personal responsibility for the safe keeping of the deposit. Any improper disposal of it on the instructions of one of the parties renders the stakeholder liable to the other for its loss[19]. Neither side, however, has any proprietary claim to the deposit; any claim is merely a contractual or quasi-contractual personal right to recover it[20]. A stakeholder, unlike an agent, can retain any profit (by way of interest or otherwise) resulting from the deposit; it is his reward for holding the stake[1]. Despite this ancient principle, the Council of The Law Society recommended that, in the case of a solicitor-stakeholder the contract should expressly regulate the position as to interest on the stake, failing which interest thereon should be treated as if it were covered by the relevant Deposit Interest Rules[2]. This recommendation has been acted upon so that Standard Condition 2.2.3. provides that, unless the deposit is to be used in respect of another purchase, the deposit is to be held by the seller's solicitor as stakeholder.

(b) Vendor's solicitor: agent or stakeholder?

Whilst the Standard Conditions of Sale provide for the solicitor to hold the deposit as stakeholder, they also provide for it to be used as part of the deposit in an associated purchase in effect, requiring the deposit to be paid to the solicitor as agent for the vendor[3]. This, indeed, is an essential feature of the Law Society's Formula C. The reason for this is not hard to discover. Suppose

---

17   *Ellis v Goulton* [1893] 1 QB 350, CA.
18   *Skinner v Trustee of Property of Reed (Bankrupt)* [1967] Ch 1194 at 1200, [1967] 2 All ER 1286 at 1289, per Cross J.
19   *Oakdown Ltd v Bernstein & Co* (1894) 49 P & CR 282 (release to vendor following wrongful repudiation); *Dimurro v Charles Caplin & Co* (1969) 211 EG 31 (vendor's solicitors not entitled to pay rent due from purchaser out of deposit held as stakeholder). *Rockeagle Ltd v Alsop Wilkinson* [1992] Ch 47, CA.
20   *Hastingwood Property Ltd v Saunders* [1991] Ch 114.
 1   *Harington v Hoggart*, supra; *Potters v Loppert* [1973] Ch 399, [1973] 1 All ER 658 (estate agent holding pre-contract deposit), but doubted by Sachs LJ in *Burt v Claude Cousins & Co Ltd* [1971] 2 QB 426 at 449–50, [1971] 2 All ER 611 at 622, CA.
 2   (1987) 84 LSG 1202. See note 16, ante.
 3   SCS 2.2.2.

the following chain of sales and purchases: A-B, B-C, C-D, D-E. If E's deposit is paid to D's solicitor as D's agent, D can use it wholly, or in part, towards the deposit to C and so on down the chain. E's deposit in effect ends up as part of B's deposit paid to A, who being the person at the end of the chain, his solicitor will hold the deposit as stakeholder. This scheme enables D, C and B to limit the amount of money that they have to borrow at high interest for their own deposits, or to lose interest on savings realised to fund the deposit. They will need only finance the difference in the amount of deposit received and the amount which has to be paid to their vendor. Whereas if the deposit was held by stakeholders, all the buyers have to find their own individual deposits.

The capacity in which a vendor's solicitor should hold the deposit is an emotive issue among practitioners, judging by the frequency with which the problem is aired in the legal journals. A strong body of opinion advocates that it can properly be held as the vendor's agent if he requires to use it in connection with a linked purchase, but not otherwise[4]. There is an obvious, albeit slight, element of risk in E's allowing his deposit to be used by D, especially when in practice it will eventually form part of the B-A deposit. Difficulties will arise when E becomes entitled to the return of his deposit. This may occur because, eg D's title is defective, or D may fail to complete the C-D purchase, so forfeiting the deposit paid to C in the process. E is unlikely to have his deposit returned promptly by D, if at all[5]. True, in both situations E has an equitable charge on D's land by virtue of the lien he possesses[6], but its enforcement is a cumbersome and dilatory process. Provided that the purchaser (E) is fully advised[7] of the risks involved, it is not thought that on balance there exist sufficient reasons on legal grounds alone to object to the deposit being held as the vendor's agent.

However, one further important consideration must not be ignored. Why should D (or his solicitor) expect E to make what is in effect an interest-free loan to D, albeit for a short period of time? E, if a first-time buyer, may well have had to borrow to finance the deposit or withdraw from savings, so losing interest. It is clearly open to E to require interest on his loan at the going rate, payable by means of a deduction from the purchase monies due on completion[8]. Alternatively, D should consider some inducement to E, eg by offering to accept less than the customary 10%. It is uncertain how far purchasers' solicitors are prepared to negotiate on this issue on their clients' behalf.

(c) Position of parties on loss of deposit through insolvency
In the event of the insolvency of the deposit-holder (not being the vendor holding the deposit personally), who bears the loss, the vendor or the

---

4 See the suggested national guidelines: (1987) 84 LS Gaz 2260, para 10 and Law Society's Formula C.

5 D will probably also default in the sale to E, leaving E to look for another house.

6 See p 241, post. The charge itself will be worthless if D is mortgaged up to the hilt, a circumstance that E will probably not know about. For a scheme which seeks to maximise E's security by additionally conferring an equitable charge on the property that D has agreed to buy (ie C's house), see (1970) 120 NLJ 1128, 1139–40 (J E Adams).

7 Cf *Desmond v Brophy* [1985] IR 449 (solicitor liable).

8 See *Kelly's Draftsman* (14th edn), 173, cl 44; (1981) 78 LS Gaz 1128 (H W Wilkinson).

purchaser? To answer this question it is necessary to distinguish cases where (i) there is a contract between the parties, and (ii) no binding contract exists.

(i) *Binding contract.* It is well settled that the vendor bears the loss, whether the deposit is held as agent[9] or as stakeholder. In the latter case his responsibility is based on the principle that he who nominates the stakeholder must also accept the risk[10]. Where the deposit-holder holds as agent, the purchaser must suffer the loss if the *vendor* becomes bankrupt, for receipt by the agent is equivalent to receipt by the principal. Normally, however, the vendor's bankruptcy will not affect the purchaser who can enforce the contract against the trustee in bankruptcy.

(ii) *'Subject to contract' deposit.* As we have seen, a pre-contract deposit paid to the vendor's estate agent is not in any strict legal sense earnest money; it is recoverable by the prospective purchaser on demand at any time before exchange of contracts[11]. The payer's rights in the event of the agent's bankruptcy were finally settled after considerable judicial controversy in *Sorrell v Finch*[12]. The House of Lords held that an estate agent has no implied or ostensible authority to receive as agent for the vendor a 'subject to contract' deposit from an intending purchaser. Unless the vendor expressly authorises the estate agent to take a deposit as his agent[13], he is not liable to the would-be purchaser for its repayment should the agent become bankrupt or otherwise default. Nor does knowledge that a deposit has been received by him of itself impose any liability on the vendor to repay it. In passing, the common use of the expression 'as stakeholder' when applied to the receipt of a pre-contract deposit[14] is quite inappropriate. In no sense can the estate agent be described as an agent for both parties when he must return the money on demand without consulting the vendor. Once contracts have been exchanged the agent's retention of the deposit will be inconsistent with the terms of the contract, which is rarely amended to take account of this situation. For practical reasons estate agents prefer to hang on to any deposit they have received!

The Estate Agents Act 1979 was passed to regulate the business activities of estate agents. By virtue of s 13 deposits received by an estate agent are deemed

---

9　*Ojelay v Neosale Ltd* [1987] 2 EGLR 167, CA.
10　*Annesley v Muggridge* (1816) 1 Madd 593 at 596, per Plummer V-C; *Rowe v May* (1854) 18 Beav 613. A party suffering loss through the bankruptcy of the vendor's solicitor can obtain redress from the Compensation Fund administered by The Law Society.
11　Cf *Chillingworth v Esche* [1924] 1 Ch 97, CA.
12　[1977] AC 728, [1976] 2 All ER 371, HL, overruling *Goding v Frazer* [1966] 3 All ER 234, and *Burt v Claude Cousins & Co* [1971] 2 QB 426, [1971] 2 All ER 611, CA.
13　*Ryan v Pilkington* [1959] 1 All ER 689, CA. Such express authority in no way affects the would-be purchaser's right to reclaim the deposit on withdrawal before exchange of contracts.
14　A prospective purchaser should ensure that it is received, not as stakeholder, but as his agent. He may then qualify for interest on its repayment: Estate Agents (Accounts) Regulations 1981, r 7, SI 1981 No 1520, which preserves the common law rule excluding interest on money held by a stakeholder. See p 236, ante.

to be trust moneys, and therefore do not form part of his assets on insolvency. But there is still no statutory obligation on them to take out insurance cover against loss of deposits through fraud or dishonesty[15].

4.   Forfeiture and recovery of deposit

(a) Forfeiture
The vendor is entitled to forfeit the deposit if the purchaser is in breach of contract and that breach is of such a nature as to discharge the vendor from the contract. This right does not depend on any express contractual stipulations[16]. It can be exercised notwithstanding that the vendor suffers no loss because eg he resells the property at a higher price.

(i) *Recovery of unpaid deposit.*   The purchaser's failure to pay a contractual deposit constitutes a fundamental breach of contract, enabling the vendor to rescind and recover damages. But what is the measure of his damages? Is he limited to the loss of the bargain (plus out-of-pocket expenses), or can he recover the amount of the unpaid deposit, even though it exceeds his actual loss? After some uncertainty it has now been established in *Damon Cia Naviera SA v Hapag-Lloyd International SA*[17] that the unpaid deposit is recoverable. Though the required deposit no longer bears the character of a pledge because of the purchaser's default, the vendor has still lost the benefit or value of the security itself. For this he is entitled to be compensated in damages[18]. Moreover, his right to receive the deposit accrues before, and is not affected by, the subsequent termination of the contract due to the buyer's fundamental default[19]. He cannot, however, also claim damages for the wrongful repudiation of the contract, ie the loss of the bargain, unless his actual loss exceeds the unpaid deposit. When non-payment results from dishonour of a deposit cheque, the vendor has an alternative cause of action on the cheque itself[20]. The vendor's rights can be pursued whether the whole or merely a part[1] of the deposit remains unpaid. Recovery of any unpaid balance will not be possible if the vendor has, by agreement or unequivocal conduct, waived payment of

---

15   Section 16 of the Act awaits implementation; likewise s 19 (limitation on amount of pre-contract deposits). Agents who belong to a professional body (eg the National Association of Estate Agents) are covered by an institutional bounding scheme.

16   *Hall v Burnell* [1911] 2 Ch 551.

17   [1985] 1 All ER 475, CA (sale of ships), approving *Dewar v Mintoft* [1912] 2 KB 373. The contrary decision in *Lowe v Hope* [1970] Ch 94, [1969] 3 All ER 605 was based on a misunderstanding of the effect of rescission for breach, and cannot stand in the light of *Johnson v Agnew* [1980] AC 367, [1979] 1 All ER 883, HL, p 610.

18   Per Leggatt J at first instance: [1983] 3 All ER 510 at 521.

19   Rescission for breach of contract does not divest or discharge accrued rights. Contrast rescission ab initio based on some vitiating factor affecting its formation. The difference is explored in Ch 19.

20   *Pollway Ltd v Abdullah* [1974] 2 All ER 381, CA (dishonour of cheque paid to auctioneer).

1   Cf LSC 9(2) which in effect gives the vendor a contractual right to recover the difference by requiring the purchaser to pay the balance on the vendor's service of a completion notice.

the balance[2], or even if his solicitor, without authority, accepts less than the contractual amount on exchange of contracts[3].

(ii) *Relief against forfeiture.*   Equity has shown a marked reluctance to exercise its jurisdiction to relieve against the forfeiture of a deposit in a way similar to its granting of relief against a penalty[4]. This is notwithstanding that the conventional 10% deposit will frequently bear little relation to the loss actually suffered by the vendor[5]. In the normal case where a 10% deposit has been obtained, it is unlikely that the court will intervene to prevent forfeiture, even when the vendor stands to make a substantial profit on a subsequent sale of the property[6]. In cases where more than the traditional 10% deposit has been taken, however, the courts will be prepared to intervene[7]. The leading case is *Workers Trust & Merchant Bank Ltd v Dojap Investments Ltd*[8]. The contract of sale provided for the payment of a deposit amounting to 25% of the purchase price, that price being $2,875,000. On the purchaser's breach of contract, the vendor purported to forfeit the deposit and the action was for its return. The Privy Council held that the deposit was a penalty and ordered its return. It was further held that the vendor was entitled to damages, those damages to be assessed on the basis of the actual loss suffered by the vendor from the date of rescission to the date of payment.

Giving the judgment of the Board, Lord Browne-Wilkinson considered the position of deposits for the sale of land to be 'anomalous'[9]. Nevertheless, the traditional 10% deposit was held to be acceptable but a deposit of 25% was not. In the face of this, it was argued for the vendor that, if they could not retain the 25% deposit, they should be able to obtain the traditional 10% deposit. This, too, was rejected because the contract had not provided for the payment of such a sum. The sum stipulated for by the contract was a penalty and, therefore, void, with the result that damages should be assessed in accordance with ordinary principles; to reflect the loss that had actually been occasioned by the purchaser's breach of contract. The upshot is that the Privy Council was prepared to allow a vendor to forfeit a 10% deposit, even though it was accepted that, in many cases, this would not represent a genuine pre-estimate of loss, but that if the figure was appreciably above 10%, then it was open to attack on the ground that it represented a penalty.

2   Waiver failed in *Trustbridge Ltd v Bhattessa* [1985] LS Gaz R 2580, CA.
3   The variation will bind him, if ratified (which he must do if he is to forfeit what has been paid). See p 220, ante. It has been accepted that a written contract cannot be varied orally: *McCausland v Duncan Lawrie Ltd* [1995] EGCS 133, [1996] NPC 94, CA. See p 227, ante.
4   See *Linggi Plantations Ltd v Jagaseethan* [1972] 1 MLJ 89 at 94, PC, per Lord Hailsham LC.
5   Cf Treitel, *The Law of Contract* (9th edn), 907.
6   *Windsor Securities Ltd v Loreldal and Lester Ltd* (1975) Times, 10 September (10% deposit amounting to £235,000 held forfeit).
7   See *Stockloser v Johnson* [1954] 1 QB 476 at 490–91, [1954] 1 All ER 630 at 638, CA, per Denning LJ, instancing a 50% deposit. See also *Codot Developments Ltd v Potter* [1981] 1 NZLR 729n (50% deposit); *Smyth v Jessep*[1956] VLR 230 (40%). In some Canadian jurisdictions the courts are prepared to relieve against forfeiture of even small deposits; see Butt, *Contract for Sale of Land in New South Wales*, 502 and cases cited.
8   [1993] AC 573, [1993] 2 All ER 370, PC; [1994] Conv 58 at 61 (M P Thompson).
9   [1993] AC 573 at 578, [1993] 2 All ER 370 at 373.

The approach taken in this case represents something of a half-way house. It is recognised that deposits do not represent a true pre-estimate of damages but will be allowed, provided that the element of penalty involved is not too great. While this upholds the traditional value of the deposit as a security for due performance, in some ways it is a curious compromise and is not entirely consistent with the approach which has been adopted in cases when the court is called upon to exercise its statutory jurisdiction to order the return of a deposit[10].

(b) Recovery by purchaser

If the sale goes off due to the vendor's default, the purchaser is entitled to the return of his deposit. It may be as a result of the vendor's inability to make a good title in accordance with the contract, or his failure to complete. The contract frequently regulates the right of recovery in particular instances[11]. The purchaser possesses a lien on the vendor's land for its return with interest[12], save where it is held by a stakeholder. If the vendor never receives the deposit, the purchaser cannot be regarded as his secured creditor, which is the true basis of the purchaser's right to a lien[13]. On the sale of a new house a prospective purchaser may be required to pay an initial reservation fee on terms that the builder will not offer it for sale to others provided contracts are exchanged within a specified period. The fee becomes forfeitable to the builder if the purchaser does not exchange in time or otherwise declines to proceed. An arrangement of this kind, which in effect gives the prospective purchaser something akin to a right of pre-emption, is binding upon him and he cannot recover the fee if he decided not to buy. However, as time is not of the essence of the agreement[14], equity will presumably extend the time for exchange of contracts.

(c) Instalments of purchase price

Unlike a deposit which is paid on exchange of contracts, a part payment of the purchase price is made afterwards. It is not money paid as a guarantee of performance, so the vendor possesses no right in the absence of a contrary agreement to forfeit part payments on the purchaser's default[15]. It may be that a purchaser has a lien on the land in respect of non-forfeitable instalments recoverable from the vendor[16]. A contract which provides for payment by instalments often contains a proviso that on non-payment of any instalment the vendor may rescind the contract and forfeit those already paid. The extent

10 LPA 1925, s 49(2). See p 621, post.
11 SCS 7.2(a).
12 *Whitbread & Co Ltd v Watt* [1902] 1 Ch 835, CA; *Lee-Parker v Izzet* [1971] 3 All ER 1099.
13 *Combe v Swaythling* [1947] Ch 625, [1947] 1 All ER 838. The lien takes effect as a species of equitable charge arising by implication of law, enabling the purchaser to apply for an order for sale of the vendor's land. See M & W, 914.
14 For time clauses generally, see pp 420–428, post.
15 *Harrison v Holland and Hannen and Cubitts Ltd* [1921] 3 KB 297 at 300, per Lush J; affd [1922] 1 KB 211, CA; *Mayson v Clouet* [1924] AC 980, PC.
16 *Frankcombe v Foster Investments Pty Ltd* [1978] 2 NSWLR 41 at 57, per Holland J.

to which he can enforce this term is controversial[17]. This much is clear, however. Equity will allow a purchaser who is ready and willing to perform the contract additional time to pay an outstanding instalment or complete the transaction[18], unless time is of the essence and the time stipulation has not been waived[19].

5. Reform?

Practitioners involved in conveyancing transactions often spend a disproportionate amount of time arguing about deposits. Some advocate their abolition altogether; they cause delays and make conveyancing more expensive. Others still regard them as vital to ensure that buyers adhere to their bargains[20]. Some purchasers are undoubtedly financially embarrassed to have to find a deposit of the conventional size. In many cases it bears no relationship at all to a pre-estimate of the vendor's loss should the purchaser default.

Various options for change were canvassed by the Conveyancing Standing Committee and the Law Society in a consultation paper[1]. This elicited a significant number of responses which were considered and led to the publication of a report by the same bodies[2]. It was found that there was a strong body of opinion that favoured the retention of the traditional deposit. While a number of respondents were of the view that a 10% deposit was too high a figure, 5% being more appropriate, it was considered that this was a matter for negotiation between the parties. A deposit of 10% was seen as the very top of any negotiations[3] but there was no recommendation to change the norm of a deposit of this size.

It could be that the payment of deposits will eventually be superseded by insurance schemes. One such deposit guarantee scheme for house-buyers is operated by Legal and Professional Indemnity Ltd[4]. The purchaser pays a single premium which provides a non-assignable guarantee to the vendor for the amount of the deposit. If he fails to complete, the insurers pay to the vendor's

---

17   Compare the divergent views expressed in *Stockloser v Johnson* [1954] 1 QB 476, [1954] 1 All ER 630, CA. See also *Steedman v Drinkle* [1916] 1 AC 275, PC; *Mussen v Van Diemen's Land Co* [1938] Ch 253, [1938] 1 All ER 210.

18   *Starside Properties Ltd v Mustapha* [1974] 2 All ER 567, CA.

19   Cf *Kilmer v British Columbia Orchard Lands Co* [1913] AC 319, PC (time clause waived; purchaser granted specific performance).

20   See the correspondence at (1985) 82 LS Gaz 1530; [1986] Conv 143. Cf (1983) 80 LS Gaz 2811 (J E Adams).

 1   Deposits on exchange of contracts in residential conveyancing – TIME FOR A CHANGE?, February 1988.

 2   DEPOSITS – NO TIME FOR CHANGE!, July, 1989.

 3   Ibid, p 17.

 4   Jointly underwritten by Lombard Continental Insurance and Eagle Star Insurance. The premium for a guarantee (deposit) of £10,000 costs a mere £62, £10 of which represents the solicitor's commission. Use of the scheme is subject to conditions relating to, eg amount (guarantee limited to £30,000); tenure (freehold or leasehold with 50 years unexpired); the agreed completion date (within ten weeks of exchange) and to the purchaser who must have a linked sale and purchase (though the scheme incorporates a special extension for first time buyers). Over 2,500 firms of solicitors were operating the scheme by mid-1987. For early teething troubles see (1987) 84 LS Gaz 789, 950–51.

solicitor the appropriate amount which is then recovered from the defaulting buyer[5]. All solicitors holding a current practising certificate and licensed conveyancers are authorised agents for the purpose of binding the insurers to the guarantee.

Use of the scheme in a particular case must be contractually agreed. This may prove to be a hindrance to its widespread use in cases of linked sales and purchases. Should one vendor in the chain insist on a cash deposit, others may be tempted to follow suit. Responses to the consultation paper issued by the Law Society and the Standing Committee revealed, however, a strong hostility to such schemes on the part of practitioners, who favoured the taking of cash deposits[6].

E   General effect of a contract on parties' position

It is a settled doctrine of the Court of Equity that, the moment there is a valid contract of sale, the vendor becomes in equity a trustee for the purchaser of the estate sold and the beneficial ownership passes to the purchaser[7]. The result of the doctrine of conversion is that, in the eyes of equity, the purchaser becomes the owner of the land, the vendor the owner of the purchase money. It must not be assumed merely because there is a contract for the sale of land that this doctrine automatically operates. It is subject to one obvious qualification – the contract must be one of which the court will in the circumstances decree specific performance[8]. If for some reason equity will not enforce specific performance, or if the right to specific performance has been lost by the subsequent conduct of the party in whose favour it might originally have been granted, the vendor either never was, or has ceased to be, a trustee in any sense at all[9].

It is sometimes said that the beneficial ownership passes the moment the contract is entered into[10]. This may be a satisfactory way of applying the doctrine of conversion in a succession case where the contest is between different claimants to a deceased vendor's estate. But it is something of an over-simplification in a vendor-purchaser context. The peculiar post-contract relationship between the parties is subject to the contract being eventually performed; if the contract is not performed the relationship is discharged and the vendor is treated as never being a trustee for the purchaser[11]. The true position was stated by James LJ[12], in the following terms:

---

5   Solicitors need to make their clients fully aware of this right of recovery.
6   (1989) Report, p 21.
7   *Lysaght v Edwards* (1876) 2 Ch D 499 at 506, per Jessel MR. The significance of the word 'valid' is controversial. See (1988) Law Com WP No 109, paras 1.41–1.60; (1960) 24 Conv (NS) 47 P H Pettit; (1987) 7 OJLS 60 (S Gardner).
8   *Howard v Miller* [1915] AC 318 at 326, PC, per Lord Parker; *Bushwall Properties Ltd v Vortex Properties Ltd* [1976] 2 All ER 283 at 294, CA, per Buckley LJ.
9   *Central Trust and Safe Deposit Co v Snider* [1916] 1 AC 266 at 272, PC, per Lord Parker.
10 *Lysaght v Edwards* (1876) 2 Ch D 499 at 510, 518, per Jessel MR.
11 *Plews v Samuel* [1904] 1 Ch 464 at 468, per Kekewich J.
12 *Rayner v Preston* (1881) 18 Ch D 1 at 13, CA.

> I agree that it is not accurate to call the relation between vendor and purchaser of an estate under the contract while the contract is in fieri the relation of trustee and cestui que trust. But that is because it is uncertain whether the contract will or will not be performed[13], and the character in which the parties stand to one another remains in suspense as long as the contract is in fieri. But when the contract is performed by actual conveyance then that completion relates back to the contract, and it is thereby ascertained that the relation was throughout that of trustee and cestui que trust.

The purchaser is not to be regarded as owner in equity if specific performance is not available. This may be because of some defect in the vendor's title[14], or some collateral misrepresentation, or delay sufficient to defeat the claim for the equitable remedy[15]. Acceptance by the purchaser of a defective title effects a conversion and its operation will be retrospective so that the relation between the parties is throughout one of trustee and beneficiary. Another example arises when contracts to sell land to X and then agrees to convey it to Y. The contract in favour of Y does not vest any equitable title in him. He cannot obtain specific performance, for the court will not make a decree if the sale would be in breach of a prior contract with a third party[16]. A conveyance of the land to Y may operate to defeat X's equitable interest, depending upon whether X has taken the appropriate steps to protect his interest.

It would also seem essential for the vendor himself to be a beneficial owner, or able to overreach the equitable interests affecting the land. Suppose V holds the legal title in land as a bare trustee for X absolutely. A contract for sale by V to Z without X's consent will not operate to make Z the owner in equity. This is not even something that the V-Z conveyance will achieve (unless Z takes free of X's interest through lack of notice).

Where the contract between the parties is subject to some as yet unfulfilled condition, eg the obtaining of planning permission, it seems that an equitable interest vests in the purchaser if the condition is solely for his benefit. Being in a position to waive the condition at any time, he can obtain specific performance of the contract[17]. If the condition benefits both parties, the purchaser does not obtain an equitable interest until the condition is either fulfilled[18], or waived by the vendor.

---

13   In succession disputes non-performance of the contract has been held not to cancel out the conversion effected by the contract: *Whittaker v Whittaker* (1792) 4 Bro CC 31; *Re Blake* [1917] 1 Ch 18 (non-performance of option to purchase). This suggests that the courts treat different cases in different ways.
14   *Re Thomas, Thomas v Howell* (1886) 34 Ch D 166.
15   See generally, Cozens-Hardy J in *Cornwall v Henson* [1899] 2 Ch 710 at 714.
16   *Willmott v Barber* (1880) 15 Ch D 96; *Warmington v Miller* [1973] QB 877, [1973] 2 All ER 372, CA.
17   *Wood Preservation Ltd v Prior* [1968] 2 All ER 849 at 858–59, per Goff J; affd [1969] 1 All ER 364, CA; *Nicholson v Fowler* [1981] 2 NZLR 97 (contract to buy conditional on purchaser selling existing house).
18   Similarly when the condition requires fulfilment by a third party: *Brown v Heffer* (1967) 116 CLR 344; *Shanahan v Fitzgerald* [1982] 2 NSWLR 513.

F   The vendor as trustee

The vendor has been variously described as a 'constructive'[19] or 'qualified'[20] trustee, or as a trustee 'sub modo'[1], descriptions which signify that the trusteeship is of an unusual kind. It is not one which has the normal incidents associated with the relationship of trustee and beneficiary[2]. He has a personal and substantial interest in the property, which he has an active right to protect should anything be done in derogation of it[3]. His interest is in actually obtaining the purchase money. On its receipt he becomes a bare trustee for the purchaser, assuming there has been no conveyance of the legal estate to him[4].

1.   The property subject to the trust

The vendor's trusteeship extends only to the subject matter of the contract, including physical accretions[6]. Unusually for a trustee, he is not accountable to the purchaser for gains made as legal owner between contract and conveyance. So in *Re Lyne-Stephens and Scott-Miller's Contract*[6], it was held that, on a sale of a house by a purchaser with vacant possession, the purchaser had no claim to money paid to the vendor by the outgoing tenant in respect of dilapidations. In similar vein, and of considerable importance, it was held in *Rayner v Preston*[7] that a purchaser is not entitled to insurance money paid to the vendor in respect of damage to the property occurring between contract and completion.

A new twist was given to this trusteeship in *Lake v Bayliss*[8]. Here land which V had contracted to sell to P for a non-pecuniary consideration was, in breach of contract, conveyed to P2. It was not clear from the report whether the original contract had been protected by registration[9]. Nevertheless, Walton J held that, as trustee[10], V was accountable to P for the net proceeds of the V-P2 sale, subject

19 *Shaw v Foster* (1872) LR 5 HL 321 at 326, per Lord Hathersley.
20 *Rayner v Preston* (1881) 18 Ch D 1 at 16, CA, per Cotton LJ; cf Brett LJ, at 10: 'With the greatest deference, it seems wrong to say that the [vendor] is a trustee for the [purchaser]'.
1   *Wall v Bright* (1820) 1 Jac & W 494 at 501. See also *Dowson v Solomon* (1859) 1 Drew & Sm 1 at 9 per Sir Richard Kindersley V–C.
2   See *Re Watford Corpn's and A S Ware's Contract* [1943] Ch 82 at 85 per Simonds J.
3   *Shaw v Foster*, supra, at 338 per Lord Cairns.
4   *Wall v Bright* supra at 503, per Sir Thomas Plumer MR; *Bridges v Mees* [1957] Ch 475, [1957] 2 All ER 577. As to vendor's ability to effect completion unilaterally, see *Tudor v Hamid* [1988] 1 EGLR 251, CA.
5   *Re Hamilton-Snowball's Conveyance* [1959] Ch 308 at 312, [1958] 2 All ER 319 at 321, per Upjohn J.
6   [1920] 1 Ch 472, CA; aliter if the sale had been subject to but with the benefit of the lease. See also *Re Hamilton-Snowball's Conveyance* [1959] Ch 308, supra, (purchaser no right to compensation payable on derequisitioning of property).
7   Supra. For a discussion of insurance issues, see pp 251–255, post.
8   [1974] 2 All ER 1114 (sale of land in consideration of withdrawal of writs).
9   The only reference to this was a comment that 'there was a muddle in a proper search': ibid, at 1118, per Walton J.
10 Consistent with this, it was also accepted that a vendor might, in certain circumstances be obliged to pass on to the purchaser any higher offers for the purchase of the property received after the formation of the contract: ibid, at 1118.

to P fulfilling his own contractual obligations to V. Despite its superficial attractiveness, the decision must be treated with reserve[11]. If because of non-registration, the original contract between V and P was not enforceable against P2, then specific performance of that contract would no longer be available and the consequence of that should be that P should not be regarded as the equitable owner of the property[12]. That difficulty aside, it will rarely be necessary for a purchaser to resort to this tracing remedy. Normally an action for damages for breach of contract will ensure adequate compensation for his loss[13].

2. Extent of vendor's interest

Pending completion, the vendor's rights are as follows[14]:
(i) He can retain possession of the property until payment of the purchase money, though this right may be varied by the contract.
(ii) He is entitled to a lien on the property for the security of the purchase price, or the balance. This lien arises, apparently, immediately there is a binding contract[15]. As a general rule, it remains enforceable by the vendor so long as money is outstanding, notwithstanding that he has conveyed the property to the purchaser and let him into occupation. If the purchaser is in possession, the court will restrain him from any act, such as felling timber, by which the vendor's security might be lessened[16].
(iii) Though the vendor still retains the legal estate, qua trustee, his powers as owner are suspended to some degree. Where the property sold is subject to tenancies, he should not determine a tenancy without consulting the purchaser[17]. Similarly, if a tenant quits prior to completion, the vendor should not create a new lease without the purchaser's consent[18]. The vendor should not withdraw any application for planning permission and, if he

---

11 Its weakness is palpably demonstrated by the fact that the only supporting authority relied upon was an unanswered query posed obiter by Lord Eldon in *Daniels v Davison* (1809) 16 Ves 249 at 254, and a statement, *arguendo*, by Sir George Jessel, when Solicitor-General, in *Shaw v Foster*, supra, at 327. It is apparently accepted by M & W, 602, but doubted by Emmet, para 8.002; (1974) 38 Conv (NS) 357. A similar decision was reached in *Bunny Industries Ltd v FSW Enterprises Pty Ltd* [1982] Qd R 712. Had P already performed his part of the bargain, V would have become a bare trustee for him.
12 See [1984] Conv 43 at 47–48 (M P Thompson).
13 See [1980] CLJ 58, 85 (A J Oakley), outlining circumstances when tracing would be useful: non-monetary consideration, V's bankruptcy, and P2's sale at above market value.
14 See generally, *Lysaght v Edwards* (1876) 2 Ch D 499 at 506–7, per Jessel MR.
15 *Re Birmingham, Savage v Stannard* [1959] Ch 523, [1958] 2 All ER 397. See also *UCB Bank v France* [1995] NPC 144. *Sed quaere*. See *Kettlewell v Watson* (1884) 26 Ch D 501 at 507 per Lindley LJ. Remember also that it requires protection as a C(iii) land charge or entry on the register of title to be enforceable against later purchasers. Where title is registered the lien can take effect as an overriding interest if the vendor is in actual occupation of the property: *London and Cheshire Insurance Co Ltd v Laplagrene Property Co Ltd* [1971] Ch 499, [1971] 1 All ER 766.
16 *Crockford v Alexander* (1808) 15 Ves 138.
17 *Earl Egmont v Smith* (1877) 6 Ch D 469 at 944–45, per Romer J.
18 *Abdulla v Shah* [1959] AC 124, PC, a case decided under the Indian Transfer of Property Act 1882, ss 54, 55 which imposed a statutory obligation on the vendor with regard to the property between contract and completion. Contrast *Earl Egmont v Smith*, supra.

does will be liable for any additional expense incurred by the purchaser in applying anew[19]. Again, if a business is being operated from the property, at a loss, the vendor should not continue to run the business without consulting the purchaser[20]. On the other hand, the vendor may create a mortgage for his own benefit provided, of course, he redeems it before completion[1].

(iv) The general rule that a trustee must not make any profit from his trust does not apply to the vendor. So he is entitled to retain the rents and profits until the time fixed for completion[2]. Once that date has passed without actual completion, he must account for them to the purchaser, not only for what he actually receives, but for what he should have received had he not allowed the property to lie waste[3]. The vendor is not entitled to retain rents received by him after the contractual date for completion, in satisfaction of rents accrued due before that date[4].

3. Vendor's duty to maintain

(a) Nature of duty

The law imposes a correlative duty on the vendor to maintain the property. He is liable to the purchaser if he wilfully damages or injures it[5], or if he fails to take reasonable care of it. It has been described as a duty to use reasonable care to preserve the property in a reasonable state of preservation and as it was when the contract was made[6]. In effect the vendor must treat the property as a prudent owner would do. He is not obliged to improve it. Liability can arise from the actions of trespassers who cause damage to the property, if such damage is the result of a failure to take proper care of the property[7]. Similarly, he can be liable for damage caused to the property by an outgoing tenant[8] or furniture removers[9]. It would seem, however, that, despite the vendor being entitled to possession of the property, the maxim, *res ipsa loquitur*, does not apply[10]. This leads to a further difficulty for the purchaser as, being only the owner in equity, he cannot sue any wrongdoer in respect of damage caused to the property[11]. Broken windows and slates should be replaced; reasonable steps

---

19 *Sinclair-Hill v Sothcott* (1973) 226 EG 1399.
20 *Golden Bread Co Ltd v Hemmings* [1922] 1 Ch 162.
1   See *Burges v Williams* (1912) 15 CLR 504.
2   *Cuddon v Tite* (1858) 1 Giff 395; NCS 6(3), LSC 19(1), (3).
3   *Phillips v Silvester* (1872) 8 Ch App 173.
4   *Plews v Samuel* [1904] 1 Ch 464.
5   Eg by the removal of flowering shrubs, or an ornate door (*Phillips v Lamdin* [1949] 2 KB 33, [1949] 1 All ER 770).
6   *Clarke v Ramuz* [1891] 2 QB 456, CA. See generally (1971) LSG 224 (J E Adams), (1988) Law Com WP No 109, paras 1.27–1.35.
7   *Clarke v Ramuz*, supra; *Davron Estates Ltd v Turnshire Ltd* (1982) 133 NLJ 937, CA.
8   *Royal Permanent Building Society v Bomash* (1887) 35 Ch D 390.
9   *Ware v Verderber* (1978) 247 EG 1081 (damage to spiral staircase).
10 *Sochacki v Sas* [1947] 1 All ER 344. For cogent criticism, see [1978] Conv 183. The leading case of *Scott v St Katherine Docks Co* (1865) 3 H & C 596 was not cited.
11 *Leigh and Sillavan Ltd v Aliakmon Shipping Co Ltd* [1986] AC 785, [1986] 2 All ER 145, HL. See (1987) 103 LQR 433 at 455–458 (R M Goode).

should be taken to ensure that the property does not become frozen-up during winter time, especially if the property is vacant[12]. The vendor's duty seems to extend even to keeping the garden of residential property in good order[13], and to chattels contracted to be sold[14].

This duty of preservation applies alike to freehold and leasehold property. The vendor is not absolved from performance by a contractual term which requires the purchaser to take the property as it stands[15], ie as at the date of the contract. However, with leasehold property the vendor will be obliged to comply with any repairing covenant in the lease up to the date of actual completion, so as to avoid rendering the lease voidable due to the usual forfeiture clause[16].

(b) Duration of liability
The vendor's duty lasts so long as he retains possession, notwithstanding that the date fixed for completion has expired due to the purchaser's delay[17]. References in the cases to the vendor's possession are to be understood in the wider sense of his right to possession. A vendor cannot divest himself of responsibility simply by vacating the property after exchange of contracts. Should he move out, he will be under a duty to ensure that it is adequately secured to prevent foreseeable access by vandals or squatters[18]. He is not liable for deterioration to the property occurring after the contractual date for completion if the title offered is such that the purchaser could safely take possession, but refuses to do so[19]. The vendor can discharge himself from further maintenance liability if he allows the purchaser into possession before actual completion[20]. Merely to let the purchaser have the key to enable his mortgagee to inspect the property does not suffice for this purpose[1].

(c) Vendor's right of indemnity
The vendor must bear the cost of maintenance and cannot normally look to the purchaser for an indemnity. Since he is entitled to the rents and profits, it

---

12   *Lucie-Smith v Gorman* [1981] CLY 2866 but contrast, in the context of landlord and tenant, *Wycombe Health Authority v Barnett* (1982) 264 EG 619.
13   *Foster v Deacon* (1818) 3 Madd 394 at 395, per Sir Richard Leach V-C.
14   *Ware v Verderber*, supra, at 1083, per Judge Fay QC. An agreement to sell chattels not forming part of the realty constitutes a sale of goods. They remain at the vendor's risk until the property in them passes to the purchaser, which the parties will presumably intend on completion: Sale of Goods Act 1979, ss 17(1), 20.
15   See SCS 3.2.1; *Davron Estates Ltd v Turnshire Ltd* (1982) 133 NLJ 937, CA.
16   But only when the breach first occurs after exchange; otherwise he can fall back on SCS 3.2.2 if applicable.
17   *Phillips v Silvester* (1872) 8 Ch App 173.
18   Cf *Cedar Transport Group Ltd v First Wyvern Property Trustees Co Ltd* (1980) 258 EG 1077 (empty warehouse, duty discharged by putting it in care of architects and builders).
19   *Minchin v Nance* (1841) 4 Beav 332; *Phillips v Silvester*, supra, at 178, per Lord Selbourne LC.
20   SCS 5.2.2(f), discussed at p 256, post.
1   *Lucie-Smith v Gorman* [1981] CLY 2866. As to a vendor's duty to allow such access, see *Schindler v Pigault* (1975) 30 P & CR 328.

is only reasonable that the burden of repairs should fall on him. Further the vendor has his own personal interest in maintaining the property, since it may ensure for his benefit if the purchaser defaults[2]. He cannot recover money spent on improvements[3], though there are suggestions that he may be entitled to reimbursement for exceptional outlay on permanent repairs required to preserve the property[4].

To this general rule there are two limitations: one general and one specific. The maintenance of the property ranks as a current expense payable out of rents and profits; their cost must be borne by the vendor only so long as he is entitled to them for his own benefit. Thereafter the expense must be met by the purchaser. He must bear the cost of repairs as from the date a good title is shown under an open contract, or from the date of completion on a sale with vacant possession under a contract incorporating the Standard Conditions of Sale[5]. It is still the duty of the vendor in possession to maintain the property, but he is entitled to be given credit for all proper expenditure as against the rents and profits (including any occupation rent due from the vendor himself) for which he must account to the purchaser[6].

(d) Effect of breach

Breach by the vendor of his fiduciary duty does not entitle the purchaser to decline to proceed, or even to delay completion[7]. Even though the amount of compensation has not been agreed, he should still complete on time, but without prejudice to his outstanding claim. To complete without expressly reserving his position as to compensation would normally constitute a waiver of his right of action[8]. The vendor's failure to perform his duty does not of itself disqualify him from relying on a contractual notice to complete served on a dilatory purchaser[9].

(e) Sub-sales

The relationship between the vendor and a sub-purchaser is unclear. Suppose that V agrees to sell land to P who later contracts to sell all or part of it to P2. According to what is conceived to be the better view, V does not become a constructive trustee for P2 or owe him any fiduciary duty to take reasonable care to preserve the property[10]. P2's remedy in respect of any failure by V to

---

2   *Re Watford Corpn's and Ware's Contract* [1943] Ch 82 at 85, [1943] 1 All ER 54 at 56, per Simonds J (vendor not entitled to recoup war damage contributions).
3   *Monro v Taylor* (1848) 8 Hare 51 at 60, per Wigram V-C.
4   *Phillips v Silvester*, supra, at 177, per Lord Selbourne LC.
5   SCS 6.3.1, 6.3.2.
6   *Phillips v Silvester* (1872) 8 Ch App 173 at 176, per Lord Selbourne LC. See p 436, post, for payment of rent by a vendor.
7   *Davron Estates Ltd v Turnshire Ltd* (1982) 133 NLJ 937, CA (damage by squatters).
8   *Berkley v Poulett* (1976) 241 EG 911, 242 EG 39 at 41, CA, per Stamp LJ; cf *Clarke v Ramuz* [1891] 2 QB 456, CA (purchaser unaware of damage).
9   *Prosper Homes Ltd v Hambros Bank Executor and Trustee Co Ltd* (1979) 39 P & CR 395. See further p 430, post.
10 *Berkley v Poulett*, supra, at 43, 45, per Stamp LJ; contra, per Goff LJ, at 41, if V acquires notice of the sub-contract.

perform his duty to P lies against P for P's own failure to enforce the duty against V. Similarly P2 has no ground of complaint against V should V and P agree to vary the terms of their contract in a way prejudicial to P2. A sub-sale should not be confused with an *assignment*. If P assigns the benefit of the V-P contract to P2, the latter steps into P's shoes, succeeding to P's equitable interest. V is now a trustee for P2, rather than P. Whether P2 can institute proceedings in his own name to enforce the contract against V depends on whether he has given V due notice of the assignment under the Law of Property Act 1925, s 136[11].

G   The purchaser as beneficiary

1.   His equitable interest

As explained earlier in this chapter, an enforceable contract vests an equitable interest in the purchaser. This he can devise by will, charge[12] or sell. In the event of a sub-sale, the purchaser's contract becomes a vital document of title. He can obtain an injunction to restrain the vendor from transferring the property to a third party[13], or from committing acts of waste which depreciate the property.

(a) Gains and losses

All improvements to and increases in the value of the property are retained by the purchaser, such as a sudden rise in the value of the land attributable to the discovery of minerals in the sub-soil (assuming these have not been excepted on a previous transaction). As already noticed, the purchaser is limited to physical accretions, and not to financial benefits accruing to the vendor and not forming part of the contract.

The prospect of losses is likely to be of more concern to the purchaser than the possibility of gain. As from the date of the contract the risk passes to the purchaser, subject to the vendor's duty to take reasonable care to maintain the property. He must bear all loss or damage to the property resulting from earthquake, war hazards, or fire[14] not caused by the vendor's fault or neglect. He must also accept the risk of the property being made the subject of a special listing order which effectively thwarts his redevelopment plans[15]. Similarly,

---

11   See generally, *Warner Bros Records Inc v Rollgreen Ltd* [1976] QB 430 at 443–44, [1975] 2 All ER 105 at 111, CA, per Roskill LJ.

12   *Property Discount Corpn Ltd v Lyon Group Ltd* [1981] 1 All ER 379, CA (equitable mortgage of interest under agreement to grant building lease).

13   See *Hadley v London Bank of Scotland Ltd* (1865) 3 De GJ & Sm 63 where no injunction was granted because the purchaser's own right to specific performance was uncertain.

14   *Cass v Rudele* (1692) 2 Vern 280 (earthquake), but see 1 Bro CC 157n, where the case is said to be misreported; *Paine v Meller* (1801) 6 Ves 349 (fire). For an argument to the contrary, see [1984] Conv 43 (M P Thompson).

15   *Amalgamated Investment and Property Co Ltd v John Walker & Sons Ltd* [1976] 3 All ER 509, CA. This possibility may be catered for by an express contractual term; see *Aquis Estates Ltd v Minton* [1975] 3 All ER 1043, CA (property to be free from adverse entry in purchaser's local search).

service of a compulsory purchase order after contract does not discharge the purchaser; he remains liable to the vendor for the purchase price but is entitled to receive the compensation from the acquiring authority[16]. If without fault on the part of the vendor, the purchased premises collapse and cause damage to adjoining property or to a highway user, the purchaser must indemnify the vendor against damages and expenses incurred in satisfying the injured person's claim[17].

(b) Frustration

The application of the doctrine of frustration to transactions involving land has usually been considered in relation to leases rather than contracts for sale. As to the former, the previous uncertainty has now been resolved by the House of Lords. The doctrine is capable of applying to an executed lease, though the circumstances when it can operate are likely to be exceedingly rare[18]. The fact that a lease creates an estate in land, an argument traditionally advanced against its application, is now regarded as an insufficient reason to repel the doctrine.

A fully executed contract for the sale of land cannot, of course, be frustrated[19]. As yet no English authority has applied the doctrine to such a contract which is still executory[20]. But this is not to say that the doctrine cannot be invoked as a matter of law. Take the case of coastal erosion undermining a cliff and causing property at the top to collapse into the sea, or the case of total destruction of an upstairs freehold flat[1]. These are two situations which seem tailor-made for its application. Moreover, the courts' likely disinclination to order specific performance[2] of a contract to convey land or property that no longer exists forestalls any argument that the risk has passed to the purchaser, compelling him to bear the loss.

(c) Incidence of insurance[3]

If the risk passes to the purchaser as from the date of the contract, it seems but a simple precaution to insure the property, against fire, storm damage and similar risks, remembering that if the property is vacant, certain risks such as burst pipes or malicious damage may not be covered by the normal household policy. It should be standard practice for every solicitor to ensure that the purchaser is adequately protected between contract and completion. Failure

16   *Hillingdon Estates Co v Stonefield Estates Ltd* [1952] Ch 627, [1952] 1 All ER 853.
17   *Robertson v Skelton* (1849) 12 Beav 260.
18   *National Carriers Ltd v Panalpina (Northern) Ltd* [1981] AC 675, [1981] 1 All ER 161, HL (access to warehouse blocked by local authority; no frustration).
19   Ie after completion. Contrast a lease which is partly executory in that the parties' rights and obligations remain outstanding during its currency: ibid, at 705, 179, per Lord Simon.
20   In two cases the court has been prepared to assume it could, but not on the facts: *Amalgamated Investment and Property Co Ltd v John Walker & Sons Ltd*, supra; *Universal Corpn v Five Ways Properties Ltd* [1979] 1 All ER 552, CA. For the Canadian position, see [1980] Conv 98.
1   Cf *Wong Lai Ying v Chinachem Investments Co Ltd* (1979) 13 BLR 81, PC (landslide demolishing block of flats). What of a house totally gutted by fire?
2   See the *Panalpina* case, supra at 704, 178, per Lord Simon. The point was conceded.
3   See (1988) Law Com WP No 109, Part II.

to do so appears to constitute professional negligence, rendering him liable in damages to his client for any resulting loss[4]. Many firms of solicitors have arranged automatic insurance cover for their client-purchasers' houses pending completion[5]. Some building societies effect insurance[6] on behalf of prospective borrowers on receipt of a signed acceptance of the mortgage offer. But there is no uniform procedure, so that a practitioner without a block policy needs to verify the exact position and arrange insurance if needed.

In the absence of any policy taken out by or on behalf of the purchaser, he has no legal or equitable rights to any insurance money received by the vendor[7]. The latter possibility is, effectively, what occurred in *Lonsdale & Thompson Ltd v Black Arrow Group plc*[8]. Under the terms of a lease, the landlord had covenanted to insure the property and to apply all moneys received under that policy to the reinstatement of the property. The landlord then contracted to sell the freehold and, between contract and conveyance, the premises were destroyed. The freehold was later transferred for the full contract price and the issue was whether the insurer was liable to pay for the cost of reinstatement. It was held that it was, the judge taking the view that the terms of the lease were such that the landlord was effectively taking out an insurance policy on behalf of the tenant[9]. Where the policy has not been taken out in this way, then the vendor's trusteeship does not extend to the proceeds of the policy. Nor can a purchaser who completes claim against the vendor's policy, despite the vendor having assigned to him his entire interest in it. The insurance effected by the vendor is essentially a personal indemnity against loss. Receipt of the purchase price signifies no loss. So he has nothing to assign[10]. Equally the insurers can recover insurance moneys paid to a vendor who subsequently receives the full price from the purchaser[11]. He cannot make a profit.

A vendor is under no general duty to maintain his insurance[12], except in the case of property held under a lease containing a lessee's covenant to insure. Since the vendor's failure to perform the obligation would constitute a defect in title entitling the purchaser to rescind[13], he indirectly obtains the benefit of the existing insurance. In reality, the prospect of the vendor's failing to renew his policy is remote and confined to situations where the property is free from

---

4   Cf *Carly v Farrelly* [1975] 1 NZLR 356 at 369, per Mahon J (though here express instructions had been given to attend to insurance matters).
5   But see Emmet, para 1.082, querying a solicitor's authority to insure without his client's consent.
6   The practice of building societies is to nominate the company with which insurance is to be placed, though borrowers can select a different company from a list of approved insurers. Should a mortgagor prefer to arrange his own insurance (eg because membership of a professional association entitles him to a premium discount), the cover provided must be satisfactory to the society which normally charges a small administration fee.
7   *Rayner v Preston* (1881) 18 Ch D 1, CA.
8   [1993] Ch 361, [1993] 3 All ER 648.
9   An analogy was drawn with a situation where a trade union effects insurance in its name on behalf of its members: *Prudential Staff Union v Hall* [1947] KB 685.
10   *Ziel Nominees Pty Ltd v VACC Insurance Co Ltd* (1975) 7 ALR 667.
11   *Castellain v Preston* (1883) 11 QBD 380, CA.
12   *Paine v Meller* (1801) 6 Ves 349.
13   Assuming the usual forfeiture clause; *Palmer v Goren* (1856) 25 LJ Ch 841.

mortgage. No mortgagee will permit the policy to lapse during the currency of the mortgage. These factors apart, it is not in the vendor's own interest to discontinue his insurance. The purchaser may not complete; or he may successfully rescind the contract leaving the vendor to stand the loss[14].

Since both contracting parties have insurable interests in the property, the result, of benefit to nobody save insurance companies, is that there often exists double house insurance between contract and completion.

(i) *Statutory provisions.*   Section 47 of the Law of Property Act 1925, enacts, in effect, that the purchaser is to have the benefit of any insurance money payable to the vendor after the date of the contract in respect of any damage to or destruction of the property, provided (a) there is no contrary stipulation in the contract between the parties, (b) the insurers give their consent (and in many but not all household policies it is given in general terms, though a purchaser will not know this without a specific inquiry) and (c) the purchaser pays a proportionate part of the premium from the date of the contract. In spite of this provision, the advice given in all the books is that the purchaser should insure. The section does not require the vendor to maintain the insurance or to inform the purchaser that it has lapsed. Then again the policy might be voidable at the option of the company, or the sum insured may be insufficient to afford the purchaser adequate cover.

Under the Fires Prevention (Metropolis) Act 1774, s 83, an insurance company is required, in the case of loss or damage *by fire*, to reinstate the insured property upon the request of any person interested in or entitled to it, provided the insurers have not already paid out to the insured. A mortgagee is a person interested[15], but there is no decision on the rights of a purchaser under a contract for sale. It is generally felt that the section, assuming it extends to purchasers[16], does not afford adequate protection and tends to be ignored by conveyancers.

An additional cause for extreme caution in placing reliance upon either section is that it is not clear that any insurance money is payable at all, the reason being that the vendor, who is entitled to the purchase money, will have suffered no loss for which he needs an indemnity[17].

(ii) *Contractual provisions.*   This area of law was reviewed by the Law Commission, who considered the position to be unduly uncertain, potentially unjust and conducive to wasteful expenditure. In terms of potential injustice, it was felt that the position that the risk of damage to or destruction of the property between contract and conveyance passing to the purchaser may represent a trap for him, particularly if he has entered into the contract without full advice. If he had not arranged his own insurance, he runs the risk of

14   See *Simmons v Pennington & Son* [1955] 1 All ER 240, CA.
15   *Sinnott v Bowden* [1912] 2 Ch 414.
16   Supported obiter by James LJ in *Rayner v Preston* (1881) 18 Ch D 1 at 15, CA.
17   See *Kern Corpn Ltd v Walter Reid Trading Pty Ltd* (1987) 61 ALJR 319 reaching this conclusion when dealing with an Australian statute modelled on s 83. Contrast *Lonsdale & Thompson Ltd v Black Arrow Group Ltd*, supra.

financial catastrophe if he has to pay the full contract price for a property which has been destroyed. The wasteful expenditure arises because it is unsafe either for the vendor to cancel his own insurance pending completion or for the purchaser to rely on recovering under the vendor's policy. The upshot of this is that both parties to the contract are simultaneously insuring the same property; something to the advantage of insurance companies alone. To remove these problems, the Law Commission provisionally recommended, as one possible option, a change to the law to ensure that the risk of damage to the property stayed with the vendor until completion[18].

A second option put forward was for the parties to alter the position by a term in the contract, to achieve this result, without the need for any statutory intervention. The Law Society reacted positively to this suggestion by altering the standard form contract to reflect this proposal, a response which led, in turn, to the Law Commission suspending its recommendation for legislation.

Under General Condition 5.1.1 of the Standard Conditions of Sale, the vendor undertakes to transfer the property in the same physical state as it was in at the date of the contract (except for wear and tear), which means that the vendor retains the risk until completion. If the property is damaged during this period, the following consequences ensue. If the property becomes unusable, the purchaser may rescind the contract. If, however, the reason that the property has become unusable is damage against which the vendor could not reasonably have insured, or which it is not legally possible for the vendor to make good, then the vendor can rescind the contract. The vendor is under no obligation to insure the property and the operation of s 47 of the Law of Property Act 1925 is excluded[19].

The effect of this contractual provision is that, if the property is damaged between contract and completion, the vendor is liable in damages to the purchaser. If the damage is total, the purchaser can rescind and, potentially recover damages for breach of contract. This reversal of the previous position has attracted hostility in some quarters; the basis of that hostility being, to a large extent, the position that this would put the vendor in if, as well as selling a house, he was also buying another[20]. In that event, he would be liable to the purchaser but also, face the prospect of losing his deposit to his vendor further up the chain. The position of the purchaser would also be very difficult if the property he had contracted to buy was badly damaged, or destroyed, between contract and conveyance. Indeed, there is bound to be serious disruption to the chain in the event of such an event occurring. On balance, it was felt by the Law Commission that the position where the risk of damage to the property remains with the vendor until completion would be more just[1]. It should also be remembered that, if they so choose, the parties are free to amend Condition 5.1 so that the risk passes to the purchaser from the date of the contract[2]. If this course is adopted, the purchaser is at least explicitly warned as to the

18   (1988) Law Com WP No 109.
19   SCS 5.1.2–5.1.4.
20   See, eg, (1980) 87 LSG No 11, 24 (Lesley A Palmer).
 1   (1988) Law Com WP 109, paras 3.23–3.27.
 2   See National Conveyancing Protocol, 16, 17.

nature of the risk that is being run upon entering into the contract, who would also be put on express notice of the need to insure the property.

2. Possession before completion

As we have seen, the vendor is entitled to retain possession until actual completion. The parties may agree otherwise, which sometimes happens on a sale or assignment of business premises[3]. The contract itself may incorporate a special condition authorising the purchaser to take possession. Or the vendor may, after exchange of contracts, allow the purchaser to occupy on the terms of the appropriate general condition (varied as he deems prudent). Vendors of residential property, even when they are in a position to grant possession before completion, are generally reluctant to do so. The dangers cannot be minimised, and a solicitor should advise his client fully of the risks involved. The possible incidence of the Housing Act 1988 must be considered. The purchaser may be less anxious to complete on the contractual date. In the event of delay the vendor has neither actual enjoyment nor the purchase money, though often in reality the purchaser is required to pay the balance (or at least part) as a condition of being allowed into possession. If the vendor sues for specific performance the court usually gives the purchaser the option of paying the balance with interest into court as an alternative to giving up possession[4], even where he has made extensive alterations to the property[5].

Contractual provisions regarding pre-completion possession
The Standard Conditions of Sale[6] regulate the rights of a purchaser (not being a lessee already in possession) who is permitted to occupy before actual completion. The exercise of some act of ownership in relation to the land, eg entering into a sub-sale, or granting an option to purchase part[7] does not by itself amount to occupation of the property. It is expressly provided by the Standard Conditions[8] that the buyer is not in occupation for the purpose of this condition if he merely exercises rights of access given solely to do work agreed by the seller. While looking at the operation of the Standard Conditions, it will be helpful to compare the position under an open contract.

(i) *Status.* Under an open contract the purchaser is a tenant at will[9], which suffices, *prima facie*[10], to bring him within the scope of the Rent Act 1977 or the

3 See eg *Butler v Croft* (1973) 27 P & CR 1; *Tudor v Hamid* [1988] 1 EGLR 251, CA (hotel).
4 *Greenwood v Turner* [1891] 2 Ch 144, distinguished in *Attfield v DJ Plant Hire and General Contractors Co Ltd* [1987] Ch 141, [1986] 3 All ER 273 (vendor confined to rights under NCS 8).
5 *Maskell v Ivory* [1970] Ch 502, [1970] 1 All ER 488.
6 SCS 5.2.
7 Cf *Fred Morton Holdings Ltd v Davis* (1978) 97 DLR (3d) 273. But see *Ballard v Shutt* (1880) 15 Ch D 122 (erection of 'For Sale' board on vacant land an assumption of ownership).
8 SCS 5.2.4.
9 *Ball v Cullimore* (1835) 2 Cr M & R 120.
10 Contrast *Francis Jackson Developments Ltd v Stemp* [1943] 2 All ER 601, CA, with *Dunthorne and Shore v Wiggins* [1943] 2 All ER 678, CA.

Housing Act 1988[11]. The Statutory Conditions of Sale provide that a purchaser who is let into possession is a licensee and not a tenant. Provision is also made for the purchaser to pay the vendor a licence fee[12]. A difficulty with this, however, is that it has been held by the House of Lords, that if an agreement satisfies all the terms of a tenancy, then the parties cannot turn it into a licence simply by calling it one[13]. Applying this principle, it is not easy to see why a relationship which, under an open contract, would be classified as one of landlord and tenant should be reclassified as a licence simply because that is how the conditions of sale describe it. On the other hand, in *Street v Mountford*[14], Lord Templeman expressed the view that a purchaser in occupation under a contract of sale may only be a licensee, although no reasons were given for this view and it was not made clear whether he was referring to the general law or to contracts governed by a standard form contract of sale. Despite the doubts that can be raised, it would seem that the relationship of vendor and purchaser is sufficient to mean that the effect of occupation agreements between them would be regarded as being a special case, so that the purchaser is properly regarded as a licensee.

The terms of the licence are that it is non-assignable but extends to permit members of his household to occupy the property. The licence will terminate on the earliest of three alternative events: completion of the contract, rescission of the contract[15] or the expiry of five working days' notice of termination given by one party to the other[16]. It has been held that termination of the licence is not necessarily inconsistent with his remaining in occupation thereafter qua purchaser under the contract so that he cannot thereafter assert the acquisition of title by adverse possession[17] but this seems wrong in principle[18].

(ii) *Liability for interest, repairs, etc.*   As from the date of taking possession until actual completion or until he vacates the property following rescission of the contract, the purchaser is responsible for repairs and for the discharge of all outgoings by way of rates, rent[19], insurance, and even non-recurrent outgoings such as the expenses incurred in complying with a dangerous structure notice. On the purchaser taking possession, General Condition 5.1 becomes inapplicable, with the consequence that the risk of damage to the property no longer rests with the vendor[20]. The purchaser must pay interest on the balance of the purchase money, and is entitled to the rents and profits from any part

---

11   *Chamberlain v Farr* [1942] 2 All ER 567, CA; *Bretherton v Paton* (1986) 18 HLR 257, CA (occupant *intending* to buy held a tenant, not a licensee, because of rental payments).
12   SCS 5.2.2.
13   *Street v Mountford* [1985] AC 809 at 819, 821, [1985] 2 All ER 289 at 294, 296 per Lord Templeman, HL.
14   Ibid at 827 at 300.
15   See *Walters v Roberts* (1980) 41 P & CR 210 at 218, per Nourse J.
16   SCS 5.2.2(a), (b) and (d).
17   [1982] 1 All ER 1029, CA (14 years' occupation without repudiation of contract); cogently criticised at (1983) 46 MLR 89 (M Dockray).
18   *Bridges v Mees* [1957] Ch 475, [1957] 2 All ER 577, p 54, ante, was not cited.
19   *Vangeen v Benjamin* (1976) 239 EG 647.
20   SCS 5.2.3. The purchaser is required to insure the property.

of the property not physically occupied by him[1]. These conditions basically confirm the open contract position, where the act of taking possession is an implied agreement to pay interest[2].

(iii) *Improvements.*   As previously noted, the Standard Conditions of Sale draw a distinction between taking possession and being allowed access solely to effect work to the property agreed with the vendor. Activity of this nature is not treated as occupation, and the Conditions are expressly made inapplicable[3]. But what of a purchaser permitted beneficial occupation by residing in the property or carrying on business there? The Standard Conditions do not deal with this. Perhaps the general law adequately protects the vendor in this situation. A purchaser in possession who effects substantial improvements cannot recover his expenditure if the sale goes off because of the vendor's breach of contract[4]. Should the purchaser himself default, leaving the alterations incomplete, the vendor, it seems, can recover the amount necessary to render the premises habitable[5]. Nevertheless, it is desirable to regulate this by expressly providing that the purchaser shall forgo any claim against the vendor for money spent on the property.

(iv) *Waiver of title.*   The Standard Conditions[6] also stipulate that the taking of possession does not preclude the purchaser from raising requisitions on title. This is an improvement on the open contract position. The cases, some of which are difficult to reconcile, appear to establish the following general rules. Possession does not of itself constitute acceptance[7], but will do so if the purchaser exercises acts of ownership[8] or makes structural alterations[9]. Where the contract expressly provides that he shall have possession, this is interpreted as meaning beneficial possession and acts of ownership do not constitute a waiver[10].

The Standard Conditions are confined to the taking of possession. If the purchaser is let into beneficial occupation (otherwise than under the contract) and then makes structural alterations, the general rule applies. He is deemed to have waived his right to object to irremovable defects of title of which he

---

1   SCS 5.2.2(e).
2   *Fludyer v Cocker* (1805) 12 Ves 25 at 27, per Sir William Grant MR; *Birch v Joy* (1852) 3 HL Cas 565.
3   SCS 5.2.4. Aliter, if the contract provides for vacant possession earlier than the agreed completion date: *Desai v Harris* (1987) Independent, 16 February, CA.
4   It is not normally to be regarded as in the contemplation of the parties that the purchaser will spend money on improving the property before it has been conveyed to him: per Brightman J in *Lloyd v Stanbury* [1971] 2 All ER 267 at 275; *Worthington v Warrington* (1849) 8 CB 134 (tenant in possession exercising option to purchase and making alterations).
5   Cf *Crisp v Fox* (1967) 201 EG 769 (purchaser in possession before contracts exchanged liable for damage to property when sale fell through).
6   SCS 5.2.7.
7   *Simpson v Sadd* (1854) 4 De GM & G 665, unless it is taken *after* delivery of an abstract revealing defects of title: *Bown v Stenson* (1857) 24 Beav 631.
8   *Re Barrington, ex p Sidebotham* (1834) 3 LJ Bcy 122 (leasing); *Haydon v Bell* (1838) 1 Beav 337 (mortgaging).
9   *Re Gloag and Miller's Contract* (1883) 23 Ch D 320, unless the defects of title are removable.
10   *Stevens v Guppy* (1828) 3 Russ 171.

had notice before taking possession[11]. In this situation the Standard Conditions do not appear to assist the purchaser.

H Purchaser's fiduciary duty to vendor

In rare circumstances a purchaser may be held accountable to his vendor for a failure to disclose material information within his knowledge. In one case[12] a prospective purchaser (P) before exchange of contracts applied for and was later granted planning permission to develop the vendor's (V's) land. The application, in V's name, was signed by P as 'agent' for V, but without his knowledge or authority. Since P's conduct[13], if disclosed to V, might reasonably have been likely to influence V in deciding whether or not to conclude the contract, a fiduciary relationship existed between P and V. P was duty bound to disclose the existence of the application prior to exchange. Non-disclosure rendered him liable to account to V for the profit (the enhanced value of the land) accruing from the grant of permission[14]. But V would have had no recourse against P if submission of the application had been delayed until after exchange of contracts. P's action could in no way have influenced V's decision to enter into the contract.

I Effect of death before completion

The basic rule is that the death of either, or both, of the parties before completion does not avoid a contract for sale of land. It remains enforceable by and against the deceased's personal representatives[15].

1. Death of vendor

The precise effect of the vendor's death depends on the capacity in which he is selling the land.

(i) If he is selling as sole beneficial owner, the legal estate in the land and his beneficial interest in the purchase money vest in his personal representatives who should complete the contract.

(ii) If he is one of two or more trustees for sale or personal representatives, the legal title devolves on the surviving estate owners.

---

11 *Re Gloag and Miller's Contract* (1883) 23 Ch D 320 at 329, per Fry J.
12 *English v Dedham Vale Properties Ltd* [1978] 1 All ER 382.
13 The principle extends to any action taken by P purportedly as V's agent in relation to V's property and likely to influence V, per Slade J at 399.
14 V did not learn about the grant until after completion. Had he discovered it beforehand he could, it is thought, have resisted specific performance and, perhaps, have rescinded the contract as an unconscionable bargain.
15 *Hoddel v Pugh* (1864) 33 Beav 489.

(iii) If he is a sole personal representative, the proper person to complete the chain depends on whether or not the chain of representation remains unbroken[16].

2. Death of purchaser

On the death of the purchaser the vendor can enforce the contract against his personal representatives. As between the different persons claiming through him, it is the person entitled to the property who is prima facie responsible to provide the balance of the purchase money. The vendor's lien, attaching to the land at the time of the contract, constitutes a charge on the property, which the land itself must bear in the absence of any contrary intention in the deceased's will[17]. The vendor is not however deprived of his right to enforce payment out of the deceased's other assets[18]. Should it become necessary he can enforce his lien against the devisee after an assent in the beneficiary's favour, though he cannot sue him personally for the price.

J   Effect of bankruptcy before completion

1. General position

The Insolvency Act 1986[19] introduces a new code for personal insolvency, under which acts of bankruptcy are no longer relevant. The insolvency procedure commences with the presentation of a creditor's petition for bankruptcy, followed by the making of a bankruptcy order by the court and then eventually by the appointment of a trustee in bankruptcy[20]. The bankruptcy commences on the day on which the order is made[1].

2. Bankruptcy of vendor

Bankruptcy does not terminate the contract for sale; it alters the parties' rights somewhat. Under s 306 of the Act the bankrupt's property vests automatically in his trustee immediately on his appointment taking effect[2], without any

---

16 See AEA 1925, s 7; Mellows, *The Law of Succession*, (5th edn), pp 253–255.
17 *Re Birmingham, Savage v Stannard* [1959] Ch 523, [1958] 2 All ER 397.
18 AEA 1925, s 35(3).
19 Consolidating the Insolvency Act 1985, which repealed the Bankruptcy Act 1914 (save for ss 121–123).
20 Insolvency Act 1986, ss 264(1), (2), 305(1). In certain cases the official receiver becomes trustee (see eg ss 295(4), 297(1)).
1   Ibid, s 278(a). With the abolition of the concept of the act of bankruptcy there disappears the doctrine of relation back of the commencement of bankruptcy.
2   Contrast the position on the winding-up of a company. Its property does not vest in the liquidator (unless a court order is made under s 145, ibid). It will be the company that transfers the legal title to the purchaser. See generally *Ayerst v C & K (Construction) Ltd* [1976] AC 167 at 177, [1975] 2 All ER 537 at 541, HL, per Lord Diplock. Considerable difference of opinion exists as to the need for the liquidator to join in the conveyance, and for what purposes. For a summary of the conflicting views, see a note at [1983] Conv 177.

conveyance, assignment or transfer. Property held by the bankrupt qua trustee is excluded from this general vesting[3]. With registered land the title of the trustee in bankruptcy vests without any alteration of the proprietorship register. This constitutes a notable exception to the cardinal land registration principle that the legal estate is deemed to be vested in the registered proprietor for the time being. The trustee can apply to be registered as proprietor on production of the requisite evidence of title, and he will no doubt be asked to take this step should the contract be completed[4].

A purchaser who takes a conveyance from the trustee should ask for production of the certificate of appointment and for proof of the adjudication order. Specific performance may be enforced against the trustee[5], but the purchaser cannot sue the vendor for breach of contract. His claim is provable in the bankruptcy. The trustee possesses a statutory right to disclaim onerous property, but the existence of this power does not enable him to disclaim the vendor's contract for sale merely because it would be more beneficial to the bankrupt's estate[6].

Until such time as the bankrupt's property vests in his trustee, the legal title remains in the vendor notwithstanding the presentation of a bankruptcy petition. It does not follow, however, that the purchaser can safely accept a conveyance from the vendor before the statutory vesting operates. Section 284 avoids any disposition of property by the bankrupt effected between the day of presentation and the date of vesting in the trustee, unless the court consents to or ratifies the transaction. The purchaser should, therefore, take a conveyance from the trustee after his appointment. Nevertheless a conveyance from the vendor would be valid under s 284(4) if the purchaser was in good faith and without notice of the presentation of the petition. Should he become aware of its presentation after exchange of contracts, he will not, seemingly, be bound to complete the purchase, and can recover his deposit, at least if held by a stakeholder[7].

3.   Bankruptcy of purchaser

The trustee can elect to complete the contract, or disclaim it as unprofitable in which case the vendor can forfeit the deposit and prove in the bankruptcy for any loss suffered by the disclaimer[8]. The vendor cannot initially sue the

---

3   Ibid, s 283(3)(a). See also s 313 (re-vesting of house in bankrupt when substitutionary charge obtained).
4   See LRA 1925, s 110(5).
5   *Pearce v Bastable's Trustee in Bankruptcy* [1901] 2 Ch 122; *Freevale Ltd v Metrostore (Holdings) Ltd* [1984] Ch 199, [1984] 1 All ER 495 (vendor company in receivership).
6   See the Insolvency Act 1986, s 315; *Re Bastable, ex p Trustee* [1901] 2 KB 518, CA.
7   Cf *Powell v Marshall, Parkes & Co* [1899] 1 QB 710, CA (purchaser aware of act of bankruptcy when time of essence.) Aliter, if the deposit is held by the vendor's agent, in which event he will have to prove in the bankruptcy for its recovery. In the usual situation when time is not initially of the essence, he may be able to make it so by serving a contractual notice to complete (eg under SCS 6.8); p 427, post.
8   Insolvency Act 1986, s 315(5); see *Re Parnell, ex p Barrell* (1875) 10 Ch App 512.

purchaser's trustee[9]. He should give written notice to the trustee to elect either to perform the contract or disclaim it. If he does not disclaim within 28 days he is deemed to have adopted the contract[10], and the vendor can pursue his normal remedies.

Difficulties also face a vendor desirous of completing the sale before commencement of the bankruptcy on making of the order. Unless he completes without notice of the presentation of a petition (when s 284(4) will protect him), he will be liable to refund the purchase money to the trustee once the latter's title to the purchase property takes effect[11]. Nor can the vendor treat the petition as entitling him to rescind the contract on the contractual completion date, time not being of the essence[12]. Yet he would be free to exercise any contractual right enabling him to make time of the essence by service of a notice to complete.

4. Registration of petitions and orders

It should not be overlooked that the title of the trustee in bankruptcy may be unenforceable against the purchaser because the appropriate registration provisions relating to bankruptcy proceedings have not been observed. In the case of unregistered land, both the petition and the subsequent bankruptcy order are registrable under the Land Charges Act 1972 in the registers of pending actions and of writs and orders respectively[13]. The trustee's title is void against a purchaser of the legal estate in good faith for money or money's worth unless the bankruptcy order is for the time being duly registered[14].

The provisions relating to *registered land* are complicated. In the first place registration is effected under the Land Charges Act 1972, simply to set the machinery in motion. At this early stage it will not even be known whether the debtor owns any land. On registration of the petition as a pending action, the Chief Land Registrar must as soon as practicable register a *creditor's notice* in the vendor's proprietorship register[15]. This notice ensures that any subsequent disposition affecting the land lodged for registration is subject to creditors' claims, unless entitled to priority conferred by an official certificate of search. Registration of a bankruptcy order under the Act of 1972 is followed by the registration of a *bankruptcy inhibition* against the vendor's title. Until this is vacated, no dealing with the land can be registered other than the registration of the trustee[16]. The inhibition puts a complete and effective stop on the title to the vendor's land. If no creditor's notice or inhibition appears against the

---

9   *Lowes v Lush* (1808) 14 Ves 547.
10   Insolvency Act 1986, s 316(1), (2).
11   Ibid, s 284(1), which expressly applies to money payments: sub-s (2).
12   Cf *Jennings' Trustee v King* [1952] Ch 899, [1952] 2 All ER 608 (purchaser's act of bankruptcy).
13   LCA 1972, ss 5(1), 6(1) (c).
14   Ibid, s 6(5) (as substituted by the Insolvency Act 1985, s 235; Sch 8, para 21(3)(c)).
15   LRA 1925, s 61(1)).
16   Ibid, s 61(3), (4). When one of two (or more) joint proprietors is declared bankrupt, the proper procedure is to apply for a caution or restriction after adjudication: R & R, 689–90.

title, a purchaser in good faith for money or money's worth will on registration of his disposition obtain good title against the trustee in bankruptcy, unless he has notice[17] of the petition or of the adjudication[18].

---

17   At the date of execution of the disposition; presumably the vendor's execution is meant since the purchaser often does not execute the transfer.
18   LRA 1925, s 61(6) (as amended). The purchaser is under no duty to make a land charges search: ibid. Nor does registration of the petition or of the bankruptcy order under LCA 1972, fix him with notice thereof: LRA 1925, s 110(7).

Part 4

The post-contract stage

Chapter 9

Deducing title

A Introduction

We now have reached the stage where contracts have been exchanged and the parties are bound in law to complete, subject to the exercise of any rights contractual or otherwise which they have to terminate the agreement. The aim of this part of the book is to discover the various steps in the transaction ultimately leading to the vesting of the legal title in the purchaser. This particular chapter is devoted to the vendor's obligation to establish that he is in a position to transfer what he has contracted to convey, that is, his duty to deduce title as it is termed, and the manner in which he discharges that duty in practice.

It will be apparent from the previous chapters that the vendor is under no legal obligation to establish his ownership of the estate contracted to be sold prior to the formation of a binding contract for sale. Bearing in mind the complexities of English land law and the period of 60 years' investigation of title prescribed by the common law, the evolution of such a rule was hardly surprising; had it been otherwise vendors would have been seriously inconvenienced in the sale of real property[1]. Today different considerations apply, not the least of these being the simplification of land law rules designed to facilitate transfers of land, and the spread of registration of title. As we have seen[2], it is now common practice on a sale of unregistered land, for the draft contract to be accompanied by sufficient documentation to enable the purchaser's solicitor to investigate title before exchange of contracts and, when the Conveyancing Protocol is employed, the vendor's solicitor is required to furnish his counterpart with this material[3]. This procedure is not, however, universally employed; the traditional method of deducing title still survives.

The manner of deducing title varies according to the property involved – whether it is registered, or unregistered, freehold or leasehold. This chapter sets out the position on the sale of an unregistered freehold estate, assuming that the vendor furnishes evidence of his title after exchange of contracts. The following chapter deals with leasehold estates and other cases where special considerations arise. Registered titles are considered in Chapter 11.

---

1 *Reeve v Berridge* (1888) 20 QBD 523 at 528, CA, per Fry LJ ('great practical convenience').
2 See p 143, ante, and p 373, post. And see a letter in (1983) 80 LSG 2568.
3 National Conveyancing Protocol, p 24.

B   Obligation to show good title

1.   Introduction

Every contract for the sale of land prima facie imports a term that the vendor will show a good title, or, as it is sometimes expressed, a marketable title, one which may at all times and under all circumstances be forced on the purchaser[4]. The better view is that this obligation operates as an implied term[5], though there is some authority supporting the view that it is a right given by law.

This obligation is only likely to apply in its full vigour in an open contract, when the vendor must show he is entitled to the property for a freehold estate in possession free from incumbrances. In practice, the terms of the contract between the parties will often operate to modify the duty. The vendor is free to incorporate a special condition precluding any objection by the purchaser to a particular defect, and provided the condition is not misleading, a purchaser contracting on such a basis is bound thereby[6]. Occasionally the contract may simply be for the sale of such interest, *if any*, as the vendor has in the land, or it may stipulate that no title shall be required beyond the vendor's possession at the time of sale. But, save as the contract restricts the obligation in whole or in part, the purchaser is entitled to a good title and the vendor must establish that he can convey the entirety[7] of what he has contracted to sell.

2.   What is meant by good title?

The word 'title' is an ambiguous word[8], meaning different things in different contexts. Conveyancers use the word in two main senses – first, to mean ownership, the vendor's right to the property; secondly, the evidence supporting the claim to ownership, ie the proof of 'title' in the first sense. In the expression 'good title', the word is used as equivalent to ownership; a vendor must show a title as will enable the purchaser to hold the property against any person who may probably challenge his right to it[9].

This obligation to make a good title requires the vendor to show that he alone, or with the concurrence of some person or persons whose concurrence

---

4   *Pyrke v Waddingham* (1852) 10 Hare 1 at 8, per Turner V-C; *MEPC Ltd v Christian-Edwards* [1978] 3 All ER 795 at 799, CA, per Goff LJ; affd [1981] AC 205, [1979] 3 All ER 752, HL.

5   See *Ellis v Rogers* (1884) 29 Ch D 661 at 670–1, CA, per Cotton LJ, who reviews the conflicting dicta; *Alderdale Estate Co v McGrory* [1917] 1 Ch 414 at 417, CA, per Cozens-Hardy MR. See further Farrand, 83–84.

6   See pp 169–171, ante.

7   *Sears Properties Ltd v Salt* (1967) 204 EG 359 (strip of land vested in local authority for road widening; purchaser entitled to rescind).

8   *Felkin v Lord Herbert* (1861) 30 LJ Ch 798 at 799, per Kindersley V-C. And see (1964) 80 LQR 63 (B Rudden).

9   *Jeakes v White* (1851) 6 Exch 873 at 881, per Pollock CB. And see *Re Stirrup's Contract* [1961] 1 All ER 805 at 809, per Wilberforce J. To have a good title to land is to have the essential part of ownership, namely, the right to maintain or recover possession of the land as against all others: *Williams on Real Property* (24th edn) p 703.

he can compel, can convey the whole legal estate and equitable interest in the land sold[10], free from incumbrances except for those disclosed by the contract.

(a) Legal and equitable

Strictly speaking title must be shown to both the legal estate and the equitable interest in the property. Since 1925 the legal estate has formed the basis of modern conveyancing, so that in practice it will rarely be necessary to do more than establish title to the legal estate. On a sale by a sole beneficial owner, both legal and equitable titles are in him. Even where the titles are split, eg under a settlement, or trust for sale, the purchaser need not ordinarily concern himself with the equitable interests. Provided the appropriate procedure is adopted, a conveyance of the legal estate will overreach the equitable interests and give the purchaser a title free from them[11], without the equitable owners having to join in the conveyance to transfer their interests.

It is otherwise when the equitable interests are not overreachable. Suppose X purchases property but the conveyance is taken in V's name. Assuming no question of advancement arises, V holds on a resulting trust for X. If V later contracts to sell to P, V will not be able to enforce the contract against P, because of his inability to show title to the equitable interest vested in X. Nor can V compel X to join in a conveyance of the land in order to pass his interest, unless X has requested the sale[12].

(b) Title in vendor

The legal title must be in the vendor, or in some person whom he can compel to convey. If the vendor (V) can compel a conveyance from some third party (Y), V is always in a position to obtain the legal estate[13]. The case of *Elliott and H Elliott (Builders) Ltd v Pierson*[14] illustrates this aspect of the rule.

> W Ltd owned freehold property which is leased to V, the sole director. V granted to P an option to purchase the property, which P exercised. P later repudiated the contract on the ground that V, being a mere leaseholder, had no title to the freehold.

It was held that V, being in sole and absolute control of the company, could compel it to convey the freehold to P. Other instances of the application of this rule occur in the case of a sub-sale, where the purchaser can, subject to any contrary term in the contract, call upon his vendor to convey the property to the sub-purchaser, or a sole beneficiary of full age under a bare trust. He need only show a good title in his trustee, for he can always terminate the trust by calling for the legal title to be vested in him[15].

---

10 Williams, *Title*, 565.
11 See *City of London Building Society v Flegg* [1988] AC 54, [1987] 3 All ER 435, HL.
12 *Re Baker and Selmon's Contract* [1907] 1 Ch 238 (trustee-vendor with no power of sale held able to compel concurrence of beneficiaries who requested sale); *Re Hailes and Hutchinson's Contract* [1920] 1 Ch 233 (sale with consent of concurring beneficiaries).
13 See [1979] Conv 1, pointing out that P will either take a conveyance from Y by direction of V, or one in which both V and Y join. See Hallett, 227, Form 21 (sub-sale).
14 [1948] Ch 452, [1948] 1 All ER 939; cf *Jones v Lipman* [1962] 1 All ER 442.
15 *Saunders v Vautier* (1841) Cr & Ph 240.

The decision in *Re Bryant and Barningham's Contract*[16] should be contrasted with these examples. Vendors contracted to sell as trustees for sale, but in fact no trust for sale arose till after the death of a tenant for life. Though the life tenant was willing to execute a conveyance, the court upheld the purchaser's objection that a good title had not been shown since the vendors could not compel her concurrence. A vendor cannot require his purchaser to accept one contract in substitution for another.

(c) Freedom from incumbrances

The vendor must also show he can convey the property free from incumbrances, except those subject to which the property is stated to be sold. If incumbrances exist which he fails to disclose in the contract[17], he does not show a good title, for the purchaser is entitled to assume that the property is sold free from incumbrances[18], or subject only to such as are mentioned. The purchaser can, therefore, refuse to complete, but he cannot object to an undisclosed incumbrance of which he was aware when entering into the contract[19]. Knowledge does not preclude his insisting upon a good title where:

(i)   the contract expressly provides that a marketable title shall be given[20],
(ii) he reasonably believes the incumbrance to be no longer enforceable[1],
(iii) the incumbrance is removable, that is, capable of being discharged, or removed, before completion without the concurrence of the incumbrancer (eg a mortgage), as distinct from being irremovable, such as an easement[2].

Furthermore, a vendor does not show a good title enforceable in equity if he fails to disclose in the contract a known defect in title[3].

(d) Matters of conveyance

Where there exists a defect which the vendor can remove independently of another person, it is said to constitute a matter of conveyance. Matters of conveyance do not strictly fall within the duty to show a good title, but they are still matters which the vendor must deal with in order to perform his contract. The following constitute matters of conveyance: the discharge of a mortgage affecting the property[4], the concurrence of a mortgagee who is immediately

16   (1890) 44 Ch D 218, CA.
17   Including incumbrances created before the commencement of the title. See generally, pp 157–160, ante.
18   *Phillips v Caldcleugh* (1868) LR 4 QB 159 (restrictive covenants not disclosed).
19   *Timmins v Moreland Street Property Co Ltd* [1958] Ch 110, [1957] 3 All ER 265, CA (purchaser aware of lease not disclosed by informal memorandum).
20   *Cato v Thompson* (1882) 9 QBD 616, CA; *Re Gloag and Miller's Contract* (1883) 23 Ch D 320 at 327, per Fry J.
1   *Ellis v Rogers* (1884) 29 Ch D 661, CA (restrictive covenants thought to have been extinguished).
2   *Ellis v Rogers*(1884) 29 Ch D 661 at 666, CA, per Kay J.
3   *Faruqi v English Real Estates Ltd* [1979] 1 WLR 963 (inability to produce documents imposing restrictive covenants affecting land); *Rignall Developments Ltd v Halil* [1987] 3 All ER 170 (local land charge).
4   *Re Jackson and Oakshott* (1880) 14 Ch D 851, applied in *Leominster Properties Ltd v Broadway Finance Ltd* (1981) 42 P & CR 372, p 430, post.

redeemable[5], the appointment of trustees for the purposes of giving a receipt for capital money arising on a sale of settled land[6], but not the appointment of a new trustee for sale to *replace* one of the contracting parties[7].

(e) Time for performance

At law the vendor fulfils his obligation if he establishes a good title by the contractual date for completion. Provided he can convey at the proper time, it is no defence to an action by him for specific performance or damages that he had no title at the date of the contract[8]. The cases also show that a purchaser who discovers a fundamental defect in title can, if he acts promptly, repudiate the contract even before the agreed completion date. The precise legal effects of taking that step are controversial and will be considered in a later chapter[9]. It is obviously in the vendor's interests to establish a good title by the time he submits the evidence thereof to the purchaser's solicitor.

3. Gradations of title

Over the years conveyancers and judges have employed various expressions indicating a hierarchy of titles ranging from good to bad, or from white to black through varying shades of grey.

(a) Good title

This is not necessarily a perfect title but one that in a vendor's action for specific performance the court will enforce against a reluctant purchaser. If the title is such that it can be sold without the necessity of making special conditions of sale restrictive of the purchaser's rights, it is said to be a 'good marketable title'[10]. In a proper case the court will presume the facts on which the title depends. In *MEPC Ltd v Christian-Edwards*[11], the purchaser maintained that a good title had not been deduced because the abstract of title disclosed an outstanding contract for sale entered into as long ago as 1912. The House of Lords held that a good marketable title had been shown and decreed specific performance against the purchaser. In the circumstances the evidence overwhelmingly supported a presumption that the contract had been abandoned. Apart from this the contract, if still subsisting, was no longer

---

5   *Re Priestley's Contract* [1947] Ch 469 at 477, [1947] 1 All ER 716 at 720, per Romer J.
6   *Hatten v Russell* (1888) 38 Ch D 334.
7   *Re Priestley's Contract,* supra (contracting parties were A and B, whereas legal title in A and C; A could not compel C's retirement from the trust). Contra, when under a subsisting trust for sale, a surviving trustee, A, wishes to appoint B as a new trustee.
8   *Hoggart v Scott* (1830) 1 Russ & M 293; *Thomson v Miles* (1794) 1 Esp 184.
9   See the discussion in *Price v Strange* [1978] Ch 337 at 355, 364, [1977] 3 All ER 371 at 381, 389, CA, per Goff and Buckley LLJ. See further pp 645–648, post.
10 *Re Spollon and Long's Contract* [1936] Ch 713 at 718, [1936] 2 All ER 711 at 716–17, per Luxmoore J.
11 [1981] AC 205, [1979] 3 All ER 752, HL, a decision not favourably received by some commentators; see Emmet, para 8.034.

capable of specific enforcement. Any claim for this remedy by the persons entitled to the benefit of the contract would have been successfully met by a plea of laches.

(b) Doubtful title

Cases arise where it is doubtful as to whether the vendor can show a good title. In cases where the doubt is not capable of resolution, the title will not be forced upon the purchaser. So in *Nottingham Patent Brick and Tile Co v Butler*[12], the court refused to order specific performance against a purchaser who discovered the existence of restrictive covenants which the vendor had failed to disclose and which he alleged were not binding upon him through lack of notice. Future litigation may well have been necessary to substantiate this claim and the court will not compel a purchaser to buy a lawsuit.

In some cases, the doubt surrounding the vendor's title will be based upon an uncertain point of law[13]. At one time, there was a tendency for the courts, when faced with such a problem, to seek to resolve the point of law at issue but, if the point was regarded as being one of any difficulty, not force the title upon the purchaser taking the view that, until the point had been resolved, the purchaser's objection to the title was legitimate[14]. Latterly, however, a different, and more robust, approach has emerged. This approach is to decide the disputed point of law and, if the doubt was resolved in favour of the vendor, declare the title to be good and force the title on the purchaser[15]. This course has been adopted even in situations where, to resolve the point, previous authorities have had to be overruled[16].

This method of resolving the doubt affecting a title, which is now well established[17], is logical in that the effect of the court's decision in favour of the vendor is that the title is good and can, therefore, be forced upon a purchaser. It is nevertheless somewhat hard upon the purchaser who, until the point is resolved, is quite right to object to the title, particularly if the point is ultimately decided against the vendor. Recognising the difficulty faced by a purchaser in situations such as this, the courts have on occasion refused to award costs in favour of the vendor who, in any event, should have dealt with the particular difficulty in the contract[18].

---

12 (1886) 16 QBD 778, CA. See also *Pyrke v Waddingham* (1852) 10 Hare 1.
13 See Thompson, *Investigation and Proof of Title*, pp 11–17.
14 See *Marlow v Smith* (1723) 2 P Wms 198 at 201; *Price v Strange* (1820) 6 Madd 159 at 164, 65; *Pyrke v Waddingham*, supra, at 10, 11; *Palmer v Locke* (1881) 18 Ch D 381 at 388.
15 *Alexander v Mills* (1870) 6 Ch App 124, CA; *Re Thakwray and Young's Contract* (1888) 40 Ch D 34; *Re Carter and Kenderdine's Contract* [1897] 1 Ch 776, CA. The approach adopted in *Re Hollis Hospital Trustees and Hague's Contract* [1899] 2 Ch 540 at 545 is inconsistent with this line of authority.
16 *Re Carter and Kenderdine's Contract*, supra, overruling *Re Briggs and Spicer* [1891] 2 Ch 127.
17 *Smith v Colbourne* [1914] 2 Ch 533; *Imperial Tobacco Co Ltd v Wilmott* [1964] 2 All ER 510; *Darvell v Basildon Development Corpn* (1969) 211 EG 33.
18 *Osbourne v Rowlett* (1880) 13 Ch D 774; *Johnson v Clarke* [1928] Ch 847. See also *MEPC Ltd v Christian-Edwards* [1978] Ch 281 at 290, [1978] 3 All ER 795 at 801, CA, per Goff LJ, on appeal [1981] AC 205, [1979] 3 All ER 752, HL. Contrast *Re Carter and Kenderdine's Contract*, supra, where the vendor was awarded costs without discussion.

Costs will certainly be refused to a vendor who omits to take a relatively simple course of action to resolve a doubt affecting a title but, instead seeks to force it on a reluctant purchaser[19]. A good example of this occurred in *Horton v Kurzke*[20]. A purchaser, having contracted to buy land with vacant possession, discovered that there was a claim to grazing tenancy over part of the land. He then asked for completion to be deferred until after the resolution of arbitration proceedings under the Agricultural Holdings Act 1948. The vendor refused and served a notice to complete. He then purported to forfeit the deposit, whereupon the purchaser brought an action for specific performance with an abatement of the purchase price[1] if the claim for the tenancy was upheld. Meanwhile, the arbitrator held there to be no tenancy and the contract of sale was duly completed. The action concerned the issue of liability for costs in respect of the earlier proceedings. Goff J held that they should be borne by the vendor. The purchaser had been justified in objecting to a title which was doubtful. Furthermore the doubt could have been speedily and cheaply resolved by the vendor by arbitration proceedings and should not have been resolved in an action for specific performance.

(c) Bad title

Where it is clear that the vendor cannot convey what he has contracted to sell, because, for example, title is in some other person or the property is subject to undisclosed incumbrances, the title is bad, and unenforceable[2]. Even where the contract provides that the purchaser shall not object to the title, if he discovers aliunde that it is bad, and not merely doubtful, the court will not force the title on him, but will leave the parties to pursue their legal remedies[3].

(d) Good holding title

There are qualities of badness. Lindley LJ once remarked[15]:

> ... there are bad titles and bad titles; bad titles which are good holding titles, although they may be open to objections which are not serious, are bad titles in a conveyancer's point of view, but good in a business man's point of view ...

The learned judge had in mind cases involving some technical defect of title which no longer exposed the purchaser to any real threat of eviction. In other words the defect may be cured by undisturbed possession for at least 12 years and such a title, supplemented by a statutory declaration as to possession, may be enforced on the purchaser[5].

19 *Re Nichol's and Van Joel's Contract* [1910] 1 Ch 43, CA; *Wilson v Thomas* [1958] 1 All ER 871, [1958] 1 WLR 422.
20 [1971] 2 All ER 577, [1971] 1 WLR 769.
 1 See pp 620, post.
 2 See *George Wimpey & Co Ltd v Sohn* [1967] Ch 487, [1966] 1 All ER 232, CA (vendor's failure to procure statutory declaration of 20 years' undisputed possession as contracted); *Faruqi v English Real Estates Ltd* [1979] 1 WLR 963, p 171, ante.
 3 *Re Scott and Alvarez's Contract* [1895] 2 Ch 603, CA, p 170, ante.
 4 *Re Scott and Alvarez's Contract*, supra, at 613, CA.
 5 *Re Atkinson and Horsell's Contract* [1912] 2 Ch 1, CA. Twelve years' possession will not be sufficient in every case; see p 332, post.

4.   Length of title

Having seen that the vendor is under an obligation to show a good title, the next question is to ascertain for what period of time the law requires him to establish this. Whilst his possession of the land contracted to be sold is prima facie evidence of his seisin in fee simple, it is hardly to be expected that a purchaser, in the absence of any contrary stipulation, should be required to hand over his purchase money merely on the strength of the vendor's possession[6]. He may be only a lessee, or even just a squatter. Nor yet is it satisfactory for the vendor simply to produce as evidence of his title the document by virtue of which he acquired that title, at least not where he has owned the estate for a short time only. Production of that document and nothing more affords no guarantee that the title was sound when the vendor acquired it. Mistakes could have been made. He may have knowingly accepted a title defective in certain matters, possibly of no concern to him, but perhaps important to a purchaser. The very complexity of our land law structure renders these considerations of no small consequence.

A title may be good, or bad. The law never speaks of a perfect title. The possibility always exists that some person may claim an adverse estate or interest[7]. There can be no mathematical certainty of a good title. However, if the vendor can give proof of the exercise of acts of ownership by himself and his predecessors over a period of time, this reduces the possibility of adverse claims existing – and the more extended the period of research the greater is the assurance of safety[8]. He must give a convincing historical account of how the property came to be owned by him[9]. It is the purchaser's responsibility to investigate this account to check that the vendor can convey the subject-matter of the contract.

Over the years this period of investigation has been progressively reduced from 60 years, the period which conveyancers had customarily established, to 15 years, which is now prescribed by the Law of Property Act 1969, s 23[10], for contracts made on or after 1 January 1970. This period applies only when the contract expresses no contrary intention, ie to an *open* contract. The parties are free to stipulate for a shorter or longer period. In practice the statutory figure is used as a safe yard-stick by the vendor's solicitor when drafting the contract. Moreover, this 15 years' period relates predominantly to sales of freehold land. Different considerations apply to leaseholds, as the next chapter will show.

At the time concern was expressed that this reduction to 15 years would increase the risk of certain defects not coming to light, particularly defects

---

6   'No man in his senses would take an offer of a purchase from a man merely because he stood on the ground': per Lord Erskine in *Hiern v Mill* (1806) 13 Ves 114 at 122.

7   See eg *Wyld v Silver* [1963] Ch 243, [1963] 1 QB 169, CA (purchaser of land without notice subject to right of inhabitants to hold annual fair established by private Act of 1799, though last recorded occasion of its occurrence was in 1875).

8   Hayes, *Introduction to Conveyancing* (5th edn) (1840), 282.

9   Farrand, 95.

10   Amending LPA 1925, s 44(1), which prescribed a 30 year period, as recommended by the Law Commission. See Law Com No 9.

arising from faulty plans, from inadequate descriptions of the property, or from double conveyancing[11]. These fears appear to have been unfounded. These past two decades have not witnessed any significant increase in the number of titles accepted under the new regime being upset in subsequent litigation. This shortening of the statutory period of investigation of title can be welcomed as 'a useful step towards the simplification of conveyancing'[12].

(a) Earlier title

Complementary to the provision limiting the period of the purchaser's investigation of title is a rule exonerating him from notice of any matter of which he might have had notice had he investigated the title prior to the period of commencement fixed by statute[13]. So he is not deemed to have notice of any equitable interest which he could only have discovered by investigating the earlier title, unless he actually investigates that title or the interest, being a land charge, has been registered[14]. He will be deemed to have notice of any non-registrable matter or interest discoverable on inspection of the property.

(b) Contractual provisions

A formal contract normally provides for the title to commence with a specified document. The vendor may stipulate that less than a 15 years' title shall be deduced. What risks does the purchaser run by accepting such a condition? His position is as follows.

(i) He will be bound by any equitable interest which he would have discovered had he contracted for the full statutory period. In the words of Romer LJ[15]:

> ... if a purchaser chooses, by agreement with his vendor or otherwise, to take less than a [15] years' title, he cannot by so restricting his investigation, and by not inquiring into the title for the full period of [15 years], say that he is not affected with notice of such equities affecting the land as he would have ascertained by reasonable inquiries into the title for the earlier part of the [15] years.

(ii) Where this equitable interest takes the form of a registered land charge he cannot claim compensation under s 25 of the Law of Property Act 1969. In broad terms, this section enables a purchaser in certain circumstances to claim compensation from public funds in respect of loss caused by a land charge which he learns about for the first time after completion and which he has no means of discovering because it was registered:

---

11 (1969) 32 MLR 477, 495 (S Cretney); (1966) 110 Sol Jo 179, 201 (V Hallett & E Nugee). See also Law Com No 9, paras 23, 34–36. For examples of double conveyances, see *Re Sea View Gardens, Claridge v Tingey* [1966] 3 All ER 935; *Bligh v Martin* [1968] 1 All ER 1157; *Epps v Esso Petroleum Co Ltd* [1973] 2 All ER 465; *Jackson v Bishop* (1979) 48 P & CR 57, CA.
12 Law Com No 9, para 36.
13 LPA 1925, s 44(8).
14 By virtue of LPA 1925, s 198; see p 396, post.
15 *Re Nisbet and Potts' Contract* [1906] 1 Ch 386 at 408, CA; LPA 1925, s 199(1)(ii)(a). Cf *Hudston v Viney* [1921] 1 Ch 98 (legal mortgagee not making full investigation not bound by prior equitable charge).

> ... against the name of an owner of an estate in the land who was not as owner of any such estate a party to any transaction, or concerned in any event, comprised in the relevant title[16].

The expression 'the relevant title' is a key phrase in the understanding of the operation of s 25. It is so defined that whatever title the purchaser accepts he cannot claim compensation in respect of a land charge which he should have discovered had he investigated the full title which he was entitled to require under an open contract[8]. This should ensure that in the future purchasers' solicitors will advise their clients not to accept less than the full statutory period. The wording of s 25 needs to be noted carefully. It does not provide that compensation cannot be recovered merely on the ground that a purchaser has not investigated the relevant title. As the extract from the section indicates, what is vital is whether the charge has been registered against the name of an estate owner appearing as such within the period comprising the relevant title; for if it has not, then a search could not have been made against his name. Therefore, accepting less than the relevant title will not, it seems, debar a claim for compensation if the registered charge could not have been discovered even on an investigation of the title for the statutory period.

(iii) He cannot normally insist on seeing any documents relating to the earlier title, nor raise objections to it[18]. If before completion he discovers the existence of an incumbrance by other means (aliunde), he can object to the title on account of the vendor's failure to disclose it[19], as he can where he has contracted for a 15 years' title.

(iv) If on the other hand he contracts for a title for the full statutory period but does not discover the existence of a registered land charge until after completion, it remains binding upon him, but he may be able to claim compensation under s 25. He cannot contend that he takes free from the charge under s 44(8) of the Law of Property Act 1925, which deems him not to have notice of any matter discoverable only by investigating the earlier title. It is generally assumed that s 198 of this Act (under which registration constitutes *actual* notice) overrides the terms of s 44(8)[20]. Indeed the compensation provisions of the Law of Property Act 1969 presuppose that he remains bound.

---

16 Section 25(1)(c). If the estate owner's name appears as such within the relevant title, the purchaser can search against his name and thereby discover the existence of any registered charge. Section 25 gives effect to the recommendations of the Law Commission contained in Report No 18. He cannot claim compensation if he has actual knowledge of the charge; but for the purposes of s 25 registration of the charge does *not* constitute actual notice: s 25(2). See further, p 397, post.

17 See s 25(10) which in relation to a disposition of land made under a contract defines 'relevant title' to mean 'the title which the purchaser was, apart from any acceptance by him (by agreement or otherwise) of a shorter or an imperfect title, entitled to require'.

18 See the LPA 1925, s 45(1), discussed at p 277, post.

19 *Re Cox and Neve's Contract* [1891] 2 Ch 109.

20 Law Com No 9, para 23(c). And see *White v Bijou Mansions Ltd* [1937] Ch 610 at 621, [1937] 3 All ER 269 at 273, per Simonds J; on appeal [1938] Ch 351, [1938] 1 All ER 546, CA. Strictly there is no conflict between s 44(8) and s 198 if the former means that a purchaser is not affected with *constructive* notice of matters he is prevented by statute from investigating.

C Root of title

1. The need for a root of title

Though the statutory provisions speak of 15 years' title, in practice it will be longer. In *Re Cox and Neve's Contract*[1], North J explained the position thus:

> And, when I say a [15] years' title, I mean a title deduced for [15] years and for so much longer as it is necessary to go back in order to arrive at a point at which the title can properly commence. A title cannot commence in nubibus at the exact point which is represented by 365 days multiplied by [15]. It must commence at or before the [15] years with something which is in itself, or which is agreed shall be, a proper root of title.

The title must commence with a document at least 15 years old, known as the *root of title*, though it is not absolutely essential that the title should commence with any instrument at all[2]. Under an open contract the document must constitute a *good root of title*. In a formal contract the vendor stipulates the root of title by such a clause as: The title shall commence with a conveyance on sale dated ... and made between ... [3]. He may stipulate for a root of title which is not a good root. What constitutes a good root of title under an open contract has assumed a greater importance in view of s 25 of the Law of Property Act 1969. Though the purchaser accepts more than a 15 years' title, if it does not commence with a good root of title, sufficient under an open contract, he has not investigated *the relevant title*. It is by no means unknown even today, especially in the case of older properties located in rural areas, for the title to be deduced for a period well in excess of 30 years[4].

2. Good root of title

(a) Accepted definition

A good root of title is not defined by statute, nor, apparently, has any member of the bench hazarded any definition. The Law Commission declined to advocate a statutory definition, maintaining that practitioners should have complete freedom to negotiate the root according to the particular circumstances of each case[5]. The Commission happily accepted the description given in *Williams on Vendor and Purchaser*[6] that a good root of title:

> ... must be an instrument of disposition dealing with or proving on the face of it, without the aid of extrinsic evidence, the ownership of the whole legal and

---

1 [1891] 2 Ch 109 at 118.
2 See *Cottrell v Watkins* (1839) 1 Beav 361 at 365, per Lord Langdale MR.
3 See p 163, ante.
4 The author recalls a purchase in which he was involved in 1973 where the title commenced with an indenture dated 11 June 1900, at a time when the property was held in copyhold tenure. More recently he heard of a case of a sale of farm land in 1986 where the root of title was a mortgage in 1876.
5 Law Com No 9, para 40.
6 Fourth edn, p 124. See [1975] CLP 125 (A Prichard).

equitable estate in the property sold, containing a description by which the property can be identified and showing nothing to cast any doubt on the title of the disposing parties.

(i) *Legal and equitable estate.*   Because of the overreaching provisions of the 1925 property legislation, it will rarely be necessary for the root of title to have to deal with the equitable title. A post-1925 conveyance on trust for sale is a good root of title, even though it does not deal with the equitable interests. The following do not under an open contract rank as good roots: (1) a pre-1926 conveyance subject to a mortgage, since the legal estate was not vested in the mortgagor; (2) an equitable mortgage; (3) a lease; (4) a post-1925 will or disentailing deed, since both only operate in equity.

(ii) *Adequate description*[7].   Examples of dispositions failing this test are a conveyance or assent, which describes the land transferred by reference to a full description in the parcels clause of an earlier deed, eg the conveyance under which the testator acquired his title. An assent may also be disqualified on other grounds. It may fail to specify the estate assented to, simply vesting the property for all the estate or interest of the deceased at the time of his death; it is also necessary to check the assentor's title to make the assent against the grant of probate.

(iii) *No doubt.*   A document does not constitute a good root of title if it contains recitals which throw reasonable doubt upon the earlier title. A document is regarded as casting a doubt on the vendor's title if it depends for its effect on some earlier instrument, as where, for example, it is executed in exercise of some power[8]. The purchaser is entitled to know (in the absence of a condition to the contrary) that the power still subsisted at the time of its purported exercise, which the subsequent document does not show. Some doubts exist as to whether a conveyance in execution of a trust for sale is a good root because of the need, possibly, to go back to the deed creating the trust[9]. In practice, such a conveyance is invariably accepted without question by solicitors under an express contractual provision.

(b) Good roots of title
The best root of title and the one most commonly encountered is a conveyance on sale. This constitutes the 'best' root since a transaction on sale raises a strong inference that the title was investigated and approved. Strictly speaking, a post-1925 mortgage does not rank as a good root; not taking effect as a conveyance of the fee simple, the mortgage does not deal with the whole legal

---

7   See *Re Bramwell's Contract, Bramwell v Ballards Securities Investments Ltd* [1969] 1 WLR 1659 (description of land in root of title not identifiable with that agreed to be sold).
8   *Re Copelin's Contract* [1937] 4 All ER 447 (power of attorney); *Re W & R Holmes and Cosmopolitan Press Ltd's Contract* [1944] Ch 53, [1943] 2 All ER 716 (pre-1926 power of sale); *Gateway Developments Property Ltd v Grech* (1970) 71 SRNSW 161 (instrument exercising power of appointment).
9   Williams, *Title*, 575; Law Com No 9, para 39(b); contra, Prichard, op cit, 140.

estate. Nevertheless, it is considered by many that a mortgage is a better root than a conveyance on sale, for a mortgagee is less likely to accept a doubtful title than a purchaser[10]. Its acceptability may, however, be suspect in a particular case because the description of the property is abbreviated by referring merely to the conveyance to the mortgagor. In consequence there is no adequate description of the property, nor any reference to restrictive covenants or other adverse rights affecting the property. A voluntary conveyance at least 15 years old may be a good root, even under an open contract[11].

(c) Contractual provisions

Usually the root of title is provided for in the contract. In relation to freehold land the Standard Conditions of Sale leave the vendor to determine both the length and root of title. He may stipulate for it to commence with something less than a good root, in which case the purchaser has to decide whether to accept it. But certain rules must be observed. Any stipulation for *less* than the statutory period must be accompanied by a clear statement of the nature of the document forming the root[12]. If it is a voluntary conveyance, the condition should say so, otherwise the court will regard it as misleading and will not force the title upon the purchaser[13]. When the root of title is at least 15 years old, it is not clear to what extent the vendor is under a duty to specify its nature. However, as the Law of Property Act 1969 lays so much emphasis on the title which a purchaser could demand under an open contract[14], it seems that the vendor ought not to be entitled to conceal that the contractual root would not be a good root under an open contract, for then he would be depriving the purchaser of any opportunity to decide whether to run the risk of being outside the ambit of the Act.

3. Pre-root of title documents

(a) The statutory limitation

The fixing of a root of title limits the extent of a purchaser's investigation and absolves a vendor from establishing the title from any earlier date[15]. The Law of Property Act 1925, s 45(1) precludes a purchaser from: (i) requiring the production, or any abstract or copy, of any document dated prior to the root of title, and (ii) making any requisition, objection or inquiry with respect to the earlier title, even though the prior title is agreed to be produced. These provisions must be read in conjunction with sub-s (11), which reads:

> Nothing in this section shall be construed as binding a purchaser to complete his purchase in any case where, on a contract made independently of this section

---

10 Emmet, para 5.021. Cf 1 Williams V & P, 124, suggesting that it is a proper root if it recites the mortgagor's seisin. But a recital of seisin is not generally regarded as adequate; *Re Wallis and Grout's Contract* [1906] 2 Ch 206; M & W, 608n.
11 *Re Marsh and Earl Granville* (1883) 24 Ch D 11 at 24, per Cotton LJ.
12 See *Re Marsh and Earl Granville* (1883) 24 Ch D 11 at 22, per Baggallay LJ.
13 *Re Marsh and Earl Granville* (1883) 24 Ch D 11. See also p 279, post.
14 Page 275, ante.
15 *Re Atkinson and Horsell's Contract* [1912] 2 Ch 1 at 19, CA, per Buckley LJ.

and containing stipulations similar to the provisions of this section – specific performance of the contract would not be enforced against him by the court.

The restrictions imposed by sub-s (1) are construed as if they were express terms of the contract. They have practically the same effect as those conditions precluding inquiry into the earlier title, which were prevalent prior to the Conveyancing Act 1881, s 3(3) (the forerunner of s 45(1)). The Act of 1881 was not intended to constitute a legislative repeal of well-established doctrines[16]. A purchaser is, therefore, not debarred from showing aliunde that the pre-root title is defective, or that there are pre-root incumbrances not disclosed by the vendor. He may discover the defect as a result of inquiries made of an adjoining owner or his solicitor[17], or because the vendor accidentally produces the earlier documents for inspection[18], or through his official search certificate. The courts will not decree specific performance against the purchaser when the title is thoroughly bad[19]. Yet, since the provisions of sub-s (1) in effect operate as a contractual term, the purchaser's refusal to complete amounts at law to a breach of contract. He cannot recover his deposit[20], which the vendor would prima facie be entitled to forfeit. Now, by virtue of the Law of Property Act 1925, s 49(2), the court is empowered to order its repayment[1].

(b) Exceptions

Sub-section (1) entitles a purchaser to require the production of a pre-root of title document (or an abstract or copy) in three cases.

(i) A power of attorney[2] under which any abstracted document is executed. In *Re Copelin's Contract*[3], the root of title which was over 30 years old was executed under a power of attorney; the purchaser was held entitled to a copy or abstract of the power, even though it was a pre-root of title document. The purchaser is entitled to a copy or abstract of any power of attorney affecting the title, *notwithstanding any stipulation to the contrary*[4].

(ii) A document creating or disposing of an interest, power or obligation which is not shown to have ceased or expired, and subject to which any part of the property is disposed of by an abstracted document. It seems that this exception was intended to relate primarily to pre-root leases and mortgages, but it is wide enough to cover a document which creates subsisting covenants, or a plan on a pre-root deed, which is incorporated by reference in the subsequent description of the property[5].

16 *Nottingham Patent Brick and Tile Co v Butler* (1885) 15 QBD 261 at 272, per North J; on appeal (1886) 16 QBD 778, CA.
17 *Re Cox and Neve's Contract* [1891] 2 Ch 109 (undisclosed pre-root restrictive covenant).
18 *Smith v Robinson* (1879) 13 Ch D 148; *Waddell v Wolfe* (1874) LR 9 QB 515 (express condition); cf Walford, 73–76.
19 *Re Scott and Alvarez's Contract* [1895] 2 Ch 603, CA, p 170, ante.
20 Ibid, at 612–24, per Lindley LJ; *Re National Provincial Bank of England and Marsh* [1895] 1 Ch 190; 1 W & C, 120. But see *Re Cox and Neve's Contract*, supra, note 1 (recovery of deposit, interest and costs in case involving post-1881 contract, but no reliance placed on Conveyancing Act 1881, s 3(3), (11)).
1 Page 621, post.
2 A power of attorney arises when one person empowers another to act in his stead for certain purposes, eg to sell land, to execute a deed. See further, pp 458–463, post.
3 [1937] 4 All ER 447.
4 LPA 1925, s 125(2), as amended by the LP(Am)A 1926.
5 Emmet, para 5.041.

(iii) A document creating any limitation or trust by reference to which any part of the property is disposed of by an abstracted document. The purchaser is not affected by any trust that will be overreached by the conveyance to him[6].

(c) Contractual provisions

A purchaser's right to a pre-root of title document falling within exception (ii) or (iii) can be excluded by an express contractual provision. Under the Standard Conditions of Sale[7], the vendor must supply the original of every relevant document, or an abstract, epitome or copy with an original marking by a solicitor of examination either against the original or against an examined abstract or against an examined copy. The Condition does exonerate the vendor from compliance, if such documents are within his possession or power. If that is the case as, for example, when the property is sold subject to restrictive covenants but there is no copy of them available with the deeds[8], the matter should be dealt with by a special condition.

4. The subsequent title

Having fixed the root of title, the vendor must, subject to any contractual provision to the contrary, trace all the links in the chain of title from that document to the document or event by which the ownership became vested in him. As we have seen, the final link must show that the legal title is in himself or in some person whom he can compel to convey. To establish a good title the vendor is not obliged to prove his title in an unbroken sequence, commencing with the root and passing through a chain of events and transactions ending with that under which he claims. A defect in the intervening title may have occurred. Yet, if that defect has been cured by adverse possession, the title may be forced on the purchaser, as is shown by the majority decision in *Re Atkinson and Horsell's Contract*[9]. The vendor in this case had shown a good title because, despite the defect, there was no longer any possibility of an adverse claim being upheld. The purchaser could not be prejudiced, and he was compelled to take the property.

In short, the root of title need not necessarily have any direct connection with the title actually offered. This does not mean, however, that the title prior to the date when adverse possession began is irrelevant. It may establish that there was then no person under a disability who is now able to upset the title.

(a) Voluntary conveyances

A particular problem which existed arose when, in the chain of title, there was a voluntary conveyance, particularly if it was by means of such a conveyance

---

6 Compare this situation where the trust arises by virtue of contributions to the purchase and the conveyance does not overreach the equitable interest, p 314, post.

7 SCS 4.2.3.

8 See *Faruqi v English Real Estates Ltd* [1979] 1 WLR 963, where failure to regulate the position expressly proved fatal.

9 [1912] 2 Ch 1, CA (possession taken under mistake as to effect of will).

that title was vested in the vendor. Under s 339 of the Insolvency Act 1986, when an individual[10] is adjudged bankrupt and has, at a relevant time entered into a transaction at an undervalue[11], the trustee of the bankrupt's estate may apply to the court for an order to restore the position to that which it would have been had the individual not entered into the transaction. The relevant time is defined to mean a period of five years between the transaction and the bankruptcy petition[12]. That period is reduced to two years, if the individual can show that he was not insolvent at the time of making the transaction, or became insolvent as a result of making it[13].

Under the Act as originally enacted, the position of a purchaser was less secure than was the case under the previous statutory regime applicable to this type of situation[14]. Under s 342(2) of the Act, an order may be made affecting the property of any person, whether or not he was the person who entered into the transaction in question. The protection seemingly offered to a purchaser was provided by the provision that no order may be made so as to prejudice any interest in property which was acquired from a person other than that individual in good faith and for value without notice of the relevant circumstances. The problem was that the relevant circumstances were defined to mean the circumstances under which an order may be made under ss 339 and 340[15]. The criterion laid down by s 339 is simply that the transaction was at an undervalue. While it may well be the case that a purchaser will not have notice that a transaction was at an undervalue, in the case of a voluntary transfer, he will inevitably have notice of this from an investigation of title[16]. The risk was, therefore, that, potentially, for a period of five years after a voluntary conveyance, that transaction was liable to be set aside.

Following representations made by the Law Society, this trap has been removed. Section 2 of the Insolvency (No 2) Act 1994 inserts a new s 342(2A) into the 1986 Act. The effect of this provision is that the purchaser will be protected unless he has notice of the insolvency at the time of acquisition. As registration constitutes actual notice, a purchaser who is aware that there has been a transaction at an undervalue within the previous five years should conduct a bankruptcy search against the person who effected the transaction[17].

---

10 Similar provisions apply in respect to dispositions by companies: Insolvency Act 1986, ss 238–241.
11 As defined by Insolvency Act 1986, s 339(3).
12 Ibid, s 341.
13 Ibid, s 341(2).
14 Bankruptcy Act 1914, s 42; Law of Property Act 1925, s 172. Neither of these provisions will any longer have much, if any, relevance.
15 Section 340 deals with transactions in respect of preference.
16 See (1987) 84 LSG 2257 (I S Storey). For the position where title is registered, see p 478, post.
17 See [1994] Conv 434 (J E Adams); Emmet, para 11.050(A), where a persuasive argument is put that the trap did not in fact exist, at least in respect of transactions between two and five years of the acquisition by the purchaser.

D   Deducing title

1.   The abstract of title

It now remains to consider how in practice the vendor discharges his obligation to make title. It is his duty to deliver to the purchaser an abstract of title[18], which may be described as a summary of the documents by which any dispositions of the property have been made during the period for which title has been shown, and of all facts, such as births, marriages, deaths, or other matters, affecting the devolution of the title during the same period[19]. By perusing the abstract and later verifying it the purchaser's solicitor forms his opinion as to the title. It has to contain everything necessary to enable him to make his decision; such parts of the relevant documents as are immaterial for this purpose are mentioned in an abbreviated form, or even omitted altogether. The process of delivering an abstract of title, and its subsequent verification, is commonly termed deducing title.

The vendor's duty to supply this specially prepared document at his own expense is a long-standing one[20]. He cannot prudently deliver the actual deeds to the purchaser, even if this were possible[1]. However, the advent of sophisticated photocopying techniques now means that photographic copies of all relevant deeds and documents can be provided in place of an abstract in the traditional form. Much can be said in favour of copies rather than abstracts. A copy can be prepared far more quickly and accurately. The risk of error in abstracting is virtually eliminated, and the time spent in examining the copy against the original is greatly reduced.

Where copies are supplied in lieu of an abstract, they should be accompanied by an *epitome of title*. This epitome is not the evidence of title, simply an index which lists in chronological order all material documents, events and matters normally appearing in an abstract, and states the date and nature of each and the names of parties to documents. In addition the mode of deducing title (whether by copy or abstract) should be indicated and against each copy it should be shown whether the original will be handed over on completion[2]. If no copy document is offered as evidence, eg in the case of a probate or death certificate, the relevant particulars should be set out on a

---

18   In relation to registered titles, the vendor's obligations are quite different; see pp 334–338, post.

19   34 *Halsbury's Laws* (4th edn), para 147. For a judicial description, see Kindersley V-C in *Oakden v Pike* (1865) 34 LJ Ch 620 at 622 (a document which contains with sufficient clearness and sufficient fullness the effect of every instrument which constitutes part of the vendor's title).

20   See Williams, *The Contract of Sale of Land*, xvii, note 20.

1   Often they will be held by a mortgagee. In practice the mortgagee will normally forward the deeds to the vendor's solicitor at the commencement of the transaction to enable him to prepare the contract and the abstract. But they are held as agent for the mortgagee on terms that they will be returned on demand.

2   See (1969) 66 LS Gaz 492–93; Emmet, para 5.052. Delivery of an epitome is frequently omitted in practice.

separate sheet as in a traditional abstract, and supplied with the copy documents. Whilst it is now standard practice to provide photographic copies whenever possible[3], it will be some years before abstracts in traditional form disappear completely from the conveyancing scene. A vendor may be unable to supply photographic copies because the original deeds are not in his possession and his only evidence is an abstract; and it is not customary to produce facsimile copies of deeds already abstracted for a previous transaction. It is therefore necessary to consider briefly the form and content of an abstract.

2. Form of abstract

An abstract in traditional form follows a stereotyped pattern. The various parts of a deed are abstracted in different margins or columns. These act as starting points and enable the reader to discover more easily any particular part of the document to which he needs to refer. In general the exact wording of the document should be reproduced in narrative form, but using the past tense and the passive voice. To reduce the length of the abstract and the time spent in its preparation (though reading it is another matter, except for those well-versed in the art), many words appear in abbreviated form[4]. For the inexperienced this adds to the confusion and prolongs its reading. The description of the property in the parcels clause should always be abstracted in full, unless it merely repeats the description contained in a previously abstracted deed, when it is permissible to refer to the property as 'the before abstracted premises'. A copy of any plan forming part of an abstracted deed should also be supplied[5]. As for recitals, these are confined to the bare minimum where they refer simply to the vendor's seisin and the contract for sale[6]. One basic point tends to be overlooked. Recitals in the deed constituting the root of title should be abstracted in full, even though the purchaser is precluded from raising requisitions on the prior title.

An abstract of a conveyance is set out in Appendix E. After an abstract has been checked against the original documents, a signed and dated record of the fact is endorsed on it by the person undertaking the examination in words such as: 'Original produced at the offices of Messrs — and examined by —'. Such an abstract is termed an examined, or marked, abstract[7].

---

3 Very few typists in solicitors' offices know how to prepare an abstract in proper form.
4 Eg 'vdr' stands for 'vendor', 'prems' for 'premises', 'or' for 'other', 'tree' for 'trustee'. More misleading examples will be encountered in practice by readers not already accustomed to this strange guessing game.
5 Even one 'for identification purposes only', though this has been queried: (1977) 41 Conv (NS) 298. But see *Wigginton and Milner Ltd v Winster Engineering Ltd* [1978] 3 All ER 436, CA.
6 'Reciting seisin of the vendor and agreement for sale' suffices.
7 Copies should be examined and marked, too, but are often not. Cf LSC 12(2). Contrast (1987) 84 LS Gaz 2260, para 2 (marking of deeds as examined against the originals recommended to be undertaken by *vendor's* solicitor before forwarding draft contract).

3.   Contents of the abstract

All relevant documents and events forming part of the chain of title are abstracted in chronological order[8]. Each deed is abstracted in chief, ie as a separate document. When copies are supplied in lieu of an abstract, the vendor's solicitor must provide copies of all deeds which it would have been necessary to abstract in chief had title been deduced in the traditional way.

(a) Documents requiring to be abstracted or copied
These documents forming part of the title need to be copied or abstracted: conveyances, mortgages (including discharged ones), subsisting leases, assents, releases, grants of probate or letters of administration, vesting instruments, pre-1926 wills, and appointments of new trustees (but in relation to settled land the purchaser is concerned only with the deed of declaration[9]). Births, marriages and deaths must be recorded, as also should court orders. Discharged mortgages need to be abstracted, albeit briefly, because a purchaser is entitled to see that it has been properly discharged, or that the receipt has not operated as a transfer[10]. Equitable charges are not in general included, though this is at variance with the slender authority on the point[11]. However, it would appear advisable to abstract the charge if registered as a land charge. Since it will be revealed on the purchaser's official search certificate it is preferable to alert him to its existence when sending the abstract, rather than having inquiries raised about it just before completion.

No duty to include land charge search certificates apparently exists, but it is standard practice to do so. Indeed, if they are omitted, the purchaser's solicitor will usually ask whether one was made. Their inclusion is particularly helpful in ascertaining whether existing restrictive covenants have ceased to be binding on account of non-registration.

(b) Documents which need not be abstracted or copied

(i) *Wills.*   Where an estate owner dies after 1925, the correct procedure is simply to abstract the grant of probate or the letters of administration. The will should not ordinarily be abstracted since it operates only in equity[12]. The

---

8   In practice the abstract supplied could often consist of two or more separate ones. Thus, on a sale by V to P, an abstract of V's title would be prepared. When P later sold to P2, the existing abstract would be utilised and a continuation abstract of P's title would be provided.
9   SLA 1925, s 35, p 305, post.
10   Under LPA 1925, s 115(2), p 603–606, post.
11   *Drummond v Tracy* (1860) John 608 (letter creating charge to be repaid out of purchase money), criticised in 1 Dart, 298. For the position of an equitable chargee, see M & W, 953.
12   Compare 18 Ency F & P, 228, Williams, *Title*, 581, advocating a limited abstracting of a will, but even this is not necessary. Though exceptionally a will may require to be abstracted, it is generally unwise to give a purchaser notice of its contents, whether in the abstract or in a subsequent assent; see p 323, post. It is not uncommon (but undesirable) for an assent to be made 'upon the trusts declared by the will'. This brings the trusts on to the title and necessitates their being abstracted.

legal title vests in the personal representatives[13], and the grant of representation constitutes the sole link in the chain of title. It is not strictly essential to abstract the death, though this is frequently done. The abstract should contain a note of any endorsement on the probate or letters of administration.

(ii) *Interests to be overreached.*   The Law of Property Act 1925, s 10(1) contains an important qualification to the general rule governing the contents of an abstract. It provides that where title is shown to a legal estate, it is not necessary or even proper to include in the abstract an instrument relating only to some interest or power which will be overreached by the conveyance of the legal estate. This section fits in with the general scheme of the property legislation of 1925 to keep the equitable interests off the legal title. Therefore on a sale by a tenant for life in exercise of his statutory power of sale, or by trustees for sale or personal representatives, the equitable interests arising under the settlement, trust, or will need not be abstracted. They are not the purchaser's concern. Where overreaching powers exist, a purchaser cannot be compelled to accept a title made with the concurrence of the equitable owners[14], but he may do so if he chooses[15].

Section 10(1) is not exclusively confined to equitable interests. If A mortgages property to B, and then to C, a conveyance by B in exercise of his statutory power of sale vests in the purchaser A's legal estate, freed from C's mortgage, as well as his own[16]. B's mortgage should be abstracted or copied and the date when the mortgage money became due indicated. C's mortgage need not be disclosed even though it has been registered as a land charge, nor do the circumstances under which the power of sale became exercisable[17]. This situation is not a true case of overreaching, a term reserved for interests which remain in existence but are transferred to the proceeds of sale, for in this case C's interest is destroyed altogether. Yet this situation is clearly within the spirit of the section.

The subsection does not obviate the need to abstract any instrument creating or affecting an equitable interest[18] which will not be overreached. Thus if A holds property on trust for B who assigns his equitable interest to C, A can vest a good title in a purchaser only if C concurs in the sale, and this will entail showing the devolution of C's title in equity.

It may also be essential to bring equitable interests on to the title to show that a surviving trustee for sale is entitled to sell as beneficial owner consequent upon the determination of the trust. Suppose land is conveyed to X and Y on trust for sale for themselves as equitable tenants in common. If X dies leaving

13   AEA 1925, ss 1, 3.
14   LPA 1925, s 42(1), p 175, ante. See further, Ch 10.
15   See *Cole v Rose* [1978] 3 All ER 1121 at 1127, per Mervyn Davies QC.
16   LPA 1925, ss 88(1), 104(1), assuming, of course, B has priority.
17   LPA 1925, s 104(2), (3), exempts a purchaser from inquiring into due exercise of the power.
18   Because of their very nature equitable interests arising by operation of law by virtue of contribution to the purchase price do not get abstracted. Ordinarily such interests are overreached on a conveyance by two trustees for sale.

his interest in the land to Y, then Y becomes sole beneficial owner. He can sell as such, but to establish his title it will be necessary to abstract X's will so far as it relates to the gift to Y, as well as the grant of probate[19]. Alternatively Y can, by appointing a new trustee, keep the trust for sale alive. This method obviates the need to bring the equitable interests on to the title, but the problems of satisfying the client of the advantages of this artificial procedure may in practice prove to be unsurmountable.

(c) Fraudulent concealment

Under the Law of Property Act 1925, s 183, a vendor or his solicitor who, with intent to defraud, conceals from the purchaser any instrument or incumbrance material to the title is guilty of a criminal offence punishable by fine or imprisonment. The purchaser (or persons deriving title under him) can maintain an action for damages in respect of loss (including money spent on improvements) sustained by reason of the concealment. Neither civil nor criminal liability arises unless there is an intention to defraud[20]. It would seem that this provision is wide enough to cover concealment of a pre-root of title incumbrance[1]. It is material to the title since it is within the ambit of the vendor's duty of disclosure; and where loss can be established the measure of damages awarded under the section may, depending on the circumstances, be greater than those recoverable under the covenants for title[2].

E   The vendor's obligations

1.   Duty to supply

The vendor's obligation to prepare and deliver to the purchaser an abstract of his title is confirmed by the Standard Conditions of Sale. Sometimes the vendor's solicitor forwards the abstract on terms that it is to be held to his order (ie returnable on demand) pending completion. This restriction is inconsistent with the unqualified nature of the obligation as stated in the contract, and has been disapproved of by the Council of The Law Society[3].

In the absence of any contrary agreement, the vendor must bear the expense of preparing the abstract, including costs incurred in obtaining documents not in his possession, which are needed for this purpose[4].

---

19 Necessary to establish the validity of X's will; see LPA 1925, s 204. This is not a case where title could be made by Y under the Law of Property (Joint Tenants) Act 1964. For a more complicated illustration encountered by the author, see the 2nd edn, p 315.
20 *District Bank Ltd v Luigi Grill Ltd* [1943] Ch 78, [1943] 1 All ER 136, p 356, post.
1 1 W & C (13th edn), 340. In *Smith v Robinson* (1879) 13 Ch D 148 at 151, Fry J referring to the Law of Property Amendment Act 1859, s 24, queried whether this was so.
2 See Ch 23.
3 Law Society's Digest (Third (Cumulative) Supplement), Opinion No 95(b).
4 *Re Johnson and Tustin* (1885) 30 Ch D 42, CA.

2. Time for delivery

Under an open contract, the abstract must be delivered within a reasonable time after exchange of contracts[5]. Under the Standard Conditions of Sale, the vendor is required to deliver the abstract upon exchange of contracts[6]. This obligation is, however, inconsistent with the Conveyancing Protocol, which requires the vendor's solicitor to deliver the abstract to his opposite number prior to exchange of contracts.

Time is not of the essence with regard to the delivery of the abstract under either an open contract[7] or one governed by the Standard Conditions. The general rules relating to time clauses[8] determine the consequences of the vendor's delay. Assuming the usual case where time is not of the essence, if the vendor fails to deliver the abstract by the due date the purchaser should notify the vendor that unless the abstract is sent within a specified period, the contract is at an end[9]. In a modern conveyancing transaction of domestic property, it is hardly conceivable that a purchaser will ever need to resort to this procedure. Yet should he do so, he may repudiate the contract after expiry of the specified period, even though the date for completion has not arrived, or the vendor subsequently forwards an abstract. In this event he should take the precaution of returning the abstract on its receipt[10].

The vendor should always remember that when delivery of the abstract is delayed, the timetable for raising requisitions will be put back and to the extent to which this causes a delay in completion, the vendor may be unable to charge interest in respect thereof[11].

3. Verification of abstract

The vendor is also under an obligation to furnish satisfactory evidence of all matters included in the abstract. The purchaser's task is to verify the abstract by examining[12] it against the evidence which is produced; the vendor's duty is to produce the evidence for examination. The important question of expense will be considered at the end of this section.

---

5   *Compton v Bagley* [1892] 1 Ch 313, where Romer J indicated (at 321) that 14 days is about the time usually required for delivery.
6   SCS 4.1.1.
7   *Roberts v Berry* (1853) 3 De GM & G 284.
8   See p 421 et seq, post, for the application for these principles to a delayed completion.
9   *Compton v Bagley* [1892] 1 Ch 313. The vendor's delay does not entitle the purchaser to repudiate without first serving a notice requiring delivery: *Jones v Price* (1797) 3 Anst 724. *Behzadi v Shaftesbury Hotels Ltd* [1992] Ch 1 [1991] 2 All ER 477, CA. For the purchaser's position when the abstract delivered is incomplete, see SCS 4.1.1, p 353, post.
10   *Hipwell v Knight* (1835) 1 Y & C Ex 401 (waiver inferred from subsequent communications as to title); *Compton v Bagley* [1892] 1 Ch 313.
11   For the raising of requisitions, see p 351, post; for the vendor's right to interest in the event of delay, see pp 436–437, post.
12   For the time of conducting such examinations, see p 358, post.

(a) Production of deeds
Abstracted deeds or copies are proved by production of the originals.
Technically, this is not adequate proof. The original may be a forgery, and
how can the vendor establish otherwise? Only by proving it was duly executed.
However, he does not normally have to undertake this task. In the absence of
suspicious circumstances, a deed is presumed to have been duly executed if
produced from the proper custody, that is, if it comes from a place where it
might reasonably be expected to be found[13]. In practice the deeds are usually
produced by the vendor's solicitor, or the mortgagee's solicitor, and it is not
customary to inquire from what source they were obtained.

A deed at least 20 years old is said to prove itself. In the absence of any
suspicious circumstances the purchaser must presume it was duly executed
according to its tenor[14]. Though authority is lacking, it seems that proof of
execution cannot be required even where the deed is less than 20 years old[15]
and it is not the practice so to do unless there are suspicious circumstances.
For example, a purchaser would be entitled to an explanation (at his own
expense) of the marked difference in the vendor's signature of the conveyance
to him and the conveyance by him[16], or of suspicious alterations.

(i) *Marked abstracts.* A vendor may not have all the original deeds in his
possession – a frequent occurrence on a sale of property on a building estate.
Individual house owners will not have the deeds of the builder's title, only an
abstract or copies marked as examined against the originals at the time of the
first sale. Strictly speaking, the purchaser's solicitor should locate and examine
the original deeds; but since the purchaser must bear the expense of verifying
the abstract, it is the usual practice to accept the vendor's examined abstract.
In this way a marked abstract becomes a form of secondary evidence. The
Council of The Law Society has refused to approve this practice officially,
'having regard to the possible issue of negligence involved'[17].

(ii) *Lost deeds.* Normally the problem of missing documents is covered by
some express clause in the contract[18]. Even if this is not so, failure to produce
an original document which should be in the vendor's possession does not
afford the purchaser any ground of rescission, provided the vendor can
satisfactorily explain the loss (a statutory declaration will suffice) and can also
produce adequate secondary evidence, such as a completed copy or draft. In
the case of a missing document, its execution has to be proved[19].

13 *Croughton v Blake* (1843) 12 M & W 205 at 208, per Parke B.
14 Evidence Act 1938, s 4, reducing the common law presumption from 30 to 20 years. See *Re
    Airey, Airey v Stapleton* [1897] 1 Ch 164 (execution by attorney presumed, not the existence
    of any authority to execute).
15 See 1 Dart, 309; Williams, *Title*, 658; cf Farrand, 128. But see [1978] Conv 249, considering
    Re Beaney [1978] 2 All ER 595.
16 An actual case encountered by the author. As to expense, see p 288, post.
17 See the correspondence at (1969) 66 LS Gaz 96. The problem ceases to exist when a vendor
    can commence his title with the conveyance from the developer to the first purchaser.
18 Page 171, ante.
19 *Bryant v Busk*(1827) 4 Russ 1, though it may be presumed in the case of very old documents:
    Moulton v Edmonds (1859) 1 De GF & J 246.

(b) Proof of events

Events such as marriages or deaths are sufficiently proved by production of the appropriate certificate, though grants of representation are commonly accepted as evidence of death. A change of street name or house number is proved by a certified copy of the order made by the local authority[20].

(c) Presumptions

A purchaser may be obliged to accept as proof nothing more concrete than a presumption which the law makes[1]. In particular, s 47(6) of the Law of Property Act 1925, enacts that:

> Recitals, statements, and descriptions of facts, matters and parties contained in deeds, instruments, Acts of Parliament, or statutory declarations twenty years old at the date of the contract, shall, unless and except so far as they may be proved to be inaccurate, be taken to be sufficient evidence of the truth of such facts, matters and descriptions.

Suppose a deed of appointment of new trustees recites the death of X, a previous trustee. X's death should be abstracted in chief. If the deed is 20 years old, the fact of death is sufficiently proved by the recital; otherwise it should be proved by production of X's death certificate. This statutory presumption is likely to fall into comparative disuse consequent upon the reduction in the period of investigation of title to 15 years. The Law Commission felt there was much to be said for its abolition but, not having the courage of its convictions, it declined to recommend any change[2].

(d) Expenses of verification

Section 47(4) of the Law of Property Act 1925 throws the cost of verification on the purchaser, except in relation to documents or evidence in the possession of the vendor, his mortgagee or trustee. This covers the expenses of the production and inspection of deeds, wills, probates etc, and the expenses of all journeys incidental thereto, and also expenses incurred in searching for, procuring, making, verifying and producing certificates, declarations, evidences and information, save as above mentioned. For example, if, in the situation considered on page 287, the purchaser is not content to rely on the marked abstract, but requires to inspect the original deeds, all expenses involving their production must be borne by him[3]. This sub-section does not absolve the vendor from his obligation to procure the production of the appropriate documentary evidence, whether in his possession or not 'it merely relieves him of the burden of the *expenses* involved. It is left to the Standard Conditions of Sale to lessen the vendor's duty of production[4].

---

20   In practice a letter from the local authority is usually accepted. For proof of other matters, see Williams, *Title*, 668–83.

1   See *Emery v Grocock* (1821) 6 Madd 54 at 57, per Leach V-C.

2   Law Com No 9, paras 42–45.

3   *Re Stuart and Olivant and Seadon's Contract* [1896] 2 Ch 328, CA (root of title not in vendor's possession).

4   See p 279, ante.

Sub-section (4) proceeds on the assumption that the vendor has delivered a proper abstract. The cost of preparing the abstract, including expenses incurred in obtaining copies or abstracts of relevant documents not in his possession, falls on him[5]. He must also bear the cost of obtaining the deeds for the purpose of handing them over on completion[6], though not if his inability to obtain them is because of some defect in title which under the contract he is absolved from having to cure.

(e) Place of production

Section 47 says nothing about the proper place for production by the vendor. This is governed by the general law. Modern conveyancing practice dictates that this is at the offices of the vendor's solicitor, or his mortgagee's solicitor, especially as verification almost invariably takes place at the time of completion. This does not, however, accord with the common law rule (surely by now obsolete?) as stated by leading authorities[7].

5   *Re Johnson and Tustin* (1885) 30 Ch D 42, CA.
6   *Re Duthy and Jesson's Contract* [1898] 1 Ch 419 (deeds in possession of deceased mortgagee's solicitors who, though debt repaid, refused to hand the deeds over without authority from the mortgagee's representatives).
7   1 Dart, 415; 1 Williams V & P, 164, stating that production should be either at the vendor's own residence, or upon or near the property, or in London, as he selects.

Chapter 10

Deducing title II: particular cases

A   Leaseholds

1.   Title to be deduced

The rules governing the title to be offered on the grant of a lease or sale of an existing lease under an *open contract* are contained in the Law of Property Act 1925, s 44(2)–(4). These provisions may loosely be summarised as follows: an intending lessee or a purchaser of an existing lease is entitled to call for the lease under which the other contracting party holds, but not the freehold or other superior title. The effect of the relevant sub-sections can best be seen against the background of specific illustrations.

(i)   A contracts to grant a lease to B. B is not entitled to call for any deduction of the freehold title: sub-s (2).

(ii) B contracts to assign the lease to C. C is entitled to call for the A-B lease (the headlease), but not the freehold title: sub-s (2).

(iii) C contracts to grant an underlease to D. D can call for the A-B lease[1], and the B-C assignment, but no more.

(iv) D contracts to assign the underlease to E. E can call for the underlease, but not the title to the leasehold reversion: sub-s (3), that is, he cannot investigate the head lease, or the B-C assignment. This puts E, a purchaser of an underlease, in a position inferior to that of the original underlessee, D, in situation (iii). There is some slight authority for the view that on the sale of an existing underlease, the purchaser can call for the title of the headlease, but the generally accepted opinion is to the contrary[2]. E's rights may be enlarged by express contractual provisions, to be discussed in section 2 below.

(v)   E agrees to grant a sub-underlease to F. F is limited to the underlease and the assignment to E, but *not* the headlease which sub-s (4) precludes.

These statutory restrictions do not prevent a lessee or purchaser from showing aliunde that the superior title is bad[3]. Though on the sale of an existing leasehold interest the title must commence with the lease (or underlease), it is not essential to show a complete chain of transactions ending with the

---

1   *Gosling v Woolf* [1893] 1 QB 39, more fully reported at (1893) 68 LT 89.
2   Walford, 118; Emmet, para 5.103; *Becker v Partridge* [1996] 2 QB 155, [1966] 2 All ER 266 at 269, CA, per Danckwerts LJ. Contra, *Drive Yourself Hire Co (London) Ltd v Strutt* [1954] 1 QB 250 at 278, [1953] 2 All ER 1475 at 1485, CA, per Romer LJ, citing *Gosling v Woolf*, supra.
3   *Jones v Watts* (1890) 43 Ch D 574, CA, but vague allegations that the property is subject to restrictive covenants do not suffice; see also *Becker v Partridge*, supra.

assignment to the vendor, provided the title is deduced for a period of at least 15 years prior to the contract[4].

2.   Contractual variations of statutory provisions

These statutory provisions regulate the position under an open contract, and apply only if and so far as a contrary intention is not expressed in the contract[5]. In practice it is the lessee or purchaser who seeks to enlarge the grantor's obligations, depending on the subject-matter of the contract.

(a) Grant of new lease
It is not customary to insist upon an investigation of any superior title in the case of short leases at a rack rent (a rent representing the full annual value of the land and buildings). The parties frequently dispense with a formal contract in these situations. On the grant of a long lease at a ground rent (ie a rent representing the annual value of the land only) the position is very different. In some parts of the country developers sell their houses by way of long leases for 99 or 999 years at a ground rent plus a premium which represents the price of the house. In theory no purchaser ought to proceed unless he peruses the freehold title, for by accepting the lease without such investigation he exposes himself to the risk that the lessor's title to grant the lease is defective. His need to obtain the freehold title is all the more urgent if, as is the usual case, he is obtaining a mortgage. The mortgagee is not bound by the terms of the contract between the lessor and the lessee-mortgagor who may find himself considerably embarrassed if, having accepted the open contract position, his mortgagee requires the freehold title to be deduced. It is the common, but by no means universal, practice on the grant of a long term of years for the contract to provide for an abstract of the freehold title to be supplied (often at the buyer's expense!), but the lessee's right to raise objections is expressly excluded. Alternatively the abstract may be delivered with the draft contract so that the lessee's solicitor has the opportunity to peruse the freehold title before his client contracts to take a lease. On the grant of an underlease the underlessee is entitled under the general law to an abstract or copy of the headlease.

   Under the Standard Conditions of Sale, on the grant of a lease of over 21 years, the vendor is obliged to deduce a title that will enable the purchaser to register the lease with an absolute title. This, in practice, means that the open contract position is reversed in the case of leases that will require substantive registration.

Duty of solicitor. A solicitor acting for a proposed lessee or purchaser of an existing lease is not to be deemed guilty of neglect or breach of duty by reason of his omitting, in good faith, to negative in the contract the application of the statutory provisions or to insert others in their place[6]. Failure to insist on a

---

4   *Williams v Spargo* [1893] WN 100. This assumes that the lease is at least 15 years old.
5   LPA 1925, s 44(11); *Re Pursell and Deakin's Contract* [1893] WN 152.
6   LPA 1925, s 182(1).

right for a client does not, it seems, constitute professional negligence[7]. On the other hand, where a right to inspect a superior lease exists, a solicitor failing to do so is guilty of negligence[8], as he would also appear to be if he allowed his client to sign a contract without advising him of the dangers involved in being unable to investigate a superior title.

(b) Sale of existing lease

In the past, the Law Society's Conditions of Sale imposed obligations on the vendor with regard to the title which he must deduce when selling an existing lease[9]. The Standard Conditions of Sale contain nothing relevant to this type of transaction and so the matter is governed by the open contract position.

3.   Notice

The statutory restriction on the lessee's right to investigate the superior title raises important problems in the field of notice. Prior to 1926, under the rule in *Patman v Harland*[10], an intending lessee or assign was fixed with constructive notice of matters or defects which he would have discovered had he investigated the superior title, notwithstanding that he was statutorily precluded from calling for such title. He was held to have accepted the consequences of not contracting out of the statute. This illogical rule was abrogated by s 44(7) of the Law of Property Act 1925. An intending lessee or assign who, by virtue of the statutory restrictions, is unable to call for the superior title, is not:

> ... deemed to be affected with notice of any matter or thing of which, if he had contracted that such title should be furnished, he might have had notice.

Whilst securing a measure of protection for lessees, this rule has been said to provide a remedy worse than the disease by creating insecurity of property[11]; it may result in the destruction of third party rights leaving the third party without any effective means of protection. Suppose X, the owner of a freehold property subject to a pre-1926 covenant prohibiting its use for any purpose other than as a private dwelling house, leases the property to Y for seven years. Y opens an art school on the premises[12]. Under s 44(7), Y's inability to investigate X's freehold title does not fix him with constructive notice of the covenant and, assuming he has no actual notice, he takes free from it. Thus the person entitled

---

7   Farrand, 136; cf Walford, 113. See also *Imray v Oakshette* [1897] 2 QB 218 at 229 CA per Rigby LJ where, however, the predecessor to s 182(1) (the Conveyancing Act 1881, s 66) was not cited.

8   *Hill v Harris* [1965] 2 QB 601 at 618, [1965] 2 All ER 358 at 363, CA, per Russell LJ, criticised at (1965) 29 Conv (NS) 162–63.

9   See the 3rd edition of this work, p 268.

10   (1881) 17 Ch D 353 (decided on the Vendor and Purchaser Act 1874, s 2(1)); *Imray v Oakshette* [1897] 2 QB 218, CA.

11   M & W, 726.

12   These are basically the facts of *Patman v Harland* (1881) 17 Ch D 353, where the convenantee obtained an injunction against Y. As to the position where a post-1925 restriction is concerned, see para (*a*).

to the benefit of the covenant ceases, through no fault of his own, to be able to enforce it against Y and his successors. Y would be bound if he had *actual* notice of the restriction; the burden of establishing notice lies on the person seeking to enforce the covenant[13].

Depending on the wording of the covenant, the covenantee may not even have any remedy against X. A person under a covenant not to use property in a particular way cannot commit a breach thereof except by his own act or that of his agent; but the lessee, Y, is not X's agent[14]. Furthermore, if X is a successor from the original covenantor, he is not bound at law, for the burden does not pass. Equity will not grant any injunction against X who is not in possession, and since he is only bound on the principle of *Tulk v Moxhay*[15], the court will not compel him to do anything which will involve him in expense (in the present context bringing an action against Y)[16].

(a) Limitations on s 44(5)
The protection afforded by sub-s (7) is not as comprehensive as appears at first sight. It does not relieve a lessee from constructive notice of any matter or thing discoverable on inspection of the property, or by investigating such title as he is entitled to call for either by virtue of the statute or under the contract. Thus an intending underlessee who fails to inspect the headlease cannot shelter behind it.

In particular, and this is the most serious limitation on its operation, s 44 (7), notwithstanding its unqualified language, must be read subject to s 198 (1) of the same Act. Consequently, a lessee is affected with notice of all land charges registered under the Land Charges Act 1972[17]. As to registered incumbrances (eg a post-1925 restrictive covenant), the protection afforded by sub-s (7) is illusory. An effective search can only be made if the lessee investigates the freehold title, which the statute forbids in the absence of any contractual provision to the contrary. He may therefore be bound by a registered charge which he has no means of discovering. Thus the old rule in *Patman v Harland* still lives on[18].

(b) Law of Property Act 1969
This Act, though providing for compensation in certain cases for loss due to undisclosed registered land charges, does not apply to any charge affecting a reversionary title (freehold or leasehold) which a lessee or assignee is *precluded*

---

13 *Shears v Wells* [1936] 1 All ER 832.
14 *Wilson v Twamley* [1904] 2 KB 99, CA; *Berton v Alliance Economic Investment Co Ltd* [1922] 1 KB 742 at 759, CA, per Atkin LJ.
15 (1848) 2 Ph 774.
16 *Hall v Ewin* (1887) 37 Ch D 74, CA; *Atkin v Rose* [1923] 1 Ch 522 at 534, per Lawrence J.
17 *White v Bijou Mansions Ltd* [1937] Ch 610 at 621, [1937] 3 All ER 269 at 273, per Simonds J (a case on registered land, see p 311, post); affd on other grounds [1938] Ch 351, [1938] 1 All ER 546, CA. This dictum appears to be the sole authority on the point, but it is accepted as correct by almost all commentators: M & W, 726; Emmet, para 5.152; Williams, *Title*, 569, note 7; contra (1938) 3 Conv (NS) 116.
18 But see the effect of the Law Commission's proposals, if implemented, p 301, post.

by statute from investigating[19]. The Law Commission felt that the present hardship stemmed from a general rule of long standing, rather than from the inadequacies of the registration system established by the Land Charges Act 1925[20]. Yet it is clearly arguable that compensation ought to be available when the relevant superior title has actually been investigated under a contractual right, but the registered charge remains undiscovered[1].

The Act does enable compensation to be claimed in appropriate circumstances for loss occasioned by an undisclosed land charge registered against a title which the claimant is statutorily entitled to, and does in fact, investigate. Thus an original underlessee[2] is covered in respect of an undiscoverable charge registered against the immediate leasehold interest, as is an assignee of a lease as regards a charge registered against a previous owner of the term.

(c) Restrictive covenants between lessor and lessee
The difficulties created by s 198(1) do not arise in relation to restrictions between landlord and tenant, which are not capable of registration as land charges[3]. On the grant of an underlease, an underlessee who refrains from inspecting the headlease is deemed to have constructive notice of the covenants in it[4], but not a subsequent purchaser of the underlease, save where he fails to exercise a contractual right of inspection. An injunction may be awarded against an underlessee in breach of a negative covenant in the headlease, but not against the purchaser (save as above).

4.   Duty to show good title and the statutory assumptions

Like his freehold counterpart the vendor of a leasehold interest must establish that he can assign a good title in accordance with the contract. We saw in Chapter 6 that various special considerations arise on the sale of leasehold property. The vendor must ensure that the tenure is correctly described as leasehold[5]. He must disclose unusual and onerous covenants affecting the property[6], and reveal that covenants in the headlease are more stringent than those in the underlease (if such be the case). The statutory restrictions as to title considered on page 290 do not abrogate the vendor's duty to disclose defects affecting a superior title, of which he is aware[7].

---

19 See s 25(9) and the meaning ascribed to 'registered charge' in sub-s (10). For the Act generally, see p 274, ante, and p 396, post.
20 Law Com No 18, para 37.
 1 (1969) 32 MLR 477, 485 (S Cretney).
 2 A lease granted out of a leasehold interest is expressly within the Act: s 25(9)(b).
 3 LCA 1972, s 2(5)(ii), p 388, post.
 4 See *Becker v Partridge* [1966] 2 QB 155, [1966] 2 All ER 266, CA.
 5 *Re Russ and Brown's Contract* [1934] Ch 34, CA, p 152, ante.
 6 See *Chester v Buckingham Travel Ltd* [1981] 1 All ER 386, p 152, ante.
 7 *Becker v Partridge,* supra (known breach of covenant in headlease).

Moreover, he does not discharge his obligation to show a good title if the lease has become forfeitable because of existing breaches of covenant.[8] In the absence of any contrary stipulation, the purchaser is entitled to be satisfied that all covenants have been performed to the date of completion. How can the vendor satisfy the purchaser on this point? The Law of Property Act 1925, s 47(2) enacts that on a sale of land held by lease (other than an underlease) the purchaser shall assume that the lease was duly granted and that, on production of the receipt for the last payment of rent due before completion, all covenants and provisions of the lease have been duly observed and performed up to the date of actual completion of the purchase. On the sale of an underlease, similar assumptions apply under sub-s (3), which extend to every superior lease. The presumption that the head lease was duly granted is a corollary of the rule precluding investigation of the freehold title[9].

(a) Rebuttable presumptions
These presumptions do not operate where the contrary appears. A purchaser discovering the existence of breaches of covenant by other means can object to the title, unless prohibited from raising objection thereto by a bona fide and clear special condition[10]. Even knowledge of the existence of a breach when entering into the contract was held in *Re Highett and Bird's Contract*[11] not to debar the purchaser's objection. Despite doubts as to the scope of this decision[12], the better view[13] is that a breach of covenant constitutes a removable[14] defect in title. The purchaser's notice does not constitute a waiver of his right to a good title, since he is entitled to assume that the vendor will remedy the breach before completion. A purchaser's right of objection is subject to any contrary contractual provision.

In the case of covenants to repair, the matter is governed by the Standard Conditions of Sale. General Condition 3.2 requires the purchaser to accept the property in the physical state it was in at the date of the contract. Moreover, it is also provided that the leasehold property is sold subject to any subsisting breach of a repairing covenant which renders the lease liable to forfeiture[15]. In respect of breaches of other covenants, the statutory presumptions are left

---

8 *Palmer v Goren* (1856) 25 LJ Ch 841 (breach of covenant to insure); *Becker v Partridge*, ante, (covenant not to underlet without consent); *Pips (Leisure Productions) Ltd v Walton* (1980) 260 EG 601 (writ for forfeiture issued before contract made). See also *Peyman v Lanjani* [1985] Ch 457, [1984] 3 All ER 703, CA (consent to assignment obtained by subterfuge).

9 That a purchaser of a underlease must assume the validity of the underlease is another argument against the view (see note 2, p 290, ante) that he can call for the headlease.

10 *Becker v Partridge* [1966] 2 QB 155 at 169, [1966] 2 All ER 266 at 268, CA, per Danckwerts LJ.

11 [1903] 1 Ch 287, CA, applying *Barnett v Wheeler* (1841) 7 M & W 364.

12 *Re Allen and Driscoll's Contract* [1904] 2 Ch 226 at 231, CA, per Romer LJ, limiting its application to cases of an express contract to make a good title.

13 Walford, 124–25; 1 Prideaux's Precedents 274, note 72; Farrand, 138. Contra Williams, *Title*, 557, note 3, citing *Clarke v Coleman* [1895] WN 114, CA, a decision too briefly reported to be of much value. Cf *Lockharts v Bernard Rosen & Co Ltd* [1922] 1 Ch 433 at 439, per Astbury J.

14 Not all breaches of covenant are susceptible of being remedied; eg a covenant not to use for illegal or immoral purposes: *Rugby School (Governors) v Tannahill* [1935] 1 KB 87, CA.

15 A similar condition exists in the case of a sale of a sub-lease.

to regulate the parties' rights. The effect of such a condition is to preclude objection to the title on account of breaches of covenant committed prior to the contract or to continuing breaches[16].

(b) Conclusive evidence

A condition requiring the purchaser to accept the last receipt for rent as *conclusive* evidence[17] of compliance with the covenants precludes objection to the title on account of breaches of covenant committed prior to the contract, or of continuing breaches[18]. It does not protect the vendor in relation to a breach of covenant committed subsequently to the contract, otherwise the purchaser might lose the property by the vendor's inadvertence or neglect[19]. A further limitation appears from *Beyfus v Lodge*[20], where the court refused to permit a vendor who knew about the breaches to rely on the condition. This illustrates the principle already encountered that a vendor cannot by his contract require the purchaser to assume the truth of something known to be false[1]. If the vendor is aware of the existence of a breach of covenant, he should disclose it and either bar any objection thereto or stipulate for its waiver to be assumed, though, again, the latter clause will only assist him if he has good reason for believing it to have been waived.

(c) Title of person giving receipt

Under the Standard Conditions of Sale[2] the purchaser is required to assume that the person who gave any receipt for a payment of rent was the person entitled to that rent or his agent. This does not preclude objection if the reversion's title is shown to be bad aliunde. Even in the absence of any such clause, it seems unlikely[3] that in normal cases the purchaser can insist on the reversionary title being traced from the original lessor to the person giving the receipt, for this would be in flat contradiction of the restrictions contained in s 44. Exceptionally he can require it to be deduced should the vendor allege waiver of a breach of covenant, or where the purchaser establishes clear uncertainty as to the entitlement to the reversion[4].

---

16 *Lawrie v Lees* (1880) 14 Ch D 249, CA; affd (1881) 7 App CAS 19, HL.
17 Under contracts governed by the SCS the statutory presumptions are left to regulate the parties' rights.
18 *Lawrie v Lees* (1880) 14 Ch D 249, CA; affd (1881) 7 App Cas 19, HL.
19 *Howell v Kightley* (1856) 21 Beav 331 at 336, per Romilly MR (possession deemed conclusive evidence of due performance). The contract may provide otherwise.
20 [1925] Ch 350. The vendor was refused specific performance but was entitled to forfeit the deposit. But see now the LPA 1925, s 49(2), p 621, post.
 1 Page 169, ante.
 2 SCS 6.6.
 3 The point is not free from doubt. See the authorities cited in Walford, 120–21.
 4 See 1 Dart, 172; *Pegler v White* (1864) 33 Beav 403.

5. Licence to assign

Many leases for short terms are subject to a covenant not to assign, underlet or part with possession without the lessor's consent, such consent not to be unreasonably withheld[5]. On a sale of the lease, the problem of the lessor's consent arises. Depending on the circumstances, it may be necessary to obtain more than one licence, eg on the sale of an underlease both the consent of the head lessor and of the immediate lessor may be required, the problem of the lessor's consent arises. The need to obtain the lessor's consent was, for a long time, a source of considerable delay and frustration, in that neither party to the contract was in a position to exert much leverage over the lessor[6]. This position was considered to be unsatisfactory and, implementing the Law Commission's recommendation[7] what has been described as this 'curious little Act, the Landlord and Tenant Act 1988'[8] was enacted.

Section 1(3) of the Act imposes a duty on the lessor, within a reasonable time, to give his consent to an assignment, except in a case where it is reasonable not to give consent. Furthermore, the lessor must give the tenant written notice of his decision whether or not to give consent specifying in addition (i) if the consent is given subject to conditions, what those conditions are and (ii) if consent is withheld, the reasons for withholding it. Reversing the previous position, the onus of proof is placed on the lessor to show that he has complied with the duties which the Act has imposed[9]. If the lessor is in breach of the duties imposed by the Act then he is liable in tort for breach of statutory duty[10].

A quite deliberate decision was taken not to specify what is a reasonable period in which to make the decision as to whether or not consent will be granted[11]. In judging this issue, much will depend upon the facts of individual cases so that if, as in *Midland Bank plc v Chart Enterprises Inc*[12], the landlord, when asked for consent to assign, is suspicious that there may have been breaches of covenant, he is fully entitled to take some time to make inquiries and to consider the position, although in that case, where the delay had amounted to about two and a half months, it was held that the landlord had failed to discharge the onus of proof imposed upon him to show that the delay had not been unreasonable.

A covenant against parting with possession without consent, which does not in express terms restrict an assignment, nevertheless requires consent to be obtained to any assignment (or subletting) of the premises[13]. However,

---

5   The Landlord and Tenant Act 1927, s 19(1) makes all covenants against assignment subject to this proviso, other than those expressed in absolute terms.
6   See the observations in *29 Equities Ltd v Bank Leumi (UK) Ltd* [1987] 1 All ER 108 at 114, CA, per Dillon LJ.
7   (1987) Law Com No 161.
8   *Venetian Glass Gallery Ltd v Next Properties Ltd* [1989] 2 EGLR 42 at 46 per Harman J.
9   Landlord and Tenant Act 1988, s 1(3)(6).
10   Ibid, s 4.
11   (1987) Law Com No 161, para 2.5.
12   [1990] 2 EGLR 59.
13   *Marks v Warren* [1979] 1 All ER 29; *Field v Barkworth* [1986] 1 All ER 362 (covenant against assigning 'any part' prohibits dealing with the 'whole').

provided that the tenant retains the legal possession of the property, no breach of this covenant occurs merely by allowing another person to occupy[14]. A vesting order granted by the court does not rank as an assignment within the normal covenant since it is a transfer taking effect by operation of law[15].

(a) General points
Before considering the respective rights and obligations of the parties to the contract, it will assist to note a few general points.
(i) An assignment by the existing tenant (T) without the consent of the lessor (L), is effective to vest the residue of the leasehold term in a purchaser (P), but subject to the risk of forfeiture proceedings by L if the lease contains the usual forfeiture clause[16].
(ii) In assessing the reasonableness of the landlord's refusal to consent to an assignment, the landlord will be judged on the reasons which he has given to the tenant. If, subsequently, facts come to light which would have been relevant in assessing the reasonableness, or otherwise, of withholding consent, these cannot be relied upon[17]. It is not necessary, however, for the landlord to justify as a matter of fact the issues on which he relied when refusing consent[18].
(iii) If T seeks consent but it is reasonably withheld, P is not safe in taking an assignment from T. Since an assignment in these circumstances will constitute a breach of covenant rendering the lease defensible, T is unable to show a good title to the property. A refusal of consent because the proposed assignee might eventually be eligible to acquire the freehold of the demised premises under the Leasehold Reform Act 1967, has been held to be reasonable[19].
(iv) The vendor's (ie T's) execution of a declaration of trust of the premises in P's favour does not breach the covenant against assigning without consent[20], even if P enters into occupation. This device cannot be recommended as a satisfactory means of avoiding the necessity of L's consent. In the absence of any contractual stipulation to the contrary[1], T could never compel P to accept such a declaration in lieu of an assignment of the term.
(v) If L unreasonably refuses consent, an assignment by T to P does not constitute a breach of covenant. Nevertheless, specific performance will

---

14 *Jackson v Simons* [1923] 1 Ch 373.
15 *Marsh v Gilbert* (1980) 256 EG 715.
16 See *Old Grovebury Manor Farm Ltd v W Seymour Plant Sales and Hire Ltd (No 2)* [1979] 3 All ER 504, CA; *Hemingway Securities Ltd v Dunraven Ltd* [1995] 09 EG 322 (underlease).
17 *CIN Properties Ltd v Gill* (1992) 67 P & CR 288. See [1995] Conv 316 (Letitia Crabb).
18 *International Drilling Fluids Ltd v Louisville Investments (Uxbridge) Ltd* [1986] Ch 513 at 520, [1986] 1 All ER 321 at 325, CA, per Balcombe LJ; *Air India v Balabel* [1993] 2 EGLR 66, CA.
19 *Norfolk Capital Group Ltd v Kitway Ltd* [1977] QB 506, [1976] 3 All ER 787, CA; *Bickel v Duke of Westminster* [1977] QB 517, [1976] 3 All ER 801, CA; *West Layton Ltd v Ford* [1979] QB 593, [1979] 2 All ER 657, CA. See generally on the question of the reasonableness of refusing consent, *International Drilling Fluids Ltd v Louisville Investments (Uxbridge) Ltd* [1986] Ch 513, [1986] 1 All ER 321, CA. See also the Sex Discrimination Act 1975, s 31(1), and the Race Relations Act 1976, s 24(1).
20 *Gentle v Faulkner* [1900] 2 QB 267, CA (trust for benefit of creditors).
1 As to which see *Pincott v Moorstons Ltd* [1937] 1 All ER 513, CA.

not normally be decreed against an unwilling purchaser[2]. P himself may obtain specific performance if the grounds of refusal are so unreasonable that T can clearly assign without consent[3]. In cases of wrongful refusal, the vendor's proper course is to obtain a declaration of unreasonableness from the court, and then to launch specific performance proceedings[4].

(b) Rights of parties under general law
The Standard Conditions of Sale deal expressly with the position of the parties relative to the right to assign. The parties' rights under the general law can, therefore, be summarised briefly[5]. In the absence of express contractual provisions, the contract will be unconditional on the question of the licence. The vendor is obliged to use his best endeavours to obtain it, and the purchaser is required to assist in this, eg, by providing satisfactory references[6]. The vendor's failure to obtain the licence by the contractual date for completion constitutes a breach of contract[7]. It was formerly the case that the tenant's damages would be limited by the anomalous rule in *Bain v Fothergill*[8], to recovery of the deposit plus interest and the costs of investigating title. With the abolition of the rule by s 3 of the Law of Property (Miscellaneous Provisions) Act 1989, there is now no such restriction and damages fall to be assessed in accordance with general principles. If the licence cannot be obtained because the landlord has unreasonably refused his consent, then, on principle, it would seem that the liability of the landlord to pay damages under s 4 of the Landlord and Tenant Act 1988, would extend to cover the damages payable by the tenant to the proposed assignee, such loss being well within the contemplation of the parties.

(c) Standard Conditions of Sale – vendor's obligations
General Condition 8.3.2 of the Standard Conditions of Sale requires the vendor to apply for the consent at his expense, and to use his best endeavours to obtain it. The purchaser must provide all information and references reasonably required. The obligation to use best endeavours is construed reasonably by the courts, so that the vendor would not be regarded as having breached this requirement by failing to institute litigation against the landlord in order to obtain consent[9], nor has he to allow the purchaser the opportunity

---

2   *Re Marshall and Salt's Contract* [1900] 2 Ch 202. Cf *White v Hay* (1895) 72 LT 281.
3   *Curtis Moffat Ltd v Wheeler* [1929] 2 Ch 224 at 236, per Maugham J.
4   Cf *Theodorou v Bloom* [1964] 3 All ER 399n (declaration obtained by purchaser).
5   See generally *Bickel v Courtenay Investments (Nominees) Ltd* [1984] 1 All ER 657 at 660, per Warner J.
6   *Sheggia v Gradwell* [1963] 3 All ER 114 at 121, CA, per Harmen LJ.
7   Contrast *Lehmann v McArthur* (1868) 3 Ch App 496, where the agreement was simply 'subject to the landlord's approval' and the vendor, having failed to obtain a licence, despite reasonable efforts, was entitled to treat the contract as at an end.
8   (1874) LR 7 HL 158, p 584, and see post, p 655. See eg *Re Marshall and Salt's Contract* [1900] 2 Ch 202; *Vangeen v Benjamin* (1976) 239 EG 647 (grant of underlease).
9   *Lehmann v McArthur* (1868) 3 Ch App 496; *Fischer v Toumazos* [1991] 2 EGLR 204 at 207, CA, per Dillon LJ.

to obtain it[10]. The terms on which a licence is granted are not the purchaser's concern so long as they do not prejudice him[11]. Similarly, the obligation on the purchaser to supply all information reasonably required does not impose an absolute obligation to supply all information that will satisfy the lessor[12]. The vendor cannot require the purchaser to submit to an interview with the lessor's agents[13] or to provide a guarantee for payment of the rent[14].

Some uncertainty exists as to whether procurement of the licence is strictly a matter of title or of conveyance[15]; the better view is that it is a term of the contract relating to title[16]. Failure to obtain it by the time for completion[17] amounts to a defect in title which the vendor cannot remove at his own volition. Because the word 'lease' is defined to include sub-lease and an agreement for a sub-lease[18], General Condition 8.3 applies *mutatis mutandis* to a contract to grant an underlease which requires the head lessor's consent.

(d) Consequences of failure to obtain licence

It was previously the case that, under the National Conditions of Sale[19], the vendor had the right to rescind if the licence could not be obtained. This led to the somewhat unfortunate decision in *29 Equities Ltd v Bank Leumi (UK) Ltd*[20] that whether or not a licence could be obtained was a question of fact to be determined, not on the contractual completion date, but on the date when the vendor purported to rescind[1]. Under the Standard Conditions of Sale the position is clear. Under General Condition 8.3.4, unless there has been a breach of obligation with regard to the obtaining of the licence, then if three working days before completion date, either the consent has not been given or has been given subject to a condition to which the purchaser reasonably objects, then either party has the right to rescind the contract. In that event, the vendor must return the purchaser's deposit and the purchaser must return all documents supplied to him by the vendor and cancel any registration of the contract[2].

One final point. The vendor's failure to obtain a licence is not a defect of title which the purchaser can waive in the expectation of being able to insist upon an assignment without consent[3]. A court of equity will not decree specific

10 *Lipmans Wallpaper Ltd v Mason and Hodghton Ltd* [1969] 1 Ch 20 at 35, [1968] 1 All ER 1123 at 1129, per Goff J.
11 *Re Davies' Agreement* (1969) 21 P & CR 328.
12 *Shires v Brock* (1977) 247 EG 127, CA.
13 *Elfer v Beynon-Lewis* (1972) 222 EG 1955.
14 *Butler v Croft* (1973) 27 P & CR 1.
15 See *Property and Bloodstock Ltd v Emerton* [1968] Ch 94 at 118, [1967] 3 All ER 321 at 329, CA, per Danckwerts LJ; *Ellis v Lawrence* (1969) 210 EG 215, per Stamp J.
16 *Property and Bloodstock Ltd v Emerton*, supra, at 121, 331, per Sachs. See also *Bain v Fothergill*, supra.
17 This is the relevant time: *Ellis v Rogers* (1884) 29 Ch D 661, CA; *Day v Singleton* [1899] 2 Ch 320 at 327, CA, per Romer LJ.
18 SCS 1.1.1(h).
19 NCS (20th edn) 11(5).
20 [1987] 1 All ER 108, CA.
1 For the resultant difficulties, see the 3rd edition of this work at p 275.
2 SCS 7.2.
3 *Lipmans Wallpaper Ltd v Mason and Hodghton Ltd* [1969] 1 Ch 20, [1968] 1 All ER 1123.

performance if it involves the vendor in breaking a pre-existing contract, and it is not within the purchaser's competence to waive a term which partially benefits the vendor[4].

(e) Covenant to surrender

A covenant not to assign without consent is sometimes coupled with a proviso whereby the tenant, on wishing to assign, must first offer in writing to surrender the lease to the lessor. The object of this clause[5] is to give the benefit of any increase in the value of the lease to the lessor, not to the tenant who would ordinarily be free to assign it at a premium. The lessor is given a limited period in which to accept the offer, failing which he is deemed to have rejected it. If he accepts, the question of consent never arises. If it is declined, the tenant must then apply for his licence to assign. The tenant's covenant to surrender is registrable as a Class C(iv) land charge[6].

6. Law Commission reforms

As we have seen, the general law confers no right on an intending lessee to investigate the freehold title when a lease is granted by a fee simple owner. In effect he has to accept the lease blindly, unless the lessor agrees to make his title available for perusal. In theory this defect is offset to a limited degree by the lessor's covenant for quiet enjoyment, but in reality this covenant provides little effective protection. In its Report on Obligations of Landlords and Tenants the Law Commission considered the position to be far from satisfactory. It put forward 'a recommendation for radical reform', whereby every lease or tenancy should imply a new enlarged covenant for quiet enjoyment, to have effect notwithstanding anything to the contrary in the lease[7]. Under its terms the lessee (T) would be entitled peacefully to hold and enjoy the demised premises for the purposes of the lease without interruption or disturbance by the lessor (L), or by any person lawfully asserting or enforcing a title or right whether derived from or *superior* to L's title. It would not extend to an interruption or disturbance by someone other than L in consequence of a 'defect in the title of the landlord' of which L had no notice, or of which T did have notice when the lease was granted. The expression 'defect in the title of the landlord' would be statutorily defined to include, for example, lack of title, lack of power to grant the lease (eg because of a covenant in a mortgage affecting the freehold), or a restriction affecting the use of the

---

4 Cf *Warmington v Miller* [1973] QB 877, [1973] 2 All ER 372, CA (absolute covenant against underletting; specific performance of agreement for underlease refused).
5 *Bocardo SA v S and M Hotels Ltd* [1979] 3 All ER 737 at 745, CA, per Browne LJ. But see Hallett, 483, note 1. The covenant is not invalidated by the Landlord and Tenant Act 1927, s 19(1) (p 297, ante): ibid. But such a clause in a lease of business premises is void under the Landlord and Tenant Act 1954, s 38 (1): *Allnatt London Properties Ltd v Newton* [1984] 1 All ER 423, CA.
6 *Greene v Church Comrs for England* [1974] Ch 467, [1974] 3 All ER 609, CA, p 387, post.
7 Law Com No 67, para 62 and Draft Bill, cl 5.

premises for the purpose of the lease[8]. Similarly, 'notice' would be defined to exclude constructive or statutory notice in circumstances where L or T could not reasonably be expected to discover what it was of which he would otherwise be deemed to have notice.

It has not been the Commission's intention to propose a statutory right for T to investigate L's freehold title. The aim is to encourage L to disclose his title to enable T to discover possible defects in it. This investigation would serve a different purpose from that undertaken on a sale of freehold land (para 47). L would furnish his title to protect himself from potential liability under his implied covenant, not to establish that he owns and is therefore able to demise the subject matter of the contract. It would not be necessary for L's solicitor to submit an abstract of title or even copies of relevant documents. Simply to make the title available for investigation at his offices would suffice. Nor, seemingly, would L be under any duty to reply to T's observations or requisitions on title, as the object of the exercise would merely be to enable T to acquire notice.

Compared with the present law these changes would mark a significant improvement in the position of every prospective lessee. Nevertheless, the Report fails to deal adequately with several important consequential issues. The Commission deliberately refrained from specifying what title L should allow T to inspect. Another vital omission relates to the question of remedies[9]. It is uncertain what T's precise rights would be if, on investigating the title, he discovered prior to the grant of the lease the existence of a statutory defect in title. Nor is it clear how the proposed definition of 'notice' interrelates with the provisions of s 27 of the Law of Property Act 1969. Hopefully these difficulties[10] will receive further consideration before legislation is introduced in Parliament. When this will be remains a matter of speculation, though implementation in the near future seems remote.

B   Settlements

1.   General scheme for settled land

The reader will already be conversant with the machinery and operation of the Settled Land Act 1925. It is not proposed to repeat in detail material that is fully covered in standard real property textbooks[11]. However, certain aspects of this machinery are clearly relevant to conveyancing and they must be discussed.

---

8   Thus abrogating the decision in *Hill v Harris* [1965] 2 QB 601, [1965] 2 All ER 358, CA, p 171, ante. See also *Stokes v Mixconcrete (Holdings) Ltd* (1978) 38 P & CR 488, CA.
9   Save to state (para 30) that until the proposals for new and reformed remedies take effect, breach of all the new implied covenants put forward in the Report would entitle the tenant to remedies which the law currently provides for breach of covenant.
10   More fully explored in the second edn, pp 314–16.
11   See M & W, Chap 8; C & B, 165–193.

It will be recalled that it is the policy of the Act that a purchaser of settled land should not concern himself with the beneficial interests arising under the settlement. To achieve this end the Act requires all post-1925 settlements to be created according to the statutory pattern and provides that a conveyance by the tenant for life (or statutory owner) operates to overreach the beneficial interests, thus giving the purchaser a title free from them, provided – and this is vital – the purchase money is paid to or by the direction of the trustees of the settlement or into court[12]. As to the mode of creation, two documents are necessary: a vesting deed and a trust instrument (or in the case of a testamentary settlement, the will). If effected in any other way the instrument does 'not operate to transfer or create a legal estate'[13].

(a) Vesting deed
The purchaser's main preoccupation is with the vesting deed which contains all the information which he requires. It describes[14] the settled land, declares in whom the legal estate is vested and summarises those parts of the trust instrument of concern to him, such as naming the trustees of the settlement. As a general rule, so long as the land remains settled, the existence of a vesting deed is vital. Under s 13 of the Settled Land Act 1925[15], no disposition of the legal estate can be effective until the execution of a vesting deed. The section expressly excludes from its application a disposition in favour of a purchaser without notice of the existence of a settlement, and a disposition by a personal representative, such as a sale by him of the land in the course of administration. Moreover, the purchaser must assume that the statements and particulars in the vesting deed are correct. He cannot call for production of the trust instrument to verify the accuracy of the information in the vesting deed[16]. Exceptionally the Act does permit the purchaser to peep behind the curtain to see the trust instrument[17]. But these are all abnormal situations, rarely encountered today, where, for one reason or another, no proper vesting deed is executed in the course of creating the settlement. In practice, this will usually occur when, as a result of some informal arrangement[18], a life interest is created and the provisions of the Settled Land Act become applicable.

---

12   SLA 1925, ss 18(1)(b), 72 (2).
13   SLA 1925, s 4(1). It may constitute a trust instrument under s 9(1).
14   See SLA 1925, s 5(1).
15   As amended by the LP(Am)A 1926, Schedule.
16   SLA 1925, s 110(2). For certain theoretical difficulties regarding this provision, see Emmet, para 22.050; M & W, 335–36.
17   SLA 1925, s 110(2), proviso (a)–(d).
18   Notable examples include *Bannister v Bannister* [1948] 2 All ER 133, CA and *Binions v Evans* [1972] Ch 359, [1972] 2 All ER 70, CA. See also *Martin v Martin* [1978] Fam 12, [1977] 3 All ER 762, CA (court order on divorce); *Ungurian v Lesnoff* [1990] Ch 206 (constructive trust); *Costello v Costello* (express, although probably unintended, settlement): see [1994] Conv 391 (M P Thompson)). Contrast *Griffiths v Williams* (1977) 248 EG 947, CA and *Ivory v Palmer* [1975] ICR 340, CA (accommodation supplied as part of contract of employment) where such problems were avoided. See generally, (1977) 93 LQR 561 (A Hornby).

(b) Provisions for protection of purchaser

A sale of the settled land by the tenant for life must be made for the best consideration in money that can reasonably be obtained[19]. Any purported disposition of the land which is not authorised by the Act or by any additional powers in the settlement is void as a transfer of the legal estate in the land[20]. This provision operates to avoid an unauthorised transaction even though the other party is unaware that the land is settled[1]. Some protection is, however, conferred upon a purchaser of settled land by s 110(1) of the Act[2]. This enacts that on a sale, a purchaser dealing in good faith is to be conclusively taken to have given the best consideration that could reasonably be obtained, and to have complied with all the requisitions of the Act. Provided that he acts in good faith, he can claim this protection whether or not he knows that he is dealing with a tenant for life[3]. In this context, good faith means, or at least involves, a belief that all is being regularly and properly done. The fact that he acquires the land at an undervalue is not, by itself, evidence of bad faith[4]. In the absence of good faith, a transaction which does not comply with the requirements of the Act can be upset by the beneficiaries under the settlement, even though the land has subsequently become vested in a purchaser without notice of the defect[5]. The protection afforded by s 110(1) is not, however, all embracing. If the transaction entered into is not one which the tenant for life is empowered by the Act to make, then the purported transaction is, in effect, *ultra vires*, the tenant for life and, as a result of s 18 of the Act, void[6]. Section 110(1) only appears to give protection when the transaction in question is within the tenant for life's powers but there is some defect in the way those powers have been exercised.

2.   Devolution of settled land

It will be helpful to trace the devolution of settled land in two typical situations. Suppose that T (a testator) dies leaving realty to A for life remainder to C absolutely. T appoints E as his executor. If after A's death C contracts to sell the land to P, the following should be abstracted (together with earlier deeds to complete a proper chain of title):

(i)   *grant of probate to E;*

---

19   SLA 1925, s 39(1).
20   SLA 1925, s 18(1)(a).
 1   *Weston v Henshaw* [1950] Ch 510; *Bevan v Johnston* [1990] 2 EGLR 33, CA.
 2   *Re Morgan's Lease, Jones v Norsesowicz* [1972] Ch 1, [1971] 2 All ER 235 where *Mogridge v Clapp* [1892] 3 Ch 382 was preferred to *Weston v Henshaw*, supra.
 3   Per Kay J, in *Mogridge v Clapp*, supra, at 401 (decision on SLA 1882, s 54). See eg *Chandler v Bradley* [1897] 1 Ch 315 (bribe paid to life tenant as inducement to grant lease; lessee not in good faith).
 4   *Hurrell v Littlejohn* [1904] 1 Ch 689.
 5   *Re Handman and Wilcox's Contract* [1902] 1 Ch 599, per Buckley J (assignment of lease not granted at best rent). The CA left this point open, but declined to force the title on an unwilling purchaser.
 6   See cases cited in note 1, supra.

(ii) *vesting assent by E in A's favour*, which will contain the particulars prescribed by s 7 of the Act, thus alerting P to the existence of a settlement;

(iii) *grant of representation to A's estate*: since the land has ceased to be settled, the legal estate vests in A's general representatives who should vest it in C;

(iv) *assent to C*: the settlement has now terminated, so this document will make no mention of the trustees of the settlement. Section 110(7) of the Act requires P to assume that C is entitled to the land absolutely and beneficially, free from all limitations, powers and charges under the settlement. In other words, P must accept that the settlement is at an end so that he can safely pay the purchase money to C.

If instead the limitations in T's will were to A for life, *remainder to B for life*, remainder to C absolutely, the main difference in the devolution of the title would occur on A's death. Where land remains settled on the death of a life tenant[8], he is deemed, in the absence of any express appointment in their favour, to have appointed the trustees of the settlement as his special executors[9]. They should, therefore, take out a grant of probate to A's estate, limited to settled land, and then by means of a *vesting* assent (containing the relevant s 5 particulars) transfer the legal estate to B. The subsequent links in the chain follow (iii) and (iv) above (B being substituted for A). Failure to adopt the correct procedure on the death of A may not be fatal. A purchaser is entitled to rely on an order of the court (such as a grant of probate) even if made without jurisdiction[10]. So, a grant to A's general personal representatives, instead of to the trustees of the settlement, would not constitute a defect in title provided the grant extended to settled land[11].

Should at any stage it have been necessary to appoint fresh trustees of the settlement, the deed of declaration should be abstracted, but not the deed of appointment which does not concern P. The deed of declaration merely declares who are the trustees consequent upon the appointment[12]. P must assume the truth of the particulars contained in it[13].

3. Termination of settlements

The purchaser, being ignorant of the beneficial interests, has no means of knowing whether the settlement has terminated. He lacks any assurance whether it is safe to deal with a person claiming to be absolutely entitled to land which, according to the purchaser's knowledge, is still settled. The Settled Land Act 1925, s 17, resolves this difficulty by requiring the trustees on request

---

7 See *Re Bridgett and Hayes' Contract* [1928] Ch 163; SLA 1925, s 7 (5).
8 As to which see *Re Taylor's Estate* [1929] P 260.
9 AEA 1925, s 22. The grant to A's general representatives would be 'save and except settled land'.
10 LPA 1925, s 204, applied in *Re Bridgett and Hayes' Contract* [1928] Ch 163.
11 Aliter if the grant was 'save and except settled land'; see eg *Re Powell's Estate* [1935] P 114.
12 SLA 1925, s 35.
13 SLA 1925, s 110(2)(d).

to execute a deed of discharge declaring they are discharged from the trusts, whenever the settled land vests in a person free from all equitable interests and powers under the trust instrument. Suppose X owns land subject only to a family charge in favour of Y. The land is settled by virtue of s 1(1)(v), and X has the legal estate vested in him[14]. On Y's death X becomes solely entitled, but a purchaser from him could only discover the termination of the settlement from the deed of discharge.

In two situations no deed of discharge is required. One occasion has already been encountered, the simple assent or conveyance not naming any settlement trustees. The other arises where land ceases to be settled before any vesting instrument is executed[15]; it is pointless to inform the purchaser of the termination of something the existence of which he is unaware.

C   Trusts for sale[16]

A trust for sale may exist by virtue of (i) some statutory provision, as in the case of beneficial co-ownership and intestacies[17], or (ii) an express trust which may arise under a will or be created by a conveyance in circumstances where there would otherwise be a statutory trust. By virtue of s 1(1) of the Bodies Corporate (Joint Tenancy) Act 1899, land can be conveyed to an individual and a body corporate, eg a limited company, as trustees for sale for themselves as joint tenants[18]. On the dissolution of the company the property devolves on the surviving joint tenant.

1.   Conveyance by all trustees necessary

The essence of a trust for sale is that the trustees are under a *duty* to sell, though s 27(1) of the Law of Property Act 1925, implies a power to postpone sale unless a contrary intention appears. Accordingly, whereas one trustee can call on his co-trustees to perform the duty and sell[19], all of them must be agreed if they are to exercise their power to postpone. In the case of a *statutory* trust for sale this principle must be read subject to s 26 (3) of the Act. This sub-section requires the trustees, so far as practicable, to consult with the beneficiaries and, so far as is consistent with the general interest of the trust, to give effect to their wishes. In the event of a dispute the wishes of the majority (according to the value of their combined interests) are to prevail. Thus a majority of beneficiaries who are also trustees for sale will normally[20] be able

---

14   SLA 1925, s 29(1), (ix).
15   Cf *Re Alefounder's Will Trusts, Adnams v Alefounder* [1927] 1 Ch 360.
16   See (1989) Law Coun No 181, *Trusts of Land.*
17   LPA 1925, s 36(1) (joint tenancy); SLA 1925, s 36(4) (tenancy in common); AEA 1925, s 33 (intestacy). And see *Bull v Bull* [1955] 1 QB 234, [1955] 1 All ER 253, CA.
18   The common law permitted a body corporate to be a tenant in common.
19   *Re Mayo, Mayo v Mayo* [1943] Ch 302, [1943] 2 All ER 440.
20   But see *Smith v Smith and Smith* (1975) 120 Sol Jo 100.

to insist on a postponement of the sale. Similarly, a beneficial tenant in common (not being a trustee for sale) who is entitled to the larger share in the beneficial entitlement can effectively override the wishes of his co-tenant as to a sale[1]. The necessity to consult the beneficiaries arises not only when the trustees intend to sell, but also on the exercise of any statutory or extended power vested in them[2]. A purchaser is not concerned to see that the provisions of sub-s (3) have been observed. Section 26(3) does not apply to an express trust for sale unless the contrary appears in the document of creation. It is not the practice to *adopt* sub-s (3) into express trusts.

(a) Refusal to sell

One trustee for sale cannot convey (or mortgage[3]) trust land without the concurrence of his co-trustees, nor has he any implied authority on behalf of the others to enter into a binding contract to sell the property[4]. The Law of Property Act 1925, s 30[5], provides a solution to the troublesome situation that arises when one trustee declines to agree to a proposed sale. It enacts that:

> If the trustees for sale refuse to sell or to exercise any of the powers conferred by [ss 28 or 29] any person interested may apply to the court for a vesting or other order for giving effect to the proposed transaction and the court may make such order as it thinks fit.

The court has no power to vary the beneficial interests under this provision. It enables an interested person[6] to apply to the court to force a sale. It does not permit an application to *prevent* a sale taking place. No statutory power is needed for this; a beneficiary can always seek the court's assistance to restrain a threatened sale in breach of trust[7]. The Act contains no guidelines for the exercise of this judicial discretion. The courts look at all the circumstances to decide whether it would be inequitable to order a sale. The s 30 discretion is not fettered by s 26(3) of the Act[8]. The courts recognise the primacy of the duty to sell; they also investigate the existence of any 'secondary or collateral object besides that of sale'[9]. If there is such a purpose still capable of fulfilment, then a sale will not ordinarily be ordered. Another test, often adopted in bankruptcy cases[10], simply asks whose voice ought to prevail in equity. Though

---

1 See eg *Bull v Bull* [1955] 1 QB 234, [1955] 1 All ER 253, CA.
2 *Re Jones, Jones v Cusack-Smith* [1931] 1 Ch 375.
3 Cf *First National Securities Ltd v Hegerty* [1985] QB 850, [1984] 3 All ER 641, CA (co-owner's signature of mortgage deed forged; no legal charge created); p 556, post.
4 See pp 120–121, ante.
5 Which applies equally to disputes relating to jointly owned registered land.
6 Such as a beneficiary under the trust, a co-owner's trustee in bankruptcy, or an equitable chargee, but not (perhaps) a trustee with no beneficial interest in the land (see Law Com Working Paper, No 94 (Trusts), para 3.9). See also pp 311–312, post.
7 *Waller v Waller* [1967] 1 All ER 305 (sale of matrimonial home restrained by wife).
8 *Smith v Smith and Smith*, supra.
9 *Jones v Challenger* [1961] 1 QB 176 at 181, [1960] 1 All ER 785 at 789, CA, per Devlin LJ.
10 *Re Turner (a bankrupt)* [1975] 1 All ER 5 at 7, per Goff J; *Re Densham (a bankrupt)* [1975] 3 All ER 726; *Re Holliday (a bankrupt)* [1981] Ch 405, [1980] 3 All ER 385, *Re Lowrie (a bankrupt)* [1981] 3 All ER 353.

differently framed, these two tests are in reality one and the same[11]. In one case[12] four persons, A, B, C and D, each of whom owned separate but neighbouring properties, bought a plot of land which they desired to retain as an open space. The plot was conveyed to them as joint tenants, and they covenanted *inter se* to keep it as an open space. A later sold his own property and applied, against the wishes of the others, to have the land sold. His application failed. It was clearly inequitable to allow the voice of a trustee in breach of his obligation to prevail. It could also be said that the original purpose of the acquisition was still capable of performance.

(i) *Co-habitees.*   The court's help is frequently sought by one of two co-habitees who, having purchased a house for their joint occupation, later part company. Their separation indicates that the purpose of the trust is exhausted. A sale will generally be ordered at the request of the one who no longer lives in the house[13], but not always. No order will be granted when there are dependent children (whether of the relationship or not) living in the house with the trustee resisting the sale[14]. Nor should it be overlooked that the house will often have been bought as a residence for the surviving co-habitee after the other's death. In *Stott v Ratcliffe*[15], X, who was separated but not divorced from his wife, W, set up home with Y in a house that was vested in their joint names. X died intestate. As administratrix of X's estate, W sought an order for sale. Her application was dismissed. The purpose of the trust had not been exhausted, since the house was acquired so as to provide a secure home for Y during her own lifetime[16].

(ii) *Family-sharing.*   Another not uncommon occasion for dispute arises when members of a family combine together to purchase a house as a residence for themselves. Should the house sharing arrangement not work satisfactorily so that one co-owner is forced to leave, the other who remains in occupation not unnaturally declines to concur in any sale of the house. Since the purpose of the trust has come to an end, the courts will usually order a sale[17]. However, despite the collateral purpose failing, the court still retains a discretion to reject the application if in the circumstances an order for sale would be

11   *Cousins v Dzosens* (1981) Times, 12 December; affd [1984] LS Gaz R 2855, CA, per HH John Waite QC.
12   *Re Buchanan-Wollaston's Conveyance* [1939] Ch 738, [1939] 2 All ER 302, CA; *Re Hyde's Conveyance* (1952) 102 L Jo 58, unreported (applicant acting out of spite to defeat purpose); *Chhokar v Chhokar* [1984] FLR 313, CA (wife resisting sale sought by accomplice to whom husband had sold property at undervalue).
13   *Bernard v Josephs* [1982] Ch 391, [1982] 3 All ER 162, CA.
14   *Re Evers's Trust* [1980] 3 All ER 399, CA; *Dennis v McDonald* [1982] Fam 63, [1982] 1 All ER 590, CA.
15   (1982) 126 Sol Jo 310, CA; Cf *Diwell v Farnes* [1959] 2 All ER 379, CA; *Jones v Jones* [1977] 2 All ER 231, CA (father providing three-quarters of purchase price and buying house in own name for son and his family to live in; step-mother inheriting house on father's death refused order for sale).
16   But a change of circumstances (eg Y's subsequent marriage to or co-habitation with another man) might produce a different result.
17   *Smith v Smith and Smith* (1975) 120 Sol Jo 100; *Fuller v Rooney* (1961) 178 EG 65; *Mudge v Gibbon* (1962) 181 EG 275 (express provision for sale in event of dispute).

inequitable[18], perhaps because the one seeking a sale was primarily responsible for the break-down of relations[19]. Similarly, in *Charlton v Lester*[20], the judge refused an order for sale on the application of two trustees, because the third (the mother of one of them) had agreed to the purchase only on the basis of a clear understanding that she would always be allowed to keep the house as her home where she had lived as a protected tenant prior to its acquisition.

(iii) *Spouses*[1].   The principles discussed in (i) and (ii) have frequently been applied in the past in disputes between spouses[2]. In practice, however, a sale is nowadays almost invariably sought as part of matrimonial proceedings between them. On divorce the courts have wide powers to make property adjustment orders under the Matrimonial Causes Act 1973, including the power to order one (ex) spouse to transfer property to the other[3]. The court can also order a sale of property on divorce[4]. Occasionally there may still be situations when a spouse has to initiate proceedings under s 30 of the Law of Property Act 1925. For example, the parties may split up without any intention to seek a divorce or judicial separation, or the spouse desiring a sale may remarry before applying for relief under the Act of 1973[5].

One form of property adjustment order commonly encountered is the *Mesher*[6] order (as it is often called). The former matrimonial home is vested in the parties on trust for sale in equal shares, subject to a proviso that no sale is to occur before a stated event, such as the wife's remarriage or co-habitation, or until the youngest child attains 18. When, as is usual, the order is expressed to be 'until further order', the court has jurisdiction to direct a sale within the original period of postponement, without the applicant having to resort to s 30 proceedings[7].

The *Mesher* order has, however, proved to be not without its own difficulties, in particular, that it has a tendency to store up trouble for the future[8]. An

---

18   *Rivett v Rivett* (1966) 200 EG 858, per Goff J; *Bernard v Josephs* [1982] Ch 391 at 411, [1982] 3 All ER 162 at 176, CA, per Kerr LJ.
19   Cf *Cullingford v Cullingford* (1967) 204 EG 471.
20   (1976) 238 EG 115; *Re Mott* [1987] CLY 212.
1   See [1981] Conv 404 (M Hayes & G Battersby); [1984] Conv 103 (M P Thompson).
2   See eg *Jones v Challenger* [1961] 1 QB 176, [1960] 1 All ER 785, CA; *Rawlings v Rawlings* [1964] P 398, [1964] 2 All ER 804, CA; *Bedson v Bedson* [1965] 2 QB 666, [1965] 3 All ER 307, CA.
3   Sections 23, 24. For the statutory guidelines relevant to the exercise of the courts' powers, see s 25 (as substituted by the Matrimonial and Family Proceedings Act 1984, s 3). The interests of any children under 18 are now of primary consideration. See generally, Bromley and Lowe, *Family Law* (8th edn), 758f.
4   Section 24A, added by the Matrimonial Homes and Property Act 1981, s 7. A non-party to the marriage, who has a beneficial interest in the home, has a right to make representations about the proposed order: sub-s (6), added by the 1984 Act, Sch 1, para 11.
5   Matrimonial Causes Act 1973, s 28 (3) (as amended). The application must be initiated (though not necessarily determined) before remarriage: *Jackson v Jackson* [1973] Fam 99, [1973] 2 All ER 395.
6   See *Mesher v Mesher and Hall* [1980] 1 All ER 126n, CA.
7   By virtue of s 24A: *Thompson v Thompson* [1986] Fam 38, [1985] 2 All ER 243, CA.
8   See the criticisms collected in *Clutton v Clutton* [1991] 1 All ER 340 at 345–6, CA, per Lloyd LJ.

alternative order which may be made, which also involves a postponement of
the sale of the property is the *Martin*[9] order. This entails an order postponing
a sale until the wife died, remarried or started cohabiting with another man.

(b) Form of order

Under s 30 the court can make 'such order as it thinks fit'. The usual form is
for the property to be sold with vacant possession coupled with an order for
the reluctant trustee to concur in the sale. Should the defendant trustee be in
occupation (as will often be the case) the court can require him to deliver up
possession by a certain date[10]. This works more unfavourably towards an
occupying trustee, because it results in his having to move out earlier than if
he had simply been ordered to concur in the sale. An order of this type may
be necessary to facilitate the sale if there is any likelihood that the trustee
might be obstructive. Bearing in mind that a sale pursuant to s 30 may entail
consequences which neither party wants[11], the courts will in an appropriate
case exercise the discretion so as to facilitate the purchase of the property by
the occupying co-owner[12].

If one co-owner ousts the other, the court may order the occupier to pay
an occupation rent[13]. Although the court has no ancillary power, on an
application under s 30, to order an occupation rent to be paid, this result can
be achieved indirectly, by the court indicating that a sale will be ordered unless
the person who is to remain in occupation undertakes to pay a rent[14]. This
approach will be taken whenever it is necessary in order to do equity between
the parties that an occupation rent should be paid[15].

(c) Trusts for sale created by will

A trust for sale not infrequently arises under a will. A testator may leave land
on trust for sale and provide for the proceeds to be divided between certain
beneficiaries. A direction to sell as soon as possible after the testator's death
signifies a contrary intention for the purposes of s 25(1) of the Law of Property
Act 1925. The trustees have no implied power to postpone the sale[16]. In the
case of a testamentary trust for sale the prima facie object of the trust is the
sale of the property. An occupying beneficiary under the trust cannot restrain

---

9   See *Martin v Martin* [1978] Fam 12, [1977] 3 All ER 762, CA.
10   *Re McCarthy (a bankrupt)* [1975] 2 All ER 857. Time to find alternative accommodation may
     be allowed: *Cousins v Dzosens* (1981) Times, 12 December (sale postponed for seven months
     to allow woman to be rehoused by Housing Association).
11   See *Bernard v Josephs* [1982] Ch 391 at 410, [1982] 3 All ER 162 at 175, CA, per Kerr LJ.
12   *Bernard v Josephs*, supra (four months given to buy out plaintiff); *Ali v Hussein* (1974) 231
     EG 372; *Pariser v Wilson* (1973) 229 EG 786 (option to purchase included in order by
     consent).
13   *Dennis v McDonald* [1981] 2 All ER 632; varied [1982] Fame 63, [1982] 1 All ER 590, CA.
     Voluntary non-occupation gives rise to no rent entitlement: *Jones v Jones* [1977] 2 All ER 231
     at 235, CA, per Lord Denning MR.
14   *Dennis v McDonald*, supra.
15   *Re Pavlou* [1993] 3 All ER 955, [1993] 1 WLR 1046, at 1050,959 per Millett J.
16   *Re Rooke's Will Trusts* [1953] Ch 716, [1953] 2 All ER 110; *Re Atkin's Will Trusts* [1974] 2 All
     ER 1 (direction to sell on death of life tenant; duty to sell within one year thereof).

a sale by the trustees, who are entitled to an order of possession against him[17]. The position is different when the beneficiary (eg the deceased's widow) has the right to occupy under a residence clause in the will, which directs that the property is not to be sold during her lifetime (or widowhood) without her written consent. Should a proposed sale by the trustees be opposed by the widow, resort must be had to s 30 of the Act[18]. The widow cannot prevent a sale if the executors require to dispose of the property for the payment of debts, ie for administration purposes.

(d) Bankruptcy of co-owner

On the bankruptcy of one of two (or more) co-owners, the bankrupt possesses no right against his trustee in bankruptcy to remain in occupation of any jointly-owned property. His beneficial interest vests in the trustee[19]. In practice the trustee will be anxious to have the entirety of the property sold, not simply the bankrupt's beneficial interest. This will normally be resisted by the other co-owner, in which case the trustee will be obliged to seek an order for sale under s 30 of the Law of Property Act 1925. No rule of law exists that the court must exercise its discretion in his favour. However, he is under a statutory duty to realise the bankrupt's assets for the benefit of his creditors, and the trustee's voice will usually be allowed to prevail. There may be exceptional circumstances justifying a refusal to grant an order[20].

When a matrimonial home is involved, the provisions of the Insolvency Act 1986 come into play. On any application for a sale order, the court is required under s 336(4) of the Act to have regard to certain factors in deciding how to exercise its discretion under s 30. These are: the creditors' interests, the spouse's conduct so far as contributing to the bankruptcy, the needs of any children, and all the circumstances of the case other than the bankrupt's own needs. Spouse includes a former spouse. Where, however, the application is made more than one year after the bankrupt's property vested in the trustee, the court is required to assume that the creditors' interests outweigh all other considerations, unless the circumstances are exceptional[1]. The facts that a sale will result in the bankrupt's wife not having enough money after the sale to be able to acquire another property, or that schooling problems may be caused to the children, are not exceptional circumstances. Rather they 'are the melancholy consequences of debt and improvidence with which every

---

17 *Barclay v Barclay* [1970] 2 QB 677, [1970] 2 All ER 676, CA.

18 Cf *Newcomb v Miller* (1962) 186 EG 331 (provision for occupation pending execution of trust; sale decreed).

19 Not the legal estate held as trustee for sale: Insolvency Act 1986, s 283(3)(a). For the effect of bankruptcy generally, see pp 259–262, ante.

20 See *Re Holliday (a bankrupt)* [1981] Ch 405, [1980] 3 All ER 385, CA (husband initiating own bankruptcy); *Mott, Re, ex p trustee of the property of the Bankrupt* [1987] CLY 212 (aged parent resisting sale sought by co-owner son's trustee). Contrast *Re Lowrie (a bankrupt)* [1981] 3 All ER 353, and other cases cited in note 10, p 307, ante.

1 Insolvency Act 1986, s 336(5). A bankrupt's spouse's existing rights under MHA 1983 are now binding on the trustee: s 336(2). The bankrupt may also have rights of occupation enforceable against his trustee if there are dependent children living with him in the house: s 337.

civilised society is familiar'[2]. What might constitute exceptional circumstances is if the house was specially adapted to meet the particular needs of a handicapped child[3].

Although the existence of an underlying purpose to provide a family home will be a relevant factor in the exercise of the court's discretion, when the dispute as to whether or not the property should be sold is between the co-owners of it, this will not normally be relevant when it is the trustee in bankruptcy who is seeking a sale. The underlying purpose of providing a home is regarded as having ended when one co-owner is divested of his beneficial interest in the property as a result of bankruptcy[4]. In unusual cases, the existence of a continuing underlying purpose may enable a petition for sale to be resisted. In *Abbey National plc v Moss*[5] an elderly widow was persuaded by her daughter to transfer the house from her sole name into the joint names of the two of them in order to simplify transfer on her death. It was expressly agreed that the house was not to be sold in the mother's lifetime. The daughter then forged her mother's signature on a mortgage, which purported to have been executed by them both and the action arose when the bank, as a creditor sought to have the property sold. The Court of Appeal, by a majority, refused to order a sale. It was held that the collateral purpose of the trust for sale, to provide a home for the mother, continued to survive and its continuing existence militated against the court ordering a sale. The case is clearly unusual, however, and in the more normal situation where one of two co-owners becomes insolvent, it is unlikely that a sale will be refused after a year from the bankruptcy.

On a sale of the property, the bankrupt's spouse is entitled to her (or his) share of the proceeds of sale[6], and the same will apply between co-habitees.

Charging orders. For the purpose of enforcing a court judgment awarding payment of money, the court can make a charging order on the debtor's property, which has the same effect as an equitable charge in writing created by him[7]. A charging order may now be imposed on the debtor's beneficial interest under a trust for sale[8]. Such a charge entitles the chargee to apply to the court under s 30 for a sale of the land, itself, in order to enforce the charge[9]. Although, unlike a trustee in bankruptcy, a judgment creditor owes no duty to

2   *Re Citro* [1991] Ch 142, [1990] 3 All ER 952 at 157, 962, CA, per Nourse LJ.
3   *Re Bailey (a bankrupt)* [1977] 2 All ER 26 at 284,32, [1977] 1 WLR 278, DC, per Walton J.
4   *Re Citro*, supra.
5   (1993) 26 HLR 249, CA. See [1994] Conv 331 (D N Clarke).
6   Unless the trustee is able to have the spouse's interest set aside under ss 339 or 423 of the Act. Cf *Re Densham (a bankrupt)* [1975] 3 All ER 726; *Re Windle (a bankrupt)* [1975] 3 All ER 987, both decisions on the Bankruptcy Act 1914, s 42 (now replaced by s 339). And see *Re Pittortou (a bankrupt)* [1985] 1 All ER 285.
7   Charging Orders Act 1979, ss 1(1), 3(4). As to its protection by registration, see s 3(2), (3), and p 391, post.
8   Ibid, s 2(1)(a)(ii); *National Westminster Bank Ltd v Stockman* [1981] 1 All ER 800. The contrary decision in *Irani Finance Ltd v Singh* [1971] Ch 59, [1970] 3 All ER 199, CA, has been abrogated.
9   *Harman v Glencross* [1986] Fam 81 at 101, [1986] 1 All ER 545 at 560, CA, per Fox LJ, applied in *Midland Bank plc v Pike* [1988] 2 All ER 434, [1986] 2 FLR 143.

the general body of creditors, the approach of the courts to an application for a sale of the property is the same as that taken as if the application is made by the trustee in bankruptcy[10].

2.   Statutory provisions protecting purchasers

(a) Generally

Various statutory provisions exist for the protection of a purchaser buying from trustees for sale. The trust is deemed to be subsisting until the land has been conveyed to or under the direction of the beneficiaries[11]. The purchaser can therefore rely on the trust notwithstanding notice that the proceeds of sale have become absolutely vested in a sole beneficiary of full age. But when the entire legal and equitable interests have become vested in a single person, the trust for sale ceases to exist[12]. A purchaser may, however, have to investigate the title to the equitable interests to satisfy himself of this[13]. With a statutory trust for sale the purchaser is not concerned to see that the sale by the trustees accords with the beneficiaries' wishes. If consents are made requisite to the execution of a trust for sale, the consent of any two persons is deemed sufficient[14].

(b) Overreaching

A purchaser of a legal estate from trustees for sale is not concerned with the trusts affecting the proceeds of sale[15], even though he has express notice of them because they are declared by the instrument creating the trust for sale[16]. As a matter of strict conveyancing practice it may be better to have two deeds, but this counsel of perfection is virtually ignored today and it is commonplace to declare the beneficial interests in the conveyance of the land to the trustees, at least where they hold for themselves in equity[17].

A conveyance in execution of the trust for sale overreaches all equitable interests arising thereunder, provided the proceeds of sale are 'paid to or applied by the direction of [not] fewer than two persons as trustees for sale' or a trust corporation[18]. This overreaching of beneficial interests takes effect

---

10 *Lloyds Bank plc v Byrne* (1991) 23 HLR 472, CA; *Abbey National Building Society v Moss*, supra. For the resolving of conflicts between the chargee and the debtor's wife who seeks a property adjustment order on divorce, see *Harman v Glencross*, supra, distinguishing *First National Securities Ltd v Hegerty* [1985] QB 850, [1984] 3 All ER 641, CA. See Thompson, *Co-Ownership*, 101,102.

11 LPA 1925, s 23.

12 *Re Cook, Beck v Grant* [1948] Ch 212, [1948] 1 All ER 231.

13 See p 284, ante. Cf the position on termination of a settlement, p 305 ante.

14 LPA 1925, s 26(1), (3).

15 LPA 1925, s 27(1), provided there is an effective conveyance: *Ahmed v Kendrick* (1987) Times, 12 November, CA (co-owner forging transfer; no overreaching, therefore beneficial interests held by purchaser and other co-owner).

16 LPA 1925, ss 2(1)(ii), 27(1).

17 See pp 558–560, post.

18 LPA 1925, ss 2(1)(ii), 27(2), as amended by the LP(Am)A 1926, Schedule. Strictly the beneficiaries' interests are overreachable ab initio without the aid of any statute, for under the doctrine of conversion their rights attach to the proceeds, not to the land. See *Irani*

notwithstanding occupation by a beneficiary under the trust. The Law of Property Act 1925, s 14, by which the interest of a person in possession of land is not to be affected by Part I of the Act, does not nullify the overreaching provisions in Part I. So, an occupying beneficiary cannot resist the purchaser's (or mortgagee's) claim for possession[19]. A purchaser who, knowing of the existence of the trust, fails to comply with this requirement does not obtain a good title and takes subject to the rights of the beneficiaries. There is no power to overreach *prior* legal rights, nor, it seems, prior equitable rights, notwithstanding that trustees for sale have all the powers of a tenant for life under the Settled Land Act 1925[20]. A sole trustee for sale can pass a good title in a transaction where no capital money arises. He can grant a valid lease provided no fine is taken, or effect an exchange of land where no equality money is received.

If a new trustee becomes necessary so as to comply with s 27(2), the appointment ought preferably to be contained in a separate deed, and not incorporated in the conveyance to the purchaser, particularly when the trust for sale relates to other land. A sound case can be made for effecting the appointment by a separate deed in every case, though it is common practice to include it in the purchase deed[1].

3.   Sale by sole trustee for sale

The safeguard of having at least two trustees or a trust corporation for the receipt of capital money has been called a fairly obvious reform[2]. A purchaser cognisant of the trust for sale will always insist on compliance with the statutory requirement, unless the Law of Property (Joint Tenants) Act 1964, considered below, is applicable. But many situations arise where a trust for sale exists, of which a purchaser is completely unaware. An apparent sole owner may in fact be a trustee for sale because eg his spouse has contributed to the purchase price[3], or to the making of substantial improvements to the property[4]. The application of s 27(2) of the Law of Property Act 1925 to this kind of situation has never been directly before the courts. It is significant that no paralysing provision, of the type found in the context of the Settled Land Act 1925[5] exists

---

Finance Ltd v Singh [1971] Ch 59 at 79–80, [1970] 3 All ER 199 at 203, CA, per Cross LJ; approved by Lord Oliver in *City of London Building Society v Flegg* [1988] AC 54, [1987] 3 All ER 435 at 447–448, HL.

19   *City of London Building Society v Flegg*, supra. See [1988] Conv 108 (M P Thompson).
20   LPA 1925, s 28 (1); *Re Ryder and Steadman's Contract* [1927] 2 Ch 62 at 82, CA, per Sargant LJ. Cf LPA 1925, s 2 (2) (ad hoc trust for sale).
1   See the correspondence in (1979) 123 Sol Jo 14, 30, 62, 77.
2   1 W & C (12th edn) 268.
3   *Waller v Waller* [1967] 1 All ER 305; *Bull v Bull* [1955] 1 QB 234, [1955] 1 All ER 253, CA (mother and son); *Eves v Eves* [1975] 3 All ER 768, CA (man and mistress).
4   See the Matrimonial Proceedings and Property Act 1970, s 37. See also *Hussey v Palmer* [1972] 3 All ER 744, CA (mother-in-law paying for extension to house owned by son-in-law).
5   SLA 1925, s 18(1)(a).

to render ineffective a conveyance not complying with s 27(2). A conveyance of land by a sole trustee for sale does vest the legal estate in the purchaser, but, if he has notice, actual or constructive, of the beneficial interests existing behind the trust for sale he will be bound by them[6]. What amounts to constructive notice in this situation is somewhat problematic and is fully considered in Chapter 13. Should the purchaser, by enquiry, discover the existence of an equitable interest, he cannot be compelled to take a conveyance from the sole trustee-vendor, with the beneficiary joining in[7]. He is within his legal rights to insist on the appointment of a second trustee[8] to obtain a good receipt and a conveyance having overreaching effect.

4. Sale by surviving trustee for sale

Once the legal estate and the equitable interests existing under a trust for sale have become vested in one and the same person in the same right, the trust for sale determines[9]. The Law of Property (Amendment) Act 1926, catered for this situation by adding to s 36(2) of the main Act a proviso that nothing in the Act should affect the right of a survivor of joint tenants, who was *solely and beneficially* interested, to deal with the legal estate as if it were not held on trust for sale[10]. However, a purchaser could never be sure that the vendor was solely and beneficially interested. There might have been a severance in equity, unknown to the surviving joint tenant, and notwithstanding the Act it became the tendency to preserve the trust for sale by appointing a new trustee.

(a) Law of Property (Joint Tenants) Act 1964
Adoption of this procedure is no longer necessary. The Law of Property (Joint Tenants) Act 1964, s 1, enacts that in favour of a purchaser of a legal estate a survivor of two or more joint tenants shall 'be *deemed* to be solely and beneficially interested if he conveys as beneficial owner or the conveyance includes a statement that he is so interested'. If the survivor has himself died, his personal representative can include in the conveyance a statement of the *survivor's* beneficial entitlement[11]. The Act is retrospective, being deemed to have come into operation on 1 January 1926 (s 2).

The Act does not apply in the following situations:
(i) if a memorandum of severance has been endorsed on or annexed to the conveyance to the joint tenants – this notifies the purchaser that the

---

6 See, eg, *Kingsnorth Finance Ltd v Tizard* [1986] 2 All ER 54, [1986] 1 WLR 783.
7 LPA 1925, s 42, but consider the common practice, discussed at p 191 ante, of joining the beneficiary as a party to the contract.
8 Preferably the other beneficiary so as to show his consent, otherwise the purchaser may become involved in proceedings to restrain the sale.
9 *Re Cook, Beck v Grant* [1948] Ch 212, [1948] 1 All ER 231.
10 According to Harman J in *Re Cook, Beck v Grant* [1948] Ch 212 at 214, [1948] 1 All ER 231 at 232, this sentence was an afterthought introduced ex cautela because of some danger, real or imaginary, thought to exist after the Act of 1925 had come into force.
11 See s 1(2). The personal representative must, of course, convey as such.

survivor is not solely and beneficially interested and reminds him of the
need to have another trustee appointed;

(ii) if a bankruptcy petition or receiving order has been registered under the
Land Charges Act 1972[12];

(iii) where the title to the land is registered[13].

The existence of a severance in equity[14] will not prevent a purchaser obtaining
a good title from a surviving joint tenant who conveys as beneficial owner,
provided no notice of severance is annexed to the conveyance. The Act was
not intended to be applicable where there never was a joint tenancy in equity[15].
For example, land is conveyed to A and B, and the conveyance expressly
declares that they hold as tenants in common in equity. On A's death B cannot
make a good title under the Act, for the conveyance discloses that he and A
were tenants in common. Should B wish to sell as a beneficial owner, he will
have to establish his right to do so. He may, for example, show that he inherited
A's share under A's will. But if the conveyance to A and B is silent as to their
beneficial entitlement, B can (it seems) utilise the Act, though this is not what
Parliament envisaged. This point is elaborated below.

(b) Difficulties raised by the Act

Though laudably brief, the Act is hardly a model of good draftsmanship[16]. It
creates several problems. It is uncertain whether a purchaser can safely rely
on the Act where no memorandum is endorsed, but he has express notice of
severance from other sources. Perhaps the better view[17] is that the Act affords
no protection in these circumstances. Its purpose was to remove difficulty where
no evidence of severance was forthcoming, and it can hardly be intended to
operate when the purchaser knows the survivor is not so entitled. This argument
may also offer a solution in the following situation. Suppose that land is vested
in A and B as beneficial joint tenants but C, a non-party to the deed, contributes
to the purchase, so acquiring an equitable interest in it. A dies and B later
purports to convey the land to P as beneficial owner. The B-P conveyance
cannot overreach C's interest; the purchase money is not paid to two trustees
for sale. Notwithstanding the 1964 Act, it is thought that B will not take free
from C's interest if he has actual notice of it. It ought also to follow that P will
take subject to C's interest, should C's occupation be such as to give P
constructive notice thereof if P fails to make reasonable inquiries.

A defect of far greater consequence is that the Act may tend to increase
fraud at the expense of the beneficiaries – in marked contrast to the provisions
of s 27(2) of the Law of Property Act 1925, which were designed to minimise
fraud and mistake. The Act of 1964 can be used, it seems, in cases where

---

12   See p 391, post. Bankruptcy effects an involuntary severance.
13   Section 3. For the position on a sale of registered land, see p 348, post.
14   For severance by statutory notice, see LPA 1925, s 36(2), and *Harris v Goddard* [1938] 3 All
     ER 242, CA.
15   37 *Halsbury's Statutes* (4th edn), 389n.
16   (1964) 28 Conv (NS) 329, 330; (1966) 30 Conv (NS) 27 (P R Jackson).
17   Contra, M & W, 441. It is, however, significant that the Act says the survivor is *deemed* entitled,
     not that the statement in the deed is to be taken as *sufficient evidence* of his entitlement; cf
     AEA 1925, s 36 (7), p 323, post.

originally the legal joint tenants were tenants in common in equity, or where they had no equitable interest but held on trust for others. Take the example given at the end of para *(a)* above. Suppose that A dies, leaving his share in the property to a third party, C. B then contracts to convey the land to P 'as beneficial owner'. The curtain principle ensures that P has no means of knowing that B really holds on trust for himself and C. Since the conveyance to A and B says nothing as to B's entitlement in equity, P must assume that B is solely and beneficially interested and able to deal with the legal title as if it were not held on trust for sale. The Act may have remedied a constant nuisance in conveyancing[18], but at the expense of exposing the beneficiaries to a greater risk of fraud. Previously cautious conveyancing practice, by insisting upon the appointment of a second trustee, did at least pay lip-service to s 27(2) and in so doing reduced the prospect of malpractice. Nowadays a surviving trustee can cheerfully disregard such restrictions, unless the purchaser knows the true position. Bringing the equitable interests on to the title seems the only safe antidote to prevent abuse of the Act.

One final problem warrants discussion. Again an illustration will help. Land is conveyed to A and B as beneficial joint tenants. A dies without severing the joint tenancy in equity. B then dies, leaving the property to C absolutely. B's executor assents to the property vesting in C. Subsequently C contracts 'as beneficial owner' to sell the land to P. How can C satisfy P that B was solely and beneficially entitled at the time of his death? The assent to C may contain a statement that B was so entitled[19]. Though this will not assist C, who is not a purchaser, the declaration may well avail P, notwithstanding that P was not a party to the assent. The validity of this point is uncertain, however[20]. More than likely the assent will not include any statement of B's entitlement. In this case it would appear to be advisable for B's executor to join in the C-P conveyance for the sole purpose of declaring that B was solely and beneficially interested. Failing this, the only safe way is for C to insert in the contract for sale a special condition requiring P to assume that B was so entitled at the time of his death.

5. The Trusts of Land and Appointment of Trustees Act 1996

The existence of two systems of creating settlements of land has, for a long time, been the subject of critical comment, the main thrust of this criticism being that it causes unnecessary complication[1]. The Law Commission accepted this point of view and proposed a new trust of land to replace both the trust for sale and the strict settlement.[2] This proposal has now been enacted as the Trusts of Land and Appointment of Trustees Act 1996, which is expected to come into force in 1997.

18 M & W, 440.
19 The Act is to be construed as one with the LPA 1925; see s 4(1). Accordingly 'conveyance' includes an assent.
20 Cf (1977) 41 Conv (NS) 423, 424–26 (P W Smith).
 1 See, eg, (1961) 24 MLR 123 (G A Grove).
 2 (1989) Law Com No 181.

Under the terms of the Act, it will be impossible, except in certain very limited circumstances, to create a Settled Land Act settlement[3]. Instead a new trust of land, replacing both the trust for sale and the strict settlement, will be created. Under this new trust, the trustees will have the power either to sell or to retain the land and will be under no duty to sell it. The doctrine of conversion will be abolished. The resolution of disputes as to whether or not the property is to be sold will be dealt with under the Act which, unlike s 30 of the Law of Property Act 1925, which it will replace, lists criteria to which the courts must have regard when exercising their discretion. These criteria include the welfare of children living in the property and the interests of secured creditors.

The new trust of land, when the legislation is brought into force, will, to a considerable extent simplify the law and remove some of the more artificial aspects of the existing trust for sale. It will remain the case, however that, because settlements existing at the time when the Act is brought in to force will remain unaffected, familiarity with the law relating to such settlements will continue to be necessary for some time to come.

D   Transactions by personal representatives

1.   Devolution on death and power to act generally

On death, if the deceased dies testate, his real property devolves on his personal representative[4], and he possesses, in relation to both realty and personality, a statutory power of sale for administration purposes[5]. If the deceased dies intestate after 1 July 1995, his estate will, pending a grant of administration, vest in the Public Trustee[6]. The difference between the legal position of an executor appointed by will and that of an administrator must not be overlooked. The former derives his title from the will, whereas the latter derives his title from the grant of administration. This has important consequences.

(a) Executor
Even prior to obtaining a grant of probate an executor has power to do all the acts which are incident to his office, except such as necessitate production of a grant in order to prove his title[7]. For instance, he can exercise the statutory power of appointing a new trustee[8], exercise an option to purchase vested in

3   Settlements existing at the date of the coming in to force of the Act will be unaffected.
4   AEA 1925, s 1(1). For this purpose 'real estate' includes leaseholds: s 3(1)(i). At common law only the personal estate (including leaseholds) devolved on him.
5   Ibid, s 39(1)(iii), giving all the statutory powers conferred on trustees for sale by LPA 1925, s 28(1), as amended. Further, he has the same common law power of sale as was exercisable by a personal representative before 1926 in relation to the deceased's leaseholds: AEA 1925, s 2(1).
6   Law of Property (Miscellaneous Provisions) Act 1994, s 14. Previously the deceased's estate devolved on the President of the Family Division of the High Court: AEA 1925, s 9.
7   *Re Stevens, Cooke v Stevens* [1897] 1 Ch 422 at 429, per North J; affd [1898] 1 Ch 162, CA.
8   Under the Trustee Act 1925, s 36 (1); *Re Crowhurst Park, Sims-Hilditch v Simmons* [1974] 1 All ER 991; but the new trustee needs the grant of representation to prove his title: ibid.

the deceased[9], serve a notice to quit, or enter into a binding contract to sell land forming part of the deceased's estate[10]. However, neither he nor a successor in title would be able in court to establish or rely on his title to act without producing a grant of representation. Whilst in theory a conveyance of land executed before a grant would vest the legal title in the purchaser, in practice no purchaser would complete the transaction until a grant had been obtained, and the executor could never compel the purchaser to accept the title without first taking out a grant.

It was previously the case that one of two (or more) executors could enter into a binding contract to sell the deceased's freehold land[11]. The position now is that all the executors must be parties to the contract[12]. If one executor purports to contract on behalf of himself and his co-executor, there is no enforceable contract and the purchaser is left to his remedy in damages against the signatory for damages for breach of warranty of authority[13].

(b) Administrator

A person entitled to a grant of administration has no power to act qua administrator before a grant is made to him. When granted, letters of administration relate back to the date of the deceased's death, enabling him (eg) to sue for trespass to land or for breach of covenant committed during the interval between death and the grant[14]. This doctrine of relation back does not operate to validate acts, such as issuing a writ[15] or making a contract for sale, done at a time when he lacked the authority to act. Although it is uncertain, at common law, whether on appointment, one administrator can, without the concurrence of his co-administrator, enter into a binding contract to sell land forming part of the estate[16], it is thought that such uncertainty will be resolved to achieve a result consistent with that pertaining to executors. All administrators must sign the contract.

2. Power to assent

Section 36(1) of the Administration of Estates Act 1925, empowers a personal representative to assent to the vesting of a legal estate in the beneficiary or other person entitled thereto. This power is confined to estates which have *devolved* upon the representative. The consequence is as follows. Suppose that

---

 9 Barnsley, *Land Options*, (2nd edn) 97; cf *Kelsey v Kelsey* (1922) 91 LJ Ch 382 (notice validly served *on* executors before grant).
10 See (1977) 41 Conv (NS) 300.
11 *Fountain Forestry Ltd v Edwards* [1975] Ch 1, [1974] 2 All ER 280.
12 Law of Property (Miscellaneous Provisions) Act 1994, s 16 amending AEA 1925, s 2(2).
13 *Sneesby v Thorne* (1855) 7 De GM & G 399; *Fountain Forestry v Edwards,* supra. Cf *Collier v Hollinshead* (1984) 272 EG 941 (lease by one executor binding on co-executor held to have adopted transaction).
14 *R v Inhabitants of Horsley* (1807) 8 East 405 (trespass to land); *Re Pryse's Goods* [1904] P 301 at 305, CA, per Stirling LJ.
15 *Ingall v Moran* [1944] KB 160, [1944] 1 All ER 97, CA.
16 See the authorities reviewed by Brightman J in *Fountain Forestry Ltd v Edwards,* supra.

B, a beneficiary under T's will, survives T but dies before the property is vested in him, and that T's personal representatives assent to the property vesting in B's own representatives. When the latter come to vest the property in the person entitled under B's will or intestacy, they should, strictly speaking, do so by way of a conveyance under seal. Technically s 36(1) does not apply, for the legal title did not devolve on B's representatives, it was vested in them. However, it was held in *Re Stirrup's Contract*[17] that if in such circumstances B's representatives execute an assent under seal, that document is effectual to pass the legal title to the ultimate beneficiary, and a purchaser from him has no right to have the formal defect rectified. An assent under hand would probably not have been effective[18].

3.   Form of assent

To be operative, s 36(4) requires the assent to be in writing, signed by the personal representative, and to name the person in whose favour it is given[19]. An assent therefore constitutes an exception to the basic rule which demands a deed to convey a legal estate[20]. Prima facie it relates back to the deceased's death and the statutory covenants for title may be implied in it as in a conveyance by deed[1]. All proving executors must execute the assent.

(a) Express assent

A simple assent of freehold land by a sole executor may be as follows:

> I, AB of [etc] as the personal representative of XY late of [etc] do this   day of   198– hereby as such personal representative assent to the vesting in CD of [etc] of ALL THAT [parcels] for an estate in fee simple[2] and I acknowledge the right of the said CD to production of the probate of the will of the said XY and to delivery of copies thereof[3].

An assent in this form will normally be executed under hand only. Alternatively, it may be an inter partes document between AB and CD. This form is frequently adopted when the assent is by deed because, for example, the beneficiary enters into an indemnity covenant to observe restrictive covenants created by the testator. Unless absolutely vital, it is safer not to include recitals in an assent[4].

---

17   [1961] 1 All ER 805, applying LPA 1925, ss 63(1), 205(1)(ii).
18   Contra, (1961) 25 Conv (NS) 491 (L Elphinstone).
19   Suggestions that the beneficiary should be named and not merely described as 'the beneficiary' or 'myself' are not thought to be sound, provided the assentee's name appears elsewhere in the document. See Emmet, para 11.112.
20   LPA 1925, s 52(1), (2)(a).
  1   AEA 1925, s 36(2), (3). See p 664, post.
  2   Or 'for all the estate and interest of the said XY at the time of his death'. The wording in the text is preferable. And see p 276, ante.
  3   This follows the statutory precedent (see LPA 1925, Sch 5, Form No 8) with the addition of an acknowledgement for production. An assent by a personal representative in his own favour should not include any acknowledgement. Not being given 'to another', it cannot, if included, take effect under LPA 1925, s 64 (1), p 579, post.
  4   See p 323, post. In some cases they may be unavoidable, eg to take advantage of the Law of Property (Joint Tenants) Act 1964; see (1977) 41 Conv (NS) 423 (P W Smith).

(b) Implied assent
A written assent is necessary to pass a *legal* estate[5]. For many years practitioners had acted on the assumption, though without clear supporting authority, that a written assent was unnecessary where there was no 'passing' of the legal estate, but merely a change in the capacity in which the estate was held. An assent could be implied from the circumstances[6]. However, this implied assent myth was exploded by Pennycuick J in *Re King's Will Trusts, Assheton v Boyne*[7], where in the space of one judgment the learned judge cast into the melting pot of uncertainty many titles that had previously been accepted as sound on the basis that no assent was necessary. The decision was not welcomed by conveyancers[8] and prompted a provisional recommendation by the Law Commission for a change in the law[9]. On consultation, however, it transpired that the decision was not as problematic as has been thought, largely as a result of the relaxed attitude taken by the land registry[10]. Despite this approach, the fact remains that the decision can cause a defect in title to occur and two situations where problems can occur require discussion.

(i) *Executor and beneficiary the same person.* Suppose that T (a testator) devised realty to B and appointed B as his executor. B proved the will after T's death. Whilst it was clearly desirable (and recognised to be so) for B to execute an assent in his own favour so as to furnish documentary evidence of the change of capacity, it was not considered fatal if no assent was executed. B already had the legal estate qua executor; there was no 'passing' within s 36(4), merely a change of character from personal representative to beneficial owner. On completion of his administrative duties B came to hold the legal estate as beneficial owner without any written assent. Pennycuick J dismissed this argument rather summarily. In his view sub-s (4) contemplates that a person may by assent vest an estate in himself in another capacity; this vesting necessarily implies a divesting of the estate in the original capacity[11]. In this situation, therefore, B should execute an assent in his own favour.

The inconveniences created by this ruling readily become apparent when considering how title should be made on B's death intestate. In the absence of any assent the legal estate is at the time of B's death vested in B as T's executor. Technically, T's estate is unadministered and before title can be made a grant

5　But not an equitable interest: *Re Hodge* [1940] Ch 260; *Re Edwards' Will Trusts* [1982] Ch 30, [1981] 2 All ER 941, CA, though Buckley LJ appears to have overlooked (at p 949) the point that an administrator has no common law power to make an assent; see [1982] Conv 4. No assent is necessary before a personal representative becomes a trustee on completion of his administrative duties. The change in capacity is automatic: *Eaton v Daines* [1894] WN 32; *Re Ponder* [1921] 2 Ch 59 (administrator). But see Parry & Clark, *The Law of Succession* (7th edn), 379–80.
6　As was the position before 1926; see *Wise v Whitburn* [1924] 1 Ch 460.
7　[1964] Ch 542, [1964] 1 All ER 833.
8　See Emmet, para 11.121; Farrand (2nd edn), 115–119; (1964) 28 Conv (NS) 298 (J F Garner). See also [1976] CLP 60 (E C Ryder). The shortening of the period of investigation of title may cause problems associated with the decision to diminish.
9　(1987) Law Com WP No 105, para 4.23.
10　See (1989) Law Com No 184, para 1.6.
11　[1964] Ch 542 at 549, [1964] 1 All ER 833 at 836.

of administration de bonis non to T's estate is required. If this is not appreciated and, for instance, B's own administrator conveys the property to C, C will not obtain a good legal title[12]. No problem arises if B dies testate, leaving an executor who proves B's will. This executor becomes T's executor by representation[13] in relation to T's unadministered estate (ie the outstanding legal estate), and a conveyance by B's executor passes the legal estate to C. Similarly, if during his lifetime but without executing any assent in his own favour, B conveys the property to C as 'beneficial owner', this conveyance is effective to vest in C a good title to both the legal and the equitable interests. By virtue of s 63(1) of the Law of Property Act 1925, B's conveyance is effectual to pass to C all the estate, right and title which B has in the property, including the legal estate vested in him as personal representative.

(ii) *Personal representative and trustee.*   The actual decision in *Re King's Will Trusts* concerned the effectiveness of a deed of appointment of an additional trustee, executed by a surviving executor who had not executed any assent in his own favour. Pennycuick J held that no legal estate vested in the appointee, and he rejected an argument that the appointment itself operated as an assent[14]. This decision may usefully be contrasted with *Re Cockburn's Will Trusts, Cockburn v Lewis*[15]. Here it was held that personal representatives, having completed their administrative duties, became trustees and were empowered by s 36 of the Trustee Act 1925 to appoint new trustees of the will, and such appointment was effective, apparently without any assent, to confer on the new trustees the powers and discretions contained in the will. Yet, somewhat illogically, they have no power to deal with the legal estate in the land forming part of the trust until an assent is executed in their favour[16].

Despite its unpopularity the decision in *Re King's Will Trusts* is logically correct[17]. Its hostile reception is to be interpreted as conveyancers' outrage at the upsetting of an established but erroneous practice. Take the illustration on page 321. If B's title depends on an implied assent of the legal estate in himself, a purchaser from him has no means of knowing that B is beneficially entitled under T's will[18], unless he calls for production of the will itself. But

12   To remedy the defect it will be necessary to trace the person entitled to take out a grant of representation to T's estate in accordance with the Non-Contentious Probate Rules 1987, SI 1987 No 2024, r 20 – an exercise possibly resulting in expense and delay. The technical defect in C's title will be cured by his possession of the land for 12 years.

13   See AEA 1925, s 7.

14   On the basis of the vesting declaration implied in the appointment by s 40(1)(b) of the Trustee Act 1925. It is sometimes asserted that the legal title ought to have been held to have vested in the additional trustee under LPA 1925, s 63(1) (cf *Re Stirrup's Contract* [1961] 1 All ER 805, p 320, ante, which was not cited to Pennycuick J), but it is arguable that s 63(1) cannot conveniently be applied where X wishes to vest an estate in X and Y, as distinct from Y alone.

15   [1957] Ch 438, [1957] 2 All ER 522.

16   Ryder, op cit, 72; but see [1984] Conv 423 (C Stebbings).

17   The decision was not challenged in *Re Edwards' Will Trusts* [1982] Ch 30, [1981] 2 All ER 941, CA. See also *Beebe v Mason* (1980) 254 EG 987, CA (absence of written assent no bar to sole executor-beneficiary's claim to possession qua resident landlord under Rent Act 1977, s 12(1)(c), Sch 2, para 1).

18   Cf AEA 1925, s 36 (7), p 323, post (written assent to be sufficient evidence of beneficiary's entitlement).

this is contrary to the scheme of the Administration of Estates Act 1925, under which the grant of probate acts as a curtain screening the beneficial interests created by the will.

(c) Will creating trust for sale

When the will creates a trust for sale, it becomes necessary to decide whether the assent should be made upon the trust for sale contained in the will, or on an independent trust for sale created by the assent[19]. The former method results in the abstracting of the will on any subsequent sale in execution of the trust in order to establish that the property is subject to a trust for sale. The main drawback of the latter scheme is that the appointment of new trustees of the will and of the assent must be by separate instruments, notwithstanding that the same persons must be appointed as new trustees of both the will and the assent[20].

4. Statutory provisions protecting purchasers

Since 1925, a will no longer constitutes a document of title and a purchaser is not concerned with the beneficial interests arising thereunder. Where the executor has assented to the vesting of the testator's property in a beneficiary, the assent will be abstracted but not the will. How then can a purchaser from that beneficiary be sure the assent was made in favour of the proper person? The Administration of Estates Act 1925, s 36(7), enacts that in favour of a purchaser the assent shall be taken as sufficient evidence that the person in whose favour it is made is the person entitled to have the legal estate conveyed to him, unless notice of a previous assent or conveyance affecting the legal estate has been annexed to or endorsed on the grant.

(a) Sufficient evidence

This provision does not debar objection to the title, if a defect is otherwise discovered. 'Sufficient' does not mean 'conclusive'. In *Re Duce and Boots Cash Chemists (Southern) Ltd's Contract*[1], the land was in fact settled and a recital in the assent showed this, but the operative part of the document purported to vest the property in a beneficiary absolutely. It was held that a purchaser was not precluded from objecting to the title. Although a copy of the will is annexed to the grant by the Probate Registry, a beneficiary will not, unless he is also the executor, have the original grant, only an examined abstract or photocopy (without the copy will) which the purchaser will inspect. He is, therefore, not able to obtain independent confirmation of the beneficiary's entitlement by

---

19 Executors apparently have power to create an independent trust for sale; see LPA 1925, Sch 5, Form No 9.
20 Trustee Act 1925, s 35(1); LPA 1925, s 24(1). The respective merits of the two methods are considered in Hallett, 110–13. Another problem area with assents is the appropriate form to adopt in favour of a surviving tenant in common; see (1973) 37 Conv (NS) 42 (A M Pritchard); 2nd edn, 334–35.
1 [1937] Ch 642, [1937] 3 All ER 788.

peeping inside the grant[2].

Somewhat curiously, an assent relating to land formerly settled is rendered unchangeable; if it does not name any trustees of the settlement, a purchaser is *bound and entitled* to assume that the assentee is entitled absolutely and beneficially[3]. Why other assents are to be regarded merely as 'sufficient evidence' is not apparent.

(b) Endorsements

Section 36(5) of the Act enables a person in whose favour an assent or conveyance of a legal estate is made by a personal representative to have notice thereof endorsed on or annexed to the grant of probate. It appears to be good conveyancing practice for the solicitor acting for the personal representative to make the endorsement without being requested to do so[4]. Every assentee should ensure that this simple precaution is taken. Otherwise he runs the risk of losing his estate to a subsequent purchaser[5] to whom the representative states in writing[6] (invariably in the conveyance) that he has not given or made any previous assent. The purchaser is entitled to rely on this statement, though false, as sufficient evidence[7] that no assent has been given, unless there is an endorsement. Under s 36(6) the conveyance operates to transfer the legal estate to the purchaser as if no previous assent had been made.

This statement of no previous assent applies in favour only of a purchaser, not an assentee (sub-s (11)). Yet it is commonplace to incorporate such a statement in the assent itself. This seems a misguided practice, serving little effective purpose[8]. It affords no protection to the assentee against either a prior purchaser or an earlier assentee. Nor is it of assistance to a purchaser from the assentee, for the statement is of value only when inserted in a conveyance by *the personal representative* to a purchaser.

5. Conveyance by personal representative to purchaser

A personal representative possesses a statutory power of sale [9] in relation to the deceased's property, as we have previously noticed. Various provisions exist

---

2 On a sale by an executor-beneficiary, his solicitor needs to ensure that the purchaser's solicitor sees no more that he is entitled to (ie, not the annexed copy will). Cf *Smith v Robinson* (1879) 13 Ch D 148 (purchaser free to object to pre-root of title defect discovered when vendor's solicitor inadvertently produced earlier document for inspection).
3 SLA 1925, s 110(5), p 304, ante.
4 Emmet, para 11.118, citing The Law Society's Digest, Opinion no 642.
5 This can occur not infrequently, though inadvertently, when land vested in the beneficiary is later conveyed in error to a purchaser. Cf *Bligh v Martin* [1968] 1 All ER 1157.
6 In addition to criminal liability attaching to a false statement made knowingly, the representative would seem to owe the assentee a duty of care when making the statement. But would the failure to have a notice endorsed amount to contributory negligence?
7 But not conclusive; cf s 36(7), discussed above. So a purchaser would not get a good title despite the absence of any endorsement, if the prior assent had been abstracted.
8 See 8 Ency F & P, 707 (by way of caution only), 769, Forms 2:9, 2:10; cf Hallett, 84, 101, Form 2.
9 AEA 1925, s 39(1)(iii), p 315, ante.

for the purchaser's protection. He is not concerned to inquire why the property is being sold[10], nor is the purchase invalidated by reason only that he has notice that all the debts and other liabilities have been discharged[11]. On a conveyance to a purchaser it is customary to endorse notice of it on the probate. Failure to do this is not prejudicial[12] as it might be for a beneficiary. Whenever the title comprises a dealing with land by personal representatives, a later purchaser will always be concerned to check the existence of endorsements. For this reason it is that since 1925 a grant of representation has become a document of title[13].

A sole personal representative *as such* can give a valid receipt for purchase money, even though he may hold on trust for sale (eg on an intestacy)[14]. But the limitations on this power must be noted. He must be acting *as such*, ie in his capacity as personal representative. Suppose A and B hold land on trust for sale for C and D in equity. A dies, then B. X, B's sole proving executor, could not pass a good title by himself. A sale by him would not be qua executor of B but qua trustee, executing the trust for sale on the instructions of C and D. His conveyance would vest the legal title in the purchaser, but it would not overreach the rights of the beneficiaries. X should therefore appoint another trustee[15].

E Mortgages[16]

1. Sale by legal mortgagee

(a) The power of sale
By virtue of s 101(1) of the Law of Property Act 1925, every legal mortgagee has a statutory power of sale when the mortgage money has become due, ie when the legal date of redemption has passed. However, this power does not become properly exercisable unless and until one of the conditions laid down by s 103 of the Act has been satisfied, namely:
(i)   notice requiring payment of the mortgage money has been served on the mortgagor who has defaulted in payment for three months; or
(ii) some interest under the mortgage is in arrears for at least two months; or
(iii) a breach by the mortgagor of some provision in the Act or in the mortgage (other than the covenant for payment of principal and interest).
In practice most mortgagees are content to rely on their statutory power of sale. It is commonplace to extend[17] or modify the circumstances when it can

---

10   Trustee Act 1925, s 17. 'Trustee' includes 'personal representative'; ibid, s 68(17).
11   AEA 1925, s 36(8).
12   Ibid, s 36(6) (without prejudice to any previous disposition made in favour of another purchaser).
13   *Re Miller and Pickersgill's Contract* [1931] 1 Ch 511.
14   LPA 1925, s 27 (2).
15   Cf *Re Myhill, Hull v Myhill* [1928] Ch 100. See also the Trustee Act 1925, s 18(2), (3), which expressly makes X's right to exercise any power or trust vested in the surviving trustee, B, subject to the restrictions imposed in regard to receipts by a sole trustee not being a trust corporation.
16   See (1991) Law Com No 204.
17   Variations or extensions operate in the like manner as if contained in the Act: s 101(3).

be exercised. Building societies frequently provide for the statutory power to apply free from the restrictions imposed by s 103. Some societies expressly reserve a right to sell if the mortgagor commits an act of bankruptcy. The mortgagee is authorised to sell by public auction or private contract, subject to such conditions respecting title or other matters as he thinks fit, with power to vary or rescind the contract and to re-sell, without being answerable for loss occasioned thereby[18]. He is perfectly entitled to sell under conditions of sale in common use[19], and may leave the whole of the purchase price outstanding on mortgage[20]. The mortgagee does not need the consent of the mortgagor or of the court to sell, but a court order for possession will be necessary before a sale with vacant possession whenever the mortgagor is in occupation. In the case of residential property the mortgagor has certain statutory rights under the Administration of Justice Act 1970[1]. The ability to sell with vacant possession may also be thwarted by occupants claiming equitable rights enforceable against the mortgagee[2].

(b) Exercise of power

(i) *Genuine sale.*   Provided the power of sale has become exercisable, the court will not inquire into the mortgagee's motive in selling[3]. There must, however, be a genuine sale. It has long been the rule that a mortgagee cannot sell to himself, either alone or with others, neither to a trustee for himself, nor to a person employed in the conduct of the sale[4]. There is no inflexible rule that he cannot sell to a company in which he has an interest[5]. Nevertheless, such a transaction will be set aside unless the mortgagor and the company establish that the sale was in good faith and at the best price reasonably obtainable at the time of sale. A sale by auction does not necessarily prove the validity of the transaction[6].

18   LPA 1925, s 101(1)(i); *Wright v New Zealand Farmers' Co-operate Association of Canterbury Ltd* [1939] AC 439, [1939] 2 All ER 701, PC (recession on purchaser's default and re-sale at a loss; mortgagee not accountable for difference).

19   *Falkner v Equitable Reversionary Society* (1858) 4 Drew 352 (condition empowering rescission on ground of objectionable requisition upheld).

20   *Northern Developments (Holdings) Ltd v UDT Securities Ltd* [1977] 1 All ER 747, (1976) 32 P & CR 376 at 380, per Megarry J.

1   Section 36, as extended by the Administration of Justice Act 1973, s 8.

2   Eg an equitable tenancy in common held by a spouse or other person contributing to the acquisition of the property. See further pp 361–372, post.

3   *Nash v Eads* (1880) 25 Sol Jo 95, CA (mortgagee selling out of spite).

4   *Farrar v Farrars Ltd* (1888) 40 Ch D 395 at 409, CA, per Lindley LJ; *Martinson v Clowes* (1882) 21 Ch D 857, CA (purchase by mortgagee's secretary). A local authority mortgagee may in certain limited situations and with leave of the county court vest the property in itself instead of selling: Housing Act 1985, s 452(1), Sch 17, which reverses the ruling in *Williams v Wellingborough Borough Council* [1975] 3 All ER 462, CA. This power does not relate to mortgages granted to secure tenants under Pt V of the Act (the right to buy provisions). The mortgagee may purchase the property when the sale is under the direction of the court: *Palk v Mortgage Services Ltd* [1993] Ch 330, [1993] 2 All ER 481, CA.

5   *Farrar v Farrars Ltd,* supra; *Tse Kwong Lam v Wong Chit Sen* [1983] 3 All ER 54, PC, unless mortgagee and purchaser are both companies controlled by the same person: *Australian and New Zealand Banking Group Ltd v Bangadilly Pastoral Co Pty Ltd* (1978) 139 CLR 195.

6   Ibid, at 59, 60, per Lord Templeman. See further p 328, post, note 6.

(ii) *Duty of care.*   The mortgagee is not a trustee of the power of sale for the mortgagor. He is perfectly justified in giving priority to his own interests if they clash with the mortgagor's. Salmon LJ expressed the mortgagee's position in the following terms[7]:

> Once the power has accrued, the mortgagee is entitled to exercise it for his own purposes whenever he chooses to do so. It matters not that the moment may be unpropitious and that by waiting a higher price could be obtained. He has the right to realise his security by turning it into money when he likes.

This is not to say that he can ignore the mortgagor's interests completely. For as Salmon LJ concluded, both on principle and authority, the mortgagee owes a duty to him to take reasonable precaution to obtain the true market value of the property[8] at the date of sale. Although there has been judicial support for the view that the mortgagee owes a duty of care with regard to the timing of the sale[9], it is now clear that there is no such duty and that the mortgagee can sell at any time to suit his own interests[10], provided, of course, that the power of sale has become exercisable. Building Societies are under a statutory duty to obtain the best price reasonably obtainable[11] but it is doubtful if this duty differs from the duty imposed upon other mortgagees by the common law.

(iii) *Scope of duty.*   It was thought at one time that the origin of the mortgagee's liability was tortious in nature and that people other than the mortgagee could possibly bring an action if they were within a sufficient degree of proximity to the mortgagee[12]. It is now well established that the basis of liability is equitable[13]. This means that one cannot address the issue of liability solely on the ground of foreseeability of damage. Although the basis of holding the mortgagee liable to a surety seemed to be based on tortious principles[14], such liability is now explained on equitable principles because 'Equity intervenes to protect a surety'[15]. A similar duty is owed to subsequent mortgagees of whom the mortgagee has notice[16]. There is no liability, however, to an equitable co-owner of the property of whom the mortgagee has notice[17]. The mortgagee is liable for the negligence of a receiver acting as his agent[18], and of professional

7   *Cuckmere Brick Co Ltd v Mutual Finance Ltd* [1971] Ch 949 at 965, 968, [1971] 2 All ER 633 at 643, 646, CA.
8   Or the best price reasonably obtainable as Lord Templeman expressed it in *Lam's* case, ante, at 59.
9   *Standard Chartered Bank Ltd v Walker* [1982] 3 All ER 938 at 942, CA, per Lord Denning MR.
10 *Bank of Cyprus (London) Ltd v Gill* [1980] 2 Lloyd's Rep 51, CA; *China and South Sea Bank Ltd v Tan Soon Gin* [1990] 1 AC 536; [1989] 3 All ER 839, PC.
11 Building Societies Act 1986, Sch 4, para 1. See [1982] Conv 246, on the possible consequences of non-compliance.
12 See (3rd edn) p 298.
13 *China and South Sea Bank Ltd v Tan Soon Gin*, supra; *Downsview Nominees Ltd v First City Corpn Ltd* [1993] AC 295, [1993] 3 All ER 626, PC.
14 *Standard Chartered Bank Ltd v Walker*, supra.
15 *China and South Sea Bank Ltd v Tan Soon Gin*, supra, at 544, 841 per Lord Templeman.
16 See LPA 1925, s 105.
17 *Parker-Tweedale v Dunbar Bank* [1991] Ch 12, [1990] 2 All ER 577, CA.
18 *American Express International Banking Corpn v Hurley* [1985] 3 All ER 564. The mortgagee is entitled to an indemnity in the absence of an express exclusion. The receiver himself owes a duty to the mortgagor and and surety.

advisers, such as surveyors and estate agents[19]. It has been held that an agent is liable in negligence to the mortgagor for selling the property at an undervalue[20], although now that a more restrictive view is taken as to when a plaintiff can recover damages in respect of pure economic loss[1], it is perhaps, questionable whether this authority would be followed today.

(iv) Breach of duty. In deciding whether the mortgagee has breached his duty of care, the facts must be looked at broadly; he will not be adjudged to be in default unless he is plainly on the wrong side of the line[2]. Mortgagees have been held to have fallen short by failing to advertise the mortgaged property as having the benefit of planning permission for flat development[3], for ignoring professional advice to sell with vacant possession[4], and for failing to protect vacant premises from vandalism[5]. On a sale by public auction a breach of duty may be evidenced by organising the sale at short notice and with minimum publicity, or by fixing a reserve price without taking expert advice[6].

A mortgagee will also be liable if he instructs a valuer to sell the property on a 'crash sale' basis. The property must be properly exposed to the market[7].

(c) Protection of purchaser

The power of sale is treated in law as exercised when the mortgagee enters into a binding contract to sell the property. The contract precludes redemption pending completion so long as it subsists, provided the sale is not tainted with any irregularity[8]. On exercise of the power a purchaser is not concerned to inquire whether any case has arisen to authorise the sale, or due notice has been given, or the power is otherwise properly and regularly exercised, and the conveyance is deemed to have been made in exercise of the statutory power unless a contrary intention appears[9]. A purchaser from a mortgagee who abstains from inquiry as to the exercisability of the power is not deemed to have constructive notice of any irregularity. But he must otherwise be in good faith[10]. The fact that a sale is made at an undervalue does not per se show that the purchaser is in bad faith[11], unless the price is so low as to be itself evidence

19   *Cuckmere Brick Co Ltd v Mutual Finance Ltd* [1971] Ch 949, [1971] 2 All ER 633, CA.
20   *Garland v Ralph Pay Ransom* (1984) 271 EG 106.
1   See *Murphy v Brentwood District Council* [1991] 1 AC 398, [1990] 2 All ER 908, HL.
2   *Cuckmere Brick Co Ltd v Mutual Finance Ltd,* ante, at 969, 646, per Salmon LJ. Liability was not established in *Palmer v Barclays Bank Ltd* (1971) 23 P & CR 30; *Waltham Forest London Borough v Webb* (1974) 232 EG 461; *Bank of Cyprus (London) Ltd v Gill* [1980] 2 Lloyd's Rep 51, CA.
3   *Cuckmere Brick Co Ltd v Mutual Finance Ltd,* ante.
4   *Holohan v Friends Provident and Century Life Office* [1966] IR 1.
5   *Norwich General Trust v Grierson* [1984] CLY 2306.
6   See *Standard Chartered Bank Ltd v Walker* [1982] 3 All ER 938, CA; *Tse Kwong Lam v Wong Chit Sen* [1983] 3 All ER 54, PC.
7   *Predeth v Castle Phillips Finance Co Ltd* [1986] 2 EGLR 144, CA. See [1986] Conv 442 (M P Thompson).
8   *Property and Bloodstock Ltd v Emerton* [1968] Ch 94, [1967] 3 All ER 321, CA.
9   LPA 1925, s 104(2), (3). The mortgagee will be liable in damages to 'any person damnified' by an unauthorised or irregular exercise of the power of sale: sub-s (2).
10   'Purchaser' means 'a purchaser in good faith ...': LPA 1925, s 205(1)(xxi).
11   *Lord Waring v London and Manchester Assurance Co Ltd* [1935] Ch 310.

of fraud[12]. If on the other hand he has *actual* notice of some impropriety the cases indicate that he cannot invoke the statutory protection[13]. It is also enacted that the purchaser's title shall not be impeached on the ground that the sale is irregular or improper[14]. This provision is of limited application; it operates only where *a conveyance is made* in exercise of a power of sale. It is conceived that the court could, at the suit of the mortgagor, restrain the mortgagee from completing an irregular sale, irrespective of the purchaser's lack of knowledge of the impropriety as between the mortgagor and mortgagee[15]. Even *after* completion the court has power to intervene in a proper case to set aside the conveyance to the purchaser if the parties have been guilty of fraud or collusion, or the purchaser had actual knowledge of some irregularity[16]. The conveyance would not be completely devoid of effect, for equity would treat the purchaser as having taken a transfer of the mortgage[17]. In effect he would acquire the property subject to the mortgagor's right of redemption.

When the property is conveyed at an undervalue in breach of the mortgagee's tortious duty, the mortgagor's primary remedy is to sue for damages. He may have the transaction set aside if the purchaser had notice of the breach of duty[18]. The court will be more willing to intervene in this manner where there exists a special relationship between the parties and they fail to establish the validity of the transaction. But even here relief is discretionary[19].

(d) Consumer Credit Act 1974

This Act applies to certain non-exempt mortgages where the loan does not exceed £15,000[20]. It excludes from its scope mortgages granted by building societies, local authorities and other specified institutional lenders, such as insurance companies[1]. Any mortgage regulated by the Act is enforceable only on an order of the court: s 126. No sanction is prescribed for breach of this requirement. It is expressly enacted by s 157(2) that nothing in the Act is to affect the operation of the provisions of s 104 of the Law of Property Act 1925.

---

12 *Warner v Jacob* (1882) 20 Ch D 220 at 224, per Kay J.
13 *Bailey v Barnes* [1894] 1 Ch 25 at 30, CA, per Stirling J; *Lord Warning v London and Manchester Assurance Co Ltd*, supra, at 310 per Crossman J; M & W, 938.
14 LPA s 104 (2).
15 See on a similarly worded statutory provision *Forsyth v Blundell* (1973) 129 CLR 477 (mortgagee acting with calculated indifference to mortgagor's interests); *Holohan v Friends Provident and Century Life Office* [1966] IR 1.
16 See *Jenkins v Jones* (1860) 2 Giff 99; *Selwyn v Garfit* (1888) 38 Ch D 273, CA, both cases involving express powers of sale. See also the authorities cited in note 13, ante.
17 *Selwyn v Garfit* (1888) 38 Ch D 273, CA.
18 *Cuckmere Brick Co Ltd v Mutual Finance Ltd* [1971] Ch 949 at 971, [1971] 2 All ER 633 at 648, CA, per Cross LJ.
19 *Tse Kwong Lam v Wong Chit Sen* [1983] 3 All ER 54 at 63, PC, per Lord Templeman (mortgagor's inexcusable delay in prosecuting claim barring equitable relief).
20 The limit as from 20 May 1985: SI 1983, No 1878. For earlier mortgages the original limit of £5,000 applies. The Act is aimed at second mortgages by which home owners may be tempted to borrow imprudently for personal needs: M & W, 931.
1 Section 16(1). Banks are also exempt. To the surprise of the Building Societies Association, some building society mortgages below £15,000 have been brought within the Act by the Building Societies Act 1986. See also p 595, post.

Seemingly, therefore, a purchaser will be able to acquire a good title to the land despite the lack of a court order. He will not, it is thought, be under a duty to ascertain that the necessary order has been granted; but if the failure to obtain one were to come to his notice, he could properly object to the title which the court would not enforce against him in its absence.

(e) Effect of conveyance

At the most the mortgagee possesses a term of years absolute in the mortgagor's land, and where the mortgage is created by way of legal charge his interest ranks merely as a legal interest. Nevertheless, in both cases a conveyance by the mortgagee in exercise of his statutory power of sale operates to vest in the purchaser the mortgagor's fee simple estate, subject to any legal mortgage having priority, but free from all subsequent mortgages and the mortgagor's equity of redemption[2]. In *Duke v Robson*[3], a contract for sale entered into by a mortgagee in exercise of his power of sale was held to override a prior contract for sale of the mortgaged property made by the mortgagor, notwithstanding that it had been registered as a C(iv) land charge. The court declined to restrain the mortgagee from performing his contract.

In the case of leasehold property the assignment is similarly effectual to pass to the assignee the unexpired residue of the mortgagor's term of years[4], creating privity of estate between the lessor and the assignee and rendering the covenants in the lease enforceable against the latter.

2.   Equitable mortgages

The power of sale exists only when the mortgage is made by deed. It was formerly the case that an equitable mortgage could be created by deposit of deeds[5]. This is no longer the case, it having been held that the effect of s 2 of the Law of Property (Miscellaneous Provisions) Act 1989 is that this age old practice is no longer sufficient to create an equitable mortgage because the contract to create a legal mortgage is not in writing signed by both parties[6]. Even under the old law, an equitable mortgagee would not have the power of sale unless the deposit was accompanied by a deed. If, now, there is a deposit of title deeds and a deed setting out the intention to create an equitable mortgage, then, it is thought, the courts will hold, first that an equitable mortgage has been created, and second, that a power of sale will arise once the money has become due.

2   LPA 1925, ss 88(1), 104(1).
3   [1973] 1 All ER 481, CA; cf *Lyus v Prowsa Developments Ltd* [1982] 2 All ER 953 at 957, per Dillon J.
4   LPA 1925, s 89(1); *Rust v Goodale* [1957] Ch 33, [1956] 3 All ER 373.
5   See, eg, *Re Wallis & Simmonds (Builders) Ltd* [1974] QB 94, [1974] 1 All ER 561.
6   *United Bank of Kuwait v Sahib* [1996] 3 All ER 215, CA. For criticism of the first instance decision, which was upheld on appeal, see [1994] Conv 465 (M P Thompson).

A basic difficulty, however, will still face an equitable mortgagee. He has no statutory power to convey the mortgagor's *legal* estate[7], unless his power to sell has been extended by means of one or other of the usual devices[8]: either (i) a declaration of trust by the mortgagor that he holds the mortgaged property on trust for the mortgagee, or (ii) the creation of a power of attorney in the mortgagee's favour enabling him to vest the legal estate in the purchaser. This power of attorney enables the mortgagee to convey the legal estate without first having to call upon the mortgagor to execute a legal mortgage[9]. To ensure that the conveyance operates under the statute to give the purchaser a title free from subsequent charges, it is essential that the vendor is expressed to *convey* as mortgagee in exercise of his statutory power of sale. If he merely *releases* unto the purchaser the land discharged from his mortgage, the conveyance will be construed as an ordinary sale by the mortgagor (acting albeit by the mortgagee-attorney) with the concurrence of his mortgagee. The purchaser will then only acquire the same title as the mortgagor has, freed from the mortgagee's mortgage but subject to any subsequent charges[10].

Where the mortgage is not made by deed the mortgagee can only enforce a sale, in the absence of the mortgagor's concurrence, under an order of the court. On the mortgagee's application the court may direct a sale on such terms as it thinks fit[11]. It may make a vesting order in favour of a purchaser or appoint a person to convey to him, or vest in the mortgagee a legal term of years absolute to enable him to effect a sale[12] and make title out of court.

F   Title by adverse possession

1.   Formal contracts

Where it is appreciated that the vendor's title is wholly dependent on the Limitation Act 1980, a formal contract should provide that the vendor shall convey such title as he has in the property. He should also offer in support a statutory declaration that he has been in undisturbed possession of the property

---

7   *Re Hodson and Howes' Contract* (1887) 35 Ch D 668, CA. In *Re White Rose Cottage* [1965] Ch 940 at 951, [1965] 1 All ER 11 at 15, CA, Lord Denning MR suggested obiter that the LPA 1925, s 104 empowered an equitable mortgagee to convey the legal estate, and that *Re Hodson and Howes' Contract* was not authoritative on s 104. The validity of this opinion awaits further judicial confirmation. It is thought that the view is difficult to reconcile with LPA 1925, ss 88 and 89; see (1965), 29 Conv (NS) 222, and Emmet, para 25.125.

8   See Fisher and Lightwood's *Law of Mortgage* (9th edn) pp 49–51.

9   *Re White Rose Cottage* [1965] Ch 940 at 956, [1965] 1 All ER 11 at 18, CA, per Harman LJ. It is usual for the memorandum of deposit to contain an undertaking by the mortgagor to execute a legal mortgage when called upon, although this is implied from the mere fact of deposit: *Pryce v Bury* (1853) 2 Drew 41.

10   *Re White Rose Cottage* [1965] Ch 940, [1965] 1 All ER 11, CA. For a precedent, see 19 Ency F & P, 1347, Form 7:K:31.

11   LPA 1925, s 91(2).

12   LPA 1925, s 90(1). The vesting order has the same effect as a conveyance by the mortgagor: ibid, s 9(1).

or of the rents and profits for so many years without acknowledging the right of any person. Where only a small plot of land is involved the contract may simply stipulate that no title shall be required beyond the vendor's possession[13]. The vendor must ensure he is in a position to procure the proferred declaration. In *George Wimpey & Co v Sohn*[14]:

> ... vendors contracted to convey all such right title and interest as they had in certain property and in support they agreed to make or procure a declaration of undisputed possession for 20 years.

This condition was held to constitute a warranty[15] as to the evidence to be furnished in support of their title, and their failure to fulfil that obligation exactly entitled the purchaser to rescind. Even had the vendors established 12 years' adverse possession, the purchaser could still have declined to accept the title. As Harman LJ explained, a vendor who offers only such right as he has must abide by a condition which obliges him to support it in a certain way; he cannot affect to perform his contract by an assertion of a different right and the production of different evidence[16].

(a) Title part documentary, part possessory

The decision in *Re Atkinson and Horsell's Contract*[17] shows that if at some point in the title offered there is a defect but thereafter the vendor can establish a good possessory title, the title can be forced on the purchaser – even in the absence of any contractual provision. According to *Games v Bonnor*[18], the vendor can enforce the contract if his possessory title has accrued before the commencement of his action, even though he did not have good title at the contractual date for completion, unless the purchaser has in the meantime effectively rescinded the contract for want of title.

In the absence of any contractual provision, the purchaser is entitled to have the possessory title verified by proper evidence. At least 12 years' uninterrupted adverse possession without any acknowledgement of the disseisee's title must be proved. Such possession following a defect occurring more than 12 years previously will suffice if the disseisee was a sole beneficial owner[19], but not necessarily if he was merely a limited owner. Thus, where the land is subject to a settlement, 12 years' adverse possession against the life tenant, though sufficient to bar his equitable title, does not extinguish his legal estate which remains vested in him until all the beneficiaries under the settlement have been barred[20]. As for the ultimate remainderman, his title is not extinguished unless he fails to take action within twelve years of the

---

13   For specimen clauses see 18 Ency F & P, 645–47.
14   [1967] Ch 487, [1966] 1 All ER 232, CA.
15   Cf *Re Spencer and Hauser's Contract* [1928] Ch 598.
16   At 505 and 237, respectively. *Re Atkinson and Horsell's Contract* [1912] 2 Ch 1, CA, was distinguished on the ground that there the vendor's title could not be questioned.
17   [1912] 2 Ch 1, CA, p 279, ante.
18   (1884) 54 LJ Ch 517, CA.
19   Even if he dies during the relevant twelve years and is succeeded by a person under a disability time does not stop running; Limitation Act 1980, s 28(2).
20   Limitation Act 1980, s 18(2).

dispossession *or* within six years of his own interest falling into possession, whichever is the longer period[1].

One consequence of the reduction in the period of investigation of title will be to increase the risk of defects remaining undiscovered, particularly where dispossession of a trustee occurred before the root of title and the beneficiaries' rights remain unbarred[2]. It also follows that if the purchaser discovers a defect during his investigation, it is less likely to have been cured by adverse possession than previously when 30 years was the statutory period[3].

2.   Open contracts

A title resting solely on the vendor's possession (or that of his predecessors) for at least twelve years, though supported by statutory declarations, does not suffice to establish a good title under an open contract. He must show that the possession has extinguished the interests of all claimants to the original title. This entails tracing the title from a good root to the point when the then legal owner was dispossessed. Thereafter possession for at least twelve years may, depending on the facts, constitute a good title if verified by sufficient evidence. On the other hand, adverse possession for even 30 years (the maximum period for the recovery of land in cases of disability[4]) may not be adequate to bar all rightful claims[5]. The land may be subject to a settlement, in which case, as we have just seen, time may not begin to run against a remainderman until his interest falls into possession.

1   Limitation Act 1980, s 15(2).
2   The Law Commission was unable to suggest any solution to the question whether the loss should fall on the purchaser or the beneficiaries; Law Com Report No 9, para 46(2).
3   For the position when title deeds are lost, see pp 171–172, ante.
4   Limitation Act 1980, s 28(4).
5   Statements to the contrary, eg Williams, *Title*, 570–72, 18 Ency F & P, 645, note 12, are misleading.

Chapter 11

Deducing title III: registered land

A   Introduction

As we saw in the first chapter, one of the primary objectives of registered conveyancing is to abolish the repeated investigation of title each time a property is sold. The effect of a person being registered as proprietor of freehold land with an absolute title is to vest the fee simple in him, subject to the various matters set out in the Land Registration Act 1925[1]. This vesting is backed by the State guarantee. The purchaser's principal concern is the state of the vendor's title at the time of the sale, which, subject to qualifications previously noted[2], he can ascertain by inspecting the vendor's register of title. As the leading authority on registered conveyancing emphasises[3], the purchaser can quickly and safely accept the evidence of title offered by the vendor *without the need to investigate the past history of the title*[4]. But this in no way obviates the need for a purchaser of registered land to check that the title offered accords with the title contracted to be sold. For example, in *Faruqi v English Real Estate Ltd*[5], a purchaser contracted to buy at an auction land which was sold 'subject to the entries on the register of title'. On later inspecting these he discovered that the land was subject to restrictive covenants imposed by an old deed, no copy or abstract of which had been produced to the Registry on first registration. The vendor could not provide any details of the covenants, and the purchaser was held entitled to recover his deposit.

The absence of any need to investigate the past history of the title does not absolve a vendor from having to establish his title by the production of proper evidence. His obligations are defined by the Act, obligations which vary according to the type of title involved.

---

1   LRA 1925, ss 5, 20. References in this chapter to the Act are to be taken as references to the Land Registration Act 1925, unless otherwise indicated.
2   Pages 42–45, ante.
3   R & R, 2.01 (italics supplied). Compare the more restrained exposition of the advantages of the land registration system contained in this latest work with the fulsome praise appearing in the 3rd edn (1972) (pp 9–10). Are successive Chief Land Registrars becoming less enamoured with the system or more conscious of its defects?
4   The position is otherwise in the case of titles less than absolute; see p 338, post.
5   [1979] 1 WLR 963; *Re Stone and Saville's Contract* [1963] 1 All ER 353 (failure to disclose restrictive covenants).

B Freehold land

1. Absolute titles

The vendor's obligations on a sale or other disposition of registered land are contained in s 110 of the Act. Certain documents must be supplied to the purchaser (other than a lessee or chargee), notwithstanding any stipulation to the *contrary*, others must be furnished in the absence of any contrary agreement. Save for documents falling within either of these categories, s 110 (3) enacts that it is not necessary for the vendor to furnish the purchaser with any abstract or other written evidence of title, or any copy or abstract of the land or charge certificate.

(a) Documents that must be supplied (s 110(1))
The vendor is obliged to supply at his own expense[6] the following documents: (i) a copy of the subsisting entries on the register; (ii) a copy of the filed plan; and (iii) copies or abstracts of documents noted on the register. Documents in groups (i)-(iii) have to be furnished 'if required'. This is a puzzling limitation, since it is difficult to imagine a situation where a purchaser will be happy to contract, let alone complete, without wanting to see copies of (i) and (ii).

(i) *Inspection of the register.* It was formerly the case that, because the register of title was private, the vendor had to furnish the purchaser with authority to inspect the register. This is no longer the case. Section 112 of the Land Registration Act 1925[7] provides that any person may inspect and make copies of any entry on the register. The vendor's authority to inspect is, therefore, no longer necessary.

(ii) *Copy of subsisting entries.* Somewhat surprisingly, the Act does not require the vendor to furnish office copy entries issued by the Registry. Some practitioners are content to supply their own photocopies of the entries in the land or charge certificate. This practice cannot be recommended. Office copies are preferable for a number of reasons. First, under s 113 of the Act they are admissible in evidence to the same extent as the originals and a person suffering loss by reason of an inaccuracy is entitled to an indemnity. Second, they will be up to date. Unless the land certificate has recently been compared with the register an adverse entry, such as a caution or a notice protecting a spouse's statutory right of occupation may have been entered against the title and the solicitor may not be aware of this. Such an entry is not likely to come to light until shortly before the completion date and there may well be a resultant

---

6 Unless the purchase price does not exceed £1,000 (a figure unchanged since 1925!); s 110(1)(a). Even in such cases the vendor normally bears the cost.
7 This section was inserted into the Act by LRA 1988, s 1. See also Land Registration (Open Register) Rules 1991, r 2.

delay, to the annoyance of both parties, while the vendor seeks to clear the offending blot on his title.

Under a contract governed by the Standard Conditions of Sale, the vendor is, on exchange of contracts, obliged to furnish the purchaser with office copy entries[8] and this obligation will not be met by the sending of a photocopy of the land certificate[9]. If the Conveyancing Protocol is used, the vendor is required to furnish office copies with the draft contract[10].

(iii) *Copy of filed plan.*   This is needed because registered land is always described by reference to a plan[11]. On a transfer of part of the land comprised in a registered title, a careful comparison of the intended transfer plan with the filed plan should always be undertaken[12].

(iv) *Copies or abstracts of documents noted on the register.*   Where, for instance, the charges register refers to a deed or transfer that imposes restrictive covenants without reproducing the covenants verbatim, the purchaser should call for a copy or abstract of the deed. Section 110(4) of the Act provides that as between vendor and purchaser any abstract filed in the Registry, or copy of, or extract from, a deed referred to on the register, must be assumed to be correct and to contain all material parts of the original document. The purchaser is not entitled to its production, but this does not relieve him of the necessity of inspecting the abstract or copy. The vendor's obligations do not extend to providing copies of charges or incumbrances to be discharged or overridden at or prior to completion, eg a mortgage, or to matters not affecting the land to be sold, eg on a transfer of part of the registered property. He must, of course, supply a copy or abstract of any mortgage subject to which the property is sold.

(b) Copies to be supplied in the absence of contrary agreement (s 110(2))
The vendor must at his own expense furnish copies, abstracts and evidence (if any) in respect of appurtenant rights and interests as to which the register is not conclusive. The register is conclusive as to appurtenant rights, particulars of which appear as part of the description of the property. It is not conclusive if the Registrar has merely entered a note that the proprietor claims that an appurtenant right exists, eg by prescription[13].

---

8   SCS 4.2.1. In the event of a delayed completion causing financial loss to the purchaser, could he charge his own solicitor with professional negligence for not insisting on office copies, even in the absence of a contractual right to them? And consider the letters in (1982) 79 LSG 298, (1984) 81 LSG 2425, 2737.
9   *Wood v Berkeley Homes (Sussex) Ltd* (1992) 64 P & CR 311, CA.
10   National Conveyancing Protocol, p 24.
11   But see Ruoff and West, *Concise Land Registration Practice* (3rd edn), 86, suggesting that a copy of the filed plan is not often required on a transfer of the whole of the registered land; *sed quaere*, and cf R & R, 17.04.
12   The recent case of *AJ Dunning & Sons (Shopfitters) Ltd v Sykes & Son (Poole) Ltd* [1987] Ch 287, [1987] 1 All ER 700, CA, p 680, post, illustrates the dangers of failure to do this.
13   LRR 1925, r 254(1), (2).

Evidence of matters excepted from the effect of registration must be produced. These include (i) overriding interests and (ii) matters excepted on registration with a possessory or qualified title. As to the former it has been said[14] that it is seldom necessary or profitable to pursue this subject beyond the register, considering that overriding interests are matters on which abstracts of title under the unregistered system cannot be relied on for complete information, and that it is the practice to note on the register at the time of first registration any appearing in the abstracts that seem to be of importance. It is clear, however, that a vendor who is aware of some overriding interest not mentioned on the register should disclose it in the contract and, apart from any excluding provision, must satisfy the purchaser by proper evidence of its nature.

Special stipulations can be inserted in the contract restricting or excluding the purchaser's rights in relation to matters mentioned in this section. In any case, his right is limited to such abstracts and evidence as he would have been entitled to if the land had not been registered.

(c) Sub-sales

Particular difficulty may be encountered in complying with these obligations in the case of a sub-sale or resale. Suppose A transfers part of his land to B who contracts to sell that land to C before the Registry have completed B's registration. Being a sale of part of A's land, a new register has to be opened for B's title, but B cannot fulfil his statutory duty of supplying C with copy entries of a non-existent register. Instead B supplies an office copy of A's register, and C applies for an official certificate of search, which will reveal the existence of the A-B transfer and will also indicate whether it is in order and whether or not it contains restrictive covenants or easements affecting C's land. C can then ascertain from B the precise terms of B's transfer and ultimately complete his own transaction in the normal way, after having made a second official search to secure the statutory protection for his transfer[15].

A further potential difficulty which can arise is a result of s 110(5) of the Act[16]. This section provides that when the vendor is not himself registered as the proprietor of the land he shall, notwithstanding any stipulation to the contrary, either procure the registration of himself as a proprietor of the land or procure a disposition from the proprietor to the purchaser. The difficulty potentially arises if there has been a transfer from the head vendor to the intermediate vendor, who has applied to be registered as proprietor. If, as was previously the case, there was a considerable delay in the application for registration being processed then the intermediate vendor could not comply with the terms of the section. Now that the average time for effecting registration is only three weeks[17], this problem should be academic.

---

14 Brickdale, 259. And see p 51, ante.
15 See Registered Land Practice Note M.1.
16 See Thompson, *Investigation and Proof of Title*, 75.
17 Land Registry Annual Report 1994–95, p 57.

2.   Possessory titles

Where land is registered with a possessory title, the vendor must supply copy entries and an authority to inspect the register in the normal way. In relation to the estates and interests excepted from the effect of registration, the purchaser can call for the same evidence of title as he would have been entitled to had the land not been registered[18]. Since the State indemnity does not extend to excluded matters, he needs to ascertain to what extent the title might be upset by some claim arising under any excepted estate. However, the vendor is free to contract out of this additional statutory obligation altogether, and it is common practice for the contract to preclude a purchaser from calling for evidence of excepted matters[18]. In the absence of any contrary stipulation, the title prior to first registration should be deduced in the normal unregistered manner so as to show that the title will not be disturbed. Thereafter the abstract will consist of a copy of the subsisting entries (as required by s 110(1) of the Act), save that as regards any incumbrance subsisting at the date of first registration the ordinary abstract should be continued to the date when it was discharged or to the date of the sale. A purchaser of a possessory title should consider the possibility of the title being converted into absolute[20].

3.   Building estates

The advantages of registration of title are particularly demonstrated in the case of building estates. On a sale of property on a registered building estate, the developer's obligations as to title remain the same; however the normal procedure has been adapted under special arrangements[1] devised by the Registry to ensure that individual sales-off proceed smoothly.

(a) Approved lay-out plan

The developer may obtain official approval of his estate lay-out plan. This plan indicates each individual plot and the extent of its boundaries. It has two main advantages. First, it enables negotiations between vendor and purchaser to proceed without an office copy of the filed plan in a manner to be described. Secondly, the purchaser, when applying for an official search of the register, need only refer to the plot number on the plan instead of having to provide a separate plan. This procedure can only operate effectively provided no departure from the approved plan is undertaken without the Registry's knowledge. Failure to notify the Registry promptly of any alteration may result in the cancellation of applications for the registration of transfers based upon the old plan.

---

18   LRA 1925, s 110(2). For the effect of registration with a possessory title, see pp 33–35, ante.
19   See eg 18 Ency F & P, 657, Forms 3:B:20C and E.
20   Page 36, ante.
 1   For full details, see Registered Land Practice Notes B.6 and B.7, Practice Leaflet No 7, and R & R, 18.01–18.13.

(b) Dispensing with filed plan – Form 102
The transfer of newly developed properties on a building estate to individual purchasers poses problems not normally encountered in the usual transaction involving a single property. The developer's solicitor may be faced with the task of supplying numerous office copies of the filed plan which, for practical reasons, is never likely to show land recently removed from the title. The Registry is faced with the difficulty of producing plans copied from an original which is constantly in use for recording transfers of part. The purchaser's solicitor, when confronted with a filed plan covering a large area of land, may be unable to ascertain that his client's land is within the vendor's title.

Where the lay-out plan has been officially approved, the purchaser's solicitor can, prior to exchanging contracts, apply to the Registry for a certificate of official inspection of a filed plan[2]. This document (known as Form 102) certifies that the purchaser's plot is comprised within the vendor's title and states whether or not the plot is affected by any colour or other reference shown on the plan and mentioned in the entries on the register. The theory is that the purchaser can dispense with an inspection of the filed plan, for the certificate furnishes him with the required information. It does not confer any priority for the subsequent registration of the transfer, but its accuracy is guaranteed under s 83(3) of the Act[3] so that a purchaser suffering loss through an error in the certificate is entitled to be indemnified in respect thereof.

That this procedure has undoubted merits cannot be denied. Yet allegations have been made that it is not always self-sufficient, for the purchaser needs to inspect the plan to discover, eg the extent of restrictive covenants or the existence of rights of way[4]. This is a valid criticism, and a purchaser desiring maximum protection should insist upon a copy of the filed plan. There is nothing in the relevant Rules to relieve the vendor of his statutory obligation to supply an office copy of this plan.

One defect has been acknowledged. Form 102 does not show the extent of the vendor's title. The purchaser cannot satisfy himself that the vendor has power to grant the easements provided for in the contract, such as rights of way or drainage. However, it is possible when applying for the certificate to ask the Registry to confirm that the proposed rights are within the vendor's title. Vendors' solicitors can make arrangements for this information to be automatically included within the certificate[5].

(c) Approved transfers
The Registry is willing to approve a standard form of transfer for the estate, thereby enabling attention to be drawn to unusual features in the lay-out plan or the proposed contents. Approval of the transfer facilitates the proof of easements. A written assurance will be given by the Registry to the vendor that

2 Land Registration (Official Searches) Rules 1993, No 3276, r 10. In practice the purchaser's solicitor obtains this as a matter of conveyancing convenience, though strictly the vendor should apply for it under s 110(1) in place of a copy of the filed plan.
3 Ibid, r 10(3), (7). For s 83(3), see p 97, ante.
4 See the correspondence in (1969) 66 LS Gaz 93, 227.
5 See Practice Note B.7.

easements granted in the standard form will be registered as appurtenant to purchasers' individual titles. A purchaser relying upon this assurance is relieved of the duty of investigating the vendor's power to grant the easements[6].

4. The title shown procedure

The Registry has introduced a procedure, known as the title shown procedure, for adoption on the sale and subsequent first registration of the title of individual properties on large building estates. It is confined to unregistered land within an area of compulsory registration. The procedure has no statutory basis, and vendors cannot, therefore, insist on its use as of right. The prospective vendor deduces his title to the Registrar in the normal way. If he is satisfied as to the title, a letter is written to the vendor's solicitor stating the terms upon which an absolute title will be granted to subsequent purchasers. This letter is not just a mere opinion as to title. If copied and issued to prospective purchasers, it can be relied upon by them and the normal deduction and investigation of title can be dispensed with; the purchaser knows that the title is acceptable to the Registrar. There must, of course, be a conveyance to the purchaser. All proper searches must be undertaken, and a normal application for first registration submitted to the Registry. The contract for sale should provide for the adoption of this procedure.

This procedure is used when an established estate is being disposed of, as when a vendor offers to sell the freehold reversion to existing lessees. The Registry is only willing to operate the scheme in relation to estates comprising at least 70 houses, where the vendor's title is derived from a single conveyance in his favour. In the case of new development, a builder who has acquired his land prior to the introduction of compulsory registration can achieve the same result by registering his title voluntarily once the area has been made one of compulsory registration, notwithstanding the Land Registration Act 1966[7].

C   Leasehold titles

1.   The vendor's obligations

(a) Grant of lease
It was previously the case that the Land Registration Act 1925 did not alter the basic principles laid down by the Law of Property Act 1925[8] governing the investigation of title on the grant or sale of an existing lease. Difficulties could then arise as to the ability of a purchaser to inspect the register in respect of the superior freehold title[9]. Now that the register is open to public inspection,

---

6   This will have been done by the Land Registry.
7   The Act does not prohibit voluntary registration *within* compulsory areas. Should this step be taken, the individual sales-off will lead to first registration of title. For the voluntary registration of certain building estates within non-compulsory areas, see p 26, ante.
8   Section 44 (2)–(4), p 290, ante.
9   See the 3rd edition of this work, pp 309–10.

these difficulties have, to a large extent, disappeared. Until the register became open to public inspection, the purchaser was not entitled to office copies of the lessor's registered freehold title[10]. As any person may now make an official search of the register, this problem no longer exists. If the term of the lease is to exceed 21 years, under the Standard Conditions of Sale, the seller must deduce a title which will enable the buyer to be registered with an absolute leasehold title[11].

(b) Sale of existing registered lease

As was the case before the register became public, the purchaser is entitled to inspect the register and to obtain office copy entries and a copy of the filed plan. The vendor must also supply a copy or abstract of the lease which, in effect, constitutes the root of title as in unregistered conveyancing. This is necessary because the property register contains merely brief particulars of the lease, such as the date, parties, term and rent. The Registry does not retain the original lease; at the most a copy is held there, and then not always[12].

Apart from any contractual stipulation to the contrary[13], the assignee cannot investigate the freehold title. This will only be a problem if the freehold title is not registered. In the sale of land registered with an *absolute* leasehold title, the purchaser need not concern himself with the superior title; the title is guaranteed even against defects affecting the superior title and all restrictions affecting the reversion are entered on the lessee's title[14].

(c) Grant of underlease

The position on the grant of an underlease was previously somewhat obscure, it being unclear whether the grantee had the statutory right to call for information as to the *lessee's* registered title[15]. Again, this uncertainty is dispelled by the opening of the register to public inspection.

(d) Non-registrable leases

On the sale of a lease for a term not exceeding 21 years (which cannot, it will be recalled, be substantively registered), title must be deduced in the normal unregistered manner. To this extent, unless and until the provisions regulating these leases are modified[16], registration of title will never entirely supplant the unregistered system with its deducing and investigation of title.

10 LRA 1925, s 110 applies only in favour of a purchaser other than a lessee or a chargee. See now Land Registration (Official Searches) Rules 1993, r 2.
11 SCS 8.2.4.
12 An assignee of a lease applying for first registration, unlike an original lessee, is not required to supply a copy of a lease. The Registry is not prepared, except in exceptional circumstances, to supply an office copy of any filed copy lease: R & R 21.22.
13 Cf LSC (1984 rev) 8(2).
14 See section 2, post.
15 See the 3rd edition of this work, p 310.
16 In its Report No 125, the Law Commission declined to recommend any reduction in the length of the term laid down as the criterion for registrability on the grounds of doubtful benefit to tenants and increased financial burdens on the Registry: paras 4.27–29.

2.   Notice of superior title

As in unregistered conveyancing[17] an intending lessee or purchaser of registered leasehold property may be deemed to have notice of matters affecting a superior title, even though he has no means of ascertaining what they are. The problem exists in relation to good leasehold titles. By virtue of s 50(2) of the Act, on notice of a restrictive covenant (other than one between landlord and tenant) being entered on the register, the proprietor and the persons deriving title under him are deemed to be affected with notice of it. In *White v Bijou Mansions Ltd*[18], Simonds J held that this provision extended to a purchaser of leasehold property without actual knowledge of the existence of the covenants affecting the registered freehold title. Consequently, restrictive covenants noted against a registered freehold title are binding upon a lessee or a purchaser from him, a situation which was made worse by the fact that he was not permitted by statute to inspect the register of the freehold title. Now that the register is open to public inspection, that particular problem has disappeared. The difficulty does not arise with absolute leasehold titles. Not only has the Registrar (at some time) approved the freehold title, but also on first registration a note will have been made on the lessee's title of all restrictive covenants appearing on the register of the superior title[19].

Restrictive covenants made between a lessor and a lessee cannot be noted on the register of title[20]. An underlessee is therefore bound by such covenants in the headlease if he has actual or constructive notice of them.

3.   Miscellaneous matters

A purchaser of a registered leasehold will be concerned to check that the rent is not in arrears and the covenants duly performed. He is entitled to the same evidence by way of proof as in unregistered conveyancing[1]. Where the lease contains a covenant against alienation without consent, the Registrar does not need to call for evidence of compliance before registering the transferee. Registration of an unlicensed transaction vests the legal title in the transferee. However, the entry on the transferor's title, excepting from the effect of registration all rights arising under an unlicensed transaction[2], ensures that the transferee cannot claim any indemnity if his title is upset by the lessor. The discussion in chapter 10 relating to licences to assign is also relevant to purchasers of registered leases containing the restriction.

---

17   If the freehold title is unregistered, the position of a lessee whose title is registered is the same vis-à-vis the freehold as if the lease were not registered.
18   [1937] Ch 610, [1937] 3 All ER 269; affd [1938] Ch 351, [1938] 1 All ER 546, CA.
19   See R & R, 5.09.
20   LRA 1925, s 50(1).
 1   LPA 1925, s 45(2), p 295, ante.
 2   LRR 1925, r 45.

D   Transmission on death

1.   Death of sole proprietor

On the death of a sole proprietor beneficially entitled, his personal representative can apply to be registered on production of the grant and the land certificate[3]. Without being registered himself, he can assent to the property vesting in the beneficiary, or can transfer it to a purchaser for value, leaving the beneficiary or purchaser to seek substantive registration. However, a purchaser from the personal representative cannot be compelled to accept a title in this way. Section 110(7) of the Act enacts that a vendor selling on the basis of his entitlement to be registered cannot by contractual stipulation[4] prevent the purchaser from insisting that the vendor first procures his own registration as proprietor. The purchaser can therefore require the personal representative to seek registration. This is, in fact, an unnecessary step, especially as the Registrar is not entitled to call for information concerning the reason why any transfer is made and must assume that the personal representative is acting correctly and within his powers[5].

Opinions differ as to whether the assent or transfer should contain an acknowledgement for production of the grant of representation in order to obviate any difficulty in lodging the grant at the Registry when registration is sought. However, the point would appear to be academic in view of the Registry's willingness to accept in lieu of the original grant an official copy (obtainable from the Probate Registry) or even a plain copy (such as a photographic copy), if certified by a solicitor as being a correct copy of the original grant[6].

(a) Endorsement of notice of assent

Though there appears to be no express provision in the Act excluding the operation of s 36 (6) of the Administration of Estates Act 1925[7], it is generally agreed that in relation to registered land an assentee who registers his title cannot be prejudiced by a failure to have notice of his assent endorsed on the grant. His registration as proprietor vests the legal title in him and a subsequent disposition of the land by the personal representative in favour of a purchaser cannot deprive him of his title[8]. Indeed it would be contrary to the whole

---

3   LRR 1925, r 168(1).
4   This limitation is sometimes overlooked in practice; see eg *Walia v Michael Naughton Ltd* [1985] 3 All ER 673 at 679.
5   LRR 1925, r 170(1)–(5). See R & R, 27.03, suggesting that it is difficult to envisage circumstances when a purchaser would need to rely on his strict legal right.
6   See Practice leaflet No 6; R & R, 27.15; 19 Ency F & P, 1082, note 6. Cf Potter, 69–70; Emmet, para 11.117.
7   See p 324, ante.
8   R & R, 27.12 (endorsement a needless precaution); 3 K & E, 279. Were the subsequent purchaser to be registered as proprietor in error, the assentee could seek rectification under LRA 1925, s 82(1)(e). It may be advisable to endorse notice of an assent for record purposes.

tenor of the Act if it were possible for a registered proprietor not guilty of any fraud to suffer rectification at the instance of some person whose alleged title only arose by virtue of some dealing effected after the assentee's registration. In any event a subsequent purchaser would not normally be able to claim the protection of s 36(6). His official certificate of search would reveal the existence of the assentee's registration with the result that a denial of any previous assent, given in the transfer to the purchaser, could not operate as 'sufficient evidence' of its correctness. For this reason it is not considered necessary to incorporate in a transfer from a personal representative any statement that he has not given or made any previous assent or transfer[9].

(b) Registration of personal representative or assentee as proprietor
On registration, the personal representative holds the land upon the trusts and for the purposes upon and subject to which the same is applicable by law and subject to minor interests binding upon the deceased. Save as to these matters, he is, as regards any registered dealings, in the same position as if he had acquired the land under a transfer for value[10]. An assentee, being a mere volunteer, is bound by all minor interests subject to which the deceased held the land.

2. Death of joint owner

On the death of one of two or more joint proprietors, his name will be deleted from the register on production of satisfactory proof of death[11] and the land certificate. This may also necessitate the removal of the restriction sometimes registered against joint proprietors[12].

E   Settlements

1. The curtain principle

As regards registered land, the Settled Land Act 1925 takes effect subject to the provisions of the Land Registration Act 1925[13], but the latter Act in no way alters the substantive law governing settlements. It merely adapts the Settled Land Act machinery to the scheme of registered conveyancing. The mode of creation remains unchanged, except that a vesting deed affecting registered

---

9   A prior unregistered assent will not normally affect a subsequent registered purchaser of land included within the assent. But an interesting question arises whether an unregistered assentee in actual occupation can enforce his equitable interest under the will against the subsequent proprietor by virtue of s 70(1)(g) of the Act. It is arguable that his failure to endorse the probate coupled with the purchaser's reliance on the statement (if made) of no previous assent deprives the assentee of his 'rights' under the general law so as to make para (g) inapplicable.

10   LRA 1925, s 43, a most obscurely drafted section; see R & R, 27.16; 3 K & E, 274.

11   LRR 1925, r 172.

12   See p 348, post.

13   SLA 1925, s 119(3).

land must be in the statutory form[14]. The prescribed form contains all the details required by the Settled Land Act 1925, s 7, and also includes a request for the entry of an appropriate restriction (the significance of which is considered in the next section). Registration of the proper person as proprietor is determined by the general law.

The curtain principle is preserved by the register of title and the beneficial interests are kept off the title. This principle is maintained in two ways. A purchaser is debarred from calling for production of any settlement or copy filed in the Registry; he is not affected with notice of its contents[15]. Secondly, the beneficial interests arising under the settlement take effect under s 86(2) of the Act as minor interests and not otherwise[16]. They require protection on the register, as will be explained, but the beneficial limitations are never revealed by it[17].

Protection of beneficial interests

By virtue of s 86(3) of the Act the beneficiaries' rights are protected by means of an entry in the proprietorship register of a restriction which binds the proprietor during his life. The Rules prescribe three different restrictions according to the circumstances[18]. The form (Form 9) for use when the tenant for life is registered as proprietor is as follows:

> No disposition by the proprietor of the land under which capital money arises is to be registered unless the money is paid to AB and CD (the trustees of the settlement of whom there must be two and not more than four individuals, or a trust corporation) or into court. Except under an order of the Registrar, no disposition is to be registered unless authorised by the Settled Land Act 1925.

Whilst it is clearly not the Registrar's duty to ensure that the appropriate restriction is entered, the Act deals with the question of this responsibility somewhat haphazardly. It may be the person applying for registration, or the deceased's personal representatives at the request of the statutory owners, or the trustees of the settlement – all depending on the circumstances[19]. As successive situations occur it may be necessary for an application to be made to vary the form of the restriction to meet the new circumstances.

14 LRR 1925, rr 99–101; Forms 21–24.
15 LRA 1925, ss 88(1), 110(1)(b).
16 Ie, not as overriding interests, even if coupled with actual occupation. But see the Law Commission's recommendation to bring such rights within the ambit of a revised s 70(1)(g): Report No 158, para 2.69. See p 67.
17 The priority of dealings with the beneficial interests, which take place off the register, is now governed by LPA 1925, s 137 (the rule in *Dearle v Hall* (1823–1828) 3 Russ 1): LRA 1986, s 5, abolishing the Minor Index Register which had previously determined questions of priority under LRA 1925, s 102(2).
18 LRR 1925, r 58.
19 See generally LRA 1925, s 87(6): LRR 1925, rr 56, 171(1). No restriction will have been entered if the proprietor is unaware that the land is settled because of an inadvertent settlement, p 16, ante. A registered transferee from him will acquire a good title under s 20(1) of the Act, free from the interests of the beneficiaries, whose occupation will not avail them (note 16, supra).

2.   Changes of ownership

(a) Sale of settled land

The existence of the restriction warns a purchaser that he is dealing with settled land and notifies him of the need to pay the purchase money to the appropriate persons. Though the restrictions forbid registration of any disposition not authorised by the Settled Land Act 1925, this is to be read as referring to the statutory powers as extended by the settlement[20]. The register does not reveal these extended powers. A purchaser's only means of discovering them is to inspect the vesting instrument (which will set them out), which he can do by virtue of his authority to inspect the register.

(b) Death of life tenant

If the settlement continues the trustees of the settlement, as special personal representatives, will execute a vesting assent in favour of the succeeding life tenant by means of a document in the prescribed form. This contains an application for entry of the appropriate restriction[1]. If the settlement terminates the deceased's general personal representatives, as in unregistered conveyancing, will execute an ordinary assent in favour of the person absolutely entitled. No deed of discharge is required[2]. The assent and the grant of probate (or copy) should be lodged at the Registry. The Registrar acts on the assent without question, registers the assentee as proprietor and automatically deletes the existing restriction[3].

3.   Appointment of new trustees

New or additional trustees are appointed by deed in the manner prescribed by the Settled Land Act 1925. No deed of declaration is required. Its place is taken by an application to the Registry to modify the existing restriction by substituting the names of the new and continuing trustees in place of the previous ones[4]. This application should be signed by the life tenant, the previous trustees and the new and continuing ones, or by their respective solicitors. In the case of a deceased trustee his death certificate requires production.

4.   Termination of settlement otherwise than by death of life tenant

A deed of discharge executed by the trustees is required on all occasions when it is necessary in unregistered conveyancing. When lodged at the Registry, the Registrar is entitled to act upon it in the same way as would a purchaser of

---

20   LRR 1925, r 58 (2).
1   LRR 1925, r 170(3), Form 57.
2   As is also the case in unregistered conveyancing; SLA 1925, s 110(5), p 304, ante.
3   There is no need for the assent to include a request for its removal: R & R, 31.21.
4   LRR 1925, r 235(2), prescribing Form 77.

unregistered land. He must assume that the settlement has determined; accordingly he will cancel the restriction protecting the minor interests[5].

F Trusts

1. Trusts for sale

Whenever registered land is transferred to joint owners[6], they hold on trust for sale under the general law. They are registered as proprietors[7] subject to an obligatory restriction which the Registrar automatically enters save in one situation[8]. If one of the proprietors refuses to join in a proposed transfer, an order for sale must be sought under s 30 of the Law of Property Act 1925[9].

(a) The obligatory restriction
Except where the proprietors are entitled jointly in equity so that the survivor can give a valid receipt for capital money, the Registrar is obliged to enter a compulsory restriction, the modern form[12] of which reads:

> No disposition by one proprietor of the land (being the survivor of joint tenants and not being a trust corporation) under which capital money arises is to be registered except under an order of the Registrar or of the court.

This restriction is entered whenever the proprietors hold as tenants in common in equity, or for persons other than themselves. Its existence reminds a purchaser of the need to comply with s 27(2) of the Law of Property Act 1925. A sole surviving trustee cannot therefore pass a good title; if he proposes to sell, a new trustee must first be appointed. No application for entry of the restriction need be made. Every application for registration contains a question whether the survivor of joint proprietors can give a valid receipt, and the Registrar decides whether or not to enter the restriction, according to the reply given to that question. If the consent of some third person has to be obtained, a restriction to that effect is also entered.

A protective restriction should be sought by a person who contributes (otherwise than by loan or gift) to the purchase of property vested in joint proprietors. This will ensure that his interest is brought to the attention of a purchaser or mortgagee from the proprietors, so that his consent to the transaction can be obtained[11].

---

5   LRA 1925, s 87(4). And see SLA 1925, s 17, p 304, ante.
6   See p 565, post, discussing express declarations of beneficial entitlement in registered land transfers.
7   LRA 1925, s 94(1). If there are more than four, the first four named will be registered: ibid, s 95; Trustee Act 1925, s 34.
8   LRA 1925, s 58(3).
9   See pp 306–311, ante.
10   The form of restriction prescribed by LRR 1925, r 213 is no longer used: R & R, 38.15.
11   But the restriction will not, it seems, prevent a disposition by the joint proprietors being effective to overreach his beneficial interest; see the discussion of *City of London Building Society v Flegg* [1988] AC 54, [1987] 3 All ER 435, HL, on p 64, ante. Nor will his overriding interest, if he is in actual occupation, survive the overreaching effect of their disposition; ibid.

(b) Law of Property (Joint Tenants) Act 1964
This Act does not apply to registered land; see s 3. The powers of a sole surviving trustee of registered land to pass a good title depend on the presence or absence of the restriction. Even if the survivor is not solely and beneficially entitled, a transferee for value prima facie[12] takes free from interests of the beneficiaries should no restriction be entered.

(c) Single trustee for sale
The obligatory restriction procedure operates effectively in cases where it is apparent that there must be a trust for sale, either because one is expressly created, or because property is transferred to joint proprietors. However, as previously noted[13], a sole owner may strictly be a trustee for sale, in which case he ought to apply for entry of a restriction. But in practice he will usually be quite ignorant of his fiduciary character. In the absence of any protective entry against the title, a purchaser from a single trustee for sale will prima facie take free from the beneficiaries' interests in equity unless, perhaps, he has notice of them at the time of the transfer[14]. Moreover, if supported by actual occupation, a beneficiary's interest is capable of enforcement as an overriding interest under s 70(1)(g) of the Act, notwithstanding that it takes effect behind a trust for sale[15]. Additionally, the beneficiary himself can apply for entry of a restriction, provided the land certificate is produced at the Registry, otherwise he may lodge a caution[16].

2.   Dealings affecting equitable interests

Subsequent events affecting the equitable interests may render necessary cancellation of an existing restriction or require the entry of one for the first time. The need to cancel arises where a sole survivor, originally entitled in equity to an undivided share, becomes solely and beneficially entitled (eg under the will of his deceased co-proprietor). Although s 78(4) of the Act provides that the obligatory restriction cannot be withdrawn, this must be deemed subject to the proviso that the land remains subject to a trust for sale. To obtain cancellation of the restriction, the equitable title should strictly be produced to the Registrar, though in practice a statutory declaration by the survivor setting out the details is acceptable[17].

---

12   LRA 1925, s 20(1). But see para (*c*) as to the possible effect of the purchaser's notice or the beneficiary's occupation.
13   Page 314, ante.
14   See *Peffer v Rigg* [1978] 3 All ER 745, doubted p 77, ante.
15   *Williams & Glyn's Bank Ltd v Boland* [1981] AC 487, [1980] 2 All ER 408, HL. Similarly a beneficiary under a bare trust: *Hodgson v Marks* [1971] Ch 892, [1971] 2 All ER 684, CA.
16   *Elias v Mitchell* [1972] Ch 652, [1972] 2 All ER 153. Contrast the unregistered land position. The beneficiary cannot register his interest under the LCA 1972 (cf *Taylor v Taylor* [1968] 1 All ER 843, CA), but his occupation will normally operate to give constructive notice of his rights, p 378, post.
17   LRR 1925, r 214; R & R, 32.11.

On severance of a joint tenancy in equity, a restriction should be entered to ensure that the survivor cannot make title by himself. The application can be made either by the registered proprietors or by the person effecting the severance, or in the case of bankruptcy, by the trustee or even the Registrar acting on his own initiative.

Subsequent dealings with the equitable interests, such as a sale by one of several equitable tenants in common to another or to a third person, operate behind the curtain and do not appear on the register. They need not result in any alteration in the legal title, though a registered proprietor ceasing to have any beneficial interest may prefer to retire from the trust. In this event the Registrar must give effect on the register to any express or implied vesting of the trust property in the continuing trustees[18].

---

18   LRA 1925, s 47(1). For the vesting of trust property on the retirement of a trustee, see the Trustee Act 1925, s 40(2).

Chapter 12

Investigation and acceptance of title

A   Investigation of title

It is the purchaser's task to investigate the title which the vendor has deduced. Basically this involves three things:
(i)   perusing the abstract and raising requisitions on title;
(ii) comparing the abstract with the original documents;
(iii) searching in the appropriate registers.

The first two of these processes are the concern of this chapter; official searches and the related topic of notice will be considered in the next chapter.

1.   Perusal of the abstract

A study of the abstract or copy documents enables the purchaser's solicitor to ascertain whether the vendor is able to convey what he is contractually bound to convey. The solicitor cannot be completely satisfied on this until the deeds have been examined and the results of all necessary searches are to hand. In theory the examination of the deeds should be undertaken after perusal of the abstract and before the purchaser's solicitor asks his questions (requisitions), but in practice this is almost invariably done on completion of the transaction.

The simplification of our land law and the reduction in the period of investigation of title has, compared with a hundred years ago, greatly reduced the likelihood of the practitioner encountering a thoroughly bad title[1]. Yet this consideration should never be an excuse for the purchaser's solicitor to undertake the investigation of title in a perfunctory manner. It is his duty to ensure that a good title is shown in accordance with the contract. He should satisfy himself on the following matters: that the abstract commences with the proper root of title; that particular documents are in law capable of having their supposed effect (which entails consideration of whether the executing parties had power to buy, convey[2], or otherwise deal with the property); that

---

1   The Royal Commission on Legal Services observed that it is now rare to encounter a modern title with a serious and previously undetected defect or to find the documentary evidence of title inadequate: 1 Report, 245, para 21.5.
2   He should be watchful for conveyances in breach of trust.

there are no subsisting incumbrances save for those mentioned in the contract; that all abstracted mortgages have been duly discharged; and that all documents are in order as to stamping, execution[3], registration, or other formal requirements. The identity of the property must be carefully checked[4].

Where the title is registered, it can readily be appreciated how much simpler this task is, particularly in relation to absolute titles. The purchaser is not concerned with the devolution of the title. He must still ensure that the office copy entries do not reveal anything inconsistent with the description of the property in the contract. Requisitions may still have to be raised, but they are the exception rather than the rule.

Should the vendor's title prove to be defective, the purchaser is much more favourably placed if he discovers the defect before, rather than after, completion[5]. Thus he may well be entitled to rescind the contract should the vendor be unable to remedy a defect discovered prior to completion, but thereafter he cannot as a general rule reopen the transaction. He cannot, for instance, recover the purchase money because he finds that the title is defective. What his remedies are in such situations is considered in Chapters 21 to 23. An alternative open to the purchaser in the case of a known technical defect is defective title insurance available from major insurance companies[6]. The vendor's offer of an indemnity may, depending on the circumstances, amount to sufficient answer to the purchaser's objection to the title[7].

2. Requisitions on title

Queries about or objections to the title, discovered by perusing the abstract, are brought to the vendor's attention by means of requisitions on title. They are technically more than mere questions, for they require the vendor to remove the defect or the doubt revealed by the abstract – hence their name.

(a) Nature of requisitions
The matters on which requisitions are raised in practice are legion. They may concern flaws or defects in the title[8], or inconsistencies between the contract description of the property and that deduced. The proper course here is to state the defect or objection and either ask how the vendor proposes to rectify it or state the purchaser's requirements. Over the years conveyancing practice has extended the scope of post-contract inquiries and demands. Often they do no more than remind the vendor of his contractual obligations, or draw attention to matters on which the purchaser requires to be satisfied, eg the

3 Especially when executed under a power of attorney. See further pp 456–463, post.
4 Re Bramwell's Contract, Bramwell v Ballard's Securities Investments Ltd [1969] 1 WLR 1659.
5 Even better still if, resulting from a pre-contract investigation, the defect is discovered before the purchaser has signed any contract to buy.
6 Eg for lost documents, or a title based in part on adverse possession. The vendor should finance the expense involved, but cannot be compelled to do so.
7 Re Heaysman's and Tweedy's Contract (1893) 69 LT 89, CA; Manning v Turner [1956] 3 All ER 641 (insurance to cover contingent estate duty liability).
8 For typical illustrations, see 18 Ency F & P, 783–804.

obtaining of a licence to assign, the discharge of mortgages, the production of receipts and the observance of covenants. These are not strictly requisitions on title. Other inquiries may relate to the evidence of facts, the existence of official search certificates or the clarification of mistakes in the abstract. Some so-called requisitions are simply requests for information about various aspects of completion, such as details of the vendor's solicitor's bank account to enable a direct bank transfer of funds prior to completion, or the form of the undertaking to repay the vendor's mortgage, given on completion[9].

Standard form printed requisitions obtainable from law stationers have largely been superseded by preliminary inquiries, which were considered in Chapter 7. As we saw, some of the questions raised are really matters of title[10], which it is advisable to have resolved before exchange of contracts. It is customary to seek confirmation that if the preliminary inquiries were repeated as requisitions, the replies would be the same, practice which, though judicially approved[11], has been criticised[12] on the grounds that it duplicates work and lets in many improper requisitions by the back door. A short form of printed requisitions is available for use when preliminary inquiries have been answered. This form deals with routine matters: the production of receipts (eg for rates), the discharge of subsisting mortgages, completion and the mode of payment of the purchase money. Requisitions founded on the abstract or the contract must, of course, be added.

Improper or unnecessary requisitions. The purchaser should not raise requisitions which infer that relevant matters might have been suppressed from the abstract[13]. He is precluded by statute from making requisitions to the earlier title[14], but as we have seen he is not debarred from proving aliunde that the title is defective. One point to be borne in mind is that some contracts allow the vendor to rescind the contract in certain circumstances if he is unable or unwilling to comply with a particular requisition[15]; indeed such a clause used to be included in both the Law Society's and the National Conditions of Sale. The current edition of the Standard Conditions of Sale does not include such a condition but the parties are, of course, free to include such a clause if they wish to do so. If there is such a clause in the contract, then this factor ought to suffice to confine the purchaser's requisitions to matters of substance upon which he is likely to insist if an unsatisfactory answer is given.

9   As to which see pp 441–444, post.
10 See p 191, ante.
11 *Goody v Baring* [1956] 2 All ER 11 at 16–17, per Danckwerts J.
12 (1959) 23 Conv (NS) 153–54; cf Emmet, paras 5.076–77. And see *Hamp v Bygrave* (1982) 266 EG 720 (request for confirmation negates any intention that replies to inquiries amount to collateral warranties).
13 *Re Ford and Hill* (1879) 10 Ch D 365, CA; *Re Chafer and Randall's Contract* [1916] 2 Ch 8 at 15, per Younger J, adverting to the vendor's statutory liability (p 285, ante) to supply an abstract of all material documents. An example of such a requisition, sometimes encountered when the abstract reveals an unencumbered property, is a request for confirmation that there is no existing mortgage. But see NCS 9(2) (vendor required to deal with requisitions relating to occupiers' rights).
14 LPA 1925, s 45(1), p 277, ante.
15 See p 357, post.

(b) Time for making requisitions

Where the contract is silent on this point, requisitions must be delivered within a reasonable time. This is clearly unsatisfactory and so the Standard Conditions of Sale set out a timetable[16] to govern these matters. The buyer may raise requisitions for up to six working days from date of the contract or the delivery of the seller's evidence of title on which the requisitions are to be raised, whichever is the later. The reason for the alternative dates is that, if the National Conveyancing Protocol has been used, the evidence of title should have been delivered to the purchaser's solicitor prior to contracts being exchanged. The seller is then required to reply to the requisitions within four working days of their receipt and the buyer then has three working days in which to make written observations on the vendor's replies.

The purchaser is not relieved from complying with these time limits merely because a complete abstract has not been supplied. However, time does not begin to run in respect of any requisition that could not have been made on an imperfect (ie, incomplete) abstract until the vendor has supplied the missing part[17]. This timetable is a workable one when the completion date is a few weeks from the date of exchange of contracts. They will have little meaning, however, when exchange is delayed and the parties have perforce to agree a completion date soon after the date of the contract. Practitioners anticipating a delayed exchange will proceed with a pre-contract investigation of title, in which event the contractual time limits for raising and answering requisitions have no application.

(c) Time of the essence

The Standard Conditions of Sale do not expressly state that time is of the essence in respect of the delivery of requisitions but that is the effect, because the purchaser loses the right to raise requisitions or make observations on the vendor's replies once the relevant time period has expired[18]. He cannot resist an action for specific performance on the ground of an objection to title raised out of time[19], though equity may refuse to decree specific performance if the title is clearly bad. A contractual provision that objections not made within the specified period are deemed to be waived and the title accepted has been construed as equivalent to making time of the essence[20].

The existence of the essential time clause for raising requisitions must not be overlooked by a solicitor acting for a purchaser whose mortgagee is separately represented. He may need the assistance of the vendor's solicitor to reply to the mortgagee's requisitions. Unless these are submitted within the contractual time limit, the vendor's solicitor can decline to reply, so causing

---

16 SCS 4.1.1.

17 SCS 4.1.1.

18 Ibid. See *Sinclair-Hill v Sothcott* (1973) 26 P & CR 490.

19 *Oakden v Pike* (1865) 34 LJ Ch 620. For a recent example see *Re Martins Bank Ltd's Contract, Thomas v Williams* (1969) 21 P & CR 221.

20 *Oakden v Pike* (1865) 34 LJ Ch 620. This seems to be the true basis of this decision. It is not authority, it is submitted, for the widely, but mistakenly, held view that the time for submission of requisitions is always of the essence, even without express mention; cf 1 Dart, 173; Walford, 47–48; 42 *Halsbury's Laws* (4th edn), para 108, note 3.

difficulties for the purchaser, though usually he will do so by way of courtesy. It is clearly prudent for the purchaser's solicitor, before the time limit expires, to seek an extension for any requisitions raised by the mortgagee. This is normally granted in practice.

(d) Requisitions not subject to a time limit
A clause making time of the essence does not prevent the raising of requisitions out of time in three cases.

(i) *Objections going to the root of the title.*   The purchaser can object that the vendor has no title at any time before completion. This is a fundamental objection importing that the vendor has broken or has no means of performing his contract, and the matter ceases to be simply one of objection and answer[1]. Apart from situations where the vendor has no title, eg because he has no power to sell[2], it is difficult to state with accuracy when an objection can be said to go to the root of the title for this purpose. It is not thought that it extends to an objection that the title is defective on account of some adverse third party right, such as a restrictive covenant or easement[3]. Requisitions on such matters are more likely to fall within exception (ii).

(ii) *Defects not discoverable on perusal of the abstract[4].*   The purchaser is not bound by the time limits in respect of requisitions on matters discovered aliunde as a result of his own inquiries[5] or searches (eg the search in the land charges register), or on inspection of the deeds. He ought, however, to raise his requisitions on such matters within a reasonable time of their discovery[6]. It is customary for the purchaser's solicitor, when raising requisitions, to reserve the right to make additional requisitions arising out of the usual searches and inspection of the deeds. The traditional reply, 'Noted subject to contract', does not entitle the vendor to refuse to answer any requisitions so arising.

(iii) *Matters of conveyance[7].*   Requisitions on such matters are strictly unnecessary. They are often made simply as reminders, but are not subject to any time limit[8], unless the Conditions of Sale are, exceptionally, expressed to include such matters. Perhaps the commonest example of a matter of

1   *Want v Stallibrass* (1873) LR 8 Exch 175 at 181, per Kelly CB.
2   *Want v Stallibrass,* supra; *Saxby v Thomas* (1890) 63 LT 695 (vendor declining to obtain necessary consents); revsd on other grounds (1891) 64 LT 65, CA. Cf *Rosenberg v Cook* (1881) 8 QBD 162, CA (vendor having possessory title only; objection out of time not sustained).
3   See *McFadden v Pye* (1978) 93 DLR (3d) 198 (undisclosed easement restricting intended building operations not going to the root). Cf Emmet, para 5.080, suggesting the contrary; but the cases cited in support are both examples of defects not discoverable from the abstract.
4   *Warde v Dixon* (1858) 28 LJ Ch 315.
5   *Re Cox and Neve's Contract* [1891] 2 Ch 109 (belated requisition as to undisclosed restrictive covenant upheld). Neither NCS 9 nor LSC 15 bars out of time requisitions concerning defects discovered aliunde.
6   Ibid, at 119, per North J.
7   See p 268, ante.
8   *Re Scott and Eave's Contract* (1902) 86 LT 617.

conveyance is the discharge of a subsisting mortgage, provided (as will usually[9] be the case) the vendor can discharge it as of right. Technically, the purchaser is entitled to have the mortgage discharged by the time of completion. In practice, his solicitor accepts an undertaking from the vendor's solicitor to do this after completion and to forward the mortgage deed duly vacated[10].

3. Vendor's replies

(a) Extent of vendor's duty

Requisitions of a general nature may be ignored. In *Re Ford and Hill*[11], the vendors were held entitled to decline to answer a requisition seeking information as to any undisclosed 'settlement, deed, fact, omission or incumbrance affecting the property'. Following this decision the rule came to be stated[12] that the vendor was bound to answer all specific questions put to him in respect of the property or the title, unless expressly absolved by the contract. This formulation of the duty was considered to be too widely drawn by Dillon J in *Luff v Raymond*[13], a case involving the sale of a mortgage secured on registered land. The vendor's failure to reply to a requisition about the mortgagor's insurance policy was held not to be a breach of contract which entitled the purchaser to delay completion until it had been answered to his satisfaction. The vendor's strict legal obligation appears to be confined to answering requisitions relating to the title deduced to the property as described in the contract, but subject to its terms. It should not be overlooked that a reply to a requisition can amount to a professional undertaking by the solicitor[14].

A reply which seeks to conceal the true position, rather than explain it, will not count as a reply for the purposes of the relevant contractual provisions[15]. Where necessary a solicitor should always confirm the accuracy of his answers before replying to the requisitions. It has been suggested that a reply 'not so far as we are aware' should not be accepted if what is being sought is the vendor's confirmation[16]. A reply which accords with the general conveyancing practice does not give rise to any action by the vendor against his solicitor even though the answer enables the purchaser to resile from the contract[17]. Answers to requisitions submitted out of time should not be given without preserving the vendor's rights under the contract, otherwise he may be held to have waived them[18]. Simply to state that the replies are given 'as a matter of

---

9 But not when the legal date for redemption has been postponed, as in *Twentieth Century Banking Corpn Ltd v Wilkinson* [1977] Ch 99, [1976] 3 All ER 361.
10 For undertakings to discharge mortgages, see p 441, post.
11 (1879) 10 Ch D 365, CA.
12 1 Dart, 148, adopted by Emmet (17th edn), 160. But see the 19th edn, para 5.077.
13 [1982] LS Gaz R 1330.
14 Eg in relation to the discharge of mortgages on completion; see p 441, post.
15 *Pratt v Betts* (1973) 27 P & CR 398 at 404, CA, per Stamp LJ.
16 Emmet, (17th edn), 161.
17 *Simmons v Pennington & Son* [1955] 1 All ER 240, CA.
18 *Cutts v Thodey* (1842) 13 Sim 206. See also *Ogilvy v Hope-Davies* [1976] 1 All ER 683 (abstract delivered piecemeal; waiver of time limit inferred from request that purchaser raise his requisitions all at the same time). One consequence of a waiver might be to invalidate a notice to complete (see p 428, post) served by the vendor if the purchaser delays completion.

courtesy' may suffice for this purpose. But there is no hard and fast rule. In one case[19] where the purchaser had already accepted the title before exchange of contracts, the vendor's solicitor's replies to out-of-time requisitions raised by a mortgagee were held not to constitute a waiver of the time stipulation. He was merely responding to the purchaser's solicitor's request for assistance in a transaction with a third party (the mortgagee).

(b) Failure to reply

The Standard Conditions of Sale impose a limit of four working days for the vendor's written replies[20]. Time is not expressly made of the essence but it is conceived that, because by necessary implication, time is of the essence with regard to the purchaser, time is also of the essence with regard to the vendor's obligation to reply. Seemingly, the purchaser can treat the vendor's default as a refusal to answer, enabling him to terminate the contract and recover his deposit on general principles[1]. In *Re Stone and Saville's Contract*[2], it was held that a notice to complete served by the vendor on the purchaser at a time when requisitions going to the root of the title remained unanswered entitled him to treat the contract as repudiated by the vendor. The purchaser was not, in the circumstances, required to serve a notice of his own.

The Law Society's Conditions impose a limit of four working days for the vendor's written replies. Time is made of the essence seemingly, the purchaser can treat the vendor's default as a refusal to answer, enabling him to terminate the contract and recover his deposit on general principles.

(c) Inaccurate replies

Little appears to have been said[3] about the standard of care that should be exercised when replying to requisitions, or about the purchaser's rights in the event of a reply proving to be erroneous. If he discovers the inaccuracy before completion, the purchaser should be able to re-open the question, whether it goes to the root of the title or not, even though the time for raising observations or replies has elapsed. The vendor can hardly rely upon his contractual rights where he has misled the purchaser. It is perhaps more likely that the error will be discovered only after completion. Whatever rights a purchaser may have, it seems he must be content with damages; he cannot have the transaction set aside, even if the reply is fraudulent. A statutory action for damages may lie if the false reply involves the concealment of any instrument or incumbrance material to the title; however, success requires proof of the defendant's intent to defraud[4]. An action

---

19   *Luck v White* (1973) 26 P & CR 89.
20   SCS 4.1.1.
 1   The vendor is in fundamental breach, provided the requisition is one that he is under a duty to answer; and see *Re Ford and Hill* (1879) 10 Ch D 365 at 372, CA, per Bramwell LJ.
 2   [1963] 1 All ER 353, CA.
 3   For the fullest treatment, see Farrand, 119–20.
 4   See LPA 1925, s 183 (2), p 285, ante; *District Bank Ltd v Luigi Grill Ltd* [1943] Ch 78; [1943] 1 All ER 136, where Lord Clauson assumed with considerable reservation (see [1943] 1 All ER at 139) that a failure to disclose the payment of rent in advance when answering

in deceit may possibly lie[5] but this, though seemingly wider than the statutory remedy, also requires a fraudulent intent. In the absence of fraud, the circumstance may be such as to give rise to an action on the covenants for title. However, as with preliminary inquiries[6], it would appear that a duty of care is owed when replying to requisitions, a duty which is owed separately by the vendor or his solicitor depending on the nature of the requisition raised. The purchaser could, therefore, sue for damages in respect of a negligent reply to a requisition if he could show that he had suffered financial loss resulting from it.

(d) Observation on replies

Having considered the vendor's replies, the purchaser has a further period of three working days in which to submit any observations, should he still not be satisfied[7]. If as a result of a requisition a supplementary abstract is delivered, a question on that abstract constitutes an original requisition which the purchaser should raise within the appropriate time limit[8]. The purchaser should always consider his position carefully before raising further observations. A purchaser who discovers a fundamental defect in the vendor's title may be able to repudiate the contract, even before the completion date, provided he acts promptly. He will be deemed to have waived this right if, for instance, he seeks explanations or demands the getting in of outstanding interests[9].

(e) Rescission by vendor

For many years, it was the practice to insert into formal contracts a clause entitling the vendor to rescind the contract if the purchaser raises or persists in any objection to the title which the vendor is, on reasonable grounds, unable or unwilling to remove. The current edition of the Standard Conditions of Sale does not include such a clause. It is, of course, open to the parties to insert such a clause and the effect of the different clauses of this type will be considered in a later chapter.

4. Registered land

On a purchase of registered land there will be far less need to raise requisitions on title, for registration will have eliminated any flaws or technical defects in the vendor's title. Suggestions have sometimes been made that a purchaser

requisitions came within s 183. Maybe the section adds nothing to the liability incurred by the original omission from the abstract: Farrand, loc cit.

5 *Gray v Fowler* (1873) LR 8 Exch 249 at 282, per Blackburn J, who suggested that a purchaser might recover damages in deceit for loss resulting from being induced to act on the vendor's representation, known by the vendor to be false, that the abstract was perfect.

6 In one respect there may be a difference. It does not seem open for the vendor's solicitor to give the replies 'without responsibility'.

7 SCS 4.1.1.4.

8 *Re Ossemsley Estates Ltd* [1937] 3 All ER 774, CA.

9 *Elliott and H Elliott (Builders) Ltd v Pierson* [1948] Ch 452 at 456, [1948] 1 All ER 939 at 942, per Harman J. See further pp 645–648, post.

who tries to invent a requisition upon title properly so called is attempting the impossible[10]. Statements of this nature are based on a misconception of the true function of a requisition. Whether the title to the land is registered or unregistered, the purchaser must satisfy himself that the title deduced accords with the title contracted to be conveyed. Thus it is quite proper to raise objections about restrictive covenants entered in the charges register, though not disclosed by the contract[11] or disclosed in an insufficiently candid manner[12]. It may be necessary to raise requisitions about, for example, overriding interests (as to which the register of title is not conclusive), subsisting tenancies, identity, and cautions, though normally matters of this nature are resolved by pre-contract inquiries since the copy entries are normally forwarded with the draft contract. In the case of a possessory title requisitions may have to be raised upon the earlier title, unless these are precluded by the contract. The purchaser should ensure that the vendor complies with any restriction affecting his powers of disposition. Thus the existence of a restriction in Form 62[13] may necessitate the appointment of another trustee. The vendor's attention should be directed to this, though strictly it is a matter of conveyance.

5.   Examination of original documents

It is the duty of the vendor to verify the contents of the abstract or the copy documents; certain aspects of this duty were considered in Chapter 9. Verification takes place when the purchaser examines the original documents in the vendor's possession. This section is concerned with two additional matters: (a) the object of examination and (b) the time when it should be undertaken.

(a) Object

Since the abstract does not constitute the vendor's evidence of title[14], it is essential to compare it with the actual deeds and documents in his possession. Indeed it has been said that the real proof of title only begins on verification and the most careful scrutiny of the abstract may be completely worthless if the purchaser's solicitor is lax in examining the evidence in its support[15]. The object of this examination may be said to be fourfold[16] – to ascertain:

(i)   that what has been abstracted is correctly abstracted;
(ii) that what is omitted from the abstract is immaterial;

---

10   See R & R (4th edn), 320, omitted from the current edn, 17–14; and see 18 Enc F & P, 174.
11   Page 158, ante. And see *Walia v Michael Naughton Ltd* [1985] 3 All ER 673 (requisition as to execution of unregistered transfer to vendor).
12   See *Faruqi v English Real Estates Ltd* [1979] 1 WLR 963.
13   Page 347, ante.
14   But see p 287, ante, as to examined abstracts.
15   1 Williams, V & P, 180. Yet, somewhat surprisingly, one of the suggested national guidelines advocates that copies or abstracts of deeds not to be handed over on completion should be marked as examined against the originals by the *vendor's* solicitor before being sent to the purchaser's solicitor: (1987) LS Gaz 2260, para 2.
16   1 Dart, 425.

(iii) that all documents are perfect respecting execution, attestation, and stamps;

(iv) that there are no memoranda endorsed on the deeds, nor any circumstances attending the mode of execution or attestation calculated to arouse suspicion.

When the abstract comprises photocopies of the relevant documents the task of examination is greatly facilitated. The above four points will not necessarily be applicable in every case. But the purchaser's solicitor ought never to dispense with an examination of the original deeds. An inspection may, for example, reveal that part of a deed, or a memorandum endorsed on it, has inadvertently been omitted from the copy. Much of what appears in the next paragraph, which is concerned primarily with the position when an abstract in traditional form has been supplied, is also relevant in situations where photocopies have been provided.

The description of the property sold should always be carefully checked (especially where the abstract refers to it as 'the before abstracted premises'), and the wording of covenants watched. It is important to look for possible memoranda often endorsed on the back of a deed. Those most likely to be encountered in practice relate to restrictive covenants, the grant of easements, sales-off, the appointment of new trustees, and in the case of a grant of probate, assents affecting the deceased's property. Besides examining all abstracted deeds, search certificates and other certificates produced as evidence of abstracted facts should be inspected. It would also seem prudent to inspect any other documents and papers in the packet of deeds relating to the period of title which the purchaser has investigated. In this way information relating to some third party right might come to light or the existence of a material document omitted from the abstract discovered. He need not concern himself with deeds dated prior to the time fixed for the commencement of the title, for he is not deemed to be affected with notice of any matter or thing relating to the earlier title unless he actually investigates it[17]. Nevertheless, he is not precluded from taking objection to the title if he does inspect a deed prior to the root of title and thereby discovers a defect[18].

That the examination of the abstract against the deeds is a very vital part of the transaction has already been stressed. Unfortunately, even before the advent of photocopies, the verification of the abstract was all too frequently performed in a rather cursory fashion, or by some inexperienced person. Nowadays, particularly where photocopies have been supplied, the examination is a very perfunctory affair. When completion takes place 'through the post' it is sometimes dispensed with altogether[19] – a practice which clearly bears the stamp of professional negligence, but which practitioners happily adopt as a means of simplifying conveyancing procedures and reducing costs. The thoroughness of the examination varies according to the circumstances,

---

17   LPA 1925, s 44(8), p 273, ante.

18   *Smith v Robinson* (1879) 13 Ch D 148 (discovery of counterpart lease in bundle of deeds when examining abstract).

19   Alternatively the vendor's solicitor is asked to act as the purchaser's agent on completion, and to undertake the examination on his behalf. But see note 15, ante.

depending in part on whether an abstract in conventional form or simply copies need to be verified. A verbatim check of a traditional abstract is desirable when the original deeds are not to be handed over on completion, eg on a sale-off, for the abstract will be used as the purchaser's principal documentary evidence of title on future sales[20]. On the purchase of a typical suburban house, the title to which has been deduced several times before, it should be sufficient merely to check that the vital parts of the abstracted deeds (eg date, stamp duty, parties, descriptions and execution) have been correctly abstracted. Copies can be verified much more speedily.

(b) Time

The former practice was to examine the deeds before raising requisitions. Technically this is the correct procedure, for requisitions should strictly relate to those queries which a purchaser is not able to resolve on verification of the abstract. Nowadays it is the almost invariable practice to leave the inspection of deeds until the time of actual completion, a procedure which does not meet with the approval of the Council of The Law Society[3]. Doubtless the increasing pressures of business life, coupled with the belief that the inspection of deeds is unlikely to reveal anything adverse especially if the title has been examined on previous sales within a comparatively short period of time, have encouraged solicitors to adopt this time-saving practice. The discovery on completion of a serious defect is likely to result in delay, to the annoyance and inconvenience of both parties. Yet in practice an inspection at this late stage does not seemingly operate to the parties' detriment, largely because so few major defects are in fact discovered. Of course it is conceivable that defects might well be overlooked, which would not have been missed had more time been available to consider the matter. The practice, often adopted in the case of trivial defects, of completing subject to the vendor's solicitor's undertaking not to account to his client for the purchase money until the defect is rectified, is open to serious objection[2].

It would not appear to be too late to raise an objection on completion, notwithstanding that the time for raising requisitions has elapsed. A defect only discoverable by inspection of the deeds would rank normally as a defect not discoverable on the face of the abstract itself, and in respect of such defects the usual time clause does not apply. Some support for this view is afforded by the decision in *Pagebar Properties Ltd v Derby Investment Holdings Ltd*[3]. In this case a purchaser was held to be entitled to object to the existence of a lease which his solicitor did not discover until he examined the deeds on completion. However, according to the Council of The Law Society[4], a solicitor may be

---

20   Page 282, ante. For the marking of abstracts as examined, see p 287, ante.
1   Law Society's Digest, Third Cumulative Supplement, Opinion No 95 (a); Emmet, para 5.087.
2   A procedure not open to the vendor's solicitor when his client is involved in a chain transaction.
3   [1973] 1 All ER 65.
4   See note 1, ante. It is significant that Goulding J seems to have accepted that the purchaser could object only if there was no fault on his part (see at 70). It is arguable that a failure to examine the deeds within the period allowed for raising requisitions constitutes fault, and so bars the purchaser's objection. The purchaser was not at fault in the *Pagebar* case; his

guilty of negligence if, as a result of a belated examination of the deeds, he is out of time with his requisitions.

(c) Registered land

Under s 113 of the Land Registration Act 1925, office copies of and extracts from the register of title are admissible in evidence to the same extent as the originals. A purchaser is entitled to compensation for loss resulting from any inaccuracy in them. Since the accuracy of office copies supplied by the vendor is guaranteed, verification against the actual register or the land certificate is technically unnecessary, provided the purchaser makes an official search[7] of the register prior to completion to ensure that the entries are up to date. Nevertheless, a brief comparison of the copy entries with the land, or charge, certificate is sometimes undertaken on completion.

6.   Investigation of title by mortgagee

The possibility of a mortgagee having to exercise his power of sale on the mortgagor's subsequent default makes it essential for him to ensure that he is lending on a good marketable security. He needs, therefore, to investigate the mortgagor's title in the same way as if he were a purchaser. Even in the case of a temporary loan secured on property, it may be unwise not to effect a land charges search against the mortgagor[6]. Moreover, in the usual situation the mortgage is granted contemporaneously with the mortgagor's purchase of the property, so that the mortgagee must also satisfy himself as to the soundness of the vendor's title. Institutional lenders frequently instruct the purchaser's solicitor or licensed conveyancer[7] to act, in which case there is no separate investigation on the mortgagee's behalf. A number of issues of concern to an intending mortgagee will be considered.

(a) Freedom from rights of occupiers

The House of Lords' decision in the *Boland* case[8] alerted mortgagees to the reality of being bound by the equitable interests of persons in occupation at the time the mortgage was created. The decision generated considerable controversy and it was felt that building societies, and other institutional lenders, would have to take considerable precautions when lending money by way of mortgage to ensure that they would not be bound by the equitable rights of co-owners with the result that possession could not be obtained in the event of mortgage default. As will be seen, however, these fears have proved

solicitor had, prior to exchange of contracts, inspected counterparts of the leases which were stated by the contract to affect the property.
5   See p 407, post. For s 113, see p 335, ante.
6   As the mortgagee discovered in *Perez-Adamson v Perez-Rivas* [1987] Fam 89, [1987] 3 All ER 20, CA (bank without express notice bound by wife's registered lis pendens).
7   Many building societies have appointed licensed conveyancers to their panels, enabling them to act.
8   [1981] AC 487, [1980] 2 All ER 408, HL.

to have been greatly exaggerated and there has emerged in the resultant case law a clear distinction between situations where the mortgage is used to finance the purchase of the house and is, therefore, contemporaneous with the conveyance or transfer and situations when the mortgage is created some time after the house has been acquired. Before considering this distinction, it is convenient to refer to one other important limitation on the impact of *Boland*.

(b) Two trustees

In *Boland* itself, Mr Boland was the sole registered proprietor of the house but, in equity, he and his wife were tenants in common. When the mortgage was created, Mrs Boland was in actual occupation of the house and her interest was held to be an overriding interest which was binding on the bank. The fact that there was only one legal owner was crucial. In *City of London Building Society v Flegg*[9] a house was in the joint names of a couple, the Maxwell-Browns, who held the property on trust for sale for themselves and Mrs Maxwell-Brown's parents, the Fleggs. They created a number of mortgages until, finally, a mortgage was created in favour of the plaintiffs, the prior mortgages being redeemed. It was held that, because the mortgage was executed by two trustees for sale, the interests of the Fleggs were overreached and took effect only against the equity of redemption. In cases where there is co-ownership of the legal estate then, provided that the mortgagee deals with all the legal co-owners, no concern needs be paid to the possibility of other occupiers of the property having equitable rights in it.

While this decision is a logical application of basic principles[10], some disquiet was felt at the outcome of the case, in that the parents lost their home as a result of transactions affecting the property in which they lived and about which they knew nothing. This consideration led the Law Commission to recommend the statutory reversal of the decision in *Flegg*, so that the rights of co-owners in actual occupation of the property would be protected against a mortgagee even when the mortgage was created by two legal owners[11]; a proposal, it is suggested, which has much to commend it, particularly when regard is had to the type of mortgage which may potentially be affected by the decision in *Boland*.

(c) Acquisition mortgages

The decision in *Boland* occasioned building societies considerable disquiet, the worry being that if a house was being bought ostensibly by one person, but a second person was going to move into the house having made a contribution to the purchase price, then the latter would have an equitable interest in the house, binding on the mortgagee who had lent money in order to finance the

---

9   [1988] AC 54, [1987] 3 All ER 435, HL. See [1988] Conv 108 (M P Thompson).
10   See (1986) 130 NLJ 208 (D J Hayton).
11   (1989) Law Com No 188. Contrast the approach taken earlier by the Commission when, reacting to the decision in *Boland*, it recommended that that decision be reversed by legislation so that the rights of co-owners would only be binding upon a mortgagee if protected by registration: (1982) Law Com No 115.

purchase. Various precautions were taken to try and minimise the risk of being bound by such an interest. In the light of developments subsequent to *Boland*, however, it seems that it will only be in very rare situations that a mortgagee who lends money in order to finance the acquisition of the home, the mortgage then being created at the same time as the conveyance or transfer, will be bound by the interest of a beneficial co-owner of the property.

In *Bristol and West Building Society v Henning*[12] a house was being conveyed into the sole name of Mr Henning but it was accepted that Mrs Henning had a beneficial interest in it, she having contributed to the lump sum put down on the house by her partner[13]. The balance of the purchase price was provided by Bristol & West Building Society who addressed no enquiries to Mrs Henning. When Mr Henning defaulted on the mortgage, the society sought possession, this action being resisted by Mrs Henning who argued that the society had constructive notice of her equitable interest in the house and was therefore bound by it. The Court of Appeal decided in favour of the society.

It was held that, although Mrs Henning had given no thought to the issue of whether or not her interest would have priority over that of the mortgagee, because she knew that a mortgage was being created and she benefited from that mortgage because the house could not have been bought at all without it, the intention which must be imputed to her was that the building society's mortgage should have priority to her equitable interest in the house.

Although the reasoning has been criticised on the basis that, in this area of law, the approach of the courts is to infer the intentions of the parties rather than imputing to them intentions which they never actually had[14], nevertheless, the result seems sensible in that it is difficult to see why a person in the position of Mrs Henning, who both knows of and will benefit from the mortgage should be able, subsequently, to assert rights binding upon that mortgagee. More importantly, the approach taken in *Henning* was tacitly approved by the House of Lord in *Abbey National Building Society v Cann*[15], although the case was not actually cited, and approved and extended in the controversial case of *Equity and Law Home Loans Ltd v Prestidge*[16].

A house was in the sole legal name of Mr Prestidge but his partner, a Mrs Brown, was an equitable tenant in common. The property had been bought with the aid of a £30,000 mortgage in favour of the Britannia Building Society. Some time later Mr Prestidge approached the plaintiffs seeking a loan of over £42,000, the purpose of the loan being, so he said, to effect improvements to the property. Prior to granting the loan, Equity & Law enquired of Mr Prestidge as to whether anyone over the age of 17 was living in the property and he replied, truthfully, that he shared the property with Mrs Brown and, on further enquiry, revealed that she had not consented to the mortgage but that he was confident that she would do so. Equity & Law then granted him the loan and

---

12   [1985] 2 All ER 606, CA, followed in *Paddington Building Society v Mendelsohn* (1985) 50 P & CR 244, CA (registered land).
13   The couple were not in fact married but nothing turned on this point.
14   See (1986) 49 MLR 245, [1986] Conv 52 (M P Thompson); (1986) 16 Fam Law 315 (J Martin).
15   [1991] 1 AC 56, [1990] 1 All ER 1085, HL.
16   [1992] 1 All ER 909, [1992] 1 WLR 137, CA.

a mortgage was created in their favour. £30,000 of the money was used to discharge the mortgage in favour of Britannia and the remainder was retained by Mr Prestidge. He defaulted on the mortgage and the plaintiffs sought possession, an action resisted by Mrs Brown, who argued that her equitable interest was binding upon the mortgagee.

The Court of Appeal granted possession. Starting from the premise, accepting the decision in *Henning*, that Britannia could have obtained possession, that mortgage having been used to finance the purchase of the home and being known about by Mrs Brown, it was held that, because part of the money advanced had been used to redeem the mortgage, allowing Equity & Law to take on the position of Britannia, Mrs Brown would not be placed in any worse position than she would have been in had the second mortgage not been created. Accordingly, it was held that Equity & Law had priority up to the sum of £30,000, the size of the original mortgage, her equitable interest having priority over the mortgagee in respect of the remainder of the sum borrowed.

The actual decision in this case has been criticised on the basis that it effectively allowed the second mortgagee to be subrogated to the position of the first mortgagee without the normal rules of subrogation being satisfied[17]. Nevertheless, the decision provides strong support for the *Henning* line of authority of not allowing the rights of a co-owner to have priority over a mortgage of which she knew and from which she benefited. As such, it is now abundantly clear that it is most unlikely that a mortgagee, when the mortgage is contemporaneous with the acquisition of the house, will ever be bound by the interest of a beneficial co-owner, it being highly unlikely that the co-owner will think that the house is being bought outright without the need of mortgage finance[18].

A further potential worry for institutions lending money in order to finance the purchase of a home was the so-called registration gap. The perceived problem was that, when title to land was registered, the legal title does not actually pass until the transferee applied to be registered as proprietor of the land. As there is frequently a gap between the actual transfer and the application for registration, the worry was that, during that period, a co-owner could go into actual occupation of the property and consequently be able to establish an overriding interest binding on the mortgagee who would only acquire a legal charge over the property when the purchaser was registered as proprietor. In *Abbey National Building Society v Cann*[19], the House of Lords held that, for the purpose of s 70(1)(g) of the Land Registration Act 1925, the relevant time for the person claiming to be in actual occupation was the date of the transfer and not the date of registration[20]. Consequently, where registered land is concerned, a co-owner can only assert an overriding interest binding upon a mortgagee where the mortgage is created contemporaneously with the transfer if, first, she did not know that a mortgage was being created to finance the

---

17   [1992] Conv 206 at 211, 212 (M P Thompson).
18   For a rare example of this, see *Lloyds Bank plc v Rosset* [1991] 1 AC 107, [1990] 1 All ER 1111, HL.
19   Supra. See [1991] Conv 116 (S Baughen).
20   See an argument anticipating this decision at [1986] Conv 309 (P Sparkes).

purchase of the home and, second, she was in actual occupation of the home prior to the execution of a transfer; an unlikely combination of circumstances which effectively means that mortgagees lending money to enable the house to be bought can view the decision in *Boland* with equanimity.

A further potential problem for mortgagees which was removed in *Abbey National Building Society v Cann* was that of tenancies which the purchaser had purported to create prior to becoming the owner of the legal title. Because the purchaser did not own the legal title when he purported to create the tenancy, the effect of the transaction was to create a tenancy by estoppel, that tenancy being automatically fed when the transferee acquired the legal title. The difficulty was that theory used to recognise the passing of the legal estate to the purchaser and the grant of the mortgage as being two separate transactions separated by a *scintilla temporis*. The result of this doctrine was that the tenancy by estoppel was fed a split second before the creation of the mortgage with the result that the mortgagee was bound by the lease[1]. While appreciating the logic of this argument, the House in *Cann* considered it to be practically inconvenient, and also considered that the clothing of the purchaser with the legal estate and the creation of the legal mortgage occurred simultaneously, with the result that the mortgagee would not be bound by a lease created in the circumstances outlined above.

(d) Mortgages not contemporaneous with acquisition

When a mortgage is created after the property has been acquired, the mortgagee faces a number of problems in ensuring that he gets a good title. First, if he is dealing with only one legal owner, he must ensure that there are no other co-owners living in the property whose interests may be binding upon him. If such a person is discovered, then that person's consent to the mortgage having priority to her interest must be obtained. As will be seen, care must be taken when obtaining that consent to ensure that it is not liable to be set aside as having been obtained by some vitiating factor such as misrepresentation or undue influence. Alternatively, the house may be in joint names. In which case, clearly, both parties must sign the mortgage deed. Difficulties may then arise in ensuring the validity of the signatures. There are essentially two potential problems: forgery and the existence of a vitiating factor.

(e) Forgery

Situations have occurred when a house is in joint names and one co-owner, with the assistance of an accomplice, forges the signature of the other co-owner when purporting to create a mortgage. The consequence of this differs, depending upon whether or not title is registered. Where title is unregistered, the mortgage deed is ineffective to affect the legal estate. Instead, the mortgage operates against the forger's equitable interest in the property[2]. If, prior to

---

1   *Church of England Building Society v Piskor* [1954] Ch 553, [1954] 2 All ER 85, CA.
2   If the purchaser is involved and is a party to the fraud, the whole transaction is a nullity: *Penn v Bristol and West Building Society* [1996] 2 FCR 729, [1995] 2 FLR 938.

the forgery, the forger was a beneficial joint tenant of the property, the effect of the forgery is to sever the joint tenancy, the mortgage then taking effect against his beneficial half share in the property[3]. Where title is registered, the position is different.

If, after the forged mortgage deed has been executed, the mortgagee is registered as proprietor of a registered charge then, despite the basis of the registration being a forged deed, the very fact of registration will be enough to vest in the chargees a legal mortgage. In such a case, when the forgery comes to light, the remedy for the innocent co-owner will be to seek rectification of the register; a remedy which should, ordinarily, be available[4], in which case, assuming, as is likely to be the case, that the mortgagee has not been guilty of a lack of proper care, an indemnity will be payable to compensate for the loss of the mortgage[5].

(f) Misrepresentation and undue influence

When a house is mortgaged, some time after its acquisition, there can be many reasons why this course of action is taken. The mortgage could be to secure an overdraft or to finance borrowing for a variety of purposes. The *Boland* problem arose when the house was in sole legal ownership and the other, equitable, co-owner was not consulted by anyone about the mortgage. Problems can also arise, however, when there is legal co-ownership, if it is not clear that both co-owners have given a fully informed, or freely given, consent to the mortgage.

At one time it was thought the mortgage would be liable to be set aside against one of the co-owners in one of two situations. These were where the person seeking the loan had been entrusted with the task of obtaining the requisite signature to the mortgage deed and that person had obtained the signature either by the use of undue influence or by misrepresenting the nature of the transaction, the person guilty of such wrongdoing being regarded as the agent of the mortgagee[6] or, alternatively, that the mortgagee had actual notice that one co-owner had exercised undue influence on the other and that the transaction was to the manifest disadvantage to that person[7]. Other than that, the mortgage was thought to be secure, even if undue influence had been used in order to obtain the signature[8]. A different approach was taken, however, in the leading case of *Barclays Bank plc v O'Brien*[9].

Mr and Mrs O'Brien were joint legal owners of their matrimonial home. Mr O'Brien was closely associated with a company which had an overdraft

3   *First National Securities Ltd v Hegerty* [1985] QB 850, [1984] 3 All ER 641, CA. For the remedies open to the mortgagee, see Thompson, *Co-Ownership*, 99–102.
4   See *Norwich and Peterborough Building Society v Steed (No 2)* [1993] Ch 116, [1993] 1 All ER 330 at 138, 347–8, CA, per Scott LJ.
5   Ibid.
6   *Avon Finance Co Ltd v Bridger* [1985] 2 All ER 281, CA; *Kingsnorth Trust Ltd v Bell* [1986] 1 All ER 423, [1986] 1 WLR 119, CA.
7   *Bank of Credit and Commerce International SA v Aboody* [1990] 1 QB 923, [1992] 4 All ER 955, CA.
8   See, for example, *Coldunell Ltd v Gallon* [1986] QB 1184, [1986] 1 All ER 429, CA; *Midland Bank plc v Perry* (1988) 56 P & CR 202, CA; *Lloyds Bank plc v Egremont* [1990] FCR 770, [1990] 2 FLR 351, CA.
9   [1994] 1 AC 180, [1993] 4 All ER 417, HL.

facility with the bank. He argued to stand as surety for the company's overdraft and to mortgage the matrimonial home as security. At this time the level of indebtedness was £60,000 and it was envisaged that the loan would only be outstanding for a month. The agreement to create a mortgage on the house was not, at this time, implemented. When the mortgage was in fact created, the debt had risen to £135,000 and the mortgage, itself, contained an all moneys clause so that, when the bank eventually came to enforce its security, the amount owing was £154,000.

When the mortgage deed was signed by Mr and Mrs O'Brien, the bank official did not follow his instructions, which were to explain to her the nature and effect of the mortgage and to recommend to her that she obtained independent legal advice prior to signing it. Instead, she simply signed the mortgage deed, together with a side letter acknowledging that she had had the mortgage explained to her and had understood it. This was not, in fact, the case. She thought, as her husband had encouraged her to believe, that the mortgage was only to secure a short term loan of £60,000, rather than to secure an open-ended liability. The House of Lords held that the mortgage was void against her.

Lord Browne-Wilkinson, who gave the only speech, sought to tackle the issue from first principles. First, he rejected the argument, which had found favour in the Court of Appeal[10], that there was a special rule of equity that, where a wife was acting as a surety for her husband's debts, the creditor owed a duty to ensure that she fully understood the effect of the transaction and had been separately advised. Neither did he accept that the relationship of husband and wife automatically gave rise to a presumption that, in a transaction between them, he had exercised undue influence upon her, or that some other vitiating factor, such as misrepresentation, was present. Rather, he accepted that, where there was a close relationship between two parties, relationships, which he made clear, could include unmarried cohabitation relationships[11], either heterosexual or homosexual, and a joint transaction was entered into which was for the sole benefit of one of the parties, a presumption of undue influence, or the existence of some other vitiating factor used in order to obtain the requisite consent, would arise. In such circumstances, the person who was not benefited by the transaction would have an equitable right to set the transaction aside against his or her partner. This equity would then be binding upon the mortgagee if it had notice, actual or constructive, of the possibility of some vitiating factor being present in the transaction between the two mortgagors[12]. To avoid being fixed with constructive notice, the mortgagee should advise the non-benefiting mortgagor of the nature of the transaction and should also recommend that independent legal advice be taken prior to signing the mortgage. Because the bank official had not taken these steps, it was held that the mortgage was not binding upon Mrs O'Brien.

10 [1993] QB 109, [1992] 4 All ER 983, CA.
11 See also *Massey v Midland Bank plc* [1995] 1 All ER 929, Sub nom *Midland Bank plc v Massey* [1994] 2 FLR 342, CA.
12 For a discussion of the correct way of interpreting the role of notice in cases such as *O'Brien*, see [1994] Conv 140 (M P Thompson); [1994] Conv 421 (C Harpum and M Dixon); [1995] Conv 250 (P Sparkes); (1995) 15 LS 35 (G Battersby).

The two key elements of the decision relate to whether the transaction is for the sole benefit of one of the parties and, if so, whether the mortgagee has notice of the possible presence of some vitiating factor. These matters will be addressed in turn.

(i) *The nature of the transaction.*   It was made clear in *O'Brien* that the fact that the transaction involves a husband and wife, or other people who are in a relationship where one party reposes trust in the other, does not, of itself, give rise to a presumption that undue influence has been exercised. It is important to have regard to the nature of the transaction involved. In *CIBC Mortgages plc v Pitt*[13], the matrimonial home was in the joint name of Mr and Mrs Pitt. At the time that the transaction was entered into, the house was valued at £270,000 and was subject to a mortgage of £16,700. Mr Pitt was keen to borrow money against the security of the house to enable him to invest in the stock market. Mrs Pitt was highly reluctant to mortgage the house for this purpose but, after considerable pressure from her husband, agreed to be a party to the mortgage. When the mortgage was applied for, the purpose of the loan was expressed to be to pay off the existing mortgage and to buy a holiday home. The company lent the Pitts £150,000 and took a mortgage on the matrimonial home. The mortgage deed was signed by Mrs Pitt, who did not read the documents before signing them. She was not counselled to take independent advice prior to signing and she did not appreciate the size of the loan. Mr Pitt used the money to embark on a series of speculative, leveraged, share purchases which, after the stock market crash, became substantially worthless and were sold off by other creditors. He was unable to pay the mortgage instalments and so the mortgagee sought possession of the house which had fallen in value so that the amount owing on the mortgage exceeded its value. Mrs Pitt argued that the mortgage was not binding upon her because her signature had been obtained as a result of the undue influence exerted by her husband.

The House of Lords accepted that undue influence had been used but, nevertheless, upheld the validity of the mortgage. This was because the mortgagee was not affected by it. Mr Pitt was not the mortgagee's agent and the mortgagee was not considered to have constructive notice of the use of undue influence by him. The reason for this was because, unlike the situation in *O'Brien*, the transaction appeared to be a joint venture; it was not one which was solely, or substantially, for his benefit.

The purpose of the loan, as this is presented to the mortgagee, is of critical importance in determining whether the lender is put on notice that undue influence may have been exercised or some misrepresentation have taken place. What should trigger alarm bells is if the purpose of the loan appears to be for the benefit of only one of the mortgagees. In addition, if the purpose of the loan, while ostensibly for the benefit of both parties is an inherently risky transaction, it is thought that the lender will also be put on notice. So, if in *Pitt*, the couple had told the truth about what the loan was for then, because what was planned was a highly risky venture, it is conceived that the lender

---

13   [1994] 1 AC 200, [1993] 4 All ER 433, HL.

would have been put on notice and would have had to take precautions to ensure that the mortgage was valid as against Mrs Pitt[14].

It may not always be easy to determine if a particular transaction is for the sole benefit of one of the borrowers. This is especially the case when the purpose of the loan is for the benefit of a company with which both the parties are involved[15]. In such cases, the well-being of the company may be a matter of mutual interest to both parties to the mortgage. The approach which is adopted is to consider the degree of involvement of the wife in the company. In *Goode Durrant Administration v Biddulph*[16], a wife had a 5% stake in a company in which her husband had a 90% stake. A mortgage which made her personally liable for a loan in excess of £300,000, taken out for the benefit of the company, was held to be to her manifest disadvantage with the result that the lender was put on notice that some vitiating factor may have been present when her consent to the mortgage was obtained. Conversely, if the wife appears to have a financial interest in a company which seems to be on a par with that of her husband, the lender will not be put upon enquiry[17]. If there is doubt as to the degree of involvement, the mortgagee should err on the side of caution and counsel the wife to obtain independent legal advice prior to signing the mortgage.

(ii) *The effect of the vitiating factor.* An important issue, particularly when the vitiating factor is misrepresentation, is whether the mortgage is void as against the misrepresentee, or whether it can be upheld up to the limit of the wife's understanding. The point is now settled that the mortgage is void[18]. In *TSB Bank plc v Camfield*[19], the husband's company needed an overdraft of £30,000. This was agreed to by the bank provided it got security for the loan. Mrs Camfield, as a result of an innocent misrepresentation made to her by her husband, thought that her liability under the mortgage was limited to £15,000, whereas, in fact, her liability was unlimited. It having been accepted by the bank that it had constructive notice of the misrepresentation[20], it was argued that the mortgage should be valid against her to the limit of her understanding of the transaction: £15,000. This was rejected by the Court of Appeal[1] who held that the effect of the misrepresentation was to invalidate, totally, the mortgage as against her.

(iii) *The necessary precautions.* In *O'Brien*, Lord Browne-Wilkinson described the steps that the mortgagee should take to prevent being fixed with constructive notice of the vitiating factor. He considered that the mortgagee

---

14 This argument was suggested to the author by Professor Michael Furmston.
15 See Anthony Mann QC speaking at a meeting of the Chancery Bar Association, summarised at [1994] Conv 349.
16 [1995] 1 FCR 196, [1994] 2 FLR 551.
17 *Barclays Bank plc v Sumner* [1996] EGCS 65.
18 *Bank Melli Iran v Samadi-Rad* [1995] 3 FCR 735, [1995] 2 FLR 367, CA.
19 [1995] 1 All ER 951, [1995] 1 WLR 430; CA. See [1995] Conv 325 (A Dunn); (1995) 111 LQR 555 (P Ferguson).
20 This concession was, on the facts, almost certainly, wrongly made.
1 Applying *Allied Irish Bank plc v Byrne* [1995] 1 FCR 430, [1995] 2 FLR 325.

should see the wife separately from her husband, to explain the nature of the transaction and advise her to obtain independent legal advice prior to signing the mortgage[2]. While this is a counsel of perfection, it has become clear from subsequent authority that lesser precautions will be adequate. In *Banco Exterior Internacional v Mann*[3], the bank offered a company, owned by Mr Mann, a loan of £175,000 to be secured, *inter alia*, by a second charge on the matrimonial home. The loan was made conditional on the nature of the loan being explained to Mrs Mann by her solicitor and the solicitor certifying that he had done so. The documentation was sent to the company's solicitor who saw the Manns together. She then signed a document waiving any rights she might have in the house under s 70(1)(g) of the Land Registration Act 1925. The solicitor then wrote that this document had been signed in his presence and that Mrs Mann appeared fully to understand it. On the liquidation of the company, the bank sought possession and this was resisted by Mrs Mann.

It was conceded that the presumption that Mr Mann had exerted undue influence upon his wife had not been rebutted. The issue was whether the bank had constructive notice of that undue influence which, in turn, depended upon whether the precautions taken by the bank were adequate. The Court of Appeal, Hobhouse LJ dissenting, held that they were and that the mortgage was binding upon Mrs Mann. The majority view was that the bank was entitled to rely on the solicitor's professional integrity and competence. If he certified that he had advised the wife and that she had understood the transaction, the bank need not enquire further, even if the solicitor was closely associated with the company which needed the money. It may be best practice for the bank to interview the wife separately, but if a solicitor attests that she has been advised and understands the transaction, this is good enough.

This line has been consistently taken[4]. Most recently, it was held in *Halifax Mortgage Services Ltd v Stepsky*[5] that even if the solicitor who is advising the wife, and who was also appointed to act for the building society in respect of the mortgage, actually knows that the purpose of the loan is being misrepresented to the wife but, nevertheless, does not mention this to the mortgagee, the knowledge of the solicitor is not to be imputed to the mortgagee. It would seem clear, therefore, that the security of the mortgagee will normally[6] be safe, if a solicitor certifies that the wife has been advised as to the transaction and that she has understood it, even if the solicitor is closely associated with the husband and has not, in fact, seen the wife on her own.

(iv) *The role of solicitors.*   Where the principles laid down in *Barclays Bank plc v O'Brien* are potentially applicable, it seems clear that the mortgagee will be

---

2   [1994] 1 AC 180 at 196; [1993] 4 All ER 417 at 429–430.
3   [1995] 1 All ER 936, CA.
4   *Midland Bank plc v Serter* (1995) 27 HLR 647, CA; *Bank of Baroda v Rayarel* [1995] 2 FCR 631, [1995] 2 FLR 376, CA.
5   [1996] Ch 207, [1996] 2 All ER 277, CA. In this case, the purpose of the loan, as represented to the building society, would not, of itself, have raised an inference of undue influence.
6   Difficulties can arise if the solicitor is the mortgagee's agent: see *Allied Irish Bank plc v Byrne* [1995] 2 FLR 325.

exonerated from constructive notice if a solicitor certifies to having advised the wife as to the nature of the transaction. When the solicitor who is advising the wife is also the husband' solicitor, or otherwise connected with the company for whom the loan is being raised, potential difficulties arise with regard to conflict of interest between the wife and his other client. The position, unfortunately, is not entirely clear.

In *Clark Boyce v Mouat*[7], an elderly woman was seeking to mortgage her house to secure a loan of $NZ100,000 for her son, who needed the money to inject capital into his business. The usual family solicitor was approached but he declined to act. A different firm was then engaged and the mother and son saw the solicitor together. He advised her to get independent advice and offered to effect an introduction to another solicitor but she declined. He did not advise her as to the prudence of the arrangement but simply told her that her house would be at risk if the repayments were not made. After the mortgage was created, the son went bankrupt leaving the mother facing action by the mortgagee to recover a sum of $NZ100,000. She sued the solicitor alleging breach of contract and breach of fiduciary duty, the essence of her claim being that the solicitor was liable for not ensuring that she had independent legal advice, not refusing to act for her and not informing her that another solicitor had refused to act for her son. Reversing the New Zealand Court of Appeal, the Privy Council held in favour of the solicitor.

While accepting that there was a conflict of interest between the mother and the son, this was not considered to constitute an absolute prohibition against the same solicitor acting for both parties. What was necessary was that the informed consent of both parties should be obtained. This, it was accepted, might entail the solicitor being disabled from giving advice to one party which conflicts with the interest of the other.

This, with respect, seems to take a rather relaxed view of the duty of a solicitor and also sits uneasily with the later decision of the Court of Appeal in *Mortgage Express Ltd v Bowerman*[8]. In this case, a solicitor was acting for a purchaser of a flat and the mortgagee, the transaction involving the purchaser being a sub-sale. The solicitor discovered that both the valuation of the property and the purchase price being paid by his client were considerably in excess of what the vendor was paying for the property. He was held to be liable to the mortgagee for not informing them of this information. Had they known of this information, a second valuation would have been commissioned as a matter of urgency and the probability was that the mortgagee would not have lent the purchaser the money[9].

In this case, the solicitor did not acquire the information from his client. It was recognised, however, that circumstances may arise when a solicitor is acting for both purchaser and mortgagee, that the purchaser tells the solicitor something which might affect the mortgagee's decision to lend the money.

7   [1994] 1 AC 428, [1993] 4 All ER 268, PC. See [1994] Conv 404 (R Tobin).
8   [1995] QB 375, [1995] 12 EG 144, CA.
9   This will not affect the measure of damages when the value of the property has fallen because of a depressed market. See *Banque Bruxelles Lambert SA v Eagle Star Insurance Co Ltd* [1996] 3 WLR 87, HL.

Because information given to the solicitor by a client is confidential, the solicitor cannot pass on this information without his client's consent. If that consent is not forthcoming, however, the solicitor should decline to continue to act for the purchaser because a conflict of interest has arisen[10]. It would seem, notwithstanding the decision in *Mouat*, which preceded the decision in *O'Brien*, that in the present context, when the potential conflict of interest is apparent from the outset that it would be unwise for the same solicitor to act for both husband and wife and that, while the interest of the mortgagee will be secure, the solicitor may be liable to the wife for failing to advise fully of the dangers involved in a particular transaction[11].

B Acceptance of the title

The culmination of these processes of deducing, investigation and verification is the acceptance of the title by the purchaser. Except where there is an express acceptance (which is rare), or the purchaser is contractually bound to accept the vendor's title, a final acceptance does not in practice occur until completion of the transaction. In whatever manner acceptance takes place (and this will be considered shortly), it only relates to the title shown by the abstract. The purchaser can still raise objections not arising on the abstract[12], or on matters of conveyance. The purchaser's conduct may amount to a waiver of defects disclosed by the abstract, or of irremovable objections of which he has knowledge. In each case the question is whether the facts establish an intention to waive[13]. No intention to waive will be inferred if the purchaser continues to insist upon his objections or acts without prejudice to his right to require a good title[14].

(a) Conduct amounting to acceptance

(i) *Failure to send requisitions.* Certain old cases establish that a failure to raise requisitions or request an abstract constitutes a waiver of the right to investigate the title[15]. This matter is now governed, inferentially, by the Standard Conditions of Sale which preclude the raising of requisitions outside the stated time limit[16].

---

10 See also *Halifax Mortgage Services Ltd v Stepsky* [1996] Ch 1 at 17–18, [1995] 4 All ER 656 at 671–672 per Mr Edward Nugee QC, affirmed [1996] 2 All ER 277, CA. See also *The Guide to the Professional Conduct of Solicitors* (1990) Annex 241.

11 See also *Massey v Midland Bank plc* [1995] 1 All ER 929 at 934, CA, per Steyn LJ; *Banco Exterior Internacional v Mann* [1995] 1 All ER 936 at 950, CA, per Sir Thomas Bingham MR.

12 *Bown v Stenson* (1857) 24 Beav 631; *Becker v Partridge* [1966] 2 QB 155, [1966] 2 All ER 266, CA; *Peyman v Lanjani* [1985] Ch 457, [1984] 3 All ER 703, CA.

13 *Flexman v Corbett* [1930] 1 Ch 672 at 682–83, per Maugham J.

14 *Burroughs v Oakley* (1819) 3 Swan 159, an important case on waiver.

15 *Fleetwood v Green* (1809) 15 Ves 594; *Sibbald v Lowrie* (1853) 23 LJ Ch 593. In these and similar cases the purchaser had been allowed into possession.

16 Page 353, ante. See *Sinclair-Hill v Sothcott* (1973) 26 P & CR 490.

(ii) *Delivery of draft conveyance.* Under traditional conveyancing procedures, the purchaser's solicitor submits a draft conveyance for approval by his opposite number when he delivers his requisitions. Under Condition 4.5.1 of the Standard Conditions of Sale the purchaser does not prejudice his right to raise requisitions by adopting this procedure. Even in the absence of such a clause, submission of a draft document for approval does not of itself operate as a waiver[17], and in any case it is common practice to make its submission 'subject to the vendor's replies to requisitions being satisfactory'.

(iii) *Taking possession.* Entry into possession does not under the Standard Conditions of Sale operate as an acceptance of title or waiver of the right to raise requisitions[18], neither does the purchaser's possession under an express condition in the contract[19]. If the contract is silent on this question, the position is not absolutely clear. Taking possession, though not by itself conclusive of an acceptance, may well have this effect if coupled with other circumstances. For example, a purchaser who makes structural alterations to the property after receiving notice of an adverse incumbrance not disclosed in the contract will be held to have waived his right to object to the title on that account[20]. On the other hand, in *Peyman v Lanjani*[1], the purchaser's conduct in taking possession of demised premises and paying part of the purchase money did not debar an objection that the lease was voidable, since he was not aware at the time of his legal right to rescind.

(b) Receipt of abstract prior to exchange of contracts
Reference has already been made[2] to the familiar practice of forwarding the abstract of title with the draft contract. When this happens the purchaser's solicitor usually investigates the title before exchange of contracts, adding any 'requisitions' to his preliminary inquiries. When the vendor deduces his title pre-contract, a special condition is sometimes inserted in the contract whereby the purchaser is deemed to have accepted the title so deduced[3]. In the absence of such a term the purchaser's solicitor can decline to investigate the title pre-contract, though clearly it is not in his client's interests to defer this, should exchange of contracts appear likely to be delayed. A solicitor who decides not to conduct a pre-contract investigation of title is well advised to preserve his client's rights to object to defects discovered by the post-contract examination[4]. Perhaps he ought also to obtain his client's authority to adopt this course of

17 *Burroughs v Oakley* (1819) 3 Swan 159.
18 SCS 5.2.7.
19 *Stevens v Guppy* (1828) 3 Russ 171.
20 *Re Gloag and Miller's Contract* (1883) 23 Ch D 320 (purchaser's knowledge of restrictive covenants). The mere taking of possession *with knowledge of* the encumbrance would bar his right to object if it were an irremovable defect, but not in the case of a removable defect such as a mortgage: ibid, at 327–28, per Fry J.
 1 [1985] Ch 457, [1984] 3 All ER 703, CA (lease voidable because of vendor's previous deception of landlord).
 2 See p 142, ante.
 3 See the Bristol Law Society's protocol: (1985) 82 LS Gaz 3158, 3159.
 4 But failure to do so is not likely to be prejudicial; see p 144, ante.

action, at least if he suspects there may be difficulties with the title. It does not follow, however, that a purchaser whose solicitor exchanges contracts without expressly preserving the right to raise objections later will be deemed thereby to have accepted the title. The terms of the contract must be considered. Thus, Condition 3.1.1 stipulates what the purchaser takes subject to the list of such matters in Conditions 3.1.2 and does not include matters disclosed in any abstract or document delivered pre-contract. Apart from specific provisions of this type, the contractual term regulating the raising of requisitions is itself a prima facie denial of any acceptance[5], but this can be rebutted by clear evidence, eg from the correspondence passing between the solicitors, that the purchaser has accepted the title.

(c) Purchase subject to specific defect
A purchaser who discovers a defect in the title may elect to purchase the property subject to that defect. The vendor cannot resist specific performance on the ground that he has contacted to give a good title; such a term, being for the purchaser's benefit alone, can be waived by him[6].

5   *Luck v White* (1973) 26 P & CR 89 at 93, per Goulding J. See eg LSC 15(2) (requisition to be raised within six days of contract date when abstract delivered beforehand).
6   *Bennett v Fowler* (1840) 2 Beav 302 at 304, per Lord Langdale MR; *Valley Ready Mix Ltd v Utah Finance and Development (NZ) Ltd* [1974] 1 NZLR 123 (purchaser accepting title subject to undisclosed tenancy).

Chapter 13

Searches for incumbrances

A Introduction

One final step must be undertaken before completion, the search for registered land charges, or where the title is registered, the search for adverse entries on the register of title. A search in the Companies Register is also required when the vendor is a limited company. A second search for local land charges is rarely made, as the responsibility for charges registered after the contract normally falls on the purchaser[1].

There is no guarantee that the purchaser's investigation of title will disclose all incumbrances affecting the land. Indeed the complexities of our land law are such that the vendor himself may not be aware of them all. Discovery of an incumbrance aliunde prior to completion may entitle the purchaser to rescind the contract. Once completion has taken place, the question of its enforceability becomes vital. Whether or not he takes subject to a third party right depends on two principal considerations: notice and the nature of the right. Irrespective of notice he takes subject to existing *legal* estates and interests. These confer rights in rem enforceable against the whole world, though Parliament has made limited encroachments upon this basic principle[2]. As to *equitable* interests, a bona fide purchaser for value of the legal estate takes free from any equitable interest of which he has no notice. This doctrine of notice has been severely curtailed by the system of registration under the Land Charges Act 1972, but by no means eclipsed. Not all equitable interests are governed by the Act, and the cases suggest that such interests are more numerous than was once suspected[3]. This continuing influence of the doctrine of notice is unfortunate; for, despite the drawbacks of the system of registration, the Act does provide a simple criterion for determining the question of enforceability.

Exceptionally a legal owner may be postponed to a later incumbrancer (legal or equitable) on the ground of fraud, estoppel, or gross negligence in relation to the title deeds, a possibility most likely to occur within the field of mortgages when a prior mortgagee may be postponed to a subsequent mortgagee[4].

1 Page 205, ante.
2 See eg AEA 1925, s 36(6) p 324, ante; LPA 1925, s 88(1), p 330, ante; and LCA 1972, s 2(4)(i), p 385, post.
3 The main culprits being estoppel interests under a constructive trust. See also *Poster v Slough Estates Ltd* [1969] 1 Ch 495, [1968] 3 All ER 257; *Shiloh Spinners Ltd v Harding* [1973] AC 691, [1973] 1 All ER 90, HL, p 393, post.
4 See *Snell's Principles of Equity* (29th edn), 59; *Walker v Linom* [1907] 2 Ch 104 (trustees failing to obtain title deeds postponed to subsequent equitable incumbrancer).

The doctrine of notice plays little part in the system of land registration. The only kind of notice recognised has been said to be by entry on the register of title[5]. A transferee for value takes subject to all overriding interests and to all minor interests duly protected on the register, whether he knows of them or not[6]. He does, however, take free from the rights of a person in actual occupation of the land if inquiry is made of such person and the rights are not disclosed[7].

B   The purchaser without notice

Equity's jurisdiction has always stopped short of the purchaser of a legal estate whose conscience is not affected by notice of an equitable right. The plea of purchase for valuable consideration without notice is an absolute, unqualified, unanswerable defence, and an unanswerable plea to the jurisdiction of the Court of Chancery[8]. Various aspects of this defence require closer examination.

1.   Purchaser for value

In legal terminology a purchaser is a person who acquires an interest in land otherwise than by operation of law and includes a lessee or mortgagee. 'Value' means any consideration in money, money's worth (such as securities, other land, the discharge of an existing debt[9]) or marriage, provided it is a *future* marriage. A donee, and a devisee under a will, though technically purchasers, never come within the scope of the equitable doctrine since they give no value. They take subject to prior equitable interests, even those of which they have no notice. A squatter is similarly bound[10]; he is not a purchaser, acquiring his title by operation of law.

Equity only protects the purchaser for value if he is bona fide[11]. Fraud or sharp practice deprives him of his special privileges. Fraud in the legal sense is not necessary. Negligence so gross as to justify a court of equity in concluding that there has been fraud in an artificial sense of the word suffices, such as omitting to make any investigation of the title of the property[12].

2.   Legal estate

Subject to the question of conscience, equity always accords due preference to the legal title whenever the contest is between a legal owner and an equitable

---

5   *Williams and Glyn's Bank Ltd v Boland* [1981] AC 487 at 504, [1980] 2 All ER 408 at 412, HL, per Lord Wilberforce.
6   LRA 1925, ss 20(1), 59(6). But see *Peffer v Rigg* [1978] 3 All ER 745; *Lyus v Prowsa Developments Ltd* [1982] 2 All ER 953; pp 77–78, ante; pp 475–476, post.
7   LRA 1925, s 70(1)(g), pp 55–63, ante. See *UCB Bank plc v French* [1995] NPC 144.
8   *Pilcher v Rawlins* (1872) 7 Ch App 259 at 269, per James LJ.
9   *Thorndike v Hunt* (1859) 3 De G & J 563.
10   *Re Nisbet and Potts' Contract* [1906] 1 Ch 386, CA (restrictive covenant).
11   *Midland Bank Trust Co Ltd v Green* [1981] AC 513 at 528, [1981] 1 All ER 153 at 157, HL, per Lord Wilberforce.
12   See *Oliver v Hinton* [1899] 2 Ch 264, CA.

owner. Where the rival claimants are both equitable owners, equity adopts the rule *qui prior est tempore, potior est iure*. The purchaser of an equitable interest is normally bound by a prior equitable interest, with or without notice, though he takes free from a mere equity of which he is unaware. This rule is subject to various qualifications, in particular the equitable doctrine enshrined in *Bailey v Barnes*[13] that a subsequent equitable incumbrancer who gets in the legal title takes precedence over the prior incumbrancer, save where he has notice, actual or constructive[14], of the prior interest.

3. Without notice

Notice may be actual, constructive or imputed.

(a) Actual notice

This arises where the existence of the equitable interest is within the purchaser's own knowledge. Notice at the time of the conveyance is what counts; lack of notice when entering into the contract is immaterial[15]. Apparently a purchaser is not bound to attend to vague rumours or to statements by mere strangers; to be binding the notice should proceed from some person interested in the property[16]. This expression of the rule is perhaps too narrow. A purchaser would seem under a duty to investigate information emanating from a reasonable source, otherwise he might be fixed with constructive notice of matters he would have discovered on inquiry.

(b) Constructive notice

In their concern to ensure that too many purchasers of a legal estate did not escape through the net, Chancery judges developed a complicated doctrine of constructive notice. Apart from this doctrine, a purchaser would have had every incentive to refrain from making inquiries, for the less he knew the better. Constructive notice is the knowledge which the courts impute to a person upon a presumption so strong of the existence of the knowledge that it cannot be allowed to be rebutted, either from his knowing something which ought to have put him to further inquiry or from his wilfully abstaining from inquiry, to avoid notice[17]. The doctrine is now clothed in statutory form. The Law of Property Act 1925, s 199, re-enacting s 3 of the Conveyancing Act 1881, provides that a purchaser is not prejudicially affected by notice of any instrument, matter or fact unless it is within his own knowledge, or *would have come to his knowledge if such inquiries and inspections had been made as ought reasonably to have been made*

---

13   [1894] 1 Ch 25, CA.
14   *McCarthy and Stone Ltd v Julian S Hodge & Co Ltd* [1971] 2 All ER 973 (equitable mortgage created by vendor after contracting to sell land).
15   *Taylor Barnard Ltd v Tozer* (1983) 269 EG 225.
16   *Barnhart v Greenshields* (1853) 9 Moo PCC 18 at 36, per Lord Kingsdown; *Lloyd v Banks* (1868) 3 Ch App, 488.
17   *Hunt v Luck* [1901] 1 Ch 45 at 52, per Farwell J; affd [1902] 1 Ch 428, CA. The doctrine does not require any fraudulent intent on the purchaser's part.

by him: sub-s (1)(a)(ii). This really does no more than state the law as it was prior to 1882. Its negative form has been said to show that a restriction rather than an extension of the doctrine of notice was intended by Parliament[18] – an important consideration that has been ignored in recent years. A purchaser is not affected with notice of anything which he could not have discovered by making proper inquiries. If a reasonable, though misleading, reply is given to a requisition, the purchaser is not bound to assume that it is incorrect or pursue his inquiry further[19]. Constructive notice can arise in three ways.

(i) *Failure to make proper investigation of title.*   This has already been considered in Chapter 9.

(ii) *Notice from the possession of deeds.*   A purchaser (including a mortgagee) is bound to inquire for the title deeds and should insist on their production. If he does not do so, or accepts an unsatisfactory explanation for their non-production, he will take subject to the rights of the person having their custody. An explanation that the deeds were deposited at a bank for safe custody has been held to be insufficient to protect a purchaser[20]. Notice of a deed forming part of the title is notice of its contents[1]. It may also constitute notice of the contents of documents referred to in it[2]. Where a vendor in good faith informed the purchaser that an original deed had been lost and produced what purported to be a true copy, the purchaser was held bound by restrictive covenants not disclosed by the copy[3].

(iii) *Failure to inspect property.*   Every prudent purchaser should, and does, inspect the property, but he will frequently not appreciate the legal significance of what he sees. For example, when a person buys property where a visible state of things exists that could not legally do so without it being subject to some burden, he is taken to have notice of the nature and extent of that burden[4]. If the vendor is not himself in possession, the purchaser should make inquiries of every occupier whose interest is not satisfactorily accounted for in the contract. Such occupation is prima facie inconsistent with the vendor's title and requires an explanation. Thus, occupation by a tenant has been held to fix a purchaser with notice of the tenant's rights including an option to

---

18   *Bailey v Barnes* [1894] 1 Ch 25 at 35, CA, per Lindley LJ. See also s 199(3). As early as the 1850s, eminent Chancery judges were advocating the expendiency of confining the doctrine within its then boundaries: *Ware v Lord Egmont* (1854) 4 De GM & G 460 at 473, per Lord Cranworth LC; *Montefiore v Browne* (1858) 7 HL Cas 241 at 269, per Lord Chelmsford LC.
19   *Re Alms Corn Charity, Charity Comrs v Bode* [1901] 2 Ch 750 at 762, per Stirling LJ.
20   *Maxfield v Burton* (1873) LR 17 Eq 15 (purchaser under marriage settlement).
 1   *Peto v Hammond* (1861) 30 Beav 495; *Parker v Judkin* [1931] 1 Ch 475, CA.
 2   *Coppin v Fernyhough* (1788) 2 Bro CC 291; cf *Land Revenue Collector, Singapore v Hoalim* [1978] AC 525, PC.
 3   *Hooper v Bromet* (1903) 89 LT 37; varied (1904) 90 LT 234, CA; *Re Childe and Hodgson's Contract* (1905) 50 Sol Jo 59 (failure to call for deed referred to in contract).
 4   *Allen v Seckham* (1879) 11 Ch D 790 at 795, CA, per Brett LJ. See *Morland v Cook* (1868) LR 6 Eq 252 (sea wall); *Davies v Sear* (1869) LR 7 Eq 427 (archway).

purchase[5], but not with notice of his right in equity to have the lease rectified[6], nor with notice of the lessor's title or rights[7].

A person can be in occupation of property although his residence there is not continuous and uninterrupted[8]. He is still to be regarded as in occupation despite a temporary absence due to holidays or hospitalisation[9]. What constitutes occupation becomes a vital issue should the vendor or mortgagor also be living in the property. This question frequently arises when a matrimonial or quasi-matrimonial home is involved, since a wife or mistress, not being a legal co-owner, will often have an equitable interest in it by virtue of contributing to its acquisition[10]. Until *Caunce v Caunce*[11] in 1969 there appears to have been no reported judicial consideration of the nature of a purchaser's duty of inquiry in cases of joint occupation. Here Stamp J formulated the proposition that failure by a purchaser or mortgagee to inquire did not fix him with notice of the equitable interest of any other person in occupation whose presence was wholly consistent with the title offered. This would occur in the familiar situation when a vendor, himself in occupation, contracts to sell with vacant possession on completion. The mere presence of some other occupier implies nothing to negative the title offered and so demands no explanation. Indeed, to make inquiries of other occupants in such circumstances carries the implication that the purchaser suspects the vendor of deliberately failing to discharge his duty of disclosure. Stamp J's statement of principle was in complete accord with judicial explanations of the rule applied in cases of non-occupying vendors; but it was destined to be short-lived. *Caunce v Caunce* was adversely commented upon in *Hodgson v Marks*[12] and by the House of Lords in *Boland's* case[13], both registered land decisions. Despite the difference between the two systems as to what kind of notice binds a purchaser and the kind of inquiries he has to make[14], the courts have been content to apply to unregistered land the principles enunciated in *Boland's* case in relation to s 70(1)(g) of the Land Registration Act 1925. So, basing himself on that decision, Oliver LJ has stated the rule in these terms[15]:

---

5   *Daniels v Davison* (1809) 16 Ves 249. Registration would now govern enforceability.
6   *Smith v Jones* [1954] 2 All ER 823, p 700, post.
7   See generally *Hunt v Luck* [1902] 1 Ch 428, CA.
8   *Kingsnorth Finance Ltd v Tizard* [1986] 2 All ER 54 (wife visiting matrimonial home regularly and leaving most of wardrobe there but sleeping elsewhere); cf *Hoggett v Hoggett* (1979) 39 P & CR 121, CA.
9   *Chhokar v Chhokar* [1984] FLR 313, CA.
10 See further pp 562–565, post.
11 [1969] 1 All ER 722 (bank not bound by wife's equitable interest). And see (1976) 36 MLR 25, 32–35 (R H Maudsley).
12 [1971] Ch 892 at 934–35, [1971] 2 All ER 684 at 690, CA, per Russell LJ; p 58, ante.
13 [1981] AC 487 at 505–6, [1980] 2 All ER 408 at 413–14, HL, per Lord Wilberforce. Arguably these later cases misinterpreted Stamp J's judgment. It was plainly wrong to hold (see p 728) that the wife's occupation was not inconsistent with the title offered as she was ostensibly in residence as her husband's spouse. But this ought not to have resulted in the general disavowal of the wider principle, except purely on policy grounds.
14 *National Provincial Bank Ltd v Ainsworth* [1965] AC 1175 at 1261, [1965] 2 All ER 472 at 503, HL, per Lord Wilberforce. For the position under LRA 1925, s 70(1)(g), see p 58, ante.
15 *Midland Bank Ltd v Farmpride Hatcheries Ltd* (1980) 260 EG 493 at 498, CA. This effectively extends the doctrine of constructive notice, contrary to what Parliament envisaged; p 378, ante.

A purchaser who is put on notice that someone other than the vendor himself is in occupation of the property sold, either because he actually knows of such occupation or because he does not bother to inspect the property, has constructive notice of the occupier's interest if he does not bother to inquire what it is.

The vexed problem of striking a balance between the need to preserve the rights of occupiers and to facilitate and simplify conveyancing transactions has been a delicate one for the courts to resolve. They have eventually thrown their weight behind the occupier, responding to social changes evidenced in the widespread development of shared property ownership. This affords an example of judicial willingness to reach a solution in conflict within a primary objective of the 1925 property legislation[16]. A purchaser from a sole legal and beneficial owner in occupation of the land sold is obliged to investigate the equitable title. Simply to investigate the legal title as deduced in the abstract will not suffice to satisfy him that the vendor has a good title, despite having contracted to buy with vacant possession.

When the vendor is also in occupation, the circumstance of another's occupation does not of itself fix the purchaser with notice of that other's rights[17]. Otherwise he could be bound by rights not discoverable by making a reasonable inspection. He is required to make such inquiries as a reasonable purchaser would make. What these should be depend on the circumstances of each case. The authorities indicate that a heavy burden may rest on a purchaser or mortgagee. In *Kingsnorth Finance Ltd v Tizard*[18], a mortgagee was held to be bound by an occupying wife's equitable interest, even though an inspection by his agent failed to reveal her occupation. The inspection was not of such a kind 'as ought reasonably to have been made', because it had been pre-arranged with the mortgagor for a Sunday afternoon when the mortgagor knew that his wife would not be at home. This is thought to go too far; it suggests that the inquirer should assume the role of a furtive private investigator. It seems to be accepted, however, that the duty to look for signs of occupation by someone else does not entail opening drawers and cupboards[19] – welcome news for all occupiers. Nor should there be a duty to inquire of a vendor's marital status, unless there are relevant suspicious circumstances[20]. A more realistic approach was adopted in *Midland Bank Ltd v Farmpride Hatcheries Ltd*[1]. A majority of the

---

16   Contrast the House of Lords' determination not to allow the Court of Appeal decision in *City of London Building Society v Flegg* [1986] Ch 605, [1986] 1 All ER 989, CA; revsd [1988] AC 54, [1987] 3 All ER 435, HL, to undermine one of the fundamental objectives of the 1925 legislation.

17   *Kingsnorth Trust Ltd v Tizard* [1986] 2 All ER 54 at 63, per Judge Finlay QC; cf *Cavander v Bulteel* (1873) 9 Ch App 79 at 83, per James LJ, arguendo. But see the more stringent rule required by LRA 1925, s 70 (1) (g): *Hodgson v Marks*, supra, note 12, at 932, 688, per Russell LJ.

18   [1986] 2 All ER 54, noted [1986] Conv 283. Cf *Northern Bank Ltd v Henry* [1981] IR 1.

19   Ibid, at 61, per Judge Finlay QC.

20   Eg a discrepancy between information revealed on a mortgage application form and that imparted to the mortgagee's agent: *Kingsnorth Trust Ltd v Tizard*, supra.

1   (1980) 260 EG 493, CA (occupation by mortgagor's managing director under service agreement). But why was it never argued that the occupier's interest was not of a proprietary nature?

Court of Appeal held that a mortgagee who negotiated with the agent of the mortgagor (a company) need not make any inquiry of the agent. He was entitled to assume that the agent would disclose any interest of his own adverse to his principal's title. In any event the agent would be estopped from asserting his interest in priority to the mortgagee[2], as might a wife present at negotiations with the mortgagee for a loan to her husband if she fails to disclose her own equitable interest in the house[3].

Though seen as an unwelcome development, conveyancers have readily adapted to the need to make more extensive inquiries on behalf of their clients, following Lord Wilberforce's condemnation of their previous easy-going practice[4]. It is now standard procedure on a purchase of land to ask the vendor in preliminary inquiries for the names of other adult occupants, and to inquire if any such person has a legal or equitable interest in the property[5]. Of course, a negative response given in good faith will not protect the purchaser if it proves to be incorrect. To be safe the inquiries should be directed to the occupier. Even then there is no certainty that the purchaser will receive an informed reply. The cases show that it is far from easy to determine, especially in disputes not involving spouses, whether a contribution to a purchase or improvement of property was intended as a gift, loan or the acquisition of a beneficial interest[6].

A satisfactory solution to the continuing problem of ensuring adequate protection for both purchasers and mortgagees and also for equitable owners in occupation is proving singularly elusive to find. The Law Commission is no nearer to finding an acceptable formula[7]. The Government's attempt in 1987 to deprive occupiers other than spouses of the protection currently afforded by their occupation of land turned out to be an unmitigated disaster when its Land Registration and Law of Property Bill was withdrawn because of concerted opposition to its ill-judged provisions. In the meantime, practitioners and their clients must continue to make the most of a trying and time-consuming exercise, which can occasionally produce quite unforeseen consequences[8].

---

2   Ibid, per Buckley LJ, and Shaw LJ who, unlike the majority, took the view that the mortgagee was prima facie bound because he did not inquire of the occupier.
3   Cf *Ulster Bank Ltd v Shanks* [1982] NI 143. Seemingly the wife was aware of her equitable interest in the house.
4   *Boland's* case [1981] AC 487 at 508, [1980] 2 All ER 408 at 415, HL.
5   See p 191, ante.
6   See eg *Hussey v Palmer* [1972] 3 All ER 744, CA; *Dewar v Dewar* [1975] 2 All ER 728; *Re Sharpe (a bankrupt)* [1980] 1 All ER 198.
7   See the proposed registration requirement advocated for co-ownership situations in Report No 115, paras 72–84, which despite its alleged overwhelming advantages (para 83) remains unadopted. See Report No 155, Annual Report 1984–85, para 1.38.
8   See the letter in (1979) 123 Sol Jo 520.

(c) Imputed notice

Actual or constructive notice possessed by the purchaser's agent is imputed to the purchaser. This rule is of particular importance in conveyancing transactions since the majority of vendors and purchasers employ a solicitor or licensed conveyancer. The agent's notice is imputed to the principal only if it is acquired in the same transaction[9]. Knowledge obtained in a previous transaction does not suffice. In the *Tizard* case[10], the mortgagee was held to have knowledge of the mortgagor's marital status, discovered (but not subsequently reported) by its surveyor when inspecting the property for the purpose of preparing a valuation report.

Where, as is commonly the case, a solicitor is acting for a purchaser and a mortgagee, the mortgagee will not have imputed notice of matters communicated to him by the purchaser. He owes a duty of confidentiality to his client[11]. If the information received from the purchaser indicates a conflict of interest with the mortgagee, then the solicitor should either get the purchaser's consent to his passing that information on to the mortgagee, or decline to continue to act[12].

4.   Successors in title

If A, a purchaser without notice of an equitable interest, later conveys to B, B can shelter behind A's lack of notice and take free from that interest, irrespective of his own notice. This consequence is not because of any special indulgence towards the successor, rather the need to protect A, the original purchaser without notice, so as not to 'clog the sale of estates'[13]. In effect, A's lack of notice enables him to deal with his land unincumbered by the equitable interest[14]. There appears to be no authority to the effect that a volunteer from A, eg A's devisee, also takes free from the equitable interest, but it would seem to follow on principle since he succeeds to A's unincumbered estate. It is thought, however, that a squatter would be bound; he is not a successor in title of the former dispossessed owner and equity's reason for protecting the successor is inapplicable in the case of a squatter.

One important qualification exists to this rule. A man cannot profit from his own wrong. A trustee selling trust property in breach of trust to a purchaser without notice continues to hold the property subject to the trusts if he later acquires the property[15]. This exception does not in terms cover the situation where V conveys land subject to an enforceable equitable interest to P, a

9   LPA 1925, s 199(1)(ii)(b); LPA 1969, ss 24(4), 25(11). The notice must be that of the solicitor personally, not that of his firm: *Winkworth v Edward Baron Development Co Ltd* [1987] 1 All ER 114, HL.
10   [1986] 2 All ER 54. The fact of agency was conceded by counsel for the plaintiffs.
11   See *Halifax Mortgage Services Ltd v Stepsky* [1996] Ch 207, [1996] 2 All ER 277, CA.
12   *Mortgage Express Ltd v Bowerman* (1995) 12 EG 144.
13   *Lowther v Carlton* (1741) 2 Atk 242, per Lord Hardwicke.
14   *Wilkes v Spooner* [1911] 2 KB 473 at 484, CA, per Vaughan Williams LJ.
15   *Re Stapleford Colliery Co, Barrow's Case* (1880) 14 Ch D 432 at 445, CA, per Jessel MR, applied in *Gordon v Holland* (1913) 108 LT 385, PC.

purchaser without notice, and later reacquires it from P, for V is not a trustee for the equitable owner. Yet V ought on principle to be bound; he should not be able to purge his own conscience by conveying to a purchaser without notice.

C System of registration of charges

1. Scheme of Land Charges Act 1972[16]

The scheme of the Land Charges Act 1972 is to require[17] the owner of a registrable interest to protect his rights by registering it in an appropriate register maintained at a central Registry and open to public inspection. The Act achieves its objective indirectly by providing that failure to register avoids the interest in certain circumstances. A purchaser who does not search the register takes subject to all registered interests, for registration constitutes *actual* notice[18]. Hence the importance of the search for incumbrances.

It is tempting to interpret the Act as operating within the equitable doctrine of notice; it simply provides a statutory procedure for giving notice by way of registration. The Act does more than this. It extends the scope of the equitable rule by embracing some legal interests and in some cases confers protection on a mere equitable owner. It does not, however, apply to all *equitable* interests and those outside the Act continue to be governed by the equitable rule. Some commentators prefer therefore to treat the Act as establishing a separate system[19].

A system of registration is workable only so long as registered interests are readily discoverable. From the very outset the Land Charges Act 1925 suffered from one fundamental defect, and the Act of 1972, being merely a consolidating measure, makes no attempt to remedy it. Charges are registered not against the burdened land, but against the estate owner. A purchaser can make an effective search only if he knows the names of all estate owners since 1925. This knowledge he is invariably denied, for the vendor need only deduce title for a period of 15 years. In consequence a purchaser may be bound by a charge the existence of which he has no practical means of discovering. Only the extension of the system of registration of title will eliminate the problem, and even then not completely so long as certain leasehold estates are incapable of registration. The Law of Property Act 1969[20] introduced a temporary solution by giving a statutory right to compensation in certain cases.

Under s 1(1) of the Act five separate registers are maintained in the Land Charges Department at the Land Registry in Plymouth. These are:

---

16 Replacing the LCA 1925. In the rest of this chapter references to 'the Act' are to be taken as references to the LCA 1972, unless the context otherwise requires.
17 But he owes no duty to the other party to register: *Wright v Dean* [1948] Ch 686, [1948] 2 All ER 415 (lessee's failure to register option no bar to recovery of damages from lessor).
18 LPA 1925, s 198, p 396, post.
19 M & W, 134.
20 Section 25, implementing the Law Commission's recommendations in Law Com No 18, paras 17–27. See further p 274, ante, and p 397, post.

(a) a register of land charges;
(b) a register of pending actions;
(c) a register of writs and orders affecting land;
(d) a register of deeds of arrangement affecting land;
(e) a register of annuities.
There is also kept at the Registry a register of agricultural charges required to be registered under the Agricultural Credits Act 1928[1].

2.   Register of land charges

Land charges comprise by far the most important category of registrable interests. They are divided into six classes, A, B, C, D, E, and F which was added to the original list by the Matrimonial Homes Act 1967. These six classes comprehend charges on or obligations affecting land[2], other than local land charges which are regulated by the Local Land Charges Act 1975[3]. To constitute a land charge for the purposes of the Act of 1972, there must be a charge on *land*. In general terms this is defined by s 17(1) to mean corporeal land or corporeal hereditaments, but not the proceeds of sale of land. Thus a charge on an undivided share of land is not a registrable land charge[4].

Our attention must now be turned to the individual classes which are defined in s 2 of the Act. Unfortunately, uncertainty exists as to the precise scope of some of the classes, and there could well be some overlap between them[5]. This is a major defect of the Act. It is highly desirable that a solicitor, who has to apply the Act in day to day conveyancing transactions, should be able to tell at a glance what obligations require registration, and the importance of giving to the section a plain and ordinary interpretation has been stressed[6].

(a) Class A, s 2(2)
This category consists of financial charges on land created pursuant to the application of some person under the provisions of a statute. It covers, for example, a charge obtained by a landlord in respect of compensation paid to a tenant for improvements to business premises[7].

---

1   These relate to charges in favour of a bank on farming stock and other agricultural assets; they do not directly affect the land.
2   LCA 1972, s 2(1). New registrations for the year ending 1995 were: A–0; B–3,625; C(i)–32,295; C(ii)–22; C(iii)–1,611; C(iv)–15,518; D(i)–281; D(ii)–9,518; D(iii)–615; F–1,950.
3   Save for certain dual status local land charges registered as such before the LLCA 1975 came into force: LCA 1972, s 3A, added by the LLCA 1975, s 17 (1). For the LLCA 1975, see Ch 7.
4   *Re Rayleigh Weir Stadium* [1954] 2 All ER 283. See also *Georgiades v Edward Wolfe & Co Ltd* [1965] Ch 487, [1964] 3 All ER 433, CA (charge on deposit and proceeds of sale of land not registrable). Cf the position under LRA 1925, p 74, ante.
5   *Shiloh Spinners Ltd v Harding* [1972] Ch 326 at 345, [1971] 2 All ER 307 at 316, CA, per Russell LJ.
6   *Shiloh Spinners Ltd v Harding* [1973] AC 691 at 721, [1973] 1 All ER 90 at 99, HL, per Lord Wilberforce; ironically the interest (an equitable right of entry) was held to be outside the Act.
7   Landlord and Tenant Act 1927, s 12 and Sch 1, para (7). For other examples, see LCA 1972, Sch 2.

(b) Class B, s 2 (3)
This group comprises charges (not being local land charges) similar to those within Class A, save that they are imposed automatically by statute. Most of the charges which would qualify for inclusion within this Class are excluded because they are registrable as local land charges. The central Registry attracts few Class B registrations. An example occurs under the Legal Aid Act 1974, which creates a charge in favour of The Law Society on property recovered or preserved for an assisted litigant[8]. A recent addition has been made to the list by the Health and Social Services and Social Security Adjudications Act 1983[9].

(c) Class C, s 2 (4)
The following constitute Class C land charges: a puisne mortgage, a limited owner's charge, a general equitable charge and an estate contract[10].

C(i) *Puisne mortgage.* This is any legal mortgage not being a mortgage protected by a deposit of documents relating to the legal estate affected. If a mortgagee has the title deeds, their non-production by the mortgagor will give notice of the mortgage to persons subsequently dealing with the land; protection by registration is unnecessary. It is not clear whether all the documents relating to the estate must be deposited with the mortgagee, though it is clearly preferable for him to hold all of them.

C(ii) *Limited owner's charge.* This is defined as any *equitable* charge acquired by a tenant for life or statutory owner under the Capital Transfer Tax Act 1984, by reason of his discharge of capital transfer tax or other liabilities. Such a charge arises where a life tenant discharges tax[11] payable on the death of the previous life tenant out of his own pocket instead of resorting to the settled property.

C(iii) *General equitable charge.* This is a comprehensive class of *equitable* charge *not included in any other class of land charge*. Certain charges are expressly excluded, including (a) an equitable charge protected by a deposit of deeds relating to the legal estate affected; and (b) a charge arising or affecting an interest under a trust for sale or settlement.
   The following appear to be registrable within this class: equitable charges of a legal estate, a vendor's lien for unpaid purchase money[12], annuities charged on land created after 1925[13], an equitable rentcharge. An equitable mortgage, the basis of which is a contract to execute a legal mortgage, is seemingly registrable, not as a C(iii), but as a C(iv) land charge because of the express

---

8 Section 9, see *Hanlon v Law Society* [1981] AC 124, [1980] 2 All ER 199, HL.
9 Section 22(8) (charge for arrears of contributions for accommodation provided by local authority). The charge is created by a simple written declaration by the authority: s 22(7).
10 For the registration of pre-1926 charges, see ss 2(8), 3(3).
11 LCA 1972, s 3(4)(ii), as amended by CTTA 1984, Sch 8, para (3). This tax is now called Inheritance Tax: Finance Act 1986, s 100.
12 See *Uziell-Hamilton v Keen* (1971) 22 P & CR 655.
13 For annuities created before the Act, see p 390, post.

exclusion from Class C(iii) of any charge included within another class[14]. The position of an equitable mortgage protected by a deposit of deeds is uncertain[15]. To require registration as a C(iv) would run counter to the general scheme of the 1925 legislation, which excludes from registration all mortgages secured by a deposit of deeds. The better view is that such equitable mortgages are not registrable. In practice, a purchaser with notice of an equitable mortgage (either from non-production of the deeds or registration as a C(iii) land charge) will insist upon its discharge, rather than rely on its being void against him for non-registration as a C(iv)[16].

It should be noted, however, that a simple deposit of title deeds will not, after 1989 be effective to create an equitable mortgage. The basis of a deposit of title deeds amounting to an equitable mortgage is that the deposit constituted part performance of a contract to create a mortgage. Because of s 2 of the Law of Property (Miscellaneous Provisions) Act 1989 a contract to create a mortgage must now be in writing and cannot be created simply by a deposit of title deeds[17]. In practice, however, a purchaser is unlikely to take the risk that the deposit of deeds was not effective to create an equitable mortgage and will continue to insist upon its discharge.

C(iv) *Estate contract.*   An estate contract is defined as:

> …a contract by an estate owner or by a person entitled at the date of the contract to have a legal estate conveyed to him to convey or create a legal estate, including a contract conferring either expressly or by statutory implication a valid option to purchase, a right of pre-emption or any other like right.

In addition to the rights included by express reference, this definition embraces (inter alia) a contract for the sale of land, an agreement for a lease, an option to renew a lease[18], an equitable mortgage, a boundary agreement if there is a contract to convey land but not an agreement which merely confirms existing boundaries[19], and a contract to grant a legal easement[20]. A conditional contract appears to be registrable, at least if the condition is one to be satisfied, not by

---

14   *Shiloh Spinners Ltd v Harding* [1972] Ch 326 at 345, [1971] 2 All ER 307 at 316, CA, per Russell LJ; *Williams v Burlington Investments Ltd* (1977) 121 Sol Jo 424, HL. The point is not finally settled; see M & W, 176. But an equitable charge on an *equitable* interest in land ranks as a C(iii): *Property Discount Corpn Ltd v Lyon Group Ltd* [1981] 1 All ER 379 at 384, CA, per Brightman LJ.

15   See M & W, 998, C & B, 674. The Committee on Land Charges (the Roxburgh Committee) (1956) recommended legislation to make it clear that such mortgages were not registrable: Cmd 9825, para 16.

16   See (1962) 26 Conv (NS) 445, 446–49 (R G Rowley).

17   *United Bank of Kuwait plc v Sahib* [1996] 3 All ER 215, CA. For critical comment, see [1994] Conv 485 (M P Thompson).

18   *Beesley v Hallwood Estates Ltd* [1960] 2 All ER 314; affd on other grounds [1961] 1 All ER 90, CA; *Taylors Fashions Ltd v Liverpool Victoria Trustees Co Ltd* [1982] QB 133n, [1981] 1 All ER 897. See also *Markfaith Investment Ltd v Chiap Hua Flashlights Ltd* [1991] 2 AC 43, PC.

19   *Neilson v Poole* (1969) 20 P & CR 909, p 544, post.

20   See the Roxburgh Committee, loc cit; *E R Ives Investments Ltd v High* [1967] 2 QB 379 at 403, [1967] 1 All ER 504 at 513, CA; Winn LJ accepted as correct counsel's submission that an agreement for a right of way should have been registered as an estate contract.

the parties, but by some extraneous person or event[1]. Once an option to purchase has been registered, it is not necessary, separately, to register the contract of sale that arises upon the exercise of the option[2].

It was formerly the case that a written instrument was not a prerequisite for registrability[3] but an enforceable oral contract was not registrable[4]. In the case of contracts made after 1989, they must now actually be in writing and so an oral agreement for the sale of land, which now lacks contractual status[5], is plainly not registrable.

The statutory definition expressly includes a right of pre-emption. According to the rather unsatisfactory majority decision in *Pritchard v Briggs*[6] such a right is immediately capable of protection as an estate contract, even though an equitable interest in land arises only when it is later converted into an option to purchase on the grantor's desire to sell. The Act in effect invests the right with a special registrable quality, despite the fact that initially it lacks the proprietary characteristic normally associated with registrability. A lessee's covenant to offer to surrender his lease in certain eventualities ranks as an estate contract and is registrable as a C(iv)[7]. This will apply even to a covenant in a lease of *registered* land, not capable of substantive registration because it is granted for a term not exceeding 21 years – a point likely to be overlooked in practice.

To qualify as 'any other like right' the contract must be akin to an option to purchase or right of pre-emption. The expression covers a right to call for a surrender of a lease[8] and, seemingly, a unilateral contract to enter into a formal contract[9], but not an equitable right of entry[10].

This C(iv) class of charge is not confined to cases where a contracting party is to receive the legal estate. A contract between A and B whereby A contracts to convey a legal estate to B's nominee suffices[11], but not a contract whereby A agrees that B has power to accept offers to purchase made by third parties[12]. Provided the grantor possesses some estate in the land affected (estate ownership of *other* land does not suffice), it is immaterial that at the time of the contract he does not own the estate the subject of the contract[13]. A contract to convey unspecified land which may be acquired in the future is not

1   *Haslemere Estates Ltd v Baker* [1982] 3 All ER 525 at 534, per Megarry V-C.
2   *Armstrong & Holmes Ltd v Holmes and Dodds* [1994] 1 All ER 826; [1994] Conv 483 (N P Gravells).
3   *Universal Permanent Building Society v Cooke* [1952] Ch 95 at 104, [1951] 2 All ER 893 at 898, CA, per Jenkins LJ. See also *Lloyds Bank plc v Carrick* (1996) 14 LS Gaz R 30, CA.
4   *Mens v Wilson* (1973) 231 EG 843; *Jones v Morgan* (1973) 231 EG 1167.
5   Law of Property (Miscellaneous Provisions) Act 1989, s 2.
6   [1980] Ch 338, [1980] 1 All ER 294, CA, Goff LJ dissenting, discussed pp 229–230, ante.
7   *Greene v Church Comrs for England* [1974] Ch 467, [1974] 3 All ER 609, CA. See p 301, ante.
8   An alternative ground for the decision in *Greene's* case, supra.
9   See *Daulia Ltd v Four Millbank Nominees Ltd* [1978] Ch 231, [1978] 2 All ER 557, CA.
10 *Shiloh Spinners Ltd v Harding* [1973] AC 691, [1973] 1 All ER 90, HL.
11 *Turley v Mackay* [1944] Ch 37, [1943] 2 All ER 1.
12 *Thomas v Rose* [1968] 3 All ER 765.
13 See the controversial case of *Sharp v Coates* [1949] 1 KB 285, [1948] 2 All ER 871, CA (contract by yearly tenant to grant term of years on becoming freeholder).

registrable; there must be identifiable land affected by the contract to facilitate registration of the relevant particulars[14].

Registration of sub-contracts.   This problem was considered in *Barrett v Hilton Developments Ltd*[15]. Suppose V contracts to convey land to P, and before completion P contracts to sell it to P2. The P-P2 contract ranks as an estate contract since P is entitled at its date to have a legal estate conveyed to him. Registration is required by s 3(1) of the Act to be in the name of the estate owner, ie the owner of the legal estate, V. Registration against P's name is totally ineffective. Moreover the circumstances existing at the time of registration alone are relevant. P's subsequent acquisition of the legal title does not validate a prior ineffectual registration against his name. This may constitute a potential trap for P2, who may not become aware of V's identity until P delivers the abstract of title some time later. P2 can, of course, ascertain the estate owner's name by raising a preliminary inquiry of P before contracting with him, assuming (which may not be the case) P2 is aware that he is involved in a sub-sale. These difficulties highlight the inherent weakness of a scheme requiring registration against names, rather than against land[16].

(d) Class D, s 2(5)
This class comprises three groups.

D(i) *Inland Revenue charge.*   The Commissioners for Inland Revenue may register a charge for unpaid inheritance tax (formerly capital transfer tax). It can be registered in respect of freehold land only; leaseholds and undivided shares in land are expressly exempted[17].

D(ii) *Restrictive covenant.*   This is described as a covenant or agreement restrictive of the user of land, other than one made between lessor and lessee[18], or entered into before 1926. Restrictive obligations imposed by a local authority are registered as local land charges[19]. A covenant to observe and perform existing restrictive covenants by way of indemnity does not require registration.
    The application of the registration provisions to restrictive covenants arising under building schemes is obscure. If the Act is relevant, total

---

14   *Thomas v Rose* [1968] 3 All ER 765 at 769, per Megarry J.
15   [1975] Ch 237, [1974] 3 All ER 944, CA; *Property Discount Corpn Ltd v Lyon Group Ltd* [1980] 1 All ER 334 (developer under building agreement granting equitable charge). Cf the position in registered land, where an entry protecting a sub-contract can only be made against the title of the registered proprietor.
16   The effectiveness of P2's registration appears to depend on due registration of the V-P contract. If V conveys, not to P, but to X, a purchaser for value, P2's contract cannot be specifically enforced if P fails to protect the V-P contract. For some other problems see Emmet, para 19.002.
17   LCA 1972, s 2(5) (as amended); see CTTA 1984, s 237(1), (3), Sch 8, para 3, p 342, note 14, ante.
18   Including a covenant affecting land not demised by the lease, p 392, post.
19   LLCA 1975, s 1(1)(b). The exception as between lessor and lessee is preserved: s 2(a).

enforceability by the purchasers and their successors inter se cannot be achieved unless the common vendor registers the covenants against each purchaser. There is much to be said for the view that a building scheme is outside the Act as it creates reciprocity of obligation between the purchasers[20]. This argument at least has the merit that the common vendor cannot destroy the scheme, in whole or in part, by failing to register.

D(iii) *Equitable easement.*   Like some of the other classes, this category, has been criticised on the grounds of vagueness. The Roxburgh Committee[1] suggested its abolition, but the Law Commission recommended a reprieve, particularly in view of' the then annual rate of registrations[2]. For the purposes of the Act an equitable easement is:

> ...an easement, right or privilege over or affecting land created or arising on or after 1 January 1926, and being merely an equitable interest.

This class clearly covers the *grant* of an easement for life, or for a determinable period, eg a right of way until a road is adopted. A *contract* to create an easement would seem to be registrable either as a D(iii) land charge[3] or as an estate contract[4]. Although Lord Denning MR expressed the view that an equitable easement is some proprietary interest in land such as would before 1926 have been recognised as capable of being conveyed or created *at law* but, which since 1925, only takes effect as an equitable interest[5], this seems to be an unduly restrictive approach[6] and one which did not secure the support of the other members of the court. Nevertheless, despite the apparent width of the words 'right or privilege' they are construed narrowly, so that, to be recognised as an equitable easement, the right in question must display the essential characteristic of an easement. Consequently, the definition has been held not to include a requisition of land under Defence Regulations[7], rights arising under proprietary estoppel[8], a tenant's right to remove fixtures at the end of a lease[9], or an equitable right of re-entry[10]. Such rights are enforceable against purchasers upon the application of the old doctrine of notice.

---

20   (1928) 78 Law Jo 39; contra, Emmet, para 17.043. Recent decisions on mutual benefits and burdens, especially *E R Ives Investments Ltd v High* [1967] 2 QB 379, [1967] 1 All ER 504, CA, perhaps add some weight to this argument.
1   Cmnd 9825, para 16.
2   Law Com No 18, para 65. The figure for the year ending 31 March 1986 was 2,063. The figure for the year 1994/95 was 615.
3   *E R Ives Investments Ltd v High* [1967] 2 QB 379 at 403, [1967] 1 All ER 504 at 509, CA, per Danckwerts LJ. See [1986] Conv 31 at 34–7 (M P Thompson).
4   *Huckvale v Aegean Hotels Ltd* (1989) 58 P & CR 163 at 165. See also (1947) 11 Conv (NS) 165 at 176 (E O Walford).
5   *E R Ives Investments Ltd v High,* supra at 395 and 508.
6   See M P Thompson, loc cit.
7   *Lewisham Borough Council v Maloney* [1948] 1 KB 50, [1947] 2 All ER 36, CA.
8   *E R Ives Investments Ltd v High,* supra.
9   *Poster v Slough Estates Ltd* [1969] 1 Ch 495, [1968] 3 All ER 257.
10   *Shiloh Spinners Ltd v Harding* [1973] AC 691, [1973] 1 All ER 90, HL.

(e) Class E, s 2(6)

Annuities created before 1926 but not then registered in the existing register of annuities are registrable as Class E annuities.

(f) Class F, s 2(7)

The Matrimonial Homes Act 1983, s 1(1) gives a spouse having no legal estate in the matrimonial home certain statutory rights of occupation[11] during the subsistence of the marriage. By virtue of s 2(1) these rights constitute a charge on the property, registrable as a Class F charge. Registration is intended to protect the right of occupation; the courts will not allow it to be used for an ulterior purpose[12]. Ownership of an equitable interest in the house does not preclude registration of the charge (s 1(11)). Registration does not give the charge priority over an existing mortgage[13]. These statutory rights are now enforceable against the other spouse's trustee in bankruptcy, irrespective of registration[14]. The Class F charge differs from the majority of land charges which are created by some transaction entered into by the estate owner, so that he should in theory be aware of the likelihood of the charge being registered against him. However this charge is created by a statute, and the non-owning spouse may register it without notifying the estate owner. As we have already seen[15], this situation can create difficulties for the estate owner should he subsequently contract to sell the property in ignorance of the registration.

3.   The other registers

(a) Register of pending actions[16]

Pending land actions and bankruptcy petitions are registrable under s 7(1) of the Land Charges Act 1972, in the register of pending actions. This covers any action pending in court relating to land or any interest in or charge on land (s 17(1)). The action must be one which claims some proprietary right in land[17], such as: a claim to an easement[18], or proceedings to forfeit a lease[19], or an application under the Matrimonial Causes Act 1973 for a property adjustment order[20]. In contrast a summons seeking a declaration of equal beneficial

---

11   But not in respect of a non-matrimonial home: *S v S* (1980) 10 Fam Law 153.
12   *Barnet v Hassett* [1982] 1 All ER 80 (attempt to freeze proceeds of sale).
13   Section 2(10). The spouse has a right to pay the mortgage instalments and is entitled in some circumstances to be notified of and made a party to possession proceedings: ss 1(5), 8(2), (3).
14   Insolvency Act 1986, s 336(2).
15   See *Watts v Waller* [1973] QB 153, [1972] 3 All ER 257, CA; *Wroth v Tyler* [1974] Ch 30, [1973] 1 All ER 897, pp 165–166.
16   See [1995] Conv 309 (J Howell).
17   *Calgary and Edmonton Land Co Ltd v Dobinson* [1974] Ch 102, [1974] 1 All ER 484.
18   *Allen v Greenhi Builders Ltd* [1978] 3 All ER 1163.
19   *Selim Ltd v Bickenhall Engineering Ltd* [1981] 3 All ER 210; aliter if the action is for damages for breach of covenant: *Regan & Blackburn Ltd v Rogers* [1985] 2 All ER 180.
20   *Whittingham v Whittingham* [1979] Fam 9, [1978] 3 All ER 805, CA; *Perez-Adamson v Perez Rivas* [1987] Fam 89, [1987] 3 All ER 20, CA. Cf *Sowerby v Sowerby* (1982) 44 P & CR 192.

entitlement to a house is not registrable; there is no action affecting an interest in land[1]. Registration of a bankruptcy petition, which is usually sought by the registrar of the court where the petition is filed, is essentially a temporary measure pending registration of the receiving order. It is registered against the bankrupt, whether or not he is known to own any land.

(b) Register of writs and orders
The following are registrable in this register under s 6(1) of the Act:
(a) any writ or order affecting land issued for the purpose of enforcing a judgment or recognisance;
(b) an order appointing a receiver[2] or sequestrator of land;
(c) a bankruptcy order, whether or not the bankrupt's estate is known to include land[3].
A court order charging the land of a judgment debtor with the payment of the money due falls within (a)[4], but not a Mareva injunction which is interlocutory in character, continuing only until judgment is given[5].

(c) Register of deeds of arrangement
As an alternative to bankruptcy an insolvent debtor may make an arrangement with his creditors whereby he is released from their claims, though unable to discharge them in full. This arrangement often takes the form of a transfer of the debtor's property to a trustee for the benefit of his creditors. If the transfer (known as a deed of arrangement) affects land it should be registered[6].

It should be noted that any registration effected under ss 6 or 7 of the Act automatically lapses after five years but it may be renewed from time to time for a further period of five years[7].

4. Interests outside the registration system

Not all equitable interests are embraced by the Land Charges Act 1972.

1 *Taylor v Taylor* [1968] 1 All ER 843, CA; *Haslemere Estates Ltd v Baker* [1982] 3 All ER 525 (claim based on proprietary estoppel to non-existent charge on land which plaintiff hoped court would create).
2 *Clayhope Properties Ltd v Evans* [1986] 2 All ER 795, CA (receiver appointed to manage tenanted property).
3 Amended by the Insolvency Act 1985, Sch 8, para 21(3)(a).
4 Charging Orders Act 1979, s 3(2). A beneficial interest under a trust for sale can now be the subject of a charging order: *National Westminster Bank Ltd v Stockman* [1981] 1 All ER 800. Registration will be against the trustees holding the legal title (p 396, post), should they not be the same persons as the beneficiaries.
5 *Stockler v Fourways Estates Ltd* [1983] 3 All ER 501.
6 LCA 1972, s 7(1). They also require registration under the Deeds of Arrangement Act 1914.
7 LCA 1972, s 8. For some problems relating to re-registration, see [1982] Conv 399.

(a) Interests that are overreached
Registration is inapplicable to interests arising under a settlement or trust for sale. These are not intended to be enforceable against a purchaser of the land, being transferred to the proceeds of sale on a conveyance in the prescribed manner.

(b) Equitable interests expressly excluded by Act
The following interests, all expressly excluded, continue to be governed by the rules of notice – actual, constructive and imputed:
(i)   pre-1926 equitable easements,
(ii) pre-1926 restrictive covenants,
(iii) restrictive covenants (whenever made) between lessor and lessee.

Covenants affecting leasehold land are usually contained in the lease which every prudent purchaser will inspect, thus obtaining actual notice[8]. It has been held that a covenant given by a lessor to his lessee and affecting the lessor's adjoining land is not registrable on the ground that the benefit is annexed to the leasehold interest in the demised land[9]. This is perhaps an unfortunate decision. Unless the restriction is brought on to the title of the adjoining land, which is unlikely, a purchaser of that land will not discover its existence. He will therefore take free from it unless he also purchases the freehold reversion of the demised land. The only sure way that the lessee can give the purchaser notice of his rights is to have a memorandum of the covenants endorsed on the deeds relating to the adjoining land, but he has no statutory right to require this[10].

(c) Sale followed by compulsory registration of title
Section 14(3) of the Act renders it unnecessary to register any land charge created by a conveyance or other instrument which leads to compulsory first registration of title under s 123 of the Land Registration Act 1925. Such charges will be entered on the register of title on first registration. The exemption applies only to charges affecting the estate conveyed, and not, for example, to a land charge affecting the vendor's unregistered land, such as an option to purchase the freehold reversion granted by a lease caught by s 123.

(d) Equitable interests arising under a bare trust
Where X holds a fee simple estate in trust for Y absolutely, there is neither a trust for sale nor a settlement, so that the overreaching provisions of the property legislation of 1925 are inapplicable; nor does Y's equitable fee simple constitute a charge or obligation affecting land so as to make it registrable as a Class C or D land charge. The enforceability of his interest against a purchaser for value from X is governed by the ordinary rules of notice. His occupation of the land would normally be sufficient to fix the purchaser with constructive notice, even when X is also in occupation.

---

8   For the position of an underlessee and a purchaser from him, see p 294, ante.
9   *Dartstone Ltd v Cleveland Petroleum Co Ltd* [1969] 3 All ER 668.
10 Cf LPA 1925, s 200, which does not apply to a lessee.

(e) Mere equities
A purchaser for value of any interest (legal or equitable) takes free from a mere equity of which he has no notice. A mere equity is an equitable right falling short of an equitable interest. Essentially it is a right to equitable relief, such as a right to have a deed set aside for fraud or rectified for mistake[11].

(f) Estoppel interests and contractual licences
Equity will always restrain a legal owner from exercising his legal rights if it would be unconscionable[12] on his part to do so. Illustrations of this principle have occurred in several well known recent cases, where X has expended money on Y's land (or even on his own land) in the expectation created or encouraged by Y that he (X) will be allowed to enjoy the fruits of that expenditure and equity has refused to allow Y to defeat X's expectation[13]. The court decides in each case how X's rights are to be satisfied[14]; sometimes the court orders a conveyance[15], sometimes an injunction which has the effect of creating a permanent right over land[16], sometimes compensation only. So viewed X's rights amount to an equity (and it is variously described as an equity arising out of acquiescence or an equity by estoppel) as distinct from an equitable interest. It is therefore unenforceable against a purchaser for value without notice of any interest in the land affected.

The problem of notice was considered for the first time in the *Ives* case where both Lord Denning MR and Danckwerts LJ held that the defendant's equity arising out of acquiescence, a right of way over the plaintiff's yard, was not capable of registration as a land charge[17]. The estoppel right was regarded as being binding upon the purchaser because he had notice of it[18]. It has also been held that an estoppel right is binding upon a volunteer[19]. This indicates that the right is proprietary in nature and so, in principle, a purchaser with notice will be bound by it[20]. The view that such an interest cannot be registered

---

11   See p 696, post.
12   See eg *Binions v Evans* [1972] Ch 359 at 368, [1972] 2 All ER 70 at 76, CA, per Lord Denning MR.
13   Eg *Inwads v Baker* [1965] 2 QB 29, [1965] 1 All ER 446, CA; *E R Ives Investments Ltd v High* [1967] 2 QB 379, [1967] 1 All ER 504, CA; *Hussey v Palmer* [1972] 3 All ER 744, CA; *Dodsworth v Dodsworth* (1973) 228 EG 1115, CA; *Taylors Fashions Ltd v Liverpool Victoria Trustees Co Ltd* [1982] QB 133n, [1981] 1 All ER 897; *Greasley v Cooke* [1980] 3 All ER 710, CA; *Re Basham* [1987] 1 All ER 405 (acting in belief of future rights). See Hanbury & Martin, *Modern Equity* (14th edn), 877 ff.
14   *Inwards v Baker* [1965] 2 QB 29 at 37, [1965] 1 All ER 446 at 449, CA, per Lord Denning MR.
15   *Dilwyn v Llewelyn* (1862) 4 De GF & J 517; *Pasco v Turner* [1979] 2 All ER 945, CA.
16   *Ward v Kirkland* [1967] Ch 194, [1966] 1 All ER 609 (drainage right); *Crabb v Arun District Council* [1976] Ch 179, [1975] 3 All ER 865, CA (right of way).
17   See note 13, ante. Winn LJ held that the agreement for the right of way was void for non-registration, but the statute had no impact on the estoppel created by the conduct of the plaintiff's predecessor. See also the *Taylor Fashions* case, ante.
18   In *Lloyds Bank plc v Carrick* (1996) 14 LS Gaz R 30, CA, it was considered to be very doubtful whether the Court of Appeal could now hold that an estoppel right was not binding upon a purchaser with notice.
19   *Voyce v Voyce* (1991) 62 P & CR 290, CA; [1992] Conv 52 at 56, 57 (J Martin).
20   See also (1995) 58 MLR 637 at 642 (G Battersby); (1994) 12 LS 147 at 155 (S Baughen).

as a land charge seems to be clearly correct. Until a court has determined what remedy is appropriate to satisfy the equity, the right is inchoate.

For a period of time, it was unclear whether an irrevocable contractual licence to occupy land was an interest in land[1], or gave rise to a constructive trust[2]. Such authorities were highly controversial, not least because they were difficult to reconcile with earlier, binding authority[3]. The authorities were subjected to an extensive review, albeit obiter[4], in *Ashburn Anstalt v Arnold*[5] and the conclusion reached that statements to the effect that contractual licences created interests in land were wrong. This now seems to be the prevailing judicial view. In *IDC Group Ltd v Clark*[6], Sir Nicolas Browne-Wilkinson V-C opined that *Ashburn Anstalt* had:

> ...put what I hope is the *quietus* to the heresy that a mere licence creates an interest in land. [The Court of Appeal] also put the *quietus* to the heresy that parties to a contractual licence necessarily become constructive trustees.

In the light of these comments, it now seems impossible to argue that a purchaser will be bound by a contractual licence merely because he has notice of it. He will only be bound if he expressly agrees to take subject to the right of the licencee, in which case a constructive trust will be imposed upon him[7].

D   Effect of registration and non-registration

1.   Manner of registration

The Land Charges Act 1972, s 1, requires the Chief Land Registrar to maintain an index (which can include any device or combination of devices serving that purpose) whereby all entries in the different registers can be readily traced. Since computerisation in 1974 all relevant data are recorded on tape fed into and processed by the Department's computer. Applications for registration should be made on, and furnish the particulars required by, the prescribed forms[8]. The appropriate form for land charges (other than Class F) is Form K1. This calls for the following information: the chargee's name and address, the type of charge, details of the instrument of creation[9], particulars of the land affected (including a short description identifying its location), and the full name, address and occupation of the estate owner. Needless to say, all

---

1   See *Errington v Errington and Woods* [1952] 1 KB 290, [1952] 1 All ER 149, CA, *Binions v Evans* [1972] Ch 359, [1972] 2 All ER 70, CA.
2   *Re Sharpe* [1980] 1 All ER 198.
3   Notably, *King v David Allen & Sons Billposting Ltd* [1916] 2 AC 54, HL (Ir).
4   The court held that there was a tenancy binding on the purchaser. The subsequent overruling of this finding in *Prudential Assurance Co v London Residuary Body* [1992] 2 AC 386, [1992] 3 All ER 504, HL, does not invalidate the analysis of the authorities on licences.
5   [1989] Ch 1 [1988] 2 All ER 147, CA. See [1988] Conv 201 (M P Thompson).
6   [1992] 1 EGLR 187 at 189; affd on appeal [1992] 2 EGLR 184, CA, where Nourse LJ stated, at 185, that a licence is personal to the parties.
7   *Ashburn Anstalt v Arnold*, supra.
8   LCA 1972, s 1(2); Land Charges Rules 1974, SI 1974, No1286, r 5, and Sch 2.
9   If not created by an instrument, short particulars of its effect must be given: s 3(5).

information given in the form should be accurate. The applicant must also certify that the estate owner's title is not registered at the Land Registry, a requirement that has been relaxed for Class F applications (Form K2)[10].

Applications not made by a practising solicitor or licensed conveyancer must be supported by a statutory declaration in Form K14, unless relating to a Class F charge. Applications are acknowledged in such a way as to give full details of the actual registration.

Registration must be in the name of the estate owner, ie the legal owner, whose estate is intended to be affected[11]. No guidance is given in the Act as to what is meant by 'name'. The Registry will not accept an application for registration against a surname only[12]. In *Diligent Finance Co Ltd v Alleyne*[13] the court held that in the absence of contrary evidence the proper registration name was the one in which the conveyancing documents were taken – not the name on the birth certificate nor the name by which a person was commonly known. These last two possibilities were rightly discounted since a purchaser would have no ready means of discovering them[14]. Consequently a wife's Class F registration against her husband's name, Erskine Alleyne[15], was unenforceable against a later mortgagee who had obtained a clear certificate of search against Erskine Owen Alleyne, the name appearing in the title deeds. The court did not consider what contrary evidence might suffice to displace their prima facie ruling. This case establishes a satisfactory working rule for land charges created by a document, when registration against the grantor's name appearing therein ought normally to suffice, but it clearly highlights the difficulties facing a spouse seeking to register a Class F charge which arises under a statute. The spouse may never have seen the deeds of the property and consequently has no means of knowing that the name by which the other spouse is known differs from that in the deeds. A registration in an incorrect name may not always be invalid. According to Russell LJ in *Oak Co-operative Building Society v Blackburn*[16], yet another case which demonstrates the problems that may arise under a system of registration against names, registration in a version of a person's name is valid against someone who makes no search, or who searches in the wrong name.

Ideally, registration should be effected immediately after creation of the interest concerned. Registration against a subsequent estate owner is valid

---

10 Land Charges Rules 1974, r 13(2). See Ruoff, *Searching without Tears*, 76 and (1976) 40 Conv (NS) 104.
11 LCA 1972, s 3(1), and s 17(1) applying the meaning assigned to the same expression by LPA 1925, s 205(1)(v). See *Barrett v Hilton Developments Ltd* [1975] Ch 237, [1974] 3 All ER 944, CA, p 344, ante.
12 See the Registrar's letter at (1977) 74 LS Gaz 534. Bankruptcy petitions are an exception: Ruoff, op cit, 66.
13 (1972) 23 P & CR 346.
14 And see *Standard Property Investment plc v British Plastics Federation* (1985) 53 P & CR 25 (name as disclosed by conveyance to purchaser taken as correct name for registration purposes in preference to fuller names appearing in building society mortgage).
15 This was the name by which he was known to his wife.
16 [1968] Ch 730 at 743, [1968] 2 All ER 117 at 122, CA. In this case the estate owner's true name was Francis David Blackburn, registration was effected in the name of Frank David Blackburn and a search certificate was requested in the name of Francis Davis Blackburn.

unless the charge has become void against him (or a predecessor) for want of registration. Registration against one of two or more joint owners is ineffective[17]. Similarly registration against the name of a deceased estate owner used not to be possible, as he has ceased to be an estate owner[18]. Registration against his personal representatives was what was required. In the absence of a grant of representation registration against the President of the Family Division of the High Court was seemingly necessary[19]. It is now provided by s 15 of the Law of Property (Miscellaneous Provisions) Act 1994[20] that registration can be made against the name of a deceased estate owner. It should be appreciated, however, that where the death of the estate owner occurred prior to 1 June 1995, when the new provision came into force, that land charges may have had to be registered against personal representatives or the President. The Act does not forbid registration by an estate owner against his own name, and there may exist unusual situations where this should be considered[1].

The Registrar is not concerned to inquire into or verify the accuracy or validity of an application, but it is within his power to reject an application which on its face is outside the Act because, eg, it relates to registered land[2]. Registration can thus be obtained of a matter not properly registrable, such as an estate contract when no binding contract exists. Non-registrable matters are sometimes registered in an endeavour to provide a purchaser who obtains a search certificate with actual knowledge. There is a feeling that such use of the Act is improper and, for solicitors, unprofessional. The court has an inherent jurisdiction to order the removal of an improperly registered charge[3].

2. Actual notice

Subject to various statutory exceptions[4], the Law of Property Act 1925, s 198 (1) enacts that registration constitutes '*actual* notice of [the] instrument or matter ... to all persons and for all purposes connected with the land affected[5]. Registration operates to make the protected interest binding on the purchaser, provided it is otherwise enforceable. Registration does not confer validity; it gives notice of the existence of a right whose validity is determined by the general law. A purchaser would not be deemed to have notice of a matter which, though registered, was not properly registrable, but its disclosure on

---

17   *Snape v Snape* (1959) 173 EG 679.
18   2 W & C, 22; see further [1979] Conv 249 (A M Prichard); [1986] Conv 237.
19   This is the Registry's view; see (1986) 83 LSG 2127, also revealing an average weekly trawl of six applications for registrations against deceased owners. How many practitioners would think to search against the President? There are a mere 20 such registrations: loc cit.
20   A new s 3(1A) is introduced into LCA 1972.
 1   Consider the situation in *Wright v Dean* [1948] Ch 686, [1948] 2 All ER 415, p 383, ante, note 17. See also *UCB Bank plc v French* [1995] NPC 144, [1996] Conv 44 at 49 (M P Thompson).
 2   See LCA 1972, s 14 (1); Land Charges Rules 1974, rr 13 (1), 22.
 3   *Heywood v BDC Properties Ltd (No 2)* [1964] 2 All ER 702, CA.
 4   See LPA 1925, ss 94(2), 96(2), (as amended); LPA 1969, ss 24(1), 25(2).
 5   But not where the title to the land is registered; see generally LCA 1972, s 14(1); LRA 1925, ss 59(6), 110(7).

his search certificate would give him actual knowledge. Nor does registration govern the priority of competing equitable interests[6], which continues to be decided by general principles. So, where the contest is between a purchaser under a contract for sale and the vendor's spouse entitled to statutory rights of occupation, the purchaser does not obtain priority because he registered his contract before the spouse registered a Class F charge[7]. But he will take free from the spouse's rights if no Class F charge has been registered before completion.

Section 198 fixes a purchaser with notice of a registered charge, despite its being registered against an estate owner whose name he could not discover on an investigation of the title for the full statutory period. If such a charge comes to light *after* completion, the Law of Property Act 1969, entitles him to claim compensation for loss sustained thereby, provided certain conditions are met[8]. The measure of compensation is left to be assessed according to general principles. Basically he should recover the difference between what he paid for the land and its value as affected by the charge. He can also claim the costs of obtaining compensation, and any expenditure incurred for the purpose of securing that the estate is no longer affected by the charge or affected to a lesser extent[9].

Section 198 (1) is not, however, unlimited in its sphere of operation, despite the all-embracing nature of its language ('notice ... to all ... for all purposes'). It forms part of the machinery introduced in 1926 for the protection of third party rights affecting land. Registration should, therefore, be understood as constituting actual notice for all purposes for which such notice is material, ie for the purpose of enforcing third party rights in land[10]. So, s 198(1) has little or no role to play as between vendor and purchaser, for notice is not to be equated with knowledge[11].

3. The consequences of non-registration

Section 199(1)(i) of the Law of Property Act 1925 enacts that a purchaser is not prejudicially affected by notice of any instrument or matter capable of registration, which is void or unenforceable against him by reason of non-

6 But see LPA 1925, s 97 (priority of registrable mortgages determined by date of registration).
7 The contrary was indicated in *Watts v Waller* [1973] QB 153 at 177, [1972] 3 All ER 257 at 270, CA, per Sachs LJ. See also the obiter comments of Stephenson LJ in *Pritchard v Briggs* [1980] Ch 338 at 423, [1980] 1 All ER 294 at 332, CA, which are difficult to reconcile with the general principle stated in the text.
8 Section 25(1), (2), p 274, ante.
9 Section 25(4), eg the costs of an application under LPA 1925, s 84. For the first claim, see Chief Land Registrar's Report (1988–89) para 56.
10 *Rignall Developments Ltd v Halil* [1987] 3 All ER 170 at 178, per Millett J. See *Wrekin District Council v Shah* (1985) 150 JP 22 (registration not notice for purpose of establishing mens rea).
11 See per Millett J, at 177–78, supra, disagreeing strongly with Eve J's contrary conclusion in *Re Forsey and Hollebone's Contract* [1927] 2 Ch 379, CA (as to which see p 208, ante). So far as land charges are concerned, Eve J's ruling has been reversed by LPA 1969, s 24.

registration. The precise effect of non-registration is governed by the Land Charges Act 1972, and varies according to the particular matter in question.

(a) Avoidance of land charges

Unless registered in the appropriate register before the completion of the purchase, a land charge becomes void against a purchaser of *any* interest in the land affected[12]. But in the case of a land charge falling within Class C(iv) or Class D, non-registration avoids it only against a purchaser of a *legal estate for money or money's worth*[13]. Registration must be effected before completion of the purchase, but a last minute registration may be thwarted if the purchaser is protected by a clear certificate of search[14]. The reference in each case to the appropriate register indicates that to be effective it must be registered as a land charge of the appropriate class[15]. Failure to register is immaterial as between the original parties to the transaction.

Non-registration frees the purchaser's estate from the unprotected interest. The intention of the Land Charges Act 1972 is that the land or the relevant interest in it shall pass unincumbered. The Act does not regulate the problem of the purchaser's residual personal liability, if any. That issue is dealt with, though not completely, by the Law of Property Act 1925, s 199(1), a provision described as complementary to the Land Charges Act 1925, s 13(2)[16] and designed to put the effect of s 13 into perspective.

(b) Avoidance of other matters

A *pending land action, writ or order* (other than a bankruptcy order), *deed of arrangement* and *annuity* are all void against a purchaser unless they are for the time being duly registered, save that non-registration avoids a pending land action only if the purchaser is without express notice[17]. A *bankruptcy petition* and a *bankruptcy order* are void against a purchaser of a legal estate in good faith for money or money's worth unless they are for the time being duly registered[18]. The title of the trustee in bankruptcy is only avoided against such a purchaser if neither the petition nor the order is registered at the date of the conveyance[19].

(c) Meaning of 'purchaser'

The Land Charges Act 1972, s 17(1), defines this word to mean 'any person (including a mortgagee or lessee) who for valuable consideration takes any

---

12 LCA 1972, s 4(2), (5), (8).
13 LCA 1972, s 4(6). Rather confusingly an unregistered D(i) is made void against a purchaser of an (= any?) interest in the land: Finance Act 1975, s 51(1), Sch 12, para 18(5).
14 See p 406, post.
15 Cf ss 5 (8), 6 (4), 7 (2), which speak of registration 'under this section'.
16 Now LCA 1972, s 4. See on this inter-relation *Midland Bank Trust Co Ltd v Green* [1980] Ch 590 at 626, [1979] 3 All ER 28 at 35–36, CA, per Eveleigh LJ; revsd [1981] AC 513, [1981] 1 All ER 153, HL. The suggestion in M & W, 184, that s 199(1)(i) is 'seemingly redundant' is unsound. See further p 402, post.
17 LCA 1972, ss 5(7), 6(4), 7(2), Sch 1, para 4.
18 LCA 1972, ss 5(8), 6(5), as amended by the Insolvency Act 1985, Sch 8, para 21(2), (3).
19 LCA 1972, s 6(6).

interest in land or in a charge on land'. Valuable consideration denotes an advantage conferred or detriment suffered; it precludes any inquiry as to adequacy[20]. It covers lessee's covenant to pay an annual rent of £30[1]. Failure to register avoids the land charge or other matter against a purchaser of even an equitable interest, save in those cases where the Act requires him to be a purchaser of a legal estate[2]. In these cases also, he must purchase for 'money or money's worth', an expression narrower than 'valuable consideration' because it does not comprehend a future marriage. A sale at a gross undervalue suffices to constitute 'money' for this purpose[3].

(d) Effect of actual notice – is good faith necessary?

Registration is the sole criterion for determining the question of enforceability. Actual knowledge of an unprotected land charge is irrelevant[4]. The definition of 'purchaser' in the Act contains no element of good faith. In *Midland Bank Trust Co Ltd v Green* the omission of this requirement was held to be deliberate[5] and avoided any necessity to inquire into a purchaser's motives and state of mind. Lord Wilberforce re-emphasised the principle that it is not improper (or 'fraud') to take advantage of legal rights conferred by Parliament[6]. So, in that case a conveyance deliberately intended by both parties (a husband and wife) to defeat an unregistered option was effective to vest in the purchasing wife a title free from it. Similarly in *Hollington Bros Ltd v Rhodes*[7], the purchaser was not bound by an unprotected right, even though the conveyance was expressed to be subject to the interest and whose owner was also in occupation of the land. This result is open to the criticism that it operates unduly harshly on an occupying incumbrancer who fails to register[8], and puts him at a disadvantage compared with an occupant whose equitable interest is not capable of registration.

Recent developments suggest that in exceptional circumstances the courts may be willing to spell out a constructive trust in the incumbrancer's favour.

---

20 *Midland Bank Trust Co Ltd v Green* [1981] AC 513 at 531, [1981] 1 All ER 153 at 159, HL, per Lord Wilberforce.

 1 *Vartoukian v Daejan Properties Ltd* (1969) 20 P & CR 983. The court ought strictly to have considered whether the covenant amounted to money or money's worth.

 2 Ie under ss 4(6), 5(8), 6(5); *McCarthy and Stone Ltd v Julian S Hodge & Co Ltd* [1971] 2 All ER 973 (unregistered C(iv) not void against equitable mortgagee).

 3 *Midland Bank Trust Co Ltd v Green*, supra (land worth £40,000 conveyed for £500 to vendor's wife).

 4 Cf LCA 1972, s 5(7) (express notice of unregistered pending land action).

 5 This is underlined by ss 5(8), 6(6) of the Act, which expressly require good faith. Cf the registered land position where, according to some authorities, good faith is needed; but see p 476, post.

 6 [1981] AC 513 at 530, [1981] 1 All ER 153 at 158–59, HL, per Lord Wilberforce, approving *Re Monolithic Building Co* [1915] 1 Ch 643 at 663, CA, per Cozens-Hardy MR. See also *Lloyds Bank plc v Carrick* [1996] 14 LS Gaz R 30, CA.

 7 [1951] 2 All ER 578n.

 8 M & W, 186–87; Law Com No 18, paras 51–53. But see *Green's* case, supra, at 528 and 156, per Lord Wilberforce (the Act provides 'a simple and effective protection'). LPA 1925, s 14, does not assist here. Conjecturally s 14 ought to have been enacted in LCA 1925, not Pt I of LPA 1925: M & W, loc cit. Cf LRA 1925, s 70(1)(g) which produces a quite different result.

This may occur when there is a clear understanding or contractual arrangement between vendor and purchaser to preserve or give effect to the third party right[9]. A contract or conveyance whereby land is expressly sold or conveyed subject to but with the benefit of the unregistered right may suffice for this. However, merely to convey land subject to an adverse interest will not be adequate; this will normally signify nothing more than the fulfilment by the vendor of his duty of disclosure[10].

(e) Extent of avoidance
Once a land charge becomes void against a purchaser for non-registration, it remains unenforceable against his successors in title whether or not for value[11]. A purported registration after the land has vested in a purchaser who takes free of the charge does not operate to revive the avoided charge against a later purchaser. A subsequent registration may nevertheless be effective against a purchaser of a different estate. Suppose B conveys freehold land to A, subject to restrictive covenants imposed by that conveyance. A mortgages the land to C. B's failure to register the covenants before completion of the mortgage makes them void against C and C's successors in title, such as a purchaser to whom C sells the land in exercise of his statutory power of sale. But D, a purchaser from A, is bound provided the covenants are registered before completion of the A-D purchase, because D derives title from A, not C.

(f) Lack of registration not fatal
There are other situations to note when failure to register does not operate to defeat the interest against a successor in title.
(i) A donee, devisee, squatter or other person not ranking as a purchaser for the purposes of the Act is bound, even in the absence of registration or notice. The same is true of a purchaser of an equitable interest in the case of Class C (iv), and D(ii) and (iii) charges.
(ii) The courts are reluctant to allow a sham transaction to be used to defeat a non-registered interest. To be a sham the parties must intend that the document is not to create the rights and obligations which it gives the appearance of creating[12]. Examples might occur where a person conveys land to a company controlled by him in breach of an existing contract for sale[13], or when a husband attempts to destroy his wife's statutory rights of occupation by selling the home

9　Cf *Lyus v Prowsa Developments Ltd* [1982] 2 All ER 953 (unprotected contract affecting registered land binding), applying *Binions v Evans* [1972] Ch 359, [1972] 2 All ER 70, CA.
10　Ibid, at 960, per Dillon J; *Miles v Bull (No 2)* [1969] 3 All ER 1585 (registered land); *Ashburn Anstalt v Arnold* [1987] 2 EGLR 71, CA (registered land).
11　This is taken to be the effect of the Act, though nowhere is it explicitly stated. See *Kitney v MEPC Ltd* [1978] 1 All ER 595 at 599, 605, CA, per Goff and Buckley LJJ. Presumably only successors with a proprietary interest in the land would be entitled to take free.
12　*Snook v London and West Riding Investments Ltd* [1967] 2 QB 786, at 802, [1967] 1 All ER 518 at 528, CA, per Diplock LJ. See generally [1985] CLJ 280 (M P Thompson).
13　Cf *Jones v Lipman* [1962] 1 All ER 442 (a registered land case).

to a relative at a nominal price but he continues living there as if he were still the legal owner[14].

(iii) In *ER Ives Investments Ltd v High*[15], Winn LJ held that an equitable easement void for want of registration could still be enforceable against the purchaser, if he was estopped by his conduct from denying the grantee's right of enjoyment. The Act has no impact on an estoppel. Similarly in *Taylor Fashions Ltd v Liverpool Victoria Trustees Co Ltd*[16] the defendants could not take advantage of the non-protection of an option to renew a lease because they had later encouraged the tenant to incur expenditure and alter his position irrevocably by leasing adjacent premises from the defendants on the faith of the supposition that the option was valid.

4.   Indirect action

Failure to register deprives the incumbrancer of the right to enforce it against the land. Other remedies may, however, be open to him. Unregistered restrictive covenants may be indirectly enforceable through the medium of indemnity covenants[17]. An action for breach of contract may lie against the grantor of the interest[18], or against his own legal adviser for negligently failing to protect it[19]. However, the defeated incumbrancer will be more concerned to proceed against the purchaser, seeking to obtain the land, if possible, through the application of tortious principles[20]. The precise impact of the law of torts is uncertain[1]. In *Midland Bank Trust Co Ltd v Green (No 3)*[2], it was held that the husband and wife were liable to their son for a conspiracy to defraud. The case was litigated, however, on the issue as to whether a husband and wife could be liable in tort for conspiring together. The substantive point as to whether there actually was an actionable conspiracy seemed to have been assumed. It is suggested that this assumption was incorrect[3]. To be liable in conspiracy, the parties must intend to injure a third party[4]. Yet in *Midland*

---

14   *Miles v Bull* [1969] 1 QB 258 at 261–62, [1968] 3 All ER 632 at 635–36, per Megarry J, citing as an example *Ferris v Weaven* [1952] 2 All ER 233. This situation might need to be treated as exceptional in the light of the decision in *Green's* case, ante.

15   [1967] 2 QB 379, [1967] 1 All ER 504, CA.

16   [1982] QB 133n, [1981] 1 All ER 897.

17   See further, p 509, post.

18   *Wright v Dean* [1948] Ch 686, [1948] 2 All ER 415 (grantor of unregistered option liable in damages).

19   *Midland Bank Trust Co Ltd v Hett, Stubbs and Kemp* [1979] Ch 384, [1978] 3 All ER 571. It was this failure to register that precipitated the unfortunate and costly litigation culminating in the various *Green* decisions. Contrast *Bell v Peter Brownes Co* [1990] 2 QB 495, [1990] 3 All ER 124, CA.

20   Cf *Esso Petroleum Co Ltd v Kingswood Motors (Addlestone) Ltd* [1974] QB 142, [1973] 3 All ER 1057 (transfer of registered land in breach of unprotected covenant; re-transfer ordered); *Midland Bank Trust Co Ltd v Green* [1980] Ch 590 at 629, [1979] 3 All ER 28 at 37–38, CA, per Eveleigh LJ, obiter.

1   See (1977) 41 Conv (NS) 318 (R J Smith); (1982) 45 MLR 241 (N Cohen).

2   [1982] Ch 529; [1981] 3 All ER 744, CA.

3   See [1985] CLJ 280 at 293–295 (M P Thompson).

4   See *Lonhro Ltd v Shell Petroleum Co Ltd (No 2)* [1982] AC 173 at 189, [1981] 2 All ER 456 at 464, HL, per Lord Diplock.

Bank Trust Co Ltd v Green[5] itself, Lord Wilberforce, in rejecting an approach of equating fraud with a motive of defeating an unregistered interest, was of the view that, in the present context, such an approach was unworkable. There may have been a number of motives for doing what the Greens did. If this is true when considering the Land Charges Act, it would seem to be equally true in the context of conspiracy. Neither should there be any role for the application of the tort of inducing breach of contract. To be liable for such a tort, the tortfeasor must know of the existence of the contract. Yet the effect of s 199 of the Law of Property Act 1925 is that a purchaser is not to be prejudicially affected by notice of any matter which is void against him for lack of registration. In short, it is submitted that when the principles of property law lead to the conclusion that a particular interest is not binding upon a purchaser, the law of tort should not undermine the protection that the purchaser has by imposing personal liability upon him.

5. Priority notices

A person intending to register a contemplated charge may give a priority notice before the registration is to take effect[6]. A priority notice should be lodged in a situation like that discussed on p 400. Unless this procedure is adopted, B (the vendor) cannot register the covenants before completion of the mortgage to C if, as is usual, the conveyance and mortgage are completed simultaneously[7]. The covenants will therefore become void against C and his successors. The successful operation of this procedure involves strict observance of the prescribed time limits. B must lodge his priority notice at the Registry at least 15 working days before completion[8]. After completion an application for substantive registration pursuant to the notice must be presented within 30 working days after the notice was entered on the register. Registration then takes effect as if it had been made at the time when the covenants were created, ie on the completion of the B-A conveyance. Since this precedes momentarily the A-C mortgage, the covenants are deemed to be registered before completion of the mortgage. The existence of the priority notice will be revealed on any official search certificate made by the mortgagee, so he has notice of the intended registration.

Priority notices are not limited to restrictive covenants. They apply to any contemplated charge, instrument or other matter (including a vendor's lien) and are commonly used prior to registration of equitable easements.

6. Cancellation of entries

As we have seen earlier, some registrations automatically lapse after five years unless renewed. In the case of land charges an application for cancellation in

5 [1981] AC 513 at 531, [1981] 1 All ER 153 at 159, HL.
6 LCA 1972, s 11(1), (3), (6)(b); Land Charges Rules 1974, r 4, prescribing Form K6.
7 See NCS 19(4) (purchaser to notify vendor of intended contemporaneous mortgage).
8 This minimum period is essential to ensure disclosure by the purchaser's search.

form K11, signed by the applicant (the chargee) or his solicitor, must be submitted to the Registry. Sufficient evidence of his title must be supplied, except where he is the person on whose behalf the entry was made and he is still entitled to its benefit[9]. Many entries remain uncancelled despite the discharge of the interest protected. These commonly create problems on a subsequent transaction. Apparently a purchaser whose search certificate reveals an entry relating to a discharged mortgage cannot require the vendor to cancel the entry before completion, unless he created it. Production of the discharged mortgage is adequate notice that it is no longer subsisting[10].

Section 1(6) of the Act authorises the court to order the vacation of any entry in the register. Where an entry is disputed its vacation can normally be obtained only after the court has determined the merits of the case[11]. However, since registration, particularly of an estate contract, can constitute a weapon of considerable nuisance value, a speedier remedy by way of summary application exists where there are no substantial grounds for supporting the registration. In *Hooker v Wyle*[12], the court vacated a C(iv) registration because it was plain that the contract had come to an end and nothing remained for which registration could be maintained. Should there be a triable issue, the court may permit the entry to subsist, provided the person registering undertakes to pay the estate owner damages for any loss caused by its presence if it is later held to have been wrongly registered[13].

In relation to pending land actions, s 7(10) of the Act empowers the court to vacate a registration and order the payment of costs and expenses if the proceedings are not prosecuted in good faith[14]. This provision confers no jurisdiction to vacate a registration which is invalid because the list is not capable of protection as a matter of law. Here the court can resort to its inherent jurisdiction to order removal of the entry[15]. Save for s 5(10) there is no provision in the Act imposing liability for registering a charge without reasonable cause. The Law Commission has suggested that this omission should be rectified[16]. This apart, a malicious registration may give rise to an action in tort for slander of title. To succeed the estate owner must prove that he has suffered actual damage resulting from the registration and that the defendant acted with a dishonest or otherwise improper motive[17].

---

9   Land Charges Rules 1974, rr 10, 11 (prescribing Form K13 for Class F charges). For a vendor's duty to discharge a Class F charge when selling with vacant possession, see p 166, ante.

10   See The Law Society's Digest (Third Supplement), Opinion Nos 136, 139.

11   *Re Engall's Agreement* [1953] 2 All ER 503.

12   [1973] 3 All ER 707 (expiry of notice to complete); *Heywood v BDC Properties Ltd* [1963] 2 All ER 1063, CA (no binding contract).

13   Cf *Tucker v Hutchinson* (1987) 54 P & CR 106, CA. See further in relation to cautions affecting registered land, pp 80–81, ante.

14   Eg because the action is frivolous, vexatious and an abuse of the process of the court: *Calgary and Edmonton Land Co Ltd v Discount Bank (Overseas) Ltd* [1971] 1 All ER 551. Section 10 (5) does not curtail the general power under s 1 (6): *Northern Development (Holdings) Ltd v UDT Securities* [1977] 1 All ER 747.

15   *Heywood v BDC Properties Ltd (No 2)* [1964] 2 All ER 702, CA (but no costs); *Stockler v Fourways Estates Ltd* [1983] 3 All ER 501.

16   Working Paper No 67, para 125. Contrast LRA 1925, s 56(3), p 75, ante.

17   See *Almas v Spenceley* (1972) 25 DLR (3d) 653.

E   Searches for incumbrances

1.   Purpose and mode of search

The primary object of a search is to discover the existence of any registered entry affecting the land. If some incumbrance not disclosed on investigation of the title is discovered, the purchaser will call upon the vendor to cancel the entry or secure its discharge if he can. A search certificate that reveals no entries may mean that a registrable interest of which he is aware has not been registered and so is, or will become, void against him for want of registration[18]. A search is usually effected by means of a written requisition for a search to be made by the Registry, which issues an official certificate of the result. Searches are also often requested by telephone[19]. The result of a telephone search is automatically followed up with an immediate official certificate from the Registry.

(a) Application
A written application for an official search in the index to all the registers must be made on the prescribed Form K 15. This has to specify certain essential particulars: (1) the full names to be searched; (2) the county[20] in which the land is situated; and (3) the period of ownership to be covered by the search. A short description of the land may be added. On the grant of a mortgage it is common practice for the mortgagee's solicitor to require a search to be made against the borrower to verify that no bankruptcy proceedings have been instituted against him. Form K16 is used for a 'bankruptcy only' search. Such searches cannot be made by telephone or telex. In the year 1994/95, bankruptcy only searches accounted for almost 57% of all searches[1].

(b) Against whom to search
Strictly, a search should be made against every person appearing as an estate owner during the period of investigation of title, including the vendor. In practice it is not customary to search against a person in respect of whom a search was made on the occasion of a previous transaction. Nevertheless, an element of danger exists in relying on a search obtained by someone else, unless the certificate (or a photocopy) is checked to ensure that the search was made against the correct name. The names included in Form K17 should correspond exactly with the names appearing on the title. Where there is a change of name or a variation in spelling, it is a wise step to search each different

---

18   See also MHA 1983, s 8(3), (4) (mortgagee's search for Class F charge to determine duty to notify spouse of proceedings for possession of mortgagor's house).

19   LCA 1972, ss 9, 10(1). Two other methods sometimes used exist: (i) personal attendance at the Registry; (ii) telex. See generally, Ruoff, *Searching without tears*.

20   Problems arise when property situated in one county has a postal address in another; see the letter in (1975) 119 Sol Jo 8. Any former county name is also required; see Ruoff, op cit, 28–32, 39–43. There is obvious potential for error here.

1   Land Registry Annual Report, p 29.

name or variation[2]. The Registry searches names precisely as they appear in the application. The applicant must ensure that each name is correctly presented, taking care that the forename(s) and surname are listed on the appropriate lines of the form[3].

Against each estate owner's name must be added the period (in whole years) to be searched. This will be the period during which he or she owned the land, though it is arguable that 1926 should be quoted as the commencement of every period of estate ownership[4]. Regardless of the stated period of ownership, the certificate will disclose any subsisting bankruptcy entries against any name searched.

(c) Result of official search

Section 10(3)(a) of the Act requires the Registrar to issue a certificate setting out the result of the search. The computer prints the certificate. Its form is dictated by the existence or absence of any entries to be disclosed[5]. When no entries are revealed Form K 17 is issued, which certifies that there are no subsisting entries. A certificate in Form K 18 is sent if any entries are disclosed. The details recorded include the chargor's name and address, the nature of the charge, its official reference number and date of registration. Whenever more than 25 entries exist against a particular name the Registry will edit the certificate by excluding irrelevant entries, provided a description of the land was given in the application.

The certificate shows the date of commencement of the priority period and also its expiry. The certificate is dated one working day before that on which it is issued, so it covers all entries bearing dates of registration up to and including the date of the certificate. Office copies of any entries can be obtained using Form K19. In respect of entries clearly affecting the land sold it is thought to be the vendor's solicitor's duty to obtain office copies[6]. It is a common practice, especially with bankruptcy entries, for the vendor's solicitor to certify that a particular entry does not relate to the vendor or his land; but this step ought not to be taken without first checking an office copy or consulting the vendor, where appropriate.

2.   Advantages of official search certificate

(a) Priority over late registrations

A purchaser who obtains an official certificate of the result of a search is not affected by any entry made in the register after the date of the certificate and

---

2   Had this precaution been taken by the mortgagee in *Standard Property Investment plc v British Plastic Federation* (1985) 53 P & CR 25, note 14, p 395, ante, he would have discovered the prior charge registered against a shorter version of the mortgagor's name.
3   For example, Martin Oliver could easily be transposed to appear as Oliver Martin.
4   (1971) 35 Conv (NS) 155 (J E Adams); contra, Ruoff, op cit, 25. And see (1980) 124 Sol Jo 633, discussing searching problems raised by *Property Discount Corpn Ltd v Lyon Group Ltd* [1980] 1 All ER 334; affd [1981] 1 All ER 379, CA.
5   See generally Land Charges Rules 1974, r 17 (1)–(3).
6   Aliter if the certificate reveals an entry which it is stated *may* affect the property (a not infrequent occurrence): Law Society's Digest, Vol 1, Opinion No 123.

before completion of the purchase, *provided the purchase is completed before the expiration of the fifteenth day (excluding days when the Registry is not open to the public) of the certificate's date*[7].

Protection lasts for 15 working days or until earlier completion. The certificate confers no protection in relation to incumbrances registered within the 15 days' period but after completion of the purchase[8]. Should the period of protection expire before completion takes place, a fresh application must be made; dating the conveyance with some date falling within the protection period, a practice once commonly adopted, is not sufficient[9].

(b) Conclusiveness

Unless a purchaser can rely upon the certificate, the system of official searches would break down. Section 10(4) of the Act provides that the certificate, according to its tenor, shall be conclusive, affirmatively or negatively, as the case may be. If any entry is not disclosed and a clear certificate is issued, the purchaser is entitled to assume that no charge is registered against the named estate owner. He takes free from the registered charge and, though this point has not yet been decided, his successor in title also, presumably, takes free because he acquires his predecessor's unincumbered estate. To this extent actual registration does not prevail against an inaccurate certificate and the loss is made to fall upon the chargee who loses his incumbrance. A purchaser can, however, only rely on s 10(4) if his application gives no reasonable scope for misunderstanding so that the blame for the non-disclosure of the relevant entry rests fairly and squarely on the Registry officials[10]. Should the purchaser not search against the correct name of the estate owner, a clear search certificate which he may receive is not conclusive, even against an incumbrancer who has himself registered his charge but in a version of the estate owner's full name[11]. Where the result of a search is given over the telephone, it is the confirmatory printed certificate, *not* the telephone reply, which is conclusive as to the information disclosed.

Section 10(6) of the Act exempts (fraud apart) any officer, clerk or person employed in the Registry from liability for loss suffered by reason of (a) any discrepancy between the particulars shown in the result of the search certificate and those given by the applicant in his requisition, or (b) the communication of the result of a search otherwise than by issuing a certificate (eg by telephone). Exemption (a) will apply in this situation. Suppose that a search is requested against XY and the result of the certificate shows no entries against XZ. No action will lie against the Registry officials for loss caused by this discrepancy.

---

7   LCA 1972, s 11(5), (6)(a), unless pursuant to a priority notice registered before the certificate date.
8   This is an important consideration when determining the priority of two registrable mortgages created by a mortgagor within the space of a few days.
9   See further, p 454, post.
10   *Du Sautoy v Symes* [1967] Ch 1146 at 1168, [1967] 1 All ER 25 at 37, per Cross J (insufficiently clear description of land).
11   *Oak Co-operative Building Society v Blackburn* [1968] Ch 730, [1968] 2 All ER 117, CA, note 16, p 395, ante.

It will be necessary to effect a second search against XY. Should the purchaser's solicitor complete the purchase without noticing the difference, the purchaser will be bound by any charge registered against XY. He cannot rely upon s 10(4) to give him a clear title because his search certificate is not conclusive against XY. It behoves practitioners, on receipt of every search certificate, to check that the particulars on which the search has been made by the Registry correspond exactly with those in the application. It is clearly advisable to keep a copy of this, but few do.

(c) Erroneous certificates
By virtue of s 12 of the Act a solicitor or other person obtaining an official search certificate is not answerable for any loss arising from any error in it, neither is any trustee or executor for whom he is acting. Criminal liability attaches to any Registry official who is wilfully negligent in the making of any certificate or is party to any act of fraud or collusion affecting it: s 10(5). On the other hand it is a matter of continuing regret that Parliament has not seen fit to provide for the payment of statutory compensation whenever s 10(4) of the Act renders duly protected interests unenforceable against the purchaser. He may be able to maintain an action in negligence against the Registrar[12], but a remedy in damages is a poor substitute for the loss of his interest. For example, financial relief may be totally inadequate compensation for loss of a right to restrain by injunction breach of a restrictive covenant.

F Registered land searches

1. Official searches

The copy of the subsisting entries in the vendor's register of title, upon which the purchaser conducts his investigation of the title[13], may be out of date by the time he comes to complete. The Land Registration (Official Searches) Rules 1993[14] enable the purchaser, for a modest fee, to obtain an official certificate of search. This not only reveals any adverse entry made after the date of the office copy entries, but also confers priority over late entries, in much the same way as the official certificate under the Land Charges Act 1972. The prescribed forms of application (to be submitted in duplicate) are Forms 94A or 94B, depending on whether the whole, or part only, of the land

---

12 See the obiter discussion in *Ministry of Housing and Local Government v Sharp* [1970] 2 QB 223, [1970] 1 All ER 1009, CA, as to the Registrar's liability for issuing an inaccurate certificate under LCA 1925, s 17(2) (now s 10(3) of the 1972 Act); approved in *Murphy v Brentwood District Council* [1991] 1 AC 398 at 486, [1990] 2 All ER 908, at 934, HL, per Lord Oliver. The Registrar has always been prepared in appropriate circumstances to accept responsibility for mistakes in official search certificates: Law Com No 18, paras 49–50. Apart from cases of loss falling within s 10(6) of the Act (see above) the introduction of the computerised system has not changed this policy: Ruoff, op cit, 3.
13 See p 335, ante.
14 SI 1993, No 3276.

comprised in the title is being purchased. The applicant must indicate the date of commencement of the search, being either the day after the issue of an office copy of the subsisting entries or the last date when the land certificate was officially examined with the register. It was formerly the case that the register was private and so it used to be necessary for the purchaser to be furnished with authority to search the register. Now that the register is open, the purchaser is entitled to requisition an official search.

It is now possible to apply for a search with priority in a number of ways. Provision is made in the rules for searches to be made by personal attendance, fax, telephone and by computer from a distant terminal[15], the final method currently having only a limited application, being subject to a pilot scheme. When searching by telephone, the search must be of the whole land and must contain all the particulars as are appropriate for an application made in Form 94A. The person searching, as is the case if the search if made by fax or by computer, must have a credit account at the Land Registry.

2.   Effect of official certificate

(a) Date of delivery
The 1993 Rules contain provisions for determining when a search application is to be regarded as having been delivered at the appropriate district registry. For example, by virtue of r 2(3)(a) an application duly delivered at 9.15 on a Tuesday is deemed to have been delivered immediately before 9.30 on that day, whereas one delivered at noon on Tuesday is deemed to have been delivered immediately before 9.30 on the Wednesday. This curious rule is designed to eliminate difficulties that would otherwise arise from the simultaneous receipt of conflicting applications[16].

(b) Freedom from subsequent entries
If the application is in order, an official certificate of search in documentary form will be issued. In the case of a search in respect of part of the land the result will be communicated in Form 94B. In addition to this, as searches can now be applied for without using writing, the result of such a search can also be communicated without writing[17]. This will give the result of the search as at the time and date of its deemed delivery: r 4(1). It may reveal the following[18]:
(i)   entries affecting the land made in the register since the date specified in the application;
(ii) applications for registration pending but not completed[19];
(iii) unexpired official certificates of search relating to the title.

---

15   Land Registration (Official Searches) Rules 1993, r 3(3).
16   For the priority of competing applications deemed to have been delivered at the same time, see the 1993 Rules, r 8.
17   Ibid, rr 4, 14. See R & R, 30.09.
18   See R & R, 30.09.
19   Including an application to note a contract for sale still awaiting protection by entry of a notice: *Smith v Morrison* [1974] 1 All ER 957 at 965–66.

Rule 3 provides that where a purchaser obtains an official search, any entry made in the register during the priority period is postponed to a subsequent application to register the instrument effecting the purchase, provided the application is deemed to be delivered at the proper registry *within the priority period* and it is in due course completed by registration. In effect, the purchaser takes free from the interest which the subsequent entry seeks to protect, but – and this is vital – not only must completion have taken place, the application for substantive registration must be delivered at the Registry within the priority period. In *Howell v Montey*[20] a purchaser applied for registration outside the priority period conferred by the official search. During the priority period a creditor of the vendor sought to register a notice to protect a charging order *nisi*. The only reason that the purchaser was not bound by the charging order was that the court, in the exercise of its discretion, declined to make the charging order absolute. Had the right not been one where, ultimately, its enforceability was dependent upon a court's discretion, the purchaser would simply have been bound by it. The priority period lasts for 30 working days[1]. It runs from the time when the search application is deemed to have been delivered and ends immediately after 9.30 am on the thirtieth day thereafter (r 2(1)). An application for registration of a transfer which under the deeming provisions is delivered at the same time as the expiry of the priority period is nevertheless deemed to be delivered within the period (r 8(5)). The application therefore will have priority over a competing application lodged contemporaneously. The expiration date is stamped on the certificate, but it has no legal effect and an error gives rise to no claim for indemnity.

Under rule 6 an official search made on behalf of an intending mortgagee automatically ensures protection for the transfer on which the mortgage is dependent. Where on a purchase and mortgage the same solicitor acts for both parties, only one search on the mortgagee's behalf need be obtained. Should different solicitors be acting, it is conceived that the purchaser's solicitor should still search on his client's behalf, rather than leave the task to another.

(c) Delayed completion
If it becomes apparent that the application for registration cannot be submitted within the priority period, eg because completion has been delayed, a second search should be requested, even though the priority under the first certificate still subsists. The second certificate will confer a further 30 working days' protection; it does not extend the period granted by the first one. The purchaser will not, of course, take free from any adverse entry disclosed by the second certificate, which he will need to investigate.

(d) Meaning of purchaser
The protection afforded by r 6 is conferred on a purchaser, defined by r 2 (1) to mean any person (including a lessee or chargee) who in good faith and for

---

20   (1990) 61 P & CR 18, CA. See also p 475, post.
 1   'Day' means a day when the Registry is open to the public: r 2(1). For a search under LRA 1925, s 112B the period is 15 working days: MHA 1983, s 8(5), adopting the shorter period prescribed by LCA 1972.

valuable consideration acquires or intends to acquire a legal estate in land. The significance of 'good faith ' in this context is not immediately apparent, especially as various provisions of the main Act define the effect of registration of a disposition without any reference to this qualification[2]. An honest doubt as to the validity of a competing unprotected claim was held in *Smith v Morrison*[3] not to amount to bad faith within r 6. Mere notice of an unprotected interest ought not of itself to be equated with bad faith. The elaborate system of registration of incumbrances and the official search procedure appear to exclude the doctrine of notice, save where it is expressly preserved[4]. It would be absurd if a third party incumbrancer could torpedo the statutory scheme and obtain priority, not by protecting his interest on the register in the proper way, but simply by giving express notice of it to a purchaser before completion of the transaction[5]. The present state of the law is far from satisfactory. Hopefully, a robust construction of 'good faith' will be adopted, consistent with the clear policy of the Act[6]. Different considerations ought quite properly to operate when there exists some ulterior motive for the transaction[7], but such a design is not likely to be present in the ordinary conveyancing transaction.

(e) Non-priority searches – r 9
Forms 94A and 94B are designed for use by a purchaser as defined by r 2(1). Any other person (eg an assentee, or chargee who merely intends to protect his security by notice of deposit) can for a modest fee apply for an official search on Form 94C. He must have an authority to inspect the register. The certificate (in Form 94D) does not confer priority for the registration of any dealing, and it so states (r 10).

3.   Erroneous certificates

A solicitor or other person is not answerable for loss that may rise from an error in an official certificate of search obtained by him, and this protection extends to any fiduciary owner for whom he acts[8]. The Land Registration Act 1925, contains no provision similar to s 10(4) of the Land Charges Act 1972, which makes the certificate conclusive according to its tenor. In *Parkash v Irani*

---

2 LRA 1925, ss 20(1), 23(1), 59(6); *De Lusignan v Johnson* (1973) 230 EG 499; *Miles v Bull (No 2)* [1969] 3 All ER 1585. See pp 475–477, post. Contra, *Peffer v Rigg* [1978] 3 All ER 745, p 77, ante.
3 [1974] 1 All ER 957 (purchaser aware of alleged prior contract).
4 LRA 1925, s 61(6) (bankruptcy proceedings).
5 In *Smith v Morrison*, ante, it was common ground that the date for testing the issue of good faith was completion date. This would appear to be correct, despite the purchaser's non-acquisition of the legal title until registration.
6 For the Law Commission's recommended solution, see Report No 158, paras 4.14–17, p 78, ante.
7 *Jones v Lipman* [1962] 1 All ER 442 (sham transaction). And see *Lyus v Prowsa Developments Ltd* [1982] 2 All ER 953.
8 LRR 1925, r 295.

Finance Ltd, a purchaser of registered land took subject to a caution which his certificate of search failed to disclose. This was so even though s 79(6) of the Act of 1925 does not say in terms that a purchaser is affected by notice of matters protected by caution, for this is implicit in the scheme of the Act and in the subsection itself[9]. The purchaser's remedy is to claim an indemnity under s 83(3) of the Act[10].

4. Search in Land Charges Register

A purchaser of registered land need not make a search in the Land Charges Registry[11]. The Land Registration Act 1925 provides its own machinery for the protection of matters which in the case of unregistered land require registration under the Land Charges Act 1972, and the enforceability of any such matter affecting a registered title is determined solely by whether it is duly protected by notice, caution or inhibition under the former Act. Furthermore, the Act expressly exempts a purchaser from any obligation to make a search in the Land Charges Registry[12], though in passing it should be observed that a purchaser of a qualified or possessory title ought to make such a search in respect of estates excepted from the effect of registration. On a contemporaneous purchase and mortgage the mortgagee will often make a 'bankruptcy only' search against the purchaser under the Land Charges Act 1972. The register of title cannot provide information about the financial standing of a proposed borrower who is not yet registered as proprietor[13].

G   Search in the companies register

1. Registration of financial charges: unregistered land

On a purchase of land from a company the purchaser needs to make a search in the register of companies maintained under s 397 of the Companies Act 1985. This search will reveal (i) any charge on land to secure money created by a company before 1 January 1970, and (ii) floating charges whenever made. Charges within (ii) are discussed below. Until 1970, fixed (ie non-floating) company charges on land could be protected under what was then s 97 of the Companies Act 1948, as an alternative to registration under the Land Charges Act 1925. This method of protection under the Companies Act has been removed by s 3(7) of the Land Charges Act 1972[14] for all fixed financial charges

---

9   [1970] Ch 101 at 110, [1969] 1 All ER 930 at 935, per Plowman J. It is expressly so stated in relation to notices: LRA 1925, ss 48 (1), 50 (2).

10   In the year 1994/95, over £122,000 was paid by way of indemnity, of which one claim alone amounted to over £113,000: Land Registry Annual Report 1994/95, p 29.

11   The contrary suggestion in *City Permanent Building Society v Miller* [1952] 2 All ER 621 at 625, CA, per Lord Evershed MR cannot be sustained. See further R & R, 30.31.

12   LRA 1925, ss 61(6), 110(7).

13   Wontner, *Guide to Land Registry Practice* (15th edn), 191.

14   Re-enacting LPA 1969, s 26.

created after 1969. Their enforceability against a purchaser[15] is now determined solely by registration as a land charge, where necessary[16].

Company searches are normally effected by a firm of law agents who make a personal search of the company's file in the register and then confirm the result in writing. Their report, or certificate, is not conclusive as to the contents of the register, nor does it confer any priority. It is, therefore, necessary to organise the search for a date as close as possible to the date of completion. A purchaser also needs to ascertain that no winding up proceedings are pending. In a winding up by the court a disposition of the company's property after commencement of the winding up is void unless the court directs otherwise[17]. A search of the *London Gazette* (again performed by agents) will reveal the existence of any winding up petition.

2.   Registered land

A company charge affecting registered land is treated no differently from one created by an individual. It does not bind a purchaser unless it is properly protected under the Land Registration Act 1925, irrespective of its registration under the Companies Act 1985[18]. A company search, in so far as it is made to discover registered charges, is unnecessary. Moreover, the better view is thought to be that there is no need to effect a companies search to discover the existence of possible winding up or dissolution proceedings. Registration as proprietor is effective to vest the legal title in the purchaser, even though the company had, unknown to him, no title to pass on completion because of its earlier dissolution[19]. But not all practitioners are convinced[20].

3.   Floating charges

A floating charge has been judicially explained[1] as one which presently affects all the items expressed to be included in it but not specifically affecting any item until the happening of an event which causes the security to crystallise as regards all the items. It floats over the company's assets, enabling the company to deal with them in the ordinary course of business. It becomes a fixed charge on the occurrence of an event causing it to crystallise[2], eg liquidation, or the appointment of a receiver.

---

15 Other than a mortgagee, whose position is also governed by s 395 of the Companies Act 1985.
16 Ie if not protected by a deposit of deeds (p 385, ante).
17 Companies Act 1985, s 522. For the commencement of the winding up, see s 524.
18 LRA 1925, s 60(1).
19 Ibid, ss 20(1), 23(1). See this issue considered generally at p 476, post. Similarly if registration were effected after a winding up by the court.
20 See R & R, 30.36 (advocating a search by an intending chargee from a company); Emmet, para 7.001 (now beyond doubt no search is necessary). See also the correspondence in (1976) 73 LS Gaz 893, 968, 1035–36, 1080; (1977) 74 LS Gaz 108, 132, 192.
 1 *Evans v Rival Granite Quarries Ltd* [1910] 2 KB 979 at 1000, CA, per Buckley LJ.
 2 See *Re Brightlife Ltd* [1987] Ch 200, [1986] 3 All ER 673.

A floating charge affecting unregistered land continues to be registrable under s 397 of the Companies Act 1985, not in the land charges register[3]. Strictly speaking a floating charge should be abstracted, for the purchaser requires to know the events on which it will crystallise. Though the company can convey the land without the chargee's concurrence, the purchaser is entitled to evidence of non-crystallisation. The practice varies as to the kind of evidence produced. Some practitioners are happy to accept a certificate to that effect signed by an officer of the company, whereas others insist, and perhaps more correctly, on a certificate from the chargee. The purchaser must bear the expenses of obtaining the certificate[4]. If the charge has crystallised the mortgagee must join in to release the property.

A floating charge affecting registered land requires protection on the register by means of a notice or a caution, failing which a purchaser is not bound despite registration under s 395. Apparently the Registrar will cancel the entry of the charge on production of a certificate of non-crystallisation, signed by the company's solicitor[5].

4.   Registration under the Companies Act 1985, s 395

The Land Charges Act 1972 does not abrogate the need for registration at the companies register for the purposes of s 397. This section avoids (inter alia) a company charge on land[6], whether fixed or floating, against the liquidator or any creditor, including a mortgagee, unless particulars of it in the prescribed Form 47 are received by the registrar of companies within 21 days of its creation[7]. Failure to register does not avoid the debt; it avoids the security and all ancillary rights[8]. The lender becomes a mere unsecured creditor in the event of the company's liquidation. However, an unregistered charge is not void against persons who are not creditors, including, it seems, a purchaser of the land subject to the charge.

The duty to register is cast on the company (s 399(1)), but registration by or on behalf of the chargee is statutorily permissible. A solicitor acting for a company taking a secured loan owes a duty of care to any guarantors to ensure due registration[9]. The registrar's certificate of registration acts as 'conclusive evidence' that the registration requirements have been satisfied (s 401(2)),

---

3   Its very nature makes this highly impracticable, for a fresh registration would be necessary on every change in the company's landed assets. But this is the very problem facing the mortgagee where the company later acquires registered land.
4   LPA 1925, s 45 (4) (b), p 288, ante.
5   R & R, 24.22; 18 Ency F & P 735, Form 3:B:17.
6   Including an equitable charge: *Re Wallis and Simonds (Builders) Ltd* [1974] QB 94, [1974] 1 All ER 561, but not a vendor's lien for unpaid purchase money: *London and Cheshire Insurance Co Ltd v Laplagrene Property Co Ltd* [1971] Ch 499, [1971] 1 All ER 766.
7   See further (1987) 137 NLJ 548 (changes in registration procedures effective as from 1 August 1987).
8   *Re Molton Finance Ltd* [1968] Ch 325, [1967] 3 All ER 843, CA (no right to retain deposited deeds).
9   *Re Foster* (1984) 129 Sol Jo 333.

notwithstanding the particulars were inaccurate or delivered out of time[10]. The court is empowered by s 404 of the Act to extend the time for registration in various situations, eg where the delay was accidental or due to inadvertence. Any court order authorising late registration is made without prejudice to the rights of intervening secured creditors. A belated registration will not ordinarily be permitted when the company is already in liquidation[11].

This duality of registration produces at least one anomaly. A purchaser, not being a mortgagee, takes subject to a mortgage duly registered as a C(i) or C(iii) charge, whereas a mortgagee (who ranks as a creditor within s 395) is not bound if the mortgage, albeit protected as a land charge, is not also registered under s 395.

10   *Re CL Nye Ltd* [1971] Ch 442, [1970] 3 All ER 1061, CA; *R v Registrar of Companies, ex p Central Bank of India* [1986] QB 1114, [1986] 1 All ER 105, CA.
11   *Re Ashpurton Estates Ltd* [1983] Ch 110, sub nom *Victoria Housing Estates Ltd v Ashpurton Estates Ltd* [1982] 3 All ER 665, CA; but see *Re R M Arnold & Co Ltd* (1984) 128 Sol Jo 659. Extension applications are likely to increase following the registrar's change of practice (noted at [1986] 1 All ER 118) in not now accepting for registration any original or amended Form 47 not timeously delivered. The registrar cannot grant extensions.

Chapter 14

Completing the transaction

A Introduction

The stage has now been set for forging the final link in the chain of procedures – completion, an expression which usually refers to the complete conveyance of the estate and final settlement of the business[1]. For the parties this normally signifies cash for the vendor and keys (ie possession) for the purchaser. From the legal standpoint, the vital element in the case of unregistered land is the passing of the legal estate[2]. Not even payment of the whole of the purchase price coupled with possession of the premises constitutes completion, in the absence of any conveyance of the legal estate[3]. On a sale of registered land the legal title does not vest in the purchaser until registration[4]. It is the purchaser's responsibility to effect registration; therefore completion also occurs on the purchaser's payment of the balance of the price in exchange for the land or charge certificate and a duly executed transfer document.

As a general rule the parties' respective obligations regarding completion are dependent and concurrent. Almost invariably completion is a bilateral or consensual act; both parties have their own respective duties to discharge[5]. The case of *Tudor v Hamid*[6] shows that very exceptionally completion may be effected by the vendor's unilateral action. Here P, having accepted V's title, was allowed into possession of a leasehold hotel before completion on payment of the entirety of the purchase money. Because of a dispute P later declined to complete, whereupon V's solicitors engrossed the assignment which was then executed by V. It was held that the deed operated to pass the legal estate in the property to P[7].

Needless to say, before proceeding to complete, the purchaser's solicitor should satisfy himself that his searches have not expired, that there are no

---

1   *Killner v France* [1946] 2 All ER 83 at 86, per Stable J. For a full discussion see [1991] Conv 15, 81 and 185 (D G Barnsley).
2   This is subject to the peculiar effect of the law relating to escrows, pp 449–453, post.
3   *Killner v France*, supra; *Maktoum v South Lodge Flats Ltd* (1980) Times, 22 April; *Lloyds Bank plc v Carrick* [1996] 14 LS Gaz R 30.
4   LRA 1925, ss 19(1), 22(1), p 419, post, and s 110(6) (referring to completion of the purchase).
5   See eg *Noble v Edwardes* (1877) 5 Ch D 378, CA; 2 Williams V & P, 796, 993–94.
6   [1988] 1 EGLR 251, CA.
7   V's execution of the deed was unconditional (ie not in escrow, p 449, post), and in the circumstances P's non-execution was immaterial. V's unilateral action would not have been possible if the title had not been accepted, or the form of the assignment not previously agreed.

outstanding requisitions and that he has the balance of the purchase money. Ideally he should also allow sufficient time to enable the purchaser's cheque for any part of the balance due to be cleared[8]. In some respects completion can be the most frustrating and harassing part of the whole transaction. Solicitors and their clients work for completion to take place on the specified day, only to learn of some delay a few days beforehand. Transactions involving residential property frequently involve a chain of vendors and purchasers. The failure by one person in the chain to complete on time is very likely to prevent completion of other dependent transactions. Delay of only two or three days' duration can create endless complications.

B   Place and manner of completion

Completion usually takes place at the offices of the vendor's solicitor. The Standard Conditions of Sale provide that completion is to take place either at the seller's solicitor's office or at some other place that the seller reasonably requires[9]. When the deeds are held by a mortgagee who is separately represented, completion will normally take place at the offices of his solicitor, a rather inconvenient practice when the parties' solicitors are in the same provincial town and the mortgagee's solicitor practises elsewhere[10]. The majority of building societies instruct the vendor's solicitor to act on the redemption of the vendor's existing mortgage, thereby enabling completion at his offices. This convenient practice may not survive the development of conveyancing services by building societies, resulting in mortgagees instructing their own in-house solicitor to act on redemption. It is not customary for the parties themselves to attend completion.

The Conveyancing Committee wisely declined to recommend the adoption of any general practice that on the sale of residential property completion should take place there to ensure vacant possession. This procedure would virtually eliminate the risk of the purchaser being bound by the adverse rights of occupiers; it would not result in any simplification of the conveyancing process. In the Committee's view it should suffice if, on or before completion, the purchaser or his agent were to enter the property and telephone his solicitor with instructions to complete[11]. This suggestion is not without its own practical difficulties. Solicitors usually act on the basis that the vendor will duly discharge his obligation to give vacant possession on the completion day, without verifying in advance of actual completion that the property has been vacated. Despite the obvious risks involved, this procedure gives rise to surprisingly few problems in practice.

8   See *Boodle Hatfield & Co v British Films Ltd* [1986] FLR 134 (cheque dishonoured), p 439, post.
9   SCS 6.2.
10   Assurance companies, banks and local authorities generally have separate solicitors.
11   Report II, paras 6.36, 9.39. Cf NCS 5(4), proviso, which is rarely resorted to.

Postal completions

It is at completion time that the element of professional trust between solicitors is seen at its highest. Traditionally completion necessitated attendance at the vendor's (V's) solicitor's offices by the purchaser's (P's) solicitor. He would examine the deeds (unless already examined) and hand over a banker's draft for the balance of the purchaser money, receiving in exchange the documents of title, including the conveyance to P, and the keys (or some of them). This procedure was clearly not feasible when P's solicitor practised in another part of the country. In this situation he would instruct a local solicitor to attend and act on his behalf at completion. Nowadays it is standard practice in such cases, even when the title is unregistered, to complete by post rather than by agent's attendance. The Standard Conditions are, however, silent as to this matter and so, if the parties do wish to complete by post, a special condition of sale should be included in the contract to this effect. Completion by P's solicitor's personal attendance is now virtually confined to cases where the respective solicitors practice in the same locality.

The widespread use of postal completions prompted The Law Society to introduce in 1984 a Code in an attempt to regularise procedures. Adoption of it is not compulsory. Solicitors are still free to make their own individual arrangements. Its use in a particular transaction requires the express agreement of the parties' solicitors, preferably in writing. Where adopted it is to apply without variation except so far as recorded in writing beforehand. The essence of the Code is that V's solicitor agrees to act as agent for P's solicitor without fee or disbursement. In view of the general prohibition against acting for both parties (subject to minor exceptions), the Society's willingness to sanction this form of agency agreement to operate at what is the most vital part of the transaction appears most surprising. Practitioners are warned to ensure that no circumstances exist that are likely to create a conflict between the Code and their client's interests. If some unforeseen snag or problem subsequently gives rise to conflict, V's solicitor ought, consistently with the duty to his own client, to refuse to continue to act as agent for the other side, despite the probable delay in completion. Uncertainty also exists as to whether a purchaser's solicitor, himself an agent, can lawfully appoint a sub-agent without his client's express (or perhaps implied) authority. Few practitioners do in fact seek their client's instructions. There is little doubt that postal completions have much to commend them in terms of business efficiency, an important consideration in the search for a cheaper and speedier conveyancing process. Yet solicitors should not ignore the potential hazards. In particular, bearing in mind the theoretical importance of the examination of documents of title, P's solicitor ought not readily to entrust this task to his opposite number in any unregistered land transaction where the title is not straightforward.

The provisions[12] of the Code are set out below.

---

12 See (1984) 81 LS Gaz 858. Paras 10 (arbitration of disputes) and 11 (definition clause) are not reproduced.

1. Adoption hereof must be specifically agreed by all the solicitors concerned and preferably in writing[13].
2. On completion the vendor's solicitor will act as agent for the purchaser's solicitor without fee or disbursements.
3. The vendor's solicitor undertakes that on completion, he:
    (1) will have the vendor's authority to receive the purchase money; and
    (2) will be the duly authorised agent of the proprietor of any charge upon the property to receive the part of the money paid to him which is needed to discharge such charge.
4. The purchaser's solicitor shall send to the vendor's solicitor instructions as to:
    (1) documents to be examined and marked;
    (2) memoranda to be endorsed;
    (3) deeds, documents, undertakings and authorities relating to rents, deposits, keys, etc; and
    (4) any other relevant matters. In default of instructions, the vendor's solicitor shall not be under any duty to examine, mark or endorse any documents.
7. The purchaser's solicitor shall remit to the vendor's solicitor the balance due on completion, specified in the vendor's solicitor's completion statement or with written notification; in default of either, the balance shown due by the contract. If the funds are remitted by transfer between banks[14], the vendor's solicitor shall instruct his bank to advise him by telephone immediately the funds are received. The vendor's solicitor shall hold such funds to the purchaser's solicitor's order pending completion.
6. The vendor's solicitor, having received the items specified in paras 4 and 7, shall forthwith, or at such later times as may have been agreed, complete. Thereupon he shall hold all documents and other items to be sent to the purchaser's solicitor as agent for such solicitor.
7. Once completion has taken place, the vendor's solicitor shall as soon as possible thereafter on the same day confirm the fact to the purchaser's solicitor by telephone or fax and shall also as soon as possible send by first class post or document exchange written confirmation to the purchaser's solicitor, together with the enclosures referred to in para 4 hereof. The vendor's solicitor shall ensure that such title deeds and any other items are correctly committed to the post or document exchange. Thereafter, they are at the risk of the purchaser's solicitor.
8. If either the authorities specified in para 3 or the instructions specified in para 4 or the funds specified in para 7 have not been received by the vendor's solicitor by the agreed completion date and time, he shall forthwith notify the purchaser's solicitor and request further instructions.
9. Nothing herein shall override any rights and obligations of parties under the contract or otherwise.

Some specific comments are needed.

---

13 It is understood that solicitors often dispense with any written agreement, or agree a postal completion in writing but without reference to the Code.
14 See p 434, post.

(i) *Mortgagee's agent (para 3(2)).* This requirement was introduced in response to the Privy Council decision in *Edward Wong Finance Co Ltd v Johnson, Stokes and Master*[15]:

> Mortgagees' solicitors, who also acted for P, paid over the mortgage advance on completion to V's solicitor in return for his undertaking to forward to them the documents of title, including the discharge of an existing mortgage on the property in favour of a bank. V's solicitor absconded with the money. The bank refused to discharge its mortgage, not having received the redemption monies. In consequence the mortgagees failed to obtain the agreed security for their advance to the purchaser. Their solicitors were held guilty of negligence, notwithstanding they had acted in accordance with the general practice of' the profession in Hong Kong.

One way to avoid a similar occurrence is to ensure that V's solicitor, if also acting for V's mortgagee, is the mortgagee's agent to receive on completion the amount required to redeem the mortgage. The purchaser. is protected because the mortgagee cannot refuse to discharge the mortgage if its agent fails to account for the redemption monies. A note to the Code warns that V's solicitor must confirm before he agrees to use it that he will be the mortgagee's authorised agent for the purposes of the Code. Many building societies do in fact appoint V's solicitor as their agent. It has been argued that consistently with the advice tendered in the *Wong* case[16] P's solicitor ought to obtain confirmation of the agency appointment directly from the mortgagee. The Code itself does not require this, nor do practitioners adopt such a precautionary measure. In the event of V's solicitor not giving the necessary confirmation, P's solicitor, instead of arranging for an inter-bank transfer of funds, should provide two banker's drafts on completion, one in *favour of the mortgagee* for the amount required to redeem V's mortgage, the other for the balance of the purchase money in favour of V's solicitor.

(ii) *Detailed instructions (para 4).* P's solicitor should instruct his opposite number to undertake all such acts that he would have done, had he attended completion in person. In addition to matters expressly referred to in the paragraph, common tasks should include checking the execution of the conveyance or transfer, and where possible verifying V's signature to detect possible forgery, eg by comparing it with the signature on the previous purchase deed[17].

(iii) *Completion (para 6).* P's solicitors should ensure that his instructions and the transmission of the required funds are received in time for V's solicitor to complete on the contractual date. His obligation, assuming he is able to comply with the instructions, is to complete 'forthwith' unless some later time has

---

15 [1984] AC 296, PC.
16 Supra, at pp 307–308, per Lord Brightman. See [1984] Conv 158, 159, arguing that the Code 'seems seriously flawed'. This criticism could be met by production of a photocopy of the appointment.
17 Possible only in unregistered land transactions. Since registered land transfers are kept in the Registry (p 44, ante), V's solicitor will not have the transfer of V's earlier purchase.

been agreed. When funds are remitted by inter-bank transfer, he should not act until advised by his bank that the purchase money has been received[18]. Paragraph 7 spells out his duties as agent once completion has taken place. Since only V's solicitor will be present at completion, the traditional exchange between solicitors of deeds in return for the purchase money will not take place. However, the normal completion tasks will still require to be attended to: examining deeds, endorsing memoranda, dating the conveyance or transfer, preparing undertakings. The Standard Conditions of Sale do not deal with this matter and uncertainty exists as to the precise moment when it legally occurs. This could be crucial in the event of a last-minute withdrawal by one of the parties.

It is thought that completion cannot be said to have taken place until such time as V's solicitor has performed all tasks that would ordinarily have been undertaken on a completion effected by personal attendance. On this view dating the conveyance to P, often treated in practice as the final act of completion, would not be sufficient if a required undertaking to discharge an existing mortgage had not been prepared and signed.

The use of the word 'forthwith' in the Code also creates problems. Suppose that after receiving confirmation of receipt of funds from his bank but before effecting completion V's solicitor receives instructions from V not to proceed, so that completion is delayed or never takes place. If 'forthwith' is construed as meaning immediately, rather than within a reasonable period, then V's solicitor would be in breach of the agency arrangements and liable to P for loss sustained by his failure to complete timeously. However, the Code is not intended to override the parties' contractual rights and obligations (see para 9).

C   Date of completion

1.   Formal contracts

Where a date has been agreed by the parties, it is expressly inserted in the contract[19], often with varying degrees of precision. Usually a specific date appears; sometimes expressions such as 'on or before', or, less frequently, 'on or about', a certain date are to be found. The reason for using such formulae is patent. The parties have fixed their latest date but are hoping to effect completion earlier. It is equally obvious that their adoption achieves nothing. One party cannot complete before the specified date without the other's concurrence, and the parties are free to arrange an earlier completion without

---

18   Solicitors not infrequently anticipate this 'phone call when the vendor is involved in a chain transaction. Suppose A is selling to B, and B to C. B's solicitor may instruct his bank to transfer funds necessary to complete the A–B purchase on the strength of confirmation from C's solicitor that the latter has requested his bank to remit funds to complete the B–C sale. In effect B's solicitor is using client's money on B's behalf before it has been credited to his bank account in breach of the Solicitor's Accounts Rules 1986.

19   It should not be forgotten that quite often completion takes place within a few days of, or even on the same day as, exchange of contracts; see p 216, ante, and a letter at (1986) 83 LS Gaz 3120.

resort to any special term. Solicitors are best advised to avoid using these expressions[20]. On the sale of a new house it is quite common to provide that completion shall take place not later than a specified period after notification to the buyer that the house has been structurally completed.

No date mentioned
Failure by the parties to agree a date does not mean there is no effective completion date. The matter is governed by Condition 6.1.1 of the Standard Conditions of Sale which provides that the completion date is 20 working days from the date of the contract[1]. If they have agreed a date which is not recorded in the written agreement, then the effect of s 2 of the Law of Property (Miscellaneous Provisions) Act 1989 is to deprive their agreement of contractual effect. Solicitors have no general authority to insert a completion date into the contract, a practice sometimes resorted to when the parties have failed to agree a date. They will need to ratify their solicitors' action if the date inserted is to become a term of the contract[2].

The application of a general condition is not by implication excluded[3] even where the contract suggests that the parties contemplated the insertion of an agreed date. In one case[4] where the contract provided for completion 'on the   day of   1979', it was held there was no insistence between the general condition and the passage left blank so as to oust the operation of the former. But suppose the contract provides for completion 'on the   day of August 198–' and when calculating the period under the relevant general condition, the date is sometime in September. An inconsistency does result; neither the general nor the special condition can operate, so that the date will have to be determined as an open contract.

2. Open contracts

Where the contract fixes only the property, the price and the parties, and no completion date has been agreed, it is well established that completion takes place within a reasonable time. What constitutes a reasonable time is measured by the legal business which has to be performed in connection with investigating the title and preparing the necessary conveyancing documents[5].

3. Delay in completion

(a) Differing attitudes of law and equity to time clauses
In practice the cherished hopes of vendor and purchaser that completion will take place on the agreed date are not always realised. To understand the

---

20 See p 423, post, as to whether the phrase 'on or before' makes time of the essence.
1 The contract date is defined by SCS 2.1.
2 See p 220, ante.
3 See the strange decision in *Walters v Roberts* (1980) 41 P & CR 210 (completion date 'to be agreed'; not void for uncertainty, but NCS 5(1) inapplicable).
4 *Smith v Mansi* [1962] 3 All ER 857, CA. See also *Lee Parker v Izzet* [1971] 3 All ER 1099.
5 *Johnson v Humphrey* [1946] 1 All ER 460 at 463, per Roxburgh J.

consequences of delay and the rights of the parties in that event it is essential to understand the differing attitudes of law and equity to time clauses.

The common law always regarded the completion date as an essential part of the contract and held the parties to their bargain. A party who failed to complete on the appointed day committed a fundamental breach, entitling the other party, if he so wished, to treat the failure as a repudiation of the contract. True to character equity, refraining from following the harsh rule of law, exercised a jurisdiction akin to that of relieving forfeitures, or of permitting the redemption of mortgages after the contractual date had passed[6]. To use a time-hallowed expression, time was not prima facie of the essence of the contract. Courts of equity decreed specific performance of a contract, notwithstanding that the suitor had failed to observe the time stipulator and further, by way of ancillary relief, restrained proceedings at law brought by the other party. Yet equity only adopted this attitude if the time clause could be disregarded without injustice to the parties, not where it was contrary to the express wishes of the parties, or inequitable to hold the time limit as non-essential. Equity's rule has now been clothed, somewhat in artistically, in the following form[7]:

> Stipulations in a contract, as to time or otherwise, which according to rules of equity are not deemed to be or to have become of the essence of the contract, are also construed and have effect at law in accordance with the same rules.

This provision tended to be misunderstood in the past, giving rise to the view that where time was not of the essence equity merely regarded the agreed completion date as a target date. Completion was required, it was said, to take place on the fixed date or within a reasonable time thereafter; a mere failure to complete timeously did not constitute a breach of contract. It has now been established by the House of Lords in *Raineri v Miles*[8] that whether or not time is of the essence, failure to complete on the agreed date is a breach of contract, and the injured party is entitled to damages properly attributable to the delay[9]. What further remedies may be available to him depend largely[10] on whether or not the date for completion is of the essence.

---

6   *Stickney v Keeble* [1915] AC 386 at 401, HL, per Lord Atkinson. The judgment of Lord Parker contains a helpful survey of the legal and equitable positions: see at 415–16. See also *United Scientific Holdings Ltd v Burnley Borough Council* [1978] AC 904, [1977] 2 All ER 62, HL.
7   LPA 1925, s 41, replacing s 25(7) of the Judicature Act 1873.
8   [1981] AC 1050, [1980] 2 All ER 145, HL (sale of house with vacant possession on completion); see per Lord Fraser at 1093–94 and 163, discussing the earlier contrary authorities. See further as to damages, p 659, post.
9   There was authority for the view that, if the delay was occasioned by a defect in the vendor's title, damages would be limited by the rule in *Bain v Fothergill* (1874) LR 7 HL 158 (post p 655): ibid per Lord Edmund-Davies at 1086, 158 but contrast [1982] Conv 191 (M P Thompson). As the rule has now been abolished by the Law of Property (Miscellaneous Provisions) Act 1989, s 3, the point is academic.
10 But not entirely; consider the vendor's right to charge interest (pp 436–437, post) and the right to sue for specific performance (Ch 20).

(b) Time of the essence

Here the rule is strict. Failure to complete on the due date constitutes fundamental breach of contract both at law and in equity. The party at fault cannot enforce the contract specifically[11], whereas the other party is free to pursue his remedies for the breach. Thus he may elect to rescind the contract on the very next day, if he so chooses. According to Lord Romilly MR in *Parkin v Thorold*[12] time is regarded as essential to the contract in two situations: (i) where the parties make it so in the contract, and (ii) by necessary implication.

(i) *Act of the parties.*   This may be done by providing in specific terms that time is of the essence. Alternatively such an intention may be gathered from other terms of the contract, as in *Barclay v Messenger*[13] where the agreement provided that if the purchaser should fail to pay the balance purchase moneys on a given date, the agreement should become null and void. Sir George Jessel MR said[14] he did not know how making time of the essence could have been more strongly expressed than that. The problem becomes one of construing the contract, which may incorporate provisions negating any intention to make time of the essence. Thus a stipulation for the payment of interest in the event of delay contemplates a possible postponement of completion[15]. Suggestions have been made that the use of the 'on or before' formula may make time of the essence[16]. It is thought that this is not so. Not only is there judicial authority against the view[17], but the dictum cited in its support does not establish the proposition, when read in its context[18]. Furthermore, where the phrase appears in a contract governed by one of the standard forms, several of the general conditions will operate to prevent time from being essential. Under the Standard Conditions of Sale time is not of the essence in respect of the completion date.[19]

---

11   In Australia it has been held that in exceptional circumstances to prevent injustice the court may relieve a purchaser against the consequences of failure to comply with an essential time clause: *Legione v Hateley* (1983) 152 CLR 406 (vendor making 'ill-merited windfall'); *Ciavarella v Balmer* (1983) 153 CLR 438. This equitable jurisdiction has not as yet been exercised in this country.

12   (1852) 16 Beav 59 at 65; *British and Commonwealth Holdings plc v Quadrax Holdings Inc* [1989] QB 842 at 857; [1989] 3 All ER 492 at 504, CA, per Sir Nicolas Browne-Wilkinson. See (1954) 18 Conv (NS) 452 (G Boughen Graham).

13   (1874) 43 LJ Ch 449.

14   Supra, at 455; *Harold Wood Brick Co Ltd v Ferris* [1935] 2 KB 198, CA (completion on 31 August but 'in any event' not later than 15 September; time essential).

15   *Webb v Hughes* (1870) LR 10 Eq 281; *Patrick v Milner* (1877) 2 CPD 342. Cf *Harold Wood Brick Co Ltd v Ferris*, supra (interest provision not fatal).

16   (1956) 20 Conv (NS) 347; Farrand, 182; [1980] Conv 238f. See p 421, ante.

17   *James Macara Ltd v Barclay* [1945] KB 148 at 156, [1944] 2 All ER 589 at 593, CA, per Uthwatt J delivering the opinion of the court.

18   *Patrick v Milner* (1877) 2 CPD 342 at 348, per Grove J. The context makes it clear that the reason why time might otherwise have been of the essence was not because of the words 'on or before', but simply because the sale concerned a reversionary interest where time is prima facie of the essence (see per Lopes J, at p 350).

19   SCS 6.1.1.

(ii) *Necessary implication.*   As to this head, Lord Romilly said:

> The implication that time [is] of the essence of the contract is derived from the circumstance of the case, such as where the property sold is required for some immediate purpose, such as trade or manufacture, or where the property is of a determinable character, as an estate for life.

Other judges have spoken of a third category, where time is deemed of the essence by virtue of the surrounding circumstances[20], but this situation is clearly covered by Lord Romilly's second head. Time has been held to be of the essence in respect of transactions involving wasting properties such as a short leasehold[1], property used for trade purposes[2], the sale of a shop as a going concern[3]. In each case delay might prejudice the parties. Equity refused to intervene, leaving the aggrieved person to pursue his legal remedies unhindered. In *Tilley v Thomas*[3] time was held to be of the essence on the purchase of a house required for immediate residence on the day possession was agreed to be given. The circumstances relied upon by the court differ little from those operating in house sales today, especially when the parties are involved in a chain transaction. Yet despite this authority the general view seems to be that the completion date is not ordinarily regarded as essential by implication in contract for the sale of a private house with vacant possession[5].

The rule that time may be of the essence by implication is ousted if express contractual provisions indicate to the contrary. In *Ellis v Lawrence*[6] General Conditions of Sale, regulating the payment of interest and the service of a contractual notice to complete in the event of delay, were held to show that time was not of the essence in a contract for the sale of premises on which the vendor conducted an ironmongery business. Again, in *British and Commonwealth Holdings plc v Quadrax Inc*[7], the failure to include a completion date in the contract meant that time was not of the essence in circumstances where, otherwise, it would have been.

20   *Roberts v Berry* (1853) 3 De GM & G 284 at 292, per Turner LJ; *Stickney v Keeble* [1915] AC 386 at 416, HL, per Lord Parker.
 1   *Hudson v Temple* (1860) 30 LJ Ch 251, applied in *Pips (Leisure Productions) Ltd v Walton* (1980) 43 P & CR 415 (sale of 21 years' lease with 15 to run). How long has the unexpired residue to be before time ceases to be of the essence? Cf *Brewer v Broadwood* (1882) 22 Ch D 105 (sale of agreement for 90 years' lease with obligation to build within limited period; time essential).
 2   *Cowles v Gale* (1871) 7 Ch App 12 (public house); *Woods v Tomlinson* [1964] NZLR 399 (timber felling).
 3   *Smith v Hamilton* [1951] Ch 174 at 179, [1950] 2 All ER 928 at 932, per Harman J.
 4   (1867) 3 Ch App 61. The house was in fact held on a lease for 49 years of which 19 remained unexpired, but this factor does not appear to have been the basis of the decision. See *Jamshed Khodaram Irani v Burjorji Dhunjibhai* (1915) 32 TLR 156 at 157, PC, per Lord Haldane, who cited *Tilley's* case as an illustration where equity inferred an intention that time was essential from what passed between the parties before signing contracts.
 5   Relying on *Smith v Hamilton*, supra, at 179 and 932. Interestingly in *Raineri v Miles* [1981] AC 1050, [1980] 2 All ER 145, HL, Lord Edmund-Davies (at pp 1082 and 155) considered it arguable that the surrounding circumstances might have made time of the essence. But this was said without reference to the terms of LSC (1973 Revision) governing the contract, which would have negatived such a result. See also [1980] Conv 238f.
 6   (1969) 210 EG 215; *F and B Entertainments Ltd v Leisure Enterprises Ltd* (1976) 240 EG 455 (price increase if completion delayed).
 7   [1989] QB 842, [1989] 3 All ER 492, CA.

(c) Time not of the essence

Where time is not originally of the essence, failure to complete on the agreed date does not entitle the aggrieved party to decline to proceed with the contract. It was thought that there was one exception to this rule. This was where the delay has been so protracted as to justify his treating the default as a repudiation of the contract. A protracted delay means one which is an unreasonably long time and is a question of fact to be decided in all the circumstances of the case[8]. So, in *Howe v Smith*[9] a purchaser's delay for three months, despite the vendor's urgent requests for completion, was, of itself, sufficient for the vendor to treat the contract as rescinded. Not only did the delay bar the purchaser's claim for specific performance, it also defeated any right to recover the deposit which he claimed when the vendor later resold the property.

This rule, that in the event of an unreasonable delay the innocent party was entitled to treat the contract as having been repudiated, seemed to be firmly established. In *Graham v Pitkin*[10] the existence of any such rule was denied, it being said that delay was only a factor in determining whether a party in default did not intend to proceed and had repudiated the contract[11]. Whatever may be meant by this, the statement has been cogently criticised[12]. There was little discussion of authority; in particular *Howe v Smith* was not cited and so, arguably, the statement was made *per incuriam*[13]. The approach is also inconsistent with the general attitude adopted in the modern Court of Appeal decision in *Behzadi v Shaftesbury Hotels Ltd*[14] where Nourse LJ, having described the approach of equity to the question of delay as being more tolerant than that of the common law, observed that 'the authorities show that [equity's] patience is exhaustible'[15], a comment which seems to indicate that in his view that, in the event of an unreasonable delay, the innocent party can rescind the contract. The statement in *Graham v Pitkin* is, it is submitted, contrary to principle and, being both *obiter* and a Privy Council case, which is persuasive, but not binding, authority, need not be followed by English courts; an approach which, it is hoped will be taken. It is unfortunate, however, that what was once relatively clear has now become uncertain.

In the absence of an unreasonable delay, the contract remains fully effective. If, for example, the vendor fails to complete on the agreed date, but can do so a week later, the purchaser must complete or risk proceedings for specific performance. The vendor's initial breach (for which he is liable in damages) is no bar to his obtaining specific performance.

When completion is delayed the innocent party will normally be anxious to take action long before delay becomes protracted. If he wishes to be rid of

8   *Cole v Rose* [1978] 3 All ER 1121 at 1129, per Mervyn Davies QC.
9   (1884) 27 Ch D 89, CA; *Farrant v Olver* (1922) 91 LJ Ch 758; cf *Cole v Rose, supra* (nine weeks' delay not unreasonable).
10   [1992] 2 All ER 235, [1992] 1 WLR 403, PC.
11   Ibid at 406, 238 per Lord Templeman.
12   See [1992] Conv 318 at 324–329 (C Harpum). See also correspondence at [1994] Conv 342 (D G Barnsley); [1995] Conv 83 (C Harpum); ibid at 94 (D G Barnsley). Both correspondents are highly critical of Lord Templeman's approach.
13   See the correspondence referred to in n 12.
14   [1992] Ch 1, [1991] 2 All ER 477, CA.
15   Ibid at 12, 486.

the contract, he must first serve on the other party a notice requiring completion by a specified date, failing which he will treat the non-performance as a repudiation of the contract. The purpose of giving such a notice is to put an end to the defaulter's right to seek specific performance, so leaving the server free to rescind at law without fear of equitable intervention. To be a valid notice the server must himself be ready and willing to complete at the time of service[16]. The notice is commonly, and conveniently, said to make time of the essence (in respect of the date which it fixes, not the original contract date). This is, however, rather misleading; for in the absence of an express power one party to a contract cannot by notice unilaterally introduce a new term into it[17]. Though the notice calls for completion, it needs to be emphasised that serving it is the first step towards terminating the contract. It is not a prerequisite for a writ for specific performance, but often the procedure is adopted as an inducement to the defaulting party to complete without court proceedings. In practice most notices are served pursuant to an express term in the standard form contracts. First, however, consideration must be given to the service of completion notices under the general law.

(d) Making time of the essence; open contract position
Two issues arise for discussion: (i) how soon after the agreed completion date can the innocent party serve his notice? and (ii) How long should he allow for completion to take place?

(i) *Time for service.*   On this point considerable uncertainty at one time existed. According to a considerable body of judicial authority, the innocent party cannot serve his notice until there has been delay by the other party, variously described as gross, vexatious, improper or unreasonable[18]. Under an open contract, it is clear that the innocent party must wait until there has been an unreasonable delay before serving a notice to complete[19], the reason for this being that, until such a period has elapsed, the date for completion has not passed and the guilty party is not in breach of his obligations under the contract[20]. What, until recently, was considerably less clear was the position when, as is usual the parties had fixed a date for completion. Several cases supported the view that, even in this situation, the innocent party must wait until a reasonable time had elapsed since the agreed date of completion before serving a notice to complete and that the length of time stipulated by that

16   *Quadrangle Development and Construction Co Ltd v Jenner* [1974] 1 All ER 729 at 731, CA, per Russell LJ. For what this involves, see p 429, post.
17   *United Scientific Holdings Ltd v Burnley Borough Council* [1978] AC 904 at 946, [1977] 2 All ER 62 at 85, HL, per Lord Simon.
18   See *Taylor v Brown* (1839) 2 Beav 180 at 183, per Lord Langdale MR; *Wells v Maxwell* (1863) 33 LJ Ch 44 at 50, per Knight-Bruce LJ.
19   *Green v Sevin* (1879) 13 Ch D 589.
20   See *Behzadi v Shaftesbury Hotels Ltd* [1992] Ch 1 at 12–13, [1991] 2 All ER 477 at 486, CA, per Nourse LJ. It is thought to be doubtful whether a notice to complete can validly be served before the time for completion. Contrast *Parkin v Thorold* (1852) 16 Beav 59; *Bernard v Williams* [1928] All ER Rep 698, 139 LT 22.

notice must, itself, also be reasonable[1]. The better view, which was supported by Commonwealth authority[2], was that a notice can be given under the general law as soon as the completion date has passed[3]. After a thorough review of the authorities, the better view was accepted as being correct by the Court of Appeal in *Behzadi v Shaftesbury Hotels Ltd*[4] and the position is now clear: as soon as the date fixed for completion has passed[5], the innocent party may serve a notice to complete on the other. The period specified in the notice must be reasonable.

(ii) *Length of notice.* To be effective the notice must limit a reasonable time for performance. In determining this issue of reasonableness the court considers all the circumstances of the case – what at the date of notice remains to be done to complete, the reasons for the delay and the attitude of the innocent party to it[6]. The purchaser's ability to raise the purchase money within the allotted time ought not in principle to be a relevant factor, but the cases are not entirely consistent on the point[7]. Notices giving as little as six days have been upheld[8], others allowing six weeks declared invalid[9].

(e) Contractual notices to complete
The service of a notice to quit is governed by the Standard Conditions of Sale. Condition 6.8 enables either party, once the date of completion has passed, to serve upon the other a notice to complete the contract in conformity with the condition. This contractual power to serve a notice in no way excludes or limits the server's existing rights under the general law. He can still sue for

1 *Smith v Hamilton* [1951] Ch 174, [1950] 2 All ER 928, The same approach was adopted in *Rightside Properties Ltd v Gray* [1975] Ch 72, [1974] 2 All ER 1169; *McKay v Turner* (1975) 240 EG 377; *Inns v D Miles Griffiths, Piercy & Co* (1980) 255 EG 623; *Dimsdale Developments (South East) Ltd v De Haan* (1983) 47 P & CR 1.
2 *Neeta (Epping) Pty Ltd v Phillips* (1974) 131 CLR 286; *Winchcombe Carson Trustee Co Ltd v Ball-Rand Pty Ltd* [1974] 1 NSWLR 477 (where the English authorities are thoroughly reviewed); *O'Sullivan v Moodie* [1977] 1 NZLR 643; *Louinder v Leis* (1982) 149 CLR 509, noted (1983) 99 LQR 5, where the contrary view expressed in *Smith v Hamilton*, supra, is described as 'heresy'.
3 Although clear authority was hard to find, see the very clear statement by Lord Diplock in the *Burnley* case, ante n 17, at pp 928 and 71, echoed by Lord Fraser at pp 962 and 97–98; cf Lord Simon at pp 946 and 85, citing *Smith v Hamilton*, supra. See further [1978] Conv 144, 157–59 (C T Emery); Farrand, 185.
4 [1992] Ch 1 [1991] 2 All ER 477, CA. *Smith v Hamilton* was overruled.
5 Under the general law, the purchaser has until midnight of the day fixed for completion to tender the purchaser money: *Afovos Shipping Co SA v Pagnan* [1983] 1 All ER 449, [1983] 1 WLR 195, HL; *Camberra Investment Ltd v Chan Wai-Tek* [1989] 1 HKLR 568, CA of Hong Kong. See [1992] Conv 402 (H W Wilkinson). Under the Standard Conditions of Sale, for the purposes of apportionment and compensation for delayed completion, payment tendered after 2.00 pm on the date for completion is deemed to have been paid on the next working day: SCS 6.1.1.
6 *Stickney v Keeble* [1915] AC 386, HL.
7 *Re Roger Malcolm Developments Ltd's Contract* (1960) 176 EG 1237; *Chintamanie Ajit v Sammy* [1967] 1 AC 255, PC; cf *Green v Sevin* (1879) 13 Ch D 589 at 601, per Fry J.
8 *Ajit v Sammy*, supra; *Nott v Riccard* (1856) 22 Beav 307 (14 days).
9 *Pegg v Wisden* (1852) 16 Beav 239. For the consequences of acting on an invalid notice, see p 433, post.

damages for delay, notwithstanding service of a notice with which the delaying party complies[10]. Nor does it, apparently, preclude service of a notice taking effect under the general law[11]. A decree of specific performance does, however, override the right to serve a contractual notice, since the terms of the contract are superseded by the order of the court[12].

Service of a completion notice can be a tricky affair, fraught with potential hazards for the unwary. It should not be undertaken lightly. The cases indicate that practitioners tend to resort to the procedure in a rather cavalier fashion, without due regard to the provisions of the relevant condition, or to the consequences of giving the notice[13] or acting on it. This area of law has proved to be a fruitful source of litigation, especially at times of spiralling house prices when vendors are anxious to find any legitimate reason to be rid of an existing contract in order to resell at a higher price.

(i) *Form of notice.* The Condition simply requires service of a notice. This may be a formal document based on one of the precedents in the standard books[14], but this is not essential. In *Babacomp Ltd v Rightside Properties Ltd*[15] a letter which said: 'Please treat this letter as Notice to Complete the contract in accordance with its terms' sufficed. However, wording employed in a notice served on a party's solicitor might not be adequate for the purposes of one served on a person acting for himself. In such a situation the notice ought to spell out clearly the consequences of non-compliance[16]. In all cases it needs to be unambiguous in its contents. A notice which suggests that notwithstanding a failure to complete the server might still be willing to perform the contract on terms may not be upheld[17].

(ii) *Consequences of serving notice.* The Standard Conditions of Sale provide that, on the service of a valid notice to complete, the parties are to complete the contract within ten working days of giving the notice, the day the notice is served being excluded. For this purpose, time is of the essence of the contract. It is further provided that if the buyer has not paid a deposit he shall forthwith pay a deposit of 10% and, if he has paid a deposit of less than 10%, he will pay a further deposit equal to the balance of 10%[18].

---

10   *Raineri v Miles* [1981] AC 1050, [1980] 2 All ER 145, HL; *Woods v Mackenzie Hill Ltd* [1975] 2 All ER 170. See NCS 22(1); LSC 23(4)(b).

11   *Dimsdale Developments (South East) Ltd v De Haan* (1983) 47 P & CR 1, p 433, post.

12   *Singh v Nazeer* [1979] Ch 474, [1978] 3 All ER 817.

13   Contractual notices can be found served prematurely (eg *Hooker v Wyle* [1973] 3 All ER 707 at 709), or on behalf of the wrong persons (*Woods v Mackenzie Hill Ltd*, supra) and frequently because the server is not ready and willing to complete (see p 429, post).

14   See eg Ency F & P Additional Forms, [94] 2 and 3; *Kelly's Draftsman* (14th edn), 456, Form 107.

15   [1974] 1 All ER 142, CA; *Hooker v Wyle*, supra (letter upheld sent 'as formal notice to complete the transaction' under LSC 19 (1970 ed)); *Dimsdale Developments (South East) v De Haan*, supra.

16   See *Plowman v Dillon* [1985] 2 NZLR 312 (notice served on lay-purchaser acting for himself upheld).

17   See the discussion in *Balog v Crestani* (1975) 132 CLR 289 at 297, per Gibbs J.

18   SCS 6.8.3; 6.8.4.

Several points call for comment. Since the parties have agreed in advance to the procedure, no objection can be taken to the introduction into the contract of a new term resulting from action taken by one of them. The notice binds both parties. Time becomes of the essence for server and recipient alike[19]. Once given it cannot be unilaterally withdrawn by the server (unlike a notice under the general law). The parties may agree before its expiry that time shall no longer be essential, so effecting a variation of the contract. But failing this the party who serves a notice may find himself hoist by his own petard and in fundamental breach should he be unable to complete by the required date. Moreover, the obligation on the recipient is to complete within, not necessarily at the end of, the 16 days' period. He is, therefore, entitled to nominate the date for completion, with perhaps unforeseen consequences for the server[20]. By providing a fixed contractual period, the Conditions avoid the difficulties inherent in the uncertain requirement of reasonable notice prescribed by the general law. It is preferable not to specify in the notice the final date for completion or even to refer to the period within which it should be effected, just in case an inaccurate statement invalidates the notice[1].

(iii) *Server ready and willing to complete.* A notice is not valid and effective unless the party giving it is at the time of service ready, able and willing to complete[2]. The expression 'ready and willing', found in the National Conditions, necessarily connotes 'not only the disposition but the capacity to do the act' in question[3]. The significance of this qualification tends to be overlooked in practice. Vendors' notices not infrequently fail because the title is defective, eg it is subject to an adverse third party right[4], or to an undisclosed tenancy[5], or because he has not answered the purchaser's requisitions[6], or not obtained the lessor's licence to assign[7]. But if the vendor satisfactorily meets an objection to the title, his notice will not be declared bad merely because a document necessary to remedy the defect has not actually been obtained, provided it is clear that he will be able to hand it over on completion[8]. A notice has been

19 *Quadrangle Development and Construction Co Ltd v Jenner* [1974] 1 All ER 729, CA.
20 *Oakdown Ltd v Bernstein & Co* (1894) 49 P & CR 282, considered p 431, post.
 1 The court will lean towards saving the notice if it has not misled the recipient: *Dimsdale's case*, ante (notice given under NCS 22 (19th edn) to complete within 28 days 'from the date hereof' upheld though day of service to be excluded); cf *Rightside Properties Ltd v Gray* [1975] Ch 72, [1974] 2 All ER 1169.
 2 SCS 6.8.1. As to whether this readiness needs to be maintained throughout the period covered by the notice, see p 431, post.
 3 *De Medina v Norman* (1842) 11 LJ Ex 320 at 322, per Lord Abinger CB.
 4 *Horton v Kurzke* [1971] 2 All ER 577 (grazing rights).
 5 *Pagebar Properties Ltd v Derby Investment Holdings Ltd* [1973] 1 All ER 65; *Pratt v Betts* (1973) 27 P & CR 398, CA; *Chung v Pericleous* [1981] CLY 2277 (sub-vendor entitled only to equitable interest); *Walia v Michael Naughton Ltd* [1985] 3 All ER 673 (defective power of attorney).
 6 *Re Stone and Saville's Contract* [1963] 1 All ER 353.
 7 *Jneid v Mirza* [1981] CA Transcript 306. For the vendor's contractual rights on failing to obtain the required licence, see p 300, ante.
 8 *Edwards v Marshall-Lee* (1975) 235 EG 901 (offer to produce duly receipted mortgage created by previous owner). See also *Naz v Raja* (1987) Times, 11 April, CA (failure to supply authority to inspect register not fatal).

disallowed when given by a purchaser who was refusing to complete until the vendor procured a licence to assign[9]. On the other hand, a vendor's notice is not prejudiced by a breach of his trustee's duty to preserve the property pending completion[10]. In one case involving the sale of registered land a notice served by a vendor who was not then registered as the proprietor[11] was not fatal to the notice[12]. The fact that the purchaser might have been entitled to rescind the contract for misrepresentation at the time of the vendor's notice does not invalidate it[13]. Similarly, the fact that the purchaser could rescind on account of a substantial misdescription of the property, again, did not invalidate a notice to complete served by the vendor[14]. Neither will the failure by the vendor to deliver a completion statement invalidate a notice; the sending of such a notice being regarded as a matter of practice rather than a matter of law[15].

This requirement of readiness at the time of service raises an interesting question. What precisely does it entail? Must the vendor have vacated the property, or discharged existing mortgages? Does the purchase money have to be with the purchaser's solicitor? A strict interpretation would preclude the service of an effective notice in many domestic conveyancing transactions. The courts have sensibly adopted a more liberal approach. In *Cole v Rose*[16] a distinction was drawn between outstanding matters of substance and mere administrative arrangements respecting completion, which do not operate to defeat the notice. Examples of such matters are: preparing a completion statement, executing the conveyance, or the discharge of a mortgage which the vendor's solicitor has undertaken to redeem on completion[17]. In this case the vendor's notice was held to be invalid because at the time of service his solicitors did not have sufficient information about certain puisne mortgages to enable them to undertake their discharge on completion This was a matter of substance. Another example might be the vendor's non-payment of rent on a sale of leasehold land. The breach of covenant, whilst easily remediable, renders his title defective (assuming the lease contains the usual forfeiture clauses)[18]. Vacating the property is thought to be an administrative

9   *Re Davies' Agreement* (1969) 21 P & CR 328.
10   *Prosper Homes Ltd v Hambros Bank Executor and Trustee Co Ltd* (1979) 39 P & CR 395; *Re Prestbury Investments Ltd's Contract* (1960) 177 EG 75 (demolition of houses on redevelopment site).
11   He did have a duly executed and stamped transfer from the proprietor, awaiting submission to the Registry.
12   *Naz v Raja* supra. The purchaser had not requested the vendor to procure his own registration; see LRA 1925, s 110(5). Had he done so, at least before expiration of the notice, the result would have been different.
13   *McGrath v Shah* (1987) Times, 22 October; aliter if the purchaser has already rescinded the contract at the date of the notice: *Walker v Boyle* [1982] 1 All ER 634 at 641, per Dillon J.
14   *Bechal v Kitsford Holdings Ltd* [1988] 3 All ER 985, [1989] 1 WLR 105 (60% discrepancy in area). For criticism, see Emmet, para 8.047.
15   *Carne v Debono* [1988] 3 All ER 485, [1988] 1 WLR 1107, CA. Even if an inaccurate statement is sent, the purchaser is still bound to attend for completion.
16   [1978] 3 All ER 1121; *Holt v Tew* [1984] 1 NZLR 570. See [1982] Conv 62 (P Butt).
17   *Cole v Rose*, supra, at 1126 (as to building society mortgage); *Edwards v Marshall-Lee*, supra. This point is now covered by SCS 6.8.2(b), provided the completion money suffices to discharge the mortgages. See also [1978] Conv 326; [1979] Conv 161.
18   See p 295, ante.

arrangement, unless there is in occupation some other person who claims an adverse interest and is refusing to move out.

To what extent it is necessary for a purchaser to have his funds immediately available is uncertain. The source of the funding could well be a relevant factor. A purchaser can hardly be said to be ready to complete if he is financing the purchase partly from the proceeds of sale of an existing house still owned and occupied by him. Similarly, the purchaser's lack of readiness would be apparent if the conveyance had not been engrossed and forwarded to the other side for execution[19]. In this situation such default would not under the Standard Conditions of Sale prevent a notice served by the vendor from being effective[20]. The rule is thought to be the same even in the absence of any express term. Otherwise a contracting party bent on delaying completion could prevent service of a valid notice simply by failing to perform some obligation on which the innocent party's own ability to complete depended.

(f) Non-compliance with notice

An illustration will help to explain the rights of the parties on expiration of the notice without completion taking place[1]. Suppose X serves a valid notice to complete on Y which expires (say) on 31 May. Y fails to complete. The precise position of X and Y depends of course on which of them is the vendor.

(i) *Termination of contract.*   Provided X's own conduct has not substantially contributed to Y's inability to complete[2], Y's failure constitutes a fundamental breach of contract since time has become of the essence of completion. X, being himself able and ready to complete, is entitled to treat the contract as terminated, ie to rescind for breach, in which case he can pursue his normal contractual remedies. These are more fully considered in Part VI. Briefly X (if the vendor) can forfeit the deposit, subject to the court's power to order its return under s 49(2) of the Law of Property Act 1925. He is also at liberty to resell the property, either as absolute owner or in exercise of a contractual right of resale[3]. As purchaser X can recover his deposit with interest and damages for breach of contract. Whether vendor or purchaser, X can also sue for specific performance, but this is an unusual course of action to pursue after service and expiry of a completion notice.

The consequences of the rule that time is also of the essence for the server, X, are well illustrated by *Finkielkraut v Monohan*[4], where X having served his

---

19   The contrary decision in *McKay v Turner* (1975) 240 EG 377 is thought to be wrong on this point.

20   SCS 6.8.2(a) (party deemed ready if could be so but for other's default).

1   The position is basically the same on a delayed completion in a transaction where time is originally of the essence.

2   *Schindler v Pigault* (1975) 30 P & CR 328; *Oakdown Ltd v Bernstein & Co* (1984) 49 P & CR 282.

3   See p 648, post; SCS 7.5.2. It is incorrect to talk about rescinding the contract when the vendor elects to resell under an express contractual power. He is in fact affirming it by carrying it out in an authorised manner; *Howe v Smith* (1884) 27 Ch D 89 at 105, CA, per Fry LJ.

4   [1949] 2 All ER 234, applied in *Quadrangle Development and Construction Co Ltd v Jenner* [1974] 1 All ER 729, CA.

notice was unable to complete by the expiry date. His action for specific performance was dismissed. Moreover, his default discharged Y (the purchaser), entitling him to recover his deposit without having to serve his own notice.

(ii) *Extending time.*   It may not be in X's best interest to take the ultimate step of rescission. He may be involved in a linked transaction (eg the purchase of another house) which could be jeopardised if he were to end the contract with Y. In practice, the server of a notice is often prepared to allow further time for completion whenever there is a reasonable likelihood of it taking place in the near future. An extension of time to a new fixed date substitutes the extended date for the original one, without destroying the essential character of time[5]. Y's consent is not required, but he must be informed of the extension. Also, though Y provides no consideration for the extension, X will presumably be estopped from seeking to take action before the extended date elapses, since Y will ordinarily have acted to his detriment in relying on it. An extension cannot be granted by the server, X, for his own benefit, that is where he finds himself unable to complete on the expiry date. In such a situation it would be open for Y to extend the time, provided he was himself ready and willing to complete by the due date[6].

An extension must be distinguished from what is somewhat elliptically termed *waiver* of time being of the essence[7]. Waiver occurs when the server elects to treat the contract as still subsisting; he waives the breach of contract. To constitute a waiver X must encourage Y to think that he (Y) will be given time indefinitely to complete and will not be cut off without further notice. Mere inactivity by X is not enough unless it lasts for an unreasonably long time[8]. Positively encouraging the purchaser to remedy his default amounted to a waiver in *Luck v White*[9], as did the taking of possession on the completion date (time being originally of the essence) in *Ellis v Lawrence*[10], whereas negotiations for a new agreement have been held to indicate that the previous contract has been treated as at an end[11]. Once waived, time can only be re-made of the essence by the service of a fresh notice by either party. This may be given in exercise of the contractual power or under the general law. The latter may be preferable since a period shorter than that prescribed by the contract may well be reasonable in the circumstances[12].

(iii) *Consequences of nominating intermediate date.*   The point has already been made that since the obligation cast on Y is to complete within the prescribed

---

5   *Buckland v Farmer and Moody* [1978] 3 All ER 929, CA.
6   But what happens when neither party can complete on the expiry date? Is the contract discharged and not enforceable by either party since both of them are in fundamental breach? They would be free to agree upon a further extension, or to waive the time clause.
7   *Rawlplug Co Ltd v Kamvale Properties Ltd* (1968) 20 P & CR 32 at 37, per Megarry J.
8   *Buckland v Farmer and Moody,* ante, at 942, per Goff LJ (no waiver from ten weeks' silence).
9   (1973) 26 P & CR 89; *King v Wilson* (1843) 6 Beav 124 (negotiations to cure defect in title).
10   (1969) 210 EG 215; *Wendt v Bruce* (1931) 45 CLR 245.
11   *Rawlplug Co Ltd v Kamvale Properties Ltd,* supra; *Prosper Homes Ltd v Hambros Bank Executor and Trustee Co Ltd* (1979) 39 P & CR 395.
12   *Chancery Lane Developments Ltd v Wades Departmental Stores Ltd* (1986) 53 P & CR 306, CA.

period, he is at liberty to nominate any date for completion within that period. The precise consequences of this step are not entirely clear. Seemingly the nominated day, say, 24 May using the illustration on page 431, does not become of the essence; for if for some reason Y is unable to complete then, he has until 31 May to do so. But what if X is not ready to complete on 24 May? Is he in fundamental breach? Not according to Scott J in *Oakdown Ltd v Bernstein & Co*[13]. In his opinion, by serving the notice X imposes on himself a mirror obligation to that which it imposes on Y. X is not in breach of his obligation unless he fails to complete within the period, any more than Y's non-completion on 24 May would have repudiatory effect. This notion of equality of treatment has much to commend it, yet it is not without difficulties. It appears that X would be able to veto Y's call for completion on 24 May, so compelling it to take place on 31 May if X saw this to be in his best interests. This is plainly not what is envisaged by the standard contractual clauses. The party who sets in motion the contractual process ought not to be able to rely on some later event to destroy his original readiness and so prevent completion on the nominated day[14]. The uncertainties[15] created by the existing conditions could be avoided by providing that time shall be of the essence in relation only to the last day of the prescribed period.

(g) Acting on invalid notice

(i) *Server.*   Non-compliance with a notice to complete prima facie enables the server to rescind the contract for fundamental breach. He is, however, ill-advised to take this step without ensuring that his notice was effective from the outset. Hasty action may pave the way for the defaulting party to turn the tables. In *Rightside Properties Ltd v Gray*[16] the vendor, not appreciating that his notice was invalid, sought to terminate the contract on the purchaser's failure to complete. Since time had never been made of the essence, the purchaser's default was not a fundamental breach. Consequently the vendor's own action constituted a wrongful repudiation, entitling the purchaser to damages.

In such circumstances the server of the notice may be able to justify his own purported rescission on one, perhaps two, other grounds. First, the other party's delay, if protracted, will of itself enable him to treat the contract as

13   (1984) 49 P & CR 282 at 294–96; [1985] Conv 309. Here X's notice served under NCS 22 (19th ed) expired on 9 April (a public holiday). Y nominated 8 April, a day not acceptable to X or his solicitor as it was a religious festival. X offered completion on 13 April. Y declined whereupon X forfeited the deposit. However X, not having completed within the period, was himself in fundamental breach and not entitled to retain Y's deposit. This particular problem would not now arise under the present SCS since the period is calculated by reference to working days.
14   Scott J declined to apply dicta to the effect that the server must be ready and willing to complete *at any time* during the period: the *Quadrangle* case, p 431, ante, at 732, 733, per Russell and Buckley LJJ; *Hooker v Wyle* [1973] 3 All ER 707 at 714, per Templeman J.
15   See also Scott J's tentative discussion (at p 296) of the position if Y, whose intention to complete on the nominated day is frustrated by X's failure, is subsequently unable to complete on the expiry date, by which time X is ready and willing. One possible solution would be to regard neither party in fundamental breach.
16   [1975] Ch 72, [1974] 2 All ER 1169 (notice not of proper duration).

discharged without reference to the invalid notice[17]. Secondly, the notice may be effective under the general law to make time of the essence; this argument is available only when the contractual notice is invalid because it does not limit the prescribed period[18]. In *Dimsdale Developments (South East) Ltd v De Haan*[19] Mr Godfrey QC held that an invalid notice served pursuant to National Condition 22 was capable of taking effect as an ordinary notice under the general law. The standard contractual clauses providing for special completion notices do not operate to exclude the server's general law rights. This decision is, with respect, rather questionable. The innocent party's various remedies are undoubtedly cumulative. Yet it does not follow from this that a notice expressly given under a contractual power can also be treated as the unintended exercise of some other right available to him under the general law. The contrary obiter opinion expressed by Walton J in *Rightside Properties Ltd v Gray*[20] is perhaps preferable, a view supported by a dictum in *Delta Vale Properties Ltd v Mills*[1], where Slade LJ expressed the view that, whereas a notice which gave a period longer than that specified in the contract would be adequate, one which gave a shorter period would not be.

(ii) *Recipient.* The extent to which it is open to the server of a notice (X) to deny its validity is an issue that has yet to come before the English courts. Suppose that the recipient, Y, rescinds the contract on account of X's non-completion by the expiry date. Can X maintain that Y's action is itself a repudiation of the contract on the ground that the notice was invalid because of X's own lack of readiness to complete when serving it? On general principles it appears that X would be estopped from denying its validity. Mere service of the notice prima facie implies a representation that X is ready and willing, irrespective of any assertion to that effect in the notice. And Y has clearly acted to his detriment in relying on it. On the other hand, the estoppel argument would not be available to Y if the notice was invalid on its face (eg an insufficient period for compliance) or where facts within Y's knowledge indicated X's lack of readiness (eg unanswered requisitions at the time of service).

D   Payment of purchase price

1 .   Mode of payment

This matter is governed by the Standard Conditions of Sale[2]. In practice the manner of completion determines the mode of payment. On postal

---

17   See *Cole v Rose* [1978] 3 All ER 1121 where on the facts the delay was not unreasonable.
18   The requirement for the server's readiness applies equally to notices served under the general law; p 426, ante.
19   (1983) 47 P & CR 1, p 379, criticised at [1984] Conv 311 (M P Thompson).
20   Supra, at 81 and 1178 ('a totally astonishing proposition'), though here the contractual term (Statutory Conditions of Sale, Cl 9) contained no express saving of other rights. Cf *McKay v Turner* (1975) 240 EG 377 (notice purportedly given under LSC 19 (1973) still good under general law as contract not in circumstances subject to LSC).
1   [1990] 2 All ER 176 at 181, [1990] 1 WLR 445 at 452, CA.
2   SCS 6.7 (listing four possible methods).

completions payment is made by telegraphic transfer of funds, whereby the balance due is paid direct to the vendor's solicitor's bank by means of a credit transfer from the purchaser's solicitor's bank[3]. This method facilitates the same-day completion of several linked transactions. When completion is effected by personal attendance, payment by banker's draft[4] is the norm. Despite pressure from the profession, the Council of the Law Society has refused to sanction the use of cheques on completion. To take a cheque on completion without his client's authority would clearly be negligent if it were later dishonoured after the solicitor had parted with the deeds[5]. However, acceptance of a building society's cheque is commonplace, as is the purchaser's solicitor's cheque (drawn on his clients' account) in localities where a conveyancing protocol operates (eg in the Isle of Wight). Where, exceptionally, the whole of the purchase price is paid to the vendor's solicitor prior to completion, he holds it as agent for the vendors in the absence of any express or implied contrary agreement. Should he receive it as a stakeholder, he is entitled to release it to the vendor when the latter has fully performed his obligation to transfer the property[6].

2. Apportionments

When calculating the balance due, the deposit must be brought into account. Often on the sale of a freehold house there are no apportionments to make. It is no longer the practice to apportion the payment of council tax. Difficulties may sometimes be encountered on the assignment of leasehold property in relation to service charges payable under the lease, but not ascertained at the time of completion. Apportionments are calculated on an estimated basis, and the parties are contractually bound to make any necessary adjustments when the actual amount is notified.

The rule under the general law is that income (eg rents) and outgoings are apportioned as at the date for completion. The Standard Conditions of Sale adopt this general position, except where the whole property is sold with vacant possession. Here the date of actual completion governs apportionment, irrespective of whether the vendor remains in occupation[7]. Where the buyer is the tenant of the seller and completion is delayed, the seller may serve notice on the buyer, before the actual date for completion, that he intends to take the net income from the property[8]. If he exercises this option, then

---

3 The clearing banks have developed a system for the same-day transfer of funds electronically, known as Clearing House Automated Payment System (CHAPS); see (1984) 81 LS Gaz 181. Many firms arrange with their bankers to have certain payments that are credited to their clients' account (cheques, drafts etc) treated as cleared funds before they have actually been cleared through the banking system. This permits money to be transmitted to complete a purchase as soon as it is received by their own bank. This facility is an automatic feature of the Trustee Savings Bank's Speedsend service for solicitors: (1983) 80 LS Gaz 2963.
4 Technically an order for the payment of money, drawn by one bank on another, but otherwise resembling a cheque. It is treated as equivalent to cash.
5 *Pape v Westacott* [1894] 1 QB 272, CA.
6 *Tudor v Hamid* [1988] 1 EGLR 251, CA (purchaser taking possession before completion).
7 SCS 6.3.2.
8 Ibid 7.3.4.

apportionment is from the date of actual completion[9]. Apportionments are calculated by the vendor's solicitor a few days before actual completion and incorporated into a Completion Statement sent to the purchaser's solicitor; he then has a few days to check the figures and obtain any extra money from his client. The Standard Conditions of Sale make provision[10] for situations when a sum to be apportioned is difficult to calculate. A provisional apportionment is made. A final apportionment is then made and the balance is paid over no more than ten working days later. If there is further delay, then the balance carries interest from that date at the contract rate.

3.   Charging interest

(a) Standard Conditions

The purchaser's delay in completing prima facie entitles the vendor to charge interest on the balance of the purchase money[11]. Express provision for the payment of interest is made by the Standard Conditions of Sale, which seek to operate even-handedly between vendor and purchaser. The position is governed by Condition 7.3, a provision which rests upon the concept of comparative default. If there is default by either party with the result that completion is delayed, then the party whose total period of default is the greater is to pay compensation to the other. The compensation payable is calculated at the contract rate on the purchase price[12]. Where the purchaser is in default, compensation is calculated on the basis of the purchase price less any deposit which has already been paid for the period by which the buyer's default exceeds that of the seller or, if shorter, the period between completion date and actual completion[13].

Where the buyer is the tenant of the seller, then the seller has available to him an alternative option to claiming interest. In the event of delayed completion, the vendor may give notice to the purchaser that he intends to take the net income from the property until completion. The exercise of this right, which precludes him from also claiming interest[14], may be a valuable right where the property consists of a block of flats or multiple dwellings producing considerable income. One important limitation must be observed. Wilberforce J held in *Re Hewitt's Contract*[15] that the right to income is linked to the right to interest; if the vendor would be debarred from obtaining interest, he cannot elect to claim the income.

---

9   Ibid 6.3.2. He is also precluded from obtaining compensation for late completion under Condition 7.3.1 of the contract: SCS 7.3.4.

10   Ibid 6.3.5.

11   See *Harvela Investments Ltd v Royal Trust Co of Canada (CI) Ltd* [1986] AC 207 at 236, [1985] 2 All ER 966 at 978, HL, per Lord Templeman (a well-recognised principle).

12   The contract rate is defined by SCS 1.1.1(g) to mean the Law Society's interest rate from time to time.

13   SCS 7.3.2.

14   SCS 7.3.4

15   [1963] 3 All ER 419 (a decision on an earlier condition of sale).

(b) Meaning of default
Under the Standard Conditions of Sale, it is necessary to establish which of the parties is in default with regard to the delay in completion. According to Bowen LJ, in an often repeated dictum:

> Default is a purely relative term, just like negligence. It means nothing more, nothing less, than not doing what is reasonable under the circumstances – not doing something which you ought to do, having regard to the relations that you occupy towards the other persons interested in the transaction.[16]

Decided cases are of limited assistance, for it is a question of fact depending on the circumstances of each case. In *Re Hewitt's Contract*, vendors who had simply underestimated the time necessary to complete were held responsible for the delay since the circumstances occasioning it were foreseeable. In the past, a delay occasioned by a defect in the vendor's title was not considered to amount to default by the vendor[17], at least if the vendor had exercised reasonable care when entering into the contract[18]. This reasoning appeared to be coloured, however, by the common law rule that a purchaser was not, in general, entitled to damages for loss of bargain in the event of the contract going off owing to a defect in the vendor's title[19]. Now that that rule has been abolished by legislation[20], it seems likely that this reasoning would not survive so that, if the delay in completion was caused by a defect in the vendor's title, the vendor would be regarded as being in default and, consequently, liable to pay interest to the purchaser.

(c) No operative conditions
Under an open contract, the purchaser must pay interest from the time that he could prudently take possession, that is, from the time when a good title has been shown[1]. From that time, he is also entitled to the rent and profits including an occupation rent should the vendor retain possession. Where the vendor is responsible for the delay in completion, and the interest would exceed the amount of the income, the purchaser can require the vendor to accept rent and profits in lieu of interest[2]. It should also be appreciated, however, that delay occasioned by the vendor is a breach of contract, for which the vendor will be liable in damages[3].

---

16 *Re Young and Harston's Contract* (1885) 31 Ch D 168, CA (vendor's departure abroad two days before completion without executing the conveyance). But see Wilberforce J's critical comments in *Re Hewitt's Contract* [1963] 3 All ER 419 at 423.

17 See *London Corpn and Tubbs' Contract* [1894] 2 Ch 524, CA, a case where the contract referred to wilful default on the part of the vendor and, in any event, the main cause of delay appeared to be the purchaser's inability to produce the purchase money.

18 *Re Woods and Lewis' Contract* [1898] 2 Ch 211, CA.

19 *Bain v Fothergill* (1874) LR 7 HL 158. See *Re Woods and Lewis' Contract*, supra, at p 214 per Chitty LJ; at p 216 per Collins LJ.

20 Law of Property (Miscellaneous Provisions) Act 1989, s 3. See p 655, post.

1   *Re Keeble and Stillwell's Fletton Brick Co* (1898) 78 LT 383; see *Bannett v Stone* [1903] 1 Ch 509 at 524, CA, per Cozens-Hardy LJ, for a useful survey of the position.

2   *Esdaile v Stephenson* (1822) 2 Sim & St 122; *Re Hewitt's Contract* [1963] 3 All ER 419 at 425 per Wilberforce J.

3   See *Raineri v Miles* [1981] AC 1050; [1980] 2 All ER 145, HL, p 659, post.

4.   Receipt for payment

When completion takes place otherwise than through the post, the balance of the purchase money (adjusted where necessary) is handed over on completion in return for the deeds of the property. A receipt is invariably embodied in the conveyance. Under s 67 of the Law of Property Act 1925, this is a sufficient discharge without any further receipt being endorsed on the deed – as was the practice prior to 1881. By virtue of s 69 of the Act, a receipt in the deed is sufficient authority for payment to the solicitor or licensed conveyancer[4] producing it; consequently the money can safely be handed over on completion in the vendor's absence. Despite doubts to the contrary, it is thought that the protection afforded by s 69 extends to members of the solicitor's firm, such as his managing or articled clerk[5]. Suffice it to say that in practice the section causes no problems.

5.   Vendor's lien

If the vendor completes without having received the total purchase money, he has an equitable lien, arising by operation of law, on the land for the unpaid balance[6]. This lien is more than a mere equity, it creates a charge upon and interest in the property sold, in the same manner as if it had been expressly created[7].

Although the authorities are not entirely consistent, the generally accepted view is that the lien arises immediately there is a binding contract of sale and is discharged on completion to the extent that the money is paid[8]. The vendor may waive or abandon his lien, expressly or impliedly from the circumstances of the case. It has been held that no lien arises where the vendor takes a legal mortgage on the property for the amount unpaid[9]. The mere taking of a personal security like a promissory note does not prima facie exclude the lien; it depends whether the court infers from the circumstances whether the vendor intends to rely on the security of the estate, or the purchaser's personal credit[10].

A third party who, acting on behalf and at the request of a purchaser, uses his own money on completion to pay part of the purchase price is prima facie

4   By virtue of the AJA 1985, s 34(1)(a).
5   In *Day v Woolwich Equitable Building Society* (1888) 40 Ch D 491 (decided on the Conveyancing Act 1881, s 56) no significance was attached to the fact that payment was made, not to the solicitor, but to his clerk.
6   *Mackreth v Symmons* (1808) 15 Ves 329; *Capital Finance Co Ltd v Stokes* [1969] 1 Ch 261 at 278, [1968] 3 All ER 625 at 629, CA, per Harman LJ.
7   *Re Stucley, Stucley v Kekewich* [1906] 1 Ch 67 at 83, CA, per Cozens-Hardy LJ.
8   *Re Birmingham, Savage v Stannard* [1959] Ch 523, [1958] 2 All ER 397; *UCB Bank plc v French* [1995] NPC 144, CA; *Barclays Bank plc v Estates & Commercial Ltd* [1996] 11 LS Gaz R 30, CA. For a different view, see [1996] Conv 44 (M P Thompson).
9   *Capital Finance Co Ltd v Stokes,* supra; *Burston Finance Ltd v Speirway Ltd* [1974] 3 All ER 735; *Nationwide Anglia Building Society v Ahmed* (1995) 70 P & CR 381, CA.
10   *Winter v Lord Anson* (1827) 3 Russ 488 at 491, per Lord Lyndhurst LC (purchaser's bond conditioned for payment of balance did not negative existence of lien); *Hughes v Kearney* (1803) 1 Sch & Lef 132 (promissory note). For a useful review of the authorities, see *Barclays Bank plc v Estates and Commercial Ltd,* supra, per Millett LJ.

entitled by subrogation to the vendor's lien. In *Boodle Hatfield & Co v British Films Ltd*[11] solicitors completed their client's purchase before his cheque for part of the completion money had been cleared. The cheque was later dishonoured. They were held to have a lien on the purchaser's property. Nothing in the completion arrangements made with their client indicated that they had waived their right. Notwithstanding this decision, it would seem prudent for solicitors, faced with a similar situation, to stipulate expressly for the lien and to obtain written confirmation.

The equitable doctrine of subrogation can also operate to enable a person to be subrogated to the rights of a mortgagee. A good example of this occurred in *Boscawen v Bajwa*[12]. B, the registered proprietor of a property, mortgaged it to the Halifax Building Society. He then believed he had entered into a contract of sale but, unknown to the parties at the outset, the documentation did not satisfy s 2 of the Law of Property (Miscellaneous Provisions) Act 1989, so that no contract existed. The bank, who had made a mortgage offer to finance the proposed purchase, then advanced £140,000 to the purchaser's solicitor to be held on terms that it was to be used to complete the purchase of the property and if, for some reason, completion did not occur, to return the money to the bank. The money[13] was paid to B's solicitors who, in turn paid the money to the Halifax and the mortgage was redeemed. The proposed sale did not in fact take place and the issue arose as to the rights of the bank. It was held that the bank was in equity subrogated to the rights of the Halifax, so that it had a charge against the property having priority over a subsequent judgment creditor of B. For subrogation to occur, it was not necessary that the bank did not intend to succeed to the rights of the Halifax; it was sufficient that they intended to lend the money only upon the basis that it would have security for its loan. This equitable doctrine will not operate, however, when its application would produce an unjust result, eg when the third party has obtained all he has bargained for[14].

(a) Enforcement of lien

A lien does not give any right to possession; it confers a right of action for foreclosure[15] or for an order for the sale of the property[16]. It is enforceable against the purchaser though the conveyance to him contains a receipt clause for all the money[17], against volunteers, and sometimes against a subsequent purchaser.

---

11   [1986] FLR 134 (a registered land case), noted at [1986] Conv 149.
12   [1995] 4 All ER 769, CA.
13   Slightly less than the full £140,000 was in fact transferred but this is not material for present purposes.
14   For cases where on the facts mortgagees were not subrogated to the vendor's security rights, see *Paul v Speirway Ltd* [1976] Ch 220, [1976] 2 All ER 587; *Orakpo v Manson Investments Ltd* [1978] AC 95, [1977] 3 All ER 1, HL.
15   *Hughes v Griffin* [1969] 1 All ER 460 at 461, CA, per Harman LJ. This is equivalent to seeking cancellation of the contract by the court; see *Lysaght v Edwards* (1876) 2 Ch D 499 at 506, per Jessel MR; *Baker v Williams* (1893) 62 LJ Ch 315.
16   *Williams v Aylesbury and Buckingham Rly Co* (1873) 28 LT 547.
17   *Winter v Lord Anson* (1827) 3 Russ 488.

The Law of Property Act 1925, s 68, provides that a receipt for consideration money in the body of a deed is, in favour of a subsequent purchaser (including a mortgagee) without notice that all the money has not been paid, sufficient (but not conclusive) evidence of the payment of the whole. Nevertheless, as the section itself envisages, the enforceability of a vendor's lien ultimately rests on the doctrine of notice rather than on a purchaser's reliance upon a receipt clause. The prima facie sufficiency of the receipt is displaced if the vendor, having parted with the deeds on completion, registers the lien as a Class C (iii) land charge, for this will give the purchaser actual notice[18]. Similarly, if he retains the deeds their non-availability[19] will constitute constructive notice of the vendor's rights.

(b) Registered land

It is commonplace for registered land transfers to include the usual receipt clause[20]. Nevertheless, the decision in *London and Cheshire Insurance Co Ltd v Laplagrene Property Co Ltd* [1] suggests that s 68 will rarely assist a subsequent purchaser. There must be reliance on a receipt clause, and this entails at least seeing an accurate record of the deed, if not the actual document itself. However, seldom in practice do purchasers inspect transfer documents (or copies) relating to previous transactions. There is simply no need to do so. Reliance cannot even be placed on the entry 'Price paid £...' which may[2] appear in the proprietorship register, since this does not purport to record receipt of the money.

If the holder of the lien is in actual occupation of the land, then the lien will take effect as an overriding interest and be binding upon a subsequent purchaser[3]. Otherwise it will be void as against a purchaser for want of registration. A recent attempt was made in *UCB Bank plc v French*[4] to argue that the unpaid vendor's lien was binding upon a mortgagee in circumstances where the mortgage was being used to finance the purchase of the property. The argument was that the lien arose upon exchange of contracts and therefore pre-dated the acquisition of an interest by the mortgagee. As the vendor had remained in occupation, not having been paid the full purchase price, it was

---

18   LPA 1925, s 198, p 396, ante. Conversely, non-registration would entitle the subsequent purchaser to take free, even if he had actual knowledge (eg because of the absence of a receipt clause) that the whole price had not been paid. This does not seem to be what s 68 intended. Further, it is uncertain to what extent a vendor's lien is affected by the peculiar effect of the law of escrows, as illustrated in *Thompson v McCullough* [1947] KB 447, [1947] 1 All ER 265, CA, discussed p 451, post. If non-payment of the price in full prevents the legal title passing to the purchaser, the lien cannot strictly be registered against him for he is not an estate owner within the LCA 1972 s 3(1), p 395, ante.

19   In this situation the lien is not registrable as a land charge.

20   The published forms include the clause but not, perhaps significantly, the statutory form prescribed by LRR 1925, Sch, Form 19.

1   [1971] Ch 499, [1971] 1 All ER 766 (sale followed by lease back to vendor).

2   Formerly compulsory, but now only if the proprietor so requests: LRR 1976, r 2(2).

3   *London & Cheshire Insurance Co Ltd v Laplagrene Property Co Ltd*, supra; *Barclays Bank plc v Estates and Commercial Ltd* [1996] 11 LS Gaz R 30, CA.

4   [1995] NPC 144, CA. See also *Nationwide Anglia Building Society v Ahmed* (1995) 70 P & CR 381, CA.

contended that she had an overriding interest binding upon the bank. Although the argument was accepted in principle, it was rejected on the facts, the reason being that, in answer to preliminary inquiries, the vendor had stated that the property was being sold with vacant possession and was not subject to any adverse rights or overriding interests. These replies had been passed on to the mortgagee and so it was held that she could not claim an overriding interest under s 70(1)(g) of the Land Registration Act 1925, because enquiry had been made of her and she had not revealed the existence of her right. While the decision seems to clearly correct on the facts, it seems unfortunate that a mortgagee is even potentially at risk of being bound by an unpaid vendor's lien in circumstances such as occurred in the *French* case. To avoid such a risk, it has been argued that, as a matter of both principle and convenience, the vendor's lien should not arise until completion[5]. Current authority is, however, against this view.

One further point should be considered in passing. Since no legal title vests in the purchaser on a sale of registered land until he is registered as proprietor, the question is sometimes raised whether he is technically safe in handing over the purchase money on completion. The better view would seem to be that if he obtains a clear certificate of search and applies for registration within the protection period, he may with practical safety pay the purchase money in exchange for a duly executed transfer and the land or charge certificate[6]. This is the procedure invariably adopted in practice. The Standard Conditions of Sale make no special provision for completion of sales of registered land[7].

E   Title deeds

1.   Collection on completion

Unless the purchaser is acquiring part only of the vendor's land, he is entitled on completion to receive all the deeds, documents, searches and other relevant papers relating to the title. If the title is registered, a purchaser of the whole of the vendor's interest receives the land (or charge) certificate which is subsequently forwarded to the Land Registry for registration purposes. On a transfer of part, the certificate is not handed over; it is the vendor's duty to deposit it at the Registry for completion of the purchaser's registration[8].

Retaining mortgage deed to effect post-completion discharge

(i) *Undertakings to redeem.*   Unless he has contracted to buy subject to existing mortgages, the purchaser is legally entitled to require the vendor to repay any

5   [1996] Conv 44 at 46–50 (M P Thompson).
6   Brickdale, 38; contra Williams, *Sale of Land*, p 80, note (s).
7   Cf 3 K & E, 346–47, 373.
8   LRA 1925, ss 64(1), 110(6). See generally pp 473–475, post.

mortgage or charge affecting the property on or before completion, and to hand over the deeds, duly receipted. Since the redemption of the vendor's mortgage is a matter of conveyance, not title, the purchaser is under no duty to raise this matter in his requisitions[9]. Often the vendor is in no position to fulfil his strict legal obligation. The normal expectation is to discharge any existing mortgage out of the proceeds of sale received on completion. It is considered highly inconvenient to have to redeem it beforehand by means of a temporary bank loan. The practice has therefore developed whereby the vendor's solicitor undertakes to discharge the mortgage after completion. He retains the deed so that a vacating receipt can later be endorsed and executed by the mortgagee. The procedure has the backing of the Council of the Law Society on the ground that it facilitates conveyancing[10]. Nevertheless a purchaser is not obliged to accept an undertaking to redeem. In two situations he should insist on a pre-completion repayment, namely where the vendor is acting for himself or he is represented by an unqualified conveyancer.

A mortgage of registered land is usually discharged in the manner provided for by the 1925 Rules, ie by the mortgagee signing an instrument known as Form 53[11]. The charge certificate is handed over on completion with an undertaking to forward Form 53, duly executed , on its receipt from the mortgagee. There is no need to wait for this document before applying for registration of the purchaser as proprietor; the Registry automatically stands the case over without any loss of priority until the discharge is received.

(ii) *Form.*   The Law Society Council has recommended[12] use of the following form of undertaking:

> In consideration of your today completing the purchase of ... we hereby undertake forthwith to pay over to the ... building society the money required to redeem the mortgage dated ... and to forward the receipted mortgage to you as soon as it is received by us from the building society.

Should the vendor's solicitor propose to use some other form of wording, as he is free to do, he is well-advised to ascertain in advance that the purchaser's solicitor is willing to accept an undertaking in such terms. It will be observed that the undertaking creates contractual obligations; for the purchaser waives his entitlement to have the mortgage redeemed before completion. The Council's form has been subjected to criticism because it imposes no specific time limit for returning the vacated mortgage, but it is unrealistic to expect a

---

9   See p 355, ante.
10   (1970) 67 LS Gaz 753. This is limited to building society mortgages. As regards other mortgages, presumably the previous opinion (see (1949) 46 LS Gaz 230) still holds good, namely a purchaser's solicitor should obtain his client's authority to accept an undertaking, otherwise he may be liable in negligence if it is not discharged. This recommendation is rarely followed in practice.
11   LRR 1925, r 151. The Registrar can act upon other sufficient proof of repayment, eg an endorsed vacating receipt. See pp 603–606, post, for such receipts and Form 53.
12   See (1986) 83 LS Gaz 3127. See also (1973) 70 LS Gaz 1346, 1360 (J E Adams); (1980) 77 LS Gaz 259 (J E Adams).

solicitor to undertake to do something over which he has no control. A reply to a requisition may itself amount to an undertaking to redeem. If in response to a requisition as to the discharge of mortgages before completion or the furnishing of an undertaking in lieu the vendor's solicitor replies 'this will be done' or 'agreed', he will have undertaken to do one or the other should the matter proceed to completion. Following completion, it is no valid excuse for non-compliance that at the time he was unaware of the existence of any charge on the property, even though the purchaser's solicitor may have had that knowledge[13].

This practice of giving undertakings is universal and in the vast majority of cases operates smoothly. Yet theoretical hazards exist. Occasionally they materialise, as the case of *Edward Wong Finance Co Ltd v Johnson, Stokes and Master*[14] graphically illustrates. The requirement for the vendor's solicitor to be the mortgagee's duly authorised agent to receive the redemption monies on completion should be insisted upon in all cases, and not merely for postal completions, as laid down by the Code of Practice regulating this mode of completion. Where appropriate it would seem advisable to adapt the common form of undertaking by adding confirmation of the solicitor's authority. Problems have also occurred in the past because a mortgagee has refused to discharge the mortgage when, in reliance on an inaccurate redemption statement, an incorrect amount has been remitted on redemption. The Building Societies' Association has now agreed[15] that in such cases societies will nevertheless duly discharge the mortgage, thus ensuring that the solicitor is able to honour his undertaking. He will be expected to pursue his client actively for the shortfall due to the society.

(iii) *Execution in advance of redemption.* The need to give undertakings to repay would largely disappear if mortgagees were prepared to execute a vacating receipt in anticipation of actual redemption. The mortgage could then be handed over on completion with the other deeds. Very few institutional lenders adopt this practice[16], preferring to discharge the mortgage after actual receipt of the redemption money. However, in *Rourke v Robinson*[17], Warrington J held that on repayment it is the mortgagee's *contemporaneous* duty to hand to the mortgagor the mortgage deed duly discharged. There seems to be no objection in law to the deed being receipted in escrow in advance of actual repayment[18]. The present cautious policy by lenders has no legal basis, and can no longer be justified in those many instances when the vendor's solicitor is expressly authorised to receive the redemption money as the mortgagee's agent. Surprisingly, the Conveyancing Committee did not specifically highlight this aspect of building society procedure as ripe for reform in the interests of speedier conveyancing.

13 See *The Professional Conduct of Solicitors* (The Law Society, 1986), para 15.14, comment 2(b).
14 [1984] AC 296, PC, discussed on p 419, ante.
15 See (1985) 82 LS Gaz 2720, 2721–22. But see (1987) 84 LS Gaz 1376, 1538, 1618 (letters).
16 The Abbey National plc is a notable exception.
17 [1911] 1 Ch 480.
18 Ibid, at p 486; *Lloyds Bank Ltd v Bullock* [1896] 2 Ch 192. Cf the correspondence in (1978) LS Gaz 79, 164, 374. For escrows, see p 449, post.

2.   Vendor's statutory entitlement to retain deeds

The Law of Property Act 1925, s 47(9), permits a vendor to keep documents of title when he retains any part of the land to which they relate. Thus he may keep documents showing title to, and extinguishment of, an easement formerly appurtenant to the land sold over the servient land still held by him[19]. His statutory entitlement can be varied by contract. When the vendor does retain documents the conveyance to the purchaser contains an acknowledgment of the latter's right to their production and to delivery of copies. This acknowledgement has effect as provided by s 64 of the Law of Property Act 1925[20].

No acknowledgement is required on a transfer of part of registered land. The land certificate is sufficient proof of title without reference to the vendor's earlier title[1].

3.   Endorsements on deeds

The Law of Property Act 1925, s 200, provides that on a sale of part of the land comprised in the vendor's title, the purchaser is entitled, notwithstanding any contrary stipulation, to require a memorandum to be endorsed on some deed relating to the common title and retained by the vendor, giving notice of restrictive covenants or easements created by the conveyance to him and affecting land retained by the vendor. The purchaser has the right to select which deed shall bear the endorsement; usually the conveyance to the vendor is chosen. The endorsement does not affect the validity of the rights granted, nor obviate the need to register restrictive covenants. The existence of an endorsement is of advantage when title is later deduced by the vendor to his retained land. The section does not apply to a lessee or mortgagee, nor to dispositions of registered land.

It should be observed that the provision does not assist a purchaser where the vendor conveys part of his land without granting rights affecting his retained land. It is, however, common practice to endorse a memorandum of a sale-off, a procedure which is clearly desirable for it considerably reduces the risk of the sale being overlooked on a subsequent sale of the retained land[2]. A purchaser desirous of having notice endorsed ought to raise the matter by way of requisition; the vendor's solicitor rarely refuses to comply with the request.

---

19   *Re Lehmann and Walker's Contract* [1906] 2 Ch 640. An executor may retain the grant of probate under s 45(9)(b) when disposing of the deceased's landed property.
20   See further pp 578–580, post.
 1   R & R, 17.29, list two principal exceptions: on a transfer of part (i) of a possessory title and (ii) of leasehold property.
 2   *Re Sea View Gardens, Claridge v Tingey* [1966] 3 All ER 935; *Epps v Esso Petroleum Co Ltd* [1973] 2 All ER 465 p 88, ante, illustrate some problems that can result from failure to endorse notice of a sale-off. For endorsements on grants of representation, see p 324, ante.

A memorandum of severance of an equitable joint tenancy should be endorsed on or annexed to the conveyance which vests the legal estate in the joint tenants[3].

4. Custody of deeds

In the absence of any mortgage affecting the property, the purchaser is entitled to the personal custody of his deeds[4]. Co-purchasers are entitled to joint custody. An unauthorised deposit of the deeds by one of them alone by way of security is ineffective to create any equitable charge over the property[5].

(a) Mortgagees

On the grant of a first legal mortgage it is the invariable practice for institutional lenders to take possession of the title deeds as part of their security. Indeed any first mortgagee has by statute the same right to their possession as if his security included the fee simple[6]. Before 1926, a mortgagee of the freehold, as owner of the fee, was also treated as owner of the deeds. On this basis it has been held that the mortgagee owes no duty of care to the mortgagor in respect of their custody, because in law they belong to him[7]. At best the mortgagor can seek compensation in equity for their loss, but such relief is available only on redemption.

(b) Solicitors

A solicitor possesses a common law lien on his client's deeds so long as fees due to him in his professional capacity remain unpaid. It is merely passive and possessory in character, and (unlike a vendor's lien) creates no equitable charge on his client's interest in the property[8]. A solicitor acting for both mortgagor and mortgagee loses his lien as against the mortgagor once the mortgage is completed. It does not even revive on redemption of the mortgage[9].

---

3   Law of Property (Joint Tenants) Act 1964, s 1(1). Unlike other endorsements, it requires signature (by at least one of the equitable joint tenants).
4   But see *Clayton v Clayton* [1930] 2 Ch 12.
5   *Thomas Guaranty Ltd v Campbell* [1985] QB 210, [1984] 2 All ER 585, CA.
6   LPA 1925, s 85(1) proviso; s 86(1) proviso (mortgage of leasehold). For the position in registered land, see p 487, post.
7   *Browning v Handiland Group Ltd* (1976) 35 P & CR 345 (mortgagee losing deeds). Sed quaere. Section 85(1) merely confers a right to their *possession*. If the mortgagee no longer has the fee simple estate, why should he still be treated as owner of the deeds so as to absolve him from any duty of care?
8   *Barratt v Gough-Thomas* [1951] Ch 242 at 250, [1950] 2 All ER 1048 at 1053, CA, per Lord Evershed MR.
9   *Barratt v Gough-Thomas*, supra. See generally on solicitors' liens, *Cordery on Solicitors* (7th edn), 273–87.

F   The purchase deed[10]

1.   Introduction

The remaining document which the purchaser's solicitor takes up on completion is the grant to the purchaser, whether it be a conveyance, transfer, lease, assignment or other assurance. This document has previously been executed by the vendor and possibly by the purchaser, whose solicitor should satisfy himself that the vendor's execution is in order. The signature may not tally with the name appearing in the body of the deed. It may even be desirable to compare the vendor's signature with that on the conveyance to him[11]. The advisability of acquainting a party to a deed, especially the purchaser, with its contents and effect needs hardly to be stressed, though this may not be without its problems[12].

A party to a deed having more than one capacity (eg a trustee-vendor who in a combined document appoints a new trustee, both of whom then convey to the purchaser[13]) does not have to execute it twice. The better view seems to be that, unless the document indicates he has executed in one capacity only, then he is estopped from denying that the one execution covers both capacities[14]. Execution in each capacity eliminates any doubt. The purchaser's execution of a conveyance of an unincumbered fee simple is unnecessary, and the prescribed forms of transfer for registered land make no provision for it. One can be added if desired[15]. It is usual for the purchaser to execute the conveyance or transfer where eg it contains covenants by him with the vendor, or a clause in which joint purchasers declare their entitlement in equity[16]. The purchaser's non-execution of the deed in no way affects his ability to enforce against the vendor any covenants which the vendor has entered into with him[17]. Equally, if he takes the benefit of the deed, he is also bound by it[18]. But it does not follow that the vendor is in exactly the same position as if the purchaser had executed the conveyance. His non-execution will prevent any covenant by him taking effect and being enforced at law by the vendor[19]. It will, however,

10   For the form and contents of a typical conveyance, see Ch 17.
11   The author recalls an occasion when there was a marked disparity between the vendor's two signatures, attributable to his intervening illness. The purchaser's solicitor refused to complete without a statutory declaration setting out the circumstances.
12   Page 558, post.
13   See 19 Ency F & P, 991, Form 7:D:3.
14   *Young v Schuler* (1883) 11 QBD 651, CA (evidence admitted that agent's single signature of guarantee was both for principal and on own behalf) is not inconsistent with this view, since his 'pp' signature prima facie indicated he had signed for his principal only.
15   LRR 1925, r 98, referring to Forms 19 and 20, although the printed stationers forms do.
16   On the question whether such a declaration is conclusive if the purchasers have not executed the deed, see *Robinson v Robinson* (1976) 241 EG 153, pp 559–560, post.
17   *Morgan v Pike* (1854) 14 CB 473. The rule for leases is different. A lessor who has not executed the lease cannot sue his tenant for breach of covenant because no leasehold term is created by it: *Pitman v Woodbury* (1848) 3 Exch 4; *Swatman v Ambler* (1852) 8 Exch 72.
18   *Naas v Westminster Bank Ltd* [1940] AC 366 at 373, [1940] 1 All ER 485 at 489, HL, per Lord Maugham. So a mortgagee, who does not normally execute the mortgage, is bound by a proviso for reduction of the interest rate on punctual payment.
19   *Formby v Barker* [1903] 2 Ch 539 at 549, 555, CA, per Vaughan Williams and Stirling LJJ; *Re Rutherford's Conveyance* [1938] Ch 396 at 404, [1938] 1 All ER 495 at 501, per Simonds J.

be enforceable in equity[20], though it is unclear to what extent damages for its breach are recoverable[1]. Exceptionally equity may relieve an executing party from the consequences of his execution if the other party's non-execution materially affects the substance of the transaction[2]. For example, in *Evans v Bremridge*[3], it was the intention that a deed of suretyship would be executed by two joint and several co-sureties, but only one did. The lender was held unable to enforce the deed against the surety who had executed. It was important to him that his co-surety signed; for if the covenant had been enforced against him, he would have been charged upon a contract into which he did not enter[4].

2. Requirements for valid execution

For centuries, it was well settled that three things were of the essence and substance of a deed, namely, writing on paper or parchment, sealing and delivery[5]. At common law, signature was not essential. However, with the spread of education the signature became important for the authentication of documents and became obligatory for deeds executed after 1925[6]. Implementing the recommendations of the Law Commission[7], major changes were made to the requirements for the valid execution of deeds by s 1 of the Law of Property (Miscellaneous Provisions) Act 1989, to which attention must now be turned.

(a) The new formalities

Under s 1(1) of the Act, any rule of law restricting the substance on which a deed may be written is abolished. So too is the rule of law that required a seal for the valid execution of an instrument as a deed by an individual[8], thereby ridding the law of good deal of artificiality in terms of deciding as to what constitutes a seal[9]. Finally, the requirement that, to give authority to another person to deliver a deed, that authority must, itself, be given by deed is also abolished.

---

20 Cf *May v Belleville* [1905] 2 Ch 605 (reservation binding purchaser and successors with notice); *Re Rutherford's Conveyance*, supra, at 405, at 501, per Simonds J.

1 See *Witham v Vane* (1881) 44 LT 718 at 719, CA, per James LJ (no equitable enforcement of obligation to pay money); rvsd on other grounds (1883) 32 WR 617 HL; cf *Formby v Barker*, supra, at 549, per Vaughan Williams LJ (enforcement of negative covenant 'even by an action for damages'). A positive obligation might possibly be enforced indirectly under the rule in *Halsall v Brizell* [1957] Ch 169, [1957] 1 All ER 371.

2 See *Naas v Westminster Bank Ltd*, ante, note 18, at 404–6, 509–10, per Lord Wright.

3 (1856) 8 De GM & G 100. Contrast *Cooper v Evans* (1867) LR 4 Eq 45.

4 See also *Peto v Peto* (1849) 16 Sim 590; *Bolitho v Hillyar* (1865) 34 Beav 180; *Woollam v Barclays Bank plc* [1988] EGCS 22 (husband not bound by charge which co-owner wife refused to execute).

5 *Goddard's Case* (1584) 2 Co Rep 4b at 5a.

6 LPA 1925, s 73, repealed by Law of Property (Miscellaneous Provisions) Act 1989, s 4, Sch 2.

7 (1987) Law Com No 163.

8 This does not include a corporation sole: LP(MP)A 1989, s 1(10).

9 See 3rd edition of this work, p 395.

Under s 1(2) of the Act, it is provided that an instrument shall not be a deed unless it makes clear on its face that it is intended to be a deed and is validly executed as a deed by the person making it or, if more than one party, each of the parties. Valid execution by the party occurs if, and only if, it is signed by him in the presence of a witness who attests the signature, or at his direction and in his presence and in the presence of two witnesses who each attest the signature. It must then be delivered as a deed by him or by some person authorised to do so on his behalf[10]. What do these requirements entail?

(b) Signed

There appeared to have no reported case on the meaning of 'signed' under the previous statutory provision relating to the signing of deeds[11]. Like its predecessor, s 1(1)(4) of the 1989 Act permits the signing to include the making of one's mark (usually the signing of the cross). The question remains as to whether the court will continue to operate a liberal construction of the word 'signature' as was the case in the past, when an engraved facsimile of the ordinary signature was held to suffice[12]. The Court of Appeal has, however, in *Firstpost Homes Ltd v Johnson*[13] indicated that, for the purpose of s 2 of the 1989 Act, it is not prepared to give a strained or artificial construction as to what amounts to a signature. Accordingly, one would envisage that a similar approach will be taken to this matter with regard to s 1, so that it is likely that a person must write his own name with his own hand upon it[14]. This is subject to the exception provided by the statute that the signature can be performed by someone else acting under the direction of the person executing the deed; the reason for this being to allow for situations where, due to infirmity, a person cannot himself sign the document. If a transfer of registered land incorporates a plan, the plan must also be signed by the transferor and by or on behalf of the transferee[15].

(c) Attestation of execution

At common law, attestation was unnecessary for a deed's validity, but the custom has long been to execute deeds in the presence of a witness and to indicate in an attestation clause signed by the witness that this formality had been observed. The Law of Property Act 1925 recognised this practice, but without making it compulsory, by entitling the purchaser at his own expense to have the execution attested by his appointee including his solicitor[16]. The position has now changed

10   LP(MP)A 1989, s 1(3).
11   LPA 1925, s 73.
12   *Bennett v Brumfitt* (1867) LR 3 CP 28 (document signed for purposes of the Parliamentary Voting Act 1843); applied in *Goodman v J Eban Ltd* [1954] 1 QB 550, [1954] 1 All ER 763, CA.
13   [1995] 4 All ER 355, [1995] 1 WLR 1567, CA.
14   *Goodman v J Eban Ltd*, supra, at 561, 768, per Denning LJ.
15   LRR 1925, r 79.
16   LPA 1925 s 75. This statutory right existed only in respect of 'a sale' (defined by s 205(1)(xxiv), and therefore appeared not to extend to mortgagees.

and the signature must now be witnessed and attested. Where the signature is made under the direction of the person executing the deed, there must be two witnesses who must each attest the signature[17]. Section 75 of the Law of Property Act 1925 has not been repealed so that the purchaser can still insist upon his appointee attesting the signature.

(d) Delivered

This requirement is equally as vital as the two preceding elements. It is the final formality. Until delivery a document is inoperative. This concept of legal delivery is totally mystifying to lay people, and its legal significance is not fully appreciated by practitioners. It does not connote a physical handing over to the other side. The maker of a deed may retain it in his own possession and yet deliver it in law, provided he makes clear that he intends it as his deed presently binding on him[18]. Delivery is therefore a question of the grantor's intention, which need not be communicated to the grantee. A deed of gift of unregistered land may be perfectly valid and effective to vest the legal title in the donee, despite the latter's ignorance of the transfer[19]. Delivery of a document as a deed requires that the party whose deed it is stated to be should by words or conduct expressly or impliedly acknowledge his intention to be immediately bound by its provisions[20]. The most expressive mode of indicating this intention is to hand the document over, saying: 'I deliver this as my deed'[1]. But the ceremony whereby an executing party utters such words as he places a finger on the paper wafer (as a token adoption of it as his seal) has largely fallen into disuse. Consequently delivery is now usually inferred from conduct, eg from the mere facts of signing and sealing[2].

Delivery may be absolute or conditional. If absolute, the deed becomes immediately effective to pass the property; if conditional, the delivery (and consequently the document) does not become effective until the condition is fulfilled.

(e) Escrows

A deed may be delivered on condition that it is not to be operative until some event happens or some condition is performed. Such a document is termed an escrow, which may be said to be a deed subject to a limping restriction on its operative effect. It does not become binding unless and until the condition is satisfied. Indeed the weight of opinion favours the view that a document,

---

17 LP(MP)A 1989, s 1(3).
18 *Alan Estates Ltd v WG Stores Ltd* [1982] Ch 511 at 526, [1981] 3 All ER 481 at 490, CA, per Sir Denys Buckley; *Xenos v Wickham* (1867) LR 2 HL 296 at 312, per Blackburn J; *Sheppard's Touchstone*, Vol 1, p 57. See also (1970) 28 CLJ 52 (D E C Yale).
19 See *Hughes v Griffin* [1969] 1 All ER 460, CA; *Palfrey v Palfrey* (1973) 229 EG 1593, CA; *Ross v Ross* (1977) 80 DLR (3d) 377. See also *Tudor v Hamid* [1988] 1 EGLR 251, CA; p 415, ante.
20 12 *Halsbury's Laws* (4th edn), para 1329.
 1 Per Blackburn J in *Xenos v Wickham* (1867) LR 2 HL 296 at 312 (an oft-cited dictum).
 2 As in *Hall v Bainbridge* (1848) 12 QB 699. For deeds executed after 1989, sealing is not necessary.

while it remains in escrow, is not a deed at all[3]. Nevertheless, an escrow is not devoid of all effect. The grantor cannot revoke it, or alter its terms. He must wait to see whether or not the condition is fulfilled[4]. It remains effective despite his death prior to its fulfilment[5].

In a classic judicial understatement Stuart-Smith J has recently observed'[6] that the law of escrow is steeped in much ancient learning and has been found on occasions not altogether satisfactory in modern times. Delivery as an escrow is a question of the grantor's intention at the time of delivery. No special form of words is necessary. Nor is it essential for the grantee to concur in the delivery in escrow, though it seems that the maker should make his intention clear if he physically hands the document to him[7]. The conditions may be express or implied. In the absence of evidence on the question of intention, the court will assume that delivery was absolute[8], but frequently the circumstances suffice to raise the inference of an escrow. Where a transaction is effected by way of lease and counterpart, it was thought at one time that the lease was delivered by the lessor as an escrow conditional upon the lessee's execution of the counterpart[9]. This view was not accepted as a general proposition, however, in *Longman v Viscount Chelsea*[10]. In this case, the parties anticipated that there would be an exchange of lease and counterpart. In such circumstances, the signing and sealing of the lease did not amount to the delivery of a deed in escrow. *Beesly v Hallwood Estates Ltd*[11] was confined to its own facts. In that case, both parties acted upon the erroneous assumption that an option to renew a lease was binding on the purchaser of the reversion. In the event, neither party envisaged that the exchange of lease and counterpart was an integral part of the creation of a new lease, so that the signing and sealing[12] of the lease was held to effect the delivery of the lease in escrow. Ordinarily, however, when the parties do envisage an exchange, there will be no inference that the lease has been delivered in escrow prior to that exchange.

In a typical sale and purchase of unregistered land, the manifest intention of the vendor who executes the conveyance in advance of completion is that it shall not be operative to pass the legal title beforehand. Apart from special circumstances[13], the inference is inescapable that he executes the conveyance

---

3   Contra, per Sir Denys Buckley in *Alan Estates Ltd v WG Stores Ltd* [1982] Ch 511 at 527, [1981] 3 All ER 481 at 491, CA, who, whilst conscious of the opposing authorities (eg *Xenos v Wickham*, supra, at 332, per Lord Cranworth LC), suggested that differences of description might be no more than a matter of semantics.

4   See *Venetian Glass Gallery Ltd v Next Properties Ltd* [1989] 2 EGLR 42 at 45, per Harman J.

5   *Perryman's Case* (1599) 5 Co Rep 84a; *Graham v Graham* (1791) 1 Ves 272.

6   *Bentray Investments Ltd v Venner Time Switches Ltd* [1985] 1 EGLR 39, 274 EG 43 at 47; *Alan Estates Ltd v WG Stores Ltd*, supra, at 520, 486, per Lord Denning MR ('a relic of medieval times').

7   *Bentray Investments Ltd v Venner Time Switches Ltd*, supra, at 47.

8   *D'Silva v Lister House Development Ltd* [1971] Ch 17, [1970] 1 All ER 858; *Venetian Glass Galley Ltd v Next Properties Ltd* [1989] 2 EGLR 42 at 45 per Harman J..

9   *Beesley v Hallwood Estates Ltd* [1961] Ch 105, [1961] 1 All ER 90, CA.

10 (1989) 58 P & CR 189, CA.

11 Note 9, supra.

12 In the case of individuals, sealing is no longer necessary.

13 As in *Tudor v Hamid* [1988] 1 EGLR 251, CA (vendor in receipt of whole purchase price in advance of completion).

as an escrow conditional on payment of the purchase money[14]. Should the vendor allow part of the price to remain unpaid upon completion, the purchaser, it seems does not obtain the legal title unless the vendor has agreed to allow that part to remain outstanding on mortgage, or lien, even though the purchaser has the title deeds including the (as yet) ineffective conveyance executed by the vendor[15]. It was previously the case that a solicitor could not on completion deliver the conveyance on the vendor's behalf without his client's authority under seal[16]. The law has now changed that so where a solicitor, or licensed conveyancer, purports to deliver an instrument as a deed on behalf of a party to the instrument, it shall be conclusively presumed in favour of the purchaser that he is authorised so to deliver the instrument[17].

(i) *Relation back.*   As soon as the condition is fulfilled, the deed automatically takes effect without any re-delivery as *from the date of its original delivery as an escrow.* In the case of a conveyance of unregistered land, the legal estate is passed retrospectively as at that date. The purchaser's title is said to 'relate back' to that time[18]. The operation of the doctrine in relation to leases is illustrated by *Alan Estates Ltd v WG Stores Ltd*[19]. Under the terms of an undated lease originally delivered as an escrow a tenant was obliged to pay rent from 'the date hereof'. Notwithstanding that the conditions attached to it were not fulfilled until a year later, the lease was held to have legal effect from the date of its delivery as an escrow. The tenant therefore became liable for rent as from that earlier date. Another instructive case is *Beesly v Hallwood Estates Ltd*[20]:

> X Ltd, thinking that an option to renew exercised by their tenant, Y, was binding on them, executed a further lease of the property in Y's favour. At about the same time Y executed a counterpart lease. Later X Ltd discovered the option was unenforceable for want of registration and refused to continue.

The Court of Appeal held that the company had delivered the lease as an escrow, conditional upon Y's execution of the counterpart, which Y had done. Fulfilment of this condition made the company's lease fully binding. The decision would have been the same had X Ltd attempted to resile after sealing the lease but *before* Y had executed her counterpart, for having delivered it, it was not recallable by them. This would not have been the case had Y never executed the counterpart at all.

14   *Glessing v Green* [1975] 2 All ER 696 at 700, CA, per Sir John Pennycuick; *Kingston v Ambrian Investment Co Ltd* [1975] 1 All ER 120, CA.
15   See *Thompson v McCullough* [1947] KB 447, [1947] 1 All ER 265, CA.
16   *Re Seymour* [1913] 1 Ch 475 at 481, CA, per Joyce J.
17   LP(MP)A 1989, s 1(5).
18   See the discussion of the doctrine by Lord Denning MR and Sir Denys Buckley in *Alan Estates Ltd v WG Stores Ltd* [1982] Ch 511 at 521, 528, [1981] 3 All ER 481 at 486, 492, CA. It is far from clear how this retrospective vesting affects the scheme of registration and making searches under the LCA 1972. Ignoring the probability of the purchaser being protected by a clear certificate, would the doctrine operate to defeat as against the purchaser a land charge registered after delivery of the conveyance as an escrow but before completion of the purchase?
19   Supra; cf *Terrapin International Ltd v IRC* [1976] 2 All ER 461 (document not executed for stamp duty purposes until date escrow condition fulfilled); [1982] Conv 409 (P H Kenny).
20   [1961] Ch 105, [1961] 1 All ER 90, CA; *Kingston v Ambrian Investment Co Ltd*, supra.

This doctrine of relation back applies only for such purposes as are necessary to give efficacy to the transaction. Whilst the conditions are in suspense the grantee (whether purchaser or lessee) acquires no title to enable him to deal with third parties. He cannot lease or mortgage the property; nor can he issue notices to quit or collect rents from tenants[1]. Third party transactions (eg a mortgage) become effective when the grantee acquires his title, but their title would not appear to vest retrospectively[2]. As for the grantor, though the legal title is still with him, he also can do nothing with the property inconsistent with his ability to implement the grant immediately on fulfilment of the condition attaching to the escrow[3]. Any attempted dealing with the land will be ineffective.

(ii) *Non-fulfilment of condition.*   If the condition of the escrow is not fulfilled, the document does not become a binding deed. The grantor can renounce it without taking court action. It is not the non-fulfilment of the condition itself that destroys the document's binding quality, but the grantor's renunciation consequent thereon. Should he subsequently change his mind, the document can only be reconstituted a deed by a *re-execution*, ie signed, sealed and delivered afresh. Re-delivery alone, even unconditionally, will not suffice.

The effect of renunciation would appear to depend on the precise circumstances of each case. According to Lord Denning MR, on renunciation 'the transaction fails altogether'[4]. Clearly the grantee's belated attempt to fulfil the condition cannot bring the doctrine of relation back into play. But the extent to which his contractual rights are affected ought to be determined by ordinary rules of contract[5].

How long must the grantor wait before being entitled to renounce? No problem arises when he has expressly limited a period. In cases where the condition is implied the point is one of considerable difficulty on which the courts disagree. One view[6] favours a period of unreasonable delay, after which the grantor may be released in equity from his obligations. In *Glessing v Green*[7] the court declined to invoke this equitable principle of imprecise application. The time limit is a vital, albeit inferred, element of the condition itself. On a sale of land the implied condition attaching to the vendor's execution of the conveyance is taken to be completion in due course. This rather uncertain

---

1   *Alan Estates Ltd v WG Stores Ltd*, ante at 521, 486, per Lord Denning MR; *Security Trust Co v Royal Bank of Canada* [1976] AC 503, [1976] 1 All ER 381, PC (ineffective debenture).
2   Cf *Thompson v McCullough*, ante, note 15 (subsequent fulfilment of condition inoperative to validate notice to quit served during period of suspense).
3   *Alan Estates Ltd v WG Stores Ltd*, ante, at 527–28, 492, per Sir Denys Buckley; *Hooper v Ramsbottom* (1815) 6 Taunt 12 (purchaser not bound by intervening charge).
4   *Alan Estates Ltd v WG Stores Ltd*, ante, at 520, 486. Cf *Glessing v Green* [1975] 2 All ER 696, CA (no antecedent contract; vendor retaining property free from any rights purchaser possessed by reason by escrow).
5   Would a tenant be deprived of his right to sue for breach of contract if the lessor declined to hand over the lease following the lessee's execution of the counterpart, albeit outside the period permitted by the condition?
6   *Beesly v Hallwood Estates Ltd* [1961] Ch 105 at 118, 120, [1961] 1 All ER 90 at 94, 95, CA, per Harman LJ and Lord Evershed MR, respectively.
7   [1975] 2 All ER 696 at 701, CA, per Sir John Pennycuick, delivering the judgment of the court, and applying *Kingston v Ambrian Investment Co Ltd* [1975] 1 All ER 120, CA.

period the court linked to the expiration of a (presumably valid) notice to complete served by the vendor. The court's approach has been welcomed[8], on the basis that conveyancing transactions should run more smoothly now that the device of a notice to complete regulates both the escrow and the contract positions. The decision appears to make little practical difference to the vendor's position in cases where there is an antecedent contract, the almost invariable situation. Irrespective of his rights flowing from non-fulfilment of the escrow condition, the purchaser's failure to comply with the notice to complete entitles the vendor to rescind the contract, and this is effectively what he is seeking.

(f) Execution by corporations

The reforming provisions of s 1 of the Law of Property (Miscellaneous Provisions) Act 1989 apply only to individuals and so leave the position with regard to companies unaffected. The execution of a deed by a corporation aggregate requires the affixing of its seal. This is no mere empty formality, since a corporation, for obvious reasons, cannot sign documents. The Law of Property Act 1925, s 74(1) provides[9]:

> In favour of a purchaser a deed shall be deemed to have been duly executed by a corporation aggregate if its seal be affixed thereto in the presence of and attested by its clerk, secretary or other permanent officer or his deputy, and a member of the board of directors, council or other governing body of the corporation, and where seal purporting to be the seal of a corporation has been affixed to a deed, attested by persons purporting to be persons holding such offices as aforesaid, the deed shall be deemed to have been executed in accordance with the requirements of this section, and to have taken effect accordingly.

This section has a substantive effect. Thus a lease sealed and attested in accordance with s 74(1) can effectively bind a lessor-company even though its seal has been affixed without the authority of a resolution of the board of directors[10]. This produces the absurd result that a company will be bound by a deed executed even against the decision of its board, and requires that a company cannot safely seal a deed until after the passing of an appropriate resolution. It was thought that sealing, prima facie. imported delivery, either unconditionally or in escrow[11], but in *Longman v Viscount Chelsea*[12], Nourse LJ gave this view fairly short shrift.

Where the title is registered, the Land Registry requires satisfying that a deed not executed in accordance with s 74(1) was executed in the manner

---

8   See (1975) 39 Conv (NS) 430, 432–33. But the application of this principle by analogy to a case where there is no antecedent contract (as in *Glessing v Green*) must surely be wrong. No notice to complete can be served when there is no contract between the parties.
9   As an alternative to any other legitimate mode of execution (sub-s (6)), eg as permitted by the articles of association.
10 *D'Silva v Lister House Development Ltd* [1971] Ch 17, [1970] 1 All ER 858. A subsequent confirmatory resolution was alleged to have been passed in error.
11 See the authorities cited in Emmet, para 20.003.
12 (1989) 58 P & CR 189 at 199, citing with approval Williams, *Title*, 656–7.

prescribed by the articles[13]. This seems to be an unnecessary precaution in view of the presumption, albeit rebuttable, that the formalities regarding use of the seal are taken as having been duly observed[14].

3. Date of deed

Whilst the invariable practice is to date the conveyance or transfer, the date is not of the substance. As *Goddard's* case[15] shows, a deed with an incorrect or impossible date, or even no date at all, can still be completely effective. The prescribed forms of transfer of registered land provide for the dating of the document[16]. If two documents bear the same date, eg the conveyance to and mortgage by the purchaser, the court presumes they have been executed in such order as to give effect to the parties' manifest intention[17].

The date usually inserted in the purchase deed is that of the day of actual completion in the erroneous belief that this is when a conveyance of unregistered land operates to vest the legal estate in the purchaser. There is, however, an abundance of ancient authority to the effect that a deed takes effect from the time of delivery, not from its date[18]. The date is only prima facie evidence of the true time of execution; as soon as the contrary appears, the apparent date is to be utterly disregarded[19]. Wright J once said that it is such weak evidence that a court ought not to act upon it[20]. This used to present a theoretical difficulty in that the date of delivery was when the document was executed by the vendor, this taking effect as delivery in escrow, so that the date of the deed should be backdated to the time when the vendor executed the deed and deposited it with his solicitor. Now that the solicitor has authority to deliver the deed[1], the insertion of the completion date will be the true date of the deed.

Backdating
When completion is delayed, a solicitor sometimes finds that his land charges search certificate has expired by the time the parties are ready to complete. The once prevalent practice of backdating the conveyance in an endeavour to obtain the protection afforded by a clear certificate has largely disappeared now that a telephone or teleprinter search can be requisitioned at the last

---

13 R & R, 15.13.
14 *Parker v Judkin* [1931] 1 Ch 475, CA.
15 (1584) 2 Co Rep 4b, p 447, ante; see *Alan Estates Ltd v WG Stores Ltd* [1982] Ch 511, [1981] 3 All ER 481, CA (no date).
16 See LRR 1925, Schedule, Forms 19, 23, 24, 33, 34.
17 *Gartside v Silkstone and Dodworth Coal and Iron Co* (1882) 21 Ch D 762 at 767–68, per Fry J.
18 *Clayton's Case* (1585) 5 Co Rep 1a; *Hatter v Ashe* (1696) 3 Lev 438; *Alan Estates Ltd v WG Stores Ltd*, supra, discussed p 451, ante.
19 *Browne v Burton* (1847) 17 LJQB 49 at 50, per Patterson J. The date of a deed is taken as the relevant date for stamping requirements, p 556, post.
20 *Re Slater, ex p Slater* (1897) 76 LT 529 at 530.
 1 LP(MP)A 1989, s 1(5).

moment[2]. In any event the practice is thought to be quite ineffective to achieve the desired result. Merely dating the deed with some date falling within the protection period cannot alter the fact, where this is the case, that completion is effected after its expiration. And protection is conferred only when *the purchase is completed* before the expiry of the relevant 15 days' period[3]. Moreover, it seems possible that a deed, if back dated for this purpose, could be held to be a forgery on the ground that it bears a false date[4], even though the date is not essential to the operation of a deed.

Ante-dating so as to obtain protection against intervening incumbrances does not arise with registered titles. Protection is determined, not by the completion date, but by the date of lodgement of the transfer for registration.

4.   Alterations in deeds

Alterations in or additions to a deed are rebuttably presumed to have been made before execution[5]. If proved to have been made afterwards, their effect on the parties' rights depends on their materiality. A non-material alteration does not affect a deed's validity, such as, adding the names of tenants occupying the property conveyed[6], or altering the Christian names of one of the parties[7]. A material alteration is one which varies the rights, liabilities or legal position of the parties, or varies the document's legal effect[8]; it avoids the deed but only to a limited degree and not retrospectively. A party making (or authorising) an alteration cannot enforce any term of the deed against a non-consenting party[9]. A material alteration by the purchaser does not operate to divest the title, otherwise this would be a facile way of getting rid of onerous estates[10]; but a similar alteration by a mortgagee prevents him from enforcing his security[11]. A party bound by deed cannot evade his liabilities thereunder by

2   Page 404, ante. Since the result is not conclusive, an element of risk always attaches to these informal methods of searching.
3   LCA 1972, s 11(5), p 406, ante.
4   The Forgery and Counterfeiting Act 1981, s 9(1)(g), makes an instrument false (hence a forgery (s 1)) if it purports to have been made on a date when it was not so made. See *R v Ritson* (1869) LR 1 CCR 200; *R v Wells* [1939] 2 All ER 169, CCA. A forged conveyance passes no legal estate: *Re Cooper* (1882) 20 Ch D 611, CA; but it may still have some effect. Cf *Ahmed v Kendrick* (1987) 56 P & CR 120, CA (forger's beneficial interest passing).
5   *Re Spollon and Long's Contract* [1936] Ch 713, [1936] 2 All ER 711, the reason being, according to Co Litt 225b, that a deed cannot be altered after execution without fraud or wrong and the presumption is against there.
6   *Adsetts v Hives* (1863) 33 Beav 52, unless essential to identify the property conveyed; *Sommerville v Roynat Ltd* (1982) 136 DLR (3d) 33 (altering date).
7   *Re Howgate and Osborn's Contract* [1902] 1 Ch 451, where Kekewich J concluded that the original names were merely a misdescription so that the conveyance had always been to A, B and C, though C was wrongly called C. Aliter if C and D were two different people and C had fraudulently been substituted for D.
8   See *Norton on Deeds*, (2nd edn) p 44.
9   *Ellesmere Brewery Co v Cooper* [1896] 1 QB 75.
10 *Doe d Lewis v Bingham* (1821) 4 B & Ald 672 at 678, per Best J.
11 *Malicki v Yankovich* (1981) 125 DLR (3d) 411 (adding land to mortgage).

materially altering it. If the deed is incorrect, the proper course is to seek rectification. The effect of alterations by strangers is obscure.

If a mistake or omission is discovered in an instrument delivered for registration, it can only be corrected in accordance with the Rules. Minor clerical errors can be corrected by the Chief Land Registrar under r 13. Where a material alteration has to be made after the document has been lodged for registration, it can be withdrawn and returned for amendment and re-execution[12], otherwise, if registration has been effected, a deed of rectification is required.

G   Powers of attorney

A person (the donor of the power) can generally speaking authorise an attorney (the donee) to perform any act which the donor of the power can do. Powers of this nature are governed by the Powers of Attorney Act 1971, and the Enduring Powers of Attorney Act 1985. Both statutes give effect to recommendations in two Law Commission Reports on the topic[13]. These Acts replace and extend the previous legislation on the subject contained in the Law of Property Act 1925, and the Trustee Act 1925.

1.   Form of power

The power may be a wide one, including dealing with property by sale or lease, with power to execute deeds giving effect to such dealings, or it may be limited to the execution or delivery of a particular document. To encourage greater standardisation of powers of attorney, the Powers of Attorney Act 1971 provides a simple statutory form which, if adopted, confers on the donee a general power 'to do on behalf of the donor anything which he can lawfully do by an attorney'[14]. If a more limited power is intended it will be necessary to spell out the specific powers which it is sought to confer, remembering always that a power is strictly construed according to its terms[15]. It is no longer the case that powers need, themselves, to be created by deed[16].

Once created, the contents of the power may be proved by means of a photocopy duly certified by a solicitor or stockbroker as a true and complete copy of the original[17]. This facilitates the verification of title to land. Where a conveyance is executed by an attorney, the power becomes a document of title; he can retain the original, handing the certified copy to the purchaser. If the purchaser later splits up his land and conveys plots to X and Y, he can

---

12   LRR 1925, r 86.
13   Law Com No 30; Law Com No 122. See (1971) 68 LS Gaz 434 (C K Liddle).
14   Section 10(1), and Sch 1. A form 'to the like effect but expressed to be made under [the] Act' confers the same general power.
15   See eg *Re Dowson and Jenkin's Contract* [1904] 2 Ch 219, CA.
16   Law of Property (Miscellaneous Provisions) Act 1989, s 1(3).
17   Section 3(1). The reasons for limiting the class of persons qualified to certify are contained in Law Com No 30, para 7.

make certified photocopies of the certified photocopy. Under s 3(2) of the Act these are to be accepted by X and Y as equivalent to the original power.

2. Appointment of attorney by trustee

The maxim *delegatus non potest delegare* restricts the appointment of agents by a trustee, though various statutory encroachments were made upon this principle by the Trustee Act 1925. Section 9 of the Act of 1971 replaces the former power (contained in s 27 of the Trustee Act 1925) to delegate during absence abroad by a much wider provision which applies to any trust whenever created. This enables a trustee (and other fiduciary owners such as a tenant for life) by power of attorney to delegate for a period not exceeding 12 months the exercise of all or any of the trusts, powers and discretions vested in him. The instrument creating the power must be executed in the presence of an attesting witness, and various notices of its making must be given. Non-compliance does not invalidate the title of a person dealing with the attorney. The donor of the power remains liable for the donee's acts or defaults in the same manner as if they were his own.

A trustee cannot delegate to his sole co-trustee not being a trust corporation[18]. This restriction does not apply when one of three (or four) trustees appoints one of the others as his attorney[19]. Furthermore, the statutory form of power prescribed by s 10 of the Act cannot be employed by a trustee-donor to delegate his fiduciary functions (s 10(2)), regardless of whether he is also a beneficial owner of the land. In *Walia v Michael Naughton Ltd*[9] registered freehold land was transferred to A, B and C. Pursuant to s 10, A executed a general power in B's favour. Later they purported to transfer the land as beneficial owners to a purchaser. The court rejected an argument that the s 10 power was valid on the ground that the vendors, selling as beneficial owners, were not exercising a fiduciary function. A was undoubtedly exercising a trustee's function because it was as trustee that the legal title was vested in him jointly with B and C. Prior to this decision it was quite common for vendors to proffer and purchasers (and the Land Registry[20]) to accept a general power when vendors conveyed as beneficial owners. Unregistered titles previously accepted on this basis are now clearly and inconveniently bad, though the defect is of a highly technical nature. On future purchases practitioners will now need to be specially vigilant when perusing titles disclosing conveyances executed by attorneys[1].

---

18 Section 9(2). But see the Enduring Powers of Attorney Act 1985, s 3 (3), p 462, post.
19 *Walia v Michael Naughton Ltd* [1985] 3 All ER 673 at 678, per Judge Finlay QC. Does s 9(2) also prohibit two trustees from appointing a single donee as attorney for both of them? Would this breach the payment to two trustees rule? See [1978] Conv 85.
20 See (1977) 41 Conv (NS) 369; [1980] Conv 191, 193 (P W Smith).
 1 Cf [1986] Conv 136, 137 (N S Price), suggesting that a purchaser might well ignore the defect; in reality there is no prospect of the title being upset by a superior claim. To cure the defect a confirmatory conveyance from the trustees to the original purchaser would be required. If they initially conveyed as beneficial owners, it might be (see p 665, post) that the purchaser could not rely on any convenant for further assurance.

3.   Execution of deed by attorney

Section 7(1) of the Act permits an attorney when executing a deed to sign with his own name, except in cases where an instrument has to be executed in the name of the estate owner. If he adopts this procedure, the deed should state that he executes as attorney, ie he signs his own name, adding 'as attorney on behalf of B' (the donor). He may sign with the donor's name, in which case the form is 'B by his attorney A'.

An attorney can execute a deed on behalf of a corporation. As an alternative to the method prescribed by s 7, he can adopt the procedure permitted by the Law of Property Act 1925, which allows him to sign in the corporation's name in the presence of at least one witness and to affix his own seal[2].

4.   Protection of attorney and purchasers

At common law a power of attorney is revoked by the donor's death, insanity, marriage or bankruptcy[3], and by its very nature is revocable by him at any time unless coupled with an interest[4]. For a purchaser the inherent danger in taking a conveyance from an attorney is the revocability of the power. Sections 4 and 7 of the Act considerably simplify the former provisions in the Law of Property Act 1925, which were considered difficult to construe and unsatisfactory in result. The new rules apply to all powers whenever created, but do not determine the validity of transactions effected before the commencement of the Act. These will continue to be governed by the law as laid down by the Act of 1925[5].

The following paragraphs relate solely to the position under the new Act. It is necessary to distinguish between (a) powers given by way of security, and (b) other powers.

(a) Security powers
Under s 4(1) where power is expressed to be irrevocable and is given to secure a proprietary interest of the donee[6], then so long as the donee has the interest the power cannot be revoked either by the donor without his consent or by the donor's death, incapacity or bankruptcy. Section 4 will apply, for example, to an irrevocable power of attorney contained in an equitable mortgage whereby the mortgagee (the donee of the power) is empowered to convey the legal estate if the mortgagor (the donor) defaults under the terms of the

---

2   Section 7(2) expressly preserves the alternative modes of execution under LPA 1925, s 74(3), and (4) (which applies where a corporation is attorney).
3   See *Tingley v Müller* [1917] 2 Ch 144 at 183, CA, per Bray J. See now as to mental incapacity the Enduring Powers of Attorney Act 1985, discussed pp 460–463, post.
4   *Walsh v Whitcomb* (1797) 2 Esp 565.
5   Sections 124, 126–28, as to which see Emmet (15th edn), 246–50; Law Com No 30, paras 29–31.
6   Or the performance of an obligation owed to him – which will not usually occur in a conveyancing context.

mortgage[7]. A third party who deals with the donee of the power has no means of knowing that the power has not been revoked with his concurrence. Section 5(3) protects any person dealing with the attorney (not merely a purchaser) who is, in effect, entitled to assume that the power is still fully operational unless he knows that it has been revoked with the attorney's concurrence. In the absence of such knowledge his title will always be good despite the revocation of the power. The subsection only applies where a power is *expressed to be* irrevocable *and to* be given by way of security[8]. What the power says rather than what it does seems to be vital here.

(b) Other powers

In relation to other powers s 5(2) operates to preserve the validity of the transaction between the attorney and a third party in the absence of the latter's knowledge of revocation. However, under sub-s (5) knowledge of the occurrence of an event (such as death) which has the effect of revoking the power is equivalent to knowledge of revocation, notwithstanding that the third party was unaware that the event had that effect. If he has knowledge, he does not, of course, obtain any title to the property. Again it should be noted that sub-s (2) applies in favour of any person dealing with the attorney, not merely a purchaser.

The validity of the third party's title depends on his absence of knowledge of revocation, but how is a purchaser from him to be satisfied that he had no such knowledge? Section 5(4) gives the answer by providing that it is to be *conclusively presumed* in favour of a *purchaser* that the third party did not know that the power had been revoked if (i) the transaction between the donee and the third party was completed within a year from when the power came into operation[9] or (ii) if outside that period, the third party makes a statutory declaration, before or within three months of the completion of the purchase, that he did not know of the revocation. Unless the case falls within (i), it clearly behoves the purchaser to obtain at his own expense the desired declaration at the time of the purchase. Indeed it would seem advantageous for the third party himself to make an appropriate declaration immediately after the transaction between himself and the attorney. Such a declaration would seem to be within s 5 (4), since it will have been made before the completion of any subsequent purchase, and the Act does not specify any period prior to completion within which it has to be made[10]. Unless the third party is able in

---

7   See *Sowman v David Samuel Trust Ltd* [1978] 1 All ER 616, [1978] 1 WLR 22.
8   Cf s 4(1): 'Where a power ... is expressed to be irrevocable and is given to secure ...'. Many powers of attorney given in equitable mortgages, based on pre-Act precedents, fall foul of s 5(3) because they are not *expressed* as security powers. See eg 14 Ency F & P, 620, Form 7:8. Cf the Cumulative Noter-up, which warns of the need to amend the form. For possible abuse of the Act by dressing-up ordinary powers as security powers, see (1971) 68 LS Gaz 437, 524; cf ibid, 482.
9   This will be the date of the power unless it otherwise provides.
10 This interpretation disposes of the difficulties said to arise from the failure of s 5(2) to provide how the third party can establish his ignorance of any revocation.

this way to anticipate a future sale, the Act appears to leave unresolved the problem of what happens in a case falling outside situation (i) above where the third party dies and his personal representative conveys to a purchaser. He cannot declare as to the state of the deceased's knowledge and unless it can be established that the power had not in fact been revoked (eg by a declaration to that effect by the donor) , he may have difficulty in satisfying a purchaser of the soundness of the title.

(c) Registered land

Where the land is registered and the transaction between the attorney and the person dealing with him is not completed within 12 months from when the power came into operation, the latter must furnish[11] the Registrar with a statutory declaration that at the time of completion he did not know of the revocation of the power or of any event which had that effect. In the case of a security power he must declare that he did not know that the power was not given by way of security and did not know that it had been revoked with the donee's consent. Production of the appropriate declaration is vital if the third party is to be registered as proprietor even in cases where the transaction with the attorney results in a first compulsory registration of title. The power, or a copy, must accompany the application for registration[12].

On a subsequent sale of the land by the third party, the purchaser need not obtain a statutory declaration under s 5(4), as might be the case (depending on the circumstances) if the land were unregistered. He will rely on the entries on the register of title. In fact he will be unaware that his vendor acquired title under a document executed by an attorney.

(d) Protection of attorney

Section 5 (1) of the Act regulates the position of the attorney. If he acts in ignorance that the power has been revoked, he does not incur any liability either to the donor or to any other person, but under s 5(5) he is deemed to know of' the revocation if he knows of an act having that effect.

5.   Enduring powers of attorney (EPA)

The purpose of the Enduring Powers of Attorney Act 1985 is to enable a person to create a power of attorney, called an enduring power of attorney (EPA), that will not be revoked by his subsequent mental incapacity. To be valid it must be created at a time when the donor is of sound mind. The form and execution of the power are statutorily prescribed, and it must contain an express statement that he intends it to continue despite his subsequent mental

---

11   LRR 1925, r 82(4), (6), as substituted by the Land Registration (Powers of Attorney) Rules 1986, S.I. 1986 No 1537.
12   LRR 1925, r 82(1).

incapacity[13]. More than one attorney may be appointed (s 11(1)), but the instrument will fail as an EPA if it confers a right to appoint a substitute (s 2(9)). The power may confer general authority to do anything which the donor can lawfully do by an attorney: s 3(1), (2). The attorney is empowered within prescribed limits to use the donor's property to benefit other people, including himself, unless the instrument of creation expressly restricts these rights: s 3(4), (7). Alternatively the power to act may be limited to specified property or specified occasions.

(a) Registration of power
So long as the donor remains mentally capable an EPA operates basically as an ordinary power effective under the Act of 1971. The onset of mental incapacity does not revoke the power. The attorney's authority is *suspended* until it is duly registered: s 1(1)[14]. The lynch-pin of the whole scheme is registration of the power with the Court of Protection. Once the attorney has reason to believe that the donor is or is becoming mentally incapable[15], he is under a statutory obligation as soon as practicable to apply for registration: s 4(1), (2). This imposes an almost intolerable burden on the attorney. How is he to judge when the donor is becoming incapable? He is not required to substantiate his belief by psychiatric reports. To delay the application may result in suspension of his power to act under s 1(1). Yet hasty action may result in objections, based on prematurity, by the donor or specified relatives to whom notice of an intended application must first be given[16].

Registration of the power precludes any subsequent revocation by the donor during a lucid interval, unless it is confirmed by the court; nor can he extend or restrict the scope of the authority: s 7(1)(a), (c). No disclaimer of the power is valid until the attorney gives notice to the court: 7(1)(b). The court has jurisdiction to cancel the registration in certain circumstances, eg on being satisfied that the donor is and is likely to remain mentally capable: s 8(4).

(b) Protection of attorney and third parties
The Act sets up a complicated scheme for the protection of attorneys and those dealing with them. The possibility of the attorney acting without authority can arise in a variety of different situations too numerous to discuss fully here.

---

13   See s 2 (1), (2); Enduring Powers of Attorney (Prescribed Form) Regulations 1990, operative from 31 July 1990. All the marginal notes to the form must be included, it being insufficient merely to explain their content to the donor: Practice Direction [1989] 2 All ER 64. A power executed in the form prescribed by the Enduring Powers of Attorney (Prescribed Forms) Regulations 1987 before 31 July 1991 is capable of being a valid enduring power of attorney: r 5(a).
14   Application to register confers a limited authority to act pending registration: s 1(2).
15   Defined in s 13(1) as 'incapable by reason of mental disorder of managing and administering his property and affairs'.
16   See s 6(4), (5) also enabling objection on grounds of fraud, invalidity, unsuitability. Sub-sections (6)–(8) deal with the consequences of an objection being upheld. See *Re K* [1988] Ch 310, [1988] 1 All ER 358 (objection not sustained).

For example, he may act at a time when the power is suspended because of the donor's supervening incapacity of which he is unaware. Or he may act after registration in ignorance of the fact that the power was invalid, eg because it was executed by the donor when already mentally incapable. In both these situations the transaction between the attorney and a third party is fully effective and binding if the latter is without knowledge of the incapacity[17]. So far as a purchaser from the third party is concerned, the Act adopts the protection rules contained in s 7(4) of the Act of 1971. It will therefore be conclusively presumed in his favour that the prior transaction with the third party was valid provided – (i) it was made within a year of registration of the power, or (ii) the third party makes an appropriate statutory declaration that he had no reason to doubt the attorney's authority to dispose of the property[18].

(c) Exercise of donor's trustee's powers

By virtue of s 3(3) of the Act the attorney is authorised to 'execute or exercise all or any of the trusts, powers or discretions vested in the donor as trustee'. His trustee functions are automatically conferred on the attorney, unless the power says otherwise. The fact that the donor might not have been aware of, or intended, this consequence is quite immaterial. Not surprisingly, this provision has attracted justifiable criticism[19]. It was introduced at a late stage in the Bill's passage through Parliament. It did not feature in the recommendations of the Law Commission, which took the view that powers granted by trustees pursuant to s 25 of the Trustee Act 1925, should be denied EPA status[20].

The new sub-section seems to have been inspired by the restrictive decision in *Walia v Michael Naughton Ltd*[1]. Apparently it is intended to deal with cases where a matrimonial home is vested jointly in husband (H) and wife (W). Without s 3(3) it would not be possible for (say) H to appoint W as his attorney so as to enable her to sell the house, since delegation to a sole co-trustee is not permissible. What is more, it empowers the attorney without the concurrence of any other person to give a valid receipt for capital money. An EPA in W's favour puts her in a position of being able by herself to transfer a good title to a purchaser[2]. This provision does not, of course, enable the attorney to give a sole receipt when there is another trustee for sale apart from the donor. Suppose the house is vested in the joint names of H and W, and H executes an

---

17   Section 1(1)(c) (applying s 5 of the Powers of Attorney Act 1971); s 9(3). Equally the attorney's lack of knowledge protects him from liability: s 9(2).
18   See s 9(4). The declaration must be made before or within three months of completion. Section 5(4) is discussed on p 459, ante. For the evidence to be produced on registration of a registered land transaction involving an EPA, see LRR 1925, r 82(5) (as substituted, note 11, ante).
19   For a trenchant attack see (1986) 130 SJ 23 (R T Oreton) ('a legislative blunder'); cf Lord Hailsham LC at HL Debates, 24 June 1985, vol 465, col 549 ('a rather technical amendment').
20   Law Com No 122, para 4.2, enshrined in s 2(8) of the Act.
1   [1985] 3 All ER 673, p 457, ante; see HL Debates, ante, note 19.
2   The legal title being in H and W, they will both be the conveying parties, though W will effectively be the sole vendor as she does not need H's consent to sell (even during a lucid period).

EPA in favour of his brother, B. In this event a conveyance from B (as H's attorney) and W will be required to pass a good legal title to the purchaser.

Sub-section (3) has been attacked on the grounds that it is drafted in unduly wide terms to the potential prejudice of beneficiaries under the trust. It goes far beyond matrimonial home trusts. It also enables a single attorney of a trustee for sale to do what the trustee acting solely cannot himself do, namely give a valid receipt for capital money[3]. In view of its general application to all trusts, this extensive power would seem to be quite unjustified. Such far-reaching consequences were probably not envisaged by the parliamentary draftsman, and it is not easy to see how the courts will be able to place a narrow construction on its operation.

H   Post-completion matters

One obvious task for both solicitors to perform after completion is to report to their respective clients. The vendor's solicitor has to account to his client for the purchase money after deduction of costs and disbursements. However, in most house sales, the money received on completion will often be utilised in part by the solicitor for other purposes – in discharge of the vendor's mortgage, or towards the price of another property which he is purchasing. On a transfer of registered land it is the responsibility of the purchaser's solicitor to effect registration of the purchaser as proprietor, or to apply for compulsory first registration if the transaction falls within s 123 of the Land Registration Act 1925[4]. There may well be other important matters to attend to before the practitioner can finally shut his file.

1.   Notification of change of ownership

On a sale or other disposition of leasehold property it may be necessary to give notice of the assignment to the lessor (or his solicitor) under a covenant in the lease or by virtue of a statutory requirement[5]. This obligation must not be confused with the licence to assign which should be procured before the assignment is completed. Strictly speaking it is the vendor's duty to give the notice and pay any registration fee, subject to any contractual stipulation to the contrary. Even in the absence of any such clause it is in practice more convenient for the purchaser to give the notice, especially when the covenant also requires production of the assignment to the lessor for registration

---

3   The argument that technically there will be a payment to two trustees, since both will be parties to the conveyance qua legal owners, carries very little weight in the light of the closing words of sub-s (3).

4   See further, Ch 15. For the position where there is a contemporaneous mortgage, see p 488, post.

5   Landlord and Tenant Act 1927, s 19(1)(b). The covenant often extends to notifying a superior lessor of the grant, or assignment, of an underlease. See *Portman v J Lyons & Co Ltd* [1937] Ch 584, [1936] 3 All ER 819.

purposes. In the case of registered leasehold property, production of the transfer or a copy, or the land (or charge) certificate after registration, operates as sufficient compliance with a covenant requiring production[6]. The Landlord and Tenant Act 1987, s 3, requires an incoming landlord to notify his tenant in writing and to give his name and address. Notification of change of ownership may be desirable, or necessary, in other cases, eg for water service charges, or for the automatic transfer of a water abstraction licence under s 49, 50 of the Water Resources Act 1991.

2.   Undertakings

It is commonplace for a vendor's solicitor in the course of the transaction to enter into written undertakings to do or refrain from doing certain acts. It may be to hold title deeds to the order of a mortgagee, to discharge a mortgage on completion[7], or to account to a third person for the net proceeds of sale. An undertaking is any unequivocal declaration of intention addressed to someone who reasonably places reliance on it and made by a solicitor whereby he becomes personally bound[8]. The words 'I/We hereby undertake' are not necessary to give rise to an undertaking[9]. It may be given orally or in writing. As a matter of good conveyancing practice an oral undertaking should always be confirmed by writing forthwith by the recipient[10]. It is no answer to a complaint that a solicitor has acted in breach of an undertaking that there was no consideration for it, though if given for consideration it ought to be expressly stated in the undertaking itself[11].

Modern conveyancing procedures rely heavily on this system of undertakings. They have been said to be an important means of avoiding difficulties in conveyancing transactions[12]. Breach of an undertaking is a serious matter. Not only does it amount to professional misconduct leading to possible disciplinary action by the Law Society, it can also be enforced against the solicitor personally[13]. The court can order him to implement his undertaking, and non-compliance is punishable by committal for contempt. The basis of this Jurisdiction is the enforcing, not of legal rights, but of honourable conduct by the courts' own officers[14]. The court will not, however, call upon a solicitor

6   LRR 1925, r 91(1).
7   See further, p 443, ante.
8   *The Professional Conduct of Solicitors* (1986), para 15.01.
9   See *John Fox v Bannister King & Rigbeys* [1987] QB 925n, [1987] 1 All ER 737, CA.
10   *Udall v Capri Lighting Ltd* [1988] QB 907, [1987] 3 All ER 262 at 271, CA, per Kerr LJ.
11   *John Fox v Bannister King & Rigbeys*, supra, at 743, per Sir John Donaldson MR; *The Professional Conduct of Solicitors*, para 15.05 comment.
12   Royal Commission Report on Legal Services, para 21.25.
13   *Geoffrey Silver and Drake v Baines* [1971] 1 QB 396, [1971] 1 All ER 473, CA; *Re Mallows* (1960) 176 EG 1117. Enforcement by means of an action at law may also be possible, if a cause of action exists. See generally *The Professional Conduct of Solicitors*, Ch 15; *Cordery on Solicitors* (7th edn), 121–24. See also *Al-Kandari v J R Brown & Co* [1988] QB 665, [1988] 1 All ER 833, CA.
14   *Re A Solicitor* [1966] 3 All ER 52 at 55, per Pennycuick J. It will only be enforced under this inherent jurisdiction if given by a solicitor qua solicitor: *United Bank of Kuwait v Hammoud* [1987] NLJ Rep 921.

to perform an act which it is impossible for him to carry out[15]. Where it is inappropriate for the court to compel compliance, eg on the grounds of impossibility, it has power to order him to compensate a person who has suffered loss in consequence of his failure to implement the undertaking. This jurisdiction is not confined to cases where he has been guilty of dishonourable conduct. The mere failure to perform the undertaking is prima facie regarded as sufficient misconduct to require the solicitor to make good the loss[16].

Frequently in practice undertakings are given without proper thought as to whether they can be honoured. A solicitor ought not to give a personal undertaking, the performance of which does not lie within his sole control[17], although undertakings to use one's best endeavours to bring about a given result are often encountered. An undertaking expressed to be given on behalf of a client should be avoided. There can be no guarantee that the client can or will implement it. Yet the solicitor will be held personally liable to honour it; liability may only be evaded if it is expressly disclaimed in the undertaking[18].

Undertakings by licensed conveyancers

In their dealings with licensed conveyancers solicitors have been advised that it should normally be possible to act as if the conveyancer were a solicitor and bound by the same professional obligations as a solicitor[19]. A licensed conveyancer is required to comply fully with every undertaking given in the course of the provision of conveyancing services, whether given for consideration or not. He will also be held personally liable to honour his undertaking[20]. Failure to do so will result in disciplinary proceedings. Basically a solicitor should be able to rely on an undertaking given by a licensed conveyancer with confidence. Yet there are some significant differences to note. Licensed conveyancers are not officers of the court. They are not, therefore, amenable to the court's extraordinary jurisdiction. The ultimate sanction, imprisonment for contempt of court, does not exist; nor can the court as an aspect of its supervisory jurisdiction make any order for the payment of compensation. The Council of Licensed Conveyancers has no power to order a conveyancer to make good the loss occasioned by his breach of duty[1]. These considerations may prompt solicitors to be wary of accepting an undertaking from a licensed conveyancer in relation to any matter that is other

---

15   *Re A Solicitor*, ante (no order to forward lost deed); *Udall v Capri Lighting Ltd*, ante, at 267, per Balcombe LJ.

16   See generally the propositions stated by Balcombe LJ in the *Udall* case, at 268–69; *John Fox v Bannister King & Rigbeys*, ante.

17   See eg the *Udall* case, supra (undertaking to procure second charges on clients' residences).

18   *The Professional Conduct of Solicitors*, para 15.07. This is an example where the professional obligation is more onerous that the legal requirement.

19   See the Council Statement published in (1987) 84 LS Gaz 1202.

20   Licensed Conveyancers Rules of Conduct, Practice and Discipline, 1986, r 30(1)(a), (2).

1   For orders that the Council has power to make, see AJA 1985, s 26 (2). Equally, neither the Council of the Law Society nor the Disciplinary Tribunal has power to award compensation on breach of an undertaking.

than routine. Certainly the absence of that special relationship with the court, which operates to impose on solicitors higher standards than the law applies generally, makes it unwise to accept any undertaking not supported by consideration[2]. A solicitor should not, of course, take an undertaking from an *unqualified* conveyancer[3], or from a lay person acting for himself.

3.   Registration and cancellation of land charges

One important point that is sometimes overlooked is the registration of land charges created by the conveyance, such as restrictive covenants in favour of the vendor[4]. A purchaser's solicitor who has registered the contract as an estate contract should as a matter of good conveyancing practice effect its cancellation after completion[5] if only to avoid possible queries about the registration on a subsequent sale of the property.

4.   Stamping documents

A document liable to the payment of stamp duty should be presented for stamping within 30 days of its execution, which for present purposes is taken to be when it is delivered, or if it is delivered subject to conditions, when the conditions are fulfilled[6]. If presented late it can only be stamped on payment of the unpaid duty with interest, a fixed penalty of £10 and a further penalty equal to the amount of the unpaid duty. The Commissioners of Inland Revenue are empowered to mitigate or remit any penalty. An improperly stamped document is not admissible in evidence, but it will be received in evidence on a solicitor's undertaking to pay the duty and penalties except where the document cannot be legally stamped after execution[7]. A purchaser is entitled to have every deed forming a link in the chain of title properly stamped[8]. When investigating an unregistered title, a purchaser's solicitor should check the stamp duty on all abstracted documents and to this extent it is necessary to be aware of heads of charge and rates of duty that have since been abolished or reduced. A condition of sale framed so as to preclude any objection as to the absence or insufficiency of stamp upon any instrument executed after 16 May 1888, is void[9].

---

2   See per Sir John Donaldson in the *Fox* case, note 9, ante.
3   See the Law Society's Guidance Notes at (1986) 83 LS Gaz 492.
4   This not necessary when the sale is followed by compulsory first registration of title: LCA 1972, s 14(3), p 392, ante. Restrictive covenants created on a sale of registered land are automatically entered on the register by the Registry, p 498, post.
5   Law Society's Digest, 3rd Cumulative Supplement, Opinion No 940 (b).
6   Finance Act 1994, s 239(1).
7   Stamp Act 1891, s 14. It is unprofessional to take the point per se.
8   See *Whiting to Loomes* (1881) 17 Ch D 10, CA (discharged mortgage).
9   Stamp Act 1891, s 117.

(a) Rates of duty
Full details of rates of duty must be sought in a standard work on stamp duties. A few points may usefully be mentioned in relation to the more common conveyancing transactions encountered in practice.

(i) *Conveyances on sale.* A conveyance on sale is exempt from duty where the consideration is £30,000[10] provided the conveyance contains a 'certificate for value' clause to the effect that the transaction does not form part of a larger transaction or series of transactions in respect of which the aggregate amount of the consideration exceeds £30,000. Duty at 1% is charged when the consideration exceeds this amount[11]. On a sub-sale duty is levied on the consideration moving from the sub-purchaser, not on the original purchase price[12]. Duties which vary according to the amount of the consideration are termed ad valorem duties.

(ii) *Mortgages.* Mortgages are not subject to stamp duty. The head of charge under which duty was formerly leviable was abolished by the Finance Act 1971, s 64.

(iii) *50p fixed duty.* Many documents which were previously subject to a fixed duty of 50p are now exempt from stamp duty altogether, either by virtue of the Finance Act 1985, s 87[13], or the Stamp Duty (Exempt Instruments) Regulations 1987[14]. For instruments covered by the Regulations, exemption is subject to certification. The required certificate must be signed by or on behalf of the grantor, and should be included in, endorsed on or physically attached to, the document. It must also specify the category listed in the Schedule to the Regulations within which the instrument falls. Without the appropriate certificate the document is not duly stamped. Documents coming within the Regulations, if executed on or after 1 May 1987, include: an assent, an appointment of new trustees, the grant of an easement for no consideration in money or money's worth, a transfer of property in consideration of marriage or in connection with divorce, and an instrument which varies a disposition taking effect on death. Some deeds still attract this small duty, such as duplicate and counterpart leases and a declaration of trust.

Voluntary dispositions are now exempt from both ad valorem duty (by virtue of s 82 of the Act of 1987) and the fixed duty of 50p (if duly certified). However, one point is in danger of being overlooked, especially with gifts between spouses. Where property subject to a mortgage is transferred by way

---

10 For the period between 16 June 1992 and 20 August 1992, the threshold figure was raised to £350,000: see Stamp Duty (Temporary Provisions) Act 1992, s 1.
11 See Finance Act 1963, s 55(1); Finance Act 1984, s 109(1). The practice of 'altering' the purchase price to a lower figure by 'finding' fittings and chattels so as to avoid stamp duty should neither be adopted by the parties nor condoned by their solicitors; see *Saunders v Edwards* [1987] 2 All ER 651, CA, p 168, ante.
12 Stamp Act 1891, s 58(4).
13 Such as a power of attorney and an acknowledgement for production of deeds.
14 SI 1987 No 516, made under the Finance Act 1985, s 87.

of gift, the mortgage debt outstanding is treated as consideration under the Stamp Act 1891, s 57. Suppose that H voluntarily transfers his solely-owned house subject to a mortgage of £70,000 into the joint names of himself and W. Duty will be levied at the rate of 1% on half of the unpaid loan. No duty would be payable if it did not exceed £60,000, assuming the deed included an appropriate certificate for value clause.

(b) Production of documents to Commissioners
Irrespective of whether stamp duty is leviable, certain documents must be produced within 30 days of execution to the Commissioners of Inland Revenue; such documents are a conveyance on sale of the fee simple, a grant of a lease for at least seven years or the transfer on sale of any such lease. In addition, the transferee or lessee must furnish the Commissioners with a statement of certain particulars regarding the instrument[15]. A document produced in accordance with the statutory provisions is stamped with a special stamp (a 'Particulars Delivered' or 'PD' stamp as it is commonly called) denoting it has been produced. Without this stamp (where required) the document is not deemed duly stamped and therefore may not be received in evidence. Failure to comply with the Act also renders the grantee liable on summary conviction to a fine not exceeding £400. The Finance Act 1985[16] amended the 'PD' procedures for certain documents dated on or after 1 January 1986, designed to save time and reduce costs. In the case of conveyances and assignments on sale of registered land or land being compulsorily registered for the first time, which are exempt from ad valorem duty, the required particulars are submitted to the appropriate district Land Registry, which is obliged to forward them to the Commissioners. Other documents needing to be produced, including transfers not containing a 'certificate for value' clause and all conveyances of unregistered land not leading to first registration, have to be sent to the Stamp Office for stamping in the usual way.

I   Merger of contract in conveyance

On completion of the transaction the contract is said to merge in the conveyance. The conveyance puts an end to the contractual obligations which are thereby satisfied. After completion the purchaser cannot bring an action on the contract. Unless he is able to establish grounds for rescission or rectification, or prove the existence of some collateral warranty, his only remedy is to sue on the covenants for title.

This important doctrine of merger is not absolute. It does not apply where the contractual obligation is of such a kind that it cannot have been the parties' intention that it should be extinguished by the conveyance[17]. It therefore becomes necessary to construe the contract to see whether it was intended to

15   Finance Act 1931, s 28, Sch 2.
16   Section 89; see the Stamp Duty (Exempt Instruments) Regulations 1985.
17   *Clarke v Ramuz* [1891] 2 QB 456 at 461, CA, per Bowen LJ.

survive and to what extent. In cases of dispute resort must be had to general principles. No merger was held to have occurred in respect of these contractual terms – for vacant possession on completion[18], for compensation for misdescription[19], for the erection and completion of a house in a proper manner[20]. In these cases an action for damages was maintainable after completion. Similarly, in *Mason v Schuppisser*[1], a contractual right of re-purchase in favour of the vendor was not destroyed by execution of the conveyance to the purchaser, which omitted to reserve it.

The doctrine of merger applies to sales of registered land[2]. It is conceived that merger occurs on completion of the transaction, not on subsequent registration. Support for this view is derived from s 110(6) of the Land Registration Act 1925. This subsection requires the vendor, on a sale of the entirety of the land within his title, to deliver the land (or charge) certificate to the purchaser on completion, in order to enable him to be registered as the new proprietor. Although the Act clearly envisages that he will subsequently apply for registration, this does not form part of the parties' contractual obligations. In theory, the purchaser may elect to enter into possession by virtue of his unregistered transfer, without proceeding to acquire the legal estate by registration[3].

The difficulties of construction referred to above would seem to be alleviated by Condition 7.4 of the Standard Conditions of Sale which provide, somewhat laconically, that completion does not cancel any liability to perform outstanding obligations under the contract.

18 *Hissett v Reading Roofing Co Ltd* [1970] 1 All ER 122.
19 *Palmer v Johnson* (1884) 13 QBD 351, CA.
20 *Lawrence v Cassel* [1930] 2 KB 83, CA; *Hancock v B W Brazier (Anerley) Ltd* [1966] 2 All ER 901, CA.
 1 (1899) 81 LT 147; *Eagon v Dent* [1965] 3 All ER 334 (assignment failing to incorporate contractual indemnity).
 2 *Knight Sugar Co Ltd v Alberta Rly and Irrigation Co* [1938] 1 All ER 266, PC (a decision on a colonial statute similar to the LRA 1925); noted at (1938) 2 Conv (NS) 262.
 3 Cf the position under the Torrens system of land registration, where strictly speaking it is the transferor's duty to procure registration. Here no merger takes place until registration. See *Montgomery and Rennie v Continental Bags (NZ) Ltd* [1972] NZLR 884 (mistake as to identity of land sold discovered after completion but before registration; purchaser able to rescind and recover purchase money).

Chapter 15

Registered titles: first registration and registration of dealings

A   Freehold titles

1.   Compulsory first registration

(a) The application

Now that registration of title is compulsory throughout the whole of England and Wales, every conveyance of freehold unregistered land should be completed by registration. The application for registration has to be made within three months of the date of the conveyance, or of any authorised extension, otherwise it becomes void as regards the grant of the legal estate[1]. The consequences of this avoidance are discussed later in this chapter.

(i) *Title applied for and form of application.*   The purchaser normally seeks registration with an absolute title. Where the title is based upon adverse possession, or the title deeds have been lost or destroyed[2], a possessory title should be sought, though the Registrar is empowered to issue an absolute title if satisfied as to the soundness of the applicant's title. The appropriate application form for a solicitor or licensed conveyancer is Form 1B[3]. This contains a lengthy certificate as to the soundness of the title, including the existence of incumbrances. The solicitor will already have approved the title on his client's behalf, so signing this certificate should create no additional complications. The form should also disclose the capacity in which the land is held, eg as sole beneficial owner. Where there are joint applicants, it should be stated whether they hold as joint tenants or tenants in common; if the latter the obligatory restriction in Form 62 will be entered on the register[4]. With other limited owners, an application should be made for entry of the appropriate restriction or information given to enable the proper restriction to be entered.

(ii) *Accompanying documents.*   All deeds and documents in the applicant's possession or under his control must be forwarded with the application,

---

1   LRA 1925, s 123. For the effects of registration and the meaning of 'on sale' see Ch 2. References in this chapter to 'the Act' or 'the Rules' are references to LRA 1925 and LRR 1925, respectively, unless otherwise stated.
2   See Practice Leaflet No 4.
3   See (1987) 136 NLJ 226; R & R, 12.04. Form 1A is for use by an applicant in person.
4   See p 347, ante.

470

including preliminary inquiries, requisitions and replies, the contract for sale, search certificates, opinions of counsel on the title. Abstracts should be marked as having been verified in the usual way. This obligation to produce deeds is not limited solely to those within the title investigated by the purchaser, which is sometimes overlooked[5]. A certified copy of the conveyance to the applicant, and of any mortgage created by him, must also be supplied. When the land to be registered is a sale-off of part of a larger area, the Registry has been known to ask for certified copies of conveyances of previous sales of other parts[6], presumably to ensure that there are no boundary discrepancies resulting from the various sales. It is permissible on a sale of freehold land leading to compulsory first registration for the purchaser to take a transfer in the normal Land Registry form, as if the title were already registered, instead of a conveyance in the usual unregistered form[7]. An application for a possessory title must be supported by adequate statutory declarations[8].

(iii) *Death of applicant.* An application does not abate in the event of the applicant's death before completion of registration; it may be continued by any person entitled to apply for registration who desires to adopt it[9], eg the deceased's personal representatives. It seems that an application can be pursued in the name of the purchaser, even though he dies before submission of any application. Registration of the deceased applicant as first proprietor would not be a nullity[10].

(b) Completion of registration
Receipt of the application is followed by an examination of title by the Registry officials and the raising of requisitions if the title is not in order[11]. Apparently, applications often contain errors or omissions. The need for the Registry to raise requisitions in such cases inevitably adds to the delay in processing the application[12]. The Registrar may grant an absolute title, notwithstanding the title is open to objection, if satisfied that the proprietor's possession is unlikely to be disturbed. In the case of a serious defect in the title, only a qualified or

---

5 Registered Land Practice Note, A.5. The entry of incumbrances on the register is made by reference to the deed of creation; hence the Registry's need to see all relevant documents.
6 This would not be necessary if the earlier sales-off had given rise to compulsory first registrations.
7 LRR 1925, r 72. See p 544, post.
8 LRR 1925, r 37, referring to Form 4. And see R & R, 732–42.
9 LRR 1925, r 305.
10 Unless for some reason the conveyance fails to vest the legal title in him so that registration has a curative effect under s 5 of the Act. In this event, the earliest time that there can be any vesting is the day on which the application is delivered (LRR 1925, r 42). If death occurs before this date, it is difficult to see how a title can vest in a deceased person.
11 See generally LRA 1925, s 13; LRR 1925, rr 25–28, and 29 as substituted by LRR 1925, r 3. Rule 29 enables the Registrar to register as absolute the title to a single house on production of the solicitor's certificate as to title contained in Form 1B. See also (1976) 40 Conv (NS) 122 (C T Emery).
12 Writing in 1990, the Registrar indicated that 30% of all applications were defective: (1990) 134 SJ 849, 851. In an attempt to reduce the number of common mistakes, the Registry has issued a checklist for practitioners' use: (1990) 87 LSG 19/14.

possessory title will be granted. When he has approved the title and determined what class of title to grant, the registration is regarded by virtue of r 42 as being completed as of the day on which the application was delivered[13]. A land certificate is then issued to the proprietor, the form and contents of which have previously been considered in Chapter 2. Where the purchase is accompanied by a mortgage, a charge certificate is issued to the mortgagee and the land certificate is retained at the Registry until the mortgage is discharged[14]. The entries in the land or charge certificate and the filed plan should always be checked to ensure that they correctly reflect the applicant's title. Mistakes are known to occur, but many practitioners fail to carry out this obvious task. When the purchaser and his mortgagee are separately represented the purchaser's solicitor has no opportunity to verify the contents of the charge certificate. He can, however, apply for office copies of the plan and entries to be issued to him on completion of the registration. This request should be lodged with the application for registration which in this situation is submitted by the mortgagee's solicitor[15], but again this procedure is seldom adopted.

Before returning all original deeds not retained in the Registry to the applicant's solicitors, the Registry, as a means of protection against fraud or mistake, places its official stamp on the conveyance to the purchaser. The only way to eliminate fraud completely would be for the Registry to stamp all the deeds[16], but this it is unable to do because of staffing difficulties. This omission is unlikely to promote widespread fraudulent conduct on the part of proprietors seeking to deal with their land on the basis that it is still unregistered. A search in the public index map will always reveal whether or not the title to a particular piece of land has been registered. Pre-registration deeds ought not to be destroyed, especially when they contain information not recorded in the register, eg positive covenants, or a large scale plan of the property which it might be prudent to retain.

(c) Dealings by person entitled to be registered

A person having the right to apply for first registration may deal with the land before he is himself registered in the same way as if he were the registered proprietor[17]. No dealing (other than a lease) can be accepted for registration until an application has been made for first registration, but where the dealing takes the form of a sub-sale, the sub-purchaser is deemed to be the applicant for first registration. Where a conveyance leading to first registration is followed immediately by a mortgage, the mortgagee's solicitor applies on behalf of the purchaser-mortgagor for first registration of the estate on which the mortgage has been created.

---

13   As to when this is deemed to be, see LRR 1925, r 24 (2), as substituted by LR (Delivery of Applications) Rules 1986, r 4.
14   LRA 1925, s 65.
15   See Registered Land Practice Note H.3. See para (c) below.
16   As envisaged by LRA 1925, s 16. But see R & R, 268.
17   LRA 1925, s 123(2); LRR 1925, rr 72, 73.

(d) Effect of failure to register

Section 123 of the Act provides a sanction against non-registration. On the expiration of two months from the date of the conveyance (or of any authorised extension) the conveyance becomes 'void so far as regards the grant or conveyance of the legal estate in the freehold ... comprised in the conveyance'. The section does not apply to a partial failure to register, as where some of the land conveyed is omitted in error from the filed plan[18].

This not very happily drafted provision raises several interesting problems[19]. It is not a punitive measure, seeking to deprive a purchaser of his rights acquired by purchase. It operates rather as a potent inducement for him to register. Failure to seek registration timeously does not avoid the conveyance in toto. The purchaser loses the legal estate, but the deed remains effective for other purposes, such as the enforcement of covenants. Rather surprisingly, the section does not state in whom the legal title vests on avoidance[20]. The general consensus of opinion is that it revests in the vendor. Not that he holds it for his own use and benefit, for having received the purchase money he becomes a bare trustee of the legal estate for the benefit of the purchaser in equity[1].

The Chief Land Registrar is always willing to make an extension order if some quite ordinary but reasonable excuse for the delay in submission of the application is given by the applicant's solicitor and the proper fee is paid[2]. Indeed, it is understood that district land registries are prepared to accept as a matter of course an application up to a year late; an explanation is called for only when it is delayed beyond that period. In both situations, however, the applicant must supply up to date land charges searches. The order does not, itself, re-vest the legal title in the purchaser. It simply ensures that the Registrar will consider the application in the normal way. The subsequent registration operates to vest the legal title in him, without any reconveyance from the vendor[3]. In the unlikely event of an order being refused, a purchaser who seeks registration must first acquire the legal title again. This should present no problem, for he can call upon the vendor-trustee to vest it in him under the well-known rule in *Saunders v Vautier*[4].

2. Transfers

(a) Application for registration

Unlike unregistered conveyancing, completion (in the sense in which this word is used in the preceding chapter) of a sale of registered land does not result in

---

18   This is a case for rectification: *Proctor v Kidman* (1986) 51 P & CR 67, CA (boundary dispute).
19   See further (1968) 32 Conv (NS) 391 (D G Barnsley).
20   This omission is cured in the Law Commission's draft Bill, cl 13(1) (legal title reverts to grantor).
1   See *Pinekerry Ltd v Needs (Kenneth) (Contractors) Ltd* (1992) 64 P & CR 245 at 247 per Scott LJ, CA.
2   See R & R, 11.13.
3   LRA 1925, ss 5, 69(2).
4   (1841) Cr & Ph 240. Section 123 can, in theory, be used to evade the obligation to register, altogether. The issue is discussed more fully in the 3rd edn, at 419, and at (1968) Conv (NS) 391, 398–400. Any wholesale circumvention of s 123, using the device considered there, is extremely unlikely.

the legal estate vesting in the purchaser. Section 19(1) of the Land Registration Act 1925, provides that:

> The transfer of the registered estate in the land or part thereof shall be completed by the registrar entering on the register the transferee as the proprietor of the estate transferred, but until such entry is made the transferor shall be deemed to remain proprietor of the registered estate...

It is the purchaser's responsibility to seek registration. His application should be made on printed Form A4, which is the appropriate form for use for every kind of application affecting the *whole* of the land comprised in a title; on a transfer of part of a registered estate, Form A7 should be used. Care should be taken to ensure the form is completed correctly. An error or omission may produce a requisition from the Registry, so delaying the registration process. In the case of a transfer to joint purchasers, a statement as to the nature of their beneficial entitlement, similar to that made on a first registration is required.

The application must be accompanied by the following documents (where relevant): (i) the land (or charge) certificate[5]; (ii) a discharge (Form 73) in respect of the transferor's mortgage; (iii) the transfer[6] and, if it imposes restrictive covenants, a certified copy of the transfer; (iv) the mortgage created by the transferee; (v) a certified copy of the mortgage; and (vi) a remittance to cover the Land Registry fees. As to the transfer deed, though forms are specified by the Rules, the Registrar permits alterations and additions to a considerable extent, provided the general principles on which the register is maintained are not violated[7]. Thus trusts are not normally allowed to be mentioned, nor references to unregistered documents.

On receipt of the application at the proper district Registry, it is entered in a 'day list' and dated as of the day on which it is deemed to have been delivered[8]. Entry in this list is conclusive evidence of the sufficiency of the application as to form, despite irregularities in it or in the transfer deed[9]. Where two or more applications relating to the same title are delivered at the same time by the same person, they rank for priority purposes as he shall specify. When different applicants are involved, they are to agree the order of priority. Failing agreement the issue can be determined by the Registrar or the court, having regard (presumably) to general equitable principles[10].

---

5   If the land certificate is on deposit at the Registry, the deposit number must be quoted.
6   This is retained in the Registry after completion of the registration process: LRR 1925, r 90.
7   R & R, 17–20; LRR 1925, rr 74, 78.
8   LRR 1925, r 83(1) as amended by LRR 1990, s 10. An application duly delivered after 9.30 am on one day is deemed to have been delivered immediately after 9.30 am on the *next* day when the Registry is open to the public: r 85 (as substituted by the LR (Delivery of Applications) Rules 1986, r 5.
9   *Smith v Morrison* [1974] 1 All ER 957 (incorrect form and failure to lodge documents).
10   Rule 84(1)–(3) (substituted by LRR 1978, s 9. Simultaneous hostile applications would occur where, eg an application to enter a notice or caution is deemed to be delivered at the same time as an application to register a transfer not submitted within the priority period conferred by an official search certificate.

(b) Time for application

Unlike applications for first registration of title, no sanction is imposed to compel the transferee to seek registration within a stated time, or even at all. The transferee may rely on his equitable title[11]coupled with actual occupation of the land. No useful purpose is served by not registering. A purchaser from an unregistered transferee has a statutory right under s 110(5) of the Act to require him to procure registration and in practice no mortgagee would allow the transferee to remain unregistered.

It is absolutely vital that the application is duly received by the Registry within the 30 working days' priority period conferred by the official certificate of search. It is the responsibility of the purchaser's solicitor (or that of his mortgagee) to ensure that this is done. A failure to apply for registration within the priority period runs the risk that the purchaser will be bound by some third party right not protected on the register until after the date of the purchaser's search, or even after the date of the purchase[12]. The application need not be delayed because a discharge of a registered charge (Form 73) signed by the mortgagee has not been received; the mortgagee's solicitor's undertaking to discharge the mortgage should be forwarded with the application which is treated as in order if the discharge is subsequently lodged. Similarly, priority is not prejudiced merely because the Registry raises some requisition, provided the requisition is satisfactorily complied with within one month.

(c) Completion of registration

When the transferee has been entered as the new proprietor, the land certificate, amended and brought up to date, is returned to him (or his solicitor), unless he has obtained a mortgage in which case it is retained in the Registry. On a transfer of part of the land comprised in a registered title, that land is removed from the vendor's title and a new land certificate is issued to the purchaser with a new title number. A note is made on the vendor's property register that the land edged green on the filed plan has been removed from his title and registered under the purchaser's new number shown in green on the plan. The vendor's amended certificate is then returned to him, unless it is deposited in the Registry, as is usually the case on the development of a building estate where transfers of part are frequently made.

(d) Effect of registration

Section 20(1) of the Act provides that in the case of an absolute freehold title a disposition of registered land for valuable consideration operates on

---

11 See eg *Hart v Emelkirk Ltd* [1983] 3 All ER 15 (transfer of freehold reversion not registered).
12 See *Elias v Mitchell* [1972] Ch 652, [1972] 2 All ER 153; *Watts v Waller* [1973] QB 153, [1972] 3 All ER 257, CA. For a more recent example of delay in registration, see *City of London Building Society v Flegg* [1988] AC 54, [1987] 3 All ER 435, HL. See [1988] Conv 108 at 114 (M P Thompson). See also the 3rd edn, p 421.

registration to confer on the transferee an estate in fee simple together with appurtenant rights[13], but subject to (i) the incumbrances and other entries[14] on the register, and (ii) overriding interests affecting the land. Subject to (i) and (ii) the registered transferee takes free from 'all other estates and interests whatsoever'. Section 20 imports no element of good faith on the transferee's part[15]. He takes free from an unprotected minor interest, despite actual knowledge of it[16]. It is not fraudulent to rely on the legal rights conferred by a statute[17]. Nevertheless, the courts have, at times, seemed reluctant to allow purchasers to use s 20 to be used for what has been perceived to be fraud[18], the court being willing to impose a constructive trust. It is evident, however, that there is now considerable reluctance to adopt this approach, such a trust now being imposed only when the purchaser expressly undertakes to take subject to a particular interest[19].

The effect of registration is to vest in the transferee not merely the legal estate but also the equitable title to the land, subject only as is expressed in the section. The fact that the transferor's title was in some way defective, eg because he had no legal authority to hold land[20] or his title rested on a forged instrument, is quite immaterial. It is specifically enacted that the disposition operates in like manner as if the transferor were (subject to any contrary entry) *entitled to the registered land in fee simple in possession for his own benefit.* These words make it clear that a transferor can transmit a better title than he possessed. The section may go even further. Although the opposite view has been voiced[1], the tenor of sub-s (1) suggests that, like its counterpart, s 7, it is effective to vest both the legal and equitable titles, despite some defect in the transferor's own title. Suppose A forges a transfer for value from B (the registered proprietor) in favour of C[2]. On C's subsequent registration, he would

13   Including rights and interests which would, under LPA 1925, have been transferred had the land not been registered, eg under s 62. The transfer itself is deemed to imply the general words; see LRA 1925, s 19(3).
14   Only valid rights and claims are protected: *Kitney v MEPC Ltd* [1978] 1 All ER 595, CA.
15   Cf Land Registration (Official Searches) Rules 1993, r 2(1) (purchaser entitled to rely on clear official search certificate if in good faith); p 409, ante.
16   *Miles v Bull (No 2)* [1969] 3 All ER 1585 (unprotected Class F charge); *de Lusignan v Johnson* (1973) 230 EG 499 (mortgagee taking free from unprotected contract). The rule is the same in unregistered land: p 399. The position is otherwise when the transaction is a sham: *Jones v Lipman* [1962] 1 All ER 442. See (1978) 42 Conv (NS) 52 at 58 (Jill Martin).
17   *Re Monolithic Building Co Ltd* [1915] 1 Ch 643 at 663, CA, per Lord Cozens-Hardy MR.
18   *Peffer v Rigg* [1978] 3 All ER 745; *Lyus v Prowsa Developments Ltd* [1982] 2 All ER 953. For criticism, see [1985] CLJ 280 (M P Thompson).
19   *Ashburn Anstalt v Arnold* [1989] Ch 1, [1988] 2 All ER 147, CA. See [1988] Conv 201 at 205–6 (M P Thompson).
20   See *Morelle Ltd v Wakeling* [1955] 2 QB 379, [1955] 1 All ER 708, CA (corporation without licence to hold land). See also p 102, note 15 (transferor a minor).
1   Ibid, at 411 and 721, per Lord Evershed MR. And see *A-G v Odell* [1906] 2 Ch 47, CA (forged transfer); (1985) 101 LQR 79 (R J Smith) arguing that s 20(1) confers deferred, not immediate, indefeasibility.
2   If C is aware that the transfer is forged then, unless he secures his own registration as proprietor, the transfer will be a nullity. See *Penn v Bristol and West Building Society* [1995] 2 FLR 938.

acquire the entirety of B's interest, legal and equitable, subject, of course, to B's claim for rectification under s 82(1) of the Act[3].

(i) *Transferee's position before registration.* By virtue of s 19(1) of the Act the legal estate remains vested in the vendor until the purchaser is registered as the new proprietor. Registration takes effect as of the day on which the application is deemed to be delivered at the Registry, for this is when registration is completed[4]. This date is given in the particulars recorded in the proprietorship register. Until registration the purchaser would appear to be in a position analogous to that of a beneficiary under a bare trust, having a right to obtain the legal title by applying for registration. In the meantime his equitable interest constitutes a minor interest and if he is in actual occupation his rights rank as an overriding interest. The absence of any legal estate until registration precludes the exercise of any right dependent upon the existence of a legal title for its validity[5]. Thus he cannot serve a valid notice to quit[6]. However, this fundamental defect in the scheme of registration is largely mitigated by s 37 of the Act, which permits a person entitled to be registered as proprietor to dispose of or charge the land in the prescribed manner. Under s 37(2) the disposition or charge takes effect as if he were registered as proprietor[7]. Apart from this provision it would be impossible for a purchaser to raise money on the security of his property until he had been registered as proprietor.

(ii) *Death prior to registration.* If the transferee dies before the registration is complete, it is clear that the Registrar cannot register as proprietor a deceased person. The deceased's equitable interest will pass to his personal representatives, entitling them to continue with the application. It seems perfectly proper for the Registrar to register them as proprietors, once they have substantiated their own title by production of the grant of representation.

It is not thought that the death of the transferor before the transferee's registration prevents the transfer operating as the instrument of a living proprietor[8]. Re-execution of the transfer by the deceased's personal representatives is not, therefore, necessary. In any event, the transferee's subsequent registration will operate under s 20(1) to the vest the title in him.

---

3 See *Norwich and Peterborough Building Society v Steed (No 2)* [1993] Ch 116 at 132, [1993] 1 All ER 330 at 342, CA, per Scott LJ.

4 LRR 1925, r 83(2), as substituted by LRR 1978, r 5.

5 Approved in *Crumpton v Unifox Properties Ltd* (1992) 25 HLR 121 at 129, CA, per Staughton LJ).

6 *Smith v Express Dairy Co Ltd* [1954] JPL 45.

7 This does not mean that s 37 operates to vest a legal title in the second transferee or the chargee immediately, even when the subsequent disposition is not capable of registration. Suppose V transfers to P who, prior to registration, creates a short term lease in favour of T. T cannot obtain a legal lease until P is registered as proprietor, notwithstanding s 37(2). See *Grace Rymer Investments Ltd v Waite* [1958] Ch 831, [1958] 2 All ER 777, CA, where a similar argument based on s 27(3) (p 489, post) was rejected; see per Evershed MR, at 850, and 783, respectively.

8 The weight of Australian authority supports this view. See the authorities collected by Brennan J in *Corin v Patton* (1990) 169 CLR 540, 566.

(e) Status of Land Registry transfer

Nowhere in the Land Registration Act 1925, nor in the Rules, is the precise function of the transfer expressly stated. It must be in the prescribed form[9]. This must on its face indicate that it is intended to take effect as a deed. Although clearly a deed, it passes no legal estate, for this passes on registration. It constitutes an authority to the Registrar to enter the transferee's name on the register as proprietor. The transfer is insufficient in the absence of the land certificate; yet without the transfer the purchaser cannot obtain the legal title and, to this extent, it plays just as important a role as does the conveyance in unregistered conveyancing.

A transfer creates rights and obligations enforceable by the parties and a person not a party to a transfer can enforce a covenant made with him[10]. It also seems effective to confer an equitable interest, at least where the transferor is a beneficial owner and the transfer is for value. In one case[11] X executed a transfer of property in favour of himself and Y. This was held to confer on Y an equitable interest in half the proceeds of sale, entitling Y to be registered as joint proprietor with X. Therefore, despite the absence of a specifically enforceable contract for sale, an executed transfer will, on completion of the purchase, vest a good equitable title in the purchaser.

(f) Voluntary transfers

Registration of a transfer made without valuable consideration has the same effect as a transfer for value, save for one important qualification: the donee takes the legal estate subject to any minor interests binding on the transferor[12], even though they are not protected on the register. This includes the possibility of the donor's trustee in bankruptcy seeking, in certain circumstance, to set aside the transaction[13]. No note of the trustee's right is entered on the register, so that a subsequent purchaser, in good faith, will take free of any such right[14]. 'Valuable consideration' includes marriage consideration but not, apparently, nominal consideration of £1[15].

The problem of incomplete gifts of registered land was considered for the first time by an English court in *Mascall v Mascall*[16].

> F executed a transfer of his house by way of gift to his son, S, and handed it to him along with the land certificate. Later they quarrelled. Before S was registered

---

9   LRA 1925, s 18(1). LRR 1925, r 98.
10   Ibid (transfer of equity of redemption incorporating covenant by transferee to pay mortgage debt). Vaisey J considered the transfer was analogous to a deed-poll, rather than a deed inter partes.
11   *Pilewska v Haduch* (1962) 184 EG 11. See also *Barclays Bank plc v Khaira* [1992] 1 WLR 623, 629–31 (unregistered transfer between spouses sufficing to create/transfer equitable interest). But see *Morelle Ltd v Wakeling* [1955] 2 QB 379 at 389, CA, per Romer LJ, arguendo (transfer gives rise to personal equity against transferor).
12   LRA 1925, s 20(4).
13   Insolvency Act 1986, ss 339, 340.
14   Insolvency Act 1986, as amended by Insolvency (No 2) Act 1994, s 2. See R & R, 20.02.
15   LRA 1925, s 3(xxxi); *Peffer v Rigg* [1978] 3 All ER 745, although in this case the sum of £1 was paid as part of a wider divorce settlement.
16   (1984) 50 P & CR 119, CA; cf *Harden v Thompson* (1969) 212 EG 1364 (no perfected gift on evidence despite transfer being with donee).

as the new owner F's solicitor managed to obtain possession of the certificate from the Stamp Office where both documents had been lodged. F sought a declaration that the F-S transfer was void. HELD: the gift was complete in equity. S had within his control everything necessary to register his title, ie the transfer and the land certificate, without any further assistance from F. Accordingly F held the legal title in trust for S[17].

Once perfected the donor cannot recall the gift. But the donee's possession of *both* a duly executed transfer and the land certificate are essential to make it complete. The former without the latter[18] does not suffice unless, it would seem, the land certificate is deposited at the Registry because the property is subject to a registered charge[19]. The court will not enforce performance of a gratuitous promise to hand over the outstanding land certificate, nor can the Registrar compel its production under s 64(2) of the Act in order to perfect the gift. An executed but undelivered transfer vests no equitable title in the donee[20].

B   Leasehold titles

The benefits of the system of land registration, designed as it is to facilitate the transfer of interests in land, are not so great in relation to leases as they are to freeholds. A lease has a limited life-span and it may contain terms which reduce the chances of dealing with it. Nevertheless, this is no justification for the haphazard and illogical manner in which the Act of 1925 deals with leases. There are perplexing anomalies and inconsistencies capable[19]. It is easy to be misled by the vast jungle of statutory regulation. The Land Registration Act 1986 makes limited but nevertheless welcome improvements to the law, inspired by the Law Commission in its Land Registration Report, Law Com No 125. The Act came into operation on 1 January 1987 (the appointed day)[1]. For present purposes leases fall into two main categories[2]:
(1) leases capable of substantive registration;
(2) leases which are not capable of substantive registration but which take effect as overriding interests.

---

17   This decision accords with the rule in several Commonwealth jurisdictions: *Anning v Anning* (1907) 4 CLR 1049; *Scoones v Galvin and the Public Trustee* [1934] NZLR 1004; *Hooper v Hooper* [1953] 4 DLR 443; *Corin v Patton* (1990) 169 CLR 540.
18   Required for production purposes: LRA 1925, s 64(1)(a); cf *Scoones v Galvin,* supra.
19   See LRA 1925, s 65; cf *Macleod v Canada Trust Co* (1979) 108 DLR (3d) 424 at 431. Would donor's attempted revocation before registration be effective if he had previously given a direction under r 269 that the certificate was on deposit solely for the purposes of s 65?
20   Cf *Macedo v Stroud* [1922] 2 AC 330 at 338, PC, per Viscount Haldane.
 1   LRA 1986 (Commencement) Order 1986, SI 1986 No 2117.
 2   A third group comprising leases needing protection by a notice on the superior title (sometimes termed 'noted leases') will gradually disappear now that the Act of 1986 has become operative. It is confined to certain leases created before the appointed day, principally inalienable leases, and leases granted either rent-free or at a premium. See p 482, post, for the new law regarding such leases.

Unfortunately, the position becomes somewhat blurred because leases within group (1), which have not been substantively registered, may yet come within group (2) and be protected under s 70(1)(g) by virtue of the lessee's occupation. Similarly, the grant of a lease of *registered* land (often termed a dispositionary lease) possesses hybrid characteristics. It not only creates a new estate in land, which may result in an application for first registration, it is also a disposition or dealing with registered land[3].

1.   First registration

(a) Leases capable of substantive registration

After the appointed day substantive registration is necessary in the following instances, if the lessee is to obtain the legal estate:

(1) the grant of a lease of *unregistered* land for a term of more than 21 years[4];
(2) the assignment on sale of *unregistered* land for a term having more than 21 years to run[5];
(3) the grant of a lease of land *already registered* for a term of more than 21 years.

Grants and assignments of leases made *before* the appointed day are still subject to the 40 years' limit prescribed by s 123(1) of the 1925 Act. Previously the differing periods of 40 and 21 years caused much confusion, which, happily, will evaporate now that the dividing line between registrable and non-registrable leases is drawn at 21 years for all purposes.

(i) *Reversionary title unregistered.* Transactions (1) and (2) fall within s 123(1) of the Act. Failure to register results in a divesting of the legal estate[6]. As between the lessor and the unregistered lessee, the latter seems to hold, not under an equitable lease, but under a legal periodic tenancy arising by virtue of his entry into possession coupled with the payment and acceptance of rent[7]. Even though the lease is unregistered, the lessee's rights will rank as an overriding interest if he is in actual occupation or in receipt of the rents and profits.

(ii) *Reversionary title registered (transaction (3)).* The registered proprietor of freehold land may grant a lease of the registered land for any term of years

---

3   LRA 1925, s 18(1)(e), (5), hence the use of the expression 'dispositionary' lease.
4   When a lease is granted pursuant to the right to buy provisions in the Housing Act 1985, s 118, the obligation to register applies even though it is for a term of 21 years or less: LRA 1986, s 2(3), amending the Housing Act 1985, s 154(1). As to the reason for this, see Law Com No 125, para 4.42.
5   LRA 1986, s 2(1), substituting in (1) and (2) 21 years for 40 years laid down in LRA 1925, s 123(1).
6   Cf *British Maritime Trust Ltd v Upsons* [1931] WN 7 (sub-lessee from unregistered lessee deprived of legal title by s 123(1)). But as the superior lease was itself an unregistered disposition of registered land, s 123 should have been irrelevant; see this page, para (ii).
7   *Bishop of Bangor v Parry* [1891] 2 QB 277 (lease avoided by Charitable Trusts Amendment Act 1855); (1968) 32 Conv (NS) 391, 404–6. For the consequences of failure to register after an assignment of an existing term, see R & R, 205; (1968) 32 Conv (NS) at 406–9.

absolute for any purpose, and in any form which sufficiently refers to the registered land[8]. This requires a reference to the title number of the superior estate and there must be an identifying plan if part only of the superior estate is subject to the lease. Such a lease ranks as a disposition of registered land. If granted for more than 21 years it requires completion by substantive registration of the lessee as proprietor of the new term[9]. Presumably the lessor holds the leasehold term in trust for the lessee until registration. The lessee must therefore register his title to obtain a legal estate. The rights of a lessee of an unregistered dispositionary lease constitute an overriding interest if he is himself in actual occupation or is in receipt of the rents and profits, but not where he allows another sole occupation on a rent free basis[10]. The time limits and penalties imposed by s 123 do not apply to the grant of a dispositionary lease, not even to a lease of land within a compulsory area for a term exceeding 21 years. The avoiding provisions of the section are inapplicable to situations where the lessee cannot, by virtue of s 19(1), obtain any legal title until registration.

Section 19(2) requires notice of the lease to be entered on the lessor's register of title when a dispositionary lease is registered. The noting of leases on the superior title will be considered later in this chapter. One point calls for comment. According to the official view, notation is an essential element in completion of the registration process, and so a prerequisite for obtaining the legal title[11]. Consequently, if by an oversight the Registry omits to enter notice, the lessee holds only an equitable title. It is considered that this view is not warranted by the Act. The vital thing in the completion process is the entry on the register of the lessee as proprietor of the leasehold estate. It is difficult to see why the recording of something which operates by way of notice only (see s 52(2) of the Act) should be held to be so fundamental to the process of substantive registration. Furthermore, the Registry's view is incompatible with a basic concept of our system; for under s 2(1) only legal estates can be substantively registered.

(b) Leases incapable of substantive registration
Certain leases cannot be the subject of an application for substantive registration. These are:
(1) a lease granted for a term not exceeding 2 1 years;
(2) an equitable lease;

---

8   LRA 1925, ss 18(1)(e), 21(1)(d) (grant of sub-lease by leaseholder).
9   LRA 1925, ss 19(1), 22(1). A dispositionary lease granted for a term not exceeding 21 years cannot be registered: ibid, s 19(2)(a). Its effect may still be devastating; see *Freer v Unwins Ltd* [1976] Ch 288, [1976] 1 All ER 634, p 95, ante.
10 *Strand Securities Ltd v Caswell* [1965] Ch 958, [1965] 1 All ER 820, CA.
11 R & R, 515. (Two processes needed to make registration effectual.) If the mere omission of notice prevents the acquisition of any legal title, this may affect the rights of the parties inter se and clearly governs the nature of subsequent dealings by the lessee. The lessee can seek rectification of the register and, if he suffers loss, is entitled to be indemnified: LRA 1925, ss 82(1)(b), (h), 83(2).

(3) a lease with 21 years (or less) to run at the time of application for *first* registration[12]; and

(4) a mortgage term where there is a subsisting right of redemption.

All *legal* leases for 21 years or less and granted on or after 1 January 1987 now take effect as overriding interests under s 70(1)(k) of the Land Registration Act 1925[13]. Gratuitous leases and leases at a premium are no longer excluded from para (k)[14]. By virtue of s 19(2) of the Act a non-registrable lease within para (k) operates 'as if it were a registered disposition immediately on being granted'. It is therefore deemed to be completed, and the lessee acquires the legal estate at once, presumably for the class of title enjoyed by his lessor. The lease is subject to incumbrances and entries on the register of title[15] at the time of its creation, and to overriding interests then affecting it[16]. The precise status of an *assignment* of a para (k) lease is obscure. Unlike the original grant, it does not seem to take effect as a registered disposition, but apparently it will be subject only to such incumbrances and interests as were binding on the lessee when granted[17].

An equitable lease ranks as a minor interest. If not protected on the register it is unenforceable against a subsequent purchaser of the superior title. Yet, despite lack of notice thereon, such a lease will usually be protected as an overriding interest under s 70(1)(g) because of the lessee's occupation. It cannot constitute a lease within para (k) which is confined solely to legal leases[18]. Mortgage terms are considered later in this chapter.

(c) Application for substantive registration
The procedure on application is much the same as that for freehold titles. The appropriate form must be selected, depending on whether the transaction is the grant of a lease (Form 3B) or an assignment (Form 2B). A certified copy of the lease must be supplied by an applicant who is an original lessee; in other cases the lease must be produced if it is in the applicant's possession or control.

(i) *Title applied for.*   Where the freehold title out of which the leasehold estate is created is itself registered with an absolute title, or where the lessee can deduce the unregistered freehold title to the Registrar, application for

12   LRA 1925, s 8(1)(a). This is a small category, eg a non-dispositionary lease for (say) 22 years of land in a compulsory area, granted before the appointed day. For group (3) leases created after that day, see LRA 1986, s 2(2).
13   Unless granted pursuant to Pt V of the Housing Act 1985: LRA 1986, s 2(4), adding a new sub-s (7) to s 154 of the Housing Act 1985. These leases are substantively registrable.
14   LRA 1986, s 4(1), amending para (k). Inalienable leases have also been removed from the list of non-registrable leases: ibid, s 3(i); see p 2, ante.
15   That is the lessor's title and also the register of any superior title, such as the freehold when the lessor is not himself the registered freeholder.
16   LRA 1925, s 20 (1); *Freer v Unwins Ltd* [1976] Ch 288, [1976] 1 All ER 634.
17   Cf LRA 1925, ss 50(2), 52 (1). Section 19(2) merely governs the grant of such a lease, whilst s 22 (dispositions of leasehold land) offers no guidance. Section 101(6) confirms the assignability of the lease, by means of a disposition off the register, but is silent as to its effect. Title will be deduced in the usual unregistered manner.
18   Because of the word 'granted'; see p 64, ante.

registration with an absolute title is made. Such applications have been encouraged by the Chief Land Registrar and are the usual form of application[19]. It should also be remembered that, under the Standard Conditions of Sale, the vendor, on the grant of a new lease which is to exceed 21 years, is required to deduce a title which will enable the lessee to be registered with an absolute leasehold title[20]. Even when application is made for registration with a good leasehold title, it is the practice of the Chief Land Registrar, on his own initiative, to register the applicant with an absolute leasehold title whenever the lease is granted by the lessor out of a registered absolute title[1]. Although the lessee does not, in the absence of an appropriate contractual provision, have the right to investigate the lessor's reversionary title, when that title is registered, this problem can be overcome because, after the register was made open, he can always inspect and obtain office copies of the lessor's title[2]. Where only a possessory title is sought, the Registrar may grant a good leasehold title without the applicant's consent.

(ii) *Notices and advertisements.* On an application to register a lease of land already registered, notice must be given to the proprietor of the freehold (and of any superior leasehold) estate. If no valid objection is made within seven days, or the proprietor consents in writing, the lease is noted against the freehold and superior leasehold titles[3]. The lessor's deposit of his land certificate at the Registry signifies consent, in which event no notice is served.

(d) Completion of registration

On substantive registration of a leasehold estate a new title is opened with its own title number. A land certificate is issued to the lessee, containing short particulars of the lease – the date, parties, term and rent. The various provisions of the lease, such as the covenants, do not appear on the register. The lease constitutes an integral part of the title; it is returned with the certificate and a note of registration is endorsed on the lease.

The effect of registration according to the particular type of leasehold title granted has already been considered[4]. On first registration of a dispositionary lease the legal title vests on the date the completed application is deemed to have been delivered at the Registry[5], subject as is variously stated in the Act.

(e) Entry of notice of lease on lessor's title

Registration of the lessee as proprietor of the leasehold estate does not of

19   R & R, 5.09.
20   SCS 8.2.4.
 1   R & R 21.05.
 2   LRA 1988, s 1(1).
 3   LRR 1925, r 46(1), (2).
 4   Pages 33–36, ante.
 5   LRR 1925, r 83 (2), p 477, ante. On first registration of a lease of land formerly unregistered, the legal title will already be vested in the lessee under the grant, except where s 123 has operated to divest the legal title.

itself bring the fact that a lease has been granted on to the register of the reversionary title. This is achieved by the entry of a notice on the register of the freehold (or superior leasehold title) which, with one exception, is done automatically when the lease is registered[6]. In the absence of such a notice a subsequent purchaser of the freehold reversion will take free from the leasehold interest[7]. According to s 72 (2) of the Act it operates by way of notice only and does not confer validity on any lease otherwise invalid. The entry gives notice not merely of the existence of the lease, but also of its contents[8]. It is not, therefore, strictly necessary to apply for any separate notice protecting an option to renew or to purchase the reversion[9], though the Registry does this as a matter of course.

No notice can, of course, be entered if the freehold title is not registered. It will be the Registry's task to do this on the occasion of the registration of the freehold. A notice is not required in the case of a lease which takes effect as an overriding interest within s 70(1)(k)[10]. A pre-appointed day lease, excluded from para (k) because it was granted without a rent or at a premium, may continue to be protected by any existing notice (entered pursuant to s 48 of the Act). However, if not so protected, the lease now ranks as an overriding interest within para (k), provided that the land was subject to it immediately before the commencement of the Land Registration Act 1986[11].

(f) Production of the lessor's land certificate

Section 64 (1) (a) of the Land Registration Act 1925 requires production of the land certificate to the Registrar 'on every entry in the register of a disposition' by the registered proprietor. In *Strand Securities Ltd v Caswell*[12] the Court of Appeal held that this paragraph did not apply to an application to register a new leasehold title. The court declared as erroneous the Registrar's established practice of requiring the lessor's certificate before treating as complete the lessee's application for first registration of his lease. A lessee has no right under the general law to call for his lessor's land certificate[13] and consequently the Registrar should not be entitled to insist on its production. Though the *Strand* case was concerned with a lease at a rack rent, the tenor of

---

6   LRA 1925, ss 19(2), 22(2); LRR 1925, r 46.
7   LRA 1925, s 20(1). The lessee's rights will usually be preserved under s 70 (1)(g) of the Act.
8   A certified copy of the lease (r 186(2)) is filed in the Registry so becoming part of the register. See *Kitney v MEPC Ltd* [1978] 1 All ER 595, CA (unenforceable option granted by lease not validated by notice), p 29, ante.
9   The option may also be an overriding interest within s 70(1)(g): *Webb v Pollmount Ltd* [1966] Ch 584, [1966] 1 All ER 481, p 55, ante.
10   Though not necessary for its protection, entry of a notice is permitted by s 70 (3), in which case the lease ceases to be an overriding interest.
11   Section 4 (4). It will not be so subject if there has been a dealing for value with the reversion before the Act came into effect. For the operation of sub-s (4), see the explanatory note in Law Com No 125, p 57. Often the lessee's occupation will confer protection under s 70 (1) (g).
12   [1965] Ch 958, [1965] 1 All ER 820, CA. See R & R, 21–14; Emmet 9–018.
13   LRA 1925, s 110 (6) does not apply as between lessor and lessee.

the judgments clearly indicates that the decision is of general application.

In practice, the parties normally make arrangements before completion of the lease for the deposit of the lessor's certificate at the Registry and cases of non-co-operation are rare. If, of course, the superior title is subject to a registered charge, the lessor's land certificate will be held on deposit in the Registry and the necessary entry can be made against the lessor's title[14]. Acting on their recommendations, the Law Commission's draft Bill provides that the land or charge certificate should be produced at the Registry on the grant of every derivative lease leading to substantive registration and that this obligation should apply on the grant of a registrable lease[15]. This extension should ensure that, in future, a lessee can no longer be prejudiced by the lessor's failure or delay in lodging his certificate at the Registry.

2. Transfers of registered leases

Although a particular form of transfer is prescribed for an assignment of leasehold property, it is the practice to adopt the statutory form for freehold transfers[16]. Covenants for indemnity, similar to those operative in unregistered conveyancing, are automatically implied[17]; these can be varied or negatived as desired. Registration of the transfer is effected in much the same way as a transfer of freehold land. No legal title vests in the assignee until he is registered as the proprietor, though this will vest retrospectively as of the day when his application is deemed to have been delivered at the Registry. It is essential to register the transfer of a registered lease, even though at the time of application less than 21 years remain unexpired. Section 8(1)(a) of the Act does not bar the application, since it is concerned solely with first registrations.

Section 23 of the Act deals with the effect of registration of the transfer[18]. Under sub-s (1) a disposition[19] for valuable consideration of an absolute leasehold is deemed, on registration, to vest in the transferee the estate transferred together with all implied or expressed rights and privileges attached to the estate, but subject to: (i) the implied and express covenants and obligations incident to the estate; (ii) the incumbrances and other entries on the register; and (iii) overriding interests affecting the estate. The transfer operates as if the transferor were absolutely entitled to the estate for his own benefit. The transfer of a good leasehold title has the same effect by virtue of s 23(2), save that the disposition does not prejudice the enforcement of any right or interest affecting or in derogation of the lessor's title to grant the lease. Where the disposition is not for value then, in both cases, the transferee holds the

14 LRA 1925, s 65. The Registrar can compel production of the charge certificate (LRR 1925, r 266), at least where the lease has been granted with the chargee's consent.
15 See Law Com No 158, paras 4.110, 113; Report No 173, draft Bill, cl 55(6), (7) (defining vendor to mean any person contracting to make a registrable disposition).
16 Form 19, as opposed to Form 32 prescribed by r 115.
17 LRA 1925, s 24, p 682, post.
18 Cf the effect of first registration; see pp 32–35, ante.
19 This includes an express surrender of the term: *Spectrum Investment Co v Holmes* [1981] 1 All ER 6.

estate subject to minor interests binding on the transferor; see sub-s (5).

An assignment of *part* of the land comprised in a registered leasehold title necessitates an application for first registration. Such a transaction normally results in an informal or equitable apportionment of the rent (ie without the consent of the lessor). Particulars of the apportionment and any modification of the implied covenants are entered on the register of title.

3.   Determination of leases

The Registrar is required to notify in the prescribed manner on the register the determination of a lease, on satisfactory proof of its termination[20]. In the case of a registered lease[1] an application must be made to the Registrar. The following documents and evidence must be produced: (1) the lease and counterpart lease; (2) the land certificate of the leasehold title; (3) the land certificate of the superior title, if registered, and if unregistered, adequate evidence of the lessor's title (eg a marked abstract); and (4) evidence of the determination. The leasehold title is then closed and the notice of the lease on the freehold title (if itself registered) is cancelled.

The nature of the evidence of determination[2] depends on the reason for it. In the case of *merger*, the Registrar may treat a lease as merged where the titles to the lease and the superior estate have become vested in the same person in the same capacity, as where the freehold estate is transferred to the registered tenant. The application to close the leasehold title can be incorporated in the application for registration of the ex-tenant as proprietor of the freehold. In the case of a *surrender*, the deed of surrender must be produced; a surrender by operation of law, eg by vacating the premises and handing over the keys, must be supported by a statutory declaration of the facts. A lease determined by effluxion of time will only be cancelled if the Registrar is satisfied that it has not been statutorily extended, eg under the Landlord and Tenant Act 1954.

C   Mortgages and charges[3]

A registered proprietor may by deed charge his land with the payment of any principal sum of money either with or without interest. In addition he can, subject to any entry to the contrary on the register, mortgage his land by deed or otherwise in any manner which would have been permissible if the land had not been registered and with like effect[4]. A mortgage of registered land

---

20   LRA 1925, s 46. See Practice Leaflet No 1.
1   The procedure differs somewhat when the lease is merely noted: R & R, 21–37.
2   LRR 1925, rr 200–8; R & R, 21–29ff.
3   See Law Com No 158, paras 4.62ff, aspects of which are discussed in the notes below. One recommendation proposed in Working Paper No 67, para 76, has already reached the statute book; AJA 1977, s 26, abolished the rarely used mortgage caution.
4   LRA 1925, ss 25 (1), 66 (p 490, post), 106(1) as substituted by AJA 1977, s 16(1).

may take one of several forms:

(1) a legal mortgage completed by the registration of the lender as proprietor of the charge[5], known as a registered charge;

(2) a lien created by a deposit of the land certificate with the lender, together with a written document, complying with s 2 of the Law of Property (Miscellaneous Provisions) Act 1989[6];

(3) a mortgage or charge protected by a notice or caution[7]. This category covers a variety of mortgages, including an unregistered 'legal' mortgage[8], an equitable mortgage of a legal estate, an equitable mortgage of an equitable interest (eg a tenant in common's interest under a trust for sale[9], or a trust of land) and an equitable charge.

Of these differing methods, the creation of a registered charge is that most frequently encountered in practice.

1. Registered charges

(a) Form of charge

A charge of registered land may be in any form, provided it adequately identifies the land comprised in it[10], and for this purpose a description by reference to the title number suffices, though usually the address of the property is included. No mandatory form of instrument is prescribed, though a simple form (Form 45) may be used, if desired. This merely contains a charging clause, to which is added a statement of the sum loaned, the interest and dates of payment[11]. Special stipulations may be added, and certain covenants on the part of the mortgagor are automatically implied (unless there is a contrary entry on the register), including a covenant for payment of principal and interest[12].

In practice institutional lenders prefer to employ their ordinary form of mortgage, adapted to meet the special requirements of registered titles. The substantive provisions of the Act and the Rules apply alike to whichever form of mortgage is used.

(b) Completion by registration

An application for registration must be submitted in the same manner as for a transfer. The land certificate, the charge and a certified copy must be lodged

---

5 Under the Law Commission's draft Bill, cl 6(2), protection by substantive registration would be available for equitable mortgages by deed, if affecting a legal (ie, registered) estate. See further Report No 158, paras 4.76–78. They will continue to be protectable as minor interests as well.

6 See p 491, post.

7 For the Law Commission's proposed new scheme for the protection of minor interests, see p 79, ante.

8 Ie, one capable of registration but not so registered. It cannot take effect as a legal mortgage, despite being created by a so-called 'legal charge'. See below and also p 492, post.

9 Seemingly protectable by a caution, following *Elias v Mitchell* [1972] Ch 652, [1972] 2 All ER 153. When the Draft Bill, cl 33(5)(d) is implemented, protection will be by means of a restriction only. See also Report No 158, para 4.85.

10 LRA 1925, s 25(2).

11 LRR 1925, r 139(2) as substituted by Land Registration (Charges) Rules 1990, r 1.

12 LRA 1925, s 28(1)(a).

at the Registry. Where the mortgage is in conjunction with a transfer of the property to the borrower, a single application suffices for both transactions[13]. Registration is effected by the Registrar entering in the mortgagor's charges register the name of the mortgagee as the proprietor of the mortgage together with particulars of it[14]. The mortgage, it is to be observed, is not registered as a separate title, but the mortgagee is issued with a charge certificate which contains a copy of the filed plan and of the subsisting entries on the register. The original mortgage deed is bound up with the certificate. Section 67 of the Act requires the land certificate to be retained at the Registry until cancellation of the charge.

In the case of a second mortgage, a modified charge certificate is issued, containing an epitome of the entries, but without any copy of the plan. Production of the prior charge certificate is unnecessary and that of the land certificate impossible.

Charges by limited companies.   When a mortgage is created by a company, a certificate of registration under s 395(1) of the Companies Act 1985 should be lodged with the application, otherwise a note is made on the register that the charge is subject to the provisions of that section[15]. A certificate that the charge does not contravene the company's memorandum or articles of association is also required.

It was formerly the case that a restriction was entered on the registration of a company as the proprietor of land that, except under the registrar's order, no charge by a company was to be registered unless a duly signed certificate of non-contravention of the company's articles of association was furnished. This is no longer necessary because of the protection afforded in respect of ultra vires to anyone acting in good faith[16]. No such restriction is now entered[17].

Since a registered charge must be a charge on specific land, a floating charge (which is a charge on all the company's property for the time being) cannot be registered. It can be protected on the register by means of a notice (if the land certificate is produced), or by a caution[18].

(c) Effect of registration
The charge constitutes a disposition of registered land. When registered, it

13   If the mortgagee is separately represented, his solicitor submits the application.
14   LRA 1925, s 26(1). For the form of the entries, reference should be made to the illustration on pp 48–49, ante.
15   LRR 1925, r 145. Under s 395(1) a charge on land created by a company is void against the company's liquidator unless registered with the registrar of companies within 21 days of creation.
16   Companies Act 1985, ss 35, 35A and 35B, inserted by Companies Act 1989, s 108(1).
17   R & R, 23–17.
18   The Law Commission takes the view that, prior to crystallisation, a floating charge needs no protection on the register of title, unless it prevents, or restricts, the company's freedom to create fixed charges ranking in priority to, or pari passu with, the floating charge. Such clauses should be protected by entry of a restriction. Once crystallised, the floating charge is no different from any other equitable charge and should be protected on the register in the normal way: Report No 158, paras 4.92–93; draft Bill, cl 33(5)(b).
19   LRA 1925, ss 18(4), (5); 20(1). In s 20(1) 'legal estate' includes a legal charge: s 3(xi).

operates to confer a legal charge on the chargee[19]. The fact that the mortgagee's title is defective does not prevent the chargee from obtaining a valid legal mortgage; the aggrieved person must then seek rectification[20]. As a disposition of the land by the registered proprietor, it takes effect subject to overriding interests and to minor interests noted on the register. A potential problem occurred when a tenant went into occupation under a tenancy created by the mortgagor prior to the completion of the purchase and the mortgage. It used to be the case that the tenancy by estoppel was fed in the *scintilla temporis* which was previously held to exist between the completion of the purchase and the creation of the mortgage[1]. This trap was removed, however, in *Abbey National Building Society v Cann*[2], where it was held that the transfer and the mortgage were to be regarded as occurring simultaneously. If the mortgagor is registered with a good leasehold, qualified or possessory title, the charge takes effect subject to the provisions of the Act affecting land registered with such a title[3].

Though the mortgagee cannot obtain a legal interest before registration, this does not mean that the mortgage deed is wholly ineffective until then[4]. Section 27(3) provides that the mortgage takes effect from the date of its delivery, so that pending registration the provisions of the mortgage are fully operative as between the parties. This subsection does not, however, enable the mortgagee to exercise the powers conferred by law on the owner of a legal mortgagee – only a registered proprietor has these[5]. A registered chargee can transfer the charge to another, a power which cannot be negatived by the mortgage provisions[6].

(d) Further charges

Special rules regulate the priority of further advances on the security of registered land. Where a prior mortgagee is under an *obligation* noted on the register to make further advances, a subsequent registered chargee takes subject to any further advances, even though his charge is registered before the prior mortgagee makes the further advance[7]. In cases where the mortgagee merely secures further advances, the prior mortgagee does not obtain priority in respect of further advances made by him after notification from the Registry on the prospective entry on the register of another charge[8].

---

20   *Norwich and Peterborough Building Society v Steed (No 2)* [1993] Ch 116, [1993] 1 All ER 330, CA (rectification refused when mortgage executed under a power of attorney obtained by fraud).

1   *Church of England Building Society v Piskor* [1954] Ch 553, [1954] 2 All ER 85, CA.

2   [1991] 1 AC 56, [1990] 1 All ER 1085, HL.

3   LRA 1925, s 26(3).

4   See *Grace Rymer Investments Ltd v Waite*, supra, at 850, 783–84, per Lord Evershed MR.

5   *Lever Finance Ltd v Trustee of Property of Needleman* [1956] Ch 375, [1956] 2 All ER 378 (appointment of receiver). See LRA 1925, s 34(1).

6   LRA 1925, ss 25(3)(i), 33.

7   LRA 1925, s 30(3), as added by LP(Am)A 1926, s 5. Section 94 of the LPA 1925 does not apply to registered charges (see sub-s (4) thereof).

8   LRA 1925, s 30(1), (2). A mortgage in favour of a bank to secure an overdraft is a common example of a charge to secure further advances. The honouring of each cheque by the bank constitutes a further advance.

(e) Discharge of registered charge

The provisions in the Law of Property Act 1925 governing mortgages do not apply to registered charges[9]. The discharge of a registered charge can only be effected by a discharge entered on the register. The Rules prescribe a suitable form (Form 73) which consists of a simple admission by the mortgagee that the charge of which he is the proprietor has been discharged. Use of this form is not obligatory. Rule 151 gives the Registrar a wide discretion to accept other evidence of repayment, such as an acknowledgement for receipt of all moneys outstanding endorsed on the mortgage deed.

The charge certificate, together with Form 53 (or other satisfactory evidence) must be delivered to the Registry. The entry relating to the mortgage in the charges register is deleted, and the charge certificate is cancelled, whereupon the charge is deemed to have ceased and any term or sub-term granted by the mortgage is extinguished and merges in the registered estate without any surrender[10]. The proprietor's land certificate is brought up to date and sent to him or his solicitors. Often in practice, however, the discharge of an existing mortgage is part of a transaction which culminates in the issue of a new charge to the purchaser's mortgagee and, consequently, the land certificate remains notionally at the Registry.

A discharge of a building society mortgage may be either in Form 53 or by way of an endorsed receipt in accordance with the Building Societies Act 1986[11]. Rule 152(2) requires Form 53, where used, to be executed under the society's seal and countersigned by the secretary, but the Registrar accepts the form if it is countersigned by a person acting under the authority of the board of directors, the mode prescribed for statutory receipts under the 1986 Act.

2.   Deposit of land certificate

(a) Procedure for creation

For centuries, a method of creating an equitable charge was by deposit of title deeds[12]. Similarly, where title was registered, a charge could be created by the deposit of the land certificate with the chargee; a practice which appeared to be confirmed by s 66 of the Act. It now transpires that the mere deposit of the land certificate will not be sufficient to create a charge. The point arose in *United Bank of Kuwait plc v Sahib*[13]. One of two co-owners[14] deposited the land certificate with a creditor. Later a charging order was made against him and the issue was one of priority. It was held that the deposit of the land certificate did not create an equitable charge or mortgage, with the consequence that the later creditor had priority.

---

9   LPA 1925, s 115(10). For s 115, see p 603, post.
10   LRA 1925, s 35; LRR 1925, r 267.
11   See s 13(7), Sch 4, para 2(1), (4).
12   *Russel v Russel* (1783) 1 Bro CC 269.
13   [1996] 3 All ER 215, CA, affirming [1995] 2 All ER 973, criticised at [1995] Conv 465 (M P Thompson).
14   Nothing, for present purposes, turned on the fact that the deposit was by only one of the co-owners.

The reason for the decision was the underlying basis of the doctrine of equitable mortgages by deposit of title deeds. The view had always been taken that there existed a contract to create a legal mortgage. This contract had to satisfy the formal requirements for contracts for the sale or disposition of an interest in land; that is there must either have been a written memorandum of the agreement or an act of part performance[15]. The deposit of title deeds was taken to be an act of part performance by both parties with the result that there existed a specifically enforceable contract to create a mortgage, which, in turn, led to the creation of an equitable mortgage[16]. The Court of Appeal held that this, rather fictitious, doctrine had not survived the implementation of s 2 of the Law of Property (Miscellaneous Provisions) Act 1989.

This section, it will be recalled, requires that a contract for the sale or disposition of an interest in land must be in writing. There is now no such thing as an oral contract to create a mortgage. Consequently the deposit of title deeds can no longer be seen as part performance; there cannot be part performance of a non-existent contract. To create a mortgage by deposit of the land certificate, it is now necessary not only to deposit the certificate with the chargee; the terms of the mortgage must be in writing in a document signed by both parties.

As the deposit of the land certificate with the lender remains at the heart of this method of creating a charge, the existence of a prior registered charge precludes the creation of a mortgage of this type because the land certificate will already be in the registry. It does not seem necessary to deposit other relevant title deeds, eg the lease, in the case of a leasehold title, although this is highly desirable[17].

(b) Nature of protection

The depositee may give written notice of the deposit to the Registrar, who acknowledges its receipt and enters notice of the deposit in the proprietor's charges register[18]. This notice (not the applicant's notice) operates as a caution[19], thus entitling him to oppose any application to register a disposition or transmission of which he is notified. The notice does not itself disclose the details of the charge.

The depositee in fact enjoys a position superior to that of an ordinary cautioner. No disposition or transmission or any other entry for which production of the land certificate is required can be registered without his surrendering the certificate. This produces an anomaly as regards the creation of leases by the depositor. The grant of a lease under seal for (say) 22 years can rank as an equitable lease only; the lessee cannot, without the consent of the

---

15 LPA 1925, s 40, replacing the Statute of Frauds 1677, s 4.
16 See, eg, *Re Alton Corpn* [1985] BCLC 27 at 33 per Sir Robert Megarry V-C.
17 R & R, 25.02.
18 LRR 1925, r 239. The notice is usually given on Form 85A, which is submitted in duplicate. The Registrar returns the copy by way of acknowledgement. The form printed on the reverse side can be used to request withdrawal of the notice.
19 Under LRA 1925, s 54. For cautions generally see pp 73–76, ante.

depositee[20], procure registration of his disposition. On the other hand, a similar grant but for 20 years takes effect as a registered disposition under s 19(1) of the Act, and the lessee acquires a legal lease.

(c) Withdrawal of notice

The notice may be withdrawn on a written request signed personally by the person entitled to the lien or his successor in title[1]. In the case of a limited company, the signature of a responsible official (eg a director) is accepted. In all cases the land certificate must accompany the written request.

(d) Notice of intended deposit

Where a purchaser not yet registered as proprietor borrows money on this form of security, he may give to the Registrar notice of intended deposit. The notice is signed by the intending proprietor, it names the person with whom the deposit is to be made and to whom the land certificate should be sent after entry of the notice[2]. In practice, the lender's solicitor will attend completion of the purchase, collect the necessary documents and forward to the Registry the application for registration together with the notice signed by the purchaser. A notice of intended deposit operates in the same way as a notice of deposit and is similarly withdrawn.

3.   Unregistered mortgages

When early repayment of a loan is anticipated, the mortgagee may opt not to register his charge but to rely on the inferior protection afforded by s 106 of the Act (as amended). Sometimes he may have no choice except to resort to this section, as where the land certificate is in the hands of a prior chargee under s 66. According to s 106, the mortgage ranks as a minor interest unless and until it becomes a registered charge. Till then it takes effect only in equity and is capable of being overridden unless protected either by (i) a notice under s 49 (which necessitates production of the land certificate), or (ii) a caution under s 54[3].

The question can arise as to the issue of priority between two, unregistered mortgages. The issue arose in *Mortgage Corpn Ltd v Nationwide Credit Corpn Ltd*[4]. The first mortgage had not been registered when a further mortgage was created, which the mortgagee sought to protect by the registration of a notice. The question arose as to which of the mortgages had priority. It was held that the first did. Until there had been substantive registration, both mortgages operated only in equity. As between competing equitable interests, the general

---

20   LRR 1925, r 244. The terms of the deposit will determine whether the lease binds the chargee.
1   LRR 1925, r 246.
2   LRR 1925, rr 241, 242, applicable also to an intended deposit on first registration.
3   Section 106(2), (3), without specifying which para of s 49(1). Presumably (c) is envisaged. For the drawbacks of equitable mortgages, see p 330, ante.
4   [1994] Ch 49, [1993] 4 All ER 623, CA.

rule is whichever is first in time is first in right[5]. Protection of an equitable interest by registration of a notice does not affect this principle. It was argued that the earlier right should have been displaced owing to the negligence of the holder of it in failing to protect it by registration. This failed on the facts, because the later mortgagee was well aware of the prior right. On different facts, however, such an argument may well prevail.

D   Settlements and trusts for sale

These have been considered in Chapter 11 and no further comment is necessary. When the provisions of the Trusts of Land and Appointment of Trustees Act 1996 are brought into force, however, it will no longer be possible to create either a trust for sale or a strict settlement. Instead, a trust of land will be created and the title vested in the trustees with an appropriate restriction entered.

E   Easements[6]

The various provisions in the Land Registration Act 1925 and the Rules relating to easements are not entirely consistent and free from ambiguity. It is essential to distinguish between (i) easements existing at the time of first registration, and (ii) easements created afterwards by or in favour of a registered proprietor. In both cases two plots of land are inevitably involved, but it does not follow that the titles to both are registered, which adds to the difficulties.

1.   Easements existing at first registration

(a) Adverse easements
Here we are considering easements which adversely affect the servient land. Where at the time of first registration any easement created by an instrument and appearing on the title adversely affects the land, the Registrar is required by s 70 (2) of the Act to enter a note thereof on the register. This mandatory provision[7] is of rather limited application. It does not extend to easements arising by virtue of the Law of Property Act 1925, s 62, nor to prescriptive easements. The omission of such easements from the register of the servient title will not normally prejudice the dominant owner. If they exist as legal

---

5   See *Barclays Bank v Taylor* [1974] Ch 137, [1973] 1 All ER 752, CA.
6   The Law Commission's proposal for the total assimilation of easements and covenants, mooted as long ago as 1971 (see Working Paper No 36, paras 9, 84), has presumably been abandoned in view of Report (No 127) devoted exclusively to covenants. The suggested reform of these does, however, rely heavily on analogies with the existing law of easements: para 4.22.
7   *Re Dances Way, West Town, Hayling Island* [1962] Ch 490 at 510, [1962] 2 All ER 42 at 51, CA, per Diplock LJ. Section 70(2) is not qualified by r 41 which gives a discretionary power to enter easements not appearing on the title: per Diplock LJ.

easements under the general law, they constitute overriding interests and registration of the servient owner as proprietor takes effect subject to overriding interests[8]. The Registrar is empowered to enter notice of the burden of these easements if admitted or proved to his satisfaction, but an easement not created by an instrument cannot be noted against the title to the servient land if the proprietor shows sufficient cause to the contrary, after notice has been served on him[9].

The entry must, so far as practicable and convenient, be made either by reference to the instrument of creation or by setting out an extract therefrom[10]. Once noted against the servient title, the easement ceases to be an overriding interest. The Registry may cancel the entry of any easement on the application of the servient proprietor, if it appears it was wrongly made[11].

(b) Appurtenant easements

First registration with an absolute title vests in the proprietor all easements, rights, privileges and appurtenances appertaining or reputed to appertain to the land, without these being expressly mentioned on his register of title[12]. The benefit of an easement may be entered as appurtenant to the registered estate if capable of subsisting as a legal easement[13]. It is entered in the property register as part of the description of the land. Registration guarantees its validity and confers on the proprietor a title to the easement of the same kind as the title to the dominant land.

An application by the dominant owner for entry of an appurtenant easement is entirely optional, even where the servient land is unregistered. A purchaser of registered land with appurtenant, but unregistered, easements cannot compel the vendor under s 110(5) of the Act to procure registration of himself as proprietor of those easements[14].

2.   Easements created after first registration

The creation of an easement by a registered proprietor constitutes a disposition of the registered land and must be completed by registration in the same way as a transfer of corporeal land[15], if the grantee is to have a legal easement. What is meant by 'completed by registration' in this context is not certain. Clearly it does not mean substantive registration as this is not possible with easements. Though the wording of the relevant proviso is

8   LRA 1925, s 5.
9   LRA 1925, s 70(3); LRR 1925, rr 41, 197. The entry of trivial rights is not necessary: r 199, eg rights of way over roads found to be adopted by the time of first registration.
10   LRR 1925, r 41(2). See Registered Land Practice Note, I.2 (description of easements on register).
11   *Re Dances Way, West Town, Hayling Island* [1962] Ch 490, [1962] 2 All ER 42, CA.
12   LRA 1925, ss 5, 72, p 28, ante.
13   LRR 1925, r 257; see also rr 251–56. See p 22, ante.
14   *Re Evans' Contract, Evans v Deed* [1970] 1 All ER 1236. For s 110(5), see p 475, ante.
15   See LRA 1925, ss 18(1)(c), 19(2), 21(1)(b), 22(2).

ambiguous, registration is commonly thought to entail the entry of notice against the title of the servient land and (if the dominant land is also registered) registration of the easement as appurtenant to the dominant land[16]. The view has been expressed that an easement arising under s 62 of the Law of Property Act 1925 is not regarded as an easement created by a registered disposition[17].

(a) Servient title registered

Where the easement is created on a transfer of part of the land within a registered title, the Registrar makes the relevant entries as a matter of course. When a proprietor creates an easement by deed of grant independently of any transfer of the land, the grantee (whether or not his own land is registered) must apply for notice to be entered against the servient title. He must therefore ensure that the servient owner lodges the land certificate at the Registry to enable the required entry to be made[18]. Entry of the notice forms an integral part of the registration process. The absence of this notice prevents the acquisition of any legal easement and operates to defeat the easement on a subsequent registered transfer for value of the servient land[19]. If the grantee's title is also registered, it seems that he must register the easement as appurtenant to his own title.

(b) Only dominant title registered

Where only the dominant land is registered, the grantee may apply to have the easement entered as appurtenant to his title, and should do so if he wishes its validity to be guaranteed. It will be necessary to deduce to the Registrar the title to the unregistered servient land. Should there be doubts as to the grantor's title, a note is entered on the grantee's register of title to the effect that the deed purported to grant the right. However, application for entry of an appurtenant easement is not obligatory. As the servient land is not registered, the grant of the easement does not constitute a disposition by a registered proprietor so that the necessity for 'completion by registration' does not arise. When the servient land is subsequently registered, the easement will automatically be registered against the servient title under s 70(2) of the Act as part of the registration process.

---

16   LRA 1925, s 19 (2), proviso (c). See R & R, 9–13, 12–34; 25 Ency F & P, 209, para 158–1; Registered Land Practice Note, I.1. Cf Potter, 273; 3 K & E, 58. Pending 'completion by registration', such express easements should be treated as minor interests only, according to a Law Commission recommendation: Report No 158, para 2.26.

17   3 K & E, 58, a suggestion based, seemingly, on the view that such easements take effect as implied grants. Sed quaere. See note 1, infra.

18   Where he ranks as a purchaser (see s 3 (xxi) he can compel production of the land certificate (if outstanding) under s 110(6)).

19   LRA 1925, s 20(1). For equitable easements, see section 4, post.

3. Easements created otherwise than by express grant

(a) Implied easements

Easements may be acquired on registration under the rule in *Wheeldon v Burrows*[20], or by virtue of s 62 of the Law of Property Act 1925,[1] in the same way as if the land were not registered[2]. There is no need to note these against the servient title, and they take effect as overriding interests[3]. They may be noted as appurtenant to the dominant title, on an application by the owner stating the nature of the right and furnishing evidence of its existence, but not until the Registrar has given notice to the proprietor of the servient land. If the Registrar is satisfied as to the existence of the right he enters notice of it as a burden on the register of the servient land[4].

(b) Prescription

The rules somewhat obscurely provide that an easement acquired by prescription, capable of taking effect at law, 'shall take effect at law also' and if it is an overriding interest, the Registrar may enter notice of it against the servient title[5]. He can himself determine the validity or otherwise of the claim, but he must, before entering notice on the register, notify the servient owner who can show cause why it should not be made. A prescriptive easement may be registered as part of the description of the dominant land. This operates to guarantee its validity; consequently, unless the court has previously determined the matter, the Registrar will only make the entry if satisfied of its acquisition.

4. Equitable easements

An equitable easement may arise through lack of form (ie absence of a grant under seal), because it is not equivalent to a fee simple or term of years absolute (eg a right of way granted over a road until adoption by the highway authority), or because, being granted by a registered proprietor, the disposition is not completed by registration. Prima facie they rank as minor interests and require protection on the register to be enforceable against later purchasers of the servient land. Equitable easements created by an instrument are automatically noted against the servient title on first registration. In other cases notice may be entered[6] on production of the land certificate of the servient title; if the

---

20   (1879) 12 Ch D 31, CA.
1   As to whether s 62 operated by way of express, rather than implied, grant, see p 551, post.
2   LRA 1925, s 20(1). The general words implied in conveyances under the LPA 1925, apply to dispositions of a registered estate: LRA 1925, s 19(3).
3   LRR 1925, r 258, p 53, ante. No change is proposed by the Law Commission in the status of these easements, or of those arising by prescription, whether existing prior to first registration of the servient land, or arising later: paras 2.27–30, 2.35.
4   LRR 1925, rr 252, 253; R & R, 12–34. Once entered on the register these easements cease to be overriding: see LRA 1925, s 3(xvi).
5   LRR 1925, r 250(2), referring to s 70(3), p 53, ante. It will be recalled that a right claimed under the Prescription Act 1832 is inchoate till litigated; see M & W, 880.
6   Under LRA 1925, s 49(1)(c).

proprietor does not concur only a caution can be entered. However, as we saw in Chapter 3, an equitable easement may be enforceable as an overriding interest in two situations: (i) if it qualifies for protection under s 70(1)(g) of the Act; or (ii) when it falls within r 258 as interpreted by Scott J in *Celsteel Ltd v Alton House Holdings Ltd*[7]. The Law Commission is of the opinion that all equitable easements should no longer rank as overriding interests[8]. It sees no sufficient reason why the position of a purchaser of registered land should be any worse than in unregistered conveyancing; protection on the register of title as a minor interest should be required in all cases.

F   Covenants

1.   Positive covenants

As a general rule only the covenantor and his estate can be rendered liable for breach of positive covenants. Consequently the land registration system does not require that their existence should be revealed on the register[9]. To assist practitioners in their task of deciding upon the necessity for indemnity covenants, the Registrar has, as a special concession, permitted a limited reference to these covenants on the register[10]. In the case of positive covenants (including express covenants of indemnity) *created after* first registration, a note is made in the proprietorship register to the effect that the transfer contains a purchaser's personal covenant. The covenants themselves are set out verbatim on a separate sheet entitled 'Personal Covenants'. This is bound up in the land certificate but does not form part of the register of title. When a subsequent transfer includes a further purchaser's indemnity covenant, a copy is added to the Personal Covenants sheet[11]. No reference is made in the register of the existence of positive covenants created prior to first registration[12].

2.   Restrictive covenants

(a) First registration
All restrictive covenants (other than those between lessor and lessee) appearing to the Registrar to be existing at the time of first registration are noted in the charges register of the new title. The covenants are either set out in a schedule attached to the register, or a copy of the deed creating them is bound up in the certificate[13]. In some circumstances the Registrar may feel that the applicant

---

7   [1985] 2 All ER 562, discussed p 53, ante.
8   Report No 158, para 2.33; draft Bill, cl 7(2)(a).
9   See also p 44, ante.
10   Registered Land Practice Note 0.1; R & R, 17.11, 17.51. Since transfers are retained in the Registry, it is impossible to tell whether any previous transfer contained an indemnity covenant.
11   Should the chain be broken on failure to take an indemnity, the earlier covenants are removed from the land certificate.
12   Except in the case of a rentcharge deed creating both positive and negative covenants, when usually the entire deed is issued with the land certificate.
13   See further Registered Land Practice Note J.1.

has been unable to disclose all possible restrictions, eg on a purchase of land from a squatter or where the deeds have been lost or destroyed. To minimise the risk of an indemnity becoming payable under the Act, the Registrar places a 'protective' entry on the title. This indicates that the land is subject to such restrictive covenants as may have been imposed thereon before a specified date, so far as they are subsisting and capable of being enforced[14].

One point is often overlooked by solicitors when making an application for first registration. Whilst the Registrar does not inquire whether a restrictive covenant is still enforceable, he can be requested to omit from the register any restrictive covenant that is void for non-registration as a land charge. This request must be supported by an official certificate of search against the correct name of the covenantor, which does not disclose the registration of the restriction as a land charge. However entry of a previously avoided covenant does not revive it, as the next section will show.

It will be recalled that the Land Charges Act 1972[15] excludes from the operation of the Act restrictive covenants (and other land charges) which are created by an instrument leading to compulsory registration and affect the land to be registered. There is, therefore, no need to register such restrictions as land charges to ensure their continuing enforceability.

Effect of notice[16]. Entry of the notices fixes the proprietor and those deriving title under him with notice of the covenant as an incumbrance on the land. The only ones not so bound are incumbrancers and persons who at the time when the notice is entered may not be bound by the covenant. This exception includes a lessee who was not a party to the covenant and who took his lease before the date when the notice was entered[17]. The notice in no way guarantees or establishes the enforceability of the covenant; this question must be determined by general principles of land law. Thus in one case a positive covenant was noted on the register; it was held that the entry did not make it enforceable against a purchaser from the covenantor who had omitted to take an indemnity covenant from the purchaser[18]. A lessee is deemed to have notice of restrictive covenants already entered against the freehold title, even though he has no right, apart from contract, to investigate the superior title[19]. Now that the register is open to inspection, however, this problem should disappear.

14   See R & R, 12.19. A vendor should deal with this by way of a special condition in the contract; see *Faruqi v English Real Estates Ltd* [1979] 1 WLR 963.
15   Section 14(3), p 392, ante, which applies to documents executed on or after 27 July 1971.
16   LRA 1925, ss 50(2), 52(1), (2).
17   *Freer v Unwins Ltd* [1976] Ch 288, [1976] 1 All ER 634 (rectification of freehold title by entry of covenants after lease and assignment; assignee not bound).
18   *Cator v Newton and Bates* [1940] 1 KB 415, [1939] 4 All ER 457, CA; *Willée v St John* [1910] 1 Ch 325, CA.
19   *White v Bijou Mansions Ltd* [1937] Ch 610, [1937] 3 All ER 269; affd [1938] Ch 351, [1938] 1 All ER 546, CA. Cf *Freer v Unwins Ltd*, supra. But see p 342, ante.

(b) Covenants created on subsequent dealing

A registered proprietor is statutorily empowered[20] to impose restrictive covenants binding upon registered land, either in a transfer of the land or by a separate deed of covenant. On a transfer of part, the Registrar automatically makes the appropriate entry in the covenantor's charges register whether the parties expressly apply for it or not, even in cases where the covenants are imposed on the vendor's retained land. Covenants created by a separate deed of covenant require production of the land certificate at the Registry before notice can be entered. There appears to be no express prohibition preventing a covenantee unable to secure production of the certificate from lodging a caution against dealings.

3.   Entry of the benefit of covenants

The provisions of the Act and the Rules relating to the benefit of restrictive covenants are most unsatisfactory and the practice at the Registry tends to be unhelpful. It is apparently not possible, save in very exceptional cases, to state on the register that land has the benefit of restrictive covenants, the reason being that they may not always remain enforceable. Yet, surely, the test ought to be whether they are enforceable at the time of application. There would seem to be many more cases than the Registry is prepared to admit, where a proprietor can readily establish that his land is benefited, eg on a transfer of part where covenants are imposed for the benefit of the vendor's retained land. In such a case a note of the benefit should be made in the vendor's property register. Indeed s 40(3) provides that entries *shall be made* on the register of all obligations acquired by the proprietor for the benefit of the registered estate[1]. The fact that, on first registration, the benefit of the covenants will not be entered on the register makes it imperative to return the pre-registration deed.

For similar reasons the Registry also refuses to make any entry that a transfer assigns the benefit of existing covenants, whether negative or positive (such as an option in gross). This practice also seems to be unwarranted by the Act. The question whether the benefit of covenants not annexed to the land has passed to a successor of the covenantee can be of considerable importance. The fact that the transfer assigning the benefit is retained in the Registry should

---

20   LRA 1925, s 40.

1   R & R, 35–23, where it is stated that there is nothing in the Act or Rules authorising the Registrar to make an entry of the benefit of restrictive covenants. This is plainly inconsistent with s 40(3) and r 3(2)(c) which provides for entry of such notes as have to be entered relating to inter alia covenants for the benefit of the land. Neither of these provisions is even considered by R & R in relation to the problem under discussion. The argument in Brickdale, 328, that r 3(2) does not authorise the entry of equitable interests because the rule applies only to legal rights within r 252 appears unsound. Can the Registry's restrictive policy still be justified after *Federated Homes Ltd v Mill Lodge Properties Ltd* [1980] 1 All ER 371, CA? And see Conveyancing Committee Report II, 57, para 4.56, supporting entry of the benefit as 'useful for practical purposes', but conscious, too, of the Registry's likely opposition.

be adequate justification for noting that the transfer purported to assign them to the proprietor. At the most the entry would only provide notice. There could be no claim for an indemnity, should it be that the proprietor was unable to enforce the covenants; unlike easements, covenants cannot be registered as appurtenant to the dominant land. In relation to matters which might adversely affect a registered estate, the Registry is always anxious to ensure that the register conveys as much information as a perusal of the title deeds would reveal. It is unfortunate that a similar policy is not adopted for appurtenant rights.

4.   Release and discharge

Any release or modification of restrictive covenants should be noted on the register[2]. Where the covenant is discharged or modified by an order under the Law of Property Act 1925, s 84, or the court refuses to grant an injunction to enforce the same, the entry is either cancelled, or reference is made to the order and a copy is filed at the Registry[3].

G   Transmissions of registered land

The title to registered land may alter consequent upon some event other than a registered disposition. This is known as a transmission, an expression nowhere defined in the Act or Rules. A transmission can occur in three situations:
(1) on death, by registration of a personal representative or beneficiary;
(2) on bankruptcy, by registration of the official receiver or trustee in bankruptcy;
(3) on liquidation of a company, by registering the resolution or order appointing the liquidator.
These situations have already been discussed in earlier parts of this book[4], and nothing further need be added here, save to mention that in each case the land certificate must be produced at the Registry before the transmission can be registered[5].

---

2   LRR 1925, r 212.
3   LRA 1925, s 50(3).
4   Pages 260–262, ante (bankruptcy and liquidation), pp 343–344 (death).
5   LRA 1925, s 64(1)(b).

Part Five
Conveyancing documents

Chapter 16

Drafting and construction of deeds generally

A Forms of conveyance past and present

Section 51(1) of the Law of Property Act 1925 enacts that:

> All lands and all interests therein lie in grant and are incapable of being conveyed by livery or livery of seisin, or by feoffment, or by bargain and sale and a conveyance of an interest in land may operate to pass the possession or right to possession thereof, without actual entry, but subject to all prior rights thereto.

This provision conceals a wealth of legal history pertaining to the mode of land transfer over the centuries. A brief survey of the different forms of conveyance may not be amiss, though rarely will the average practitioner ever encounter these ancient forms.

At common law the 'most ancient method of conveyance, the most solemn and public'[1] was the *feoffment with livery of seisin*. Originally a feoffment took the form of a public and oral delivery by the grantor (the feoffor) to the grantee (the feoffee) of actual seisin. This entailed the entry on the land by both parties (or their attorneys) and a symbolic handing to the feoffee of some twig, or clod of earth, accompanied by suitable words explaining the purpose of the ceremony. Subsequently it became the practice to evidence the transaction in writing, called a charter of feoffment. A written document was made essential by the Statute of Frauds 1677, but it was not until the Real Property Act 1845 that a deed was required. In addition, s 2 of this Act also enabled a conveyance of land to be effected by a deed of grant without livery. Hitherto a *deed of grant* had been the appropriate mode of transfer for incorporeal rights only, such as rents, reversions, advowsons. These were said to lie in grant; not being an object of the senses, they could not lie in livery.

The disadvantages of the ancient mode of transfer by livery of seisin, particularly the publicity and the need for the parties' presence on or near the land, were such that long before 1845 other forms of land transfer had been devised and were in operation. One such method recognised by the common law was the lease *and release*. X leased land to Y for one year; no feoffment was required because the lease created mere personal property.

---

1   2 *Blackstone's Commentaries*, 310.

The following day X released his reversion to Y by a deed of release, thus vesting the freehold estate in Y without any livery of seisin. The drawback to this simple device was the need for Y's actual entry on the land before the release took effect; the release was only operative in favour of a lessee who had an actual term of years and at common law he had no estate prior to entry, only an interesse termini[2].

After the passing of the Statute of Uses 1535, this particular disadvantage could be avoided by creating a term by means of an assurance taking effect by virtue of the statute. X bargained and sold (ie contracted to sell) land to Y for one year. In equity this operated to create a use in Y's favour, which the statute executed, giving Y a legal term. Actual entry was unnecessary for the statute enacted that the cestui que use should be deemed 'in lawful possession' for the equivalent legal estate. Having a legal term, the release by X of his reversion became immediately effective without Y's entry. This mode of transfer became the classical form of assurance[3] of land until it was rendered virtually obsolete by the Real Property Act 1845, which, as we have seen, enabled land to be conveyed by a simple grant.

Section 51(1) abolishes these ancient forms of conveyance. Now all land lies in grant only. Section 52(1) of the Act further provides that, save for certain statutory exceptions, all conveyances of land or of any interest therein are void for the purpose of conveying or creating a legal estate unless made by deed. The requirements for a valid deed have been fully considered in Chapter 14. In the case of registered land, however, it is not the transfer deed, but the act of registration that vests the legal title in the transferee[4].

Cases where a deed is not required

Exceptionally a legal estate may pass or be created without any deed and s 52 (2) of the Act provides for seven such occasions which must briefly be considered.

(a) Assents by personal representatives
This exception has previously been encountered[5] and needs no further comment.

(b) Certain disclaimers
The most important example within this group occurs in the Insolvency Act 1986, s 178, which enables a trustee in bankruptcy to disclaim onerous property forming part of the bankrupt's estate, eg land burdened with onerous covenants. The disclaimer which must be in writing operates to determine the

---

2   A legal proprietary interest in land (but not an estate) which conferred a right to possession.
3   M & W, App 3, 1171.
4   Page 475, ante.
5   Page 320, ante.

rights and liabilities of the bankrupt in respect of the property, but not so as to affect the position of the third persons[6].

(c) Implied surrenders

A surrender occurs when the owner of a smaller estate or interest in land yields up his interest to the person entitled to the immediate estate in remainder or in reversion, as where a tenant surrenders his lease to the land prior to the time of its determination. The effect of this surrender is to pass to the landlord the tenant's estate which thereupon merges with the freehold reversion. An express surrender must be by deed[7] but a surrender by operation of law, or implied surrender as it is frequently termed, takes effect without any deed. Delivery of possession by the tenant which is accepted by the landlord effects an implied surrender[8]; so does the tenant's acceptance of a new lease to commence during the currency of an existing lease.

(d) Short term leases

By virtue of s 54(2) of the Act a legal lease may be created by parol, or by writing not under seal, provided it takes effect in possession for a term not exceeding three years at the best rent reasonably obtainable without taking a fine. This provision includes periodic tenancies, notwithstanding that they may endure for more than three years[9], but not a lease for l 4 years determined by the tenant at the end of any year[10]. The assignment of an informal lease must, however, be by deed to vest the legal estate in the assignee[10a].

(e) Receipts not required by law to be under seal

This refers to the statutory receipt endorsed on a mortgage under s 115 of the Law of Property Act 1925, which is effective to discharge the mortgage and extinguish the mortgagee's interest without any reconveyance or surrender.

(f) Court vesting orders

A vesting order made by the court for the purpose of conveying or creating a legal estate operates to vest that estate in the same manner as if it had been a conveyance executed by the estate owner[11].

(g) Conveyances taking effect by operation of law

Within this category come probates and letters of administration, and the appointment of a trustee in bankruptcy under the Insolvency Act 1986.

6   See eg *Re Bastable, ex p Trustee* [1901] 2 KB 518, CA. See further in relation to bankruptcy, pp 259–262, ante.
7   See *Tarjomani v Panther Securities Ltd* (1982) 46 P & CR 32.
8   *Dodd v Acklom* (1843) 6 Man & G 672 (return of keys).
9   *Hammond v Farrow* [1904] 2 KB 332 (yearly tenancy).
10   *Kushner v Law Society* [1952] 1 KB 264, [1952] 1 All ER 404.
10a See *Crago v Julian* [1992] 1 All ER 744, [1992] 1 WLR 372, CA.
11   LPA 1925, s 9(1). For an example of the court's power to make a vesting order, see ibid, s 30 (refusal of trustees for sale to exercise duties).

B　Drafting the conveyance

1.　Responsibility for drafting

Traditionally it has been the purchaser's responsibility to prepare at his own expense the conveyance for execution by the necessary parties. A draft is submitted in duplicate and sent to the vendor's solicitor for approval, usually at the same time as any requisitions on title. When this has been approved and any amendments made by the vendor's solicitor accepted, it is engrossed[12] and after execution by the purchaser (where necessary) is tendered to the vendor for his execution[13]. The time for delivery of the draft and the engrossment are normally regulated by the contract[14], though the relevant time limits are frequently ignored. Although submission of the draft conveyance or the engrossment does not generally constitute an acceptance of the title[15], it is common practice to tender these documents without prejudice to any outstanding requisitions. Should the vendor require the execution of a duplicate conveyance (eg because the conveyance imposes restrictive covenants for his benefit or reserves easements in his favour) he ought to stipulate for this expressly in the contract, failing which he cannot require the purchaser to prepare a duplicate at his own expense.

It is the general practice on the grant of a lease for the lease to be drafted by the lessor's solicitor; the lessor retains the freehold reversion in the property and it is for him to indicate what he is willing to grant and upon what terms. On the creation of a mortgage the mortgage deed is drafted and engrossed by the mortgagee's solicitor, but at the mortgagor's expense.

2.　Form of deed

As an aspect of the purchaser's duty to prepare the conveyance he can, if he wishes, call for a transfer to his nominee. He may also within limits insist on taking separate conveyances of different parts of the land and apportioning the purchase price between them[16]. The nature and form of the conveyance are for the purchaser, or rather his solicitor, to decide, and this is very much a matter of the draftsman's individual preference. The deed should give effect to the contract, and it is clearly advisable to have that document and the answers to preliminary inquiries (for these might amplify the contract) before him

---

12　Often on sales of registered land the document forwarded as the draft, if approved as drawn, will be executed by the vendor. In some areas where a local protocol operates (eg the Isle of Wight) a draft conveyance or transfer is submitted by the *vendor's* solicitor along with the draft contract. This is not intended to prejudice the right of the purchaser's solicitor to submit his own draft – a right which this author would almost certainly prefer to exercise.

13　For a case where the deed was, quite properly in the circumstances, engrossed by the vendor's solicitor for execution by the vendor in order to effect a unilateral completion, see *Tudor v Hamid* [1988] 1 EGLR 251, CA, p 415, ante.

14　See SCS 4.1.2.

15　See p 372, ante.

16　*Bushwall Properties Ltd v Vortex Properties Ltd* [1975] 2 All ER 214 at 222, per Oliver J, citing 1 Dart, 461; revsd on other grounds [1976] 2 All ER 283, CA.

when drafting the deed. The fact that the draft is approved on behalf of the vendor should not be used as an excuse for sloppy draftsmanship.

The drafting of a conveyance relating to the average dwelling-house presents no difficulties, though even here attention must always be paid to the description of the property. Drafting a lease or a conveyance creating covenants, granting easements, or involving some complicated commercial transaction, may not be so straightforward. In every situation the draftsman must ensure that the document gives full effect to his client's rights, as governed by the contract, and in a way most beneficial to him, especially in relation to fiscal matters. In practice constant use is made of the many standard conveyancing precedents, though the very plethora of these may tend towards his undoing. Whenever a precedent is adopted, care must be exercised to ensure that all aspects of the transaction in question are provided for, otherwise the precedent must be suitably adapted. At least one precedent book warns of the dangers of using in the same draft bits from different collections of precedents[17]. On a transfer of registered land use of the prescribed forms is mandatory[18], which eases the draftsman's task greatly. Necessary additions are permitted. Leases and charges of registered land commonly follow the form adopted in unregistered conveyancing. A call for the standardisation of leases and mortgages was made by the Royal Commission on Legal Services[19].

The advent of computerised conveyancing systems has revolutionised conveyancing procedures, with resultant and welcome savings in time and costs. Yet the benefits of modern technology, though clearly substantial, should not be overrated. Word processors and databases need sensible handling. Despite facilities to make 'one-off' amendments to standard documents stored in a system's memory, the ease with which it is possible to obtain an attractively produced document ready for execution may well increase the temptation to utilise the closest suitable precedent, without ensuring that it really meets the needs of the transaction in question. Practitioners' misuse of existing precedent books bears witness to their general reluctance to engage in adaptation exercises. These systems are alleged to take all 'the donkey work' out of drafting[20]. True though this may be, is it in the long-term interests of the legal profession? They could well give birth to a generation of conveyancers so dependent on a word-processor that they are incapable of undertaking an original piece of drafting.

Indeed the standard of legal draftsmanship has been in decline for several years, perhaps accelerated by the spread of land registration. A few examples will suffice. In *Akerib v Booth Ltd*[1] Danckwerts LJ spoke of a lease so inartistically drawn as to be calculated to bring tears to the eyes of any competent equity draftsman. A correspondent to a legal journal complained about a draft lease of a snack bar which prohibited the tenant from keeping any food on the

---

17 1 Prideaux's Precedents, 21. See generally pp 11–22 on drafting hints.
18 LRR 1925, rr 98, 114; p 474, ante.
19 Report, Vol 1, Annex 21.1, paras 13, 14.
20 By a contributor to *Lawbase Magazine*, p 8, published by Oyez Longman in 1984 in conjunction with the launch of their Lawbase Residential Conveyancing System.
1 [1961] 1 All ER 380 at 383, CA.

premises[2]! And finally, the original author recently encountered a case where
on the grant of a long lease of a house the solicitor used as his precedent the
lease of the adjacent property which the lessor had granted 40 years previously.
Yet no account was taken of the changed circumstances since then. In
consequence the later lease, whilst reserving a yearly rent of £20, merely
required the lessee to maintain on the land a house of the clear annual letting
value of £18 (the figure specified in the earlier deed). How many more glaring
mistakes and crass errors of this nature lie undetected in conveyancing
documents?

3.   Vendor's right to submit draft

Section 48(1) of the Law of Property Act 1925 entitles a vendor to furnish a
form of instrument from which the draft is to be prepared and to charge a
reasonable fee therefor, provided the right has been reserved in the contract.
Advantage is frequently taken of this power on the grant of a lease or
underlease, or on the sale of land forming part of a housing estate. In these
situations the contract usually provides that the conveyance or lease shall be
in the form of the draft annexed to the contract. The purchaser's solicitor
needs to check the proposed draft very carefully and make any objections to
its form before exchange of contracts. Experience suggests that the document
supplied is often drafted principally with the developer in mind. Covenants
may be couched in language too wide for the protection of his legitimate
interests, and provisions which may relate to the majority of plots on the estate
may not be applicable to the purchaser's particular plot[3]. It is on the
development of building estates that conveyancing practice may be seen at its
worst. Many (though by no means all) developers' solicitors adopt a take-it-or-
leave-it attitude without permitting any meaningful variations to their hallowed
drafts or attempting to justify their form. Regrettably some practitioners, faced
with this prevalent practice and pressed by clients who are not interested in
legal niceties or trivia, bow to the inevitable and meekly accept the forms
supplied. Neither attitude has anything to commend it, and such practices do
nothing to enhance the conveyancer's reputation.

4.   Approval of draft by vendor

Since the form of the conveyance is for the purchaser to determine, it is idle
for the vendor to raise objections as to form save where it involves a matter of
substance affecting him[4]. The rule has sensibly been expressed as follows[5]: no
alterations should be made except those necessary to correct clerical errors,

2   (1984) 81 LS Gaz 2821.
3   Eg clauses purporting to reserve rights in respect of overhanging eaves and protruding
    foundations will be irrelevant to a corner plot not overhung by any adjacent house.
4   See *Cooper v Cartwright* (1860) John 679 at 685, per Page-Wood V-C.
5   1 Prideaux's Precedents, 21, adding that to pass a draft without alteration is not a sign of
    weakness, rather the reverse, which is salutary advice.

to protect one's own client and to make the draft work. Basically the vendor's solicitor needs to ensure that the draft does not give the purchaser more, nor the vendor less, than his entitlement under the contract. Technically it is not the vendor's responsibility to alter the draft in favour of the purchaser where, for instance, it omits some matter contained in the contract for the purchaser's own benefit, for he is entitled to assume that the purchaser has decided to rely on his contractual rights[6]. In reality the omission is more likely to be the result of an oversight, and it is worthwhile remembering that a failure to correct the position before completion may give rise to a subsequent claim against the vendor for rectification of the conveyance.

C Wording of conveyancing documents

Lawyers are conservative creatures and of all lawyers conveyancers tend to be the most conservative. Nowhere is this most displayed than in legal documents. They are accused of being so wrapped up in the language of their profession that they have eschewed any kind of prose style that might commend itself to those outside the magic circle of the law. In April 1984, the National Consumer Council launched a savage attack on legal draftsmanship. It published guidelines on writing legal documents, specifically for lawyers. The Council claimed that lawyers have an almost universal reputation for mystifying their work. The wordy, repetitive phrases of today's legal documents still conjure up 'a musty Dickensian image and make them unintelligible to most non-lawyers', the people who are the consumers[7]. Strong criticism, some of it quite justified. But will the profession respond[8]? The spread of registration of title and the increased use of relatively simple forms have already spurred some practitioners to abandon traditional methods of drafting, and to prepare deeds more meaningful to those executing them. The past decade has witnessed the publication of a new set of forms, Practical Conveyancing Precedents[9], the wording of which is claimed to make the documents clearer, more straight-forward, and easier to read and understand. Similarly the publishers of the fifth edition of the well used Encyclopaedia of Forms and Precedents are aiming to eliminate archaic language or at least reduce it whenever possible, so as to make their precedents more readily understandable by practitioner and client alike. Nevertheless, the forms still betray a predominantly conservative approach to drafting.

6 Subject to the doctrine of merger (see p 468, ante) but in the situation under consideration this would not appear to be the vendor's concern.
7 *Plain English for Lawyers*, p 4; (1984) 81 LS Gaz 2131. See also *Plain Words for Consumers* from the same stable. Cf the equally critical comments of Megarry J in *Cresswell v Potter* [1978] 1 WLR 255n at 260.
8 It is noteworthy that the Standard Conditions of Sale consciously seek to use plain English, in a praiseworthy attempt to make the contract of sale more readily comprehensible.
9 Published by Longman Group. Their Lawbase Residential Conveyancing package (note 20, supra) utilises these precedents, which will probably become more widely accepted than the seldom seen revolutionary precedents from Parker's, *Modern Conveyancing Precedents* (1964).

Every draftsman is free to choose his own form and draft it according to his own particular tastes. Should he be of the old school of thought, he ought at least to consider whether many of his time-hallowed expressions are worth preserving, such as: 'messuage or dwellinghouse', 'delineated and described', 'covenants conditions and agreements'. The slavish adoption of a precedent form, even one of ancient lineage, without considering whether its language accords with modern conditions, must be deprecated. Whilst it may be important to indicate whether a right of way is to be vehicular, or on foot, or both, it is quite absurd today to grant a right of way 'with or without horses, carts, carriages'[10]. It would be a step in the right direction if a consistent attempt were made to introduce punctuation. Its absence can be as frustrating for the conveyancer as it is incomprehensible to his client. Yet property lawyers, unlike their commercial brothers, are generally loath to punctuate forms. Significantly, the policy of the new edition of the Encyclopaedia continues to be one of non-punctuation[11], which many would perhaps see as a retrograde decision. The practitioner is free to add his own punctuation to suit his preference. Yet is this always wise, bearing in mind that he is not the author of the form, the meaning of which can be so easily varied according to what punctuation is used and where? For the draftsman who still adheres to the traditional form and language of yesterday, there exists scope for improvement in the drafting of documents to make them more intelligible to his clients. On the other hand his more adventurous colleague, eager to embrace the modern approach, must resist the temptation to sacrifice certainty on the altar of simplicity.

D   Construction of deeds

Not only is the conveyancer required to draft deeds, he is also called upon to interpret documents drafted by others. A brief introduction to the 'basic rules of construction' is therefore necessary[12]. Particular problems of construction relating to some specific matters are also considered in the next chapter[13].

1.   The intention of the parties

When construing a deed the aim is always to discover the intention of the parties as expressed in the document. The question to be asked is: 'What is the meaning of what the parties have said?' not 'What did the parties mean to

10   1 Prideaux's Precedents, 433, Form 6.
11   4 Ency F & P, 16 (publishers' note). It is used freely in Prideaux's Precedents and to a variable extent in *Practical Conveyancing Precedents*, but not in Hallett, *Conveyancing Precedents* (1965). And see Parker, op cit, p 7, who maintains, quite rightly, that punctuation in a disguised form has long been resorted to by the use of capital letters to introduce new sentences.
12   For a fuller understanding of this important topic, see *Norton on Deeds* (2nd edn); Odgers, *The Construction of Deeds and Statutes* (5th edn).
13   Pages 534–537, post (parcels clause).

say?'[14]. For the purposes of interpretation the parties' expressed meaning is equivalent to their intention[15], and the court will give effect to that meaning, rather than to their presumed intention, even though to do so may defeat their real intention or produce some consequence which they did not have in mind[16]. In arriving at the true meaning the deed must be construed as a whole. As was said in an ancient case, every part of a deed must be compared with the other and one entire sense made thereof[17]. When a deed contains two irreconcilable provisions, the court adopts the earlier clause or expression. This 'absolutely last resort in construction' was applied in *Joyce v Barker Bros (Builders) Ltd*[18]. Here Vinelott J construed a conveyance of a house to spouses 'as beneficial joint tenants in common in equal shares' as creating a beneficial joint tenancy by striking out the last five plainly inconsistent words from the declaration. Problems of interpretation also arise from the use of standard form printed documents which are imperfectly adapted to meet the requirements of the particular transaction. The aim of the court in such cases is to give effect to the document's basic intent, and any clause inconsistent therewith is disregarded[19].

2.   Ordinary meaning

The rule of construction governing the meaning of the words used was stated in *Grey v Pearson*[20] in these terms. The grammatical and ordinary sense of the words is to be adhered to unless that would lead to some absurdity, or some repugnance or inconsistency with the rest of the deed, in which case the grammatical and ordinary meaning may be modified so as to avoid that result. Prima facie the ordinary meaning of a word is that which the ordinary usage of society applies to it, what may be said to be the popular sense. This meaning will be displaced if the context shows that the words were not intended to be used in their ordinary meaning. Thus a reservation of 'minerals' prima facie includes every substance which can be got from underneath the surface of the earth for profit; but when the word appears in a reservation of 'mines and minerals, sand, quarries of stone, brickearth and gravel pits', there is a clear indication that the draftsman was using 'minerals' in a special limited sense[1].

---

14   Norton, op cit, p 50.
15   *Shore v Wilson* (1842) 9 Cl & Fin 355 at 525, HL, per Coleridge J.
16   See eg *Re Hopkin's Lease, Caerphilly Concrete Products Ltd v Owen* [1972] 1 All ER 248, CA (perpetually renewable lease); distinguished in *Marjorie Burnett Ltd v Barclay* (1980) 125 Sol Jo 199.
17   *Throckmerton v Tracy* (1555) 1 Plowd 145 at 161, per Staunford J.
18   (1980) 40 P & CR 512 at 514, applying *Slingsby's Case* (1587) 5 Co Rep 18b, but not followed in *Martin v Martin* (1987) 54 P & CR 238. It is difficult to conceive how conveyancers can still be exhibiting such elementary confusion more than 60 years after the passing of LPA 1925.
19   *Avon Holdings Ltd v Scandix Designs Inc* (2 September 1981, CA Unbound Transcript 250) (covenant by corporate tenant to occupy flat as residence treated as surplusage).
20   (1857) 6 HL Cas 61 at 106, per Lord Wensleydale.
1   See *Hext v Gill* (1872) 7 Ch App 699 at 712, per Mellish LJ; *Waring v Foden* [1932] 1 Ch 276, CA (sand and gravel excluded); *Earl of Lonsdale v A-G* [1982] 3 All ER 579 (oil and natural gas not included).

Section 61 of the Law of Property Act 1925 provides that (unless the context otherwise requires) in deeds, contracts and other instruments executed after 31 December 1925, 'month' means calendar month[2], 'person' includes a corporation, the singular includes the plural and the masculine the feminine, and vice versa.

3.   Admissibility of extrinsic evidence

The general rule is that extrinsic evidence is not admissible to add to, vary or contradict the terms of a deed. Its construction cannot be controlled by the parties' previous negotiations[3], or the terms either of the contract[4] or the draft conveyance. In *City and Westminster Properties (1934) Ltd v Mudd*[5] the question arose whether a clause in a lease which restricted the use of the demised premises to showrooms, workrooms and offices only, prevented the lessee using them as a residence. Harman J held that he could not call in aid the fact that express words of prohibition as to residence had originally appeared in the draft, but were later deleted and omitted from the lease as executed. The court is also not entitled to take account of the parties' conduct subsequent to their execution of the deed[6], except, it seems, in cases involving a disputed title to land.

The rule excluding extrinsic evidence is subject to several well recognised exceptions. First, it is allowed to explain the meaning of the words used or to resolve a latent ambiguity in the deed. Thus to determine the meaning of 'repair' in a repairing covenant it is necessary to have regard to the age, character and condition of the building at the time of the lease[7]. Secondly, it is permissible to look at the surrounding circumstances existing at the time of the deed in order to place the court as far as possible in the position of the parties[8]. So, the court can receive evidence of the factual background known to the parties at or before the time of execution. This exception is sometimes described as construing a document in or against its 'factual matrix'. However, the dangers of using this expression were stressed in *Plumb Bros v Dolmac (Agriculture) Ltd*[9], because it suggests the need to inquire, improperly, into the parties' subjective intentions. Frequent recourse is had to this exception when construing the grant of an easement or interpreting the scope of covenants.

---

2   Prima facie at common law 'month' meant lunar month: *Phipps & Co (Northampton and Towcester Breweries) Ltd v Rogers* [1925] 1 KB 14, CA.
3   *Prenn v Simmonds* [1971] 3 All ER 237, HL.
4   *Doe d Norton v Webster* (1840) 12 Ad & El 442 (conveyance of house with 'appurtenances' held to include garden, even though conditions of sale expressly excluded it).
5   [1959] Ch 129, [1958] 2 All ER 733; *Rabin v Gerson Berger Association Ltd* [1986] 1 All ER 374, CA (counsel's opinion inadmissible).
6   *L Schuler AG v Wickman Machine Tool Sales Ltd* [1974] AC 235, [1973] 2 All ER 39, HL. See p 537, post.
7   *Brew Bros Ltd v Snax (Ross) Ltd* [1970] 1 QB 612, [1970] 1 All ER 587, CA.
8   *Baird v Fortune* (1861) 5 LT 2, HL; *Roe v Siddons* (1888) 22 QBD 224 at 233, CA, per Lord Esher MR.
9   (1984) 271 EG 373 at 374, CA, per May LJ.

Thus the nature of the demised premises is a very relevant consideration in the construction of a user clause affecting the property[10].

Finally, extrinsic evidence is always admissible to show that a deed is not binding on the ground of, for example, fraud, or that on account of some mutual mistake the deed does not record the real contract between the parties. The introduction of extrinsic evidence in such circumstances does not really constitute an exception because it is not adduced for the purposes of construing the deed. Again, evidence may be given of a collateral contract not to enforce a certain clause in the deed. This was the basis of the actual decision in *Mudd's* case[11], where the lessor's action for forfeiture of the lease for breach of covenant was dismissed on the ground that the lessee had executed the lease in reliance on a promise by the lessor's agent that the lessor would not enforce the covenant as to user against him personally.

4. Miscellaneous rules

A passing mention must also be made of a few specific rules of interpretation that the courts have recourse to when resolving problems of construction.

(a) Contra proferentem
Where a document is ambiguous and capable of two possible interpretations, the court will resort to the contra proferentem principle. The construction that is more against the interests of the party proferring the document will be preferred[12]. This rule, described as a last ditch argument[13], is sometimes utilised in disputes as to the effect of an exception or reservation in a conveyance.

(b) Expressum facit cessare tacitum
An express provision automatically ousts the implication of any provision to like effect. For example, at common law the use of the word 'demise' in a lease of land automatically implied in the lessee's favour a covenant for quiet enjoyment, but where the lessor enters into an express covenant for quiet enjoyment there is no room for the implied covenant[14].

(c) Falsa demonstratio non nocet
A false description contained in a document does not normally prejudice its intended effect. Thus where land is conveyed by a composite description part of which is true and part inaccurate, then, provided the true part describes

---

10   *Levermore v Jobey* [1956] 2 All ER 362, CA; *City and Westminster Properties (1934) Ltd v Mudd* [1959] Ch 129, [1958] 2 All ER 733.
11   Ante; *Brikom Investments Ltd v Carr* [1979] QB 467, [1979] 2 All ER 753, CA.
12   *Macey v Qazi* (1987) Times, 13 January, CA; *Tudor v Hamid* [1988] 1 EGLR 251, CA.
13   *Gruhn v Balgray Investments Ltd* (1963) 185 EG 455, CA, per Harman LJ (lessor's determination clause); *St Edmundsbury and Ipswich Diocesan Board of Finance v Clark (No 2)* [1975] 1 All ER 772, CA (reservation of right of way).
14   See *Miller v Emcer Products Ltd* [1956] Ch 304 [1956] 1 All ER 237, CA.

the land with sufficient certainty, the false part will be rejected. Further consideration is given to the operation of this rule in Chapter 17.

(d) Certum est quod certum reddi potest

No draftsman should leave the interpretation of his document to inference. Nevertheless, a lack of precision or certainty in it may not necessarily defeat the document since what is capable of being rendered certain is to be treated as certain[15].

5.   Effect of recitals on construction of deed

The construction of a deed may be assisted by the recitals, ie those clauses, introduced by the word 'whereas', which explain the purpose of the deed or set out the grantor's title to make the grant. As the recitals constitute merely a subordinate part of the deed and are not even an essential part of it[16], they cannot control the operative part of the deed (ie that part which carries out the object of the instrument) if that part uses language which admits of no doubt[17]. Thus land described with certainty in the parcels clause of the conveyance cannot be cut down or extended by recitals showing that something less, or more, was intended to pass.

Where the operative part of the deed is ambiguous or doubtfully expressed, recourse may be had to the recitals to discover its true meaning. Not that the recitals must be looked at to the exclusion of other subsidiary parts of the deed, since any question of construction renders it essential to refer to the whole of the instrument; but it is more likely that the recitals leading up to the operative part will furnish the key to its true construction than the other subsidiary clauses[18]. For example, the interpretation of a conveyance of land described in general terms may be assisted by a recital expressed in specific terms which reveals that only certain specific property was intended to pass[19]. It is also permissible to resort to the recitals to resolve some uncertainty or ambiguity arising in a covenant. If both the recitals and the operative part are clear and unambiguous, but they are inconsistent with each other, the operative part prevails[20].

6.   Correction of errors

Since a deed is construed to give effect to the parties' expressed intentions as appearing from the whole of its contents, the court will make any corrections

---

15   See *Owen v Thomas* (1834) 3 My & K 353; *Shardlow v Cotterell* (1881) 20 Ch D 90, CA.

16   *Earl of Bath and Earl of Montague's Case* (1693) 3 Cas in Ch 55 at 101, per Holt CJ.

17   *Bailey v Lloyd* (1829) 5 Russ 330 at 344, per Leach MR; see also Lord Esher MR's three rules enunciated in *Re Moon, ex p Dawes* (1886) 17 QBD 275 at 286, CA.

18   *Orr v Mitchell* [1893] AC 238 at 254, HL, per Lord Macnaghten.

19   *Jenner v Jenner* (1866) LR 1 Eq 361; see also p 536, post.

20   See the third of Lord Esher's rules propounded in *Re Moon, ex p Dawes*, note 17, ante.

which a perusal of the document shows to be necessary[1]. Incorrect grammar and spelling may be corrected, repugnant words rejected and words that have obviously been left in by mistake ignored. Words omitted by inadvertence may even be supplied, but not where this will alter the legal effect of the deed[2]. In short, the normal run-of-the-mill typographical error which is frequently encountered in practice will not be allowed to defeat the intentions of the parties[3]. If through some mutual mistake the deed fails to carry out the contract between the parties, then the proper course is to execute a confirmatory deed. Should there be a dispute between them, rectification proceedings[4] will be necessary.

1   See *Gwyn v Neath Canal Co* (1868) LR 3 Exch 209 at 215, per Kelly CB.
2   *Re Ethel and Mitchells and Butlers' Contract* [1901] 1 Ch 945 ('in fee' not read as 'in fee simple' so that only life estate passed).
3   The original author recalls a case where a conveyance recited a deed of 30 September 1961 and contained an acknowledgement by the vendor for production of 'the said conveyance' of 30 September 1962. The mortgagee's solicitor insisted on the execution of a separate acknowledgement for the deed of 1961. This would appear to have been completely unnecessary. There was clearly a typing error and the reference to 'the said conveyance' showed that the parties intended the acknowledgement to relate to the deed previously referred to. No possibility of doubt existed as to which 'said' deed was intended, since the convenyance did not refer to any other deeds.
4   See Ch 24, post.

Chapter 17

Form and contents of conveyance

A Introduction

A conveyance is divided into a number of constituent parts as follows:
1. the commencement, including the date and the parties;
2. the recitals;
3. the testatum, commencing with the words 'Now this deed witnesseth' and ending with 'hereby conveys unto the purchaser';
4. the parcels;
5. the habendum[1] ('To hold' etc);
6. the testimonium, linking the contents of the deed with the signatures.

Depending on the nature of the transaction, other clauses may have to be added after the habendum, such as a declaration of the parties' beneficial entitlement, or covenants. An illustration of a simple conveyance drafted in the traditional style is given below.

> THIS CONVEYANCE is made the 21st day of May 1992[2] BETWEEN ABEL SMALL of 'Fairhaven' Mead Road Oadby in the County of Leicester (hereinafter called 'the vendor') of the one part and DAVID LARGE of 32 Church Lane in the City of Leicester (hereinafter called 'the purchaser') of the other part
> WHEREAS the vendor is seised of the property hereinafter described for an estate in fee simple in possession subject as hereinafter appears and has agreed with the purchaser for the sale to him of the said property for a like estate at the price of £50,000
> NOW THIS DEED WITNESSETH as follows:
> 1. In pursuance of the said agreement and in consideration of the sum of £50,000 paid to the vendor by the purchaser (the receipt whereof the vendor hereby acknowledges) the vendor as beneficial owner HEREBY CONVEYS unto the purchaser ALL THAT [parcels] TO HOLD unto the

---

1 That part of the deed which precedes the habendum is technically called 'the premises', an expression which has come to mean in popular language simply land or buildings. See *Gardiner v Sevenoaks RDC* [1950] 2 All ER 84 at 85, per Lord Goddard CJ.
2 Dates and other figures (save for house numbers) are often expressed in words, not numbers.

purchaser in fee simple[3] SUBJECT to the covenants on the part of the grantee and the conditions contained in the Conveyance[4]

2. With the object and intent of affording to the vendor a full and sufficient indemnity in respect of the said covenants and conditions but not further or otherwise the purchaser hereby covenants with the vendor to observe and perform the said covenants and conditions and to indemnify the vendor against all actions claims demands and liability in respect thereof

IN WITNESS whereof the parties hereto have hereunto set their respective hands and seals the day and year first before written

SIGNED, etc.

By way of comparison a transfer of the same land would, if the title were registered, be in the following form.

H. M. LAND REGISTRY

LAND REGISTRATION ACTS 1925 TO 1986

TRANSFER OF WHOLE

County and District: Leicester

Title Number: LT 12345

Property: 'Fairhaven', Mead Road, Oadby

Date: 21 May 1992

1. In consideration of fifty thousand pounds (£50,000) the receipt whereof is hereby acknowledged I, ABEL SMALL, of 'Fairhaven', Mead Road, Oadby, Bank Manager[5], as beneficial owner hereby transfer to DAVID LARGE of 32 Church Lane, Leicester, Schoolmaster, the land comprised in the title above mentioned

2. [Covenant for indemnity as before, but suitably amended[6]]

Signed, etc.

This chapter looks principally at the contents of a conveyance of freehold land, and of a transfer of registered land. From time to time reference will also be made to other types of documents which operate to vest a legal estate in the grantee.

---

3 Compare the modern rendering of this clause adopted in *Practical Conveyancing Precedents* (p 510, ante), which reads 'As they agreed and in consideration of the sum of £— which the Purchaser paid to the Vendor (and which the Vendor has received) the Vendor as beneficial owner conveys unto the Purchaser All that — To hold it in fee simple.'

4 Sometimes there is added, unnecessarily, a qualifying phrase, such as, 'so far as the same are still subsisting and are capable of being enforced'. Contrast 19 Ency F & P, 884, note 12. The deed creating the covenants would usually have already been mentioned, with its date and the parties, perhaps in the parcels clause. For ease of subsequent reference it would be termed simply, 'the Conveyance'.

5 As to the need to add the descriptions of the parties, see p 518, post.

6 By referring to 'the covenants and conditions referred to in entry no — of the charges register of the above mentioned title'.

B Description of document

It is customary today to describe a document affecting unregistered land according to the nature of the transaction effected, eg as a conveyance, lease, assignment, assent, deed of appointment, mortgage, and so on, or it may simply be styled 'This deed'[7]. At one time a deed made between two or more parties (a deed inter partes) was termed an indenture, ie a document that had been indented by cutting the top of the first page or sheet in a wavy line. In contrast a deed poll, ie document made by one party only, was so named because the top was polled or shaved. A deed between parties now has the effect of an indenture though not indented or expressed to be an indenture[8]. A transfer of registered land bears no descriptive title, but is required by way of a heading to contain a reference to the county and district (or London borough), the title number and the property. It has been judicially stated that a registered land transfer is in form analogous to a deed poll, rather than a deed inter partes[9].

C Date of deed

The dating of deeds was discussed in Chapter 14[10], where we saw that though a deed should in strict legal theory be dated with the date of its delivery, in practice it is the date of actual completion that normally appears in the document.

D Parties

1. Mode of description

(a) Name, address and occupation

The surname and Christian or forenames should appear in full. Where the name of a party differs from that given in an earlier deed, it is advisable to draw attention to the discrepancy by means of a simple statement when reciting the earlier deed that the vendor was therein called by such and such a name. The need to ensure accuracy when naming the parties cannot be too highly stressed. A wrong name or spelling may give rise to subsequent inconvenience, even litigation. Cases are known where the purchaser's names as disclosed in the conveyance to him differ significantly from those given in the subsequent mortgage by him[11], which is quite inexcusable. In particular it should be

---

7   LPA 1925, s 57. To be valid, the document must make clear on its face that it is intended to be a deed: Law of Property (Miscellaneous Provisions) Act 1989, s 1(2)(a).
8   LPA 1925, s 56(2).
9   *Chelsea and Walham Green Building Society v Armstrong* [1951] Ch 853 at 857–58, [1951] 2 All ER 250 at 252–53, per Vaisey J; p 478, ante.
10 Page 454, ante.
11 See *Standard Property Investment plc v British Plastic Federation* (1987) 53 P & CR 25 (house conveyed to RC and HC, whilst mortgage by them in the names of RDC and HCC).

remembered that the name in the conveyance will, prima facie, be taken as the estate owner's proper name for the registration of land charges[12].

The address of every executing party is also given in the deed. However, the once standard practice of adding every party's occupation (or status, if a woman) is now virtually obsolete, except in registered land dispositions. Inclusion of the transferee's description continues to be necessary since the proprietorship register is required to contain this information[13], though sometimes it can be found omitted.

On the grant of a lease it is usual to incorporate within the parties' description words of definition to include the reversioner for the time being and the lessee's successors in title[14].

(b) Parts of a deed

In a deed inter partes the various persons who join therein for differing purposes or representing different interests are expressed to be of a separate part – the vendor 'of the one part' and the purchaser 'of the other part'. Often in modern documents the different parts are signified simply by (1), (2), etc. The party of the 'one' (or 'first', 'second', as the case may be) part may comprise two or more persons, eg joint tenants, who are considered as one person in law as regards estate ownership. A person who executes a deed in more than one capacity (eg a vendor life tenant who is also a trustee of the settlement) will be a party to the conveyance in more than one part.

The form of a registered land transfer differs from that of a conveyance. There is no reference to the parties at the beginning of the document; they are mentioned as required. It is also expressed in the first person: 'I XY of — hereby transfer'. This personal element is readily abandoned whenever the transfer contains additional clauses, in which XY usually appears as 'the transferor', or 'the vendor'.

2. Who are necessary parties

In a straightforward case the only parties are the vendor and the purchaser, lessor and lessee, mortgagor and mortgagee. There may only be a single party to the document, as where an executor assents to the vesting of land in himself as sole beneficiary. The circumstances of a particular case may render it necessary to join other people as parties in order to give effect to the transaction between the two main parties. For example, the existence of a mortgage which is not to be redeemed on completion requires the mortgagee to join in the deed to release the land conveyed from the charge, if the purchaser is to take free from it. Two other situations require separate discussion.

---

12 See p 395, ante.
13 LRR 1925, r 6.
14 As to the effect of such a definition on the transfer of the benefit of covenants, see *Griffith v Pelton* [1958] Ch 205, [1957] 3 All ER 75, CA (option to purchase); *Coastplace Ltd v Hartley* [1987] QB 948 (covenant of surety). But see *Kumar v Dunning* [1989] QB 193, [1987] 2 All ER 801 at 812, CA, per Browne-Wilkinson V-C.

(a) Equitable owners

Any equitable owner whose interest will not be overreached by the conveyance must join in to vest his interest in the purchaser. Seldom is this likely to occur. A vendor who is not beneficially entitled in equity usually has power by his conveyance to overreach equitable interests because he is selling under the Settled Land Act 1925, or under his statutory power as personal representative or mortgagee, or, in the case of joint vendors, in execution of a trust for sale. In other cases the purchaser can require the vendor to overreach the equitable interest by means of an ad hoc settlement or trust for sale[15]. Yet it may be simpler in some instances, eg where A holds in trust for B, for the purchaser to accept a conveyance made with B's concurrence rather than insist on the cumbersome overreaching procedure.

(b) Purchaser's nominee

In the absence of any agreement to the contrary a purchaser can require the vendor to convey the land to such person or persons as he may direct, save where this would be to the prejudice of the vendor because, for example, the purchaser has agreed to enter into personal covenants and the personality of the covenantor is fundamental to the transaction[16].

On a sub-sale, the conveyance is usually made direct to the sub-purchaser, so as to save the expense of a second conveyance and (where applicable) double stamp duty[17]. The original purchaser is a necessary party to this deed if (i) he has resold at a higher price, in which case he must join in to acknowledge receipt of the increase, or (ii) he has contracted to assume some personal liability and the vendor is unwilling to accept the sub-purchaser as covenantor.

E   Recitals

Recitals, though not a necessary part of any deed, are commonly inserted in conveyances. They are introduced by the word 'whereas', and fall into two main classes: (1) narrative recitals which set out the vendor's or grantor's title to make the assurance; and (2) introductory recitals which explain the purpose or operation of the deed. They are also used to state matters of fact, which by virtue of various statutory provisions[18] are to be accepted as evidence of the matter stated. It is not considered good draftsmanship to recite the contract as a document[19], though it is the practice to refer to the fact of agreement. Frequently the only recital in a straightforward conveyance of a dwelling house is the one appearing in the precedent on page 516. There are, however, many transactions apart from sales where it is desirable to incorporate appropriate recitals, as a reference to any standard precedent book will show. A deed

---

15   SLA 1925, s 21; LPA 1925, ss 2(2), 42(1), p 176, ante.
16   For the position on sale of leaseholds, see *Curtis Moffat Ltd v Wheeler* [1929] 2 Ch 224.
17   See p 466, ante.
18   Page 523, post.
19   1 Dart, 475.

expressed to be supplemental to a previous instrument is read and has effect as if it contained a full recital of the previous deed[20].

1. Narrative recitals

The general rule as to narrative recitals is that they should be limited to such matters as are necessary to explain the operative part of the conveyance[1]. A recital of the steps by which the vendor became entitled to convey is generally unnecessary. A simple recital of the vendor's seisin suffices. Recitals are commonly encountered on a sale by personal representatives. Thus a conveyance by executors often recites: (i) the seisin of the testator at the time of his death; (ii) the date of his will, his death and the grant of probate to the vendors; (iii) a statement that no previous assent or conveyance has been given[2]; and (iv) the agreement for sale[3].

Recitals are not generally incorporated in the grant of a lease. The practice on the assignment of a lease varies. Traditionally it has been the custom to recite the lease (including a verbatim description of the demised property taken from the lease), then the assignment to the vendor. Any intervening dealings are covered by a blanket recital such as: 'by virtue of divers mesne assurances acts in the law and events and ultimately by —' followed by the vendor's assignment. Some draftsmen, preferring not to bring the history on the title, simply recite that the vendor is possessed of the property assigned for a legal estate for the residue of the term granted by the lease[4].

The case of *Re Duce and Boots Cash Chemists (Southern) Ltd's Contract*[5] reveals the dangers of inserting recitals in an assent. It is safer to adopt a general practice of not having recitals in an assent unless absolutely necessary[6]. A precedent of an assent is given on p 320.

The once familiar recital of the conveyance to the vendor has been superseded by the commonplace recital of seisin, the form of which differs according to the draftsman. The various precedent books do not agree on any uniform wording, though the import is basically the same in each case. A typical recital where the land is not conveyed free from incumbrances may read:

> WHEREAS the vendor is seised of the property hereinafter described for an estate in fee simple in possession subject as hereinafter mentioned but otherwise free from incumbrances and ...

Some draftsmen feel that if the vendor is the beneficial owner, the recital should say so by adding words such as 'for his own sole benefit'[7]; others prefer

20 LPA 1925, s 58.
 1 18 Ency F & P, 288.
 2 For the purposes of AEA 1925, s 36(5), p 323, ante.
 3 19 Ency F & P, 1075, Form 27, where the statement of no prior assent appears in the operative part of the deed.
 4 Compare the precedent in Hallet, 321, Form 81, with 19 Ency F & P, 1464, Form 8:A:3.
 5 [1937] Ch 642, [1937] 3 All ER 788.
 6 See 8 Ency F & P, 772, Form 2:12 (assent of property subject to mortgage where mortgagee takes new covenant from beneficiary and releases testator's estate).
 7 Hallett, 192, Form 2.

a recital that the vendor is 'the estate owner in respect of the fee simple in possession of the property hereinafter described'. The view has been expressed[8] that a vendor's solicitor should not permit his client to execute a conveyance containing an unqualified recital of seisin free from incumbrances, if he holds subject to an interest the existence of which would mean that a vendor selling under an open contract could not show good title to an unincumbered fee simple estate. The reason for this is that an unqualified recital may operate as an absolute warranty of title wider than that imported by the usual covenants for title. It may even be that a purchaser has no right to insist on the inclusion of the phrase 'but otherwise free from incumbrances', for this conflicts with the usual contractual provision[9] that the land is sold subject to any easements, liabilities, and other rights affecting the same. A vendor who contracts to convey an unincumbered fee simple cannot object to an unqualified recital.

2.   Introductory recitals

Besides indicating the intended operation of the conveyance or other instrument, for example, to give effect to an agreement for sale or for the grant of a right of way, introductory recitals also explain the reason for joining the various parties. A typical illustration arises where a mortgagee joins in a conveyance of land by the mortgagor. After reciting seisin of the vendor subject to the mortgage, and the state of the mortgage debt, there is usually a recital to this effect:

> The vendor has agreed with the purchaser for the sale to him of the said property at the price of £— and it has been agreed that the sum of £— part of the said purchase price shall be paid to the mortgagee in part discharge of the principal money owing to him under the mortgage and that the mortgagee shall join in these presents in manner hereinafter appearing.

3.   Recitals in land registry transfers

Recitals in a registered land transfer are generally regarded as unnecessary and inconsistent with the principles on which the register is maintained[10]. They are missing from the statutory forms set out in the Schedule to the Land Registration Rules 1925. Certainly narrative recitals giving details of the devolution of the title have no place in a transfer, but in as much as the general law governing the effect of recitals applies equally to those contained in a registered land transfer, it may be desirable to incorporate a recital for some collateral purpose[11]. For instance, they may be used to explain why a particular party executed the transfer or to show that, although no monetary consideration passed between the parties, the transfer was not a deed of gift.

---

8   Emmet, para 12.006.
9   SCS 3.1–3.5, p 155, ante.
10   Ruoff, *Concise Land Registration Practice* (2nd edn), p 86; Hallett, 1318, note 1.
11   3 K & E, 125–26, adopting much the same view as that originally expressed by Potter, 79–81. For precedents incorporating recitals, see 3 K & E, 420, 428, Forms XVI and XXII.

Where recitals are incorporated the parties should be set out after the usual headings as in an ordinary conveyance.

4. Effect of recitals

(a) Recitals as evidence
By virtue of the Law of Property Act 1925, s 47(6), recitals contained in any instrument 20 years old at the date of the contract are to be taken as sufficient evidence of the truth of the facts recited, unless proved to be inaccurate. An example of the operation of this provision occurred in *Re Marsh and Earl Granville*[12]. Here a recital that trustees had caused property to be put up for sale 'in pursuance of the trust for sale conferred on them' was held to be sufficient evidence of the non-exercise of a power of revocation which the settlor had reserved. A recital in a deed of appointment of a new trustee of land as to the reasons for a vacancy (eg that a trustee refuses or is unfit to act) must be accepted by a purchaser as conclusive evidence of the matter stated[13].

(b) Estoppel
A recital in a deed may operate by way of estoppel against (but not for) the party making it in any action upon that deed but not in any collateral proceedings[14]. This is a doctrine whereby falsehood is made to have the effect of truth and the courts are not disposed to extend the rule[15]. The estoppel binds the party making the statement and his successors in title and operates in favour of the other party and his successors[16]. Where A purports to convey land to which he has no title to B in a conveyance containing a recital of A's alleged seisin, A is estopped from denying that he had the title; if A subsequently acquires title to that land, the estoppel is said to be fed and the estate automatically vests in B without the need for any confirmatory conveyance from A[17]. The estoppel binds any person, even a purchaser for value without notice, to whom A conveys the land after his acquisition of a good title.

To found an estoppel there must be a recital of a particular fact[18] expressed in precise and unambiguous terms. Thus no estoppel is created by a general recital, or by one that merely infers the vendor's seisin without saying so expressly[19]. In *Heath v Crealock*[20] a recital that the vendor was 'well entitled' to

---

12 (1882) 24 Ch D 11 (decided on the Vendor and Purchaser Act 1874, s 2).
13 Trustee Act 1925, s 38; SLA 1925, s 35(3).
14 *Carter v Carter* (1857) 3 K & J 617.
15 *Onward Building Society v Smithson* [1893] 1 Ch 1 at 13–14, CA, per Lindley LJ.
16 *Palmer v Ekins* (1728) 2 Ld Raym 1550; *Poulton v Moore* [1915] 1 KB 400, CA. The benefit does not pass to a volunteer: *General Finance, Mortgage and Discount Co v Liberator Permanent Benefit Building Society* (1878) 10 Ch D 15 at 24, per Jessel MR.
17 *Poulton v Moore* [1915] 1 KB 400 at 414–15, CA, per Phillimore LJ. Even in the absence of a recital of seisin, equity will compel A to make good the conveyance to B, if A later acquires title; see pp 672–673, post.
18 *Bensely v Burden* (1830) 8 LJOS Ch 85 at 87, per Lord Lyndhurst LC.
19 *Onward Building Society v Smithson* [1893] 1 Ch 1, CA. See also *Re Distributors and Warehousing Ltd* [1986] 1 EGLR 90.
20 (1874) 10 Ch App 22; *District Bank Ltd v Webb* [1958] 1 All ER 126 ('seised in unincumbered fee simple in possession' inadequate).

certain property was held insufficient to constitute an estoppel. An estoppel may also arise from a clear and distinct averment in the operative part of a deed, despite the absence of any recital covering the point. In *Taylor Fashions Ltd v Liverpool Victoria Trustees Co Ltd*[1] a covenant in a lease referred to the tenants exercising 'their option to have granted to them' a new lease of adjacent property. Oliver J was prepared to hold that the clause estopped the lessor from asserting that the option mentioned was invalid and incapable of effective exercise through want of registration. The existence of an estoppel may always be negatived by the deed itself, for example, where the truth appears elsewhere in the instrument[2].

(c) Creation of covenant

No technical words are required to create a covenant and a recital that shows an intention that one of the parties shall do or not do a thing will operate as a covenant unless the deed expresses a contrary intention. Suppose that a deed of exchange of land by adjoining owners for the purpose of straightening a common boundary recites that one party has agreed to erect and maintain a boundary fence. In the absence of any covenant appearing in the operative part of the deed, the recital itself constitutes a covenant on his part[3]. The rule expressed by the maxim *expressum facit cessare tacitum* prevents the recital operating as such if the deed contains an express covenant to erect and maintain a fence.

(d) Construction

Recitals may assist in the construction of the operative part of the deed; this was considered in the previous chapter.

F   The consideration

After the recitals comes the operative part of the deed introduced by the words 'NOW THIS DEED WITNESSETH as follows'. The requirement in s 5 of the Stamp Act 1891 that all the facts and circumstances affecting the liability of any instrument to stamp duty must be fully and truly set forth makes it essential to state the consideration (if any) in the deed. This explains the reason for the words, 'in consideration of the sum of £— paid by the purchaser to the vendor'. In a registered land transfer the statement of consideration appears immediately after the usual heading and the date. The consideration may take forms other than the payment of money to the vendor. For instance, an assignment of leasehold property may be made in consideration of the

---

1   [1982] QB 133n, [1981] 1 All ER 897. The lessor was held to be estopped because it had encouraged the tenants to spend money in the belief that the option was enforceable.
2   Co Litt 352b; *Right d Jefferys v Bucknell* (1831) 2 B & Ad 278 at 281, per Lord Tenterden CJ. Cf *Morton v Woods* (1869) LR 4 QB 293, ExCh.
3   For examples, see *Re Weston, Davies v Tagart* [1900] 2 Ch 164 (agreement in separation deed by spouses to live apart); *Buckland v Buckland* [1900] 2 Ch 534.

assignee's taking upon himself the rent and covenants in the lease[4]. In a deed of gift it is common practice to state that the deed is made in consideration of the natural love and affection which the donor has for the donee. No resulting trust for the grantor is implied merely by reason that the property is not expressed to be conveyed for the grantee's use or benefit[5].

G   Receipt clause

Prior to 1882 the vendor was accustomed to endorse a separate receipt for the purchase money on the conveyance, a practice which is no longer necessary. A receipt in the body of the deed now operates as a sufficient discharge to the person making payment without any further receipt being endorsed[6]. It will be recalled that special considerations apply to the receipt of capital money arising on the sale of settled land or land held on trust for sale. To overreach the beneficial interests it must be paid to, or applied by the direction of, not fewer than two trustees of the settlement, or two trustees for sale, or (in either case) to a trust corporation. A sole personal representative is empowered to give a valid receipt for the proceeds of sale[7]. The written receipt of a mortgagee is a sufficient discharge for money arising under the power of sale, and a person paying the same to him is not concerned to inquire whether any money remains due under the mortgage[8].

1.   Statutory effects of receipt clause

To operate as a sufficient discharge there must be a receipt, that is, an acknowledgement by the vendor that he has received the money. A statement that the consideration has been paid to the vendor, or that a building lease was granted in consideration of moneys already expended by the lessee[9] does not suffice. As between the vendor and the purchaser the receipt acts as a *sufficient* discharge; it is not conclusive evidence of payment. The equitable rule is thus preserved that evidence of non-payment is admissible. The vendor retains his equitable lien for unpaid purchase money, notwithstanding that the conveyance contains an acknowledgement of its receipt[10], unless there are circumstances which negative the existence of a lien.

As against a subsequent purchaser without notice of non-payment, s 68 (1) of the Law of Property Act 1925 enacts that the receipt is sufficient evidence

---

4   Cf *Johnsey Estates Ltd v Lewis & Manley (Engineering) Ltd* [1987] 2 EGLR 69, CA, where there was also a nominal £1 consideration; p 594, post.
5   LPA 1925, s 60(3). For a precedent of a deed of gift, see Hallett, 232, Form 25.
6   LPA 1925, s 67(1), (2).
7   See p 324, ante.
8   LPA, s 107(1).
9   *Renner v Tolley* (1893) 68 LT 815.
10   *Winter v Lord Anson* (1827) 3 Russ 488; see p 441, ante. At common law a receipt in a deed operated to estop the person who had given it from asserting non-payment: *Baker v Dewey* (1823) 1 B & C 704. The equitable rule now prevails.

that the money has been paid. The difficulties surrounding this provision have already been discussed[11]. In addition, under s 69 of the same Act production by the vendor's solicitor or licensed conveyancer of a deed containing a receipt for the consideration operates as sufficient authority for the purchaser to pay the money to him. This also has been considered previously[12].

2. Registered land transfers

The forms of transfer prescribed by the Land Registration Rules 1925 contain no receipt clause. Yet it is the practice to insert such a clause and the printed forms published by H M Stationery Office include an acknowledgement by the vendor of his receipt of the money. It would seem necessary to incorporate a receipt clause if it is desired to take advantage of ss 67–69. The argument that its inclusion is possibly superfluous appears unsound[13].

H   Words of grant

These words tell what the vendor or grantor does and in a normal conveyance they are comprehended within the words: 'the vendor as beneficial owner[14] HEREBY CONVEYS unto the purchaser ...'. In days of old when multiplicity of language was the order of the day the usual expression was 'grant, bargain, sell, alienate, convey, release and confirm'. Today no technical words of grant are necessary. Any word suffices to pass the legal estate if the intention is to pass it[15]. 'Conveys' is usually employed in conveyances of freehold land, 'demises' on the grant of a lease, and 'assigns' on the sale of an existing leasehold estate. In the case of registered titles the word ' transfer' is employed. The use of the word 'grant' is not necessary to convey land[16], nor does its use imply any covenant, save where otherwise provided by statute[17].

On a conveyance of the legal estate for value by a beneficial owner, no separate transfer of the equitable interest is necessary. An absolute fee simple owner does not in law hold two estates, a legal estate and an equitable estate (or, rather, interest). A person cannot be a trustee for himself[18]. He holds only

---

11   Page 440, ante.
12   Page 438, ante.
13   Farrand, 257–258, citing *Rimmer v Webster* [1902] 2 Ch 163 at 173–74, per Farwell J. But the learned judge held, not that the statutory form of transfer which stated the fact of payment without acknowledging its receipt brought into play the forerunner of s 68, but that it would suffice to create an estoppel. For a case where s 68 was considered in relation to a transfer of registered land, see *London and Cheshire Insurance Co Ltd v Laplagrene Property Co Ltd* [1971] Ch 499, [1971] 1 All ER 766, discussed at p 440, ante.
14   The significance of this, and expressions such as 'as trustee', 'as mortgagee', etc, is considered in Ch 23.
15   *Re Stirrup's Contract* [1961] 1 All ER 805 at 809, per Wilberforce J.
16   LPA 1925, s 51(2). The word 'grant' became commonplace following the Real Property Act 1845, s 2, p 503, ante.
17   LPA 1925, s 59(2). Examples of statutes which otherwise provide are the Queen Anne's Bounty Act 1838, s 22 and the Lands Clauses Consolidation Act 1845, s 132.
18   *Re Selous* [1901] 1 Ch 921 at 922, per Farwell J; *Selby v Alston* (1797) 3 Ves 339.

the legal estate, which gives him the whole right of property in the land. He holds no separate equitable interest; that is absorbed in the legal estate. Provided the appropriate formalities are complied with, he can declare himself to be a trustee of the legal estate for the benefit of another so as to vest the entire equitable interest in that person[19].

I Parcels clause

1. Introduction

The parcels clause which is commonly introduced by the words 'ALL THAT ...' contains a physical description of the land which is the subject of the conveyance. Doctrinally, of course, the deed operates to vest in the purchaser, not the land, but an estate in the land delimited by the parcels clause; it is the province of the habendum clause[20] to describe the quantum or size of estate which the grantee is to acquire. Also included within the parcels are easements and other rights which are granted to the purchaser, and exceptions and reservations in favour of the vendor.

The need to strive for complete accuracy when describing the land to be conveyed cannot be stressed too frequently. Buckley LJ once observed[1] that it is:

> ... a very dangerous practice for a conveyancer to frame a conveyance with parcels which are not adequately described. Perhaps the most important feature of all the features of a conveyance is to be able to identify the property to which it relates.

Every conveyancer would heartily endorse this comment. Yet in practice the parcels clause does not always receive the careful attention that its importance warrants. Recent instances of judicial condemnation of the sloppy drafting of the parcels are not hard to find[2]. It is clearly impracticable on the grounds of expense alone to expect every purchaser to have a detailed survey undertaken so as to check that the actual boundaries of the plot correspond with the description given in the muniments of title. To this extent the system of land registration, which describes every registered title by reference to an official (and expertly) prepared plan, solves many, but not all[3], of the problems that may arise from inadequately drafted parcels. Every purchaser's solicitor should at the very least check with his client that the description of the land in the

---

19 LPA 1925, s 53(1)(b). See generally the illuminating judgment of Hope JA in *DKLR Holding Co (No 2) Pty Ltd v Stamp Duties Comr* [1980] 1 NSWLR 510 at 518–23; *Vandervell v IRC* [1967] 2 AC 291 at 311, [1967] 1 All ER 1 at 6, HL, per Lord Upjohn; cf [1966] Ch 261 at 287, [1965] 2 All ER 37 at 44, CA, per Diplock LJ.

20 Page 556, post.

1 *Kingston v Phillips* [1976] CA Transcript 279, cited by Griffiths LJ in *Scarfe v Adams* [1981] 1 All ER 843 at 852, CA.

2 See eg *Kingston v Phillips*, supra; *Scarfe v Adams*, supra, at 845, per Cumming-Bruce LJ ('a cautionary tale to be marked and digested by every conveyancing solicitor and legal executive'); *Neilson v Poole* (1969) 20 P & CR 909 at 915, per Megarry J.

3 See p 542, post.

contract and the conveyance corresponds with the land which the purchaser thinks he is buying. Once the contract has been signed, a purchaser will not normally have any redress if he discovers that he is not getting what he thought he was purchasing, save where the contract itself contains a misdescription as to quantity or quality. It is also equally essential for the vendor's solicitor when drafting the contract to ensure that the description of the property in the particulars is accurate and accords with what the vendor intends to sell[4]. Care taken in drafting an accurate description is clearly in the interests of the parties, especially on a subdivision of land. Boundary quarrels are a frequent source of dispute between neighbours, sometimes generating litigation many years after completion.

2.   Mode of description

(a) General position
The aim of the description should be to enable the purchaser to identify on the spot the extent of the land which it embraces and where the boundaries lie[5]. When framing the parcels clause it should be the draftsman's duty to ensure that: (i) the description in the deed (including any plan) is not inconsistent with the physical features and boundaries of the land; (ii) the totality of the description is not self-contradictory; and (iii) the extent of the land can be determined without the need to resort to extrinsic evidence. On a conveyance of land leading to first registration, it is vital to ensure that the deed contains sufficient particulars of the land by plan or otherwise, to enable the property to be fully identified on the Ordnance map or the Registry's general map[6].

The description will vary according to the type of property conveyed[7]. It was once standard practice to incorporate a very detailed verbal[8] description of land comprising residential property. The address and area of the land would be given, and also the length and direction of each boundary including a statement of who owned the adjacent land in some such manner as, 'bounded on or towards the north (on which side it measures 90 feet) by land owned by XY (or contracted to be sold to XY) ...' and so on. And to put the matter beyond all doubt there was usually an accompanying plan, often expressed to delineate the plot more particularly. Verbosity of this kind belongs to a past age, although it had its virtues. Nowadays parcels clauses are much shorter and, sadly, not so reliable. Whilst the description of the typical suburban house still tends to be partly verbal and partly visual, no attempt is made to give the plot dimensions other than its area, though sometimes these appear on the plan. A terraced house with clearly defined boundaries may be adequately described simply as: 'ALL THAT house known as — together with the land forming the site thereof and occupied therewith'.

4   See eg *Lloyd v Stanbury* [1971] 2 All ER 267. See further p 150, ante.
5   Cf *Eastwood v Ashton* [1915] AC 900 at 912, HL, per Lord Parker.
6   LRR 1925, rr 20 (iii), 50–54. But see p 543, post, and *Proctor v Kidman* (1986) 51 P & CR 67, CA.
7   For different forms of parcels clauses, see 15 Ency F & P, 590–602; Hallett, 181–86.
8   'Verbal' here signifies the written description in the deed as opposed to the plan.

A more detailed description may be essential in a conveyance of industrial or agricultural land. Lengthy or involved descriptions can conveniently be placed in a schedule at the end of the deed. Thus, on the sale of a farm it may be desired to give the name or Ordnance Survey map number[9] and the area of particular fields, and it is clearly preferable to tabulate such information in schedule form.

In practice the description in the parcels clause frequently corresponds with that contained in the contract, which often simply repeats the description taken from the conveyance to the vendor[10]. Nevertheless, the draftsman should always ensure that the description reproduced from an earlier conveyance is accurate and up-to-date. The possibility of some boundary adjustment occurring during the intervening years should not be discounted[11]. There is no absolute rule that a vendor can insist on a repetition of the exact words employed in the contract and refuse to convey by any other description. The true rule appears to be that the purchaser is entitled to insert in the conveyance such a description as will clearly identify the land intended to be transferred. Where the contract description is misleading, inadequate or obsolete, he can insert his own accurate description according to its condition at the date of the conveyance. It is a convenient practice to connect the modern description with the former one in some appropriate way so as to produce a continuous description of the property[12]. The purchaser's right to supplement a verbal description by a plan raises problems for consideration later in the chapter.

The drafting of the parcels clause requires special care in two particular instances.

(b) Subdivisions

The division of land or buildings into two or more separate properties often shows conveyancing draftsmanship at its most inept. In *Scarfe v Adams*[13] Cumming-Bruce LJ gave this salutary warning in a case where a single house and its curtilage had been divided into two:

> ...it is absolutely essential that each parcel conveyed shall be described in the deed with such particularity and precision that there is no room for doubt about the boundaries of each... The plan or other drawing bound up with the deed must be on such a large scale that it clearly shows with precision where each boundary runs.

Obviously the line of the internal boundaries of the two sections was of vital importance. Yet no internal walls were shown on the plaintiff's deed plan, which was described as worse than useless because its scale was too small. The

9   The map edition should, of course, be specified and preferably not an out-of-date one!
10 This in turn has usually been copied verbatim from the parcels in the first conveyance of the land as a separate property.
11 See *Wallington v Townsend* [1939] Ch 588, [1939] 2 All ER 225, p 150, ante; *Hopgood v Brown* [1955] 1 All ER 550, CA.
12 *Re Sansom and Narbeth's Contract* [1910] 1 Ch 741 at 747–49, per Swinfen Eady J, adopting a passage from 1 Williams, V & P (1st edn), 557; see now 4th edn, Vol 1, 651.
13 [1981] 1 All ER 843 at 845, CA (a registered land case).

court was compelled to look outside the deed at the auction particulars to determine where the boundary lay. The case of *Kingston v Phillips*[14] provides another horror story. Here a large country house was divided into three lots. The plaintiffs' part was conveyed to them in the following terms:

> ...All that parcel of land being part of the C– House Estate at C– in the County of Wiltshire all which premises are by way of identification only more particularly delineated on the plan annexed hereto and thereon coloured pink. And also all that dwelling house together with the outbuildings ... being part of C– House.

This verbal description was almost devoid of any particularity. The property conveyed was simply expressed to be *part* of C– House. But there was the plan to make everything clear. Alas this was not so. It, too, was quite useless; it showed inaccurate contours of the house, with unreliable coloration and was drawn on too small a scale to plot the boundaries between the plaintiff's section and the adjacent lots. Again recourse to extrinsic evidence was necessary to resolve the uncertainties.

(c) New development

Somewhat different problems can arise on the conveyance of unregistered houses on a new estate[15]. Not only may there be no physical features on the land at the date of the deed, or at best a flimsy post and wire fence, but builders are notorious for adjusting plot boundaries, even after exchanging contracts, without advising their solicitors. Coupled with their reluctance to give plot measurements on plans in the mistaken belief that this will facilitate revision of the estate layout plan, it is not surprising that boundary disputes occur. *Spall v Owen*[16] is a typical case. The land conveyed to the plaintiff was described as, 'All that piece ... of freehold land ... known as plot no 1' on a named estate road. The plot was further identified in a deed plan which was identical to that annexed to the contract. After contracts had been exchanged the builder erected fencing around the plot, which did not follow the boundary lines shown on the plan. The plaintiff claimed the additional land which the fencing gave him. His action was dismissed. The identity of plot no 1 was governed by the plan which excluded the disputed strip, not by the fencing. Whilst the primary description of the land as 'plot no 1' was, according to Peter Gibson J, a singularly unsatisfactory mode of identification, its use was suggestive of a plan. The deed plan was the same as the contract plan. Since at the time of the contract there were no physical boundaries on the ground to indicate where plot no 1 ended and the adjoining plots began, the parties could not have intended by the phrase 'known as plot no 1' anything other than the plot as delineated on the deed plan. Had the fencing been in place before exchange of contracts, that physical boundary on the ground would probably have determined the issue[17].

---

14   [1976] CA Transcript 279, note 1, p 527, ante.
15   For the position when the title is registered, see pp 338–340, ante.
16   (1981) 44 P & CR 36. As to the vendor's duty of care when preparing the plan, see *Jackson v Bishop* (1979) 48 P & CR 57, CA, p 150, ante.
17   Cf *Willson v Greene* [1971] 1 All ER 1098, distinguished in *Spall v Owen*, supra.

3. Plans[18]

(a) Use of plans

It is common practice on a subdivision of land or on the development of a building estate to describe the land by the additional means of a plan annexed to the conveyance. Established property is often conveyed by reference to a plan on an earlier deed. Unfortunately the preparation of the plan is sometimes marked by a total disregard for accuracy. Plans not drawn to scale are hastily prepared or copied by a junior member of the office, using unsuitable drawing implements. The Royal Commission on Legal Services[19] censured conveyancing plans because they were too small[20], or lacked measurements or failed to reveal the point from which they were taken[1], or wrongly depicted the size, shape and extent of the property[2].

Every draftsman proposing to convey land by reference to a plan ought to ask himself three basic questions. First, its *purpose* – is it intended to control the verbal description, or merely be supplemental to it? Secondly, its *meaningful significance* – is it drawn to an adequate scale with accurate measurements so as to enable the boundaries to be clearly identified? Thirdly, its *accuracy* – is the plan consistent with the verbal description, the contract plan[3], and the physical features of the land including the boundaries apparent on inspection of the site[4]? Consideration of these issues may be viewed as counsel of perfection; yet there can be no justification for the sloppy and haphazard way in which parcels clauses are not infrequently drafted. The taking of the most elementary precautions would do much to reduce the volume of litigation involving boundary disputes, such as ensuring that on the division of land into two separate units, the common boundary between them is shown identically on the plans of the two conveyances[5].

Sensible conveyancing practice dictates that express reference should be made in the parcels clause to any plan drawn on or bound up inside the deed. This is not always the case. A plan forming part of a conveyance, but not referred to in it, may be looked at to identify the land conveyed, provided the description of the parcels read in the light of the other admissible evidence still leaves it

---

18   See (1981) 258 EG 927 (S Murdoch).
19   Royal Commission Report, Vol 1, 284–85, Annex 21.1, para 10. The Land Registry estimates that one in eight plans which it sees is seriously defective: Law Com Report No 125, p 6, note 9.
20   *Kingston v Phillips*, ante; *Scarfe v Adams*, ante; *Mayer v Hurr* (1983) 49 P & CR 56, CA.
1   Cf *Harding v Weir Estates Co Ltd* (1961) 179 EG 11; *Jackson v Bishop*, supra (stated boundary lengths not consistent with scaled-up measurements).
2   See eg *Smout v Farquharson* (1972) 226 EG 114, CA; *Darby v Thorner* [1983] CA Transcript 490; *Graham v Philcox* [1984] QB 747, [1984] 2 All ER 643, CA.
3   *Willson v Greene*, ante (contract plan showing 'kinky' boundary replaced on deed plan by straight-line boundary).
4   That these issues should not be ignored even when the draftsman formulates a description which adopts by reference the plan on some previous conveyance of the same property is illustrated by *Hopgood v Brown* [1955] 1 All ER 550, CA (earlier deed plan becoming inaccurate due to neighbour's encroachment).
5   See *Lamb v Lamb* (18 November 1982, CA Unbound Transcript 676), where the two conveyances were only a week apart and the defective plans gave rise to litigation 30 years later. And see *Ray v Druce* [1985] Ch 437, [1985] 2 All ER 482.

uncertain as to what is included[6], but only where there is ambiguity or doubt. It is not customary to have the plan signed by the executing parties, except in the case of a plan used on a transfer of registered land when signature is required[7].

(b) Importance of plan

Often it is necessary to determine the relationship between the plan and the verbal description in the parcels clause. A properly incorporated plan forms part of the description and must be considered when determining the extent and effect of the grant. The parcels may indicate that the plan is to rank as the primary description. In the absence of words suggesting otherwise the plan is prima facie regarded as being an alternative visual description, not intended to contradict the verbal description, and the court will endeavour to give effect to both. In *Truckell v Stock*[8] the question arose whether the conveyance of a house passed to the purchaser the eaves and footings projecting beyond the area of the land as depicted on the deed plan. The court refused to recognise any inconsistency between the plan which indicated the boundary at ground level and the verbal description referring to a 'dwelling-house', which was taken to mean all parts of the house including the protruding eaves and footings (but not the intervening column of air). In the event of a conflict, however, it becomes necessary to decide which prevails – the plan or the verbal description.

(i) *Plan prevails.*   The conveyance may describe the property as 'more particularly delineated [or described] on the plan drawn hereon and thereon edged red'. Such words tend to show that in case of conflict or uncertainty the plan is to prevail[9]. Even without any guiding phrase, the plan will prevail if it is clear and unambiguous, whereas the verbal description is vague and requires extrinsic evidence to render it certain[10].

(ii) *Plan not prevailing.*   The verbal description has been held to prevail when the plan was drawn on so small a scale that the boundaries could not be ascertained with sufficient precision[11]. The plan may also be displaced by a clear and complete verbal description, as in *Willis v Watney*[12] where an uncoloured yard on the deed plan was held to have passed to the purchaser because the parcels expressly referred to 'yards'. One method commonly adopted is to state that the plan is for 'the purpose of identification only', with

---

6   *Leachman v L & K Richardson Ltd* [1969] 3 All ER 20, distinguishing the contrary opinion, relied on by *Norton on Deeds*, 238, in *Wyse v Leahy* (1875) IR 9 CL 384.

7   LRR 1925, rr 79, 113.

8   [1957] 1 All ER 74, CA. Cf *Grigsby v Melville* [1973] 3 All ER 455, CA, p 537, post.

9   *Neilson v Poole* (1969) 20 P & CR 909 at 916, per Megarry J. See eg *Wallington v Townsend* [1939] Ch 588, [1939] 2 All ER 225; *Smout v Farquharson* (1972) 226 EG 114, CA; *Baxendale v Instow Parish Council* [1982] Ch 14, [1981] 2 All ER 620.

10   *Eastwood v Ashton* [1915] AC 900 at 912, HL, per Lord Parker, though in this case the property was also more particularly described in a plan. See p 534, post.

11   *Taylor v Parry* (1840) 1 Man & G 604. See *Scarfe v Adams* [1981] 1 All ER 843, CA.

12   (1881) 51 LJ Ch 181; cf *Smith v Sun Garage (Kingsdown) Ltd* (1961) 179 EG 89.

or without additional words such as 'and not by way of limitation or enlargement'. The true legal significance of this and similar qualifying expressions seems to elude many practitioners. The original author has seen a deed plan ostensibly for identification purposes only, which nevertheless gave the precise plot measurements in feet and inches calculated to the centre of a boundary hedge. Often the phrase 'for the purpose of identification only' can be found linked with the expression 'more particularly delineated', suggesting that draftsmen thoughtlessly employ this combination of words out of habit. For as Megarry J observed in *Neilson v Poole*[13], when used together they tend to be mutually stultifying and do not give the plan any predominance over the verbal description. Put simply, the two phrases should never be used in conjunction with one another.

Formerly it was thought that the words 'for the purpose of identification only' limited the use of the plan to ascertaining the situation of the land; it could not control the parcels or assist in identifying the exact boundaries[14]. However, in *Wiggington & Milner Ltd v Winster Engineering Ltd*[15], the Court of Appeal sensibly held that such a plan could be looked at to elucidate the identity of the property whenever the parcels clause left the boundaries ill-defined or uncertain[16]. An identification-only plan cannot override the verbal description. For example, if such a plan shows a boundary line differing from some physical feature on the ground which the conveyance otherwise indicates as the intended boundary, the latter prevails over the former[17]. From the purchaser's standpoint, introducing a plan for identification only is not objectionable, provided the land is adequately described and the boundaries clearly defined by the wording of the parcels clause. But as we have noted, a plan limited by such words is commonly used alongside a vague and almost meaningless verbal description, so that the court has to resort to extrinsic evidence to determine the extent of the property conveyed. Moreover the insertion of qualifying words is sometimes interpreted by builders as conferring a power to adjust the boundaries after exchange of contracts. However, all may not always be lost for the purchaser who discovers after completion that his plot has been reduced in size. In *Willson v Greene*[18] Foster J held that where the parcels are approximate a boundary marked out and agreed by the parties supersedes a plan which is for identification only.

(c) Purchaser's entitlement to plan

The question sometimes arises whether the purchaser is entitled to have the land conveyed by reference to a plan, in a case where the vendor has contracted

13 (1969) 20 P & CR 909 at 916.
14 See the authorities collected and discussed by Buckley LJ in *Wigginton & Milner Ltd v Winster Engineering Ltd* [1978] 3 All ER 436 at 442–45, CA.
15 Supra, applied in *Tebaldi v Wiseman and Kemp* (1983) 133 NLJ 1042; *Graham v Philcox* [1984] QB 747, [1984] 2 All ER 643, CA; *Scott v Martin* [1987] 2 All ER 813, CA.
16 Where the parcels are unambiguous, it is inappropriate to have regard to the plan: *Hatfield v Moss* [1988] 2 EGLR 58, CA.
17 Per Bridge LJ in the *Wigginton* case, supra, at 447.
18 [1971] 1 All ER 1098; *Sharwood Properties (Ealing) Ltd v Maclellan* (1971) 219 EG 830 (boundary fixed by common vendor and defendant's predecessor). Cf *Spall v Owen* (1981) 44 P & CR 36.

to sell by means of a verbal description. It is the vendor's duty to convey the property under a description which is a sufficient and satisfactory identification of the land sold. If he can do this without a plan the purchaser cannot insist on a plan in the conveyance[19], for this would involve the vendor in unnecessary expense in having the accuracy of the plan checked by his own surveyor. On the question of the sufficiency or otherwise of the verbal description, each case must depend on its particular facts. Where the description in the contract fails to identify the boundaries (eg by measurements) and there are insufficient physical features on the land itself to enable them to be located, the purchaser would seem to be within his rights to insist upon a plan. In this situation the vendor cannot insist on the insertion in the conveyance of such restrictive words as 'for the purposes of identification only'[20]. The vendor cannot refuse to convey by reference to a plan if the property is so described in the contract, and it seems he cannot object to one prepared by the purchaser should the latter show that the contract plan is inaccurate.

4.   Construction of parcels

The previous section looked at one aspect of this topic, the conflict between the verbal and visual descriptions in the deed. Problems of construction also occur in other situations. The conveyance may adopt more than one mode of verbal description; if they are inconsistent, which prevails? Or the parcels clause when read with the plan may still be sufficiently imprecise that it is necessary to look outside the deed to ascertain the exact boundaries of the plot. Notwithstanding the spread of land registration, the principles developed by the courts will continue to be relevant to the solution of boundary disputes, even after the land has been registered[1]. The dangers of a multiple description were considered by Lord Sumner in *Eastwood v Ashton*[2], a leading case on the construction of the parcels. He said:

> As long as only one species of description is resorted to in describing parcels no harm is done, and often good, by copious enumeration of particulars all belonging to that species. If the description is by name, certainty is increased by naming every close which has a separate name; if by metes and bounds, by setting out every bound; if by ad measurement, by stating not only acres and roods, but also poles. To do this is always troublesome and often impracticable, but at least it is not a cause of uncertainty. If, however, several different species of description are adopted, risk of uncertainty at once arises, for if one is full, accurate, and adequate, any others are otiose if right, and misleading if wrong.

In this case the House of Lords had to decide whether a small strip of land some 150 feet long by 36 feet wide was included in a conveyance of a farm containing over 84 acres. The parcels were described by reference to four

---

19   *Re Sharman and Meade's Contract* [1936] Ch 755, [1936] 2 All ER 1547. Contrast *Re Sansom and Narbeth's Contract* [1910] 1 Ch 741. The two decisions are not easy to reconcile.
20   *Re Sparrow and James' Contract* (1902) [1910] 2 Ch 60.
1   See *Proctor v Kidman* (1986) 51 P & CR 67, CA.
2   [1915] AC 900 at 915–16, HL.

matters: (i) the name of the farm; (ii) its acreage; (iii) the names of the occupants; and (iv) a plan drawn to scale and endorsed on the deed. Their Lordships held that the description by reference to the plan, which showed that the strip of land was included, must prevail. It was the only certain and unambiguous description; the remaining descriptions could only be rendered certain by extrinsic evidence. The description by name was too vague and by itself gave no indication whether any particular plot of land was comprised within the farm. The description by area could be disregarded; it was merely approximate (ie stated to be 'or thereabouts') and could be satisfied either with or without the inclusion of the small strip of land. The reference to occupation[3] was in fact erroneous since the person named as the occupant of the part which included the disputed strip had sub-let to others who were in occupation. Where there is a conflict between two descriptions, the court will prefer the one more likely to accord with the parties' real intentions[4].

(a) Falsa demonstratio non nocet

A description of the land conveyed, sufficient of itself to render certain what is intended to be conveyed, will prevail and the addition of a wrong name or of an erroneous statement as to quantity, occupancy, locality, or an erroneous enumeration of particulars will be ignored[5]. This rule which applies alike to deeds and wills[6] is often expressed in the terms of the Latin maxim *falsa demonstratio non nocet* – a false description does not vitiate. The order in which the conflicting descriptions occur is not decisive. The court can reject a false statement even though it precedes the true description, but the maxim cannot be applied unless and until the court has decided which of two or more conflicting descriptions ought to be considered as the true one[7].

Where the grant is expressed in *general* terms coupled with a particular description, the latter is not rejected as a false description but is treated as restricting the generality of the grant. Thus in *Homer v Homer*[8], a testator devised to X all his land 'situate at G in the occupation of S'. It was held that the devise did not pass land at G occupied by J. Similarly where general words of description in the parcels refer to a schedule containing a definite and specific enumeration of particulars, and the enumeration omits something which might

---

3 A description by occupation is one so inconclusive and liable to error that it will readily yield to any more accurate and convincing description: per Lord Wrenbury, at 919. But see *Gresty v Meacock* (1961) 180 EG 653, CA, where the words 'in the occupation of the purchaser' were the only description capable of determining whether a disputed plot of land passed.

4 *IS Mills (Yardley) Ltd v Curdworth Investments Ltd* (1975) 235 EG 127, CA (parcels construed by reference to surrounding circumstances to include storeroom excluded from plan). See also *Mid Kent Water plc v Batchelor* [1994] 1 EGLR 185.

5 *Cowen v Truefitt Ltd* [1898] 2 Ch 551 at 554, per Romer J; affd on other grounds [1899] 2 Ch 309, CA.

6 Many of the reported cases relate to the construction of wills; see *Portman v Mill* (1839) 8 LJ Ch 161; *Hardwick v Hardwick* (1873) LR 16 Eq 168 (location and occupation wrongly stated). For a recent application of the rule in a registered land case, see *A J Dunning & Sons (Shopfitters) Ltd v Sykes & Son (Poole) Ltd* [1987] Ch 287, [1987] 1 All ER 700, CA, p 543, post.

7 *Eastwood v Ashton* [1915] AC 900 at 912–13, HL, per Lord Parker.

8 (1878) 8 Ch D 758, CA.

otherwise be covered by the general description, the designation by schedule is read as restrictive of the general description and only the property mentioned in the schedule will pass[9]. The court does not readily infer an error or falsehood[10]; consequently any doubt as to whether words are a false demonstration or words of restriction will be resolved in favour of the latter.

(b) Recitals and other clauses explaining the parcels

If still unable to determine from the parcels clause the extent of the land conveyed, the court will endeavour to ascertain the parties' intentions by looking at the other provisions in the deed. *Proctor v Kidman*[11] is an interesting case. Land conveyed by V to P was intended to include a track along one of its boundaries. However the deed plan, for identification purposes only, excluded this track which was shown as being on V's adjacent land to the north. The court held that the track passed to P. Not only did the conveyance purport to reserve for V a right of way along it, it also contained a declaration of V's ownership of the boundary fence sited at the northern edge of the track. Both the reservation and the declaration were quite meaningless if the track were to form part of V's retained land.

The recitals may throw light on the extent of the parcels. For instance, a recital may show an intention to convey specific property (eg all V's land in the County of Leicestershire) whereas the parcels describe the property in terms sufficiently general to include other property not within the recital (eg all V's land and V has land in an adjoining county). Here the recital will limit the grant and only the specific property passes[12]. A recital cannot control the operative words of the conveyance if they are clear and unambiguous. Therefore parcels described with certainty are not extended, or cut down, by a recital showing that more, or less, was intended to be conveyed[13]. Recitals may also assist the court in deciding which of two or more possible constructions that may be given to the parcels is the correct one[14].

(c) Extrinsic evidence

Whilst the draftsman may fail to define the land with precision, the court is not at liberty, as Megarry J once observed[15], to leave the plot conveyed fuzzy at the edges with uncertain boundaries. It is a question of fact whether a particular plot of land is or is not included within the description in the parcels. Should doubt continue to exist after looking at the parcels and the remainder of the deed, recourse may be had to extrinsic evidence to identify the land. But –

9   *Re Brocket, Dawes v Miller* [1908] 1 Ch 185 at 196, per Joyce J; cf *Re McManus, ex p Jardine* (1875) 10 Ch App 322.
10   *Morrell v Fisher* (1849) 4 Exch 591 at 606, per Alderson B.
11   (1986) 51 P & CR 67, CA; *Scarfe v Adams* [1981] 1 All ER 843, CA (declaration that internal dividing wall to be party wall relevant).
12   *Jenner v Jenner* (1866) LR 1 Eq 361; *Re Earl of Durham, Earl Grey v Earl of Durham* (1887) 57 LT 164.
13   *Re Medley, ex p Glyn* (1840) 1 Mont D & De G 29. See further p 514, ante.
14   See *Eastwood v Ashton*, ante.
15   *Neilson v Poole* (1969) 20 P & CR 909 at 915.

and this fundamental rule must be stressed – the court will never allow such evidence to contradict the terms of a deed which clearly define the extent of the land, however inconvenient the consequences for one of the parties[16]. Subject to this, the court will turn to any relevant evidence which may help to provide a solution. In recent cases the courts have relied upon auction particulars forming the basis of the contract of sale[17], a photograph of the property appearing in the sale particulars[18], and the vendor's planning application for permission to sub-divide a large house into smaller lots[19]. Physical features on the land can also assist the court in its quest, eg staked boundary pegs indicating a boundary line agreed by the parties before the contract[20]. Parol evidence from the parties as to the intended area to be conveyed may be admitted[1]. So, when land is conveyed or demised by reference to its name together with the land occupied by the grantor, evidence will, in the event of uncertainty, be allowed to establish the extent of his occupation[2].

Apparently the court can have regard to the conduct of the parties contemporaneous with or subsequent to the execution of the deed. As a general rule for the construction of contracts this principle has been discredited[3]; but it still has a role to play when the title to land is concerned. Evidence of what a common vendor has done in subsequent conveyances of his retained land is relevant, at least if it constitutes an admission against the interests of himself and his successors[4]. Similarly, when the parcels are ambiguous it is legitimate to interpret the deed by the extent of the possession which proceeds on it[5]. Evidence may, therefore, be given that the claimant of a disputed strip did or did not assume possession of it under the conveyance whose construction is under consideration.

A final and obvious point should be made. Many of these problems could have been avoided had the practitioner only directed his mind to the need for clarity and certainty when drafting the parcels clause.

5. Boundaries

(a) Extent of land conveyed
Unless the deed shows to the contrary, a conveyance of land includes everything directly beneath the surface of the land conveyed and the space directly above it. This is a prima facie rule only, and is subject to various well known statutory

---

16 *Grigsby v Melville* [1973] 3 All ER 455, CA, discussed below, section 5(a).
17 *Scarfe v Adams* [1981] 1 All ER 843, CA.
18 *Mayer v Hurr* (1983) 49 P & CR 56, CA.
19 *Kingston v Phillips* [1976] CA Transcript 279. See also *Scott v Martin* [1987] 2 All ER 813, CA (reference to planning permission to determine width of purchaser's right of way not defined in parcels clause).
20 *Willson v Greene* [1971] 1 All ER 1098. As to the role of existing boundary fences as an aid to construction, see *Smout v Farquharson* (1972) 226 EG 114, CA.
1 *Bisney v Swanston* (1972) 225 EG 2299, CA.
2 *Magee v Lavell* (1874) LR 9 CP 107.
3 *L Schuler AG v Wickman Machine Tool Sales Ltd* [1974] AC 235, [1973] 2 All ER 39, HL, disapproving *Watcham v A-G of East Africa Protectorate* [1919] AC 533, PC.
4 *Neilson v Poole* (1969) 20 P & CR 909.
5 The *Schuler* case, supra, at 272, 63, per Lord Kilbrandon.

and common law exceptions[6]. A contrary intention would appear in the conveyance when the vendor retained for himself part of a building, such as an underground cellar, that would otherwise pass to the purchaser. In *Grigsby v Melville*[7] a house was conveyed to a purchaser. Under the sitting room was a cellar connected by steps to the adjoining house owned by the vendor. There was no access to this cellar from the house conveyed. The conveyance was held to have vested the cellar in the purchaser by virtue of the general rule stated above. The vendor had not expressly retained (ie excepted) the cellar for himself. Moreover the court refused to admit evidence of the state and history of the two houses to show that the cellar was not included, for that would have been evidence contradicting the plain language of the deed.

(i) *Demise of part of a building.*   A well-drawn lease of premises forming part of a larger building should deal specifically with the ownership of such matters as the outer walls and the roof. Failing express provisions, a demise of part of a building divided horizontally or vertically includes the external walls enclosing the demised part[8], but not the roofing in the case of a top-floor flat[9]. Where the demise of a flat does include the roof and roof space, it will also include the air space above the roof[10]. The lease of a flat in a building prima facie entitles the tenant to occupy all the space between his floor and the underneath of the floor of the flat above[11].

(ii) *Projections.*   On the conveyance of property which overhangs the vendor's adjacent land, the purchaser should ensure that the vendor grants to him a right to maintain the projections (usually overhanging eaves and protruding footings) over the vendor's land with a right of entry for the purposes of repair. Failure to make express provision for these matters may not be fatal, though it could give rise to future difficulties. In *Truckell v Stock*[12], as we have seen, the reference in the parcels clause to 'a dwelling house' showed that the parties intended all its parts including the projection to pass. An extreme case producing an unexpected result is *Laybourn v Gridley*[13]. Here the purchaser's conveyance operated to pass an overhanging loft of the vendor's adjacent

---

6   Eg as to mineral rights. See generally M & W, 61–67.

7   [1973] 3 All ER 455, CA, applying *Mitchell v Mosley* [1914] 1 Ch 438, CA.

8   *Sturge v Hackett* [1962] 3 All ER 166 at 172, CA, per Diplock LJ; *Straudley Investments Ltd v Barpress Ltd* [1987] 1 EGLR 69, CA (lease of row of buildings included roof and exterior walls).

9   *Cockburn v Smith* [1924] 2 KB 119 at 134, CA, per Sargant LJ. Cf *Douglas-Scott v Scorgie* [1984] 1 All ER 1086, CA.

10   See *Davies v Yadegar* [1990] 1 EGLR 71, CA.

11   *Graystone Property Investments Ltd v Margulies* (1983) 47 P & CR 472, CA (void space above false ceiling); *Tebaldi v Wiseman and Kemp* (1983) 133 NLJ 1042 (staircase down to tenant's basement flat).

12   [1957] 1 All ER 74, CA, p 472, ante; *Corbett v Hill* (1870) LR 9 Eq 671. As to the effect of acquiring title by adverse possession, see *Williams v Usherwood* (1981) 45 P & CR 235, CA (possessory title to driveway not vesting ownership of neighbour's overhanging eaves).

13   [1892] 2 Ch 53, cited by Stamp LJ in *Grigsby v Melville,* supra, note 16, at 461, as an illustration of 'the unhappy fact that conveyances sometimes do convey that which was not intended to be, or exclude that which should have been, conveyed'. Cf Brightman J at [1973] 1 All ER 385 at 390.

property. The parcels clause indicated that the deed plan was to prevail, and this clearly showed the loft as within the coloured area which delineated the property conveyed. Where a house is built flush with the plot boundary, no reservation of a right of access over the adjoining land for the purposes of inspecting and maintaining the flank wall will be implied[14].

When there is no right of access to neighbouring land for the purpose of effecting repairs to the property, the position of a purchaser has been improved by the enactment of the Access to Neighbouring Land Act 1992. Under s 1 of the Act, if a person does not have access to neighbouring land for the purpose of effecting repairs to his property, he may apply to the court for an order[15]. In deciding whether to make such an order, the court must be satisfied that the works are reasonably necessary for the preservation of the whole or part of the dominant land and cannot be carried out, or would be substantially more difficult to carry out, without access to the neigbouring land.

The Act is relevant to all neighbouring properties and is not confined to situations where the vendor retains land contiguous to the purchaser's property. In the latter instance, it is clearly preferable for the question of access to be dealt with expressly, rather than leaving the purchaser, or his successor in title, to have to make an application under the Act.

(b) Walls, fences, hedges[16] and ditches
The necessity for a landowner to know the exact boundaries of his land is all too obvious in these days of land scarcity and high density development, when a matter of a few feet can be of vital importance to a householder contemplating an extension to his property. Yet as has been noticed the deeds often fail to delineate plot boundaries with anything like the desired precision. Moreover, whilst an accurate plan can identify the line of the boundary on the ground, it does not settle the question of ownership of boundary structures. The general difficulty in defining boundaries and showing title to walls and fences is reflected in the Standard Conditions of Sale which relieve the seller from proving the exact boundaries of the property, proving who owns fences, ditches, hedges and walls and separately identifying parts of the property with different titles[17]. Under this condition, however, the purchaser may, if it is reasonable require the vendor, at his expense, to make or obtain a statutory declaration relevant to the above matters. The form of the declaration is to be agreed with the purchaser, who must not unreasonably withhold his consent. Where these questions cannot be resolved by the deeds, or by a statutory declaration, help may be had from various legal presumptions.

A boundary wall built exclusively on the land of one person belongs to him. The adjoining owner has no rights in respect of it unless he can prove an easement of support. A demise of a building bounded by an outside wall prima

---

14   *Kwiatkowski v Cox* (1969) 213 EG 34.
15   Any such order is registrable under the Land Charges Act 1972 or the Land Registration Act 1925 as appropriate: Access to Neighbouring Land Act 1992, s 4.
16   See generally Powell-Smith, *Law of Boundaries and Fences* (2nd edn); Conveyancing Committee Report II, 106, paras 6.34–6.47.
17   SCS 4.3.1.

facie includes both sides of it[18]. In the case of a wall which straddles the boundary (termed a party wall), s 38 of the Law of Property Act 1925 operates to sever it vertically as between the adjoining owners, each of whom becomes sole owner of his respective section[19]. Their rights of support and user over the rest of the structure remain unaffected. An agreement and declaration, commonly inserted in modern conveyances, that dividing walls and fences are deemed to be party walls and fences suffices to make s 38 applicable. Such a declaration normally provides for the adjacent owners to contribute equally to the cost of repairs[20], without imposing any duty to maintain. No obligation to repair exists at common law[1], though one owner is entitled to repair the other's half of the wall so far as is reasonably necessary for the enjoyment of his own rights in the wall, albeit at his own expense[2].

On the development of a building estate it is common practice for conveyances of individual plots to impose on each purchaser an obligation to erect and maintain one or more dividing fences (appropriately marked, often by a 'T' mark, on the deed plan)[3]. The convention, as yet lacking judicial recognition, is that a 'T' mark on one side of a boundary indicates that the owner of that side also owns the fence or other structure. It is always preferable for the deed to indicate which fences are included in the grant. The covenant to repair is not enforceable by the neighbouring owner. Alternatively, dividing fences may be declared to be party fences, repairable at the joint expense of each neighbour. One party can enforce the obligation to contribute against the other but not, as a matter of contract, against a successor in title, for the burden of a positive covenant does not run at law[4]. The common belief that a fence belongs to the owner of the land on whose side the posts and rails are placed is without legal foundation.

Where two plots of land are separated by a hedge or bank and ditch the boundary prima facie runs along the edge of the ditch away from the hedge or bank. The person who made the ditch is presumed to have dug it at the extremity of his land and thrown the soil on his own land to form the bank. This has been described as a convenient rule of common sense which, nevertheless, rests on rather slender foundations; it assumes what may not be true, that when the ditch was dug there was no common ownership of the two

---

18   *Goldfoot v Welch* [1914] 1 Ch 213; *Re Webb's Lease, Sandom v Webb* [1951] Ch 808, [1951] 2 All ER 131, CA (no right for landlord to maintain hoarding on wall).
19   Prior to 1926 such walls prima facie belonged to the owners as tenants in common. The London Building Acts (Amendment) Act 1939, Pt VI, regulates the rights of adjoining owners in relation to party structures within Inner London.
20   See eg 18 Ency F & P, 431.
1   See *Sack v Jones* [1925] Ch 235.
2   *Jones v Pritchard* [1908] 1 Ch 630 at 638, per Parker J; *Leigh v Dickeson* (1884) 15 QBD 60, CA. A duty to fence can arise by prescription: *Lawrence v Jenkins* (1873) LR 8 QB 274. See now the Party Wells Act 1996.
3   For a full discussion of the various possibilities, see (1971) 68 LS Gaz 275, 375 (J E Adams).
4   It is arguable that the successor may be bound on the principle of mutual benefits and burdens; see *Halsall v Brizell* [1957] Ch 169, [1957] 1 All ER 371. This doctrine is, however, construed narrowly. See *Rhone v Stephens* [1994] 2 AC 310 at 322; [1994] 2 All ER 65 at 73, HL, per Lord Templeman.

pieces of land[5]. The presumption does not apply where the title deeds show the actual boundary, and it can be rebutted by contrary evidence; but apparent acts of ownership by the adjoining owner, such as cleaning the ditch, are not sufficient[6].

(c) Highways

A person owning land adjoining a public or private road is presumed to own also the soil of one-half of the road co-extensive with his land (*usque ad medium filum viae*). This is not a mere conveyancing presumption. It is a rule of construction that a house includes a moiety of the road in which it is situated[7]. The presumption is rebuttable, but not simply by showing that the land is described as bounded by the road, or is edged in colour on the deed plan but the road is uncoloured[8]. It may, however, be rebutted by express negative words in the conveyance, by showing that the site of the road was not vested in the vendor, or by evidence of surrounding circumstances leading to the inference that no part of the road was intended to pass[9]. It is readily rebutted on the sale of plots forming part of a building estate, for the developer needs to retain ownership of the soil of the intended roads for the purposes of construction and subsequent dedication to the public[10]. The owner of land which includes the site of a road still retains ownership of the sub-soil, even after its dedication to the public. The effect of dedication is simply to vest in the highway authority a fee simple estate in the surface of the road and so much above and below as may be necessary for it to carry out its statutory duties[11].

A similar presumption applies on the conveyance of land abutting a non-tidal river so as to pass to the grantee the bed of the river up to the medial line and with it the right to fish in the water above that half of the bed[12].

(d) Accretion and erosion

Where land is granted with a water boundary, the grantee's title extends to that land as added to or detracted from by accretion or diluvion (ie, erosion)[13].

5 *Fisher v Winch* [1939] 1 KB 666 at 669–70, [1939] 2 All ER 144 at 145, CA, per Sir Wilfrid Greene MR, a case dealing with the different rule applicable to a boundary described by reference to the Ordnance Survey map, when it runs along the centre of the hedge or ditch.
6 *Henniker v Howard* (1904) 90 LT 157, DC.
7 *Central London Rly Co v City of London Land Tax Comrs* [1911] 2 Ch 467 at 474, CA, per Cozens-Hardy MR; affd sub nom *City of London Land Tax Comrs v Central London Rly Co* [1913] AC 364, HL. For a discussion of the origins of this rule see Cozens-Hardy MR, loc cit. *Lang v House* (1961) 178 EG 801 (private road).
8 *Norton on Deeds* (2nd edn), p 252; *Dwyer v Rich* (1871) IR 6 CL 144 at 149, Ex Ch, per Fitzgerald J.
9 See *Pryor v Petre* [1894] 2 Ch 11, CA; *Mappin Bros v Liberty & Co Ltd* [1903] 1 Ch 118.
10 *Leigh v Jack* (1879) 5 Ex D 264, CA, Cotton LJ doubting (at 274) its application to building estates; *Giles v County Building Constructors (Hertford) Ltd* (1971) 22 P & CR 978.
11 *Tithe Redemption Commission v Runcorn UDC* [1954] Ch 383, [1954] 1 All ER 653, CA.
12 See *Hesketh v Willis Cruisers Ltd* (1968) 19 P & CR 573, CA; *Rice v Dodds* (1969) 213 EG 759.
13 *Southern Centre of Theosophy Inc v State of South Australia* [1982] AC 706, [1982] 1 All ER 283, PC. The opinion of Lord Wilberforce contains a full discussion of the authorities. See also [1986] Conv 247 (W Howarth).

This rule of convenience and fairness applies to land abutting a canal, inland lake or pond, as well as the sea-shore and rivers[14]. The accretion must occur by gradual imperceptible means, though changes caused partly by human action (other than deliberate conduct by the claimant) do not exclude the doctrine. Clear words in the conveyance can, however, suffice to oust its application[15].

(e) Boundary agreements

The parties to a boundary dispute may settle their differences by entering into a boundary agreement. This can take one of two forms[16]. It may constitute a contract to convey land, as where they agree that in return for a concession by A in one place, straightening the boundary, B will make a concession in another place. Such an agreement should be registered as a land charge, and if unregistered the agreement is statutorily avoided against a subsequent purchaser. It is also quite possible, however, that the agreement between the two land owners will fail to comply with the terms of s 2 of the Law of Property (Miscellaneous Provisions) Act 1989 and, therefore, lack contractual effect. However, it is unlikely that a landowner would be allowed by equity to revoke the agreement without giving up the land his predecessor had acquired. Indeed revocation may not even be open to a subsequent purchaser since he would seem to be estopped from denying that the boundaries were otherwise than as set out in the agreement[17]. Alternatively the agreement may do nothing more than identify on the ground what is described in words or delineated in plans. This is not registrable as there is no contract to convey. Boundary agreements are usually of an informal nature, and the courts tend to regard them as falling into the second category unless there is clear evidence that the agreement is intended to convey land.

6.   Registered land

(a) Description of registered land

According to s 76 of the Land Registration Act 1925, registered land may be described on the register of title in one of three different ways, regard being had to ready identification of parcels, correct descriptions of boundaries and, so far as may be, uniformity of practice. Only one of the three permissible methods is used in practice, namely the verbal description used in conjunction with the filed plan (which is preferred to the general map)[18], thus:

> The freehold land shown and edged with red on the plan of the above Title filed at the Registry registered on .... known as 'Fairhaven', Mead Road, Oadby.

14   The contrary decision in *Trafford v Thrower* (1929) 45 TLR 502 (rule not applied to Norfolk Broads) was considered to be wrongly decided in the *Theosophy* case, supra.
15   As in *Baxendale v Instow Parish Council* [1982] Ch 14, [1981] 2 All ER 620 (grant of foreshore).
16   *Neilson v Poole* (1969) 20 P & CR 909 at 918–20, per Megarry J.
17   *Hopgood v Brown* [1955] 1 All ER 550, CA.
18   See p 45, ante.

The description of every registered title by means of an accurate and expertly prepared plan based on the Ordnance Survey map achieves one of the principal objectives of the system of registered conveyancing, that of certainty, and enables the system to score over the unregistered system in a vital respect[19]. But the advantages of the filed plan should not be over-emphasised. In particular, the plan which is drawn to a scale of 1/1,250 (104.166 feet to 1 inch)[20] does little more than indicate the location of the land. It is too small to show short distances or record kinks in an otherwise straight boundary, and no measurements or dimensions appear on the plan. The Registry will always consider a request for a plan on a larger scale and will provide an enlargement when, for example, there are small buildings, such as a washhouse or garage, physically separated from the main plot, which would not be clearly visible on the normal size plan. Furthermore, criticism is sometimes made of the Registry's plans because they are not as informative as the best plans used in unregistered conveyancing. Information recorded on deed plans, of assistance in determining the ownership of boundary structures, is not reproduced on the register of title or the filed plan and is therefore lost on first registration. This information can, however, be readily obtained by consulting the pre-registration deeds[1]. It is the Registry's practice to make an entry on the register of any declaration as to the ownership of boundary structures contained in a transfer of registered land, and any 'T' marks are shown on the filed plan[2].

On a transfer of the whole of the land comprised within a registered title the prescribed form of transfer describes the property simply as 'the land comprised in the title above referred to'. On a sale of part the wording is:

> ...the land shown and edged with red on the accompanying plan and known as ... being part of the land comprised in the title above referred to[3].

In *A J Dunning & Sons (Shopfitters) Ltd v Sykes & Son (Poole) Ltd*[4] the court was faced with a situation where the plan on a transfer of part included land[5] no longer within the vendor's registered title because of a prior sale-off. Which took priority – the plan or the reference in the document to the land comprised within the vendor's title? It was held by a majority that the colouring on the plan was the dominant description. The reference to the property comprised

---

19 See R & R, 4–01.
20 For farms and smallholdings, the scale is even smaller, a mere 1/2500. For the introduction of metrication, see Land Registry Practice Leaflet for Solicitors No 11.
1   Though some would argue that if the theory of the registered system is that the land certificate replaces the title deeds, the register of title ought to record all information that a perusal of the deeds would reveal relative to the title. But see pp 45–46, ante.
2   'T' marks not expressly referred to in pre-registration deeds are ignored unless the applicant makes a specific request for them to be added to the filed plan; see Law Com Report No 125, Appendix 3, para 5.
3   LRR 1925, r 98, prescribing Form 20. A particular verbal description which is desired to be entered on the register may be added in a schedule.
4   [1987] Ch 287, [1987] 1 All ER 700, CA. The case concerned the operation of the covenants for title.
5   Comprising no more than 100 square feet, but vital to the purchaser's plans. Because of a fencing mistake it appeared that the disputed plot was still part of the vendor's retained land.

in the title number was subordinate, believed to be accurate but to be rejected as *falsa demonstratio* in so far as it was inaccurate in relation to the disputed land. It is, therefore, a wise precaution on any transfer of part to compare the transfer plan with the filed plan.

A printed note to the standard form in use for a transfer of part (Form 20) stresses that the plan should be drawn to a suitable scale (generally not less than 1/2,500). Where necessary, the position of the part transferred should also be related by means of figured dimensions to existing physical features on the ground, eg road Junctions, walls and fences. The Registry does not always seem to insist on these requirements being fulfilled; otherwise the problems that arose in *Scarfe v Adams*[6] would presumably have been avoided. Rule 79 permits a plan to be dispensed with when the property can be clearly defined by means of a verbal reference to the filed plan. Occasionally the Registrar will sanction the parties' own professionally drawn plan to be used as an adjunct to or even in place of the filed plan[7].

If on the occasion of first registration the purchaser chooses to take a transfer in registered land form[8] instead of a traditional conveyance, he should ensure that the transfer contains a full verbal description of the land conveyed. A reference to the description in a previous deed forming part of the title deduced might suffice, provided it is still accurate and up-to-date. Simply to annex a plan, particularly one expressed to be for identification purposes only, without any explanatory verbal description, is quite inadequate[9].

(b) Boundaries

(i) *General boundaries.*   The filed plan merely indicates the general boundaries of the registered land. It does not profess to determine whether it includes a hedge or part of an adjoining road, or runs along the centre of a wall or fence, and this rule applies irrespective of whether the plan includes or excludes the whole or part of a wall, fence, ditch or road[10]. In the absence of assistance from the transfer or conveyance leading to first registration, recourse must be had to the general presumption to ascertain the exact line of the boundary. It is arguable that the general boundaries rule allows the hedge and ditch presumption to apply, notwithstanding that the Ordnance Survey map which is the basis of every filed plan runs the boundary line through the centre of the hedge[11]. The Law Commission has recommended retention of the general boundaries rule[12]. Its existence can be brought onto the register without costly surveys of adjoining properties or elaborate investigative procedures. An improvement in

---

6   [1981] 1 All ER 843, CA, p 529, ante.
7   See Registered Land Practice Notes, 6, 45, 46; R & R, 4–05.
8   Allowed by LRR 1925, r 72.
9   An actual case encountered by the original author, which resulted in a builder erecting houses on land that he did not own and was unable to sell.
10   LRR 1925, r 278(1), (2), (4). It is not the Registry's practice to include the half in width of an adjoining road.
11   See p 541, note 5, ante.
12   Report No 125, paras 2.22–28. But see the critical comment at [1984] Conv 2.

conveyancing practice is seen as the best solution to reduce the number of boundary disputes. The Commission also saw no future in attempting to simplify a rarely used procedure for fixing the exact plot boundaries[13].

Sometimes the filed plan shows the boundaries by dotted lines, in which case a note is added that they have been plotted from the deed plan and are liable to revision on survey. This is a common occurrence on building estates when individual plots are transferred before the erection of the fences. The Registry is reluctant to plot the boundaries from the survey or site pegs, for not infrequently these do not coincide with the fences subsequently erected.

(ii) *Inconsistencies.* Though happily such occurrences are rare, it does occasionally happen that a discrepancy exists between the verbal description contained in the property register and the filed plan or between the latter and a plan on the transfer. Conflicts falling within the first category are decided by the Registrar[14]. In *Lee v Barrey*[15]:

> ...the defendant proprietor built a house within the boundaries indicated by the filed plan (which showed a straight boundary), though according to the transfer plan (which showed an angled boundary) part of the house was built on the plaintiff's adjacent plot. *Held*: the transfer plan prevailed, and therefore the defendant had trespassed on the plaintiff's land.

Not only did the filed plan indicate no more than the general boundaries, it also showed them as dotted lines, subject to revision on survey. In such circumstances the plan in the land certificate did not override the transfer plan which accurately recorded the bargain between the common vendor and the defendant. This case was suggested[16] as indicating a breakdown in the operation of the machinery of registered conveyancing; the land certificate was not as reliable as it was made out to be and a prudent purchaser ought to examine the plan on the previous transfer. The Chief Land Registrar sought to allay these fears by an admission, now apparently withdrawn[17], that the Registry neglected to apply its own procedures to the transaction. The modern practice in the case of inconsistencies of this type is not to allow registration to proceed without clarification of the parties' intentions[18]. More recently in *Proctor v Kidman*[19] the court declined to allow the filed plan to overrule the conveyance leading to first registration. A strip of land which the parties intended should pass to the purchaser was held to form part of his registered title, notwithstanding that the strip was not shown as included within the plan. Parker

13 LRR 1925, rr 276, 277; R & R, 4–22. Though a mere 20 titles (out of 8.3 million then registered) have fixed boundaries (Report, para 2.18), the Commission, oddly, saw no reason to press for its abolition.
14 LRR 1925, r 285. According to LRA 1925, s 76, the plan operates to assist the identification of the land, suggesting that in cases of conflict the verbal description should prevail. See [1979] Conv 316–319, 398–99.
15 [1957] Ch 251, [1957] 1 All ER 191, CA; *Re Boyle's Claim* [1961] 1 All ER 620.
16 (1957) 21 Conv (NS) 162–63. The defendant was compensated for his loss.
17 See Registered Land Practice Notes (1972) edn no 27, the significant passage of which is omitted from the relevant note C.3 in the latest (1986) edition.
18 R & R, 4–21.
19 (1986) 51 P & CR 67, CA.

LJ observed (at p 77) that any system of land registration can from time to time produce bizarre results, but to give an incorrect plan a force and effect which overrode the parties' intentions was unsustainable[20].

7.   Easements

(a) Existing easements

An easement passes automatically without express mention on a conveyance of the dominant land to which it is appurtenant, and a failure to mention it in the parcels in no way prejudices the purchaser. It is conceived that an equitable easement also passes automatically with the dominant land[1]. In practice, it is customary to mention existing easements, introducing them by the words 'TOGETHER WITH'. These may be incorporated by reference to the deed of creation and do not have to be set out again in extenso. The burden of a legal easement binds the servient land and is enforceable against any subsequent owner or occupier thereof, irrespective of notice, whether the land is registered or unregistered. The enforceability of equitable easements affecting unregistered land is governed either by registration or notice[2].

(b) Easements created on sale

Where the conveyance to the purchaser creates easements in his favour[3], they may be set out in the parcels, similarly introduced by 'TOGETHER WITH', or alternatively, and preferably if they are lengthy, they may be set out in full in a subsequent clause of the deed[4] or in a schedule – which is the invariable practice in a transfer of registered land. Easements are commonly granted on the sale or lease of land forming part of a building estate.

Easements may also be created by a deed of grant independently of the conveyance of land. In the case of registered land the grant must be completed by registration, otherwise the easement operates merely in equity[5]. It should also be remembered that the effect of a conveyance may be to pass to the grantee as an easement some right or privilege not previously existing as such, either by virtue of the general words implied by s 62 of the Law of Property Act 1925, or under the rule in *Wheeldon v Burrows*[6].

---

20   This seems too alarmist. The court was unnecessarily preoccupied with the jurisdictional aspects of LRA 1925, s 82(1)(a), which could have been avoided by relying on para (h). Contrast the converse situation. Had *excess* land been conveyed to and registered in the purchaser contrary to the parties' intentions, then in no way could those intentions have overriden the vesting of the excess in the purchaser under s 5 of the Act. See p 30, ante. Cf *Blacklocks v J B Developments (Godalming) Ltd* [1982] Ch 183, [1981] 3 All ER 392 (where a third party was involved).
1   See *Gale on Easements* (14th edn), p 69.
2   See p 389, ante. As to the registered land position, see p 496, ante.
3   The vendor can also create or reserve (this being the technical expression) easements in favour of himself; see p 548, post.
4   In which case the parcels clause should merely state 'together with the rights and easements mentioned in clause ... hereof'.
5   Page 494, ante.
6   (1879) 12 Ch D 31 at 49, CA, per Thesiger LJ. For the operation of this rule see M & W, 861–64. See p 551, post, for s 62.

(c) Some points to consider when granting easements

When creating a new easement the practitioner should exercise the same care as is required when drafting the description of the land conveyed. However, the cases again reveal that the standard of draftsmanship leaves much to be desired on occasions[7]. It is beyond the scope of this book to discuss in detail the various considerations which should be borne in mind when preparing the grant. A few general points will be made, applicable alike to grants and reservations. First, as a matter of sound conveyancing practice, it is always desirable to identify the dominant land, eg by delineating it on a deed plan. This removes the element of doubt and reduces the risk of litigation[8], though the grant of an easement will not fail simply because the deed fails to specify the dominant tenement. Problems of the extent of the benefited land sometimes arise in relation to rights of way. The case of *Bracewell v Appleby*[9] establishes that an easement of way granted to plot A does not confer any right to an adjacent plot B, also owned by the grantee. If the dominant land is not clearly identified, it is arguable that the right of way is appurtenant to the larger area[10]. Secondly, the application of the perpetuity rule to the grant of an easement to arise in the future should not be overlooked. The draftsman needs to ensure that such an easement is limited to take effect within the period of 80 years now permitted by the Perpetuities and Accumulations Act 1964. If not so limited the grant is not void ab initio (as at common law). Under s 3 of the Act it is not avoided until it becomes certain that vesting must occur outside the 'wait and see' period, which would be 21 years from the death of the last survivor of the original parties to the grant[11]. The Act is not retrospective. All future easements granted before 16 July 1964, the date of commencement, are consequently void if falling foul of the rule at common law[12].

Finally, the grant of an easement ordinarily carries with it such ancillary rights as are reasonably necessary to its exercise or enjoyment. Thus the grantee of a right of way or drainage has the right to enter the servient owner's land to effect necessary repairs, but at his own expense. Apart from special local custom or express contract the servient owner is under no obligation to the grantee

---

7 See, eg *Celsteel Ltd v Alton House Holdings Ltd* [1985] 2 All ER 562 (deed plan not identifying drives over which rights of way exercisable); *Beatty v Curston* [1982] CA Transcript 262 (vendor on sale-off reserving right of way over retained land).

8 *Johnstone v Holdway* [1963] 1 QB 601, [1963] 1 All ER 432, CA; *Shannon Ltd v Venner Ltd* [1965] Ch 682, [1965] 1 All ER 590, CA.

9 [1975] Ch 408, [1975] 1 All ER 993. Enlargement of the dominant land may not preclude acquisition under LPA 1925, s 62: *Graham v Philcox* [1984] QB 747, [1984] 2 All ER 643, CA; cf *Nickerson v Barraclough* [1981] Ch 426, [1981] 2 All ER 369, CA; p 552, post. See also *National Trusts for Places of Historic Interest or Natural Beauty v White* [1987] 1 WLR 907.

10 At least if the grantee already owns the adjacent land. See Emmet, para 15.071.

11 If both original parties are companies, the period is 21 years: s 3(4)(b). The 80 years' period is an alternative to a 'royal lives' clause, still permissible at common law.

12 *Dunn v Blackdown Properties Ltd* [1961] Ch 433, [1961] 2 All ER 62 (drainage rights not saved by LPA 1925, s 162(1)(d)); *Newham v Lawson* (1971) 22 P & CR 852 (prescriptive right to light acquired despite avoidance of grant for perpetuity). For a fuller treatment of the consequences of avoidance, see the second edition, p 523; (1964) 61 LS Gaz 59.

to repair[13]. Authority exists for the proposition that the benefit of the grantor's covenant to repair runs with the easement, but it is uncertain whether this represents the law in England[14]. The benefit can, of course, be expressly assigned on a conveyance of the dominant land. The grant of a right of way does not constitute or imply any warranty that it will be adequate for the grantee's needs[15]. Nor does the servient owner owe any duty under the Occupiers' Liability Act 1957 to persons using a right of way across his land[16].

8. Exceptions and reservations

(a) Nature

The parcels clause not only describes the land intended to be conveyed to the grantee, it also delimits what is not to pass to him. The vendor may wish to retain for himself a specified part – certain fields from the conveyance of a farm, or the underlying mines and minerals. What the vendor retains is termed an *exception*. An exception of mines and minerals results in the surface and the subjacent minerals becoming separate tenements severed in title[17]. The grantor retains all his original rights in relation to the property excepted together with all incidentals necessary for its enjoyment.

Exceptions and reservations, though commonly bracketed together as if similar in nature, are in truth essentially different and should not be confused. An exception always refers to something in esse; it forms part of the land granted, at least before the conveyance takes effect. A *reservation* refers to some newly created right; it is not, therefore, in esse prior to the conveyance. The term 'reservation' is commonly used today[18] to connote an incorporeal right over land granted, of which the grantor desires to have the benefit, such as a right of way, or sporting rights.

(b) Creation

(i) *New rights.* Newly created exceptions and reservations are normally introduced within the parcels by the words 'Excepting and reserving'. Exceptions correctly form part of the parcels, whereas reservations should strictly appear immediately after the habendum (ie 'To hold') clause. The

13 See generally *Duke of Westminster v Guild* [1985] QB 688 at 700, [1984] 3 All ER 144 at 152, CA, per Slade LJ, citing *Jones v Pritchard* [1908] 1 Ch 630 at 637–39 per Parker J (a helpful discussion).
14 *Gaw v Córas Iompair Éireann* [1953] IR 232; contrast *Grant v Edmondson* [1931] 1 Ch 1, CA (rentcharge). The burden of the covenant, being positive, does not bind the grantor's successors.
15 *Stokes v Mixconcrete (Holdings) Ltd* (1978) 38 P & CR 488, CA; cf *Beaumont v Dukes* (1822) Jac 422 (express representation about access to be provided).
16 *Holden v White* [1982] QB 679, [1982] 2 All ER 328, CA. These people now come within the scope of the Occupiers' Liability Act 1984, and are owed the duty imposed by s 1(4).
17 *Duke of Hamilton v Graham* (1871) LR 2 Sc & Div 166; see also LPA s 205(1)(ix) ('land' includes mines and minerals whether or not held apart from the surface).
18 For its strict technical meaning, see *Mason v Clarke* [1954] 1 QB 460 at 467, [1954] 1 All ER 189 at 192, CA, per Denning LJ.

expression 'reserving' is appropriate only to the creation of new rights. Use of an incorrect introductory expression will not preclude the court from giving effect to the parties' intentions. In one case the court upheld a right of way in favour of the grantee's successors in title, notwithstanding that in the deed of creation the right was introduced by the words 'save and except'[19]. As an alternative to an express reservation the vendor may take advantage of s 65 (2) of the Law of Property Act 1925, which enacts:

> A conveyance of a legal estate expressed to be made subject to another legal estate[20] not in existence immediately before the date of the conveyance, shall operate as a reservation, unless a contrary intention appears.

This provision seems not to have been recognised as a legitimate means of creating easements in a vendor's favour until the recent instructive case of *Wiles v Banks*[1]. Here a conveyance from V to P was expressed to be subject to a right of way for the owner or occupier (O) of certain adjacent property along a track across the land conveyed. Prior thereto, O had used the track on payment of a nominal annual sum. The court held that the conveyance was effective to grant an easement of way over the track in O's favour. Though not a party to the V-P deed, he was capable of taking an interest in P's land by virtue of s 56 of the Act. A contrary intention suffices to negative its operation. This need not appear in the deed itself; a consideration of surrounding circumstances may suffice to indicate such intention. Despite statutory backing for this 'subject to' formula, it remains a most inept way of creating new rights and is, perhaps, best not adopted.

On the sale of properties by a common vendor to different purchasers, it is standard practice for each conveyance to provide for the reservation in the vendor's favour of all quasi-easements and other rights in the nature of easements used or enjoyed over the land conveyed for the benefit of the retained property. Such general words were held in *Pitt v Buxton*[2] to be capable of constituting an express regrant of an easement over the purchaser's land, its nature and extent being determined by the de facto user obtaining at the date of the conveyance. However, a general clause of this nature does not operate to withdraw by implication part of the structure of a house that is being conveyed[3].

(ii) *Vendor's entitlement.*   A vendor who seeks to rely on the reservation of an easement must be able to point to a reservation expressed in clear and

---

19   *British Railways Board v Glass* [1965] Ch 538, [1964] 3 All ER 418, CA; *A-G for New South Wales v Dickson* [1904] AC 273, PC ('reserving' held to operate as exception).
20   Including legal easements by virtue of LPA 1925, ss 1(2)(a), 205(1)(x).
1   (1984) 50 P & CR 80, CA. Section 65(2) is not cited by M & W, or in 14, 42, *Halsbury's Laws*, Easements, Sale of Land, or Jackson, *The Law of Easements and Profits*, or in previous editions of this book. According to 1 W & C, 146, its object is *not* to supply a new form of a reservation to be created de novo. And see *St Edmundsbury and Ipswich Diocesan Board of Finance v Clark (No 2)* [1975] 1 All ER 772 at 775, CA, per Sir John Pennycuick.
2   (1970) 21 P & CR 127, CA, applied in *Pallister v Clark* (1975) 30 P & CR 84, CA (general words in agreement and declaration sufficient to create reservation). For a precedent see 19 Ency F & P, 923, Form 7.A.33.
3   *Grigsby v Melville* [1973] 3 All ER 455, CA (underground cellar).

unambiguous language[4]. Moreover his entitlement to have an exception or reservation in his favour stems from the contract. A vendor intending to reserve a right of way over the land granted cannot insist on the conveyance incorporating the reservation if he has failed to provide for such a right in the contract[5]. Where the owner of two adjoining properties conveys one of them there is no *implied* reservation of any rights over the land sold, save for easements of necessity and reciprocal rights of support; but the court will imply the appropriate reservation if the circumstances of the case raise a necessary inference that the common intention of the parties was to reserve some easement in favour of the grantor[6]. A conveyance which fails to give effect to a reservation provided for in the contract operates to extinguish the intended right, and the vendor's only remedy is to seek rectification of the conveyance[7]. It hardly needs to be stressed that the vendor's solicitor must ensure that the words of the reservation inserted in the conveyance are ample enough to give his client what he wants[8]. The vendor should retain documentary evidence of his title to the exception or reservation and the contract should stipulate for the conveyance to be executed in duplicate.

(iii) *Existing rights.*   On a subsequent transaction it is not technically correct to repeat verbatim the exceptions and reservations appearing in the previous conveyance. This may have the unintended effect of creating new rights in favour of the subsequent vendor, should he own adjacent land. The correct procedure is to refer to them in the habendum, prefaced by words 'subject to the exceptions and reservations... '. If the 'excepting and reserving' formula is adopted, the court will not as a matter of construction recognise the creation of new rights if it is clear that the parties merely intended a reference to existing rights[9].

(c) Reservation operating without regrant
At common law the reservation of an easement or profit operated as a regrant by the purchaser, and as such necessitated his execution of the deed to make it effective at law (unlike an exception). This requirement has been abolished by s 65(1) of the Law of Property Act 1925, which enacts that reservation now operates at law 'without any execution of the conveyance by the grantee ... or any regrant by him'. This is apparently the sole change in the law made by sub-s (1). Despite the words 'without ... any regrant', the Court of Appeal has held that a reservation continues to operate by way of regrant. So, where a conveyance by X (as trustee) and Y (as beneficial owner) reserved a right of

---

4   *Broomfield v Williams* [1897] 1 Ch 602 at 616, CA, per Rigby LJ.
5   *Simpson v Gilley* (1922) 92 LJ Ch 194; *Grigsby v Melville*, supra.
6   *Re Webb's Lease, Sandom v Webb* [1951] Ch 808 at 823, [1951] 2 All ER 131 at 141, CA, per Jenkins LJ.
7   *Teebay v Manchester, Sheffield and Lincolnshire Rly Co* (1883) 24 Ch D 572.
8   For cases of ineffective drafting, see *Cordell v Second Clanfield Properties Ltd* [1969] 2 Ch 9, [1968] 3 All ER 746; *MRA Engineering Ltd v Trimster Co Ltd* (1987) 56 P & CR 1, CA (failure to reserve right of way on sale-off).
9   *Re Dances Way, West Town, Hayling Island* [1962] Ch 490, [1962] 2 All ER 42, CA.

way in Y's favour over land conveyed to Z, the deed operated to vest in Y a legal easement. Although Y merely held an equitable interest in the dominant land, Z was the effective grantor and he was the legal owner of the servient land[10]. It follows, therefore, that in cases of uncertainty or ambiguity the easement is to be construed against the purchaser, as grantor. Megarry V-C has championed the view that the wording of s 65(1) 'without any regrant' changes the substantive law, one consequence of which would be that the contra proferentum rule, when applicable, would operate against the vendor in favour of the purchaser. Despite there being 'much force in the reasoning'[11], the argument is not one that has found favour with other judges.

9. General words

By virtue of s 62(2) of the Law of Property Act 1925[12], a conveyance of land *with houses or other buildings thereon* is deemed to include and operates to convey with the land, houses or other buildings:

> ... all outhouses, erections, fixtures, cellars, areas, courts, courtyards, cisterns, sewers, gutters, drains, ways, passages, lights, watercourses, liberties, privileges, easements, rights, and advantages whatsoever, appertaining or reputed to appertain to the land, houses or other buildings conveyed, or any of them, or any part thereof, or, at the time of conveyance, demised, occupied, or enjoyed with, or reputed or known as part or parcel of or appurtenant to, the land, houses, or other buildings conveyed, or any of them, or any part thereof.

These are known as the general words which were expressly included in a conveyance before they came to be statutorily implied. Nowadays in the absence of a contrary intention any such matter as is referred to in the subsection is deemed to be included within the parcels, and so passes to the purchaser. For the purposes of the section, 'conveyance' includes a written tenancy agreement for a term not exceeding three years[13], but not an agreement for a lease for seven years[14]. The section applies to registered land[15]. It does not operate to convey chattels, so that greenhouses resting on the land by their own weight without being secured cannot constitute 'erections' and do not pass without express mention[16]. Nor does the section pass other land not included in the parcels, even though it has previously been enjoyed with the land conveyed. As is well known, the section operates to transform into legal easements reputed

---

10   *Johnstone v Holdway* [1963] 1 QB 601, [1963] 1 All ER 432, CA, applied in the *St Edmundsbury* case [1975] 1 All ER 772, CA.

11   *St Edmundsbury* case, supra, at 782, per Sir John Pennycuick, disapproving of *Cordell v Second Clanfield Properties Ltd*, ante, and Megarry J's first instance decision on this point at [1973] 3 All ER 902; see also M & W, 858–59.

12   Sub-s (1) deals with the conveyance of *land* and sub-s (3) with the conveyance of a *manor*. Section 62 replaces the Conveyancing Act 1881, s 6.

13   *Wright v Macadam* [1949] 2 KB 744, [1949] 2 All ER 565, CA. But an oral tenancy is not a 'conveyance': *Rye v Rye* [1962] AC 496, [1962] 1 All ER 146, HL.

14   *Borman v Griffith* [1930] 1 Ch 493. And see LPA 1925, s 205(1)(ii).

15   LRA 1925, ss 19(3), 22(3).

16   *H E Dibble Ltd v Moore* [1970] 2 QB 181, [1969] 3 All ER 1465, CA; *Deen v Andrews* (1986) 52 P & CR 17 (prefabricated greenhouse).

rights, or rights which merely existed as liberties or privileges whose enjoyment had previously been permissive or precarious[17], though it is submitted that it does not apply where the user has been objected to continually. The section only passes what actually exists already; so, user of an unmade lane for sporting and agricultural purposes cannot be converted into a right of way for all purposes[18]. It cannot create an easement out of some facility enjoyed with land other than the land conveyed[19]. The way in which s 62 works can be seen in *Graham v Philcox* [20], though this is not strictly a case of upgrading but of enlargement. The rather complicated factual situation can be reduced to the following.

> L leased a first-floor flat of a house to T together with a right to use a drive on L's adjacent land. After L's death his executors conveyed the entire house to P[1] (the plaintiff), subject to T's tenancy which he subsequently surrendered. P then converted the house into a single residence, and claimed a right to use the drive which had become vested in the defendant. He succeeded.

The effect of s 62(2) was to enlarge the right of way so that after the conveyance it endured for the benefit of the entire house, not just that part (the flat) comprising the original dominant tenement. It was the fact of user with the land conveyed at the relevant time that mattered, rather than the title under which it had been enjoyed. For a fuller consideration of the working of s 62, reference should be made to standard real property books[2]. The following points require some discussion here.

(a) Rights known to the law

The section applies only to a right or advantage capable of existing at law as an easement. It cannot pass, for example, a right to wind and air coming in an undefined channel[3], or a right to protection from the weather[4]. It is debatable whether the benefit of covenants is intended to pass by virtue of the general words. A right under covenant cannot 'appertain' to land within s 62 unless it is annexed to land[5]. So, if and so far as the general words do embrace covenant rights, s 62 does not enlarge the category of covenants capable of passing

---

17   See *Ward v Kirkland* [1967] Ch 194 at 230, [1966] 1 All ER 609 at 620, per Ungoed-Thomas J (right to enter land to repair wall).
18   *Nickerson v Barraclough* [1981] Ch 426 at 446, [1981] 2 All ER 369 at 383, CA, per Eveleigh LJ.
19   *Nickerson v Barraclough*, supra.
20   [1984] QB 747, [1984] 2 All ER 643, CA, noted at [1985] Conv 60.
1   P was in fact a purchaser twice removed from the conveyance by L's executors.
2   M & W, 864–69; C & B, 503–6; Jackson, op cit, 92ff; (1966) 30 Conv (NS) 340 (P Jackson).
3   Cf *Webb v Bird* (1862) 13 CBNS 841.
4   *Phipps v Pears* [1965] 1 QB 76, [1964] 2 All ER 35, CA. See also *Green v Ashco Horticulturist Ltd* [1966] 2 All ER 232; *Regis Property Co Ltd v Redman* [1956] 2 QB 612, [1956] 2 All ER 335, CA; *Anderson v Bostock* [1976] Ch 312, [1976] 1 All ER 560.
5   And as such the benefit will pass without any help from s 62, either on general principles as in *Kumar v Dunning* [1989] QB 193, [1987] 2 All ER 801, CA (surety covenant), or by virtue of LPA 1925, s 78(1) (p 571, post). In *Kumar v Dunning* Browne-Wilkinson V-C assumed without deciding that rights under covenant are within s 62. See also *Pinemain Ltd v Welbeck International Ltd* (1984) 272 EG 1166 at 1170, per Judge Nugee QC.

automatically without express assignment. It cannot be relied on to pass the benefit of a purely personal covenant.

(b) Title of vendor
The statute does not pass by implication any right which the vendor is not capable of granting expressly[6]. This is an important and obvious restriction that is not always fully appreciated, even by the judiciary, it seems. Lord Edmund-Davies's dictum in *Sovmots Investments Ltd v Secretary of State for the Environment*[7] to the effect that s 62 can operate when there is diversity of ownership of the two tenements prior to conveyance is difficult to follow. Unity of ownership of both plots is essential; if the grantor does not own the servient land, he is without power, express or implied, to grant rights over it. Suppose that the owner of Blackacre grants to the owner of the adjoining land, Whiteacre, a licence to cross Blackacre. A subsequent conveyance of Whiteacre will not convert this privilege into an easement for the benefit of the purchaser. In practice the operation of s 62 is usually confined to situations when there is a severance of land in common ownership, or where a lessor sells to, or renews the lease of, his tenant[8].

(c) Diversity of occupation
In the *Sovmots* case the House of Lords approved obiter the proposition established in *Long v Gowlett*[9] that s 62 does not apply unless there is diversity of *occupation* before the conveyance. For example, if the owner and occupier of two adjacent properties, Blackacre and Whiteacre, crosses Blackacre to reach Whiteacre, a conveyance of Whiteacre will not pass any right over Blackacre under the section. That right, it is said, has not been enjoyed with Whiteacre (the quasi-dominant plot) but was exercised by virtue of the vendor's own occupation of Blackacre (the servient land)[10]. The necessity for such diversity has been attacked[11] as being an unwarranted gloss on the statute, not the least because of the difficulty of distinguishing the contrary decision in *Broomfield v Williams*[12]. Here the Court of Appeal held that the statutory general words operated to pass to the purchaser of a house a right of light over the vendor's

---

6 Section 62 (5); *Quicke v Chapman* [1903] 1 Ch 659, CA; *MRA Engineering Ltd v Trimster Co Ltd* (1987) 56 P & CR 1, CA.
7 [1979] AC 144 at 176, [1977] 2 All ER 385 at 397, HL, adopted by C & B, 505.
8 See also *Goldberg v Edwards* [1950] Ch 247, CA (privilege afforded to tenant allowed into possession before grant of formal lease converted into easement); *Lyme Valley Squash Club Ltd v Newcastle under Lyme Borough Council* [1985] 2 All ER 405 (right of light acquired for building erected on land before conveyance). But what of the peculiar doctrine of relation back governing escrows (p 451, ante)?
9 [1923] 2 Ch 177.
10 *Long v Gowlett*, supra, at 200–1, per Sargant J; *Sovmots* case, supra, at 169, 391 per Lord Wilberforce; at 184, 404, per Lord Keith ('a self-evident proposition').
11 See Gale, op cit, 125–26; Jackson, op cit, 97–103; [1978] Conv 449, [1979] Conv 311 (P Smith). Contra, (1977) 41 Conv (NS) 415, [1979] Conv 113 (C Harpum).
12 [1897] 1 Ch 602, CA. In *Long v Gowlett*, supra, at 202, Sargant J accepted the binding force of *Bromfield v Williams* as regards any easement on the same footing as light, ie one that is continuous and apparent.

adjacent land, although the vendor had previously lived in the house. Simply to state[13] that the easement of light is an exception to many rules is hardly convincing. The judges in *Broomfield v Williams* gave no hint that they were dealing with an exceptional situation. Indeed, Rugby LJ[14] thought that the case was governed by *Kay v Oxlye*[15], a decision on express general words involving a right of way. What is of significance about *Kay v Oxlye* is Blackburn J's clear rejection of the argument that unity of possession by a common occupier prevented the exercise of a right over one plot from being regarded in law as appurtenant to the other. Despite the previous uncertainty, it now seems to be clear that, to for an easement to be created under s 62, there must either have been diversity of occupation prior to the conveyance, or the quasi-easement must have been continuous and apparent[16]; any other rule would cause s 62 to operate as a terrible potential trap to a vendor selling off part of his land.

(d) Contrary intention

Section 62 applies only if and so far as a contrary intention is not expressed in the conveyance (sub-s (4)). A statement on the deed plan which shows the vendor's adjacent land as 'building land' does not suffice to prevent the acquisition of a right of light over that land[17]; nor does the express grant of a limited easement operate as a contrary intention to exclude wider rights passing under the general words[18]. The vendor's right to have a contrary intention inserted in the conveyance depends on the terms of the contract. The necessity for a solicitor, when he is drafting the contract, to consider carefully the implications of s 62, has been considered in an earlier chapter[19]. The vendor can insist on the insertion in the conveyance of appropriate words modifying or excluding the operation of the section whenever the general words will give the purchaser more than his entitlement under the contract[20]. An omission of such a clause through some mutual mistake may lead to rectification of the conveyance[1].

But what if the contract is silent as to the purchaser's rights? According to Forbes J's helpful analysis in the *Sovmots* case at first instance[2], the position appears to be as follows. The vendor impliedly contracts to sell (i) all appurtenant easements, and (ii) rights in the nature of quasi-easements necessary for the reasonable enjoyment of the property for the use intended

---

13   Per Lord Edmund-Davies in the *Sovmots* case, supra at 176, 398, citing M & W, 866.
14   [1897] 1 Ch 602 at 617.
15   (1875) LR 10 QB 360, especially at 365, per Blackburn J.
16   See [1979] Conv 113 (C Harpum); [1995] Conv 239 at 241 (M P Thompson), discussing *Wheeler v J J Saunders Ltd* [1996] Ch 19, [1995] 2 All ER 697, CA (a case on *Wheeldon v Burrows*).
17   *Broomfield v Williams* [1897] 1 Ch 602, CA; *Pollard v Gare* [1901] 1 Ch 834.
18   *Hansford v Jago* [1921] 1 Ch 322; *Gregg v Richards* [1926] Ch 521, CA.
19   Pages 172–174, ante. For relevant contractual clauses, see SCS 3.4.2.
20   *Re Walmsley and Shaw's Contract* [1917] 1 Ch 93.
1   *Clarke v Barnes* [1929] 2 Ch 368; cf *Slack v Hancock* (1912) 107 LT 14 (rectification refused).
2   [1977] QB 411 at 439–443, [1976] 1 All ER 178 at 199–202, relying heavily on M & W (3rd edn) 835; see now 5th edn, 867–68. On appeal [1979] AC 144, [1977] 2 All ER 385, HL.

by the parties and actually used for the benefit of the land sold at the time of the contract. The parties' intentions, if not ascertainable from the contract, are to be gleaned from the surrounding circumstances[3]. This produces the same result as would the operation of the rule in *Wheeldon v Burrows*[4] on the subsequent grant, not because the grant determines what must be presumed to be the contract, but due to a direct coincidence[5] of the rules governing both contract and conveyance in this situation. The vendor does not, however, contract to convey quasi-easements of mere convenience, unless specifically included in the contract. Nor can the purchaser claim all those rights which would pass under s 62; a contract to sell Blackacre with no additional words entitles the vendor to exclude the appropriate parts of s 62.

10. The 'all estate' clause

Section 63(1) of the Law of Property Act 1925, which replaces the Conveyancing Act 1881, s 63, provides that every conveyance is effectual to pass 'all the estate, right, title, interest[6], claim and demand'[7] which the conveying parties have, or have power to convey, in the property. It does not apply if there is a contrary intention and has effect subject to the terms and provisions in the deed itself (sub-s (2)).

The section operates to pass to the grantee every estate or interest held by the grantor in the land, although not expressly mentioned in the conveyance, or not vested in him in the capacity in which he is made a party to the deed[8]. A conveyance of the fee simple may, therefore, pass to the purchaser an outstanding term of years vested in the vendor, which has not merged with the freehold[9]. In *Re Stirrup's Contract*[10] Wilberforce J held that an assent under seal executed by personal representatives was effective because of s 63 to pass the legal estate vested in them, though technically they had no power to execute an assent, since the title had not devolved on them as required by s 36(1) of the Administration of Estates Act 1925. Similarly the section ensures that a conveyance by an executor-beneficiary as 'beneficial owner' vests in the purchaser both the legal and equitable titles in the property, notwithstanding that he has not executed an assent in his own favour. It may also be of assistance to a mortgagee who unwittingly advances money on the strength of a forged mortgage deed. Suppose that A and B are beneficial joint tenants of certain land, and a mortgage thereof in favour of C purports to be executed by A and B, but in fact B's signature is forged. The mortgage cannot operate as a charge

3   See *Borman v Griffith* [1930] 1 Ch 493, as explained by Forbes J.
4   (1879) 12 Ch D 31, CA.
5   See *Wheeler v J J Saunders Ltd* [1996] Ch 19, [1995] 2 All ER 697, CA; criticised at [1995] Conv 239.
6   *Boots the Chemist Ltd v Street* (1983) 268 EG 817 (benefit of right to rectification).
7   See *Hill v Booth* [1930] 1 KB 381, CA ('demand' does not cover unpaid balance of premium reserved on grant of lease).
8   *Taylor v London and County Banking Co* [1901] 2 Ch 231 at 255–56, CA, per Stirling LJ, citing *Drew v Earl of Norbury* (1846) 3 Jo & Lat 267 at 284, per Lord St Leonards.
9   *Burton v Barclay* (1831) 7 Bing 745; see also *Thelluson v Liddard* [1900] 2 Ch 635.
10 [1961] 1 All ER 805, p 320, ante. 'Conveyance' includes an assent: LPA 1925, s 205(1)(ii).

on the legal estate, but by virtue of s 63 it is effective to create a valid equitable charge on A's beneficial interest in the land[11].

In relation to registered land, there is no provision in the Land Registration Act 1925 exactly corresponding to s 63. However, the all estate clause would appear to be implied[12] by the wide words of ss 20(1) and 23(1) of that Act, which provide that registration confers on the proprietor the legal estate together with 'the appropriate rights and interests which would, under the Law of Property Act 1925, have been transferred if the land had not been registered'.

J   Habendum clause

The habendum determines the size or quantum of the estate to be acquired by the grantee. In the normal conveyance it often appears in this form: 'TO HOLD[13] unto the purchaser in fee simple'. In a lease it is usually drafted in some such form as 'TO HOLD unto the lessee for the term of ... years from the date hereof', and in an assignment of an existing leasehold term as 'TO HOLD unto the purchaser for all the residue now unexpired of the term created by the lease'. A term of years commencing *from* a specified date is generally reckoned as exclusive of that day, whereas a term to start *on* a certain day includes that day[14]. Though the term may be expressed to run from some date anterior to the date of the lease, the lessee's actual interest therein only takes effect from the date of delivery (taken to be the date of the deed). Thus in *Roberts v Church Comrs for England*[15] a lease dated 29 October 1972, which granted a term of 21 and a quarter years from 27 March 1970, was held not to create a long tenancy (ie one for a term exceeding 21 years) for the purposes of s 3(1) of the Leasehold Reform Act 1967; consequently the tenant was not entitled under the Act to acquire the freehold. The lease may quite properly

11   *First National Securities Ltd v Hegerty* [1985] QB 850, [1984] 1 All ER 139; affd [1985] QB 861, [1984] 3 All ER 641, CA. The contrary decision in *Cedar Holdings Ltd v Green* [1981] Ch 129, [1979] 3 All ER 117, CA, based on the view that an interest in the proceeds of sale of land is not within s 63, was considered to be wrongly decided on that point by Lord Wilberforce in *Williams and Glyn's Bank Ltd v Boland* [1981] AC 487 at 507, [1980] 2 All ER 408 at 415, HL; *Thames Guaranty Ltd v Campbell* [1985] QB 210 at 227–29, [1984] 2 All ER 585 at 598–99, CA, per Slade LJ; *Ahmed v Kendrick* (1987) 56 P & CR 120, CA, note 12, infra, but without referring to the views of Lord Oliver in *City of London Building Society v Flegg* [1988] AC 54, [1987] 3 All ER 435 at 443–44, 447, HL, which offer support for the view that the *Cedar Holdings* case (not cited in *Flegg*) might after all have been correctly decided on the s 63 point.

12   And see *Ahmed v Kendrick*, supra (husband forging wife's signature to transfer; transfer, though not completed by registration, still effective to pass husband's beneficial interest under trust for sale to purchaser).

13   Originally the clause commenced 'To have (habendum) and to hold (tenendum)', the purpose of the latter being to signify the tenure by which the estate was to be held, eg *tenendum in libero socagio*; see 2 *Blackstone's Commentaries*, 298–99.

14   *Meggeson v Groves* [1917] 1 Ch 158; *Clayton's Case* (1585) 5 Co Rep 1a.

15   [1972] 1 QB 278, [1971] 3 All ER 703, CA; *Bradshaw v Pawley* [1979] 3 All ER 273 at 276–77, per Megarry V-C; *Keen v Holland* [1984] 1 All ER 75, CA.

contain contractual provisions which are to take effect by reference to some earlier date. The covenant to pay rent is a common example.

No habendum clause appears in the prescribed forms of registered land transfers[16]. The size of the estate acquired by the transferee is indicated, if only indirectly. The transfer relates to 'the land comprised in the title above mentioned' and this is a sufficient reference to the register of title which contains particulars of the registered estate. The habendum is strictly a non-essential part of the deed even at common law. In the absence of any habendum, the grantee took the quantum of estate mentioned in the premises (ie that part of the deed preceding the habendum)[17]; otherwise he took a mere life estate. It might be thought there is even less need today for the habendum in the normal conveyance of freehold land, since it is enacted that the deed operates to pass the fee simple or other the grantor's whole interest without any words of limitation unless a contrary intention appears[18]. Nevertheless it is still the practice to retain the expression 'in fee simple' in the habendum. Indeed this appears to be highly desirable, for the omission of these three words may well render nugatory the implied statutory covenants for title[19]. The habendum is the proper place to refer to existing exceptions and reservations, restrictive covenants and other liabilities and incumbrances subject to which the property is conveyed. The object of qualifying the habendum in this way is to limit the operation of the vendor's covenants for title. The purchaser is entitled to a conveyance expressed to be subject only to such restrictive covenants and other adverse rights as are mentioned in the contract[20]. The omission of some adverse interest or incumbrance from the habendum does not affect the question of its enforceability, which is determined by general principles, but it may render the vendor liable on his covenants for title.

Over the years various rules have been laid down by the courts to resolve conflicts between the premises and the habendum. These are of little practical importance today and only one need be mentioned. The habendum cannot be read so as to enlarge the description of the parcels; consequently land not included in the parcels does not pass though it is named in the habendum[1]. This rule does not prevent the passing of land or appurtenant rights referred to only in the habendum, which are deemed to be included within the parcels by virtue of the general words and so pass to the grantee in any event.

K Reddendum clause

On the grant of a lease the habendum is followed by the reddendum clause which specifies the amount of the rent and the time when it is payable[2].

16 See LRR 1925, Schedule, Forms 19, 32.
17 *Goodtitle d Dodwell v Gibbs* (1826) 5 B & C 709.
18 LPA 1925, s 60(1).
19 1 K & E, 537; p 671, post.
20 *Re Wallis and Barnard's Contract* [1899] 2 Ch 515.
 1 *Sheppard's Touchstone*, p 75; *Norton on Deeds* (2nd edn), pp 311–12.
 2 See further, p 586, post.

L   Declaration of beneficial entitlement

1.   Co-ownership

Prior to 1926 the habendum was frequently followed by a declaration of uses operating under the Statute of Uses 1535. Nowadays this position is often filled by a clause which says how joint purchasers are to hold the property in equity and enlarges their powers qua trustees. What commonly used to be the position was that an express trust for sale was created, the conveyance declaring that:

> ...the purchasers shall hold the said property upon trust to sell the same with power to postpone the sale thereof and shall hold the net proceeds of sale and other money applicable as capital and the net rent and profits thereof until sale upon trust for themselves as joint tenants [or tenants in common].

When the Trusts of Land and Appointment of Trustees Act 1996 comes into force, this formula will no longer be appropriate as the trust for sale, together with the strict settlement, will have been abolished and replaced with a new trust of land, whereby the trustees will have power to sell or retain the land. This new device does not substantially alter the rights of the co-owners; rather it puts the law on a more realistic footing, in that it was frequently difficult to explain to a couple why the house that they were buying as a home had to be held upon a trust for sale.

2.   Declaring the beneficial entitlement[3]

(a) Practitioner's duty

The question of the equitable ownership is of prime importance to all co-purchasers. When acting on a joint purchase the responsibility rests with the practitioner to take the initiative and obtain from his clients full instructions as to the nature and extent of the beneficial interests. Failure to do so may amount to professional negligence[4]. It is not even safe to assume, merely because the conveyance is being taken in joint names, that the legal owners are to be the persons entitled in equity. One person may be joining in the transaction to enable another to obtain a loan, there being no intention that he should acquire any beneficial interest[5].

Traditional conveyancers may prefer to declare the beneficial interests in a separate document, so keeping them off the legal title altogether[6]. This procedure should be adopted whenever the legal and equitable titles are to be vested in different people, and, preferably, when the legal owners are to hold in unequal undivided shares. Often the legal and equitable owners will be the same people. Here it is standard practice to declare the beneficial interests in the conveyance to them. This may be either in the clause creating

---

3   See (1983) 127 Sol Jo 554 (D G Barnsley).
4   *Walker v Hall* [1984] FLR 126 at 129, CA, per Dillon LJ. And see *Bernard v Josephs* [1982] Ch 391 at 403, [1982] 3 All ER 162 at 170, CA, per Griffiths LJ.
5   See *Wilson v Wilson* [1969] 3 All ER 945; *Brown v Staniek* (1969) 211 EG 283; *Pink v Lawrence* (1977) 36 P & CR 98, CA; *Hoare v Hoare* (1982) 13 Fam Law 142.
6   See the comments of Buckley J in *Wilson v Wilson*, supra at 948; Emmet, para 23.005.

an express trust for sale, or (where there is no such clause) in the habendum, eg 'TO HOLD unto the purchasers in fee simple as tenants in common in equal shares'. No real harm can ensue from the adoption of this procedure.

(b) Conclusiveness of declaration

An effective declaration of beneficial entitlement concludes the question of title between the purchasers[7]. Once declared the trust can only be got rid of by rescinding the clause because of fraud or mistake, or by rectifying it[8]. These situations apart, oral evidence is not admissible to displace or vary the express trust, nor can the doctrine of constructive trusts be utilised to contradict the declaration[9]. Hence the need for the draftsman to ensure that the clause gives effect to his clients' ascertained (rather than their presumed) intentions. So, a declaration that A and B are beneficial joint tenants is binding between them, despite their unequal contribution to the purchase price[10], and on severance they become equitable tenants in common in *equal* shares[11]. Such a declaration would not, of course, be binding on a third party claiming to have contributed to the purchase; nor is it to be regarded as conclusive if it does not exhaustively declare the beneficial interests. A declaration that A and B hold as beneficial tenants in common says nothing as to the quantum of their respective shares; either of them can adduce evidence to show that the holding is on some basis other than 50/50. Whether they are joint tenants or tenants in common, the parties are free to vary their interests subsequently. In one situation a statutory variation may occur[12].

(i) *Purchasers' execution of conveyance.* To be binding the trusts affecting the beneficial interests must be effectively declared. Authority exists for saying that oral evidence is admissible to vary the declared equitable title if the purchasers have not executed the deed[13]. The necessity for such execution seems in conformity with s 73(1)(b) of the Law of Property Act 1925. However, the decision in *Pink v Lawrence*[14] indicates that notwithstanding non-execution

---

7   *Goodman v Gallant* [1986] Fam 106, [1986] 1 All ER 311, CA, discussing the earlier authorities and laying to rest a heresy, propounded by Lord Denning MR in *Bedson v Bedson* [1965] 2 QB 666 at 681–82, [1965] 3 All ER 307 at 314, CA. See also *Barton v Morris* [1985] 2 All ER 1032 (partnership property held as beneficial joint tenants). Contrast *City of London Building Society v Flegg* [1988] AC 54, [1987] 3 All ER 435 at 438, HL, per Lord Templeman.

8   *Pink v Lawrence*, supra, at 101, per Buckley LJ. See also *Thames Guaranty Ltd v Campbell* [1985] QB 210, [1984] 2 All ER 585, CA.

9   *Brykiert v Jones* (1981) 2 FLR 373, CA.

10   *Goodman v Gallant*, supra; *Turton v Turton* [1988] Ch 542, [1987] 2 All ER 641, CA (nil contribution by spouse).

11   *Goodman v Gallant*, supra.

12   Matrimonial Proceedings and Property Act 1970, s 37 (spouse's substantial contribution to improvement of property). Presumably the acquisition of 'an enlarged share' operates to sever a beneficial joint tenancy.

13   *Crisp v Mullings* (1974) 233 EG 511; on appeal (1975) 239 EG 119, CA; *Robinson v Robinson* (1976) 241 EG 153.

14   (1977) 36 P & CR 98, CA; *Wilson v Wilson* [1969] 3 All ER 945 (estoppel not binding when deed rectifiable). A marginal note to Land Registry Form 19 (JP), warning that transferees *must* execute the document, is hortative, not mandatory.

they will be estopped from asserting that the position is otherwise, since the declaration was presumably inserted at the behest of the purchasers or their solicitors.

(ii) *Rectification.* A claim for rectification may succeed if the declaration fails to give effect to the agreed intentions of the co-owners. Rectification was ordered in *Wilson v Wilson*[15] when a solicitor acting for X and Y (two brothers) failed to appreciate the true position and vested property in them as beneficial joint tenants. In fact there never was any intention that X should acquire any beneficial interest; he merely joined in the transaction to enable Y to obtain a mortgage. It is not sufficient to support a plea of rectification for a co-owner merely to allege that he did not understand the legal effect of the declaration[16].

(c) Type of equitable holding
The inclusion of an express declaration calls for a decision as to whether the co-owners are to hold in equity as joint tenants or tenants in common (and if the latter, in what proportions). The fundamental difference between the two forms of holding is well known to lawyers[17], but not necessarily to their clients. Appropriate advice needs to be given and instructions obtained. The draftsman should never assume that a beneficial joint tenancy will be in his clients' preferred interests; their particular circumstances (eg relationship or inequality of contribution) may make the automatic right of survivorship inappropriate or undesirable. Spouses often hold as equitable joint tenants, at least initially. Yet valid reasons may exist for them to take as beneficial tenants in common. They may prefer to have the testamentary flexibility that a tenancy in common provides. This form of holding also affords greater scope for inheritance tax savings, and some commentators openly advocate it for spouses[18]. The practitioner should always be ready to advise on the tax implications of his clients' purchase.

3.   Ascertaining the beneficial entitlement in absence of a declaration

The draftsman should avoid creating a potential source of litigation for his clients. If the deed contains no clause declaring the beneficial interests, the question of the equitable ownership remains in doubt. Should a dispute arise the co-owners are put to the expense of having the issue determined by the

---

15   Supra; *Re Colebrook's Conveyances* [1973] 1 All ER 132, p 698, post. Cf *Goodman v Gallant*, supra, where a claim for rectification was not pursued (see at 117, 319).
16   *Pariser v Wilson* (1973) 229 EG 786.
17   Or should be. But see *Joyce v Barker Bros (Builders) Ltd* (1980) 40 P & CR 512 (conveyance to spouses as 'beneficial joint tenants in common in equal shares'; not followed in *Martin v Martin* (1987) 54 P & CR 238, where the same contradictory expression was held to give rise to a beneficial joint tenancy.
18   See Ray, *Practical CTT Planning* (2nd edn), 83; (1985) 135 NLJ 1073, 1205; (1986) 136 NLJ 13, 127. For a different view, see [1987] Conv 29, 275 (M P Thompson). Contrast [1987] Conv 273 (A M Prichard).

courts. The probable outcome, particularly in cases involving non-spouses, is that they will see a large part of their share in the equity swallowed up in legal costs[19]. It is not intended to consider the detailed principles applied by the courts to determine questions of beneficial ownership, but certain basic propositions may usefully be stated[20]. It will be necessary to distinguish between cases where the property is taken in joint names or in a single name only.

(a) Joint names
1.   Prima facie joint tenancy at law will be reflected in joint tenancy in equity[1].
2.   Rarely will this be determinative. Parol evidence is admissible as to the intended beneficial ownership, and where such evidence is not forthcoming (as frequently occurs) the courts will often be able to draw an inference as to their intentions from their conduct[2].
3.   A conveyance of the legal title into joint names does not necessarily mean equal shares in equity[3].
4.   The court has regard to the respective contributions made by the purchasers to the acquisition of the property[4], by way of contribution to the purchase price or the mortgage instalments. The contribution may be indirect because the parties pool their resources so that the mortgage is repaid from this common fund.
5.   The beneficial interests crystallise at the time of acquisition[5], but to ascertain the parties' intentions the court must take account of contributions made subsequent to the purchase.
6.   Where the purchasers are spouses their contributions are likely to point to an intention to share equally in equity.
7.   In the case of an unmarried couple living together as man and wife, the same considerations apply to determine their beneficial entitlement as govern disputes between spouses, except that the court has to be satisfied that the relationship was intended to involve the same degree of commitment as marriage.
8.   When a man purchases a house which is conveyed into the joint names of himself and his partner in order to obtain a mortgage on their joint incomes, he will not ordinarily be able to claim the entire beneficial interest for himself. The fact that the house could not be purchased without his partner incurring liability under the mortgage is ground for inferring that she was intended to

19   A factor that clearly disturbed Griffiths LJ in *Bernard v Josephs* [1982] Ch 391 at 403, [1982] 3 All ER 162 at 170, CA (co-habitees). With spouses the courts have a wide discretionary power under the Matrimonial Causes Act 1973 to adjust their property rights on divorce.
20   See Hanbury and Martin, *Modern Equity* (14th edn) Ch 11; Bromley and Lowe *Family Law* (8th edn) Chapters 17 & 18; Cretney and Masson, *Principles of Family Law* 227–252.
1   *Pettitt v Pettitt* [1970] AC 777 at 813–14, [1969] 2 All ER 385 at 406, HL, per Lord Upjohn.
2   Per Lord Upjohn, loc cit, adding that ultimately resort to the presumptions could be had. Cf Lord Diplock at 824, 415, doubting their usefulness today, at least as between spouses.
3   *Bernard v Josephs*, supra, at 398, 166, per Lord Denning MR.
4   See generally for the points made in the text the judgment of Griffiths LJ in *Bernard v Josephs*, supra, at 403–4, 169–71.
5   Subject, of course, to any subsequent variation proved to the court's satisfaction.

have some beneficial interest in it, though not necessarily a half share[6]. In this situation it seems that credit is to be given for the sum representing the mortgage liability undertaken, not simply the actual payments made[7].

(b) Conveyance in sole name

When a person pays the purchase price, takes a conveyance and grants a mortgage in his sole name, the prima facie inference is that he intends to acquire the sole beneficial interest as well as the legal estate[8]. Nevertheless, it is frequently the case that another person who shares the house with him asserts that she has a beneficial interest in the property. The case law on this topic is now vast and little more than an outline of the main themes can be given here.

To establish a beneficial interest the claimant will rely primarily on the law of trusts, although estoppel may also be relevant. The most straightforward situation is where there is a declaration as to the beneficial ownership which, being a trust relating to land must, in order to be effective, be evidenced in writing and signed by the person declaring the trust[7]. More commonly, there will be no such writing and the doctrines of resulting and constructive trusts will come into play, the principles of which are, to a large extent founded on the two well-known cases of *Pettitt v Pettitt*[10] and *Gissing v Gissing*[11].

(i) *Resulting trusts.*   The basis of the resulting trust is to establish that the claimant has made a financial contribution to the acquisition of the house. Such expenditure can take the form of a contribution to the original down payment on the property[12]. It can also amount to regular payments of mortgage instalments. What will not suffice, however, is household work of a non-financial kind. In *Burns v Burns*[13] an unmarried couple had lived together for 19 years. The house was in his name and, for most of that period, she stayed at home looking after the house and their two children. When the relationship came

---

6   *Crisp v Mullings* (1975) 239 EG 119, CA; *Bernard v Josephs*, supra (equal shares); *Walker v Hall* [1984] FLR 126, CA (25% share only). As to the date for valuing the shares, see *Turton v Turton* [1988] Ch 542, [1987] 2 All ER 641, CA. See also Law Com Working Paper No 94, para 16.9, advocating a deemed beneficial joint tenancy in the absence of an express declaration.

7   *Marsh v Von Sternberg* [1986] 1 FLR 526 (engaged couple), preferring the approach of *Walker v Hall*, ante, to *Young v Young* [1984] FLR 375, CA (no beneficial interest despite liability under mortgage and small capital repayment).

8   *Gissing v Gissing* [1971] AC 886 at 910, [1970] 2 All ER 780 at 793, HL, per Lord Diplock. In disputes involving the ownership of the family it is usually, but not invariably, the case that the legal title is in the name of the man and that the claimant is the woman. For this reason, the text will assume that the man and woman occupy these roles.

9   LPA 1925, s 53(1)(b).

10   [1970] AC 777, [1969] 2 All ER 385, HL.

11   Supra.

12   This will include a person's entitlement to a discount under the right to buy legislation: *Springette v Defoe* [1992] 2 FLR 388.

13   [1984] Ch 317, [1984] 1 All ER 244, CA, a case described as having checked any tendency discernible in earlier CA decisions to depart from a strict application of the principles of *Gissing* and *Pettitt*: per Nouse LJ in *Winkworth v Edward Baron Development Co Ltd* (1985) 52 P & CR 67 at 74, CA; revsd [1987] 1 All ER 114, HL. See also [1984] Conv 381.

to an end, she claimed to have a beneficial interest in the house but this claim was rejected by the Court of Appeal. The work she had done was not referable to the acquisition of an interest in the home and, therefore, no resulting trust arose.

The importance of what might be termed 'purchasing behaviour' was stressed by the House of Lords in *Lloyds Bank plc v Rosset*[14]. Lord Bridge said:

> ... direct contributions to the purchase price by the partner who is not the legal owner, whether initially or by payment of mortgage instalments, will readily justify the inference necessary to the creation of a constructive trust[15]. But, as I understand the authorities, it is at least doubtful whether anything less will do.

This dictum perhaps goes too far in that it has long been recognised that indirect contributions to the acquisition of the house will suffice to give rise to a resulting trust. Such cases involve situations where both parties are in paid employment and the salary of one goes towards meeting the mortgage payments, while the other salary meets all the other household expenditure. Where the mortgage could not be serviced without this financial contribution, the other party will acquire a beneficial interest in the house[16]. It does emphasise, however, that to acquire an interest under a resulting trust general household work will not be sufficient. The trust enables the claimant to acquire a beneficial share commensurate with the size of her financial contribution[17].

(ii) *Constructive trusts.*   An alternative method by which an interest in the house can be obtained is through the imposition of a constructive trust. In the case of resulting trusts, the courts seek to infer the intention of the parties with regard to the beneficial ownership of the property by paying regard to the financial contribution made by each of them to its acquisition; in accordance with normal resulting trust principles, the quantum of the beneficial interest is determined by the proportionate size of the contribution. In such cases, it is evident that the parties have not come to any actual agreement as to the beneficial ownership; inferences are drawn from the purchasing conduct of the parties. In some cases, however, the parties have considered the beneficial ownership but have not complied with the requisite statutory formalities to implement their agreement. The enforceability of such agreements is the province of the constructive trust[18].

A leading case is *Re Densham*[19]. A husband and wife agreed to share the ownership of the home equally. There was no written evidence of this agreement. She contributed approximately one-ninth of the purchase price. On his bankruptcy, among the questions to be decided was the size of her interest in the house. Goff J held that she was entitled to a half share under a constructive trust, whereas, had there been an actual agreement between the

---

14   [1991] 1 AC 107 at 133, [1990] 1 All ER 1111 at 1119, HL.
15   This seems to be a slip for resulting trust: see [1990] Conv 314 at 317 (M P Thompson).
16   See *Gissing v Gissing* [1971] AC 886 at 908, [1970] 2 All ER 780 at 792, HL, per Lord Diplock.
17   The more discretionary approach adopted in *Midland Bank plc v Cooke* [1995] 4 All ER 562, CA seems impossible to reconcile with the principles laid down in *Rosset*.
18   See *Lloyds Bank plc v Rosset* [1991] 1 AC 107 at 132; [1990] 1 All ER 1111 at 1119, HL, per Lord Bridge, where there is an unfortunate conflation of constructive trusts and estoppel.
19   [1975] 3 All ER 726, [1975] 1 WLR 1519.

parties, she would have been entitled to only a one-ninth beneficial share in the house under a resulting trust. The importance of this distinction was that, as against the trustee in bankruptcy, the difference between one half and one ninth was liable to be set aside as a voluntary settlement[20].

The basis of the imposition of the constructive is that the oral agreement as to the beneficial ownership is unenforceable owing to non-compliance with s 53(1)(b) of the Law of Property Act 1925. Where, however, the person claiming an interest has, in reliance on the agreement, contributed to the purchase price, it would be fraudulent of the legal owner to rely on the statute to deny the other an interest in the property. A constructive trust is imposed to give effect to the actual agreement of the parties[1]. The size of the beneficial interest is determined by what the parties have actually agreed, not the size of the beneficial contributions[2].

A number of cases have applied this principle, sometimes when the legal owner gives some pretext to his partner as to why the house is not being put into joint names[3]. The very fact that some pretext has been given leads the court to infer that there is an agreement between the parties to share the beneficial interest in the home; were that not so, no such pretext would have been necessary. The finding of this agreement is not, of itself, sufficient, however, for the claimant to establish an interest in the home[4]. The claimant must show that it is inequitable for the legal owner to rely on the statute and deny her a beneficial interest in the house. To do this, the claimant must show detrimental reliance on that agreement. As the basis of the constructive trust is the prevention of unjust enrichment, it is conceived that the conduct in question must be referable to the acquisition of the house and be of value in money, or money's worth, to the legal owner[5].

(iii) *Estoppel.* The final method by which an interest may be acquired is through estoppel; a doctrine which bears a close affinity to the constructive trust, as just described. The essence of the doctrine is that one party has acted in reliance on an expectation of acquiring an interest in another's property in circumstances which makes it unconscionable for the latter to deny some satisfaction to the former's expectation[6]. A person who moves in with a partner and then spends her energies looking after the home and, possibly, children, may plausibly argue that she has an expectation of security of occupation and has relied upon that expectation by foregoing her own career prospects and,

---

20 Bankruptcy Act 1914, s 42. See now Insolvency Act 1986, s 339.
 1 See *Rochefoucauld v Boustead* [1897] 1 Ch 196.
 2 For an unusual example, see *Ungurian v Lesnoff* [1990] Ch 206 (life interest). The view expressed in *Drake v Whipp* [1996] 1 FLR 826 at 830, CA, per Peter Gibson LJ, that in constructive trust cases the court can adopt a broad brush approach to determining the parties' respective shares seems unsound.
 3 *Eves v Eves* [1975] 3 All ER 768, CA; *Grant v Edwards* [1986] Ch 638, [1986] 2 All ER 426, CA.
 4 *Midland Bank plc v Dobson* [1986] 1 FLR 171, CA.
 5 In *Grant v Edwards*, supra, Browne-Wilkinson V-C inclined to the view that any detrimental act relating to the joint lives of the parties would suffice. Such comments seem more apposite, however, to estoppel.
 6 See *Taylors Fashions Ltd v Liverpool Victoria Trustees Ltd* [1982] QB 133n, [1981] 1 All ER 897.

perhaps, giving up previously secure accommodation of her own thereby causing an estoppel right to arise in her favour. The cases on this are not easy to reconcile[7]. The main points of difference between estoppel and the constructive trust, as outlined above, are that, with estoppel, it is not necessary to spell out the precise metes and bounds of the claimant's expectation and that the reliance need not confer a financial benefit on the other party. The reliance may include the giving up of secure accommodation in the expectation of having security in the new home[8].

At present, it is unclear how liberal the courts will be in accepting behaviour such as looking after the house, the legal owner and, perhaps, looking after the children of the relationship. If a liberal line is taken, then some of the rigidity of the *Rosset* approach could well be loosened.

4. Trustees' powers

Where land was held upon trust for sale, the purchasers had vested in them all the powers conferred by statute on the tenant for life and on trustees of a settlement[9]. Wide those these powers are, they do authorise a mortgage of the property in order *to raise the purchase money*. To overcome possible objections from mortgagees it became established practice to incorporate a declaration that:

> … the purchasers or other the trustees for the time being of this deed shall have full power to charge lease or otherwise dispose of all or any part of the property hereby conveyed with all the powers in that behalf of an absolute owner.

When the Trusts of Land and Appointment of Trustees Act 1996 is brought into force, such a declaration will become unnecessary. Under s 6(1) of the Act, the trustees of land will have in relation to the land subject to the trust all the powers of an absolute owner.

5. Registered land

On a transfer of registered land to joint proprietors, the standard practice was to utilise Form 19 (JP), introduced by the Registry in 1974 for the greater convenience of solicitors. This form contains a printed clause whereby the transferees declare that 'the survivor of them can/cannot give a valid receipt for capital money arising on a disposition of the land'. Deletion of the word 'can' suffices to indicate that the parties are held as tenants in common and the Registry is protecting the beneficial interests by means of the obligatory restriction

---

7 Contrast *Maharaj v Chand* [1986] AC 898, [1986] 3 All ER 107, PC with *Coombes v Smith* [1986] 1 WLR 808.

8 See *Jones (AE) v Jones (FW)* [1977] 2 All ER 231, [1977] 1 WLR 438, CA. See also *Wayling v Jones* (1993) 69 P & CR 170; [1995] Conv 409 (C Davis).

9 LPA 1925, s 128(1); *Re Suenson-Taylor's Settlement* [1974] 3 All ER 397 (no power to mortgage land to purchase additional property). See further Emmet, para 23.037.

in Form 62[10]. Conversely, if the word 'cannot' was deleted it was thought safe to assume that the proprietors were joint tenants. While it is safe for a purchaser to rely on the register, the use of Form 19 (JP) is not, however, conclusive as between the joint proprietors. In the somewhat inconvenient decision in *Huntingford v Hobbs*[11], the majority of the Court of Appeal held that such a declaration, as between the parties themselves, did not amount to a declaration of trust. The parties should, therefore, sign a document stating their beneficial entitlement.

A matter of some debate was whether any express extension of the trustees' powers was necessary in registered land transactions[12]. Once the Trusts of Land and Appointment of Trustees Act 1996 comes into force, this point will become academic as the trustees will have all the powers of an absolute owner[13].

M   Covenants

1.   Creation of new covenants

The practitioner is frequently called upon to draft a deed which imposes covenants on one or both of the parties. Whether any, and if so what, particular covenants are necessary depends on the nature of the transaction. The right of either party to impose covenants depends largely on the contract which should, wherever possible, set out the actual words of the covenant to be inserted in the deed. Care should be taken to ensure that the conveyance gives effect to all the terms of the contract, for on completion the contract merges in the conveyance, save for those terms that are expressly or impliedly to remain effective thereafter[14]. It is not proposed to cover ground already familiar to the reader, such as the rules governing the enforceability of covenants[15], but to concentrate on matters likely to concern the draftsman.

The Royal Commission on Legal Services observed that many thousands of words of restrictive covenants clutter the titles of house property and bedevil modern conveyancing. In many cases these covenants are difficult to construe and there is doubt as to whether they are enforceable or whether anyone has power to release them[16]. This undesirable state of affairs has arisen because over the years it has been the invariable practice on the development of residential estates to impose on individual purchasers a host of detailed restrictions designed to preserve estate amenities. The Commission queried whether such estate schemes were necessary under modern planning law. However, this view pays insufficient attention to their potential advantages if purchasers and their successors in title could enforce the restrictions inter se

10   Page 347, ante. In the absence of any appropriate declaration in the transfer, the form of the application for registration (A4) requests information as to the survivor's power in relation to capital money.
11   [1993] 1 FCR 45, [1993] 1 FLR 736, CA.
12   See 3rd edn, p 501.
13   Trusts of Land and Appointment of Trustees Act 1996, s 6.
14   For the doctrine of merger, see p 468, ante.
15   See further M & W, 760ff. For a brief account, refer to Law Com No 127, paras 3.17–3.29.
16   Report, Vol 1, 283, Annex 21.1, para 3. Obsolete restrictive covenants are also impeding the computerisation of Land Registry records, p 499, ante.

through the medium of a building scheme[17]. Unfortunately there seems a general reluctance on the part of builders of houses in the lower or middle price ranges (or their legal advisers) to impose these schemes. In consequence, the restrictions become of little practical value once the builder has finished the estate and sold all the houses.

(a) Words of creation

No technical language is necessary to create a covenant, provided the words used indicate an agreement to do or refrain from doing something. The usual expression in a conveyance or transfer is that the purchaser 'hereby covenants with the vendor that … '. Lengthy covenants are often set out in a schedule to the deed, in which event a typical clause imposing restrictive covenants might be in the following form[18]:

> For the benefit and protection of the land of the vendor coloured brown on the plan annexed hereto and each and every part thereof and so as to bind so far as may be the land hereby conveyed into whosoever hands the same may come the purchaser hereby covenants with the vendor that the purchaser and the persons deriving title under him will at all times hereafter observe the restrictions set out in the schedule hereto …

If the schedule also contains positive covenants, it will read 'observe and perform the restrictions and stipulations set out in …'. However, negative and positive covenants ought not to be lumped together indiscriminately in the same schedule, but rather set out in different ones[19].

In the absence of express words of obligation a covenant will arise by construction where the deed shows an intention that a party is to be bound. The words 'provided' or 'on condition that' have been held to create a covenant, but in each case it is necessary to look at the whole of the instrument to ascertain the parties' intention[20]. Similarly a covenant arises where, for instance, a purchaser is granted a right to enter adjoining land for certain purposes, 'the purchaser making good all damage caused thereby'. A recital may operate as a covenant. It is not, however, sufficient to convey land subject to restrictions contained in a schedule to the deed without imposing on the purchaser a covenant to observe them. As between the vendor and the purchaser, the latter is apparently under an equitable obligation to observe them, but no covenant in the strict sense exists and a purported assignment of the benefit of the restrictions is totally ineffective[1]. The wording of a covenant may be so framed as to result in the creation of an easement[2].

17 As to which see M & W, 790–93. See also p 583, post.
18 Adapted from 19 Ency F & P, 887, Form 7:A:20.
19 See *Shepherd Homes Ltd v Sandham (No 2)* [1971] 2 All ER 1267 (single positive covenant embracing three negative obligations).
20 *Sheppard's Touchstone*, 162; *Brookes v Drysdale* (1877) 3 CPD 52; *Landau v Curton* (1962) 184 EG 13.
 1 *Re Rutherford's Conveyance* [1938] Ch 396, [1938] 1 All ER 495. It is at most an equitable burden which cannot be forced into the legal category of covenant: ibid, at 405, 501, per Simonds J. The benefit of it cannot, it seems, pass under LPA 1925, s 78(1), p 571, post.
 2 *Dowty Boulton Paul Ltd v Wolverhampton Corpn (No 2)* [1976] Ch 13, [1973] 2 All ER 491, CA (covenant to allow airfield to be used for test flights).

(b) Covenanting parties

(i) *Covenantee.*   Usually the covenantee is a party to the deed creating the covenant, but he need not be. At common law, in an indenture inter partes the covenantee had to be named as a party to it in order to take the benefit of the covenant. Section 56(1) of the Law of Property Act 1925, replacing s 5 of the Real Property Act 1845, enacts that:

> A person may take the benefit of any covenant or agreement over or respecting land or other property, although he may not be named as a party to the conveyance or other instrument.

The scope of this enactment has been the subject of differing judicial views[3]. It is accepted, however, that there must be *actual words of covenant with* the intended covenantees[4]. A vague indication that they are to have the benefit is inadequate. Whereas a covenant by A with C (a non-party to the instrument of creation) suffices[5], a covenant by A with B (a party) for the benefit of C (a non-party) is not effective. An example of the latter encountered by the author occurred when a purchaser of a new house covenanted with the vendor to maintain protective fencing around an area of woodland forming part of the property to the satisfaction of the local council (a non-party) as well as of the vendor. Moreover, the intended covenantees must be in existence and identifiable at the time the covenant is made[6]. So, when in a lease the word 'lessor' is defined to include his 'successors in title' or 'the persons deriving title' under him, a subsequent purchaser of the freehold reversion cannot claim to be a covenantee within the scope of s 56[7].

To take advantage of s 56 a draftsman should use words such as:

> The purchaser hereby covenants as a separate covenant with the owners or occupiers for the time being of the land adjoining or adjacent to the land hereby conveyed[8] [or of the land coloured brown on the plan annexed hereto] ...

The effect of the section is to make existing owners of the designated land original covenantees, just as much as if they were named as parties to the deed. They can enforce the covenants notwithstanding their non-execution of the document[9].

Unlike a deed inter partes, a deed poll could always be sued on at common law by a person with whom a covenant was made. In *Chelsea and Walham Green*

---

3   See the conflicting opinions in *Beswick v Beswick* [1968] AC 58, [1967] 2 All ER 1197, HL, as to whether its operation is confined to covenants respecting land or extends to personal property.

4   *White v Bijou Mansions Ltd* [1937] Ch 610 at 625, [1937] 3 All ER 269 at 277, per Simonds J; *Beswick v Beswick*, supra, at 106, 1224, per Lord Upjohn; *Lyus v Prowsa Developments Ltd* [1982] 2 All ER 953.

5   See *Stromdale and Ball Ltd v Burden* [1952] Ch 223, [1952] 1 All ER 59.

6   *Kelsey v Dodd* (1881) 52 LJ Ch 34 at 39, per Jessel MR, approved in *Forster v Elvet Colliery Co Ltd* [1908] 1 KB 629, CA.

7   *Pinemain Ltd v Welbeck International Ltd* (1984) 272 EG 1166; *Re Distributors and Warehousing Ltd* [1986] 1 EGLR 90. Successors may be able to claim the benefit of the covenant under LPA 1925, s 78(1) or s 141(1).

8   See *Re Ecclesiastical Comrs for England's Conveyance* [1936] Ch 430.

9   See p 446, ante.

Building Society v Armstrong[10] a registered land transfer contained a covenant with a building society for the repayment to it of money due under a mortgage subject to which the land was transferred. The society was not a party to the transfer, yet it was held entitled to sue on the covenant, for the transfer was analogous to a deed poll.

(ii) *Covenantor.* For obvious reasons the covenantor must be a party to the instrument. Moreover, his execution of the deed is essential if the covenant is to give rise to liability at law[11]. By virtue of s 79(1) of the Law of Property Act 1925, a covenant made by A with B, relating to A's land, is deemed to be made by A on behalf of himself, his successors in title and persons deriving title under him, and it has effect as if such successors and other persons were expressed, unless a contrary intention appears. Prior to the Act words of similar import were specifically required if it was intended to bind the covenantor's land, and not merely the covenantor personally[12]. Such words are no longer necessary. The effect of s 79(1) is to show a prima facie intention that the covenant runs with A's land. The words in the specimen clause on page 567 'so as to bind the land ... into whosoever hands the same may come' are strictly otiose. Nor is there any need to refer expressly to 'the persons deriving title' under the covenantor. The tendency in practice, however, is to include both expressions so as to establish beyond question that the covenants are not merely personal to A. Any intention to create mere personal covenants should be clearly stated, eg by providing that the burden is not to run with the land. This would amount to a contrary intention for the purposes of s 79; an express exclusion is not essential[13].

Since the covenantor (A) is deemed to covenant for himself and his successors in title, he assumes a personal or vicarious liability for the actions of his successors[14]. A's liability for breach of covenant does not cease when he conveys the land to a purchaser – hence the need to take an indemnity covenant. It may be limited *expressly* to the duration of A's interest in the land[15], but unless the contract so provides a covenantor is not entitled to a qualified covenant[16].

(c) Making positive covenants run
Notwithstanding the wide judicial interpretation now given to the corresponding s 78, it is clear that s 78 does not extend the class of covenants

---

10 [1951] Ch 853, [1951] 2 All ER 250. For deed polls, see p 518, ante.
11 Page 447, ante.
12 See *Re Fawcett and Holmes' Contract* (1889) 42 Ch D 150, CA.
13 *Re Royal Victoria Pavilion, Ramsgate* [1961] Ch 581, [1961] 3 All ER 83 (covenant to 'procure' certain state of affairs).
14 *Tophams Ltd v Sefton* [1967] 1 AC 50 at 81, [1966] 1 All ER 1039 at 1053, HL, per Lord Wilberforce; M & W, 773. Contra, Preston & Newsom, *Restrictive Covenants* (6th edn), 104, citing *Powell v Hemsley* [1909] 1 Ch 680 at 688–89, per Eve J; affd [1909] 2 Ch 252, CA.
15 By some such qualification as: 'but so that the purchaser shall not be liable for any breach of such restrictions occurring after he shall have parted with all interest in the land hereby conveyed'.
16 *Pollock v Rabbits* (1882) 21 Ch D 466, CA.

capable of running with the land and, in particular, it does not abrogate the basic common law rule that positive covenants do not run with land[17]. The reader will be familiar with the equally fundamental proposition that as between lessor and lessee the burden of any covenant which touches and concerns the land runs with the lease. In respect of leases created after 1 January 1996, the requirement that the covenant touches and concerns the land, if it is to bind the assignee has been removed[18]. There are, however, several ways, noted in standard land law textbooks[19], whereby the burden of positive covenants can be made to run indirectly with freehold land. Of these the draftsman whose client is anxious to ensure the continuing enforceability of positive covenants ought to consider the possibility of creating an 'estate rentcharge' within the Rentcharges Act 1977. Though this Act forbids the creation of new rentcharges, estate rentcharges form an exempt category (s 2(3)(c)). Such rentcharges, usually for a nominal amount only, are created for the purpose of making covenants performed by the owner of the land affected thereby enforceable by the covenantee (the rent owner) against the owner for the time being of the land[20].

(d) Joint and several covenants
A covenant by two or more persons is generally framed as a joint and several covenant. The covenantee can elect how he will sue upon the covenant. He can sue both or all covenantors together, or he may sue just one of them, charging the entire liability on that particular covenantor. This form of liability may be indicated by other expressions, eg 'A and B covenant for themselves and each of them'. The covenant operates as a several covenant where joint covenantors limit their liability to their own acts or defaults.

At common law a single covenant could not be made with covenantees jointly and severally; it had to be one or the other. Now, by virtue of s 81(1) of the Law of Property Act 1925, a covenant made after the Act with two or more jointly is to be construed as being made with each of them.

(e) Registration of restrictive covenants
By way of reminder, restrictive covenants affecting unregistered land should be registered as class D (ii) land charges, otherwise they become unenforceable against a later purchaser of the burdened land. It is thought that this vital precaution is not infrequently ignored in practice. It is not unknown for the non-registration point to be overlooked even in legal proceedings, with disastrous consequences for the defendant[1]. In the case of registered land, restrictive covenants created on a transfer of land are automatically entered

---

17   *Rhone v Stephens* [1994] 2 AC 310, [1994] 2 All ER 65, HL.
18   Landlord and Tenant (Covenants) Act 1995, s 3.
19   See eg M & W, 767–70.
20   Section 2(4)(a). See further Law Com No 68, pp 16–17, para 49. The eventual implementation of the reform of the law of covenants (p 576, post) will result in the prohibition of new estate rentcharges: Law Com No 127, 155, para 24.42.
1   *Balchin v Buckle* (1982) 126 Sol Jo 412, CA (covenants treated as registered).

on the register of title as part of the registration process. In other cases application for entry of a notice must be made.

(f) Construction of covenants
It is the draftsman's responsibility to make the covenants 'express, so as to state what they really mean'; a covenanting party cannot seek the assistance of the courts to supply something for which he has not stipulated in order to secure benefit which is supposed to have been intended[2]. Even tautology has some virtue in serving the useful purpose of clarity[3]. He should eschew any desire to frame the covenant in broad general terms in case it might be held void for uncertainty[4]. The normal rules for the interpretation of documents apply. The covenant will be construed against the covenantor.

The courts are not infrequently called upon to construe covenants designed to restrict building on land. In *Re Enderick's Conveyance*[5] a covenant not to use the burdened land 'for any purpose other than that of a single private dwellinghouse' prevented the erection of a second house on another part of the land. Whether a particular structure constitutes a building other than a dwellinghouse is a question of fact and degree[6].

2. Transfer of benefit of covenants

A covenant relating to freehold land is capable of being enforced by persons other than the original covenantee. The question is: by which persons and in what circumstances?

(a) Automatic statutory annexation
Until recently this was a highly technical area of law, subject to fine distinctions. Moreover, though a covenant could run with land both at law and in equity, there existed considerable diversity between the two sets of rules, adding to the complexity and uncertainties bedevilling this important topic. However, the law has now been radically altered, especially as regards negative covenants, following the interpretation placed on s 78(1) of the Law of Property Act 1925, by the Court of Appeal in *Federated Homes Ltd v Mill Lodge Properties Ltd*[7]. It is a well-established legal principle that the benefit of a covenant (negative or positive) annexed to freehold land passes automatically on a conveyance of that land without express mention. It runs irrespective of the purchaser's

---

2 *Kemp v Bird* (1877) 5 Ch D 974 at 976, CA, per James LJ.
3 *Re Enderick's Conveyance* [1973] 1 All ER 843 at 848, per Goulding J.
4 See eg *Brigg v Thornton* [1904] 1 Ch 386, CA; *National Trust for Places of Historic Interest or Natural Beauty v Midlands Electricity Board* [1952] Ch 380, [1952] 1 All ER 298.
5 Supra.
6 *Harlow v Hartog* (1977) 245 EG 140 (enclosed swimming pool); *Landau v Curton* (1962) 184 EG 13 (games room); *Windsor Hotel (Newquay) Ltd v Allen* [1981] JPL 274, CA (stone barbecue).
7 [1980] 1 All ER 371, CA (covenant not to build more than 300 houses on land). Brightman LJ gave the leading judgment.

knowledge because he has bought something which inheres in or is annexed to the land[8]. According to s 78(1):

> A covenant relating to any land of the covenantee shall be deemed to be made with the covenantee and his successors in title and the persons deriving title under him or them, and shall have effect as if such successors and other persons were expressed.

The court held that s 78 effected a statutory annexation of the covenant to the covenantee's land, with the result that it passed automatically to and was enforceable by a subsequent purchaser. In the view of Brightman LJ (at p 379) it followed from the language of the section that the covenant ran with the land because ex hypothesi every successor in title thereto had the right by statute to the covenant. Though the covenant before the court was negative in nature, the decision applies also to positive obligations, for the section speaks simply of a covenant. One requirement only needs to be fulfilled to achieve this statutory annexation. The covenant must 'relate' to the covenantee's land. In other words it must touch and concern that land, that is, affect it as regards mode of occupation or be such as per se (and not merely from collateral circumstances) affects its value[9]. Statutory annexation is achieved despite the failure of the instrument of creation to disclose any intention by the parties that the benefit should run[10]. It may even be no longer essential for the deed itself to signify what land is intended to be benefited[11], provided this can be ascertained by extrinsic evidence. Before the *Federated Homes* case, the current understanding of the law rendered it essential for the draftsman to ensure that the conveyance made clear in an appropriate manner[12] the intention to annex. For the avoidance of any doubt the skilled conveyancer would also define the benefited land in the deed itself (as in the clause on page 567). One effect of the decision will be to ease considerably the draftsman's task, since effective annexation does not now depend on suitable drafting.

Reaction to the case has been mixed[13]. Several different lines of attack have been directed at it. In particular, it is difficult to resist the conclusion that the parliamentary draftsman did not intend to achieve a statutory annexation, otherwise he would surely have said so expressly in view of the

---

8   *Rogers v Hosegood* [1900] 2 Ch 388 at 407, CA, per Collins LJ.
9   *Smith and Snipes Hall Farm Ltd v River Douglas Catchment Board* [1949] 2 KB 500 at 506, [1949] 2 All ER 179 at 183, CA, per Tucker LJ (covenant to improve and maintain river banks).
10   A necessary requirement for the passing of the benefit in equity, and also at law (as to which see Tucker LJ in *Smith's* case, loc cit).
11   This issue was left open in the *Federated Homes* case since the conveyance adequately described the benefited land (see at 379). This was not a requirement for the benefit to pass at law: *Smith's* case, supra, at 508, 184, per Tucker LJ.
12   As to which see *Drake v Gray* [1936] Ch 451 at 466, [1936] 1 All ER 363 at 377, CA, per Greene LJ. Occasionally annexation might be implied: *Shropshire County Council v Edwards* (1982) 46 P & CR 270.
13   See M & W, 785–86 (strongly in favour); also C & B, 623–5, Law Com No 125, p 16, para 3.27 (guarded acceptance). Contra, (1981) 97 LQR 32 (G H Newsom), as to which see *Roake v Chadha* [1983] 3 All ER 503 at 507–8, per Judge Baker QC; (1980) 43 MLR 445 (D J Hayton). See also (1982) 2 Legal Studies 53 (D J Hurst).

clear words of annexation found in the two preceding sections 76(6) and 77(5)[14]. Moreover, if the wording of s 78(1) has a substantive effect, ought not the corresponding s 79, relating to the burden, to be similarly interpreted? Yet authority exists for the proposition that s 79 is a word-saving provision only[15], not intended to change the law so as to facilitate the running of the burden of positive covenants.

Despite its suspect parentage, the decision, if not the reasoning[16], is to be welcomed. It goes a long way towards assimilating the law on positive and negative covenants; it will eliminate the complexity and semantic confusion surrounding the rules governing the effective annexation of restrictive covenants. It should also reduce the volume of litigation in a troublesome area of property law, a significant consequence not to be overlooked. Assuming the decision remains unchallenged by the House of Lords, the following points should be noted.

1. The effect of statutory annexation seems prima facie to annex the covenant to every part of the benefited land, unless a contrary intention clearly appears[17]. This reverses the previous law, under which it was necessary to show an intention to annex the covenant not simply to the covenantee's land as a whole, but (eg) to each and every part of it[18]. A subsequent purchaser of part only of the land will ordinarily be able to enforce the covenant, without having to rely on any express assignment.

2. The benefit of the covenant passes not only to the covenantee's successors in title (ie a subsequent purchaser of the freehold), but also to a person deriving title under him, such as a lessee[19] or mortgagee. In the case of covenants restrictive of the use of land it passes even to 'occupiers for the time being' of the land[20]. How the courts will interpret 'occupiers' in this context is uncertain. Will it be limited to persons having at least some recognised equitable interest

14 Unless he considered that this had already been achieved by the precursor of s 78, namely s 58 (1) of the Conveyancing Act 1881. Such judicial opinion as exists on the point is against this view: Hurst, op cit, 65ff; cf M & W, 786, note 6.

15 *Tophams Ltd v Sefton* [1967] 1 AC 50 at 73, 81, [1966] 1 All ER 1039 at 1048, 1053, HL, per Lords Upjohn and Wilberforce. Brightman LJ merely observed, without elaboration, that s 79 involved quite different considerations (at 380). In fact the two provisions are not drafted in equivalent terms. Compare s 79(1) ('a covenant ... deemed to be made by the covenantor *on behalf of* himself and his successors ...') with s 78(1) ('a covenant ... deemed to be made *with* the covenantee *and* his successors ...'). See Hurst, loc cit.

16 The decision is not without further difficulties, which hardly justify the comment in M & W, 786, note 6, that the judgment of Brightman LJ is clear and straightforward. Consider: (i) the action was against the original covenantor; on the facts the benefit should have passed at law without the need to resort to s 78 (1); (ii) Brightman LJ indicated (at 379) there was sufficient in the conveyance for an express annexation, albeit not to individual parts, but this was not a fatal objection (at 381); (iii) reliance on *Smith's* case, supra, note 9 was misplaced because there s 78(1) was relied on solely to establish that the positive covenant passed to a derivative owner (a tenant), the covenant otherwise running at law: per Somervell LJ at 510, 186. See further Hurst, op cit, 61–63.

17 *Federated Homes* case, ante, at 381, per Brightman LJ. See *Williams v Unit Construction Co Ltd* (1955) 19 Conv (NS) 262, CA (tenant of one of four houses able to enforce road repairing covenant); *Allen v Veranne Builders Ltd* [1988] NPC 11.

18 See *Russell v Archdale* [1964] Ch 38, [1962] 2 All ER 305.

19 *Smith and Snipes Hall Farm Ltd v River Douglas Catchment Board*, ante.

20 LPA 1925, s 78(1); *Federated Homes* case, ante, at 379, per Brightman LJ.

in land? Can Parliament really have intended to confer a right of enforcement on a mere licensee or squatter?

3.   The decision will greatly reduce the number of occasions when success for a plaintiff depends on establishing an express assignment of the benefit or even a chain of assignments[1].

4.   Section 78(1) applies only to covenants created after the Act. Pre-1926 covenants continue to be subject to the rules in force prior to the *Federated Homes* case, unless s 58(1) of the Conveyancing Act 1881, the forerunner of s 78(1), is to be similarly interpreted[2].

(b) Express assignment of benefit

An express assignment of the benefit of a covenant is unnecessary when the covenant is annexed to the land. Unlike s 79(1) of the Act, which yields to a contrary intention, s 78(1) is subject to no such limitation. Nevertheless, it is not to be applied blindly without reference to the terms of the covenant. In *Roake v Chadha*[3] s 78 was held not to achieve an automatic annexation because the covenant specifically precluded the benefit from passing except by way of express assignment. This seems a sensible decision, and the court was surely right to refuse to override the parties' clear intentions. This device should not be overlooked by draftsmen anxious to curtail the automatic effect of s 78(1).

For the section to apply the covenant must relate to (ie touch and concern[4]) the covenantee's land. It is of no consequence that the covenantor is a stranger to the land or owns no adjacent land burdened by the covenant[5]. The benefit of a covenant not relating to land does not pass automatically but requires an express assignment of it in the purchaser's favour. This point could well be overlooked by the busy practitioner, especially in relation to positive covenants. Two points deserve mention. A landlord's covenant to sell the freehold reversion to his tenant does not run with the demised premises[6]. Sound conveyancing practice dictates that an express transfer of the option is included in an assignment of the lease. On the other hand, a surety's covenant guaranteeing payment of rent by a tenant has now been held to run with the reversion; it is enforceable by a purchaser of the freehold despite the absence of any express assignment of it[7]. A covenant personal to the covenantee cannot, of course, be assigned[8].

---

1   Because there had been no effective express annexation; see *Russell v Archdale,* supra; *Re Pinewood Estate, Farnborough* [1958] Ch 280, [1957] 2 All ER 517.

2   But see note 12, ante. Rubin J declined to consider the validity of the argument in *Shropshire County Council v Edwards* (1982) 46 P & CR 270 (1908 restrictive covenant).

3   [1983] 3 All ER 503.

4   See the meaning of this phrase considered in relation to a surety's covenant guaranteeing payment of rent by a tenant in *Kumar v Dunning* [1989] QB 193, [1987] 2 All ER 801 at 809–10, CA, per Browne-Wilkinson V-C.

5   *Smith's* case, ante.

6   *Woodall v Clifton* [1905] 2 Ch 257, CA. Absence of an express assignment is not necessarily fatal. The option may have passed automatically: *Griffith v Pelton* [1958] Ch 205, [1957] 3 All ER 75, CA (lease containing conventional definition clause), or by virtue of a latter separate assignment. See p 518, ante; Barnsley, *Land Options,* 49–59.

7   *Kumar v Dunning,* ante; see further p 591, post.

8   *Formby v Barker* [1903] 2 Ch 539, CA.

3. Indemnity covenants

Existing covenants subject to which unregistered land is sold should be introduced within the operative part of the deed in the habendum. The covenantor's continuing liability for breach of covenant renders it essential for a vendor to obtain an indemnity covenant from the purchaser whenever he is (i) the original covenantor who will remain liable on the covenants after the conveyance, or (ii) a successor in title who entered into an effective indemnity covenant when he acquired the land. The need is the same whether the covenants are negative or positive[9], and even if in the case of the former, the restrictions will be unenforceable in equity for want of registration[10]. In some cases an indemnity is implied by statute. These will be considered later.

(a) Express indemnity covenant

The vendor's right to an indemnity covenant is governed by the Standard Conditions of Sale[11]. It is provided that, if after completion, the seller will remain bound by any obligation affecting the property, but there is no implied indemnity covenant, then the purchaser will covenant in the transfer to indemnify the vendor against any breach of that obligation and to perform[12] it from then on. The purchaser is also obliged, if required by the vendor, to execute and deliver to the seller on completion a duplicate transfer prepared by the buyer. Even failing any contractual stipulation, the court will require the purchaser to enter into a suitable indemnity[13]. The precedent on page 517 includes a typical indemnity covenant. It is standard practice to preface the covenant with the words: 'With the object and intent of affording the vendor a full indemnity but not otherwise'. This limitation makes it clear that the covenant is to operate by way of indemnity only and is not intended to enable the vendor himself to enforce the original covenants[14]. If he requires the purchaser to observe the original restrictions for the benefit of his own retained land, clear provision for this must be made in the contract and in the conveyance.

The original covenantor (V) cannot insist upon an indemnity on a subsequent sale if his liability is expressly limited to the duration of his ownership of the burdened land. The implications of this limited liability are not always fully appreciated. Not infrequently an indemnity covenant is

---

9   An indemnity covenant worded so as to indemnify the vendor against breaches of covenant 'in so far as the same affect the property' will not be construed to refer only to those covenants which can run with the land, so that positive covenants will be embraced by such an expression: *TRW Steering Systems Ltd v North Cape Properties Ltd* (1993) 69 P & CR 265, CA.
10   The possibility of an action at law for damages still remains; cf *Wright v Dean* [1948] Ch 686, [1948] 2 All ER 415 (option void for non-registration; grantor liable for damages).
11   SCS 4.5.4.
12   A mere covenant of indemnity becomes valueless on the purchaser's insolvency, but if he covenants to observe and perform the court can restrain a breach if the covenantee complains, but not otherwise.
13   *Moxhay v Inderwick* (1874) 1 De G & Sm 708.
14   See *Re Poole and Clarke's Contract* [1904] 2 Ch 173, CA. Even if the covenant is not so framed it will still be construed as an indemnity only: *Reckitt v Cody* [1920] 2 Ch 452.

(unnecessarily) obtained, or given, when V conveys to a purchaser (P1). However, the mere existence of P1's covenant of indemnity with V does not entitle P1 to insist upon an indemnity on a sale to P2. There is no possibility of P1's having to indemnify V in respect of breaches of covenant committed by P2, since the covenantee is precluded from suing V after V has parted with his interest in the land.

(b) Implied indemnity covenants
An indemnity covenant may be statutorily implied in certain circumstances. The occasion most likely to be encountered is on the assignment of land comprised within a lease. In this case, provided the transfer is for valuable consideration, the purchaser impliedly covenants to pay the rent, and to observe and perform all the covenants, agreements and conditions contained in the lease[15]. An express indemnity is required when the transaction is not for value, eg on an assent of leasehold property to a beneficiary[16]. No indemnity covenant is implied, and one should be stipulated for on a conveyance of a freehold (or leasehold) reversion. Condition 3.3.2(d) of the Standard Conditions of Sale, if applicable, regulates the vendor's rights in this situation by providing that the purchaser shall keep the vendor indemnified against all claims by the tenant for compensation or otherwise. This clause extends to all claims arising out of the landlord-tenant relationship, as the decision in *Eagon v Dent*[17] illustrates. L granted T an underlease conferring an option to renew which T failed to register. L assigned the leasehold reversion to A who declined to renew T's lease. T sued L for breach of covenant[18]. L was held entitled by virtue of a forerunner of Condition 3.3.2(d).

4. Covenants for title

These are fully discussed in Chapter 23.

5. Reform

After an exercise lasting over 17 years, the Law Commission published in 1984 its long-awaited Report[19] on the reform of the law of covenants affecting freehold land. The complexity and detail of the suggested scheme makes it impossible to do more than give the briefest of outlines. The Commission,

---

15 LPA 1925, s 77(1)(c), Sch 2, Part IX. The indemnity relates to positive and negative covenants. See further, p 664, post, note 18.
16 As to the personal representatives' right to require an indemnity, see AEA 1925, s 36(10).
17 [1965] 3 All ER 334.
18 T's claim was maintainable despite his failure to register the option: *Wright v Dean* [1948] Ch 686, [1948] 2 All ER 415.
19 Law Com No 127 (Positive & Negative Covenants), discussed at (1984) 47 MLR 566 (P Polden) (a critical assessment); (1984) 134 NLJ 459, 481 (H H Wilkinson).

adopting 'the easement analogy', proposes the replacement of positive and negative covenants by a new interest in land, termed a land obligation[20], capable of taking effect as a legal interest if duly created, but nevertheless requiring protection on the register of title in the case of registered titles[1] or registration as a new Class C land charge for unregistered land. As an appurtenant right the benefit of the obligation would pass automatically like an easement, without the need for any express assignment. The rules for the running of the burden are more complicated. The extent to which subsequent owners and occupiers would be bound would depend not simply on proper protection of the interest or lack of it, but also on the particular type of land obligation involved[2]. A most welcome recommendation is the suggested abolition of the continuing liability of an original covenantor once he has disposed of the land.

The Commission has sought to devise a comprehensive code covering all aspects of the proposed new law, including matters such as creation, transmission, enforcement, liability for particular contraventions, remedies, extinguishment, equitable variations and discharge by the Lands Tribunal. The draft Bill appended to the Report contains 25 sections, no fewer than 138 sub-sections and 3 Schedules. Its provisions are perforce highly technical and exceedingly detailed and complex. The Commission's deliberations have resulted in a scheme more rational and more related to the needs of a modern society than the existing law, but in no sense can it be said to simplify. the law. This must be seen as a major defect in the proposals. It was not an unreasonable expectation that the Commission would be able to come up with a set of reforms less formidable than its draft code, which, if implemented, will take practitioners years to master, and students, perhaps never.

A further disturbing feature is that the new code will apply only to rights constituting land obligations created after the date when legislation comes into force. Faced with the perennial problem that bedevils much land law reform – what to do with existing rights? – the Commission regretfully concluded that it would not be possible to transform existing covenants into land obligations enforceable under the new law, desirable though that objective was. The present law will, therefore, remain relevant for the indefinite future, hardly a pleasing prospect for the conveyancer. Meanwhile the Report gathers dust, despite pleas to the Lord Chancellor for its speedy implementation[3]. No sign of legislation appears on the horizon. Indeed it might well be premature to introduce the code (whether as proposed or in some modified form) in

---

20 Two types are proposed: (1) neighbour obligations and (2) development obligations to be imposed pursuant to a development scheme, a much wider and more flexible concept than the present-day building scheme.

1 Requiring (in the case of neighbour obligations) entry of a notice against the servient title and inclusion as an appurtenant right on the dominant title. They would not constitute overriding interests. But see the alternative proposal if manpower problem at the Registry would make the preferred recommendation unworkable: para 9.25–9.26.

2 Eg a restrictive and access obligation would bind a tenant under a lease for 21 years or less, but not other neighbour obligations (such as an obligation to maintain a boundary wall).

3 From the Council of the Law Society. See the correspondence published at (1984) 81 LS Gaz 2666, giving reasons for the delay in implementation.

advance of the implementation of the Commission's own deliberations on condominium schemes[4].

N   Acknowledgement for production of deeds

On completion the purchaser has a prima facie right under the general law to take possession of the deeds relating to the property, subject to his mortgagee's right to keep them during the mortgage[5]. The Law of Property Act 1925, s 45 (9) enables a vendor to retain possession of the deeds in certain circumstances[6], and in this event the conveyance to the purchaser will incorporate an acknowledgement of his right to the production and delivery of copies of the documents retained. The purchaser's right to this acknowledgement stems from the general law[7]; it does not depend on any statutory or contractual provision[8]. Section 64 of the Act governs the effect of a statutory acknowledgement[9]. It does not confer any right to damages for loss or destruction of or injury to the documents (sub-s (6)); it merely gives a right to specific performance of the obligations at the expense of the person requesting the same. Consequently there is usually coupled with the acknowledgment an undertaking to keep the documents safe, whole, uncancelled and undefaced unless prevented from so doing by fire, or other inevitable accident (sub-s (9)). An action for damages lies for breach of this undertaking, but since destruction does not affect title, merely its proof, damages will apparently be limited to the cost of executing the necessary statutory declarations and exhibits[10]. The acknowledgement and undertaking may be the subject of a separate document, but normally they are contained in the conveyance to the purchaser in some such form as:

> The vendor hereby acknowledges the right of the purchaser to the production of the documents referred to in the schedule hereto (the possession of which is retained by the vendor) and to delivery of copies thereof and hereby undertakes for the safe custody of the same.

It has become customary for fiduciary vendors (personal representatives, trustees and mortgagees) not to enter into the undertaking for safe custody.

---

4   See Cmnd 179 (1987) (Commonhold). The Landlord and Tenant Act 1987 implements the recommendations of the Nugee Committee relating to flat management. Parts of this Act came into force on 1 February 1988; see SI 1987 No 2177.

5   LPA 1925, s 85(1) proviso, p 445, ante.

6   As to which see p 445, ante.

7   *Cooper v Emery* (1844) 1 Ph 388.

8   Under the Standard Conditions of Sale, the vendor must not retain the documents of title after the purchaser has tendered the purchase price. This obligation does not apply in respect to documents of title relating to land being retained by the vendor after completion: SCS 6.5.1, 6.5.2.

9   The full obligation is contained in sub-s (4). Note that there is no right to take one's own copies, and there is an exemption for fire and other inevitable accident: sub-s (2). The statutory acknowledgement replaces in less onerous terms the former express covenant for production given by a vendor: sub-s (8). See generally 1 W & C, 141–45.

10   Williams, *Title*, 799, note (18). Cf *Barrett v Brahms* (1966) 111 Sol Jo 35.

This practice, though without apparent legal foundation[11], has in fact received statutory recognition[12].

In merely referring to 'documents', the section introduces some uncertainty as to what it covers. Clearly it relates to deeds affecting the land convened, and to probates and letters of administration now that they may be endorsed with notice of assents and conveyances[13]. It is not considered necessary, nor is it the practice, to include planning permissions or certificates of search in an acknowledgement. Illogically, although a vendor must hand over all deeds in his possession, authority exists for saying that a purchaser is not entitled to an acknowledgement for documents dated prior to the date fixed for commencement of the title[14].

The statutory acknowledgement and undertaking are only effective when given by the person retaining the deeds 'to another'. An executor's acknowledgement for production of the probate contained in an assent whereby he vests the property in himself beneficially is valueless[15]. A subsequent purchaser should endeavour to obtain one in the conveyance to him. Failing this, he might have an equitable right to its production. Under s 45(7) of the Act a vendor's inability to furnish an acknowledgement is not to be an objection to the title in any case where the purchaser will, on completion, have an equitable right to the production of documents. The law relating to this equitable right is obscure and ill-defined[16]. Equally worthless is an acknowledgement by a mortgagor-vendor in a conveyance of part of the mortgaged property. The absence of a proper acknowledgement in this situation has been held to prevent the vendor from showing a good marketable title[17]. Normally the mortgagee holds the deed. He is the proper person to give the acknowledgement, but he cannot be compelled to do so. If he does, its obligations devolve on the mortgagor when the documents come into his possession. Mortgagees do not enter into any undertaking for safe custody. It is uncertain whether, apart from express stipulation, the purchaser can insist on the vendor's covenanting to give the undertaking when the deeds come into his possession[18].

The statutory obligations only bind the person having possession or control of the deeds so long as they are in his possession or control. The duties imposed by the undertaking are similarly imposed on the possessor only: see s 64(2), (9).

---

11 See Farrand, 313–14; cf 1 W & C, 144. Yet a fiduciary owner who subsequently acquires possession of the deeds comes under the obligations of sub-s 9 if a previous owner has given the undertaking.

12 See the Leasehold Reform Act 1967, s 10 (1), (6) (leasehold enfranchisement).

13 *Re Miller and Pickersgill's Contract* [1931] 1 Ch 511. See p 323, ante.

14 Emmet, para 21.022, citing *Re Guest and Worth* (unreported).

15 Despite, it is thought, the rule that a person with different capacities may have power to contract in a representative capacity with himself as an individual. See 9 *Halsbury's Laws* (4th edn), para 204; *Rowley Holmes & Co v Barber* [1977] 1 All ER 801.

16 For cases see *Fain v Ayers* (1826) 2 Sim & St 533; *Re Jenkins and Commercial Electric Theatre Co's Contract* [1917] WN 49; 1 Dart V & P, 483; cf Emmet, para 21.023.

17 *Pratt v Betts* (1973) 27 P & CR 398, CA, applying *Re Pursell and Deakin's Contract* [1893] WN 152. LPA 1925, s 45(7) was not considered.

18 Under LSC 17(5) a non-fiduciary vendor can be required to covenant.

The benefit of the acknowledgement runs with the land under sub-s (3) in favour of any successor (other then a lessee at a rent), whether of the whole or part of the original purchaser's land. If A conveys part of his land to B who later conveys a smaller portion to C, the benefit of A's acknowledgement to B will pass to C who will, however, require an acknowledgement from B for the A-B conveyance. There is no corresponding provision for the running of the benefit of the undertaking; it is thought that it runs under s 78(1) of the Act[19].

O   Certificate for value

The purpose of the certificate for value clause has already been explained[20]. This clause is usually in the following form:

It is hereby certified that the transaction hereby effected does not form part of a larger transaction or of a series of transactions in respect of which the amount or value or the aggregate amount or value of the consideration exceeds £60,000.

P   Testimonium and execution

The testimonium links the contents of the deed with the parties' seals and signatures, as follows:

IN WITNESS whereof the parties hereto have hereunto set their respective hands and seals the day and year first before written

Underneath towards the left hand side of the page appears the attestation clause and the executing party signs his name on the right hand side, thus–

SIGNED AND DELIVERED by the said
ABEL SMITH in the
presence of: JOHN BROWN
} Abel Smith
John Brown

The requirements of a valid execution and the necessity for any attestation have already been considered in Chapter 14[1]. Any schedules appended to the deed are sandwiched between the testimonium and the attestation clause. A registered land transfer contains no testimonium. The signatures and seals appear immediately after the certificate of value clause (if any), except where there are schedules to the transfer, which are also placed before the attestation clause.

---

19   Farrand, 313; Walford, 209. Title deeds to real estate devolved on the heir prior to 1926 (*Atkinson v Baker* (1791) 4 Term Rep 229) and so come within the definition of 'land' in LPA 1925, s 205(1)(ix); the requirement of s 78(1) (covenant relating to any *land* of the covenantee) is satisfied.
20   Page 467, ante.
 1   Pages 447–449, ante.

Chapter 18

Documents for particular transactions

A Introduction

A cursory glance at any book of conveyancing precedents will soon indicate the vast number of different transactions for which the conveyancer may be required to draft a suitable document. The aim of this chapter is not to furnish the reader with a selection of simple precedents, but to consider mainly (though not exclusively) the contents of conveyances and other documents relating to some of the transactions to which we have had occasion to refer in the preceding chapters, and to draw attention to particular problems for which special provision should be made in the deed. This chapter concentrates upon the contents of deeds relating to unregistered land. However, though we have seen that the form of a transfer of registered land is much simpler than that of a conveyance, especially in relation to the description of the land transferred and the absence of any need to have recitals, any special provisions which a particular transaction renders necessary must be incorporated in a transfer of registered land just as in a conveyance of unregistered land.

A precedent of a simple conveyance of freehold land by a beneficial owner appears on page 516. This form, suitably amended, can be used for straightforward transactions by vendors who are only limited owners. One point in particular should be remembered. When the vendor is not a beneficial owner, the conveyance should make reference to the authority, statutory or otherwise, which enables him to convey free from the rights of the beneficiaries. Thus in a conveyance in execution of an express trust for sale, the vendors should be expressed to convey 'as trustees in execution of the said trust for sale'. Similarly a conveyance by a mortgagee[1] will recite the mortgage and the agreement of sale, and state in the operative part that:

> ... the vendor as mortgagee in exercise of the power of sale conferred on him by the Law of Property Act 1925 HEREBY CONVEYS unto the purchaser ALL THAT [parcels] TO HOLD unto the purchaser in fee simple discharged[2] from all right of redemption and claims under the before recited mortgage.

---

1 See 19 Ency F & P, 1340, Form 7:K:26; Hallett, 273, Form 52.
2 It is customary to insert the words 'discharged etc,' since they occur in the statutory form of conveyance by a mortgagee (see LPA 1925, Sch 5, Form No 4), but their inclusion does not seem essential in view of s 88(1)(b) of the Act.

Incumbrances subject to which the property is conveyed are introduced by the usual words 'SUBJECT to' which appear in the habendum immediately after 'in fee simple'. The words 'discharged etc,' come at the end of the clause after the incumbrances. Where the land is conveyed subject to restrictive covenants, the purchaser need not enter into any indemnity covenant[3] with the mortgagee; the latter does not require any indemnity from the purchaser, not having given any similar covenant to the mortgagor.

In the following pages it is proposed to enlarge upon the contents of the documents listed below:

A conveyance of a new house on a building estate.
Conveyances of the freehold reversion.
A lease, and other documents relating to leasehold land.
A building society mortgage and related documents.

The form and contents of a simple assent in favour of a beneficiary entitled to property under the will of a deceased testator are discussed in Chapter 10[4].

B   Conveyance of new house on building estate

The conveyancer is frequently involved in the drafting or approval of conveyances of new residential property. In practice the reader will encounter a wide variety of such conveyances, some more complex in their provisions than others. In keeping with the general policy of this chapter, it is proposed to draw attention to those matters for which it is normally necessary to provide in a straightforward conveyance of a new house, rather than to comment upon a specific precedent. Some points have already been touched upon in the preceding chapter, but the following discussion affords an opportunity to bring together several topics previously considered in isolation.

1.   Parcels clause

Nothing further need be said about the description of the property, save to stress the point made in Chapter 17 that it is vital to ensure that the description is accurate and that any plan which is intended to control the parcels faithfully represents the actual boundaries of the plot[5].

2.   Easements and reservations

It is usually essential for the conveyance to grant and reserve rights of way and use of sewers and other services. At the time of the conveyance the estate roads are probably still under construction and the site of these roads is still vested in the vendor. The purchaser should be granted a right of way for all

---

3   See pp 575–576, ante.
4   See p 320, ante.
5   See pp 528–534, ante.

purposes connected with the use of the land conveyed with or without vehicles along the estate roads[6] (an expression which will require amplification in the actual deed) or along a road or roads suitably indicated on the deed plan or named in the deed. In addition to this right of way there is grant of a right, frequently expressed (as is the right of way) to be in common with the vendor and all others entitled to use the like rights, to connect with and to use the sewers, drains, watercourses, pipes, cables, wires and other services 'now laid or hereafter to be laid' in, under or over the vendor's adjacent land (and, sometimes, adjoining land which the developer hopes subsequently to acquire). The use of the 'now or hereafter' formula renders it essential to see that the easement is limited to take effect within the perpetuity period[7]. There will be a reservation of a similar right to use the sewers, etc, under the purchaser's land.

Where the building erected on the purchaser's plot overhangs the adjacent land the conveyance should grant adequate rights to maintain footings, foundations, eaves and gutters in, under or over the adjacent land, and to enter that land for the purposes of maintenance and repair, on condition that any resulting damage to the adjacent property is made good by the purchaser.

3. Covenants

As we have already observed, it is the invariable practice on any residential development to subject individual purchasers to numerous detailed restrictions. The following are only illustrative of the many that find their way into present day conveyances: not to use otherwise than as a single private dwelling; not to create nuisances or annoyance; not to add to or alter the existing buildings without the vendor's written consent; not to display advertisements (other than for sale or to let notices); not to station caravans and other vehicles (other than private cars) on the land; not to plant poplars and certain other trees within specified distances of adjacent buildings. These and similar restrictions which can do much to preserve the amenities of a building estate serve a useful purpose if imposed so as to create a building scheme, thereby enabling one owner to enforce the restrictions against his neighbour. If this is the intention it should be so stated in the conveyance[8]. Alas, in practice the conveyance is more likely to contain a clause which expressly negates any intention to create such a scheme. In effect, the restrictions are imposed solely for the benefit of the vendor's retained land, which he clearly has a legitimate interest to protect. Yet it is to be regretted that so many practitioners representing builders are reluctant to consider the wider implications of estate development. In the absence of an enforceable scheme the restrictions become virtually obsolete once the estate has been completed. An individual house owner may justly feel aggrieved when advised that he cannot take legal action against a neighbour who is in breach of covenant. He may well question the reason for imposing

6   See *White v Richards* (1993) 68 P & CR 105, CA.
7   See p 547, ante.
8   Eg by a suitably drafted recital, see 19 Ency F & P, 906, Form 7:A:27.

the restrictions in the first place and is hardly likely to be satisfied when told they were imposed for the vendor's benefit[9].

Little need be said about a purchaser's positive covenants. A covenant to maintain boundary fences is often encountered. On some estate developments the vendor lays out the front garden with trees, shrubs and flowering plants, and the purchaser is commonly required to maintain and replace these when necessary. The only obligation usually entered into by the vendor is the covenant to construct the road upon which the property abuts to the satisfaction of the local highway authority. The wording of this covenant needs watching. Unless the vendor also covenants to repair and maintain the road until its adoption[10], the liability for maintenance pending adoption falls on the individual purchasers.

4. Other clauses

Attention needs to be drawn to some miscellaneous clauses frequently encountered. It is advisable to regulate the rights of adjoining owners as regards walls, fences, spouts, pipes, drains and similar matters used and enjoyed in common. The difficulties created by the standard form declaration that these are to be maintained and repaired at the joint expense of the persons entitled to use them have previously been considered[11]. It is standard practice for the vendor to reserve the right[12] to modify, waive or release the restrictions affecting any land forming part of the development and to prevent the purchaser's acquisition of any right of light or air which will restrict or interfere with the use of the vendor's adjoining land for building or other purposes. Such a clause would appear to be ineffective to prevent the acquisition of a right of light over land not owned by the vendor at the time but subsequently acquired by him, though frequently the clause professes to extend to land 'now or hereafter' belonging to the vendor.

C Conveyances of freehold reversion

1. Sale to stranger

On a sale of freehold land subject to an existing lease, the conveyance normally contains a recital of the vendor's seisin subject to the lease and the habendum will read as follows: 'TO HOLD unto the purchaser in fee simple subject to but with the benefit of the before recited lease'. The Law of Property Act

---

9 Even under the Law Commission's proposed scheme of land obligations, the imposition of a development scheme will not be obligatory.
10 Construction of the estate roads is normally covered by an agreement made with the highway authority under s 38 of the Highways Act 1980, supported by a bond guaranteeing payment of the costs if the developer defaults; see the 2nd edn, pp 200–201.
11 Page 540, ante.
12 Such a provision is not inconsistent with the existence of a building scheme: *Re Elm Avenue (6, 8, 10 and 12), New Milton* [1984] 3 All ER 632.

1925, s 141 operates to pass automatically to the purchaser the benefit of the rent reserved by the lease and the lessee's covenants having reference to the subject matter thereof, without the need for any express assignment. It also vests in him the right to sue and re-enter (assuming there is the usual forfeiture clause) for rent in arrears at the time of the conveyance[13]. The section does not extend to covenants entered into with the lessor by a third party, such as a surety who guarantees payment of the rent and performance of the covenants. The House of Lords has now held in *P & A Swift Investments (a firm) v Combined English Stores Group plc*[14] that such a covenant by a surety touches and concerns the land (the reversion) and, therefore, passes automatically on a conveyance of the freehold reversion. The absence of an express assignment of the benefit of surety's covenant is no bar to an action against him by the new freehold owner.

In the case of leases granted before January 1996, the privity of contract rule will ensure that the original lessor remains liable to the original lessee on the covenants in the lease, despite a sale of the reversion. No statutory indemnity is implied in the conveyance. However, under the Standard Conditions of Sale, the vendor is entitled to require the purchaser to indemnify him against all claims arising from the lease after completion[15]. With regard to leases created after 1 January 1996, the privity of contract rule with regard to the assignment of leases and reversions has been significantly affected by the Landlord and Tenant (Covenants) Act 1995 the main effects of which will be considered later in this Chapter[16].

2. Sale to lessee

When the purchaser of the freehold reversion is the lessee himself, his solicitor should consider the need for including in the conveyance a formal declaration that the lessee's leasehold term shall merge and be extinguished in the fee simple estate. Merger depends on the intention, expressed or implied, of the parties[17]. Where merger is capable of taking place, an appropriate declaration is desirable, if such be the intention, for it obviates any requisitions on title on this point when the purchaser comes to sell his property. In the absence of any expressed intention, the court considers what is most advantageous for the party owning the two estates[18]. There can be no implied merger if the leasehold estate is subject to incumbrances, eg a mortgage, or if he holds the two estates

---

13 *London and County (A and D) Ltd v Wilfred Sportsman Ltd* [1971] Ch 764, [1970] 2 All ER 600, CA.
14 [1989] AC 632, [1988] 2 All ER 885, HL, approving *Kumar v Dunning* [1989] QB 193, [1987] 2 All ER 801. Several first instance decisions had previously been to the contrary: *Pinemain Ltd v Wellbeck International Ltd* (1984) 272 EG 1166; *Re Distributors and Warehousing Ltd* [1986] 1 EGLR 90; *Coastplace v Hartley* [1987] QB 948.
15 SCS 3.3.2(d).
16 Below pp 589–594.
17 See LPA 1925, s 185, which applies the equitable rule to all cases of merger. The rule at law was independent of intention.
18 *Ingle v Vaughan Jenkins* [1900] 2 Ch 368.

in different capacities. A declaration of merger should not be included if it is intended to preserve the enforceability of restrictive covenants entered into by the lessor in the lease in respect of the lessor's adjoining land[19]. Seemingly an express merger does not affect a charge of the leasehold title[20]. Nor in the case of registered land can merger take place if any incumbrance remains outstanding on the register of the leasehold title[1]. Merger would require closure of the leasehold title, and this would operate to destroy the chargee's interest.

Where the lessee purchases in exercise of an option in his favour, it is the practice to treat the conveyance as being in pursuance of an ordinary agreement for sale, so that there is no need to recite the option. Special problems arise where the conveyance takes effect under the Leasehold Reform Act 1967, and the reader is referred to specialist books on this aspect[2].

D   Documents relating to leasehold land

1.   Form of lease

The form of a lease differs in some important respects from that of a conveyance, as the following precedent shows:

> THIS LEASE made the .... day of ....
> 199........................ BETWEEN AB of (etc) (hereinafter called 'the landlord' which expression shall where the context so admits include the person for the time being entitled to the reversion immediately expectant on the determination of the term hereby granted) and XY of (etc) (hereinafter called 'the tenant' which expression shall where the context so admits include his successors in title)
>
> WITNESSETH as follows:
>
> 1. In consideration of the rent and the tenant's covenants hereinafter reserved and contained the landlord HEREBY DEMISES unto the tenant ALL THAT [parcels] TO HOLD unto the tenant from the .... day of .... for a term of .... years YIELDING AND PAYING therefor during the said term the rent of £........................ by equal half yearly payments on .... and on .... the first of such payments or a proportionate part thereof to be made on ....

[Then follow the covenants and the other provisions of the lease.]

The following miscellaneous points should be noted. Recitals are not normally included in leases. Where there is consideration other than the rent and lessee's covenants, such as the payment of a premium, the deed should so state. The word 'demise' is generally used as the operative word of grant. The landlord is not expressed to demise in any stated capacity. The reason for this

---

19   *Golden Lion Hotel (Hunstanton) Ltd v Carter* [1965] 3 All ER 506 (covenants destroyed).
20   See Emmet, para 26.095.
 1   R & R, 21.30.
 2   See generally, Hague, *Leasehold Enfranchisement* (2nd edn).

is that the covenants for title[3] implied by s 76 of the Law of Property Act 1925 in a conveyance by a person who conveys and is expressed to convey in a certain capacity do not apply to 'a demise by way of lease at a rent'[4]. The quantum of the lessee's estate is indicated by the habendum clause. It should be remembered that a lease takes effect from the date of its delivery, notwithstanding that the term is expressed to commence from some earlier date[5]. The words 'Yielding and Paying' introduce the reddendum clause which specifies the amount of the rent, and the frequency with which and the time when it is payable. In leases of business or industrial premises it is very common to provide for the rent to be subject to periodic reviews in accordance with an agreed formula. These rent review clauses have generated much litigation during recent years, but happily consideration of the cases is beyond the scope of this book[6].

A lease of registered land normally follows the form of a lease of unregistered land, save that the deed must contain the usual heading and the parcels clause must sufficiently refer in the prescribed manner to the registered land[7].

2. Contents of lease

Considerable variation exists in the precise contents of a formal lease, depending on the length of the term and the type of property demised. Thus the provisions of a lease of an agricultural holding will differ from those of a lease of an office block or factory. Similarly the obligations imposed on a lessee of residential property may well vary according to whether the lease is granted at a rack rent, ie a rent representing the full annual value of the land and buildings, or at a nominal (or ground) rent, ie rent representing the annual value of the land only, plus a premium (representing the value of the house). Leases of this second kind are normally for a long term of years, eg 99 or 999 years, and are frequently encountered in parts of the country. Such a lease would usually contain covenants by the lessee: to pay the rent and rates; to repair; to insure (sometimes in a named insurance office) and to apply the insurance moneys in rebuilding; to allow the lessor to enter to view the state of repair; not to make alterations without consent; to register assignments with the lessor; to use solely as a private residence; to yield up the property on the determination of the term. In addition the lessor will covenant for quiet enjoyment, and there will be a proviso for re-entry in the event of non-payment of rent or other breach of covenant[8]. Any unusual clause in a draft lease should put a practitioner on inquiry, and the proper discharge of his duty requires

3 See p 664, post.
4 LPA 1925, s 76(5).
5 See p 556, ante.
6 See Clarke & Adams, *Rent Reviews & Variable Rents* (2nd edn).
7 LRA 1925, s 18(1)(e), p 542, ante, s 76 (p 481, ante). In practice these specific requirements are ignored where the lease takes effect as an overriding interest.
8 See 11 Ency F & P, 349, Form 3:14. For leases of other types of property, refer to 22 Ency F & P (4th edn), Forms C22–31.

him to alert his client to its effect and to warn him of the risks inherent in entering into the transaction[9].

3.   Grant of underlease

In certain areas of the country[10] it is relatively common for a housing estate to be developed by way of lease and underlease. The freeholder, F, demises the land to D, the developer, for (say) 999 years at an annual rent of £1,000. D builds 50 houses on the land and sub-demises individual properties for a term of 990 years at a premium (representing the cost of the house) plus a yearly rent of £40[11]. It is essential that the underlease confers adequate protection for each 'purchaser' in the event of D's failure to perform the covenants in the headlease and the consequent risk of forfeiture proceedings by F. It should contain a covenant by D to pay the head rent and to perform the covenants so far as they relate to the remainder of the land comprised in the head lease. This is a purely collateral covenant which does not touch and concern the land demised by the underlease; it does not bind an assignee of the head-lease[12]. D's covenant is not merely for indemnity; it constitutes a covenant to perform the obligations in the headlease and is enforceable by the underlessee irrespective of whether the head lessor is seeking to enforce the covenant[13].

In practical terms D's covenant may be worthless should he go into liquidation or otherwise default in payment of the rent. In theory any one of the underlessees may find himself faced with a demand for £1,000. It is, therefore, usual to confer additional remedies[14] on each underlessee. Until he is fully re-imbursed all money, loss or damage, paid or sustained, he is empowered: (i) to retain the rent reserved by his own underlease; (ii) to receive or collect the rents reserved by the underleases already granted or thereafter to be granted; and (iii) to enter upon the remainder of the land still occupied by the underlessor and to receive and distrain for the rents and profits. The efficacy of these various rights is suspect, to say the least. Remedy (iii) will

---

9   *Simple Simon Catering Ltd v J E Binstock Miller & Co* (1973) 228 EG 527, CA; *County Personnel (Employment Agency) Ltd v Alan R Pulver & Co* [1987] 1 All ER 289, CA.

10   In Lancashire tiers of leases are often encountered. The occupier, despite holding under a long lease, may in fact be a sub-under-underlessee (or assignee). The Royal Commission advocated the compulsory enfranchisement of all the leases except for the occupation lease as a cure for the conveyancing complications that these tiers can create: Report, Vol 1, 283, Annex 21.1, para 4.

11   Even in the long leases it is now standard practice to provide for the ground rent to be increased at intervals in accordance with a simple formula, eg after the first 50 years and thereafter every 25 years. Cf 12 Ency F & P, 469, Form 3:99 (999 years' lease).

12   *Dewar v Goodman* [1909] AC 72, HL, but questioned by Browne-Wilkinson V-C in *Kumar v Dunning* [1989] QB 193, [1987] 2 All ER 801 at 811, CA. Nor is D's covenant annexed to the land by virtue of LPA 1925, s 189(2) which, apparently, is confined to situations where land charged with a single rent is subdivided (rather than sub-let): *Kumar v Dunning*. Sed quaere.

13   *Ayling v Wade* [1961] 2 QB 228, [1961] 2 All ER 399, CA (underlessor's failure to repair). The court distinguished *Harris v Boots Cash Chemists (Southern) Ltd* [1904] 2 Ch 376, and *Reckitt v Cody* [1920] 2 Ch 452, where similar covenants were construed as indemnity covenants only.

14   For a precedent, see 11 Ency F & P, 330, Form 2:46.

probably be valueless, for the undeveloped or partly developed sections of the estate are not likely to be income-producing, and the power of collection in (ii) may prove worthless since there is no means of enforcing payment from a defaulter. However, irrespective of any express powers, an underlessee who pays the head rent under threat of forfeiture is entitled in equity to a contribution from his co-underlessees, since he has borne a burden for the benefit of others amongst all of whom exists community of interest[15].

Whether the term created by the sub-lease is for a short or a long period, the underlessor must ensure that in relation to the property underleased the sub-lessee is under an obligation to observe covenants at least as stringent as those in the head lease (other than that for payment of rent). Here the underlease repeats verbatim the relevant covenants in the headlease. An indemnity covenant should, in addition, be taken from the underlessee. Without it the underlessor cannot recover the costs of proceedings for relief against forfeiture incurred by him as a result of the underlessee's default[16].

4.   Assignment of existing lease

An assignment of an existing leasehold term is similar in form to a conveyance of freehold land, subject to such alterations as are dictated by the difference in the tenure of the land transferred. As we saw on page 521, considerable variation exists in practice in the mode of reciting the vendor's estate ownership. The operative part of the deed will be in some such form as this:

> ... the vendor as beneficial owner HEREBY ASSIGNS unto the purchaser ALL THAT the property comprised in the lease[17] TO HOLD unto the purchaser for all the residue now unexpired of the term of years created by the lease SUBJECT to the rent reserved by and to the lessee's covenants and the conditions contained in the lease.

Where part only of the property comprised in a lease is assigned, the rent reserved thereby is usually apportioned informally, that is, without the consent of the lessor, between the land assigned to the purchaser and that retained by the vendor. The lessor is not bound by this informal apportionment and he can distrain on any part of the land for the whole rent[18]. The position between the vendor and purchaser is largely regulated by statute, which implies in an assignment for value mutual covenants by the parties to pay the apportioned part of the rent and perform the covenants in respect of the land vested in each of them[19]. Advantage is sometimes taken of the statutory power whereby

---

15 *Whitham v Bullock* [1939] 2 KB 81 at 88, [1939] 2 All ER 310 at 316, CA, per Clauson LJ.
16 *Clare v Dobson* [1911] 1 KB 35. A mere covenant to perform the covenants in the head lease implies an obligation to indemnify: *Hornby v Cardwell* (1881) 8 QBD 329, CA.
17 This wording is adopted where the property has already been fully described in the recital of the lease. Alternatively, a full description of the property may be given in the parcels clause or in a schedule.
18 As to the rights inter se of the assignees of part, see *Whitham v Bullock* [1939] 2 KB 81, [1939] 2 All ER 310, CA.
19 LPA 1925, s 77(1)(D). The vendor's covenant is implied only where he assigns 'as beneficial owner', a limitation sometimes overlooked in practice.

each party charges his land with the payment of all money which may become
payable under his implied covenant[20]. These mutual charges cannot be insisted
upon unless the contract so provides. The existence of the charge enables the
court to order a sale in appropriate circumstances.

(a) The original tenant's continuing liability – some problems[1]

For centuries, a central tenet of Landlord and Tenant law was that the original
parties to the lease were liable to each other for the duration of that lease[2].
This was so on the basis of privity of contract so that, even when a tenant had
assigned the lease, he could still be sued by the original landlord for arrears of
rent incurred by the assignee. While it is true that the assignee would also be
liable, this may not be of much value to the landlord if, as became increasingly
common, the assignee was insolvent. Moreover, the landlord did not have to
exhaust his remedies against the assignee before bringing an action against
the original tenant[3] who, accordingly, could find himself having to pay a
substantial amount of money in rent arrears built up by an assignee of a lease
which had been assigned years previously. This liability could be extensive, in
that if the rent was revised upwards pursuant to a rent review, even after the
lease had been assigned, the original tenant was liable to the original landlord
in respect of the higher rent[4]. Indeed, in *Selous Street Properties Ltd v Oronel
Fabrics Ltd*[5] it was held that the original tenant was liable for an increased rent,
the rent having been increased as a result of improvements carried out to the
property after the lease had been assigned.

Although this decision was doubted in *Friends' Provident Life Office v British
Rlys Board*[6], on the basis that the original tenant should only be liable to pay
an increased rent if the lease to which he was privy contemplated an upwards
revision of the rent, as will be the case when the lease contains a rent review
clause, the dangers for the original tenant, particularly in the case of a lease of
commercial premises were considerable. This particular problem has now been
regulated by statute, whereby a tenant who, after assignment of the lease,
remains liable on the covenants in it, will not be liable to pay a higher rent in
respect of a variation of the lease to which the landlord could have refused[7].
This relates to a situation where the landlord agrees to an easing of use
restrictions imposed by the lease in return for a higher rent and confirms the
position in *Friends' Provident.*

The Law Commission considered the whole position to be unsatisfactory
and proposed wide-ranging reform[8]. After a considerable delay, reform was

20   LPA 1925, s 77(7).
 1   See (1984) 81 LSG 2214 (K Reynolds & S Fogel): a highly informative discussion.
 2   The liability would not extend to any statutory continuation of the original lease: see *City of
     London Corpn v Fell* [1994] 1 AC 458, [1993] 4 All ER 968, HL.
 3   *Norwich Union Life Insurance Society v Low Profile Fashions Ltd* (1991) 64 P & CR 187, CA.
 4   *Centrovincial Estates plc v Bulk Storage Ltd* (1983) 46 P & CR 393.
 5   [1984] 1 EGLR 50, (1984) 270 EG 643.
 6   [1996] 1 All ER 336 at 351, CA, per Sir Christopher Slade.
 7   Landlord and Tenant (Covenants) Act 1995, s 18.
 8   (1988) Law Com No 174.

implemented by the Landlord and Tenant (Covenants) Act 1995, although in a very different form from that proposed by the Law Commission[9]. It is now necessary to distinguish between leases created before 1 January 1996, when the Act came into force and those created afterwards.

(b) Pre-1996 leases

The main aim of that Act was to free the original tenant from the dangers occasioned by the doctrine of privity of contract. It is not retrospective and so, in respect of leases created before 1996, the original tenant will remain liable to the original landlord in respect of obligations imposed by the original lease. The Act does, however, make some alterations to his position.

(i) *Procedure.* Where the landlord seeks to enforce a covenant in relation to a fixed charge[10] against the original tenant, he must now follow a specified procedure. What he must now do is serve on the tenant, and the same applies to a guarantor of the tenant, a notice within six months of the money becoming due which states that the money is due and that the landlord intends to recover from the tenant[11]. A failure to adhere to this timetable will mean that the landlord will lose his right to proceed against the tenant in respect of a fixed charge.

(ii) *Overriding leases.* A second innovation which applies to leases created both before and after the coming into force of the Act is the tenant's right, in certain circumstances, to the, somewhat misleadingly named, overriding lease. Under s 19 of the Act, where a tenant has made full payment in respect of an obligation in the lease which has since been assigned, he is entitled to an overriding lease. An overriding lease is a tenancy of the reversion expectant on the term equivalent to the relevant term plus three days or the longest period which will not displace the landlord's reversion. This lease is subject to the same covenants as the original lease. The point of this provision is that the original tenant becomes the landlord of the defaulting tenant and can, therefore, pursue remedies against that person. The *quid pro quo* for this is that he becomes liable on all the covenants in the lease.

To acquire an overriding tenancy, the tenant must serve a notice on the landlord requesting the grant of such a tenancy. The landlord must then comply with this request within a reasonable time. Once the request has been made, the tenant should protect his claim by registration. If title is unregistered, an estate contract should be registered; if title is registered, the claim should be protected on the register of title[12].

---

9 For excellent discussions of the background and the changes introduced by the Act, see (1996) 59 MLR 78 (M Davey) and [1996] CLJ 313 (S Bridge).
10 Defined to mean a payment in repsect of rent, a service charge or liquidated damages: Landlord and Tenant (Covenants) Act 1995, s 17(4).
11 Ibid, s 17(2).
12 Ibid, s 20(6).

(c) Post–1996 tenancies
The main thrust of the new Act is to ease the position of the original tenant
when he has assigned the lease. Some changes are also made to the position
of the landlord. It is convenient to treat separately the position when the lease
is assigned and that when the reversion is assigned.

(d) New leases: the position of tenants
The main provisions of the Act apply to what are termed new leases. These are
leases created after the Act came into force (1 January 1996) other than leases
created pursuant to a contract entered into before that date[13]. Also defined as
a new lease is a lease created before 1996 which is varied after that date when
the effect of the variation is that there is a deemed surrender and regrant of a
new tenancy[14].

(i) *Release from liability.*   On a total assignment of a new lease, s 5 of the Act
provides that the tenant is released from liability to the landlord on tenant
covenants and ceases to have the benefit of the landlord's covenants. This
does not absolve him from liability in respect of breaches of covenant which
occurred before the assignment[15]. The assignee is then liable on all the tenant's
covenants, the previous rule that he would only be bound by covenants which
touched and concerned the land having been abolished[16].
     The position of the tenant may not, however, be entirely straightforward.
Although contracting out of the Act is prohibited[17], s 16 of the Act provides
that there is no bar to the tenant, when assigning the lease, from guaranteeing
performance of the covenants in the lease. For such a guarantee to be valid,
the lease must contain a qualified covenant against assignment and the
condition imposed for consent to be given, ie that the tenant enters such a
guarantee must be lawful within the terms of the Landlord and Tenant Act
1988.

(ii) *Consents to assign.*   As a major concession to commercial landlords,
amendments were made to s 19 of the Landlord and Tenant Act 1927
concerning the giving of a consent to an assignment of a non-residential lease.
Section 22 of the Act amends the 1927 Act to allow the landlord, when the
tenant has given a qualified covenant against assignment, to stipulate in advance
when consent will not be given to an assignment. This will enable landlords to
include in the original lease a term that consent will not be given to an
assignment unless the tenant guarantees the performance of the covenants in
the lease. In this way, the tenant's continuing liability on the covenants can be
restored. Whether such clauses become commonplace will depend to a

---

13   Ibid, s 1. This includes leases created after 1996 pursuant to an option or right of pre-
     emption created before that date.
14   Ibid, s 1(6). For a helpful discussion of this issue, see [1995] Conv 124 (A Dowling).
15   Ibid, s 24.
16   Ibid, s 2. See p 594, post.
17   Ibid, s 25.

considerable extent upon the respective bargaining strength of the parties; something which is heavily influenced by the prevailing state of the property market.

(e) New leases: the position of landlords

Unlike the position with tenants, the starting point of the Act insofar as landlords are concerned is not to free them from continuing liability under the landlord covenants upon an assignment of the reversion. He will remain liable on the covenants unless he is released from them. To obtain a release from his covenants, he must, within four weeks, beginning with the date of the assignment, serve a notice on the tenant informing him of the assignment and seeking a release. Such a release will then occur if either, the tenant agrees or fails to reply within four weeks. If the tenant does object, the landlord can apply to the court to determine if the objection is reasonable and, if it is held that it is not, then a release will be given[18].

A former landlord, who has assigned the lease without obtaining a release from his covenants, may on the occasion of a further assignment, seek a release from his liability on the covenants[19]. Again, he has only four weeks in which to do this. An obvious difficulty facing such a person is finding out that such an assignment has taken place. A way of circumventing this difficulty is, when assigning the reversion, to include a covenant by the purchaser that he will notify him in the event of a future assignment of the reversion.

(f) Liability of assignee (A)–effect of statutory indemnity covenants

The 1995 Act has altered the position of assignees both in regard to the issue of what covenants in the original lease will be binding upon him and, also, the scope of the implied statutory covenants. Because the Act does not operate retrospectively, the old law as it relates to assignments which took place before 1996 will continue to be relevant for some time to come. It is therefore necessary to consider the two positions separately.

(i) *Pre-1996 assignments.* The position under the general law was that, on an assignment of a lease from T to A, A assumed a primary liability to L in respect of covenants which touched and concerned the land. This liability ceases once A assigns the leasehold term to A2, save in respect of breaches committed while it was vested in him. Moreover, at common law A is not liable to indemnify T in respect of rent which T has been called upon to pay after the A-A2 assignment because of A2 's default[20]. However, the effect of the implied statutory indemnity covenants must not be overlooked. By virtue of the Law of Property Act 1925[1], A covenants with T on the occasion of the T-A assignment that he 'will at all times ... duly pay all rent becoming due under the lease ...'.

---

18 Ibid, s 8.
19 Ibid s 7.
20 *Wolveridge v Steward* (1833) 1 Cr & M 644.
1 Section 77(1)(C), Sch 2, Pt IX. On the question whether s 77(1)(C) operates as an indemnity covenant only, see Emmet, para 26.143, and p 576, note 15, ante.

He also covenants to observe and perform the lessee's covenants contained therein, and to indemnify T in the usual manner. So, if L recovers unpaid rent from T, T can seek redress from A under the covenants, even though it is A2 who defaults in payment of the rent. These statutory covenants are implied only in an assignment for valuable consideration. According to the recent decision in *Johnsey Estates Ltd v Lewis & Manley (Engineering) Ltd*[2], the mere assumption by A of a liability to L at common law in respect of the covenants in the lease is itself valuable consideration. The assignor (T) obtains an obvious benefit because he ceases to be primarily liable to L and he gains the benefit of another party being also liable. The fact that a nominal sum of £1 is expressed as the consideration for the assignment does not prevent it being one for valuable consideration[3]. The transaction in the *Johnsey* case was of a commercial nature; no element of bounty was involved. The case is not, therefore, an authority governing the position where there is a purely voluntary assignment, though the reasoning is apt to cover such a situation[4]. To extend it to voluntary assignments would, within the context of leasehold transactions, deprive the words of s 77(1)(C) 'for valuable consideration' of any meaning. All assignments by their very nature would incorporate the covenants by implication. Yet s 77(4) envisages the need to incorporate them by making express reference to s 77 when a transaction is not for valuable consideration. These factors suggest that despite the *Johnsey* case it remained prudent to have express covenants or to adopt the s 77(4) procedure whenever the assignment is by way of gift[5].

(ii) *Post-1996 assignments.*   The 1995 Act affects assignees of the lease in two ways. First the requirement that the covenant touches and concerns the land, criterion which for many years was a source of difficulty, has been abolished. The assignee will be liable on all tenants' covenants after the assignment[6]. Second, the statutory indemnity covenant is also abolished[7]. The reason for this is that, because the original tenant, on assignment, ceases to be liable on the covenants contained in the original lease and, therefore, does not need to be indemnified. Where the tenant has guaranteed the performance of the covenant, he may still claim as a matter of law, an indemnity from the occupying tenant or sub-tenant who is actually responsible for the breach[8].

2   (1987) 284 EG 1240, CA, adopting *Price v Jenkins* (1877) 5 Ch D 619 at 621, CA, per James LJ.
3   The trial judge held that £1 was not valuable consideration within LPA 1925, s 205(1)(xxi). There was no cross-appeal against this ruling, and the Court of Appeal did not have to consider the point.
4   See *Price v Jenkins*, supra, at 620, per James LJ, arguendo: 'Can an assignment of leasehold property ever be, strictly speaking, voluntary?' Subsequent cases tended to regard *Price v Jenkins* as a decision on a particular statute, the Fraudulent Conveyances Act 1584–5: *Re Ridler* [1911] 2 Ch 530. It was followed by Kekewich J in *Harris v Tubb* (1889) 42 Ch D 79, where a voluntary assignee of leaseholds was held to be a purchaser for value and so entitled to take free from a lien (binding the assignor) of which he had no notice.
5   The point is left open in 19 Ency F & P, 1462, note 6. Hallett, 325, Form 83, 326, note (ii), adopts a more cautious stance.
6   Landlord and Tenant (Covenants) Act 1995, s 2.
7   Ibid, s 14.
8   Emmet, para 26.122A.

E   Mortgages

It is not intended in this section to attempt to consider the different types of mortgage that the practitioner may encounter in a conveyancing transaction. Attention will be focused mainly on building society mortgages. The majority of house purchases are financed by means of a loan from this source, though in recent years banks have begun to play a significant role in the residential mortgage market[9].

1.   Types of mortgage

A building society mortgage will take one of two main forms: a capital and interest repayment mortgage, or an endowment repayment mortgage. With the former, the loan (ie the capital) and the accrued interest are gradually repaid by monthly repayments. In the early years most of each monthly payment comprises interest charged, and only a small proportion represents a repayment of capital. But over the years as more capital becomes repaid, so reducing the amount of interest charged, a greater fraction of each payment constitutes a repayment of capital. In the case of an endowment mortgage the entire loan remains outstanding throughout the life of the mortgage. It is repaid on redemption in one lump sum from the proceeds of a life assurance policy taken out by the borrower and charged to the society as additional security. The sum assured by the policy is equivalent to the amount borrowed. In addition to the monthly payments to the building society, which go solely to discharge accrued interest, the borrower has to pay the insurance premiums in respect of the policy. To borrowers who can afford the extra outlay, this method of financing a loan is attractive because on maturity of the policy he will receive for himself a tax-free capital sum representing the value of the annual bonuses added to the policy[10].

The Building Societies Act 1986 permits building societies to grant index-linked mortgages[11]. These are designed to ensure that the real value of the

---

9 Various different types of financial institutions also lend money on the security of a second mortgage. These mortgages are regulated by the Consumer Credit Act 1974, if the loan does not exceed £15,000: SI 1983 No 1878. Local authorities, insurance companies and, apparently, banks are exempted from the Act's operation; see s 16, and Law Com Working Paper No 99, para 3.42. The position in relation to building societies is complex. The blanket exemption conferred by s 16 has been removed by the Building Societies Act 1986, Sch 18, para 10. As a result certain mortgages for £15,000 or less now fall within the 1974 Act, such as loans for home improvements to an existing house-owner whose property is not subject to any mortgage.

10 Assuming it is a full 'with profits' policy. With a 'low-cost' endowment (as it is termed) the basic sum assured is less than the amount borrowed, and the accrued bonuses are expected to make up the difference on maturity. This type of policy is cheaper to finance because the premiums are lower but it is unlikely to leave much of a surplus in the borrower's hands after repayment of the loan. An endowment mortgage qualifies for relief under AJA 1973, s 8(1): *Bank of Scotland v Grimes* [1985] QB 1179, [1985] 2 All ER 254, CA.

11 Section 10(10). Such mortgages are valid under the general law: *Multiservice Bookbinding Ltd v Marden* [1979] Ch 84, [1978] 2 All ER 489 (repayments linked to value of Swiss franc), and were even permissible under the Building Societies Act 1962: *Nationwide Building Society v Registry of Friendly Societies* [1983] 3 All ER 296.

mortgage advance is repaid by adjustments to the capital element of the debt, which takes account of inflation. The rate of interest is substantially lower than that ordinarily charged by societies; in consequence, the monthly repayments are appreciably lower in the early years of the loan because of the low interest rate. This enables some borrowers unable to afford a loan on the usual terms to obtain a mortgage. To date very few societies have ventured into this field to fund private domestic home loans, but this type of mortgage will become increasingly more common in the corporate housing sector, eg to finance loans to housing associations.

2.   Form of mortgage deed

Until about the mid-1970s it was standard practice for each building society to produce its own mortgage form containing all the mortgage terms and conditions. Considerable variation in format, style and content existed in the different deeds used by societies. Borrowers were confronted by a formidable looking document, which solicitors made no attempt to explain in detail, though some did attempt to explain those obligations most likely to concern their clients.

Calls[12] for the simplification and standardisation of mortgage deeds have borne fruit. Several of the leading societies have collaborated in the production of a simple standard form of document reproduced overleaf[13]. This form, which has the backing of the Building Societies Association, is intended for use in both registered and unregistered land transactions. The document has already been introduced by the Halifax Building Society and the Abbey National is expected to follow suit in the near future. It is hoped that eventually other societies will adopt this form. Even before its introduction many of the larger societies had already reduced their mortgage deeds to a single sheet containing similar clauses.

(a) General features of standard mortgage deed
It will immediately be apparent that the deed makes no provision for recording the financial terms of the mortgage: the sum borrowed, the rate of interest, or the date and amount of each monthly payment. This may seem unusual, but in fact it was already standard practice among societies using the single-page format of mortgage deed not to include such information (save for the amount of the loan). The terms and conditions governing the mortgage are merely incorporated by reference (cl 1). This is clearly unsatisfactory, especially as the borrower may find himself bound by rules of the society adopted or amended after the date of the mortgage. Each mortgagor will have his own copy of the mortgage conditions in the form of a separate booklet received along with his mortgage offer. He can in theory acquaint himself with these in

12   See Royal Commission Report, Vol 1, 286, Annex 21.1, para 14; Conveyancing Committee Report II, paras 6.39–42; 7.19–20 (advocating the statutory imposition of a standard form).
13   The 'HMLP' Code enables the Land Registry to identify the lending society. The letters 'CHFAD', if added, indicate that the mortgage secures further advances.

advance of signing the document; but few who try will profit from the exercise. A practitioner who permits his client to execute the deed without drawing his attention to the more important terms is plainly in breach of duty[14]. No standardisation of mortgage conditions is as yet envisaged by building societies[15].

MORTGAGE DEED

Account number:	Date:
Society:	HMLR Codes:
Mortgage conditions:	
Borrower:	
Property:	
	Title No.:

1. This Mortgage incorporates the Mortgage Conditions a copy of which has been received by the Borrower.
2. The Borrower as beneficial owner charges the Property by way of legal mortgage with the payment of all moneys payable by the Borower to the Society under the Mortgage Conditions.

Signed sealed and delivered by the Borrower in the presence of the Witness.

Borrower	Seal	Witness (signature, name and address)
	(LS) (LS)	

14 Cf *Forster v Outred & Co* [1982] 2 All ER 753, CA; *Cornish v Midland Bank plc* [1985] 3 All ER 513, CA.
15 For the Law Commission's provisional views on standardisation and the statutory implication of commonplace mortgage obligations, see Working Paper No 99, paras 5.29–44.

(b) Common-form mortgage provisions
Consideration must now be given to the more commonplace terms and
conditions binding the borrower; these will be continued either in the mortgage
deed itself or in a separate booklet incorporated by reference.

(i) *The charge.*   Every building society mortgage includes a clause whereby
the borrower charges his property by way of legal mortgage with the payment
of all monies payable by him to the society. The legal charge is preferred to a
mortgage by demise. The property constitutes the security for the mortgage
advance, the interest, other sums for which the borrower becomes liable under
the terms of the deed (eg insurance premiums for a policy effected by the
society in relation to the property) and also further advances if the deed is
expressed to be made for securing them[16]. In the case of a mortgage to a bank,
intended to secure an overdraft, the property will stand charged with the
payment of all present or future actual or contingent liabilities of the debtor
to the bank.

(ii) *Capital and interest payments.*   Provision is made, usually in the incorporated
mortgage conditions rather than in the deed itself, for the date of payment of
each monthly instalment[17]. Interest accrues daily and is calculated with yearly
rests on the amount outstanding on the last day of the preceding year. So, in
the case of a mortgage granted during 1994, interest for the first partial year
ending 31 December 1985 would be calculated on the full sum loaned; interest
for 1986 would be calculated on the amount outstanding on 31 December
1995, and interest for 1996 based on the debt outstanding on 31 December
1995, and so on. Nowadays it is standard practice to reserve the right to vary
the rate of interest. But an increase, or decrease, in the rate does not necessarily
result in an immediate change in the amount of a borrower's monthly
repayments. Many societies, conscious of the need to prune their ever-
increasing administrative costs, have adopted a system of annual reviews.
Monthly repayments are fixed for a 12 months' period. Any adjustments
necessary because of alterations in the rate during the period are reflected in
the required monthly repayments for the ensuing 12 months. Depending on
interest rate trends, banks and insurance companies are sometimes prepared
to grant fixed interest rate mortgages. A competitive rate is fixed for an initial
period of (say) three years[18]. Thereafter the mortgagor is given an option either
to continue on the same basis for a further three years, but probably at a
different fixed rate depending on the prevailing market conditions, or else to
switch to a variable rate mortgage.

16   This obviates the need to execute a separate deed of further charge securing the amount of
the additional loan.
17   Eg the first day in each month. The initially monthly repayment figure is not stated in the
deed but is notified to the borrower in the offer of advance. Tax relief on house purchase
loans up to £30,000 is allowed on the annual interest paid to the society. The borrower pays
a net monthly sum because the MIRAS ('mortgage interest relief at source') scheme permits
him to deduct relief at the standard rate from the gross amount of each payment.
18   These mortgages are usually required to be in conjunction with an endowment policy. To
deter borrowers from a premature redemption if a general drop in interest rates make the

With a bank mortgage securing an overdraft on a current account held at the bank, the mortgagor assumes a liability to repay on demand. The mortgage does not require periodic payments of capital, or even of interest. Accrued interest is added, usually quarterly, to the account, and does not become payable until the bank makes a demand for repayment of the moneys owing to it[19].

(iii) *Leasing-power excluded.* Mortgagees, building societies included, invariably exercise their statutory right to exclude the borrower's leasing powers conferred by s 99 of the Law of Property Act 1925. This ensures that the borrower does not without its consent create a tenancy binding on the society in the event of an enforced sale. An unauthorised lease, though not binding on the society unless estopped from asserting this[20], remains valid as between the borrower and his lessee. The standard building society exclusion clauses are couched in much wider terms and prohibit without the society's prior written consent a wide range of transactions, such as a letting, mortgage, charge, licence, or parting with possession[1].

A similar clause sometimes encountered seeks to restrain the borrower from disposing of the property subject to the mortgage without the society's written consent. Some societies take the step of registering a restriction under s 58 of the Land Registration Act 1925, to protect their rights under the clause. The aim of this clause is to ensure that the borrower does not diminish the society's security by placing it in a less tenable position with regard to the covenants in the deed. A typical transaction caught by the restriction occurs when a married man wishes to transfer the matrimonial home into the joint names of himself and his wife. The society's consent will normally be forthcoming, but on terms that the wife covenants with the society to pay the monthly instalments and to abide by the mortgage conditions. Failure to seek consent does not invalidate the transfer, but it operates to put the borrower in default of his mortgage obligations, with the consequential right for the society to take action if it chooses. It is not thought that the restriction constitutes a clog on the equity[2].

fixed rate no longer competitive, lenders impose an early redemption penalty of two or three months's interest; this effectively cancels out the benefits derived from the lower rate initially charged. Unlike building societies, banks calculate interest on a daily basis on the reducing balance, which means that repaid capital is taken into account immediately.

19 Such a mortgage strictly constitutes a collateral security for a pre-existing debt. Compare a building society loan, which is created by virtue of the mortgage deed itself: *Barclays Bank Ltd v Beck* [1952] 2 QB 47 at 54, [1952] 1 All ER 549 at 553, CA, per Denning LJ. For the application of AJA 1973, s 8, to this type of mortgage, see *Habib Bank Ltd v Tailor* [1982] 3 All ER 561, CA.

20 See *Stroud Building Society v Delamont* [1960] 1 All ER 749; *Chatsworth Properties Ltd v Effiom* [1971] 1 All ER 604, CA.

1 This will be interpreted as parting with 'legal' possession, and will not be broken merely by permitting another to use and occupy: *Richards v Davies* [1921] 1 Ch 90 at 96, per Lawrence J; (1963) 27 Conv (NS) 159, 171–72 (D G Barnsley). But sometimes the prohibition extends to not *sharing occupation*, which seems unduly restrictive and technically requires consent for members of the family (eg, aged parents) to live there. Further, the society can have no legitimate interest in calling for consent to the creation of a second mortgage.

2 See Wurtzburg and Mills, *Building Society Law* (14th edn), 186–87. See also the correspondence in (1974) 118 Sol Jo 326, 351, 368, 398, 423.

As a result of provisions contained in the Housing Act 1988, mortgagees may now be more willing to consent to the mortgagor letting the property than was previously the case. Under Schedule 2 to the Act, a court must order possession under s 7 if the mortgagee's power of sale has arisen, the mortgagee requires possession in order to sell the property with vacant possession and the tenant was informed, prior to the commencement of the lease, that possession could be obtained on this ground. This latter requirement can be dispensed with by the court if it considers it just and equitable to do so. This sensible provision enables a mortgagee to consent to a letting of the property safe in the knowledge that possession can be obtained if the mortgagor defaults. If the mortgagor is going to work abroad for a year, it should be easier for him to persuade the mortgagee to consent to a letting of the property during that absence.

(iv) *Miscellaneous provisions.*   Other commonplace provisions include covenants by the borrower to observe and be bound by the society's rules in force from time to time; to keep the property in good and substantial repair; not without prior written consent to make structural alterations or institute any change of use; to observe and perform restrictive and other covenants affecting the property.

(v) *Society's powers and remedies.*   Standard mortgage conditions always provide for a date[3] when the mortgage money becomes due for the purposes of the Law of Property Act 1925; it may be 28 days after the date of the mortgage, or when the first monthly payment falls due. The statutory power of sale is often made applicable free from the restrictions imposed by s 103 of the Act. It is also made exercisable on the occurrence of other events, such as the borrower's bankruptcy. Despite these extensions, societies commonly undertake not to exercise the power of sale or enforce their right to take possession unless the borrower defaults for two months in making his monthly payments or is in breach of some obligation under the mortgage. On the happening of either event the whole of the principal money still outstanding is expressed to become immediately payable. In the case of the normal bank mortgage to secure an overdraft the principal sum does not become due and cannot be sued for until the bank makes a written demand for payment[4].

The usual modification of a building society's right to enter into possession has been noted. The general rule is that apart from contract and statute a legal mortgagee has, as an incident of his interest in the land, an unqualified right to possession. To this principle a single exception exists; the court will not permit the mortgagee to exercise his right in the face of a concrete offer by the mortgagor to redeem[5]. In an instalment mortgage the court is quite

---

3   A purely artificial date which 'contributes towards making the mortgage deed incomprehensible': Law Com Working Paper No 95, para 3.58. For the consequences of providing for a deferred redemption date, see *Twentieth Century Banking Corpn Ltd v Wilkinson* [1977] Ch 99, [1976] 3 All ER 361.
4   See *Habib Bank Ltd v Tailor* [1982] 3 All ER 561, CA.
5   See *Mobil Oil Co Ltd v Rawlinson* (1981) 43 P & CR 221 at 224–25, per Nourse J, discussing the authorities.

ready to find an implied term limiting the mortgagee's right to possession[6]. In the case of residential property his right is controlled by the Administration of Justice Act 1970[7], but other types of property, such as commercial premises, are not within the Act.

(c) Execution
The rules governing execution of a mortgage are no different from those relating to deeds generally. However, various factors affecting the execution of a mortgage may operate to prevent the mortgagee from obtaining the security for which he had bargained. We have already seen, in the context of unregistered land that a mortgage of land purporting to be granted by the legal owners, A and B, whose signature is a forgery, is totally ineffective to create any charge on the legal estate[8]. If title is registered, however, and the mortgagee secures registration of the charge, he will acquire a legal mortgage and the dispute will be resolved in rectification proceedings. Where forgery occurs, B incurs no liability to the mortgagee because she did not execute the mortgage. Unless the mortgage is registered as a registered charge, the document creates merely an equitable charge on A's beneficial share in the property[9]. Should C wish to enforce his security, he should seek a charging order under the Charging Orders Act 1979. The court has a wide discretion as to whether or not to make an order[10]. If made, the mortgagee may apply under s 30 of the Law of Property Act 1925 or, in the future, under s 14 of the Trusts of Land and Appointment of Trustees Act 1996[11] for a sale of the property, but an order for sale is not automatic[12].

The effectiveness of the mortgagee's security may also be affected by either undue influence or misrepresentation having occurred before one of the legal co-owners was prevailed upon to sign the mortgage. This important issue has been considered elsewhere[13].

3. Endowment mortgages

The nature of an endowment policy mortgage was briefly explained on page 595. The policy is assigned to the society by way of mortgage. When it matures, or on the prior death of the life assured, the sum assured is utilised to redeem

6 *Western Bank Ltd v Schindler* [1977] Ch 1 at 22, [1976] 2 All ER 393 at 406, CA, per Goff LJ.
7 Section 36, as amended by AJA 1973, s 8; see *Western Bank Ltd v Schindler*, supra.
8 Unless the mortgagee admits the validity of the mortgage: see *Winkworth v Edward Baron Development Co Ltd* [1987] 1 All ER 114, HL (husband forging wife's signature).
9 See p 556, ante; *First National Securities Ltd v Hegerty* [1985] QB 850, [1984] 3 All ER 641, CA (mistress impersonating wife). If A and B are joint tenants, A's conduct operates to sever the joint tenancy.
10 See s 1(5). *Harman v Glencross* [1986] Fam 81, [1986] 1 All ER 545, CA.
11 For the criteria to which the court should have regard, see Trusts of Land and Appointment of Trustees Act 1996, s 15.
12 See pp 311–312, ante.
13 Pages 366–372, ante.

the mortgage[14]. The borrower[15] is entitled to the accrued bonuses. Since the life policy constitutes collateral security, some societies will not release the mortgage advance until it is either in their possession or held by their solicitors. Others will proceed to completion provided the policy is in force. A borrower's solicitor owes his client a duty of care to ensure that any policy forming part of the security is in force and the insurers on risk before he completes the transaction[16]. One society (the Halifax) allows the policy to be issued up to six months after completion of the mortgage, but if it has not been issued within this period the mortgage automatically reverts to a normal repayment mortgage.

(a) Legal assignment

Until quite recently it was standard practice for building societies to take a legal assignment of the policy. The borrower (or policy owner, if different) assigned the policy to the society subject to re-assignment on redemption of the principal mortgage. Normally the policy was assigned in a separate deed; sometimes one mortgage deed charged the land and also assigned the policy. To protect its rights and complete its legal title notice of assignment[17] should be given to the assurance company issuing the policy (the life office, as it is commonly called) by the society's solicitor after the mortgage has been completed.

(b) Equitable assignment

Whilst many societies still insist on a legal assignment, others are content to rely on the deposit of the policy with them sufficing to create an equitable assignment[18]. The mortgage of one leading society provides that every life policy deposited with it shall be treated as deposited by way of charge to secure all moneys payable under the mortgage[19]. In the case of an equitable assignment, notice to the life office is not essential to perfect the society's title, but it is general practice to give notice of deposit to preserve priority against subsequent assignees[20]. Under the standard form policy conditions

14   On redemption before maturity, eg on a sale of the property, the loan will be repaid out of the proceeds. The policy can be used in connection with a mortgage on any newly-acquired property. If, as will often be the case, the new mortgage is for a larger amount, the borrower will be obliged either to take out a second policy to cover the excess or to opt for a hybrid form of mortgage, part endowment and part repayment covering the additional amount.
15   Assuming he is the policy-owner, but he may not be. The policy may be owned by his wife who has assured his life, or perhaps her own.
16   *McLellan v Fletcher* [1987] NLJ Rep 593.
17   LPA 1925, s 136(1). This enables the society to sue at law on the policy in its own name. This subsection does not affect the provisions of the Policies of Assurance Act 1867. For this Act and its uncertain interaction with s 136, see MacGillivray & Parkington, *Insurance Law* (6th edn), paras 1320–1330.
18   *Maugham v Ridley* (1863) 8 LT 309.
19   Another society makes it a condition of an endowment-loan offer that the policy is to be deposited with it, and the borrower undertakes to execute a legal assignment on request. The mortgage deed itself contains no express reference either to the deposit or to the policy.
20   See generally as to equitable assignments of choses in action, Snell, 77–82.

applying to the mortgage the borrower appoints the society irrevocably to be his attorney and in his name to assign, transfer, surrender or otherwise deal with the policy.

(c) Borrower's obligations in relation to policy

Whether the assignment be legal or equitable, the borrower enters into various obligations relating to the policy. He covenants not to allow it to become void or voidable, and to pay the premiums punctually. If he fails to keep up the policy the society may do so, its costs and expenses being added to the mortgage debt. Should the society be forced to sell the primary security (the house), it can also sell the policy or surrender it to the insurers.

(d) Redemption of mortgage

When the mortgage is redeemed before the policy matures[1], it is necessary for the society to execute a deed of re-assignment of the policy to the borrower and also to notify the life office of the fact. In practice the re-assignment is endorsed on the deed of assignment in some such form as: 'X Building Society re-assigns the policy to the policy owner discharged from this deed'.[2] No deed of re-assignment is required when the policy has merely been deposited by way of equitable assignment, but notice of release from the charge needs to be given to the life office.

It is frequently overlooked in practice that documents which assign, or charge, or re-assign a life policy constitute documents of title relating to it. Ideally they should be kept with the policy. This is important because when a claim is made on the policy, the life office is entitled to production not only of the policy but also of all documents of title affecting it, including the mortgage and any deed of re-assignment. The steps to be adopted[3] on redemption of an endowment policy mortgage differ according to whether the title to the land is or is not registered, and whether the policy has been mortgaged by a separate deed or a combined one covering both the land and the policy. If the title is unregistered a deed which separately assigns the policy should be kept with it[4], and in no circumstances handed to the purchaser's solicitor on completion with the deeds of the property. Where a mortgage of *registered land* also assigns

---

1 See note 14, p 601, ante.
2 Some societies incorporate the re-assignment in an endorsed vacating receipt: 'X Building Society hereby acknowledges to have received all moneys intended to be secured by the within-written deed and hereby re-assigns to the assignor the policy referred to therein'. The re-assignment is executed under seal.
3 See the recommended procedures published at (1958) 55 LS Gaz 149.
4 If, following redemption, the policy is re-mortgaged in connection with the borrower's new purchase, the policy documents should be kept with the deeds of the new property, rather than handed to the borrower who may well mislay them, despite a warning to keep them safe.

a life policy[5], any potential problems as to future production of the deed to the life office can easily be avoided. The Registry will always comply with an express request to return the charge to the mortgagor or his solicitor. Indeed, it will be automatically returned whenever the application to register the discharge is not accompanied by any other application, but this is rarely the case[6]. Alas, practitioners rarely request return of the charge, which languishes in the Registry's files. Non-production of relevant title documents does not deprive the assured of his policy moneys. However, it is likely to delay settlement of his claim until the insurers receive a letter of disclaimer from the society confirming that it has no further interest in the policy[7].

4. Discharge of mortgages

Frequently a borrower redeems his mortgage long before expiry of the repayment period negotiated with his lender. The procedure of building societies on early redemption varies. The rules of some societies provide for the giving of written notice of intention to redeem (usually a month), but in practice they tend not to enforce this requirement. Some charge interest up to and including the day on which redemption takes place; others calculate it to the last day of the month in which it occurs. The borrower is entitled to proper documentary evidence of the discharge of his mortgage[8]. This may take one of several forms.

(a) Statutory receipt under the Law of Property Act 1925, s 115
Under this section a receipt endorsed on the mortgage for all money thereby secured and executed by the mortgagee operates to discharge the mortgaged property from all principal and interest secured by it. The receipt need not be under seal[9]. Though s 1 17(1) provides that the receipt should state the name of the person who pays the money, this is not apparently an essential requirement. In *Edwards v Marshall-Lee*[10], a simple receipt not naming the payers

---

5 Contrast the position here if the title is unregistered when the redeeming mortgagor's solicitor should either (i) produce the mortgage deed to the insurers for inspection on the occasion of redemption, for having once seen the deed most life offices do not require further production on the making of a claim; or (ii) obtain from the purchaser an acknowledgement for its production and an undertaking for safe custody (see p 512, ante) – a cumbersome procedure which would require an express contractual stipulation. There is no statutory entitlement to retain the deed; the policy is not 'land' within LPA 1925, s 45(9)(a): *Re Williams and Duchess of Newcastle's Contract* [1897] 2 Ch 144.
6 See R & R, 24.20.
7 Despite receipt of a notice of re-assignment at the time of redemption, some offices demand a statutory declaration verifying the loss of relevant documents.
8 Notwithstanding that on repayment of a mortgage by demise, the term becomes satisfied and ceases: LPA 1925, s 116; see 1 W & C, 225. The Law Commission would like to see the introduction of a single prescribed form of receipt to replace those currently in use: Working Paper No 99, para 9.45.
9 *Simpson v Geoghegan* [1934] WN 232.
10 (1975) 235 EG 901.

was held to be a valid discharge of a legal charge. A statutory form of receipt is provided (see Sch 3, Form No 2) and this can be varied as may be deemed expedient (s 115(5)). When the receipt shows that payment has been made by some third person, and not the person entitled to the immediate equity of redemption (ie the borrower), it operates as a transfer of the mortgage to such person, unless expressly providing otherwise (sub-s (2))[11]. This provision apart, it is a general principle that where A pays off B's mortgage, A is presumed, unless the contrary appears, to intend the mortgage to be kept alive for his benefit[12].

The borrower's right to require a re-assignment, surrender or release is expressly preserved (sub-s (4)). A release is essential where, eg, part only of the property is discharged from the mortgage on repayment of part of the outstanding debt. Even on payment in full banks tend to execute a formal release under seal, in lieu of the statutory receipt, whereby the bank as mortgagee releases unto the mortgagor all the premises charged by the mortgage from all moneys secured by it.

(b) Building society statutory receipt
Building societies prefer not to use the s 115 form of receipt, adopting instead the form permitted by the Building Societies Act 1986. Such a receipt states simply that the society 'hereby acknowledge to have received all moneys intended to be secured by the within written deed'.[13] The society's seal is affixed in the presence of, and the receipt countersigned by, a person authorised by the board of directors. The receipt operates in the same way as one given under s 115(1) of the Act of 1925[14], but it cannot operate as a transfer, nor does it name the payer. This special building society form is equally applicable to mortgages either of registered or unregistered land, but in the case of the former, societies use the form discussed in *(c)* below.

Authority exists for the proposition that the statutory receipt, once given, precludes the society from pursuing any further claim against the borrower in respect of the debt, even though less than the sum required to redeem was received due to an error[15]. This may not, however, represent the modern position. By virtue of s 115(1), the receipt operates 'as a discharge of the mortgaged property from all principal money and interest'; this suggests that the borrower still remains personally liable for any underpayment, notwithstanding the receipt[16].

11 See *Simpson v Geoghegan*, ante, discussed in Emmet, para 25.087, advocating a formal transfer of the mortgage in such circumstances.
12 *Butler v Rice* [1910] 2 Ch 277, applied in *Ghana Commercial Bank v Chandiram* [1960] AC 732, [1960] 2 All ER 865, PC.
13 The wording prescribed by the Building Societies (Supplementary Provisions as to Mortgages) Rules 1986, Sch Pt II; see the Building Societies Act 1986, Sch 4, para (2)(1).
14 See Sch 4, para (2) (2) of the 1986 Act, re-enacting s 37(2) of the Building Societies Act 1962.
15 *Harvey v Municipal Permanent Investment Building Society* (1884) 26 Ch D 273, CA, a decision on the Building Societies Act 1874, s 42 (receipt expressed to vacate the *debt*).
16 See Wurtzburg & Mills, op cit, 206. This appears to be the view of the Building Societies Association. See their policy statement advocating member societies to seal a receipt when a solicitor remits an incorrect sum in reliance on an inaccurate statement, leaving the solicitor to pursue the borrower for the shortfall: (1985) 82 LS Gaz, 2720–22, paras 9–13.

The general reluctance of building societies to seal vacating receipts in advance of actual receipt of the redemption moneys has been discussed elsewhere[17].

(c) Registered land

Discharge of a registered land charge is governed by the Land Registration Act 1925, s 35. The appropriate document is Form 53 (Co)[18] which after the usual heading and date states that the society:

> ... hereby admits that the charge dated ... and registered on ... of which it is proprietor has been discharged.

(d) Date of receipt

When, as is often the case, redemption is followed by a conveyance of the land, the receipt or Form 53 should be dated with the same date as or one day earlier than that of the deed to the purchaser. But what happens if a subsequent date is inadvertently inserted? This does not in the case of unregistered land constitute a defect in title to which a subsequent purchaser can object. Somewhat ludicrously the receipt operates as a transfer of the mortgage to the vendor who has paid it off! Nevertheless, a recital of seisin free from incumbrances in the conveyance following redemption creates an estoppel preventing the vendor from exercising any rights under the transferred mortgage[19]. Problems of this nature are unlikely to arise with registered land; presumably the Registry would spot the discrepancy and have the error corrected before proceeding with the application to discharge the mortgage.

(e) Disposal of title deeds

If redemption is not accompanied by another transaction affecting the property, the mortgagee will ordinarily return the deeds to the borrower, unless there is a subsequent mortgagee of whom he has actual notice, and to whom the deeds should be delivered. Registration of this second charge under the Land Charges Act 1972 does not constitute notice for this purpose, hence the prior incumbrancer is under no obligation to effect a search of the register before parting with the deeds[20].

---

17 See p 443, ante.

18 For use when a company or corporation including a building society is the chargee. The discharge of registered charges is more fully discussed in Ch 15, p 443, ante.

19 *Cumberland Court (Brighton) Ltd v Taylor* [1964] Ch 29, [1963] 2 All ER 536 (receipt dated two days later). There are other valid grounds for denying any continuing enforceability to the transferred mortgage: Emmet, para 25.086.

20 LPA 1925, s 96(2) as amended by LP(Am)A 1926, Sch. Compare the position when a mortgagee distributes any surplus proceeds of sale after an enforced sale: M & W, 941.

Part Six

Remedies

Chapter 19

The rights of the parties on breach of contract: an introduction

The vast majority of vendor-purchaser transactions proceed smoothly to completion without any major dispute arising between the parties. Sometimes, however, the contract is never completed; sometimes it is completed only after litigation between the parties and occasionally it may be necessary to have recourse to the courts after completion of the transaction. Part VI of this book deals with the various rights of the parties on non-performance of the contract. Several factors may determine what these are: which party is in default, why the contract has been broken, and whether a particular remedy is available under the general law or only exercisable by virtue of some contractual provision. There is also an important distinction to be drawn between their rights whilst the contract is still executory and the position after completion. It will be helpful to give a brief survey of the principal remedies available to the parties, leaving the detailed consideration for subsequent pages.

A Remedies under uncompleted contract

The injured party may wish to pursue one of three main remedies: specific performance, an action for damages, or rescission.

1. Specific performance

This is a remedy peculiar to contracts relating to land and is not generally applicable to other contracts. The plaintiff seeks a decree from the court ordering the other party to perform the contract specifically.

2. Rescission

Over the years the word 'rescission' has proved to be 'a fertile source of confusion'[1]. It has different meanings and its sense must be gleaned from the context in which it is used. It is vital to distinguish between rescission ab initio and rescission for breach. *Rescission ab initio* describes the effect of the relief

---

1 *Johnson v Agnew* [1980] AC 367 at 392, [1979] 1 All ER 883 at 889, HL, per Lord Wilberforce.

that is normally available when the formation of a contract is affected by some vitiating factor such as fraud, mistake or misrepresentation. The court annuls the contract in every respect so as to produce a state of affairs as though it had never come into existence[2]. As a result the parties are restored to the position which they occupied before the contract was made, a process known as *restitutio in integrum.*

In contrast, the expression *rescission for breach* connotes the consequence of an innocent party's acceptance of the repudiation of the contract by the other party's breach of some essential term. Acceptance of a repudiatory breach does not result in rescission ab initio. The contract has come into existence and is determined, but only so far as it is still executory. Both parties are discharged from further performance of their contractual obligations. Rights that have already accrued are not lost, and the innocent party's entitlement to damages for breach remains intact[3].

3. Damages

Here the injured party seeks compensation for the loss occasioned by the breach.

These three remedies are discussed in Chapters 20, 21 and 22. A plaintiff may seek more than one remedy in the same action. A claim for specific performance may be linked with an alternative claim for damages or rescission[4]. He must elect at the hearing which remedy he intends to pursue and judgment for one will bar the others.

4. Forfeiture of deposit

As we saw in Chapter 8[5], the deposit acts as a guarantee of performance. On breach by the purchaser, the vendor may be entitled to forfeit the purchaser's deposit. Compared with the purchaser the vendor is in a much superior position. Forfeiture of the deposit frequently enables him to obtain adequate compensation (and often more) without the assistance of the court, save where the right to forfeit is disputed. However, a purchaser entitled to repayment of his deposit can recover it only by taking legal proceedings, should the vendor refuse to return it voluntarily. The court has a statutory discretion to order the return of the deposit to the purchaser, notwithstanding the vendor has a prima facie right to forfeit it[6].

---

2   *Buckland v Farmer and Moody* [1978] 3 All ER 929 at 938, CA, per Buckley LJ.
3   It was at one time thought that rescission of a contract for the sale of land following breach of an essential clause terminated the contract ab initio, so preventing the innocent party from obtaining damages: *Henty v Schröder* (1879) 12 Ch D 666; *Barber v Wolfe* [1945] Ch 187, [1945] 1 All ER 399; *Horsler v Zorro* [1975] Ch 302, [1975] 1 All ER 584; 2 Williams V & P, 993, 1004. This fallacy has been finally laid to rest by the House of Lords in *Johnson v Agnew*, ante.
4   *Farrant v Oliver* (1922) 127 LT 145; *Lowe v Hope* [1970] Ch 94, [1969] 3 All ER 605.
5   See further pp 239–242, ante, and p 621, post.
6   LPA 1925, s 49(2). See further p 622, post.

5.   Vendor and purchaser summons

A statutory procedure exists for the settling of disputes between vendor and purchaser that may arise during the course of the transaction. Under the Law of Property Act 1925, s 49(1):

> A vendor or purchaser of any interest in land may apply in a summary way to the court in respect of any requisitions or objections, or any claim for compensation or any other question arising out of or connected with the contract ... and the court may make such order upon the application as to the court may appear just ...

This procedure enables either party to obtain a decision upon some particular point, without having to commence an action for specific performance. For example, the summons may ask the court to declare whether the vendor has sufficiently answered a requisition, whether he has a right to rescind under the contract, or whether he has discharged his obligation to show a good title in accordance with the contract. There is no jurisdiction to determine the existence or validity of the contract. The court can order the return of the deposit with interest and costs (including costs of the summons) if the vendor is held to have failed to show a good title[7], and the costs can be ordered to be a charge on the vendor's interest in the property[8]. The court has no power on a vendor-purchaser summons to award damages for the purchaser's delay in completion[9].

In contrast with former days, this procedure is infrequently used today, doubtless because of the spread of land registration and the comparative simplicity of the present day title to unregistered land. In February 1970, a specially expedited procedure for the hearing of these summonses was cancelled only three years after its introduction on account of there being too few cases to justify it[10].

B   Post-completion remedies

Once the contract is executed and the legal title vested in the purchaser, the parties' remedies in the event of a dispute are somewhat restricted. Usually it is the purchaser who wishes to sue and in the main he is confined to his action (if any) on the covenants for title. The following remedies briefly mentioned in this section may be available to the parties, depending on the circumstances. Chapters 23 and 24 deal with post-completion rights in greater detail.

---

7   *Re Hargreaves and Thompson's Contract* (1886) 32 Ch D 454, CA.
8   *Re Higgins and Percival* (1888) 57 LJ Ch 807.
9   *Re Wilsons and Stevens' Contract* [1894] 3 Ch 546.
10   See *Practice Directions* at [1967] 1 All ER 656 and [1970] 1 All ER 671. Recent instances of the use of this procedure occurred in *Faruqi v English Real Estates* [1979] 1 WLR 963; *MEPC Ltd v Christian-Edwards* [1981] AC 205, [1979] 3 All ER 752, HL; *Walia v Michael Naughton Ltd* [1985] 3 All ER 673.

1.   Covenants for title

The doctrine of merger, whereby on completion the contract is superseded by the conveyance, ensures that the purchaser's only mode of redress if his title proves to be defective is an action for damages on the covenants for title implied in the conveyance. Fraud apart, he cannot recover the purchase price even though the conveyance turns out to be worthless[11]. Notwithstanding completion a purchaser can, however, still maintain an action for damages for breach of contract if he establishes a breach of some collateral warranty, or breach of a contractual term that has survived completion, eg a clause which provides for compensation for errors in the contract[12]. Similarly completion of the transaction is no bar to the vendor's right to sue for any unpaid purchase money, or to enforce his seller's lien.

2.   Setting the transaction aside

The right to set aside the transaction on account of some vitiating factor, such as fraud or common mistake of a fundamental nature, survives completion. The court can, on sustaining the plaintiff's plea, set aside the conveyance or declare it to be void, and may order it to be delivered up and cancelled. Usually it is the purchaser who will institute such proceedings, but a vendor or grantor may also be desirous of having the deed set aside on account of eg undue influence, or because he was mistaken as to the nature of the document which he executed . The setting aside of a transaction after completion is commonly termed rescission[13].

3.   Rectification

Where the conveyance does not correctly give effect to the terms of the contract, either party may seek equity's aid to rectify it so as to make it accord with their real intention. Equally it may be that the written contract fails to express what the parties orally agreed. In no sense is this a remedy which can only be sought after completion, but it is considered in Chapter 24 for the sake of convenience.

---

11   *Clare v Lamb* (1875) LR 10 CP 334.
12   *Palmer v Johnson* (1884) 13 QBD 351, CA. For the doctrine of merger, see p 468, ante.
13   But see p 687, post.

Chapter 20

Specific performance

A General nature of remedy

1. Introduction

Land has a special character of its own, and in the eyes of equity a purchaser ought not to have to be content simply with the common law remedy of damages for breach of a contract for the sale or leasing of land. Damages do not constitute adequate compensation for him. The main part of the doctrine of specific performance is that the purchaser is actually to get the land[1]. Nevertheless, this remedy is available to a vendor, even though his claim is essentially monetary[2]. In practice, a vendor is usually content to forfeit the deposit and resell the property. In some situations a decree of specific performance is of no avail to him, as where the purchaser has no funds to pay for the property. A contract for a loan, whether secured or unsecured, will not as a general rule be specifically enforceable; equity tends to regard the award of damages for breach of this type of contract as a sufficient remedy[3]. This rule does not prevent specific performance being decreed of a contract for the purchase of land, one of whose terms provides for part of the purchase price to remain outstanding on mortgage, for the contract is in substance and in fact one for the sale and purchase of land[4]. The court may occasionally in an appropriate case decree specific performance of a contract to build, or to do repairs[5], and there now exists a statutory jurisdiction to order specific performance of a landlord's repairing covenant (whether express or implied) in a lease of a *dwelling*[6]. As evidence of the courts' greater willingness to award specific performance, in *Co-operative Insurance Society Ltd v Argyll Stores (Holdings)*

---

1 *Re Scott and Alvarez's Contract* [1895] 2 Ch 603 at 615, CA, per Rigby LJ.
2 *Adderley v Dixon* (1824) 1 Sim & St 607.
3 *Rogers v Challis* (1859) 27 Beav 175, unless the money has actually been advanced on the strength of the borrower's promise to execute a mortgage: *Hermann v Hodges* (1873) LR 16 Eq 18. But see *Luff v Raymond* [1982] LS Gaz R 1330 (performance of contract to transfer mortgage decreed); *Wight v Haberdan Pty Ltd* [1984] 2 NSWLR 280 (decree granted; damages inadequate to satisfy demands of justice).
4 *Starkey v Barton* [1909] 1 Ch 284.
5 See the discussion in *Price v Strange* [1978] Ch 337 at 359, [1977] 3 All ER 371 at 385, CA, per Goff LJ; *Jeune v Queens Cross Properties Ltd* [1974] Ch 97, [1973] 3 All ER 97 (repairs); *Posner v Scott-Lewis* [1987] Ch 25, [1986] 3 All ER 513 (employment of resident porter); contra, *F W Woolworth plc v Charlwood Alliance Properties Ltd* [1987] 1 EGLR 53 (covenant to use premises as retail store).
6 Landlord and Tenant Act 1985, s 17; *Francis v Cowlcliffe Ltd* (1976) 33 P & CR 368 (maintenance of service lift).

Ltd[7], the Court of Appeal, by a majority, granted specific performance of a covenant by a tenant to keep open a shop, notwithstanding the previously received wisdom that specific performance would not be ordered of a tenant's covenant[8]. This case did involve, however, a particularly blatant breach of covenant and it remains to be seen whether the courts become more willing to enforce tenant's covenants by ordering specific performance.

2. Breach of contract unnecessary

A claim for specific performance can be linked in the same action with an alternative claim for damages for breach of contract. Since the court is empowered to grant either form of relief[9], it is perfectly proper for the plaintiff to seek these apparently inconsistent remedies, but he must elect at the trial which he desires to pursue. Once a contracting party has chosen to put an end to the contract by accepting the other's repudiation, he cannot thereafter seek specific performance. It may be counterclaimed by a purchaser in a vendor's action for damages, and vice versa.

This equitable remedy is fundamentally different from the action at law for damages, where a breach of the contract is a condition precedent to the right to sue. An award of specific performance is not necessarily dependent upon a breach of contract by the defendant, and a writ can be validly issued before the contractual date for completion has arrived[10], though the court will not compel performance before the proper day. A vendor seeking specific performance is under no obligation to mitigate his loss by re-selling, even when the purchaser refuses to complete, for this would require him to take action which would preclude him from performing his contract with the purchaser[11].

3. Discretionary remedy

Specific performance has been described as 'special and extraordinary in character'[12]. It lies in the discretion of the court to grant or withhold the relief claimed. This is not exercised capriciously or arbitrarily, but according to fixed and settled principles of equity. As long ago as 1804, it was said that in an unobjectionable case it would be decreed as much of course as damages were granted at law[13]. In the exercise of its discretion the court may award specific

7 [1996] 3 WLR 27, CA.
8 See, eg, *Hill v Barclay* (1810) 16 Ves 402.
9 Supreme Court Act 1981, s 49(2).
10 *Manchester Diocesan Council for Education v Commercial and General Investments Ltd* [1969] 3 All ER 1593, following *Hasham v Zenab* [1960] AC 316, PC (vendor tearing up contract within minutes of signing it); *Oakacre Ltd v Clare Cleaners (Holdings) Ltd* [1982] Ch 197, [1981] 3 All ER 667, p 623, post.
11 *Ellis v Lawrence* (1969) 210 EG 215.
12 44 *Halsbury's Laws* (4th edn), 275, para 401; *Hope v Walter* [1900] 1 Ch 257 at 259, CA, per Lindley, MR.
13 *Hall v Warren* (1804) 9 Ves 605 at 608, per Grant MR.

performance, but on terms, eg as to the payment of interest on the purchase money at a reasonable rate[14], or subject to an abatement (reduction) in the purchase price[15].

As a condition precedent to any claim for specific performance, the plaintiff must establish two basic requirements. First, there must be a concluded contract[16], the terms of which are sufficiently certain for the court to order their' performance. Specific performance cannot be decreed of negotiations subject to contract[17]. Moreover, the contract must be capable of being specifically performed. Equity does nothing in vain and will not make any decree if in the meantime the vendor has conveyed the property to a third person, unless that transaction was merely a sham and the vendor has it in his power to compel the third person to convey to the purchaser[18]. The court will not refuse a decree simply because the plaintiff's interest is of a transient nature[19].

Secondly, the plaintiff must himself be able and willing to perform his own part of the contract, and it is standard practice for his statement of claim to contain an allegation to this effect. This requirement must not be pushed too far. For example, if the vendor repudiates the contract and the purchaser elects to sue for specific performance, he is not obliged to prove his actual readiness to complete the contract. Equity is not so esoteric as to place on the purchaser the burden of showing that at a time after repudiation he was in a position to complete a contract which it was clear would not be performed[20].

B   Refusal of specific performance

1.   Defences available at law

The grounds upon which equity refuses a decree of specific performance fall into well established categories. The court will not enforce a contract where the defendant raises a defence which would be a complete answer to a claim at law, as where the contract is void for mistake[1], illegal, voidable for misrepresentation, or contrary to public policy[2]. Equity sometimes goes further and may refuse a decree where the mistake or misrepresentation[3] is not of

---

14 *Harvela Investments Ltd v Royal Trust Co of Canada (CI) Ltd* [1986] AC 207, [1985] 2 All ER 966, HL (sale of shares specifically enforced; vendor disallowed interest at penal contract rate).
15 See *Topfell Ltd v Galley Properties Ltd* [1979] 2 All ER 388. This jurisdiction is commonly exercised in cases of partial performance, discussed at p 620, post.
16 See *Harrison v Battye* [1974] 3 All ER 830, CA (defective exchange of contracts).
17 *Cohen v Nessdale Ltd* [1982] 2 All ER 97, CA.
18 *Jones v Lipman* [1962] 1 All ER 442 (conveyance to company controlled by vendor).
19 *Verrall v Great Yarmouth Borough Council* [1981] QB 202, [1980] 1 All ER 839, CA (contractual licence to hire hall for two day conference).
20 *Rightside Properties Ltd v Gray* [1975] Ch 72 at 86–88, [1974] 2 All ER 1169 at 1182, per Walton J.
1 *Jones v Clifford* (1876) 3 Ch D 779 (sale of land already owned by purchaser).
2 *Sutton v Sutton* [1984] Ch 184, [1984] 1 All ER 168 (agreement for house transfer after divorce ousting court's jurisdiction under the Matrimonial Causes Act 1973, ss 23 and 24).
3 See *Holliday v Lockwood* [1917] 2 Ch 47.

such a nature as to entitle the plaintiff to rescind the contract. In the case of mistake a purchaser may be able to resist specific performance if he has been misled by the vendor in some way[4], but not when the mistake is entirely his own. In *Tamplin v James*[5], the purchaser bid for a public house at an auction under the mistaken impression that the lot included land at the rear. Specific performance was decreed against him, there being no misdescription or ambiguity in the particulars of sale.

There are various defences to a claim for specific performance, which are not generally available at law, these being: delay, want of mutuality, hardship, inequitable conduct and doubtfulness of the vendor's title[6].

2. Delay

Delay defeats equity. The plaintiff must pursue his remedy promptly. A claim for specific performance of a contract for the sale of land is not subject to the normal six years' limitation period[7], yet in practice a much shorter period may operate to bar the plaintiff's claim. A year's delay has been held to be fatal[8], and even a shorter period where time was of the essence[9]. However, the modern approach appears to be that delay of itself is not a bar unless the defendant has been prejudiced thereby[10]. Delay in the prosecution of proceedings once instituted may disentitle a plaintiff to relief[11]. Similarly, enforcement of the decree after a long lapse of time will be refused without an adequate explanation for the delay if it has resulted in detriment to the defendant[12].

In one important respect laches is no bar, that is where the purchaser takes possession of the land under the contract. In *Williams v Greatrex*[13], a delay of ten years did not debar a purchaser in possession from successfully claiming a decree. He had not been sleeping on his rights, but relying on his equitable title without thinking it necessary to perfect his legal title. There must, however, be acquiescence by the vendor in the purchaser's continued possession throughout the period.

---

4   *Goddard v Jeffreys* (1881) 30 WR 269 at 270, per Kay J; *Denny v Hancock* (1870) 6 Ch App 1.
5   (1880) 15 Ch D 215, CA; *Van Praagh v Everidge* [1902] 2 Ch 266 (purchaser buying wrong lot); revsd on other grounds [1903] 1 Ch 434, CA. Cf *Malins v Freeman* (1836) 2 Keen 25. For hardship, see p 617, post.
6   For the consequences of misdescription, see pp 636–644, post.
7   Limitation Act 1980, s 36.
8   *Watson v Reid* (1830) 1 Russ & M 236.
9   *Glasbrook v Richardson* (1874) 23 WR 51 (sale of leasehold colliery; delay of 14 weeks fatal).
10   *Lazard Bros & Co Ltd v Fairfield Properties Co (Mayfair) Ltd* (1977) 121 Sol Jo 793 (two years' delay no bar).
11   *Towli v Fourth River Property Co Ltd* (1976) Times, 24 November (nine years' delay from writ to hearing: 'a disgrace'); cf *Du Sautoy v Symes* [1967] Ch 1146, [1967] 1 All ER 25.
12   *Easton v Brown* [1981] 3 All ER 278 (purchaser acting reasonably in waiting eight years for co-operation of occupying spouse before enforcing order).
13   [1956] 3 All ER 705, CA. This had been a long established exception in the case of leases: *Clarke v Moore* (1844) 1 Jo & Lat 723.

3. Want of mutuality

It was once commonly stated[14] that to be specifically enforceable the contract had to be mutually binding when made, ie the court would refuse the remedy to one party where it could not be claimed by the other. This view has now been rejected by the Court of Appeal in *Price v Strange*[15]. Want of mutuality is not an absolute bar, it is merely a relevant factor to be considered by the court in exercising its discretion.

A striking example of want of mutuality used to arise when contracts for the sale of land were governed by s 40 of the Law of Property Act 1925. Under that provision, specific performance was available against the party who had signed the memorandum but, in the absence of an act of part performance, was not available against the other party if he had not signed. This, somewhat anomalous, position no longer exists because, to be valid, a contract for the sale of land must be in writing and signed by both parties or their agents[16]. It is, therefore, no longer possible for a contract for the sale of land to be unilaterally enforceable.

4. Hardship

Being a discretionary remedy, equity may refuse to grant specific performance if to do so would work hardship on the defendant. Hardship is often pleaded in connection with some other factor, such as mistake[17] or misrepresentation, but it appears to be a sufficient defence by itself. In one case no decree was ordered on a sale of land without any definite means of access[18]. It will not be granted where it would subject the purchaser to forfeiture[19] or expose him to civil or criminal proceedings[20], or require the vendor to embark upon uncertain litigation[1].

The excessiveness or inadequacy of the consideration is not of itself a sufficient ground to refuse relief[2], though it may be evidence of fraud, or undue influence if the parties stand in a fiduciary relationship. The court will not withhold specific performance merely because the transaction turns out unfavourably to the party against whom it is sought[3], or because the purchaser's

---

14 Relying on Fry's *Specific Performance* (6th edn, 1921), pp 219–228.
15 [1978] Ch 337, [1977] 3 All ER 371, CA; *Lyus v Prowsa Developments Ltd* [1982] 2 All ER 953.
16 Law of Property (Miscellaneous Provisions) Act 1989, s 2.
17 See *Tamplin v James* (1880) 15 Ch D 215, CA, p 616, ante.
18 *Denne v Light* (1857) 8 De GM & G 774.
19 See *Dowson v Solomon* (1859) 1 Drew & Sm 1; *Becker v Partridge* [1966] 2 QB 155, [1966] 2 All ER 266, CA, p 271, ante. In such cases the purchaser may be entitled to rescind the contract.
20 *Pegler v White* (1864) 33 Beav 403; *Hope v Walter* [1900] 1 Ch 257, CA (property used as brothel; liability to prosecution under Criminal Law Amendment Act 1885).
 1 *Wroth v Tyler* [1974] Ch 30, [1973] 1 All ER 897 (proceedings necessary to terminate wife's statutory rights of occupation).
 2 *Western v Russell* (1814) 3 Ves & B 187; *Fragomeni v Fogliani* (1968) 42 ALJR 263 (purchaser mistaken as to price to which committing himself when signing contract); *Mountford v Scott* [1975] Ch 258, [1975] 1 All ER 198, CA (sale price insufficient to buy another suitable house).
 3 *Haywood v Cope* (1858) 25 Beav 140 (lessee ignorant of mining matters).

financial arrangements have collapsed, leaving him penniless[4]. Normally the hardship must have existed at the time of the contract. This is not an invariable rule as is seen from the tragic case of *Patel v Ali*[5].

> The defendant, a married woman with young children, and her co-owner agreed to sell their house, but completion was unavoidably delayed. She later contracted bone cancer resulting in the amputation of a leg, and became heavily dependent on the assistance of neighbouring family and friends. Goulding J held that in view of the unforeseen post-contract change in the defendant's personal circumstances, it would inflict hardship amounting to an injustice on her to decree specific performance of the contract, so causing her to lose her essential assistance. The purchaser was left to his remedy in damages.

Hardship must not be confused with impossibility. No decree will be made if supervening events render performance impossible, as where the vendor has in the meantime conveyed the property to a third person[6].

Hardship on third parties

The court will not decree specific performance of a contract which would, if enforced, involve a breach of trust[7] or breach of an existing contract with another person[8], or operate to the prejudice of third parties. Where land is vested in A and B, the court will not decree specific performance of a contract for sale made by A alone without B's knowledge or consent, since this would clearly be prejudicial to the non-contracting co-owner, B[9]. This defence can be raised even by the party in default. For this reason it has been suggested that in these cases the court refuses to intervene, not on the ground of hardship, but because equity will not act inconsistently with its own principles so as to defeat a prior equity[10].

5. Inequitable conduct

He who comes to equity must come with clean hands. In the exercise of its discretion the court will consider all the circumstances of the case, including

---

4　*Nicholas v Ingram* [1958] NZLR 972; *Francis v Cowlcliffe Ltd* (1976) 33 P & CR 368 (defendant embarking on expensive development scheme without adequate finances). See also *Co-operative Insurance Society Ltd v Argyll Stores (Holdings) Ltd* [1996] 3 All ER 934, [1996] 1 EGLR 71, CA. (Prospective tenant in receivership; no bar to specific performance of a contract to create a lease).

5　[1984] Ch 283, [1984] 1 All ER 978; *Roberts v O'Neill* [1983] IR 47 at 56, per McCarthy J (post-contract hardship resulting from inflation insufficient).

6　*Denton v Stewart* (1786) 1 Cox Eq Cas 258; *Beston v Stutely* (1858) 27 LJ Ch 156 (agreement for lease; refusal of existing lessee to surrender term).

7　*Rede v Oakes* (1864) 4 De GJ & Sm 505; *Jacobs v Bills* [1967] NZLR 249.

8　*Willmott v Barber* (1880) 15 Ch D 96 (contract to assign lease containing covenant not to assign); *Warmington v Miller* [1973] QB 877, [1973] 2 All ER 372, CA. It is immaterial that the prior contract has not been registered as a land charge, or protected on the register of title.

9　*Watts v Spence* [1976] Ch 165, [1975] 2 All ER 528, p 138, ante. See also *Thomas v Dering* (1837) 1 Keen 729; *Cedar Holdings Ltd v Green* [1981] Ch 129, [1979] 3 All ER 117, CA; *Thames Guaranty Ltd v Campbell* [1985] QB 210, [1984] 2 All ER 585, CA, p 620, post.

10　2 Williams V & P, 1052.

the conduct of all parties, and their mental and physical condition. When the court's aid is sought by way of specific performance, the principles of ethics have a more extensive sway than when a contract is sought to be rescinded[11]. It will not assist a plaintiff if there is evidence of fraud or sharp practice[12], duress, undue influence, misrepresentation[13], non-disclosure, or if the transaction is otherwise unconscionable[14]. Where impropriety on both sides is alleged, the court does not seek to balance the misconduct of one against the other[15]. A plaintiff who commits a breach of an essential term of the contract will be denied relief. Thus a vendor who by notice makes time of the essence as regards the completion date is not entitled to a decree if he fails to complete on that date[16]. Non-essential or trivial breaches are no bar to relief[17]. In the absence of any legal duty of disclosure[18], mere silence is no bar to specific performance, even in relation to material matters like the identity of the other contracting party[19] or the value or fitness of the property which, if known to the defendant, would have induced him not to enter into the contract[20]. This is simply another aspect of the caveat emptor rule that has been encountered before.

Illegal conduct

As we have already seen, equity follows the law and refuses to enforce an illegal contract. Where a purchaser buys land, intending to use it for an illegal purpose but without disclosing this to the vendor, the vendor can compel specific performance and the purchaser cannot allege his own unlawful intent as a defence[1]. A purchaser intending to use land for a purpose not authorised under the planning legislation is not, it seems, debarred from claiming this remedy unless, perhaps, both parties know of the proposed unauthorised use and that the purchaser has no intention of seeking permission[2]. In *Ailion v Spiekermann*[3], a vendor who contracted to sell a protected tenancy for an illegal premium was ordered to assign the tenancy without its payment, despite the buyer's awareness of the illegality. The contract to assign was not illegal and the statutory prohibition[4] was designed to protect the assignee.

11 Kerr, *Fraud and Mistake* (7th edn), p 562.
12 *Pateman v Pay* (1974) 232 EG 457.
13 *Walker v Boyle* [1982] 1 All ER 634 at 644, per Dillon J.
14 See *Conlon v Murray* [1958] NI 17 (suspicious circumstances arising from extraordinary haste in rushing through transaction); *Knupp v Bell* (1968) 67 DLR (2d) 256; *Hart v O'Connor* [1985] AC 1000, [1985] 2 All ER 880, PC; *Watkin v Watson-Smith* (1986) Times, 3 July. See also the observations of Evershed J in *Hawkins v Price* [1947] Ch 645 at 660.
15 *Sang Lee Investment Co Ltd v Wing Kwai Investment Co Ltd* (1983) 127 Sol Jo 410, PC.
16 See the discussion on pp 423, 427–432, ante. The rule is not so strict in Australia: *Legione v Hateley* (1983) 152 CLR 406.
17 *Dyster v Randall & Sons* [1926] Ch 932 (non-submission of plans for approval).
18 *Beyfus v Lodge* [1925] Ch 350 (failure to disclose disrepair notices).
19 *Dryster v Randall & Sons* [1926] Ch 932 (purchaser an undischarged bankrupt).
20 *Haywood v Cope* (1858) 25 Beav 140 (lessor's knowledge that mine unproductive no bar).
1   *Doe d Roberts v Roberts* (1819) 2 B & Ald 367; 2 Williams V & P, 841.
2   *Best v Glenville* [1960] 3 All ER 478 at 481, CA, per Ormrod LJ. And see *Williams v Greatrex* [1956] 3 All ER 705, CA (erection of buildings without statutory licence no bar).
3   [1976] Ch 158, [1976] 1 All ER 497; aliter, perhaps, if the vendor is ignorant of the law, or the buyer tempts him with his cheque book (at p 163).
4   See now the Rent Act 1977, ss 120, 123; as amended by the Housing Act 1988, s 15.

6. Defective title

Where the vendor is unable to make a title in accordance with the contract, the purchaser can not only resist specific performance, he may also be entitled to rescind the contract. Rescission is considered in Chapter 21. A purchaser cannot resist specific performance on the ground of some defect which he is contractually bound to accept. One exception to this principle exists. The court will not enforce the contract if the title is clearly bad and will expose the purchaser to immediate eviction. The essence of the doctrine of specific performance is that the purchaser is actually to get the land, it is therefore inapplicable in any case where he cannot get the land in any substantial sense, not even a good holding title[5].

The court will not compel a purchaser to complete a contract if the vendor's title is doubtful, that is, one not shown to be good or bad. The title may be considered doubtful because it depends upon the construction of a will[6], or of some ill-drafted document, or on facts which are difficult to establish. Thus a purchaser will not be compelled to accept a title depending on the fact that the vendor had no notice of an equitable incumbrance[7]. The court will, however, endeavour to resolve the doubt one way or the other, if possible[8]. A purchaser cannot set up the doubtfulness of the vendor's title as a defence if the doubt relates to some matter to which he is by the contract precluded from objecting.

Partial performance
Where the vendor is unable to make a good title to the whole of the land which he has contracted to sell, the purchaser is prima facie entitled to enforce the contract specifically as to such interest that the vendor has with an appropriate reduction in the purchase price. The court in effect executes the contract 'cy près'. The vendor is not permitted to plead his own want of title as a defence to the purchaser's claim. This doctrine of partial performance applies when there is some deficiency in the area of the land, or in the vendor's interest in it, as where land sold free from incumbrances is subject to mortgages which he cannot redeem[9]. *Thames Guaranty Ltd v Campbell*[10] provides another illustration. H and W (spouses) were co-owners of a house. Without W's consent, H deposited the deeds with the plaintiff bank as security for a loan. As the

---

5   *Re Scott and Alvarez's Contract, Scott v Alvarez* [1895] 2 Ch 603 at 613, CA, per Lindley LJ (condition restricting objections to intermediate title), p 170, ante. See also *Faruqi v English Real Estates Ltd* [1979] 1 WLR 963, p 622, post.
6   *Wilson v Thomas* [1958] 1 All ER 871 (sale of reversionary interest; latent ambiguity in description of beneficiary in will). See generally *Mullings v Trinder* (1870) LR 10 Eq 449.
7   *Nottingham Patent Brick and Tile Co v Butler* (1885) 15 QBD 261, p 160, ante; *Re Handman and Wilcox's Contract* [1902] 1 Ch 599, CA.
8   See the authorities discussed by Roxburgh J in *Wilson v Thomas* [1958] 1 All ER 871.
9   *Grant v Dawkins* [1973] 3 All ER 897; *Thellusson v Liddard* [1900] 2 Ch 635 (vendor selling freehold having only equitable leasehold); *Basma v Weekes* [1950] AC 441, [1950] 2 All ER 146, PC.
10 [1985] QB 210, [1984] 2 All ER 585, CA.

deposit could not create any equitable charge binding the legal title, the bank sought an order charging H's equitable interest in the house. Whilst recognising that the factual situation fell within the scope of the doctrine, the court, exercising its discretion, declined to uphold the bank's claim on the ground that an order would substantially prejudice W.

7.   Consequences of refusal of decree

(a) Position at law and statutory power to return deposit
Equity's refusal to grant a decree leaves the parties to their common law remedies. The contract remains fully binding at law. A purchaser may successfully resist specific performance. Yet his failure to complete will constitute a breach of contract, in respect of which the vendor can claim damages at law or forfeit the deposit, unless the circumstances are such as to permit rescission by the purchaser. The obvious injustice of this rule, seen in operation in cases such as *Re Scott and Alvarez's Contract*[11] and *Beyfus v Lodge*[12], has now been mitigated by s 49(2) of the Law of Property Act 1925. This provision enables the court, if it thinks fit, to order the repayment of any deposit where it refuses to grant specific performance. There is no need for a purchaser to rely on the subsection if it is not he, but the vendor, who is in default, though in the past the courts have tended on occasions to apply s 49(2) when the purchaser has been legally entitled to its recovery[13].

In *Universal Corpn v Five Ways Properties Ltd*[14], the court held that it possessed an unqualified discretion to order return of the deposit when this would be the fairest course between the parties. There need be no equitable disfavour or misconduct affecting the vendor's behaviour[15]. It can be exercised despite the fact that the contract contains an express power which, in the events that happen, operates to confer on the vendor a right to forfeit the deposit[16]. The discretion must be exercised judicially with regard to all relevant considerations, including, according to Megarry J[17], the conduct of the parties (especially the applicant), the gravity of the matters in question and the amounts at stake. Return of the deposit has been ordered in two cases[18] where on the purchaser's default the vendor has been in a position to resell the property at a handsome profit. It is not thought that the court would order its return when the amount

---

11   [1895] 2 Ch 603, CA.
12   [1925] Ch 350. And see *Wood v Scarth* (1855) 2 K & J 33; subsequent proceedings at (1858) 1 F & F 293.
13   See *Charles Hunt Ltd v Palmer* [1931] 2 Ch 287 (actionable misrepresentation); *Finkielkraut v Monohan* [1949] 2 All ER 234 (non-completion when time of the essence); *Shires v Brock* (1977) 247 EG 127, CA; *George Wimpey & Co Ltd v Sohn* [1967] Ch 487, [1966] 1 All ER 232, CA.
14   [1979] 1 All ER 552, CA.
15   As was thought in *Cole v Rose* [1978] 3 All ER 1121 at 1130, per Mervyn Davies QC.
16   *Maktoum v South Lodge Flats Ltd* (1980) Times, 22 April. But see *Michael Richards Properties Ltd v Corpn of Wardens of St Saviour's Parish, Southwark* [1975] 3 All ER 416 at 425, per Goff J.
17   *Schindler v Pigault* (1975) 30 P & CR 328 at 336.
18   *Maktoun v South Lodge Flats Ltd*, supra; *Dimsdale Developments (South East) Ltd v De Haan* (1983) 47 P & CR 1.

of the deposit represents no more than adequate compensation for the vendor's loss resulting from the purchaser's breach[19]. The wording of s 49(2) does not envisage a power to return less than the entire deposit[20]. Nevertheless this restriction was neatly avoided in *Dimsdale Developments (South East) Ltd v De Haan*[1]. The judge expressed willingness to return the deposit provided the purchaser submitted to a deduction therefrom of a sum covering the extra expenses (eg legal fees, bank interest) incurred by the vendor following the purchaser's default.

The operation of s 49(2) is well illustrated by *Faruqi v English Real Estates Ltd*[2]. Here registered land was sold at auction subject to entries on the register of title, which referred to certain restrictions. The vendor knew he could not produce any copy of the deed creating these covenants, and when the purchaser became aware of this he declined to complete. At law the contract was good and the purchaser was bound to take the title because the contract expressly provided that the property was sold subject to the entries on the register. However, equity would not force the title on the purchaser on account of the vendor's failure to disclose a known defect in title. Walton J exercised his statutory discretion in the purchaser's favour, and the practical effect of this was to put a complete end to the contract[3]. The purchaser also claimed the costs of investigating the title and of providing insurance. These sums were not recoverable because the vendor had not broken his contract at law. This highlights one significant difference between the position of the purchaser where he is able to establish a successful claim to rescission at law and when he is dependent on the court's intervention under the statute[4].

(b) Damages in equity

Where the court has jurisdiction to entertain an application for specific performance it may, by virtue of s 70 of the Supreme Court Act 1981, grant damages in addition to or in substitution for a decree of specific performance[5]. Damages under the Act are not as of right. Provided there exists jurisdiction to enforce the contract specifically, damages *may* be awarded if a decree is refused on some discretionary ground such as hardship[6] or delay[7]. This statutory

19 See *Safehaven Investments v Springbok* (1995) 71 P & CR 59.
20 *James Macara Ltd v Barclay* [1944] 2 All ER 31 at 32, per Vaisey J. Nor does it extend to part payments.
1 (1983) 47 P & CR 1.
2 [1979] 1 WLR 963.
3 At 969, per Walton J, referring to *Schindler v Pigault* (1975) 30 P & CR 328 at 337, per Megarry J.
4 See *Schindler v Pigault*, supra, at 336–37, though the reference to rescission entitling the purchaser to be restored to his pre-contract position is not good law in the light of *Johnson v Agnew* [1980] AC 367, [1979] 1 All ER 883, HL.
5 Equity's power to grant damages alone was first conferred by the Chancery Amendment Act 1858 (Lord Cairns' Act). Beforehand equity exercised jurisdiction to award compensation by way of abatement of the price (see eg p 638, post) or damages in addition to, but never independently of, a decree of specific performance: *Joliffe v Baker* (1883) 11 QBD 255 at 267–68; *Phelps v Prothero* (1855) 7 De GM & G 722. See generally [1981] Conv 286 (T Ingham & J Wakenfield).
6 *Wroth v Tyler* [1974] Ch 30, [1973] 1 All ER 897, p 165, ante.
7 *McKenna v Richey* [1950] VLR 360.

discretion may be exercised even though no cause of action exists at law[8], a consideration that is sometimes overlooked. So, it used to be the case that damages could be awarded under the Act in the case of a parol contract for the sale of land which was supported by an act of part performance. Now that s 2 of the Law of Property (Miscellaneous Provisions) Act 1989 has removed the possibility of parol contracts for the sale of land, this possibility has now ended. What the court cannot do is award damages in lieu of specific performance when it has become impossible to enforce the contract specifically. This situation will occur, for example, when the vendor has conveyed the land to another purchaser who is not bound by the plaintiff's interest, or the contract is incapable of specific performance because of lapse of time[9]. Damages awarded in equity under the Act are assessed in the same manner as damages at common law. The subject of damages is dealt with in Chapter 22. Damages in addition to specific performance are not infrequently awarded for delay in completion[10]. The court can award such damages, despite the fact that the action was instituted before the contractual completion date had passed and thus before the cause of action in damages had accrued[11]. A claim for damages at law could not succeed in these circumstances.

C   Enforcement of order

1.   Form of order

The judgment generally commences with a declaration that the court orders and adjudges the agreement 'to be specifically performed and carried into execution'. Then follow directions, varying according to the circumstances, for an inquiry as to damages, the payment of interest, the taking of accounts, an inquiry into the vendor's title[12] (unless this has been accepted or the right to a reference waived), the preparation and execution of the conveyance to be settled by the judge, and for the simultaneous delivery at a time and place to be appointed of the executed conveyance and the other title deeds in exchange for the purchase money, interest and costs[13]. If the purchaser is in possession of the property, he is put to his election to give up possession or to

---

8   *Price v Strange* [1978] Ch 337 at 358–59, 369, [1977] 3 All ER 371 at 384, 393, CA, per Goff & Buckley LJJ. See *Eastwood v Lever* (1863) 4 De GJ & Sm 114 (action for breach of restrictive covenant where no privity at law).

9   *Lavery v Pursell* (1888) 39 Ch D 508 (expiry of time limit for removal of building materials from demolished house).

10   *Scott v Bradley* [1971] Ch 850, [1971] 1 All ER 583; *Ford-Hunt v Singh* [1973] 2 All ER 700. For an unusual example see *Grant v Dawkins* [1973] 3 All ER 897 (house sold free from incumbrances mortgaged for more than purchase price).

11   *Oakacre Ltd v Claire Cleaners (Holdings) Ltd* [1982] Ch 197, [1981] 3 All ER 667. The action must have been commenced as a properly constituted action for specific performance.

12   See further 44 *Halsbury's Laws* (4th edn), paras 534–40. The court does not inquire whether the vendor has a good title before making the order; but if the title is not established to the court's satisfaction, the purchaser is not obliged to take the property. He can apply to be discharged from the contract: *Halkett v Earl of Dudley* [1907] 1 Ch 590 at 601, per Parker J.

13   See the form of the order in *Palmer v Lark* [1945] Ch 182, [1945] 1 All ER 355.

pay the balance due into court[14]. The court's order is final and will not ordinarily be varied unless, exceptionally, a supplemental order is granted on the basis of new facts[15].

2. Effect of order

After a decree of specific performance the contract continues to exist, it does not merge in the order. This does not mean, however, that the exercise of rights conferred by the contract remain unaffected by the order. The court has become seised of the matter and the future performance of the contract is within the court's own control. Neither party is competent to exercise a contractual right of rescission without the court's approval, and a notice to complete served under the contract is invalid and of no effect[16].

3. Enforcement of order

Having obtained his decree the plaintiff must then seek an order fixing a time and place for completion, though this will have to await the outcome of the inquiry (if any) into the title. Unjustified delay in prosecuting the order may result in the court's refusal to enforce it[17]. Since the carrying out of the contract is in the court's hands, the defendant's non-compliance with the order does not entitle the plaintiff of his own accord to treat the contract as rescinded. Even when it is the party obtaining the order who fails to comply with it, the restriction on terminating the contract without a court order applies equally to the other party[18]. The legal position following non-compliance by the defendant varies according to whether the plaintiff is the vendor or the purchaser.

(a) Non-compliance by purchaser
On default by the purchaser the vendor has a choice. He may either (i) apply to the court to dissolve the order and terminate the contract, or (ii) proceed to enforce the order in an appropriate way. If he adopts the first course he is entitled to recover damages for breach of contract. The purchaser's failure to complete constitutes a repudiation of the contract, which the court can permit him to accept. If the court then discharges the contract, the vendor's entitlement to damages follows on ordinary principles of contract law[19]. As an alternative to damages he may be content with an order for forfeiture of the deposit[20]. The vendor is not entitled, however, to sell to a third party in

---

14 *Greenwood v Turner* [1891] 2 Ch 144; *Maskell v Ivory* [1970] Ch 502, [1970] 1 All ER 488. But
    see *Attfield v D J Plant Hire and General Contractors Co Ltd* [1987] Ch 141, [1986] 3 All ER 273.
15 *Ford-Hunt v Singh* [1973] 2 All ER 700 (order for inquiry into damages).
16 See generally *Singh v Nazeer* [1979] Ch 474, [1978] 3 All ER 817.
17 See p 616, ante.
18 As is shown by *Singh v Nazeer*, ante.
19 *Johnson v Agnew* [1980] AC 367, [1979] 1 All ER 883, HL. See also p 610, ante.
20 *Hall v Burnell* [1911] 2 Ch 551.

pursuance of a contractual right of resale unless the court first dissolves the order for specific performance or the agreement of the defaulting purchaser is obtained[1].

The court will not make an order dissolving the decree if to do so would in the circumstances be unjust to the other party. In *Johnson v Agnew*[2], the vendor obtained a decree of specific performance after the purchaser's failure to complete following the expiry of the vendor's completion notice. Performance of the contract was later rendered impossible when the land was sold by mortgagees. The House of Lords held that the ultimate impossibility of completion was the purchaser's fault. The decree was discharged and the vendor awarded common law damages for breach of contract.

If the vendor elects to enforce the order, various courses of action are open to him, though in practice they may not prove to be very efficacious. He can levy an execution on the purchaser's goods, apply for a charging order on any land he owns[3], or seek a writ of sequestration.

(b) Non-compliance of vendor
When the vendor is guilty of non-compliance, the purchaser is likewise put to his election. He can ask the court to discharge the contract, recovering his deposit and damages (if any) caused by the vendor's breach. Should he choose instead to enforce the order, he occupies a more favourable position. He can apply to the court for an order vesting the land in him or for the appointment of a third person to convey it to him[4].

---

1 *GKN Distributors Ltd v Tyne Tees Fabrication Ltd* (1985) 50 P & CR 403.
2 [1980] AC 367, [1979] 1 All ER 883, HL.
3 Under the Charging Orders Act 1979. The order for payment of the price is a final judgment on which a bankruptcy petition may be presented; see *Re A Debtor* [1912] 3 KB 242, CA.
4 Trustee Act 1925, ss 48–50. The procedure by way of vesting order is the more convenient; see *Jones v Davies* (1940) 84 Sol Jo 334.

Chapter 21

Rescission

A   Introduction

As we saw in Chapter 19[1] rescission is a word used by lawyers in more than one sense. Some further comment about its two chief usages is necessary before specific instances giving rise to a right of rescission are discussed in more detail.

1.   Rescission ab initio

In certain circumstances a contracting party may be entitled to set the contract aside and to be restored as far as possible to the state of affairs which existed before the making of the contract. Even before 1877 rescission was available at law as well as in equity. For example, at common law a contract could be rescinded for fraud. Money paid under a rescinded contract (such as a deposit) was recoverable by an action for money had and received. However, rescission was only possible at law provided both parties could be put in status quo as before the contract. This requirement was very strictly interpreted with the result that a purchaser or tenant who had entered into occupation of the property could not rescind[2]. On the other hand equity, by virtue of its superior machinery, particularly in relation to the taking of accounts and the making of allowances, was able to give relief by way of rescission wherever by the exercise of its powers it could do what was practically just, although not able to restore the parties precisely to their pre-contract position[3]. Additionally equity permitted rescission in circumstances unknown to the common law, notably for innocent misrepresentation; moreover, it was possible only in equity to bring an action to enforce rescission by a judgment. Consequently rescission ab initio came to be regarded as essentially an equitable remedy. Yet rescission can be exercised without recourse to the courts, for it is not strictly a judicial process but the act of the party rescinding[4]. In practice the courts' aid is often sought to enforce or uphold the plaintiffs right, or to obtain consequential relief.

---

1   See p 616, ante.
2   *Hunt v Silk* (1804) 5 East 449; *Blackburn v Smith* (1848) 2 Exch 783, both cases involving a breach of contract; see p 640, post.
3   *Erlanger v New Sombrero Phosphate Co* (1878) 3 App Cas 1218 at 1278, per Lord Blackburn. See pp 701–702, post.
4   *Horsler v Zorro* [1975] Ch 302 at 310, [1975] 1 All ER 584 at 590, per Megarry J.

2.   Rescission for breach

(a) Innocent party put to election

Acceptance of a repudiatory breach of contract is, as we have noticed, frequently termed rescission, but the consequences of rescission in this sense are vastly different from those resulting from rescission ab initio. An example may help to illustrate the position of the parties on rescission for breach. Suppose there is a contract for the sale of land by V to P, which P indicates by words or conduct that he no longer intends or is unable to perform. V thereupon becomes entitled to treat this wrongful repudiation by P as terminating the contract. If V adopts this course, both he and P are discharged from further liability to perform their respective obligations under the contract. V can also pursue any appropriate remedy. He may sue at once for damages for its breach without waiting for the completion date to elapse. It must be stressed that P's repudiation does not of itself operate to discharge the contract. There has to be acceptance of the repudiation by V, who must communicate this to P, either expressly or impliedly (eg by re-advertising the property for sale). Thereafter the acceptance cannot be retracted. However, V has an option. He may elect to ignore the repudiation, in which case the contract remains subsisting for the benefit of both parties. They continue to be bound by their own obligations under it, and V must await the agreed completion date before taking legal action, should P still not perform the contract. Moreover, the party in default (P) can avail himself of any defence to an action for breach of contract occasioned by his eventual non-performance, just as if his previous default had never occurred[5].

This rule that the innocent party can keep the contract alive can produce some startling consequences when pushed to its logical conclusion. For example, can he insist on fulfilling his part of the bargain, despite the known repudiation by the other party, and recover the full contract price, rather than damages for the breach ? In *White and Carter (Councils) Ltd v McGregor*[6], a bare majority of the House of Lords on an appeal from Scotland answered this point in the affirmative. On the basis of this decision it would seem that, despite P's wrongful repudiation, V could perform his part of the contract by executing the conveyance unconditionally, thus vesting the legal estate (in the case of unregistered land) in P. He could then sue P for the full price or exercise his equitable lien, and he need not be limited to damages for loss of profit nor have to resort to equity for a decree of specific performance[7].

---

5   *Avery v Bowden* (1855) 5 E & B 714.
6   [1962] AC 413, [1961] 3 All ER 1178, HL (continued display of advertisements after promoter's cancellation of contract).
7   This conclusion is supported by *Tudor v Hamid* [1988] 1 EGLR 251, CA, discussed at p 415, ante, where the whole of the purchase money had been paid prior to completion to the vendor's solicitors as stakeholders, and they were held to be justified in paying it over to the vendor after completion had been unilaterally effected. And see Farrand, 213. It is not open to P to disclaim the conveyance in an attempt to cause the legal title to revest in V. Disclaimer does not apply between vendor and purchaser; p 706, post.

The *White* case has not on the whole been well received. It is difficult to reconcile with the principle of mitigation, for the innocent party is actually aggravating the damage. The doctrine does, however, appear to be subject to qualifications. It does not apply where the innocent party cannot complete the contract without the assent or co-operation of the defaulting party[8]. This limitation might well operate in the situation mentioned above, if, for example, the title had not been accepted by P, or the form of the conveyance not agreed. Recently in *Clea Shipping Corpn v Bulk Oil International Ltd*[9], Lloyd J held that exceptionally the court has power to refuse to allow the innocent party to elect not to accept the repudiation, if he has no legitimate interest in performing the contract rather than claiming damages.

(b) Trivial breach

Repudiation is a drastic conclusion which should only be held to arise in clear cases of a refusal, in a matter going to the root of the contract, to perform contractual obligations[10]. Not every breach of contract entitles the innocent party to treat it as discharged. He can take this step when there has been a breach of an essential term (as it is sometimes alternatively expressed) but not otherwise. It is outside the scope of this book to explore in detail how the courts determine the essentiality of contractual terms. Whether in any given case a breach of contract constitutes a fundamental breach justifying rescission depends on the construction of the contract and on all the facts and circumstances of the case[11].

Breach of a non-essential term gives rise to an action for damages; it does not enable the injured party to treat the contract at an end. A non-essential breach has been held to occur where there was failure to complete on the agreed date and time was not of the essence[12], and where the purchaser delayed completion insisting bona fide on a wrong interpretation of the contract[13]. Similarly, a purchaser who in good faith relies on an express stipulation in the contract to terminate it is not by that fact alone to be regarded as having repudiated it, even though it later appears that he was mistaken as to his rights[14]. A party who wrongfully treats the contract as discharged is himself in breach. In *Cornwall v Henson*[15], the purchaser's failure to pay the last of 12 equal instalments of the purchase price was held not to amount to repudiation. The vendor was therefore liable to pay damages to him for having in the meantime let the land to a tenant.

8   *White and Carter (Councils) Ltd v McGregor*, supra, at 428–29, 1181–82, per Lord Reid.
9   [1984] 1 All ER 129.
10 *Woodar Investment Development Ltd v Wimpey Construction UK Ltd* [1980] 1 All ER 571 at 576, HL, per Lord Wilberforce.
11 *Suisse Atlantique Société d'Armement Maritime SA v NV Rotterdamsche Kolen Centrale NV* [1967] 1 AC 361 at 422, [1966] 2 All ER 61 at 86, HL, per Lord Upjohn.
12 *Raineri v Miles* [1981] AC 1050, [1980] 2 All ER 145, HL; p 422, ante.
13 *Luff v Raymond* [1982] LS Gaz R 1330; *Luck v White* (1973) 26 P & CR 89 (purchaser disputing interest payable on late completion; no repudiation).
14 *Woodar Investment Development Ltd v Wimpey Construction UK Ltd*, supra.
15 [1900] 2 Ch 298, CA.

(c) Vendor's position on rescission

(i) *Generally.* It is now clearly established by the decision in *Johnson v Agnew*[16] that a vendor rescinding for fundamental breach by the purchaser can recover damages consequent thereon. It goes without saying that he is entitled to recover possession of the land if the purchaser has been allowed into occupation, and presumably he can charge him with an occupation rent[17]. The purchaser must also account for rents and profits actually received by him[18]. Once the vendor has accepted the purchaser's repudiation he cannot thereafter claim specific performance[19]. Save for the question of damages the contract is at an end and both parties are discharged from further performance. One consequence of the contract's termination is that the vendor is restored to his former position as owner of the property free from the contract. He can resell it without recourse to the courts and independently of any special contractual clause[20]. In practice, standard form contracts invariably contain an express power of resale in certain situations, so the vendor may be able to pursue alternative remedies though not necessarily with the same results[1].

(ii) *Forfeiture of deposit.* On rescission the vendor will normally be entitled to forfeit the deposit paid on exchange of contracts[2]. This right exists irrespective of any express provision[3]. The deposit, besides being part payment of the price, is an earnest or guarantee of the contract's fulfilment. He cannot retain other sums paid on account of the purchase price, but may recover as damages any shortfall in the deposit that remains unpaid[4]. A vendor in a position to forfeit the deposit will not usually be interested in seeking damages for breach, unless the loss on a subsequent resale exceeds the amount of the deposit. A purchaser is not able to recover a forfeited deposit on the ground that the vendor's title is later discovered to have been defective[5].

(d) Purchaser's position on rescission
The purchaser is similarly entitled to claim damages if he elects to rescind following the vendor's repudiatory breach. He can recover his deposit with interest and the costs of investigating the title, as well as damages for loss of

---

16 [1980] AC 367, [1979] 1 All ER 883, HL. For damages, see Ch 22.
17 The contrary decisions in *Hutchings v Humphreys* (1885) 54 LJ Ch 650 and *Barber v Wolfe* [1945] Ch 187, [1945] 1 All ER 399 can no longer be accepted as sound law in the light of *Johnson v Agnew*, supra.
18 *King v King* (1833) 1 My & K 442; *Clark v Wallis* (1866) 35 Beav 460.
19 He may prefer to keep the contract alive and to sue for specific performance or damages in the alternative, but he must elect at the trial which remedy to pursue.
20 *Howe v Smith* (1884) 27 Ch D 89, CA, p 648, post.
 1 See pp 649–652, post.
 2 Subject to the court's power to order its return: LPA 1925, s 49(2), p 621, ante.
 3 *Hall v Burnell* [1911] 2 Ch 551, p 239, ante. The contract may show an intention to exclude forfeiture: *Palmer v Temple* (1839) 9 Ad & El 508 (term that purchaser to pay £1,000 as liquidated damages).
 4 See the discussion at pp 240–241, ante.
 5 *Soper v Arnold* (1889) 14 App Cas 429, HL.

the bargain. Prior to 1989, the purchaser would often be denied damages for loss of bargain by the anomalous rule in *Bain v Fothergill*[6], but this rule has now been abolished by s 3 of the Law of Property (Miscellaneous Provisions) Act 1989[7]. He may claim a lien on the land for his deposit, which is enforceable in like manner as a vendor's lien for unpaid purchase money[8]. Should he have enjoyed personal possession, he is chargeable with an occupation rent[9] or with interest payable under a contractual term[10]. The contract may also bar the purchaser's right to rescind in particular circumstances[11].

B   Scope of chapter

This chapter is concerned with the parties' rights to rescind whilst the contract is still executory. Rescission after completion is considered in Chapter 24 which also contains a discussion of various bars operating to preclude rescission. A right to rescind my arise for any of the following reasons:
1.   misrepresentation;
2.   mistake;
3.   misdescription;
4.   defective title;
5.   failure to complete;
6.   by virtue of some express contractual term.

This is not intended to be an exhaustive list of circumstances justifying rescission, but it does represent the main situations likely to be encountered by the conveyancer. Non-disclosure could be added to the list, but this can be adequately subsumed in heading 4. Of these six situations, the first two are examples of rescission ab initio, whereas items 3, 4 and 5 are instances of rescission for breach[12]. An express contractual right to rescind (item 6) operates in a manner similar to rescission ab initio[13], though here the terms on which it is exerciseable and with what consequences will be governed by the contract.

C   Misrepresentation

A purchaser acquires a prima facie right to rescind the contract if he has been induced to enter into it by a false representation made by the vendor, who

---

6   (1874) LR 7 HL 158.
7   See p 655, post.
8   *Whitbread & Co Ltd v Watt* [1902] 1 Ch 835, CA. For the vendor's lien, see p 438, ante. It requires protection in the appropriate way.
9   Cf *Allen v Smith* [1924] 2 Ch 308.
10   Eg SCS 5.1, p 256, ante. The contract is not retrospectively terminated, so accrued rights remain unaffected.
11   See pp 649–650, post.
12   Rescission for misdescription under the rule in *Flight v Booth* (1834) 1 Bing NC 370 presents certain difficulties of categorisation; see p 640, post.
13   *Johnson v Agnew* [1980] AC 367 at 393, [1979] 1 All ER 883 at 889, HL, per Lord Wilberforce.

intends him to act on it. The reader will already be familiar with the basic elements of misrepresentation[14], and it is not intended to do more here than to draw attention to one or two particular aspects. There must be a statement of fact which excludes representations of law, opinion and future intention. To describe business premises as office premises constitutes a representation not merely as to their physical state but as to the availability of planning permission for such use[15]. Failure to disclose a material fact in the contract does not amount to a misrepresentation. The omission renders no stated fact untrue[16]. A statement of future conduct may amount to a statement of present intention and thus a misrepresentation of fact if at the time of making the statement the vendor had no such intention. An expression of opinion may also involve an implied assertion that the speaker knows nothing leading to the contrary conclusion. In *Smith v Land and House Property Corpn*[17], the description of a tenant who was considerably in arrears with his rent as 'most desirable' was held an actionable misrepresentation. No action lies in respect of 'puffing'. Words are not essential for a representation, conduct may suffice as where a vendor conceals defects in his house by covering up areas of dry rot infestation[18]. The false statement must induce the contract, but it is sufficient if it is one of several factors having this effect[19]. In the absence of evidence of non-reliance, inducement to enter into the contract will be readily inferred if it is a material representation calculated to induce the purchaser to contract[20]. No right to rescind arises if the purchaser, or his solicitor[1], knew at the time of the contract that the representation was untrue, or if he did not in fact rely on it. The purchaser is invariably the party seeking rescission for misrepresentation. A contract for the sale of land is not uberrimae fidei[2]. Although the purchaser is under no duty to disclose information which could influence the price, statements made by him and intended to induce the vendor to believe in the existence of a non-existing fact which might affect the price may suffice for the court to refuse to award the purchaser specific performance[3], and in extreme cases may warrant setting the contract aside for fraud[4].

At law misrepresentation gave rise to a right to rescind the contract only if it was made fraudulently, that is, with knowledge of its falsity or in reckless

14 See further Treitel, *The Law of Contract* (9th edn) Ch 9. See also the discussion in Ch 7, pp 193–197, ante.
15 *Laurence v Lexcourt Holdings Ltd* [1978] 2 All ER 810; *F and B Entertainments Ltd v Leisure Enterprises Ltd* (1976) 240 EG 455 (misrepresentations as to service of rent review notice).
16 *Beyfus v Lodge* [1925] Ch 350 at 361, per Russell J.
17 (1884) 28 Ch D 7, CA; *Registered Holdings Ltd v Kadri* (1972) 222 EG 621 (property described as 'nice house'); *Reece v Seru Investments Ltd* (1972) 225 EG 89 (recently decorated house stated to be 'as good as it looks').
18 *Gordon v Selico Co Ltd* [1986] 1 EGLR 71, CA (grant of long lease); *Ridge v Crawley* (1959) 173 EG 959, CA (papering over wall cracks).
19 See eg *Walker v Boyle* [1982] 1 All ER 634 at 641, per Dillon J.
20 *Redgrave v Hurd* (1881) 20 Ch D 1 at 21, CA, per Jessel MR.
1 *Strover v Harrington* [1988] Ch 390, [1988] 1 All ER 769.
2 Exceptionally the purchaser's conduct may give rise to a fiduciary relationship: *English v Dedham Vale Properties Ltd* [1978] 1 All ER 382, p 258, ante.
3 *Walters v Morgan* (1861) 3 De GF & J 718. And see p 619, ante.
4 *Coaks v Boswell* (1886) 11 App Cas 232 at 236, HL, per Lord Selbourne.

disregard whether it was true or false. In equity, however, rescission was available in respect of an innocent misrepresentation. The Misrepresentation Act 1967 leaves a purchaser's right to rescind for misrepresentation prior to completion basically[5] unaltered, save that s 2(2) of the Act[5] gives the court a discretion to award damages in lieu of rescission in cases where a person is entitled to rescind a contract by reason of a non-fraudulent misrepresentation. The subsection does not, of course, empower the court to award damages as an alternative to rescission where it is sought on the grounds of the vendor's failure to make a good title, or because of a substantial misdescription.

D   Mistake

The reader will already be familiar with the intricacies and controversies surrounding the law of mistake in contract. For a detailed exposition of the law on this complicated topic, reference should be made to textbooks on the law of contract[6]. This section purports to do nothing more than remind the reader of some basic principles. At the outset it is necessary to appreciate the differing attitudes of law and equity to the problem of mistake. At law mistake, if operative, makes the contract void ab initio. It prevents any real consensus existing between the parties; there is no contract. This differentiates mistake from other vitiating factors like fraud, misrepresentation or duress, which make a contract voidable not void. Strictly speaking, therefore, it is inept to speak of rescinding a contract void for mistake, though the expression is commonly used to denote the process of setting the alleged contract aside, whereby each party restores what he has received and recovers what he gave. Since the contract is void, no title can be acquired under it and this can operate to the detriment of a third party[7].

On the other hand, equity is prepared to afford relief in cases where the mistake does not fall within the narrow confines of the common law. Relief may take one of three forms: (i) a refusal of specific performance, the effect of which is to leave the parties to their common law rights; (ii) rescission which may be granted unconditionally or on terms and is subject to the usual bars[8]; and (iii) rectification of a written document to accord with the true terms agreed between the parties[9]. Only rescission will be considered here.

1.   Mistake at law

According to Lord Atkin in *Bell v Lever Bros Ltd*[10], mistake, if it operates at all, does so to negative or nullify consent and he instanced three particular forms

---

5   Page 193, ante. For rescission after completion, see s 1(b) of the Act, p 691, post.
6   See Trietel, op cit, Ch 8.
7   See eg *Cundy v Lindsay* (1878) 3 App Cas 459, HL.
8   See pp 700–706, post.
9   See pp 696–700, post.
10   [1932] AC 161 at 217, HL.

of mistake which it will be convenient to adopt for present purposes. These are mistakes as to: (i) the existence of the subject-matter of the contract; (ii) the identity of the contracting parties; and (iii) the quality of the subject-matter.

(a) Existence of subject-matter
Within this category come cases where, unknown to both parties, the subject-matter of the contract has ceased to exist or has never, in fact, existed. An example of the latter type of case occurred in *Associated Japanese Bank (International) Ltd v Crédit du Nord SA*[11], where a contract of guarantee had been entered into in respect of a sale and leaseback arrangement concerning four machines which never, in fact, existed. The contract was held to be void for mistake. In the conveyancing context, a similar situation would arise where the land was already owned by the purchaser – cases of res extincta, or res sua[12]. Here the parties have contracted on the basis of a fundamental assumption which is false. For example, a contract for the sale of a life interest is void if the life tenant is already dead[13], and notwithstanding completion of the transaction the conveyance will be set aside and the purchaser is entitled to recover the price as money paid under a mistake of fact. The same appears to be true where prior to the contract the land has been completely swept away by a flood[14]. Several cases establish that a contract is void both at law and in equity where the purchaser or tenant is already the owner or lessee of the subject-matter of the contract[15].

A mistake of private rights is for these purposes regarded as a mistake of fact, not law. Where, however, unknown to both parties the title is not in the vendor but in some third party, there is a valid contract, albeit unenforceable by the vendor, and the purchaser is entitled to recover damages for the vendor's breach of contract[16]. A mistake by one party as to the subject-matter does not avoid the contract. Thus if a purchaser bids for one lot at an auction, thinking that it is another, the contract will normally be enforced against him, his mistake being no defence to the vendor's action for specific performance[17]. The minds of the parties are not strictly ad idem, but the purchaser is not allowed to give

11 [1988] 3 All ER 902, [1989] 1 WLR 255.
12 Perhaps the true basis of the decision in these cases is not so much the fact of a common mistake as the absence of any contractual subject-matter, although in the *Associated Japanese* case the contract of guarantee of the payment of rent by the tenant could be regarded as separate from the lease itself.
13 *Strickland v Turner* (1852) 7 Exch 208; *Scott v Coulson* [1903] 2 Ch 249, CA.
14 *Hitchcock v Giddings* (1817) 4 Price 135 at 141, per Richards CB. Similarly, perhaps, a house totally destroyed by fire: 2 Williams V & P, 772.
15 *Cooper v Phibbs* (1867) LR 2 HL 149 (agreement for lease of fishery); *Jones v Clifford* (1876) 3 Ch D 779. Cf *Bligh v Martin* [1968] 1 All ER 1157 (lessee already owning freehold of part of land leased to him; no rescission); see pp 692–693, post.
16 As to the measure of damages, see p 656, post. He may choose to waive the defect and complete the purchase. He may think it worthwhile to do this to enter into occupation, taking his chance of its ripening into a title acquired by adverse possession. If the want of title is not discovered until after completion, he can sue on the covenants for title.
17 *Van Praagh v Everidge* [1902] 2 Ch 266; revsd [1903] 1 Ch 434, CA, on the ground there was no enforceable contract; *Tamplin v James* (1880) 15 Ch D 215, CA, p 616, ante.

evidence of the state of his mind. It is imperative that contracts should be observed wherever possible and the purchaser (or the vendor) is not to be freed from his bargain when to all outward appearances he has agreed on the same terms on the same subject-matter[18]. The contract is therefore valid at law. There may be circumstances sufficient in equity to justify a refusal of specific performance because the other party has contributed to the mistake or, being aware of it, deliberately refrains from disabusing the mistaken party.

(b) Identity

It is clear that a mistake as to the identity of the other contracting party operates to avoid the contract if personal considerations are fundamental to its formation. The defence has been difficult to establish in relation to contracts relating to land. It has been raised unsuccessfully by vendors in several cases where the apparent purchaser has been an agent for some undisclosed principal[19]. Equity adopts a similar attitude on the question of identity. In *Dyster v Randall & Sons*[20], Lawrence J enforced a contract at the instance of a purchaser who was an undischarged bankrupt. Although the contract had been made on his behalf by an agent who knew that the vendor would not have contracted with the undisclosed principal, it was not one where personal considerations formed a material ingredient. However, in the exercise of its discretionary jurisdiction, equity is more willing than the common law to take account of personal attributes. Where a lease is concerned the tenant's solvency must necessarily be of primary importance and his insolvency may be a ground for refusing specific performance[1].

(c) Quality

According to Lord Atkin[2], a mistake as to the quality of the subject-matter only avoids the contract at law if it makes the actual subject-matter something essentially different from what it is supposed to be. The cases suggest that rarely will mistake as to quality be regarded at law as so fundamental as to avoid the contract[3]. In *Solle v Butcher*[4], the parties mistakenly thought that a flat was free from rent control and the lease they entered into on this assumption was upheld at law, though relief was given in equity. It follows that a mistake by one party as to quality or as to some element affecting the value of the land, such as the presence of subjacent minerals, will not affect the contract at law, even though he would not have entered into the contract had

18   See Blackburn J's classic explanation in *Smith v Hughes* (1871) LR 6 QB 597 at 607.
19   See eg *Smith v Wheatcroft* (1878) 9 Ch D 223; *Nash v Dix* (1898) 78 LT 445 (purchaser not an agent but a person buying for resale). It is generally agreed that *Sowler v Potter* [1940] 1 KB 271, [1939] 4 All ER 478 cannot be supported on the ground of mistake.
20   [1926] Ch 932.
 1   *Dyster v Randall & Sons*, supra, at 939, citing *O'Herlihy v Hedges* (1803) 1 Sch & Lef 123.
 2   *Bell v Lever Bros Ltd* [1932] AC 161 at 218, HL.
 3   In *William Sindall plc v Cambridgeshire County Council* [1994] 3 All ER 932, [1994] 1 WLR 1016, CA, an analogy was drawn with the doctrine of frustration; at 956, 1039, respectively, per Evans LJ.
 4   [1950] 1 KB 671, [1949] 2 All ER 1107, CA.

he been aware of the true facts. If the mistake finds its way into the contract and becomes a term, eg an error as to quantity, there is a misdescription which, as will be seen, may entitle the purchaser to rescind, but this is quite different from avoiding the contract for mistake.

2. Mistake in equity

In cases of res extincta or res sua equity follows the law and treats the contract as a nullity. In the exercise of its jurisdiction to set aside the contract equity goes further than the common law and may impose terms on the parties. Equity may also intervene where the contract is valid at law. The rule enunciated by Denning LJ in *Solle v Butcher*[6] is as follows:

> A contract is also liable in equity to be set side if the parties were under a common misapprehension either as to the facts, or as to their relative respective rights, provided that the misapprehension was fundamental and that the party seeking to set it aside was not himself at fault.

Despite uncertainty as to its precise scope, this equitable jurisdiction has been invoked in a few later cases. In *Grist v Bailey*[7], a house valued at £2,270 with vacant possession was sold for only £850 as both parties believed it to be subject to a statutory tenancy. In fact the occupier was not able to claim the protection of the Rent Acts. Goff J held there was a fundamental common mistake, insufficient to avoid the contract at law, but within the equitable rule propounded by Lord Denning. He dismissed the purchaser's action for specific performance and ordered rescission of the contract, but on terms that the vendor entered into a new agreement at the vacant possession price. On the need for an absence of fault the learned judge, though unsure of what it comprehended, felt that there must be some degree of blameworthiness beyond the mere fault of making a mistake[8]. However, in *Laurence v Lexcourt Holdings Ltd*[9], Judge Brian Dillon QC went far towards nullifying this qualification. The parties to an agreement for a lease of premises erroneously believed that unlimited planning permission for their use as offices had been granted, whereas permission for only three years was available. Had the intending lessee followed normal conveyancing procedures and effected the usual searches and inquiries, he would have discovered the true position. Yet this imprudence was held not to amount to fault, and the agreement was set aside[10]. These cases were doubted, however, in *William Sindall plc v Cambridgeshire County Council*[11]. Hoffmann LJ was critical of the reasoning, in that regard was

---

5   See eg *Cooper v Phibbs* (1867) LR 2 HL 149.
6   [1950] 1 KB 671 at 693, [1949] 2 All ER 1107 at 1120, CA.
7   [1967] Ch 532, [1966] 2 All ER 875. See also *Peters v Batchelor* (1950) 100 L Jo 718, CA; *Magee v Pennine Insurance Co Ltd* [1969] 2 QB 507, [1969] 2 All ER 891, CA (motor insurance policy).
8   [1967] Ch 532 at 542, [1966] 2 All ER 875 at 880-81.
9   [1978] 2 All ER 810.
10 The learned judge was clearly reluctant to enforce the agreement specifically, especially as the lessor's own forgetfulness was the primary cause of the mistake, and the lessee was neither responsible for this nor the forgetfulness.
11 [1994] 3 All ER 932, [1994] 1 WLR 1016, CA.

not had to the issue of upon whom either the contract, or the general law, placed the risk of the property being less valuable than the purchaser had hoped and, in particular, did not relate to the principle of *caveat emptor*[12]. This approach is in keeping with the view that there is no scope for equity's intervention where the mistake does not exist at the date of the contract, or it relates merely to the parties' expectations[13]. It seems probable that the role for a separate, equitable, doctrine of mistake is likely to be diminished in the future.

E   Misdescription

1.   Nature of misdescription

An error or misstatement appearing in the contract and relating to the property to be sold amounts to a misdescription. Whilst such errors can occur when land is sold by private treaty, they arise more frequently on a sale by public auction. Inaccurate statements appear in the advertised sale particulars which form part of the contract of sale. Mistakes as to the area of the property or the nature of the vendor's interest (eg describing leasehold land as freehold[14] or selling as leasehold property held on an underlease[15]), or the net annual rental of the property[16], or the terms of restrictions affecting it[17] all constitute misdescriptions. Representations as to the quality of the land may also be misdescriptions. In *Re Puckett and Smith's Contract*[18], it took the form of a statement in the sale particulars that the land possessed a 'valuable prospective building element' whereas an underground culvert crossed the land, creating a substantial drawback to its use for building purposes. In *Charles Hunt Ltd v Palmer*[19], the vendor described two leasehold shops sold at auction as 'valuable business premises'. The purchaser was held entitled to recover his deposit on discovery that the lease prohibited their use without the lessor's consent for any business other than a ladies' outfitter, fancy draper and manufacturer of ladies' clothing. In a more recent case the particulars of sale of a house purchased at auction contained a full description of its accommodation. Part of the property was in fact subject to an undisclosed closing order. The purchaser was held entitled to rescind the contract on the ground of

---

12   Ibid, at 952 and 1035; see also at 959 and 1040 per Evans LJ.
13   *Amalgamated Investment and Property Co Ltd v John Walker & Sons Ltd* [1976] 3 All ER 509, [1977] 1 WLR 164, CA (warehouse bought for redevelopment subjected to listed building control *after* contract).
14   *Drewe v Corp* (1804) 9 Ves 368; *Turner v West Bromwich Union Guardians* (1860) 3 LT 662 (copyhold land described as freehold).
15   *Re Beyfus and Master's Contract* (1888) 39 Ch D 110, CA, p 152, ante; *Dobell v Hutchinson* (1835) 3 Ad & El 355.
16   *Palmer v Johnson* (1884) 13 QBD 351, CA; *Re Englefield Holdings Ltd and Sinclair's Contract* [1962] 3 All ER 503; see also *Ridley v Oster* [1939] 1 All ER 618 ('freehold decontrolled properties' subject as to part to controlled tenancies).
17   *Flight v Booth* (1834) 1 Bing NC 370; *Re Courcier and Harrold's Contract* [1923] 1 Ch 565.
18   [1902] 2 Ch 258, CA; *Re Chifferiel* (1888) 40 Ch D 45 (unmade road stated to be made up).
19   [1931] 2 Ch 287.

misdescription, rooms which were the subject-matter of a closing order could not properly be described as 'accommodation'[20]. Like misrepresentation, there must be a statement which purports to be of fact; on the other hand laudatory expressions extolling the virtues of the property, not uncommonly encountered in sales by public auction, will be treated as mere 'puff'. Descriptions such as 'fertile and improvable'[1] and 'valuable and extensive, very suitable for development'[2] have been treated as falling within this category.

Misdescription should be contrasted with misrepresentation. The essence of a misdescription is that it is contained in the contract itself, usually in the particulars of sale. The vendor is unable to convey what he has contracted to sell and he is, therefore, in breach of contract. A misrepresentation *induces* the contract without causing any breach (save where it is later incorporated as a term). Nevertheless, fundamental though this difference is, the distinction between them is not always so clear cut and frequently becomes blurred. Misrepresentation is sometimes applied in a loose sense to misdescription situations, both judicially and extra-judicially[3].

2. Position of the parties under the general law

It has long been the practice for vendors to safeguard their position by expressly regulating in the contract the purchaser's rights in the event of misdescription. Only a brief survey need be given of the parties' rights under the general law. These may be summarised as follows depending on the nature of the misdescription, whether it was slight or substantial.

(1) Any misdescription trivial or substantial precluded the vendor's enforcement of the contract at law. His own breach of contract disentitled him to damages if the purchaser refused to complete the transaction because of the error.

(2) A misdescription in a material and substantial point was said to result in the contract being 'avoided altogether'[4]. The purchaser was entitled to rescind the contract at law and recover his deposit in an action for money had and received. Nor yet would equity decree specific performance against him, for the court would not compel him to take something materially different from what he had agreed to buy.

(3) As an alternative to rescission the purchaser could seek the assistance of equity for a decree of specific performance, with a reduction in the purchase

20 *Registered Holdings Ltd v Kadri* (1972) 222 EG 621.
1 *Dimmock v Hallet* (1866) 2 Ch App 21.
2 *Watson v Burton* [1956] 3 All ER 929 at 931, per Wynn-Parry J (mis-statement of area).
3 See eg *Re Terry and White's Contract* (1886) 32 Ch D 14 at 29, CA, per Lindley LJ; *Re Davis and Cavey* (1888) 40 Ch D 601 at 609, per Stirling J; *Walker v Boyle* [1982] 1 All ER 634 at 643–44, per Dillon J, adverting to his earlier decision in *Laurence v Lexcourt Holdings Ltd* [1978] 2 All ER 810. See also Walford, 222, who does not distinguish between them; Williams, *Contract of Sale of Land*, 107, 108 (substantial deficiency said to enable purchaser to rescind for *misrepresentation*); 42 *Halsbury's Laws* (4th edn) para 58, but cf para 122, note 4.
4 *Flight v Booth* (1834) 1 Bing NC 370 at 377, per Tindal CJ. The precise significance of this puzzling phrase is considered below. For the meaning of substantial in this context, see section 3, infra.

price by way of compensation for the deficiency. This jurisdiction has been said to be based upon the principle of equitable estoppel. A vendor representing and contracting to sell an estate cannot afterwards assert that he has not got what he has contracted to sell, and the purchaser can call upon him to convey what he actually has[5]. The limits of this jurisdiction are somewhat ill-defined. Generally it was immaterial whether the misdescription was slight or substantial, though equity would not intervene where the error was so great as to 'affect the whole foundation and substance of the contract'[6]. Specific performance with compensation was allowed where there was a deficiency of 28 acres out of a total of 217[7], and where a vendor purporting to sell the fee simple was only a life tenant[8]. It was rejected where the amount of the compensation was difficult to assess[9], and where it would have caused great hardship to the vendor to enforce the contract against him[10]. In cases of refusal the purchaser must elect to rescind the contract or submit to its performance on payment of the full price.

(4) An *insubstantial* error which the vendor innocently made did not entitle the purchaser to be relieved of his contract. He had to be content with damages[11]. On the other hand equity would enforce the contract against him, provided the vendor allowed compensation for the deficiency[12].

3.   Contractual restrictions on purchaser's rights

This survey demonstrates the weakness of the vendor's position under the general law. Clauses designed to ameliorate his lot have been in vogue for well over 170 years. Different conditions have been employed over the years. One provision common to many clauses was a term that no error or misdescription was to annul the contract. The Standard Conditions of Sale do not use this language, although, as will be seen, its effect as drafted is to restrict the right of the purchaser to rescind the contract. Sometimes compensation could be

---

5   *Mortlock v Buller* (1804) 10 Ves 292 at 315–16, per Lord Eldon LC. Cf [1981] CLJ 47, 53–54 (C Harpum) arguing that this rationale is not entirely satisfactory.
6   *Re Terry and White's Contract*, ante, at 22, CA, per Lord Esher MR; *Rutherford v Acton-Adams* [1915] AC 866 at 870, PC, per Viscount Haldane (indicating no restrictions other than hardship and (presumably) other general bars applicable to specific performance). Dicta in *Rutherford v Acton-Adams* [1915] AC 866 at 870, PC, per Viscount Haldane (indicating no restrictions other than hardship and (presumably) other general bars applicable to specific performance). Dicta in *Rudd v Lascelles* [1900] 1 Ch 815 at 819, per Farwell J and elsewhere, limiting equitable relief to cases of insubstantial error, appear contrary to principle; see Harpum, op cit, 59ff.
7   *Hill v Buckley* (1811) 17 Ves 394.
8   *Barnes v Wood* (1869) LR 8 Eq 424; *Burrow v Scammell* (1881) 19 Ch D 175.
9   *Rudd v Lascelles*, supra (restrictive covenants), criticised by Harpum, loc cit. It is unlikely that a court today would shrink from the task of assessment in this situation; cf *Wrotham Park Estate Co v Parkside Homes Ltd* [1974] 2 All ER 321.
10   *Earl of Durham v Sir Francis Legard* (1865) 34 Beav 611; *Rudd v Lascelles*, supra.
11   See *Belworth v Hassell* (1815) 4 Camp 140 (contract for sale of unexpired term of eight years, though only seven years seven months remained). A purchaser who wrongfully repudiated because of an insubstantial error would himself now be liable to the vendor in damages: *Le Mesurier v Andrus* (1986) 25 DLR (4th) 424 (deficiency of only 0.16%).
12   *Halsey v Grant* (1806) 13 Ves 73 at 76, per Lord Erskine; *M'Queen v Farquhar* (1805) 11 Ves 467.

claimed for the deficiency, but in its most extreme form, the clause would preclude both rescission and compensation. Strictly speaking the cases, and there are many of them, are essentially decisions on the construction of the particular wording before the court. They do, however, establish general principles relevant to the operation of the conditions which have been in common use. The Standard Conditions of Sale allow for compensation in certain situations, so no attempt will be made in the following discussion to consider the parties' rights under a no-compensation clause.

(a) No annulment of contract

A principal objective of some clauses commonly used in the past was to preclude the purchaser from rescinding the contract, by providing that no error, misstatement or omission in any preliminary answer or in the sale plan or Special Conditions should annul the sale[13]. Nevertheless, despite the unequivocal language of the condition, the courts have steadfastly declined to enforce the provision. The leading authority is *Flight v Booth*[14]. This was a common law action by a purchaser to recover his deposit on account of a misstatement in the contract particulars of restrictive covenants affecting the property. After adverting to the discrepancy between the decided cases, Tindal CJ considered it a safe rule to adopt that:

> …where the misdescription, although not proceeding from fraud, is in a material and substantial point, so far affecting the subject-matter of the contract that it may reasonably be supposed that, but for such misdescription, the purchaser might never have entered into the contract at all, in such case the contract is avoided altogether, and the purchaser is not bound to resort to the clause of compensation. Under such a state of facts, the purchaser may be considered as not having purchased the thing which was really the subject of the sale.[15]

The misdescription was held to be fatal. The purchaser's claim succeeded. He was entitled to rescind the contract and recover his deposit: he was not obliged to accept compensation as provided by the contract. This principle has been consistently acted upon in numerous later cases, the judgments of which are replete with the statement that a substantial misdescription entitles the purchaser to rescind the contract. But in what sense? Attempts to supply a rationale for the rule consistent with general contractual principles have been described as unconvincing[16]. Is the rule to be understood as entitling a purchaser to rescind ab initio, or for breach? The former may perhaps be suggested by expressions such as 'avoided altogether' or by the statement that a material misdescription occasioned by negligence only, not by fraud, would 'vitiate' the whole contract[17]. A substantial but non-fraudulent misdescription

13 NCS (20th edn) 19 LSC (1984) 7. For the less stringently framed SCS see p 642, post.
14 (1834) 1 Bing NC 370. And see *Jones v Edney* (1812) 3 Camp 285 (tied public house described as free).
15 At 377, a negative but pregnant proposition, easy to understand though often difficult to apply: *Re Fawcett and Holmes' Contract* (1889) 42 Ch D 150 at 156–57, CA, per Lord Escher MR.
16 *Beard v Drummoyne Municipal Council* (1969) 71 SRNSW 250 at 264–65, per Walsh JA.
17 Per Tindal CJ, loc cit, language echoed by Lindley LJ in *Re Terry and White's Contract* (1886) 32 Ch D 14 at 29, CA; see also per Lord Esher MR at 22 (contract to be treated 'as if it had never existed').

was to be equated at law with fraud and with like consequences for enforcement of the contract. However, as we have seen, a misdescription results in a breach of contract, and the rule in *Flight v Booth* applies where the purchaser is substantially deprived of the subject-matter of the contract. It should be borne in mind that when *Flight v Booth* was decided, rescission in toto, or ab initio, was regarded as vital in a case of an essential breach of contract[18] if the plaintiff was to be able to recover money paid under it in an action at law for money had and received[19]. This readily explains the language adopted by Tindal CJ[20].

(b) Tests for determining substantiality

For the rule to apply there must be a misdescription 'in a material and substantial point', so far affecting the transaction that the purchaser can be considered 'as not having purchased the thing which was really the subject of the sale'. This is a question of fact and degree. The test appears to be an abstract one, the standard is general, not individual[1]. The court has to consider every incident differentiating the property offered from that actually bought, if the sum of these really alters the subject-matter, the purchaser may rescind[2]. Relevant factors are the magnitude of the discrepancy, and the difference in value between the property as it really is and as it is wrongly described. But value is not the dominant consideration[3]. Indeed the circumstance that the market value of the property is not affected by the error does not necessarily lead to the conclusion that the misdescription is not sufficiently material to attract the rule. Ultimately the question depends on the court's view of the importance of the error. In *Jacobs v Revell*[4] the purchaser was held entitled to rescind when it was discovered that the vendor did not have a good title to approximately one acre out of five. In *Re Fawcett and Holmes' Contract*[5], the

---

18 A heresy which survived well into the 1970s in the case of contracts for the sale of land; see note 3, p 610, ante.

19 For examples see *Hunt v Silk* (1804) 5 East 449; *Blackburn v Smith* (1848) 2 Exch 783; Goff & Jones, *Law of Restitution* (2nd edn), 372. It would follow, therefore, that any contractual no-annulment clause would be treated as falling automatically with the contract: *Re Terry and White's Contract*, supra, per Lindley LJ, loc cit. But this cannot be the position today if a substantial misdescription is viewed as permitting rescission for breach. On what basis ought the courts to continue to uphold no-annulment clauses? Or is the rule in *Flight v Booth*, as some have maintained, an early example of the now discredited doctrine of fundamental breach, whereby the courts declined to give effect to an exemption clause in the face of a fundamental breach: *Yeoman Credit Ltd v Apps* [1962] 2 QB 508 at 523, [1961] 2 All ER 281 at 291, CA, per Harman LJ; *Chitty on Contracts* (25th edn), vol 1, para 1084, suggesting in the light of *Photo Production Ltd v Securicor Transport Ltd* [1980] AC 827, [1980] 1 All ER 556, HL, that the effect of a no-annulment clause might now depend on its construction, rather than on any substantive rule of law. This would permit the court, if it chose, to uphold such a clause allowing compensation, despite a substantial misdescription that would otherwise justify rescission.

20 But it is more difficult to justify the continued use of 'annul' in these no-annulment clauses.

1   *Ridley v Oster* [1939] 1 All ER 618 at 622, per Oliver J, note 16, p 636, ante.

2   See generally *Lee v Rayson* [1917] 1 Ch 613 at 618–19, per Eve J; *Re Fawcett and Holmes' Contract* (1889) 42 Ch D 150 at 157, CA, per Lord Esher MR.

3   *Lee v Rayson*, supra, per Eve J, loc cit.

4   [1900] 2 Ch 858; *Watson v Burton* [1956] 3 All ER 929 (40% over-statement).

5   (1889) 42 Ch D 150, CA; *Flewitt v Walker* (1885) 53 LT 287.

purchaser was held to have got substantially what he bargained for, although 339 square yards of the 1,372 square yards which he had contracted to buy had been sold-off by a previous owner. To describe as leasehold property land held on an underlease is a fatal error, justifying rescission[6]. A material misdescription may arise because the property sold does not possess some important physical attribute which the contract states that it has. Thus rescission was allowed in *Brewer v Brown*[7] when property was described as enclosed by a rustic wall with tradesman's side entrance, but in fact the wall belonged to an adjoining owner and the entrance was used on sufferance.

The purpose to which the purchaser proposes to put the land, if known to the vendor, is also a relevant consideration. In *Re Puckett and Smith's Contract*[8], the existence of the underground culvert was a serious drawback to the use of the land for building purposes, whereas in *Re Brewer and Hankins's Contract*[9], the land was acquired for residential purposes so that the existence of an undisclosed sewer made very little difference and the purchaser was obliged to accept compensation.

(c) Construction of compensation clauses[10]

The common form compensation clause usually conferred on either party a right to claim compensation for the deficiency. An initial question of construction always faced the courts when the claim was disputed. What did the condition cover? A wide variety of different expressions has been used in the past. Sometimes the condition referred simply to an 'error' or to a 'misdescription', sometimes both expressions were used in conjunction. An 'error' includes an omission[11]. Again, the error, etc, might be expressed to be in relation to the property or contained in the particulars, or both. Some examples will illustrate the nature of the problem. An 'error in the description of the property' has been held to cover some mistake about its physical nature, not an error as to the vendor's title to it[12]. In *Re Courcier and Harrold's Contract*[13], the relevant expression was 'any error, mis-statement or omission in the particulars'. The condition was held not to be confined to physical misdescriptions. It covered a mis-statement of the covenants affecting the property, even though these were reproduced not in the particulars strictly so-called, but in a part of the document headed 'Conditions of Sale'. Depending on the wording, the condition might be construed to extend to defects of

6   *Re Beyfus and Master's Contract* (1888) 39 Ch D 110, CA.
7   (1884) 28 Ch D 309; see also *Duke of Norfolk v Worthy* (1808) 1 Camp 337; *Price v Macaulay* (1852) 2 De GM & G 339; *Stanton v Tattersall* (1853) 1 Sm & G 529.
8   [1902] 2 Ch 258, CA, p 636, ante.
9   (1899) 80 LT 127, CA; *Shepherd v Croft* [1911] 1 Ch 521; *Re Belcham and Gawley's Contract* [1930] 1 Ch 56.
10 See (1983) 57 ALJ 93 (P Butt) which, though concentrating on the New South Wales form of contract, contains an excellent analysis of the relevant English cases.
11 *Ashburner v Sewell* [1891] 3 Ch 405 at 409, per Chitty J.
12 *Re Beyfus and Master's Contract*, supra; *Travinto Nominees Pty Ltd v Vlattas* (1973) 129 CLR 1 (sale of land subject to lease; non-disclosure of option to renew in lease).
13 [1923] 1 Ch 565. See p 146, ante.

title. A failure to exclude mines and minerals from the description of the property sold was held in *Re Jackson and Haden's Contract*[14] to constitute 'an … omission in the particulars', entitling the purchaser to take it at a reduced price. But not every defect of title can be classed as an error or misdescription[15].

We must now turn to consider the clause found in the Standard Conditions of Sale.

4.   Standard Conditions of Sale

Condition 7 is in the following terms:

> 7.1.1. If any plan or statement in the contract, or in the negotiations leading up to it, is or was misleading or inaccurate due to an error or omission, the remedies available are as follows.
>
> 7.1.2. When there is a material difference between the description or value of the property as represented and as it is, the injured party is entitled to compensation.
>
> 7.1.3. An error or omission only entitles the injured party to rescind the contract;
> (a) where it results from fraud or recklessness, or
> (b) where he would be obliged, to his prejudice, to transfer or accept property differing substantially (in quantity, quality or tenure) from what the error or omission had led him to expect.

The following discussion is confined to the operation of the clause in relation to contractual misdescriptions, though its scope is wider than this, extending to errors, etc, in negotiations leading up to the formation of the contract.

(a) Rescission
In contrast to its predecessors, the Standard Conditions of Sale do not start from a position prohibiting the purchaser from rescinding the contract. Instead, the circumstances when he can do so are elaborated. A blanket prohibition on the purchaser's right to rescind was, as we have seen, ineffective to prevent rescission by the purchaser where the misdescription was so fundamental as to fall within the rule in *Flight v Booth*[16]. Condition 7.1.3(b) gives effect to this rule.

(b) Compensation
Clause 7.1.2. entitles the injured party to damages in respect of any material difference between the description or value of the property as represented

---

14 [1906] 1 Ch 412, CA; *Ashburner v Sewell*, supra; *Re Belcham and Gawley's Contract* [1930] 1 Ch 56 (non-disclosure of underground sewer).

15 *Phillips v Caldcleugh* (1868) LR 4 QB 159 (non-disclosure of restrictive covenants); *Ex p Riches* (1883) 27 Sol Jo 313, CA; *Debenham v Sawbridge* [1901] 2 Ch 98 (part of house belonging to third party), a decision not easy to reconcile with *Re Jackson and Haden's Contract*, supra.

16 (1834) 1 Bing NC 370, where there was a compensation clause.

and as it is. The clause does not, therefore extend to trivial or minor errors. In such cases, the purchaser must take the property as described. As for small deficiencies in area, it should not be forgotten that words of approximation, such as 'more or less', or 'thereabouts' are commonly introduced into the contract description. Generally speaking, these words cover merely trifling discrepancies[17]. What will be regarded as within the permitted tolerance may well vary according to the location of the property, whether, for instance, it is a suburban house, or a rural property.

Although the purchaser is entitled to compensation in respect of material differences, this does not deprive him of his right to rescind the contract if the error is sufficiently substantial. In such a case, however, he is not bound to rescind. Subject to this point, either party can specifically enforce the contract against the other, making or allowing compensation for the deficiency[18]. Even in the case of a misdescription justifying rescission, the purchaser is entitled to his contractual right to compensation, although the vendor would prefer to return the deposit and retain the land[19]. This contractual right to compensation operates within the general framework of specific performance and subject to the court's discretion to deny equitable remedies in suitable circumstances, eg on the ground of hardship. For the purchaser, it replaces the equitable right which he would otherwise have[20]. The condition does not purport to confer any right to damages or compensation on a *non-completing* purchaser.

An error may fall within the terms of this clause and yet not be sufficiently substantial to justify rescission. In *Re Belcham and Gawley's Contract*, the existence of public sewers running beneath the house did not cause the property to be substantially different from that agreed to be sold; but the vendor's failure to disclose them did materially affect its description, thereby entitling the purchaser to compensation. This contractual right does not merge on completion, and an action may lie in respect of errors not discovered until afterwards[2].

An error, etc, in the contract enables the purchaser to claim compensation. This expression is apt to include the sale plan, and the Special Conditions, which includes the particulars of sale. It therefore covers a misdescription in the physical subject matter as well as defect in the title, such as a failure in the contract to disclose in the particulars some third party right affecting the property[3].

17 *Davis v Shepherd* (1866) 1 Ch App 410 at 418 per LJ; *Winch v Winchester* (1812) 1 Ves & B 375 (deficiency of 5 acres out of 21 within tolerance – an extreme case); *Portman v Mill* (1826) 2 Russ 570; *Belfrage v McNaughton* [1924] VR 441; Butt, op cit, 99.
18 It is debatable whether a court would be willing to order return of the deposit under LPA 1925, s 49(2), p 621, ante, if the purchaser, despite being able to rely on *Flight v Booth* refused to complete and the vendor sues for specific performance or forfeits the deposit on account of the purchaser's breach of contract.
19 *Beard v Drummoyne Municipal Council* [1970] 1 NSWR 432, 71 SRNSW 250.
20 See p 638, ante. On the question whether it is in total derogation of the equitable right, see Butt, op cit, 94.
 1 [1930] 1 Ch 56; *St Pier v Shirley* (1961) 179 EG 837 (failure to exclude cellar vested in adjacent owner).
 2 *Bos v Helsham* (1866) LR 2 Exch 72; *Palmer v Johnson* (1884) 13 QBD 351, CA. The purchaser may have an alternative claim on the covenants for title.
 3 See p 641, ante; *Re Belcham and Gawley's Contract*, supra. Not every title defect will be covered; see *Debenham v Sawbridge* [1901] 2 Ch 98; cf *St Pier v Shirley*, supra.

(i) *Effect of parties' knowledge.* The vendor's knowledge of the error does not necessarily debar his right to seek compensation. The cases[4] suggest, however, that this principle is confined to innocent non-disclosures. Errors or mis-statements made fraudulently or recklessly are expressly excluded by Condition 7.1.3(a). As for the purchaser, the better view appears to be that his knowledge of the error at the time of contract does deprive him of his right to compensation[5]. He should not be in a position to obtain a reduction in the purchase price when his knowledge gave him an opportunity, before entering into the contract, to adjust his offer accordingly.

(ii) *Error to vendor's prejudice.* Compensation is to be allowed by *either* party. This introduces a principle of mutuality and envisages the payment of compensation by the purchaser. Suppose the actual area of the land sold is greater than that stated in the contract. It seems clear that if the purchaser wants the property he is bound by the clause and must pay compensation[6]. But can the vendor enforce the contract, requiring the purchaser to pay for the excess? Little authority exists on this point[7]. Probably the condition will in these circumstances be limited to slight errors, for it is unlikely that a court would order the purchaser to pay a price greatly in excess of the contract figure.

5.   Misrepresentation Act 1967

Clauses regulating a purchaser's rights in respect of misdescription do not fall within s 3 of the Misrepresentation Act 1967[8]. A misdescription is not ordinarily a misrepresentation made before the contract, it actually constitutes a term of the contract. However, in the Standard Conditions of Sale the same clause that deals with misdescription also restricts the purchaser's rights in respect of misrepresentation[9]. Section 3 enacts that a contractual provision which excludes or restricts the liabilities or remedies of the contracting parties for misrepresentation 'shall be of no effect' except to the extent to which it satisfies the test of reasonableness laid down in s 11(1) of the Unfair Contract Terms Act 1977. Prima facie it would seem that s 3 makes the whole clause of no effect, including those provisions relating to misdescription. Nevertheless, it is conceived that the courts could enforce that part relating to misdescription on the basis that it was fair and reasonable. Alternatively they might sever the

4   *Shepherd v Croft* [1911] 1 Ch 521 (failure to reveal underground watercourse), followed in *Re Belcham and Gawley's Contract*, supra.
5   *Cobbett v Locke-King* (1900) 16 TLR 379; *Re Edwards v Daniel Sykes & Co Ltd* (1890) 62 LT 445; contra, *Lett v Randall* (1883) 49 LT 71. Cf the rule on knowledge of an adverse irremovable unincumbrance freehold, p 157, ante.
6   *Leslie v Tompson* (1851) 20 LJ Ch 561 at 562, per Turner V-C.
7   *Leslie v Tompson*, supra (excess and deficiency both compensatable for different lots in same sale); *Price v North* (1837) 2 Y & C Ex 620 (vendor's claim stale); 1 Williams V & P, 728.
8   As substituted by s 8(1) of the Unfair Contract Terms Act 1977. Nor are they subject to the requirement of reasonableness under s 3 of the 1977 Act, which does not extend to any contract relating to the creation or transfer of an interest in land: s 1(2), Sch 1, para 1(b).
9   See p 195, ante, for a discussion of SCS 7 in relation to misrepresentation.

various parts of the Condition, leaving the compensation provisions outside the operation of s 3.

A misrepresentation inducing a contract may in effect become a misdescription if it is later incorporated into the contract as a term. Section 1(a) of the 1967 Act preserves the purchaser's right to rescind for misrepresentation, notwithstanding it has become a term. To the extent that the standard form misdescription clause restricts the purchaser's remedies in relation to an incorporated misrepresentation it is subject to the test of reasonableness. This would become a relevant consideration in a case where in the circumstances the condition operates to limit the purchaser to compensation but denies him the right of rescission. The importance of the matter misrepresented would be a relevant factor in determining whether the clause should be upheld[10].

F   Defective title

It is the vendor's duty to show a good title to the property in accordance with the contract. Failure in this respect constitutes a breach of contract. When the failure goes to the root of the contract then, subject to any express contractual terms, the purchaser is entitled to rescind the contract, recover his deposit with interest and damages for its breach. The vendor's title will be defective where, for example, part of the land sold is vested in a third party[11], or the vendor's lease has been forfeited by the lessor[12]. Similarly, non-disclosure of a latent defect in title, eg a restrictive covenant, renders the title defective[13]. The purchaser's rights may be affected by the terms of the contract. As we have seen Condition 7 of the Standard Conditions of Sale extends to 'omissions'. It therefore covers certain defects in title[14], though the clause will not preclude rescission where the non-disclosure prevents the purchaser getting substantially what he agreed to buy.

1.   Nature of purchaser's right

The purchaser's right to rescind for a fundamental defect in title arises at the latest on the contractual date for completion. He is not obliged to allow the vendor further time to perfect his title. Even though time is not of the essence, he is free to rescind without first serving a notice to complete[15].

10   See generally *Chitty on Contracts*, op cit, para 1804.
11   *Sears Properties Ltd v Salt* (1967) 204 EG 359.
12   *Pips (Leisure Productions) Ltd v Walton* (1980) 43 P & CR 415; *Peyman v Lanjani* [1985] Ch 457, [1984] 3 All ER 703, CA (licence to assign procured by fraud).
13   *Phillips v Caldcleugh* (1868) LR 4 QB 159; *Carlish v Salt* [1906] 1 Ch 335; *Beyfus v Lodge* [1925] Ch 350. For the duty of disclosure, see pp 153–159, ante.
14   Page 643, ante; *Re Belcham and Gawley's Contract* [1930] 1 Ch 56 (underground sewer); cf *Phillips v Caldcleugh*, supra. A non-disclosure may sometimes give rise to a positive misdescription: *Re Puckett and Smith's Contract* [1902] 2 Ch 258, CA, p 636, ante.
15   *James Macara Ltd v Barclay* [1945] KB 148, [1944] 2 All ER 589, CA (third party right preventing vacant possession).

Suppose the purchaser purports to rescind before the agreed completion date. In the oft-quoted words of Sir John Romilly[16]:

> ...when a person sells property which he is neither able to convey nor has the power to compel a conveyance of it from any other person, the purchaser, as soon as he finds that to be the case, may say, 'I will have nothing to do with it'.

Considerable controversy surrounds the true nature of this right. In *Halkett v Earl of Dudley*[17], Parker J expressed the view that it is no more than an equitable right, arising out of want of mutuality, which bars the vendor's claim to specific performance, even if he later succeeds in curing the defect[18]. It is a 'special right arising out of the difficulty of making title to land'[19]. Parker J's statement of principle has been applied in at least two subsequent first instance decisions[20], and was expressly adopted, albeit obiter, by Goff and Buckley LJJ in *Price v Strange*[1]. Despite the purchaser's repudiation in equity the contract remains subsisting at law. Should the vendor subsequently acquire a good title before the contractual completion date, he can recover damages for breach of contract if the purchaser fails to complete[2]. Moreover, as was held in *Procter v Pugh*[3] where the purchaser repudiated the contract on the ground of non-disclosure of restrictive covenants, the vendor is still free to exercise his own contractual right to rescind.

Notwithstanding this weight of authority, the view has been subjected to considerable criticism, notably by Cyprian Williams[4] who maintained that rescission on account of a substantial defect of title was a right enjoyed at law and exercisable even before the agreed completion date. Cases can be cited to support this opinion, the latest being *Pips (Leisure Productions) Ltd v Walton*[5]. However, this view pays insufficient regard to the cardinal rule, stressed by Buckley LJ, that the vendor's obligation at law is to convey a good title when

---

16 *Forrer v Nash* (1865) 35 Beav 167 at 170.
17 [1907] 1 Ch 590 at 596.
18 See *Bellamy v Debenham* [1891] 1 Ch 412, CA (vendor without title to mines).
19 Per Goff LJ in *Price v Strange* [1978] Ch 337 at 355, [1977] 3 All ER 371 at 381, CA, following Harman J in *Elliott and H Elliott (Builders) Ltd v Pierson* [1948] Ch 452 at 455, [1948] 1 All ER 939 at 942.
20 *Procter v Pugh* [1921] 2 Ch 256; *Elliott and H Elliott (Builders) Ltd v Pierson*, supra.
1   Supra, at 355, 364 and 381, 389, respectively.
2   *Halkett v Earl of Dudley* [1907] 1 Ch 590 at 596; *Price v Strange*, supra, at 364, 389, per Buckley LJ; contra *Brewer v Broadwood* (1882) 22 Ch D 105 (purchaser's rescission good defence to vendor's action for damages). Aliter if the defect is not cured until after the contractual date: *Bellamy v Debenham*, supra.
3   [1921] 2 Ch 256.
4   1 V & P, 203–5. Sargant J referred to these criticisms in *Procter v Pugh*, supra, but rejected them without consideration. This prompted Harman J's comment in *Elliott's* case, supra, at 456, 942, that despite Mr Williams' counter-attack the field remained in possession of the judiciary.
5   (1980) 43 P & CR 415 at 424, per Megarry V-C, obiter (the purchaser not rescinding until long after the completion date). See also *Roper v Coombes* (1827) 6 B & C 534; *Weston v Savage* (1879) 10 Ch D 736; *Brewer v Broadwood*, supra; *Re Hucklesby and Atkinson's Contract* (1910) 102 LT 214 at 217, per Eve J. Emmet, para 5.001, regards *Pips* case as correctly stating the law, without adverting at all to the contrary view; cf Farrand, 111–12.

completion becomes due[6]. It should follow that at law a vendor cannot, merely because the title is defective, be treated as in breach until that date has elapsed. It may be that where, notwithstanding a fundamental defect, the vendor insists that the purchaser must take the title disclosed by the abstract and none other, he indicates that he will not make such a title as he is contractually obliged to make. Such conduct, evincing an intention not to perform the contract, would justify the purchaser's rescission at law[7] even before the contractual completion date.

2. Exercise of right

Whatever the true nature of the purchaser's right, he must exercise it categorically and expeditiously. There must be a definite repudiation in unequivocal terms. When he rescinds the purchaser is not inviting the vendor to agree to any course of action, he is exercising a unilateral right[8]. The clearest way of intimating this is for him to say, 'I rescind'. An offer to cancel by consent does not suffice[9]. He must not delay exercising his right, otherwise he will be held to have elected to treat the contract as subsisting. Waiver will be inferred if he calls upon the vendor to perfect his title by getting in outstanding interests or requiring the concurrence of third parties who can complete the title[10]. Registration of the contract as a land charge is sufficient affirmation to bar rescission[11]. The issue of a vendor and purchaser summons, asking for a declaration that a requisition has not been answered and for return of the deposit, is not inconsistent with an allegation that the contract has been rescinded[12]. The purchaser should, however, beware of acting too precipitously. The abstract may disclose a prima facie defect in the title, eg because it is incomplete, but if the purchaser repudiates before giving the vendor a reasonable opportunity of showing there is no defect, he does so at his own risk[13]. Where the purchaser elects to proceed with the contract, it subsists for all purposes. The vendor can obtain specific performance if he subsequently cures the defect[14]. He can exercise the usual contractual right of rescission if the purchaser still persists in his objection to the title[15]. It also follows that

---

6   Note 2; *Stickney v Keeble* [1915] AC 386 at 403, HL, per Lord Atkinson; *Svanosio v McNamara* (1956) 96 CLR 186 at 211.

7   *Re Atkinson and Horsell's Contract* [1912] 2 Ch 1 at 12–13, CA, per Fletcher Moulton LJ. Perhaps cases such as *Weston v Savage* and *Brewer v Broadwood*, supra, may be explained on this basis. See (1977) 41 Conv (NS) 18, 21–22 (C T Emery).

8   *Re Stone and Saville's Contract* [1962] 2 All ER 114 at 121, per Buckley J; affd [1963] 1 All ER 353, CA.

9   *Re Atkinson and Horsell's Contract* [1912] 2 Ch 1, CA; *Re Hailes and Hutchinson's Contract* [1920] 1 Ch 233.

10   *Murrell v Goodyear* (1860) 1 De GF & J 432.

11   *Elliott and H Elliott (Builders) Ltd v Pierson* [1948] Ch 452, [1948] 1 All ER 939.

12   *Re Stone and Saville's Contract* [1963] 1 All ER 353, CA.

13   *Re Hucklesby and Atkinson's Contract* (1910) 102 LT 214 at 217, per Eve J (sub-vendor failing to abstract contract between legal owner and himself).

14   *Salisbury v Hatcher* (1842) 2 Y & C Ch Cas 54. It suffices if title is acquired by the date of the certificate as to title: *Eyston v Simonds* (1842) 1 Y & C Ch Cas 608.

15   *Re Deighton and Harris's Contract* [1898] 1 Ch 458, CA, unless on the facts he is held to have waived his right: *Bowman v Hyland* (1878) 8 Ch D 588 at 590, per Hall V-C.

should the vendor fail to make a good title by the agreed completion date, the purchaser is then entitled to rescind for breach of contract. But once he allows the vendor further time to remove the defect, he cannot later repudiate the contract without first limiting a reasonable time for the title to be made good[16].

G   Failure to complete: rescission for breach

Failure to complete on the *contractual* date may or may not constitute a fundamental breach of contract entitling the injured party to rescind. Where time is of the essence of the contract he may rescind the contract on the very next day if he wishes, and the normal consequences will flow from that rescission. If time is not of the essence he may be able to pursue alternative remedies. For instance, protracted delay by the purchaser may amount to a repudiation of the contract, entitling the vendor to rescind without the need to serve any notice to complete. Since rescission terminates the contract he is at liberty to resell under his own absolute title and to forfeit the deposit; in addition he can claim as damages any deficiency resulting from the resale[17].

In practice most injured parties will prefer to act more expeditiously by exercising a contractual right to make time of the essence by notice. Various aspects relating to notices to complete have already been discussed[18]. Here it is proposed to consider in greater detail the consequences of non-compliance with a valid contractual notice.

1.   Purchaser's failure to comply with contractual notice

In the event of the purchaser's default, the Standard Conditions of Sale[19] provide for (i) forfeiture of the deposit, (ii) resale of the property if the vendor chooses, and (iii) the recovery of damages. The purchaser is required to return any documents he received from the vendor and to cancel any registration of the contract. It is expressly provided that the seller retains his other rights and remedies[20]. Previous editions of standard contracts of sale made provision for the vendor to recover liquidated damages[1]. The effect of this was to put the vendor to his election. He could sell as absolute owner without recourse to the contract and pursue a claim at common law for unliquidated damages for breach[2]. When exercising his contractual right of resale, because the liquidated damages clause referred to the vendor recovering the difference between the contract price and the money actually obtained on the resale, the vendor should seek to obtain a reasonable price for the property as part of his duty to mitigate

---

16   *Murrell v Goodyear*, supra; *Halkett v Earl of Dudley* [1907] 1 Ch 590 at 596, per Parker J.
17   *Howe v Smith* (1884) 27 Ch D 89, CA, p 629, ante.
18   Pages 426–433, ante.
19   SCS 7.5.
20   SCS 7.5.3.
 1   NCS (20th edn) 22(3); LSC (1984 rev) 23(4)(5).

his loss. It would not seem to be necessary to go so far as to impose upon him a duty akin to that of a mortgagee exercising his power of sale[3].

The need for an election to be made meant that if a vendor elected to exercise his remedies under the contract, he could not recover damages additional to those allowed under the respective liquidated damages clause[4]. Under the Standard Conditions of Sale, the vendor is spared the possible dilemma of election. This is because the question of damages is left at large by the relevant condition and all other rights and remedies are expressly preserved. The contractual clause, therefore, provides the basis for a speedy settlement of the vendor's claim.

2. Vendor's failure to comply with notice

The situation where a vendor fails to comply with a notice to complete served by the purchaser is dealt with by Condition 7.6 of the Standard Conditions of Sale. In this circumstance the purchaser may rescind the contract. If he adopts this course, he is entitled to the return of his deposit with accrued interest. He must also return any documents received from the vendor and, at the vendor's expense, secure the cancellation of any registration of the contract. His other rights and remedies remain unaffected, so that he can also, in an appropriate case, sue for damages.

H   Contractual rights of rescission

In the past, a standard condition in formal contracts of sale allowed the vendor to rescind the contract, on favourable terms, if the purchaser insisted upon any objection or requisition which the vendor was unable or unwilling to comply with. No such position exists under an open contract. Although the earliest editions of the Standard Conditions of Sale contained a clause to this effect, the current edition does not. Consequently, unless a Special Condition of Sale is introduced to enable the vendor to rescind in the face of an unwelcome requisition or objection, he will have no such right.

It is, of course, possible that a vendor may introduce such a clause. In the past such clauses as were found in the General Conditions varied in their wording and some of the decisions as to their efficacy depended upon such variations[5]. Some general principles emerged, however, as to when a vendor would not be allowed to rely on his contractual right to rescind the contract and it may be useful to refer to them here, as, although cases on general

---

2   For examples, see *Howe v Smith,* supra; *Harold Wood Brick Co Ltd v Ferris* [1935] 2 KB 198, CA.
3   See *Jampco Pty Ltd v Cameron (No 2)* [1985] 3 NSWLR 391, now following *Bullion Sale International Pty Ltd v Fitzgerald* [1983] Qd R 215 (point conceded).
4   *Talley v Wolsey-Neech* (1978) 38 P & CR 45, CA; *Wallace-Turner v Cole* (1982) 46 P & CR 164; *Sakkas v Donford Ltd* (1982) 46 P & CR 290. Contra *Bruce v Waziri* (1982) 46 P & CR 81, discussed at [1984] Conv 81–83.
5   See 3rd edn, pp 576–578.

conditions, they would seem to be equally applicable if a vendor is given a contractual right to rescind by a Special Condition.

(a) Limitations

The reservation of this right of rescission has been attacked as a violation of one of the first principles of the law of contract[6]. It is often expressed in unqualified terms, yet the courts have consistently refused to countenance any improper use of the power. In *Re Dames and Wood*[7] Lindsay LJ said:

> The power so reserved to the vendor must be exercised with reference to the object with which it was inserted, an object perfectly well known to everybody who has any experience in real property transactions. The vendor cannot say, 'I will not complete and will throw up the contract for sale', he must exercise the power bona fide for the purpose for which it was made part of the contract.

The language used by judges in the cases is not always easy to reconcile, but the underlying principles are now well established. The difficulty often lies in determining whether the facts of a particular case bring it within the limitations imposed by the courts. The vendor's inability to rely on the clause leaves the way open for the purchaser to pursue his remedies. He may seek specific performance with abatement[8], or claim the return of his deposit and damages (if available) on the ground that the title is defective.

The following restrictions on the exercise of the right exist.

(i) *Unreasonable exercise.* It is variously stated that the vendor must not act capriciously or arbitrarily, expressions which mean no more than that he must not act without reasonable cause[9]. He cannot use the power as a device for terminating the contract simply because he has decided not to sell, or has received a higher offer from a third party[10]. The requisition to which he takes umbrage must be one of some substance in the sense that compliance will involve him in considerable expense, or even litigation. In *Re Weston and Thomas' Contract*[11], the vendor's purported rescission, following the purchaser's insistence on the discharge of a contingent liability in respect of succession duty, was held unreasonable because neither difficulty, delay nor expense was involved in assessing and commuting the duty.

(ii) *Recklessness.* Recklessness in entering into the contract precludes the exercise of the right. A vendor is under a duty to his purchaser to satisfy himself before signing the contract that he can convey what he has contracted to sell[12]. In this context 'recklessness' connotes

---

6   Williams, *The Contract of Sale of Land*, xi. See Farrand, 122–124.
7   (1885) 29 Ch D 626 at 634, CA; see also *Selkirk v Romar Investments Ltd* [1963] 3 All ER 994 at 999, PC, per Viscount Radcliffe.
8   As in *Re Jackson and Haden's Contract* [1906] 1 Ch 412, CA, note 14, infra.
9   *Qunion v Horne* [1906] 1 Ch 596 at 604, per Farwell J.
10 *Smith v Wallace* [1895] 1 Ch 385.
11 [1907] 1 Ch 244; *Quinion v Horne* [1906] 1 Ch 596.
12 *Baines v Tweddle* [1959] Ch 679 at 695, [1959] 2 All ER 724 at 732, CA, per Romer LJ.

... an unacceptable indifference to the situation of a purchaser who is allowed to enter into a contract with the expectation of obtaining a title which the vendor has no reasonable anticipation of being able to deliver[13].

Recklessness may exist in the making of some untrue statement of fact about the property, without having any or at the most only insubstantial grounds for believing it is true. Such conduct need not involve any element of fraud or dishonesty. Recklessness was established in *Re Des Reaux and Setchfield's Contract*[14], where the vendor agreed to sell a house knowing of his lack of title but hoping to make it good with the concurrence of the legal owner. More recently in *Baines v Tweddle*[15], a vendor contracted to convey mortgaged property free from incumbrances without first inquiring whether the mortgagees would join in the conveyance to release the land. He was held unable to rescind on learning of their refusal to concur. Similarly, a vendor could not, it is thought, resort to the clause if, being a co-owner, he had agreed to sell on his own without seeking his co-owner's consent[16], or if he (or even his solicitor) was aware of the registration of a Class F charge but had nevertheless entered into the contract without ascertaining that it would be duly released before completion.

A vendor is not denied his right of rescission where he makes an untrue statement under a genuine belief that it is true and there exists some substantial ground for his belief[17]. For instance, if in *Baines v Tweddle*[18] the vendor had, before signing the contract, received some assurance from the mortgagees that they would join in the conveyance and they had later changed their mind, he could have relied on the clause. The court also considered, but did not answer, the interesting question whether the vendor would have been entitled to rescind had he been erroneously informed by his solicitor that the mortgagees would concur. Is he only to be affected by his own personal default, or do the general principles of agency apply? The doctrine of imputed notice is one of general application in a conveyancing context[19]; it is also arguable that as a matter of policy a purchaser should not be prejudiced by the default of the vendor's solicitor. The vendor will normally be able to recover from his solicitor any loss resulting from his inability to rely on a special condition allowing him to rescind.

(iii) *No title.* The case of *Bowman v Hyland* establishes that a vendor who has no title at all to the property cannot shelter behind the normal rescission

13 *Selkirk v Romar Investments Ltd* [1963] 3 All ER 994 at 999, PC, per Viscount Radcliffe.
14 [1926] Ch 178; *Re Jackson and Haden's Contract*, ante (contract description of land sold wide enough to cover minerals to which vendor knew he had no title).
15 [1959] Ch 679, [1959] 2 All ER 724, CA. The relevant rescission clause (LSC (1953 ed) 10 (1)) referred to any requisition as to title, conveyance or otherwise.
16 *Noske v McGinnis* (1932) 47 CLR 563; cf *Watts v Spence* [1976] Ch 165, [1975] 2 All ER 528, but the purchaser's rescission for misrepresentation would preclude reliance on the clause.
17 *Duddell v Simpson* (1866) 2 Ch App 102; *Merrett v Schuster* [1920] 2 Ch 240.
18 See Lord Evershed MR, [1959] Ch 679 at 689–90, [1959] 2 All ER 724 at 728, CA.
19 See *Strover v Harrington* [1988] Ch 390, [1988] 1 All ER 769 (knowledge of misrepresentation imputed).

clause for it is not framed with reference to this particular situation[20]. An objection that the vendor has no title at all is one going to the root of the contract and it has recently been queried whether such objections come within the scope of the condition. In *Baines v Tweddle*[1], Pearce LJ doubted whether the standard condition applied 'where the defect in title is, in view of all the circumstances, so radical and extensive'. This suggests further judicial restrictions on the exercise of his right. However, there is clear authority that provided he can show title to part of the land agreed to be sold, he is not debarred from exercising his right if the purchaser objects that he has no title to the remainder[2].

(iv) *Contract already at an end.*   The vendor may find himself deprived of his contractual right if the purchaser has already validly rescinded the contract on the ground of, for instance, misrepresentation[3]. Recourse by the vendor to the rescission clause becomes impossible once the contract has ceased to exist[4].

2.   Other contractual rights

For contracts governed by the Standard Conditions of Sale the provisions of Condition 7.2 apply in two other situations encountered elsewhere in this book. Provided that the vendor has applied for a landlord's consent to an assignment, or underletting, and has used all reasonable efforts to obtain it, then either party is entitled to rescind the contract if three working days before the completion date, the consent has not been given, or it has been given but subject to a condition to which the purchaser reasonably objects[5]. If the purchaser exercises his right to rescind, he is, under Condition 7.2, entitled to his deposit but to no more.

---

20   (1878) 8 Ch D 588 (contract for sale of freehold; vendor possessing fag-end of long lease expiring after the contract). Where the title is vested in a third party, 'the matter is not one capable of being complied with as between vendor and purchaser': per Hall V-C, at 590.
1   Ante at 69, 734; see also at 687–88 and 727, per Lord Evershed MR.
2   *Heppenstall v Hose* (1884) 51 LT 589 (vendor no title to 1.5 acres out of 5).
3   See *Holliwell v Seacombe* [1906] 1 Ch 426.
4   This will be so whether the purchaser rescinds because of some vitiating factor or for fundamental breach. Cf *Proctor v Pugh* [1921] 2 Ch 256, p 646, ante, where the purchaser's rescission because of a defective title (undisclosed restrictive covenants) was held to operate in equity only and did not debar the vendor's reliance on the rescission clause.
5   SCS 8.3.4.

Chapter 22

Damages

A Introduction

Breach of a contract for the sale or purchase of land gives rise to a right of action at common law for damages. It may take different forms, with varying consequences. Breach of a term which goes to the root of the contract entitles the innocent party to treat himself as discharged from the contract and to recover damages. Alternatively, instead of electing to rescind, he may affirm the contract, in which case he can sue for damages if the other party eventually fails to perform it[1]. Breach of a non-essential term merely gives rise to an action for damages. A repudiatory breach of contract can, of course, be committed before the agreed completion date, as well as afterwards. It may occur beforehand should one party expressly refuse to proceed with the contract; or it may be inferred from conduct as, for instance, where the vendor puts it out of his power to perform the contract by conveying the property to another person. In both situations the innocent party is put to his election. Damages are not confined solely to cases where the contract is not performed. A purchaser may seek damages after completion but, because of the rule that on conveyance the contract and any remedies under it become merged in the conveyance, damages are not normally recoverable after completion. There are exceptions to this rule, and damages may be obtained in the event of:

(i)   a fraudulent misrepresentation inducing the contract, and now by virtue of the Misrepresentation Act 1967, damages may be recoverable in certain circumstances notwithstanding that the misrepresentation is not made fraudulently[2];
(ii) a breach of collateral warranty[3];
(iii) a breach of some contractual term which has not merged in the conveyance[4].

In addition the normal remedy for breach of the statutory covenants for title sounds in damages; covenants for title are considered in Chapter 23.

---

1   The measure of damages will not necessarily be the same as those recoverable on rescission for breach. In practice a party who affirms the contract despite a fundamental breach will normally seek in the first instance to enforce it by specific performance.
2   Section 2(1), (2), p 661, post.
3   See p 180, ante.
4   See p 468, ante.

B   Damages recoverable by vendor

In relation to damages contracts for the sale of land are no different from other contracts; the general common law rule applies. The injured party is entitled to be placed in the same position as if the contract had been performed, so far as money can do this, provided the damage suffered is not too remote. The normal contractual rule formulated in *Hadley v Baxendale*[5] governs the question of remoteness. Only such damages are recoverable as may fairly and reasonably be considered as arising naturally, ie according to the usual course of things, from the breach, or such as may reasonably be supposed to have been within the contemplation of both parties when they made the contract as the probable result of it.

The vendor's damages are measured by the amount of the loss actually sustained. He is not entitled to recover the purchase price as damages, save where the conveyance has been executed and the legal title vested in the purchaser; he cannot have both the land and its value. Consequently he is limited to recovering the difference in value, if any, between the contract price and the value of the property taken usually, but not invariably, at the time of the breach[6]. This later value is determined by the price obtained, or obtainable, on a resale within a reasonable time of the breach, but excluding any inflated price which the property might fetch by nursing it[7]. In assessing damages, credit must be given for any deposit that has been paid[8]. Where the loss is covered by the amount of the deposit a vendor is often content to rescind the contract and forfeit the deposit (which he can also do notwithstanding that he manages to resell at the same or a higher price, so not sustaining any loss). The vendor is not entitled to recover in addition to damages his expenses incurred in connection with the abortive sale (eg legal fees). However, as an alternative to suing for damages for loss of profit, he may elect to claim for wasted expenditure and recovery is not limited to post-contract expenses[9], but he cannot forfeit the deposit and also recover his expenses[10]. Should the vendor resell the property at a lower figure, he can claim the expenses of the resale in addition to the difference in price but again the defaulting purchaser's deposit must be brought into account[11].

To succeed in a claim for damages for non-performance the vendor must show that he can give a good title and that he is ready and willing to complete, otherwise he cannot establish a breach of contract by the purchaser since he himself is unable to perform what is a condition precedent to performance by the other party. Thus in *Noble v Edwardes*[12], a vendor's claim for damages for

---

5   (1854) 9 Exch 341. See further p 656, post.
6   *Laird v Pim* (1841) 7 M & W 474; *Watkins v Watkins* (1849) 12 LTOS 353. As to the appropriate date for assessment, see p 657, post.
7   *Keck v Faber, Jellett and Keeble* (1915) 60 Sol Jo 253.
8   *Ockenden v Henley* (1858) EB & E 485; *Shuttleworth v Clews* [1910] 1 Ch 176.
9   *Anglia Television Ltd v Reed* [1972] 1 QB 60, [1971] 3 All ER 690, CA, p 658, post.
10   In *Essex v Daniell* (1875) LR 10 CP 538 recovery of expenses was allowed apparently on the basis of a contractual provision.
11   *Ockenden v Henley* (1858) EB & E 485.
12   (1877) 5 Ch D 378, CA, especially at 393, per James LJ. But see now the effect of LPA 1925, s 41, p 422, ante; *Stickney v Keeble* [1915] AC 386 at 404, HL, per Lord Atkinson.

failure to complete, time being of the essence, was rejected on the ground that he could not make a good title on the completion date.

C   Damages recoverable by purchaser

1.   The rule in *Bain v Fothergill*

For over two hundred years, there existed a rule, known as the rule in *Bain v Fothergill*[13], which limited the damages available to a purchaser when the vendor's inability to perform the contract was a result of a defect in his title. The rule originated at a time when making title to land was considerably more complex than is the case in modern times and so its survival and continued application came to be a matter of fierce criticism[14]. The Law Commission advocated abolition of the rule[15] and this recommendation was 'to the relief of all and in the interests of justice'[16] implemented by s 3 of the Law of Property (Miscellaneous Provisions) Act 1989 which abolished the rule with respect to contracts entered into after the Act came into force[17]. Consistent with the ethos underlying the repeal of the rule, the condition which was formerly found in standard form contracts of sale, which allowed the vendor to rescind on favourable terms should the purchaser object to the title on grounds that the vendor was unable or unwilling to rectify[18], has also been removed from the current edition of the Standard Conditions of Sale. Unless a Special Condition is included in the contract, restricting the purchaser's rights with regard to damages, the position is now that damages are assessed according to general principles of contract law.

2.   Recovery of substantial damages

When the contract is not completed owing to a defect in the vendor's title, the purchaser is now entitled to damages for loss of bargain. Substantial damages may also be sought by the purchaser where, though the contract is performed, there has been delay in completion[19] or the vendor fails to give vacant possession in accordance with the contract[20]. To succeed in a claim for damages the

---

13   (1874) LR 7 HL 158. Although always referred to by references to this case, the rule itself originated earlier in *Flureau v Thornhill* (1776) 2 Wm Bl, 1078. For a discussion of the ambit and the effect of the rule, see 3rd edn, pp 584–87, (1986) Law Com WP No 98.
14   See (1977) 41 Conv (NS) 341 (A Sydenham) [1983] Conv 435 (C Harpum), (1985) 82 LSG 2402. For lone academic support, see [1978] Conv 338. For judicial condemnation, see, eg, *Sharneyford Supplies Ltd v Edge* [1987] Ch 305, [1987] 1 All ER 588, CA, per Balcombe LJ at 318–19, 594 (impossible to justify), per Kerr LJ at 325, 600 (referring to 'the basic injustice of the rule').
15   (1987) Law Com No 166.
16   *Newbury v Turngiant* (1991) 63 P & CR 458, CA, at 470, per Dillon LJ.
17   For what must surely be the last application of the rule, see *Seven Seas Properties Ltd v Al-Essa* [1989] 1 All ER 164, [1988] 1 WLR 1272, CA.
18   See p 649, ante.
19   *Raineri v Miles* [1981] AC 1050, [1980] 2 All ER 145, HL.
20   *Beard v Porter* [1948] 1 KB 321, [1947] 2 All ER 407, CA, p 659, post.

purchaser must establish his own ability to perform the contract. Strictly speaking he should prove a tender of both the conveyance for execution and the balance of the purchase money. In practice it suffices if the purchaser pleads that he is ready and willing to complete[1].

(a) Measure of damages

The damages recoverable will in the first instance be dependent on the nature of the vendor's breach of contract. Where the contract remains unperformed, the purchaser retains his money but does not obtain the property. The breach entitles him to be placed in the same position, so far as money can do this, as if it had been conveyed to him, subject only to this, that the purchaser is always entitled to the return of his deposit and interest thereon in respect of loss of its use[2]. He can recover damages for loss of bargain, that is, the difference (if any) between the purchase price of the property and its market value assessed at the appropriate date, which may or may not be the date of the breach. A resale of the property at an increased price will be accepted as prima facie evidence of its market value[3].

Loss of the bargain is loss which can be said to result from the vendor's breach of contract in the ordinary course of events; it falls within the first limb of the rule in *Hadley v Baxendale*[4]. Loss of prospective profits to be obtained from developing the property attracts the operation of the second limb of the rule; such additional loss is also recoverable if the damages are:

> ... such as may reasonably have been supposed to have been in the contemplation of both parties, at the time they made the contract, as the probable result of the breach.

In *Cottrill v Steyning and Littlehampton Building Society*[5], the vendor was aware of the purchaser's intention to develop the land, and damages were assessed by reference to the profits which both parties contemplated he would make. On the other hand in *Diamond v Campbell-Jones*[6], the vendor was ignorant of the purchaser's development projects and Buckley J held that the fact that the property was ripe for conversion was insufficient to impute such knowledge to him. It is unlikely that a purchaser will be able to recover anticipated profits on a re-sale of the property, because this will not be in the contemplation of the purchaser[7]. As has been aptly pointed out, when the purchaser intends immediately to resell the property at a profit he is in a 'Catch 22' situation[8]. If

1   *Lovelock v Franklyn* (1846) 8 QB 371.
2   The deposit is an earnest of the performance of the contract to which the innocent party is entitled.
3   *Engell v Fitch* (1869) LR 4 QB 659, Ex Ch.
4   (1854) 9 Exch 341 at 354, p 654, ante.
5   [1966] 2 All ER 295; *Jaques v Millar* (1877) 6 Ch D 153; *Wadsworth v Lydall* [1981] 2 All ER 401, CA (interest charges recoverable); *Cochrane (Decorators) Ltd v Sarabandi* (1983) 133 NLJ 558.
6   [1961] Ch 22, [1960] 1 All ER 583 (damages paid gross since liable to tax on profits of purchaser's business).
7   *Seven Seas Properties Ltd v Al-Essa (No 2)* [1993] 3 All ER 577, [1993] 1 WLR 1083.
8   Emmet, para 7.016.

he tells the vendor of his plan to resell the property then the price he has to pay for it is likely to be negotiated upwards; if he does not, then the loss of profit is unlikely to be recoverable because such a loss was not in the vendor's contemplation when the contract was made.

Damages awarded to a disappointed purchaser are not intended to place him in a better position than if the contract had been performed. Consequently he cannot have in addition to general damages his conveyancing expenses[9], for he would have had to pay these had the property been conveyed to him. Similarly, expenses not yet incurred but which would otherwise have been paid (eg land registration fees) ought also on principle to be deducted from the damages recoverable[10].

(b) Date for assessment of damages

At common law damages for breach of contract, whether claimed by the vendor or purchaser, are assessed as a general rule at the date of the breach. This follows from the basic principle considered on page 654 that damages are compensatory. Nevertheless, a rigid application of this rule is likely to cause severe hardship during times of high inflation, leaving an injured party considerably out of pocket by the time his case comes to trial. The problem is well illustrated by *Wroth v Tyler*[11], where property bought for £6,000 in 1971 was worth £7,700 at the time of the breach (the completion date) and had risen in value to £11,500 by the date of judgment some 15 months later.

The House of Lords has now held in *Johnson v Agnew*[12] that the common law rule is not inflexible. The court has power to fix such other date for assessment as is appropriate to avoid injustice to the innocent party. Depending on the circumstances the date selected may be the date of the hearing[13], the date when the contract is finally lost[14], or some other date. In one case the court moved back the date for valuing the property one year before the judgment date because of the purchaser's tardiness in bringing proceedings to a conclusion[15]. In other situations the appropriate date for calculation will clearly be the date of breach and not any later date, eg where the property decreases in value after a wrongful repudiation[16].

---

9   *Re Daniel's, Daniel v Vassall* [1917] 2 Ch 405. The cases of *Engell v Fitch* (1869) LR 4 QB 659 and *Godwin v Francis* (1870) LR 5 CP 295, where both damages and expenses were awarded (though the purchaser's entitlement to the latter was not disputed) must be regarded as wrongly decided.
10   *Ridley v De Geerts* [1945] 2 All ER 654, CA (stamp duty and other costs not deducted) should be confined to its special facts. The market was active and the purchaser could have re-sold immediately at a profit.
11   [1974] Ch 30, [1973] 1 All ER 897, where the date of hearing, not the date of breach was held to be the proper date for assessing damages awarded in lieu of specific performance. But see note 17, post.
12   [1980] AC 367, [1979] 1 All ER 883, HL.
13   *Forster v Silvermere Golf and Equestrian Centre Ltd* (1981) 42 P & CR 255; *Radford v De Froberville* [1978] 1 All ER 33 (breach of covenant to erect boundary wall).
14   *Johnson v Agnew,* supra, applied in *Domb v Isoz* [1980] Ch 548, [1980] 1 All ER 942, CA.
15   *Malhotra v Choudhury* [1980] Ch 52, [1979] 1 All ER 186, CA; *Hickey v Bruhns* [1977] 2 NZLR 71.
16   *Woodford Estates Ltd v Pollack* (1978) 93 DLR (3d) 350.

It now seems settled that damages awarded in equity in lieu of specific performance are assessed no differently from common law damages[17].

(c) Wasted expenditure

Where the purchaser cannot show he has suffered any loss of bargain, he is entitled to recover as damages[18] the expenditure thrown away by entering into the contract. They are awarded to restore as far as possible the status quo ante. He is not limited to expenditure arising after the contract. According to Lord Denning MR in *Anglia Television Ltd v Reed*[19], expenses preliminary to the contract may be claimed provided they are 'likely to be such as would reasonably be in the contemplation of the parties as likely to be wasted if the contract was broken'. The purchaser can recover his legal fees incurred prior to exchange of contracts[20] and also, seemingly, the cost of having the property surveyed. Other pre-contract expenses which purchasers sometimes imprudently incur, such as the cost of new curtains, carpets, etc, will not normally be recoverable. Nor, as *Lloyd v Stanbury*[1] shows, will a purchaser let into occupation prior to completion be able to claim the cost of improving the property, as distinct from repairs necessary for its preservation. It will not ordinarily be within the parties' contemplation that the buyer will spend money on improvements before the legal title has been conveyed to him. Even when the purchaser has suffered loss of profits, he has an unfettered choice to claim instead for his wasted expenditure[2]. He must, however, elect between them. He cannot recover both.

(d) Duty to mitigate

It should not be forgotten that an aggrieved purchaser is under a duty to take reasonable steps to mitigate his loss. He cannot recover greater damages for the breach than the loss he would have sustained had he acted reasonably to reduce, or even avoid, the loss[3]. What steps are reasonable for this purpose is a question of fact[4]. On the other hand the defaulting vendor is liable for any additional damage suffered, should the innocent party's reasonable steps eventually increase the loss[5]. The duty to mitigate applies equally to a plaintiff vendor seeking damages.

---

17 *Johnson v Agnew*, supra, at 400, 896, per Lord Wilberforce, obiter, not agreeing with contrary suggestions by Megarry J in *Wroth v Tyler*, note 11, ante.
18 What are sometimes termed damages for loss of the purchaser's reliance interest as distinct from his expectation interest (ie loss of bargain).
19 [1972] 1 QB 60 at 64, [1971] 3 All ER 690 at 692, CA (actor repudiating television contract).
20 This was already established in *Wallington v Townsend* [1939] Ch 588, [1939] 2 All ER 225.
 1 [1971] 2 All ER 267. Various items of pre-contract expenditure were held to be recoverable, including the purchaser's loss of earnings.
 2 *Anglia Television Ltd v Reed*, supra; *CCC Films (London) Ltd v Impact Quadrant Films Ltd* [1985] QB 16, [1984] 3 All ER 298.
 3 See *Raineri v Miles* [1979] 3 All ER 763 at 774, CA, per Templeman LJ; affd [1981] AC 1050, [1980] 2 All ER 145, HL. Contrast *Strutt v Whitnell* [1975] 2 All ER 510, CA, p 659, post.
 4 *Payzu Ltd v Saunders* [1919] 2 KB 581, CA (sale of goods).
 5 *Esso Petroleum Co Ltd v Mardon* [1976] QB 801, [1976] 2 All ER 5, CA.

(e) Failure to obtain vacant possession on completion
The vendor's contractual obligation to give vacant possession (where applicable) does not merge with the conveyance[6]. The purchaser is entitled to damages if vacant possession is not given on completion because eg the premises are full of rubbish[7] which substantially interferes with the enjoyment of the right of possession. In *Beard v Porter*[8], the presence of a sitting tenant (who had retracted his promise to quit) prevented the vendor from being able to give vacant possession and the purchaser was obliged to purchase a second house. He was entitled to recover (i) the difference in value between the purchase price and the value of the house subject to the tenancy, (ii) payments made for lodgings, and (iii) solicitors' charges and stamp duty incurred in buying the second house. Similarly, in *Strutt v Whitnell*[9], a purchaser who completed but was denied possession by an occupying tenant was held not to be under any duty to mitigate his loss by accepting the vendor's offer to buy back the house. In both these cases the failure to give vacant possession resulted from a defect in title (the tenancy). Yet substantial damages were recoverable the rule in *Bain v Fothergill* did not apply to a completed contract[10]. Normally the existence of the tenancy would cause the sale to go off, and the purchaser would obtain his conveyancing costs only, provided the vendor had used his best efforts to obtain vacant possession.

(f) Delay in completion
In *Raineri v Miles*[11], the House of Lords held that failure to complete on the contractual date entitled the injured party (whether vendor or purchaser) to damages for delay, assuming loss is suffered, even though time is not of the essence. These may include a sum for loss of earnings[12]. Damages may also be claimed, where appropriate and subject to the duty to mitigate, to cover the cost of a bridging loan obtained to complete a linked transaction[13], or extra legal and removal charges, or hotel accommodation expenses. When the parties are involved in a chain of transactions, eg A-B-C, B is entitled to be indemnified by C against his own liability to A if C's default has caused B to delay completion of the A-B contract[14]. Apparently a claim for damages can be maintained after completion, despite the rule that on completion the contract merges with the conveyance. Such a claim was upheld by Croom-Johnson J in *Phillips v Lamdin*[15],

---

6 Page 469, ante.
7 *Cumberland Consolidated Holdings Ltd v Ireland* [1946] 1 All ER 284, CA. See further in relation to vacant possession, pp 163–166, ante.
8 [1948] 1 KB 321, [1947] 2 All ER 407, CA. The contract provided for vacant possession to be given some four months *after* completion, which is most unusual. Evershed LJ dissented as to item (iii) on the ground that they were expenses forming part of the cost of the second purchase and not flowing from the vendor's breach.
9 [1975] 2 All ER 510, CA.
10 *Lock v Furze* (1866) LR 1 CP 441.
11 [1981] AC 1050, [1980] 2 All ER 145, HL.
12 *Phillips v Lamdin* [1949] 2 KB 33, [1949] 1 All ER 770.
13 *Wadsworth v Lydall* [1981] 2 All ER 401, CA; *Bruce v Waziri* (1982) 46 P & CR 81.
14 *Raineri v Miles*, supra.
15 [1949] 2 KB 33, [1949] 1 All ER 770.

despite counsel's argument to the contrary, but the judge did not seem consciously to be adding to the list of exceptions to the rule. His decision was approved in *Raineri v Miles* where, however, the question of merger did not arise as the purchaser's writ was issued on the day of completion. The safe course is to complete without prejudice to one's rights[16]. Where the Standard Conditions of Sale apply, the innocent party may prefer to pursue a contractual claim for compensation for loss occasioned by the delay[17]. If the delay is occasioned by a defect in the vendor's title, he will be regarded as being the party in default[18] and, consequently, liable to compensate the purchaser, the position prior to the Act being somewhat uncertain[19].

(g) Misrepresentation

(i) *Fraud.*   An action for fraud is an action in tort, not an action for breach of contract. The plaintiff-purchaser is entitled to be put in the same position in which he would have been had the representation *not been made*. He cannot claim to be put in the position he would have been in if the representation were true, ie he cannot recover damages for loss of the bargain (which would be the contractual measure of damages). Prima facie the damages recoverable are the difference between the price paid and the amount which he would have paid had he known the actual circumstances[20], this being taken to represent the actual value of the property at the time of sale. So in a recent case involving a misrepresentation as to the amount of a service charge, the purchaser was entitled to recover damages for the diminution in the value of the flat attributable to the higher charge to which it was subject[1]. A plaintiff is entitled to damages as well as rescission of the contract[2].

The purchaser can recover all non-remote consequential loss, for the vendor is bound to make reparation for all the actual damage directly flowing from the fraud[3]. The damage will be regarded as too remote in any case where the purchaser has not behaved with reasonable prudence[4] or common sense,

---

16   As in *Jones v Gardiner* [1902] 1 Ch 191, which Croom-Johnson J proposed to follow, but in this case completion took place after issue of the writ.

17   SCS 7.3, which does not merge in the conveyance: SCS 4.5.3. See p 468, ante.

18   *Newbury v Turngiant* (1991) 63 P & CR 458 at 470, CA, per Dillon LJ.

19   See [1982] Conv 191 (M P Thompson).

20   *London County Freehold and Leasehold Properties Ltd v Berkeley Property and Investment Co Ltd* [1936] 2 All ER 1039 at 1047–48, CA, per Slesser LJ.

1   *Heinemann v Cooper* (1987) 19 HLR 262, CA (innocent misrepresentation). But see *Jacovides v Constantinou* (1986) Times, 27 October (no evidence that true market price less than what purchaser paid, yet entitled to recover cost of executing works necessary to keep shop open).

2   *Archer v Brown* [1985] QB 401, [1984] 2 All ER 267.

3   *Doyle v Olby (Ironmongers) Ltd* [1969] 2 QB 158 at 167, [1969] 2 All ER 119 at 122, CA, per Lord Denning MR.

4   Cf *Hamer v James* (1886) 2 TLR 852, CA (special damage occuring after discovery of fraud, when plaintiff might have rescinded, not recoverable).

or has been the author of his own misfortune[5]. In *Doyle v Olby (Ironmongers) Ltd*[6], the plaintiff was induced by the defendant's fraud to take an assignment of a leasehold shop and the ironmongery business carried on there, which he continued to run at a loss for three years before being able to sell. He was held entitled to damages for all his loss brought about by that representation[7] based on a comparison of his position before and after it was made to him.

(ii) *Innocent misrepresentation.* The provisions of the Misrepresentation Act 1967 were noted in Chapter 7[8]. The following points are relevant here. The effect of s 2 (1) of the Act is to impose liability in damages for what may loosely be termed a negligent misrepresentation. It imports a fiction of fraud; the representor is made liable if he 'would be liable in damages ... had the misrepresentation been made fraudulently'. One consequence of this is that damages are assessed on the same tortious basis as that outlined in the previous paragraph[9]. Consequently damages for loss of the bargain (the contractual measure) ought not to be recoverable under s 2(1)[10]. As for s 2(2), in the case of a wholly innocent misrepresentation the court is given a discretion 'to declare the contract subsisting and to award damages in lieu of rescission'. The court is given some guidance in determining how to operate this new power; it must be:

> ... equitable to do so, having regard to the nature of the misrepresentation and the loss that would be caused by it if the contract were upheld, as well as to the loss that rescission would cause to the other party.

The court has therefore to balance the competing interests of the vendor and the purchaser. In the exercise of its discretion, the court will have regard to the importance of the misrepresentation, the loss which would be caused by the misrepresentation if the contract is set aside and the loss that would be caused to the misrepresentor if the contract is set aside[11]. The measure of damages, when upholding the contract, is the amount necessary to compensate for loss suffered on account of the property not having been what it was represented to be. It can never exceed the damages which would have been available if the misrepresentation had been a contractual warranty[12].

---

5 *Doyle v Olby (Ironmongers) Ltd* [1969] 2 QB 158 at 168, [1969] 2 All ER 119 at 123, CA, per Winn LJ.
6 Supra. See (1969) 32 MLR 556, discussing difficulties raised by this case.
7 For a detailed breakdown of the assessment of the damages, reference should be made to the judgment of Winn LJ, at 169–70 and 124–25, respectively.
8 See pp 193–195, ante.
9 *F and B Entertainments Ltd v Leisure Enterprises Ltd* (1976) 240 EG 455; *Chesnau v Interhome Ltd* (1983) cited in 134 NLJ Rep 341, CA; *Jacovides v Constantinou,* supra.
10 *Royscot Trust Ltd v Rogerson* [1991] 2 QB 297, [1991] 3 All ER 294, CA, disapproving dicta to the contrary.
11 See *William Sindall plc v Cambridgeshire City Council* [1994] 3 All ER 932, [1994] 1 WLR 1016, CA, at 952–95, 1035–38 per Hoffmann LJ. Had a misrepresentation occurred, rescission would not have been ordered when the loss caused would have been in the region of £18,000 in the context of a contract worth £5 million.
12 Ibid.

Chapter 23

Covenants for title

A Nature and purpose of covenants for title

On completion the transaction between the vendor and purchaser is at an end and can only be re-opened within certain well-defined limits. The finality of the conveyance was explained in *Allen v Richardson*[1] by Malins V-C, in these terms:

> I do not think there is a more important principle than that a purchaser investigating a title must know that when he accepts the title, takes the conveyance, pays his purchase money and is put into possession, there is an end to all as between him and the vendor on that purchase. If it were otherwise, what would be the consequence. A man sells an estate generally because he wants the money; if this were not the rule, he must keep the money at his banker's, and there never would be an end to the question...

A purchaser can never be absolutely sure that he will obtain a perfect title. The possibility of an adverse claim arising after completion may be remote, but it can never be discounted altogether even on the transfer of a registered absolute freehold title. The discovery of such a claim does not entitle the purchaser to recovery of the purchase money, unless there is fraud, or no conveyance of the land has yet been taken[2]. In the absence of any express warranty of ownership given by the vendor (and such warranties are nowadays never encountered in practice), the purchaser's remedy is to sue for breach of the implied covenants for title[3].

On 1 July 1995 the provisions of Part 1 of the Law of Property (Miscellaneous Provisions) Act 1994 came into force. These provisions were the product of recommendations made by the Law Commission[4] and were designed to simplify the law relating to covenants for title. Consequently, in respect of transactions effected after this date[5], the new regime will apply in respect of them. For transactions entered prior to that date, the old rules will continue to apply and so these rules will continue to be relevant for some time to come. It is therefore necessary to have regard to the traditional rules before considering the effect of the new legislation.

---

1 (1879) 13 Ch D 524 at 541; *Clare v Lamb* (1875) LR 10 CP 334 at 338–39, per Grove J.
2 *Early v Garrett* (1829) 9 B & C 928 (fraud); *M'Culloch v Gregory* (1855) 1 K & J 286 (no conveyance).
3 *Clare v Lamb* (1875) LR 10 CP 334; *Soper v Arnold* (1887) 37 Ch D 96 at 101–2, CA, per Cotton LJ; affd (1889) 14 App Cas 429, HL.
4 (1991) Law Com No 199.
5 Transitional provision exist in relation to transactions effected pursuant to a contract entered into before the Act came into force: ibid, s 11.

B   Covenants before 1995

1.   Implication of statutory covenants for title[6]

The origins of covenants for title are bound up with the feudal system. On a grant of land the lord was required to warrant his tenant's title to it. A clause of the Statute De Bigamis 1276 implied a limited warranty from the use of certain words in feoffment, and express warranties became customary after the Statute Quia Emptores 1290. It was during the sixteenth century that covenants for title began to take shape, and in course of time these became increasingly complex. Statutory covenants for title have been implied in conveyances since 1881 by the use of special words. The present position is regulated, in relation to unregistered conveyancing, by the Law of Property Act 1925, s 76 and Sch 2[7]. The appropriate expressions are: 'as beneficial owner', 'as settlor', 'as trustee', 'as mortgagee', 'as personal representative' or 'under an order of the court'. The comprehensiveness of the various covenants differs greatly according to the capacity in which the vendor is expressed to convey, and depends also on whether the land is freehold or leasehold. Where the covenants are given *by* more than one vendor, they are implied 'by each person who conveys', ie they are several covenants, whereas covenants made with more than one covenantee are made *with them jointly*[8].

(a) Conveyance of freehold land by beneficial owner
The widest covenants are implied on the part of a vendor 'who conveys and is expressed to convey as beneficial owner'. Provided the conveyance is for valuable consideration[9], s 76(1)(A) and Part I of Sch 2 imply covenants for:
(i)   good right to convey;
(ii) quiet enjoyment;
(iii) freedom from incumbrances; and
(iv) further assurance.
It is customary to think in terms of four separate and distinct covenants. In reality they are essentially parts of one entire covenant[10]; the section speaks of implying a covenant. Further, the better view is that obligation (iii) does not form an independent covenant but is strictly part of (ii)[11]. These beneficial owner covenants do not constitute an *absolute* warranty of title. They are controlled by the introductory words, which limit the vendor's liability to defects arising since the last transaction for value. This important qualification will be considered in greater detail later in the chapter.

---

6   For a historical review see Holdsworth, *History of English Law*, Vol iii, pp 159–63, 230–1.
7   Replacing with amendments the Conveyancing Act 1881, s 7, which in turn adopted in general terms the standard covenants then in vogue. See generally (1968) 32 Conv (NS) 123 (M J Russell); [1979] Conv 93 (C K Liddle). For registered conveyancng, see pp 678–683, post.
8   LPA 1925, s 76(1).
9   Including marriage but not a nominal consideration in money: LPA 1925, s 205(1)(xxi).
10   *David v Sabin* [1893] 1 Ch 523 at 531, CA, per Lindley MR.
11   This point is elaborated on p 673, post.

(b) Conveyance of freehold land by fiduciary owner[12]
Where a person conveys 'as trustee', 'mortgagee', 'personal representative', or under an order of the court, a single covenant is implied that the grantor has not himself incumbered the land. The implication of this covenant is not dependent on the transaction being for value; it may be implied in an assent by a personal representative. On a sale of settled land, the vendor should convey 'as trustee', for he is a trustee both of the legal estate and in relation to the exercise of the statutory powers[13].

Strictly speaking joint tenants should convey 'as trustees' (not as trustees for sale, an expression sometimes employed by the unwary). However, it is common practice for co-owners who are spouses to convey 'as beneficial owners' if they are the persons entitled in equity[14]. On a conveyance to a sub-purchaser (ie where A contracts to sell to B who contracts to sell to C and A conveys to C, with B joining in the conveyance) it is not uncommon for B (the original purchaser) to convey 'as trustee', but the more usual practice is for both A and B to convey as 'beneficial owner'[15].

(c) Conveyance by way of settlement
The use of the expression 'as settlor' in a conveyance by way of settlement imports a limited covenant for further assurance[16].

(d) Transfer of leasehold land by beneficial owner
On an assignment of an existing leasehold term by a beneficial owner, there are implied the four covenants outlined in paragraph *(a)* above, and by virtue of s 76(1)(B) two additional ones, namely:
(i)   that the lease is valid and subsisting;
(ii) that the rent has been paid and the covenants in the lease duly performed[17]. These six covenants are only implied on an assignment for valuable consideration[18] and never on the grant of a lease, or sub-lease[19]. The mere relationship of landlord and tenant automatically implies a qualified covenant by the lessor for quiet enjoyment[20], and quite frequently the lessor enters into an express covenant. Although a lease may be voidable at the date of the assignment by virtue of the non-performance of the repairing covenant in the

12   LPA 1925, s 76(1)(F); Sch 2, Part VI; p 677, post.
13   SLA 1925, ss 16(1), 107(1).
14   But see p 667, post on the question whether any convenants would be implied in this event. It is not unknown for co-owners, misguidedly, to convey or be asked to convey 'as trustees and as beneficial owners'.
15   See Hallett, 227; cf 19 Ency F & P, 953, Form 7:B:1. It may not always be proper for the vendor (A) to convey 'as beneficial owner', eg where he has already received the purchase money and has delivered possession to B; see (1962) 106 Sol Jo 132.
16   LPA 1925, s 76 (1) (E); Sch 2, Part V.
17   As to the interaction between an assignor's covenants for title under s 76 and the assignee's covenant of indemnity implied by s 77(1)(C) (p 576, ante), see *Middlegate Properties Ltd v Bilbao* (1972) 24 P & CR 329 (breach of repairing covenant).
18   Cf *Johnsey Estates Ltd v Lewis & Manley (Engineering) Ltd* (1987) 284 EG 1240, CA (a decision on s 77(1)(C)), p 576, ante.
19   LPA 1925, s 76(5).
20   *Markham v Paget* [1908] 1 Ch 697.

lease, a purchaser cannot maintain an action against his vendor for breach of covenant (i) above where the defect has been cured by the lessor's subsequent acceptance of rent from the purchaser[1].

(e) Transfer of leasehold land by fiduciary owner

The same covenant as that considered in paragraph (b) is implied. This follows because the word 'conveyance' is wide enough to cover an assignment of leasehold property. The two additional covenants implied by s 76(1)(B) do not apply, but perhaps the fiduciary vendor's limited covenant extends to some acts which would otherwise be within the special leasehold covenants[2].

(f) Mortgage of land

A mortgagor who 'as beneficial owner' demises or charges land by way of mortgage enters into the four beneficial owner covenants, but with this important difference – the covenants are absolute, not qualified; so the covenants are *not* limited, as in the case of a vendor's beneficial owner covenants, to defects arising since the last transaction for value[3]. It will be observed on looking at any building society mortgage that joint mortgagors regularly enter into these covenants even though their technical capacity is that of trustees[4]. Where the property mortgaged is freehold subject to a rentcharge, or leasehold, there is an additional covenant to pay the rent and perform the covenants during the continuance of the security[5].

(g) No covenants for title

The use of one of the specific capacities operates as a kind of magic formula, implying the relevant covenants. If the grantor is not expressed to convey in one of those categories, no covenant is, by virtue of the section, implied in the conveyance[6]. Use of an incorrect expression, such as, trustees for sale, absolute owner, mortgagor, is ineffective to imply any covenants. It is not customary to enter into covenants for title on a voluntary conveyance, or where the vendor only has a possessory title; in this latter case the vendor contracts to convey only such title as he has, if any.

2.   Conveys and is expressed to convey

Section 76 implies the appropriate covenant by a person *'who conveys and is expressed to convey'* in a stated capacity. Do these words require that the vendor must actually possess the capacity in which he is expressed to convey? Much

---

1   *Butler v Mountview Estates Ltd* [1951] 2 KB 563, [1951] 1 All ER 693.
2   See p 678, post.
3   LPA 1925, s 76(1)(C); Sch 2, Part III. See (1979) 123 Sol Jo 71 (M J Russell).
4   Any argument that this might result in an ineffective implication of the covenants (see section 2, below) is usually met by a provision in the mortgage conditions (see p 596, ante) whereby joint borrowers expressly covenant with the society in the terms of Parts III and IV.
5   LPA 1925, s 76(1)(D); Sch 2, Part IV.
6   LPA 1925, s 76(4).

controversy and conflict of opinion, judicial and otherwise, rages around this question. The phraseology adopted by the parliamentary draftsman appears to have been quite deliberate, and in marked contrast to the wording of s 77, where covenants are implied on the part of a person who conveys or is expressed to convey as beneficial owner[7]. Starting with dicta in *Fay v Miller, Wilkins & Co*[8], judicial opinion during the past four decades has certainly favoured an interpretation which requires the vendor to possess the actual capacity in which he is expressed to convey, failing which no covenants are implied. The most recent observations have been made by Megarry J in *Re Robertson's Application*[9], a case concerning a tenant's application to acquire the freehold under the Leasehold Reform Act 1967, which enables the landlord to convey 'as trustee', notwithstanding he is a beneficial owner. After referring to section 10 of the Act, he continued:

> In such a case it may perhaps suffice if in the conveyance the owner is merely expressed to convey 'as trustee'. Yet by the Law of Property Act 1925, section 76(1)(F), the appropriate covenant is implied by the use of this phrase only if the grantor in fact 'conveys' as trustee, as well as being expressed to convey thus: see *Fay v Miller Wilkins & Co*. If he is in fact a beneficial owner it may be said that he will not in fact be conveying as trustee and so the covenant will not be implied merely by expressing that he conveys 'as trustee'. If this is so, the covenant should be imposed by inserting words of covenant in the conveyance[10], and not by merely relying on the statutory implication.

This modern trend of judicial opinion is inconsistent with several pre-1926 decisions which proceed on the basis that the vendor's actual capacity is irrelevant, though the point seems to have been assumed rather than specifically argued. For instance, in *Wise v Whitburn*[11] a breach of the fiduciary owner's limited covenant was held to have occurred when executors, after assenting to the vesting of leasehold property in a life tenant, purported to assign it after her death to a purchaser 'as personal representatives'.

If the modern interpretation is subsequently upheld (for none of the earlier decisions were apparently cited in the more recent cases), it will have unfortunate repercussions. Prior to the Act of 1881, the vendor's actual capacity was irrelevant because he entered into express covenants, so that what was intended simply as a form of statutory shorthand to reduce the length of conveyances has effected a substantive alteration in the law[12]. Furthermore

---

7 Sub-s (1)(B)(ii), (D)(ii). See (1968) 32 Conv (NS) at 124, where the point is made that the three Conveyancing Bills in 1880–81 adopted the formula 'is expressed to convey as beneficial owner'. The words 'conveys and' were only added at the eleventh hour.

8 [1941] Ch 360 at 363, 366, [1941] 2 All ER 18 at 23, 26, CA, per Lord Greene MR, and Clauson LJ respectively. It may well be that this conclusion forms part of the ratio of this case: *Pilkington v Wood* [1953] Ch 770 at 777, [1953] 2 All ER 810 at 813, per Harman J.

9 [1969] 1 All ER 257n at 258. Cf M & W, 160, note 35, maintaining that the actual interest of the vendor should be irrelevant. And see Emmet, 16.04.

10 Megarry J approved a form of conveyance incorporating such a clause which at the worst would be 'mere surplusage' (at 259).

11 [1924] 1 Ch 460. See also *David v Sabin* [1893] 1 Ch 523, CA (life tenant conveying 'as beneficial owner'); *Eastwood v Ashton* [1915] AC 900, HL; *Parker v Judkin* [1931] 1 Ch 475, CA.

12 This is, of course, not unknown. See LPA 1925, s 78, p 571, ante as interpreted by *Smith and Snipes Hall Farm Ltd v River Douglas Catchment Board* [1949] 2 KB 500, [1949] 2 All ER 179, CA.

under this view the covenants afford no protection when it is perhaps most needed, that is where the so-called beneficial owner has previously disposed of his whole estate in the land, in which event he is not even an owner and can convey nothing[13]. Nor yet is it easy to reconcile the strict view with two post-1925 decisions involving an innocent double conveyance of land. In both cases an actionable breach of the covenants was held to have occurred when part of the land included in a conveyance to P1 was later purportedly conveyed to P2 by the common vendor 'as beneficial owner'[14]. Should the conveyance fail to give effect to the contract because the covenant which the vendor contracted to give has not in fact been implied, the purchaser should not overlook the possibility of seeking rectification of the conveyance. This remedy might mitigate the harshness of a strict interpretation of s 76, but remembering the old adage that prevention is better than cure, it is surely preferable to adopt a construction which avoids these difficulties.

The controversy on this point renders it uncertain whether any covenants for title will be implied in a conveyance by co-owners who are expressed to convey 'as beneficial owners' rather than 'as trustees'. The difficulty can be avoided by incorporating in the conveyance a clause to the effect that the same covenants are to be implied as if the vendors were and were expressed to convey 'as beneficial owners'. It is not, apparently, the general practice to adopt this precaution[15].

3.   Variations

By virtue of s 76(7) any implied covenant may be varied or extended with the like incidents, effects and consequences as if such variation were directed to be implied by the section. The need for some suitable variation is vital on the sale by a beneficial owner of leasehold property which, in breach of covenant, is in a state of disrepair. His implied covenant is in the nature of a warranty that the covenants have been duly performed and he thus renders himself liable to the purchaser, even though the latter is aware of the breach of covenant[16]. Limitation of the vendor's covenant for title in this situation is now expressly provided for by the Standard Conditions of Sale[17]. Likewise the vendor is entitled to limit the scope of his covenant if the purchaser has agreed to take the property as it stands[18]. Where the conveyance fails to give effect to

---

13   (1882) 2 LQR 511.
14   *Conodate Investments Ltd v Bentley Quarry Engineering Co Ltd* (1970) 216 EG 1407; *Jackson v Bishop* (1979) 48 P & CR 57, CA. These decisions are in line with *Eastwood v Ashton* [1915] AC 900, HL, p 672, post.
15   See eg 19 Ency F & P, 967, Form 7:C:3, containing no such clause.
16   *Butler v Mountview Estates Ltd* [1951] 2 KB 563, [1951] 1 All ER 693.
17   SCS 3.2.2. This modifies the full title guarantee to which the purchaser is entitled under SCS 4.5.2: see ibid, 4.5.3 producing a similar effect to that which existed under the old conditions of sale: NCS 11(7); LSC 8(5) which operates notwithstanding the vendor expressly contracts to convey as 'beneficial owner'. This negatives the argument that in such a case the condition does not apply. See (1974) 38 Conv (NS) 312.
18   *Michelin Tyre Co Ltd v Adlington* (1952) 161 EG 5.

some contractual variation of the normal covenant for title, a claim for rectification of the conveyance will lie[19].

C   Enforceability of covenants

1.   Burden

Even the covenant for title given by a vendor conveying 'as beneficial owner' does not constitute an absolute warranty of title. He assumes liability for the acts or omissions of himself and of certain other people for whom he is made responsible. According to Lindley LJ in the leading case of *David v Sabin*[20], this liability extends to the acts or omissions of:

(i)   the vendor himself;

(ii) any person through whom he claims otherwise than for value (and for this purpose 'value' does not include marriage[1]);

(iii) any person claiming by, through or under the vendor, or some person within (ii);

(iv) any person claiming in trust for the vendor. Groups (ii) and (iii) require further explanation.

(a) Liability for predecessors
A vendor conveying 'as beneficial owner' is not rendered liable for the acts or omissions of any person from whom he purchased the land for value. In his judgment Lindley LJ explained the position in the following terms:

> The covenant by a vendor in fee is not understood as extending to acts done previously to the last preceding sale. On each sale the title is investigated, and conveyancers are content with a series of covenants for title each of which covers the time which has elapsed since the last conveyance from a vendor in fee.

Suppose A conveys land to B who later conveys it to C, the conveyances being for value and both vendors conveying 'as beneficial owner'. The burden of A's covenant does not pass to B. Moreover, B is not liable on his own covenants given to C in respect of any incumbrance created by A which causes disturbance to C, since B derives title through A by virtue of a purchase for value. This is not to say that C has no remedy. It will be seen that the *benefit* of A's covenant implied in the A-B conveyance passes to C, enabling C to sue A. C may also be able to sue B in respect of an incumbrance which, though created by A, prevents B from fulfilling his contractual duty to give vacant possession on completion. It will be recalled that this term is not subject to the doctrine of merger[2].

Under his covenant B is made liable for the acts or omissions of a person through whom he derives title *otherwise than by purchase for value*. If in the above

---

19   *Stait v Fenner* [1912] 2 Ch 504; *Butler v Mountview Estates Ltd,* supra.
20   [1893] 1 Ch 523 at 532 et seq, CA.
 1   See LPA 1925, Sch 2 Part I. Cf note 9, p 663, ante.
 2   Page 469, ante. C may also be entitled to claim compensation under a misdescription clause (eg SCS 7.1.3) in the B–C contract, which also survives completion, unless the contrary is stated: *Palmer v Johnson* (1884) 13 QBD 351, CA. See further, pp 642–643, ante.

illustration A had devised the property to B, B would be liable for any incumbrance created by A. If this were not so, C would be without remedy; no action could be maintained against A's estate because A, having died, has not entered into any covenant. B would similarly be liable if he had acquired the land from A by way of gift or marriage settlement.

(b) Liability for persons deriving title under him
A covenantor is liable for the acts or omissions of persons claiming from him a *derivative* interest, such as his lessee, or mortgagee. In *David v Sabin*:

> A leased land to B who mortgaged the land to M by demise. B surrendered his lease to A for value without disclosing the mortgage to M, which remained unaffected by the surrender. Later A conveyed the land to B in fee 'as beneficial owner', and B conveyed to C. *Held*: the creation of the mortgage term by B was an incumbrance 'made by a person rightfully claiming through' A within the covenant for quiet enjoyment and freedom from incumbrances and A was liable to C in damages[3].

It should be noted that the covenantor is not liable for the acts of his *successors in title*. Thus had A originally conveyed (and not merely leased) the land to B who had created the mortgage term, and B had then conveyed to C without disclosing the mortgage, A would not have been liable to C for the incumbrance created by B. B would be liable for his own act.

2. Benefit

The benefit of the implied covenant is annexed and incident to, and passes with, the estate of the implied covenantee[4]. If A conveys land to B, and then B to C, C obtains the benefit of any covenant which A gave B, and C can enforce the covenant against A. A purchaser may, therefore, receive the benefit of a chain of covenants for title which previous vendors entered into at the time of their respective conveyances. In theory this affords partial relief against the principle, already noted, that covenants for title do not constitute an absolute warranty of title. Yet in practice the protection afforded by this chain of covenants is rather illusory. Previous vendors in the chain may have died[5], or merely given a fiduciary owner covenant, or the right of action may be time barred because more than 12 years have elapsed since the date of their respective conveyances. In effect the purchaser may be restricted to an action on the covenant given by his own vendor, which may not afford any redress. The benefit of the covenant is enforceable by every person in whom the covenantee's estate is, for the whole or any part thereof, from time to time vested. Therefore on a sub-division of land, a purchaser of part obtains the benefit of the covenant given by the vendor of the entirety.

---

3 There was also a breach of A's covenant for good right to convey; the grant of B's lease, which was still outstanding for M's benefit, was an act done by A within that covenant.
4 LPA 1925, s 76(6).
5 Cf *Butler v Broadhead* [1975] Ch 97, [1974] 2 All ER 401 (innocent double conveyance; purchaser unable to recover from vendor company after its dissolution).

(a) Mortgages

A mortgagee does not, it seems, receive the benefit of covenants implied on the occasion of previous transactions affecting the land. Suppose V 'as beneficial owner' conveys land to P who mortgages it to M. Since the mortgage takes effect as a demise, M cannot take the benefit of V's implied covenant with P. There is nothing in s 76(6), which in this respect merely confirms the common law rule, to extend the benefit of covenants for title to persons deriving title under the covenantee, such as his lessee or mortgagee, as distinct from successors in title to his estate. M's inability to sue V (or any earlier covenantor) would not seem to be unduly prejudicial (save where the mortgagor's covenant is worthless on account of his insolvency). The covenant for title given by P to M is *absolute*[6] with the result that P assumes responsibility for the acts and omissions of his predecessors, including those through whom he claims by purchase for value. It is not thought that the benefit of V's covenant will pass to M under the Law of Property Act 1925, s 78(1)[7].

It is generally assumed that on a conveyance of land by a mortgagee in exercise of his power of sale, the purchaser obtains the benefit of the mortgagor's absolute covenant. Though strictly speaking the purchaser obtains a larger interest than the mortgagee possessed, the conveyance by the latter operates to convey the estate in like manner as if it had been executed by the mortgagor[8]. This would appear sufficient to entitle the purchaser to the benefit of the mortgagor's covenant with the mortgagee.

(b) Burden of proof

Some limitations on the effectiveness of a chain of covenants have already been noted. There is a further hurdle to bar the progress of a purchaser seeking to enforce a covenant for title – the burden of proof. Thus in the illustration on page 669, C may have the benefit of covenants given by A and B, but the onus is on him to establish whether it is A, or B, who is liable, a task that may be well nigh impossible if the origin of the adverse claim is uncertain[9].

D   Particular covenants

1.   Good right to convey

The first section of the covenant implied in a conveyance for valuable consideration by a person who conveys and is expressed to convey as beneficial owner, reads as follows:

---

6   Page 665, ante.
7   See (1979) 123 Sol Jo 71 (M J Russell); contra, Farrand, 274f. The point is more fully discussed in the second edition of this book; see pp 625–6. See generally (1961) 28 Conv (NS) 205 (A M Prichard).
8   LPA 1925, ss 9(1)(e), 88 (1); see 2 Williams V & P, 1076.
9   *Stoney v Eastbourne RDC* [1927] 1 Ch 367, CA (no evidence when right of way dedicated to public). The potential liability on covenants is well illustrated by this case in that the property had been in the vendor's family from 1782.

That, notwithstanding anything by the person who so conveys or any one through whom he derives title otherwise than by purchase for value, made, done, executed, or omitted, or knowingly suffered, the person who so conveys has full power to convey the subject-matter expressed to be conveyed, subject as, if so expressed, and in the matter in which, it is expressed to be conveyed ...

This covenant is commonly called a covenant for title. This is somewhat misleading. Because of the opening qualification 'notwithstanding that ...'[10], the vendor does not warrant that he actually has any title. The covenant constitutes an assurance that neither the vendor nor any person for whom he is responsible has done or omitted to do any act which will prevent the purchaser acquiring 'the subject-matter expressed to be conveyed'. Herein lies one justification for the continued use of technical words of limitation. A conveyance of land to a purchaser to hold 'in fee simple' signifies that it purports to deal with a fee simple estate. In the absence of such words there passes the fee simple or other the whole interest which the vendor has power to convey[11]. In other words the 'subject-matter expressed to be conveyed' is such interest as he actually has, if any. If he has no title, the purchaser cannot sue on the covenant for the simple reason that the vendor has not covenanted that he has any title. Nor can the purchaser sue in respect of any defect or incumbrance subject to which the property is expressed to be conveyed, these for obvious reasons being outside the scope of the covenant. Where the property is not expressed in the conveyance to be conveyed subject to a specific defect or incumbrance, a purchaser is not debarred from suing on the covenant in respect thereof merely because he has knowledge of it, even if the defect appears on the face of the conveyance itself[12]. The purchaser is entitled to a conveyance expressed to be subject only to such incumbrances as are mentioned in the contract[13]. However, should the conveyance fail to convey the property subject to some incumbrance specifically referred to in the contract as affecting the property, the exercise by the incumbrancer of his rights does not amount to a breach of the implied covenant[14].

(a) Breach of covenant
A breach of the covenant occurs if the land conveyed remains subject to any outstanding estate, interest, mortgage, charge or claim, to which the

---

10 A curious formula: per Oliver LJ in *Meek v Clarke* [1982] CA Transcript 312. The word 'notwithstanding' is used in the sense of 'to the extent of': ibid, citing M & W (4th edn), 608, note 88. The various points made in this chapter relating to this case are taken from the Lexis transcript.
11 See LPA 1925, s 60(1), p 557, ante.
12 *Page v Midland Rly Co* [1894] 1 Ch 11, CA (defect disclosed by recital); *Great Western Rly Co v Fisher* [1905] 1 Ch 316.
13 *Re Wallis and Barnard's Contract* [1899] 2 Ch 515.
14 *Celsteel Ltd v Alton House Holdings Ltd (No 2)* [1986] 1 All ER 598 at 607, per Scott J, obiter (a case concerning a lessor's express covenant for quiet enjoyment); affd without reference to this point [1987] 2 All ER 240, CA. In any event rectification of the conveyance would prima facie be available to the vendor.

conveyance is not expressly made subject such as an undisclosed right of way[15], or other easement. The vendor is liable if he has previously conveyed or leased part of the land which he subsequently purports to convey to the purchaser[16]. The covenant also extends to 'omissions'. In *Eastwood v Ashton*[17]:

> V conveyed land to P. At the date of the conveyance an adverse title to a strip of land had been acquired by adjoining owners. V's failure to prevent acquisition of this adverse title constituted an omission within the covenant, for which he was liable.

But a vendor is not guilty of an omission within the covenant because he fails to perfect his title by getting in some incumbrance which was created by a previous vendor and of which he is unaware[18]. As previously mentioned the onus of proof lies on the covenantee. He must establish that the act or omission creating the defect is that of the vendor (or of someone for whom he is responsible). If, therefore, it is uncertain when adverse possession first commenced, or when a right of way became dedicated to the public[19], the plaintiff's claim will fail. He cannot show that his vendor is in breach.

There is no breach of the covenant where the purchaser is evicted by a *title paramount*. This is a vital qualification. The covenant is not a complete warranty that the vendor has a title, rather that he has done no act to affect or derogate from his title[20]. As Lord Eldon once explained, the vendor is to be taken as selling his land in the plight that he received it and not in any degree made worse by him[1]. A purchaser cannot, therefore, sue his vendor on the covenant if the vendor's interest ceased before completion (otherwise than as a result of his own act or default)[2], or even if he never had any title at all. Thus a vendor will incur no liability under the statutory covenants where the conveyance includes land which never belonged to him or his predecessors in title but is vested in an adjacent owner under an independent title, or land wrongfully occupied by the vendor and in respect of which no title has been acquired by adverse possession. Notwithstanding that the purchaser is evicted by the legal owner, he cannot point to any act or omission whereby the vendor was prevented from having full power to convey the land expressed to be conveyed.

A purchaser will not necessarily be without remedy in situations such as these. If the vendor knows he has no title, the purchaser may be entitled to

---

15   *Turner v Moon* [1901] 2 Ch 825; *David v Sabin* [1893] 1 Ch 523, CA (outstanding mortgage); 2 Williams V & P, 1078.

16   *May v Platt* [1900] 1 Ch 616; *Jackson v Bishop* (1979) 48 P & CR 57, CA (double conveyance); *A J Dunning & Sons (Shopfitters) Ltd v Sykes & Son (Poole) Ltd* [1987] Ch 287, [1987] 1 All ER 700, CA (registered land transfer including small plot not within title).

17   [1915] AC 900, HL.

18   *David v Sabin* [1893] 1 Ch 523 at 529, CA, per Romer J; at 534, per Lindley LJ, CA. Otherwise the covenant would become an unrestricted warranty of title.

19   *Stoney v Eastbourne RDC* [1927] 1 Ch 367, CA. Difficult problems arise where the defect is an easement acquired by prescription; see Prichard, op cit, p 206, note 6.

20   *Thacheray v Wood* (1865) 6 B & S 766, at 773, per Erle CJ.

1   *Browning v Wright* (1799) 2 Bos & P 13 at 22.

2   *Stannard v Forbes* (1837) 6 Ad & El 572 (assignment of leasehold term known by vendor to have determined on death of third party).

have the conveyance set aside for fraud[3]; alternatively damages may be recovered in deceit or for misrepresentation[4]. Additionally an action for damages may lie for breach of a duty to prepare an accurate contract plan used as the deed plan annexed to the conveyance[5]. Moreover, where a vendor with no title purports to convey land to a purchaser, equity will compel him to make good his contract with the purchaser if he later acquires title to the land[6]. He cannot plead that the contract has been discharged by performance, because the conveyance is defective.

(b) Limitation

Breach of this covenant occurs and is complete at the time of execution of the conveyance[7]. It is not a continuing breach. Time begins to run in the covenantor's favour as from that date, not from the time when the covenantee first learns of the breach.

(c) Measure of damages

The measure of damages, assessed as at the date of the conveyance, is the difference between the value of the property as purported to be conveyed and its value as the vendor had power to convey it[8]. In the absence of evidence to the contrary, the price actually paid is taken to be the value as purported to be conveyed. Thus, depending on particular circumstances, the purchaser can recover money paid to a third party in order to enjoy the land in the actual state in which he was entitled by the contract to enjoy it[9], or the amount by which the adverse interest diminishes the value of the property, or even the full purchase price if he suffers total eviction[10]. Though there is an absence of authority on the point, the costs of subsequent improvements to the property do not seem recoverable on a breach of the covenant for good right to convey[11].

2. Quiet enjoyment free from incumbrances

This part of the covenant reads:

> ...and that, notwithstanding anything as aforesaid, the subject-matter shall remain to and be quietly entered upon, received and held, occupied, enjoyed, and taken, by the person to whom the conveyance is expressed to be made, and any person

---

3 See p 687, post.
4 Cf *Errington v Martell-Wilson* (1980) 130 NLJ 545, p 142, ante. But see also p 660, ante.
5 *Jackson v Bishop* (1979) 48 P & CR 57, CA (estate development plan).
6 *Re Bridgwater's Settlement, Partridge v Ward* [1910] 2 Ch 342.
7 *Turner v Moon* [1901] 2 Ch 825. Cf Kelly CB's dissenting judgment in *Spoor v Green* (1874) LR 9 Exch 99 at 116.
8 *Turner v Moon* [1901] 2 Ch 825.
9 *Great Western Rly Co v Fisher* [1905] 1 Ch 316 (compensation paid for blocking up right of way).
10 *Jenkins v Jones* (1882) 9 QBD 128, CA.
11 2 Dart, 676; 2 Williams V & P, 1090. But see p 675, post, and compare the position under the Sale of Goods Act 1979, ss 12, 53(2): *Mason v Burningham* [1949] 2 KB 545, [1949] 2 All ER 134, CA (cost of overhauling stolen typewriter recoverable).

deriving title under him, and the benefit thereof shall be received and taken accordingly, without any lawful interruption or disturbance by the person who so conveys ...

And that, freed and discharged from, or otherwise by the person who so conveys sufficiently indemnified against, all such estates, incumbrances, claims and demands, other than those subject to which the conveyance is expressly made, as, either before or after the date of the conveyance, have been or shall be made, occasioned, or suffered by that person ...

This is a covenant against disturbance and for indemnity in that event. The words 'And that, freed and discharged from' are sometimes interpreted as creating a separate covenant that the estate is free from incumbrances[12]. The better view[13] may be that both parts constitute a single obligation. The vendor covenants that the land will be quietly enjoyed free from incumbrances and, in effect, he undertakes to indemnify the purchaser in the event of his enjoyment being disturbed by the enforcement of some incumbrance. In addition to assuming responsibility for the acts of predecessors in title through whom he claims otherwise than by purchase for value, the covenantor is liable for lawful disturbance caused by a person claiming through[14], under or in trust for him. He is not responsible for unauthorised wrongful or negligent acts of persons claiming under him[15]. Again it will be noticed that the covenantee cannot complain of any disturbance, claim or demand resulting from an incumbrance subject to which the conveyance is expressly made. No action lies where the liability is imposed, not as a result of the vendor's conduct, but by statute or under the common law[16]. As with the previous covenant, no protection is afforded in cases of disturbance by title paramount.

(a) Breach of the covenant

The covenantee must prove that he has actually been disturbed in his possession, or his enjoyment interrupted by the enforcement of some adverse claim. The mere existence of some incumbrance effects no breach of this covenant, though it may give rise to liability under the covenant for good right to convey. In *Howard v Maitland*[17], it was held that a court decree declaring that land in Epping Forest, including land previously conveyed by the defendant to the plaintiff, was subject to a general right of common was not actionable

12   See eg Joyce J in *Turner v Moon* [1901] 2 Ch 825 at 828. So to interpret this part of the covenant is to add little, if anything, to the covenant for good right to convey.
13   2 Williams V & P, 1080, Farrand, 265, Williams, *Title*, 755, [1979] Conv 93 (C K Liddle); contra (1970) 34 Conv (NS) 178, 187 (M J Russell), recent support for which can be found in Oliver LJ's judgment in *Meek v Clarke* [1982] CA Transcript 312.
14   This is limited to persons with a derivative title only, p 669, ante. See *Celsteel Ltd v Alton House Holdings Ltd (No 2)* [1987] 2 All ER 240, CA (lessor not liable on express covenant for quiet enjoyment for exercise of adverse rights by persons deriving title under his predecessor). And see the next note.
15   See *Williams v Gabriel* [1906] 1 KB 155 (a landlord and tenant case). The covenant for quiet enjoyment given by a vendor is very similar to that implied on the grant of a lease.
16   *Chivers & Sons Ltd v Air Ministry* [1955] Ch 585, [1955] 2 All ER 607 (liability to repair church chancel).
17   (1883) 11 QBD 695, CA.

because there had been no entry on the land nor any disturbance of the plaintiff's possession. A breach of the covenant is established on proof of the existence of some adverse right of way, a threat of eviction by some person to whom the vendor conveyed the land prior to its purported conveyance to the plaintiff[18], a decree or judgment against the purchaser recognising the existence of some third party claim[19], or the discharge by the purchaser of some mortgage or charge affecting the land, such as street works expenses operating as a charge on land[20]. Service of an enforcement notice on the purchaser consequent upon a contravention of the town planning legislation by the vendor may, perhaps, constitute a 'claim or demand' occasioned by the vendor so as to render him liable for breach of the implied statutory covenant[1].

The covenant for quiet enjoyment cannot enlarge the scope of the conveyance to the purchaser. He cannot complain that acts lawfully done by the vendor on his adjoining land amount to a breach of the covenant merely because such acts cause him inconvenience, without affecting his title or possession to the land. This rule applies whether the adjoining land was owned by the vendor at the time of the conveyance or acquired subsequently, except that in the former case the vendor may be liable, not upon the covenant, but upon the principle of non-derogation from grant[2].

(b) Measure of damages

This covenant is broken when the purchaser's quiet enjoyment is actually disturbed. For the purposes of the Limitation Act 1980, time begins to run from the occasion of the breach and, the covenant being a continuing one, a fresh cause of action accrues on every disturbance. The measure of damages is also referable to the date of the breach. It follows that where the interruption takes the form of eviction, the covenantee can recover the value of the property at the date of the breach, including any increase in value since conveyance due to a general rise in land prices. In *Bunny v Hopkinson*[3], where land was, to the vendor's knowledge, bought for building purposes, the purchaser recovered the cost of erecting the houses. However, the decision in *Rolph v Crouch*[4] suggests that the value of improvements is recoverable, though not within the vendor's contemplation. The covenantee can recover any loss which is the natural consequence of the breach, such as expenses involved in moving into other

---

18 *Conodate Investments Ltd v Bailey Quarry Engineering Co Ltd* (1970) 216 EG 1407.
19 *Howard v Maitland* (1883) 11 QBD 695 at 700, CA, per Brett MR. The vendor was not a party to the suit in Chancery establishing the right of common.
20 *Stock v Meakin* [1900] 1 Ch 683, CA. Usually the contract will regulate the parties' rights as to the discharge of charges in favour of a local authority; see NCS 16; LSC 3.
1 Emmet, para 14.009, but subject to the terms of the contract.
2 See *Davis v Town Properties Investment Corpn Ltd* [1903] 1 Ch 797, CA; *Harmer v Jumbil (Nigeria) Tin Areas Ltd* [1921] 1 Ch 200, CA (both landlord-tenant cases). See generally [1978] Conv 418 (M J Russell).
3 (1859) 27 Beav 565.
4 (1867) LR 3 Exch 44 (cost of conservatory recovered by tenant suing on covenant for quiet enjoyment in lease). Since the benefit of the covenant passes to the covenantee's successors in title, it would be improper to limit the damages to those recoverable under the normal contractual rule.

premises, or the cost of defending an action brought against him by an adverse claimant, provided he notifies the covenantor of the action to obtain his instructions as to the course to be adopted[5].

Where there is no eviction but, for example, the interruption takes the form of the exercise of a right of way, the Court of Appeal held in *Child v Stenning*[6] that the measure of damages is not the permanent injury to the land[7] but only the damage actually sustained at the commencement of the action. The court refused to accept as evidence of damage the diminution in the value of the land for building purposes. Subsequent cases have not always adhered to this principle. In *Sutton v Baillie*[8], Cave J awarded damages to a purchaser for depreciation in the value of the land by reason of the existence of rights of way. In *Turner v Moon*[9], Joyce J reached a similar decision in effect; but since the learned judge equated the covenant for freedom from incumbrances with that for good right to convey, rather than treating it as part of the covenant for quiet enjoyment, the correctness of his decision on this point may be doubted. Nevertheless, it would seem preferable to allow the recovery of permanent injury, including diminution in the value of the land, if such injury can be shown to have been suffered at the time the writ is served.

3.   Further assurance[10]

This covenant imposes on the vendor an obligation to 'execute and do all such lawful assurances and things for further or more perfectly assuring the subject matter of the conveyance' to the grantee, provided the outstanding estate is vested in him, or in some person for whom he assumed responsibility. If V conveys to P a plot of land to which V has no title, but subsequently he acquires title thereto, whether for value or not, P can call upon V to convey it to him[11]. The cost of the deed of further assurance must be borne by P, but this apart he cannot be required to compensate V in any way. If V refuses to execute the necessary deed, P can sue for specific performance. The covenant can be enforced against V's trustee in bankruptcy[12], or his successors in title, including a purchaser with notice of the covenant[13]. The purchaser can enforce the covenant notwithstanding that the legal title may have automatically vested in him under the doctrine of estoppel[14]. Indeed a conveyance from the vendor is highly desirable in order to perfect the paper title.

5   *Rolph v Crouch* (1867) LR 3 Exch 44. See generally, 2 Williams V & P, 1089–91.
6   (1879) 11 Ch D 82, CA (action for breach of covenant for quiet enjoyment in lease).
7   This could not be ascertained since it was uncertain to what extent, if at all, the incumbrancer might choose to exercise his right in the future: per Jessel MR, at 85.
8   (1891) 65 LT 528. See on the relevant cases *McGregor on Damages* (14th edn), para 773.
9   [1901] 2 Ch 825, especially at 829; see p 673, ante.
10   See [1985] Conv 398 (M J Russell).
11   Equity will compel execution of a conveyance in the absence of this covenant, p 673, ante.
12   *Re Phelps, ex p Fripp* (1846) 1 De G 293.
13   The burden of the covenant, though not running with the land, constitutes a covenant to convey which equity will specifically enforce. See 2 Williams V & P, 1085.
14   Pages 523–524, ante.

A purchaser can rely on the covenant to require the vendor to discharge an undisclosed mortgage affecting the property[15], or, it seems, to regrant a valid future easement where the vendor's original grant was void for perpetuity[16]. There is ancient authority for saying that the covenant obliges the covenantor to execute a duplicate if the original has been accidentally destroyed by the purchaser[17] or handed over to a later purchaser of part of the land sold[18]. It is, however, open to question whether the implied covenant extends to a situation where the original conveyance is fully effective to vest the legal title in the purchaser, and the need for a duplicate or confirmatory assurance stems solely from his own act or neglect occurring after the original grant. If this is so, a purchaser failing to apply for first registration of title within the statutory two months' period[19] could not rely on the covenant to re-acquire the legal estate.

4. Covenant given by fiduciary vendor

A vendor who conveys and is expressed to convey as trustee, mortgagee or personal representative covenants that he has:

> ... not executed, or done, or knowingly suffered, or been party or privy to, any deed or thing whereby the subject matter of the conveyance ... is or may be impeached, charged, affected, or incumbered in title, estate or otherwise, or whereby [he] is in anywise hindered from conveying the subject-matter of the conveyance in the manner in which it is expressed to be conveyed.

This is a somewhat limited covenant in comparison with the beneficial owner covenants just discussed. It is expressly limited to the covenantor's own acts only[20]. The restricted operation of this covenant is often advocated as a sufficient reason why beneficial co-owners (as in the usual case where the vendors are husband and wife) should convey, not as trustees, but as beneficial owners. The covenant is broken by the vendor's creation of some adverse incumbrance, or by a previous conveyance or assent by him[1] of the property. The covenantor's obligations are limited to anything 'executed, or done, or knowingly suffered'; the word 'omitted' is significantly absent. The word 'suffer' has been widely interpreted in different contexts but it does not cover the failure to prevent the acquisition of an adverse title by a squatter. In *Eastwood v Ashton*[2] the House of Lords held that such failure was an 'omission' within the covenant for good right to convey. Liability also arises if the covenantor has been 'party or privy' to a deed creating an incumbrance. In this context 'privy' means, not knowledge,

---

15 *Re Jones, Farrington v Forrester* [1893] 2 Ch 461.
16 See p 547, ante. Disposal of the servient land would render the vendor liable to an action of damages at the purchaser's instance.
17 *Bennett v Ingoldsby* (1676) Cas Temp Finch 262.
18 *Napper v Lord Allington* (1700) 1 Eq Cas Abr 166; 2 Dart, 673.
19 LRA 1925, s 123, p 473, ante; (1968) 32 Conv (NS) 391, 398 (D G Barnsley).
20 LPA 1925, s 76(1) (F).
 1 *Wise v Whitburn* [1924] 1 Ch 460, p 666, ante.
 2 [1915] AC 900, HL, p 672, ante. See particularly Lord Parker at 913. Compare on the meaning of 'suffer' Luxmoore J in *Barton v Reed* [1932] 1 Ch 362 at 375.

but participation in some act by which the parties will be bound[3]. The covenant therefore catches a mortgagee who, in exercise of his power of sale, conveys the mortgaged property to a purchaser without disclosing the existence of a right of way which the mortgagor created by a deed to which the mortgagee was a party[4].

This covenant applies alike to freehold and leasehold land. An assignment of leasehold land by a vendor 'as personal representative' implies no covenant that the lease is in full force or that the covenants in the lease have been observed and performed. However, since the fiduciary vendor's covenant extends to acts whereby the subject matter of the assignment 'is or may be impeached', it partially overlaps the special leasehold covenant implied by s 76(1)(B)[5]. But there will be no protection in respect of omissions such as a failure to repair.

E   Registered conveyancing[6]

Neither the Land Registration Act 1925 nor the Rules made thereunder deal with covenants for title in a satisfactory manner, due largely to the wholesale application of the provisions of the Law of Property Act 1925, to the somewhat different statutory rules governing the transfer of registered land. Rule 76 of the Land Registration Rules 1925[7] states that:

> For the purpose of introducing the covenants implied under paragraphs (B)(ii) and (D)(ii) of the Law of Property Act 1925 a person may, in a registered disposition
> (a)   be expressed to execute, transfer or charge as beneficial owner; or
> (b)   where the instrument effecting the disposition expressly refers to section 77 of the Law of Property Act 1925, be expressed to execute, transfer or charge as settlor, trustee, mortgagee, or personal representative of a deceased person, or under an order of the court,
> and the instrument effecting the disposition may be framed accordingly.

This provision justifies the view that the general law relating to covenants for title applies to registered land, subject only to express modifications made by the Act or the Rules. However, to what extent are covenants for title necessary on a sale of registered land, and, if implied, what measure of protection do they afford?

1.   Freehold land

It is generally agreed that the implied covenants for title serve a valid purpose where the title is qualified or possessory, as protection may be necessary in

---

3   *Woodhouse v Jenkins* (1832) 9 Bing 431 at 441, per Tindal CJ.
4   Cf *Clifford v Hoare* (1874) LR 9 CP 362, where the claim against the mortgagee only failed because there was no substantial interference with the plaintiff's interest.
5   Page 665, ante.
6   See R & R, Ch 14; [1982] Conv 145 (M J Russell).
7   As substituted by LR (Implied Covenants for Title) Rules 1995, r 3.

respect of rights or interests subsisting prior to or excepted from registration. These are likely to be the very situations when a beneficial owner is reluctant to enter into full beneficial owner covenants. On the other hand where an absolute title is transferred, the covenants for title appear at first blush to be of limited value[8]. Yet this, even if true, would afford no sufficient reason not to incorporate them, and it is standard practice to do so. The form of transfer commonly used by solicitors and obtainable from HM Stationery Office includes the expression 'as beneficial owner'[9]. An absolute title is not indefeasible. The proprietor of an absolute title who suffers rectification will turn initially to s 83 of the Act for indemnity. However, his eviction or disturbance of possession may not always constitute loss for the purposes of the Act. The existence of covenants for title may enable a purchaser to obtain redress from his vendor in circumstances where the Act affords no assistance, for example, where he suffers rectification in order to give effect to an overriding interest[10]. Another instance of their usefulness is seen in *A J Dunning & Sons (Shopfitters) Ltd v Sykes & Son (Poole) Ltd*[11] discussed below.

In the interesting but unreported case of *Meek v Clarke*[12] the purchaser, hoping to obtain a large sum by way of damages, pursued his action on the covenants for title, despite having an unanswerable claim for compensation under s 83. The facts are rather involved.

> In 1961 X, the owner of land entitled to the benefit of an easement of way across Y's land, released the right by deed. In 1973 X conveyed his land to the defendant, C, who was registered as first proprietor with an absolute title. In 1974, as a result of action taken by C's then solicitors who were ignorant of the deed of release, C's register of title was amended by the addition of the easement as an appurtenant right[13]. Later C as beneficial owner transferred the registered title (which included the easement) to the plaintiff, M. When he attempted to exercise the right of way, Y objected. Eventually Y obtained rectification of M's title by entry of a note that the easement had been extinguished.

M's claim against C was dismissed. There was no breach of the covenant for good right to convey. At the date of the C-M transfer (the relevant time to determine the issue) C was registered as proprietor of the easement. He was thus able to transfer it as part of the registered estate by virtue of s 18(1) of the Act. Even if Y's potential claim for rectification at that time could be said to have prevented C from having full power to convey, this resulted from X's act in releasing the easement. But C was not responsible for the act of X through

---

8 See *Meek v Clarke* [1982] CA Transcript 312, per Oliver LJ, note 10, p 671, ante; *Re King Robinson v Gray* [1962] 2 All ER 66 at 82, per Buckley J. See also 2 Williams V & P, 1160; 3 K & E, 127. Contrast Hallett, 1248; R & R, 16.10 (no good reason for excluding them in quite normal sales and purchases of land registered with an absolute title – a view totally vindicated by the decision in the *Dunning* case, supra).

9 A marginal note reads: 'If desired or otherwise as the case may be'. Curiously, the forms of transfer prescribed by r 89 omit the vendor's capacity.

10 See *Re Chowood's Registered Land* [1933] Ch 574 (squatter's adverse title); *Re Boyle's Claim* [1961] 1 All ER 620 (neighbour's trespassing garage). See p 97, ante.

11 Supra. This is thought to be the first reported case concerning the operation of covenants of title in a registered land transaction.

12 See note 8, ante.

whom he claimed by purchase for value. Nor was there any breach of the covenant for quiet enjoyment. M's exercise of the right of way had, at least after rectification of the register, been lawfully interrupted by Y. However, C was in no way responsible for Y's conduct. Y's claim was, in the view of Oliver LJ, claim by title paramount.

(a) Rule 77

To what extent a purchaser can sue on the implied covenants in any particular case is governed largely by r 77. The wording of this rule should be noted carefully. It provides that any implied covenant for title takes effect *as though the disposition was expressly made subject to*:

(a) all charges and other interests appearing or protected on the register at the time of the execution of the disposition[14] and affecting the covenantor's title;

(b) any overriding interests of which the purchaser has notice and subject to which it would have taken effect, had the land been unregistered.

The benefit of any implied covenant runs with the land and can be enforced by the proprietor for the time being of that land[15]. The Land Registration Act 1925, s 83(10) enables the Registrar to enforce on behalf of the Crown any implied covenant which a person indemnified under the Act could have enforced in relation to the matter in respect of which indemnity has been paid. The italicised words are important. It has been noted that the covenants for title take effect subject as the property is expressed in the conveyance. In registered conveyancing it is not customary to refer to adverse incumbrances in the transfer[16]; any reference to third party rights is unnecessary in view of s 20 (1) of the Act. Nevertheless, r 77 preserves the unregistered conveyancing position by deeming the transfer to be made expressly subject to interests and charges appearing or protected on the register, thus precluding any action by the purchaser.

The effect of r 77(1)(a) was considered in the recent *Dunning case*, particularly as to the significance of the word 'register'. Here the plan on the V-P transfer included[17] a small area of land that had been previously sold off by V and was now registered in X's name. This land was vital to P's plans and, having purchased it from X, P sought to recover from V on his beneficial owner covenants the cost of its acquisition and the incidental expenses. The claim succeeded. The court rejected an argument that 'register' meant the

---

13　This would probably not have occurred had the Registry notified Y as required by LRR 1925, r 253. For entry of appurtenant easements on the register, see p 495, ante.

14　This is significant. It does not preclude an action on the covenant in respect of eg restrictive covenants entered on the register after execution of the transfer but before the purchaser's registration as proprietor, though with the protection of a clear official certificate of search, he would take free from such restrictions provided he lodged his application in time (see p 405, ante).

15　Rule 77(2). Though this is not clearly stated, it is assumed that the benefit passes to a proprietor of part; cf LPA 1925, s 76(6), p 669, ante.

16　Save where on first registration a transfer is used instead of the normal conveyance (p 544, ante), see Hallett, 1108.

global register of all registered titles, thereby causing V's covenants to take effect subject to X's registered interest. The 'register' was held to refer only to the register of V's own individual title. V fared no better with an alternative plea that the transfer was not a registered disposition in relation to X's land with the consequence that his covenants were implied only qua the land that was effectively transferred by the transfer. The document purported to transfer the disputed area to P, and this sufficed to render V liable on his implied covenants. Had a few simple precautions been taken, this litigation could have been avoided. A search of the public index map would have revealed that the disputed plot was not part of V's registered title. Even a careful comparison of the transfer plan with the filed plan should have alerted the solicitors of both sides to the discrepancy.

(b) Overriding interests

Rule 77(1)(b) prevents recourse to the covenants for title in respect of overriding interests of which the purchaser has notice. Paragraph (b) has, not without justification, been criticised as being an ill-drafted and misconceived rule[18]. It gives rise to several problems. In unregistered conveyancing mere notice of an incumbrance is immaterial to the enforcement of the covenants[19]. It is not clear why a different rule should operate in registered conveyancing. Perhaps the rule is intended to relate to cases where the existence of the overriding interest is disclosed to the purchaser in the contract; in unregistered conveyancing the vendor would be entitled to have the property conveyed expressly subject to that interest, so excluding the operation of any covenant for title. Again r 77(1) preserves the position under the general law by deeming the disposition to take effect as though it were expressly made subject to known overriding interests. But the rule goes further. No limitation is placed on the word 'notice'. If it covers constructive as well as actual notice, occupation will generally constitute notice, so precluding any claim in respect of a right within s 70(1)(g) of the Act. Furthermore, the additional requirement in (b) that the disposition would have taken effect subject to that interest had the land been unregistered is difficult to apply in relation to certain overriding interests, such as an estate contract or an equitable lease, which may be protected as overriding interests under s 70(1)(g), as being rights of a person in actual occupation of the land. In unregistered conveyancing the enforcement of such interests is determined by their registration as land charges, yet the Land Charges Act 1972 has no application to registered titles.

Academic opinion has long been divided on the question whether the covenants for title afford any protection even in respect of overriding interests

---

17   The court had first to decide that as a matter of construction the transfer purported to include the disputed land. See p 543, ante.

18   See (1970) 34 Conv (NS) 129. Nevertheless, the rule has been reintroduced with respect to the 1994 Act: see LRR 1925, r 77A, introduced by LR (Implied Covenants for Title) Rules r 5.

19   *Great Western Rly Co v Fisher* [1905] 1 Ch 316, p 671, ante. Compare *Hissett v Reading Roofing Co Ltd* [1970] 1 All ER 122 (purchaser of registered land aware of protected tenancy; claim on covenants for title abandoned).

of which the purchaser has no notice[20]. Such has been the uncertainty that some precedent books urge the insertion in the transfer of express covenants extending to such interests[1], a recommendation that is ignored in practice. However, since rr 76 and 77 clearly point to the conclusion that the implied covenants, if introduced, are intended to apply to unknown overriding interests, the courts are unlikely to adopt arguments that would preclude this result. Indeed the arguments advanced by those denying the effectiveness of the covenants for title in this situation are no longer sustainable in the light of the *Dunning case*[2]. This decision should lay to rest the doubts that have been voiced on this issue for so long.

2.   Leasehold titles

On an *assignment* of registered leasehold property certain covenants on the part of both transferor and transferee are implied by s 24 of the Land Registration Act 1925, unless the transfer indicates to the contrary (in which event an entry negativing their implication is made on the register[3]). These covenants do not operate on the grant of a lease or underlease. The transferee's covenants implied by sub-s (1)(b), to pay the rent and perform the covenants, differ little from the indemnity covenant implied in an assignment for valuable consideration by virtue of s 77(1)(C) of the Law of Property Act 1925[4]. Close attention must be paid to the transferor's covenants. Though these are somewhat similar to those implied by s 76(1)(B) of the same Act, considered on page 664, there are several important differences. The Land Registration Act 1925, s 24(1)(a) implies a covenant on the part of the transferor with the transferee that:

> ... notwithstanding anything by such transferor done, omitted or knowingly suffered, the rent, covenants and conditions reserved and contained by and in the registered lease, and on the part of the lessee to be paid, performed, and observed, have been so paid, performed, and observed up to the date of the transfer ...

The following points are to be observed.

1. The s 24 covenant is not as wide as its unregistered counterpart. It implies no covenant that the lease is valid and subsisting, and limits the covenantor's liability to his own acts or omissions.

2. There is no express provision for the running of the benefit of the covenant[5].

---

20   See (1942) 58 LQR 356 (H Potter); Emmet, para 14.013; Farrand, 277–80; R & R, 340–42; 17 Ency F & P, 194–95; [1981] Conv 32 (P H Kenny); [1982] Conv 145 (M J Russell); Hayton, 67–71. The issue is more fully explored in the second edition of this book at 636–37.

1   Hallett, 1248, note (t); 3 K & E, 128, 408, giving a suitable clause by questioning its necessity. Express stipulation for such a clause would be needed in the contract.

2   See particularly [1987] Ch 287 at 300, [1987] 1 All ER 700 at 706, CA, per Dillon LJ.

3   LRR 1925, r 115. It is the entry that operates to negative their implication.

4   See p 576, ante.

5   Cf LPA 1925, s 76(6), though perhaps the benefit of the covenant in s 24(1)(a) will run here under LPA 1925, s 78. But see p 669, ante.

3. Under s 24 the covenant is implied irrespective of whether the assignment is for value and – this is most important – it is *not* dependent on the transferor's capacity as beneficial owner[6]. This obviously constitutes a trap for the unwary. The normal assignment of leasehold property by a fiduciary owner implies the limited covenant against personal incumbrance only (s 76(1)(F)), not the wider leasehold covenant under s 76(1)(B) given by a beneficial owner. Where the transferor is eg a trustee or personal representative, the practitioner must not overlook the fact that the s 24 covenant will be automatically implied, unless it is expressly excluded or modified, and for this to be forced on a purchaser there must be express provision in the contract[7]. The Law Commission tentatively suggests[8] the repeal of s 24, thus leaving the parties to incorporate the Law of Property Act 1925 covenants by the use of the appropriate statutory formula.

F   Covenants created after 1995[9]

The Law Commission, when reporting on the issue of covenants for title made some quite radical proposals for reform[10]. The legislation enacted was not, however, of a radical type. Instead, the main impact of the legislation is to restate the law in a more intelligible fashion than was previously the case, although there are, also, some changes of substance.

Section 1 of the Act applies to any instrument effecting or purporting to effect a disposition of property, whether or not for valuable consideration. Disposition includes the creation of a term of years but this does not extend to a lease created orally as there is then no instrument. It should also be noted that the section refers to an instrument which purports to effect a disposition, an expression which clearly resolves the problem where a person purports to convey property which he does not, in fact, own[11]. The section also applies to implied covenants in the case of voluntary disposition but, as the appropriate wording must be used for the covenants to be implied, it is unlikely that such covenants will be incorporated in a voluntary conveyance or transfer. Where the appropriate words are used, then the implied covenants will either be a full title guarantee, or a limited title guarantee. There are to be no other forms of covenants for title.

---

6   In practice the transferor is expressed is expressed to transfer 'as beneficial owner' (if such he be) in order to obtain the full beneficial owner covenants implied by LPA 1925, s 76(1)A).
7   Cf *Re King, Robinson v Gray* [1962] 2 All ER 66 (s 24(1)(a) negatived on compulsory acquisition of leasehold property from executor vendor); revsd in part on other grounds, [1963] Ch 459, [1963] 1 All ER 781, CA.
8   Law Com Published Working Paper No 32, para 61.
9   See, generally, Kenny, *Covenants for Title: Understanding the New Law*.
10   (1991) Law Com No 199.
11   See p 665, ante.

1.   Full title guarantee

Where the Standard Conditions of Sale are applicable, the purchaser is entitled to have the land transferred to him with a full title guarantee[12]. The terms of this guarantee are then elaborated by ss 2(1), 3(1) and (2) 4 and 5 of the Act which will be considered in turn.

(a) Right to disposal and further assurance
Section 2(1) of the Act implies a covenant by the vendor that he has the right (with the concurrence of any other person conveying the property) to dispose of the property as he purports to, and that that person will at his own cost do all that he reasonably can to give the person to whom he disposes of the property the title he purports to give. Section 2(2) further clarifies this latter obligation by including:
(a) in relation to registered land, doing all that he reasonably can to ensure that the person to whom the disposition is made is entitled to be registered with at least the class of title registered immediately before the disposition; and
(b) in relation to a disposition of an interest in land the title to which is required to be registered by virtue of the disposition, giving all reasonable assistance to establish to the satisfaction of the Chief Land Registrar the right of the person to whom the disposition is made to registration as proprietor.
In relation to a disposition of an interest in land there is, subject to a contrary intention, a presumption, where title is registered that the disposition is of the whole interest and, where title is not registered, if the disposition is of a leasehold interest, the disposition is of the whole unexpired term and, in any other case, is of the fee simple.

(b) Charges, incumbrances and third party rights
A conveyance with a full title guarantee requires the vendor to convey the property free:
(a) from all charges and incumbrances (whether monetary or not); and
(b) from all other rights exercisable by third parties, other than any charges, incumbrances or rights which that person does not and could not be expected to know about[13].
This extends to liabilities conferred by or under any enactment except to the extent that such liabilities and rights are, by reason of:
(a) being at the time of the disposition, only potential liabilities and rights in relation to the property; or
(b) being rights and liabilities imposed or conferred on property generally, not such as to amount to defects in title[14].
   This wide-ranging covenant goes further that the previous law, in that it makes the vendor liable for incumbrances created by predecessors in title.

---

12   SCS 4.5.2. This is subject to such matters referred to in 4.5.3.
13   Law of Property (Miscellaneous Provisions) Act 1994, s 3(1).
14   Ibid, s 3(2).

The obligation is, however, subject to an important qualification. The obligation does not extend to matters to which the disposition is expressly made subject[15]. Under the Standard Conditions of Sale[16], the property is expressly sold subject to the following incumbrances:

(i) those mentioned in the agreement;
(ii) those discoverable by inspection of the property before the contract;
(iii) those the seller does not and could not have known about;
(iv) entries made before the date of the contract in any public register except those maintained by HM Land Registry or its Land Charges Department[17] or by Companies House; and
(v) public requirements.

Under the terms of this condition, therefore, full title guarantee is qualified leaving uncertainty only surrounding the question of what the vendor could not know about. The guarantee also does not extend to any right which is, at the time of the disposition, within the actual knowledge of the purchaser or is a necessary consequence of the facts which are within his actual knowledge[18].

(c) Validity of leases

Section 4 of the Act provides that when the disposition is of leasehold property and a full title guarantee is given the vendor covenants that:

(a) the lease is subsisting at the date of the disposition; and
(b) that there is no subsisting breach of a condition or tenant's obligation, and nothing which at that time would render the lease liable to forfeiture.

This obligation is also modified substantially, however, by the Standard Conditions of Sale, which provides that the leasehold property is sold subject to any subsisting breach of condition or tenant's obligation relating to the physical state of the property which renders the lease liable to forfeiture[19]. In respect of breaches of other covenants, however, the assignor will be liable under this implied covenant should the lease be liable to forfeiture.

(d) Running of benefit

Section 7 of the Act provides for the annexation of the implied covenants. It is provided that the benefit of the covenant shall be annexed and incident to, and shall go with the estate or interest of the person to whom the disposition is made, and shall be capable of being enforced by every person in whom that estate is (in whole or part) for the time being vested.

It should be noted that the annexation is to the estate and not to the land. This means that for the benefit to pass to a successor in title, that person must possess the same estate in land as the person with whom the covenant was entered into.

15 Ibid, s 6(1).
16 SCS 3.
17 For the purpose of the 1994 Act, notice supplied by s 198 of the Law of Property Act 1925 is to be disregarded: s 6(3). A pre-root of title land charge may, therefore, be regarded as an interest that the vendor could not reasonably know about.
18 Ibid, s 6(2).
19 SCS 3.2.2.

2.   Limited title guarantee

A vendor may opt to give only a limited title guarantee. If this is done, the main difference between the ambit of this covenant and the full title guarantee is in respect of charges, incumbrances and rights to which the land is subject. The covenant which is implied in this case is restricted to one that the person disposing of the land has not since the last disposition for value:

(a) charged or incumbered the property by means of any charge or incumbrance which subsists at the time when the disposition is made, or granted third party rights in relation to the property which so subsists; or

(b) suffered the property to be so charged or subjected to any such rights, and that he is not aware that anyone else has done so since the last disposition for value[20].

Unlike the case where there is a full title guarantee, therefore, this covenant does not extend to the actions of a predecessor in title.

---

20   Law of Property (Miscellaneous Provisions) Act 1994, s 3(3).

Chapter 24

Miscellaneous post-completion remedies[1]

The finality of the transaction once it has been completed was mentioned at the commencement of the previous chapter. Nevertheless it may still be possible to have the conveyance set aside after completion on the ground of fraud, innocent misrepresentation or mistake. This is commonly termed rescission. However, whereas rescission of a contract prior to completion can be effected out of court a court order is required to set aside an executed transaction. Considerable uncertainty exists as to the true juristic nature of this right to avoid a conveyance. Some commentators maintain that the right to have a deed set aside on account of fraud or undue influence is a mere equity and is not normally assignable[2]. But this view fails to pay sufficient regard to a line of nineteenth century cases[3] which clearly establish that an owner of land induced by fraud to convey it to another retains an equitable interest in it. This interest is capable of being devised or assigned inter vivos, and exists independently of any act to be done by the party seeking avoidance. Perhaps the difference between the two conflicting views arises from concentrating on different aspects flowing from a voidable conveyance[4].

A Fraud

1. Fraudulent representations

At law to establish fraud the plaintiff had to show that the false representation inducing him to enter into the contract was made by the other party knowingly, or without belief in its truth, or recklessly, not caring whether it was true or false. The party deceived could either avoid the contract, subject to the normal limitations, or affirm it and sue to recover damages in an action of deceit.

---

1 For a more detailed analysis of the topics discussed in this chapter, reference should be made to the standard text books on Contract and Equity.
2 M & W, 145–46, relying on *Phillips v Phillips* (1861) 4 De GF & J 208 at 218, per Lord Westbury, adopted by Fry J in *Cave v Cave* (1880) 15 Ch D 639 at 649.
3 See *Uppington v Bullen* (1842) 2 Dr & War 184; *Stump v Gaby* (1852) 2 De Gm & G 623; *Gresley v Mousley* (1859) 4 De G & J 78 (sale to vendor's solicitor at gross undervalue); *Dickinson v Burrell* (1866) LR 1 Eq 337.
4 *Latec Investments Ltd v Hotel Terrigal Pty Ltd* (1965) 113 CLR 265 at 290, per Menzies J. The judgments in this case contains a most helpful consideration of the problem.

Completion of the transaction was no bar to avoiding the transaction at law, provided the parties could be restored to their former position and the purchaser could recover the purchase price in an action for money had and received. Equity exercised a concurrent jurisdiction to grant relief against fraud (but without being able originally to award damages) and it also had an exclusive jurisdiction to compel the delivery up and cancellation of documents procured by fraud.

(a) Effect of fraud

A contract induced by fraud is voidable at the instance of the party defrauded, but it is not void. Consequently, a conveyance giving effect to the contract operates to vest the legal title in the purchaser, and with it the right to lawful possession until the deed is set aside[5]. The purchaser has a choice, however. He may prefer instead to affirm the transaction and to sue for damages in deceit[6]. The right to rescind a contract for fraud has been held not to run with the land conveyed. Where A by fraud induces B to buy land and B assigns the benefit of the contract to C who later takes a conveyance direct from A, C has no right to rescind as against A. Although B may communicate the information to C, the representation is made to B who buys on the strength of it and the effect of the misrepresentation is spent when A makes the contract with B[7].

(b) Extent of jurisdiction

The jurisdiction to set aside a conveyance for fraud is not confined to cases of affirmative fraud where one party fraudulently makes an express statement which induces the other to enter into the contract. According to Grant MR in *Edwards v M'Leay*[8], equity will intervene if 'the vendor knows and conceals a fact material to the validity of the title'. In this case he failed to disclose a known defect of the title affecting part of the land, which was material to the enjoyment of the remainder. This principle was applied in a case where a lessor failed to disclose to his lessee that he had no title to part of the land comprised within the lease, as the lessor well knew[9]. Perhaps the most striking illustration of equity's intervention occurs in *Hart v Swaine*[10]:

> V agreed to sell to P land which, though copy hold, was described in the contract as freehold. V must have been aware that this was not so because on his purchase some years earlier the land had been described as partly copy hold, but V had the whole property conveyed to him as freehold.

5   See eg *Feret v Hill* (1854) 15 CB 207 (tenant procuring lease by false representation of intended user).
6   See eg *Gordon v Selico Co Ltd* [1986] 1 EGLR 71, CA. Knowledge of the fraud at the time of completion would not preclude a subsequent claim for damages, but it would bar rescission.
7   *Gross v Lewis Hillman Ltd* [1970] Ch 445, [1969] 3 All ER 1476, CA. For situations when rescission by C might be possible, see at 461 and 1483, per Cross LJ.
8   (1815) Coop G 308 at 312; affd (1818) 2 Swan 287. There appears in this case to have been an express representation of title.
9   *Mostyn v West Mostyn Coal and Iron Co* (1876) 1 CPD 145.
10   (1877) 7 Ch D 42.

Fry J upheld the purchaser's claim to have the conveyance set aside after completion. Even assuming the vendor had made the representation believing it to be true, he had, in order to secure a benefit for himself, asserted that to be true which had turned out to be false, and according to the learned judge he had 'in the view of a court of law committed a fraud'[11]. It is not easy to follow the reasoning of this case, though the actual decision is generally accepted as correct[12]. It is perhaps best explained as an illustration of misrepresentation amounting to fraud. It does not lay down any general proposition that a purchaser can, in the absence of deceit, have the transaction set aside after completion if the title turns out to be bad[13].

These decisions give warning of the care to be exercised by the vendor when instructing his solicitor to draft the contract. Any deliberate failure to disclose a material defect of title may justify rescission after completion; so also may a material representation incorporated in the contract, made recklessly with indifference as to its truth or falsity. To enter into a contract knowing that he has no title does not amount to fraud unless he has no intention of acquiring one or no reasonable belief in his ability to do so[14], and it is perfectly proper for a vendor to contract to convey such title as he has, if any.

2. Equitable fraud

Equity's understanding of fraud was much wider than that recognised at law and its courts were prepared to set aside transactions not induced by any fraudulent representation, but nevertheless procured by the exercise by one party of influence over the remind of the other[15]. This equitable doctrine applies alike to contracts and conveyances for value as it does to voluntary settlements and gifts inter vivos.

(a) Undue influence

The law on this topic was reviewed by the House of Lords in *National Westminster Bank plc v Morgan*[16]. It was there laid down that a transaction will be set aside for undue influence if it can be shown that it was to the manifest disadvantage of the person influenced, eg a purchase at a highly inflated price[17], or at a gross undervalue. The need to show that the transaction was manifestly

---

11 Per Fry J, at 47. The vendor alleged that events after his own purchase, particularly the fact that no demand for payment of any quit-rent had been made, led him to conclude that none of the land was copyhold.

12 See *Joliffe v Baker* (1883) 11 QBD 255 at 259–60, per Watkin Williams J; *Brownlie v Campbell* (1880) 5 App Cas 925 at 938, HL, per Lord Selbourne LC.

13 *Soper v Arnold* (1887) 37 Ch D 96 at 102, CA, per Cotton LJ; affd (1889) 14 App Cas 429, HL.

14 *Bain v Fothergill* (1874) LR 7 HL 158 at 207, per Lord Chelmsford.

15 A contract induced by duress in the shape of actual force or threats of personal violence is voidable at law. See *Welch v Cheesman* (1973) 229 EG 99.

16 [1985] AC 686, [1985] 1 All ER 821, HL (wife, without advice, executing mortgage over matrimonial home; transaction upheld since not disadvantageous). See generally Snell, 538–43; [1985] Con 387 (C J Barton & P M Rank).

17 *Tufton v Sperni* [1952] 2 TLR 516, CA.

disadvantageous must now be considered to be highly doubtful. Where undue influence has actually been shown to have been exercised, there is no longer any need to show that the transaction is to the manifest disadvantage of the person so influenced. Undue influence is a species of equitable fraud and, in such cases, one does not need to show manifest disadvantage[18]. Whether manifest disadvantage needs to be shown in cases of presumed undue influence was left open by the House of Lords in *CIBC Mortgages plc v Pitt*[19] but it would seem probable that this criterion will, in the future, no longer be considered essential. The basis of equity's intervention is not public policy but the prevention of the victimisation of one person by another. Sometimes undue influence will be presumed if the two parties stand in such a relationship that confidence is necessarily reposed by the one and the influence which naturally flows from that confidence is held by the other[20]. Domination of the will of the former by the latter is not, however, an essential ingredient[1]. Not every confidential relationship gives rise to the presumption. It has been held to exist between parent and child, fiancée's trustee and beneficiary, solicitor and client, religious adviser and disciple, but not between spouses[2] or banker and customer. If presumed, the onus is on the person seeking to uphold the transaction to establish that undue influence was not in fact exercised. He may show that it was the spontaneous act of the grantor resulting from a free exercise of will[3]. Proof of independent advice from a competent person usually suffices. On a transfer for value it must be shown that the full market price was paid[4].

In the absence of any presumption, equity will still set aside the transaction if affirmative proof of undue influence is forthcoming[5]. Here the onus of proof lies with the person seeking to upset the transaction, which must be shown to be wrongful in the sense of being to his manifest disadvantage. An example occurred in *Lloyds Bank Ltd v Bundy*[6] where a charge and guarantee given by a father in favour of his son's bank were set aside because the bank had failed to ensure that he obtained independent and informed advice before signing the documents.

The possibility of undue influence existing between two persons, A and B, should not be overlooked by a mortgagee on the creation of a mortgage to

---

18   *CIBC Mortgages plc v Pitt* [1994] 1 AC 200 at 208–9, [1993] 4 All ER 433 at 438–9, HL, per Lord Browne-Wilkinson.
19   Ibid.
20   *Tate v Williamson* (1866) 2 Ch App 55 at 60, per Lord Chelmsford LC. See also *Barclays Bank plc v O'Brien* [1994] 1 AC 180, [1993] 4 All ER 417, HL.
  1   *Goldsworthy v Brickell* [1987] Ch 378, [1987] 1 All ER 853, CA (business adviser securing farm lease at low rental).
  2   See *Bank of Montreal v Stuart* [1911] AC 120, PC; *National Westminster Bank plc v Morgan*, supra, at 703, 806, per Lord Scarman.
  3   *Re Brocklehurst, Hall v Roberts* [1978] Ch 14, [1978] 1 All ER 767, CA.
  4   *Wright v Carter* [1903] 1 Ch 27, CA (solicitor and client).
  5   *Bank of Montreal v Stuart*, ante (spouses).
  6   [1975] QB 326, [1974] 3 All ER 757, CA. This case did not decide that a banker-customer relationship raises a presumption of undue influence. Contrast *Cornish v Midland Bank plc* [1985] 3 All ER 513, CA, and *Woodstead Finance Ltd v Petrou* 1986 FLR 158, CA, both cases where a mortgage by a wife was held not to be disadvantageous to her in the circumstances.

secure A's indebtedness. This is a topic of considerable importance and topicality, which has been fully considered elsewhere in the book[7].

(b) Unconscionable bargains

Equity also maintains a wry eye on any transaction tainted by unfair dealing. A conveyance may be avoided where there is inequality of position between the parties, coupled with inadequacy of consideration and lack of independent advice. The party seeking to uphold the transaction must prove it was fair, just and reasonable in the circumstances[8]. In *Cresswell v Potter*[9], the plaintiff on the break-up of her marriage executed, without obtaining any advice, a release of her interest in the matrimonial home in favour of her husband for no consideration other than an indemnity against further liability in respect of the mortgage on it. Megarry J set aside the deal, observing that this branch of law was still operative and capable of development in ways of direct concern to practitioners today[10].

B   Innocent misrepresentation

Prior to the Misrepresentation Act 1967, no ground existed at law or in equity for setting aside an executed transaction for an innocent misrepresentation or an innocent concealment of some defect of title. This rule applied equally to conveyances as it did to leases[11]. Now s 1(b) of the Act permits rescission of any contract on the ground of innocent misrepresentation notwithstanding its performance, but subject to the usual bars. Whilst the Act is silent on the point, it is thought that 'rescission' of a conveyance after completion requires, to be effective, a court order setting it aside. The view that on rescission the legal estate will revest in the grantor by operation of law seems unsound[12]. It may be that a court will be more ready to exercise its discretion under s 2 (2) to award damages in lieu of rescission when a contract for the sale of land has been executed[13].

C   Mistake

Mistake can affect a transaction involving land in three different ways. First, as we saw in Chapter 21, it may affect the formation of the contract; this section

---

7   See pp 366–372 ante.
8   See *Fry v Lane* (1888) 40 Ch D 312 at 321–22, per Kay J, discussing various nineteenth century decisions.
9   [1978] 1 WLR 255n; *Watkin v Watson-Smith* (1986) Times, 3 July; cf *Backhouse v Backhouse* [1978] 1 All ER 1158; *Butlin-Sanders v Butlin* [1985] FLR 204 (transfer executed in face of legal advice upheld). See also *Hart v O'Connor* [1985] AC 1000, [1985] 2 All ER 880, PC.
10   See also *Langton v Langton* [1995] 3 FCR 521, [1995] 2 FLR 890, [1996] Conv 308 (D Capper).
11   See *Wilde v Gibson* (1848) 1 HL Cas 605 (non fraudulent concealment of right of way); *Angel v Jay* [1911] 1 KB 666 (lease).
12   See Farrand, 57; contra M & W, 621–22.
13   Emmet, para 4.012; *Chitty on Contracts* (25th edn), para 456.

is concerned primarily with the rights of the parties where relief is sought after completion of the purchase. Second, a party to a transaction may allege that he executed a document under the mistaken impression that it was a document of a totally different kind, ie he raises the plea of non est factum. Thirdly, the executed written document, be it contract or conveyance, may contain a mistake by failing to embody the parties' true agreement, so giving rise to a claim for rectification.

1.   Mistake affecting formation

(a) Total failure of consideration
Prior to *Solle v Butcher*[14], relief on account of common mistake could only be obtained after completion of a contract involving land on the narrow ground of a total failure of consideration. In effect this limited rescission to cases of res sua or res extincta, cases like *Bingham v Bingham*[15] where the purchaser was conveyed land which unknown to both parties he already owned, or like *Strickland v Turner*[16] where an assignment of an annuity was executed in ignorance of the fact that the annuitant had died before the making of the agreement for sale. In such cases the conveyance was devoid of legal effect since the vendor had nothing to sell or convey, and the purchaser could recover the purchase price in an action at law without equity's intervention. If the purchaser desired some form of relief not available at law, proceedings had to be commenced in equity[17].

Though there are dicta suggesting otherwise[18], rescission after completion was not available in the absence of a total failure of consideration. In *Re Tyrell, Tyrell v Woodhouse*[19], Cozens-Hardy J declined to be the first judge to give a decision contrary to this rule, when holding that the post-completion discovery that the land conveyed was subject to a reversionary lease (the existence of which was unknown to both parties) was no ground for setting the conveyance aside. Again rescission was not available where a tenant already owned one tenth of the land comprised within the tenancy agreement; the judge refused to dissect the agreement and to declare it void as to part only of the land included in it[20]. The same principle has been affirmed by the High Court of Australia in *Svanosio v McNamara*[1], where the plaintiff discovered after completion that the hotel he had bought was erected partly on land to which the vendor unknowingly had no title. His action to set aside the conveyance for common mistake was dismissed. A purchaser is not necessarily without

---

14   [1950] 1 KB 671, [1949] 2 All ER 1107, CA.
15   (1748) 1 Ves Sen 126.
16   (1852) 7 Exch 208.
17   *Cooper v Phibbs* (1867) LR 2 HL 149.
18   *Debenham v Sawbridge* [1901] 2 Ch 98 at 109, per Byrne J.
19   (1900) 82 LT 675; *Debenham v Sawbridge* [1901] 2 Ch 98 (discovery after completion that part of house conveyed belonged to third party: rescission denied).
20   *Bligh v Martin* [1968] 1 All ER 1157.
 1   (1956) 96 CLR 186. See also *Montgomery and Rennie v Continental Bags (NZ) Ltd* [1972] NZLR 884, note 3, p 469, ante.

remedy in this kind of situation. He may have a contractual right to claim compensation[2]. Alternatively he may be able to sue on the covenants for title, but these will not, as we have seen[3], afford any protection when the vendor (and his predecessors in title) never had any title to the missing land.

(b) Solle v Butcher

In *Solle v Butcher*[4], the Court of Appeal set aside an executed lease because the parties had made a fundamental mistake as to whether reconstruction of a flat, the subject of the letting, had taken it out of the Rent Restriction Acts. There was no total failure of consideration. The basis of equity's jurisdiction to intervene even after completion, is the existence of some common fundamental misapprehension as to the facts or the parties' respective rights, which goes to the root of the contract. It remains to be seen how extensive this principle is and in particular whether it will be held to apply generally to completed contracts for the sale of land. No reported English decision has so far held that it does[5].

Prima facie the rule as stated by Denning LJ in *Solle v Butcher*[6] appears wide enough to cover cases where the parties make a fundamental mistake as to quantity, but it is far from clear that he was purporting to lay down a rule intended to apply to conveyances of land[7]. In the Australian case of *Svanosio v McNamara*[8] the court took the view that *Solle v Butcher* did not extend to executed contracts for the sale of land. To allow the purchaser a remedy after completion in such circumstances would run counter to the hallowed principle that the purchaser must stand or fall by his investigation of the title and any loss sustained recovered under the covenants of title. However, the limitations of these covenants have already been exposed[9], and it can be argued that there is little justification today for denying all remedy to the purchaser. In some jurisdictions the principle has long been established that an error as to quantity justifies rescission even after completion if it is so substantial that in essence it alters the quality of the subject-matter of the contract (an error in substantialibus as it is termed) notwithstanding there is no total failure of consideration[10].

A mere unilateral mistake in an executed lease is no ground for rescission even in equity[11].

2 *Palmer v Johnson* (1884) 13 QBD 351, CA, note 2, p 643, ante.
3 See p 671, ante.
4 [1950] 1 KB 671, [1949] 2 All ER 1107, CA; *Curtin v Greater London Council* (1970) 69 LGR 281, CA.
5 See p 535, ante for examples of its application in cases where the mistake was discovered *before* completion.
6 [1950] 1 KB 671 at 693, [1949] 2 All ER 1107 at 1120, CA.
7 See his observations at 692 and 1121.
8 (1956) 96 CLR 186, at 199, 210.
9 See p 643, ante.
10 *Freear v Gilders* (1921) 64 DLR 274; *Hyrsky v Smith* (1969) 5 DLR (3d) 385; *Marwood v Charter Credit Corpn* (1970) 12 DLR (3d) 765; on appeal (1971) 20 DLR (3d) 563. See (1978) 56 Can Bar Rev 603 (G H L Fridman).
11 *Riverlate Properties Ltd v Paul* [1975] Ch 133, [1974] 2 All ER 656, CA.

2.   Non est factum

A party to a deed who alleges that he was induced to execute something different in character from that which he thought he was signing may be entitled to raise the plea of *scriptum predictum non est factum suum.* He thereby seeks to have the deed set aside on the ground that it is void against him as not being his deed, and being void it is ineffectual to pass the estate or interest which it purports to transfer. The plea is not confined to the blind and illiterate for whose protection it originated in the late sixteenth century. Whilst it must be kept within narrow limits, it may exceptionally be available to a person of full age. The House of Lords, decision in *Saunders v Anglia Building Society*[12] in 1970 greatly clarified the law on this topic. The facts were these:

> X, a widow aged 78, was induced to execute a deed in the belief that it was a deed of gift of her leasehold house to her nephew, Y, whereas in fact it was an assignment of the house to Z. Z mortgaged the property to a building society. X did not read the assignment; her glasses were broken at the time and she was content to trust Y who witnessed her signature to the deed. Later Z defaulted in payment of the mortgage instalments and the society commenced possession proceedings. X pleaded that the deed to Z was void so that the society acquired no rights under the mortgage deed.

As against Z the assignment was voidable as having been induced by fraud and it was held to be void against him. Their Lordships upheld the Court of Appeal's decision that X was not entitled to raise the plea against the society. The onus of establishing non est factum fell on X as the party seeking to disown the document. It required clear and positive evidence, but she had singularly failed to prove a sufficient discrepancy between her intention and her act[13]. Her evidence indicated that she would have executed the deed in Z's favour, even if the transaction had been fully explained to her.

(a) Availability

A plaintiff is not entitled to relief if (i) he has failed to exercise reasonable care when signing the document or (ii) the actual document is not fundamentally different from the document as the signer believed it to be[14]. The two separate limbs of this rule require further treatment.

(i) *Negligence.*   Common prudence dictates that every person should exercise care when signing a document, though commercial life sees this trite advice constantly ignored. Yet, surprisingly, it was the law before the *Saunders* case that negligence on the part of the person signing did not prevent his relying on the plea[15]. This oft-criticised rule has now been buried. The House of Lords laid down that in order to succeed a plaintiff must show that when signing the

---

12   [1971] AC 1004, [1970] 3 All ER 961, HL. The original plaintiff (the widow) died during the course of the litigation and the proceedings were continued by her executrix.
13   Per Lord Wilberforce at 1027 and 973.
14   Per Lord Pearson at 1034 and 979.
15   *Carlisle and Cumberland Banking Co v Bragg* [1911] 1 KB 489, CA.

document he acted with reasonable care. It therefore affords no assistance to the man who does not read the document before signing it because he was too busy or too lazy or because of the trust he placed in another[16]. What amounts to reasonable care will depend on the circumstances of the case, including the nature of the document which it is thought is being signed. The same standard of care ought not to be expected of an elderly spinster who might be none the wiser if she read the document as of a business executive[17].

(ii) *Fundamental difference.*   There must be a difference which is 'radical', or 'fundamental' or 'very substantial' – various expressions were used by their Lordships – between what the plaintiff signed and what he thought he was signing. The plaintiff's mistake in the *Saunders* case was not sufficiently fundamental. She intended to divest herself of her leasehold property by transferring it to another, albeit by way of gift rather than by an assignment ostensibly for value[15]. A sufficient difference would seem to exist for the purpose of this rule where a man is induced to execute a conveyance under the impression he is granting a lease for seven years, but perhaps not vice versa. A mistake of identity may or may not be fundamental depending on the circumstances. In the case of a deed, an error of personality is not necessarily so vital as in the case of a contract, which requires consensus[16]. The mistake as to the identity of the transferee in the *Saunders* case (ie Z in place of Y) was considered not to make the deed totally different from what she intended to sign. A mistake as to the legal effect of a document cannot give rise to a plea of *non est factum.* In *Lloyds Bank plc v Waterhouse*[20] the majority of the Court of Appeal considered that a mistake as to whether a mortgage was to secure all monies owed, as opposed to a fixed sum, was sufficiently fundamental to bring the doctrine into play, although the dissenting judgment of Woolf LJ seems preferable.

(b) Illiterate persons

The House of Lords was not directly concerned with the position of illiterate or blind people, but it seems that signers within this category must establish the same basic requirements. Because of the nature of their disability they will more readily be able to raise the plea successfully, but even they must still act responsibly and carefully according to their circumstances when putting their signature to legal documents[1]. Where a person gives a power of attorney to a person who is blind or illiterate, then his lack of care in selecting such a person

---

16   See eg *United Dominions Trust v Western* [1976] QB 513, [1975] 3 All ER 1017, CA (form signed in blank and completed by third party); *Avon Finance Co Ltd v Bridger* [1985] 2 All ER 281, CA.

17   Per Viscount Dilhorne at 1023 and 969.

18   For some of the earlier authorities, see *Bagot v Chapman* [1907] 2 Ch 222 (mortgage described as power of attorney: plea upheld); *Howatson v Webb* [1908] 1 Ch 1, CA (conveyance described as mortgage: plea defeated because it was a mere mistake as to contents), disapproved in the *Saunders* case.

19   Per Lord Hodson at 1019 and 965.

20   [1993] 2 FLR 97, CA.

 1   Per Lord Wilberforce at 1027 and 971.

as the donee is likely to prevent the donor from raising the plea of non est factum[2]. If no third party has become involved relief may be obtained on the ground of fraud, without it being necessary to rely on the plea.

3.   Rectification[3]

(a) The jurisdiction to rectify
The conveyancing process, which involves the taking of instructions, the drafting, amending and engrossing of documents, is one that not infrequently results in mistakes occurring in the documents which the parties eventually execute. It is a fundamental rule of English law that extrinsic evidence is not admissible to vary or contradict the terms of a written document. To this basic proposition an important exception exists. Where owing to some error a written document fails to record accurately the terms of the parties' true agreement, equity will rectify the document to make it accord with their agreement. This jurisdiction to rectify must not be confused with the courts' inherent power to correct obvious errors as a matter of construction of a document[4].

Equity assumes jurisdiction in a proper case to rectify conveyances, leases, voluntary deeds, contracts and other written instruments. A plaintiff can in the same action claim rectification of a written contract for the sale of land and specific performance of the contract as rectified. It is no bar to rectification that a mistake in the written agreement has been repeated in the conveyance[5]. The granting of relief in these circumstances seems at first sight to run foul of s 2 of the Law of Property (Miscellaneous Provisions) Act 1989, for the court is specifically performing a written agreement with a parol variation. The truth of the matter is that after rectification the written agreement does not continue to exist with a parol variation; it is read as if it has been originally drawn in its rectified form and it is the amended written document of which specific performance is decreed[6].

(b) Conditions of rectification
Several requirements must be satisfied to succeed in a claim for rectification.

(i) Antecedent expressed accord.   It was once thought[7] that the court could only rectify a document so as to make it accord with a complete antecedent concluded oral contract. In *Joscelyne v Nissen*[8] the Court of Appeal held that a concluded binding agreement is not essential; a claim to rectification can be based on an antecedent expressed accord reached during negotiations and adhered to in intention by the parties. Rectification can therefore be obtained

---

2   See *Norwich & Peterborough Building Society v Steed* [1991] 2 All ER 880, [1991] 1 WLR 449, CA.
3   See (1984) 81 LS Gaz 1577 (S Tromans).
4   Page 514, ante. See eg *Re Alexander's Settlement, Jennings v Alexander* [1910] 2 Ch 225.
5   *Craddock Bros Ltd v Hunt* [1923] 2 Ch 136, CA.
6   *Craddock Bros Ltd v Hunt*, supra, at 151–52, CA, per Lord Sterndale MR. See also *Wright v Robert Leonard (Development) Ltd* [1994] NPC 49, CA; [1995] Conv 484 (M P Thompson).
7   See *Craddock Bros Ltd v Hunt*, supra, at 159, per Warrington LJ.
8   [1970] 2 QB 86, [1970] 1 All ER 1213, CA. And see note 20, post.

when a formal contract fails to incorporate some term agreed in a 'subject to contract' document. Even a voluntary settlement may be rectified if it fails to express the settlor's true intentions, despite the absence of any bargain between him and the trustees[9].

(ii) *Intention to embody in writing.*   The parties must intend the written document to contain all the terms of their agreement, a requirement not difficult to establish in relation to contracts and conveyances relating to land. This intention was not present in *City and Westminster Properties (1934) Ltd v Mudd*[10]. In this case premises were let solely for business purposes, though both parties intended that the tenant should be permitted to live there. The tenant's claim for rectification of the lease by including an express proviso allowing him to reside there was rejected. There was no common intention to insert such a provision in the document; the landlords in particular had no desire to attract the provisions of the Rent Acts.

(iii) *Common mistake.*   The plaintiff must establish that owing to some common mistake in drafting the subsequent written document does not accurately express the parties' prior accord. It is no bar to the plaintiff's claim that the mistake resulted from the negligence of his solicitor[11]. Rectification will not be ordered merely because one party desires to introduce additional terms, or because (except in the special situation discussed in paragraph (iv)) he intended to incorporate a particular term but failed to do so. The plaintiff must also establish that the alleged common intention continued concurrently in the minds of both parties down to the time the relevant document was executed[12]. A plaintiff who pleads two alternative claims based on inconsistent assertions of the parties' continuing intentions plainly cannot succeed in his action[13].

The standard of proof required to establish the common intention is the ordinary civil standard of the balance of probability[14]. Though reluctant to do so, the court may act on the parol evidence of the plaintiff[15]. Rectification suits frequently come before the courts. It is commonly granted where a conveyance or other deed fails to give effect to the terms of the written contract. Here the plaintiff may be able to succeed merely on proof of the disparity, whereas a more onerous burden of proof will usually rest on the shoulders of one seeking to show that a written contract does not accord with an antecedent oral bargain[16]. A conveyance may be rectified where, for instance, by mutual

---

9   *Behrers v Heilbut* (1956) 222 LJo 290; *Re Butlin's Settlement Trust* [1976] Ch 251, [1976] 2 All ER 483.
10   [1959] Ch 129, [1958] 2 All ER 733.
11   *Weeds v Blaney* (1977) 247 EG 211, CA.
12   *Fowler v Fowler* (1859) 4 De G & J 250. A change of mind after signing contracts cannot, of course, assist a party in resisting rectification of a conveyance.
13   *C H Pearce & Sons Ltd v Stonechester Ltd* (1983) Times, 17 November.
14   *Thomas Bates & Son Ltd v Wyndham's (Lingerie) Ltd* [1981] 1 All ER 1077, CA.
15   *Smith v Iliffe* (1875) LR 20 Eq 666; *Bonhote v Henderson* [1895] 1 Ch 742; affd [1895] 2 Ch 202, CA.
16   See *Lloyd v Stanbury* [1971] 2 All ER 267 (no convincing proof of vendor's intention to exclude disputed plot from contract: rectification refused).

mistake parcels are omitted from the deed[17], or the vendor's covenants for title are wider than those provided for by the contract[18], or the statutory general words operate to pass to the purchaser an implied right of way contrary to terms of the contract[19]. In *Re Colebrook's Conveyances*[20], where land was conveyed to purchasers as joint tenants, the court rectified the deed by substituting 'tenants in common' for 'joint tenants'. Similarly rectification of a lease has been decreed so as to delete an option to purchase mistakenly granted by it[1], or to include an agreed rent review clause omitted in error[2]. The court may also rectify one part of a formal contract which, when exchanged, does not accord in a material respect with the other part[3].

(iv) *Unilateral mistake.*   Traditionally, equitable relief by way of rectification has been founded on the common mistake of both parties. However, the courts have of recent years taken the view that although only one party is mistaken, the conduct of the other party may make it inequitable for him to object to rectification. In *Thomas Bates & Son Ltd v Wyndham's (Lingerie) Ltd*[4], the defendant tenant became aware before executing his lease that owing to the landlord's mistake the document failed to carry out their common intention. He nevertheless signed the lease, without disclosing the error. His conduct was held sufficient to disentitle him to resist the landlord's claim for rectification, despite the absence of any common mistake. This decision establishes[5] that the court may order rectification even in a case of unilateral mistake. There must exist a common intention between the parties and the party seeking rectification (X) must further show:
(a) that he erroneously believed the document gave effect to the common intention;
(b) that the other party (Y) knew that it failed to do so because of X's mistake;
(c) that Y did not bring the mistake to X's notice; and
(d) that the mistake would benefit Y or (perhaps) merely be detrimental to X.
    This principle appears to be based on a species of equitable estoppel, rather than on fraud (in the equitable sense). The *Bates* case makes it clear that Y need not be guilty of any sharp practice, though it may often be present.

17   *White v White* (1872) LR 15 Eq 247; *Beale v Kyte* [1907] 1 Ch 564 (too much land conveyed); *Weeds v Blaney* (1977) 247 EG 211, CA.
18   *Stait v Fenner* [1912] 2 Ch 504; *Butler v Mountview Estates Ltd* [1951] 2 KB 563, [1951] 1 All ER 693.
19   *Clark v Barnes* [1929] 2 Ch 368.
20   [1973] 1 All ER 132; *Wilson v Wilson* [1969] 3 All ER 945 (name of co-purchaser deleted from joint tenancy clause). In both cases rectification was based on an arrangement between relatives falling short of a concluded contract.
1   *Kent v Hartley* (1966) 200 EG 1027.
2   *Central and Metropolitan Estates Ltd v Compusave* (1983) 266 EG 900.
3   See *Domb v Isoz* [1980] Ch 548, [1980] 1 All ER 942, CA; cf *Harrison v Battye* [1974] 3 All ER 830, CA, p 226, ante.
4   [1981] 1 All ER 1077, CA (no machinery in rent review clause for fixing rent in default of parties' agreement).
5   See particularly at 1086, per Buckley LJ, applying a principle enunciated by Pennycuick J in *A Roberts & Co Ltd v Leicestershire County Council* [1961] Ch 555 at 570, [1961] 2 All ER 545 at 551, approved in *Riverlate Properties Ltd v Paul* [1975] Ch 133, [1974] 2 All ER 656, CA.

The conduct need only be such as to affect the conscience of the party who has suppressed the fact that he has discovered the presence of a mistake. Actual, rather than constructive, knowledge of the mistake appears to be required[6], but the courts are likely to uphold X's claim if Y suspects the existence of an error yet deliberately refrains from checking the true position[7].

The courts' willingness to grant rectification in suitable cases of mere unilateral mistake renders it unnecessary to explore further a troublesome trilogy of nineteenth century decisions where equity put the defendant on terms either to submit to rectification or have the contract annulled, despite the absence of fraud or common mistake[8].

(c) Principle of Leuty v Hillas[9]

It occasionally happens at a sale of land by auction that vendor, V, sells adjacent properties to two different purchasers, P and P2, but owing to a common mistake land which P contracted to buy is omitted from his conveyance and included in the V-P2 conveyance. Provided P2 is aware of the error, equity treats him as a trustee of the excess land intended for P. This rather obscure rule of equity was first formulated by Lord Cranworth LC in *Leuty v Hillas*, and applied by the Court of Appeal in *Craddock Bros v Hunt*[10]. Equity imposes a trust on P2 because it is inequitable in the circumstances for him to retain land to which he knows he is not entitled. Whilst rectification proceedings could be maintained by V against P2, and by P against V, the court will order P2 to convey the excess land direct to P, without V being a necessary party to the action. This avoids circuity of action. The precise sequence of the two conveyances is perhaps immaterial, though in the two cases the V-P conveyance came first[11].

Seemingly the *Leuty v Hillas* trust principle applies only where there are two separate transactions relating to two different properties. Recently the rule was tentatively extended in *Blacklocks v J B Developments (Godalming) Ltd*[12] to cover a situation where only one plot of land was involved. Here V transferred land to P, both parties being unaware that the transfer included land to which P was not contractually entitled. Later P sold the entirety of the land to P2. Judge Mervyn Davies QC (as he then was) granted V a declaration that P2

---

6 See Tromans, op cit, 1579, citing *Agip SpA v Navigazione Alta Italia SpA* [1983] Com LR 170, CA.
7 See *Commission for the New Towns v Cooper (Great Britain) Ltd* [1995] Ch 259, [1995] 2 All ER 929, CA, a case where one party was guilty of sharp practice. See [1995] Conv 319 at 321–25 (M P Thompson).
8 See *Garrard v Frankel* (1862) 30 Beav 445; *Harris v Pepperell* (1867) LR 5 Eq 1; *Paget v Marshall* (1884) 28 Ch D 255. The precise status of these decisions is in any event uncertain in view of their strong disapproval in *Riverlate Properties Ltd v Paul*, supra.
9 (1858) 2 De G & J 110; [1983] Conv 361, 366–70 (D G Barnsley).
10 [1923] 2 Ch 136 at 158–59, CA, per Warrington LJ.
11 Where the V–P2 conveyance precedes the V–P2 conveyance, the benefit of V's accrued claim to rectify the V–P2 deed appears to pass to P under LPA 1925, s 63 (1)(note 15, post). P can thus obtain redress without recourse to any special trust created by equity.
12 [1982] Ch 183, [1981] 3 All ER 392. For additional problems relating to the registered land aspects of this decision, see p 85, ante.

held the excess land in trust for V, despite the apparent lack of evidence that P2 was aware that he had acquired land which V claimed[13]. Leaving aside this complication, it is submitted that the facts did not warrant any application of the trust principle. As between V and P, V was clearly entitled to rectification, and this equity would bind any subsequent purchaser taking with notice.

(d) Transmission to successors in title

A claim to rectify a document for mistake constitutes an equity[14], rather than an equitable interest in land. Nevertheless, the benefit is capable of passing on a conveyance of land by virtue of s 63(1) of the Law of Property Act 1925[15]. As for the burden, being a mere equity it does not bind a purchaser for value of *any* interest in the land who has no notice. He must be without notice at the time of completion[16]. Contrary to the general rule, occupation of unregistered land does not of itself fix a purchaser with constructive notice of an occupier's equity of rectification. The purchaser of a freehold reversion is clearly obliged to inspect the tenant's lease; but he is under no duty to inquire of him as to whether the document accurately sets out the parties' rights[17].

(e) Effect of order

Rectification relates back to the time when the document was executed and it is to be read as if it had been originally drawn in its rectified form. The execution of a fresh document is unnecessary. The court order operates to pass any outstanding legal estate[18]. It is the practice to indorse a copy of the order on the deed or other instrument. The court will give effect to any consequential rights following rectifications, such as the implied reservation of a right of way[19].

D   Loss of right to rescind

The right to have a transaction set aside may be barred on one or more of several grounds. These apply whether rescission is sought before or after completion. If the right of rescission has been lost, the injured party must have recourse to any alternative remedy available to him, such as an action for

---

13   A necessary ingredient if the rule is to apply: *Ellis v Hills and Brighton and Preston ABC Permanent Benefit Building Society* (1892) 67 LT 287.

14   *Phillips v Phillips* (1861) 4 De GF & J 208 at 218, per Lord Westbury; *Smith v Jones* [1954] 2 All ER 823.

15   *Boots the Chemist Ltd v Street* (1983) 268 EG 817 (purchaser of freehold reversion entitled to rectification of lease granted by vendor). For s 63, see p 699, ante.

16   *Taylor Barnard Ltd v Tozer* (1983) 269 EG 225 (no notice at time of contract immaterial); *Lyme Valley Squash Club Ltd v Newcastle under Lyme Borough Council* [1985] 2 All ER 405 (mortgagees without notice).

17   *Smith v Jones*, supra; cf *Downie v Lockwood* [1965] VR 257 at 260, per Smith J. Contrast the position under LRA 1925, s 70(1)(g) where the title is registered. And see the *Blacklocks'* case, supra.

18   *White v White* (1872) LR 15 Eq 247.

19   *Rice v Dodds* (1969) 213 EG 759.

damages in deceit[20], or an action on the covenants for title implied in his conveyance. In this section the following bars[1] to relief are considered:
1. impossibility of restitutio in integrum;
2. affirmation;
3. lapse of time;
4. intervention of third party rights.

1. Restitutio in integrum impossible

It has always been a condition of rescission both at law and in equity that the parties should be put in status quo and if this cannot be achieved rescission is not available. However, as McCardie J once remarked, the expression restitutio in integrum is somewhat vague and must be applied with care[2]. As we have already seen[3], equity by the exercise of its wider powers was able to uphold the right of an aggrieved party to rescind in a much wider variety of cases than those which the common law would recognise as admitting of rescission. In effect, rescission is possible provided the court can achieve practical justice between the parties[4]. Thus occupation by the purchaser is no bar because he can be required to pay rent for his period of occupation[5], neither is deterioration of the property caused by the purchaser, for this can be the subject of compensation. Restitution may be impossible if the plaintiff has disposed of the property or it has ceased to exist, eg where the purchaser of a mine has worked it out[6]. In one case the purchaser of leasehold business premises went into occupation before completion but later vacated them without warning on the vendor's failure to obtain the required licence to assign. The landlord re-entered, thereby occasioning a forfeiture. Restitution became impossible, and the purchaser was denied recovery of the purchase money which he had paid[7].

A contract cannot be rescinded in part and still be good for the remainder. One reason for refusing rescission here is that the parties cannot be restored to their status quo. In *Thorpe v Fasey*[8], it was held that a single contract for the

---

20   *Clarke v Dickson* (1858) EB & E 148.
1   These bars are irrelevant (except for no 2) to situations of rescission for breach, nor do they apply where rescission is sought on the ground of mistake operative at law, eg in cases of res sua or where non est factum is successfully pleaded.
2   *Armstrong v Jackson* [1917] 2 KB 822 at 828.
3   Page 626, ante.
4   See eg *O'Sullivan v Management Agency & Music Ltd* [1985] QB 428, [1985] 3 All ER 351, CA.
5   *F & B Entertainments Ltd v Leisure Enterprises Ltd* (1976) 240 EG 455.
6   *Lagunas Nitrate Co v Lagunas Syndicate* [1899] 2 Ch 392, CA.
7   *Butler v Croft* (1973) 27 P & CR 1, criticised at (1975) 91 LQR 337, 356 (M Albery) on the ground that the purchaser was exercising a contractual right of rescission and not seeking equitable relief. Cf *Alati v Kruger* (1955) 94 CLR 216.
8   [1949] Ch 649, [1949] 2 All ER 393, a difficult decision to follow. Seemingly it was a case of purported rescission for breach, in which case the restitution rule ought not to have been relevant. The vendor's alternative claim for damages also failed. The purchaser's non-completion did not constitute a repudiation of the contract as the vendor had not served any notice making time of the essence.

purchase of four separate plots of land could not be rescinded by a vendor on account of the purchaser's failure to complete, because a conveyance of one of the plots had already been taken. Perhaps a better explanation for this rule is simply that the vendor having affirmed the contract as to part cannot disaffirm it as to the balance. If the rule were otherwise the court would be re-making the bargain for the parties.

2.   Affirmation

A contract cannot be rescinded once the injured party, with knowledge of all material facts, elects to affirm the transaction. This principle applies alike whether the plaintiff seeks to rescind a voidable contract, eg on the ground of fraud, or purports to repudiate for breach of an essential term. Affirmation may be inferred from words or conduct, provided they unequivocally show to the other party that he intends to proceed with the transaction. A classic example of affirmation precluding repudiation occurred in *Aquis Estates Ltd v Minton*[9]. The purchaser of leasehold property, after discovering it had been adversely listed as an historic building, so entitling him to rescind the contract, nevertheless proceeded to exercise a contractual right to negotiate for the purchase of the freehold. By way of contrast, in *Watson v Burton*[10] a purchaser's rescission of a contract for substantial misdescription was upheld, notwithstanding that after becoming aware of the error he had paid the balance of the deposit and asked for repairs to be done. His conduct was consistent with his intention to try in the first instance to negotiate a reduction in the price.

Knowledge of the legal right to choose whether to affirm or disaffirm is a precondition to making an effective election[11]. Knowledge of facts giving rise to a right to rescind is not of itself enough. Relevant knowledge by a solicitor may suffice to deny his client relief, despite the latter's ignorance[12]. Affirmation (or election) should not be confused with estoppel. Conduct pointing to an apparent affirmation may operate as an estoppel if the other party acts to his detriment in reliance on it. Estoppel by conduct does not require any awareness of the legal right to which the known facts may give rise[13]. This is the difference.

3.   Lapse of time

The remedy of rescission is regarded as essentially an equitable one and equity requires its suitors to act with promptness. Delay of itself does not bar the claim, but it is a factor which the court cannot disregard. Coupled with other

9   [1975] 3 All ER 1043, CA (undisclosed irremovable title defect).
10   [1956] 3 All ER 929. The sale was by auction, at which the buyer paid only a nominal deposit. See also *Laurence v Lexcourt Holdings Ltd* [1978] 2 All ER 810; *Trustbridge Ltd v Bhattessa* [1985] LS Gaz R 2580, CA.
11   *Peyman v Lanjani* [1985] Ch 457, [1984] 3 All ER 703, CA.
12   *Peyman v Lanjani*, supra, at 487, 724, per Stephenson LJ; *Sargent v ASL Developments Ltd* (1974) 131 CLR 634 at 659, per Stephen J.
13   *Peyman v Lanjani*, supra, at 495, 730, per May LJ.

circumstances it may defeat the plaintiff. It may be taken as evidence of affirmation, or in the interval an innocent third party may have acquired an interest in the property, or the subject-matter of the contract may have changed, preventing substantial restoration to the status quo.

Running of time

Some uncertainty surrounds the rules determining when time begins to run. To some extent they depend on the reason why the plaintiff seeks to have the transaction set aside.

(i) *Misrepresentation.*   In the case of fraud it is clear that the injured party is not affected by mere lapse of time so long as he remains in ignorance of the fraud[14]. Time runs from discovery of the fraud and thereafter if the plaintiff delays his claim for more than six years, equity will (apart from any other reason) act by analogy to the Limitation Act 1980, and refuse to grant relief[15]. It might be thought that the same rule would apply to innocent misrepresentation, but apparently this is not so. In one case[16], the buyer of a painting was debarred from rescinding five years after entering into the contract, even though he instituted proceedings as soon as he discovered the truth. There had been ample opportunity to inspect it in the first few days after its purchase. Time would thus seem to run from when the truth could have been discovered by the exercise of reasonable diligence. Since the Misrepresentation Act 1967 puts contracts for the sale of land on the same footing in relation to innocent misrepresentation as other contracts, it would be difficult to maintain that a different rule governing the running of time should apply to land contracts.

(ii) *Mistake.*   The cases involving rectification of documents are somewhat contradictory. The better view is thought to be that time runs, not from the date of execution[17], but from the discovery of the mistake. In *Wolterbeck v Barrow*[18], rectification of a marriage settlement was decreed 34 years after its execution and four years following discovery of the mistake. In an age when most purchasers never see their deeds it would be quite unrealistic to hold that time runs from the date of completion[19]. As to other forms of mistake, direct authority is lacking. In *Beale v Kyte*[20] Neville J expressed the view obiter

---

14   *Rolfe v Gregory* (1865) 4 De GJ & Sm 576 at 579, per Lord Westbury; *Oliver v Court* (1820) Dan 301, 8 Price 127 (lapse of 12 years); *Gresley v Mousley* (1859) 4 De G & J 78 (conveyance at gross undervalue set aside 22 years later); Limitation Act 1980, s 32.
15   *Armstrong v Jackson* [1917] 2 KB 822 at 830–31, per McCardie J.
16   *Leaf v International Galleries* [1950] 2 KB 86, [1950] 1 All ER 693, CA; Treitel, *The Law of Contract* (7th edn), 297.
17   As held in *Bloomer v Spittle* (1872) LR 13 Eq 427.
18   (1857) 23 Beav 423; *Beale v Kyte* [1907] 1 Ch 564, questioning *Bloomer v Spittle*, supra.
19   It is not the practice to provide clients with photocopies of the deeds which they execute. Not only is it very doubtful whether the client would discover a mistake if instructed to check, but most clients would object that this is what they employed their solicitor to do. Treitel, op cit, 249, favours application of the rule for innocent misrepresentation.
20   Supra. Laches was not pleaded. Further support can be derived from *Rees v De Bernardy* [1896] 2 Ch 437 at 445, per Romer J.

that in all cases of mistake time runs from when the plaintiff's attention is first called to the error.

In view of the confused and uncertain state of the law, it might perhaps be argued that save in cases of fraud, it is more in keeping with equitable principles not to lay down a hard and fast rule, but to allow the court to do justice in each particular case. Irrespective of when the plaintiff commences proceedings, should hardship result to a vendor of land having to submit to rescission long after completion of the contract, the court can in the exercise of its discretion refuse to grant it. If the purchaser delays a long time after ascertaining the truth, it will be open for the court to infer affirmation.

4.　Third party rights

Equity will not allow rescission to the prejudice of a third party who has acquired an interest in the property for value and without notice of the equitable right. Where third party rights are involved the courts tend to treat a claim to set aside a transaction as a mere equity (not an equitable interest)[1]. It is, therefore, unenforceable against a purchaser of *any* interest (ie legal or equitable). Where a purchaser of land has disposed of it for value to another he is no longer able to return the land to the vendor. In this situation the intervention of the third party interest makes restoration of the status quo impossible. It does not follow that the existence of a third party right always has this effect, as is shown by cases where a vendor or grantor seeks rescission. In *Sturge v Sturge*[2]:

> X obtained rescission of a conveyance of land to his younger brothers on the ground of equitable fraud, notwithstanding that they had conveyed much of the land to purchasers. X elected to take the purchase money in lieu of land which had been sold and he agreed to confirm the conveyances to the purchasers.

Rescission and the Misrepresentation Act 1967
As we have already seen, s 1(b) of the 1967 Act enables rescission of a contract induced by an innocent misrepresentation notwithstanding that it has been performed. So far as contracts for the sale of land were concerned, the Law Reform Committee had recommended no change in the existing law[3]. It plumped for finality in conveyancing transactions, arguing that:

> The vendor will often have spent the proceeds of sale on the purchase of another house and so be unable to repay them. The purchase of a house is commonly linked with the raising of a mortgage and perhaps a sequence of other transactions. Rescission of one sale may thus start a chain reaction.

It seems to have been accepted that there may not be many occasions involving land transactions where a clear-cut case of rescission after completion can

---

1　Contrast p 687, ante. See generally *Bulley v Bulley* (1874) 9 Ch App 739; *Bainbrigge v Browne* (1881) 18 Ch D 188 at 197, per Fry J. For rectification, see p 696, ante.
2　(1849) 12 Beav 229.
3　10th Report (Innocent Misrepresentation), Cmnd 1782, para 6.

arise[4]. The suggestion has been made[5] that the existence of a mortgage will make it difficult or impossible to restore the parties to their original positions. This conclusion appears to be open to serious doubt. Suppose V conveys property to P, the contract being induced by an actionable innocent misrepresentation. P mortgages the property to M. An institutional lender will not normally object to a premature repayment and there seems no reason why the court cannot order V to repay direct to M so much of the purchase money as is necessary to redeem the mortgage, and on its discharge P can reconvey the property to V free from the charge. The fact that V has invested the money received from P in the purchase of another house should not be a bar to relief[6], for he can raise the cash by reselling the house. This seems to be the extent of the chain reaction which the Law Reform Committee feared might result. The existence of a mortgage or the likelihood of hardship being caused to a vendor in having to resell his newly-acquired property may well be factors to be considered by the court in determining whether to award damages in lieu of rescission[7].

E   Terms on which relief granted

The underlying principle in the granting of relief is the substantial restoration of the parties to their original position. Basically this entails, where rescission is sought after completion, repayment of the purchase price to the purchaser and revesting the legal estate in the vendor. The court will set aside the transaction and order the purchaser to reconvey the property to the vendor[8] at the latter's expense, or declare that the conveyance is inoperative and order a memorandum of the judgment to be endorsed on the deed[9]. Where rescission is sought on the ground of mistake, as in *Cooper v Phibbs*[10], no reconveyance is necessary since the original conveyance, being completely nugatory, passes no legal title to the plaintiff. Equity will, however, make a decree setting aside the transaction and will impose such terms as it considers necessary to do justice between the parties.

A purchaser who successfully rescinds is entitled to repayment of the purchase money with interest, and to his expenses incurred in consequence of the purchase. He must account for all rents and profits which he has received, and if he has been in occupation he is charged with an occupation rent[11]. He

---

4   See HL Debates, 18 October 1966, Vol 277, col 52.
5   (1967) 64 LS Gaz 404, (1967) 117 NLJ 413. And see M & W, 621.
6   It can hardly be argued that V could resist rescission because he had used the money to buy stocks and shares. Why should it be material that he bought a house instead?
7   Unless the operation of the doctrine of merger (p 468, ante) precludes an award of damages after completion on the ground that there ceases to be any proceedings arising out of the contract, as Lord Upjohn suggested might possibly be the case: HL Debates, 17 May 1966. Vol 274, col 943.
8   *Edwards v M'Leay* (1818) 2 Swan 287; *Sturge v Sturge* (1849) 12 Beav 229.
9   See *Hart v Swaine* (1877) 7 Ch D 42, p 688, ante.
10   (1867) LR 2 HL 149.
11   *F and B Entertainments Ltd v Leisure Enterprises Ltd* (1976) 240 EG 455.

is entitled to an allowance in respect of substantial repairs and improvements, provided they are undertaken before he discovers that the transaction is voidable[12]. He must also compensate the vendor in respect of depreciation caused by his acts. There may be circumstances when the purchaser is denied relief because he cannot obtain repayment of the purchase money from the vendor. In *Debenham v Sawbridge*[13], land had been sold by the court and the vendor, a trustee, had never received the money which had been paid into court and distributed among the beneficiaries. Byrne J considered this to be one reason for rejecting the purchaser's claim for rescission.

The allowances received and given by a purchaser are much the same when it is not he but the vendor or grantor who is entitled to have the transaction set aside. As is to be expected, the purchaser is responsible for the vendor's expenses, and he is chargeable with any depreciation caused by acts of waste or it seems, mere deterioration[14].

F   Disclaimer

Previously in this chapter we have been mainly concerned with situations where because of some vitiating element in a transaction a party to a conveyance seeks to have it set aside and thereby undo the bargain he has made. There is another way whereby a grantee of land can divest himself (otherwise than by disposition) of a legal estate in land – by disclaimer. Disclaimer is simply a right which can be exercised independently of court proceedings to renounce an estate or interest under a deed. Suppose A conveys land to B by way of gift. Delivery of the deed by A is effective to vest the legal estate in B, without B's execution of the deed, and even without his knowledge[15]. But no man is obliged to accept any assurance of land made to him without his consent, so that B has a right to refuse to accept the gift, or, in other words, to disclaim. Until he disclaims the legal estate remains vested in him.

Disclaimer need not be by deed; an estate may be disclaimed by conduct without any express declaration[16]. On disclaimer the deed becomes void and the legal estate which passed under it revests in the grantor (or his personal representatives) by operation of law[17]. The grantee cannot disclaim once he has unequivocally signified his acceptance of the grant. Acceptance may be express. It may be inferred from conduct, by acting as owner of the property in demanding rents or advertising the property for sale[18], by taking up residence there, or perhaps by merely accepting the title deeds of the property.

12   *Trevelyan v White* (1839) 1 Beav 588; *Edwards v M'Leay*, supra, at 289, per Lord Eldon LC.
13   [1901] 2 Ch 98.
14   *Ex p Bennett* (1805) 10 Ves 381; *Gresley v Mousley* (1859) 4 De G & J 78 (sale to solicitor who granted mining leases set aside).
15   See p 449, ante. See *Hughes v Griffin* [1969] 1 All ER 460, CA (donee ignorant of gift until deeds handed to him eight years after donor's execution of conveyance).
16   *Re Birchall, Birchall v Ashton* (1889) 40 Ch D 436, CA (disclaimer by trustee).
17   See generally *Sheppard's Touchstone* (7th edn), p 285; *Mallott v Wilson* [1903] 2 Ch 494 at 501, per Byrne J.
18   *Bence v Gilpin* (1868) LR 3 Exch 76.

Though direct authority is lacking, it is clear from general principles that this doctrine of disclaimer has no application between vendor and purchaser. The rule at law has always been that acceptance of the grant is implied until disagreement is signified[19]. In the case of a purchaser, prior acceptance has already been expressly given by entering into a binding contract to purchase the estate, so that an attempted disclaimer of the conveyance would be inoperative[20], even where the legal estate had become vested in him as a result of the vendor's unconditional delivery of the conveyance without payment of the balance of the purchase money[1].

19 *Thompson v Leach* (1690) 2 Vent 198 at 203, per Ventris J.
20 See 12 *Halsbury's Laws* (4th edn) 550, para 1371, citing *Bence v Gilpin* (1868) LR 3 Exch 76, where, however, assent was inferred from subsequent acts of ownership.
 1 See p 415, ante.

Appendices

Appendix A

Standard Conditions of Sale

AGREEMENT
(Incorporating the Standard Conditions of Sale (Third Edition))

Agreement date	:
Seller	:
Buyer	:
Property (freehold/leasehold)	:
Root of title/Title Number	:
Incumbrances on the Property	:
Title Guarantee (full/limited)	:
Completion date	:
Contract rate	:
Purchase price	:
Deposit	:
Amount payable for chattels	:
Balance	:

The Seller will sell and the Buyer will buy the Property for the Purchase price.

The Agreement continues on the back page.

WARNING	Signed
This is a formal document, designed to create legal rights and legal obligations. Take advice before using it.	
	Seller/Buyer

SPECIAL CONDITIONS

1. (a) This Agreement incorporates the Standard Conditions of Sale (Third Edition). Where there is a conflict between those Conditions and this Agreement, this Agreement prevails.

   (b) Terms used or defined in this Agreement have the same meaning when used in the Conditions.

2. The Property is sold subject to the Incumbrances on the Property and the Buyer will raise no requisitions on them.

3. Subject to the terms of this Agreement and to the Standard Conditions of Sale, the seller is to transfer the property with the title guarantee specified on the front page.

4. The chattels on the Property and set out on any attached list are included in the sale.

5. The Property is sold with vacant possession on completion.

(or) 5. The Property is sold subject to the following leases or tenancies:

Seller's Solicitors   :

Buyer's Solicitors   :

©1995   *OYEZ*   The Solicitors' Law Stationery Society Ltd,
Oyez House, 7 Spa Road, London SE16 3QQ

© 1995 THE LAW SOCIETY

4.95   F29334
5065046
* * * * *
3rd Edition

Standard Conditions of Sale

STANDARD CONDITIONS OF SALE (THIRD EDITION)

(NATIONAL CONDITIONS OF SALE 23rd EDITION, LAW SOCIETY'S CONDITIONS OF SALE 1995)

1.   GENERAL

1.1   Definitions

1.1.1 In these conditions:
(a) "accrued interest" means:
   (i) if money has been placed on deposit or in a building society share account, the interest actually earned
   (ii) otherwise, the interest which might reasonably have been earned by depositing the money at interest on seven days' notice of withdrawal with a clearing bank
   less, in either case, any proper charges for handling the money
(b) "agreement" means the contractual document which incorporates these conditions, with or without amendment
(c) "banker's draft" means a draft drawn by and on a clearing bank
(d) "clearing bank" means a bank which is a member of CHAPS Limited
(e) "completion date", unless defined in the agreement, has the meaning given in condition 6.1.1
(f) "contract" means the bargain between the seller and the buyer of which these conditions, with or without amendment, form part
(g) "contract rate", unless defined in the agreement, is the Law Society's interest rate from time to time in force
(h) "lease" includes sub-lease, tenancy and agreement for a lease or sub-lease
(i) "notice to complete" means a notice requiring completion of the contract in accordance with condition 6
(j) "public requirement" means any notice, order or proposal given or made (whether before or after the date of the contract) by a body acting on statutory authority
(k) "requisition" includes objection
(l) "solicitor" includes barrister, duly certificated notary public, recognised licensed conveyancer and recognised body under sections 9 or 32 of the Administration of Justice Act 1985
(m) "transfer" includes conveyance and assignment
(n) "working day" means any day from Monday to Friday (inclusive) which is not Christmas Day, Good Friday or a statutory Bank Holiday.
1.1.2 When used in these conditions the terms "absolute title" and "office copies" have the special meanings given to them by the Land Registration Act 1925.

1.2   Joint parties
If there is more than one seller or more than one buyer, the obligations which they undertake can be enforced against them all jointly or against each individually.

1.3   Notices and documents
1.3.1 A notice required or authorised by the contract must be in writing.
1.3.2 Giving a notice or delivering a document to a party's solicitor has the same effect as giving or delivering it to that party.
1.3.3 Transmission by fax is a valid means of giving a notice or delivering a document where delivery of the original document is not essential.
1.3.4 Subject to conditions 1.3.5 to 1.3.7, a notice is given or a document delivered when it is received.
1.3.5 If a notice or document is received after 4.00pm on a working day, or on a day which is not a working day, it is to be treated as having been received on the next working day.
1.3.6 Unless the actual time of receipt is proved, a notice or document sent by the following means is to be treated as having been received before 4.00pm on the day shown below:
(a) by first-class post: two working days after posting
(b) by second-class post: three working days after posting
(c) through a document exchange: on the first working day after the day on which it would normally be available for collection by the addressee.
1.3.7 Where a notice or document is sent through a document exchange, then for the purposes of condition 1.3.6 the actual time of receipt is:
(a) the time when the addressee collects it from the document exchange or, if earlier
(b) 8.00am on the first working day on which it is available for collection at that time.

1.4   VAT
1.4.1 An obligation to pay money includes an obligation to pay any value added tax chargeable in respect of that payment.
1.4.2 All sums made payable by the contract are exclusive of value added tax.

2.   FORMATION

2.1   Date
2.1.1 If the parties intend to make a contract by exchanging duplicate copies by post or through a document exchange, the contract is made when the last copy is posted or deposited at the document exchange.
2.1.2 If the parties' solicitors agree to treat exchange as taking place before duplicate copies are actually exchanged, the contract is made as so agreed.

2.2   Deposit
2.2.1 The buyer is to pay or send a deposit of 10 per cent of the purchase price no later than the date of the contract. Except on a sale by auction, payment is to be made by banker's draft or by a cheque drawn on a solicitors' clearing bank account.
2.2.2 If before completion date the seller agrees to buy another property in England and Wales for his residence, he may use all or any part of the deposit as a deposit in that transaction to be held on terms to the same effect as this condition and condition 2.2.3.
2.2.3 Any deposit or part of a deposit not being used in accordance with condition 2.2.2 is to be held by the seller's solicitor as stakeholder on terms that on completion it is paid to the seller with accrued interest.
2.2.4 If a cheque tendered in payment of all or part of the deposit is dishonoured when first presented, the seller may, within seven working days of being notified that the cheque has been dishonoured, give notice to the buyer that the contract is discharged by the buyer's breach.

2.3   Auctions
2.3.1 On a sale by auction the following conditions apply to the property and, if it is sold in lots, to each lot.
2.3.2 The sale is subject to a reserve price.
2.3.3 The seller, or a person on his behalf, may bid up to the reserve price.
2.3.4 The auctioneer may refuse any bid.
2.3.5 If there is a dispute about a bid, the auctioneer may resolve the dispute or restart the auction at the last undisputed bid.

3.   MATTERS AFFECTING THE PROPERTY

3.1   Freedom from incumbrances
3.1.1 The seller is selling the property free from incumbrances, other than those mentioned in condition 3.1.2.
3.1.2 The incumbrances subject to which the property is sold are:
(a) those mentioned in the agreement
(b) those discoverable by inspection of the property before the contract
(c) those the seller does not and could not know about
(d) entries made before the date of the contract in any public register except those maintained by HM Land Registry or its Land Charges Department or by Companies House
(e) public requirements.

3.1.3 After the contract is made, the seller is to give the buyer written details without delay of any new public requirement and of anything in writing which he learns about concerning any incumbrances subject to which the property is sold.
3.1.4 The buyer is to bear the cost of complying with any outstanding public requirement and is to indemnify the seller against any liability resulting from a public requirement.

3.2   Physical state
3.2.1 The buyer accepts the property in the physical state it is in at the date of the contract unless the seller is building or converting it.
3.2.2 A leasehold property is sold subject to any subsisting breach of a condition or tenant's obligation relating to the physical state of the property which renders the lease liable to forfeiture.
3.2.3 A sub-lease is granted subject to any subsisting breach of a condition or tenant's obligation relating to the physical state of the property which renders the seller's own lease liable to forfeiture.

3.3   Leases affecting the property
3.3.1 The following provisions apply if the agreement states that any part of the property is sold subject to a lease.
3.3.2 (a) The seller having provided the buyer with full details of each lease or copies of the documents embodying the lease terms, the buyer is treated as entering into the contract knowing and fully accepting those terms
(b) The seller is to inform the buyer without delay if the lease ends or if the seller learns of any application by the tenant in connection with the lease; the seller is then to act as the buyer reasonably directs, and the buyer is to indemnify him against all consequent loss and expense
(c) The seller is not to agree to any proposal to change the lease terms without the consent of the buyer and is to inform the buyer without delay of any change which may be proposed or agreed
(d) The buyer is to indemnify the seller against all claims arising from the lease after actual completion; this includes claims which are unenforceable against a buyer for want of registration
(e) The seller takes no responsibility for what rent is lawfully recoverable, nor for whether or how any legislation affects the lease
(f) If the let land is not wholly within the property, the seller may apportion the rent.

3.4   Retained land
3.4.1 The following provisions apply where after the transfer the seller will be retaining land near the property.
3.4.2 The buyer will have no right of light or air over the retained land, but otherwise the seller and the buyer will each have the rights over the land of the other which they would have had if they were two separate buyers to whom the seller had made simultaneous transfers of the property and the retained land.
3.4.3 Either party may require that the transfer contain appropriate express terms.

4.   TITLE AND TRANSFER

4.1   Timetable
4.1.1 The following are the steps for deducing and investigating the title to the property to be taken within the following time limits:

Step	Time Limit
1. The seller is to send the buyer evidence of title in accordance with condition 4.2	Immediately after making the contract
2. The buyer may raise written requisitions	Six working days after either the date of the contract or the date of delivery of the seller's evidence of title on which the requisitions are raised whichever is the later
3. The seller is to reply in writing to any requisitions raised	Four working days after receiving the requisitions
4. The buyer may make written observations on the seller's replies	Three working days after receiving the replies

The time limit on the buyer's right to raise requisitions applies even where the seller supplies incomplete evidence of his title, but the buyer may, within six working days from delivery of any further evidence, raise further requisitions resulting from that evidence. On the expiry of the relevant time limit the buyer loses his right to raise requisitions or make observations.
4.1.2 The parties are to take the following steps to prepare and agree the transfer of the property within the following time limits:

Step	Time Limit
A. The buyer is to send the seller a draft transfer	At least twelve working days before completion date
B. The seller is to approve or revise that draft and either return it or retain it for use as the actual transfer	Four working days after delivery of the draft transfer
C. If the draft is returned the buyer is to send an engrossment to the seller	At least five working days before completion date

4.1.3 Periods of time under conditions 4.1.1 and 4.1.2 may run concurrently.
4.1.4 If the period between the date of the contract and completion date is less than 15 working days, the time limits in conditions 4.1.1 and 4.1.2 are to be reduced by the same proportion as that period bears to the period of 15 working days. Fractions of a working day are to be rounded down except that the time limit to perform any step is not to be less than one working day.

4.2   Proof of title
4.2.1 The evidence of registered title is office copies of the items required to be furnished by section 110(1) of the Land Registration Act 1925 and the copies, abstracts and evidence referred to in section 110(2).
4.2.2 The evidence of unregistered title is an abstract of the title, or an epitome of title with photocopies of the relevant documents.
4.2.3 Where the title to the property is unregistered, the seller is to produce to the buyer (without cost to the buyer):
(a) the original of every relevant document, or
(b) an abstract, epitome or copy with an original marking by a solicitor of examination either against the original or against an examined abstract or against an examined copy.

4.3   Defining the property
4.3.1 The seller need not:
(a) prove the exact boundaries of the property
(b) prove who owns fences, ditches, hedges or walls
(c) separately identify parts of the property with different titles
further than he may be able to do from information in his possession.
4.3.2 The buyer may, if it is reasonable, require the seller to make or obtain, pay for and hand over a statutory declaration about facts relevant to the matters mentioned in condition 4.3.1. The form of the declaration is to be agreed by the buyer, who must not unreasonably withhold his agreement.

4.4   Rents and rentcharges
The fact that a rent or rentcharge, whether payable or receivable by the owner of the property, has been or will on completion be, informally apportioned is not to be regarded as a defect in title.

Left Column

4.5 Transfer

4.5.1 The buyer does not prejudice his right to raise requisitions, or to require replies to any raised, by taking any steps in relation to the preparation or agreement of the transfer.

4.5.2 If the agreement makes no provision as to title guarantee, then subject to condition 4.5.3 the seller is to transfer the property with full title guarantee.

4.5.3 The transfer is to have effect as if the disposition is expressly made subject to all matters to which the property is sold subject under the terms of the contract.

4.5.4 If after completion the seller will remain bound by any obligation affecting the property, but the law does not imply any covenant by the buyer to indemnify the seller against liability for future breaches of it:

(a) the buyer is to covenant in the transfer to indemnify the seller against liability for any future breach of the obligation and to perform it from then on, and

(b) if required by the seller, the buyer is to execute and deliver to the seller on completion a duplicate transfer prepared by the buyer.

4.5.5 The seller is to arrange at his expense that, in relation to every document of title which the buyer does not receive on completion, the buyer is to have the benefit of:

(a) a written acknowledgement of his right to its production, and

(b) a written undertaking for its safe custody (except while it is held by a mortgagee or by someone in a fiduciary capacity).

5.   PENDING COMPLETION

5.1 Responsibility for property

5.1.1 The seller will transfer the property in the same physical state as it was at the date of the contract (except for fair wear and tear), which means that the seller retains the risk until completion.

5.1.2 If at any time before completion the physical state of the property makes it unusable for its purpose at the date of the contract:

(a) the buyer may rescind the contract

(b) the seller may rescind the contract where the property has become unusable for that purpose as a result of damage against which the seller could not reasonably have insured, or which it is not legally possible for the seller to make good.

5.1.3 The seller is under no obligation to the buyer to insure the property.

5.1.4 Section 47 of the Law of Property Act 1925 does not apply.

5.2 Occupation by buyer

5.2.1 If the buyer is not already lawfully in the property, and the seller agrees to let him into occupation, the buyer occupies on the following terms.

5.2.2 The buyer is a licensee and not a tenant. The terms of the licence are that the buyer:

(a) cannot transfer it

(b) may permit members of his household to occupy the property

(c) is to pay or indemnify the seller against all outgoings and other expenses in respect of the property

(d) is to pay the seller a fee calculated at the contract rate on the purchase price (less any deposit paid) for the period of the licence

(e) is entitled to any rents and profits from any part of the property which he does not occupy

(f) is to keep the property in as good a state of repair as it was in when he went into occupation (except for fair wear and tear) and is not to alter it

(g) is to insure the property in a sum which is not less than the purchase price against all risks in respect of which comparable premises are normally insured

(h) is to quit the property when the licence ends.

5.2.3 On the creation of the buyer's licence, condition 5.1 ceases to apply, which means that the buyer then assumes the risk until completion.

5.2.4 The buyer is not in occupation for the purposes of this condition if he merely exercises rights of access given solely to do work agreed by the seller.

5.2.5 The buyer's licence ends on the earliest of: completion date, rescission of the contract or when five working days' notice given by one party to the other takes effect.

5.2.6 If the buyer is in occupation of the property after his licence has come to an end and the contract is subsequently completed he is to pay the seller compensation for his continued occupation calculated at the same rate as the fee mentioned in condition 5.2.2(d).

5.2.7 The buyer's right to raise requisitions is unaffected.

6.   COMPLETION

6.1 Date

6.1.1 Completion date is twenty working days after the date of the contract but time is not of the essence of the contract unless a notice to complete has been served.

6.1.2 If the money due on completion is received after 2.00pm, completion is to be treated, for the purposes only of conditions 6.3 and 7.3, as taking place on the next working day.

6.1.3 Condition 6.1.2 does not apply where the sale is with vacant possession of the property or any part and the seller has not vacated the property or that part by 2.00pm on the date of actual completion.

6.2 Place

Completion is to take place in England and Wales, either at the seller's solicitor's office or at some other place which the seller reasonably specifies.

6.3 Apportionments

6.3.1 Income and outgoings of the property are to be apportioned between the parties so far as the change of ownership on completion will affect entitlement to receive or liability to pay them.

6.3.2 If the whole property is sold with vacant possession or the seller exercises his option in condition 7.3.4, apportionment is to be made with effect from the date of actual completion; otherwise, it is to be made from completion date.

6.3.3 In apportioning any sum, it is to be assumed that the seller owns the property until the end of the day from which apportionment is made and that the sum accrues from day to day at the rate at which it is payable on that day.

6.3.4 For the purpose of apportioning income and outgoings, it is to be assumed that they accrue at an equal daily rate throughout the year.

6.3.5 When a sum to be apportioned is not known or easily ascertainable at completion, a provisional apportionment is to be made according to the best estimate available. As soon as the amount is known, a final apportionment is to be made and notified to the other party. Any resulting balance is to be paid no more than ten working days later, and if not then paid the balance is to bear interest at the contract rate from then until payment.

6.3.6 Compensation payable under condition 5.2.6 is not to be apportioned.

6.4 Amount payable

The amount payable by the buyer on completion is the purchase price (less any deposit already paid to the seller or his agent) adjusted to take account of:

(a) apportionments made under condition 6.3

(b) any compensation to be paid or allowed under condition 7.3.

6.5 Title deeds

6.5.1 The seller is not to retain the documents of title after the buyer has tendered the amount payable under condition 6.4.

6.5.2 Condition 6.5.1 does not apply to any documents of title relating to land being retained by the seller after completion.

6.6 Rent receipts

The buyer is to assume that whoever gave any receipt for a payment of rent or service charge which the seller produces was the person or the agent of the person then entitled to that rent or service charge.

6.7 Means of payment

The buyer is to pay the money due on completion in one or more of the following ways:

(a) legal tender

(b) a banker's draft

(c) a direct credit to a bank account nominated by the seller's solicitor

(d) an unconditional release of a deposit held by a stakeholder.

Right Column

6.8 Notice to complete

6.8.1 At any time on or after completion date, a party who is ready able and willing to complete may give the other a notice to complete.

6.8.2 A party is ready able and willing:

(a) if he could be, but for the default of the other party, and

(b) in the case of the seller, even though a mortgage remains secured on the property, if the amount to be paid on completion enables the property to be transferred freed of all mortgages (except those to which the sale is expressly subject).

6.8.3 The parties are to complete the contract within ten working days of giving a notice to complete, excluding the day on which the notice is given. For this purpose, time is of the essence of the contract.

6.8.4 On receipt of a notice to complete:

(a) if the buyer paid no deposit, he is forthwith to pay a deposit of 10 per cent

(b) if the buyer paid a deposit of less than 10 per cent, he is forthwith to pay a further deposit equal to the balance of that 10 per cent.

7.   REMEDIES

7.1 Errors and omissions

7.1.1 If any plan or statement in the contract, or in the negotiations leading to it, is or was misleading or inaccurate due to an error or omission, the remedies available are as follows.

7.1.2 When there is a material difference between the description or value of the property as represented and as it is, the injured party is entitled to damages.

7.1.3 An error or omission only entitles the injured party to rescind the contract:

(a) where it results from fraud or recklessness, or

(b) where he would be obliged, to his prejudice, to transfer or accept property differing substantially (in quantity, quality or tenure) from what the error or omission had led him to expect.

7.2 Rescission

If either party rescinds the contract:

(a) unless the rescission is a result of the buyer's breach of contract the deposit is to be repaid to the buyer with accrued interest

(b) the buyer is to return any documents he received from the seller and is to cancel any registration of the contract.

7.3 Late completion

7.3.1 If there is default by either or both of the parties in performing their obligations under the contract and completion is delayed, the party whose total period of default is the greater is to pay compensation to the other party.

7.3.2 Compensation is calculated at the contract rate on the purchase price, or (where the buyer is the paying party) the purchase price less any deposit paid, for the period by which the paying party's default exceeds that of the receiving party, or, if shorter, the period between completion date and actual completion.

7.3.3 Any claim for loss resulting from delayed completion is to be reduced by any compensation paid under this contract.

7.3.4 Where the buyer holds the property as tenant of the seller and completion is delayed, the seller may give notice to the buyer, before the date of actual completion, that he intends to take the net income from the property until completion. If he does so, he cannot claim compensation under condition 7.3.1 as well.

7.4 After completion

Completion does not cancel liability to perform any outstanding obligation under this contract.

7.5 Buyer's failure to comply with notice to complete

7.5.1 If the buyer fails to complete in accordance with a notice to complete, the following terms apply.

7.5.2 The seller may rescind the contract, and if he does so:

(a) he may

(i) forfeit and keep any deposit and accrued interest

(ii) resell the property

(iii) claim damages

(b) the buyer is to return any documents he received from the seller and is to cancel any registration of the contract.

7.5.3 The seller retains his other rights and remedies.

7.6 Seller's failure to comply with notice to complete

7.6.1 If the seller fails to complete in accordance with a notice to complete, the following terms apply.

7.6.2 The buyer may rescind the contract, and if he does so:

(a) the deposit is to be repaid to the buyer with accrued interest

(b) the buyer is to return any documents he received from the seller and is, at the seller's expense, to cancel any registration of the contract.

7.6.3 The buyer retains his other rights and remedies.

8.   LEASEHOLD PROPERTY

8.1 Existing leases

8.1.1 The following provisions apply to a sale of leasehold land.

8.1.2 The seller having provided the buyer with copies of the documents embodying the lease terms, the buyer is treated as entering into the contract knowing and fully accepting those terms.

8.1.3 The seller is to comply with any lease obligations requiring the tenant to insure the property.

8.2 New leases

8.2.1 The following provisions apply to a grant of a new lease.

8.2.2 The conditions apply so that:

"seller" means the proposed landlord

"buyer" means the proposed tenant

"purchase price" means the premium to be paid on the grant of a lease.

8.2.3 The lease is to be in the form of the draft attached to the agreement.

8.2.4 If the term of the new lease will exceed 21 years, the seller is to deduce a title which will enable the buyer to register the lease at HM Land Registry with an absolute title.

8.2.5 The buyer is not entitled to transfer the benefit of the contract.

8.2.6 The seller is to engross the lease and a counterpart of it and is to send the counterpart to the buyer at least five working days before completion date.

8.2.7 The buyer is to execute the counterpart and deliver it to the seller on completion.

8.3 Landlord's consent

8.3.1 The following provisions apply if a consent to assign or sub-let is required to complete the contract.

8.3.2 (a) The seller is to apply for the consent at his expense, and to use all reasonable efforts to obtain it

(b) The buyer is to provide all information and references reasonably required.

8.3.3 The buyer is not entitled to transfer the benefit of the contract.

8.3.4 Unless he is in breach of his obligation under condition 8.3.2, either party may rescind the contract by notice to the other party if three working days before completion date:

(a) the consent has not been given or

(b) the consent has been given subject to a condition to which the buyer reasonably objects.

In that case, neither party is to be treated as in breach of contract and condition 7.2 applies.

9.   CHATTELS

9.1 The following provisions apply to any chattels which are to be sold.

9.2 Whether or not a separate price is to be paid for the chattels, the contract takes effect as a contract for sale of goods.

9.3 Ownership of the chattels passes to the buyer on actual completion.

Appendix B

Abstract of Title in traditional form[1]

ABSTRACT OF THE TITLE of David Large[2] to freehold property known as 'Fairhaven' Mead Road Oadby in the County of Leicester

10 May 1982   OFFICIAL CERTIFICATE[3] of search in H.M. Land Charges Register No. 637112 against Abel Small revealing no subsistng entries

21 May 1982   By conveyance of this date made between the said ABEL SMALL of 'Fairhaven' Mead Road Oadby in the County of Leicester (thereinafter called 'the vendor') of the one part and DAVID LARGE of 32 Church Lane in the city of Leicester (thereinafter called 'the purchaser') of the other part

RECITING seisin of the vendor and agreement for sale

IT WAS WITNESSED as follows:
1.   IN pursuance of the said agreement and in consideration of the sum of £50,000 paid to the vendor by the purchaser (the receipt etc[5]) the vendor as beneficial owner thereby conveyed unto the purchaser ALL THAT plot of land fronting to Mead Road Oadby aforesaid containing in the whole 811 square yards and delineated and described on the plan annexed to the before abstracted Conveyance (hereinafter called 'the Conveyance')of 16 January 1970[6] and thereon edged red AND ALSO ALL THAT dwellinghouse erected thereon and known as 'Fairhaven' Mead Road Oadby aforesaid TOGETHER with the full benefit and advantage of the right of way granted by the Conveyance over and along the road shown coloured brown on the said plan
TO HOLD unto the purchaser in fee simple SUBJECT to the covenants on the part of the grantee and the conditions contained in the Conveyance
2.   COVENANT by the purchaser with the vendor to observe and perform the said covenants and conditions and to indemnify[7]
EXECUTED by both parties and ATTESTED

1   Based on the conveyance illustrated at p 516, ante.
2   The names of the parties and the properties appearing in this example are entirely fictitious. In practice the abstract would be prepared on the occasion of a sale or mortgage by David Large, and for this reason it is stated to be an abstract of his title. For ease of reading the

715

standard abbreviations have not been adopted.

3   For the abstracting of search certificates, see p 283, ante.

4   'P.D.' stands for 'Particulars delivered', for the significance of which see p 468, ante.

5   This is an adequate summary of the clause acknowledging receipt of the consideration.

6   There is no need to mention the parties to a deed that has been previously abstracted.

7   Indemnity covenants of this nature normally follow a set pattern. All that need be shown is that such a covenant was given. Had the purchase price been £40,000, the conveyancing would have incorporated the appropriate certificate for value clause resulting in stamp duty of £600 being paid (ie at the then rate of 1.5 per cent. Under the Finance Act 1980, s 95(1), this clause would have been abstracted simply as 'Certificate for value'.

Index